EIGHTH EDITION

Elementary and Middle School Mathematics

Teaching Developmentally

John A. Van de Walle
Late of Virginia Commonwealth University

Karen S. Karp
University of Louisville

Jennifer M. Bay-Williams
University of Louisville

With Contributions by
Jonathan Wray
Howard County Public Schools

PEARSON

Boston • Columbus • Indianapolis • New York • San Francisco • Upper Saddle River
Amsterdam • Cape Town • Dubai • London • Madrid • Milan • Munich • Paris • Montreal • Toronto
Delhi • Mexico City • São Paulo • Sydney • Hong Kong • Seoul • Singapore • Taipei • Tokyo

Senior Acquisitions Editor: Kelly Villella Canton
Senior Development Editor: Christina Robb
Editorial Assistant: Annalea Manalili
Senior Marketing Manager: Darcy Betts
Senior Production Editor: Gregory Erb
Editorial Production Service: Electronic Publishing Services Inc.
Manufacturing Buyer: Megan Cochran
Electronic Composition: Jouve
Interior Design: Carol Somberg
Cover Designer: Jennifer Hart

Credits and acknowledgments borrowed from other sources and reproduced, with permission, in this textbook appear on the appropriate page within text. Cover photo © Shutterstock.

Many of the designations by manufacturers and sellers to distinguish their products are claimed as trademarks. Where those designations appear in this book, and the publisher was aware of a trademark claim, the designations have been printed in initial caps or all caps.

Library of Congress Cataloging-in-Publication Data

Van de Walle, John A.
   Elementary and middle school mathematics: teaching developmentally / John A. Van de Walle, Karen S. Karp; Jennifer M. Bay-Williams; with contributions by Jonathan Wray.—8th ed.
      p.cm.
   Includes bibliographical references and index.
   ISBN-13: 978-0-13-261226-5 (pbk.)
   ISBN-10: 0-13-261226-7 (pbk.)
  1. Mathematics—Study and teaching (Elementary)   2. Mathematics—Study and teaching (Middle school)   I. Karp, Karen   II. Bay-Williams, Jennifer M.   III. Title.
   QA135.6.V36 2013
   510.71'2—dc23   2011035541

10 9 8 7 6 5 4 3 2

ISBN-10: 0-13-261226-7
ISBN-13: 978-0-13-261226-5

Elementary and Middle School Mathematics

About the Authors

John A. Van de Walle was a professor emeritus at Virginia Commonwealth University. He was a mathematics education consultant who regularly gave professional development workshops for K–8 teachers in the United States and Canada. He visited and taught in elementary school classrooms and worked with teachers to implement student-centered math lessons. He co-authored the Scott Foresman-Addison Wesley *Mathematics K–6* series and contributed to the Pearson School mathematics program enVisionMATH. Additionally, he wrote numerous chapters and articles for the National Council of Teachers of Mathematics (NCTM) books and journals and was very active in NCTM, including serving on the board of directors, chairing the educational materials committee, and speaking at national and regional meetings.

Karen S. Karp is a professor of mathematics education at the University of Louisville (Kentucky). Prior to entering the field of teacher education she was an elementary school teacher in New York. Karen is a co-author of *Feisty Females: Inspiring Girls to Think Mathematically*, which is aligned with her research interests on teaching mathematics to diverse populations. With Jennifer, Karen co-edited *Growing Professionally: Readings from NCTM Publications for Grades K–8* and co-authored (along with Janet Caldwell) *Developing Essential Understanding of Addition and Subtraction for Teaching Mathematics in Pre-K–Grade 2*. She is a former member of the board of directors of the National Council of Teachers of Mathematics (NCTM) and a former president of the Association of Mathematics Teacher Educators (AMTE). She continues to work in classrooms with elementary and middle school teachers and with teachers at all levels who work with students with disabilities.

Jennifer M. Bay-Williams is a professor of mathematics education at the University of Louisville (Kentucky). Jennifer has published many articles on teaching and learning in NCTM journals. She has also co-authored numerous books, including *Developing Essential Understanding of Addition and Subtraction for Teaching Mathematics in Pre-K–Grade 2*, *Math and Literature: Grades 6–8*, *Math and Nonfiction: Grades 6–8*, and *Navigating Through Connections in Grades 6–8*. She is the author of the *Field Experience Guide* for this book. Jennifer taught elementary, middle, and high school in Missouri and in Peru, and continues to work in classrooms at all levels with students and with teachers. Jennifer is on the board of directors for TODOS: Equity for All, is the editor for the 2012 NCTM Yearbook, and is a former president of the Association of Mathematics Teacher Educators (AMTE).

About the Contributor

 **Jonathan Wray** is the technology contributor to *Elementary and Middle School Mathematic: Teaching Developmentally* (Sixth–Eighth Editions). He is the instructional facilitator for secondary mathematics curricular programs in the Howard County public school system. He is the president elect of the Association of Maryland Mathematics Teacher Educators (AMMTE) and past president of the Maryland Council of Teachers of Mathematics (MCTM). He has been recognized for his expertise in infusing technology in mathematics teaching, receiving the Outstanding Technology Leader in Education award for his school district from the Maryland Society for Educational Technology (MSET). Jon is also actively engaged in NCTM, serving on the editorial panels of *Teaching Children Mathematics* and *ON-Math*. He has served as a primary and intermediate grades classroom teacher, gifted/talented resource teacher, elementary mathematics specialist, curriculum and assessment developer, grant project manager, and educational consultant.

Brief Contents

Detailed Contents

CHAPTER 6

Teaching Mathematics Equitably to All Children   94

CHAPTER 7

Using Technological Tools to Teach Mathematics   113

SECTION II
Development of Mathematical Concepts and Procedures

This section serves as the application of the core ideas of Section I. Here you will find chapters on every major content area in the pre-K–8 mathematics curriculum. Numerous problem-based activities to engage students are interwoven with a discussion of the mathematical content and how children develop their understanding of that content. At the outset of each chapter, you will find a listing of "Big Ideas," the mathematical umbrella for the chapter. Also included are ideas for incorporating children's literature, technology, and assessment. These chapters are designed to help you develop pedagogical strategies and to serve as a resource for your teaching now and in the future.

CHAPTER 8
Developing Early Number Concepts and Number Sense   128

CHAPTER 9
Developing Meanings for the Operations   148

CHAPTER 10

Helping Students Master the Basic Facts 171

CHAPTER 11

Developing Whole-Number Place-Value Concepts 192

CHAPTER 12

Developing Strategies for Addition and Subtraction Computation 216

CHAPTER 13

Developing Strategies for Multiplication and Division Computation   236

CHAPTER 14

Algebraic Thinking: Generalizations, Patterns, and Functions   258

CHAPTER 15

Developing Fraction Concepts   290

CHAPTER 16

Developing Strategies for Fraction Computation   315

CHAPTER 17

Developing Concepts of Decimals and Percents   338

CHAPTER 18

Proportional Reasoning   357

CHAPTER 19

Developing Measurement Concepts   375

CHAPTER 20

Geometric Thinking and Geometric Concepts   402

CHAPTER 21

Developing Concepts of Data Analysis   434

CHAPTER 22

Exploring Concepts of Probability   454

CHAPTER 23

Developing Concepts of Exponents, Integers, and Real Numbers   472

APPENDIX A

Standards for Mathematical Practice   491

APPENDIX B

Standards for Teaching Mathematics   493

APPENDIX C

Guide to Blackline Masters   495

Preface

NEW TO THIS EDITION

The eighth edition has been revised to include the following changes to better prepare teachers to teach mathematics to all learners:

- **New adaptations and accommodations for English language learners and students with disabilities** appear not only in the narrative in Section I but also in many activities through direct examples and descriptions for the various content areas in Section II. The increased emphasis on diversity will be obvious to those who have used the book in the past. Chapter 4 (Planning in the Problem-Based Classroom) has an increased focus on planning for all learners, including new coverage on considerations for students with disabilities to complement the revised section on ELLs. Chapter 6 (Teaching Mathematics Equitably to All Children) contains significant updates to each section and alignment with the research synthesis from *RtI Practice Guide for Students Struggling in Mathematics* (Gersten, Beckmann, Clarke, Foegen, Marsh, Star, & Witzel, 2009). New to this chapter are strategies for cultural/ethnic differences, including Table 6.4, "Reflective Questions to Focus on Culturally Responsive Mathematics Instruction," and additional guidance for teachers on students with disabilities, including a chart of common stumbling blocks. Importantly, in Section II the Activities feature specific adaptations and accommodations for ELLs and students with disabilities. These provide specific ways to make the activity accessible and still challenging.

- **Revised Expanded Lessons** located in the book, the *Field Experience Guide*, and on MyEducationLab (www.myeducationlab.com) now include tips and strategies for English language learners and students with disabilities.

- **Increased emphasis on student misconceptions and how to address them effectively** will better support teachers' understanding of what needs explicit attention when teaching mathematics. Since the publication of the seventh edition, an increasing body of research has emerged on students' misconceptions and naïve understandings in a variety of mathematics content. Throughout Section II, the research about misconceptions and gaps in student mathematical knowledge is presented to assist teachers in the identification and preparation for these common barriers to understanding. In such topics as fractions and decimals, related findings allow teachers to plan ahead using examples and counterexamples to strengthen student understanding as they face what may be expected areas of confusion.

- **New samples of authentic student work** illustrate student thinking. Responses to problem-based assignments present glimpses into how students think about problems and what students' written work on mathematical tasks looks like, increasing teachers' awareness of how rich students' mathematical thinking can be—and how high our expectations should be. Some student work also demonstrates naïve understandings.

- **Increased early childhood coverage** provides expanded emphasis on and reorganization of early numeracy in Chapters 8 and 9 reflecting the work of the Committee on Early Childhood Mathematics through the National Research Council. Based on learning trajectories and progressions for the core areas of number, relations, and operations, the work with early learners is seen as the essential foundation for number sense and problem solving.

- **New Formative Assessment Notes** in each chapter in Section II guide readers through ideas they can test with individual students or students in groups. Formative assessment is one of the key tools in finding out what students are thinking, and thereby identifying their areas of strength and weakness. Chapter 5, Building Assessment into Instruction, contains a more detailed description of formative assessments organized by Piaget's three major assessment areas: tasks, observation, and interviews. To bring these ideas to life and to make them more directly linked to the content, these Formative Assessment Notes are included throughout content area chapters to support teachers in the effective use of formative assessment, which is directly connected to increased student achievement.

- **New information on using NCTM standards and *Common Core State Standards*** to inform instruction appears in Chapter 1 and 2 and in relevant references in Section II. Not surprisingly, this book is aligned with the new *Common Core State Standards*, adopted by 44 of the 50 states at the time of publication. The *Common Core State Standards* and other standards documents are described in Chapter 1. The Standards for Mathematical Practice portion of the *Common Core State Standards* are addressed in Chapter 2 (connected to the *Adding it Up* mathematical proficiencies) and infused throughout the book. As essential content is described in Section II, specific standards are referenced, giving the appropriate grade level and treatment relevant to the content. In addition, chapter content has been adapted to reflect the attention given to the content in the *Common Core State Standards*. Appendix A provides the Standards for Mathematical Practice.

- **Extensively updated information on how to effectively integrate new technological tools** to support teaching and learning appears in Chapter 7 and throughout the text with marginal icons. Updated technology integration content and strategies now also appear in select Activities.

- **A reorganization of Chapters 12 and 13** emphasizes both strategies for computation and estimation for addition and subtraction in Chapter 12 and the same for multiplication and division in Chapter 13. This is a change from the seventh edition, which separated developing strategies for whole number computation and estimation for the four operations. Many reviewers suggested this change, infusing computational estimation in these new chapters, and this rearrangement links too to the developmental nature of those operations.

- **A discussion on engaging families in meaningful ways** to help students learn mathematics appears in Chapter 4.

- **Additional attention to classroom discourse** now appears in Chapter 3 (Teaching Through Problem Solving). The coverage includes how to conduct productive discussion sessions and develop effective questioning, and is illustrated with a vignette.

OTHER CHANGES OF NOTE

Much has changed on the landscape of mathematics education, and so many aspects of the book have been updated to reflect those changes. In addition to the changes listed previously, the following substantive changes have been made:

- A new section on homework and parental involvement is provided in Chapter 4.

- There is an increased focus on the research-based three-phase developmental model of developing basic facts, and added new activities to support basic fact mastery appear in Chapter 10.

- The content on algebraic thinking has been adapted to align with current research and standards. Specifically, Kaput's five areas (from his 1999 work) are now three areas (based on his 2008 work). Also, there is an increased emphasis on equivalence and variables, including adding the number-line representation of variables. Increased attention is given to making the properties (especially distributive) more explicit in response to the *Common Core State Standards.*

- Chapter 15 (Developing Fraction Concepts) has greatly expanded sections on partitioning and on equivalence to reflect three recent research reviews that have indicated that this is essential to all advanced fraction work and success in algebra.

- Chapter 16 (Developing Strategies for Fraction Computation) now includes Activities— ten new ideas for developing understanding of fraction operations.

- Chapter 18 has been shortened, had new activities added, and been refocused to address understanding of ratios more deeply (with less focus on connecting to other content areas).

- The chapter on measurement, Chapter 19, has been reorganized. Previously the development of all measurement formulas was shared at the end of the chapter; now the formulas are integrated with the corresponding measurement topic (e.g., area or volume).

- Chapter 21 gives more explicit attention to distinguishing between numerical data and categorical data.

- Chapter 23 includes a significantly revised section on order of operations and numerous new activities.

WHAT YOU WILL FIND IN THIS BOOK

If you look at the table of contents, you will see that the chapters are separated into two distinct sections. The first section, consisting of seven chapters, deals with important ideas that cross the boundaries of specific areas of content. The second section, consisting of 16 chapters, offers teaching suggestions and activities for every major mathematics topic in the pre-K–8 curriculum. Chapters in Section I offer perspectives on the challenging task of helping students learn mathematics. Having a feel for the discipline of mathematics—that is, to know what it means to "do mathematics"—is critical to learning how to teach mathematics well. In addition, understanding constructivist and sociocultural perspectives on learning mathematics and how that is applied to teaching through problem solving provides a foundation and rationale for how to teach and assess pre-K–8 students.

Importantly, you will be teaching diverse students, including students who are English language learners, are gifted, or have disabilities. You will learn how to apply instructional strategies in ways that support and challenge *all* learners. Formative assessment strategies, strategies for diverse learners, and effective use of technological tools are addressed in specific chapters in Section I (Chapters 5, 6, and 7, respectively), and throughout Section II chapters.

Each chapter of Section II focuses on one of the major content areas in pre-K–8 mathematics curriculum. It begins with identifying the big ideas for that content, and also provides guidance on how students best learn that content and many problem-based activities to engage students in understanding mathematics. Reflecting on the activities as you read can help you think about the mathematics from the perspective of the student. As often as possible, take out pencil and paper and try the problems so that you actively engage in *your learning* about *students learning* mathematics. In so doing, we hope this book will increase your own understanding of mathematics, the students you teach, and how to teach them well.

SOME SPECIAL FEATURES OF THIS TEXT

By flipping through the book, you will notice many section headings, a large number of figures, and various special features. All are designed to make the book more useful as a textbook and as a long-term resource. Here are a few things to look for.

Big Ideas ▶

Much of the research and literature espousing a student-centered approach suggests that teachers plan their instruction around "big ideas" rather than isolated skills or concepts. At the beginning of each chapter in Section II, you will find a list of the key mathematical ideas associated with the chapter. Teachers find these lists helpful for quickly getting a picture of the mathematics they are teaching.

Mathematics Content Connections ▶

Following the Big Ideas lists are brief descriptions of other content areas in mathematics that are related to the content of the current chapter. These lists are offered to help you be more aware of the potential interaction of content as you plan lessons, diagnose students' difficulties, and learn more yourself about the mathematics you are teaching.

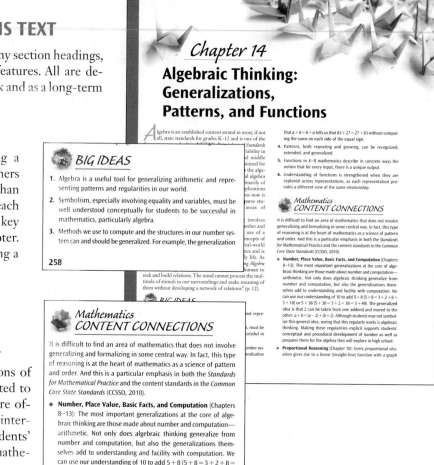

Activities ▶

The numerous activities found in every chapter of Section II have always been rated by readers as one of the most valuable parts of the book. Some activity ideas are described directly in the text and in the illustrations. Others are presented in the numbered Activity boxes. Every activity is a problem-based task (as described in Chapter 3)

Activity 14.11 explores properties of odd and even numbers using the calculator.

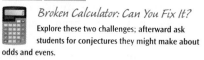

Activity 14.11

Broken Calculator: Can You Fix It?

Explore these two challenges; afterward ask students for conjectures they might make about odds and evens.

1. If you cannot use any of the even keys (0, 2, 4, 6, 8), can you create an even number in the calculator display? If so, how?
2. If you cannot use any of the odd keys (1, 3, 5, 7, 9), can you create an odd number in the calculator display? If so, how?

Cooper, 2008). The *core* of a repeating pattern is the string of elements that repeats. It is important to use knowledge of the core to extend the pattern.

Activity 14.12

Making Repeating Patterns

STUDENTS with SPECIAL NEEDS

Students can work independently or in groups of two or three to extend patterns made from simple materials: buttons, colored blocks, connecting cubes, toothpicks, geometric shapes—items you can gather easily. For each set of materials, draw or build two or three complete repetitions so the core is obvious. The students' task is to extend it. Figure 14.10 illustrates one possible pattern for

and is designed to engage students in doing mathematics. New adaptations and accommodations for English language learners and students with disabilities are included in many activities.

Investigations in Number, Data, and Space and Connected Mathematics ▶

In Section II, four chapters include features that describe an activity from the standards-based curriculum *Investigations in Number, Data, and Space* (an elementary curriculum) or *Connected Mathematics Project (CMP II)* (a middle school curriculum). These features include a description of an activity in the program as well as the context of the unit in which it is found. The main purpose of this feature is to acquaint you with these materials and to demonstrate how the spirit of the NCTM *Standards* and the constructivist theory espoused in this book have been translated into existing commercial curricula.

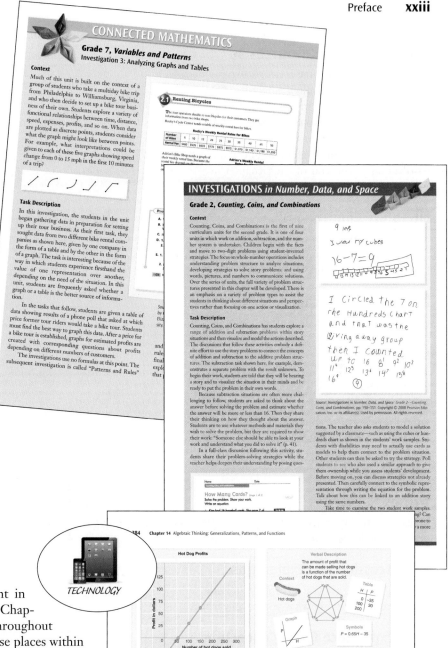

Technology Ideas ▶

Infusing technological tools is important in learning mathematics, as you will learn in Chapter 7. We have infused technology ideas throughout Section II. An icon is used to identify those places within the text or activity where a technology idea or resource is discussed. Descriptions include open-source (free) software, applets, and other Web-based resources, as well as calculator ideas.

Formative Assessment Notes ▶

Assessment should be an integral part of instruction. Similarly, it makes sense to think about what to be listening for (assessing) as you read about different areas of content development. Throughout the content chapters, you will see Formative Assessment Note icons indicating a short description of ways to assess the topic in that section. Reading these assessment notes as you read the text can also help you understand how best to help your students.

End-of-Chapter Resources ▶

The end of each chapter includes two major subsections: *Resources*, which includes "Literature Connections" (found in all Section II chapters), "Recommended Readings," and "Online Resources"; and *Reflections*, which includes "Writing to Learn" and "For Discussion and Exploration." Also found at the end of each chapter are "Field Experience Guide Connections."

Literature Connections

Section II chapters contain examples of great children's literature for launching into the mathematics concepts in the chapter just read.

Recommended Readings

In this section, you will find an annotated list of articles and books to augment the information found in the chapter.

Online Resources

At the end of each chapter, you will find an annotated list of some of the best Web-based resources along with their website addresses so that you can further explore how to infuse technological tools into instruction to support student learning.

Writing to Learn

Questions are provided that help you reflect on the important pedagogical ideas related to the content in the chapter.

For Discussion and Exploration

These questions ask you to explore an issue related to that chapter's content, applying what you have learned.

Field Experience Guide Connections

This feature showcases resources from the *Field Experience Guide** that connect to the content and topics within each chapter. The *Field Experience Guide*, a supplement to *Elementary and Middle School Mathematics*, provides tools for learning in schools, many Expanded Lessons, activities, and assessments. (For details, see the Supplements section on pages xxvi–xxvii.)

---

*The *Field Experience Guide* and access to MyEducationLab are sold separately. Please see pages xxvi–xxvii for more details.

Resources for Chapter 17   **355**

allows the problem to be worked mentally using fraction equivalents. The second number requires a substitution with an approximation or estimation as in the last activity.

1. The school enrolls {480, 547} students. Yesterday {12½ percent, 13 percent} of the students were absent. How many came to school?
2. Mr. Carver sold his lawn mower for {$45, $89}. This was {60 percent, 62 percent} of the price he paid for it new. What did the mower cost when it was new?
3. When the box fell off the shelf, {90, 63} of the {720, 500} widgets broke. What percentage was lost in the breakage?

The first problem asks for a part (whole and fraction given), the second asks for a whole (part and fraction given), and the third asks for a fraction (part and whole given).

There are several common uses for estimating percentages in real-world situations. As students gain full conceptual understanding and flexibility, there are ways to think about percents that are useful as you are shopping or in situations that bring thinking about percents to the forefront.

Tips. To figure a tip, you can find 10 percent of the amount and then half of that again to make 15 percent.

Taxes. The same approach is used for adding on sales tax. Depending on the tax rate, you can find 10 percent, take half of that, and then find 1 percent and add or subtract that amount as needed. But encourage other approaches as well. Students should realize that finding percents is a process of multiplication; therefore, finding 8 percent (tax) of $50 will generate the same result as finding 50 percent (half) of 8, or $4.

Discounts. A 30 percent decrease is the same as 70 percent of the original amount, and depending on the original amount, using one of those percents may be easier to use in mental calculations than the other. If a $48 outfit is 30% off, for example, you are paying 70%. Round $48 to $50 and you have .70 × 50 (think 7 × 5), so your cost is less than $35.

Again, these are not rules to be taught but are reasoning activities to develop that require a full understanding of percent concepts and the commutative property.

RESOURCES *for Chapter 17*

LITERATURE CONNECTIONS

In newspapers and magazines, you will find decimal and percent situations with endless real-world connections. Money-related increases and decreases are interesting to project over several years. If the consumer price index rises 3 percent a year, how much will a $100 basket of groceries cost by the time your students are 21 years old?

The Phantom Tollbooth *Juster, 1961*
References to mathematical ideas abound in this story about Milo's adventures in Digitopolis, where everything is number-oriented. There, Milo meets a half of a boy, appearing in the illustration as the left half of a boy cut from top to bottom. As it turns out, the boy is actually 0.58 since he is a member of the average family: a mother, father, and 2.58 children. The boy is the 0.58. One advantage, he explains, is that he is the only one who can drive the 0.3 of a car, as the average family owns 1.3 cars. This story can lead to a great discussion of averages that result in decimals.

An extension of the story is to explore averages that are interesting to the students (average number of siblings, etc.) and see where these odd decimal fractions come from. Illustrating an average number of pets can be very humorous!

Piece = Part = Portion: Fraction = Decimal = Percent *Gifford & Thaler, 2008*
Illustrated with vivid photos, this book shows how fractions relate to decimals and percents. Written by a teacher, connections are made through common representations, such as one

sneaker representing ½ or 0.50 or 50 percent of a pair of shoes. Real-world links such as one-seventh of a week and one-eleventh of a soccer team will connect with students. Note that some decimals and percents are rounded.

RECOMMENDED READINGS

Articles
Cramer, K., Monson, D., Wyberg, T., Leavitt, S., & Whitney, S. B. (2009). Models for initial decimal ideas. *Teaching Children Mathematics, 16*(2), 106–116.
This article describes ways of using 10 × 10 grids and decimal addition and subtraction boards to enhance students' understanding of decimals. Several diagnostic interviews and an emphasis on having students use words, pictures, and numbers are included.
Suh, J. M., Johnston, C., Jamieson, S., & Mills, M. (2008). Promoting decimal number sense and representational fluency. *Mathematics Teaching in the Middle School, 14*(1), 44–50.
A group of fifth- and sixth-grade teachers in a lesson study group explored a variety of representations to develop students' proficiency with decimals. Ideas for games and strategies for ELLs and students with special needs are shared.

ONLINE RESOURCES

Base Blocks—Decimals
http://nlvm.usu.edu
Base-ten blocks can be placed on a place-value chart. The number of decimal places can be selected, thus designating any of the four blocks as the unit. Addition and subtraction problems can be created or can be generated randomly.

This is an engaging matching game using representations of percents, fractions, and a regional model.

REFLECTIONS *on Chapter 17*

WRITING TO LEARN

1. Describe three different base-ten models for fractions and decimals, and use each to illustrate how base-ten fractions can be represented.
2. How can we help students think about very small place values such as thousandths and millionths in the same way we get students to think about very large place values such as millions and billions?
3. Use an example involving base-ten pieces to explain the role of the decimal point in identifying the units position. Relate this idea to changing units of measurement as in money or metric measures.
4. Explain how the line-up-the-decimals rule for adding and subtracting can be developed through practice with estimation.

5. Give an example explaining how, in many problems, multiplication and division with decimals can be replaced with estimation and whole-number methods.

FOR DISCUSSION AND EXPLORATION

1. A way you may have learned to order a series of decimals is to annex zeros to each number so that all numbers have the same number of decimal places. For example, rewrite

   0.34 as 0.3400
   0.3004 as 0.3004
   0.059 as 0.0590

   Now ignore the decimal points and any leading zeros, and order the resulting whole numbers. This method was found to detract from students' conceptual understanding (Roche & Clarke, 2004). Why do you think that was the case? What should you try instead?

MyEducationLab™

Go to the MyEducationLab (www.myeducationlab.com) for Math Methods and familiarize yourself with the content. Much of the site content is organized topically. The topics include all of the following to support your learning in the course:

• Learning outcomes for important mathematics methods and standards

Field Experience Guide
CONNECTIONS

Expanded Lesson 9.8 is an engaging lesson that helps students fluently convert common fractions to their decimal equivalences. In Expanded Lesson 9.10 ("How Close Is Close?") students shade 10 × 10 grids to explore density of decimals, thus learning that for any two decimals, another decimal can be found between them.

Field Experience Guide
CONNECTIONS

Expanded Lesson 9.8 is an engaging lesson that helps students fluently convert common fractions to their decimal equivalences. In Expanded Lesson 9.10 ("How Close Is Close?") students shade 10 × 10 grids to explore density of decimals, thus learning that for any two decimals, another decimal can be found between them.

Appendixes ▶

Appendix A contains a copy of the *Common Core State Standards'* Standards for Mathematical Practice, which describe what it is we want students to be able to do in order to demonstrate mathematical proficiency.

Appendix B contains the Standards for Teaching Mathematics from *Mathematics Teaching Today* (NCTM, 2007a).

Expanded Lessons ▶

An example of an Expanded Lesson can be found at the end of Chapter 4. In addition, eight similar Expanded Lessons can be found on MyEducationLab at www.myeducationlab.com. An additional 24 Expanded Lessons spanning all content areas can be found in the *Field Experience Guide*. The Expanded Lessons follow the lesson structure described in Chapter 4 and include detailed descriptions of how to teach the lesson, adapt it for ELLs and students with disabilities, and assess student understanding of the lesson. Related Blackline Masters are included as needed.

Appendix A
Standards for Mathematical Practice

Appendix B
Standards for Teaching Mathematics

Appendix C
Guide to Blackline Masters

This Appendix contains images of all of the Blackline Masters (BLM) that are listed below. The full-size masters can be found in either of two places:

- In hard copy at the end of the *Field Experience Guide* (Blackline Masters 62–77 are connected to Expanded Lessons provided in the *Field Experience Guide*.)
- On the MyEducationLab website (www.myeducationlab.com)

0.5-cm square grid 36	Clock faces 33	Looking at collections 62
1-cm isometric dot grid 39	Coordinate grid 48	Missing-part worksheet 13
1-cm isometric dot/diagonal grid 40	Create a journey story 71	More-or-less cards 1
1-cm square dot grid 37	Crooked paths 72	Motion man 52–53
1-cm square grid 35	Degrees and wedges 32	Multiplication and division recording charts 20
2-cm isometric grid 38	Design a bag 60	Number cards 2
2-cm square grid 34	Dot cards 3–8	Place-value mat (with ten-frames) 17
2 more than 63	Double ten-frame 11	Predict how many 69–70
2 less than 64	Five-frame 9	Properties of quadrilateral diagonals 75
10 × 10 grids 27	Fixed area recording sheet 74	Property lists for quadrilaterals 54–57
10 × 10 multiplication array 12	Four small hundreds charts 23	Rational number wheel 28
10,000 grid 29	Fraction names 66	Rectangles made with 36 tiles 73
Addition and subtraction recording charts 19	Geoboard pattern 49	Solving problems involving fractions 67
Assorted shapes 41–47	Geoboard recording sheets 50	Tangrams and mosaic puzzle 51
Assorted triangles 58	How long? 65	Ten-frame 10
Base-ten grid paper 18	Hundreds chart 22	Toying with measures 77
Base-ten materials 14	It's a matter of rates 68	Toy purchases 76
Blank hundreds chart (10 × 10	Little ten-frames 15–16	
	Look-alike rectangles 30	

EXPANDED LESSON

Fixed Areas

CONTENT AND TASK DECISIONS
Grade Level: 3–4

Mathematics Goals
- To contrast the concepts of area and perimeter
- To develop an understanding of the relationship between area and perimeter of different shapes when the area is fixed
- To compare and contrast the units used to measure perimeter and those used to measure area

Grade Level Guide

NCTM CURRICULUM FOCAL POINTS	COMMON CORE STATE STANDARDS
Perimeter is a **grade 3** connection within Measurement. Area is a **grade 4** focal point in Measurement: "Developing an understanding of area and determining the areas of two-dimensional shapes" (NCTM, 2006, p. 16).	Area is one of four critical themes in **grade 3**: "developing understanding of the structure of rectangular arrays and of area." Specifically, students will be able to "recognize perimeter as an attribute of plane figures and distinguish between linear and area measures" (CCSSO, 2010, p. 22).

Consider Your Students' Needs

Students have worked with the ideas of area and perimeter. Some, if not the majority, of students can find the area and perimeter of given figures and may even be able to state the formulas for finding the perimeter and area of a rectangle. However, they may become confused as to which formula to use.

For English Language Learners
- Build background for the terms *rectangle, length, width, area,* and *perimeter*. Ask students whether they have heard of these words and use their ideas to talk about their mathematical meaning.
- Use visuals (tiles) as you model the mathematical terms.

For Students with Special Needs
- Students who struggle may need to use either a computer-based program to model different areas or a geoboard.
- Sometimes the large number of color tiles used for an area of 24 or 26 can be distracting. Students may focus more on the construction than the mathematical concept. Consider using a smaller total, like 16.
- If you are using color tiles to model smaller areas, create a special set with "Area" written with a permanent marker on each. The use of these tiles to create the shapes with an area will reinforce the difference between area and perimeter.

Also note for students who confuse these two measures that the mnemonic "rim" is in the word *perimeter* to jog their memory.

Materials

Each student will need:
- 36 square tiles such as color tiles
- Two or three sheets of centimeter grid paper
- "Rectangles Made with 36 Tiles" recording sheet (Blackline Master 73)
- "Fixed Area" recording sheet (Blackline Master 74)

Fixed Area Recording Sheet

Name _____

Length	Width	Area	Perimeter

Teacher will need:
- Color tiles
- "Rectangles Made with 36 Tiles" recording sheet (Blackline Master 73)
- "Fixed Area" recording sheet (Blackline Master 74)

76

LESSON

Before

Begin with a simpler version of the task:
- Have students build a rectangle using 12 tiles at their desks. Explain that the rectangle should be filled in, not just a border. After eliciting some ideas, ask a student to come to the document camera and make a rectangle as described.
- Model sketching the rectangle on a grid. Record the dimensions of the rectangle on the recording chart—for example, "2 by 6."
- Ask, "What do we mean by perimeter? How do we measure perimeter?" After helping students define perimeter and describe how it is measured, ask students for the perimeter of this rectangle. Ask a student to come to the document camera to measure the perimeter of the rectangle. (Use either the rectangle made from tiles or the one sketched on grid paper.) Emphasize that the units used to measure perimeter are one-dimensional, or linear, and that perimeter is just the distance around an object. Record the perimeter on the chart.
- Ask, "What do we mean by area? How do we measure area?" After helping students define area and describe how it is measured, ask for the area of this rectangle. Here you want to make explicit that the units used to measure area are two-dimensional and, therefore, cover a region. After counting the tiles, record the area in square units on the chart.
- Have students make a different rectangle using 12 tiles at their desks and record the perimeter and area as before. Students will need to decide what "different" means. Is a 2-by-6 rectangle different from a 6-by-2 rectangle? Although these are congruent, students may wish to consider these as being different. That is okay for this activity.

Present the focus task to the class:
- See how many different rectangles can be made with 36 tiles.
- Determine and record the perimeter and area for each rectangle.

Provide clear expectations:
- Write the following directions on the board:
  1. Find a rectangle using *all* 36 tiles.
  2. Sketch the rectangle on the grid paper.
  3. Measure and record the perimeter and area of the rectangle on the recording chart.
  4. Find a new rectangle using *all* 36 tiles and repeat steps 2–4.
- Place students in pairs to work collaboratively, but require that each student draw his or her own sketches and use his or her own recording sheet.

During

Initially:
- Question students to be sure they understand the task and the meaning of *area* and *perimeter*. Look for students who are confusing these terms.
- Be sure students are both drawing the rectangles and recording them appropriately in the chart.

Ongoing:
- Observe and ask the assessment questions, posing one or two to a student and moving to another student (see the "Assessment" section of this lesson).

After

Bring the class together to share and discuss the task:
- Ask students what they have found out about perimeter and area. Ask, "Did the perimeter stay the same? Is that what you expected? When is the perimeter big and when is it small?"
- Ask students how they can be sure they have all of the possible rectangles.
- Ask students to describe what happens to the perimeter as the length and width change. ("The perimeter gets shorter as the rectangle gets fatter." "The square has the shortest perimeter.") Provide time to pair-share ideas.

ASSESSMENT

Observe
- Are students confusing perimeter and area?
- As students form new rectangles, are they aware that the area is not changing because they are using the same number of tiles each time? These students may not know what area is, or they may be confusing it with perimeter.
- Are students looking for patterns in how to find the perimeter?
- Are students stating important concepts or patterns to their partners?

Ask
- What is the area of the rectangle you just made?
- What is the perimeter of the rectangle you just made?
- How is area different from perimeter?
- How do you measure area? Perimeter?

495

77

SUPPLEMENTS

Field Experience Guide (Fourth Edition)

This guide has been updated to reflect current standards for students and teachers. It can be used for practicum experiences and student teaching at the elementary and middle school levels. The guide contains three parts: Part I provides tools and tasks for preservice teachers to use in classrooms; Part II provides three types of ready-to-use classroom activities: 24 Expanded Lessons, mathematics Activities, and Balanced Assessment Tasks; and Part III contains Blackline Masters to support classroom implementation of *Elementary and Middle School Mathematics* activities. This guide was designed to directly address the NCATE accreditation requirements. If *Field Experience Guide* did not come packaged with your book, you may purchase it online at www.mypearsonstore.com.

The guide contains a number of new features:

- **Focus on *Common Core State Standards* content throughout.** First, there are a number of field experiences throughout Part I that include a focus on the Standards for Mathematical Practice. All lessons and activities have grade-level suggestions that are consistent with the CCSSO recommendations.

- **New field experience activities.** New activities were added to several of the Part I chapters (see for example, Field Experience 2.3, "Levels of Cognitive Demand," and Field Experience 4.7, "Classroom Discussions—Talk Moves").

- **Revised rubrics in Part I chapters**. These focus on teaching skills and are intended to be broad enough that they can be used with any task in that chapter.

- **Grade-level guide added to Expanded Lessons**. Each Expanded Lesson is correlated to a specific grade range and to the *Curriculum Focal Points* and *Common Core State Standards*.

- **Increased focus on diversity**. Each lesson now has specific strategies for English language learners (ELLs) and students with disabilities.

MyEducationLab:
The Power of Classroom Practice

Preparing Teachers for a Changing World (Darling-Hammond & Bransford, 2005) shows that grounding teacher education in real classrooms—among real teachers and students and among actual examples of students' and teachers' work—is an important, and perhaps even essential, part of preparing teachers for the complexities of teaching in today's classrooms. MyEducationLab is an online learning solution that provides contextualized interactive exercises designed to help teacher candidates develop the knowledge and skills that teachers need. All of the activities and exercises in MyEducationLab are built around essential learning outcomes for teachers and are mapped to professional teaching standards. Utilizing classroom video, authentic student and teacher artifacts, and other resources and assessments, the scaffolded learning experiences in MyEducationLab offer you a unique and valuable education tool.

For each topic covered in the course-specific site you will find all of the following features and resources.

Connection to National Standards

Now it is easier than ever to see how coursework is connected to national standards. Each topic and activity on MyEducationLab lists intended learning outcomes connected to the National Council of Teacher of Mathematics *Mathematics Teaching Today* standards and the *Common Core State Standards* (Standards for Mathematical Practice and Standards for Mathematical Content).

Assignments and Activities

Designed to enhance your understanding of concepts covered in class, these assignable exercises show mathematical concepts and instruction in action. The questions provided help teacher candidates deepen mathematics knowledge necessary for teaching as well as pedagogical content knowledge and present a unique opportunity to practice synthesizing and applying concepts and strategies they read about in the book. (Correct answers for these assignments are available to the instructor only.) Assignments are built around authentic classroom video, IMAP video, enVision Math and other curriculum samples, and childrens' work samples.

Building Teaching Skills and Dispositions

These unique and powerful learning units help teacher candidates practice and strengthen skills that are essential to effective teaching. These Building Teaching Skills have a unique three part structure. Part I, "Your Own Understanding," builds and assesses a teacher candidate's content knowledge, including mathematics knowledge for teaching. Part II, "Connection to Students," provides opportunity for analysis of *student work, student solutions, and student thinking* related to the same content in Part I. Part III, "Connections to Teaching Practices," provides opportunities for teacher-candidates to practice the skills necessary to facilitate student understanding of mathematics.

Resources Specific to Your Text

On MyEducationLab you will also find book-specific resources including Blackline Masters, Expanded Lesson activities, and artifact analysis activities.

Course Resources

The Course Resources section of MyEducationLab is designed to help you put together an effective lesson plan; prepare for and begin your career; navigate your first year of teaching; and understand key educational standards, policies, and laws.

It includes the following:

- The **Lesson Plan Builder** is an effective and easy-to-use tool that you can use to create, update, and share quality lesson plans. The software also makes it easy to integrate state content standards into any lesson plan.

- The **Preparing a Portfolio** module provides guidelines for creating a high-quality teaching portfolio.

- **Beginning Your Career** offers tips, advice, and other valuable information on:

  - *Resume writing and interviewing*: Includes expert advice on how to write impressive resumes and prepare for job interviews.

  - *Your first year of teaching*: Provides practical tips to set up a first classroom, manage student behavior, and more easily organize for instruction and assessment.

  - *Law and public policies*: Details specific directives and requirements you need to understand under the No Child Left Behind Act and the Individuals with Disabilities Education Improvement Act of 2004.

Certification and Licensure

The Certification and Licensure section is designed to help you pass your licensure exam by giving you access to state test requirements, overviews of what tests cover, and sample test items.

The Certification and Licensure section includes the following:

- **State certification test requirements:** Just click on a state and you will be taken to a list of state certification tests.

- **Licensure exams:** By clicking on the exams you need to take, you will find

  - Basic information about each test

  - Descriptions of what is covered on each test

  - Sample test questions with explanations of correct answers

- **National Evaluation Series™ :** NES from Pearson is an advanced system for educator certification. In MyEducationLab, students can see the tests in the NES, learn what is covered on each exam, and access sample test items with descriptions and rationales of correct answers. You can also purchase interactive online tutorials developed by Pearson Evaluation Systems and the Pearson Teacher Education and Development group.

- **ETS Online Praxis Tutorials:** Here you can purchase interactive online tutorials developed by ETS and by the Pearson Teacher Education and Development group. Tutorials are available for the Praxis I exams and for select Praxis II exams.

Visit www.myeducationlab.com for a demonstration of this exciting new online teaching resource.

SUPPLEMENTS FOR INSTRUCTORS

Qualified college adopters can contact their Pearson sales representatives for information on ordering any of the supplements below. The instructor supplements are also available for download at www.pearsonhighered.com/educator.

Instructor's Resource Manual/Text Bank The Instructor's Resource Manual for the eighth edition includes a wealth of resources designed to help instructors teach the course, including chapter notes, activity suggestions, suggested assessments, and test questions.

MyTest Pearson *MyTest* is a powerful assessment generation program that helps instructors easily create and print quizzes and exams. Questions and tests are authored online, allowing flexibility and the ability to efficiently create and print assessments anytime, anywhere. Instructors can access Pearson MyTest and their test bank files by going to www.pearsonmytest.com to log in, register, or request access.

PowerPoint Presentation Ideal for instructors to use for lecture presentations or student handouts, the PowerPoint presentation provides dozens of ready-to-use graphic and text images tied to the text.

ACKNOWLEDGMENTS

Many talented people have contributed to the success of this book, and we are deeply grateful to all those who have assisted over the years. Without the success of the first edition, there would certainly not have been a second, much less eight editions. John worked closely with Warren Crown, John Dossey, Bob Gilbert, and Steven Willoughby, who gave time and great care in offering detailed comments on the original manuscript.

In preparing this eighth edition, we have received thoughtful input from the following educators who offered comments on the seventh edition or on the manuscript for the eighth:

Margaret Adams, *University of North Carolina at
   Charlotte*
Joohi Lee, *University of Texas at Arlington*
Sandra J. Phifer, *Metropolitan State College of Denver*
Diana Piccolo, *Missouri State University*
Janet Lynne Tassell, *Western Kentucky University*

Each reviewer challenged us to think through important issues. Many specific suggestions have found their way into this book, and their feedback helped us focus on important ideas. We are indebted to these committed professionals.

We received indispensable support and advice from colleagues at Pearson. We are privileged to work with our acquisitions editor, Kelly Villella Canton, who continues to offer us invaluable advice and encouragement in our every step of the revision process. She is able to respond to complicated questions with insightful approaches and a comforting grace. We also are fortunate to work with Christina Robb, our senior development editor, who was able to keep us on track and focused on the important decisions that would make the book a better product for pre-service and in-service teachers. We also wish to thank Karla Walsh and the rest of the production and editing team at Electronic Publishing Services Inc. Our thanks also goes to Elizabeth Todd Brown and Elizabeth Popelka, who helped write some of the supplementary materials.

We also would each like to thank our families for their many contributions and support. On behalf of John, we thank his wife of more than 40 years, Sharon. Sharon was John's biggest supporter in this process and remained a sounding board for his many decisions as he wrote the first six editions of this book. We also thank his daughters, Bridget (a fifth-grade teacher in Chesterfield County, Virginia) and Gretchen (an associate professor of psychology at Rutgers University–Newark). They were John's first students and he tested many ideas that are in this book by their sides. We can't forget those who called John "Math Grandpa": his granddaughters, Maggie, Aidan, and Gracie.

From Karen Karp: I would like to express thanks to my husband, Bob Ronau, who as a mathematics educator graciously helped me think about decisions while offering insights and encouragement. In addition, I thank my children, Matthew, Tammy, Joshua, Misty, Matt, Christine, Jeffrey, and Pamela for their kind support and inspiration. I also am grateful for my wonderful grandchildren, Jessica, Zane, and Madeline, who have helped deepen my understanding about how children think.

From Jennifer Bay-Williams: I am so grateful to my husband, Mitch, who offers support, guidance, and wisdom to my writing, and my children, MacKenna (8 years) and Nicolas (6 years), who enjoy doing a little extra math from time to time. My parents, siblings, and nieces and nephews have all contributed ideas and support to the writing of this edition. Finally, I want to thank Brandy Jones, who has been invaluable in helping me find research to inform my writing for this edition.

Most importantly, we thank all the teachers and students who gave of themselves by assessing what worked and what didn't work in the many iterations of this book. In particular for the eighth edition, we thank teachers who generously tested activities and provided student work for us: Kyle Patterson, Kim George, Kelly Eaton, Sarah Bush, and Elizabeth Popelka. If future teachers learn how to teach mathematics from this book, it is because teachers and children before them shared their best ideas and thinking with the authors. We continue to seek suggestions from teachers who use this book, so please email us at teachingdevelopmentally@gmail.com with any ideas or insights you would like to share.

Chapter 1

Teaching Mathematics in the 21st Century

In this changing world, those who understand and can do mathematics will have significantly enhanced opportunities and options for shaping their futures. Mathematical competence opens doors to productive futures. A lack of mathematical competence keeps those doors closed.... All students should have the opportunity and the support necessary to learn significant mathematics with depth and understanding.

NCTM (2000, p. 50)

Someday soon you will find yourself in front of a class of students, or perhaps you are already teaching. What general ideas will guide the way you will teach mathematics? This book will help you become comfortable with the mathematics content of the pre-K–8 curriculum. You will also learn about research-based strategies for helping students come to know mathematics and be confident in their ability to do mathematics. These two things—your knowledge of mathematics and how students learn mathematics—are the most important tools you can acquire to be an effective teacher of mathematics. What you teach, however, is largely influenced by state and national standards, as well as local curriculum guides.

For more than two decades, mathematics education has been undergoing steady change. The impetus for this change, in both the content of school mathematics and the way mathematics is taught, can be traced to various sources, including knowledge gained from research. One significant factor in this change has been the professional leadership of the National Council of Teachers of Mathematics (NCTM), the world's largest mathematics education organization, with more than 90,000 members (www.nctm.org). Another factor is the public or political pressure for change in mathematics education due largely to less-than-stellar U.S. student performance in national and international studies. The federal legislation commonly referred to as the No Child Left Behind Act (NCLB) presses for higher levels of achievement, more testing, and increased teacher accountability. Although all agree that we should have high expectations for students, there seems to be little consensus on what the best approach is to improve student learning. According to NCTM, "Learning mathematics is maximized when teachers focus on mathematical thinking and reasoning" (NCTM, 2009, n.d.).

As you prepare to help students learn mathematics, it is important to have some perspective on the forces that effect change in the mathematics classroom. This chapter addresses the leadership that NCTM provides for mathematics education as well as other important influences.

Ultimately, it is you, the teacher, who will shape mathematics for the students you teach. Your beliefs about what it means to know and do mathematics and about how students make sense of mathematics will affect how you approach instruction.

The National Standards-Based Movement

The momentum for reform in mathematics education began in the early 1980s in response to a "back to basics" movement that emphasized "reading, writing, and arithmetic." As a result, problem solving became an important strand in the mathematics curriculum. The work of Jean Piaget and other developmental psychologists helped to focus research on how students can best learn mathematics.

This momentum came to a head in 1989, when NCTM published *Curriculum and Evaluation Standards for School Mathematics* and the standards movement or reform era in mathematics education began. It continues today. No other document has ever had such an enormous effect on school mathematics or on any other area of the curriculum.

In 1991, NCTM published *Professional Standards for Teaching Mathematics*, which articulates a vision of teaching mathematics based on the expectation described in the *Curriculum and Evaluation Standards* that significant mathematics achievement is a vision for all students, not just a few. In 1995, NCTM added to the collection the *Assessment Standards for School Mathematics*, which focuses on the importance of integrating assessment with instruction and indicates the key role that assessment plays in implementing change (see Chapter 5).

In 2000, NCTM released *Principles and Standards for School Mathematics* as an update of its original standards document. Combined, these two standards documents have prompted a revolutionary reform movement in mathematics education, not just in the United States and Canada but throughout the world.

As these documents influenced state policy and teacher practice, ongoing debate continued about the U.S. curriculum. In particular, many argued that instead of hurrying through many topics every year, the curriculum needed to address content more deeply. Guidance was needed in deciding what mathematics content should be taught at each grade level. In 2006, NCTM released *Curriculum Focal Points*, a little publication with a big message—the mathematics taught at each grade level needs to focus, go into more depth, and explicitly show connections. The standards movement had gained significant momentum and engaged more than just the mathematics education community as business and political leaders became interested in a national vision for K–12 mathematics curriculum.

In 2010, the Council of Chief State School Officers (CCSSO) presented *Common Core State Standards*—grade-level specific standards that incorporated ideas from *Curriculum Focal Points* as well as international curriculum documents. A large majority of U.S. states adopted these as their standards. In less than 25 years, the standards movement transformed the country from having little to no national vision on what mathematics should be taught and when, to a widely shared vision of what students should know and be able to do at each grade level.

In the following sections, we discuss these more recent documents because their message is critical to your work as a teacher of mathematics.

Principles and Standards for School Mathematics

Principles and Standards for School Mathematics (NCTM, 2000) provides guidance and direction for teachers and other leaders in pre-K–12 mathematics education.

The Six Principles

One of the most important features of *Principles and Standards for School Mathematics* is the articulation of six principles fundamental to high-quality mathematics education:

- Equity
- Curriculum
- Teaching
- Learning
- Assessment
- Technology

According to *Principles and Standards*, these principles must be "deeply intertwined with school mathematics programs" (NCTM, 2000, p. 12). The principles make it clear that excellence in mathematics education involves much more than simply listing content objectives.

The Equity Principle

> Excellence in mathematics education requires equity—high expectations and strong support for all students. (NCTM, 2000, p. 12)

The strong message of the Equity Principle is high expectations for all students. All students must have the opportunity and adequate support to learn mathematics "regardless of personal characteristics, backgrounds, or physical challenges" (p. 12). The significance of high expectations for all is interwoven throughout the document.

The Curriculum Principle

> A curriculum is more than a collection of activities: it must be coherent, focused on important mathematics, and well articulated across the grades. (NCTM, 2000, p. 14)

Coherence speaks to the importance of building instruction around "big ideas"—both in the curriculum and in daily classroom instruction. Students must be helped to see that mathematics is an integrated whole, not a collection of isolated bits and pieces.

Mathematical ideas can be considered "important" if they help develop other ideas, link one idea to another, or serve to illustrate the discipline of mathematics as a human endeavor.

The Teaching Principle

> Effective mathematics teaching requires understanding what students know and need to learn and then challenging and supporting them to learn it well. (NCTM, 2000, p. 16)

What students learn about mathematics depends almost entirely on the experiences that teachers provide every day in the classroom. To provide high-quality mathematics education, teachers must (1) understand deeply the mathematics content they are teaching; (2) understand how students learn mathematics, including a keen awareness of the individual mathematical development of their own students and common misconceptions; and (3) select meaningful instructional tasks and generalizable strategies that will enhance learning. "Teachers' actions are what encourage students to think, question, solve problems, and discuss their ideas, strategies, and solutions" (p. 18).

The Learning Principle

> Students must learn mathematics with understanding, actively building new knowledge from experience and prior knowledge. (NCTM, 2000, p. 20)

The learning principle is based on two fundamental ideas. First, learning mathematics with understanding is essential. Mathematics today requires not only computational skills but also the ability to think and reason mathematically to solve new problems and learn new ideas that students will face in the future.

Second, students *can* learn mathematics with understanding. Learning is enhanced in classrooms where students are required to evaluate their own ideas and those of others, are encouraged to make mathematical conjectures and test them, and are helped to develop their reasoning and sense-making skills.

The Assessment Principle

> Assessment should support the learning of important mathematics and furnish useful information to both teachers and students . . . Assessment should not merely be done *to* students; rather, it should also be done *for* students, to guide and enhance their learning. (NCTM, 2000, p. 22)

Ongoing assessment highlights for students the most important mathematics concepts. Assessment that includes ongoing observation and student interaction encourages students to articulate and, thus, clarify their ideas. Feedback from daily assessment helps students establish goals and become more independent learners.

Assessment should be a major factor in making instructional decisions. By continuously gathering data about students' understanding of concepts and growth in reasoning, teachers can better make the daily decisions that support student learning. For assessment to be effective, teachers must use a variety of assessment techniques, understand their mathematical goals deeply, and have a research-supported notion of students' thinking or common misunderstandings of the mathematics that is being developed.

The Technology Principle

> Technology is essential in teaching and learning mathematics; it influences the mathematics that is taught and enhances students' learning. (NCTM, 2000, p. 24)

Calculators, computers, and other emerging technologies are essential tools for doing and learning mathematics. Technology permits students to focus on mathematical ideas, to reason, and to solve problems in ways that are often impossible without these tools. Technology enhances the learning of mathematics by allowing for increased exploration, enhanced representation, and communication of ideas.

The Five Content Standards

Principles and Standards includes four grade bands: pre-K–2, 3–5, 6–8, and 9–12. The emphasis on preschool recognizes the need to highlight the critical years before students enter kindergarten. There is a common set of five content standards throughout the grades:

- Number and Operations
- Algebra
- Geometry
- Measurement
- Data Analysis and Probability

Each content standard includes a set of goals applicable to all grade bands followed by grade-band chapters that provide specific expectations for what students should know. Although the same five content standards apply across all grades, you should not infer that each strand has equal weight or emphasis in every grade band. Number and Operations is the most heavily emphasized strand from pre-K through grade 5 and continues to be important in the middle grades, with a lesser emphasis in grades 9–12. This is in contrast to Algebra, which moves from an emphasis related to number and operations in the early grades and builds to a strong focus in the middle and high school grade bands. Section II of this book (Chapters 8 through 23) is devoted to elaborating on these content standards.

The Five Process Standards

Following the five content standards, *Principles and Standards* lists five process standards:

- Problem Solving
- Reasoning and Proof
- Communication
- Connections
- Representation

The process standards refer to the mathematical processes through which students should acquire and use mathematical knowledge. The statement of the five process standards can be found in Table 1.1.

TABLE 1.1

THE FIVE PROCESS STANDARDS FROM *PRINCIPLES AND STANDARDS FOR SCHOOL MATHEMATICS*	
Problem Solving Standard Instructional programs from prekindergarten through grade 12 should enable all students to—	• Build new mathematical knowledge through problem solving • Solve problems that arise in mathematics and in other contexts • Apply and adapt a variety of appropriate strategies to solve problems • Monitor and reflect on the process of mathematical problem solving
Reasoning and Proof Standard Instructional programs from prekindergarten through grade 12 should enable all students to—	• Recognize reasoning and proof as fundamental aspects of mathematics • Make and investigate mathematical conjectures • Develop and evaluate mathematical arguments and proofs • Select and use various types of reasoning and methods of proof
Communication Standard Instructional programs from prekindergarten through grade 12 should enable all students to—	• Organize and consolidate their mathematical thinking through communication • Communicate their mathematical thinking coherently and clearly to peers, teachers, and others • Analyze and evaluate the mathematical thinking and strategies of others • Use the language of mathematics to express mathematical ideas precisely
Connections Standard Instructional programs from prekindergarten through grade 12 should enable all students to—	• Recognize and use connections among mathematical ideas • Understand how mathematical ideas interconnect and build on one another to produce a coherent whole • Recognize and apply mathematics in contexts outside of mathematics
Representation Standard Instructional programs from prekindergarten through grade 12 should enable all students to—	• Create and use representations to organize, record, and communicate mathematical ideas • Select, apply, and translate among mathematical representations to solve problems • Use representations to model and interpret physical, social, and mathematical phenomena

Source: Standards are listed with permission of the National Council of Teachers of Mathematics (NCTM). NCTM does not endorse the content or validity of these alignments. Reprinted with permission from *Principles and Standards for School Mathematics,* copyright © 2000 by the National Council of Teachers of Mathematics, Inc. www.nctm.org.

The process standards should not be regarded as separate content or strands in the mathematics curriculum. Rather, they direct the methods of doing all mathematics and, therefore, should be seen as integral components of all mathematics learning and teaching. To teach in a way that reflects these process standards is one of the best definitions of what it means to teach "according to the *Standards*."

The Problem Solving standard describes problem solving as the vehicle through which students develop mathematical ideas. Learning and doing mathematics *as you solve problems* is probably the most significant message in the *Standards* documents.

The Reasoning and Proof standard emphasizes the logical thinking that helps us decide if and why our answers make sense. Students need to develop the habit of providing a rationale as an integral part of every answer. It is essential for students to learn the value of justifying ideas through logical argument.

The Communication standard points to the importance of being able to talk about, write about, describe, and explain mathematical ideas. Learning to communicate in mathematics fosters interaction and exploration of ideas in the classroom as students learn through active discussions of their thinking. No better way exists for wrestling with or cementing an idea than attempting to articulate it to others.

The Connections standard has two parts. First, it is important to connect within and among mathematical ideas. For example, fractional parts of a whole are connected to concepts of decimals and percents. Students need opportunities to see how mathematical concepts build on one another in a network of connected ideas.

Second, mathematics should be connected to the real world and to other disciplines. Students should see that mathematics plays a significant role in art, science, language arts, and social studies. This suggests that mathematics should frequently be integrated with other discipline areas and that applications of mathematics should be explored in real world contexts.

The Representation standard emphasizes the use of symbols, charts, graphs, manipulatives, and diagrams as powerful methods of expressing mathematical ideas and relationships. Symbolism in mathematics, along with visual aids such as charts and graphs, should be understood by students as ways of communicating mathematical ideas to others. Moving from one representation to another is an important way to add depth of understanding to a newly formed idea.

Members of NCTM have free online access to the *Principles and Standards* as well as the three previous standards documents. Nonmembers can sign up for 120 days of free access to the *Principles and Standards* at www.nctm.org.

Curriculum Focal Points: A Quest for Coherence

Curriculum Focal Points for Prekindergarten through Grade 8 Mathematics: A Quest for Coherence (NCTM, 2006) pinpoints mathematical "targets" for each grade level that specify the big ideas for the most significant concepts and skills. At each grade, three essential areas (focal points) are described as the primary focus of that year's instruction. The topics relating to that focus are organized to show the importance of a *coherent* curriculum rather than a curriculum with a list of isolated topics. The expectation is that three focal points along with integrated process skills and connecting experiences form the fundamental content of each grade. Besides focusing instruction, the document provides guidance to professionals about ways to refine and streamline curriculum in light of competing priorities.

Common Core State Standards

As noted earlier, the national dialogue on improving mathematics teaching and learning extends beyond mathematics educators. State policy makers and elected officials have also considered NCTM standards documents, international assessments, and research on the best way to prepare students to be "college and career ready." The state governors (National Governors Association Center for Best Practices) and the Council of Chief State School Officers (CCSSO) collaborated with many other professional groups and entities to develop such benefits as shared expectations for K–12 students across states, a focused set of mathematics content standards and practices, and efficiency of material and assessment development (Porter, McMaken,

Hwang, & Yang, 2011). As a result, they created the *Common Core State Standards for Mathematics* (which can be downloaded at www.corestandards.org). Like *Curriculum Focal Points*, this document articulates an overview of *critical areas* for each grade from kindergarten through 8 to provide a coherent curriculum built around big ideas. These larger groups of related standards are called *domains*, and there are eleven that relate to grades K–8 (see Figure 1.1).

At this time approximately 44 of the 50 states (and Washington, D.C., and the Virgin Islands) have adopted the *Common Core State Standards*. Notice that these standards are silent on preschool-aged students, so the use of the *Curriculum Focal Points* remains significant in making curricular decisions for this age group.

Mathematical Practice. The *Common Core State Standards* goes beyond specifying mathematics content to include Standards for Mathematical Practice. These are "'processes and proficiencies' with longstanding importance in mathematics education" (CCSSO, 2010, p. 6) that are founded on the five NCTM process standards and the components of mathematical proficiency identified by NRC in their important document *Adding It Up* (National Research Council, 2001). Teachers must develop these mathematical practices in all students (CCSSO, 2010, pp. 7–8) as described briefly in Table 1.2. (A more detailed description of the Standards for Mathematical Practice can be found in Appendix A.)

Learning Progressions. The *Common Core State Standards* were developed with strong consideration given to building coherence through the research on what is known about the development of students' understanding of mathematics

Kindergarten	Grade 1	Grade 2	Grade 3	Grade 4	Grade 5	Grade 6	Grade 7	Grade 8
Counting and Cardinality								
	Operations and Algebraic Thinking					Expressions and Equations		
	Number and Operations in Base Ten					The Number System		
	Measurement and Data					Statistics and Probability		
	Geometry							
		Number and Operations—Fractions				Ratios and Proportional Relationships		Functions

FIGURE 1.1 *Common Core State Standards* domains by grade level.

TABLE 1.2

THE STANDARDS FOR MATHEMATICAL PRACTICE FROM THE *COMMON CORE STATE STANDARDS*	
K–8 Students Should Be Able To:	
Make sense of problems and persevere in solving them	• Explain the meaning of a problem • Describe possible approaches to a solution • Consider similar problems to gain insights • Use concrete objects or illustrations to think about and solve problems • Monitor and evaluate their progress and change strategy if needed • Check their answers using a different method
Reason abstractly and quantitatively	• Explain the relationship between quantities in problem situations • Represent situations using symbols (e.g., writing expressions or equations) • Create representations that fit the problem • Use flexibly the different properties of operations and objects
Construct viable arguments and critique the reasoning of others	• Understand and use assumptions, definitions, and previous results to explain or justify solutions • Make conjectures by building a logical set of statements • Analyze situations and use counterexamples • Justify conclusions in a way that is understandable to teachers and peers • Compare two possible arguments for strengths and weaknesses
Model with mathematics	• Apply mathematics to solve problems in everyday life • Make assumptions and approximations to simplify a problem • Identify important quantities and use tools to map their relationships • Reflect on the reasonableness of their answer based on the context of the problem
Use appropriate tools strategically	• Consider a variety of tools and choose the appropriate tool (e.g., manipulative, ruler, technology) to support their problem solving • Use estimation to detect possible errors • Use technology to help visualize, explore, and compare information
Attend to precision	• Communicate precisely using clear definitions and appropriate mathematics language • State the meanings of symbols • Specify appropriate units of measure and labels of axes • Use a degree of precision appropriate for the problem context
Look for and make use of structure	• Explain mathematical patterns or structures • Shift perspective and see things as single objects or as composed of several objects • Explain why and when properties of operations are true in a context
Look for and express regularity in repeated reasoning	• Notice if calculations are repeated and use information to solve problems • Use and justify the use of general methods or shortcuts • Self-assess to see whether a strategy makes sense as they work, checking for reasonableness prior to getting the answer

Source: Adapted from Council of Chief State School Officers. (2010). *Common Core State Standards.* Copyright © 2010 National Governors Association Center for Best Practices and Council of Chief State School Officers. All rights reserved.

over time (Cobb & Jackson, 2011). The resulting selections of topics at particular grades reflects not only rigorous mathematics but also what is known from current research and practice about learning progressions—sometimes referred to as *learning trajectories* (Confrey, Maloney, & Nguyen, 2011; Daro, Mosher, & Corcoran, 2011; Sarama & Clements, 2009) or teaching-learning paths (Cross, Woods, & Schweingruber, 2009). It is these learning progressions that can help teachers know what came before as well as what to expect next as students reach "key way-points" (Corcoran, Mosher, & Rogat, 2009) on the road to learning mathematics concepts. These progressions identify the interim goals students should reach on the path to desired learning targets (Daro, Mosher, & Corcoran, 2011). Although these paths are not identical for all students, they can inform the order of instructional experiences that will support movement toward understanding and application of mathematics concepts. Go to http://math.arizona.edu/~ime/progressions to find progressions for the domains in the *Common Core State Standards.*

Assessments. New summative assessments are being developed that will be aligned to the *Common Core State Standards.* The assessments will focus on both the grade-level content standards and the standards for mathematical practice. This process would eliminate the need for each state to develop their own assessments for the standards, a problem that has existed since the beginning of the standards era.

Professional Standards for Teaching Mathematics and Mathematics Teaching Today

In addition to curriculum-related standards, NCTM has developed related standards documents about teaching. *Professional Standards for Teaching Mathematics* (1991) and its companion document, *Mathematics Teaching Today* (2007a), use detailed classroom stories (vignettes) of real teachers to illustrate the careful, reflective work that is required of effective teachers of mathematics.

Mathematics Teaching Today and its predecessor are excellent resources to help you envision your role as a teacher in creating a classroom that supports teaching through problem solving. As you read the chapters in this book, you will note that the following seven standards are developed in ways that will support your growth as a teacher of mathematics. (See Appendix B for detailed descriptions of these standards.)

1. Knowledge of Mathematics and General Pedagogy
2. Knowledge of Student Mathematical Learning
3. Worthwhile Mathematical Tasks
4. Learning Environment
5. Discourse
6. Reflection on Student Learning
7. Reflection on Teaching Practice

Mathematics Teaching Today lists six major components of the mathematics classroom that are necessary to allow students to develop mathematical understanding:

- Creating an environment that offers all students an equal opportunity to learn
- Focusing on a balance of conceptual understanding and procedural fluency
- Ensuring active student engagement in the NCTM process standards (problem solving, reasoning, communication, connections, and representation)
- Using technology to enhance understanding
- Incorporating multiple assessments aligned with instructional goals and mathematical practices
- Helping students recognize the power of sound reasoning and mathematical integrity (NCTM, 2007a).

PAUSE and REFLECT

Take a moment now to select one or two of the six components that seem especially significant to you and are areas you wish to develop. Why do you think these are the most important to your teaching?

Influences and Pressures on Mathematics Teaching

National and international comparisons of student performance continue to make headlines, provoke public opinion, and pressure legislatures to call for tougher standards backed by testing. The pressures of testing policies exerted on schools and ultimately on teachers may have an impact on instruction.

National and International Studies

Large studies that tell the public how the students are doing in mathematics receive a lot of attention. They influence political decisions as well as provide useful data for mathematics education researchers. Why do these studies matter? Because international and national assessments provide strong evidence that mathematics teaching *must* change if our students are to be competitive in the global market and able to understand the complex issues they must confront as responsible citizens.

National Assessment of Educational Progress. Since the 1960s and at regular intervals, the United States gathers national data on how students are doing in mathematics (and other content areas) through the National Assessment of Educational Progress (NAEP). These data provide an important tool for policy makers and educators to measure the overall improvement of U.S. students over time. Reported in what is called the "Nation's Report Card," NAEP examines both national and state-level trends. NAEP rates fourth-, eighth-, and twelfth-grade students using four achievement levels: below basic, basic, proficient, and advanced (with proficient and advanced representing substantial grade-level achievement). The criterion-referenced test is designed to reflect current curriculum but keeps a few stable items from 1982 for purposes of comparison (Kloosterman, Rutledge, & Kenney, 2009b). In the most recent assessment in 2009, less than half of all U.S. students in grades 4 and 8 performed at the desirable levels of proficient and advanced (39 percent in fourth grade and 34 percent in eighth grade) (National Center for Education Statistics, 2009b). Although No Child Left Behind legislation specifies that all students must be at or above the proficient level by 2014, current NAEP data suggest that goal is likely unattainable. Most troubling, approximately 18 percent of fourth-grade students and 27 percent of eighth-grade students were at the below-basic level. Despite encouraging gains in the NAEP scores over the last 30 years due to important shifts to standards-based instruction (particularly at the elementary level) (Kloosterman, Rutledge, & Kenney, 2009b), U.S. students' performance still reveals some students have disappointing levels of competency. More detailed information can be found at http://nationsreportcard.gov/math_2009.

Trends in International Mathematics and Science Study (TIMSS).

In the mid-1990s, 41 nations participated in the Third International Mathematics and Science Study, the largest study of mathematics and science education ever conducted. Data were gathered in grades 4, 8, and 12 from 500,000 students as well as from teachers. The most widely reported results revealed that U.S. students performed above the international average of the TIMSS countries at the fourth grade, below the average at the eighth grade, and significantly below average at the twelfth grade (U.S. Department of Education, 1997a).

TIMSS studies were repeated in 1999 (38 countries), 2003 (46 countries), and again in 2007 (63 countries). (See http://nces.ed.gov/timss for details.) The 2007 TIMSS found that U.S. fourth and eighth graders were above the international average, but were significantly outperformed by eight countries or parts of countries (Hong Kong, Singapore, Chinese Taipei, Japan, Kazakhstan, Russian Federation, England, and Latvia) at the fourth-grade level and by five countries (Chinese Taipei, Korea, Singapore, Hong Kong, and Japan) at the eighth-grade level. Only 15 percent of U.S. fourth graders and 10 percent of U.S. eighth graders performed above the advanced international benchmark. This is in stark contrast with Singapore at 44 percent at the fourth grade and 32 percent at the eighth grade. The impressive performance by Singapore has led some educators to talk about "Singapore mathematics" as a methodology to be emulated.

A report on the original TIMSS curriculum analysis labeled the U.S. mathematics curriculum "a mile wide and an inch deep" (Schmidt, McKnight, & Raizen, 1996, p. 62), meaning it was found to be unfocused, pursuing many more topics than other countries while engaging in a great deal of repetition. They found the U.S. curriculum attempted to do everything and, as a consequence, rarely provided depth of study, making reteaching all too common.

One of the most interesting components of the study was the videotaping of eighth-grade classrooms in the United States, Australia, and five of the highest-achieving countries. The results indicate that teaching is a cultural activity and, despite similarities, the differences in the ways countries taught mathematics were often striking. In all countries, problems or tasks were frequently used to begin the lesson. However, as a lesson progressed, the way these problems were handled in the United States was in stark contrast to high-achieving countries.

Analysis revealed that although the world is for all purposes unrecognizable from what it was 100 years ago, the U.S. approach to teaching mathematics during the same time frame was essentially unchanged (Stigler & Hiebert, 2009). They found the U.S. teacher begins with a review of previous materials or homework and then demonstrates a problem. Students practice similar problems at their desks, the teacher checks the seatwork, and then assigns problems for either the remainder of the class session or homework. (Sound familiar?) In more than 99.5 percent of the U.S. lessons, the teacher reverts to showing students how to solve the problems. In not one of the 81 U.S. lessons was any high-level mathematics content observed; in contrast, 30 to 40 percent of lessons in Germany and Japan contained high-level mathematics content. Although all teachers knew the research team was coming to videotape, 89 percent of the U.S. lessons consisted exclusively of low-level content. Other countries incorporated a variety of methods, but they frequently used a problem-solving approach with an emphasis on conceptual understanding and students engaged in problem solving (Hiebert et al., 2003). Teaching in the high-achieving countries more closely resembles the recommendations of the NCTM standards than does the teaching in the United States.

Curriculum

As described in the beginning of this chapter, curriculum documents (standards) have a significant influence on what is taught, and even how it is taught. In addition, the textbook is a very influential factor in determining the what, when, and how of actual teaching. What is becoming increasingly complicated is how teachers and school systems attempt to align existing textbooks or other curriculum materials with the *Common Core State Standards*, *Curriculum Focal Points*, or other key documents.

Textbooks greatly influence teaching practice. A teacher using one textbook may be more likely to cover many topics, spend one day on each topic, use a teacher-directed instructional approach, and focus on procedures. Using a different textbook (that is more standards-based), a teacher may devote more time to a concept, teach it more deeply, and use a student-centered approach. Writing, speaking, working in groups, and problem solving are more likely to be commonplace components in current curriculum offerings. The selection of curriculum materials is an important endeavor.

In Section II of this book you will find features describing activities from two standards-based (problem-solving oriented) curriculum programs: *Investigations in Number, Data, and Space* (Grades K–5) and *Connected Mathematics Project* (Grades 6–8). These features are included to offer you some insight into how a textbook can support your implementation of the standards (both the content and the processes/practices).

A Changing World Economy

In his book *The World Is Flat* (2007), Thomas Friedman discusses the need for people to have skills that are lasting and will survive the ever-changing landscape of available jobs. These are what he calls "the untouchables"—the individuals who outlast all the ups and downs of the economy. He suggests people who fit into several broad categories that he defines will not be challenged by a shifting job market. One of his safety-ensuring categories is "math lovers." Friedman points out that in a world that is digitized and surrounded by algorithms, math lovers will always have career opportunities and options.

Now it becomes the job of the teacher to develop this passion in students. As Lynn Arthur Steen, a well-known mathematician and educator, states, "As information becomes ever more quantitative and as society relies increasingly on computers and the data they produce, an innumerate citizen today is as vulnerable as the illiterate peasant of Gutenberg's time" (1997, p. xv).

The changing world influences what should be taught in pre-K–8 mathematics classrooms. As we prepare pre-K–8 students for jobs that possibly do not currently exist, we do know that there are few jobs for people where they just do simple computation. We can predict that there will be work that requires interpreting complex data, designing algorithms to make predictions, and using the ability to approach new problems in a variety of ways.

An Invitation to Learn and Grow

The mathematics education described in the NCTM *Principles and Standards* and new *Common Core State Standards* may not be the same as the mathematics and the mathematics teaching you experienced in grades K through 8. Along the way, you may have had excellent teachers of mathematics who reflect the current reform spirit. Examples of good standards-based curriculum have been around since the early 1990s. But for the most part, after more than two decades the goals of the reform movement have yet to be realized in many of the school districts in North America.

As a practicing or prospective teacher facing the challenge of teaching standards-based mathematics from a problem-solving approach, this book may require you to confront some of your personal beliefs—about what it means to *do mathematics*, how one goes about *learning mathematics*, how to *teach mathematics through reasoning and sense making*, and what it means to *assess mathematics* so that it leads to targeted instructional change.

As part of this personal assessment, you should understand that mathematics is unfortunately seen as the subject that people love to hate. At parties or even at parent–teacher conferences, other adults will respond to the fact that you are a teacher of mathematics with comments such as "I could never do math," or "I can't even balance my checking account." Instead of just dismissing these disclosures, consider what action you can take. Would people confide that

they don't read and hadn't read a book in years? That is not likely. Families' and teachers' attitudes toward mathematics may enhance or detract from students' ability to do math. It is important for you and for students' families to know that mathematics ability is not inherited—anyone can learn mathematics. Moreover, learning mathematics is an essential life skill. You need to find ways of countering these statements, especially if they are stated in the presence of students, pointing out the importance of the topic and the fact that all people have the capacity to learn mathematics. Only in that way can the long-standing sequence that passes this apprehension from family member to child (or in rare cases teacher to student) be broken. There is much joy to be had in solving mathematical problems, and you need to model this and nurture that passion in your students.

Students and adults alike need to think of themselves as mathematicians, in the same way as many think of themselves as readers. As all people interact with our increasingly mathematical and technological world, they need to construct, modify, or integrate new information in many forms. Solving novel problems and approaching circumstances with a mathematical perspective should come as naturally as reading new materials to comprehend facts, insights, or news. Consider how important this is to interpreting and successfully surviving in our economy. Thinking and talking about mathematics instead of focusing on the "one right answer" is a strategy that will serve us well in becoming a society where all citizens are confident that they can do math.

Becoming a Teacher of Mathematics

This book and this course of study are critical to your professional teaching career. The mathematics education course you are taking now or the professional development you are experiencing will be the foundation for much of the mathematics instruction you do in your classroom for the next decade. The authors of this book take that seriously, as we know you do. Therefore, this section lists and describes the characteristics, habits of thought, skills, and dispositions you will need to succeed as a teacher of mathematics.

Knowledge of Mathematics. You will need to have a profound, flexible, and adaptive knowledge of mathematics content (Ma, 1999). This statement is not intended to scare you if you feel that mathematics is not your strong suit, but it is meant to help you prepare for a serious semester of learning about mathematics and how to teach it. The "school effects" for mathematics are great, meaning that unlike other subject areas, where students have frequent interactions with their family or others outside of school on topics such as reading books, exploring nature, or discussing current events, in the area of mathematics what we do in school is often "it" for many students. This adds to the earnestness of your responsibility, because a student's learning for the year in mathematics will likely come only from you.

If you are not sure of a fractional concept or other aspect of mathematics content knowledge, now is the time to make changes in your depth and flexibility of understanding to best prepare for your role as an instructional leader. This book and your professor will help you in that process.

Persistence. You need the ability to stave off frustration and demonstrate persistence. This is the very skill that your students must have to conduct mathematical investigations. As you move through this book and work the problems yourself, you will learn methods and strategies that will help you anticipate the barriers to student learning and identify strategies to get them past these stumbling blocks. It is likely that what works for you as a learner will work for your students. As you experience the material in this book, if you ponder, struggle, talk about your thinking, and reflect on how it all fits or doesn't fit your prior knowledge, then you enhance your repertoire as a teacher. Remember you need to demonstrate these characteristics so your students can model them. Creating opportunities for your students to struggle is part of learning (Stigler & Hiebert, 2009).

Positive Attitude. Arm yourself with a positive attitude toward the subject of mathematics. Research shows that teachers with positive attitudes teach math in more successful ways that result in their students liking math more (Karp, 1991). If in your heart you say, "I never liked math," that will be evident in your instruction. The good news is that research shows that changing attitudes toward mathematics is relatively easy (Tobias, 1995) and that attitude changes are long-lasting (Dweck, 2006). Through expanding your knowledge of the subject and trying new ways to approach problems, you can learn to enjoy mathematical activities. Not only can you acquire a positive attitude toward mathematics, it is essential that you do.

Readiness for Change. Demonstrate a readiness for change, even for change so radical that it may cause disequilibrium. You may find that what is familiar will become unfamiliar and, conversely, what is unfamiliar will become familiar. For example, you may have always referred to "reducing fractions" as the process of changing $\frac{2}{4}$ to $\frac{1}{2}$, but this phrase is not appropriate because it is misleading—the fractions are not getting smaller. Such terminology can lead to mistaken connections. ("Did the reduced fraction go on a diet?") A careful look will point out that *reducing* is not the term to use; rather, you are writing an equivalent fraction that is simplified. Even though you have used the term *reducing* for years, you need to become familiar with more precise language such as "simplifying fractions."

On the other hand, what is unfamiliar will become more comfortable. It may feel uncomfortable for you to be asking students, "Did anyone solve it differently?" especially if you are worried that you won't understand their approach. Yet this is essential to effective teaching. As you bravely use this strategy, it will become comfortable (and you will learn new things!).

Another potentially difficult change is toward an emphasis on concepts as well as procedures. What happens in a procedure-focused classroom when a student doesn't understand division of fractions? A teacher with only procedural knowledge is often left to repeat the procedure louder and slower. "Just change the division sign to multiplication, flip over the second fraction, and multiply." We know this approach doesn't work well, so let's consider an example using $3\frac{1}{2} \div \frac{1}{2} = \underline{\qquad}$. You might relate this division problem to a whole number division problem such as $25 \div 5 = \underline{\qquad}$. A corresponding story problem might be, "How many orders of 5 pizzas are there in a group of 25 pizzas?" Then ask students to put words around the fraction division problem, such as "You plan to serve each guest $\frac{1}{2}$ a pizza. If you have $3\frac{1}{2}$ pizzas, how many guests can you serve?" Yes, there are seven halves in $3\frac{1}{2}$ and therefore 7 guests can be served. Are you surprised that you can do this problem in your head?

To respond to students' challenges, uncertainties, and frustrations you may need to unlearn and relearn mathematical concepts, developing comprehensive understanding and substantial representations along the way. Supporting your mathematics content knowledge on solid, well-supported terrain is your best hope of making a lasting difference—so be ready for change. What you already understand will provide you with many "Aha" moments as you read this book and connect new information to your current mathematics knowledge.

Reflective Disposition. Make time to be self-conscious and reflective. As Steve Leinwand wrote, "If you don't feel inadequate, you're probably not doing the job" (2007, p. 583). No matter whether you are a preservice teacher or an experienced teacher, there is more to learn about the content and methodology of teaching mathematics. The ability to examine oneself for areas that need improvement or to reflect on successes and challenges is critical for growth and development. The best teachers are always trying to improve their practice through the latest article, the newest book, the most recent conference, or by signing up for the next series of professional development opportunities. These teachers don't say, "Oh, that's what I am already doing"; instead, they identify and celebrate one small tidbit that adds to their repertoire. The best teachers never finish learning all that they need to know, they never exhaust the number of new mental connections that they make, and, as a result, they never see teaching as stale or stagnant. An ancient Chinese proverb states, "The best time to plant a tree is twenty years ago; the second best time is today." So, as John Van de Walle said with every new edition, "Enjoy the journey!"

RESOURCES *for Chapter 1*

RECOMMENDED READINGS

Articles

Hoffman, L., & Brahier, D. (2008). Improving the planning and teaching of mathematics by reflecting on research. *Mathematics Teaching in the Middle School, 13* (7), 412–417.
This article addresses how a teacher's philosophy and beliefs influence his or her mathematics instruction. Using TIMSS and NAEP studies as a foundation, the authors talk about posing higher-level problems, asking thought-provoking questions, facing students' frustration, and using mistakes to enhance understanding of concepts. They pose a set of reflective questions that are good for self-assessment or discussions with peers.

Books

Lambdin, D., & Lester, F. K., Jr. (2010). *Teaching and learning mathematics: Translating research for elementary school teachers.* Reston, VA: NCTM.
Using the most current research on the teaching and learning of mathematics, this book translates research into meaningful chapters for classroom teachers. Built around major questions on a variety of topics, the authors highlight the importance of research in helping teachers be reflective and to assist in the day-to-day judgments teachers make as they support all learners.

National Research Council. (2001). *Adding it up: Helping children learn mathematics.* J. Kilpatrick, J. Swafford, & B. Findell (Eds.). Mathematics Learning Study Committee, Center for Education, Division of Behavioral and Social Sciences and Education. Washington, DC: National Academy Press.
The hallmark of this book is the formulation of five strands of "mathematical proficiency": conceptual understanding, procedural fluency, strategic competence, adaptive reasoning, and productive disposition. Educators and policy makers will cite this book for many years to come.

ONLINE RESOURCES

Dare to Compare (NCES Kids' Zone)
http://nces.ed.gov/nceskids/eyk/index.asp
See how your students perform compared to peers from around the world on items used on past administrations of the grades 4 and 8 NAEP and grades 4, 8, and 12 TIMSS.

Illuminations
http://illuminations.nctm.org
A companion website to NCTM provides lessons, interactive applets, dynamic paper, and links to websites for learning and teaching mathematics.

Illustrative Mathematics Project
http://illustrativemathematics.org
This site provides tools and support for the *Common Core State Standards.* It includes multiple ways to look at the standards across grades and domains as well as provides task and problems that will illustrate individual standards.

National Council of Teachers of Mathematics
www.nctm.org
Here you can discover everything about NCTM and its resources to support your work. Also find an overview of several standards-based documents, position statements, research-based clips and briefs, free access to interactive digital lessons, professional development resources, membership and conference information, online publications store, links to related sites, and much more.

Progressions Documents for the Common Core Math Standards
http://math.arizona.edu/~ime/progressions
This site provides the learning progressions based on mathematical structure and students' cognitive development at given grades across the domains in the *Common Core State Standards.*

REFLECTIONS *on Chapter 1*

WRITING TO LEARN

At the end of each chapter of this book, you will find a series of questions under this same heading. The questions are designed to help you reflect on important ideas of the chapter. Writing (or talking with a peer) is an excellent way to explore new ideas and incorporate them into your own knowledge base.

1. What are the five content strands (standards) defined by *Principles and Standards*? How are they emphasized differently in different grade bands?

2. What is meant by a *process* as referred to in the *Principles and Standards* process standards? Give a brief description of each of the five process standards.

3. Describe two results derived from TIMSS data—one about students' performance and one about teachers' teaching. What are the implications?

4. What are the Standards for Mathematical Practice? How do they relate to the *Common Core State Standards*?

FOR DISCUSSION AND EXPLORATION

1. Examine a textbook at any grade level of your choice. If possible, use a teacher's edition. Page through any chapter and look for signs of the five NCTM process standards or the eight CCSSO Standards for Mathematical Practice. To what extent are students who are being taught from that textbook likely to be doing and learning mathematics in ways described by those processes or practices? What would you have to do to supplement the general approach of that text?

MyEducationLab™

Go to the MyEducationLab (www.myeducationlab.com) for Math Methods and familiarize yourself with the content. Much of the site content is organized topically. The topics include all of the following to support your learning in the course:

- Learning outcomes for important mathematics methods course topics aligned with the national standards
- Assignments and Activities, tied to these learning outcomes and standards, that can help you more deeply understand course content
- Building Teaching Skills and Dispositions learning units that allow you to apply and practice your understanding of the core mathematics content and teaching skills

Your instructor has a correlation guide that aligns the exercises on the topical portion of the site with your book's chapters.

On MyEducationLab you will also find book-specific resources including Blackline Masters, Expanded Lesson Activities, and Artifact Analysis Activities.

Field Experience Guide
CONNECTIONS

The *Field Experience Guide: Resources for Teachers of Elementary and Middle School Mathematics* (FEG) is a workbook designed to respond to both the variety of teacher preparation programs and NCATE's recommendation that students have the opportunity to engage in diverse activities. At the end of each chapter in this book, you will find notes that connect chapter content to FEG activities and experiences. Many of the field experiences focus on aligning practice with both the NCTM and CCSSO standards. For example, see the observation protocol for shifts in the classroom environment (FEG 1.2), a teacher interview based on the teaching standards (FEG 1.4), and observation protocol for the process standards (FEG 4.1). Developing a reflective disposition is the purpose of FEG 3.7, 4.9, 5.5, and 6.4. These opportunities for reflection focus on your students' learning and your own professional growth.

Chapter 2

Exploring What It Means to Know and Do Mathematics

No matter how lucidly and patiently teachers explain to their students, they cannot understand for their students.

Schifter and Fosnot (1993, p. 9)

What does it mean to know a mathematics topic? Take division of fractions, for example. If you know this topic well, what do you know? The answer is more than being able to do a procedure (e.g., invert the second fraction and multiply). Knowing division of fractions means that you can think of examples or situations, use alternative strategies to solve problems, estimate an answer, draw a diagram to show what happens when a number is divided by a fraction, and describe in general what it means.

This chapter is about the learning theory of teaching developmentally and the knowledge necessary for students to learn mathematics with understanding. You might consider this chapter the what, why, and how of teaching mathematics. The *how* is addressed first—how should mathematics be experienced by a learner? Second, *why* should mathematics look this way? And, finally, *what* does it mean to understand mathematics?

What Does It Mean to Do Mathematics?

Mathematics is more than completing sets of exercises or mimicking processes the teacher explains. Doing mathematics means generating strategies for solving problems, applying those approaches, seeing if they lead to solutions, and checking to see whether your answers make sense. Doing mathematics in classrooms should closely model the act of doing mathematics in the real world.

Mathematics Is the Science of Pattern and Order

This heading is a wonderfully simple description of mathematics, found in the thought-provoking publication *Everybody Counts* (Mathematical Sciences Education Board, 1989). This emphasis challenges the popular view of mathematics as a discipline dominated by computation. Science is a process of figuring out or making sense, and mathematics is the science of concepts and processes that have a pattern of regularity and logical order. Finding and exploring this regularity or order, and then making sense of it, is what doing mathematics is all about.

Even the youngest schoolchildren can and should be involved in the science of pattern and order. Have you ever noticed that these combinations all have the same sum?

$$6 + 7$$
$$5 + 8$$
$$4 + 9$$

Do you see a pattern? What are the relationships between these examples? In multiplication, have you ever wondered why an odd number times an odd number always generates an odd answer, an even number times an even number is always an even number, and an even number times an odd number is always an odd number? Why is this true?

Patterns are central to algebra, too. Imagine sending a toy car down a ramp. Does the height of the ramp determine how far the car will roll? Through exploring different ramp heights and measuring the distance the toy cars travel, you can see whether there is a pattern, which leads to a general rule—a function—to describe the relationship between ramp height and distance traveled by the car.

Engaging in the science of pattern and order—*doing mathematics*—takes time and effort (for teachers as they plan and for students as they learn). Basic facts and basic skills such as computation of whole numbers, fractions, and decimals are important in enabling students to be able to *do* mathematics. But if taught only for the sake of doing these calculations by rote, students will be not be prepared to do the mathematics required in the 21st century. To "master" these facts and procedures by imitating a teacher's demonstration and/or through memorization is no more doing mathematics than playing scales on the piano is making music.

 PAUSE and REFLECT

Envision for a moment an elementary or middle school mathematics class where students are doing mathematics as "a study of patterns." What do you see as you observe this class? Think of three ideas, and then read about the classroom environment. ●

A Classroom Environment for Doing Mathematics

Doing mathematics begins with posing worthwhile tasks and then creating an environment where students take risks and share and defend mathematical ideas. Students are actively engaged in solving problems, and teachers are posing questions that encourage students to make connections and understand the mathematics they are exploring.

The Language of Doing Mathematics.   Children in traditional mathematics classes often describe mathematics as imitating what the teacher shows them. Instructions to students given by teachers or in textbooks ask students to listen, copy, memorize, drill, and compute. These are lower-level thinking activities and do not adequately prepare students for the real act of doing mathematics. In contrast, the following verbs engage students in doing mathematics:

compare	explain	predict
conjecture	explore	represent
construct	formulate	solve
describe	investigate	use
develop	justify	verify

These verbs lead to opportunities for higher-level thinking and encompass "making sense" and "figuring out." Children engaged in these actions in mathematics classes will be actively thinking about the mathematical ideas that are involved. In observing a third-grade classroom where the teacher used this approach to teaching mathematics, researchers found that students became "doers" of mathematics. In other words the students began to take the math ideas to the next level by (1) connecting to previous material, (2) responding with information beyond the required response, and (3) conjecturing or

predicting (Fillingim & Barlow, 2010). When this happens on a daily basis, students are getting an empowering message: "You are capable of making sense of this—you are capable of doing mathematics!"

The Classroom Environment for Doing Mathematics.   Classrooms where students are making sense of mathematics do not happen by accident—they happen because the teacher establishes practices and expectations that encourage risk taking, reasoning, sharing, and so on. The list below provides expectations that are often cited as ones that support students in doing mathematics (Clarke & Clarke, 2004, CCSSO, 2010, Hiebert et al., 1997, NCTM, 2007).

1. *Persistence, effort, and concentration are important in learning mathematics.* Engaging in productive struggle is important in learning! The more a student stays with a problem, the more likely they are to get it right. Getting a tough problem right leads to a stronger sense of accomplishment than getting a quick, easy problem correct.
2. *Students share their ideas.* Everyone's ideas are important, and hearing different ideas helps students to become strategic in selecting good strategies.
3. *Students listen to each other.* All students have something to contribute and these ideas should be considered and evaluated for whether they will work in that situation.
4. *Errors or strategies that didn't work are opportunities for learning.* Mistakes are opportunities for learning—why did that approach not work? Could it be adapted and work or is a completely different approach needed? Doing mathematics involves monitoring and reflecting on the process—catching and adjusting errors along the way.
5. *Students look for and discuss connections.* Students should see connections between different strategies to solve a particular problem, as well as connections to other mathematics concepts and to real contexts and situations. When students look for and discuss connections, they see mathematics as worthwhile and important, rather than an isolated collection of facts.

Notice who is doing the thinking, the talking, and the mathematics—the students. Mathematics requires effort, and it is important that students, families, and the community acknowledge and honor the fact that effort is what leads to learning in mathematics (National Mathematics Advisory Panel, 2008). In fact, a review of research on what connects mathematics teaching practice to student learning found that two things result in conceptual understanding: *making mathematics relationships explicit* and *engaging students in productive struggle* (Bay-Williams, 2010; Hiebert & Grouws, 2007).

The teacher's role is making mathematical relationships explicit is to be sure that students are making the connections that are implied in a task. For example, asking students to relate today's topic to one they investigated last week, or by asking "How is Lisa's strategy like Marco's strategy?" when the two students have picked different ways to solve a problem, are ways to be "explicit" about mathematical relationships. The focus is on students' applying their prior knowledge, testing ideas, making connections and comparisons, and making conjectures.

Have you ever just wanted to think through something yourself, without being interrupted or told how to do it? Yet, how often in mathematics class does this happen? As soon as a student pauses in solving a problem the teacher steps in to show or explain. While this may initially help the student reach the answer, it does not help the student learn mathematics—engaging in productive struggle is what helps students learn mathematics. Notice the importance of both words in "productive struggle." Students must have the tools and prior knowledge to solve a problem, and not be given a problem that is out of reach, or they will struggle without being productive; yet students should not be given tasks that are straightforward and easy, or they will not be struggling with mathematical ideas. When students (even very young students) know that struggle is expected as part of the process of doing mathematics, they embrace the struggle and feel success when they reach a solution (Carter, 2008).

An Invitation to Do Mathematics

The purpose of this section is to provide you with opportunities to engage in the science of pattern and order—to *do* some mathematics. If possible, find one or two peers to work with you so that you can experience sharing and exchanging ideas. For each problem posed, allow yourself to try to (1) make connections within the mathematics (i.e., make mathematical relationships explicit) and (2) engage in productive struggle.

We will explore four different problems. None requires mathematics beyond elementary school mathematics—not even algebra. But the problems do require higher-level thinking and reasoning. Try out your ideas! Have fun!

Problems

1. Start and Jump Numbers: Searching for Patterns

You will need to make a list of numbers that begin with a "start number" and increase by a fixed amount we will call the "jump number." First try 3 as the start number and 5 as the jump number. Write the start number at the top of your list, then 8, 13, and so on, "jumping" by 5 each time until your list extends to about 130.

Examine this list of numbers and record the patterns you see. Share your ideas with the group, and write down every pattern you agree really is a pattern.

◉ STOP

Do not read on until you have listed as many patterns as you can identify. ●

A Few Ideas. Here are some questions to guide your pattern search:

- Do you see at least one alternating pattern?
- Have you looked at odd and even numbers?
- What can you say about the numbers in the tens place?
- Have you tried doing any adding of numbers? Numbers in the list? Digits in the numbers?
- Do the patterns change when the numbers are greater than 100?

◉ STOP

If there is an idea in this list you haven't tried, try that now. ●

Don't forget to think about what happens to your patterns after the numbers are more than 100. How are you thinking about 113? One way is as 1 hundred, 1 ten, and 3 ones. But, of course, it could also be "eleventy-three," where the tens digit has gone from 9 to 10 to 11. How do these different perspectives affect your patterns? What would happen after 999?

When you added the digits in the numbers, the sums are 3, 8, 4, 9, 5, 10, 6, 11, 7, 12, 8, and so on. Did you look at every other number in this string? And what is the sum of the digits for 113? Is it 5 or is it 14? (There is no "right" answer here. But it is interesting to consider different possibilities.)

Next Steps. Sometimes when you have discovered some patterns in mathematics, it is a good idea to make some changes and see how the changes affect the patterns. What changes might you make in this problem?

◉ STOP

Try some ideas now before going on. ●

Your changes may be even more interesting than the following suggestions. But here are some ideas:

- Change the start number but keep the jump number equal to 5. What is the same and what is different?
- Keep the same start number and explore with different jump numbers.
- What patterns do different jump numbers make? For example, when the jump number was 5, the ones-digit pattern repeated every two numbers—it had a "pattern length" of 2. But when the jump number is 3, the length of the ones-digit pattern is 10! Do other jump numbers create different pattern lengths?

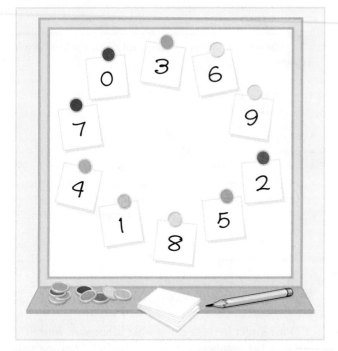

FIGURE 2.1 For jumps of 3, this cycle of digits will occur in the ones place. The start number determines where the cycle begins.

- For a jump number of 3, how does the ones-digit pattern relate to the circle of numbers in Figure 2.1? Are there similar circles of numbers for other jump numbers?
- Using the circle of numbers for 3, find the pattern for jumps of multiples of 3, that is, jumps of 6, 9, or 12.

Using Technology. Calculators facilitate exploration of this problem. Using the calculator makes the list generation accessible for young children who can't skip count yet, and it opens the door for students to work with bigger jump numbers, such as 25 or 36. Most simple calculators have an automatic constant feature that will add the same number successively. For example, if you press 3 **+** 5 **=** and then keep pressing **=**, the calculator will keep counting by fives from the previous answer (the first sequence of numbers you wrote). This also works for the other three operations. A nice online calculator that can be projected in the classroom (and/or used with an interactive whiteboard) while children use their own handheld calculators can be found at www.online-calculator.com/full-screen-calculator.

2. Two Machines, One Job

Ron's Recycle Shop started when Ron bought a used paper-shredding machine. Business was good, so Ron bought a new shredding machine. The old machine could shred a truckload of paper in 4 hours. The new machine could shred the same truckload in only 2 hours. How long will it take to shred a truckload of paper if Ron runs both shredders at the same time?

STOP

Do not read on until you get an answer or get stuck. Can you check that you are correct? Can you approach the problem using a picture? ●

A Few Ideas. Have you tried to predict approximately how much time you think it should take the two machines? For example, will it be closer to 1 hour or closer to 4 hours? What facts about the situation led you to this estimated time? Is there a way to check your estimate? Checking a guess in this way sometimes leads to a new insight.

Some people draw pictures to solve problems. Others like to use something they can move or change. For example, you might draw a rectangle or a line segment to stand for the truckload of paper, or you might get some counters (chips, plastic cubes, pennies) and make a collection that stands for the truckload.

STOP

Go back and try an approach that models the situation. ●

Consider Solutions of Others. There are many ways to model and solve the problem, and understanding other people's ways can develop our own understanding. See below one explanation for solving the problem, using strips (adapted from Schifter & Fosnot, 1993):

> "This rectangle [see Figure 2.2] stands for the whole truckload. In 1 hour, the new machine will do half of this." The rectangle is divided in half. "In 1 hour, the old machine could do $\frac{1}{4}$ of the paper." The rectangle is divided accordingly. "So in 1 hour, the two machines have done $\frac{3}{4}$ of the truck, and there is $\frac{1}{4}$ left. What is left is one-third as much as what they already did, so it should take the two machines one-third as long to do that part as it took to do the first part. One-third of an hour is 20 minutes. That means it takes 1 hour and 20 minutes to do it all."

As with the teachers in these examples, it is important to decide whether your solution is correct through justifying why you did what you did; this reflects real problem solving (rather than checking with an answer key). After you have justified that you have solved the problem in a correct manner, try to find other ways that students might solve the problem—in considering multiple ways, you are making mathematical connections.

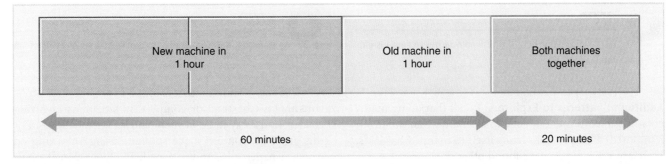

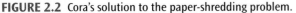

FIGURE 2.2 Cora's solution to the paper-shredding problem.

3. One Up, One Down

For Grades 1–3. When you add 7 + 7, you get 14. When you make the first number 1 more and the second number 1 less, you get the same answer:

↑ ↓
7 + 7 = 14 and 8 + 6 = 14

It works for 5 + 5 too:

↑ ↓
5 + 5 = 10 and 6 + 4 = 10

Does this work any time the numbers are the same? Does it work in other situations where the addends are not the same? Explore and develop your own conjectures.

For Grades 4–8. Does the one up, one down pattern apply to multiplication?

↑ ↓
7 × 7 = 49
8 × 6 = 48

↑ ↓
5 × 5 = 25
6 × 4 = 24

In these two multiplication examples, One Up, One Down resulted in an answer that is *not* equal, but is one less than the original problem. Does this work any time the original numbers are the same? Does it work in other products where the original numbers are not the same? Explore and develop your own conjectures.

 STOP

Explore the multiplication problem, responding to the questions posed. ●

A Few Ideas. Multiplication is more complicated. Why? Use a physical model or picture to compare the before and after products. For example, draw rectangles (or arrays) with a length and height of each of the factors (see Figure 2.3(a)), then draw the new rectangle (e.g., 8-by-6-unit rectangle). See how the rectangles compare.

You may prefer to think of multiplication as equal sets. For example, using stacks of chips, 7 × 7 is seven stacks with seven chips in each stack (set) (see Figure 2.3(b)). The expression 8 × 6 is represented by eight stacks of six (though six stacks of eight is a possible interpretation). See how the stacks for each expression compare.

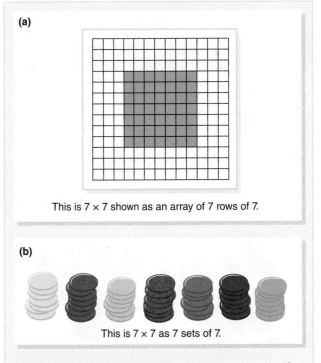

(a)

This is 7 × 7 shown as an array of 7 rows of 7.

(b)

This is 7 × 7 as 7 sets of 7.

What happens when you change one of these to show 6 × 8?

FIGURE 2.3 Two physical ways to think about multiplication that might help in the exploration.

STOP

Work with one or both of these approaches to gain insights and make conjectures. ●

Additional Patterns to Explore. Recall that doing mathematics includes the tendency to extend beyond the problem posed. This problem lends itself to many "what if?"s. Here are a few. If you have found other ones, great!

- Have you looked at how the first two numbers are related? For example, 7 × 7, 5 × 5, and 9 × 9 are all products with like factors. What if the product were two consecutive numbers (e.g., 8 × 7 or 13 × 12)? What if the factors differ by 2 or by 3?
- Think about adjusting by numbers other than one. What if you adjust two up and two down (e.g., 7 × 7 to 9 × 5)?
- What happens if you use big numbers instead of small ones (e.g., 30 × 30)?
- If both factors increase (i.e., one up, one up), is there a pattern?

Have you made some mathematical connections and conjectures in exploring this problem? In doing so you have hopefully felt a sense of accomplishment and excitement—one of the benefits of *doing* mathematics.

4. The Best Chance of Purple

Three students are spinning to "get purple" with two spinners, either by spinning first red and then blue or first blue and then red (see Figure 2.4). They may choose to spin each spinner once or one of the spinners twice. Mary chooses to spin twice on spinner A; John chooses to spin twice on spinner B; and Susan chooses to spin first on spinner A and then on spinner B. Who has the best chance of getting a red and a blue? (Lappan & Even, 1989, p. 17)

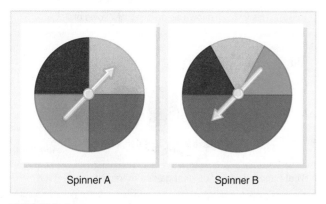

FIGURE 2.4 You may spin A twice, B twice, or A then B. Which option gives you the best chance of spinning a red and a blue?

STOP

Think about the problem and what you know. Experiment. ●

A Few Ideas. Sometimes it is tough to get a feel for problems that are abstract or complex. In situations involving chance, find a way to experiment and see what happens. For this problem, you can make spinners using a drawing on paper, a paper clip, and a pencil. Put your pencil point through the loop of the clip and on the center of your spinner. Now you can spin the paper clip "pointer." Try at least 20 pairs of spins for each choice and keep track of what happens.

Consider these issues as you explore:

- For Susan's choice (A then B), would it matter if she spun B first and then A? Why or why not?
- Explain why you think purple is more or less likely in one of the three cases compared to the other two. It sometimes helps to talk through what you have observed to come up with a way to apply some more precise reasoning.

STOP

Try these suggestions before reading on. ●

Strategy 1: Tree Diagrams. On spinner A, the four colors each have the same chance of coming up. You could make a tree diagram for A with four branches, and all the branches would have the same chance (see Figure 2.5). Spinner B has different-sized sections, leading to the following questions:

- What is the relationship between the blue region and each of the others?
- How could you make a tree diagram for B with each branch having the same chance?
- How can you add to the diagram for spinner A so that it represents spinning A twice in succession?
- Which branches on your diagram represent getting purple?

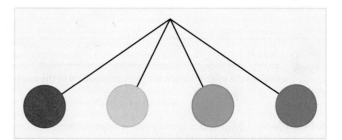

FIGURE 2.5 A tree diagram for spinner A in Figure 2.4.

- How could you make tree diagrams for John's and Susan's choices?
- How do the tree diagrams relate to the spinners?

Tree diagrams are only one way to approach this. If the strategy makes sense to you, stop reading and solve the problem. If tree diagrams do not seem like a strategy you want to use, read on.

Strategy 2: Grids.   Suppose that you had a square that represented all the possible outcomes for spinner A and a similar square for spinner B. Although there are many ways to divide a square into four equal parts, if you use lines going all in the same direction, you can make comparisons of all the outcomes of one event (one whole square) with the outcomes of another event (drawn on a different square). When the second event (in this case the second spin) follows the first event, make the lines on the second square go the opposite way from the lines on the first. Use transparencies and create squares to represent each spinner (see Figure 2.6). Place one over the other, and you will see 24 little sections.

Why are there six subdivisions for the spinner B square? What does each of the 24 little rectangles stand for? What sections would represent purple? Did 24 come into play in another strategy? Can you connect the tree diagram strategy to the rectangle strategy?

Where Are the Answers?

No answers or solutions are given in this text. How do you feel about that? What about the "right" answers? Are your answers correct? What makes the solution to any investigation "correct"?

In the classroom, the ready availability of the answer book or the teacher's providing the solution or verifying that an answer is correct sends a clear message to students about doing mathematics: "Your job is to find the answers that the teacher already has." In the real world of problem solving outside the classroom, there are no teachers with answers and no answer books. Doing mathematics includes using justification as a means of determining whether an answer is correct. The answer, then, to the question, is that the answers lie in your own reasoning and justification.

What Does It Mean to Learn Mathematics?

Now that you have had the chance to experience doing mathematics, you may have a series of questions: Can students solve such challenging tasks? Why take the time to solve these problems—isn't it better to do a lot of shorter problems? Why should students be doing problems like this, especially if they are reluctant to do so? In other words, how does "doing mathematics" relate to student learning? The answer lies in learning theory and research on how people learn.

Learning theories have been developed through analysis of students (and adults) as they develop new understandings. Here we describe two theories (constructivism and sociocultural theory) that are most commonly used by researchers in mathematics education to understand how students learn mathematics. These theories are not competing, but are compatible (Norton & D'Ambrosio, 2008). Learning theories might be thought of as tools or lenses for interpreting how a person learns (Simon, 2009). For example, constructivism might be the best tool, or lens, for thinking about how a student might internalize an idea, and sociocultural theory might be a better tool for analyzing influence of the social/cultural aspects of the classroom.

Constructivism

Constructivism is rooted in Jean Piaget's work, which was developed in the 1930s and translated to English in the 1950s. At the heart of constructivism is the notion that learners are not blank slates but rather creators (constructors) of their own learning. Integrated *networks*, or *cognitive schemas*, are both the product of constructing knowledge and the tools with which additional new knowledge can be constructed. As learning occurs, the networks are rearranged, added to, or otherwise modified. This is an active endeavor on the part of the learner (Baroody, 1987; Cobb, 1988; Fosnot, 1996; von Glasersfeld, 1990, 1996).

All people, all of the time, construct or give meaning to things they perceive or think about. As you read these words, you are giving meaning to them. Whether listening passively to a lecture or actively engaging in synthesizing findings in a project, your brain is applying prior knowledge (existing schemas) to make sense of the new information.

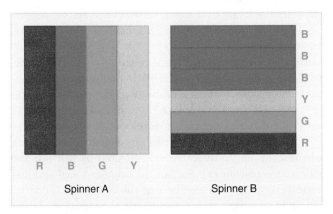

FIGURE 2.6 A square shows the chance of obtaining each color for the spinners in Figure 2.4.

Through *reflective thought* (effort to connect existing ideas to new information), people modify their existing schemas to incorporate new ideas (Fosnot, 1996). This can happen in two ways—*assimilation* and *accommodation*. Assimilation occurs when a new concept "fits" with prior knowledge and the new information expands an existing network. Accommodation takes place when the new concept does not "fit" with the existing network (causing what Piaget called *disequilibrium*), so the brain revamps or replaces the existing schema. Though learning is constructed within the self, the classroom culture contributes to learning while the learner contributes to the culture in the classroom (Yackel & Cobb, 1996).

Construction of Ideas. To construct or build something in the physical world requires tools, materials, and effort. The tools we use to build understanding are our existing ideas and knowledge. The materials we use to build understanding may be things we see, hear, or touch, or our own thoughts and ideas. The effort required to connect new knowledge to old knowledge is reflective thought.

In Figure 2.7, blue and red dots are used as symbols for ideas. Consider the picture to be a small section of our cognitive makeup. The blue dots represent existing ideas. The lines joining the ideas represent our logical connections or relationships that have developed between and among ideas. The red dot is an emerging idea, one that is being constructed. Whatever existing ideas (blue dots) are used in the construction will be connected to the new idea (red dot) because those were the ideas that gave meaning to it. If a potentially relevant idea (blue dot) is not accessed by the learner when learning a new concept (red dot), then that potential connection will not be made.

Sociocultural Theory

In the same way that the work of Piaget relates to constructivism, the work of Lev Vygotsky, a Russian psychologist, has greatly influenced sociocultural theory. Vygotsky's work also emerged in the 1920s and 1930s, but was not translated into English until the late 1970s. There are many concepts that these theories share (for example, the learning process as active meaning-seeking on the part of the learner), but sociocultural theory has several unique features. One is that mental processes exist between and among people in social learning settings, and that from these social settings the learner moves ideas into his or her own psychological realm (Forman, 2003).

Second, the way in which information is internalized (or learned) depends on whether it was within a learner's zone of proximal development (ZPD) (Vygotsky, 1978). Simply put, the ZPD refers to a "range" of knowledge that may be out of reach for a person to learn on his or her own, but is accessible if the learner has support from peers or more knowledgeable others. "[T]he ZPD is not a physical space, but a symbolic space created through the interaction of learners with more knowledgeable others and the culture that precedes them" (Goos, 2004, p. 262). Researchers Cobb (1994) and Goos (2004) suggest that in a true mathematical community of learners there is something of a common ZPD that emerges across learners and there are also the ZPDs of individual learners.

Another major concept in sociocultural theory is *semiotic mediation*. Semiotic refers to the use of language, and other ways to convey cultural practices, such as diagrams, pictures, and actions visuals, and mediation means that these semiotics are exchanged between and among people. So, semiotic mediation is the "mechanism by which individual beliefs, attitudes, and goals are simultaneously affected and affect sociocultural practices and institutions" (Forman & McPhail, 1993, p. 134). In mathematics, semiotics include mathematical symbols (e.g., the equal sign), and it is through classroom interactions and activities that the meaning of these symbols are developed.

Social interaction is essential for mediation. The nature of the community of learners is affected by not just the culture the teacher creates, but the broader social and historical culture of the members of the classroom (Forman, 2003). In summary, from a sociocultural perspective, learning is dependent on the new knowledge falling within the ZPD of the learner (who must have access to the assistance),

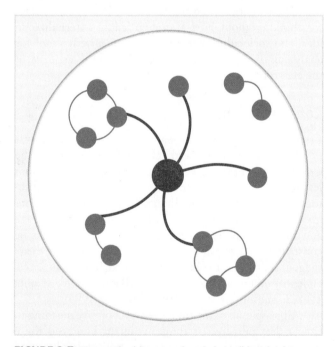

FIGURE 2.7 We use the ideas we already have (blue dots) to construct a new idea (red dot), in the process developing a network of connections between ideas. The more ideas used and the more connections made, the better we understand.

and occurs through interactions that are influenced by tools of mediation (words, pictures, etc.) and the culture within and beyond the classroom.

Implications for Teaching Mathematics

It is not necessary to choose between a social constructivist theory that favors the views of Vygotsky and a cognitive constructivism built on the theories of Piaget (Cobb, 1994; Simon, 2009). In fact, when considering classroom practices that maximize opportunities to construct ideas, or to provide tools to promote mediation, they are quite similar. Classroom discussion based on students' own ideas and solutions to problems is absolutely "foundational to children's learning" (Wood & Turner-Vorbeck, 2001, p. 186).

Remember that learning theory is not a teaching strategy—theory *informs* teaching. This section outlines teaching strategies that are informed by constructivist and sociocultural perspectives. You will see these strategies revisited in Chapters 3 and 4, where a problem-based model for instruction is discussed, and in Section II, where you learn how to apply these ideas to specific areas of mathematics.

Importantly, if these strategies are grounded in how people learn, it means *all* people learn this way—students with special needs, English language learners, students who struggle, and students who are gifted. Too often, when teachers make adaptations and modifications for particular learners, they abandon these problem-based strategies for methods that involve fewer opportunities for students to connect ideas and build knowledge—thereby impeding, not supporting, learning.

Build New Knowledge from Prior Knowledge.   Consider the following task.

> Four children had 3 bags of M&Ms. They decided to open all 3 bags of candy and share the M&Ms fairly. There were 52 M&M candies in each bag. How many M&M candies did each child get? (Campbell & Johnson, 1995, pp. 35–36)

Note: You may want to select a nonfood context, such as decks of cards, or any culturally relevant or interesting item that would come in similar quantities.

 STOP

Consider how you might introduce division to third graders and what your expectations might be for this problem as a teacher grounding your work in constructivist or sociocultural learning theory. ●

The student work samples in Figure 2.8 are from a classroom where students are asked to develop strategies for doing mathematics using their prior knowledge and

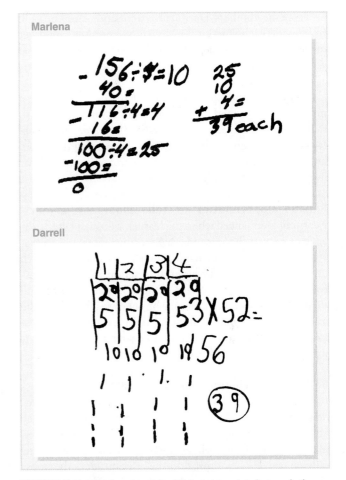

FIGURE 2.8 Two fourth-grade children invent unique solutions to a computation.

Source: Reprinted with permission from P. F. Campbell and M. L. Johnson, "How Primary Students Think and Learn," in I. M. Carl (Ed.), *Prospects for School Mathematics* (pp. 21–42), copyright © 1995 by the National Council of Teachers of Mathematics, Inc. www.nctm.org.

explain their reasoning. From a constructivist and sociocultural perspective, this classroom culture allows students to access their prior knowledge, use cultural tools, and build new knowledge.

Marlena interpreted the first task as "How many sets of 4 can be made from 156?" She used facts that were either easy or available to her: 10 × 4 and 4 × 4. These totals she subtracted from 156 until she got to 100. This seemed to cue her to use 25 fours. She added her sets of 4 and knew the answer was 39 candies for each child. Marlena is using an equal subtraction approach using known multiplication facts. While this is not the most efficient approach, it demonstrates that Marlena understands the concept of division and, with the assistance of others, can move toward more efficient approaches.

Darrell's approach reflects the sharing context of the problem. He formed four columns and distributed amounts to each, accumulating the amounts mentally and orally as he wrote the numbers. Darrell used a counting-up approach, first giving each student 20 M&Ms, seeing they could get more, distributed 5 to each, then 10, then singles until he reached the total. Like Marlena, Darrell used facts and procedures that he knew.

Note that this approach, in which students explore a problem and the mathematical ideas are later connected to that experience, is called a *problem-based* or *inquiry* approach. It is through inquiry that students are activating their own knowledge and trying to assimilate or accommodate (or internalize) new knowledge.

Provide Opportunities to Talk about Mathematics.
Learning is enhanced when the learner is engaged with others working on the same ideas. A worthwhile goal is to create an environment in which students interact with each other and with you. The rich interaction in such a classroom allows students to engage in reflective thinking and to internalize concepts that may be out of reach without the interaction and input from peers and their teacher. In discussions with peers, students will be adapting and expanding on their existing networks of concepts.

Build In Opportunities for Reflective Thought.
Classrooms need to provide structures and supports to help students make sense of mathematics in light of what they know. For a new idea you are teaching to be interconnected in a rich web of interrelated ideas, children must be mentally engaged. They must find the relevant ideas they possess and bring them to bear on the development of the new idea. In terms of the dots in Figure 2.7 we want to activate every blue dot students have that is related to the new red dot we want them to learn. Interestingly, this practice, grounded in learning theory, also has been established through research studies. Recall the research finding, stated earlier, that making mathematical relationships explicit is connected with improving student conceptual understanding (Hiebert & Grouws, 2007).

A key to getting students to be reflective is to engage them in interesting problems in which they use their prior knowledge as they search for solutions and create new ideas in the process. The problem-solving (inquiry) approach requires not just answers but also explanations and justifications for solutions.

Encourage Multiple Approaches.
Teaching should provide opportunities for students to build connections between what they know and what they are learning. The student whose work is presented in Figure 2.9 may not understand the algorithm she is trying to use. If instead she were asked to use her own approach to find the difference, she might be able to get to a correct solution and build on her understanding of place value and subtraction.

Even learning a basic fact, like 7 × 8, can have better results if a teacher promotes multiple strategies. Imagine a

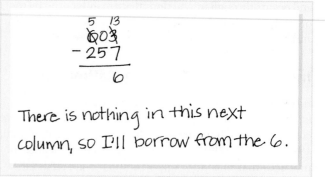

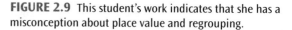

FIGURE 2.9 This student's work indicates that she has a misconception about place value and regrouping.

class where students discuss and share clever ways to figure out the product. One student might think of 5 eights (40) and then 2 more eights (16) to equal 56. Another may have learned 7 × 7 (49) and added on 7 more to get 56. Still another might think "8 sevens" and take half of the sevens (4 × 7) to get 28 and double 28 to get 56. A class discussion sharing these ideas brings to the fore a wide range of useful mathematical "dots" relating addition and multiplication concepts.

In contrast, facts such as 7 × 8 can be learned by rote (memorized). This knowledge is still constructed, but it is not connected to other knowledge. No blue dots! Rote learning can be thought of as a "weak construction" (Noddings, 1993). Students can recall it if they remember it, but if they forget, they don't have 7 × 8 connected to other knowledge pieces that would allow them to redetermine the fact.

Engage Students in Productive Struggle.
Related to supporting multiple approaches, it is important to allow students the time to struggle with the mathematics they are exploring. As Piaget describes, learners are going to experience disequilibrium in developing new ideas. Let students know this disequilibrium is part of the process. Susan Carter, a National Board Certified Teacher who learned to engage her students in productive struggle, writes of her transformation,

> I repeated the mantras of ineffective teachers: "This is too hard for them!" or "My kids just don't have the background for this kind of assignment."... Imagine my heartbreak when I realized the disservice I was doing to my students, especially the ones who needed it most. By substituting a focus on happiness for a focus on engagement with the ideas, I deprived students of what they needed most: worthwhile mathematical tasks and the support to think through them. The more I challenged myself...the closer I moved to an understanding of the necessity of struggle in learning." (Carter, 2008, p. 135)

This is not just one teacher's "aha"; this is one of the findings mentioned earlier as key to developing conceptual understanding (Hiebert & Grouws, 2007). This means redefining what we think of as "helping" students—rather than showing students how to do something, your role in helping students is to ask probing questions that keep students engaged in the productive struggle until they reach a solution. This communicates high expectations and maximizes students' opportunities to learn with understanding.

Treat Errors as Opportunities for Learning. When students make errors, it can mean a misapplication of their prior knowledge in the new situation. Remember that from a constructivist perspective, the mind is sifting through what it knows in order to find useful approaches for the new situation. Knowing that children rarely give random responses (Ginsburg, 1977; Labinowicz, 1985) gives insight into addressing student misconceptions and helping students accommodate new learning. For example, students comparing decimals may incorrectly apply "rules" of whole numbers, such as "the more digits, the bigger the number" (Martinie, 2007; Resnick, Nesher, Leonard, Magone, Omanson, & Peled, 1989). Often one student's misconception is shared by others in the class, and discussing the problem publicly can help other students understand (Hoffman, Breyfogle, & Dressler, 2009). This public negotiation of meaning allows students to construct deeper meaning for the mathematics.

Figure 2.9 is an example of a student incorrectly applying what she learned about regrouping. If the teacher tries to help the student by re-explaining the "right" way to do the problem, the student loses the opportunity to reflect on and correct her misconceptions. If the teacher instead asks the student to explain her regrouping process, the student must engage her reflective thought and think about what was regrouped and how to keep the number equivalent.

Scaffold New Content. The practice of *scaffolding*, often associated with sociocultural theory, is based on the idea that a task otherwise outside of a student's ZPD can become accessible if it is carefully structured. For concepts completely new to students, the learning requires more structure or assistance, including the use of tools like manipulatives or more assistance from peers. As students become more comfortable with the content, the scaffolds are removed and the student becomes more independent. Scaffolding can provide support for those students who may not have a robust collection of "blue dots."

Honor Diversity. Finally, and importantly, these theories emphasize that each learner is unique, with a different collection of prior knowledge and cultural experiences. Since new knowledge is built on existing knowledge and experience, effective teaching incorporates and builds on what the students bring to the classroom, honoring those experiences. Thus, lessons begin with eliciting prior experiences, and understandings and contexts for the lessons are selected based on students' knowledge and experiences. Some students will not have all the "blue dots" they need—it is your job to provide experiences where those blue dots are developed and then connected to the concept being learned.

Classroom culture influences the individual learning of your students. As stated previously, you should support a range of approaches and strategies for doing mathematics. Students' ideas should be valued and included in classroom discussion of the mathematics. This shift in practice, away from the teacher telling one way to do the problem, establishes a classroom culture where ideas are valued. This approach values the uniqueness of each individual.

What Does It Mean to Understand Mathematics?

Both constructivist and sociocultural theories emphasize the learner building connections (blue dots to the red dots) among existing and new ideas. So you might be asking, "What is it they should be learning and connecting?" Or "What are those red dots?" This section focuses on mathematics content required in today's classrooms.

It is possible to say that we know something or we do not. That is, an idea is something that we either have or don't have. Understanding is another matter. For example, most fifth graders know something about fractions. Given the fraction $\frac{6}{8}$, they likely know how to read the fraction and can identify the 6 and 8 as the numerator and denominator, respectively. They know it is equivalent to $\frac{3}{4}$ and that it is more than $\frac{1}{2}$.

Students will have different *understandings*, however, of such concepts as what it means to be equivalent. They may know that $\frac{6}{8}$ can be simplified to $\frac{3}{4}$ but not understand that $\frac{3}{4}$ and $\frac{6}{8}$ represent identical quantities. Some may think that simplifying $\frac{6}{8}$ to $\frac{3}{4}$ makes it a smaller number. Some students will be able to create pictures or models to illustrate equivalent fractions or will have many examples of how $\frac{6}{8}$ is used outside of class. In summary, there is a range of ideas that students often connect to their individualized *understanding* of a fraction—each student brings a different set of blue dots to his or her knowledge of what a fraction is.

Understanding can be defined as a measure of the quality and quantity of connections that an idea has with existing ideas. Understanding is not an all-or-nothing proposition. It depends on the existence of appropriate ideas and on the creation of new connections, varying with each person (Backhouse, Haggarty, Pirie, & Stratton, 1992; Davis, 1986; Hiebert & Carpenter, 1992).

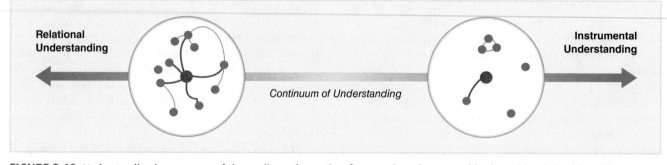

FIGURE 2.10 Understanding is a measure of the quality and quantity of connections that a new idea has with existing ideas. The greater the number of connections to a network of ideas, the better the understanding.

Relational Understanding

One way that we can think about understanding is that it exists along a continuum from a relational understanding—knowing what to do and why—to an instrumental understanding—doing something without understanding (see Figure 2.10). The two ends of this continuum were named by Richard Skemp (1978), an educational psychologist who has had a major influence on mathematics education.

In the $\frac{6}{8}$ example, the student who can draw diagrams, give examples, find equivalencies, and approximate the size of $\frac{6}{8}$ has an understanding toward the relational end of the continuum, while a student who only knows the names and a procedure for simplifying $\frac{6}{8}$ to $\frac{3}{4}$ has an understanding closer to the instrumental end of the continuum.

Multiple Representations. The more ways children are given to think about and test an emerging idea, the better chance they will correctly form and integrate it into a rich web of concepts and therefore develop a relational understanding. Figure 2.11 illustrates five representations for demonstrating an understanding of any topic (Lesh, Cramer, Doerr, Post, & Zawojewski, 2003). Lesh and colleagues have found that children who have difficulty translating a concept from one representation to another also have difficulty solving problems and understanding computations. Strengthening the ability to move between and among these representations improves student understanding and retention. Discussion of oral language, real-world situations, and written symbols is woven into this chapter, but here we elaborate on how manipulatives and models can help (or fail to help) children construct ideas.

Tools and Manipulatives. A *tool for a mathematical concept* refers to any object, picture, or drawing that represents the concept or onto which the relationship for that concept can be imposed. *Manipulatives* are physical objects that students and teachers can use to illustrate and discover mathematical concepts, whether made specifically for mathematics (e.g., connecting cubes) or for other purposes (e.g., buttons).

It is incorrect to say that a tool "illustrates" a concept. To illustrate implies showing. Technically, all that you actually see with your eyes is the physical object; only your mind can impose the mathematical relationship on the object (Suh, 2007b; Thompson, 1994).

Manipulatives can be a testing ground for emerging ideas. It is sometimes difficult for students (of all ages) to think about and test abstract relationships using only words or symbols. For example, students exploring the relationship between perimeter and area might use color tiles (squares of various colors), a geoboard (pegs on a grid) with rubber bands, or toothpicks to make the rectangles. A variety of tools should be accessible for students to select and use freely.

Examples of Tools. Physical materials or manipulatives in mathematics abound—from common objects such as lima

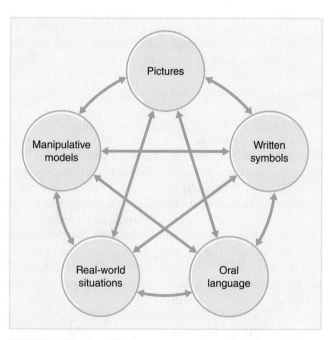

FIGURE 2.11 Five different representations of mathematical ideas. Translations between and within each can help develop new concepts.

beans and string to commercially produced materials such as wooden rods (e.g., Cuisenaire rods) and blocks (e.g., pattern blocks). Figure 2.12 shows six tools, each representing a different concept, giving only a glimpse into the many ways each manipulative can be used to support the development of mathematics concepts and procedures.

STOP

Consider each of the concepts and the corresponding model in Figure 2.12. Try to separate the physical tool from the relationship that you must impose on the tool in order to "see" the concept. ●

The examples in Figure 2.12 are models that can show the following concepts:

a. The concept of "6" is a relationship between sets that can be matched to the words *one, two, three, four, five,* or *six*. Changing a set of counters by adding one changes the relationship. The difference between the set of 6 and the set of 7 is the relationship "one more than."

b. The concept of "measure of length" is a comparison. The length measure of an object is a comparison relationship of the length of the object to the length of the unit.

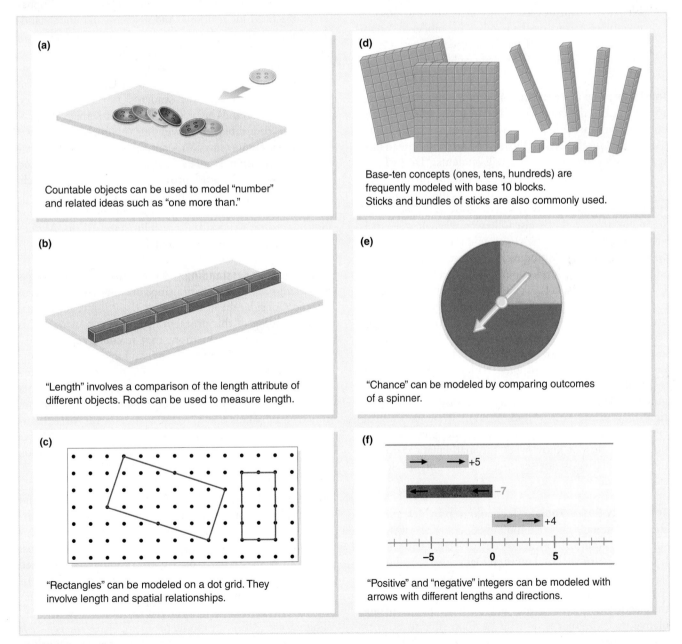

(a) Countable objects can be used to model "number" and related ideas such as "one more than."

(b) "Length" involves a comparison of the length attribute of different objects. Rods can be used to measure length.

(c) "Rectangles" can be modeled on a dot grid. They involve length and spatial relationships.

(d) Base-ten concepts (ones, tens, hundreds) are frequently modeled with base 10 blocks. Sticks and bundles of sticks are also commonly used.

(e) "Chance" can be modeled by comparing outcomes of a spinner.

(f) "Positive" and "negative" integers can be modeled with arrows with different lengths and directions.

FIGURE 2.12 Examples of tools to illustrate mathematics concepts.

c. The concept of "rectangle" includes both spatial and length relationships. The opposite sides are of equal length and parallel and the adjacent sides meet at right angles.

d. The concept of "hundred" is not in the larger square but in the relationship of that square to the strip ("ten") and to the little square ("one").

e. "Chance" is a relationship between the frequency of an event happening compared with all possible outcomes. The spinner can be used to create relative frequencies. These can be predicted by observing relationships of sections of the spinner.

f. The concept of a "negative integer" is based on the relationships of "magnitude" and "is the opposite of." Negative quantities exist only in relation to positive quantities. Arrows on the number line model the opposite of relationship in terms of direction and size or magnitude relationship in terms of length.

Ineffective Use of Tools and Manipulatives. In addition to not making the connection between the model and the concept, there are other ways that models or manipulatives can be used ineffectively. One of the most widespread misuses occurs when the teacher tells students, "Do as I do." There is a natural temptation to get out the materials and show children exactly how to use them. Children mimic the teacher's directions, and it may even look as if they understand, but they could be just following what they see. It is just as possible to move blocks around mindlessly as it is to "invert and multiply" mindlessly. Neither promotes thinking or aids in the development of concepts (Ball, 1992; Clements & Battista, 1990; Stein & Bovalino, 2001). For example, if you have carefully shown and explained how to get an answer to a multiplication problem with a set of base-ten blocks, then students may set up the blocks to get the answer but not focus on the patterns or processes that can be seen in modeling the problem with the blocks.

Conversely, leaving students with insufficient focus or guidance results in nonproductive and unsystematic investigation (Stein & Bovalino, 2001). Students may be engaged in conversations about the model they are using, but if they do not know what the mathematical goal is, the manipulative is not serving as a tool for developing the concept.

Technology-Based Tools. Technology provides another source of models and manipulatives. There are websites, such as the National Library of Virtual Manipulatives, that have a range of manipulatives available (e.g., geoboards, base-ten blocks, spinners, number lines). Virtual manipulatives are a good addition to physical models. In some cases, the electronic version allows users to interact with a manipulative in a way that is difficult or impossible to do with hands-on tools, and it may be accessed at home. Also, some students with physical disabilities may be better able to work with electronic versions of manipulatives.

 It is important to include calculators as a tool. The calculator models a wide variety of numeric relationships by quickly and easily demonstrating the effects of these ideas. For example, you can skip-count by hundredths from 0.01 (press 0.01 [+] .01 [=], [=], [=] . . .) or from another beginning number such as 3 (press [+] 0.01 [=], [=], [=] . . .). How many presses of [=] are required to get from 3 to 4?

Mathematics Proficiency

Much work has emerged since Skemp's classic work emphasized the need for relational and instrumental understanding, based on the need to develop a robust understanding of mathematics. Mathematically proficient people exhibit certain behaviors and dispositions as they are "doing mathematics." *Adding It Up* (National Research Council, 2001), an influential report on how students learn mathematics, describes five strands involved in being mathematically proficient: (1) conceptual understanding, (2) procedural fluency, (3) strategic competence, (4) adaptive reasoning, and (5) productive disposition. Figure 2.13 illustrates these interrelated and interwoven strands, providing a definition of each. These five proficiencies are the foundation for the Standards for Mathematical Practice described in the *Common Core State Standards* (CCSSO, 2010). The Standards for Mathematical Practices can be found in Table 1.2 on page 6.

Conceptual Understanding. Conceptual understanding is knowledge about the relationships or foundational ideas of a topic. Consider the task of adding 37 + 28. The conceptual understanding of this problem includes such ideas as this being a combining situation; that it could represent 37 people and then 28 more arriving; and that this is the same as 30 + 20 + 7 + 8, since you can take numbers apart, rearrange, and still get the same sum. Additionally, students might understand that the value is larger than 50, but not much larger. (This relates to the Standards for Mathematical Practice in the *Common Core State Standards*: "1. Make sense of problems and persevere in solving them"; "7. Look for and make use of structure" [CCSSO, 2010].)

Procedural Fluency. Procedural fluency is knowledge and use of rules and procedures used in carrying out mathematical processes and also the symbolism used to represent mathematics. A student may choose to use the traditional algorithm (see Figure 2.14b) or employ an invented approach (see Figure 2.14 (c) or (d)). A student who is procedurally fluent might move part of one number to another (see 2.14(c)) or use a counting-up strategy (see 2.14(a)). This choice will vary with the problem. He or she is *flexible* in ways to compute an answer. Note that the ability to

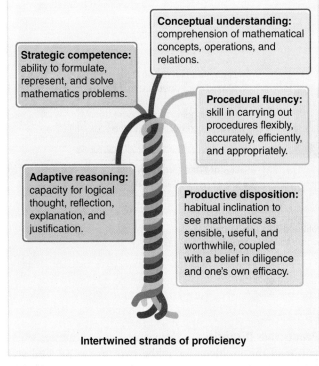

FIGURE 2.13 *Adding It Up* describes five strands of mathematical proficiency.

Source: National Research Council. (2001). *Adding It Up: Helping Children Learn Mathematics*, p. 5. Reprinted with permission from the National Academy of Sciences, courtesy of the National Academies Press, Washington, DC.

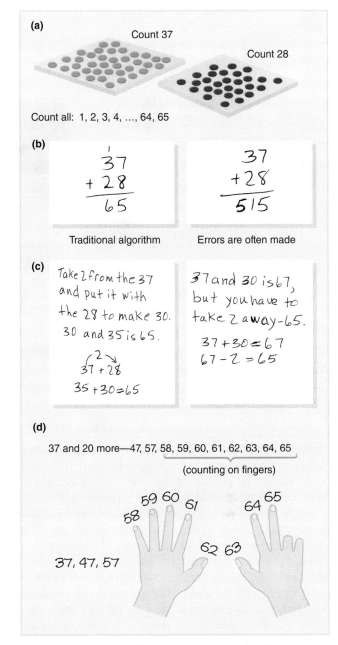

FIGURE 2.14 A range of computational examples showing different levels of understanding.

employ invented strategies, such as the ones described here, requires a conceptual understanding of place value and multiplication.

The ineffective practice of teaching procedures in the absence of conceptual understanding results in a lack of retention and increased errors. Think about the following problem: 40,005 – 39,996 = ___. A student with weak procedural skills may launch into the standard algorithm, regrouping across zeros (this usually doesn't go well), rather than notice that the number 39,996 is just 4 away from 40,000, and therefore notice that the difference between the two numbers is 9. Much research supports the fact that conceptual understanding is critical to developing procedural proficiency (Bransford et al., 2000; National Mathematics Advisory Panel, 2008; NCTM, 2000). The *Principles and Standards* Learning Principle states it well:

> The alliance of factual knowledge, procedural proficiency, and conceptual understanding makes all three components usable in powerful ways. (p. 19)

Students can also have weak understanding of concepts—for example, only understanding the ideas when tied to a context. It is important to note that having deep conceptual and procedural understanding is important in having a relational understanding (Baroody, Feil, & Johnson, 2007). One way to explore all the interrelated ideas for a topic is to create a network or web of associations, as demonstrated in Figure 2.15 (page 28) for the concept of ratio. Note how much is involved in having a relational

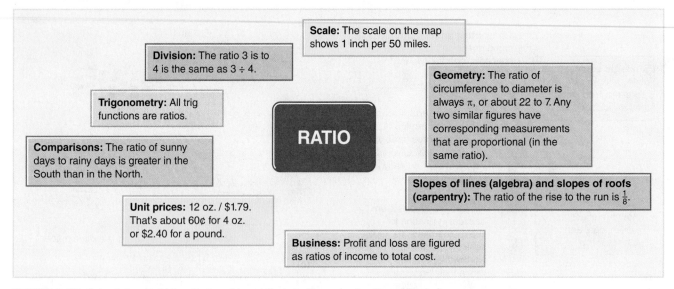

FIGURE 2.15 Potential web of ideas that could contribute to the understanding of "ratio."

understanding of ratio. (This relates to the Standards for Mathematical Practice in the *Common Core State Standards*: "2. Reason abstractly and quantitatively"; "6. Attend to precision"; "7. Look for and make use of structure" [CCSSO, 2010].)

Strategic Competence. In solving Problems 1 through 4 earlier in the chapter, did you design a strategy? If it didn't work, did you try something else? Perhaps you decided to draw a diagram or to fold paper to help you model the task. If you did any of these things, and if you changed out one strategy for a different one, then you were demonstrating strategic competence. Think of the value of this strand, not just in mathematics, but as a life skill. You have a problem; you need to figure out how you will solve it. If at first you don't succeed, try, try again. (This relates to the Standards for Mathematical Practice in the *Common Core State Standards*: "4. Model with mathematics"; "5. Use appropriate tools strategically" [CCSSO, 2010].)

Adaptive Reasoning. When you finished one of the problems, did you wonder whether you had it right? Did you have a way of convincing yourself or your peer that it had to be correct? Conversely, did you head down a wrong path and realize it wasn't working? This capacity to reflect on your work, evaluate it, and then adapt, as needed, is adaptive reasoning. (This relates to the Standards for Mathematical Practice in the *Common Core State Standards*: "2. Reason abstractly and quantitatively"; "3. Construct viable arguments and critique the reasoning of others"; "8. Look for and express regularity in repeated reasoning" [CCSSO, 2010].)

Productive Disposition. What was your reaction when you read the problem about the two machines? Did you think, "I can't remember the way to do this type of problem"? Or, did you think, "I can solve this, let me now think how"? The first response is the result of a history of learning math in which you were shown how to do things, rather than challenged to apply your own knowledge. The latter response is a productive disposition—a "can do" attitude. If you were committed to making sense of and solving those tasks, knowing that if you kept at it, you would get to a solution, then you have a productive disposition. This relates to the perseverance we just talked about in Chapter 1. What more important thing can we instill in students than a "can do" attitude? (This relates to the Standards for Mathematical Practice in the *Common Core State Standards*: "1. Make sense of problems and persevere in solving them"; "8. Look for and express regularity in repeated reasoning" [CCSSO, 2010].)

The last three of the five strands develop only when students have experiences with solving problems as part of their daily learning in mathematics (i.e., a problem-based or inquiry approach to instruction). Note how close these practices are to the teaching suggestions offered in the earlier section on learning theory.

Benefits of Developing Mathematical Proficiency

To teach for mathematical proficiency requires a lot of effort. Concepts and connections develop over time, not in a day. Tasks must be strategically selected to help students build connections. The important benefits to be derived from relational understanding make the effort not only worthwhile but also essential.

Effective Learning of New Concepts and Procedures.
Recall what learning theory tells us—students are actively building on their existing knowledge. The more robust their understanding of a concept, the more connections students are building, and the more likely it is they can connect new ideas to the existing conceptual webs they have. Fraction knowledge and place-value knowledge come together to make decimal learning easier, and decimal concepts directly enhance an understanding of percentage concepts and operations. Without these and many other connections, children will need to learn each new piece of information they encounter as a separate, unrelated idea.

Less to Remember.
When students learn in an instrumental manner, mathematics can seem like endless lists of isolated skills, concepts, rules, and symbols that must be refreshed regularly and often seem overwhelming to keep straight. Constructivists talk about teaching "big ideas" (Brooks & Brooks, 1993; Hiebert et al., 1996; Schifter & Fosnot, 1993). Big ideas are really just large networks of interrelated concepts. Frequently, the network is so well constructed that whole chunks of information are stored and retrieved as single entities rather than isolated bits. For example, knowledge of place value subsumes rules about lining up decimal points, ordering decimal numbers, moving decimal points to the right or left in decimal-percent conversions, rounding and estimating, and a host of other ideas.

Increased Retention and Recall.
Memory is a process of retrieving information. Retrieval of information is more likely when you have the concept connected to an entire web of ideas. If what you need to recall doesn't come to mind, reflecting on ideas that are related can usually lead you to the desired idea eventually. For example, if you forget the formula for surface area of a rectangular solid, reflecting on what it would look like if unfolded and spread out flat can help you remember that there are six rectangular faces in three pairs that are each the same size.

Enhanced Problem-Solving Abilities.
The solution of novel problems requires transferring ideas learned in one context to new situations. When concepts are embedded in a rich network, transferability is significantly enhanced and, thus, so is problem solving (Schoenfeld, 1992). When students understand the relationship between a situation and a context, they are going to know when to use a particular approach to solve a problem. While many students may be able to do this with whole-number computation, once problems increase in difficulty and numbers move to rational numbers or unknowns, students without a relational understanding are not able to apply the skills they learned to solve new problems.

Improved Attitudes and Beliefs.
Relational understanding has an affective as well as a cognitive effect. When ideas are well understood and make sense, the learner tends to develop a positive self-concept and a confidence in his or her ability to learn and understand mathematics. There is a definite feeling of "I can do this! I understand!" There is no reason to fear or to be in awe of knowledge learned relationally. At the other end of the continuum, instrumental understanding has the potential of producing mathematics anxiety, a real phenomenon that involves fear and avoidance behavior.

Connecting the Dots

It seems appropriate to close this chapter by connecting some dots, especially because the ideas represented here are the foundation for the approach to each topic in the content chapters. This chapter began with discussing what *doing* mathematics is and challenging you to do some mathematics. Each of these tasks offered opportunities to make connections between mathematics concepts—connecting the blue dots.

Second, you read about learning theory—the importance of having opportunities to connect the dots. The best learning opportunities, according to constructivism and sociocultural theories, are those that engage learners in using their own knowledge and experience to solve problems through social interactions and reflection. This is what you were asked to do in the four tasks. Did you learn something new about mathematics? Did you connect an idea that you had not previously connected?

Finally, you read about understanding—that having relational knowledge (knowledge in which blue dots are well connected) requires conceptual and procedural understanding as well as other proficiencies. The problems that you solved in the first section emphasized concepts and procedures while placing you in a position to use strategic competence, adaptive reasoning, and a productive disposition.

This chapter focused on connecting the dots between theory and practice—building a case that your teaching must focus on opportunities for students to develop their own networks of blue dots. As you plan and design instruction, you should constantly reflect on how to elicit prior knowledge by designing tasks that reflect the social and cultural backgrounds of students, to challenge students to think critically and creatively, and to include a comprehensive treatment of mathematics.

RESOURCES *for Chapter 2*

RECOMMENDED READINGS

Articles

Berkman, R. M. (2006). One, some, or none: Finding beauty in ambiguity. *Mathematics Teaching in the Middle School, 11*(7), 324–327.

This article offers a great teaching strategy for nurturing relational thinking. Examples of the engaging "one, some, or none" activity are given for geometry, number, and algebra activities.

Carter, S. (2008). Disequilibrium & questioning in the primary classroom: Establishing routines that help students learn. *Teaching Children Mathematics, 15*(3), 134–137.

This is a wonderful teacher's story of how she infused the constructivist notion of disequilibrium and the related idea of productive struggle to support learning in her first-grade class.

Hedges, M., Huinker, D., & Steinmeyer, M. (2005). Unpacking division to build teachers' mathematical knowledge. *Teaching Children Mathematics, 11*(9), 478–483.

This article describes the many concepts related to division.

Suh, J. (2007). Tying it all together: Classroom practices that promote mathematical proficiency for all students. *Teaching Children Mathematics, 14*(3), 163–169.

As the title implies, this is a great resource for connecting the NRC's Mathematics Proficiencies (National Research Council, 2001) to teaching.

Books

Lampert, M. (2001). *Teaching problems and the problems of teaching.* New Haven, CT: Yale University Press.

Lampert reflects on her personal experiences in teaching fifth grade and shares with us her perspectives on the many issues and complexities of teaching. It is wonderfully written and easily accessed at any point in the book.

ONLINE RESOURCES

Classic Problems
www.mathforum.org/dr.math/faq/faq.classic.problems .html

A nice collection of well-known problems ("Train A leaves the station at . . .") along with discussion, solutions, and extensions.

Constructivism in the Classroom
http://mathforum.org/mathed/constructivism.html

Provided by the Math Forum, this page contains links to numerous sites concerning constructivism as well as articles written by researchers.

Utah State University National Library of Virtual Manipulatives
http://nlvm.usu.edu/en/nav/vlibrary.html

A robust collection of virtual manipulatives. Many do not have corresponding, hands-on counterparts. A great site to bookmark and use.

REFLECTIONS *on Chapter 2*

WRITING TO LEARN

1. How would you describe what it means to "do mathematics"?
2. What is reflective thought? Why is reflective thinking so important in the development of conceptual ideas in mathematics?
3. What does it mean to say that understanding exists on a continuum from relational to instrumental? Give an example of an idea, and explain how a student's understanding might fall on either end of the continuum.
4. Explain why a tool for a mathematical idea is not really an example of the idea. If it is not an example of the concept, what does it mean to say we "see" the concept when we look at the tool?

FOR DISCUSSION AND EXPLORATION

1. Consider the following task and respond to these three questions.
   - What features of "doing mathematics" does it have?
   - To what extent does it lead students to develop a relational understanding?
   - To what extent does it develop mathematical proficiency? (See Figure 2.13 on page 27.)

Some people say that to add four consecutive numbers, you add the first and the last numbers and multiply by 2. Is this always true? How do you know? (Stoessiger & Edmunds, 1992)

2. Not every educator believes in the constructivist-oriented approach to teaching mathematics. Some of their reasons include the following: There is not enough time to let kids discover everything. Basic facts and ideas are better taught through quality explanations. Students should not have to "reinvent the wheel." How would you respond to these arguments?

MyEducationLab™

Go to the MyEducationLab (www.myeducationlab.com) for Math Methods and familiarize yourself with the content. Much of the site content is organized topically. The topics include all of the following to support your learning in the course:

- Learning outcomes for important mathematics methods course topics aligned with the national standards
- Assignments and Activities, tied to these learning outcomes and standards, that can help you more deeply understand course content
- Building Teaching Skills and Dispositions learning units that allow you to apply and practice your understanding of the core mathematics content and teaching skills

Your instructor has a correlation guide that aligns the exercises on the topical portion of the site with your book's chapters.

On MyEducationLab you will also find book-specific resources including Blackline Masters, Expanded Lesson Activities, and Artifact Analysis Activities.

Field Experience Guide
C O N N E C T I O N S

An environment for doing mathematics is the focus of Chapter 1 of the *Field Experience Guide*. Activities include observation protocols, teacher and student interviews, teaching, and a project. The act of doing mathematics is also the focus of an observation targeting higher-level thinking (FEG 2.2). In addition, Chapter 4 of the guide includes experiences related to teaching for understanding and learning mathematics developmentally.

Chapter 3

Teaching Through Problem Solving

We only think when we are confronted with problems.

John Dewey

For more than two decades since the publication of the original NCTM *Standards* document (NCTM, 1989), evidence has continued to mount that problem solving is a powerful and effective vehicle for learning. As *Principles and Standards* (NCTM, 2000) states:

> Solving problems is not only a goal of learning mathematics but also a major means of doing so.... Problem solving is an integral part of all mathematics learning, and so it should not be an isolated part of the mathematics program. Problem solving in mathematics should involve all the five content areas described in these Standards.... Good problems will integrate multiple topics and will involve significant mathematics. (p. 52)

In a classic publication on the types of teaching related to problem solving, Schroeder and Lester (1989) identified three types of approaches to problem solving:

1. *Teaching for problem solving.* This approach can be summarized as teaching a skill so that a student can later problem solve. Teaching for problem solving often starts with learning the abstract concept and then moving to solving problems as a way to apply the learned skills. For example, students learn the algorithm for adding fractions and, once that is mastered, solve story problems that involve adding fractions. (This approach is used in many textbooks and is likely familiar to you.)

2. *Teaching about problem solving.* This second approach involves teaching students *how* to problem solve, which can include teaching the process (understand, design a

strategy, implement, look back) or strategies for solving a problem. An example of a strategy is "draw a picture," in which students use a picture or diagram to help solve a problem. See "Teaching about Problem Solving" in this chapter.

3. *Teaching through problem solving.* This approach generally means that students learn mathematics *through* real contexts, problems, situations, and models. The contexts and models allow students to build meaning for the concepts so that they can move to abstract concepts. Teaching *through* problem solving might be described as upside down from teaching *for* problem solving—with the problem(s) presented at the beginning of a lesson and skills emerging from working with the problem(s). For example, in exploring the situation of combining $\frac{1}{2}$ and $\frac{1}{3}$ feet of ribbon to figure out how long the ribbon is, students would be led to discover the procedure for adding fractions.

A Shift in the Role of Problems

Teaching *for* problem solving (first approach described earlier) is engrained in mathematics teaching practice as the historic way to teach mathematics: The teacher presents the mathematics; the students practice the skill, and finally, students solve story problems that require using that skill. Unfortunately, this approach to mathematics teaching has not been successful for many students in understanding or remembering mathematics concepts. Why? Because teaching *for* problem solving:

- Requires that all students have the necessary prior knowledge (the blue dots described in Chapter 2) to understand the teacher's explanations, which is rarely, if ever, the case.

- Typically involves the teacher presenting one way to do the problem/procedure, which likely will not make sense to many learners, disadvantaging students who could solve the problem differently.
- Can communicate that there is only one way to solve the problem, a message that misrepresents the field of mathematics and disempowers students who naturally may want to try to do it their own way.
- Positions the student as a passive learner, dependent on the teacher to present ideas, rather than as an independent thinker with the capability and responsibility for solving the problem.
- Separates learning skills and concepts from problem solving, which does not improve student learning (Cai, 2010).
- Decreases the likelihood a student will attempt a new problem without explicit instructions on *how* to solve it. But that's what doing mathematics is—figuring out an approach to solve the problem at hand.

Some teachers may think that showing students how to solve a set of problems is the most helpful approach for students, preventing struggling while saving time. However, it is the struggle that leads to learning, so teachers must resist the natural inclination to take away the struggle. The best way to help students is to not help too much. In summary, teaching *for* problem solving—in particular modeling and explaining a strategy for how to solve the problem—can actually make students worse at solving problems and doing mathematics, not better.

Students learn mathematics as a *result* of solving problems. Mathematical ideas are the *outcomes* of the problem-solving experience rather than elements that must be taught before problem solving (Hiebert et al., 1996, 1997). Furthermore, the process of solving problems is completely interwoven with the learning; children are *learning* mathematics by *doing* mathematics and by doing mathematics they are learning mathematics (Cai, 2010).

Learning by doing, or teaching *through* problem solving, requires a paradigm shift. That is, a teacher is changing more than just a few things about her teaching; she is changing her philosophy of how she thinks children learn and how she can best help them learn. At first glance, it may seem that the teacher's role is less demanding because the students are doing the mathematics, but the teacher's role is actually very demanding in such classrooms. Teachers must select high-quality tasks that allow students to learn the content by figuring out their own strategies and solutions. Teachers must ask well-designed questions that allow students to verify and relate their strategies. Teachers must listen to student responses and observe student work, determining in the moment how to extend and formalize student thinking. See Appendix B, Standards for Teaching Mathematics, for more details on all that is involved in effective mathematics teaching.

Teaching about Problem Solving

Teaching about problem solving can (and should) be embedded within teaching content, but it requires that you devote time to teaching students the processes and the strategies for how to solve problems.

Four-Step Problem-Solving Process

George Polya, a famous mathematician, wrote a classic book, *How to Solve It* (1945), which outlined four steps for problem solving. These widely adopted steps for problem solving have appeared and continue to appear in many resource books and textbooks. Explicitly teaching these four steps to students can improve their ability to think mathematically. The four steps are described very briefly in the following list:

1. *Understanding the problem.* First you must be engaged in figuring out what the problem is about and identifying what question or problem is being posed.

2. *Devising a plan.* In this phase you are thinking about how to solve the problem. Will you want to write an equation? Will you want to model the problem with a manipulative? (See the next section, "Problem-Solving Strategies.")

3. *Carrying out the plan.* This is the implementation of your strategy/approach.

4. *Looking back.* This phase, arguably the most important as well as most skipped, is the moment you determine whether your answer from step 3 answers the problem as originally understood in step 1. Does your answer make sense? If not, loop back to step 2 and select a different strategy to solve the problem or loop back to step 3 if you just need to fix something within your strategy.

Most recently, the ideas of Polya have been infused in the interwoven Strands for Mathematical Proficiency (National Research Council, 2001) and the Standards for Mathematical Practice (CCSSO, 2010). Specifically, as previously described in Chapter 2, students who are mathematically proficient have *strategic competence* (see Polya's step 2) and *adaptive reasoning* (see Polya's step 4). Polya's steps are further extended and explained in the Standards for Mathematical Practice, including *reason abstractly and quantitatively* (see Polya's steps 2–4), *construct viable arguments* (see Polya's step 3), and *look for and express regularity in repeated reasoning* (see Polya's steps 1–4).

The beauty of Polya's framework is its generalizability; it can and should be applied to many different types of problems, from simple computational exercises to authentic and worthwhile multistep problems. As noted earlier, it is important to remember that these four steps should not be taught in isolation, but embedded in the learning of mathematics concepts.

Problem-Solving Strategies

Strategies for solving problems are identifiable methods of approaching a task that are completely independent of the specific topic or subject matter. Students select or design a strategy as they devise a plan (see Polya's step 2). When students discover important or especially useful strategies, the method should be identified, highlighted, and discussed. Labeling a strategy provides a useful means for students to talk about their methods, which can help students make connections between and among strategies and representations. The following labeled strategies are commonly encountered in grades K–8, though not all of them are used at every grade level.

- *Draw a picture, act it out, use a model.* The strategy of using models and manipulatives is described in Chapter 2. "Act it out" extends models to a real interpretation of the problem situation.
- *Look for a pattern.* Pattern searching is at the heart of mathematics (and is one of the Standards for Mathematical Practice). Patterns in number and in operations play a huge role in helping students learn and master basic skills starting at the earliest levels and continuing into middle and high school.
- *Guess and check.* This might be called "Try and see what you can find out." This is not as easy as it may sound, as it involves making a strategic attempt (guess), reflecting (quantitative analysis), and adjusting. The quantitative analysis (the answer is too small or too big) supports student sense making and is a bridge to algebra (Guerrero, 2010).
- *Make a table or chart.* Charts of data, function tables, and tables involving ratios or measurements are a major form of analysis and communication. The chart is used to search for patterns in order to solve the problem.
- *Try a simpler form of the problem.* This strategy involves simplifying the quantities in a problem so that the resulting task is easier to understand and analyze. This can lead to insights that can be applied to the original, more complex quantities in a problem.
- *Make an organized list.* Systematically accounting for all possible outcomes in a situation can show the number of possibilities there are or verify that all possible outcomes have been included.
- *Write an equation.* In this strategy, the story problem, once understood, is converted into numbers or symbols, and the equation is solved.

It is important not to "proceduralize" problem solving. In other words, don't take the problem solving out of problem solving by telling students the strategy they should pick and how to do it. Instead, pose a problem that lends itself to the strategy you would like them to develop (e.g., make an organized list) and allow students to solve the problem in a way that makes the most sense and is best supported by their own reasoning. During the sharing of results, highlight student work that uses a list or, if no one uses a list, ask, "Could we have made an organized list to solve the problem more efficiently? What would that look like? Give it a try!"

Teaching Through Problem Solving

Mathematics concepts and procedures are best taught through problem solving. This statement reflects the NCTM's *Principles and Standards* and represents current thinking of researchers in mathematics education (Cai, 2003, 2010; NCTM, 2000; Stein, Remillard, & Smith, 2007). In his summary of the review of research, Cai (2010) explains that there are two roles in the effective implementation of teaching through problem-solving: selecting tasks and orchestrating classroom discourse. The sections "Selecting Worthwhile Tasks" and "Orchestrating Classroom Discourse," which follow, address these two topics.

What Is a Problem?

Teachers can and should pose tasks or problems that engage students in thinking about and developing the important mathematics they need to learn. Let's examine why this approach better supports student learning. As discussed in Chapter 2, the two research-supported ways to develop conceptual understanding are engaging students in productive struggle and making relationships explicit. Selecting problems that will do this is paramount to effective teaching.

A *problem* is defined here as any task or activity for which the students have no prescribed or memorized rules or methods, nor is there a perception by students that there is a specific "correct" solution method (Hiebert et al., 1997). Note that a problem may or may not have words. A story problem may be "routine," such that students can tell right away whether it is a multiplication, division, addition, or subtraction problem. Or the story problem may be "non-routine," meaning that they don't initially know how to solve it. Conversely an equation with no story or even no words can be problematic or nonroutine. Consider the following:

$$10 + \underline{\quad} = 4 + (3 + \underline{\quad})$$

Find numbers for each blank to make the equation true.

Find different pairs of numbers that will make the equation true.

What is the relationship between the two numbers for any correct solution? Why?

This problem is "nonroutine" if, when the students first read it, they do not know how they are going to find the answer.

Features of a Problem

To be considered a "problem," the learner must find it problematic. The following features of a problem can be used as a guide in assessing whether a task is a problem:

- *It must begin where the students are.* The design or selection of the task must take into consideration the students' current understanding. They should have the appropriate ideas to engage and solve the problem and yet still find it challenging and interesting.

- *The problematic or engaging aspect of the problem must be due to the mathematics that the students are to learn.* Engaging contexts are important in students finding mathematics meaningful. But the context is not the focus—the content is. A good problem has interesting *mathematics*. The previous section's example problem is interesting and engaging because the students can play with the numbers and discover that there is always a difference of three between the two values.

- *It must require justifications and explanations for answers and methods.* In a good problem, neither the process nor the answer is straightforward, so justification is central to the task. Students should understand that the responsibility for determining whether answers are correct and why they are correct rests within themselves and their mathematical reasoning. This is how mathematical proficiency is developed!

In teaching *through* problem solving, problems (tasks or activities) are the vehicle by which the desired content is learned. So, the need to incorporate the three features described above is central to setting up meaningful learning environments where students engage in and make sense of mathematics.

Examples of Problems

Students can develop conceptual or procedural knowledge through problem solving. The first three examples here focus on concepts; the later three focus on procedures.

Concepts. Concepts are developed by building on what concepts students already have. In starting where the students are (i.e., what they already understand) and then using problematic and engaging tasks related to the new concept, students develop new concepts. Through justification and explanation these ideas are solidified and connected to other concepts. A few examples are shared below.

Concept: Partitioning
Grades: K–1

Think about six bowls of cereal placed at two different tables. Draw a picture to show a way that six bowls might be placed at two tables. Can you find more than one way? How many ways do you think there are?

At the kindergarten or first-grade level, the teacher may want students simply to find one or two ways to decompose 6. In first or second grade, the teacher may challenge children to find all of the combinations and be able to justify how they know they found all the ways. In a class discussion following work on the task, students are likely to develop an orderly process for listing all the ways: As one table grows from 0 to 6 bowls, the other table begins at 6 and shrinks by ones to 0 (seven ways!).

Concept: Fractions Greater Than 1
Grades: 3–5

Place an X on the number line about where $\frac{11}{8}$ would be. Explain why you put your X where you did.

$$\vdash\!\!-\!\!-\!\!-\!\!-\!\!-\!\!-\!\!-\!\!-\!\!-\!\!-\!\!-\!\!-\!\!-\!\!-\!\!-\!\!-\!\!-\!\!-\!\!\dashv$$

0   2

Note that the task can be solved in variety of ways—for example, with a ruler or by folding a strip of paper. Students will have to justify where they placed their mark. In the follow-up discussion, the teacher will be able to help the class refine ideas about fractions greater than 1 (for example, that 11 eighths are equivalent to a whole and 3 more eighths).

Concept: Comparing Ratios and Proportional Reasoning
Grades: 6–8

Jack and Jill were at the same spot at the bottom of a hill, hoping to fetch a pail of water. They both begin walking up the hill, Jack walking 5 yards every 25 seconds and Jill walking 3 yards every 10 seconds. Assuming constant walking rate, who will get to the pail of water first?

Students can solve this problem in a variety of ways, including acting out the problem, creating a table, or comparing ratios. Students may also use a rate approach, determining the number of yards walked per minute for each person. The discussion about this task will focus on how students compared the ratios, which is the essence of proportional reasoning. This task is one of four used to introduce proportional reasoning in Expanded Lesson 9.11 in the *Field Experience Guide*.

Procedures. A distinction of teaching *through* problem solving is that it is the *student* who determines the approach to the computation. Some teachers will use teaching *through* problem solving for concepts, but not for procedures. This creates a disconnect for students—why wouldn't they use their own strategies for procedures when they were designing strategies for the related concepts? Students can invent their own strategies for doing procedures and this should be valued and encouraged by teachers. (This point is elaborated throughout Section II of this book.) A few examples are shared below.

Procedure: Adding Two-Digit Whole Numbers
Grades: 1–2

What is the sum of 48 and 25? How did you figure it out?

Even though there is no story or situation to resolve, this is a problem because students must figure out *how* they are going to approach the task. (They have not been taught the standard algorithm at this point.) Students work on the problem using manipulatives, pictures, or mental strategies. After students have solved the problem in their own way, the teacher gathers the students together to hear one another's strategies and solutions. This list below contains just some of the approaches created by students in one second-grade classroom (Russell, 1997):

$$4\boxed{8} \ + \ 2\boxed{5} \quad \text{(Boxed digits help ``hold'' them.)}$$
$$40 \ + \ 20 \ = \ 60$$
$$8 \ + \ 2 \ = \ 10 \quad \boxed{3} \quad \text{(The 3 is left from the 5.)}$$
$$60 \ + \ 10 \ = \ 70$$
$$70 \ + \ 3 \ = \ 73$$

$$40 \ + \ 20 \ = \ 60$$
$$60 \ + \ 8 \ = \ 68$$
$$68 \ + \ 5 \ = \ 73$$

$$48 \ + \ 20 \ = \ 68$$
$$68 \ + \ 2 \ (\textit{``from the 5''}) \ = \ 70$$
"Then I still have that 3 from the 5."
$$70 \ + \ 3 \ = \ 73$$

$$25 \ + \ 25 \ = \ 50 \quad \boxed{23}$$
$$50 \ + \ 23 \ = \ 73$$

Teacher: Where does the 23 come from?
"It's sort of from the 48."
How did you split up the 48?
"20 and 20 and I split the 8 into 5 and 3."

$$48 \ - \ 3 \ = \ 45 \quad \boxed{3}$$
$$45 \ + \ 25 \ = \ 70$$
$$70 \ + \ 3 \ = \ 73$$

In a similar way, decimal operations can be invented and discussed. Procedures for fractions, poorly understood by many people, can be explored through problem solving.

Procedure: Division of Fractions
Grades: 5–7

Clara has 2 whole pizzas and $\frac{1}{3}$ of another. All of the pizzas are the same size. If each of her friends will want to eat $\frac{1}{4}$ of a pizza, how many friends will she be able to feed with the $2\frac{1}{3}$ pizzas?

In addition to operations of whole numbers and rational numbers, procedures related to measurements can be taught through problem solving.

Procedure: Area of a Rectangle
Grades: 3–4

Find the area of the cover of your math book by covering it with color tiles. Repeat for the areas of books of various sizes. What patterns do you notice in covering the book? Is this pattern or rule true for covering any rectangle?

Most formulas can be developed through problem solving. For example, students can look at circular container lids to explore how the diameter relates to the circumference of a circle, or cut parallelograms to create rectangles in order to see how these formulas are related (see Chapter 19 for more on learning measurement through problem solving).

What is abundantly clear is that the more problem solving students do, the more willing and confident they are to solve problems and the more methods they develop for attacking future problems (Boaler, 1998, 2002; Boaler & Humphreys, 2005; Buschman, 2003a, 2003b; Cai, 2003; Lesh & Zawojewski, 2007; Silver & Stein, 1996; Wood, Cobb, Yackel, & Dillon, 1993).

Selecting Worthwhile Tasks

As noted in the list of features of a problem, task selection must include consideration of the students' ability; the task must be problematic for the student. Standard 3 in the NCTM's *Professional Standards for Teaching Mathematics* (see Appendix B) provides a good list of important considerations when selecting tasks. There are various things to consider, including the level of cognitive demand, the potential of the task to have multiple entry and exit points, and whether the task is relevant to students. Fortunately, you don't need to start from scratch—you have a textbook, which can be a source for selecting tasks.

Levels of Cognitive Demand

First and foremost in selecting tasks is to be sure the task is cognitively demanding, meaning it involves higher-level thinking. (See Standard 3, Worthwhile Mathematical Tasks, in *Professional Standards for Teaching Mathematics*.) Low cognitive demand tasks (also called routine problems or lower-level tasks) involve stating facts, following known procedures (computation), and solving routine problems. Higher-level thinking tasks, on the other hand, involve making connections, analyzing information, and drawing conclusions (Smith & Stein, 1998). For example, if you ask students to find the area of a rectangle, there is a different level of thinking than if you ask students to create a "blueprint" of a room and to figure the area of the floor. Table 3.1 provides a well-known framework that is useful in helping to determine whether a task is set up to challenge students.

TABLE 3.1

LEVELS OF COGNITIVE DEMAND	
Low-Level Cognitive Demand	**High-Level Cognitive Demand**
Memorization Tasks • Involve either producing previously learned facts, rules, formulas, or definitions or memorizing • Are routine—involving exact reproduction of previously learned procedure • Have no connection to related concepts	**Procedures with Connections Tasks** • Focus students' attention on the use of procedures for the purpose of developing deeper levels of understanding of mathematical concepts and ideas • Suggest general procedures that have close connections to underlying conceptual ideas • Are usually represented in multiple ways (e.g., visuals, manipulatives, symbols, problem situations) • Require that students engage with the conceptual ideas that underlie the procedures in order to successfully complete the task
Procedures Without Connections Tasks • Use of the procedure is specifically called for • Are straightforward, with little ambiguity about what needs to be done and how to do it • Have no connection to related concepts • Are focused on producing correct answers rather than developing mathematical understanding • Require no explanations or explanations focus on the procedure only	**Doing Mathematics Tasks** • Require complex and nonalgorithmic thinking (i.e., nonroutine—there is not a predictable, known approach) • Require students to explore and to understand the nature of mathematical concepts, processes, or relationships • Demand self-monitoring or self-regulation of one's own cognitive processes • Require students to access relevant knowledge in working through the task • Require students to analyze the task and actively examine task constraints that may limit possible solution strategies and solutions • Require considerable cognitive effort

Source: Adapted from Smith, M. S., & Stein, M. K (1998). Selecting and Creating Mathematical Tasks: From Research to Practice. *Mathematics Teaching in the Middle School, 3*(5): 344–350. Reprinted with permission.

As you read through the descriptors for the tasks that are low-level cognitive demand and those that are high-level cognitive demand, you will notice that the low-level tasks are routine and straightforward. In other words, they do not engage students in productive struggle. Conversely, with the high-level (nonroutine) tasks, students not only engage in productive struggle as they work, but they are also challenged to make connections to concepts and to other relevant knowledge. Hopefully, this is a connection for you to the research on learning described in Chapter 2—that students develop conceptual understanding when they engage in productive struggle and make mathematical connections (Hiebert & Grouws, 2007).

Multiple Entry and Exit Points

Because your students will likely have a big range in "where they are" mathematically, it is important to use problems that have multiple entry points, meaning that the task has varying degrees of challenge within it or it can be approached in a variety of ways. One of the advantages of a problem-based approach is that it can help accommodate the diversity of learners in every classroom because students are encouraged to use a variety of strategies that are supported by their prior experiences. Students are told, in essence, "Use the ideas *you* own to solve this problem." In the examples posed above, some students may use less efficient approaches (for example, counting or building all), but they will develop more advanced strategies during the lesson through other students' sharing their approaches and the teacher's effective questioning. Having a choice of strategies can lower the anxiety of students, particularly ELLs (Murrey, 2008).

Figure 3.1(a) provides a high cognitive demand task that has multiple entry and exit points, as illustrated by the range of solutions provided in Figure 3.1(b).

These solutions vary in the prior knowledge applied to the problem. During a classroom discussion, the teacher's role is to ensure that the strategies are strategically shared (perhaps sharing some less advanced strategies first or related strategies together). In doing this, all students can advance their knowledge of fraction concepts (Smith, Bill, & Hughes, 2008).

Tasks should have multiple exit points, or various ways that students can demonstrate understanding of the learning goals. For example, students might draw a picture, write an equation, use manipulatives, or act out a problem involving perimeter of a rectangle to demonstrate that they can find the perimeter for any sized rectangle. These options are particularly important for teachers to get a better sense of what ELL students know; their use of a visual or model may convey more than what they can communicate with their limited language skills. Students with learning disabilities may also struggle with language expression and be able to demonstrate their knowledge more effectively with a picture. Asking students to both explain and illustrate a solution is one way to more effectively assess whether the student learned what you intended.

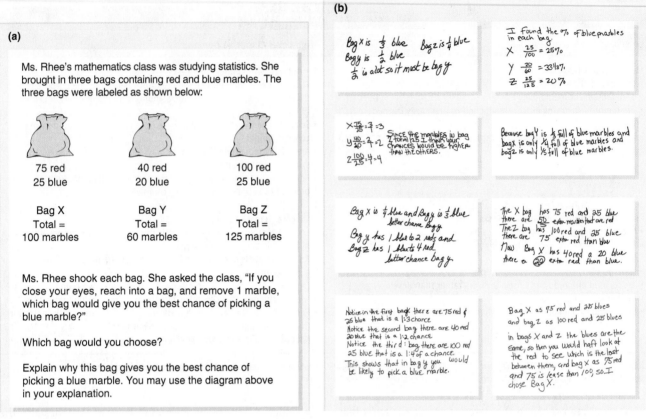

FIGURE 3.1 A task with multiple entry and exit points, as illustrated by the range of student solutions.

Source: Smith, M. S., Bill, V., & Hughes, E. K. (2008). Thinking Through a Lesson: Successfully Implementing High-Level Tasks. *Mathematics Teaching in the Middle School, 14*(3), 132–138. Reprinted with permission.

PAUSE and REFLECT

See if you can think of more than one path to solving any of the six examples in the previous section. Try to think of an approach that is less sophisticated and another that is more sophisticated. Reflect on how the two are related to each other.

Relevant Contexts

Certainly one of the most powerful features of teaching through problem solving is that the problem that begins the lesson can get students excited about learning mathematics. Compare these two sixth-grade introductory tasks on ratios:

> "Today we are going to explore ratios and see how ratios can be used to compare amounts."
>
> "In a minute, I am going to read to you a passage from Harry Potter about how big Hagrid is. We are going to use ratios to compare our heights and widths to Hagrid's."

Contexts can also be used to learn about cultures, such as those of students in your classroom. Contexts can also be used to connect to other subjects. Children's literature and links to other disciplines are explored here for their potential to engage students in learning mathematics.

Children's Literature. Children's literature is a rich source of problems at all levels, not just primary. Children's stories can be used in numerous ways to create a variety of reflective tasks, and there are many excellent books to help you in this area (Bay-Williams & Martinie, 2004, 2009; Bresser, 1995; Burns, 1992; Karp, Brown, Allen, & Allen, 1998; Sheffield, 1995; Theissen, Matthias, & Smith, 1998; Ward, 2006; Welchman-Tischler, 1992; Whitin & Whitin, 2004; Whitin & Wilde, 1992, 1995).

An example of literature lending itself to mathematical problems is the very popular children's picture book *Two of Everything* (Hong, 1993). In this magical Chinese folktale, a couple finds a pot that doubles whatever is put into it. (Imagine where the story goes when Mrs. Haktak falls in the pot!) In a second-grade classroom, the students can calculate how many students would be in their class if the whole class fell in the Magic Pot. Figure 3.2 illustrates different ways that students solved the problem (multiple entry points) and different ways they explained and

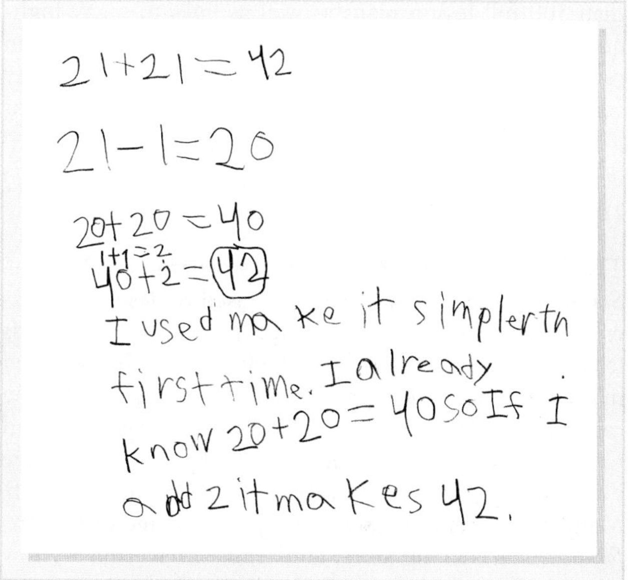

$21 + 21 = 42$

$21 - 1 = 20$

$20 + 20 = 40$

$1 + 1 = 2$

$40 + 2 = \boxed{42}$

I used make it simpler th first time. I already know $20 + 20 = 40$ so If I add 2 it makes 42.

Robbie adds tens and ones to solve.

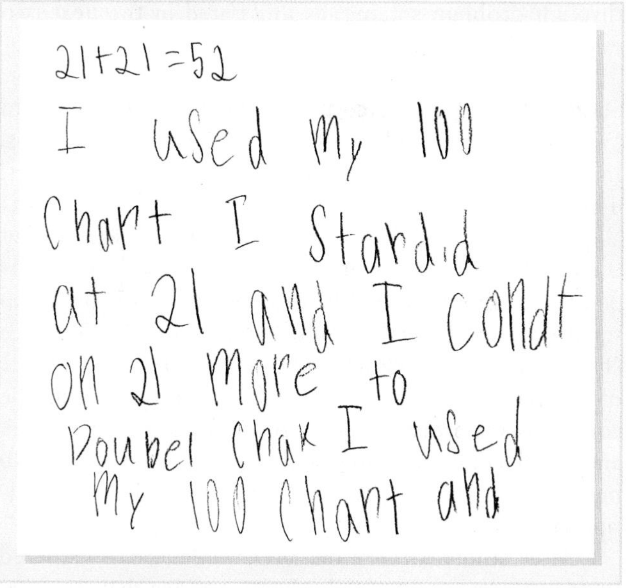

$21 + 21 = 52$

I used my 100 Chart I stardid at 21 and I condt on 21 more to Doubel chak I used My 100 chart and

Kylee uses a hundreds chart and counts on.

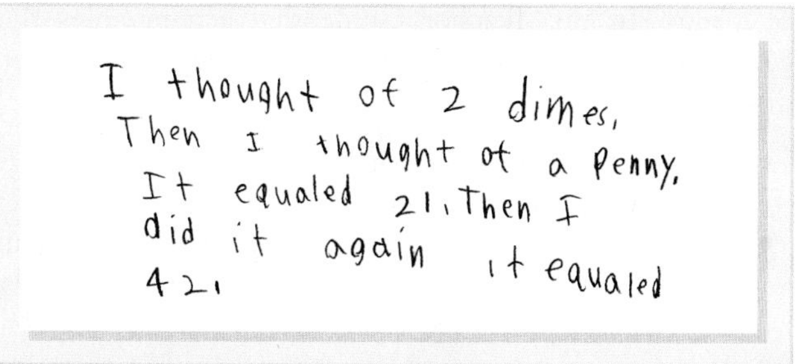

I thought of 2 dimes, Then I thought of a Penny, It equaled 21, Then I did it again it equaled 42.

Benjamin uses the context of money to combine.

FIGURE 3.2 Second graders use different problem solving strategies to figure out how many students there would be if their class of 21 were doubled.

illustrated how they figured it out (multiple exit points). Notice that the student using the hundreds chart has a wrong answer. The teacher will need to follow up to determine whether this was a copy error or a misconception.

The great thing about literature is that there are often several tasks that can be launched from the story. In this case, the Magic Pot can start doing other unexpected things, like tripling what is put in, or increasing what is put in by 5, and so on—making it a wonderful context for input-output activities to build a foundation for the later study of functions (see Suh, 2007a, and Wickett, Kharas, and Burns, 2002, for more ideas on this book).

In *Harry Potter and the Sorcerer's Stone* (Rowling, 1998), referred to earlier, the lesson is based on the author's description of Hagrid as twice as tall and five times as wide as the average man. Students in grades 2–3 can cut strips of paper that are as tall as they are and as wide as their shoulders are (you can cut strips from cash register rolls). Then they can figure out how big Hagrid would be if he were twice as tall and five times as wide as they are. In grades 4–5, students can create a table that shows each student's height and width and look for a pattern (it turns out to be about 3 to 1). Then they can figure out Hagrid's height and width and see whether they keep the same ratio (it is 5 to 2). In grades 6–8, students can create a scatter plot of their widths and heights and see where Hagrid's data would be plotted on the graph. Measurement, number, and algebra content are all embedded in this example.

Whether students are 6 or 13, literature resonates with their experiences and imaginations, making them more enthusiastic about solving the related mathematics problems and more likely to learn and to see mathematics as a useful tool for exploring the world. Several recent teacher resources focus on using nonfiction literature in teaching mathematics (Bay-Williams & Martinie, 2009; Petersen, 2004; Sheffield & Gallagher, 2004). Nonfiction literature can include newspapers, magazines, and the Web—all great sources for problems that have the added benefit of students learning about the world around them.

For example, the British *Manchester Evening News* (Leeming, 2007) reported that the Cool Cash lottery scratch card had to be recalled—the integer values were too difficult for many people:

> To qualify for a prize, users had to scratch away a window to reveal a temperature lower than the value displayed on each card. As the game had a winter theme, the temperature was usually below freezing. [The scratch card company] received dozens of complaints on the first day from players who could not understand how, for example, –5 is higher than –6. . . . [One person] said: "On one of my cards it said I had to find temperatures lower than –8. The numbers I uncovered were –6 and –7 so I thought I had won, and so did the woman in the shop. But when she scanned the card the machine said I hadn't.

Can you think of a good task that could be launched from having read this article? One task is to ask students to prepare an illustration and explanation that can help grown-ups understand the value of negative numbers.

In Section II, each end-of-chapter resources section includes "Literature Connections," quick descriptions of picture books, poetry, and novels that can be used to explore the mathematics of that chapter. Literature ideas are also found in articles in NCTM journals.

Links to Other Disciplines. Finding relevant contexts for engaging all students is always a challenge in classes of diverse learners. Using contexts familiar for all students can be effective but are sometimes hard to find. An excellent source for problems, therefore, is the other subject matter that students are studying. Elementary teachers can pull ideas from the topics being taught in social studies, science, and language arts; likewise, middle school teachers can link to these subjects through their grade-level colleagues. Other familiar contexts such as art, sports, and pop culture can also be valuable.

In kindergarten, students can link their study of natural systems in science to mathematics, for example, by sorting leaves based on color, smooth or jagged edges, feel of the leaf, and shape. Students learn about rules for sorting and can use Venn diagrams to keep track of their sorts. They can observe and analyze what is common and different in leaves from different trees. Sorting and measuring, topics in both mathematics and science, are more concepts to explore with leaves. Older students can find the perimeter and area of various types of leaves and learn about why these perimeters and areas differ.

AIMS (Activities in Mathematics and Science), a series of teacher resource books integrating mathematics and science, has fantastic ideas in every book. See www.aimsedu .org for more information. In *Looking at Lines* (AIMS, 2001), a middle school AIMS book, students hang paper clips from a handmade balance to learn about linear equations (mathematics) and force and motion (science).

Social studies is rich with opportunities to do mathematics. Time lines of historic events are excellent opportunities for students to work on the relative sizes of numbers and to make better sense of history. Students can explore the areas and populations of various countries, provinces, or states and compare the population densities, while in social studies they can talk about how life differs between regions with 200 people living in a square mile and regions with 5 people per square mile.

The Web can be a great resource for finding problems that have multiple entry and exit points, are relevant, and are engaging for students. *Illuminations* (http://illuminations .nctm.org), a resource website of NCTM, is perhaps the best portal for finding high-quality lessons on the Internet. Besides over 100 activities that use applets, there are more than 500 full lesson plans as well as links to many high-quality websites (they only link to sites that have been reviewed and are considered "first rate"). Searchable by content and by grade band, it is a site you'll definitely want to bookmark!

Using Textbooks

Textbooks (curriculum) range in their instructional design. *Standards-based curricula* is a term used to describe curricula that were developed to reflect professional standards (such as the NCTM standards), and tend to be designed in the teaching *through* problem solving model. This is the case with the *Investigations in Number, Data, and Space* and *Connected Mathematics Project* (CMP II) series, which are illustrated here, as well as in activities on MyEducationLab. Many mainstream textbooks are still designed in a teach-*for*-problem-solving style, and tend to have mostly low cognitive demand tasks. Regardless of what you start with, it is possible to pose worthwhile tasks and teach through problem solving, as illustrated in the next two examples.

Standards-Based Curriculum. The CMP II lesson in Figure 3.3 is the first lesson on multiplication of fractions. In the problem, a familiar context is used: a pan of brownies. This context helps students use prior knowledge to think about and solve the problem. The lesson begins with posing the problem, "How much of the pan have we sold?" Students work in groups on Questions A through D using the square pan as a model. Notice how the questions are (1) grounded in the context of brownies, (2) placed in order of increasing difficulty, and (3) focused on connecting the concept to the procedure. Parts A and B are very conceptual and visual (concrete), and C and D connect those visuals to more abstract thinking by developing an algorithm for multiplying fractions.

After students work on A–D, students are gathered back as a whole group and asked questions that focus on the concept of multiplication of fractions—taking a part of a part. In the Teacher Guide that accompanies the curriculum, the following questions are suggested for the discussion:

- How did you decide what fraction of a whole pan is being bought?
- Can someone suggest a way to mark the brownie pan so it is easy to see what part of the whole pan is being bought?
- What number sentences [equations] could I write for Question A?

This is just one lesson in a series of lessons to build meaning for multiplication of fractions, all designed in the teaching through problem solving style.

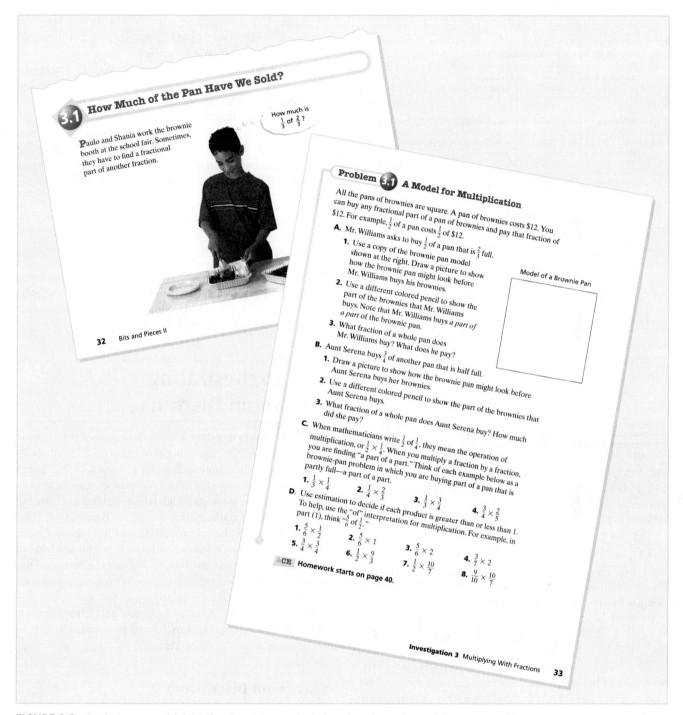

FIGURE 3.3 First lesson on multiplying fractions in a standards-based mathematics program.

Source: Connected Mathematics: Bits and Pieces II: Student Edition by G. Lappan, J. Fey, W. Fitzgerald, S. Friel, and E. Phillips, pp. 32–33. Copyright © 2006 by Michigan State University. Used by permission of Pearson Education, Inc. All rights reserved.

Adapting a Non-Problem-Based Task. Many traditional textbooks are designed for teacher-directed classrooms, a contrast to the approach you have been reading about. In order to incorporate a teaching through problem solving approach, focus on the big ideas of the unit. (Big ideas are found in the *Common Core State Standards* and in state standards, and are listed at the start of each chapter in Section II of this book.) Second, find an important task. This may be done by (1) adapting the best or most important tasks in the chapter to a problem-based format or (2) creating or finding a task in another resource.

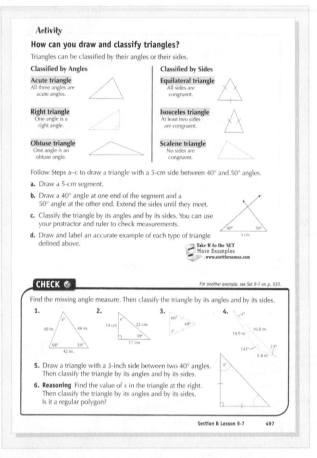

FIGURE 3.4 A first-grade lesson from a traditional textbook.

Source: Scott Foresman–Addison Wesley Math: Grade 1 (p. 137), by R. I. Charles et al. Copyright © 2004 Pearson Education, Inc., or its affiliate(s). Used by permission. All rights reserved.

Figure 3.4 shows a page from a first-grade traditional textbook. The lesson addresses an important idea: the different classifications of triangles. The expectation for students is limited to labeling already-drawn triangles.

 PAUSE and REFLECT

How can students be challenged to wrestle with this task? How might a different approach allow for multiple entry points? If this problem is redesigned to be more open-ended (multiple entry and exit points), how will it affect the challenge and learning in the lesson? How can this be adapted for students with disabilities? ●

One possibility is to provide a set of triangles and have pairs of students work to separate them into groups based on features of the triangles. To provide more structure, students can be asked to sort by sides and sort by angles. They can share and compare with another group of students. Then the vocabulary can be connected to the students' groups. Students can then be given uncooked spaghetti and asked higher-level questions: "Can you build two triangles of different sizes that are both isosceles?" "Can you create

a triangle with three obtuse angles? Why or why not?" "If a triangle is classified as [right], then which classifications for sides are possible or impossible?"

Notice how these adaptations fit with the features of a problem. Students are developing a deeper understanding of triangles and are more able to see the relationships between the classifications.

In summary, selecting worthwhile tasks is complex and an ongoing priority for teachers. Researchers suggest using a process that will help in the selection of worthwhile tasks (Barlow, 2010; Breyfogle & Williams, 2008–2009):

- Identify the mathematical goals (objectives).
- Create (find) the problem.
- Anticipate student solutions.
- Implement and reflect on the problem.

Do you notice the parallels to Polya's process for solving problems? They are parallel processes: You engage in problem solving as you make decisions about the mathematics tasks your students will explore.

Orchestrating Classroom Discourse

Classroom discourse refers to the interactions that occur throughout a lesson. Learning how to orchestrate an effective classroom discussion is quite complex and requires attention to various elements. The goal of discourse is to keep the cognitive demand high while students are learning and formalizing mathematical concepts (Breyfogle & Williams, 2008–2009; Kilic et al., 2010; Smith, Hughes, Engle, & Stein, 2009). Note that the purpose is not for students to tell their answers and get validation from the teacher. Discourse can occur before, during, or after solving a problem, but the after phase is particularly important as it is this discussion that is supposed to help students connect their problem to more general or formal mathematics, and to make connections to other ideas.

Classroom Discussions

The value of student talk in mathematics lessons cannot be overemphasized. As students describe and evaluate solutions to tasks, share approaches, and make conjectures, learning will occur in ways that are otherwise unlikely to take place. Students—in particular English language learners, other students with more limited language skills, and students with learning disabilities—need to use mathematical vocabulary and articulate mathematics concepts in order to learn both the language and the concepts of mathematics. Students begin to take ownership of ideas (strategic competence) and develop a sense of power in making sense of mathematics (productive disposition). As they listen to other students' ideas, they come to see the varied approaches in how mathematics can be solved and see mathematics as something that they can do.

Discourse should occur throughout a lesson. When a problem is introduced, students can be asked *what* strategies they might use and why. By joining a group, you can model questions you want the students to ask each other and themselves. You can also model think-alouds, in which you discuss how you thought about the problem. These are critical for students with learning disabilities to support their thinking about a strategy because it makes explicit the reasoning process. In the upper grades, each group can have a designated monitor, whose job is to be the reflective questioner (first modeled by you). In the discussion that occurs after students have solved the problem(s), students can reflect not just on their own strategy, but other's strategies. Questions asking students if they would do it differently next time, which strategy made sense to them (and why), what caused problems for them, and how they overcame these stumbling blocks, are critical in developing mathematically proficient students. While many good questions are specific to the task being solved, some general questions can help students build understanding:

- What did you do that helped you understand the problem?
- Was there something in this problem that reminded you of another problem we've done?
- Did you find any numbers or information you didn't need? How did you know that the information was not important?
- How did you decide what to do?

- How did you decide whether your answer was right?
- Did you try something that didn't work? How did you figure out it was not going to work out?
- Can something you did in this problem help you solve other problems?

Notice these questions focus on the process as well as the answer, and what worked as well as what didn't work. A balanced discussion helps students learn how to *do mathematics*.

In *Classroom Discussions*, a teacher resource describing how to implement effective discourse in the classroom, Chapin, O'Conner, and Anderson (2009) write, "When a teacher succeeds in setting up a classroom in which students feel obligated to listen to one another, to make their own contributions clear and comprehensible, and to provide evidence for their claims, that teacher has set in place a powerful context for student learning" (p. 9). This is true for every student. There are no exceptions! Struggling learners often struggle because they have been denied the opportunity to explore and connect ideas. These authors share five "talk moves" that help a teacher to get students talking about mathematics (see Table 3.2).

The following exchange illustrates an example of discourse with a small group of students discussing how to solve 27 − 19 = ____. The teacher is asking two students (Tyler and Aleah) to reconcile that they got different answers.

TYLER: Well, I added one to nineteen to get twenty. So then I did twenty-seven take away twenty and got seven. But I added one, so I needed to take one away from the seven, and I got six.

TABLE 3.2

PRODUCTIVE TALK MOVES FOR SUPPORTING CLASSROOM DISCUSSIONS		
Talk Moves	**What It Means and Why**	**Example Teacher Prompts**
1. Revoicing	This move involves restating the statement as a question in order to clarify, apply appropriate language, and to involve more students. It is an important strategy to reinforce language and enhance comprehension for ELLs.	"You used the hundreds chart and counted on?" "So, first you recorded your measurements in a table?"
2. Rephrasing	Asking students to restate someone else's ideas in their own words will ensure that ideas are stated in a variety of ways and encourage students to listen to each other.	"Who can share what Ricardo just said, but using your own words?"
3. Reasoning	Rather than restate, as in talk move 2, this move asks the student what they think of the idea proposed by another student.	"Do you agree or disagree with Johanna? Why?"
4. Elaborating	This is a request for students to challenge, add on, elaborate, or give an example. It is intended to get more participation from students, deepen student understanding, and provide extensions.	"Can you give an example?" "Do you see a connection between Julio's idea and Rhonda's idea?" "What if . . ."
5. Waiting	Ironically, one "talk move" is to not talk. Quiet time should not feel uncomfortable, but should feel like thinking time. If it gets awkward, ask students to pair-share and then try again.	"This question is important. Let's take some time to think about it."

Source: Based on Chapin, S., O'Conner, C., & Anderson, N. (2009). *Classroom Discussions: Using Math Talk to Help Students Learn* (2nd ed.). Sausalito, CA: Math Solutions. Reprinted with permission.

TEACHER: What do you think of that, Aleah?

ALEAH: That is not what I got.

TEACHER: Yes, I know that, but what do you think of Tyler's explanation?

ALEAH: Well, it can't be right, because I just counted up. I added one to nineteen to get twenty and then added seven more to get twenty-seven. So, I counted eight altogether. Six can't be right.

TEACHER: Tyler, what do you think of Aleah's explanation?

TYLER: That makes sense, too. I should have counted.

TEACHER: So, do you think both answers are right?

TYLER: No.

ALEAH: No. If it was twenty-seven minus twenty, the answer would be seven, because you count up seven. So, if it is nineteen, it has to be eight.

TYLER: Oh, wait. I see something I did get the seven. . . . See, I got the twenty-seven take away twenty is seven. But then . . . I see . . . it's twenty-seven take away nineteen. I took away twenty! I took away too many so I have to add one to the seven. I get eight, just like Aleah! (Kline, 2008, p. 148)

While this conversation is with two children, a similar style can be used in whole-class discussions, pushing students to help students make sense of what is correct and incorrect about their strategies.

PAUSE and REFLECT

What talk moves do you notice in this vignette? See if you can identify two. ●

Considerable research into how mathematical communities develop and operate provides us with additional insight for developing effective classroom discourse (e.g., Rasmussen, Yackel, & King, 2003; Stephan & Whitenack, 2003; Wood, Williams, & McNeal, 2006; Yackel & Cobb, 1996). Suggestions from this collection of research include the following recommendations:

• Encourage student–student dialogue rather than student–teacher conversations that exclude the rest of the class. "Juanita, can you answer Lora's question?" "Devon, can you explain that so that LaToya and Kevin can understand what you are saying?" When students have differing solutions, have students work these ideas out as a class. "George, I noticed that you got a different answer than Tomeka. What do you think about her explanation?"

• Encourage students to ask questions. "Pete, did you understand how they did that? Do you want to ask Antonio a question?"

• Ask follow-up questions whether the answer is right or wrong. Your role is to understand student thinking (not to lead students to the correct answer). So follow up with probes to learn more about their answers. Sometimes you will find that what you assumed they were thinking is not correct. And if you only follow up on wrong answers, students quickly figure this out and get nervous when you ask them to explain their thinking.

• Call on students in such a way that, over time, all students are able to participate. Use time when students are working in small groups to identify interesting solutions that you will highlight during the sharing time. Be intentional about the order in which the solutions are shared; for example, select two that you would like to compare presented back-to-back. All students should be prepared to share their strategies.

• Demonstrate to students that it is okay to be confused and that asking clarifying questions is appropriate. This confusion, or disequilibrium, just means they are engaged in doing real mathematics and is an indication they are learning.

• Move students to more conceptually based explanations when appropriate. For example, if a student says that he knows 4.17 is more than 4.1638, you can ask him (or another student) to explain why this is so. Say, "I see *what* you did but I think some of us are confused about *why* you did it that way."

• Be sure *all* students are involved in the discussion. ELLs, in particular, need more than vocabulary support; they need support with mathematical discussions (Moschovich, 1998). For example, you can use sentence starters or examples to help students know what kind of responses you are hoping to hear and to reduce the language demands. Sentence starters can also be helpful for students with disabilities because it adds structure. You can have students practice their explanations with a peer. You can invite students to use illustrations and actual objects to support their explanations. These strategies benefit not just the ELLs and other students in the class who struggle with language, but are useful for everyone to use so that every student can understand the discussion.

Questioning Considerations

Questions are important. If you don't ask students to think, they aren't going to. While this may sound simple, questioning is actually very complex and something that effective teachers continue to improve throughout their career. Here are some of the major considerations in questioning that influence student learning.

1. *The "level" of the question.* Questions are leveled in various models. For example, Bloom's Taxonomy includes six levels (knowledge, comprehension, application, analysis, synthesis, evaluation), with each one more cognitively demanding than the previous (Bloom, Engelhart, Furst, Hill, & Krathwohl, 1956). Smith and Stein's (1998) Levels of Cognitive Demand include two low-level demand categories and two high-level demand categories. Regardless of the taxonomy or specific categories, the key is to ask higher-level questions. This is critical if students are to think at higher levels, and yet too few higher-level questions are used in mathematics teaching.

2. *Type of knowledge that is targeted.* Both procedural and conceptual knowledge are important, and questions must target both. If questions are limited to procedural questions, such as "How did you solve this?" or "What steps did you use?" then students will be thinking about procedures, but not about related concepts. Questions focused on conceptual knowledge include, "Will this rule always work?" "How does the equation you wrote connect to the picture?" and "Why use common denominators to add fractions?"

3. *Pattern of questioning.* As Herbel-Eisenmann and Brey-fogle (2005) articulate, "Thinking about the questions we ask is important, but equally important is thinking about the *patterns of questions* that are asked" (p. 484). One common pattern of questioning goes like this: teacher asks a question, student answers the question, teacher confirms or challenges answer. This "initiation-response-feedback" or "IRF" pattern does not lead to classroom discussions that encourage all students to think. Another pattern is "funneling," when a teacher continues to probe students in order to get them to a particular answer. This is different than a "focusing" pattern, which uses probing questions to negotiate a classroom discussion and help students understand the mathematics (Herbel-Eisenmann & Breyfogle, 2005). The talk moves described above are intended to help facilitate a focusing discussion.

4. *Who is thinking of the answer.* As if it is not enough to develop higher-level questions, focusing on both procedures and concepts, and think about your questioning patterns, you must be sure that such efforts engage all students. When that great question is asked, if only one student responds, then students will quickly figure out they don't need to think of the answer and all your effort to ask a great question is wasted. Instead, use strategies to be sure everyone is accountable to think of the answer. Ask students to "talk to a partner" about the question. Employ the talk tools described above.

5. *How you respond to an answer.* When you confirm a correct solution, rather than use one of the talk moves above, you lose an opportunity to engage students in meaningful discussions about mathematics, and thereby limit the learning opportunities. Save the positive reinforcement for later in the day and, while in the middle of a lesson, use student answers to find out if other students think the answer is correct, whether they can justify why, and if there are other strategies or solutions to the problem.

Metacognition

Metacognition refers to conscious monitoring (being aware of how and why you are doing something) and regulation (choosing to do something or deciding to make changes) of your own thought process. Metacognition is connected to learning (Bransford, Brown, & Cocking, 2000). Good problem solvers monitor their thinking regularly and adjust as

needed (adaptive reasoning) (Schoenfeld, 1992). Metacognitive behavior can be learned (Campione, Brown, & Connell, 1989; Garofalo, 1987; Lester, 1989; Thomas, 2006) and making it a part of classroom discourse is one way to make this happen. The THINK framework can be used to ensure students are developing metacognitive skills (Thomas, 2006):

> *Talk* about the problem.
> *How* can it be solved?
> *Identify* a strategy to solve the problem.
> *Notice* how your strategy helped you solve the problem.
> *Keep* thinking about the problem. Does it make sense? Is there another way to solve it?

Notice how closely the THINK framework is like Polya's four steps of problem solving. In studies, students who used the THINK framework improved in their problem solving more than those who did not use it (Thomas, 2006). Posting mnemonics like the THINK framework in your classroom and using the prompts as you introduce, solve, and reflect on a problem illustrate the value of such thinking and encourages students to initiate the questions on their own.

Having students "look back" (Polya's fourth step) can help students become more metacognitive. Wieser (2008) found out that even if students get the answer right, they may think it was hard. After a test, this fifth-grade teacher asks her students to complete a one-page reflection where, for each test question, they write whether they think they got it right or wrong. In addition, students write which questions were the easiest, the hardest, and whether there were any questions for which they changed their answer due to checking their work. In addition to prompting students to think about what they understand and what they need more help with, this type of reflection is a great formative assessment for the teacher.

How Much to Tell and Not to Tell

When teaching through problem solving, one of the most perplexing dilemmas for teachers is how much to tell. On one hand, telling can diminish what is learned and lower the level of challenge in a lesson by eliminating the productive struggle that is key to conceptual understanding (Hiebert & Grouws, 2007). On the other hand, to tell too little can sometimes leave students floundering in what you might think of as "not productive" struggle.

One way to frame this dilemma is shared by researchers who have analyzed classroom practices as it relates to student learning: "Information can and should be shared as long as it does not solve the problem [and] does not take away the need for students to reflect on the situation and develop solution methods they understand" (Hiebert et al., 1997, p. 36). They go on to suggest three things that teachers do need to tell students:

- *Mathematical conventions.* The symbols used in representing "three and five equals eight" as "$3 + 5 = 8$" are conventions (+ and =). Terminology and labels are also conventions. As a rule of thumb, symbolism and terminology should be introduced *after* concepts have been developed and then specifically as a means of expressing or labeling ideas. Sometimes students with disabilities benefit from preteaching on terminology and the meaning of symbols to support participation in the problem-solving process.

• *Alternative methods.* When an important strategy does not emerge naturally from students, then the teacher should introduce the strategy, being careful to introduce it as "another" way, not the only or the best way.

• *Clarification or formalization of students' methods.* You should help students clarify or interpret their ideas and point out related ideas. A student may add 38 and 5 by noting that 38 and 2 more is 40 with 3 more making 43. This strategy can be related to the Make 10 strategy used to add 8 + 5. The selection of 40 as a midpoint in this procedure is an important place-value concept. Drawing everyone's attention to this connection can help other students see the connection, not to mention build the confidence of the students who originally proposed the strategy.

Writing to Learn

There are many reasons to use writing in a mathematics classroom. The most important is that it improves student learning and understanding (Bell & Bell, 1985; Pugalee, 2005; Steele, 2007), although there are other interrelated reasons as well:

• *The act of writing is a reflective process.* As students make an effort to explain their thinking and defend their answers, they will spend more focused time thinking about the ideas involved.

• *A written report is a rehearsal for the discussion period.* It is difficult for students to explain how they solved a problem 15 minutes after they have done so. Students can always refer to a written report when asked to share. Even a kindergarten child can show a picture and talk about it.

• *A written report is also a written record that remains when the lesson is finished.* The reports can be collected and looked at later. The information can be used for planning, for finding out who needs help or opportunities to extend their knowledge, and for evaluation and parent conferences.

It is important to help students understand what they are trying to accomplish in their written report. When you ask students to explain how they got their answer, they may just repeat each step, rather than explaining why they did what they did. Figures 3.5 and 3.6 illustrate a range of quality in student explanations. Modeling for students how to explain their thinking is essential. Using student work samples, such as those illustrated, can help students understand your expectations for them. To help elicit better explanations, you might consider the following two possibilities:

• Give students a template to begin their report: "I (We) think the answer is ____. We think this because _____."

• Give the following instruction: "Use words, pictures, and numbers to explain how you got your answer and why you think your answer makes sense and is correct."

Posting different solutions and asking students to reflect on which is clearest and why is a good way to teach good mathematical writing skills (Kinman, 2010) and build metacognitive skills, as discussed above. Writing helps students focus on the need for precise language in mathematics, see how the order of words in a sentence matters, and understand that illustrations can support a good explanation.

Writing for different audiences can also be valuable. First graders writing to third graders, such as in a pen pal structure can lead students to explain more and enjoy the process (Lampe & Uselmann, 2008).

Graphic Organizers. Writing can also be used to help students connect representations. A common graphic organizer is the four-box table. In each box, students record the problem, an explanation, and illustration, and the general math concept (Wu, An, King, Ramirez, & Evans, 2009; Zollman, 2009). The requirements for each box can be adapted, as needed, for the content area; for example, in geometry you may use a box for examples and another box for non-examples:

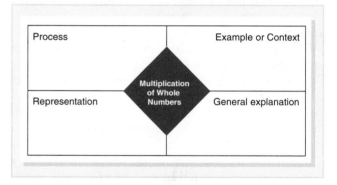

Many graphic organizers can be used for writing. They help students know what to write. In the case of the one pictured here, you don't even need a handout; just fold your paper in fourths and then dog-ear the inside corner on the fold. When you unfold, you will have a paper divided as shown here.

Technology Tools in Writing. Take advantage of the following free programs to allow students to write, edit, and submit work to you electronically:

Text Editing (real-time, collaborative writing tools)

• Google Docs and Spreadsheets (http://docs.google.com)
• Synchroedit (www.synchroedit.com)
• Zoho Writer—includes the ability to use math equations with MathType (http://zoho.com)

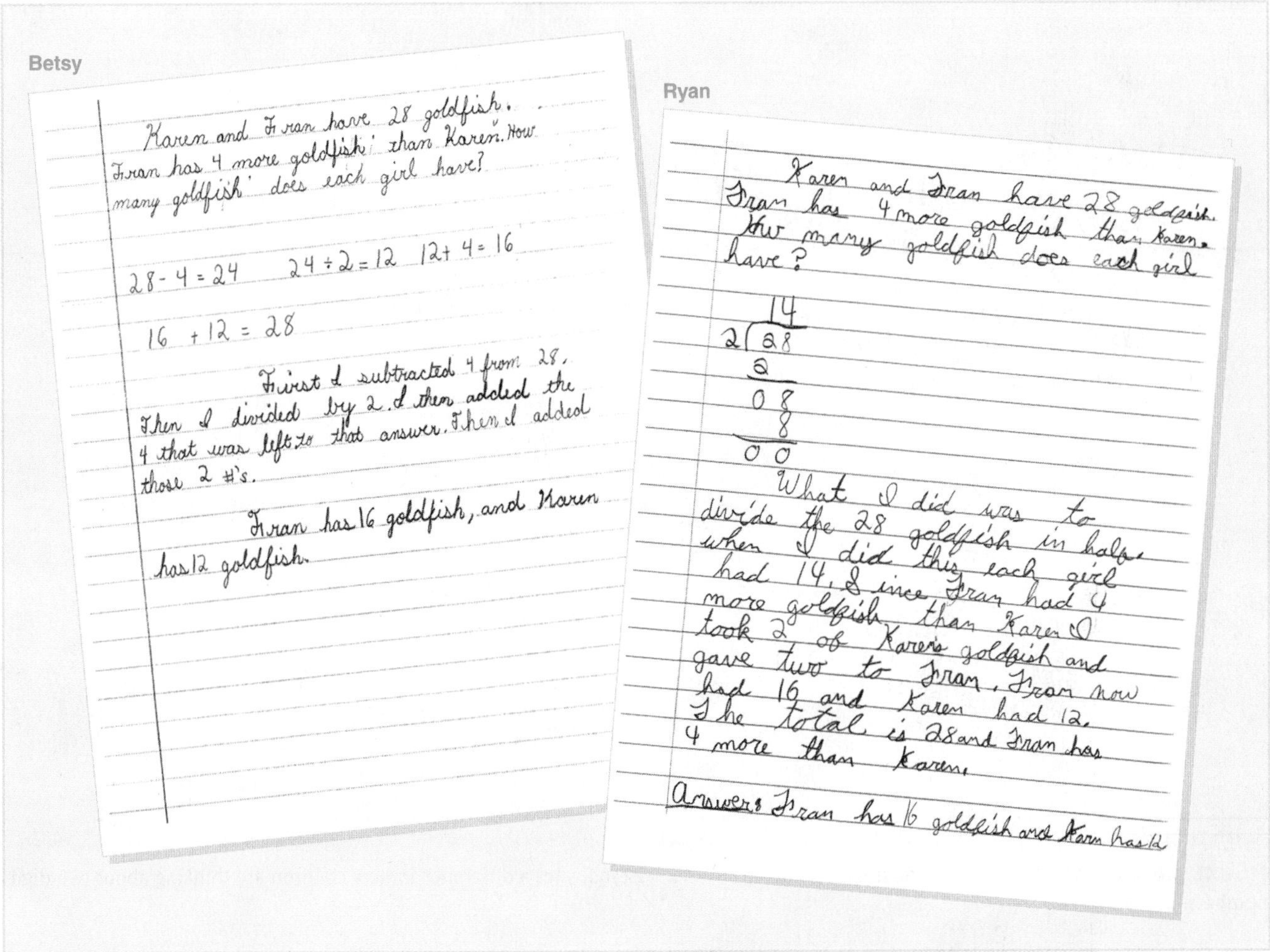

Betsy

Karen and Fran have 28 goldfish. Fran has 4 more goldfish than Karen. How many goldfish does each girl have?

$28 - 4 = 24$ $24 \div 2 = 12$ $12 + 4 = 16$

$16 + 12 = 28$

Fiirst I subtracted 4 from 28. Then I divided by 2. I then added the 4 that was left to that answer. Then I added those 2 #'s.

Fran has 16 goldfish, and Karen has 12 goldfish.

Ryan

Karen and Fran have 28 goldfish. Fran has 4 more goldfish than Karen. How many goldfish does each girl have?

$$\begin{array}{r} 14 \\ 2\overline{)28} \\ \underline{2} \\ 08 \\ \underline{8} \\ 0\ 0 \end{array}$$

What I did was to divide the 28 goldfish in half when I did this each girl had 14. Since Fran had 4 more goldfish than Karen I took 2 of Karen's goldfish and gave two to Fran. Fran now had 16 and Karen had 12. The total is 28 and Fran has 4 more than Karen.

Answer: Fran has 16 goldfish and Karen has 12

FIGURE 3.5 Betsy tells each step in her solution but provides no explanation. In contrast, Ryan's work includes reasons for his steps.

Wikis (free, asynchronous, collaborative website creation tools)

- PBworks (http://pbworks.com/content/edu-classroom-teachers)
- Wikispaces—includes the ability to use math equations (www.wikispaces.com)
- Wikidot (www.wikidot.com)

Blogging Tools

- Blogger (www.blogger.com)
- Tumblr (www.tumblr.com)
- WordPress (http://wordpress.com)

Web-based tools such as these can be used in the mathematics classroom, the computer lab, the library, and at home to allow students and teachers to collaboratively draft, read, and edit one another's mathematical ideas. Students who are reluctant to write by hand or in a word document could be motivated by the more interactive technologies, increasing the likelihood that they will produce quality written explanations.

Equity and Teaching Through Problem Solving

Teaching through problem solving provides opportunities for all students to become mathematically proficient. This view is supported by NCTM standards and by prominent mathematics educators who have worked extensively with at-risk populations (Boaler, 2008; Diversity in Mathematics Education, 2007; Gutstein, Lipman, Hernandez, & Reyes, 1997; NCTM, 2000; Silver & Stein, 1996). Teaching through problem solving:

- *Focuses students' attention on ideas and sense making.* When solving problems, students are necessarily reflecting on the concepts inherent in the problems. Emerging concepts are more likely to be integrated with existing ones, thereby improving understanding. This approach honors the different knowledge students bring to the classroom.

FIGURE 3.6 The work of two first-grade students solving 10 + 13 + 22 indicates a difference in how children are thinking about two-digit numbers.

• *Develops mathematical processes.* Students solving problems in class will be engaged in all five of the processes of doing mathematics—the process standards described by NCTM's *Principles and Standards*: problem solving, reasoning, communication, connections, and representation. These processes move mathematics into a domain that is more accessible, more interesting, and more meaningful.

• *Develops student confidence and identities.* As students engage in learning through problem solving, they begin to identify themselves as doers of mathematics (Cobb, Gresalfi, & Hodge, 2009; Leatham & Hill, 2010). Every time teachers pose a problem-based task and expect a solution, they say to students, "I believe you can do this." When students are engaged in discourse where the correctness of the solution lies in the justification of the process, they begin to see themselves as mathematicians.

• *Provides a context to help students build meaning for the concept.* Providing a context, especially when that context is grounded in an experience familiar to students, supports the development of mathematics concepts. Such an approach provides students access to the mathematics, allowing them to successfully learn the content.

• *Allows an entry and exit point for a wide range of students.* Good problem-based tasks have multiple paths to the solution. Students may solve 42 – 26 by counting out a set of 42 counters and removing 26, by adding onto 26 in various ways to get to 42, by subtracting 20 from 42 and then taking off 6 more, by counting forward (or backward) on a hundreds chart, or by using a standard computational method. Each student gets to make sense of the task using his or her own ideas. Furthermore, students expand on these ideas and grow in their understanding as they hear and reflect on the solution strategies of others. In contrast, the teacher-directed approach ignores diversity, to the detriment of most students.

• *Allows for extensions and elaborations.* Extensions and "what if" questions can motivate advanced learners or quick finishers, resulting in increased learning and enthusiasm for doing mathematics. Such problems can be configured to meet the needs of a range of learners.

• *Engages students so that there are fewer discipline problems.* Many discipline issues in a classroom are the result of students becoming bored, not understanding the teacher directions, or simply finding little relevance in the task. Most students like to be challenged and enjoy being permitted to solve problems in ways that make sense to them, giving them less reason to act out or cause trouble.

• *Provides formative assessment data.* As students discuss ideas, draw pictures or use manipulatives, defend their solutions and evaluate those of others, and write reports or explanations, they provide the teacher with a steady stream of valuable information. These products provide rich evidence of how students are solving problems, what misconceptions they might have, and how they are connecting and applying new concepts. With a better understanding of what students know, a teacher can plan more effectively and accommodate each student's learning needs.

• *Is a lot of fun!* Students enjoy the creative process of problem solving, searching for patterns, and showing how they figured something out. Teachers find it exciting to see the surprising and inventive ways students think. Teachers know more about their students and appreciate the diversity within their classrooms when they focus on problem solving.

When students have confidence, show perseverance, and enjoy mathematics, it makes sense that they will achieve at a higher level and want to continue learning about mathematics—opening many doors to them in the future. In the following section, a three-phase lesson format is explained. This lesson structure engages students in learning through problem solving.

A Three-Phase Lesson Format

In a non-problem-based lesson, teachers typically spend a small portion of a lesson explaining or reviewing an idea and then go into "production mode," where students wade through a set of similar exercises. When this explain-then-practice pattern is used, students are conditioned to wait for the teacher to tell them how to do something, rather than try to apply their own knowledge. The mathematical proficiencies described in Chapter 2, in particular adaptive reasoning, strategic competence, and productive disposition, are not developed in such a lesson; rather students are imitating what the teacher is modeling and replicating it. After a teacher explanation, teachers find themselves going from student to student to reteach the lesson, because it didn't meet the students where they were or engage students.

In contrast, teaching through problem solving, also called problem-based teaching, does start where the students are, engage students in the mathematics, and involve students in justifying their thinking. A problem-based lesson is often taught in three phases—before, during, and after (see Figure 3.7). The lesson may take a full day or even longer. Each phase of the lesson has a specific goal. How you attend to these goals may vary depending on the class, the problem itself, and the purpose of the lesson.

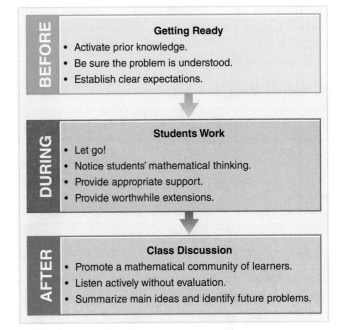

FIGURE 3.7 Teaching through problem solving lends itself to a three-phase structure for lessons.

The *Before* Phase of a Lesson

There are three related agendas for the *before* phase of a lesson:

1. *Activate prior knowledge.* This means to begin by pulling in what students' have previously learned, as well as connect to their personal experiences.
2. *Be sure the problem is understood.* This does not mean to explain *how* to solve it, just to be sure the task at hand is clear.
3. *Establish clear expectations.* This includes both how they will be working (individually, in pairs or small groups) and what product you expect to demonstrate their understanding of the problem.

These *before* phase agendas need not be addressed in the order listed. For example, for some lessons you will do a short activity to activate students' prior knowledge for the problem and then present the problem and clarify expectations. Other lessons may begin with understanding the problem and then having students brainstorm their own experiences related to the topic of the problem.

Teacher Actions in the *Before* Phase

What you do in the *before* portion of a lesson will vary with the task. For example, if your students are used to solving story problems and know they are expected to use words, pictures, and numbers to explain their solutions in writing, all that may be required is to read through the problem with them and be sure all understand it. On the other hand, if students are asked to model a problem with a new manipulative, more time is needed to familiarize students with the tool and perhaps model how the manipulative can be used to model similar problems.

1. Activate Prior Knowledge.

Activate specific prior knowledge related to today's concept. What form this preparation activity might take will vary with the topic, as shown in the following options and examples.

Begin with a Simple Version of the Task. Some tasks are more accessible if students first explore a related but simpler task.

Concept: Perimeter (Lappan & Even, 1989).
Grades: 4–6

Assume that the edge of a square is 1 unit. Add square tiles to this shape so that it has a perimeter of 18 units.

Instead of beginning your lesson with this problem, you might consider activating prior knowledge in one of the following ways:

• Draw a 3-by-5 rectangle of squares on the board and ask students what they know about the shape. (It's a rectangle. It has squares. There are 15 squares. There are three rows of five.) If no one mentions the words *area* and *perimeter*, you could write them on the board and ask if those words can be used in talking about this figure.

• Provide students with some square tiles or grid paper and say, "I want everyone to make a shape that has a perimeter of 12 units. After you make your shape, find out what its area is." After a short time, have several students share their shapes. Students can also use a virtual geoboard, like the one found at the Math Playground (www.mathplayground.com/geoboard.html).

Each of these warm-ups uses the vocabulary needed for the focus task. The second activity suggests the tiles as a possible model students may elect to use and introduces the idea that there are different figures with the same perimeter.

The following problem is designed to help students use addition to solve a subtraction problem.

Concept: Subtraction
Grades: 2–3

Dad says it is 503 miles to the beach. When we stopped for gas, we had gone 267 miles. How much farther do we have to drive?

Before presenting this problem, you can elicit prior knowledge by asking the class to supply the missing part of 100 after you give one part. Try numbers like 80 or 30 at first; then try 47 or 62. When you present the actual task, you might ask students if the answer to the problem is more or less than 300 miles.

Connect to Students' Experiences. Whether a problem begins with a context or not, bringing in students' life experiences can help them see mathematics as relevant to them and make sense of the problem to be solved.

Concepts: Ratios and Statistics
Grades: 6–7

Enrollment data for the school provide information about the students and their families—in this case, comparing the whole school to one class.

	School	*Class*
Siblings		
None	36	5
One	89	4
Two	134	17
More than two	93	3
Race		
African American	49	11
Asian American	12	0
White	219	15
Travel-to-School Method		
Walk	157	10
Bus	182	19
Other	13	0

If someone asked you how typical the class was, compared to the rest of the school, how would you answer? Write an explanation of your answer. Include one or more charts or graphs that you think would support your conclusion.

The teacher might begin the task by gathering class data and asking students to compare their own class to the class in the problem. This connects to the students and to the mathematics, as the task requires comparisons. Students might discuss (e.g., think-pair-share) what "typical" means and how they could determine what a typical class is.

Estimate or Predict. When the task is aimed at the development of a computational procedure, a useful *before* action is to have students actually do the computation mentally or suggest an estimated answer. This practice can raise curiosity as to what the answer might be.

Concept: Multiplication
Grades: 3–4

How many small unit squares will fit in a rectangle that is 54 units long and 36 units wide? Use base-ten blocks to help you with your solution. Note that base-ten blocks come in ones (one cube), tens (a row of ten cubes), and hundreds (a ten-by-ten grid). Make a plan for figuring out the total number of squares without doing too much counting. Explain how your plan would work on a rectangle that is 27 units by 42 units.

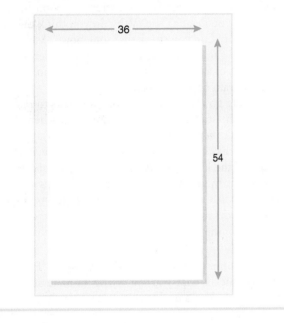

---

2. Be Sure the Problem Is Understood. Understanding the problem is not optional! You must always be sure that students understand the problem before setting them to work. It is important for you to analyze the problem in order to anticipate student approaches and possible misinterpretations or misconceptions (Wallace, 2007). Time spent at this stage of the problem-solving process is critical to the rest of the lesson. You can ask questions to clarify student understanding of the problem (i.e., knowing what it means rather than how they will solve it). For example, ask, "What do you know?" and "What do you need to know?" Wallace, a mathematics researcher and teacher, notes, "The more I questioned *prior to* giving the problem, the less help the students needed from me *during* problem solving" (p. 510).

Consider a problem-based approach to mastering the multiplication facts. The most difficult facts can each be connected or related to an easier fact already learned, called a "helping fact."

Concept: Multiplication Facts
Grades: 3–4

Use a "helping fact" (a multiplication fact you already know) to help you solve each of these problems: 4×6, 6×8, 7×6, 3×8.

For this task, it is essential that students understand the idea of using a helping fact. They have most likely used helping facts in addition. You can build on this prior knowledge by asking, "When you learned addition facts, how could knowing $6 + 6$ help you find the answer to $6 + 7$?"

In the case of a word problem, like the following one, it is important to help students understand the meaning of the sentences, without giving away how to solve the problem. This is particularly important for poor readers and for ELLs.

Concept: Multiplication and Division
Grades: 3–5

The local candy store purchased candy in cartons holding 12 boxes per carton. The price paid for one carton was $42.50. Each box contained 8 candy bars that the store planned to sell individually. What was the candy store's cost for each candy bar?

Questions to build background might include: "What is the problem asking? How does the candy store buy candy? What is in a carton? What is in a box? What does that mean when it says 'each box'?" The last question here is to identify vocabulary that may be misunderstood. It is good to first ask students what the problem is asking. Asking students to reread a problem does little good, but asking students to restate the problem or tell what question is being asked helps students be better readers and problem solvers.

If you have struggling readers or English language learners, additional support may be needed. Explicit attention to vocabulary is critical. Graphic organizers can aid in reading and understanding the text.

3. Establish Clear Expectations. There are two components to establishing expectations: (1) how students are to work and (2) what products they are to prepare for the discussion.

It is always a good idea for students to have some opportunity to discuss their ideas with one or more classmates prior to sharing their thoughts in the *after* phase of the lesson. When students work in groups, though, there is the possibility of some students not contributing or learning. On the other hand, when students work alone, they have no one to look to for an idea and no chance to talk about the mathematics and practice what they might later share with the whole group. So it is essential to have students be individually accountable and also work together.

One way to address both individual accountability and sharing with other students is a think-write-pair-share approach (Buschman, 2003b). The first two steps are done individually, and then students are paired for continued work on the problem. With independent written work to share, students have something to talk about. Although all students benefit from this strategy, it is especially helpful for K–1 students or reluctant learners who tend to passively observe in group situations.

Because teaching through problem solving focuses on processes (strategies) and solutions, it is important to model and explain what a final product might be. One expectation could be a written explanation and/or illustration of the problem. As noted earlier, writing supports student learning in mathematics, and having multiple ways to demonstrate knowledge is important for providing access to all learners. One effective strategy is to have each student write and illustrate their solution, but to present the team's solution as a group, with each person sharing a part of the presentation.

The *During* Phase of a Lesson

In the *during* phase of the lesson, students explore the focus task (alone, with partners, or in small groups). There are clear agendas that you will want to attend to:

1. *Let go!* Give students a chance to work without too much guidance. Allow and encourage students to embrace the struggle—it is an important part of doing mathematics.
2. *Notice students' mathematical thinking.* Take this time to find out what different students are thinking, what ideas they are using, and how they are approaching the problem. This is a time for observation and formative assessment.
3. *Provide appropriate support.* Consider ways to support student thinking (as needed) without taking away their thinking. Be careful not to imply that you have the correct method of solving the problem.
4. *Provide worthwhile extensions.* Have something prepared for students who finish quickly to extend their thinking.

Teacher Actions in the *During* Phase

These agendas can challenge teachers who tend to help too much. In making instructional decisions in the *during* phase you must ask yourself, "Does my action lead to deeper thinking or is it taking away the thinking?" These decisions are based on carefully listening to students and knowing the content goals of the lesson.

1. Let Go! Once students understand what the problem is asking, it is time to *let go*. While it is tempting to "step in front of the struggle" in the *during* phase, you need to hold yourself back. Doing mathematics takes time, and solutions are not always obvious. It is important to communicate to students that spending time on a task, trying different approaches, and consulting each other are important to learning and understanding mathematics. When students are stuck, you can ask questions like, "Is this like another problem we have solved?" "Did you try to make a picture?" "What is it about this problem that is difficult?" This approach is effective in helping students because you are supporting their thinking, yet you are not telling them how to solve the problem.

Students will look to you for approval of their results or ideas. Avoid being the source of right and wrong. When asked if a result or method is correct, respond by saying, "How can you decide?" or "Why do you think that might be right?" or "Can you check that somehow?" Asking "How can we tell if that makes sense?" reminds students that the correctness of an answer lies in the justification, not in the teacher's brain or answer key.

Letting go also means allowing students to make mistakes. When students make mistakes (and when they are correct), ask them to explain their process or approach to you. They may catch their mistake. In addition, in the *after* portion of the lesson, students will have an opportunity to explain, justify, defend, and challenge solutions and strategies. This process of uncovering misconceptions or computational errors nurtures the important notion that mistakes are opportunities for learning (Boaler & Humphreys, 2005).

2. Notice Students' Mathematical Thinking. "Professional noticing" means that you are trying to understand a student's approach to a problem and decide in the moment an appropriate response to extend that student's thinking (Jacobs, Lamb, & Philipp, 2010). Consequently your questions must be based on the students' work and responses to you. This is very different from listening for a known response or *the* answer, and in fact is quite difficult to do, because questions are based on what is heard or seen from the student.

The *during* phase is one of two opportunities you have to find out what your students know, how they think, and how they are approaching the task you have given them. (The other is in the *after* phase.) As students are working, any of the following prompts can help you notice what they know and are thinking:

- Tell me what you are doing.
- I see you have started to [multiply] these numbers. Can you tell me why you are [multiplying]?" [substitute any process/strategy]
- Can you tell me more about . . . ?
- Why did you . . . ?

- How did you solve it?
- How does your picture connect to your equation?

By asking questions, you find out where students are in their understanding of the concepts.

Conversely, you can inadvertently say things that shut down student thinking and damage self-esteem. "It's easy" and "Let me help you" are two such statements. Think about the message each one sends. If a student is stuck and you say, "It's easy," then you inadvertently say, "you are not very smart or you wouldn't be stuck." Similarly, saying "Let me help you" communicates that you think the student cannot solve the problem without help. The probing questions offered here, in contrast, communicate to students the real messages you want to send: "Doing mathematics takes time and thinking. You can do it—let's see what you know and go from there."

3. Provide Appropriate Support.

If a group or student is searching for a place to begin, you might suggest some broad strategies (in addition to using the probing questions listed). Jacobs and Ambrose (2008) suggest four "teacher moves" to support student thinking before giving a correct answer:

- Ensure the student understands the problem. ("What do you know about the problem?") If needed, change the context to a more familiar context so that the student does understand it.
- Change the mathematics to a parallel problem with simpler values. This is something students will eventually use as their own problem-solving strategy (as described earlier in this chapter).
- Ask students what they have tried. ("What have you tried so far?" "Where did you get stuck?").
- Suggest to the student to use a different strategy. ("Have you thought about drawing a picture?" "What if you used cubes to act out this problem?")

Concept: Percent Increase and Decrease
Grades: 6–8

In Fern's Furniture Store, Fern has priced all of her furniture at 20 percent over wholesale. In preparation for a sale, she tells her staff to cut all prices by 10 percent. Will Fern be making a 10 percent profit, less than a 10 percent profit, or more than a 10 percent profit? Explain your answer.

For this problem, consider the following suggestions that do not take away student thinking, but provide some starting point:

- "Try drawing a picture or a diagram of something that shows what 10 percent off and 20 percent more means."
- "Have you tried picking a price and seeing what happens when you increase the price by 20 percent and then reduce the price by 10 percent?"

Notice that these suggestions are not directive, but rather, they serve as starters. After offering a hint, walk away—this keeps you from helping too much and the student from relying on you too much.

4. Provide Worthwhile Extensions.

Some students will always finish earlier than their classmates. Early finishers can often be challenged in some manner connected to the problem just solved without it seeming like extra work.

Many good problems are simple on the surface. It is the extensions that are challenging. The area and perimeter task in this chapter is a case in point. Many students will quickly come up with one or two solutions. "I see you found one way to do this. Are there any other solutions? Are any of the solutions different or more interesting than others? Which of the shapes with a perimeter of 18 has the largest area and which has the smallest area? Does the perimeter always change when you add another tile?"

Questions that begin "What if . . . ?" or "Would that same idea work for . . . ?" are ways to extend student thinking in a motivating way. For example, "Suppose you tried to find all the shapes possible with a perimeter of 18. What could you find out about the areas?" As an example, consider the following task.

Concept: Percent Increase and Decrease
Grades: 6–8

The dress was originally priced at $90. If the sale price is 25 percent off, how much will it cost on sale?

This is an example of a straightforward problem with a single answer. Many students will solve it by multiplying by 0.25 and subtracting the result from $90. Ask students, "Could you find another way? Rico solved it by finding 75 percent of 90—does this work? Will it work in all situations? Why?" Or you can extend the use of different representations by asking, "How would you solve it using fractions instead of decimals? Draw me a diagram that explains what you did."

Second graders will frequently solve the next problem by counting or using addition.

Concept: Addition and Subtraction
Grades: K–2

Maxine had saved up $9. The next day she received her allowance. Now she has $12. How much allowance did she get?

"How would you do that on a calculator?" and "Can you write two equations that represent this situation?" are ways of encouraging children to connect $9 + ? = 12$ with $12 - 9 = ?$.

The *After* Phase of a Lesson

In the *after* phase of the lesson, your students will work as a community of learners, discussing, justifying, and challenging various solutions to the problem all have just worked on. Here is where much of the learning will occur, as students reflect individually and collectively on the ideas they have explored. It is challenging but critical to plan sufficient time for a discussion. The agendas for the *after* phase are easily stated but difficult to achieve:

1. *Promote a mathematical community of learners.* Engage the class in productive discussion, helping students work together as a community of learners.

2. *Listen actively without evaluation.* Take this second major opportunity to find out how students are thinking—how they are approaching the problem. Evaluating methods and solutions is the duty of your students.

3. *Summarize main ideas and identify future problems.* You can make connections between strategies or different mathematical ideas and/or lay the groundwork for future tasks and activities.

Teacher Actions in the *After* Phase

Be certain to plan ample time for this portion of the lesson and then be certain to *save* the time. Twenty minutes is not at all unreasonable for a good class discussion and sharing of ideas. It is not necessary for every student to have finished, but all students will have something to share. This is not a time to check answers but for the class to share ideas.

1. Promote a Mathematical Community of Learners. Over time, you will develop your class into a mathematical community of learners where students feel comfortable taking risks and sharing ideas, where students and the teacher respect one another's ideas even when they disagree, where ideas are defended and challenged respectfully, and where logical or mathematical reasoning is valued above all. You must teach your students about your expectations for this time and how to interact respectfully with their peers.

Earlier in the chapter, the section "Orchestrating Classroom Discourse" provided research, strategies, and recommendations. While this section is short here, this may be the most important agenda in a lesson.

2. Listen Actively Without Evaluation. Like the *during* phase, the goal here is noticing students' mathematical thinking and, in addition, making that thinking visible to other students. When you serve as a facilitator and not an evaluator, students will be more willing to share their ideas during discussions. Resist the temptation to judge the correctness of an answer. When you say, "That's correct, Dewain," there is no longer a reason for students to think about and evaluate the response. Had students disagreed with Dewain's response or had a question about it, they will

not challenge or question it since you've said it was correct. Consequently, you will not have the chance to hear and learn from them and notice how they are thinking about the problem. You can support student thinking without evaluation. "What do others think about what Dewain just said?"

Relatedly, use praise cautiously. Praise offered for correct solutions or excitement over interesting ideas suggests that the students did something unusual or unexpected. This can be negative feedback for those who do not get praise. Comments such as "Good job!" and "Super work!" roll off the tongue easily. However, there is evidence to suggest that we should be careful with expressions of praise, especially with respect to student products and solutions (Kohn, 1993; Schwartz, 1996).

In place of praise that is judgmental, Schwartz (1996) suggests comments of interest and extension: "I wonder what would happen if you tried . . ." or "Please tell me how you figured that out." Notice that these phrases express interest and value the student's thinking. For example, if Chrisstine is sharing her work (see Figure 3.8) to show how many different ways five people could be on the two stories of a house, you can ask Chrisstine to explain her thinking and ask Chrisstine and her classmates such things as, "Are all of these ways different?" or "I wonder if there are other ways?" or "I wonder if there is a way to know if we have found all the ways?" These prompts engage all students in thinking about Chrisstine's solution and extend everyone's thinking about the problem.

There will be times when a student will get stuck in the middle of an explanation. Be sensitive about calling on someone else to "help out." You may be communicating that the student is not capable on his or her own. Some teachers establish a classroom practice of the student actually asking to "phone a friend" if they get confused when explaining. Allow ample time. You can offer to give the student time and come back to them after hearing another strategy.

Kindergarten
How many ways can five people be on two stories of a house?

FIGURE 3.8 Chrisstine shows her thinking about ways to make 5.

Remember, the *after* phase is your window into their thinking and therefore an assessment of their learning. Listening actively and noticing student thinking will provide insights for planning tomorrow's lesson and beyond.

3. Summarize Main Ideas and Identify Future Problems.

The main purpose of the *after* phase is to formalize the main ideas of the lesson. In addition, it is the time to reinforce appropriate terminology, definitions, or symbols.

If a problem involves multiple methods of computing, list the different strategies on the board. These can be labeled with the student's name and an example. Ask students questions that help them understand and see connections between the strategies.

There are numerous ways to share verbally, such as a partner exchange, where one partner tells one key idea and the other partner gives an example. Following oral summaries with individual written summaries is important to ensure that you know what each child has learned from the lesson. For example, exit slips (handouts with one or two prompts that ask students to explain the main ideas of the lesson) can be used as an "exit" from the math instruction. Or be creative—ask students to write a newspaper headline to describe the day's activity and a brief column to summarize it. There are many different templates and writing starters that are engaging for students.

Finally, challenge students to think beyond the problem. Ask students to make conjectures and look for generalizations. For example, when comparing fractions, suppose that a group makes this generalization and you display it: *When deciding which fraction is larger, the fraction in which the bottom number is closer to the top number is the larger fraction. Example: $\frac{4}{7}$ is not as big as $\frac{7}{8}$ because 7 is only 1 from 8 but 4 is 3 away from* 7. This is an interesting hypothesis, but it is not correct in all instances. A problem for a subsequent day can examine this conjecture to determine whether it is always right or to find fractions for which it is not right (counterexamples).

Frequently Asked Questions

The following are questions teachers have asked about implementing a teaching through problem solving approach to instruction.

1. *How can I teach all the basic skills I have to teach?* It is tempting, especially with pressures of state testing programs, to resort to rote drill and practice to teach "basic skills." Some people believe that mastery of the basics is incompatible with a problem-based approach. However, the evidence strongly suggests otherwise. In fact, drill-oriented approaches in U.S. classrooms have consistently produced poor results in developing mathematical understanding (Battista, 1999; Hiebert & Grouws, 2007; Kamii & Dominick, 1998). Short-term gains on low-level skills may possibly result from drill, but even state testing programs require more than low-level skills.

Second, research data indicate that on basic skills, as measured by standardized tests, students in programs using a problem-based approach do as well or better than students in traditional programs (Carpenter, Franke, Jacobs, Fennema, & Empson, 1998; Hiebert, 2003; Hiebert & Wearne, 1996; Riordan & Noyce, 2001; Silver & Stein, 1996; Stein & Smith, 2010). Any deficit in skill development is more than outweighed by strength in concepts and problem solving.

Finally, traditional skills such as basic facts and procedures can be effectively learned in an approach that emphasizes understanding (Hiebert & Grouws, 2007; Huinker, 1998).

2. *Why is it often better for students to "tell" or "explain" than for me to do so?* First, students' explanations are grounded in their own understanding. Second, as students communicate their mathematical ideas in words, they are solidifying their own understanding. Third, there are implications for creating a community of learners. Students will question their peers when an explanation does not make sense to them, whereas explanations from the teacher are usually accepted without scrutiny (and possibly without understanding). Finally, when students are responsible for explaining, the class members develop a sense of pride and confidence that *they* can figure things out and make sense of mathematics. *They* have power and ability.

3. *Is it okay to help students who have difficulty solving a problem?* Of course you want to help students who are struggling. However, as Buschman (2003b) suggests, rather than propose how to solve a problem, a better approach is to try to find out *why* the student is having difficulty. If you jump in with help, you may not even be addressing the real reason the student is struggling. It may be as simple as not understanding the problem or as complex as a lack of understanding of a fundamental concept. "Tell me what you are thinking" is a good beginning.

Recall our previous discussion of the negative consequences of these two simple sentences: "It's easy!" "Let me help you." Instead, try to build on the student's knowledge. Do not rob students of the feeling of accomplishment and the true growth in understanding that come from solving a problem themselves. Remember, productive struggle is linked to student learning!

4. *Where can I find the time to cover everything?* Mathematics is much more connected and integrated than a look at the itemized objectives found on many state "standards" lists might suggest. To deal with coverage, the first suggestion is to teach with a goal of developing the "big ideas," the main concepts in a unit or chapter. Most of the skills and ideas on your list of objectives will be addressed as you progress. If you focus separately on each item on the list, then big ideas and connections, the essence of understanding, are unlikely to develop. Second, we spend far too much time reteaching because students don't retain ideas. Time spent up front to help students develop meaningful networks of ideas drastically reduces the need for reteaching and remediation, thus creating time in the long term.

5. *How much time does it take for students to become a community of learners and really begin to share and discuss ideas?* Students have to be coached in how to participate in a classroom discussion about a problem and how to work collaboratively in small groups. For the first weeks of school, time must be devoted to explicitly teaching and modeling these skills. Frequent reinforcement of participation and active listening is needed initially; then the support becomes less necessary as the community is established. Students in the primary grades will adapt much more quickly than students in the upper grades, as they have not yet developed an expectation that mathematics class is about sitting quietly and following the rules. Probing, asking good questions, and developing a community of learners require a long-term commitment. Don't give up!

6. *Can I use a combination of student-oriented problem-based teaching with a teacher-directed approach?* Switching instructional approaches is not recommended. By switching methods, students become confused as to what is expected of them. More importantly, students will come to believe that their own ideas do not really matter because the teacher will eventually tell them the "right" way to do it (Mokros, Russell, & Economopoulos, 1995). In order for students to become invested in a problem-based approach, they must deeply believe that their ideas are important and that the source of knowledge is themselves—every day.

7. *Is there any place for drill and practice?* Absolutely! The error is to believe that drill is a method of developing or reinforcing concepts. Drill is appropriate when (1) the desired concepts have been meaningfully developed, (2) flexible and useful procedures have been developed, *and* (3) speed and accuracy are needed. With drill and practice, the important thing to remember is a little goes a long way. Drilling on basic facts should take no more than 10 minutes in one sitting. Five multiplication problems can be as useful in assessing student understanding as 25 problems; therefore, not much is gained from the additional 20 problems. Also, when students are making mistakes, more drill and practice is not the solution—identifying and addressing misconceptions is far more effective. For example, some middle school students still do not know their multiplication facts. Drilling on the 144 facts won't help nearly as much as working on strategies for the targeted facts a student is forgetting (e.g., helping facts). (See Chapter 10 for more on basic facts.)

8. *What do I do when a problem-based lesson bombs?* It will happen, although not as often as you think, that students just do not know what to do with a problem you pose, no matter how many hints and suggestions you offer. Do not give in to the temptation to "tell them." Set it aside for the moment. Ask yourself why it didn't work well. Did the students have the prior knowledge they needed? Was the task too advanced? Often we need to regroup and offer students a simpler related task that gets them prepared for the one that proved too difficult. When you sense that a task is not going anywhere, regroup! Don't spend days just hoping that something wonderful might happen. Instead, consider what might be a way to step back or step forward in the content in order to support and challenge students.

RESOURCES *for Chapter 3*

RECOMMENDED READINGS

Articles

Hartweg, K., & Heisler, M. (2007). No tears here! Third-grade problem solvers. *Teaching Children Mathematics, 13*(7), 362–368.

These authors elaborate on how they have implemented the before, during, and after lesson phases. They offer suggestions for supporting student understanding of the problem, ideas for questioning, and templates for student writing. The data they gathered on the response of teachers and students are impressive!

Reinhart, S. C. (2000). Never say anything a kid can say! *Mathematics Teaching in the Middle School, 5*(8), 478–483.

The author is an experienced middle school teacher who questioned his own "masterpiece" lessons after realizing that his students were often confused. This classic article shares a teacher's

journey to a teaching through problem solving approach. Reinhart's suggestions for questioning techniques and involving students are superb.

Rigelman, N. R. (2007). Fostering mathematical thinking and problem solving: The teacher's role. *Teaching Children Mathematics, 13*(6), 308–314.

This is a wonderful article for illustrating the subtle (and not so subtle) differences between true problem solving and "proceduralizing" problem solving. Because two contrasting vignettes are offered, it gives an excellent opportunity for discussing how the two teachers differ philosophically and in their practices.

Books

Boaler, J., & Humphreys, C. (2005). *Connecting mathematical ideas: Middle school video cases to support teaching and learning.* Portsmouth, NH: Heinemann.

This book offers cases from Cathy Humphreys's classroom based on different content areas and issues in teaching. Each case is followed by a commentary. Accompanying the book are two CDs that provide videos of the cases.

Buschman, L. (2003). *Share and compare: A teacher's story about helping children become problem solvers in mathematics.* Reston, VA: NCTM.

Larry Buschman describes how he makes problem solving work in his classroom. Much of the book is written as if a teacher were interviewing Larry as he answers the kinds of questions you may also have.

Hiebert, J., Carpenter, T. P., Fennema, E., Fuson, K., Wearne, D., Murray, H., Olivier, A., & Human, P. (1997). *Making sense: Teaching and learning mathematics with understanding.* Portsmouth, NH: Heinemann.

The authors of this significant and classic book make one of the best cases for developing mathematics through problem solving.

ONLINE RESOURCES

Annenberg/CPB
www.learner.org

A unit of the Annenberg Foundation, Annenberg/CPB offers professional development information and useful information for teachers who want to learn about and teach mathematics.

Math Solutions Classroom Lessons
www.mathsolutions.com/index.cfm?page=wp9&crid=56

This is a great collection of lessons for teaching through problem solving.

NCTM's Problem Database
http://nctm.org/resources/content.aspx?id=16387

Free for all NCTM members, this resource contains thousands of problems, sorted by level and topic, from articles published in past issues of *Teaching Children Mathematics, Mathematics Teaching in the Middle School, Student Math Notes, and Figure This!*

ENC Online (Eisenhower National Clearinghouse)
www.goenc.com

Click on Digital Dozen, Lessons and Activities, or Web Links. The ENC site is full of useful information for teachers who are planning lessons and activities or searching for professional development resources.

Writing and Communication in Mathematics
http://mathforum.org/library/ed_topics/writing_in_math

This Math Forum page lists numerous articles and Web links concerning the value of writing in mathematics at all levels.

REFLECTIONS *on Chapter 3*

WRITING TO LEARN

1. Of the many suggestions provided in this chapter, which three do you want to remember when it comes to selecting a worthwhile problem?
2. Polya's four-step process maps to a *before, during,* and *after* lesson plan model. What questions might you ask students to support their thinking in each of the four steps?
3. Describe in your own words what is meant by "discourse." What are some important considerations in effectively implementing classroom discourse?
4. What are some of the benefits of having students write in mathematics class? When should the writing take place? How can very young students "write"?
5. Why are "It's easy!" and "Let me help you" not good choices for supporting students? What is a better way of supporting a student who is having difficulty solving a problem?

FOR DISCUSSION AND EXPLORATION

1. Select an activity from any chapter in Section II of this text. How can the activity be used as a problem or task for the purpose of teaching through problem solving? If you were using this activity in the classroom, what specifically would you do during the *before, during,* and *after* phases of the lesson? (Include effective questions for each phase.)
2. Find a traditional textbook for any grade level. Look through a chapter and find at least one lesson that you could convert to a problem-based lesson without drastically altering the lesson as it was written.

MyEducationLab™

Go to the MyEducationLab (www.myeducationlab.com) for Math Methods and familiarize yourself with the content. Much of the site content is organized topically. The topics include all of the following to support your learning in the course:

- Learning outcomes for important mathematics methods course topics aligned with the national standards
- Assignments and Activities, tied to these learning outcomes and standards, that can help you more deeply understand course content
- Building Teaching Skills and Dispositions learning units that allow you to apply and practice your understanding of the core mathematics content and teaching skills

Your instructor has a correlation guide that aligns the exercises on the topical portion of the site with your book's chapters.

On MyEducationLab you will also find book-specific resources including Blackline Masters, Expanded Lesson Activities, and Artifact Analysis Activities.

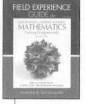

Field Experience Guide
C O N N E C T I O N S

Just as problem solving will be found throughout this book, it is found throughout the *Field Experience Guide*. The levels of cognitive demand (Table 3.1 on p. 37) are adapted to a field-based activity in FEG 2.3. FEG 2.6 provides a template for planning a problem-based lesson and FEG 4.7 focuses on using talk moves in classroom discussions. FEG 2.7 focuses on using children's literature as a context for doing meaningful, worthwhile mathematics. Chapter 9 of the guide offers 24 Expanded Lessons, all designed using the *before, during,* and *after* model. Chapter 10 of the guide offers worthwhile tasks that can be developed into problem-based lessons.

Chapter 4

Planning in the Problem-Based Classroom

Helping students become successful problem solvers should be a long-term instructional goal so that efforts are made toward this goal in every grade level, every mathematical topic, and every lesson . . . Teaching today's students to become the thinking and caring leaders who will be able to solve the world's increasingly complex and quantitative problems requires a total commitment.

Cai (2010, p. 11)

The three-phase lesson format in Chapter 3 provided a structure for problem-based lessons, based on the need for students to be engaged in problems followed by time for discussion and reflection. To successfully implement this instructional model, it is necessary to take a closer look at planning.

This chapter begins with a 10-step planning guide, focusing on teachers' thought processes as they design a lesson. Then the chapter addresses planning for short tasks, making lessons accessible to all learners, and effective homework and family engagement—each important as you plan for effective instruction.

Planning a Problem-Based Lesson

It is crucial that you give substantial thought to lesson planning. There is no such thing as a "teacher-proof" curriculum—where you can simply teach every lesson as it is written and in the order it appears. Every class of students is different. Choosing which tasks to use and how they will be presented in light of the needs of your diverse students and state and local curriculum guidelines is central to effective teaching.

Planning Process for Developing a Lesson

Planning lessons is usually couched within the planning of an instructional unit, each lesson building from the prior lesson to accomplish the unit goals and objectives. This book does not address unit development but instead focuses on how to develop a problem-based lesson within a unit. Figure 4.1 provides an outline of the considerations involved in lesson planning. Content and task decisions (the first column) are often overlooked when lessons are planned—yet this is the most important part of the planning process. Once these decisions are made, the lesson is ready to be designed (see purple-shaded steps in Figure 4.1). Here the focus is on designing activities for students that accomplish the goals outlined in Chapter 3 for the three lesson phases (*before*, *during*, and *after*). It is through these phases that the content goals are accomplished. Once the plan is drafted, it is important to review and finalize the plan, taking into consideration the flow of the lesson, the anticipated challenges, expected responses and misconceptions from students, and the questions or prompts that can best support the learner. Each of the considerations in planning a problem-based lesson is briefly discussed next. Within the considerations, an example lesson titled "Fixed Areas" is discussed to illustrate how the process is implemented (this Expanded Lesson plan is found at the end of the chapter). The *Field Experience Guide* also offers a template (FEG 2.6) that can provide support for designing a lesson.

Step 1: Determine the Mathematics Content and Learning Goals. How do you decide what mathematics your students need to learn? Every state has mathematics curriculum standards. Many have adopted the *Common Core State Standards* (CCSSO, 2010), which identifies mathematics

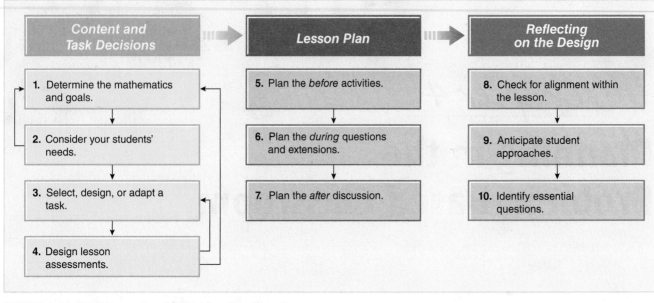

FIGURE 4.1 Planning steps for a problem-based lesson.

content by grade level. Teachers within districts determine how they will teach objectives, making use of their textbook and other resources. Each lesson within a unit is directed toward supporting the larger goal of the unit. In fact, keeping focused on the bigger mathematical goals, rather than small skills, is very important in planning. At the lesson level, it is important to ask, "What is it that my students should be able to *do* when this lesson is over?" Keep in mind that a lesson can take several days to accomplish. As you respond to this question, be sure you are focused on the *mathematics* and not the activity you want to do.

Example: Fixed Areas. In looking at the standards for fourth grade, you read, "Apply the area and perimeter formulas for rectangles in real world and mathematical problems" (CCSSO, 2010). A possible goal for one lesson on this topic is for students to explore the relationship between area and perimeter, specifically that one can change while the other stays the same.

This goal leads to the development of *observable* and *measurable* objectives. The objectives are the very things you want your students to *do* or *say* to demonstrate what they know. There are numerous formats for lesson objectives, but there is consensus that an objective must state clearly what the learner will do.

Example: Fixed Areas. Students will be able to draw a variety of rectangles with a given area and accurately determine the perimeter of each. Students will be able to explain relationships between area and perimeter. Students will write a process (their own algorithm) for finding the perimeter of a rectangle.

Non-Example: Fixed Areas. Students will understand that the perimeter can change and the area can stay the same.

Note that the "example" objectives are actions you can *see* or *hear*. The "non-example," although a reasonable goal to guide your planning, is not an objective because understanding is not observable or measurable.

Step 2: Consider Your Students' Needs. What do your students already know or understand about the selected mathematics concepts? Perhaps they already have some prior knowledge of the content you have been working on, which this lesson is aimed at expanding or refining. Be sure that the mathematics you identified in step 1 includes something new or at least slightly unfamiliar to your students. At the same time, be certain that your objectives are not out of reach.

Consider individual student needs, including learning disabilities and each person's strengths and weaknesses. In addition, language and culture must be a consideration. What might students already know about this topic that can serve as a launching point? What context might be engaging to this range of learners? What learning gaps or misconceptions might need to be addressed? What visuals or models might support student understanding? What vocabulary support might be needed?

Example: Fixed Areas. Students are likely to have prior knowledge of the terms *perimeter* and *area*. However, they may also confuse the meaning of the two. They may have a misconception that for a given area, there is only one perimeter, or vice versa.

Step 3: Select, Design, or Adapt a Task. With your goals and students in mind, you are ready to consider what focus method you will use, perhaps a task, activity, or exercises that may be in your textbook. The importance of selecting a worthwhile task cannot be overstated! See Standard 3 in NCTM's *Professional Standards for Teaching Mathematics* for a helpful list of what is important to consider. Also, recall from Chapter 3 that the following points were made regarding what makes a task worthwhile: level of cognitive demand, multiple entry and exit points, and relevance to students. Because task selection has already been addressed, it is only mentioned briefly here.

The questions to ask yourself are "Does the task you are considering (from the textbook or any other source) accomplish the content goals (step 1) and the needs of my students (step 2)?" and "Is the task worthwhile?" If the answers are yes, you can plan minor adaptations to enhance the lesson, like using a different context that better relates to your students or including a children's literature connection. If you find the task does not fit your content and student needs, then you will need to either make substantial modifications to the task or find a new task.

Step 4: Design Lesson Assessments.

You might wonder why you are thinking about assessment before you have even introduced the lesson, but thinking about what it is you want students to know and how they are going to show that to you *is* assessment. The sentence you just read may give you a déjà-vu experience related to the section on objectives—and so it should. Your assessments are derived from your objectives. It is important to assess in a variety of ways—see Chapter 5 for extended discussions of assessment strategies. Formative assessment is the type of information gathering that lets you know how students are doing on each of the objectives during the lesson. This information can be used for adjusting midstream or making changes for the next day. Formative assessment also informs the questions you pose in the discussion of the task for the *after* phase of the lesson. Summative assessment captures whether students have learned the objectives you have listed for the lesson (or unit).

Example: Fixed Areas. Objective 1: Students will be able to draw a sufficient variety of possible rectangles for a given area and determine the perimeters. *Assessment:* In the *during* phase, I will use a checklist to see whether each student is able to create at least three different rectangles with the given area and accurately record the perimeter. I will ask individuals, "How did you figure out the perimeter of that (point at one rectangle) rectangle?"

Objective 2: Students will be able to describe the relationship between area and perimeter. *Assessment:* In the *during* phase, I will ask individuals, "What have you noticed about the relationship between area and perimeter of these rectangles?" An exit slip will be used that asks students to explain the relationship between area and perimeter of a rectangle and to draw pictures to support their explanation. An exit slip is a written response turned in at the end of class—as an "exit" to the lesson.

Objective 3: Students will describe a process (their own algorithm) for finding perimeter of a rectangle. *Assessment:* In the *during* phase of the lesson, I will ask, "How are you finding perimeter? Are you seeing any patterns or shortcuts? Explain it to me." In the *after* phase, this will be the focus of a discussion.

Steps 1 through 4 define the heart of your lesson. The next three steps explain how you will carry the plan out in your classroom.

Step 5: Plan the *Before* Phase of the Lesson.

As discussed in Chapter 3 in the section titled "Teacher Actions in the *Before* Phase," the beginning of the lesson should elicit students' prior knowledge, provide context, and establish expectations. Think about the task you have selected and how you will introduce it. Questions to guide your thinking include:

- What terminology and background might students need to be ready for the task?
- What questions will you ask to help students access their prior knowledge and relevant experiences? (Will you read a children's book that connects to the task and builds student interest? Is there a current or popular event that could be used to introduce the topic?)
- What challenges might the task present to students, in particular to ELLs and/or students who have disabilities?

Consider how you will present the task. Options include having it written on paper; using their texts; using the document camera on a projection device; or having it written on the interactive whiteboard, chalkboard, or on chart paper. Be sure to tell students about their responsibilities. Students need to know (1) the resources or tools they might use; (2) whether students will work independently or in groups and, if in groups, how groups will be organized, including assigned roles; and (3) how their work will be presented (e.g., completing a handout, writing in a journal, preparing a team poster) (Smith, Bill, & Hughes, 2008).

Example: Fixed Areas. With the school play quickly approaching, I decide to use the context of the stage, asking students to think about building a stage that has an area of 36 square meters. A focus question to raise curiosity is, "Does it matter what the length and width are for the stage floor in terms of how much space we have for doing our play? Would one shape of rectangle be better or worse than another? Let's see what the possibilities are and then pick one that will best serve the performers."

I explain that students will have 20 minutes to use a virtual geoboard (www.cut-the-knot.org/Curriculum/Geometry/Geoboard.shtml) and find different rectangles with an area of 36. They will work in pairs, but each person must record each option on centimeter grid paper. Students will be told they have 20 minutes and then I will ask them to share what they feel is the best and worst stage dimensions and why.

Step 6: Plan the *During* Phase of the Lesson. While it may seem that this phase is when the students are working independently, this is a critical time for teaching. The teacher's role is to monitor and assess student progress and to provide hints as necessary. For example, you might make one quick visit to each group to verify that each understands the task and is engaged in solving the problem.

The *during* phase is the time to ask questions related to the content of the lesson. Prepare these questions in advance and as you observe, ask as many students/groups as you are able to. Also, carefully prepare prompts that can help students who may be stuck or who may need accommodations that will give them a start without taking away the challenge of the task. Have options of other materials such as color tiles for students who have learning disabilities. Prepare extensions or challenges you can pose to students who are gifted or others who finish early.

The *during* phase is your opportunity to learn what your students know and can do (see planning steps 1 and 4) and to work with individual learners. Students should become accustomed to the fact that in the *during* phase of the lesson they should be ready to explain what they are thinking and doing. This phase is also a time for you to think about which groups might share their work, and in what order, in the *after* phase of the lesson.

Example: Fixed Areas. I will make one trip around the room to see that students are actually building a rectangle and recording its dimensions. In the second round, I will ask the questions I prepared in Step 4 for each objective. If students finish early, I will ask them to consider applying their conjecture of the best dimensions for a stage that is 48 square meters.

Step 7: Plan the *After* Phase of the Lesson. The *after* phase is when you connect the task to the learning goals. Even if you see the mathematics concepts in the activity, it may not be clear to students. That means careful planning of the after phase is critical. Smith, Bill, and Hughes (2008) offer the following suggestions for guiding your thinking as you prepare for the discussion of the *after* phase:

- Which solution paths do you want to have shared? In what order do you want them shared? (Share ones that are mathematically similar together? Share less advanced strategies first?) Why?
- Consider what questions you will ask so that students will
  1. Make sense of the mathematical ideas that you want them to learn
  2. Expand on, debate, and question the solutions being shared
  3. Make connections between different strategies being shared (Remember, this is one of the big

findings in helping students develop conceptual understanding!)
  4. Look for patterns
  5. Begin to form generalizations
- How will you ensure that, over time, *each* student has the opportunities to share his or her thinking and reasoning with their peers?
- What will you see or hear that lets you know that *all* students understand?

Plan an adequate amount of time for your discussion. A rich problem can take 15 to 20 minutes to discuss.

Example: Fixed Areas. First, I will ask different groups to draw one of their rectangles, with its measurements, on the interactive whiteboard. Second, I plan to ask the following questions:

- How did you find the perimeters of these rectangles? (Collect different ideas—look for shortcuts and note those responses in words and symbols on the board.)
- What do you notice about the relationship between area and perimeter? (Students should notice that there are a number of possible perimeters for a given area and that the perimeter is less when the shape is more "square.")
- If you were the stage architect, which of the rectangles would you pick and why?

After the discussion, I will distribute the exit slip titled "Advice to the Architect" that asks students to explain the second question above to the architect, using illustrations to support the explanation.

Steps 5, 6, and 7 have resulted in a tentative instructional plan. The next three steps are designed to review this tentative plan in light of some critical considerations, making changes or additions as needed.

Step 8: Check for Alignment Within the Lesson. A well-prepared lesson that maximizes the opportunity for students to learn must be focused and aligned. There is often a temptation to do a series of "fun" activities that seem to relate to a topic but that are intended for slightly different learning goals. First, look to see that three parts of the plan are clearly aligned and balanced: the objectives, the assessment, and the questions asked in the *during* and *after* phases. If the questions are all focused on only one objective, add questions to address each objective or remove the objective that is not addressed.

Second, the lesson should have a reasonable flow to it, building in sophistication. The *before* activity should be related to the focus task in the *during* phase but will likely be less involved. The *after* phase should take students from looking at the task to generalizing ideas about mathematics concepts. If you feel like you are doing one activity and then switching to another, and you don't know how to pull it together in the end, it may be that the lesson is not aligned.

Look back to the objectives and make sure all activities support these objectives and build in critical thinking and challenges.

Example: Fixed Areas. The lesson demonstrates alignment. The objectives were used to write the assessments and the assessment questions were written to match the phases of the lesson. The lesson starts with an example to get students thinking about the use of area and perimeter, builds on this foundation by having them create as many rectangles with an area of 36 as they can, and then engages them in a discussion by focusing on generalized ideas of the relationship between area and perimeter and ways to find perimeter.

Step 9: Anticipate Student Approaches. This is something that continues to be a finding in studies on effective teaching—teachers who consider ways students might solve the task are better able to facilitate the lesson in ways that support student learning (Matthews, Hlas, & Finken, 2009; Stein et al., 2007). In reflecting on the task that is chosen, it is important to consider what strategies students might use and how you might respond. What misconceptions might students have? What common barriers might need to be addressed? Which of these do you want to address prior to the activity starting and which ones do you want to see emerge from their work?

Example: Fixed Areas. Students are likely to debate about whether the 6 by 6 square should be one of their rectangles. This will not be addressed up front, as a conversation around whether a square is a rectangle is a worthy class discussion. Second, students may initially consider a 4 by 9 rectangle different from a 9 by 4 rectangle. This will be addressed in the *before* as being considered the same for this activity—so that students don't get bogged down in making too many rectangles. Students may confuse the terms *perimeter* and *area*, so, in the *before* phase, we will discuss strategies for remembering which is which and students will be encouraged to use these appropriate terms as they work with their partner.

Step 10: Identify Essential Questions. While this might sound redundant after the previous steps, the quality of your questioning in a lesson is so critically important to the potential learning that it is a fitting last step. Using your objectives as the focus, review the lesson to see that in the *before* phase you are posing questions that capture students' attention and raise curiosity about how to solve the problem. In the *during* and *after* phases, you are using questions based on the objectives to focus students' thinking on the critical features of the task and what you want them to learn. Research on questioning indicates that teachers rarely ask higher-level questions—this is your chance to review and be sure that you have included some challenging questions that ask students to extend, analyze, compare, generalize,

and synthesize. These questions help students more deeply understand the concepts.

Example: Fixed Areas. Higher-level questions based on the objectives are posed to students in the *during* and *after* phases. Some additional questions to have prepared for early finishers or advanced students include the following:

> What if the perimeter were set at 36 meters? Would there be different possible areas?
> Which one might an architect prefer for a dance stage rather than a play stage?
> Is a square a rectangle? Explain using what you know of the characteristics of the shapes.

Applying the Planning Process

The importance of using the planning process cannot be overemphasized. Sometimes teachers spend more time on grading papers than preparing a lesson for an upcoming concept. This may result in a poor quality lesson. Then the teacher has even more work in trying to remediate students and respond to misconceptions, and perhaps even less time for planning. Avoid this frustrating cycle—prioritize planning!

A finished lesson plan often has the following components, though the order may vary:

- State and/or local mathematics standards
- Lesson goals and learning objectives
- Assessment(s)
- Accommodations and/or modifications
- Materials needed
- *Before* phase
- *During* phase
- *After* phase

Examples of Lessons: Expanded Lessons. The "Fixed Areas" Expanded Lesson has served as an example for each of the planning steps in a problem-based lesson. It is designed as a full-class lesson for fourth or fifth grade. In addition to this sample lesson, the MyEducationLab (www .myeducationlab.com) website and *Field Experience Guide* have Expanded Lessons that elaborate on activities from each content chapter in Section II of this book.

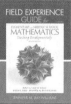

At the end of every chapter, you will find Field Experience Guide Connections that connect lessons and activities from the *Field Experience Guide* to chapter coverage.

Applying the Three-Phase Model to Short Tasks

The basic lesson structure we have been discussing assumes that a class will be given a task or problem, allowed to work on it, and end with a discussion. Not every lesson is developed around a task given to a full class. However, the basic concept of tasks and discussions can be adapted to most lessons. The three-phase format can be applied in as few as 10 minutes. You might plan two or three cycles in a single lesson. For example, consider these tasks and how you could implement the three phases—in particular, what you will ask in the *after* phase to deepen student understanding:

Kindergarten	Ms. Joy's class has three fish in their fish tank and Ms. Lo's class has five fish in their fish tank. If we combined the fish, how many would we have?
Grade 2	If you have forgotten the answer to the addition fact 9 + 8, how might you figure it out in your head?
Grade 4	On your virtual geoboard, make a figure that has only one line of symmetry. Make a second figure that has at least two lines of symmetry.
Grade 6	After playing the game "Race" four times, you notice that it took 30 minutes. If this rate is constant, how many games can you play in 45 minutes? In 2 hours?
Grade 8	Write a situation that fits each equation below: $$y = 12x$$ $$y = 30x + 5$$

An effective strategy for discussion starting in the *during* phase is *think-pair-share*. Students first spend time developing their own thoughts and ideas on how to approach the task. Then they pair with a classmate and discuss each other's strategies. This provides an opportunity to test out ideas and to practice articulating them. For ELLs and students with learning disabilities, this offers both a nonthreatening chance to speak and an opportunity to practice what they might later say to the whole class. The last step is to share the idea with the rest of the class.

Textbooks as Resources

The textbook remains the most significant factor influencing instruction in elementary and middle school classrooms. With exceptions found in occasional lessons, most traditional textbooks remain very close to a "teach by telling" instructional approach. However, standards-based textbooks are very different from traditional texts. The instructional model in standards-based mathematics texts, such as the two curriculum series featured throughout this book (*Investigations in Number, Data, and Space* and *Connected Mathematics Project II*), align to the *before, during,* and *after* lesson phases.

Research tells us that the two ways to support conceptual understanding is by engaging students in productive struggle and making mathematical relationships explicit (Hiebert & Grouws, 2007). Therefore, when reviewing a lesson in a textbook, you should be looking for these two elements, and if you don't see them, adapt the lesson to make them more prevalent. One suggestion is to emphasize the NCTM process standards or the Standards for Mathematical Practice (CCSSO, 2010; NCTM, 2000). This is particularly needed with traditional textbooks, where there are fewer opportunities to engage in discourse and reason about the mathematics.

For example, see where you can add a meaningful context (to build connections), include opportunities for open-ended questioning (to build in communication), adapt straightforward questions to make them more complex higher-level thinking questions (to enable problem solving and reasoning to occur), and consider what models or visuals you might employ (to use multiple representations). Sometimes the problems that appear in the examples section or at the end of the homework section (the story problems) are a good source for making the lesson more problem-based. See Chapter 3 for more on how to adapt a non-problem-based lesson.

Planning for All Learners

Every classroom contains a range of student abilities and backgrounds. Perhaps the most important work of teachers today is to be able to plan (and teach) lessons that support and challenge *all* students to learn important mathematics.

Interestingly, and perhaps surprisingly to some, the problem-based approach to teaching is the best way to teach mathematics and attend to the range of students. In the problem-based classroom, children are making sense of the mathematics in *their* way, bringing to the problems only the skills and ideas that they own. In contrast, in a traditional highly directed lesson, it is often assumed that all students will understand and use the same approach and the same ideas as determined by the teacher. Students not ready to understand the ideas presented must focus their attention on following rules or directions in an instrumental manner (i.e., without a conceptual understanding). This, of course, leads to endless difficulties and leaves many students with misunderstandings or in need of significant remediation.

In addition to using a problem-based approach, there are specific adaptations that can meet the needs of the diverse learners in your classroom. This is the focus of Chapter 6, but here the focus is specifically on planning (accommodations and modifications, differentiated instruction, flexible groups, and examples for ELLs and students with special needs).

Make Accommodations and Modifications

There are two paths to making a given task accessible to all students: *accommodation* and *modification*. An *accommodation* is a provision of a different environment or circumstance made with particular students in mind. For example, for a particular student you might write down instructions instead of just saying them orally. Accommodations do not alter the task. A *modification* refers to a change in the problem or task itself. For example, suppose the task begins with finding the area of a compound shape as shown here.

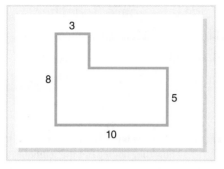

If you decide instead to focus on simple rectangular regions, then that is a modification. However, if you decide to begin with rectangular regions and build to connected compound shapes composed of rectangles, you have *scaffolded* the lesson in a way to ramp up to the original task. Scaffolding a task in this manner is an accommodation. In planning accommodations and modifications the goal is to enable each child to successfully reach your learning objectives, not to change the objectives. This is how equity is achieved in the classroom. Notice that equitable instruction targets equal *outcomes*, not equal treatment. Treating students the same when they each learn differently does not make sense.

Differentiating Instruction

Differentiating instruction means that a teacher's lesson plan includes strategies to support the range of different academic backgrounds found in classrooms that are academically, culturally, and linguistically diverse (Tomlinson, 1999). When considering what to differentiate, first consider the learning profile of each student. Second, consider what can be differentiated across three critical elements:

- *Content*—what you want each student to know
- *Process*—how you will engage them in thinking about that content
- *Product*—what they will have to show for what they have learned the content when the lesson is over

Third, consider how the physical learning environment might be adapted. This might include the seating arrangement, specific grouping strategies, and access to materials. Some common ways to differentiate include adapting the task to different levels (tiered lessons) and using centers or stations.

Content can be differentiated in many ways, including resources or manipulatives used, mathematics vocabulary developed, non-examples and examples used to develop a concept, and teacher-directed groups used to provide foundations for a new concept (Cassone, 2009).

Process can also be differentiated in various ways. Tomlinson and McTighe (2006) suggest that in thinking about process, teachers think about selecting strategies that build on students' readiness, interests, and learning preferences. In addition, the process should help students learn effective strategies and reflect on which strategies work best for them. Learning centers and tiered lessons are two ways to differentiate the process. Each is briefly addressed here. (*Products* are discussed in Chapter 5.)

Learning Centers. A mathematical concept may lend itself to having students work at different tasks at various classroom locations. Each station can use a different visual or approach the content differently. Good technology-supported tasks, especially Internet applications, can be the focus of a learning center. Because you can decide which students will be at which centers, you can differentiate content for students.

A good task for a learning center is one that can be repeated. For example, students might play a game where one student covers part of a known number of counters and the other student names the amount in the covered part.

"Fraction Game" in the NCTM Illuminations Lessons (http://illuminations.nctm.org/ActivityDetail.aspx?ID=18) can be played repeatedly, each time strengthening students' understanding of fractions.

You may want students to work at centers in small groups or individually. Therefore, for a given topic you might prepare four to eight different activities. (You can also double a station by having two activities at one center.) Place materials for the activity or game (e.g., counters and recording sheets) in a container or folder.

A good approach is to model or teach the activity to the full class ahead of time in addition to having the instructions at the center. If you do this, students will not waste time when they get to the station and you will not have to run around the room explaining what to do at each center. Also involve parents, aids, or other volunteers.

Tiered Lessons. In a tiered lesson, the teacher determines the learning goals for all students, but the task is adapted up and down to meet the range of learners. Teachers can identify the challenge of each of the defined tiers in a lesson to determine the learning needs of the students in the classroom (Kingore, 2006; Tomlinson, 1999). The adaptation is not necessarily just to the *content*; it can also be any of the following (Kingore, 2006):

1. *The degree of assistance.* This might include providing examples or partnering students.
2. *How structured the task is.* Students with special needs, for example, benefit from highly structured tasks, but gifted students often benefit from a more open-ended structure.
3. *The complexity of the task given.* This can include making a task more concrete or more abstract or including more difficult problems or applications.

4. *The complexity of process.* This includes how quickly paced the lesson is, how many instructions you give at one time, and how many higher-level thinking questions are included as part of the task.

Consider the following task:

Original Task

Eduardo had 9 toy cars. Erica came over to play and brought 8 cars. Can you figure out how many cars Eduardo and Erica have together? Explain how you know.

The teacher has distributed cubes to students to model the problem and paper and pencil to illustrate and record how they solved the problem. He asks students to model the problem and be ready to explain their solution.

Adapted Task

Eduardo had some toy cars. Erica came over to play and brought her cars. Can you figure out how many cars Eduardo and Erica have together? Explain how you know.

The teacher asks students what is happening in this problem and what they are going to be doing. Then he distributes task cards that tell how many cars Eduardo and Erica have. He has varied how hard the numbers are, giving the students who are struggling numbers less than 10 and the more advanced students open-ended cards with multiple solutions.

Card 1 (easier)

> Eduardo has 6 cars and Erica has 8 cars.

Card 2 (moderate)

> Eduardo has 13 cars and Erica has 16 cars.

Card 3 (advanced)

> Eduardo has _ cars and Erica has _ cars. Together they have 25 cars. How many cars might Eduardo have and how many might Erica have?

In each case, students must use words, pictures, models, or numbers to show how they figured out the solution. Various tools are provided (connecting cubes, counters, and hundreds chart) for their use.

There are three suggested options for how to organize the use of the task cards. First, the teacher can give everyone the cards in order. Second, the teacher can give students only one card, based on their current academic readiness (e.g., easy cards to those that have not yet mastered addition of single-digit numbers). Third, the teacher can give out cards 1 and 2 based on ability and use card 3 as an extension for those who have successfully completed card 1 or 2. In each of these cases, the teacher will know at the end of the lesson which students are able to model and explain addition problems and plan the next lesson accordingly. Notice that this tiered lesson addresses both the complexity of the task (difficulty of different cards) and the process (instructions are broken down by first starting with the no-numbers scenario).

PAUSE and REFLECT

Think of different types of learners (ELLs, students with special needs, gifted learners, unmotivated students). How does the adapted lesson above meet each of their learning needs? ●

The following example illustrates how to tier a lesson based on structure. Notice that the different tasks vary in how open ended the work is, yet all tasks focus on the same learning goal of identifying properties of parallelograms.

Topic: Properties of Parallelograms
Grade: 5–6

Students are given a collection of parallelograms including squares and rectangles as well as nonrectangular parallelograms. The following tasks are distributed to different groups based on their learning needs and prior knowledge of quadrilaterals:

● Group A, open ended: Explore the set of parallelograms. Measure angles and sides using your ruler and protractor.

- Make a list of the properties that you think are true for every parallelogram.
- Group B, slightly structured: Use your ruler and protractor to measure the parallelograms. Record any patterns that are true for all of the parallelograms related to:

  Sides   Angles   Diagonals

- Group C, highly structured: Explore the parallelograms to find patterns and rules that define the shapes as parallelograms. Use a ruler to measure the sides and a protractor to measure the angles. First, sort the parallelograms into rectangles and nonrectangles.

  1. What pattern do you notice about the measures of the *sides* of all the parallelograms in the *nonrectangle* set? What pattern do you notice about the measures of the *sides* of all the parallelograms in the *rectangle* set?
  2. What pattern do you notice about the measures of the *angles* of all the parallelograms in the *nonrectangle* set? What pattern do you notice about the measures of the *angles* of all the parallelograms in the *rectangle* set?

For many problems involving computations, you can insert multiple sets of numbers. In the following problem, students are permitted to select the first, second, or third number in each bracket. Giving a choice increases student motivation and helps students become more self-directed learners (Bray, 2009; Gilbert & Musu, 2008).

Topic: Subtraction
Grades: 2–3

Eduardo had {12, 60, 121} marbles. He gave Erica {5, 15, 46} marbles. How many marbles does Eduardo have now?

Students tend to select the numbers that provide the greatest challenge without being too difficult. In the discussions, all children benefit and feel as though they worked on the same task.

Flexible Grouping

Allowing students to collaborate on tasks provides support and challenges, increasing their chance to communicate about mathematics and building understanding. Collaboration is also an important life skill. Students feel that working in groups improves their confidence, engagement, and understanding (Nebesniak & Heaton, 2010). *Flexible grouping* means that the size and makeup of small groups vary in a purposeful and strategic manner. In other words, sometimes students are working in partner groups because the nature of the task best suits two people working together and at other times they are in groups of four because the task has enough tasks or roles to warrant a larger team. Also, groups can be selected based on the students' academic abilities, language needs, social dynamics, and behavior. It

is often effective to use mixed-ability (heterogeneous) groups, strategically placing struggling learners with more capable students who are likely to be helpful.

Groups may stay the same for a full unit so that the students become skilled at working with one another. If students are seated with their groups in clusters of four, they can still pair with one person from their group when the task is better suited for pairs.

Regardless of whether groups have two or four members or whether you have grouped by mixed ability (heterogeneous) or similar ability (homogeneous), the first key to successful grouping is *individual accountability*. That means that while the group is working together on a product, individuals must be able to explain the process, the content, and the product. While this may sound easy, it is not.

Second, and equally important, is building a sense of *shared responsibility* within a group. At the start of the year, it is important to do team building activities and to set the standard that all members will participate and that all team members are responsible to ensure that all members of their group understand the process, content, and product. Good resources for team building activities (though there are many) include *Team Building Activities for Every Group* (Jones, 1999) and *Feeding the Zircon Gorilla and Other Team Building Activities* (Sikes, 1995).

One strategy that ensures individual accountability and shared responsibility is a jigsaw grouping technique. In this strategy, students are placed in a home group and then go to an expert group to become an expert on something, returning to their home group to share what they've learned. While this was originally designed to cover large amounts of materials (in narrative form), it can be effectively used in mathematics, especially to emphasize different representations (Cleaves, 2008). As Cleaves describes, students go to expert groups to explore a problem (e.g., how three different people save money). In each group, the problem is presented with a different representation: graphs, tables, situations, or story. Students analyze the situation in the expert group and then return to their home group to share and compare the different representations and solutions.

To reinforce individual accountability and shared responsibility requires a shift in your role as the teacher. When a member of a small group asks you a question, your response is not to answer the question but to pose a question to the whole group to find out what they think. Students will soon learn that they must use teammates as their first resource and seek teacher help only when the whole group needs help. Also, when observing groups, rather than ask Angela what she is doing, you can ask Bernard to explain what Angela is doing. Having all students participate in the oral report to the whole class builds individual accountability. Letting students know that you may call on any member to explain what they did is a good way to be sure all group members understand what they did. Additionally, having students individually write and record their strategies and solutions is important. The more you use these strategies and others like them, the more effectively groups will function and the more successfully students will learn the concepts.

Avoid ability grouping! As opposed to differentiation, ability grouping means that groups are formed and those needing more support in the low group are meeting different (lesser) learning goals than students needing less support in the high group. While this may be well-intentioned, it only puts the students in the low group further behind, increasing the gap between more and less dependent students and significantly damaging students' self-esteem. Instead, use the differentiation strategies described above.

English Language Learners

Attention to the needs of the English language learner must be considered at each step of the ten-step planning guide detailed in Table 4.1.

In the NCTM's position statement on equity, the two phrases "high expectations" and "strong support" are one idea, not two (NCTM, 2008). In the following example, the teacher uses several techniques that provide support for English language learners while keeping expectations high.

Ms. Steimer is working on a third-grade lesson that involves the concepts of estimating length (in inches) and measuring to the nearest half inch. The task asks students to use estimation to find three objects that are about 6 inches long, three objects that are about 1 foot long, and three objects that are about 2 feet long. Once identified, students are to measure the nine objects to the nearest half inch and compare the measurements with their estimates. Ms. Steimer has a child from Korea who knows only a little English, and she has a child from Mexico who speaks English well but is new to U.S. schools. These two students are not familiar with feet or inches, so they will likely struggle in trying to estimate or measure in inches.

Ms. Steimer takes time to address the language and the increments on the ruler to the entire class. Because the word foot has two meanings, Ms. Steimer decides to address that explicitly before launching into the lesson. She begins by asking students what a "foot" is. She allows time for them to discuss the word with a partner and then share their answers with the class. She explains that today they are going to be using the measuring unit of a foot (while holding up the foot ruler). She asks students what other units can be used to measure. In particular, she asks her English language learners to share what units they use in their countries of origin, having metric rulers to show the class. She asks students to study the ruler and compare the centimeter to the inch by posing these questions: "Can you estimate about how many centimeters are in an inch? In 6 inches? In a foot?"

Moving to the lesson objectives, Ms. Steimer asks students to compare how the halfway points are marked for the inches and the centimeters. Then she asks students, without using rulers, to tear a piece of paper that they think is about one-half of a foot long. Students then measure their paper strips to see how close their strips are to 6 inches. Now she has them ready to begin estimating and measuring.

PAUSE and REFLECT

Review Ms. Steimer's lesson. What specific strategies to support English language learners can you identify? ●

Discussion of the word *foot* using the think-pair-share technique recognized the potential language confusion and allowed students the chance to talk about it before becoming confused by the task. The efforts to use visuals and concrete models (the ruler and the torn paper strip) and to build on students' prior experience (use of the metric system in Korea and Mexico) provided support so that the ELLs could succeed in this task. Most importantly, Ms. Steimer did not diminish the challenge of the task with these strategies. If she had altered the task, for example, not expecting the ELLs to estimate since they didn't know the inch very well, she would have lowered her expectations. Conversely, if she had simply posed the problem without taking time to have students study the ruler or to provide visuals, she may have kept her expectations high but failed to provide the support that would enable her students to succeed. Finally, by making a connection for all students to the metric system, she showed respect for the students' cultures and broadened the horizons of other students to measurement in other countries. Additional information for working with students who are English learners in mathematics can be found in Chapter 6.

Students with Special Needs

While each child has specific learning needs and strategies that work for one student may not work for another, there are some general ideas that can help in planning for students with learning needs. The following questions should guide your planning:

1. What organizational, behavioral, and cognitive skills are necessary for students with special needs to derive meaning from this activity?
2. Which students have significant weaknesses in any of these skills?
3. How can I provide additional support in these areas of weakness so that students with special needs can focus on the conceptual task in the activity? (Karp & Howell, 2004, p. 119).

Each phase of the lesson has specific considerations for students with special needs. Some strategies apply throughout a lesson. The following discussion is not exhaustive, but provides some specific suggestions for providing support and challenge to students throughout the lesson plan.

TABLE 4.1

AN AT-A-GLANCE LOOK AT GENERAL PLANNING STEPS AND ADDITIONAL CONSIDERATIONS FOR ELLS		
Steps	**General Description**	**Additional Considerations for English Language Learners**
1. Determine the mathematics and goals	• Identify the mathematical concepts that align with state and district standards. • Formulate learning objectives.	• Establish language objectives (e.g., include reading, writing, speaking, and listening) in the lesson plan. • Post content and language objectives, using kid-friendly words.
2. Consider your students' needs	• Relate concepts to previously learned concepts and experiences.	• Consider students' social/cultural backgrounds and previously learned content and vocabulary.
3. Select, design, or adapt a task	• Select a task that will enable students to explore the concept(s) selected in step 1.	• Include a context that is meaningful to the students' cultures and backgrounds. • Analyze the task for language pitfalls. Identify words that need to be discussed and eliminate terms that are not necessary to understanding the task. • Watch for homonyms, homophones, and words that have special meanings in math (e.g., *mean, similar, product*).
4. Design lesson assessments	• Determine the types of assessments that will be used for each objective. • Use a variety of assessments.	• Build in questions to diagnose understanding. Use translators if needed. • If a student is not succeeding, seek alternative strategies to diagnose whether the problem is with language, content, or both.
5. Plan the *before* activities	• Determine how you will introduce the task. • Consider warm-ups that orient student thinking.	• Build background. Link the task to prior learning and to familiar contexts. • Review key vocabulary needed for the task. List key vocabulary in a prominent location. • Provide visuals and real objects related to the selected task. • Present the task in written and oral format. • Check for understanding (e.g., ask students to pair-share).
6. Plan the *during* questions and extensions	• Think about hints or assists you might give as students work. • Consider extensions or challenges.	• Group students for both academic and language support. • Encourage students to draw pictures, make diagrams, and/or use manipulatives/models. • Maximize language. Ask students to explain and defend. • Consider using a graphic organizer. Ideas include sentence starters (e.g., "I solved the problem by . . ."), recording tables, and concept maps. • Maximize language use in nonthreatening ways (e.g., think-pair-share).
7. Plan the *after* discussion	• Decide how students will report their findings. • Determine how you will format the discussion of the task.	• Encourage students to use visuals in reports. • Give advance notice that students will be speaking, so they can plan. • Encourage students to choose the language they wish to use, using a translator if possible. • Provide appropriate "wait time."
8. Check for alignment within the lesson	• Check that all aspects of the lesson target the objectives.	• Review lesson phases to see whether key vocabulary is supported throughout the lesson. • Review lesson phases to see that visuals and other supports are in place.
9. Anticipate student approaches	• Reflect on how students will respond to the task and what misconceptions may occur. • Determine how to address these issues.	• Consider approaches that might be used in other countries and encourage students to share different approaches. • Encourage the use of pictures to replace words, as appropriate for age and language proficiency.
10. Identify essential questions	• Using your objectives as a guide, decide what questions you will ask in each lesson phase.	• If possible, translate essential questions. • Word the questions in straightforward, simple sentence structures.

Structure the Environment

- *Centralize attention.* Move the student close to the board or teacher. Face students when you speak to them and use gestures. Remove competing stimuli.
- *Avoid confusion.* Word directions carefully and specifically and ask the child to repeat them. Give one direction at a time.
- *Smooth transitions.* Ensure that transitions between activities have clear directions and limit the chances that students will get off task.

Identify and Remove Potential Barriers

- *Find ways to help students remember.* Recognizing that memory is often not a strong suit for students with special needs, develop mnemonics (memory aids) for familiar steps or write directions that can be referred to throughout the lesson. For example, STAR is a mnemonic for problem solving: **S**earch the word problem for important information; **T**ranslate the words into models, pictures, or symbols; **A**nswer the problem; **R**eview your solution for reasonableness (Gagnon & Maccini, 2001).
- *Provide vocabulary and concept support.* Explicit attention to vocabulary and symbols is critical throughout the lesson. This can be done by previewing essential terms and related prior knowledge/concepts, creating a "math wall" of words and symbols to provide visual cues and connect symbols to their meanings.
- *Use "friendly" numbers.* Instead of using $6.13, use $6.00 to emphasize conceptual understanding rather than mixing computation and conceptual goals. This technique is used when computation and operation skills are *not* the lesson objective.
- *Vary the task size.* Assign students with special needs fewer problems to solve. Some students can become frustrated by the enormity of the task.
- *Adjust the visual display.* Design assessments and tasks so that there is not too much on a single page. Sometimes the density of words, illustrations, and numbers can overload students. Find ways to put one problem on a page, increase font size, or just reduce the visual display to a workable amount.

Provide Clarity

- *Remember the timeframe.* Give students additional reminders about the time left for exploring the materials, completing tasks, or finishing assessments. This will help students with time management.
- *Ask students to share their thinking.* Use the think-aloud method or the think-pair-share strategy.
- *Emphasize connections.* Provide concrete representations, pictorial representations, and numerical representations. Have students connect the linkages through carefully phrased questions. Also connect visuals, meanings, and words. For example, as you fold a strip of paper into fourths, point out the part–whole relationship with gestures as you pose a question about the relationship between $\frac{2}{4}$ and $\frac{1}{2}$.
- *Adapt delivery modes.* Incorporate a variety of materials, images, examples, and models for students who may be more visual learners. Some students may need to have the problem or assessment read to them or generated with voice creation software. Provide written instructions with oral instructions.
- *Emphasize the relevant points.* Some students with special needs may inappropriately focus on the color of a cube instead of the quantity of cubes.
- *Utilize methods for organizing written work.* Provide tools and templates so students can focus on the mathematics rather than the organization of a table or chart. Also use graphic organizers, picture-based models, and paper with columns or grids.
- *Provide examples and non-examples.* Show examples of triangles as well as shapes that are not triangles. Help students focus on the characteristics that differentiate the examples from those that are not examples.

Consider Alternative Assessments

- *Propose alternative products.* Provide options for how to demonstrate understanding (e.g., a dictated response that is written by someone else, an audio recording of a verbal response, or a model made with a manipulative). Students may use voice recognition software or word prediction software that can generate a whole menu of word choices when they type a few letters.
- *Encourage self-monitoring and self-assessment.* Students with special needs often are not good at self-reflection. Asking them to review an assignment or assessment to explain what was difficult and what they think they got right can help them be more independent and responsible about their learning.
- *Consider feedback charts.* Monitor students' growth and chart progress over time.

Emphasize Practice and Summary

- *Help students bring ideas together.* Create study guides that summarize the key mathematics concepts and allow for review.
- *Provide extra practice.* Use a small number of carefully selected problems and allow the use of familiar physical models.

Not all of these strategies will apply to every lesson, but as you are thinking about a particular lesson and certain individuals in your class, you will find that many of these will apply and will allow a student to engage in the task and accomplish the learning goals of the lesson.

Drill or Practice?

Drill and practice, if not a hallmark of instructional methods in mathematics, is present to at least some degree in nearly every classroom. Most lessons in traditional textbooks include a long section of exercises, followed by a few story problems, usually only using mathematics taught in that lesson (rather than incorporating and connecting to past ideas). In addition, drill-and-practice workbooks and software programs abound.

A question worth asking is, "What has all of this drill accomplished?" It has been an ever-present component of mathematics classes for decades and yet the adult population is replete with those who almost proudly proclaim "I was never any good at math" and who understand little more about the subject than basic arithmetic. We must rethink the use of drill and practice.

New Definitions of Drill and Practice

The phrase "drill and practice" slips off the tongue so rapidly that the two words *drill* and *practice* appear to be synonyms—and, for the most part, they have been. In the interest of developing a new or different perspective on drill and practice, consider definitions that differentiate between these terms as different types of activities rather than link them together.

Practice refers to different problem-based tasks or experiences, spread over numerous class periods, each addressing the same basic ideas.

Drill refers to repetitive, *non*-problem-based exercises designed to improve skills or procedures already acquired.

 PAUSE and REFLECT

How are these two definitions different? Which is more in keeping with the view of drill and practice (as a singular term) with which you are familiar? How does each of these align with what we know about how people learn? ●

Using these definitions as a point of departure, it is now useful to examine what benefits we can get from each and when each is appropriate.

What Practice Provides

In essence, practice is what this book is about—providing students with ample and varied opportunities to reflect on or create new ideas through problem-based tasks. The following list of the outcomes of practice should not be surprising:

- An increased opportunity to develop conceptual ideas and more elaborate and useful connections

- An opportunity to develop alternative and flexible strategies
- A greater chance for all students to understand, particularly students with special needs
- A clear message that mathematics is about figuring things out and that it makes sense

Each of the preceding benefits has been explored in this or previous chapters and should require no further discussion. However, it is important to point out that practice can and does develop skills. The fear that without extensive drill students will not master "basic skills" is not supported by recent research on standards-based curriculum or practices (Stein & Smith, 2010). Students in practice-focused programs perform about as well as students in traditional programs on computational skills and better on problem solving and conceptual understanding.

What Drill Provides

Drill can provide students with the following:

- An increased facility with a procedure—but *only* with a procedure already learned
- A review of facts or procedures so they are not forgotten

Limitations of drill include:

- A focus on a singular method and an exclusion of flexible alternatives
- A false appearance of student understanding
- A rule-oriented or procedural view of mathematics

The popular belief is that somehow students learn through drill. In reality, drill can only help students get faster at what they already know. Drill is not a reflective activity. The nature of drill asks students to do what they already know how to do, even if they just learned it. The focus of drill is on procedural skill. Drill has a tendency to narrow the learner's thinking to one approach rather than promote flexibility.

When students successfully complete a page of exercises, teachers (and students) may believe that this is an indication that they've "got it." In fact, what they most often have is a temporary ability to reproduce a procedure recently shown to them. Superficially learned procedures are easily and quickly forgotten and confused. An approach to instruction in which students are to memorize and drill on a fact or procedure is not in the best interest of many students, including students with disabilities and those other students who are not good memorizers but are good thinkers.

When drill is a prevalent component of the mathematics classroom, it is no wonder that so many students and adults dislike mathematics. Real mathematics is about sense making and reasoning—it is a science of pattern and order. Students cannot possibly obtain this exciting view of mathematics when constantly being asked to repeat procedural skills over and over.

When Is Drill Appropriate?

In a review of research, Franke, Kazemi, and Battey (2007) report that drill improves procedural knowledge, but not conceptual understanding. But when the number of problems is reduced and time is then spent discussing problems, conceptual understanding can be increased while not diminishing procedural knowledge. The key is to keep drills short and to connect procedures to the related concepts.

When drill is appropriate—for example, practicing basic facts—a little bit goes a long way. Practicing a set of 10 facts is more effective than a page of 50 facts within a set timeframe. Drill, because it is review, is best if limited to 5 to 10 minutes. Devoting extensive time to repeating a procedure is not effective and can negatively affect students' perceptions, motivation, and understanding.

Drill and Student Misconceptions

As discussed earlier, the range of prior mathematical knowledge in classrooms is a challenge for all teachers. For those students who don't pick up new ideas as quickly as most in the class, there is an overwhelming temptation to give in and "just drill 'em." Before committing to this solution, ask yourself these two questions: *Will drill build understanding? What is this telling the child?* The child who has difficulties has certainly been shown a process before. It is naive to believe that the drill you provide will be more beneficial than the drills this child has undoubtedly experienced in the past. Although drill may provide short-term success, drill will have little effect in the long run. What children learn from more drill is: "Math is full of rules that I don't understand," which leads to not liking mathematics and believing they are not good at it.

In reality, when a student is making errors on a procedure, it is usually a conceptual issue (as in mis-*conception*). Using a medical metaphor, the drill errors are a symptom, not the problem. The problem is typically conceptual and therefore remediation should include dropping back to activities that strengthen the student's conceptual knowledge.

Homework and Parental Involvement

Homework and parental involvement can make a difference in student attitudes and learning, particularly in elementary school (Cooper, 2007; Else-Quest, Hyde, & Hejmadi, 2008; Patall, Cooper, & Robinson, 2008). The way in which parents are engaged matters. For example, students perform better when parents provide a quiet environment and rules about homework completion. Also, a parent's emotions affect student's emotions, and positive student emotions are connected to better performance (Else-Quest et al., 2008). Therefore, parents who exhibit positive interest, humor, and pride in their students' work support their child's mathematics learning.

Parents value school mathematics, but they associate mathematics with skills and seatwork (Remillard & Jackson, 2006). It is your job to help them understand the broader goals of mathematics. In addition, many parents have negative memories of their skill-driven mathematics classes, saying, "I am not good at math" or "I don't like solving math problems." Given the research just described, it is important that you help parents understand ways to really help their children. Teaching parents how to help their children has also been found to make a difference in supporting student achievement (Cooper, 2007).

How do you effectively encourage students and their families to support mathematics learning at home? There are many ways. Here we break it down into three categories: homework support, experiences beyond homework, and resources to share with parents.

Effective Homework

Homework can be a positive experience for students, families, and the teacher. Take the following recommendations into consideration when thinking about homework that you will assign to your students.

1. *Mimic the three-phase lesson model.* Complete a brief version of the *before* phase of a lesson to be sure the task is understood before students go home. At home, students complete the *during* phase. When they return with the work completed, apply the sharing techniques of the *after* phase of the lesson. Students can even practice the *after* phase with their family if this is encouraged through parent/guardian communications. Some form of written work must be required so that students are held responsible for the task and are prepared for the class discussion.

2. *Use a distributed-content approach.* Homework can address content that has been taught earlier in the year, that day's content, or upcoming content. Interestingly, research has found that distributed homework (homework that combines all three components) is more effective in supporting student learning (Cooper, 2007). The exception here is students with learning disabilities, who perform better when homework focuses on reinforcement of skills and class lessons.

3. *Promote an "ask before telling" approach with parents.* Parents may not know how to best support their child when he or she is stuck or has gotten a wrong answer. One important thing you can do is to ask parents to implement an "ask before tell" approach (Kliman, 1999). This means that before parents explain something, they should ask their child to explain how they did it. The child may self-correct (a life skill); if not, at least the parent can use what they heard from their child to provide targeted assistance.

4. *Provide good questioning prompts for parents.* Providing guiding questions for parents or guardians can help them help their child and understand your emphasis on a problem-based approach to instruction. Figure 4.2 provides guiding questions that can be included in the students' notebooks and shared with families. Translating questions for parents who are not native English speakers is important. (Often their child can help you with this task.)

Homework of this nature communicates to families the problem-based or sense-making nature of your classroom and can help them see the value in this approach. Providing guidance and support to families can make a big difference in their understanding of the approach and their ability to help their child. A final note: A little bit goes a long way—about 10 minutes a night is enough for young students.

Beyond Homework: Families Doing Math

In the same way that families support literacy by reading books with their children or pointing out letters when they encounter them, families can and should support numeracy. Because this has not been the practice in most homes, you, as the teacher, have the responsibility to help parents see the connection between literacy and numeracy. In her article, *Beyond Helping with Homework: Parents and Children Doing Mathematics at Home*, Kliman (1999) offers some excellent suggestions. Five are included here:

1. *Begin early in the year.* This might be a Family Math Night at your school, a letter sent home to the family, or a mathematics discussion at the school's Back to School Night. Too often, the discussion between teachers and parents, when they first meet, focuses only on literacy goals. This is your opportunity to promote your ideas about developing numeracy.

2. *Share anecdotes.* Ask parents to share examples of when their child has used mathematical reasoning. These stories can be shared in the moment at a parents' night or be collected and posted on a bulletin board in the classroom. If students themselves are asked to share in class "family math moments," they begin to notice the mathematics they see or hear from their families or that they themselves do at home. This is a great community-building activity that can become a weekly routine in your classroom.

3. *Story time.* It is good practice for parents to ask children about the stories they read together. Families can also ask questions that have to do with mathematics—for example, asking how much time passed between two events in the story (elapsed time is a difficult concept for students). In addition, they can ask about illustrations: "What shapes

> These guiding questions are designed for helping your child think through their math homework problems:
> - What do you need to figure out? What is the problem about?
> - What words are confusing? What words are familiar?
> - Did you solve problems like this one in class today?
> - What have you tried so far?
> - Can you make a drawing to help you think about the problem?
> - Does your answer make sense?
> - Is there more than one answer?

FIGURE 4.2 Questions for families for helping with homework.

do you see?" "How many animals do you see?" Or their questions can focus on the page numbers: "If we read from page 67 to page 81, how many pages did we read?"

4. *Scavenger hunts.* Whether riding on a bus or in a car, students can be on the hunt for mathematics. Families can adapt the usual car games of spotting things like stop lights and cows to one with math-related items: an octagon, an address between 1100 and 1250, a speed limit that is a multiple of 10, an advertisement that uses data, a license plate with a 2 and 4 on the same plate, and so on. Students can even create these as part of a project to find mathematics in their community. What a great way for you to view your students' environment through their eyes!

5. *Household chores.* From counting place settings on the dinner table to sorting laundry, there is a lot of mathematics in the mundane tasks of the home. For instance, parents or guardians can ask their children, "How many utensils will we use tonight if everyone needs a fork, spoon, and knife?" or "If each load of laundry takes 45 minutes, how long will it take us to get these three loads done?"

Adults constantly use estimation and computation in doing everyday tasks. If you get parents started talking about these instances with their children, imagine how much it can help students learn about mathematics and its importance as a life skill.

Resources for Families

As just discussed, if families are going to help their children with mathematics, you need to help the families. On your class website, provide access to homework and even possible strategies for doing the homework. If you are able to post examples of successful student solutions (in class or on your website), then families can see what you value. For each unit, send letters home that explain the big ideas of the unit as well as the mathematical practices you want to see develop. When you explain that one goal is for students to be able to approach a problem in two different ways, for example, families will be more likely to support this goal.

Check to see what online resources your textbook provides. Sometimes textbooks' websites have online resources for homework and for parents or guardians. These resources include tutorials, video tutoring, videos, connections to careers and real-world applications, multilingual glossaries, audio podcasts, and more. In addition, see the Online Resources list in the Resources for Chapter 4—several are great sites for families.

As you can tell by the discussion on homework, it is important and it needs to be reimagined. Keep in mind that in supporting families you are making a significant difference in what your students will be able to do.

RESOURCES *for Chapter 4*

RECOMMENDED READINGS

Articles

Holden, B. (2008). Preparing for problem solving. *Teaching Children Mathematics, 14*(5), 290–295.
This excellent "how to" article shares how a first-grade teacher working in an urban high-poverty setting incorporated differentiated instruction. Holden describes how she prepared her classroom and her students to be successful through six specific steps.

Reeves, C. A., & Reeves, R. (2003). Encouraging students to think about how they think! *Mathematics Teaching in the Middle School, 8*(7), 374–377.
When students (and adults) get into a habit of mind—or, in this case, a pattern for solving a problem—they often continue to use this pattern even when easier methods are available. The authors explore this idea with simple tasks you can try.

Williams, L. (2008). Tiering and scaffolding: Two strategies for providing access to important mathematics. *Teaching Children Mathematics, 14*(6), 324–330.
Using a second-grade fraction lesson and a third-grade geometry lesson as examples, Williams shares how they were tiered and then how scaffolds, or supports, were built into the lesson. A very worthwhile article.

Books

Litton, N. (1998). *Getting your math message out to parents: A K–6 resource.* Sausalito, CA: Math Solutions Publications.
Litton is a classroom teacher who has practical suggestions for communicating with family members. The book includes chapters on parent conferences, newsletters, homework, and family math night.

ONLINE RESOURCES

Illuminations
http://illuminations.nctm.org
This is a favorite of many math teachers. Click on "Lessons" and you can then select grade band and content to search for lessons—all of them excellent!

Team Building Games on a Shoestring
http://drpaulasprescriptions4pd.wikispaces.com/file/view/Teambuilding_on_a_Shoestring_sml.pdf
For a free downloadable collection, Tom Heck has created eight fun activities, all done with shoestrings.

The Math Forum: Internet Mathematics Library
http://mathforum.org/library
Here you will find links to all sorts of information that will be useful in both planning and assessment in a problem-based classroom.

Ask Dr. Math
http://mathforum.org/dr.math
Ask Dr. Math is a great homework resource for families, students, and teachers. Dr. Math has answers to all the classic math questions students have, like why a negative times a negative is a positive.

REFLECTIONS *on Chapter 4*

WRITING TO LEARN

1. What does it mean to "anticipate student approaches" (step 9) and how might you do it?
2. How might you carry out the *after* portion of a lesson when students are working at stations?
3. Why is a problem-based approach a good way to reach all students in a diverse classroom?
4. What teacher actions are needed for groups to function effectively?
5. What is the difference between making an accommodation for students and making a modification in a lesson? Explain why this distinction is important.
6. What ideas for family involvement might work in grades K–2? In grades 3–5? In grades 6–8?

FOR DISCUSSION AND EXPLORATION

1. Examine a textbook for any grade level. Look at a topic for a whole chapter and determine the two or three main objectives or big ideas covered in the chapter. Restrict yourself to no more than three. Now look at the individual lessons. Are the lessons aimed at the big ideas you have identified? Will the lessons effectively develop the big ideas for this chapter? Are the lessons problem based? If not, how can they be adapted to be problem based?

2. Take a major topic for a particular grade level (e.g., multiplication for grade 3). What ways can families be involved in supporting this learning goal? Consider the ideas discussed in the chapter, as well as considering online resources that can be used.

MyEducationLab™

Go to the MyEducationLab (www.myeducationlab.com) for Math Methods and familiarize yourself with the content. Much of the site content is organized topically. The topics include all of the following to support your learning in the course:

- Learning outcomes for important mathematics methods course topics aligned with the national standards
- Assignments and Activities, tied to these learning outcomes and standards, that can help you more deeply understand course content
- Building Teaching Skills and Dispositions learning units that allow you to apply and practice your understanding of the core mathematics content and teaching skills

Your instructor has a correlation guide that aligns the exercises on the topical portion of the site with your book's chapters.

On MyEducationLab you will also find book-specific resources including Blackline Masters, Expanded Lesson Activities, and Artifact Analysis Activities.

Field Experience Guide
C O N N E C T I O N S

Chapter 2 of the *Field Experience Guide* offers a range of experiences related to planning. In Chapter 4 of the guide, several activities focus on different types of instruction. For example, FEG 4.3 focuses on cooperative groups and FEG 4.6 focuses on small-group instruction. FEG 6.3 is a guide to preparing a Family Math Take-Home activity. Chapter 8 of the guide provides experiences focused on the needs of individual learners. For example, FEG 8.6 focuses on sheltering instruction for an English language learner. Chapter 9 in the guide offers 24 Expanded Lessons, all designed in the *before, during,* and *after* model. Chapter 10 offers worthwhile mathematics activities that can be developed into problem-based lessons, like the Expanded Lesson at the end of this chapter.

Fixed Areas

CONTENT AND TASK DECISIONS	Grade Level: 3–4

Mathematics Goals

- To contrast the concepts of area and perimeter
- To develop an understanding of the relationship between area and perimeter of different shapes when the area is fixed
- To compare and contrast the units used to measure perimeter and those used to measure area

Grade Level Guide

NCTM *CURRICULUM FOCAL POINTS*	*COMMON CORE STATE STANDARDS*
Perimeter is a **grade 3** connection within Measurement. Area is a **grade 4** focal point in Measurement: "Developing an understanding of area and determining the areas of two-dimensional shapes" (NCTM, 2006, p. 16).	Area is one of four critical themes in **grade 3**: "developing understanding of the structure of rectangular arrays and of area." Specifically, students will be able to "recognize perimeter as an attribute of plane figures and distinguish between linear and area measures" (CCSSO, 2010, p. 22).

Consider Your Students' Needs

Students have worked with the ideas of area and perimeter. Some, if not the majority, of students can find the area and perimeter of given figures and may even be able to state the formulas for finding the perimeter and area of a rectangle. However, they may become confused as to which formula to use.

For English Language Learners

- Build background for the terms *rectangle*, *length*, *width*, *area*, and *perimeter*. Ask students whether they have heard of these words and use their ideas to talk about their mathematical meaning.
- Use visuals (tiles) as you model the mathematical terms.

For Students with Special Needs

- Students who struggle may need to use either a computer-based program to model different areas or a geoboard.
- Sometimes the large number of color tiles used for an area of 24 or 26 can be distracting. Students may focus more on the construction than the mathematical concept. Consider using a smaller total, like 16.
- If you are using color tiles to model smaller areas, create a special set with "Area" written with a permanent marker on each. The use of these tiles to create the shapes with an area will reinforce the difference between area and perimeter.

Also note for students who confuse these two measures that the mnemonic "rim" is in the word *perimeter* to jog their memory.

Materials

Each student will need:

- 36 square tiles such as color tiles
- Two or three sheets of centimeter grid paper
- "Rectangles Made with 36 Tiles" recording sheet (Blackline Master 73)
- "Fixed Area" recording sheet (Blackline Master 74)

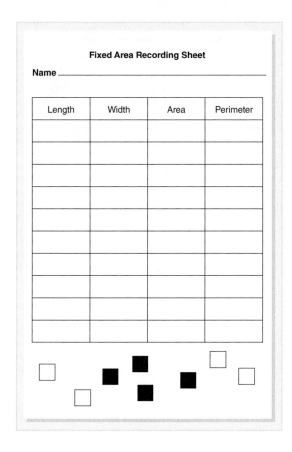

Fixed Area Recording Sheet

Name _____

Length	Width	Area	Perimeter

Teacher will need:

- Color tiles
- "Rectangles Made with 36 Tiles" recording sheet (Blackline Master 73)
- "Fixed Area" recording sheet (Blackline Master 74)

LESSON

Before

Begin with a simpler version of the task:

- Have students build a rectangle using 12 tiles at their desks. Explain that the rectangle should be filled in, not just a border. After eliciting some ideas, ask a student to come to the document camera and make a rectangle as described.
- Model sketching the rectangle on a grid. Record the dimensions of the rectangle on the recording chart—for example, "2 by 6."
- Ask, "What do we mean by perimeter? How do we measure perimeter?" After helping students define perimeter and describe how it is measured, ask students for the perimeter of this rectangle. Ask a student to come to the document camera to measure the perimeter of the rectangle. (Use either the rectangle made from tiles or the one sketched on grid paper.) Emphasize that the units used to measure perimeter are one-dimensional, or linear, and that perimeter is just the distance around an object. Record the perimeter on the chart.
- Ask, "What do we mean by area? How do we measure area?" After helping students define area and describe how it is measured, ask for the area of this rectangle. Here you want to make explicit that the units used to measure area are two-dimensional and, therefore, cover a region. After counting the tiles, record the area in square units on the chart.
- Have students make a different rectangle using 12 tiles at their desks and record the perimeter and area as before. Students will need to decide what "different" means. Is a 2-by-6 rectangle different from a 6-by-2 rectangle? Although these are congruent, students may wish to consider these as being different. That is okay for this activity.

Present the focus task to the class:

- See how many different rectangles can be made with 36 tiles.
- Determine and record the perimeter and area for each rectangle.

Provide clear expectations:

- Write the following directions on the board:
  1. Find a rectangle using *all* 36 tiles.
  2. Sketch the rectangle on the grid paper.
  3. Measure and record the perimeter and area of the rectangle on the recording chart.
  4. Find a new rectangle using *all* 36 tiles and repeat steps 2–4.
- Place students in pairs to work collaboratively, but require that each student draw his or her own sketches and use his or her own recording sheet.

During

Initially:

- Question students to be sure they understand the task and the meaning of *area* and *perimeter*. Look for students who are confusing these terms.
- Be sure students are both drawing the rectangles and recording them appropriately in the chart.

Ongoing:

- Observe and ask the assessment questions, posing one or two to a student and moving to another student (see the "Assessment" section of this lesson).

After

Bring the class together to share and discuss the task:

- Ask students what they have found out about perimeter and area. Ask, "Did the perimeter stay the same? Is that what you expected? When is the perimeter big and when is it small?"
- Ask students how they can be sure they have all of the possible rectangles.
- Ask students to describe what happens to the perimeter as the length and width change. ("The perimeter gets shorter as the rectangle gets fatter." "The square has the shortest perimeter.") Provide time to pair-share ideas.

ASSESSMENT

Observe

- Are students confusing perimeter and area?
- As students form new rectangles, are they aware that the area is not changing because they are using the same number of tiles each time? These students may not know what area is, or they may be confusing it with perimeter.
- Are students looking for patterns in how to find the perimeter?
- Are students stating important concepts or patterns to their partners?

Ask

- What is the area of the rectangle you just made?
- What is the perimeter of the rectangle you just made?
- How is area different from perimeter?
- How do you measure area? Perimeter?

Chapter 5

Building Assessment into Instruction

Assessment is a way of understanding a child in order to make informed decisions about the child.

Sattler (2008, p. 4)

What ideas about assessment come to mind from your personal experiences? Tests? Quizzes? Grades? Studying? Anxiety? All of these are common shared memories. Now suppose that you are told that the assessments you are to use should be designed to help students learn and to help you teach. How can assessment do those things?

Integrating Assessment into Instruction

The Assessment Principle in *Principles and Standards* stresses two main ideas: (1) Assessment should enhance students' learning, and (2) assessment is a valuable tool for making instructional decisions.

Assessments usually fall into two major categories: summative or formative. *Summative assessments* are cumulative evaluations that might generate a single score, such as an end-of-unit test or the standardized test that is used in your state or school districts. Although the scores are important for schools and teachers, they do not often help shape teaching decisions on particular topics or identify misunderstandings that may block future growth.

On the other hand, *formative assessments* are "along the way" evaluations that monitor who is learning and who is not, which then helps form the next lessons. Using formative assessments is a planned process of regularly checking students' understanding during instructional activities (Hattie, 2009; Popham, 2008; Wiliam, 2008). When implemented well, formative assessment can dramatically increase the speed and amount of student learning (Nyquist, 2003; Wiliam, 2007; Wilson & Kenney, 2003) by providing targeted feedback to the student and using the results and evidence collected to improve instruction—either for the whole class or individual students. Meaningful feedback from (not to) the students as to what they know and where they make errors or have misconceptions is one of the most powerful influences on achievement (Hattie, 2009). The data you collect will inform your decision making for the next steps in the learning progression. As Wiliam states, "To be formative, assessment must include a recipe for future action" (2010, p. 41).

If summative assessment could be described as a digital snapshot, formative assessment is like streaming video. One is a picture of what a student knows that is captured in a single moment of time and the other is a moving picture that demonstrates active student thinking and reasoning. In the following pages and throughout Section II of the book in the Formative Assessment Notes features, we will focus on formative approaches that include performance-based tasks, journal writings, observations of students solving problems using checklists, and diagnostic interviews.

What Is Assessment?

The term *assessment* is defined in the NCTM *Assessment Standards* as "the process of gathering evidence about a student's knowledge of, ability to use, and disposition toward mathematics and of making inferences from that evidence for a variety of purposes" (NCTM, 1995, p. 3). Note that "gathering evidence" is not the same as giving a test or quiz. Assessment can and should happen every day as an integral part of instruction. If you restrict your view of assessment to tests and quizzes, you will miss seeing how assessment can "make learning visible" (Hattie, 2009, p. 173) and thereby help students grow.

TABLE 5.1

THE NCTM ASSESSMENT STANDARDS	
The Mathematics Standard	• Use NCTM and state or local standards to establish what mathematics students should know and be able to do and base assessments on those essential concepts and processes • Develop assessments that encourage the application of mathematics to real and sometimes novel situations • Focus on significant and correct mathematics
The Learning Standard	• Incorporate assessment as an integral part of instruction and not an interruption or a singular event at the end of a unit of study • Inform students about what content is important and what is valued by emphasizing those ideas in your instruction and matching your assessments to the models and methods used • Listen thoughtfully to your students so that further instruction will not be based on guesswork but instead on evidence of students' misunderstandings or needs
The Equity Standard	• Respect the unique qualities, experiences, and expertise of all students • Maintain high expectations for students while recognizing their individual needs • Incorporate multiple approaches to assessing students, including the provision of accommodations and modifications for students with special needs
The Openness Standard	• Establish with students the expectations for their performance and how they can demonstrate what they know • Avoid just looking at answers and give attention to the examination of the thinking processes students used • Provide students with examples of responses that meet expectations and those that don't meet expectations
The Inferences Standard	• Reflect seriously and honestly on what students are revealing about what they know • Use multiple assessments (e.g., observations, interviews, tasks, tests) to draw conclusions about students' performance • Avoid bias by establishing a rubric that describes the evidence needed and the value of each component used for scoring
The Coherence Standard	• Match your assessment techniques with both the objectives of your instruction and the methods of your instruction • Ensure that assessments are a reflection of the content you want students to learn • Develop a system of assessment that allows you to use the results to inform your instruction in a feedback loop

Source: Adapted from *Assessment Standards for School Mathematics,* copyright © 1995 by the National Council of Teachers of Mathematics. Reprinted with permission.

The *Assessment Standards*

Traditionally, most mathematics tests have focused on what students *do not know* (how many wrong answers). In 1989, the NCTM *Curriculum and Evaluation Standards for School Mathematics* called for a shift away from that model and toward assessing what students *do know* (what ideas they bring to a task, how they reason, what processes they use). This shift to finding out more about students is also a theme of the *Assessment Standards for School Mathematics* (NCTM, 1995), which contains six standards for assessment that are deserving of some reflection (see Table 5.1).

Why Do We Assess?

Even a glance at the six assessment standards suggests a complete integration of assessment and instruction. *Assessment Standards* outlines four specific purposes of assessment, as depicted in Figure 5.1. With each purpose, an arrow points to a corresponding result on the outside ring.

Monitoring Student Progress.   Assessment provides both teacher and students with ongoing feedback concerning progress toward learning objectives and long-term goals. Assessment during instruction should inform each individual

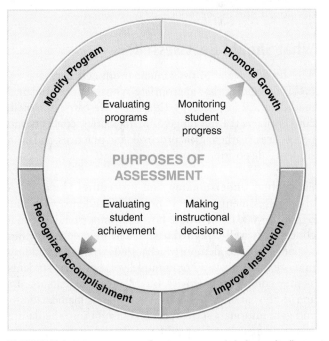

FIGURE 5.1 Four purposes of assessment and their results (in the outer ring).

Source: Adapted with permission from *Assessment Standards for School Mathematics,* p. 25, copyright 1995 by the National Council of Teachers of Mathematics. All rights reserved.

student and the teacher about problem-solving ability and growth toward understanding of mathematical concepts, mathematical practices, and procedural fluency.

Making Instructional Decisions. Teachers planning tasks to develop student understanding must have information about how students are thinking and what naïve ideas they are using. Daily problem solving and discussion provide a much richer and more useful array of data than can be gathered from a chapter test. This "on the spot" collection of evidence comes at a time when you can actually formulate plans to help students develop ideas and make changes rather than remediate after the fact.

Evaluating Student Achievement. *Evaluation* is "the process of determining the worth of, or assigning a value to, something on the basis of careful examination and judgment" (NCTM, 1995, p. 3). Evaluation involves a teacher's collecting of evidence to make an informed judgment. The evidence should take into account a wide variety of sources and types of information gathered during instruction. Most important, evaluation should reflect performance criteria about what students know and can do rather than be used to compare one student with another.

Evaluating Programs. Assessment data should be used as one component in answering the question, "How well did this lesson or unit of study achieve my goals?" For the classroom teacher, this includes evaluating the selection of tasks or problems, sequence of activities, kinds of questions developed, and use of models or representations.

What Should Be Assessed?

The broader view of assessment promoted here and by NCTM requires that appropriate assessment of students' mathematical proficiency (National Research Council, 2001) reflects the full range of mathematics: concepts and procedures, mathematical processes and practices, and even students' disposition to mathematics.

Conceptual Understanding and Procedural Fluency. A good assessment strategy provides students with the opportunity to demonstrate how they understand essential concepts. A well-designed assessment generally provides opportunities to demonstrate a student's understanding in more than one way. For example, you can assess students as they complete an activity, observing as students discuss and justify—in short, while students are doing mathematics—and gain information that provides insight into the nature of the students' understanding of that idea. And you can ask for more detail. That is something often not possible on tests.

Procedural fluency should also be assessed. This includes understanding the procedure—if a student can compute with fractions yet has no idea of why he needs a common denominator for addition but not for multiplication, then the procedure has not been "mastered" to the extent it must be for a student to have procedural fluency. Whereas a routine skill can easily be checked with a simple fact-based test, the desired conceptual connections require different assessments.

Strategic Competence and Adaptive Reasoning. Truly understanding mathematics is more than just content knowledge. The skills represented in the five process standards of *Principles and Standards* and the eight practices of the Standards for Mathematical Practice from the *Common Core State Standards* should also be assessed. These strands of mathematical proficiency are mentioned separately here to emphasize their importance, but good assessments include a blend of content and processes. One way to communicate to students that the processes/practices are important is to craft a list of rubric statements about doing mathematics that your students can understand so they recognize what you expect. Here are several examples, but consider writing your own or using those provided by your school system.

Problem Solving

- Works to make sense of and fully understand problems before beginning
- Incorporates a variety of strategies
- Assesses the reasonableness of answers

Reasoning

- Justifies solution methods and results
- Recognizes and uses counterexamples
- Makes conjectures and/or constructs logical progressions of statements based on reasoning

Communication

- Explains ideas in writing using words, pictures, and numbers
- Uses precise language, units, and labeling to clearly communicate ideas

Connections

- Makes connections between mathematics and real contexts
- Makes connections between mathematical ideas

Representations

- Uses representations such as drawings, graphs, symbols, and models to help think about and solve problems
- Moves between models
- Explains how different representations are connected

These statements should be discussed and explicitly modeled with your students to help them understand that these are processes you value. Use the statements to evaluate students' individual work, group work, and participation in class discussions. Share weak and strong examples of student work with the class to help all students see how to improve. Mathematical processes and practices must also be assessed as part of your grading or evaluation scheme, or students will not take them seriously.

Productive Disposition. Collecting data on students' ability to persevere, as well as confidence and beliefs in their own mathematical abilities, is also an important assessment. This information is most often obtained with observation, self-reported assessments, interviews, and journal writing. Information on perseverance and willingness to attempt problems is available to you every day when you use a problem-solving approach.

There are three basic methods for using formative assessment to evaluate students' understanding: observations, interviews, and tasks (Piaget, 1976). *Tasks* refers to written products and includes performance tasks, writing (e.g., journal entries, student self-assessments), and tests. Here we will discuss each in depth.

 # Performance-Based Tasks

Performance assessment tasks are tasks that are connected to actual problem-solving activities used in instruction. A good problem-based task designed to promote learning is often the most informative task for assessment.

Good tasks permit every student in the class, regardless of mathematical prowess, to demonstrate knowledge, skills, or understanding (Smith & Stein, 2011). They also include real-world or authentic contexts that interest students or relate to recent classroom events. Of course, be mindful that English language learners may need support with contexts, as those difficulties should not overshadow the attention to their mathematical ability when they work to complete a task or justify a solution.

Students who are struggling or those with disabilities should be encouraged to use ideas they possess to work on a problem even if these are not the same skills or strategies used by others in the room.

The justifications for answers, even when given orally, will almost certainly provide more information than the answers alone. Perhaps no better method exists for getting at student understanding than having students explain their thinking.

Examples of Performance-Based Tasks

Each of the following tasks provides ample opportunity for students to learn and at the same time provides data for the teacher to use in assessment. Notice that these are not elaborate tasks and yet when followed by a discussion, each could engage students for most of a period. What mathematical ideas and practices are required to successfully respond to each of these tasks? Will the task help you understand how well students understand these ideas?

Shares (Grades K–2)

Learning Targets: (1) Solve multistep problems involving the operations. (2) Use models and words to describe a solution.

Leila has 6 gumdrops, Darlene has 2, and Melissa has 4. They want to share them equally. How will they do it? Draw a picture to help explain your answer.

At second grade, the numbers in the "Shares" task should be larger. What additional concepts would be involved if the task were about sharing cookies and the total number of cookies was 34?

The Whole Set (Grades 3–4)

Learning Targets: (1) Determine a whole, given a fractional part (using a set model). (2) Make sense of quantities and their relationships in a context.

Mary counted 15 cupcakes left from the whole batch that her mother made for the picnic. "We've already eaten two-fifths," she noted. How many cupcakes did her mother bake?

In the following task, students are asked to think about the thinking of other students. Analysis of "other" students' performances is a good way to create tasks.

Decimals (Grades 4–6)

Learning Targets: (1) Compare two decimals by reasoning about their size. (2) Analyze and critique the reasoning of others.

Alan tried to make a decimal number as close to 50 as he could using the digits 1, 4, 5, and 9. He arranged them in this order: 51.49. Jerry thinks he can arrange the same digits to get a number that is even closer to 50. Do you agree or disagree? Explain.

The explanations of other students' thinking allow students to pick up alternative methods while offering evidence about students' understanding of concepts and strategy use. This observational information can be recorded over time with a checklist.

Two Triangles (Grades 4–7)

Learning Targets: (1) Classify two-dimensional shapes into categories based on their properties. (2) Attend to precision by clearly applying definitions to define categories.

Tell everything you can about these two triangles. Given what you wrote about the two triangles, determine which of the following statements are true: the large triangle is an isosceles triangle; the small triangle is an isosceles triangle; the big triangle has an area of 2 square units; the small triangle has an area of 1 square unit; the large triangle has at least one angle that measures 45 degrees; the small triangle has at least one angle that measures 30 degrees; the two triangles are similar. Explain your thinking.

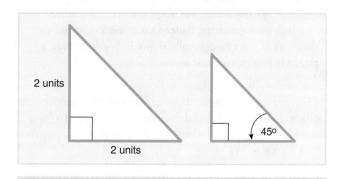

This task is a good example of an open-ended assessment. Consider how much more valuable this task is than asking for the angle measure in the triangle on the left.

Algebra: Graphing (Grades 7–8)

Learning Targets: (1) Compare and analyze quadratic functions. (2) Build a logical argument for a conjecture using reasoning.

Does the graph of $y = x^2$ ever intersect the graph of $y = x^2 + 2$? What are some ways that you could test your conjecture? Would your conjecture hold true for other equations in the form of $y = x^2 + b$? Within all quadratic functions of the form $y = ax^2 + b$, when would your conjecture hold true?

Even with a graphing calculator, proving that these two graphs will not intersect requires reasoning and an understanding of how graphs are related to equations and tables.

Public Discussion of Performance Tasks

A good performance task can be approached in more than one way. Therefore, much can be learned about students' understanding in a discussion that follows students solving the task individually. Students must develop the habit of sharing, writing, and listening to justifications. In particular, it is important for students to compare and make connections between strategies.

In addition, students should be encouraged to engage in debating mathematics ideas in order to assist them in organizing their thoughts, thinking about their position, and analyzing the positions of others. This can be developed by forcing students to take a position (e.g., Does the order of factors affect the answer in a multiplication problem?). The resulting discussions will often reveal students' misconceptions and serve as reminders about previous discussions (using ideas that came to the forefront in previous classes) (Barlow & McCrory, 2011).

Some performance assessments have no written component and no "answer" or result. For example, students may be playing a game in which dice or dominoes are being used. As students are playing, the teacher is observing the way in which students are adding the dice. As an observer, a teacher will note how students use numbers. Some will count every dot on the domino. Others will use a counting-on strategy (a student using a counting-on strategy will see four dots on one side and count on from four to tally the total number). Some will recognize certain patterns immediately without counting. Others may be unsure whether 13 beats 11. Data gathered from asking questions about and listening to a pair of students work on an activity or an extended project provide significant insights into students' thinking (Petit & Zawojewski, 2010). Especially if used for grading, it is important to keep dated written anecdotal notes that can be referred to later. (See the section "Anecdotal Notes" later in this chapter.)

One process of moving from teaching tasks to assessment tasks involves the addition of a rubric. The next section will explain how you can create and use both generic rubrics that describe general qualities of performance and topic-specific (or curriculum-based) rubrics that include criteria based on particular lesson objectives.

Rubrics and Performance Indicators

Problem-based tasks may tell us a great deal about what students know, but how do we analyze and use this information? Often there is no way to simply count the percent correct and put a mark in the grade book. It may be helpful to make a distinction between *scoring* and *grading*. "*Scoring* is comparing students' work to criteria or rubrics that describe what we expect the work to be. *Grading* is the result of accumulating scores and other information about a student's work for the purpose of summarizing and communicating to others" (Stenmark & Bush, 2001, p. 118). One valuable tool for scoring is a rubric.

A *rubric* is a framework that can be designed or adapted by the teacher for a particular group of students or a particular mathematical task (Kulm, 1994). A rubric usually consists of a scale of three to six points that is used as a rating of total performance on a single task rather than a count of how many items in a series of exercises are correct or incorrect.

Simple Rubrics.   The following simple four-point rubric was developed by the New Standards Project.

4   Excellent: Full Accomplishment
3   Proficient: Substantial Accomplishment

2   Marginal: Partial Accomplishment
1   Unsatisfactory: Little Accomplishment

This simple rubric allows a teacher to score performances by first sorting into two broad categories, as illustrated in Figure 5.2. The scale then allows you to separate each category into two additional levels as shown. A rating of 0 is given for no response or effort or for responses that are completely off task. The advantage of the four-point scale is the relatively easy initial sort into "Got It" or "Not There Yet."

Others prefer a three-point rubric such as the following example:

3   Above and beyond—uses exemplary methods, shows creativity, goes beyond the requirements of the problem

2   On target—completes the task with only minor errors, uses successful approaches

1   Not there yet—makes significant errors or omissions, uses unsuccessful approaches

These relatively simple scales are *generic rubrics*. They label general categories of performance but do not define the specific criteria for a particular task. For any given task or process, it is usually helpful to create specific performance indicators for each level.

Performance Indicators. *Performance indicators* are task-specific statements that describe what performance looks like at each level of the rubric and, in so doing, establish criteria for acceptable performance.

A rubric and its performance indicators should focus your students on the objectives and away from the self-limiting question, "How many can you miss and still get an A?" Like athletes who continually strive for better performances rather than "good enough," students should always recognize the opportunities to excel. When you take into account the total performance (processes, answers, justifications, extension, and so on), it is always possible to "go above and beyond."

When you create your task-specific rubric, what performance at different levels of your rubric will or should look like may initially be difficult to predict. Much depends on your experience with students at that grade level, students working on the same task, and your insights about the task or mathematical concept itself. One important part of helping you set performance levels is students' common misconceptions or the expected thinking or approaches to the same or similar problems.

If possible, write out indicators of "proficient" or "on target" performances before you use the task in class. This is an excellent self-check to be sure that the task is likely to accomplish the purpose you selected it for in the first place.

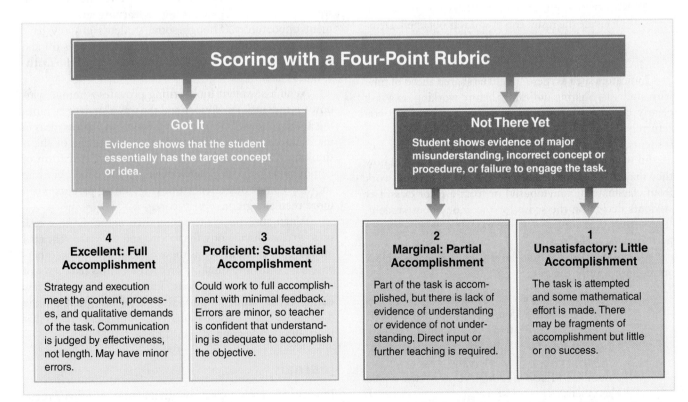

FIGURE 5.2 With a four-point rubric, performances are first sorted into two categories. Each performance is then considered again and assigned to a point on the scale.

Think about how students are likely to approach the activity. If you find yourself writing performance indicators in terms of number of correct responses, you are most likely looking at drill exercises and not the performance-based tasks for which a rubric is appropriate.

 PAUSE and REFLECT

Consider the fraction problem titled "The Whole Set" on page 81. Assume you are teaching fourth grade and wish to write performance indicators that you can share with your students using a four-point rubric (Figure 5.2). What indicators would you use for level-3 and level-4 performances? Start with a level-3 performance, and then think about level 4. Try this before reading further. ●

Determining performance indicators is always a subjective process based on your professional judgment. Here is one possible set of indicators for the "The Whole Set" task:

3 Determines the correct answer or uses an approach that would yield a correct answer if not for minor errors. Explanations and reasoning are weak. Giving a correct result and reasoning for the number eaten but an incorrect result for the total baked would also be a level-3 performance.

4 Determines the total number baked and uses words, pictures, and numbers to explain and justify the result and how it was obtained. Demonstrates a knowledge of fractional parts and the relation to the whole.

Indicators such as these should be shared ahead of time with students. Sharing indicators before working on a task clearly conveys what is valued and expected. When you return papers, it is important to review the indicators with students, including examples of correct answers and successful responses. This will help students understand how they may have done better. Often it is useful to show work from classmates (anonymously) or from a prior class. Let students decide on the score for the anonymous student. Importantly, students need to see models of what a level-4 performance looks like.

What about level-1 and level-2 performances? Here are suggestions for the same task:

2 Uses some aspect of fractions appropriately (e.g., divides the 15 into 5 groups instead of 3) but fails to illustrate an understanding of how to determine the whole. The student shows evidence that they don't understand a fraction is a number. (They may believe it is two whole numbers.)

1 Shows some effort but little or no understanding of a fractional part relative to the whole.

Unexpected methods and solutions happen. Don't box students into demonstrating their understanding only as you thought or hoped they would when there is evidence that they are accomplishing your objectives in different ways. Such occurrences can help you revise or refine your rubric for future use.

Student Involvement with Rubrics. In the beginning of the year, discuss your generic rubric (such as Figure 5.2) with the class. Post it prominently. Many teachers use the same rubric for all subjects; others prefer to use a specialized rubric for mathematics. In your discussion, let students know that as they do activities and solve problems, you will look at their work and listen to their explanations and provide them with feedback in the form of a rubric, rather than as a letter grade or a percentage.

When students start to understand what the rubric really means, begin to discuss performance on tasks in terms of the generic rubric. You might have students self-assess their own work using the generic rubric and explain their reasons for the rating.

Writing and Journals

We have been emphasizing that instruction and assessment should be integrated. No place is this more evident than in students' writing. Writing is both a learning and an assessment opportunity. Though some students initially have difficulty writing in mathematics, persistence pays off and students come to see writing as a natural part of the mathematics class.

As an assessment tool, writing provides a unique window to students' perceptions and the way a student is thinking about an idea. Even a kindergartner can express ideas in markings on paper and begin to explain what he or she is thinking. Finally, student writing is an excellent form of communication with parents during conferences. Writing shows evidence of students' thinking, telling parents much more than any grade or test score.

When students write about their solutions to a task prior to class discussions, the writing can serve as a rehearsal for the conversation about the work. Students who otherwise have difficulty thinking on their feet now have a script to support their contributions. This avoids having the few highly verbal students providing all of the input for the discussion. Call on these more reluctant talkers first so that their ideas are heard and valued.

Journals

Journals are a way to make written communication a regular part of doing mathematics. The feedback you provide to students should move their learning forward. Journals are a place for students to write about various aspects of their mathematics experiences:

- Their conceptual understandings and problem solving, including descriptions of ideas; solutions; and justifications of problems, graphs, charts, and observations
- Their questions concerning the current topic, an idea that they may need help with, or an area they don't quite understand
- Their attitudes toward mathematics, their confidence in their understanding, or their fears of being wrong

Grading journals would communicate that there is a specific "right" response you are seeking. It is essential, however, that you read and respond to journal writing. One form of response for a performance task would be to use the classroom's generic rubric along with a helpful comment.

Writing Prompts

Students should always have a clear, well-defined purpose for writing in their journals. They need to know exactly what to write about and who the audience is (you, a student in a lower grade, an adult, a new student to the school), and they should be given a definite time frame within which to write. Journal writing that is completely open-ended without a stated goal or purpose will not be a good use of time. Here are some suggestions for writing prompts to get your students thinking:

Concepts and Processes

- "I think the answer is . . . I think this because. . . ." (The journal can be used to solve and explain any problem. Some teachers duplicate the problem and have students tape it into the journal.)
- Write an explanation for a new or younger student of why 4×7 is the same as 7×4 and if this works for 6×49 and 49×6. If so, why?
- Explain to a student in class (or who was absent today) what you learned about decimals.
- What mathematics work did we do today that was easy? What was hard? What do you still have questions about?
- If you got stuck today in solving a problem, where in the problem did you get stuck?
- After you got the answer to today's problem, what did you do so that you were convinced your answer was reasonable? How sure are you that you got the correct answer?
- Write a story problem that goes with this equation (this graph, this diagram, this picture).

Productive Dispositions

- "What I like the most (or least) about mathematics is. . . ."

- Write a mathematics autobiography. Tell about your experiences in mathematics outside of school and how you feel about the subject.
- What was the most interesting mathematics idea you learned this week?

Writing for Early Learners

If you are interested in working with pre-K–1 students, the writing prompts presented may have sounded too advanced; it is difficult for prewriters and beginning writers to express ideas like those suggested. There are specific techniques for journals in kindergarten and first grade that have been used successfully.

To begin the development of the writing-in-mathematics process, one kindergarten teacher uses a language experience approach. After an activity, she writes "Giant Journal" and a topic or prompt on a large flipchart. Students respond to the prompt, and she writes their ideas, adding the contributor's name and even drawings when appropriate, as in Figure 5.3.

All students can draw pictures of some sort to describe what they have done. Dots can represent counters or blocks. Shapes and special figures can be cut out from duplicated sheets and pasted onto journal pages.

FIGURE 5.3 A journal in kindergarten may be a class product on a flipchart.

Grade 1

Read the problem. Think and use materials to help you solve it.

There were seven owls. They found some mice in the woods to eat. Each owl found five mice. How many mice did they find? How do you know? Use pictures, words, and numbers to show how you solved the problem.

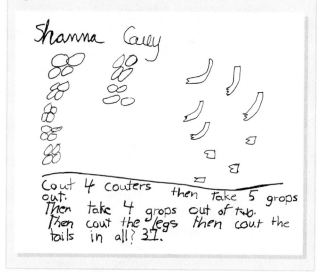

Grade 2

The farmer saw five cows and four chickens. How many legs and tails in all did he see?

FIGURE 5.4 Journal entries of students in grades 1 and 2.

The "writing" should be a record of something the student has just done and is comfortable with. Figure 5.4 shows problems solved in first and second grade.

Student Self-Assessment

Stenmark (1989) notes that "the capability and willingness to assess their own progress and learning is one of the greatest gifts students can develop. . . . Mathematical power comes with knowing how much we know and what to do to learn more" (p. 26). Student self-assessment should not be your only measure of their learning or disposition, but rather a record of how *they perceive* their strengths and weaknesses as they begin to take responsibility for their learning.

You can gather self-assessment data in several ways, including preassessments that catch areas of confusion or misconceptions prior to formally assessing students on particular content or by regularly using an "exit slip" (index card or paper slip with a quick question or two) when students are concluding the instructional period (Wieser, 2008). In each case, you can tailor your teaching to improve their understanding. As you plan for the self-assessment, consider what you need to know to help you as a teacher find instructional strategies and revised learning targets. Convey to your students why you are having them do this activity—they need to grasp that they must play a role in their mastery of mathematics rather than just focus on completing a task. Encourage them to be honest and candid.

An open-ended writing prompt such as was suggested for journals is a successful method of getting self-assessment data:

- How well do you think you understand the work we have been doing on fractions during the last few days? What is still causing you difficulty with fractions?
- Write two of the important things you learned in class today (or this week).
- Which problem(s) on the handout/quiz did you find the most challenging? Which were the easiest?

Another method is to use some form of a questionnaire to which students respond. These can have open-ended questions, response choices (e.g., *seldom, sometimes, often; disagree, don't care, agree*), concept maps, drawings, and so on. Many such instruments appear in the literature, and many textbook publishers provide examples. Whenever you use a form or questionnaire that someone else has devised, be certain to adapt it for your needs so that it serves the purpose you intend.

Students may find it difficult to write about attitudes and dispositions. A questionnaire where they can respond "yes," "maybe," or "no" to a series of statements is often a successful approach. Encourage students to add comments under an item if they wish. Here are some items you could use to build such a questionnaire:

- I feel sure of myself when I get an answer to a problem.
- I sometimes just put down anything so I can get finished.
- I like to work on really hard math problems.
- Math class makes me feel nervous.
- If I get stuck, I feel like quitting or going to another problem.
- I am not as good in mathematics as most of the other students in this class.
- Mathematics is my favorite subject.
- Memorizing rules is the only way I know to learn mathematics.
- I will work a long time at a problem until I think I've solved it.

In each case, the self-assessment supports students' movement to be active rather than passive learners. Although it takes additional time to infuse these assessments into the daily schedule, allowing students to take part in the assessment process is motivating and encourages students to monitor and adapt their approaches to learning.

Tests

Tests will always be a part of assessment and evaluation. However, a test need not be a collection of low-level skill exercises that are simple to grade. Although tests of computational skills may have a role in your classroom, the use of such tests should be only one aspect of your assessment. Like all other forms of assessment, tests should match the goals of your instruction. Tests can be designed to find out what concepts students understand and how their ideas are connected. Tests of procedural knowledge should go beyond just knowing how to perform an algorithm and should allow and require the student to demonstrate a conceptual basis for the process. The following examples will illustrate these ideas.

1. Write a multiplication problem that has an answer that falls between the answers to these two problems:

$$49 \qquad 45$$
$$\times 25 \qquad \times 30$$

2. a. In this division exercise, what number tells how many tens were shared among the 6 sets?
   b. Instead of writing the remainder as "R2," Elaine writes "$\frac{1}{3}$." Explain the difference between these two ways of recording the leftover part.

$$49R2 \qquad 49\tfrac{1}{3}$$
$$6\overline{)296} \qquad 6\overline{)296}$$

3. On a grid, draw two figures with the same area but different perimeters. List the area and perimeter of each.

4. For each subtraction fact, write an addition fact that helps you think of the answer to the subtraction.

$$\begin{array}{cccc} 12 & 9 & 9 & 14 \\ -3 & +3 & -4 & -7 \\ \hline 9 & 12 & & \end{array}$$

5. Draw pictures of arrows to show why $^-3 + {}^-4$ is the same as $^-3 - {}^+4$.

If a test is well constructed, much more information can be gathered than simply the number of correct or incorrect answers. The following considerations can help maximize the value of your tests:

1. *Permit students to use calculators.* Except for tests of computational skills, calculators allow students to focus on what you really want to test.

2. *Use manipulatives and drawings.* Students can use appropriate models to work on test questions when those same models have been used during instruction to develop concepts. (Note the use of grids and drawings in previous examples.) Simple drawings can be used to represent counters, base-ten pieces, fraction pieces, and the like (see Figure 5.5). Be sure to provide examples in class of how to draw the models before you ask students to draw on a test.

3. *Include opportunities for explanations.*

4. *Avoid always using "preanswered" tests.* Tests in which questions have only one correct answer, whether it is a calculation, a multiple-choice, or a fill-in-the-blank question, tend to limit what you can learn about what the student has learned. Rather, open-ended items allow students the opportunity to show what they know.

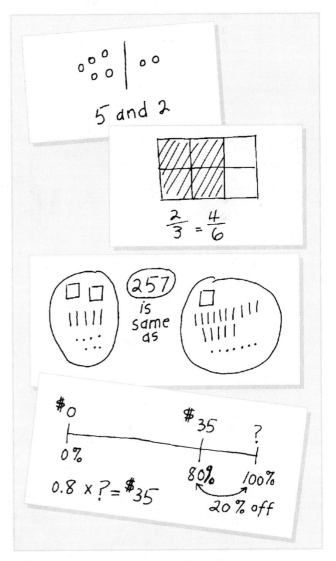

FIGURE 5.5 Students can use drawings to illustrate concepts on tests.

◆ Observations

All teachers learn useful bits of information about their students every day. When the three-phase lesson format suggested in Chapter 3 is used, the flow of evidence about student performance increases dramatically, especially in the *during* and *after* portions of lessons. If you have a systematic plan for gathering this information while observing and listening to students, at least two very valuable results occur. First, information that may have gone unnoticed is suddenly visible and important. Second, observation data gathered systematically can be added to other data and used in planning lessons, providing feedback to students, conducting parent conferences, and determining grades.

Depending on what information you may be trying to gather, a single observation of a whole class may require several days to two weeks before all students have been observed. Shorter periods of observation will focus on a particular cluster of concepts or skills or particular students. Over longer periods, you can note growth in mathematical processes or practices, such as problem solving, representation, or reasoning. To use observation effectively, you should take seriously the following maxim: *Do not attempt to record data on every student in a single class period.*

Observation methods vary with the purposes for which they are used. Further, formats and methods of gathering observation data are going to be influenced by your individual teaching style and habits.

Anecdotal Notes

One system for recording observations is to write short notes either during or immediately after a lesson in a brief narrative style. One possibility is to have a card for each student. Some teachers keep the cards on a clipboard with each taped at the top edge (see Figure 5.6). Another option is to focus your observations on about five students a day. The students selected may be members of one or two

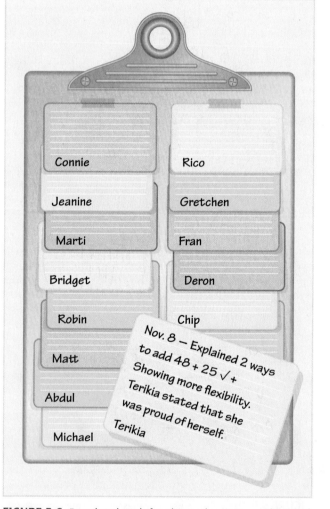

FIGURE 5.6 Preprinted cards for observation notes can be taped to a clipboard or folder for quick access.

Observation Rubric		
Making Whole Given Fraction Part		③/17
Above and Beyond Clear understanding. Communicates concept in multiple representations. Shows evidence of using idea without prompting.	Sally Latania	
Fraction whole made from parts in rods and in sets. Explains easily.	Greg	Zal
On Target Understands or is developing well. Uses designated models.	Lavant (rod) Julie (rod) George (set) Maria (set)	Tanisha (rod) Lee (set) J.B. (rod) John H. (rod)
Can make whole in either rod or set format (note). Hesitant. Needs prompt to identify unit fraction.		
Not There Yet Some confusion or misunderstands. Only models idea with help.	John S.	Mary
Needs help to do activity. No confidence.		

FIGURE 5.7 Record names in a rubric during an activity or for a single topic over several days.

cooperative groups. An alternative to cards is the use of large peel-off file labels, possibly preprinted with student names. The label notes are then moved to a more permanent notebook page for each student.

Rubrics

Another possibility is to use your three- or four-point generic rubric on a reusable form as in Figure 5.7. Include space for content-specific indicators and another column to jot down names of students. A quick note or comment may be added to a name. This method is especially useful for planning purposes.

Checklists

To cut down on writing and to help focus your attention, a checklist with several specific processes or content objectives can be devised and duplicated for each student (see Figure 5.8). Regardless of the checklist format, a place for comments should be included.

Another format involves listing all students in a class on a single page or not more than three pages (see Figure 5.9). Across the top of the page are specific abilities or deficiencies to look for. (These can be based on learning progressions or trajectories.) Pluses and minuses, checks, or codes corresponding to your general rubric can be entered in the grid. A full-class checklist is more likely to be used for long-term objectives. Topics that might be appropriate for this format include problem-solving processes, communication skills, and such subject areas as basic fact fluency or computational estimation skills. Dating entries or noting specific activities observed is also helpful.

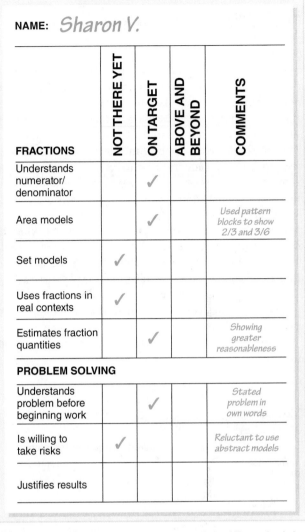

NAME: Sharon V.				
FRACTIONS	NOT THERE YET	ON TARGET	ABOVE AND BEYOND	COMMENTS
Understands numerator/ denominator		✓		
Area models		✓		Used pattern blocks to show 2/3 and 3/6
Set models	✓			
Uses fractions in real contexts	✓			
Estimates fraction quantities		✓		Showing greater reasonableness
PROBLEM SOLVING				
Understands problem before beginning work		✓		Stated problem in own words
Is willing to take risks	✓			Reluctant to use abstract models
Justifies results				

FIGURE 5.8 A focused computer-generated checklist and rubric can be printed for each student.

Topic: Mental Computation Adding 2-digit numbers **Names**	Not There Yet Can't do mentally	On Target Has at least one strategy	Above and Beyond Uses different methods with different numbers	Comments
Lalie		✓ 3-18-09 3-21-09		
Pete	✓ 3-20-09	✓ 3-24-09		Difficulty with problems requiring regrouping
Sid			✓ + 3-20-09	Flexible approaches used
Lakeshia		✓		Counts by tens, then adds ones
George		✓		
Pam	✓			Beginning to add the group of tens first
Maria		✓ 3-24-09		Using a posted hundreds chart

FIGURE 5.9 A full-class observation checklist can be used for longer-term objectives or for several days to cover a short-term objective.

Diagnostic Interviews

Diagnostic interviews are a means of getting in-depth information about an individual student's knowledge and mental strategies about concepts. These interviews, although often labor intensive, are rich assessments that provide evidence of misunderstandings and explore students' ways of thinking. In each interview, a student is given a problem and asked to verbalize his or her thinking at points in the process. Sometimes students self-correct a mistake but, more frequently, teachers can unearth a student's misunderstanding or reveal what strategies students have mastered.

The problems you select should match the essential understanding for the topic your students are studying. In every case, have paper, pencils, and a variety of materials available—particularly those models and materials you have been using during your instruction. It is often useful to have a scoring guide or rubric available to jot down notes about emerging understandings, common methods you expect students to use, or common misunderstandings that may come to light.

Here are suggested problems that can be used for diagnostic interviews.

Learning Targets: (1) Demonstrate an understanding of the addition and subtraction algorithms. (2) Explore the structure of the place-value system.

Does the 1 in each of the following problems represent the same amount? (Philipp, Schappelle, Siegfried, Jacobs, & Lamb, 2008)

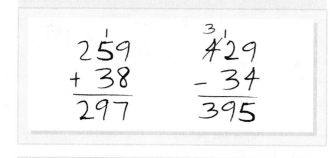

After students have given their answer, you should ask them to explain why in addition (as in the first problem) the 1 is added to the 5, but in subtraction (as in the second problem) 10 is added to the 2. This problem helps you understand whether your students are working from a procedural knowledge or if they have a conceptual knowledge of the operations of addition and subtraction. Whether the student gives attention to place-value concepts and the quantities involved in regrouping or if they believe the number is the same in each problem will provide valuable information that enhances professional judgment for your subsequent instructional decisions.

The following problem can be used in an interview to assess knowledge of comparing fractions. Figure 5.10 shows student work comparing $\frac{4}{4}$ and $\frac{4}{8}$.

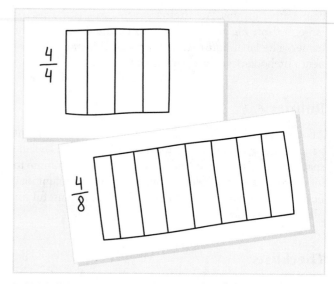

FIGURE 5.10 Student work comparing fractions.

Which is more—$\frac{4}{4}$ or $\frac{4}{8}$? (Ball, 2008)

In this case, students should be encouraged to show their thinking about this comparison. Possibly they will select an area model or a number line in their attempt to make their mental processes "visible" and justify their answer. Some students may draw diagrams of different-sized rectangles, which will reveal their understandings or misunderstandings about the whole as a constant unit for this comparison. For example, in a presentation by Deborah Ball, a noted mathematics educator, one of the students in her class drew an area model of the four-fourths and then used the same sized pieces to draw four-eighths, resulting in a whole that was twice the size of the original (2008). But he then self-corrected when he saw another student who had drawn two rectangles of the same size and divided one into fourths, shading all four, and another into eighths, shading four (or only half) of the pieces. During a diagnostic interview, the students will not be able to benefit from the explanations of other students, but these are the discoveries and results that can inform and improve your instruction. This information will also help you in redirecting or reinforcing students' thinking and strategies.

Summative Assessments: Improving Performance on High-Stakes Tests

The No Child Left Behind Act mandates that every state test students in mathematics at every grade beginning with grade 3 through grade 8. Although the method of testing and even the objectives to be tested were left up to individual states, now with the acceptance of the *Common Core State Standards*, many states will be sharing end-of-year assessments. These assessments will include performance assessments and not just rely on multiple-choice questions (Sawchuk, 2010).

Whatever the details of the testing program in your particular state, these external tests (originating from outside the classroom) impose significant pressures on school districts, which in turn put pressure on principals, who then place pressure on teachers.

External testing that has consequences for students and teachers is typically referred to as *high-stakes* testing. High stakes make the pressures of testing significant for both students (Will I pass? Will my parents be upset?) and teachers (Will my class meet state proficiency levels?). The pressures certainly have an effect on instruction.

You will not be able to avoid the pressures of high-stakes testing. The question is, "How will you respond?"

The best advice for succeeding on high-stakes tests is to teach the big ideas in the mathematics curriculum that are aligned with your state and local standards. Students who have learned conceptual ideas in a relational manner and who have learned the processes and practices of doing mathematics will perform well on tests, regardless of the format or specific objectives.

Examine lists of state objectives and identify the broader conceptual foundations on which they depend. Be certain that you provide students with an opportunity to learn the content in the standards. At the start of each chapter of Section II of this book, you will find a list of Big Ideas followed by a section called Mathematics Content Connections. These will help you explore the broader ideas behind the objectives that you need to teach so you can help students deepen their understanding of connecting ideas and strands. All programs should have a common focus on conceptual development, problem solving, reasoning, and communication of mathematical understanding. In short, a problem-based approach is the best course of action for raising scores.

Using Assessments to Grade

A grade is a statistic used to communicate to others the achievement level that a student has attained in a particular area of study. The accuracy or validity of the grade is dependent on the information used in generating the grade, the professional judgment of the teacher, and the alignment of the assessments with the true goals and objectives of the instruction. Look again at the definition of grading on page 82. Notice that it says scores are used along with "other information about a student's work" to determine a grade. There is no mention of averaging scores.

Most experienced teachers will tell you that they know a great deal about their students in terms of what the students know, how they perform in different situations, their attitudes and beliefs, and their levels of skill attainment. One idea that should be clear from the discussions in this chapter is that it is quite useful to gather a wide variety of rich information about students' understanding, problem-solving processes, and attitudes and beliefs.

For effective use of the assessment information gathered from problems, tasks, and other appropriate methods to assign grades, some hard decisions are inevitable. Some are philosophical, some require school or district policies about grades, and all require us to examine what we value and the objectives we communicate to students and parents.

What Gets Graded Gets Valued

Among the many components of the grading process, one truth is undeniable: *What gets graded* by teachers *is what gets valued* by students. Using rubric scores to provide feedback and to encourage a pursuit of excellence must also relate to grades. However, "converting four out of five [on a rubric score] to 80 percent or three out of four [on a rubric] to a grade of C can destroy the entire purpose of alternative assessment and the use of scoring rubrics" (Kulm, 1994, p. 99). Kulm explains that directly translating rubric scores to grades focuses attention on grades and away from the purpose of every good problem-solving activity—to strive for an excellent performance. The purpose of detailed rubric indicators is to instruct students on what is necessary to achieve at a high level. Early on, there should be opportunities to improve performance based on feedback.

Grading must be based on the performance tasks and other activities for which you assigned rubric ratings; otherwise, students will soon realize that these are not important scores. The grade at the end of the marking period should reflect a holistic view of where the student is now relative to your goals.

From Assessment Tools to Grades

The grades you assign should reflect all of your objectives. That means a combination of procedural skills, conceptual understandings, and mathematical processes and practices. As you assign a single grade for mathematics, different factors probably have different weights or values in making up the grade. Student X may be strong in reasoning and truly love mathematics yet be weak in computational skills. Student Y may be struggling in problem solving but possess good skills in communicating her mathematical thinking. How much weight should you give to cooperation in groups, to written versus oral evidence, to computational skills? There are no simple answers to these questions. However, they should be addressed at the beginning of the grading period and communicated to your students and their families.

The process of grading students using multiple forms of assessments has the potential to enhance your students' achievement. As you develop tools to match your instruction and provide evidence of your students' understanding, also work with colleagues. In small groups or with a grade-level partner, you can share tasks, analyze samples of students' work to try to decipher errors, and engage in discussions about how they have responded to similar student misconceptions. Working as a team to create, implement, and analyze assessments will enrich your ability to select and administer meaningful performance-based questions or tasks and enhance your professional judgment by questioning or confirming your thinking.

Using Assessments to Shape Instruction

For assessments to be useful, teachers must know what to do with the evidence revealed in an assessment or set of assessments to address the learning needs of students (Heritage, Kim, Vendlinski, & Herman, 2009). This includes shifting from one approach or strategy development to another, pointing out examples or counterexamples to students, or using different materials and prompts. Knowing how to shape the next steps in instruction for an individual when the content is not learned is critical if you are going to avoid "covering" topics and move toward student growth and progress. If instead you just move on without some students, "students accumulate debts of knowledge (knowledge owed to them)" (Daro, Mosher, & Corcoran, 2011, p. 48).

Summative assessment scores on high-stakes tests "are not of much help in designing instructional interventions to help students stay on track and continue to progress" (Daro, Mosher, & Corcoran, 2011, p. 30). But the formative assessment described throughout this book can help. In Section II, a variety of Formative Assessment Notes features suggest ways to assess areas where students struggle; in some cases, specific activities are suggested as follow-up lessons. As you learn more about your students, you will be able to target lessons that will address their naïve understandings and misconceptions through the learning supports provided in each chapter.

RESOURCES *for Chapter 5*

RECOMMENDED READINGS

Articles

Kitchen, R., Cherrington, A., Gates, J., Hitchings, J., Majka, M., Merk, M., & Trubow, G. (2002). Supporting reform through performance assessment. *Mathematics Teaching in the Middle School, 8*(1), 24–30.
Six of the seven authors are middle school teachers working together to implement a standards-based curriculum. Here they share examples of assessments they believe will help promote higher-order thinking.

Leatham, K. R., Lawrence, K., & Mewborn, D. (2005). Getting started with open-ended assessment. *Teaching Children Mathematics, 11*(8), 413–419.
These authors share examples of open-ended assessment items that include the potential for a range of responses and a balance between too much and too little information given. Teacher-author Kathy Lawrence talks personally about getting started in her third–fourth grade class of "culturally and economically diverse" students.

Books

Collins, A. (Ed.) (2011). *Using classroom assessment to improve student learning.* Reston, VA: NCTM.
Using the Common Core State Standards *as a basis for examples, this book focuses on formative assessments at the middle grade level. Emphasizing such strategies as questioning, observation protocols, interviews, classroom discussions, and exit slips, this practical guide is a worthwhile resource.*

Wright, R., Martland, J., & Stafford, A. (2006). *Early numeracy: Assessment for teaching and intervention.* London: Paul Chapman Educational Publishers.
This book includes diagnostic interviews for assessing young students' knowledge and strategy use related to numbers and the operations of addition and subtraction. Using a series of frameworks, the authors help teachers pinpoint students' misconceptions and support appropriate interventions.

ONLINE RESOURCES

Classroom-Focused Improvement Process (CFIP)
http://mdk12.org/process/cfip
The Classroom-Focused Improvement Process (CFIP) is a six-step process for increasing student achievement that is planned and carried out by teachers meeting in grade-level, content, or vertical teams as a part of their regular lesson planning cycle.

NCTM Research Clips and Briefs—Formative Assessment
www.nctm.org/news/content.aspx?id=8468
NCTM provides information on the definition of formative assessment and five key strategies for effective formative assessment, including an example of a task for a diagnostic interview. They also include an excellent set of references for further investigation.

Rubric Exemplars
www.exemplars.com/resources/rubrics/assessment.php
Here you will find example rubrics for mathematics that are aligned to NCTM and CCSSO documents, including rubrics especially for pre-K and kindergarten students.

REFLECTIONS *on Chapter 5*

WRITING TO LEARN

1. What is the difference between formative and summative assessment? Give examples of each.
2. Describe the essential features of a rubric. Give three examples of performance indicators.
3. How can you incorporate observational assessments into your daily lessons? What is at least one method of getting observations recorded?
4. How can students with limited writing skills "write" in mathematics class?
5. How do diagnostic interviews help capture student thinking?

FOR DISCUSSION AND EXPLORATION

1. Examine a few end-of-chapter tests in various mathematics textbooks. How well do the tests assess concepts and understanding? Mathematical processes and practices?

2. Access your state's department of education website and find a few released test items used by your state to determine annual yearly progress (AYP) as required by NCLB. For the released test items, first decide whether they are good problem-based tasks that would help you find out about student understanding of the concepts involved. Then, if necessary, try to improve the item so that it becomes a problem-based assessment that would be useful in the classroom.

MyEducationLab™

Go to the MyEducationLab (www.myeducationlab.com) for Math Methods and familiarize yourself with the content. Much of the site content is organized topically. The topics include all of the following to support your learning in the course:

- Learning outcomes for important mathematics methods course topics aligned with the national standards
- Assignments and Activities, tied to these learning outcomes and standards, that can help you more deeply understand course content
- Building Teaching Skills and Dispositions learning units that allow you to apply and practice your understanding of the core mathematics content and teaching skills

Your instructor has a correlation guide that aligns the exercises on the topical portion of the site with your book's chapters.

On MyEducationLab you will also find book-specific resources including Blackline Masters, Expanded Lesson Activities, and Artifact Analysis Activities.

Field Experience Guide
C O N N E C T I O N S

Assessment of student learning is the focus of Chapter 7 of the *Field Experience Guide*, where seven different opportunities are designed to help you learn to assess. Designing and using rubrics are the focus of FEG 7.4 and 7.5. Also, FEG 1.4 (a student interview on dispositions) and FEG 7.2 (assessing student understanding) are good assessment tasks to learn about student learning. Chapter 11 of the guide offers three excellent balanced assessment tasks, complete with rubrics and guidance on scoring.

Chapter 6

Teaching Mathematics Equitably to All Children

It was a wise man who said that there is no greater inequality than the equal treatment of unequals.

Supreme Court Justice Felix Frankfurter in *Dennis v. U.S.*, 339 US 162 (1950), p. 184.

Educational equity is a key component of helping all students meet the goals of the NCTM standards. The Equity Principle within *Principles and Standards for School Mathematics* states, "Excellence in mathematics education requires equity—high expectations and strong support for all students" (NCTM, 2000, p. 12). Students need opportunities to advance their knowledge supported by teaching that gives attention to their individual learning needs. In years past (and in some cases still today), some groups of students were not expected to do as well in mathematics as others, including students with special needs, students of color, English language learners, females, and students of low socioeconomic status.

Principles and Standards states, "All students, regardless of their personal characteristics, backgrounds, or physical challenges must have opportunities to study—and support to learn—mathematics" (NCTM, 2000, p. 12). Teaching for equity is much more than providing students with an equal opportunity to learn mathematics. It is not enough to require the same mathematics courses, give the same assignments, and use the identical assessment criteria. Instead, teaching for equity attempts to attain equal outcomes for all students by being sensitive to individual differences.

Many *achievement* gaps are actually *instructional* gaps or *expectation* gaps. It is not helpful when teachers establish low expectations for students, as when they say, "I just cannot put this class into groups to work; they are too unruly" or

"My students can't solve word problems—they don't have the reading skills" or "I am not doing as many writing activities during math instruction because I have so many ELLs in my class." Going in with an attitude that some students cannot "do" will ensure that they don't have ample opportunities to prove otherwise.

Recall that planning considerations for all learners were addressed in Chapter 4. In this chapter, we focus on instructional practices. You will discover many ways to create equitable mathematics classrooms and will therefore find the means of helping all students become mathematically proficient.

Mathematics for All Students

When thinking about creating and maintaining an equitable classroom environment, NCTM's position statement on equity in mathematics education (2008) states, "Excellence in mathematics education rests on equity—high expectations, respect, understanding and strong support for all students. Policies, practices, attitudes, and beliefs related to mathematics teaching and learning must be assessed continually to ensure that all students have equal access to the resources with the greatest potential to promote learning. A culture of equity maximizes the learning potential of all students."

As you work with students' areas of strength, you should identify opportunities to stretch their thinking in ways that move unfamiliar experiences to familiar ones. For example, if discussing plots or gardens with students in an urban setting, reading a story such as *City Green* (DyAnne Disalvo-Ryan, 1994) can help make the unknown known. Students can see how a land plot in an urban community can be divided and shared among neighbors. With this approach, all students can experience the background needed for the task.

Your most important challenge as a teacher is figuring out how you will maintain equal outcomes (high expectations) and yet provide for individual differences (strong support). Equipping yourself with a large collection of instructional strategies for a variety of students is critical. A strategy that works for one student may be completely ineffective with another, even for a student with the same exceptionality. Addressing the needs of *all* means providing access and opportunity for

- Students who are identified as struggling or having a disability
- Students from different cultural backgrounds
- Students who are English language learners
- Students who are mathematically gifted
- Students who are unmotivated or need to build resilience

You may think, "I do not need to read the section on culturally and linguistically diverse (CLD) students because I plan on working in a place that doesn't have any immigrants." But demographics continue to shift. Did you know that between 1980 and 2008 the Hispanic population increased from 6 percent to 15 percent of the population while the white population declined from 80 percent to 66 percent? In 2007, 14 percent of the U.S. population was born outside of the United States; this included approximately 69 percent of the Asian American population and 44 percent of Hispanic Americans (Aud, Fox, & KewalRamani, 2010).

Gifted students of all races must be identified and challenged. You may think, "I can skip the section on mathematically gifted students because they will be pulled out for math enrichment." Students who are mathematically talented need to be challenged in daily instruction, not just when they are pulled out for a gifted program.

The goal of equity is to offer all students access to important mathematics. Yet inequities exist, even if unintentionally. For example, if a teacher does not build in opportunities for student-to-student interaction in a lesson, he or she may not be addressing the needs of girls, who are often social learners, or English language learners, who need opportunities to speak, listen, and write in small-group situations. It takes more than just wanting to be fair or equitable; it takes knowing the strategies that accommodate each type of learner and making every effort to incorporate those strategies into your teaching. "Equity does not mean that every student should receive identical instruction; instead, it demands that reasonable and appropriate accommodations be made as needed to promote access and attainment for all students" (NCTM, 2000, p. 12).

Tracking Versus Differentiation

Tracking students is a significant culprit in creating inequities in the learning of mathematics. When students are placed in a lower-level track or in a "slow" group, expectations decline accordingly. Students in low tracks are frequently denied access to challenging material, high-quality instruction, and the best teachers (Burris & Welner, 2005; Futrell & Gomez, 2008). The mathematics in lower tracks or classes is often oriented toward remedial drill and low level questions. Particularly troubling is that minority and low-socioeconomic-status (low-SES) students are overrepresented in lower-level tracks (Samara, 2007; Wyner, Bridgeland, & DiIulio, 2007). And there is little evidence that tracking benefits higher-achieving students. Among major industrialized countries, only the United States and Canada seem to maintain an interest in tracking (National Research Council, 2001).

Heterogeneous classrooms, where differentiation strategies are used to provide individualized and appropriate support to students, support the learning of all students. In heterogeneous classes, expectations are often turned upside down as children once perceived as less able demonstrate understanding and work meaningfully with concepts to which they would never be exposed in a low-track class. Differentiation is addressed in Chapter 4.

Instructional Principles for Diverse Learners

Across the wonderful and myriad diversities of our students, all students learn mathematics in essentially the same way (Fuson, 2003). The authors of *Adding It Up* (National Research Council, 2001) conclude that all students are best served when attention is given to the following three principles:

1. Learning with understanding is based on connecting and organizing knowledge around big conceptual ideas.
2. Learning builds on what students already know.
3. Instruction in school should take advantage of students' informal knowledge of mathematics.

These principles, also reflected in the tenets of constructivism described in Chapter 2, apply to all learners, and therefore are essential in making decisions about how to adapt instruction to meet individual learner needs.

It is worth revisiting two ideas from Chapter 4: accommodation and modification (see pp. 64–65). An accommodation is a response to the needs of the environment or the learner; it does not alter the task. A modification changes the task, making it more accessible to the student. When modifications result in an easier or less demanding task, expectations are lowered. Modifications should be made in a way that leads to the original task, providing scaffolding or support for learners who may need it. In the sections in this chapter, we share research-based strategies that reflect these principles while providing appropriate accommodations and modifications for the wide range of students likely to appear in your classroom.

Providing for Students Who Struggle and Those with Special Needs

One of the basic tenets of education is the need for individualization of the content taught and the methods used for students who struggle, particularly those with special needs. Students with disabilities have individualized education programs (IEPs) as mandated by the Individuals with Disabilities Education Act (IDEA), which is legislation originally put into law in 1975 and amended several times since, most recently in 2004. This law guarantees students access to the general education curriculum and emphasizes the placement of students with special needs in the least restrictive environment possible, which is typically a general education classroom. This legislation also implies that educators consider individual learning needs not only in terms of *what* mathematics is taught but also *how* it is taught.

Prevention Models and Interventions for All Students

A process for achieving higher levels performance for all students includes an approach called response to intervention (RtI). This is a prevention model that emphasizes ways for struggling students to get immediate assistance and support rather than waiting for students to fail before they receive assistance. Prevention models are centered on the three interwoven elements: high-quality curriculum, instructional support (interventions), and formative assessments that capture students' strengths and weaknesses. Prevention models were designed to determine whether low achievement was due to a lack of high-quality mathematics (i.e., "teacher-disabled students") (Baroody, 2011; Ysseldyke, 2002) or due to an actual learning disability.

Response to Intervention. RtI is a tiered student support system that focuses on the results of implementing instructional interventions in a model of prevention. Many times the RtI model is represented in a triangle or pyramid format, although other models are used. Each tier in the triangle represents a level of intervention with corresponding monitoring of results and outcomes, as shown in Figure 6.1. The foundational and largest portion of the triangle (tier 1) represents the instruction that should be used with all students—instruction based on high-quality mathematics curriculum and instructional practices (i.e., manipulatives, conceptual emphasis, etc.) and on assessments. At tier 1 a balanced set of different assessments should be used to monitor progress and allow all students to demonstrate the knowledge and skills expected by grade-level standards.

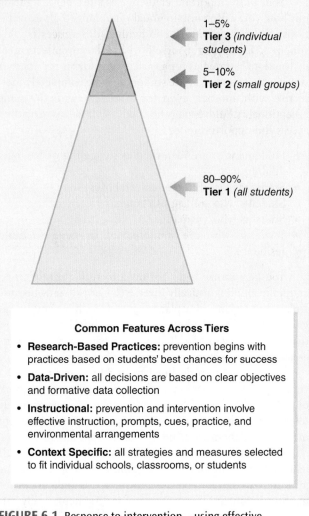

FIGURE 6.1 Response to intervention—using effective prevention strategies for all children

Source: Based on Scott, Terence, and Lane, Holly. (2001). *Multi-Tiered Interventions in Academic and Social Contexts.* Unpublished manuscript, University of Florida, Gainesville.

Tier 2 represents students who did not reach the level of achievement expected during tier 1 activities but are not yet considered as needing special education services. Students in tier 2 should receive additional targeted instruction (interventions) using more explicit instruction with systematic teaching of critical skills, more intensive and frequent instructional opportunities, and more supportive and precise prompts to students (Torgesen, 2002). If further assessment such as diagnostic interviews reveals favorable progress, the students are weaned from the extra intervention.

If challenges and struggles still exist, the interventions can be adjusted or, in rare cases, the students are referred to the next tier of support. Tier 3 is for students who need more intensive levels of assistance, which may include comprehensive mathematics instruction or a referral for special education evaluation or special education services. Strategies for the three tiers are outlined in Table 6.1.

TABLE 6.1

RTI INTERVENTIONS FOR TEACHING MATHEMATICS	
RTI Level	**Interventions**
Tier 3	**Highly qualified special education teacher:** • Works one-on-one with student • Uses tailored instruction on specific areas of weakness • Modifies instructional methods, motivates students, and adapts curricula further • Uses explicit contextualization of skills-based instruction
Tier 2	**Highly qualified regular classroom teacher, with possible collaboration from a highly qualified special education teacher:** • Conducts individual diagnostic interviews (see Chapter 5) • Collaborates with special education teacher • Creates lessons that emphasize the big ideas (focal points) or themes • Incorporates CSA/CRA (see the section "Concrete, Semi-Concrete, Abstract (CSA) Sequence" later in this chapter) • Shares thinking in a think-aloud to show students how to make problem-solving decisions • Incorporates explicit systematic strategy instruction (summarizes key points and reviews key vocabulary or concepts prior to the lesson) • Models specific behaviors and strategies, such as how to handle measuring materials or geoboards • Uses mnemonics or steps written on cards or posters to help students follow problem-solving steps • Uses peer-assisted learning, in which a student requires help that another student can provide • Tutors on specific areas of weakness outside of the regular math instruction using volunteers such as grandparents • Supplies families with additional support materials to use at home • Encourages student use of self-regulation and self-instructional strategies such as revising notes, writing summaries, and identifying main ideas • Teaches test-taking strategies and allows the students to use a highlighter on the test to emphasize important information • Slices back (Fuchs & Fuchs, 2001) to material from a previous grade to ramp back up
Tier 1	**Highly qualified regular classroom teacher:** • Incorporates high-quality curriculum and challenging standards for achievement • Builds in CCSSO Standards for Mathematical Practice and NCTM process standards • Commits to teaching the curriculum as defined • Uses multiple representations such as manipulatives, visual models, and symbols • Monitors progress to identify struggling students • Uses flexible student grouping • Fosters active student involvement • Communicates high expectations • Uses graphic organizers in the before, during, and after stages of the lesson *Before.* States purpose, introduces new vocabulary, clarifies concepts from the prior knowledge in a visual organizer, defines tasks of group members if using groups *During.* Lays out the directions in a chart, poster, or list; provides a set of guiding questions in a chart with blank spaces for responses *After.* Presents summary and list of important concepts as they relate to one another

NCTM's position statement on interventions (2011) states, "Although we do not specifically state the precise interventions, we endorse the use of increasingly intensive and effective instructional interventions for students who struggle with mathematics." Interventions are "reserved for disorders that prove resistant to lower levels of prevention and require more heroic action to preclude serious complications" (Fuchs & Fuchs, 2001).

Research into the use of prevention models such as RtI reveal that although most students remain in tier 1, approximately 15 percent of students fail to demonstrate the full growth expected and are moved to tier 2 for more intense instructional methods (Fuchs & Fuchs, 2001). Eventually nearly 40 percent of students who move to tier 2 respond to the interventions and return to tier 1. Only about 13 percent of the original group that moved to the second tier is considered for individual services—usually from a special educator—at the tier 3 level (Fuchs & Fuchs, 2005, 2007). If using an example of a group of 100 children (based on research figures), approximately 15 students would move to tier 2; then after interventions, 6 students would return to tier 1. Of the 9 students remaining in tier 2, 2 students would move to tier 3 for more individualized services.

Progress Monitoring. A key to the prevention model is the monitoring of students' progress. The data from these formative assessments are what guides the movement within tiers. Teachers can collect evidence of student knowledge of concepts through the use of diagnostic interviews. Diagnostic interviews are described throughout the book in many of the Formative Assessment Notes. Another approach is to assess students' growth toward fluency in basic facts, an area that is well documented as a barrier for students with learning disabilities (Mazzocco, Devlin, & McKenney, 2008). Combining instruction with short daily assessments of their knowledge of number combinations proved the students were not only better at remembering but better at generalizing to other facts (Woodward, 2006). The collection of information gathered from these assessments will reveal whether students are making the progress expected or if more intensive instructional approaches need to be put into practice.

Students with Mild Disabilities

Students with learning disabilities have very specific difficulties with perceptual or cognitive processing and may be identified as needing tier 3 services. These difficulties may affect memory; general strategy use; attention; the ability to speak or express ideas in writing; the ability to perceive auditory, visual, or written information; or the ability to integrate abstract ideas. Although each student will have a unique profile of strengths and weaknesses, there are ways to support students with mild disabilities in all phases of the planning, teaching, and assessing of the mathematics lesson.

NCTM has gathered a set of research-based effective strategies (NCTM, 2007b) for teaching students with difficulties in mathematics (such as students needing interventions in tier 2 or tier 3 of a prevention model such as RtI), highlighting the use of several key strategies (based on Gersten, Beckmann, Clarke, Foegen, Marsh, Star, & Witzel, 2009), including systematic and explicit strategy instruction, think-alouds, concrete and visual representations of problems, peer-assisted learning activities, and formative assessment data provided to students and teachers. These approaches, proven to be effective, in some cases represent principles quite different from those at tier 1. The strategies described here are interventions for use with the small subset of students for whom the initial interventions were ineffective.

Explicit Strategy Instruction. Explicit instruction is often characterized by highly structured, teacher-led instruction on a specific strategy. The teacher does not merely model the strategy and have students practice it, but attempts to illuminate the decision making that may be troublesome for these learners. In this model, the teaching routines used include a tightly scripted sequence from modeling to prompting students through the model to practice. Instruction is highly organized in a step-by-step format and involves teacher-led explanations of concepts and strategies, including the critical connection building and meaning making that help learners relate new knowledge with concepts they know. Let's look at a classroom teacher using explicit instruction:

> As you enter Mr. Logan's classroom, you see a small group of students seated at a table listening to the teacher's detailed explanation and watching his demonstration of equivalent fraction concepts. The students are using manipulatives, as prescribed by Mr. Logan, and moving through carefully selected tasks. He tells the students to take out the red "one-fourth" pieces and asks them to check how many "one-fourths" will exactly cover the blue "one-half" piece. As he begins, Mr. Logan often asks, "Is that a word you know?" Then, to make sure they don't allow for any gaps or overlaps in the pieces, he asks them to talk about their process with the question, "What are some things you need to keep in mind as you place the fourths on the half?" Mr. Logan writes their responses on the adjacent board as $\frac{2}{4} = \frac{1}{2}$. Then he asks them to compare the brown "eighths" and the yellow "sixths" to the piece representing one-half and records their responses. The students are taking turns answering these questions out loud. During the lesson Mr. Logan frequently stops the group, interjects points of clarification, and directly highlights critical components of the task. For example, he asks, "Are you surprised that it takes more eights to cover the half than fourths?" Vocabulary words, such as numerator and denominator, are written on the "math wall" nearby and the definitions of these terms are reviewed and reinforced throughout the lesson. At the completion of the lesson, students are given several similar examples of the kind of comparisons discussed in the lesson as independent practice.

A number of aspects of explicit instruction can be seen in Mr. Logan's approach to teaching fraction concepts. He employs a teacher-directed teaching format, prescribes the use of manipulatives, and incorporates a model-prompt-practice sequence. This sequence starts with verbal instructions and demonstrations with concrete models, followed by prompting, questioning, and then independent practice. The students are deriving mathematical knowledge from the teacher's oral, written, and visual clues.

As students solve problems, they are also given explicit strategy instruction to guide them in carrying out tasks. They are asked to read and restate the problem, draw a picture, develop a plan by identifying the type of problem, write the problem in a mathematical sentence, break the problem into smaller pieces, carry out operations, and check answers using a calculator. These self-instructive prompts, or self-questions, structure the entire learning process from beginning to end. Unlike more inquiry-based instruction, the teacher models these steps and explains components using terminology that is easily understood by students with disabilities who did not discover them independently through initial tier 1 or 2 activities. Yet, consistent with what we know about how all students learn, students are still doing problem solving (not just skill development).

Concrete models can support explicit strategy instruction. For example, a teacher demonstrating a multiplication array with cubes might say, "Watch me. Now make a rectangle with the cubes that looks just like mine." In contrast, a teacher with a more inquiry-oriented approach might say,

"Using these cubes, how can you show me a representation for 4×5?" While more structured, the use of concrete models provides access to abstract concepts.

There are a number of possible advantages to the use of explicit strategy instruction for students with disabilities. This approach helps uncover or make overt the covert thinking strategies that support mathematical problem solving. Students with disabilities may otherwise not have access to these strategies. More explicit approaches are also less dependent on the student to draw ideas from past experience or to operate in a self-directed manner.

Explicit strategy instruction can have disadvantages for students with disabilities. Some aspects of this approach rely on memory, which can be one of the weakest areas for some students with special needs. Taking a known weakness and building a learning strategy around it is not productive. There is also the concern that highly teacher-controlled approaches promote prolonged dependency on teacher assistance. This is of particular concern for students with disabilities because many of them are described as passive learners. Students learn what they have the opportunity to practice. Students who are never given opportunities to engage in self-directed learning (based on the assumption that this is not an area of strength) will be deprived of the opportunity to develop skills in this area. In fact, the best explicit instruction is scaffolded, meaning it moves from a highly structured, single-strategy approach to multiple models, including examples, and non-examples. It also includes immediate error correction with the fading of prompts to help students move to independence. Another possible challenge of explicit approaches is the depth of understanding that can be expected as a result. Experiential-based learning that centers on active problem solving and the construction of knowledge produces deeper understanding of mathematics and enhances student ability to retain, generalize, and apply information—all skills that are vital to long-term success in mathematics. Explicit instruction, to be effective, must include making mathematical relationships explicit (so that students don't just learn how to do that day's mathematics, but make connections to other mathematical ideas). Since this is one of the major findings in how students learn, it must be central to learning strategies for students with mild disabilities.

Concrete, Semi-Concrete, Abstract (CSA) Sequence.

The CSA (concrete, semi-concrete, abstract) teaching sequence (also known as CRA [concrete, representational, abstract]) has been used in mathematics education in a variety of forms for years (Heddens, 1964; Witzel, 2005). Based on Bruner's reasoning theory (1966), this model reflects a sequence that moves from an instructional focus on concrete representations (manipulative materials) and models to semi-concrete representations (drawings or pictures) and images to abstraction (using only numerals or mentally solving problems). Built into this approach is the return to visual models and concrete representations as students need or as they begin to explore new concepts or novel extensions of concepts learned previously. As students share thinking that indicates they are beginning to understand the mathematical concept, there can be a shift to semi-concrete or semi-abstract representations. This is not to say that this is a rigid approach that only moves to abstraction after the other phases. Instead, it is essential that there is parallel modeling of number symbols throughout this continuum to explicitly relate the concrete models and visual representations to the corresponding numerals. There is also direct modeling of the mental conversations that go on in the teacher's mind as he or she helps students articulate their own thinking. In the last component, students are capable of working with the abstract aspects of the concepts without the emphasis on the concrete or representational images.

Peer-Assisted Learning.

Students with special needs benefit from others' modeling and support, including modeling by their classmates or peers (Fuchs, Fuchs, Yazdian, & Powell, 2002). The basic notion is that students learn best when they are placed in the role of an apprentice working with a more skilled peer or "expert." Although the peer-assisted learning approach shares some of the characteristics of the explicit strategy instruction model described, it is distinct because knowledge is presented on an "as-needed" basis as opposed to a predetermined sequence. The students can be paired with older students or peers who have more sophisticated understandings of a concept. In other cases, tutors and tutees can reverse roles during the tasks. Having students "teach" others is an important part of the learning process, so giving students with special needs a chance to explain to another student is valuable.

Think-Alouds.

"Think-aloud" is an instructional strategy that involves the teacher demonstrating the steps to accomplish a task while verbalizing the thinking process and reasoning that accompany the steps. The student follows this instruction by imitating this process of "talking through" a solution on a different, but parallel, task. This also derives from the model in which "expert" learners share strategies with "novice" learners.

Consider a problem in which fourth-grade students are given the task of determining how much paint will be needed to cover the walls of their classroom. Rather than merely demonstrating, for example, how to use a ruler to measure the distance across a wall, the think-aloud strategy would involve the teacher talking through the steps and identifying the reasons for each step while measuring the space. As the teacher places a mark on the wall to indicate where the ruler ended in the first measurement, she states, "I used this line to mark off where the ruler ends. How should I use this line as I measure the next section of the wall? I know I have to move the ruler, but should I copy what I did the first time?" All of this dialogue occurs prior to placing the ruler for a second measurement. Often teachers share alternatives about how else they could have carried out the task. When using this metacognitive strategy, teachers try to talk about and model possible approaches in an effort to make their invisible thinking processes visible to students.

Although you will choose strategies as needed, your goal is always to work toward high student responsibility for learning. Movement to higher levels of understanding of content can be likened to the need to move to a higher level on a hill. For some, formal stair steps with support along the way is necessary (explicit strategy instruction); for others ramps with encouragement at the top of the hill will work (peer-assisted learning). Other students can find a path up the hill on their own with some guidance from visual representations (CRA/CSA approach). All people can relate to the need to have different support during different times of their lives or under different circumstances, and it is no different for students with special needs (see Table 6.2). Yet they must eventually learn to create a path to new learning on their own, as that is what will be required in the real world after schooling. Leaving students only knowing how to climb steps with support and having them face hills without stair steps or constant assistance from others will not help them attain their goals.

Students with Moderate/Severe Disabilities

Students with moderate/severe disabilities often need extensive modifications and individualized supports to understand the mathematics curriculum. This population of students may include those with severe autism, sensory disorders, limitations affecting movement, processing disorders such as intellectual disabilities, cerebral palsy, and combinations of multiple disabilities. IDEA (1990, 1997, 2004) mandated access for all students to the general grade-level curriculum, but No Child Left Behind legislation (now referred to by its original name of the Elementary and Secondary Education Act [ESEA]) has shifted emphasis from merely mandating access to instruction to requiring evidence that students learn the content. This also dramatically changes expectations for students with moderate to severe disabilities who must work toward grade-level proficiencies on state-designated alternative assessments in mathematics. To demonstrate serious intent, ESEA mandates that states include students with significant disabilities in their statewide and district assessments of student progress.

Originally, the curriculum for students with severe disabilities was called "functional," in that it often focused on

TABLE 6.2

COMMON STUMBLING BLOCKS FOR STUDENTS WITH DISABILITIES		
Stumbling Blocks	**What Will I Notice?**	**What Should I Do?**
Student has trouble forming mental representations of mathematical concepts	• Can't interpret a number line • Has difficulty going from a story about a garden plot (to set up a problem on finding area) to a graph or dot paper	• Explicitly teach the representation—for example, exactly how to draw a diagram • Using larger versions of the representation (e.g., number line) so that students can move to or interact with the model
Student has difficulty accessing numerical meanings from symbols (issues with number sense)	• Has difficulty with basic facts; for example, doesn't recognize that 3 + 5 is the same as 5 + 3, or that 5 + 1 is the same as the next counting number after 5	• Explicitly teach multiple ways of representing a number showing the variations at the exact same time • Use multiple representations for a single problem to show it in a variety of ways (blocks, illustrations, and numbers) rather than using multiple problems
Student is challenged to keep numbers and information in working memory	• Loses counts of objects • Gets too confused when multiple strategies are shared by other students during the "after" portion of the lesson • Forgets how to start the problem-solving process	• Use ten-frames or organizational mats to help them organize counts • Explicitly model how to use skip counting to count • Jot down the ideas of other students during discussions • Incorporate a chart that lists the main steps in problem solving as an independent guide or make bookmarks with questions the students can ask themselves as self-prompts
Student lacks organizational skills and the ability to self-regulate	• Loses steps in a process • Writes computations in a way that is random and hard to follow	• Use routines as often as possible or provide self-monitoring checklists to prompt steps along the way • Use graph paper to record problems or numbers • Create math walls they can use as a resource
Student misapplies rules or overgeneralizes	• Applies rules such as "Always subtract the smaller from the larger" too literally, resulting in errors such as $35 - 9 = 34$ • Mechanically applies algorithms—for example, adds $\frac{7}{8}$ and $\frac{12}{13}$ and gives the answer $\frac{19}{21}$.	• Always give examples as well as counterexamples to show how and when "rules" should be used and when they should not • Tie all rules into conceptual understanding; don't emphasize memorizing rote procedures or practices.

life-related skills such as managing money, telling time, using a calculator, measuring, and matching numbers to complete such tasks as entering a telephone number or identifying a house number. Now state initiatives and assessments have broadened the curriculum to address the five NCTM content strands that were specifically delineated by grade level in the *Curriculum Focal Points* (NCTM, 2006). For example, one emphasis is on numeracy through real-world representations as a way to prepare all students to be mathematically literate citizens. Using money to study place-value concepts or posing problems in the context of making purchases are approaches with multiple benefits for students with severe disabilities.

At a beginning level, students work on identifying numbers by holding up fingers or pictures. To develop number sense, counting up can be linked to counting daily tasks to be accomplished, and counting down can mark a period of cleanup after an activity or to complete self-care routines (brushing teeth). Students with moderate or severe disabilities should have opportunities to use measuring tools, compare graphs, explore place-value concepts (often linked to money use), use the number line, and compare quantities. When possible, the content should be connected to life skills and possible features of jobs—such as restocking supplies (Hughes & Rusch, 1989). Shopping skills or activities in which food is prepared are both options for mathematical problem solving. At other times, just linking mathematical learning objectives to everyday events

is practical. For example, when studying the operation of division, figuring how candy can be equally shared at Halloween or dealing cards to play a game would be appropriate. Students can also undertake a small project such as constructing a box to store different items as a way to explore shapes and measurements.

Do not believe that all basic facts must be mastered before students with moderate or severe disabilities can move forward in the curriculum; students can learn geometric or measuring concepts without having mastered addition and subtraction facts. Geometry for students with moderate and severe disabilities is more than merely identifying shapes, but is in fact critical for orienting in the real world. The practical aspects emerge when such concepts as parallel and perpendicular lines and curves and straight sides become helpful for interpreting maps of the local area. Using maps related to bus or subway routes as teaching materials can support students' use of public transportation. Students who learn to count bus stops and judge time can be helped to successfully navigate their world.

Table 6.3 offers ideas across the curriculum appropriate for teaching students with moderate to severe disabilities. When possible, you can blend the mathematics curriculum with the basic skills a student needs in a practical living context. If other students study the measures of various angles of triangles, the student with moderate disabilities can match right-angled triangles to a model on a mat as part of learning about right angles. In this example, the content area remains

TABLE 6.3

ACTIVITIES FOR STUDENTS WITH MODERATE AND SEVERE DISABILITIES	
Content Area	**Activity**
Number and operations	• Count out a variety of items for general classroom activities. • Create a list of supplies that need to be ordered for the classroom or a particular event and calculate cost • Calculate the number of calories in a given meal. • Compare the cost of two meals on menus from local restaurants.
Algebra	• Show an allowance or wage on a chart to demonstrate growth over time. • Write an equation to show how much the student will earn in a month or year. • Calculate the slope of a wheelchair ramp or driveway.
Geometry	• Use spatial relationships to identify a short path between two locations on a map. • Tessellate several figures to show how a variety of shapes fit together. Using tangrams to fill a space will also develop important workplace skills like packing boxes or organizing supplies on shelves.
Measurement	• Fill different-shaped items with water, sand, or rice to assess volume, ordering the vessels from least to most. • Take body temperature and use an enlarged thermometer to show comparison to outside temperatures. • Calculate the amount of paint needed to cover the walls or ceiling of the classroom, using area. • Estimate the amount of time it would take to travel to a known location using a map.
Data analysis and probability	• Survey students on favorite games (either electronic or other) using the top five as choices for the class. Make a graph to represent and compare the results. • Tally the number of students ordering school lunch. • Examine the outside temperatures for the past week and discuss the probability of the temperatures for the next days being within a particular range.

within grade-level mathematics objectives while being adapted to meet the needs of students with moderate disabilities to grow in concepts, vocabulary, and symbol use.

The following list indicates other ideas for modifying grade-level instruction.

Additional Strategies for Supporting Students with Moderate and Severe Disabilities

- *Systematic instruction.* Use repeated examples of the same problem, give repeated prompts, and provide corrective feedback.
- *In vivo.* Use real-life (in vivo) applications so students can see how mathematics concepts are useful in everyday activities.
- *Opportunities to respond.* Ensure that students have multiple opportunities to learn and practice new ideas (such as place value) or skills (such as measuring a length).
- *Visual supports.* Visual cues, color coding, and simplified numerical expressions using dots or other pictorial clues can focus students' learning.
- *Response prompt.* Ask a student, "What is three plus three?" while visually showing 3 + 3. If there is no response, say "Six" and then state to the student again, "Three plus three is six." Next give a prompt and ask again, "What's three plus three?"
- *Task chaining.* Take one step at a time on a mathematics task, giving a prompt for students at each step. Gradually fade the number of prompts based on student performance.
- *Problem solving.* State the problem. For example, after passing out an insufficient number of paper plates, ask students, "What is the problem?" The students should state a solution and suggest that more materials are needed. "How many more plates are needed?" When that amount is given, students have solved the problem. Use a visual representation showing a one-to-one correspondence between people and plates to show how to record the situation. Then write and read the corresponding equation.
- *Self-determination skills and independent self-directed learning.* Support opportunities for students to make choices by decision making and goal setting.

Students Who Are Culturally and Ethnically Diverse

We are lucky to be in a country with people from all over the world. Within our cities and towns, we have an increasing presence of foreign-born students, as well as U.S.-born students who grow up in culturally and ethnically diverse settings. You will better serve the needs of these students by valuing their culture and language and not trying to force them into local culture and language. Valuing a person's cultural background is more than a belief statement; it is a set of intentional actions that communicate to the student, "I want to know about you, I want you to see mathematics as part of your life, and I expect that you can do high-level mathematics."

You have probably heard it said that "mathematics is a universal language." This common misconception can lead to inequities in the classroom. Conceptual knowledge (e.g., what multiplication *is*) is universal. Procedures (e.g., *how* you multiply) and symbols are culturally determined, and are not universal. As you will read in Chapters 12 and 13, there are many algorithms for whole-number operations. In addition, particular mathematics practices are culturally determined. One that appears repeatedly in the research is that mental mathematics is highly valued in other countries, whereas in the United States teachers frequently request students to record every step. Compare the following two division problems from a fourth-grade classroom (Midobuche, 2001):

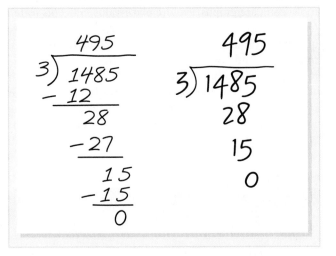

Can you follow what the first student did? If you learned division in the United States, this is likely easy to follow. But, if you learned division in another country, you may wonder why the first solution has so many numbers. Can you follow the second example? It is, in effect, the same thinking process, only the multiplication and related subtraction are done mentally. The critical equity question, though, is not whether you can follow an alternative approach, but how will you respond when you encounter a student using such an approach? Will you require the student show their steps, disregarding the way they learned it? Will you ask the student to elaborate on how they did it? Will you have the student show other students their way of thinking? The latter two questions are explicit ways that you can show that you value the student's culture. Using students' *funds of knowledge*, which means intentionally focusing on and incorporating students' family or cultural knowledge and practices (Gonzáles, Moll, & Amanti, 2005), is critical in supporting student learning of mathematics.

Culturally relevant mathematics instruction is not just for recent immigrants; it is for *all* students, including students from different ethnic groups, socioeconomic status, and so on. Culturally relevant mathematics instruction includes consideration for content, relationships, cultural knowledge, flexibility in approaches, use of accessible learning contexts, a responsive learning community, and working in crosscultural partnerships (Averill, Anderson, Easton, Te Maro, Smith, & Hynds, 2009). It is complex. A learning strategy may be highly effective in one setting, and yet not work in a different setting. Each of the following four overlapping categories offers ways to make your mathematics teaching culturally relevant.

Focus on Important Mathematics.   Too often, our first attempt to help students is to simplify the mathematics. This just lowers the chance of learning the content they must learn. For students who struggle with reading, including but not limited to ELLs, a common modification is to remove the language from the lesson. This reduces mathematics to skill development, which is rarely connected to real experiences. Culturally relevant instruction stays focused on the big ideas of mathematics (i.e., based on standards) and helps students engage in and stay focused on the big ideas. Engage students in productive struggle and in making connections between mathematics concepts.

Make Content Relevant.   There are really two components for making content relevant. One is to think about the mathematics: "Is the topic connected meaningfully to other content?" This is really important in teaching for all students, as some students in the classroom may not have learned a skill they need. Rather than assign such a student to a remedial lesson, you should instead infuse the related prior knowledge. For example, begin a lesson on finding the center of a circle by asking students to draw the diameter to locate the center. Question students as they work: "How do you know if a line is a diameter? Do all diameters have the same measure? How many diameters do you need in order to establish the center of the circle?" By incorporating the prior knowledge of diameters as they relate to circles and engaging students in explorations, the teacher was making the content relevant.

Second, making content relevant is about contexts. What contexts can bring meaning to the mathematics? There are many! Historical or cultural topics abound. Students can be personally engaged in mathematics by examining their culture's impact on the ways they use, practice, and think about mathematics. A study of mathematics within other cultures provides opportunities for students to "put faces" on mathematical contributions. Examples across the curriculum include:

- *Counting and place value.* Look at the Mayan place value system to think more deeply about reasoning about the structure of number (Farmer & Powers, 2005).

- *Geometry.* Explore Freedom Quilts (via children's literature) that helped slaves navigate the Underground Railroad (Neumann, 2005).
- *Measurement.* Explore nonstandard units used by the Yup'ik (and perhaps in your students' homes), as a way to strengthen understanding of units as they apply to measuring and to fractions (McLean, 2002).

Six areas of mathematics are found universally: counting, measuring, locating, designing and building, playing (e.g., "Mancala"), and explaining (e.g., telling stories) (Bishop, 2001). When your curriculum takes you to one of these topics, invite students and their families to share their experiences and use these experiences to engage in the content.

Incorporate Students' Identities.   This overlaps with the previous category, but is worth its own discussion. Students must see themselves in mathematics and see that mathematics is a part of their culture. You don't need to be a historian to build cultural connections—just ask your students. In a project focused on helping teachers recognize students' identities, teachers asked students to create a poster to show outsiders how many students were in their classroom. Many representations created by the K–2 students included students' skin color, hair color, and gender. These traits became part of bar graphs and sorting activities with the students' identities at the center of the learning (McCulloch, Marshall, & DeCuir-Gunby, 2009).

Both researchers and teachers have found that telling stories about their own lives, or asking students to tell stories, makes the mathematics relevant to students and can raise student achievement (Turner, Celedón-Pattichis, Marshall, & Tennison, 2009). For example, you can ask students to bring an example from a family trip to the grocery store (Butterworth & Lo Cicero, 2001). Or students can develop math story problems from photos. These photos could be pictures cut out from their community newspaper, family photographs they've brought from home, or their own pictures taken using disposable cameras you've distributed (Lemons-Smith, 2009; Leonard & Guha, 2002). Similarly, students can explore an artifact from their culture, or one that has captured their interest, presenting the mathematics of the artifact (e.g., a game or measuring device) (Neel, 2005).

The following is a teacher's story of how she incorporated family history and culture into her class by reading *The Hundred Penny Box* (Mathis, 1986). The story describes a 100-year-old woman who remembers one year's important event in her life for every one of her hundred pennies. Each penny is more than a piece of money; it is a "memory trigger" for her life.

Taking a cue from the book, I asked each child to collect one penny from each year they were alive starting from the year of their birth and not missing a year. Students were encouraged to bring in additional pennies their classmates might need. Then the students consulted with family members to create a penny time line of important events in their lives. Using information gathered at home they started with the year they were born listing their birthday and went on to record first steps, accidents, vacations, pets, and births of siblings in those early years. Then students determined how many years between certain events or calculated their age when they adopted a pet or learned to ride a bicycle. These events were to be used in the weeks and months to come as subjects of story problems and other mathematics investigations.

Another way for students to see themselves is to be sure that classroom practices reflect cultural practices. For example, research indicates that using rhythm and movement in urban, African American classrooms can engage students in mathematics and raise student achievement (Peterek & Adams, 2009). Respect code-switching (moving between languages) during discussions. Typical discourse patterns in U.S. classrooms may not feel natural to all students, so explicit guidance in how to participate can increase participation of all students.

Ensure Shared Power. You determine who has the authority in your classroom and who listens to whom. In too many classrooms, the teacher has the power—telling students whether answers are right or wrong (rather than have students determine correctness through reasoning), telling students exactly how to solve problems (rather than give

choices for how they will engage in the problem), and determining who will solve which problems (rather than allowing flexibility and choice for students). Instead, establish a classroom environment where everyone feels their ideas are worth consideration. The way that you assign groups, seat students, and call on students sends clear messages about who has power in the classroom. Distributing power among students leads to empowered students.

Each day's lesson provides new opportunities and challenges as you think about how you will make lessons culturally relevant. Table 6.4 is designed to help guide your thinking. If these reflective questions become internalized and are part of what you naturally think about as you plan, teach, and assess, then you are likely going to lead a classroom where all students are challenged and supported.

Students Who Are English Language Learners (ELLs)

Let's revisit the issue of mathematics as a universal language. As noted earlier, this holds true for concepts, but not procedures or symbols. In fact, mathematics is its own language. There are unique features of the language of mathematics that make it difficult for many students, in particular those that are learning English.

TABLE 6.4

REFLECTIVE QUESTIONS TO FOCUS ON CULTURALLY RELEVANT MATHEMATICS INSTRUCTION	
Aspect of Culturally Relevant Instruction	**Reflection Questions to Guide Teaching and Assessing**
The content of the lesson is about the importance of mathematics, and the tasks performed by students communicate high expectations.	• Does the content include a balance of procedures and concepts? • Are students expected to engage in problem solving and generate their own approaches to problems? • Are connections made between mathematics topics?
The content is relevant.	• In what ways is the content related to familiar aspects of students' lives? • In what ways is prior knowledge elicited/reviewed so that all students can participate in the lesson? • To what extent are students asked to make connections between school mathematics and mathematics in their own lives? • How are student interests (events, issues, literature, or pop culture) used to build interest and mathematical meaning?
The instructional strategies communicate the value of students' identities.	• In what ways are students invited to include their own experiences within a lesson? • Are story problems generated from students and teachers? Do stories reflect the real experiences of students? • Are individual student approaches presented and showcased so that each student sees their ideas as important to the teacher and their peers? • Are alternative algorithms shared as a point of excitement and pride (as appropriate)? • Are multiple modes to demonstrate knowledge (e.g., visuals, explanations, models) valued?
The instructional strategies model shared power.	• Are students (rather than just the teacher) justifying the correctness of solutions? • Are students invited to (expected to) engage in whole-class discussions where students share ideas and respond to each other's ideas? • In what ways are roles assigned so that every student feels that they contribute to and learn from other members of the class? • Are students given a choice in how they solve a problem? In how they demonstrate knowledge of the concept?

English language learners enter the mathematics classroom from homes in which English is not the primary language of communication. Although a person might develop conversational English language skills in a few years, it takes as many as seven years to learn "academic language," which is the language specific to a content area such as mathematics (Cummins, 1994). Academic language is harder to learn because it is not used in a student's everyday world. When learning about mathematics, students might be learning content in English that they have no words for in their native language. For example, in studying the measures of central tendency (*mean, median,* and *mode*), they may not know words for these terms in their first language, increasing the challenge for learning academic language in their second language. In addition, story problems are difficult for ELLs not just due to the language but also to the fact that sentences in story problems are often structured differently from sentences in conversational English (Janzen, 2008).

Teachers of English to Speakers of Other Languages (TESOL) argue that ELLs need to use English (and their native language) to read, write, listen, and speak as they learn appropriate content—a position similarly addressed in NCTM standards documents.

Creating effective learning for ELLs involves integrating principles of bilingual education with standards-based mathematics instruction. Among the many classroom supports for students who are learning English, the strategies discussed in this section are the ones that appear in the research literature most frequently as critical in increasing the academic achievement of ELLs in mathematics classrooms.

Honor Use of Native Language.   Research strongly supports the use of a student's native language (Haas & Gort, 2009; Moschkovich, 2009; Setati, 2005). Valuing a student's language is one of the ways you value their cultural heritage. In a mathematics classroom, students can communicate in their native language while continuing their English language development. For example, a good strategy for students working in small groups is having students discuss the problem in their preferred language. If a student knows enough English, then the presentation in the *after* phase can be shared in English. If the student knows little or no English, then he or she can explain in Spanish using a translator. Bilingual students will often code-switch, moving between two languages. Research indicates that this practice of code-switching supports mathematical reasoning because the student is selecting the language from which they can best express their ideas (Moschkovich, 2009).

Use of native language is also important for assessment. Research shows that ELLs perform better when a test is given in their native language (Robinson, 2010). If a teacher wants to understand what a student knows about mathematics, then the student should be able to communicate that understanding in the best way that she or he can, even if the teacher may need translation. Explore a multilingual math glossary at (www.glencoe.com/apps/eGlossary612/landing.php).

Native language can be a support to learning English. Because English, Spanish, French, Portuguese, and Italian all have their roots in Latin, many math words are similar across languages (Celedón-Pattichis, 2009; Gómez, 2010). For example *aequus* (Latin), *equal* (English), and *igual* (Spanish) are cognates. See if you can figure out the English mathematics terms for the following Spanish words: *división, hexágano, ángulo, triángulo, álgebra, circunferencia,* and *cubo.* Students may not make this connection if you do not point it out, so explicitly teaching students to look for cognates is important.

Write and State Content and Language Objectives.   Every lesson should begin with telling students what they will be learning. You do not give away what they will be discovering, but you state the larger purpose and provide a road map. If students know the purpose of the lesson, they are better able to make sense of the details when challenged by some of the oral or written explanations. By explicitly including language expectations, students know language they will be developing alongside the mathematical goals. Here are two examples of objectives:

1. Students will analyze properties and attributes of three-dimensional solids. (mathematics)
2. Students will describe in writing and orally a similarity and a difference between two different solids. (language and mathematics)

Build Background.   This is similar to building on prior knowledge, but it takes into consideration native language and culture as well as content. If possible, use a context and appropriate visuals to help students understand the task you want them to solve. For example, Pugalee, Harbaugh, and Quach (2009) spray-painted a coordinate axis in the field, so that students could build background related to linear equations. Students were given various equations and contexts and had to physically find (and walk to) a point on the giant axis, creating human graphs of lines. This nonthreatening, engaging activity helped students make connections between what they had learned and what they needed to learn.

Some aspects of English and mathematics are particularly challenging to ELLs (Whiteford, 2009/2010). Examples include:

- The names of teen numbers in English don't corrrespond to place value. In other languages, the teens typically follow the same pattern of the other decades. For example, the Spanish word for 16 is an amalgamation of "ten and six" (as opposed to the English reversal of "six ten").

- Teen numbers sound a lot like their decade number—if you say *sixteen* and *sixty* out loud, you will hear how similar they are. Emphasizing the *n* helps ELLs hear the difference.
- U.S. measurement systems have unrelated terminology for every new grouping and are not organized by base 10. While this is hard for all learners, having no life experiences with cups, pints, inches, miles, and other U.S. units adds to the difficulty for ELLs. Additionally, referents like *foot* and *yard* mean something else outside of mathematics, so ELLs can misinterpret the meaning of these words.

When you encounter these situations, and others, additional time is needed to build background and draw attention to how you recognize the intended meaning of the words.

Use Comprehensible Input. *Comprehensible input* means that the message you are communicating is understandable to students. Modifications include simplifying sentence structures and limiting the use of nonessential or confusing vocabulary. Note that these modifications do not lower expectations for the lesson. Sometimes teachers put many unnecessary words and phrases into questions, making them less clear to nonnative speakers. Compare the following sets of teachers' directions:

> Not Modified: You have a lab sheet in front of you that I just gave out. For every situation, I want you to determine the total area for the shapes. You will be working with your partner, but each of you needs to record your answers on your own paper and explain how you got your answer. If you get stuck on a problem, raise your hand.

> Modified: Please look at your paper. (Holds paper and points to the first picture.) You will find the area. What does *area* mean? (Allows wait time.) How can you calculate area? (*Calculate* is more like the Spanish word *calcular*, so it is more accessible to Spanish speakers.) Talk to your partner. (Points to mouth and then to a pair of students as she says this.) Write your answers. (Makes a writing motion over paper.)

Notice that three things have been done: sentences have been shortened, confusing words have been removed, and related gestures and motions have been added. Also notice the "wait time" the teacher gives. It is very important to provide extra time after posing a question or giving instructions to allow ELLs time to translate, make sense of the request, and then participate.

Another way to provide comprehensible input is to use a variety of tools to help students visualize and understand what is verbalized. In the preceding example, the teacher is modeling the instructions. When introducing a lesson, include pictures, real objects, and diagrams. For example, if teaching integers, having a real thermometer, as well as an overhead of a thermometer, will help provide a visual (and

a context). You might even add pictures of places covered in snow and position them near the low temperatures and so on. Students should be expected to include multiple representations such as drawing, writing, and explaining what they have done. Effective tools include manipulatives, real objects, pictures, visuals, multimedia, demonstrations, and children's books (Echevarria, Vogt, & Short, 2008).

Explicitly Teach Vocabulary. Intentional vocabulary instruction must be part of mathematics instruction for all students. Students can create concept maps, linking concepts and terms as they study the relationships between fractions, decimals, and percents. You can play games focused on vocabulary development (e.g., charades, "$10,000 Pyramid," "Concentration"). Mathematics word walls, when they include visuals and are used during instruction, are effective in supporting language development. Have students participate in creating and adding to the word wall. When a word is selected, students can create cards that include the word in English, translations to languages represented in your room, pictures, and a student-made description (not a formal definition) in several languages. Many websites provide translations; even if they are not completely accurate, they can help a student in the class make the translation. See, for example, www.freetranslation.com. These cards can be turned into personal math dictionaries for students (Kersaint, Thompson, & Petkova, 2009).

All students benefit from an increased focus on language; however, too much emphasis on language can diminish the focus on the mathematics. Importantly, the language support should be connected to the selected task or activity. As you analyze a lesson, you must identify terms related to the mathematics and to the context that may need explicit attention. Consider the following task, released from the 2009 National Assessment of Educational Progress (NAEP) (National Center for Education Statistics, 2009):

> **Sam did the following problems.**
> $$2 + 1 = 3$$
> $$6 + 1 = 7$$
> **Sam concluded that when he adds 1 to *any* whole number, his answer will always be odd.**
> **Is Sam correct?** _____
> **Explain your answer.**

In order for students to engage in this task, the terms even and odd must be understood. Both terms may be known for other meanings beyond the mathematics classroom (even can mean level and odd can mean strange). "Concluded" is not a math word, but must be understood if the student is to understand the meaning of the problem. In this case, rather than build meaning for this word, a new word could be used that is more familiar, like Sam has an idea (this is also a word in Spanish). Finally, you must give guidance on how students will explain – must it be in words or are pictures or diagrams acceptable?

PAUSE and REFLECT

Odd and *even* are among hundreds of words that take on different meanings in mathematics from everyday activities. Others include *product, mean, sum, factor, acute, foot, division, difference, similar,* and *angle.* Can you name at least five others? ●

As a fun way to engage students in word meanings, two middle school teachers had students perform skits, poems, or songs to address the everyday and mathematical meaning of selected words in their curriculum (Seidel & McNamee, 2005). Their list included *tangent, obtuse, acute, circular, adjacent, variable, radical, proportion, matrix, irrational,* and *factor.* With little time invested, students were able to engage in making sense of critical terminology (while poking fun at their teachers!).

Plan Cooperative/Interdependent Groups to Support Language. ELLs need opportunities to speak, write, talk, and listen in nonthreatening situations. Cooperative groups provide such an environment. In grouping, you must consider a student's language skills. Placing an ELL with two English-speaking students may result in the ELL being left out entirely. It may be better to place a bilingual student in this group or to place students that have the same first language together (Garrison, 1997; Khisty, 1997). Pairs may be more appropriate than groups of three or four. As with all group work, rules or structures should be in place to make sure that each student is able to participate and is accountable for the activity assigned.

Use Discourse That Reflects Language Needs. Discourse, or the use of classroom discussion, is explored in Chapter 4; here the focus is on the specific strategies for ELLs. *Revoicing* is a research-based strategy that helps ELLs to hear an idea more than once and to hear it restated with the appropriate language applied to the concepts. Because ELLs cannot always explain their ideas fully, rather than just call on someone else, *pressing* for details is important. This pressing is not just so the teacher can decide whether the idea makes sense; it is so that other students can make sense of the idea (Maldonado, Turner, Dominguez, & Empson, 2009). Since use of language is extra important, having opportunities for students to practice phrases or words through choral response or through pair-share is needed. Finally, students from other countries often solve or illustrate problems differently. Making their strategies public and connecting the strategies to others is interesting and supports the learning of all students, while building confidence for the ELL.

Teachers sometimes ask when they should apply these instructional strategies—what if they only have five ELLs or only one student from another culture? We suggest that these strategies must be put into action even if only one student would benefit from them. As many teachers and researchers report, these strategies are effective with all learners and therefore all will benefit from the increased attention to culture and language.

Gender-Friendly Mathematics Classrooms

Based on a large-scale study, Hyde, Lindberg, Linn, Ellis, & Williams (2008) reveal that in analyzing standardized test scores from more than 7.2 million U.S. students in grades 2–11, there were no differences in math scores for girls and boys. According to Hyde, this shows the positive results of the efforts over the past 20 years to counter the stereotype that math is a subject for boys. But Hyde also wrote that, "girls who believe the stereotype wind up avoiding harder math classes."

After high school, more males than females enter fields of study that include heavy emphases on STEM areas (science, technology, engineering, and mathematics) (Ceci & Williams, 2010). These are critical career fields linked to the economic well-being of any nation. The president of the Society of Women Engineers stated, "Why, while girls comprise 55 percent of undergraduate students, do they account for only 20 percent of engineering majors, and boys remain four times more likely to enroll in undergraduate engineering programs?" (Tortolani, 2007). It remains important to be aware of and address gender equity in your classroom. Some suggest the underrepresentation of females is due to the large proportion of males (4 to 1) at the highest performance levels of such tests as SAT Math (Wai, Cacchio, Putallaz, & Makel, 2010). This is often the population that seeks out STEM careers. In the formative years, we must challenge the gender stereotypes for both sexes and create gender-friendly environments for learning mathematics and for stimulating all students' interest in pursuing college majors and careers in mathematics-related fields.

Possible Causes of Gender Differences

Although we base much of our concerns in this area over sex differences in test scores, and what some suggest to be biologically determined basis for differences (Spelke, 2005), it is in fact the gender differences that are socially and culturally constructed that educators must examine for change. By finding some of the causes of gender differences in and out of the classroom, we can help create gender-friendly mathematics instruction for boys and girls.

Belief Systems. The belief that mathematics is a male activity persists in our society and is held by both sexes (Else-Quest, Hyde, & Linn, 2010). Stereotypes that boys are better in math shape girls' self-perceptions and motivations (Nosek, Banaji, & Greenwald, 2002). What may result is a decrease in emerging interest in math. Females report that interest is a very influential factor in their decision to pursue higher-level math courses (Stevens, Wang, Olivarez, & Hamman, 2007), often expressing that they are less proficient than males—even when they perform at similar levels (Correll, 2001). "The relative absence of females in math and science careers fuels the stereotype that girls cannot succeed in math-related areas and thus young girls are, often subtly, steered away from them" (Barnett, 2007). Yet, recent research suggests that the link between attitudes toward mathematics influencing choice of majors in STEM fields may be less of a factor (Riegle-Crumb & King, 2011).

Teacher Interactions. Teachers may not consciously seek to stereotype students by gender; however, the gender-based biases of our society may affect teacher–student interactions. According to Janet Hyde, "[b]oth parents and teachers continue to hold the stereotype that boys are better than girls [at math]" (Seattle Times News Services, 2008). Observations of teachers' gender-specific interactions in the classroom indicate that boys get more attention and different kinds of attention than girls do. Boys receive more criticism for wrong answers as well as more praise for correct answers. Boys also tend to be more involved in discipline-related attention (Campbell, 1995). Teacher attention is valued (regardless of whether it is positive or negative), with a predictable effect on both sexes. Often females in math classes go unobserved, and a study found them to be "quiet achievers" (Clarke et al., 2001). Also, female teachers with math anxiety negatively influence female students' mathematics achievement—even over just a one-year period (Beilock, Gunderson, Ramirez, & Levine, 2010). Yet females get as good or better grades in mathematics than males (Gallagher & Kaufmann, 2005; Riegle-Crumb, 2006).

What Can We Try?

As already noted, the causes of girls' and boys' perceptions of themselves vis-à-vis mathematics are partially a function of the educational environment. That is where we should look for solutions.

Awareness. As a teacher, you need to work at ensuring equitable treatment of boys and girls. As you interact with students, be sensitive to the following:

- Number and type of questions you ask
- Ability of students to act out or model mathematical situations or concepts with movements and gestures
- Amount of attention given to disturbances
- Kinds and topics of projects and activities assigned
- Praise given in response to students' participation
- Makeup and use of small groups
- Context of problems

- Characters in children's literature used in mathematics instruction (see Karp et al., 1998)
- Discussions of STEM careers to increase students' interest in these fields

Being aware of your gender-specific actions is more difficult than it may sound. To receive feedback, try video-recording a lesson. Tally the number of questions asked of boys and girls. Also note which students ask questions and what kinds of questions are being asked. Where do you stand in the room? What kind of feedback is given? You may be surprised to find gender-biased behaviors, but awareness is a step toward being more equitable.

Involve All Students. Find ways to involve all students in your class, not just those who seem eager. There are girls and boys who may tend to shy away from involvement, lack motivation, or not be as quick to seek help. Perhaps the best suggestion for involving students is to follow the tenets of this book—use a problem-based approach to instruction. Mau and Leitze (2001) suggest that when teachers are in a show-and-tell mode, there are significantly more opportunities to reinforce boys' more overt behaviors as well as girls' more passive behaviors. Instead, expect all students to talk, listen, and share their thinking. Authority resides in the students and in their arguments. Males also show strong spatial abilities (Klein, Adi-Japha, & Hakak-Benizri, 2010; Wai, Lubinski, & Benbow, 2009) and involving boys in visual representations, movements, and gestures can support their learning of mathematics.

PAUSE and REFLECT

Stop for a moment and envision the teaching model you experienced as a student. Can you remember situations in which one gender was favored, encouraged, reprimanded, or assisted by the teacher—even without consciously being aware of any differential treatment? How would these differences possibly disappear in a problem-based, student-discourse-oriented environment? ●

Reducing Resistance and Building Resilience in Students with Low Motivation

There are students who make a decision along the way in their formal education that they won't be able to learn mathematics, so why try? Teachers need to "reach beyond the resistance" and find ways to listen to students, affirm their abilities, and motivate them. Here are a few key strategies for getting there.

Give Students Choices That Capitalize on Their Unique Strengths. Students often need to have power over events by having a stake and a say in what is happening. Therefore, focus on making classrooms inviting and familiar as you connect students' interests to the content. Setting up situations where these students feel success with mathematics tasks can bring them closer to stopping the willful avoidance of learning mathematics. Schools, like families and communities, are protective support systems that can foster resilience and persistence.

Nurture Traits of Resilience. Benard (1991) suggests there are four traits found in resilient individuals—social competence, problem-solving skills, autonomy, and a sense of purpose and future. Use these characteristics to motivate students and help them reach success. Encourage your students to be successful despite risk and adversity. Get students to think critically and flexibly in solving novel problems. This skill is key to developing strategies that will serve students in all aspects of their lives. Also continue to nurture high levels of student responsibility and autonomy, intentionally fostering a disposition that students can and will be able to master mathematical concepts.

Demonstrate an Ethic of Caring. It is especially critical in mathematics, which is sometimes seen as a mechanical process, to foster a caring atmosphere. For example, work with students to identify pressures and burdens in an effort to help them navigate life stresses and create a safe refuge in the mathematics classroom. We know that "when schools focus on what really matters in life, the cognitive ends we now pursue so painfully and artificially will be achieved somewhat more naturally. . . . It is obvious that children will work harder and do things—even things like adding fractions—for people they love and trust" (Noddings, 1988, p. 32).

Make Mathematics Irresistible. Motivation is based on what students expect they can do and what they value (Wigfield & Cambria, 2010). The use of games, brainteasers, mysteries that can be solved through mathematics, and counterintuitive problems that leave students asking, "How is that possible?" help generate excitement. But the main thrust of the motivation emerges from you. Teachers communicate a passion for the content. Be enthusiastic and show that mathematics can make a difference in their lives. Well-known science educator David Hawkins stated that "some things are best known by falling in love with them" (Hawkins, 1965, p. 3).

Give Students Some Leadership in Their Own Learning. High-achieving students tend to suggest their failures were from lack of effort and see the failure as a temporary condition that can be resolved with hard work. On the other hand, students with a history of academic failure can attribute their failures to lack of ability. This internal attribution is more difficult to counteract, as they think their innate lack of mathematical ability prevents them from succeeding no matter what they do. One strategy is to help students

develop personal goals for their learning of mathematics. They might reflect on their performance on a unit assessment and what their goals are for the next unit, or they might monitor how they are doing on their basic fact memorization and set weekly targets.

Students Who Are Mathematically Gifted

Students who are mathematically gifted include those who have high ability or high interest. Some may be gifted with an intuitive knowledge of mathematical concepts, whereas others have a passion for the subject even though they may have to work hard to learn it. The National Association for Gifted Children (NAGC) describes a gifted student as "someone who shows, or has the potential for showing, an exceptional level of performance in one or more areas of expression" (NAGC, 2007). Many students' giftedness becomes apparent to parents and teachers when they grasp and articulate mathematics concepts at an age earlier than expected. They are often found to easily make connections between topics of study and frequently are unable to explain how they quickly got an answer (Rotigel & Fello, 2005).

Many teachers have a keen ability to spot talent when they note students who have strong number sense or visual/spatial sense (Gavin & Sheffield, 2010). Note that these teachers are not pointing to students who are fast and speedy with their basic facts, but those who have the ability to reason and make sense of mathematics.

Although some states require school districts to provide gifted education, there is no federal legislation that mandates special programs for gifted students. So you will see many families actively advocating for opportunities for their high-ability student.

Regardless of whether parents push for recognition of their child's gift, the students themselves do not always readily embrace the label of mathematically gifted. The media consistently portray people who do well in mathematics as looking strange or acting weird (Sheffield, 1997). Television and movie characters who are smart and successful in mathematics and science are represented as socially inept outcasts. Just as students mimic behaviors of popular media figures, they absorb these powerful negative messages about showing their intelligence in public settings. The bombardment of an anti-intellectual bias in the media needs to be countered with the consistent message that "smart wins." Showing the class "math-smart" role models in the world of television, movies, and literature, as well as the real world, encourages and supports your mathematically gifted students.

We should not wait for students to demonstrate their mathematical talent; we need to develop it through a challenging set of tasks (including the target tasks in the *Common Core State Standards* [McCallum, 2011]) and inquiry-based instruction (VanTassel-Baska & Brown 2007). Generally, the assumption in education is that good teaching is able to respond to the varying needs of diverse learners, including the talented and gifted. Yet for some gifted students who seek additional challenges in their conceptual knowledge and skills, research suggests that the curriculum should be adapted to consider level, complexity, breadth, depth, and pace (Assouline & Lupkowski-Shoplik, 2011; Renzulli, Gubbins, McMillen, Eckert, & Little, 2009; Saul, Assouline, & Sheffield, 2010).

There are four basic categories for adapting mathematics content for gifted mathematics students: *acceleration, enrichment, sophistication,* and *novelty* (Gallagher & Gallagher, 1994). In each category, students should be asked to apply rather than just acquire information. The emphasis on implementing and extending ideas must overshadow the mental collection of facts and concepts.

Acceleration. Acceleration recognizes that students may already understand the mathematics content that will be presented. Some teachers use "curriculum compacting" (Reis & Renzulli, 2005) to give a short overview of the content and assess students' ability to respond to math tasks that would demonstrate their proficiency. Teachers can either reduce the amount of time these students spend on aspects of the topic or move altogether to more advanced and complex content. Allowing students to pace their own learning can give them access to curriculum different from their grade level while demanding more independence. Moving students to higher mathematics (by moving them up a grade for example) will not succeed if the learning is still at a slow pace and the student continues to be bored. Frequently students explore similar topics as their classmates but focus on higher-level thinking, more complex or abstract ideas, and deeper levels of understanding. Research reveals that when gifted students are accelerated through the curriculum they become more likely to explore STEM fields (Sadler & Tai, 2007).

Enrichment. Enrichment activities go beyond the topic of study to content that is not specifically a part of the grade-level curriculum but is an extension of the original mathematical tasks. For example, when a second-grade class is using a spinner with three divisions of different colors to explore probability, an extension for enrichment could include challenging a group of students to create six different spinners that demonstrate the following cases: red is certain to win; red can't possibly win; blue is likely to win; red, blue, green, yellow, and orange are all equally likely to win; blue or green will probably win; and red, blue, and green have the same chance to win while yellow and orange can't possibly win. Other times the format of enrichment can involve studying the same topic as the rest of the class while differing on the means and outcomes of the work. Examples include group investigations, solving real problems in the community, writing letters to outside audiences, or identifying applications of the mathematics learned.

Sophistication. Another strategy is to increase the sophistication of a topic by raising the level of complexity or pursuing greater depth. This can mean exploring a larger set of ideas in which a mathematics topic exists. For example, while studying a unit on place value, mathematically gifted students can stretch their knowledge to study other numeration systems such as Roman, Mayan, Egyptian, Babylonian, Chinese, and Zulu. This provides a multicultural view of how our numeration system fits within the number systems of the world. In the algebra strand, when studying sequences or patterns of numbers, mathematically gifted students can learn about Fibonacci sequences and their appearances in the natural world.

Novelty. Novelty introduces completely different material from the regular curriculum and frequently occurs in after-school clubs, out-of-class projects, or collaborative school experiences. The collaborative experiences include students from a variety of grades and classes volunteering for special mathematics projects, with a classroom teacher, principal, or resource teacher taking the lead. The novelty approach allows gifted students to explore topics that are within their developmental grasp but outside the curriculum. For example, students may look at mathematical "tricks" using binary numbers to guess classmates' birthdays or solve reasoning problems using a logic matrix. They may also explore topics such as topology through the creation of paper "knots" called flexagons (see www.flexagon.net) or large-scale investigations of the amount of food thrown away at lunchtime. A group might create tetrahedron kites or find mathematics in art. Another aspect of the novelty approach provides different options for students in culminating performances of their understanding, such as demonstrating their knowledge through inventions, experiments, simulations, dramatizations, visual displays, and oral presentations.

Strategies to Avoid. There are a number of ineffective approaches that find their way into classrooms. Five common ones are:

1. *Assigning more of the same work.* This is the least appropriate way to respond to mathematically gifted students and the most likely to result in students' hiding their ability. This approach is described by Persis Herold as "all scales and no music" (quoted in Tobias, 1995, p. 168).

2. *Giving free time to early finishers.* Although students find this rewarding, it does not maximize their intellectual growth and can lead to hurrying to finish a task.

3. *Assigning gifted students to help struggling learners.* Routinely assigning gifted students to teach others what they have mastered is an error in judgment, because it puts mathematically talented students in a constant position of tutoring rather than allowing them to create deeper and more complex levels of understanding.

4. *Gifted pull-out opportunities.* Unfortunately, these programs are often unrelated to the regular math curriculum

(Assouline & Lupkowski-Shoplik, 2011). High-ability learners can't just get one-stop shopping in a pull-out program; they need individual attention to develop depth and more complex understanding.

5. *Independent enrichment on the computer.* This practice does not engage students with mathematics in a way that will enhance conceptual understanding and support their ability to justify their thinking.

Sheffield writes that gifted students should be introduced to the "joys and frustrations of thinking deeply about a wide range of original, open-ended, or complex problems that encourage them to respond creatively in ways that are original, fluent, flexible and elegant" (1999, p. 46). Accommodations and modifications for gifted students must strive for this goal.

Final Thoughts

The late Asa Hilliard, an expert on diversity, made the following statement:

> To restructure we must first look deeply at the goals that we set for our children and the beliefs that we have about them. Once we are on the right track there, then we must turn our attention to the delivery systems, as we have begun to do. Untracking is right. Mainstreaming is right. Decentralization is right. Cooperative learning is right. Technology access for all is right. Multiculturalism is right. But none of these approaches or strategies will mean anything if the fundamental belief does not fit with new structures that are being created. (1991, p. 36)

As you move into your own classroom, your high expectations for all students to succeed will make a lasting difference as you incorporate the following general strategies that support diversity:

- Identify children's current knowledge base and build instructions with that in mind
- Push all students to high-level thinking
- Maintain high expectations
- Use a multicultural approach
- Recognize, value, explore, and incorporate the home culture
- Use alternative assessments to broaden the variety of indicators of students' performance
- Measure progress over time rather than taking short snapshots of student work
- Promote the importance of effort and resilience

RESOURCES *for Chapter 6*

RECOMMENDED READINGS

Articles

National Council of Teachers of Mathematics. (2004). Teaching mathematics to special needs students [Focus Issue]. *Teaching Children Mathematics, 11*(3).
The articles in this focus issue address specific considerations for special students, strategies for differentiation, and more.

National Council of Teachers of Mathematics. (2009). Equity: Teaching, learning, and assessing mathematics for diverse populations [Focus Issue]. *Teaching Children Mathematics, 16*(3).
This issue is full of very useful articles and activities to support teachers working in diverse classrooms.

Witzel, B., & Allsopp, D. (2007). Dynamic concrete instruction in an inclusive classroom. *Mathematics Teaching in the Middle School, 13*(4), 244–248.
This article highlights the use of manipulative materials for middle grade students with high incidence disabilities such as attention-deficit hyperactivity disorder (ADHD). Two classroom vignettes address (1) linking prior knowledge to new concepts, (2) emphasizing the think-aloud model, and (3) applying multisensory prompts.

Books

Fennell, F. (Ed.) (2011). *Achieving fluency in special education and mathematics.* Reston, VA: NCTM.
This book includes information on teaching mathematics to students with disabilities by top mathematics educators. The chapters detail work in each of the five NCTM content strands as well as present models for developing a learning framework and assessing students.

ONLINE RESOURCES

Center for Applied Special Technology (CAST)
www.cast.org
This site contains resources and tools to support the learning of all students, especially those with disabilities, through universal design for learning (UDL).

LDOnline
www.ldonline.org
Offers a wealth of resources including assessment tools, teaching strategies, readings, videos, podcasts, and interesting articles on mathematical disabilities.

Special Education Resources (Guide to Online Schools)
www.guidetoonlineschools.com/library/special-education
This site contains a list of helpful resources for students receiving special education services as well as helpful technology resources.

Teaching Diverse Learners—Culturally Responsive Teaching
www.alliance.brown.edu/tdl/tl-strategies/crt-principles-prt.shtml

This site includes several characteristics of culturally relevant teaching, explaining the importance of each and giving concrete examples of how to implement each characteristic in the classroom.

National Association for Gifted Children (NAGC)
www.nagc.org

NAGC is dedicated to serving professionals who work on behalf of gifted students. See the "Tools for Educators" section for online articles and resources.

REFLECTIONS *on Chapter 6*

WRITING TO LEARN

1. How is equity in the classroom different from teaching all students equally?
2. For children with learning disabilities and special learning needs, what are two strategies to modify instruction?
3. Describe in your own words the central ideas of culturally relevant mathematics instruction.
4. What are some of the specific difficulties English language learners encounter in the mathematics class?
5. In the context of providing for the mathematically gifted, what is meant by depth? Give an example of how you might add depth to a classroom activity.

FOR DISCUSSION AND EXPLORATION

1. Develop your own philosophical statement for "all students" or "every child." Design a visual representation for your statement. Read the Equity Principle in *Principles and Standards for School Mathematics* and see whether your position is in accord with that principle.
2. What would you do if you found yourself teaching a class with one mathematically gifted student who had no equal in the room? Create a menu of six activities the student could consider on a mathematics topic of your choice. Include activities that include projects, data collection, games, integrations with other content areas, links to literature, or complex problem solving (see Wilkins, Wilkins, & Oliver, 2006, for suggestions).

MyEducationLab™

Go to the MyEducationLab (www.myeducationlab.com) for Math Methods and familiarize yourself with the content. Much of the site content is organized topically. The topics include all of the following to support your learning in the course:

- Learning outcomes for important mathematics methods course topics aligned with the national standards
- Assignments and Activities, tied to these learning outcomes and standards, that can help you more deeply understand course content
- Building Teaching Skills and Dispositions learning units that allow you to apply and practice your understanding of the core mathematics content and teaching skills

Your instructor has a correlation guide that aligns the exercises on the topical portion of the site with your book's chapters.

On MyEducationLab you will also find book-specific resources including Blackline Masters, Expanded Lesson Activities, and Artifact Analysis Activities.

Field Experience Guide
C O N N E C T I O N S

Chapter 8 of the *Field Experience Guide* focuses on diversity. Experiences include observing one child's experience (FEG 8.1), interviewing a teacher about strategies they use to meet all students' needs (FEG 8.2), and reflecting on meeting the needs of all students (FEG 8.6). The assessment tasks in Chapter 7 of the FEG also provide opportunities to focus on the needs of individual learners.

Chapter 7

Using Technological Tools to Teach Mathematics

Teachers need to carefully select and design learning opportunities for students where technology is an essential component in developing students' understanding, not where it is simply an appealing alternative to traditional instructional routines.

Fey, Hollenbeck, and Wray (2010, p. 275)

A technology-enabled learning setting is an educational environment supported by mathematical technologies, communicative and collaborative tools, or a combination of each (Arbaugh et al., 2010). *Mathematical technologies* refers to digital content accessed via computers, calculators, and other handheld or tablet devices; computer algebra systems; dynamic geometry software; online digital games; recording devices; interactive presentation devices; spreadsheets; as well as the Internet-based resources for use with these devices and tools. Communicative and collaborative tools, often referred to as *Web 2.0 tools*, encourage synchronous or asynchronous collaboration, communication, and construction of knowledge and include blogs, wikis, and digital audiocasts or videocasts.

Technology is one of the six mathematics principles in the *Principles and Standards* documents, an emphasis reinforced by NCTM's position statement on the role of technology in the teaching and learning of mathematics (NCTM, 2008b), which regards technology as an *essential tool* for both learning and teaching mathematics. The *Common Core State Standards*' Standards for Mathematical Practice promotes the strategic use of appropriate tools and technology, which includes digital applications, content, and resources (CCSSO, 2010). Thinking of technology as an "extra" added on to the list of things you are trying to accomplish in your classroom is not an effective approach. Instead, technology should be seen as an integral part of your instructional arsenal of tools for deepening student understanding. It can enlarge the scope of the content students can learn, and it can broaden the range of problems

that students are able to tackle (Ball & Stacey, 2005; NCTM, 2008b). However, it cannot be a replacement for the full conceptual understanding of mathematics content.

Pedagogical content knowledge (PCK) is the intersection of mathematics content knowledge with the pedagogical knowledge of teaching and learning (Shulman, 1986), a body of information possessed by teachers that the average person, even one strong in mathematics, would not likely know. PCK represents the specific strategies and approaches that teachers use to deliver mathematical content to students. Technological, pedagogical, and content knowledge (TPACK), as shown in Figure 7.1, describes the infusion of technology to this mix (Mishra & Koehler, 2006; Niess, 2008). We suggest that teachers consider technology as a conscious component of each lesson and a regular strategy for enhancing student learning. This chapter's emphasis on

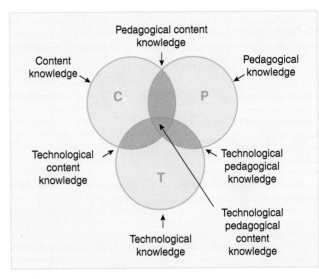

FIGURE 7.1 TPACK framework.

the importance of technology in instruction is carried over throughout the content chapters, especially in sections highlighted with the technology icon. Its value becomes evident when technological features embedded in a lesson enhance students' opportunities to learn important mathematics.

Technology-Supported Learning Activities

Grandgenett, Harris, and Hofer (2010, 2011) propose seven "genres" of mathematics activities in which teachers can combine the strategic use of technology with effective pedagogy to address important mathematics content. These activities engage learners to consider and make sense of new information, practice various techniques, interpret and explore concepts, produce artifacts and representations, apply mathematics to the real world, evaluate their work and the work of others, and create products and resources. When two or more learning activities are combined and supported by strategic digital technology use, the chance for modeling the complexity of real-world applications of mathematics increases (Checkley, 2006; Fuson, Kalchman, & Bransford, 2005). Table 7.1 provides ways to think about how digital tools, pedagogy, and content can be mixed to engage students in strategic and meaningful uses of technology and to model processes and practices that deepen student understanding.

TABLE 7.1

TECHNOLOGY-SUPPORTED LEARNING ACTIVITIES	
Description of Technology Support Activity	**Sample Digital Tools/Resources**
1. Consider and Make Sense of New Information	
Gain information from a student or teacher demonstration or presentation activity	Document camera, interactive whiteboards, presentation applications (*Keynote, PowerPoint, Prezi*), video (Animoto, Jing, YouTube, SchoolTube, TeacherTube, Vimeo), or other media tools
Gather information from reading a passage(s) from a digital or printed text	E-textbooks, portable document format (pdf) files, text files, websites
Engage in discourse with peers, teachers, or experts related to concepts, processes, or practices	Math Forum's "Ask Dr. Math," online discussion groups and social networking tools (VoiceThread), Blackboard Collaborate™, GoToMeeting, Google Voice and Video Chat, Second Life
Look for, develop, and generalize relationships in patterns and repeated calculations	Virtual manipulatives (NLVM), Illuminations activities, spreadsheets, calculators
Select and use online and research tools strategically to solve problems and deepen understanding	Online databases (ERIC, Sirs, World Book, Gale Researcher, Math Forum's MathTools, NROC), Web searching, simulations
Strive to understand the characteristics, context, or meaning of problems	Concept and mind mapping tools (*Freeplane, Inspiration, Kidspiration*)
2. Practice Various Techniques	
Use tools to compute numerous items or large quantities	Scientific/graphing calculators, spreadsheets, WolframAlpha
Do strategy-based drills and practice	AAAMath, FASTT Math, First in Math, MathXL, iFlash, computation apps on handheld/tablet devices
Do strategy-based problem-solving puzzles	Virtual manipulatives, brainteaser websites (CoolMath4Kids), online sudoku
3. Interpret and Explore Concepts	
Make conjectures, develop arguments, and highlight different approaches for solving problems	Dynamic geometry software (*Geometer's Sketchpad, GeoGebra*), widgets (Explore Learning), blogs, podcasts, wikis, concept and mind mapping tools, online discussion groups and social networking tools (VoiceThread), email
Categorize information to examine relationships	Concept and mind mapping tools, databases/spreadsheets, drawing tools
Explain relationships in representations	2-D and 3-D animations, online discussion groups and social networking tools (VoiceThread), video (iMovie, Windows Movie Maker), Global Positioning Devices (Google Earth), engineering calculation software (*Mathcad*)
Estimate and approximate values to examine relationships	Basic/scientific/graphing calculator, spreadsheets, online savings calculators, classroom response systems (clickers)
Examine and interpret a mathematics-related phenomenon	Video sharing communities (YouTube, TeacherTube, SchoolTube, iTunesU), graphing applications, portable data collection devices/tools

TABLE 7.1 (*continued*)

Description of Technology Support Activity	Sample Digital Tools/Resources
4. Produce Artifacts and Representations	
Demonstrate understanding of a mathematical concept, topic, or process	Interactive whiteboard, online discussion groups and social networking tools (VoiceThread), video (iMovie, Windows Movie Maker, YouTube), document camera, presentation software (Keynote, PowerPoint), podcasts
Produce a written document, journal entry, or report describing a concept, topic, or process	Word processing application (with Math Type), collaborative editing tools (Google docs), concept or mind mapping tools, blogs, wikis, social networking tools
Develop a mathematical representation	Spreadsheets, virtual manipulatives, concept or mind mapping software, graphing calculator
Pose a mathematical problem to illustrate a mathematics concept or relationship	Word processing application, online discussion group, social network tools, email
5. Apply Mathematics to the Real World	
Review or select a strategy to solve a problem	Online help sites (Math Forum, Math.com, WebMath), TI, Casio (calculator), Key Curriculum Press (Geometers Sketchpad), Wolfram Alpha online communities/guidebooks
Apply mathematical knowledge to test-taking situation	Test-taking and survey software, classroom response systems
Apply a mathematical representation to model a real-world situation	Spreadsheets, graphing calculators, virtual manipulatives, portable data collection devices/tools
6. Evaluate Student Work and the Work of Others	
Compare and contrast mathematical strategies or determine the most appropriate for particular situations	Inspiration, Kidspiration
Test a solution and check to see whether it makes sense within the context of a situation	Scientific/graphing calculators, spreadsheets
Make conjectures and use counterexamples to build a logical progression of statements to explore and support their ideas	Geometer's Sketchpad, GeoGebra, Excel, online calculators
Evaluate mathematical work through the use of technology-supported feedback	Online discussion groups, blogs
7. Create Products and Resources	
Engage in peer teaching of a mathematics concept, strategy, or problem	Presentation software (Keynote, PowerPoint, Prezi), interactive whiteboards, video (Animoto, Jing, YouTube, SchoolTube, TeacherTube, Vimeo)
Develop a solution pathway	Concept or mind mapping tools, collaborative writing tools (Google docs), wikis, social networking tools
Develop a creative project, invention, or artifact	Word processor, animation tools, Geometer's Sketchpad, GeoGebra
Create a mathematical process for others to use	Computer programming, iMovie, Windows Movie Maker, screencasts (Jing, Quicktime)

Source: Adapted from Grandgenett, N., Harris, J., & Hofer, M. (2011). An activity-based approach to technology integration in the mathematics classroom. *NCSM Journal of Mathematics Education Leadership, 13*(1), 19–28.

Calculators in Mathematics Instruction

In its 2011 position statement on calculator use in elementary grades, NCTM maintains its long-standing view by stating, "Calculators can promote the higher-order thinking and reasoning needed for problem solving in our information- and technology-based society, and they can also increase students' understanding of and fluency with arithmetic operations, algorithms, and numerical relationships . . . [T]he use of calculators does not supplant the need for students to develop proficiency with efficient, accurate methods of mental and pencil-and-paper calculation and in making reasonable estimations" (NCTM, 2011, p. 1).

Even with everyday use of calculators in society and the professional support of calculators in schools, use of calculators is not always central to instruction in a mathematics classroom, especially at the elementary level. Sometimes educators and students' families are concerned that just allowing students to use calculators when solving problems will hinder students' learning of the basic facts. However, rather than an either-or choice, just as with the use of other digital technologies, there are conditions when students should use technology and other times when they must call on their own resources.

Based on efficiency and effectiveness, students should learn when to use mental mathematics, when to use estimation, when to tackle a problem with paper and pencil, and when to use a calculator. Ignoring the potential benefits of calculators by prohibiting their use can inhibit students' learning. Helping students know when to grab a calculator and when not to use one is a conversation that must take place between teacher and students. Expanding students' ability to think about challenging mathematics must be balanced with the development of their computational skills.

Help families understand that calculator use will in no way prevent students from learning rigorous mathematics; in fact, calculators used thoughtfully and meaningfully enhance the learning of mathematics. Furthermore, families should be made aware that calculators and other digital technologies require students to be problem solvers. Calculators can only calculate according to input entered by humans. In isolation, calculators cannot answer the most meaningful mathematics tasks, and they cannot substitute for thinking or understanding. Sending home calculator activities that reinforce important mathematical concepts and including calculator activities on a Family Math Night are ways to educate families about appropriate calculator use.

When to Use a Calculator

If the primary purpose of the instructional activity is to practice computational skills, students should not be using a calculator. On the other hand, students should have full access to calculators when they are exploring patterns, conducting investigations, testing conjectures, solving problems, and visualizing solutions. Situations involving computations that are beyond students' ability without the aid of a calculator are not necessarily beyond their ability to think about meaningfully.

As students come to fully understand the meanings of the operations, they should be exposed to realistic problems with realistic numbers. For example, young students may want to calculate how many seconds they have been alive. They can think conceptually about how many seconds in a minute, hour, day, and so on. But the actual calculations and those that continue to weeks and years can be done more efficiently on a calculator.

Also include calculators when the goal of the instructional activity is not to compute, but computation is involved in the problem solving. For example, middle grade students may be asked to identify the "best buy" when there are different percentages off different priced merchandise. Whether purchasing a digital media player or getting a deal on ride tickets at the fair, the goal is to define the most economical relationship, given a set of choices, by calculating the various percentage discounts with a calculator.

Calculators are also valuable for generating and analyzing patterns. For example, when finding the decimal equivalent of $\frac{8}{9}, \frac{7}{9}, \frac{5}{9}$, and so on, an interesting pattern emerges. Let students explore other "ninths" and make conjectures as to why the pattern occurs. Again, the emphasis is not to determine a computational solution but instead to use the calculator to help find patterns.

Finally, calculators can be used as accommodations for students with disabilities. When used for instruction that is not centered on developing computation skills, calculators can help ensure that all students have appropriate access to the curriculum to the maximum extent possible.

Benefits of Calculator Use

Understanding how calculators contribute to the learning of mathematics includes recognizing that the "use of calculators does not threaten the development of basic skills and that it can enhance conceptual understanding, strategic competence, and disposition toward mathematics" (National Research Council, 2001, p. 354). This includes four-function, scientific, and graphing calculators. A specific discussion of graphing calculators is found later in this chapter.

Calculators Can Be Used to Develop Concepts and Enhance Problem Solving.

The calculator can be much more than a device for calculation. As shown in an analysis of more than 79 research studies, K–12 students (with the exception of grade 4) who used calculators improved their "basic skills with paper-pencil tasks both in computational operations and in problem solving" (Hembree & Dessert, 1986, p. 96). Other researchers confirm that students with long-term experience using calculators performed better overall than students without such experience on both mental computation and paper-and-pencil problems (Ellington, 2003; B. A. Smith, 1997; Wareham, 2005). There has been a call for more studies on the long-term use of calculators (National Mathematics Advisory Panel, 2008), and additional research is likely to result.

Although some worry that calculator use can impede instruction in numbers and operations, the reverse is actually the case, as shown in the following examples. In grades K–1, students who are exploring concepts of quantity can use the calculator as a counting machine. Using the automatic-constant feature (not all calculators perform this in the same way, so check how it works on your calculator), students can count. For example, press the following keys—$\boxed{0} \boxed{+} \boxed{1} \boxed{=} \boxed{=} \boxed{=}$—to count by ones, pressing the equals key for as long as the count continues. Help students try this feature. The "count by ones" on the calculator can reinforce students' oral counting and identification of patterns and can even be used by one student to count their classmates as they enter the classroom in the morning. Children's literature with repeated phrases, such as the classic *Goodnight Moon* (Brown, 1947), provides an opportunity for students to count. Students can press the equal sign each time the little rabbit says "Goodnight" in his bedtime routine. At the completion of the book, they can compare how many "goodnights" were recorded. Follow-up activities include using the same automatic-constant feature on the calculator with different stories or books to skip-count by twos (e.g., pairs of animals or people), fives (e.g., fingers on one hand or people in a car), or tens (e.g., dimes, "ten in a bed," apples in a tree).

Older students can investigate decimal concepts with a calculator, as in the following examples. On the calculator, $796 \div 42 = 18.95238$. Consider the task of using the calculator to determine the whole-number remainder. Another example is to use the calculator to find a number that when multiplied by itself will produce 43. In this situation, a student can press 6.1 $\boxed{\times}$ $\boxed{=}$ to get the square of 6.1. For students who are just beginning to understand decimals, the activity will demonstrate that numbers such as 6.3 and 6.4 are between 6 and 7. Furthermore, 6.55 is between 6.5 and 6.6. For students who already understand the density of decimals, the same activity serves as a meaningful and conceptual introduction to square roots.

Calculators Can Be Used for Practicing Basic Facts. Students who want to practice the multiples of 7 can press 7 $\boxed{\times}$ 3 and delay pressing the $\boxed{=}$. The challenge is to answer the fact to themselves before pressing the $\boxed{=}$ key. Subsequent multiples of 7 can be checked by simply pressing the second factor and the $\boxed{=}$. The TI-10 (Texas Instruments) and TI-15 calculators have built-in problem-solving modes in which students can practice facts, develop lists of related facts, and test equations or inequalities with arithmetic expressions on both sides of the relationship symbol (http://education.ti.com/educationportal/sites/US/productCategory/us_elementary.html).

A class can be split in half with one half required to use a calculator and the other required to do the computations mentally. For $3000 + 1765$, the mental math team wins every time. It will also win for simple facts and numerous problems that lend themselves to mental computation. Of course, there are many computations, such as 537×32, where the calculator team will be faster. Not only does this simple exercise provide practice with mental math, but it also demonstrates to students that it is not always effective or efficient to reach for the calculator.

Calculators Can Improve Student Attitudes and Motivation. Research results reveal that students who frequently use calculators have better attitudes toward the subject of mathematics (Ellington, 2003). There is also evidence that students are more motivated when their anxiety is reduced; therefore, supporting students during problem-solving activities with calculators is important. A student with disabilities who is left out of the problem-solving lesson due to weak knowledge of basic facts will not pursue the worthwhile explorations the teacher plans. That does not excuse them from learning their facts. As we try to increase students' confidence that they can solve challenging mathematics problems, we can expand their motivation to be persistent and stay engaged in the process of thinking about numbers. Again, the strategic use of the calculator is guided by the plans of the teacher and the eventual decision making of the students.

Calculators Are Commonly Used in Society. Calculators are used by almost everyone in every facet of life that involves any sort of exact computation. Students should be taught how to use this commonplace tool effectively and also learn to judge when to use it. Although it is available on virtually every type of digital computing device or smartphone, many adults have not learned how to use the automatic-constant feature of a calculator and are not practiced in recognizing common errors that are often made on calculators. Effective use of calculators is an important skill that is best learned by using them regularly in meaningful problem-solving activities.

Graphing Calculators

Graphing calculators help students visualize concepts as they make real-world connections with data. When students can actually see expressions, formulas, graphs, and the results of changing a variable on those visual representations, a deeper understanding of concepts can result. Graphing calculators are used in upper elementary classes through high school and beyond, but the most common use is at the secondary level. Because graphing calculators are permitted and in some cases required on such tests as the SAT, ACT, PSAT, or AP exams, it is critical for all students to be familiar with their use.

It is a mistake to think that graphing calculators are only for doing "high-powered" mathematics. The following list demonstrates some features the graphing calculator offers, every one of which is useful within the standard middle school curriculum.

- The display window permits compound expressions such as $3 + 4(5 - \frac{6}{7})$ to be shown completely before being evaluated. Furthermore, once evaluated, previous expressions can be recalled and modified. This promotes an understanding of notation and order of operations. Expressions can include exponents, absolute values, and negation signs, with no restrictions on the values used.
- Even without using function definition capability, students can insert values into expressions or formulas

without having to enter the entire formula for each new value. The results can be entered into a list or table of values and stored directly on the calculator for further analysis.

- Variables can be used in expressions and then assigned different values to see the effect on expressions. This simple method helps with the idea of a variable as something that varies.
- The distinction between "negative" and "subtract" is clear and very useful. A separate key is used to enter the negative of a quantity. The display shows the negative sign as a superscript. If $^-5$ is stored in the variable B, then the expression $^-2 - {}^-B$ will be evaluated correctly as $^-7$. This feature is a significant aid in the study of integers and variables.
- Points can be plotted on a coordinate screen either by entering coordinates and seeing the result or by moving the cursor to a particular coordinate on the screen.
- Very large and very small numbers are managed without error. The calculator will quickly compute factorials, even for large numbers, as well as permutations and combinations. For example, $23! = 1.033314797 \times 10^{40}$.
- Statistical functions allow students to examine the means, medians, and standard deviations of large and sometimes complex sets of data. Data are entered, ordered, added to, or changed almost as easily as on a spreadsheet.
- Graphs for data analysis are available, including box plots, histograms, and—on some calculators—circle graphs, bar graphs, and pictographs.
- Random number generators allow for the simulation of a variety of probability experiments.
- Scatter plots for ordered pairs of real data can be entered, plotted, and examined for trends. The calculator will calculate the equations of best-fit, linear, or quadratic functions.
- Functions can be explored in three modes: equation, table, and graph. Because the calculator easily switches from one to the other and because of the trace feature, the connections between these modes become quite clear.
- The graphing calculator is programmable. Programs are very easily written and understood. For example, a program involving the Pythagorean theorem can be used to find the lengths of sides of right triangles.
- Students can share data programs and functions from one calculator to another, connect their calculators to a classroom display screen, save information to a computer, and download software applications that give additional functionality for special uses.

Two full-color graphing calculators, the TI-Nspire™ CX (http://education.ti.com/educationportal) and the Casio PRIZM (www.casio.com), are making their way into classrooms. Student work can be transferred between the

TI-Nspire and computer via TI-Nspire Student Software. A student can explore how changing the width of a rectangle overlaid on an image of an aerial view of a building keeps the perimeter constant but affects the area. The student can simultaneously see the visual image of the rectangle that they can manipulate to desired dimensions, a table of matching values, and a graph of the resulting area. Rather than toggling from one representation to another, they can all be considered at one time, which strengthens the ability to see patterns. There are even options for writing notes to record discoveries or findings. However, these amazing devices are only as useful as the tasks teachers create for students.

Arguments against graphing calculators are similar to those for other calculators—and are equally unsubstantiated. These tools have the potential of providing students with significant opportunities for exploring real mathematics.

Portable Data-Collection Devices

In addition to the capabilities of the graphing calculator alone, portable data-collection devices and probe/sensor tools make them even more remarkable. Texas Instruments calls its version the CBL/CBR. (CBL, for *computer-based laboratory*, has become the generic acronym for such devices.) Casio's version, the Data Analyzer EA-200, is nearly identical. These devices accept a variety of probes, such as temperature or light sensors and motion detectors, that can be used to gather real data. These data can be transferred to the graphing calculator, where they are stored in one or more lists. The calculator can then produce scatter plots or prepare other analyses.

These instruments help students connect graphs with real-world events. They emphasize the relationships between variables and can dispel common misconceptions students have about interpreting graphs (Lapp, 2001). Lapp explains that students often confuse the fastest rate of change with the highest point on the graph, or they may erroneously think that the shape of the graph is the shape of the motion (like a bicycle going up the hill is faster—increasing speed—than a bicycle going downhill). The fact that the graph can be produced immediately is a powerful feature of the device so that these missteps in thinking can be tested and discussed.

A popular probe for mathematics teachers is the motion detector. Texas Instruments has a motion detector called a Ranger or CBR that connects directly to the calculator. Experiments with a motion detector include analysis of objects rolling down an incline, bouncing balls, or swinging pendulums. The device actually detects the distance an object is from the sensor. When distance is plotted against time, the graph shows velocity. Students can plot their own motion walking toward or away from the detector or match the motion shown in a graph already produced. The concept of rate when interpreted as the slope of a distance-to-time curve can become quite dramatic.

One of the most exciting aspects of digital sensors and probe software devices involves the application of skills used in science, technology, engineering, and mathematics (STEM) investigations. For example, the Concord Consortium's Technology Enhanced Elementary and Middle School Science (TEEMSS2) project promotes STEM inquiry for grades 3–8 (http://teemss.concord.org). Through curriculum and software (free after registration), they share investigations in which real-time data in physical science, life science, earth science, technology, and engineering are collected, analyzed, and shared.

Digital Tools in Mathematics Instruction

A number of powerful software tools created for use in the mathematics classroom can be purchased from software publishers as Internet-based applications accessible through Web browsers.

Applets have been around for more than a decade and exist as targeted programs that can be freely accessed and manipulated on the Internet. They are commonly referred to as *etools* or *virtual manipulatives* and the National Library of Virtual Manipulatives (http://nlvm.usu.edu) has well over 100 applets that address concepts within each content standard and are organized across K–12 grade bands. Each can be downloaded so that an Internet connection is not required for student use. Some of these applets are described briefly throughout this book and at the end of each chapter. You are strongly urged to browse and explore, as each applet offers lots of fun!

A virtual manipulative is somewhat like a physical manipulative; by itself, it does not teach. However, the user of a well-designed tool has a digital "thinker tool" with which to explore mathematical ideas.

Tools for Developing Numeration

Programs providing digital versions of popular physical manipulative models for counting, place value, and fractions are available for students to work with freely without the computer posing problems, evaluating results, or telling the students what to do.

At the primary level, there are programs that provide "counters" such as colored tiles, pictures of assorted objects, place value blocks, and more. Many of these, such as five-frames and ten-frames, are available on NCTM's Illuminations website (http://illuminations.nctm.org). Typically, students can drag counters to any place on the screen,

change the colors, and put counters in groupings. General applications such as *Kidspiration* (Inspiration Software, 2011) can also be used to "stamp" discrete objects on the screen, explore shapes, and more.

Base-ten blocks (ones, tens, and hundreds models), assorted fraction pieces, and Cuisenaire rods (centimeter rods) are available in Web-based applets. Some fraction models are more flexible than physical models. For example, a circular region might be subdivided into many more fractional parts than is reasonable with physical models. When the models are connected with fractional quantities or operations, it is possible with some programs to have fraction representations shown so that connections between concrete and abstract models can help students build conceptual knowledge. Conceptua Fractions (http://conceptuamath .com) does a nice job of connecting circular, rectangular, regional, and set models; the number line; and pattern block representations for fractions.

Some Web-based tools are designed so that students may manipulate them without constraint. For example, the Base 10 Blocks applet (http://ejad.best.vwh.net/java/ b10blocks/b10blocks.html) allows students to collect as many hundreds, tens, and ones as they wish, gluing together groups of ten or breaking a flat into ten rods or a rod into ten units.

The obvious question is, Why not simply use the actual physical models? Electronic or virtual manipulatives have some advantages that merit integrating them into your instruction—not just adding them on as extras.

- *Qualitative differences in use.* Usually it is at least as easy to manipulate virtual tools as it is to use their physical counterparts. However, control of materials on the screen requires a different, perhaps more deliberative, mental action that is "more in line with the *mental actions* that we want children to carry out" (Clements & Sarama, 2005, p. 53). For example, the base-ten rod representing a ten can be broken into ten single blocks by clicking on it with a hammer icon. With physical blocks, the ten must be traded for the equivalent blocks counted out by the student.
- *Connection to symbolism.* Most virtual manipulatives for numbers include dynamic numerals or odometers that change as the representation on the screen changes. This direct and immediate connection to numeral representation is easier than with physical models.
- *Unlimited materials with easy cleanup.* With virtual manipulatives, students can easily erase the screen and begin a new problem with the click of a mouse. They will never run out of materials. For place value, even the large 1000 cubes are readily available. And there is no storage or cleanup to worry about.
- *Accommodations for special purposes.* For English language learners or visually impaired students, some programs come with speech enhancements and available

translations so that the students can read or hear the names of the materials or the numbers. For students with physical disabilities, the digital representations that can be used with handheld or tablet devices are often easier to access and use than physical models.

Many software-based programs also offer a word-processing capability connected to the workspace, allowing students to write about what they have done or perhaps to create a story problem to go with their work. Making a screen capture or recording of student representations from the workspace, with or without a written attachment, creates a record of the work for the teacher or parent/guardian—something difficult to achieve with physical models.

Tools for Developing Geometry

Computer tools for geometric exploration are much closer to pure tools than those just described for numeration. That is, students can use most of these tools without any constraints. They typically offer significant advantages over physical models, although the use of computerized tools should "enhance teaching and learning by providing opportunities for rich mathematical thinking and discussion" (Suh, Johnston, & Doud, 2008, p. 241).

Blocks and Tiles.   Programs that allow young students to "stamp" geometric tiles or blocks on the screen are quite common. Typically, there is a palette of blocks, often the same as pattern blocks or tangrams, from which students can choose. Frequently the blocks can be made "magnetic" so that when they are released close to another block, the two snap together, matching like sides. Blocks can usually be rotated, either freely or in set increments. Figure 7.2 shows a simple-to-use applet that permits a student to slice any of the three shapes in any place and then manipulate the pieces. This is a good example of something a student can do with a computer that would be difficult or impossible with physical models.

You may find that such applets provide the ability to

- Incrementally enlarge or reduce the size of blocks
- "Glue" blocks together to make new blocks
- Reflect blocks across a line of symmetry or rotate them about a point
- Measure area or perimeter
- Create polygons with a variable number of sides
- Build and rotate three-dimensional shapes

For students who have poor motor coordination or a disability that makes physical block manipulation difficult, the digital versions of blocks are a real plus. Colorful representations can be displayed, discussed, recorded, printed, and e-mailed to parents/guardians.

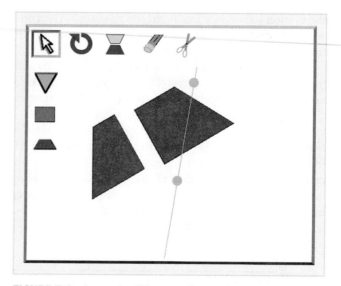

FIGURE 7.2 The Cutting Shapes Tool applet.

Drawing Programs.   For younger students, drawing shapes on a grid is easier and more useful for geometric exploration than free-form drawing. Several versions of electronic geoboards exist on which bands can be stretched to form segments between points on a grid. For an example, check NCTM's Illuminations website. The electronic geoboards offer a larger grid on which to draw, ease of use, and the ability to save and print. Some include measuring capabilities as well as the ability to reflect and rotate shapes, things that are difficult or impossible to do on a physical geoboard. An example of a good Internet applet for drawing is the Isometric Drawing Tool found at NCTM's Illuminations website (see Figure 7.3).

Dynamic Geometry Environments.   Dynamic geometry programs allow students to create shapes on the computer screen and then manipulate and measure them by dragging vertices. The most well known are *The Geometer's Sketchpad* (Key Curriculum Press) and the open-source *GeoGebra* (www.geogebra.org/cms). Dynamic geometry programs allow the creation of geometric objects so that their relationship to another screen object is established. For example, a new line can be drawn through a point and perpendicular to another line. A midpoint can be established on any line segment. Once created, these relationships are preserved no matter how the objects are moved or altered. Dynamic geometry software can dramatically change and improve the teaching of geometry in grade 3 and beyond. The ability of students to explore geometric relationships with this software is unmatched with any nondigital mode. More

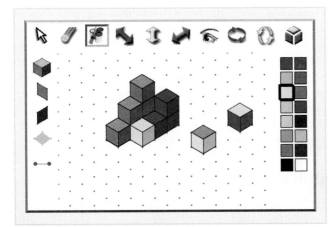

FIGURE 7.3 The Isometric Drawing Tool applet from NCTM's Illuminations website.

detailed discussion of these applications can be found in Chapter 20.

Tools for Developing Probability and Data Analysis

These computer tools allow for the entry of data and a wide choice of graphs made from the data. In addition, most produce typical statistics such as mean, median, and range. Some programs are designed for students in the primary grades. Others are more sophisticated and can be used through the middle grades. For example, students in grades 3–8 can record data, generate graphs in a variety of forms for analyzing data, and produce statistics using applications such as Excel (Microsoft) or Google's free spreadsheets (http://docs.google.com). These programs make it possible to change the emphasis in data analysis from "how to construct graphs" to "which graph best tells the story."

Probability Tools. These programs make it easy to conduct controlled probability experiments and see graphical representations of the results. For example, the National Library of Virtual Manipulatives (see Online Resources section at end of chapter) provides options for coin tossing and spinners with regions that can be customized. The young student using these programs must accept that when the computer "flips a coin" or "spins a spinner," the results are just as random and have the same probabilities as if done with real coins or spinners. The value of these programs is found in the ease with which experiments can be designed and large numbers of trials conducted, which allows more time for analyzing results.

Spreadsheet Applications and Data Graphers. *Spreadsheets* are programs that can manipulate rows and columns of numeric data. Values taken from one position in the spreadsheet can be used in formulas to determine entries elsewhere in the spreadsheet. When an entry is changed, the spreadsheet updates all values immediately.

Because the spreadsheet is among the most popular pieces of standard tool applications outside of schools, it is often available in integrated software packages or available online for free. Students as early as third grade can use these programs to organize data, display data graphically in various ways, and do numeric calculations such as finding how changing gas prices affect the family budget. Students only need to know how to use the capabilities of the spreadsheet that they will be using.

The Illuminations website from NCTM offers a couple of very nice spreadsheet applets, Spreadsheet and Spreadsheet and Graphing Tool. They can be used while connected to the Internet, or they can be downloaded to your computer. In addition, NCES Kidszone (http://nces.ed.gov/nceskids) has both graphing tools and probability simulations for elementary and middle school students.

Tools for Developing Algebraic Thinking

Very young children can use virtual pattern blocks to create patterns for copying, continuing, transforming, and analyzing (see www.mathplayground.com/patternblocks.html). Because the supply of pattern blocks is unending, students are not restricted by the number of available materials. Copies of their designs can be printed through a screen capture so that other students can be challenged to identify the pattern. Teachers of older students can use virtual pattern blocks (http://nlvm.usu.edu) on their interactive whiteboard to create a growing pattern, recording the number of squares needed at each step (or term). Students can explore the sequence of squares to make a conjecture as to how many squares will be needed at the tenth term or the nth term of the pattern.

For older students, function graphing tools permit users to create the graph of almost any function very quickly. Multiple functions can be plotted on the same axis. It is usually possible to trace along the path of a curve and view the coordinates at any point. The dimensions of the viewing area can be changed easily so that it is just as easy to look at a graph for x and y between $^-10$ and $^+10$ as it is to look at a portion of the graph thousands of units away from the origin. By "zooming in" on the intersection of two graphs, it is possible to find points of intersection without algebraic manipulation or to confirm an algebraic manipulation. Similarly, the point where a graph crosses the axis can be found to as many decimal places as is desired.

The function graphing features just described are available on all graphing calculators. Computer programs can add speed, color, visual clarity, and a variety of other interesting features to help students analyze functions.

Instructional Applications

Instructional applications are designed for student interaction in a manner that extends beyond the textbook or a tutor. In the following discussion, the intent is to provide some perspective on the different kinds of input to your mathematics program that instructional applications might offer.

Concept Instruction

A growing number of programs make an effort to offer conceptual instruction, often using real-world contexts to illustrate mathematical ideas. Using problem-solving situations, specific concepts are developed in a guided manner to support reasoning and sense making.

What is most often missing in instructional applications is a way to make the mathematics problem based on something that will engage students fully in the conceptual activity. Often when students work on a computer, there is little opportunity for discourse, conjecture, or original ideas. Additionally, some classrooms are outfitted with interactive whiteboards, but the teacher controls the program on the large display screen, with the class watching. Some software even presents concepts in such a fashion as to remove learners from thinking and constructing their own understanding. When prevented from direct contact with digital tools, just as with physical resources, students' understanding can suffer. Some applications are best used when one student controls the program on a large display screen with the class engaged in teacher-guided discussion and analysis. In this way, the teacher and/or students can pose questions and entertain discussion that is simply not possible without the aid of technology. The key is that technology should be used strategically by both the teacher and her students to improve understanding, promote engagement, and increase mathematical proficiency (NCTM, 2008b).

Problem Solving

With the current focus on problem solving, more digital publishers purport to teach students to solve problems. But problem solving is not the same as solving problems. The *Thinkport* interactives (www.thinkport.org/Classroom/math.tp) demonstrate good examples of problem solving through gaming simulations. Here the problems are not typical story problems awaiting a computation but more thoughtful simulations set in real and engaging contexts.

Dreambox Learning (www.dreambox.com) provides an adaptive, individualized program for K–3 students that enables teachers and parents to track student progress on curriculum aligned with the *Common Core State Standards* and NCTM's *Curriculum Focal Points*. Innovative tools such as the Open Number Line, Snap Blocks (algebraic thinking), Match and Make (number patterns and computation), and Quick Images (subitizing and cardinality), with corresponding lessons, are available.

Drill and Reinforcement

Drill programs give students practice with skills that are assumed to have been previously taught. In general, a drill program poses questions that are answered directly or by selecting from a multiple-choice list. Many of these programs are set in gaming formats that make them exciting for students who like video games.

Drill programs evaluate responses immediately. How they respond to the first or second incorrect answer is one important distinguishing feature. At one extreme, the answer is simply recorded as wrong with multiple opportunities to correct it. At the other extreme, the program may branch to an explanation of the correct response. Others may provide hints or supply a visual model to help with the task. Some programs also offer record-keeping features for the teacher to keep track of individual students' progress and/or build specific learning pathways based on the students' correct and incorrect responses.

One feature worth mentioning is differentiated drill, such as is found in *FASTT Math* (Tom Snyder Productions, www.tomsnyder.com/fasttmath) and *First in Math*® (Suntex International, www.firstinmath.com). The *FASTT Math* (Fluency and Automaticity through Systematic Teaching with Technology) program works to help all students develop fluency with math facts. In short sessions that are customized for individual learners, the software automatically differentiates instruction based on each student's previous performance. *First in Math* offers students a self-paced approach to practicing basic math skills and complex problem-solving tasks. Both applications provide students with the opportunity to earn electronic incentives and move on to more difficult exercises.

Guidelines for Selecting and Using Digital Resources

There is so much digital content available for mathematics today. Some commercially published digital resources can be expensive, so free open-source content should be used whenever possible. Even though many Internet-based tools are free to use, schools must still provide for Internet access and the appropriate hardware devices. In either case, it is important to make informed decisions when investing limited funds.

Guidelines for Using Digital Content

How digital content is used in mathematics instruction will vary considerably with the topic, the grade level, and the content itself. The following are offered as considerations that you should keep in mind.

- Digital content should contribute to the objectives of the lesson or unit. It should not be used as an add-on or substitute for more accessible approaches.
- For individualized or small-group use, provide specific instructions for using the resource, and provide time for students to freely explore or practice.
- Combine online activities with offline computer activities (e.g., collect measurement data in the classroom to enter into an online spreadsheet).
- Create a management plan for using the digital content. This could include a schedule for use (e.g., during centers, during small-group work) and a way to assess the effectiveness of the resource use. Although some programs include a way to keep track of student performance, you may need to determine whether the tool is effectively meeting the objectives of the lesson or unit.

How to Select Appropriate Digital Content

The most important requirements for selecting digital resources are to be well informed about the content and to evaluate its merits in an objective manner.

Gathering Information. One of the best sources of information about digital resources is the review section of NCTM journals or other journals that you respect. Many websites offer reviews on both commercially available digital resources and Internet-based tools. The Math Forum's Math Tools (Drexel University), found at http://mathforum .org, is one such site.

One important consideration is whether the digital content is accessible for all students, including individuals with disabilities. Can the text be enlarged or highlighted as it is read aloud? Are the graphics easily recognizable, containing mouse-overs (where the action is written or spoken as the mouse is moved over the image), and not dependent on color for meaning? Can the software be used with a keyboard instead of a mouse? All these questions are derived from the universal design principles defined at www.cast .org/udl/index.html.

TechMatrix at www.techmatrix.org "is a powerful tool for finding educational and assistive technology products for students with special needs" (National Center for Technology Innovation, 2010). Select mathematics under the heading "Content Area" and take a look at research-based reports related to the use of technology for students who struggle, professional development resources, and the "Ask the Tech Expert Q&A" section.

When selecting any technology tool or digital resource, it is important to evaluate it appropriately. Try first to get a preview or at least a demonstration version. Take advantage of any offer for free 30-day trial access. Before purchasing, try the digital resource with students in the grade that will be using it. Remember, it is the mathematics content you are interested in, not the game the students might be playing.

Criteria. Think about the following points as you review digital resources before purchasing or using them in your classroom. (Also see the rubric in Field Experience 5.2 in the *Field Experience Guide*.)

- How will students be challenged to learn better than opportunities without the digital access? Don't select or use a digital tool just to put your students on the computer. Go past the clever graphics and the games and focus on what students will be learning.
- How are students likely to be engaged with the *content* (not the frills)? Remember that student reflective thought is the most significant factor in effective instruction. Is the mathematics presented so that it is problematic for the student?
- How easy is the tool or resource to use? There should not be so much tedium in using the resource that attention is diverted from the content or students become frustrated.
- How does the tool or resource develop knowledge that supports conceptual understanding? In practice programs, how are wrong answers handled? Are the models or explanations going to enhance student understanding?
- What controls and assessments are provided to the teacher? Are there options that can be turned on and off (e.g., sound, types of feedback or help, levels of difficulty)? Is there a provision for record keeping so that you will know what progress individual students have made?
- Are high-quality user guides or professional development services available? Minimally, the support provided should clearly state how the resource is to operate and provide troubleshooting.
- Is the digital resource equitable in its consideration of gender and culture?
- What is the nature of the licensing agreement? For example, is a site license or district license available? If you purchase a single-user software package, it is not legal to install the software on multiple computers.
- Be sure that the digital application will run on the computers at your school. The description of system requirements should indicate the compatible platform(s)

(Windows/Macintosh) and the version of the required operating systems. School districts usually have a technology review process to address software, hardware, and network compatibility requirements.

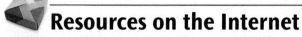

Resources on the Internet

In addition to access to Web-based applications, or applets, the Internet is a wellspring of information. Instead of using a standard search engine to find mathematics-related information, it is sometimes better to have some places to begin. Several good websites will usually provide more links to other sites than you will have time to search. One source for good websites is this book. At the end of every chapter, you will find a list of Web-based resources. Although a brief description accompanies each listing, check these out yourself—websites are frequently modified. The types of resources you can expect to find include professional information, teacher resources, digital tools, and open-source applications.

How to Select Internet Resources

The massive amount of information available on the Internet must be sifted through for accuracy and sorted by quality when you plan instruction or when the students in your class gather information or research a mathematics topic. For example, identifying a mathematics lesson plan on the Internet does not ensure that it is effective, as anyone can publish any idea they have on the Web. To use the Web as a teaching toolbox for locating successful mathematics tasks, motivating enrichment activities, or supportive strategies to assist struggling learners, it is better to go to trustworthy, high-quality websites than merely to plug a few key words into available search engines. We suggest that you add the end-of-chapter sites in this book to your computer's "bookmarks/favorites" and go to them as a first-level source of support. If you choose to explore Web pages, Web logs (blogs), or wikis (collaboratively created and updated Web pages) more broadly, take the elements enumerated in Table 7.2 into consideration. These criteria are critical for your use as a discerning educator and can be adapted or simplified for your students as they evaluate material on the Web. The main topics are adapted from a group of considerations suggested by A. Smith (1997).

Emerging Technologies

Emerging technologies refers to the ever-changing landscape of technological tools and advances. In our increasingly technological society, we must help students explore the latest technology-enabled tools with a curious mind and a reasoned approach to learning about the innovation.

Electronic Textbooks (e-Textbooks). The tight funding in schools, coupled with the success of e-readers such as Amazon's Kindle and Barnes and Noble's NOOK and digital tablets such as Apple's iPad, have pressured some schools and districts to reconsider their approach to textbook adoption. This, in turn, has forced textbook publishers to deliver programs that can be customized for districts and viewed using digital devices. Advantages to schools using e-textbooks include integrated formative assessment tools, enhanced and updated lessons using digital media, and the ability to access/store content for multiple disciplines on one device. Challenges include the costs associated with providing mobile hardware access to each student and the need for curriculum redesign, staff training, and improved networking and infrastructure stability (Fey, Hollenbeck, & Wray, 2010)

Pencasts. The Smartpen (available from Livescribe) allows students and teachers to easily capture written representations and verbal recordings and make them accessible to others via electronic media, including online and pencast PDF formats. Users need the Livescribe Smartpen, the dot paper, and a computer with which to sync pencasts. Students can revisit and share the animated Smartpen recording on a computer or handheld device/tablet such as the iPod, iPhone, or iPad.

Digital Gaming. Some experts agree that digital gaming is the direction that online educational websites are headed. Considering that many young students' first encounters with technology are digital games they played as toddlers, new games can be a familiar and attractive means to support mathematics learning. Just as in other video games, these mathematics games require resolve, concentration, and the use of a variety of strategies, imagination, and creativity to solve complex problems. Through interactive virtual worlds, students can use what they know to learn new concepts. For example, Maryland Public Television's *Thinkport* site is a leader in developing innovative websites to support instruction (www.thinkport.org/technology/learningwithgames/default.tp). One of their digital games, "Lure of the Labyrinth" (http://labyrinth.thinkport.org) is a higher-level activity geared toward middle school mathematics students. Aligned with NCTM standards, "Labyrinth" engages students in a storyline that develops critical thinking on proportionality, variables and equations, and numbers and operations. Gamers learn from experience and are the "experts" in charge of their own failure or success. As the game keeps track of progress, students can get just-in-time help when needed. If you click on "For Educators," you get a user-friendly explanation of the game as well as background on gaming, lesson plans, classroom management strategies, and the mathematics standards connection chart.

TABLE 7.2

	EVALUATING RESOURCES ON THE INTERNET		
	Criteria	**Justification**	**Evidence/Verification**
Authority	• The page should identify authors and their qualifications. • The site should be associated with a reputable educational institution or organization.	• Anyone can publish pages on the Web. You want to be sure that the information is from a reliable source and is of high quality.	• Contact information for the author or organization is easily available. Is there a link to the organization's home page? • Do the authors establish their expertise? • Use www.whois.net, a domain research service, to identify the author of the site. • Is the URL domain .org, .edu, .gov, .net, or .com?
Content	• The site should match topic of interest. • The materials should add depth to your information.	• The information should be useful facts rather than opinions. • The text should be actual information from an expert and not paraphrased from another site.	• Is it a list of links to other sites? • Are the statements verified by footnotes and research? • Do the authors indicate criteria for including information?
Objectivity	• The site should not reflect a biased point of view. • Authors should present facts and not try to sway readers.	• Websites can try to influence the readers rather than provide independent and evenhanded information sources	• Are there advertisements or sponsors either on the page or linked to the page? • Does the author discuss multiple theories or points of view?
Accuracy	• Information should be free of errors. • Information should be verified by reviewers or fact-checkers.	• Websites can be published without reviewers or accuracy checks.	• Does the page contain obvious errors in grammar, spelling, or mathematics? • Are original sources clearly documented in a list of references? • Can the information be cross-checked through another source? • Are charts, graphs, or statistical information labeled clearly?
Currency	• The site should be current and frequently revised.	• Information is changing so rapidly that pages that are not maintained and up to date cannot provide the reliable information needed. • Currency is a key advantage of the Web over print sources. If there is no evidence of currency, the site loses its potential to add to knowledge in the field.	• Look for dates and updates for the page. • Links should be current and not lead to dead sites. • References should include recent citations. • Photos and videos should be up-to-date (unless related to a historical topic).
Audience	• The site's target (i.e., whether it is for your own use or the potential use of students in your classroom) should be clear. • The site should detail whether it is a self-created site or has been created by others. • The site should be accessible by all learners, particularly those with disabilities.	• In education, the audience may be students, families, teachers, or administrators. Presenting information for a well-defined audience is critical.	• Check for suggested grade levels or ages. • Check to see that content and hyperlinks to other sites are free of offensive material (including advertisements). • Does the site allow for easy use through menus or search features that help students find information? • What is the reading level of the narrative? • Are there options for students with disabilities? Do they adhere to the principles of universal design by, for example, considering students with visual impairments (by using increased font size, synthesized speech, or a screen reader) or students with hearing impairments (by including captions for video or audio materials)? See www.udlcenter.org to learn more.

RESOURCES *for Chapter 7*

RECOMMENDED READINGS

Articles

Suh, J. M., Johnston, C. J., & Douglas, J. (2008). Enhancing mathematical learning in a technology-rich environment. *Teaching Mathematics (15)*4, 235–241.

The authors share considerations for leveraging technology-enabled learning environments by describing the teacher's role and strategies for increasing equity and access for diverse learners. Benefits of virtual manipulative use are also described.

Thompson, T., & Sproule, S. (2005). Calculators for students with special needs. *Teaching Children Mathematics, 11*(7), 391–395.

This excellent argument for the use of calculators for students who have learning problems that affect their mathematical skills can help counter any objections raised by calculator critics. Included is a framework that is easily used to make decisions about when to allow calculator use that is not only appropriate for students with disabilities but also for every student.

Books

Fey, J., Hollenbeck, R., & Wray, J. (2010). Technology and the mathematics curriculum. *NCTM Seventy-Second Yearbook.* Reston, VA: NCTM.

Fey, J., Hollenbeck, R., & Wray, J. (2010). Technology and the teaching of mathematics. *NCTM Seventy-Second Yearbook.* Reston, VA: NCTM.

These two book chapters illustrate how teachers can incorporate the effective use of technology to enhance mathematics learning and support effective teaching.

ONLINE RESOURCES

Annenberg Learner
www.learner.org

This tremendous resource lists free online professional learning activities, including information about all sorts of interesting uses of mathematics in the real world, resources for free and inexpensive materials, and information about funding opportunities.

Center for Implementing Technology in Education (CITEd): Tech Matrix
www.techmatrix.org

CITEd's Tech Matrix is a useful database of technology products that supports instruction in mathematics for students with special needs. Each product evaluation includes a link to the supplier's website.

Illuminations (NCTM)
http://illuminations.nctm.org

This is an incredible site developed by NCTM to provide teaching and learning resources such as lesson ideas and digital tools that are intended to "illuminate" *Principles and Standards for School Mathematics.* Also at this site are multimedia investigations for students and links to video vignettes designed to promote professional reflection. In addition, Calculation Nation allows students to explore mathematics topics while playing games with one another over the Web.

Inside Mathematics
http://insidemathematics.org

This site features examples of innovative teaching methods, insights into student learning, tools for mathematics instruction that teachers and specialists can use immediately, resources to support the *Common Core State Standards*, and video tours of the ideas and materials on the site.

International Society for Technology in Education (ISTE)
www.iste.org

ISTE is the professional organization for educators interested in infusing technology into instruction. It maintains exciting resources for teachers, including website links, professional development, and publications. ISTE's National Educational Technology Standards for students (NETS-S) can be found by clicking the NETS section from the home page. The standards address such topics as creativity and innovation; communication and collaboration; research and information fluency; critical thinking, problem solving, and decision making; digital citizenship; and technology operations and concepts.

The Math Forum
http://mathforum.org

The forum has resources (Math Tools) for both teachers and students. There are suggestions for lessons, puzzles, and activities, plus links to other sites with similar information. There are forums where teachers can talk with other teachers. Two pages accept questions about mathematics from students or teachers (Ask Dr. Math) and about teaching mathematics from teachers (Teacher 2 Teacher).

National Library of Virtual Manipulatives and eNLVM
http://nlvm.usu.edu

This NSF-funded site located at Utah State University contains a huge collection of applets organized by the five content strands of the *Standards* and also by the same four grade bands. The eNLVM section contains online units, customizable student activities, and tools to help teachers develop activities collaboratively.

National Science Digital Library
http://nsdl.org

The NSDL is a portal for education and research on learning in science, technology, engineering, and mathematics (STEM) and features a collection of digital learning objects connected to the *Common Core State Standards.*

REFLECTIONS *on Chapter 7*

WRITING TO LEARN

1. Explain at least three ways that technological tools have affected the mathematics curriculum and how it is taught. Give examples to support your explanation.
2. Describe some of the benefits of using calculators regularly in the mathematics classroom. Which of these seem to you to be the most compelling? What are some of the arguments against using calculators? Answer each of the arguments against calculators as if you were giving a speech at your PTA meeting or arguing for regular use of calculators before your principal.
3. Name at least three features of graphing calculators that support the improvement of mathematics learning in the middle grades.
4. What are some criteria that seem most important to you when selecting digital content?
5. What kind of information can you expect to find on the Internet that would be useful in teaching mathematics? How can you evaluate the quality of that information?
6. What are some of the emerging technologies? How can you be ready for new technologies in the future?

FOR DISCUSSION AND EXPLORATION

1. Talk with some teachers about their use of calculators in the classroom. How do they make the decision as to when to use them? Read the NCTM position statement on calculators. How do the reasons given by the teachers you talked with compare to the NCTM position?
2. Check out at least three of the websites suggested in the Online Resources section. Be sure to follow some of the links to other sites. Create your own "top ten" to bookmark as favorites on your computer.
3. Explore three or four applets from one or more of the sites listed in the Online Resources section. Select one and try it with students. Teach a lesson that incorporates the applet as either a teacher tool or student activity.

MyEducationLab™

Go to the MyEducationLab (www.myeducationlab.com) for Math Methods and familiarize yourself with the content. Much of the site content is organized topically. The topics include all of the following to support your learning in the course:

- Learning outcomes for important mathematics methods course topics aligned with the national standards
- Assignments and Activities, tied to these learning outcomes and standards, that can help you more deeply understand course content
- Building Teaching Skills and Dispositions learning units that allow you to apply and practice your understanding of the core mathematics content and teaching skills

Your instructor has a correlation guide that aligns the exercises on the topical portion of the site with your book's chapters.

On MyEducationLab you will also find book-specific resources including Blackline Masters, Expanded Lesson Activities, and Artifact Analysis Activities.

Field Experience Guide
CONNECTIONS

Technology is the focus of Chapter 5 of the *Field Experience Guide*. Projects and teaching opportunities in this section focus on the role of technology in supporting student learning. For example, in FEG 5.4 you develop a learning center involving the use of a calculator or computer. Several of the Expanded Lessons in Chapter 9—such as FEG 9.22, "Bar Graphs to Circle Graphs," and FEG 9.19, "Triangle Midsegments"—lend themselves to the use of technology.

Chapter 8
Developing Early Number Concepts and Number Sense

Young children enter school with many ideas about number. These ideas should be built upon as we work with them to develop new relationships. It is sad to see the large number of students in grades 4, 5, and beyond who essentially know little more about number than how to count. It takes time and a variety of experiences for children to develop a full understanding of number that will grow into more advanced number-related concepts. This chapter emphasizes the development of number ideas for numbers up to about 20. These foundational ideas can all be extended to larger numbers, operations, basic facts, and computation.

BIG IDEAS

1. Counting tells how many things are in a set. When counting a set of objects, the last word in the counting sequence names the quantity.

2. Numbers are related through comparisons of quantities including greater than and less than relationships. These comparisons are made through one-to-one correspondence of objects in sets. The number 7, for example, is more than 4, is two less than 9, is composed of 3 and 4, is three away from 10, and can be quickly recognized in several patterns of dots. These ideas extend to composing and decomposing larger numbers such as 17, 57, and 370.

3. Number concepts are intimately tied to operations with numbers based on situations in the world around us. Application of number relationships to problem solving marks the beginning of making sense of the world in a mathematical manner.

Mathematics CONTENT CONNECTIONS

Early number development is related to other mathematics curriculum in two ways: content that enhances the development of number (measurement, data, operations) and content directly affected by how well early number concepts have been developed (basic facts, place value, and computation).

◆ **Operations** (Chapter 9): As children solve story problems for any of the four operations, they count on, count back, make and count groups, and make comparisons. In the process, they form new relationships and methods of working with numbers.

◆ **Measurement** (Chapter 19): Selecting an appropriate unit and then determining measures of length, area, size, or weight is an important use of number. Measurement involves the counting and comparing of quantities found in the world in which the child lives.

◆ **Data** (Chapter 21): Data analysis involves counts and comparisons to both aid in developing number and connecting it to real-world situations. Comparing bar lengths on a bar graph helps young students compare quantities through an organized format.

◆ **Basic Facts** (Chapter 10): A rich and thorough development of number relationships is a critical foundation for mastering basic facts. Otherwise, facts are rotely memorized and easily forgotten. With knowledge of number relationships, facts that are forgotten can be easily constructed.

◆ **Place Value and Computation** (Chapters 11, 12, and 13): Ideas that contribute to procedural fluency and flexibility in computation are extensions of how numbers are related to 10 and how numbers can be taken apart (decomposed) and recombined (composed).

Promoting Good Beginnings

In 2007, NCTM produced a position statement emphasizing that all children need an early start in learning mathematics. This emphasis on readiness aligns with the recent findings of the National Mathematics Advisory Panel (2008) and the National Research Council (NRC) (2009). This statement suggests several research-based recommendations to help teachers develop high-quality learning activities for children aged 3 to 6:

1. Enhance children's natural interest in mathematics and their instinct to use it to make sense of their world.
2. Build on children's experience and knowledge, taking advantage of familiar contexts.
3. Base mathematics curriculum and teaching practices on a solid understanding of both mathematics and child development.
4. Use formal and informal experiences in the curriculum and teaching practices to strengthen children's problem-solving and reasoning processes.
5. Provide opportunities for children to explain their thinking as they interact with mathematics in deep and sustained ways.
6. Support children's learning by thoughtfully and continually assessing children's mathematical knowledge, skills, and strategies.

 PAUSE and REFLECT

Although all of these recommendations are critical, which two are most important for your own professional growth? ●

In 2009, the NRC established the Committee on Early Childhood Mathematics to examine research on how mathematics is taught and learned in children's early years. Unfortunately, they found a lack of opportunities for learning mathematics in early childhood settings, especially as compared to opportunities in language and literacy development. The studies showed that young children who are starting out behind their peers, such as those growing up in disadvantaged circumstances, do not catch up. They found that what a kindergartner or first-grade child knows about mathematics is a predictor of not only their math achievement (National Mathematics Advisory Panel, 2008) but also their reading achievement.

This NRC committee also identified the foundational mathematics content in number for early learners, grouping it into three core areas: number, relations, and operations. This chapter will begin with the first two core areas; then Chapter 9 will provide an intensive focus on the meaning of the operations. Please note that as you develop students' initial abilities in counting, the conversations about number relationships begin. Therefore, the activities and concepts in this chapter are not sequential but coexist in a rich environment of mathematical experiences where students see connections between and among numbers.

The Number Core: Quantity, Counting, and Knowing How Many

Families help children count their fingers, toys, people at the table, and other small sets of objects. Questions concerning "Who has more?" or "Are there enough?" are part of the daily lives of children as young as 2 or 3 years old. Considerable evidence indicates that these children have beginning understandings of the concepts of number and counting (Baroody, Li, & Lai, 2008; Clements & Sarama 2009; Gelman & Gallistel, 1978). We therefore include abundant activities to support the different experiences that young children and older students with disabilities need to gain a full understanding of number concepts.

Quantity and the Ability to Subitize

Children explore quantity before they can count. They can identify which cup is bigger or which plate of potato chips has more chips. Soon they need to attach an amount to the quantities to explore them in greater depth. When you look at an amount of objects, sometimes you are able to just "see" how many are there, particularly for a small group. For example, when you roll a die and know that it is five without counting the dots, that ability to "just see it" is called *subitizing*. There are times when you are able to do this for even larger amounts, when you break dots in a pattern of ten by seeing five in one row and mentally doubling it to get a total of 10. "Subitizing is a fundamental skill in the development of students' understanding of number" (Baroody, 1987, p. 115). Subitizing is a complex skill that needs to be developed and practiced through experiences with patterned sets.

Many children learn to recognize patterned sets of dots on standard dice due to the many games they have played. Similar instant recognition (subitizing) can be developed for other patterns (see Figure 8.1). Naming these amounts immediately without counting aids in "counting on" (from a known patterned set) or learning combinations of numbers

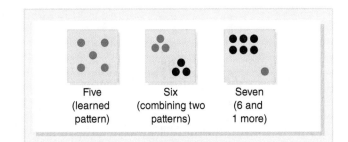

| Five (learned pattern) | Six (combining two patterns) | Seven (6 and 1 more) |

FIGURE 8.1 Recognizing a patterned set.

(seeing a pattern set of two known smaller patterns). Please note that many textbooks present illustrations of small quantities that are less than helpful in encouraging subitizing, so use objects organized in patterns that are symmetric before moving to more challenging images.

Good materials to use in pattern recognition activities include a set of dot plates. These can be made using paper plates and the peel-off dots available in office supply stores. A collection of patterns is shown in Figure 8.2. Note that some patterns are combinations of two smaller patterns or a pattern with one or two additional dots. These should be made in two colors to support early learners. Keep the patterns compact and organized. If the dots are too spread out, the patterns are hard to identify. Explore the activities "Speedy Pictures 1" and "Speedy Pictures 2" on the website www.fi.uu.nl/rekenweb/en, where students can practice

subitizing and recognizing patterned sets using flashed images of fingers, dice, beads on a frame, or eggs in a carton holding 10.

Activity 8.1

STUDENTS *with* SPECIAL NEEDS

Learning Patterns

To introduce patterns, provide each student with 10 counters and a piece of paper or a paper plate as a mat. Hold up a dot plate for about five seconds. "Make the pattern you saw on the plate using the counters on the mat. How many dots did you see? What did the pattern look like?" Spend time discussing the configuration of the pattern and how many dots. Then show the plate so they can self-check. Do this with a few new patterns each day. To modify this activity for students with disabilities, you may need to give the student a small selection of dot plates. Then instead of creating the pattern with counters, they find the matching plate.

Activity 8.2

Dot Plate Flash

Hold up a dot plate for one to three seconds. "How many dots did you see? What did the pattern look like?" Children like to see how quickly they can recognize the pattern and say how many dots. Include easy patterns first and then add more dots as their confidence builds. Students can also flash dot plates to each other as a workstation activity.

 STOP

Instant recognition activities with dot plates are exciting and can be done in 5 minutes at any time of day and at any time of year. ●

Early Counting

Meaningful counting activities begin when children are 3 and 4 years of age, but by the end of kindergarten (CCSSO, 2010), children should be able to count to 100. The counting process cannot be forced, so for children to have an understanding of counting, they must construct this idea. Only the counting sequence of number words is a rote procedure. The *meaning* attached to counting is the key conceptual idea on which all other number concepts are developed.

The Development of Verbal Counting Skills. Counting is a complex task with typical developmental progressions found in a path called a *learning trajectory* (Clements and Sarama, 2009). This trajectory can help you see what the

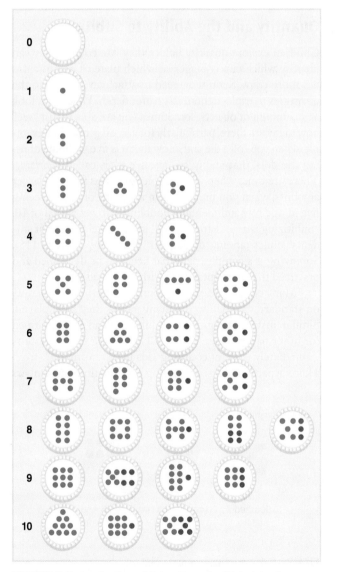

FIGURE 8.2 A collection of dot patterns for "dot plates."

TABLE 8.1

LEARNING TRAJECTORY FOR COUNTING	
Levels of Thinking	**Characteristics**
Precounter	Here the child has no verbal counting ability. A young child looking at three balls will answer "ball" when asked how many. The child does not associate a number word with a quantity.
Reciter	This child verbally counts using number words, but not always in the right order. Sometimes they say more numbers than they have objects to count, skip objects, or repeat the same number.
Corresponder	A child at this level can make a one-to-one correspondence with numbers and objects, stating one number per object. If asked "How many?" at the end of the count, they may have to recount to answer.
Counter	This student can accurately count objects in an organized display (in a line, for example) and can answer "How many?" accurately by giving the last number counted (this is called *cardinality*). They may be able to write the matching numeral and may be able to say the number just after or before a number by counting up from 1.
Producer	A student at this level can count out objects to a certain number. If asked to give you five blocks, they can show you that amount.
Counter and Producer	A child who combines the two previous levels can count out objects, tell how many are in a group, remember which objects are counted and which are not, and respond to random arrangements. They begin to separate tens and ones, like 23 is 20 and 3 more.
Counter Backwards	A child at this level can count backward by removing objects one by one or just verbally as in a "countdown."
Counter from Any Number	This child can count up starting from numbers other than one. They are also able to immediately state the number before and after a given number.
Skip Counter	Here the child can skip-count with understanding by a group of a given number—tens, fives, twos, etc.

Source: Based on Clements and Sarama (2009).

overarching goals of counting are and how you can help a child move to more sophisticated levels of thinking. Table 8.1 is adapted from their research and is a selection of levels and sublevels identified as benchmarks (pp. 30–41).

As a starting point, verbal counting has at least two separate skills. First, a child must be able to produce the standard list of counting words in order: "One, two, three, four. . . ." Second, a child must be able to connect this sequence in a one-to-one correspondence with the objects in the set being counted. Each object must get one and only one count. As part of these skills, students should recognize that each counting number identifies a quantity that is one more than the previous number and that the new quantity is embedded in the previous quantity (see Figure 8.3). This knowledge will be helpful later in breaking numbers apart.

Experience and guidance are major factors in the development of these counting skills. Many children come to kindergarten able to count sets of 10 or beyond. At the same time, children with weak background knowledge may require additional practice. The size and arrangement of the set are also factors related to success in counting. Obviously, longer number strings require more practice to learn. The first 12 counting words involve no pattern or repetition, and many children do not easily recognize a pattern in the teens. Children learning the skills of counting—that is matching oral number words with objects—should be given sets of blocks or counters that they can move or pictures of sets that are arranged in an organized pattern for easy counting.

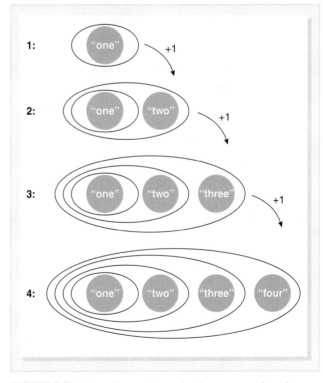

FIGURE 8.3 In counting, each number is one more than the previous number.

Source: National Research Council. (2009). *Mathematics Learning in Early Childhood: Paths Toward Excellence and Equity*, p. 27. Reprinted with permission from the National Academy of Sciences, courtesy of the National Academies Press, Washington, DC.

Meaning Attached to the Counting of Objects. Fosnot and Dolk (2001) make it clear that an understanding of cardinality and the connection to counting is not a simple task for 4-year-olds. Children will learn *how* to count (matching counting words with objects) before they understand that the last count word indicates the *amount* of the set or the set's *cardinality* as shown in Figure 8.4. Children who have made this connection are said to have the *cardinality principle*, which is a refinement of their early ideas about quantity. Most, but certainly not all, children by age $4\frac{1}{2}$ have made this connection (Fosnot & Dolk, 2001).

For many students, especially students with disabilities, it is important to have a plan for counting. The children should count objects from left to right, move the objects as they count or point and touch them as they say each number out loud. Consistently ask, "How many do you have in all?" at the end of each count.

 Young children who can count orally may not have attached meaning to their counts. Here is a **diagnostic interview** that will help you assess a child's thinking. Show a child a card with five to nine large dots in a row so that they can be easily counted. Ask the child to count the dots. If the count is accurate, ask, "How many dots are on the card?" Early on, many children will need to count again. One indication the child is beginning to grasp the meaning of counting will be that they do not need to recount. Now ask the child, "Please get the same number of counters as there are dots on the card." Here is a sequence of indicators to watch for, listed in order from a child who does not attach meaning to the count to one who is using counting as a tool:

- Does the child not count but instead make a similar pattern with the counters?
- Will the child recount?
- Does the child place the counters in a one-to-one correspondence with the dots?
- Or does the child count the dots and retrieve the correct number of counters?
- Is the child confident that there is the same number of counters as dots?

As the child shows competence with patterned sets, move to counting random dot patterns. ■

FIGURE 8.4 The student has learned cardinality if, after counting five objects, he or she can answer, "How many do you have in all?" with "Five."

 STOP

To develop the full understanding of counting, engage children in games or activities that involve counts and comparisons. The following is a suggestion. ●

 Activity 8.3

Fill the Tower

STUDENTS with SPECIAL NEEDS

Create a game board with four "towers." Each tower is a column of twelve 1-inch squares with a star at the top. Children take turns rolling a die and collecting the indicated number of counters. They then place these counters on one of the towers. The object is to fill all of the towers with counters. As an option, require that the towers be filled exactly so that a roll of 5 cannot be used to fill four empty squares. A modification for students with disabilities would be to use a die with only 2 or 3 on it. You can increase the number choices on the die when you have evidence that the student is counting accurately.

This game provides opportunities for you to talk with children about number and assess their thinking. Watch how they count the dots on the die. Ask, "How do you know you have the right number of counters?" and "How many counters did you put in the tower? How many more do you need to fill the tower?"

Regular classroom tasks, such as counting how many napkins are needed at snack time, are additional opportunities for children to learn about number and for teachers to listen to students' ideas.

Thinking about Zero. Young children need to discover the number zero (Clements & Sarama, 2009). Surprisingly it is not a concept that is easily grasped without intentionally building understanding. Three- and four-year-olds can begin to use the word *zero* and the numeral 0 to symbolize there are no objects in the set. With the dot plates discussed previously (see Figure 8.2), use the zero plate to formally discuss what it means that there is no dot on the plate. We find that because early counting often involves touching an object, zero is sometimes not included in the count. Zero is one of the most important digits in the base-ten system, and purposeful conversations about it are essential. Activities 8.1, 8.2, and 8.11 are useful in exploring the number zero.

Numeral Writing and Recognition

Kindergartners are expected to write numbers up to 20 (CCSSO, 2010). Helping children read and write the 10 single-digit numerals is similar to teaching them to read and write letters of the alphabet. Neither has anything to do with number concepts. Numeral writing does not have to be repetitious practice, but it can be engaging. For example, ask children to trace over pages of numerals, make numerals from clay, trace them in shaving cream on their desks, write them on the board or in the air, and so on.

The calculator is a good instructional tool for numeral recognition. Early calculator activities can also help develop familiarity with other symbols on the keypad so that more complex activities are possible. While these numerals may be familiar to students from other cultures, the naming of the numerals is not. Activities that move between objects, numerals, and number names are important for all learners, particularly English language learners.

Activity 8.4

Number Tubs

Give each child four to six closed margarine tubs, each containing a different number of pennies or counters. (Foam counters work well.) The tubs are then mixed up. The teacher asks the child to find the tub with a particular number of counters. After the child looks inside and counts to find the correct tub, a new twist can be added. You can allow them to mark the tubs with sticky notes to show what is inside. At first, children may make four dots to show four counters, but eventually, with your encouragement, they will write the numeral. Then the students recognize the value of writing the numbers in a form that all can understand and that doesn't require recounting.

Activity 8.5

STUDENTS with SPECIAL NEEDS

Find and Press

Give each child a calculator and ask them to press the clear key. Say a number, and have children press that number on the calculator. If you have a digital projector, you can show the children the correct key so that they can confirm their responses, or you can write the number on the board for children to self-check. Begin with single numbers. Later, progress to two or three numbers called out in succession. For example, call, "Three, seven, one." Children press the complete string of numbers as called. Some children with disabilities may need calculators with large keys spaced apart so that they can enter a number. For students with limited mobility, there is a nice online four function calculator at www.online-calculator.com/full-screen-calculator.

Perhaps the most common preschool and kindergarten exercises have children match sets with numerals. Children are given pictured sets (e.g., frogs) and asked to write or match the number that tells how many. Alternatively, they may be given a number and told to make a set with that many objects. When children are successful with these matching-numeral-to-sets activities, it is time to move on to more advanced concepts, like counting on and counting back.

Counting On and Counting Back

Although the forward sequence of numbers is relatively familiar to most young children, counting on from a particular number and counting back are often difficult skills. In particular, for English language learners counting back is more difficult (try counting back in a second language you have learned). Frequent short practice sessions are recommended.

Activity 8.6

Up and Back Counting

Counting up to and back from a target number in a rhythmic fashion is an important counting exercise. For example, line up five children and five chairs in front of the room. As the whole class counts from 1 to 5, the children sit down one at a time. When the target number, 5, is reached, it is repeated; the child who sat on 5 now stands, and the count goes back to 1. As the count goes back, the children stand up one at a time, and so on, "1, 2, 3, 4, 5, 5, 4, 3, 2, 1, 1, 2, . . ." Children find exercises such as this both fun and challenging. Any rhythmic movement (clapping, turning around) can be used as the count goes up and back.

This last activity is designed to help students become fluent with the number-word sequence in both forward and reverse order and to begin counts with numbers other than 1. Although not easy for young students, these activities do not yet address the meaning of counting on or counting back. Children will later realize that counting on is adding and counting backward is subtracting. Fosnot and Dolk (2001) describe the ability to count on as a "landmark" on the path to number sense.

Activity 8.7

Counting On with Counters

Give each child a collection of 10 or 12 counters that the children line up left to right. Tell them to count four counters and push them under their left hands or place them in a cup (see Figure 8.5). Then say, "Point to your hand. How many are there?" (Four.) "So let's count like this: fooour . . . (slowly, pointing to their hand), five, six. . . ." Repeat with other numbers under the hand.

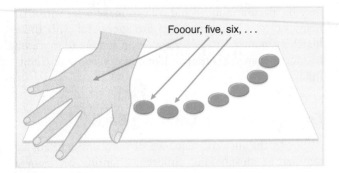

Fooour, five, six, . . .

FIGURE 8.5 Counting on: "Hide four. Count, starting from the number of counters hidden."

Activity **8.8**

STUDENTS *with* SPECIAL NEEDS

Real Counting On

This game for two requires a deck of cards (numbers 1 to 7), a die, a paper cup, and counters. The first player turns over the top number card and places the indicated number of counters in the cup. The card is placed next to the cup as a reminder of how many are inside. The second player rolls the die and places that many counters next to the cup (see Figure 8.6). Together they decide how many counters in all. A record sheet with columns for "In the Cup," "On the Side," and "In All" will support students' organization. Increase the highest number in the card deck when the children have mastered the smaller numbers. For students with disabilities, you may want to just use a single number in the cup (such as 5) and have them just count on from the number in the cup until they are fluent with that number.

Observe how children determine the total amounts in Activity 8.8. Children who are not yet counting on may empty the counters from the cup or will count up from one without emptying the counters. As children continue to

play, they will eventually count on as that strategy becomes meaningful and useful.

The Relations Core: More Than, Less Than, and Equal To

The concepts of "more," "less," and "same" are basic relationships contributing to the overall concept of number. Almost any child entering kindergarten can choose the set that is *more* if presented with two sets that are quite obviously different in number. In fact, Baroody (1987) states, "A child unable to use 'more' in this intuitive manner is at considerable educational risk" (p. 29). Classroom activities should help children build on and refine this basic notion that links to their ability to count.

Though the concept of less is logically related to the concept of more (selecting the set with more is the same as *not* selecting the set with less), the word *less* proves to be more difficult for children than *more*. A possible explanation is that children have many opportunities to use the word *more* but have limited exposure to the word *less*. To help children with the concept of less, frequently pair it with *more* and make a conscious effort to ask "Which is less?" questions as well as "Which is more?" questions. For example, suppose that your class correctly selected the set that has more from the two sets given. Immediately follow with "Which is less?" In this way, the concept can be connected with the better-known idea and the term *less* can become familiar.

For all three concepts (more/greater than, less/less than, and same/equal to), children should construct sets using counters as well as make comparisons or choices (Which is less?) between two given sets. The following activities should be conducted in a spirit of inquiry accompanied with requests for explanations. "Can you show me how you know this group has less?"

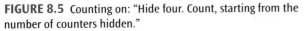

In 🥤	On side	In all
4	3	

FIGURE 8.6 How many in all? How do children count to tell the total? Empty the counters from the cup? Count up from 1 without emptying the counters? Count on?

Activity **8.9**

STUDENTS *with* SPECIAL NEEDS

Make Sets of More/Less/Same

At a workstation, provide about eight cards with pictures of sets of 4 to 12 objects (or use large dot cards); a set of counters; word cards labeled *More, Less,* and *Same;* and paper plates or low boxes to support students with disabilities. Next to each card, have students make three collections of counters: a set that is more than the amount on the card, one that is less, and one that is the same (see Figure 8.7). Start students with disabilities with matching the set that is the same.

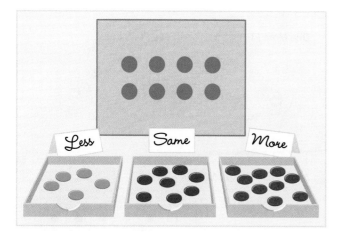

FIGURE 8.7 Making sets that are more, less, and the same.

Activity 8.10

Find the Same Amount

STUDENTS with SPECIAL NEEDS

Give children a collection of cards with sets on them. Dot cards are one option (see Blackline Masters 3–8). Have the children pick any card in the collection and then find another card with the same amount to form a pair. Continue finding other pairs. This activity can be altered to have children find dot cards that are "less" or "more." Some students with disabilities may need a set of counters with a blank ten-frame to help them "make" a pair instead of finding a pair.

Observe children as they do these tasks. (This is also a good opportunity for diagnostic interviews.) Note that some children make comparisons of more or less without assigning numerical values. Children whose number ideas are tied to counting and nothing more will select cards at random and count each dot looking for the same amount. Others will estimate and begin by selecting a card that appears to be the same number of dots. This demonstrates a significantly higher level of understanding. Also observe how the dots are counted. Are the counts made accurately? Is each dot counted only once? Does the child touch the dot? A significant milestone occurs when children recognize small patterned sets without counting.

Activity 8.11

More, Less, or the Same

This activity is for partners or a small group. Use Blackline Master 1 (make four to five of each card) to make a deck of more-or-less cards as shown in Figure 8.8. You will also need a set of number cards (Blackline Master 2) with the numbers 3 to 10 (two each). One child draws a number card and places it

---

face up. That number of counters is put into a cup. Next, another child draws one of the more-or-less cards and places it next to the number card. For the More cards, counters are added to the cup. For the Less cards, counters are removed from the cup. For Zero cards, no change is made. Once the cup has been adjusted, children predict how many counters are now in the cup. The counters are emptied and counted and a new number card is drawn.

"More, Less, or the Same" can also be played with the whole class. The words *more* and *less* can be paired or substituted with *add* and *subtract* to connect these ideas with the arithmetic operations, even if they have not yet been formally introduced.

The calculator can be used to practice relationships of one more than, two more than, one less than, and two less than. Also use it to show the pattern of adding or subtracting zero.

Early Number Sense

Howden (1989) described *number sense* as a "good intuition about numbers and their relationships. It develops gradually as a result of exploring numbers, visualizing them in a variety of contexts, and relating them in ways that are not limited by traditional algorithms" (p. 11). In *Principles and Standards for School Mathematics*, the term *number sense* is used freely throughout the Number and Operations standard.

FIGURE 8.8 Materials to play "More or Less" (see Blackline Master 1).

"As students work with numbers, they gradually develop flexibility in thinking about numbers, which is a hallmark of number sense. . . . Number sense develops as students understand the size of numbers, develop multiple ways of thinking about and representing numbers, use numbers as referents, and develop accurate perceptions about the effects of operations on numbers" (NCTM, 2000, p. 80).

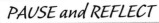 PAUSE and REFLECT

You have begun to see some of the early foundational ideas about number. Stop now and make a list of all of the important ideas that you think children should *know about* the number 8 by the time they finish first grade. (The list could be about any number from, say, 6 to 12.) Put your list aside, and we will revisit your ideas later. ●

The discussion of number sense begins as we look at the relationships and connections children should be making about smaller numbers up to 20. But "good intuition about numbers" does not end with these smaller whole numbers. Children continue to develop number sense as they use numbers in operations, build an understanding of place value, and devise flexible methods of computing and making estimates involving large numbers, fractions, decimals, and percents.

The ideas of early numeracy discussed to this point are the rudimentary aspects of number. Unfortunately, many textbooks move directly from these beginning ideas to addition and subtraction, leaving students with a very limited collection of ideas about number and number relationships to bring to these new topics. The result is that children often continue to count by ones to solve simple story problems and have difficulty mastering basic facts. Early number sense requires significant attention in pre-K–2 programs.

Relationships Between Numbers 1 Through 10

Once children acquire a concept of cardinality and can meaningfully use their counting skills, little more is to be gained from the kinds of counting activities described so far. Also, more relationships beyond the general "more or less" decision must be created for children to develop number sense, a flexible concept of number not completely tied to counting. Figure 8.9 illustrates three types of number relationships that children can and should develop:

- *One and two more, one and two less.* The two-more-than and two-less-than relationships involve more than just the ability to count on two or count back two. Children

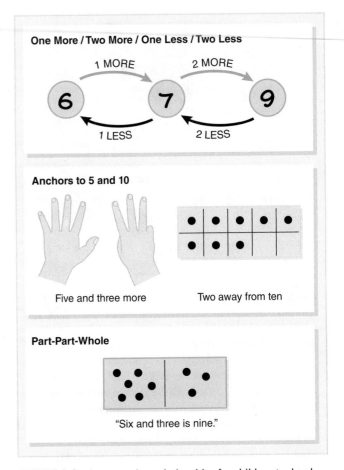

FIGURE 8.9 Three number relationships for children to develop.

should know that 7, for example, is 1 more than 6 and also 2 less than 9.

- *Anchors or "benchmarks" of 5 and 10.* Because 10 plays such a large role in our numeration system and because two fives make up 10, it is very useful to develop relationships for the numbers 1 to 10 connected to the anchors of 5 and 10.
- *Part-part-whole relationships.* To conceptualize a number as being made up of two or more parts is the most important relationship that can be developed about numbers. For example, 7 can be thought of as a set of 3 and a set of 4 or a set of 2 and a set of 5.

The principal tool that children will use as they construct these relationships is the one number tool they possess: counting. Initially, then, you will notice a lot of counting, and you may wonder if you are making progress. Have patience! As children construct new relationships and begin to use more powerful ideas, counting will become less and less necessary.

One and Two More, One and Two Less

When children count, they don't often reflect on the way one number is related to another. Their goal is only to match number words with objects until they reach the end of the count. To learn that 6 and 8 are related by the corresponding relationships of "two more than" and "two less than" requires reflection on these ideas. Counting on (or back) one or two counts is a useful tool in constructing these ideas.

Note that the relationship of "two more than" is significantly different from "comes two counts after." This latter relationship is applied to the string of number words, not to the quantities they represent. A comes-two-after relationship can even be applied to letters of the alphabet as the letter *H* comes two after the letter *F.* However, there is no numeric or quantitative difference between *F* and *H.* The quantity 8 would still be two more than 6 even if there were no number string to count these quantities. It is the numeric relationship you want to develop.

The following activity focuses on the two-more-than relationship and is a good place to begin.

Activity 8.12

Make a Two-More-Than Set

Provide students with six dot cards (Blackline Masters 3–8). Their task is to construct a set of counters that is two more than the set shown on the card. Similarly, spread out eight to ten dot cards, and ask students to find another card for each that is two less than the card shown. (Omit the 1 and 2 cards for two less than, and so on.)

In activities such as 8.12 in which children find a set or make a set, they can also add numeral cards (see Blackline Master 2) to all of the sets involved. Then they can be encouraged to take turns reading the associated number sentence to their partner. If, for example, a set has been made that is two more than a set of four, the child can say the number sentence, "Two more than four is six" or "Six is two more than four." The next activity combines the relationships.

Activity 8.13

A Calculator Two-More-Than Machine

Teach children how to make a two-more-than machine. Press 0 + 2 = . This makes the calculator a two-more-than machine. Now press any number—for example, 5. Children hold their finger over the = key and predict the number that is two more than 5. Then they press = to confirm. If they do not press any of the operation keys (+, −, ×, ÷), the "machine" will continue to perform in this way.

What is really happening in the two-more-than machine is that the calculator "remembers" or stores the last operation,

in this case "+2," and adds that to whatever number is in the window when the = key is pressed. If the child continues to press = , the calculator will continue to count by twos. At any time, a new number can be pressed followed by the equal key. To make a two-less-than machine, press 2 − 2 = . (The first press of 2 is to avoid a negative number.) In the beginning, students may accidentally press operation keys, which change what their calculator is doing. Soon, however, they get the hang of using the calculator as a function machine.

The "two-more-than" calculator will give the number that is two more than any number pressed, including those with two or more digits. The two-more-than relationship should be extended to two-digit numbers as soon as students are exposed to them. One way to do this is to ask for the number that is two more than 7. After getting the correct answer, ask, "What is two more than 37?" and similarly for other numbers that end in 7. When you try this for 8 or 9, expect difficulties and creative responses such as two more than 28 is "twenty-ten." In the first grade, this struggle can generate a "teachable moment." The "More or Less" activity can be extended to larger numbers if no actual counters are used.

Anchoring Numbers to 5 and 10

We want to help children relate a given number to other numbers, specifically 5 and 10. These relationships are especially useful in thinking about various combinations of numbers. For example, in each of the following, consider how the knowledge of 8 as "5 and 3 more" and as "2 away from 10" can play a role: $5 + 3$, $8 + 6$, $8 − 2$, $8 − 3$, $8 − 4$, $13 − 8$. For example, $8 + 6$ may be thought of as $8 + 2 + 4$ ("Up Over 10" strategy). Later similar relationships can be used in the development of mental computation skills on larger numbers such as $68 + 7$.

The most common and perhaps most important model for exploring this relationship is the ten-frame. The ten-frame is simply a 2×5 array in which counters or dots are placed to illustrate numbers (see Figure 8.10). Ten-frames can be drawn on a sheet of paper (see Blackline Master 10). Nothing fancy is required, and each child can have one. There is a nice virtual manipulative of the ten-frame with four associated games that develop counting and addition skills at http://illuminations.nctm.org/activitydetail.aspx?id=75.

For children in pre-K, kindergarten, or early first grade who have not yet explored a ten-frame, it is a good idea to begin with a five-frame. (See a virtual five-frame at NCTM's Illuminations website: http://illuminations.nctm.org/ActivityDetail.aspx?ID=74.) This row of five sections can be drawn on a sheet of paper (or Blackline Master 9 can be used). Provide children with about 10 counters that will fit in the five-frame sections and conduct the following activity.

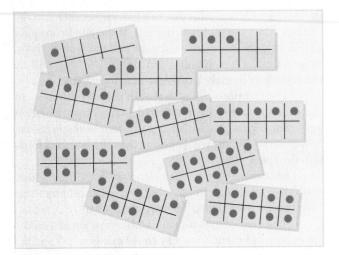

FIGURE 8.10 Ten-frames.

Five-Frame Tell-About

Explain that only one counter is permitted in each section of the five-frame. No other counters are allowed on the five-frame mat. Have children show 3 on their five-frame, as seen in Figure 8.11(a). "What can you tell us about 3 from looking at your mat?" After hearing from several children, try other numbers from 0 to 5. Children may place their counters on the five-frame in any manner. For example, with four counters, a child with two on each end may say, "It has a space in the middle" or "It's two and two." Accept all correct answers. Focus attention on how many more counters are needed to make 5 or how far away from 5 a number is. Next try numbers between 5 and 10. As shown in Figure 8.11(b), numbers greater than 5 are shown with a full five-frame and additional counters on the mat but not in the frame. In discussion, focus attention on these larger numbers as 5 and some more: "Seven is five and two more."

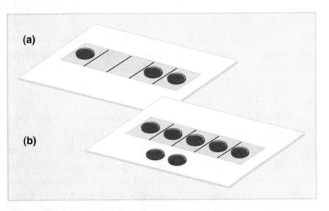

FIGURE 8.11 A five-frame focuses on the 5 anchor. Counters are placed one to a section, and students describe how they see their number in the frame.

Notice that the five-frame focuses on the relationship to 5 as an anchor for numbers and does not anchor numbers to 10. When five-frames have been used for a week or so, introduce ten-frames. Play a ten-frame version of a "Five-Frame Tell-About," but soon introduce the following rule for showing numbers on the ten-frame: *Always fill the top row first, starting on the left, the same way you read. When the top row is full, counters can be placed in the bottom row, also from the left.* This will produce the "standard" way to show numbers on the ten-frame as in Figure 8.10.

For a while, many children will continue to count every counter on their ten-frame. Some will take all counters off and begin each new number from a blank frame. Others will soon learn to adjust numbers by adding on or taking off only what is required, often capitalizing on a row of five without counting. Do not pressure students. With continued practice, all students will grow. How they are using the ten-frame provides you with insights into students' current number concept development; therefore, ten-frame questions can be used as diagnostic interviews.

Crazy Mixed-Up Numbers

ENGLISH LANGUAGE LEARNERS

This activity is adapted from the classic resource *Mathematics Their Way* (Baratta-Lorton, 1976). All children make their ten-frame show the same number. Then the teacher calls out random numbers between 0 and 10. After each number, the children change their ten-frames to show the new number. If working with ELLs, consider saying the number in their native language or writing the number. Children can play this game independently by preparing lists of about 15 "crazy mixed-up numbers." One child plays "teacher" and the rest use the ten-frames.

"Crazy Mixed-Up Numbers" is much more of a problem-solving situation than it may first appear. How do you decide how to change your ten-frame? Some children clear off the entire frame and start over with each new number. Others have learned what each number looks like. To add another dimension, have the children tell, *before changing their ten-frames,* how many more counters need to be added or removed. If, for example, the frames showed 6, and the teacher called out "4," the children would respond, "Subtract!" and then change their ten-frames accordingly. A discussion of how they know what to do is valuable.

Ten-frame flash cards are an important variation of ten-frames and can be made from cardstock (see Blackline Masters 15–16). A set of 20 cards consists of a 0 card, a 10 card, and two each of the numbers 1 to 9. The cards allow for simple practice that reinforces the 5 and 10 anchors as in the following activity.

Activity 8.16

ENGLISH LANGUAGE LEARNERS

Ten-Frame Flash

Flash ten-frame cards to the class or a small group and see how quickly the children can tell how many dots are shown. This activity is fast-paced, takes only a few minutes, can be done at any time, and is a lot of fun. For ELLs, coming up with the English word for the number may take more time, so either pair students with similar language skills, or encourage students to use their preferred language in playing the game.

Important variations of "Ten-Frame Flash" include:

- Saying the number of spaces on the card instead of the number of dots
- Saying one more than the number of dots (or two more, one less, or two less)
- Saying the "10 fact"—for example, "Six and four make ten"
- Adding the flashed card to a card they have at their desk (for challenging advanced learners)

Ten-frame tasks are surprisingly challenging for some students, as there is a lot to keep in their working memory. Students must reflect on the two rows of five, the spaces remaining, and how a particular number is more or less than 5 and how far away from 10. How well students can respond to "Ten-Frame Flash" is a good quick diagnostic assessment of their current number concept level. Consider interviews that include the variations of the activity listed above. Because the distance to 10 is so important, another assessment is to point to a numeral less than 10 and ask, "If this many dots were on a ten-frame, how many blank spaces would there be?" Or you can also simply ask, "If I have seven, how many more do I need to make ten?"

Part-Part-Whole Relationships

 PAUSE and REFLECT

Before reading on, gather eight counters. Count out the set of counters in front of you as if you were a kindergartner. ●

Any child who has learned how to count meaningfully can count out eight objects as you just did. What is significant about the experience is what it did *not* cause you to think about. Nothing in counting a set of eight objects will cause a child to focus on the fact that it could be made of two parts. For example, separate the counters you just set out into two piles and reflect on the combination. It might be 2 and 6, 7 and 1, or 4 and 4. Make a change in your two piles of counters and say the new combination to yourself. Focusing on a quantity in terms of its parts has important implications for developing number sense. A noted researcher in children's number concepts, Resnick (1983),

stated that a major conceptual achievement of young learners is the interpretation of numbers in terms of part and whole relationships.

Basic Ingredients of Part-Part-Whole Activities. Most part-part-whole activities focus on a single number for the entire activity. For example, a pair of children might work on breaking apart or building the number 7 throughout the activity. They can either build (compose) the designated quantity in two or more parts, or else they start with the full amount and separate it into two or more parts (decompose). Kindergarten children will usually begin these activities working on the number 4 or 5. As concepts develop, children can extend to numbers 6 to 12. A wide variety of materials and formats for these activities can help maintain student interest.

When children do these activities, have them say or "read" the parts aloud or write them down on some form of recording sheet (or do both). Reading or writing the combinations serves as a means of encouraging reflective thought focused on the part–whole relationship. Writing can be in the form of drawings, numbers written in blanks (a group of _____ cubes and a group of _____ cubes), or addition equations if these have been introduced ($3 + 5 = 8$ or $8 = 2 + 6$). There is a clear connection between part-part-whole concepts and addition and subtraction ideas.

Part-Part-Whole Activities. The following activity and its variations may be considered the "basic" part-part-whole task.

Activity 8.17

Build It in Parts

Provide children with one type of material, such as connecting cubes or squares of colored paper. The task is to see how many different combinations for a particular number they can make using two parts. (If you wish, you can allow for more than two parts.) Use a context that will be familiar to your students, or consider a piece of children's literature. For example, ask how many different combinations of six hats the peddler in the book *Caps for Sale* (Slobodkina, 1938) can wear, limiting the color choices to two to start. (Note that the book is also available in Spanish for some ELLs.) Each different combination can be displayed on a small mat. Here are just a few ideas, each of which is illustrated in Figure 8.12.

- Use two colors of counters such as lima beans spray painted on one side (also available in plastic).
- Make bars of connecting cubes of two different colors. Keep the colors together.
- Make combinations using two dot strips—strips of cardstock about 1 inch wide with stick-on dots.
- Make combinations of two Cuisenaire rods connected as a train to match a given amount.

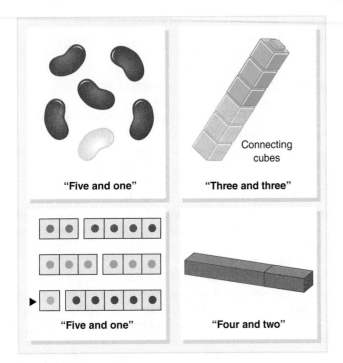

FIGURE 8.12 Assorted materials for building parts of 6.

As you observe students working on the "Build It in Parts" activity, ask them to "read" a number sentence to go with each of their combinations. Encourage students to read their number sentences to each other. Two or three students working together may have quite a large number of combinations, including repeats. Remember, the students are focusing on the combinations.

The following activity is a step toward a more abstract understanding of combinations that make 5 (or other totals). Students can do these mentally or use counters. Allowing options is both a good instructional strategy and a way to see how ready students are for addition.

Missing-Part Activities. An important variation of part-part-whole activities is referred to as *missing-part* activities. In a missing-part activity, students know the whole amount and use their already developed knowledge of the parts of that whole to tell what the covered or hidden part is. If they are unsure, they simply uncover the unknown part and say the full combination. Missing-part activities provide maximum reflection on the combinations for a number. They also serve as the forerunner to subtraction concepts. With a whole amount of 8 but with only 3 showing, the student can later learn to write "8 − 3 = 5."

Missing-part activities require some way for a part to be hidden or unknown. Usually this is done with two students working together or else in a teacher-guided whole-class lesson using a single designated quantity as the whole. The next three activities illustrate variations of this important idea. For any of these activities, you can use a context from familiar classroom events or from a children's book, such as animals hiding in the barn in *Hide and Seek* (Stoeke, 1999).

Activity 8.18

Two Out of Three

Make lists of three numbers, two of which total the whole that students are focusing on. Here is an example list for the number 5:

2–3–4

5–0–2

1–3–2

3–1–4

2–2–3

4–3–1

With the list on the board, students can take turns selecting the two numbers that make the whole. As with all problem-solving activities, students should be challenged to justify their answers.

Activity 8.19

Covered Parts

A set of counters equal to the target amount is counted out, and the rest are put aside. One student places the counters under a margarine tub or piece of cardstock. The student then pulls some out into view. (This amount could be none, all, or any amount in between.) For example, if 6 is the whole and 4 are showing, the other student says, "Four and *two* is six." If there is hesitation or if the hidden part is unknown, the hidden part is immediately shown (see Figure 8.13).

Activity 8.20

Missing-Part Cards

For each number from 4 to 10, make missing-part cards on strips of 3-by-9-inch cardstock. Each card has a numeral for the whole and two dot sets with one set covered by a flap. For the number 8, you need nine cards with the visible part ranging from zero to eight dots. Students use the cards as in "Covered Parts," saying, "Four and two is six" for a card showing four dots and hiding two (see Figure 8.13).

Activity 8.21

I Wish I Had

STUDENTS *with* SPECIAL NEEDS

Hold out a bar of connecting cubes, a dot strip, or a dot plate showing 6 or less. Say, "I wish I had six." The children respond with the part that is needed to make 6. Counting on can be used to check. The game can

focus on a single number (especially as a starting point for students with disabilities), or the "I wish I had" number can change each time (see Figure 8.13). Consider adding a familiar context, like "I wish I had six books to read."

 There are lots of ways you can use computer software to create part-part-whole activities. All that is needed is a program that permits students

TECHNOLOGY to create sets of objects on the screen. Scott Foresman's *eTools* (published by Pearson Education) is available free at www.kyrene.org/mathtools. Choose "Counters" and under "workspaces" on the bottom left, select the bucket icon. Then select the bathtub and add boat, duck, or goldfish counters. As shown in Figure 8.14, children can stamp different types of bathtub toys either in the tub (unseen) or outside the tub. The numeral on the tub shows how many are in the tub, or it can show a question mark (?) for missing-part thinking. The total is shown at the bottom. By clicking on the lightbulb, the contents of the tub can be seen, as shown in Figure 8.14(b). This program offers a great deal of diversity and challenge for both part-part-whole and missing-part activities.

(a)

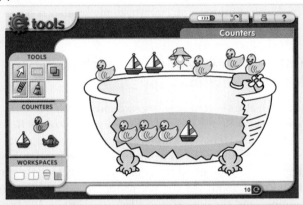

(b)

FIGURE 8.14 Scott Foresman's *eTools* software is useful for exploring part-part-whole and missing-part ideas.

Source: Scott Foresman Addison-Wesley Math Electronic-Tools CD-ROM Grade K Through 6. Copyright © 2004 Pearson Education, Inc., or its affiliate(s). Used by permission. All rights reserved.

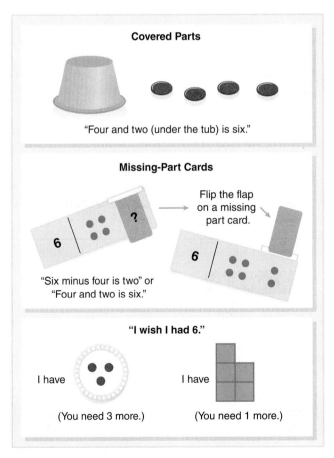

FIGURE 8.13 Missing-part activities.

⏸ **PAUSE and REFLECT**

Remember the list you made earlier in the chapter about what students should know about the number 8? Let's refer to it and see if you would add to it or revise it based on what you have read to this point. Do this before reading on. ●

Here is a possible list of the kinds of things that students should be learning about the number 8 (or any number up to about 12) while they are in pre-K (NCTM, 2006).

- Count to 8 (know the number words and their order)
- Count 8 objects and know that the last number word tells how many
- Write the numeral 8
- Recognize and read the numeral 8

The preceding list represents the minimal skills of number. In the following list are the relationships students should have that contribute to number sense:

- More and less by 1 and 2—8 is one more than 7, one less than 9, two more than 6, and two less than 10
- Patterned sets for 8 such as

- Anchors to 5 and 10: 8 is 3 more than 5 and 2 away from 10
- Part–whole relationships: 8 is 5 and 3, 2 and 6, 7 and 1, and so on (This includes knowing the missing part of 8 when some are hidden.)
- Doubles: double 4 is 8
- Relationships to the real world: my brother is 8 years old; my reading book is 8 inches wide

Dot Cards as a Model for Teaching Number Relationships

We have already seen how dot cards are valuable in developing the Number Core and early explorations in the Relations Core. Here we combine more than one of the relationships discussed so far into several number development activities by using the complete set of cards. As students learn about ten-frames, patterned sets, and other relationships, the dot cards in Blackline Masters 3–8 provide a wealth of activities (see Figure 8.15). The full set of cards contains dot patterns, patterns that require counting, combinations of two and three simple patterns, and ten-frames with "standard" as well as unusual dot placements. When children use these cards for any activity that involves number concepts, the cards help them think flexibly about numbers. The dot cards add another dimension to many of the activities already described and can be used effectively in the following activities.

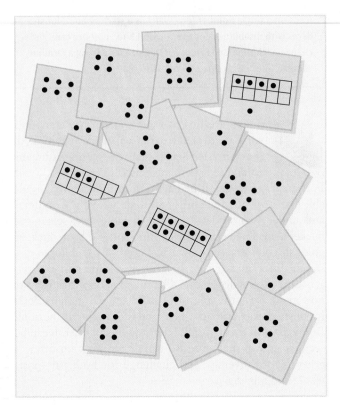

FIGURE 8.15 Dot cards can be made using Blackline Masters 3–8.

Activity 8.22

Double War

The game of "Double War" (Kamii, 1985) is played like the War card game, but on each play, both players turn up two dot cards instead of one. The winner is the player with the larger total number. Students playing the game can and should use many different number relationships to determine the winner without actually finding the total number of dots. A modification of this activity for students with disabilities would have the teacher (or another student) do a "think-aloud" and describe her thinking about the dots using relationships as she figures who wins the round. This modeling is critical for students who struggle.

STUDENTS _with_ SPECIAL NEEDS

Activity 8.23

Difference War

Deal out the dot cards to the two players as in regular War, and prepare a pile of about 40 counters. On each play, the players turn over one card from the top of the stack. The player with the greater number of dots wins as many counters from the pile as the difference between the two cards. Used cards are put aside. The game is over when the cards or counters run out. The player with the most counters wins the game. This game can also be played so the person with "less" wins the number of counters in the difference.

Activity 8.24

Number Sandwiches

Select a number between 5 and 12, and have students find combinations of two cards that total that number. They place the two cards back to back with the dot side out. When they have found at least 10 pairs, the next challenge is for the partner to name the number on the other side. The cards are flipped over to confirm. The same pairs can then be used again to name the other hidden part.

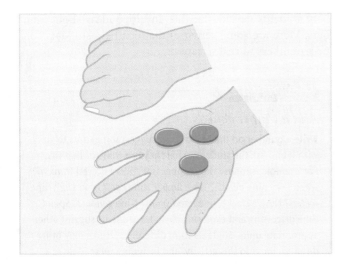

FIGURE 8.16 A missing-part number assessment. "There are eight in all. How many are hidden?"

FORMATIVE Assessment Notes To assess the important part–whole relationships, use a missing-part **diagnostic interview** (similar to Activity 8.19). Begin with a number you believe the student has "mastered," say, 5. Have the student count out that many counters into your open hand. Close your hand around the counters and confirm that the student knows how many are hidden there. Then remove some and show them in the open palm of your other hand (see Figure 8.16). Ask the student, "How many are hidden?" "How do you know?" Repeat with different amounts removed, trying three or four missing parts for each number. If the student responds quickly and correctly and is clearly not counting in any way, call that a "mastered number" and check it off on your student's assessment record. Then repeat the entire process with the next higher number. Continue until the student begins to struggle. In early kindergarten, you will find a range of mastered numbers from 4 to 8. By the end of kindergarten, students should master numbers through 10 (CCSSO, 2010). ∎

Relationships for Numbers 10 Through 20

Even though pre-K, kindergarten, and first-grade students experience numbers up to 20 and beyond daily, it should not be assumed that they will automatically extend the set of relationships they developed on smaller numbers to numbers beyond 10. And yet these numbers play a big part in many simple counting activities, in basic facts, and in much of what we do with mental computation. Relationships with these numbers are just as important as relationships involving the numbers through 10.

Pre-Place-Value Concepts

A set of ten should play a major role in students' early understanding of numbers between 10 and 20. When children see a set of six together with a set of ten, they should know without counting that the total is 16. However, the numbers between 10 and 20 are not an appropriate place to discuss place-value concepts. That is, prior to a much more complete development of place value, students should not be expected to explain the 1 in 16 as representing "one ten." Yet, this work with composing and decomposing numbers from 11 through 19 in kindergarten is seen as an essential foundation for place value (CCSSO, 2010).

 PAUSE and REFLECT

Say to yourself, "One ten." Now think about that from the perspective of a child just learning to count to 20! What could "one ten" possibly mean when ten tells me how many fingers I have and is the number that comes after nine? How can it be one of something? ●

Initially, children do not see a numeric pattern in the numbers between 10 and 20. Rather, these number names are simply ten additional words in the number sequence. In some languages, the teens are actually stated as 10 and 1, 10 and 2, 10 and 3. But since this is not the case in English, for many students, the teens provide a significant challenge.

The concept of a unit of ten is challenging for a kindergarten or early first-grade child to grasp. Although some researchers feel it is developmentally challenging (Kamii, 1985), the *Common Core State Standards* suggests that first graders should know that "10 can be thought of as a bundle of ten ones—called a 'ten'" (p. 15). The difficulty in students discussing "one ten and six ones" (what's a one?) does not mean that a set of ten should not figure prominently in the discussion of the teen numbers. The following activity illustrates this idea.

Activity 8.25

Ten and Some More

Use a simple two-part mat and a story that links to whatever counters you are using. You may want to use coffee stirrers as "sticks" with the story *Not a Stick* (Portis, 2007). Then have students count out ten sticks onto the left side of the mat. Next, have them put five sticks on the other side. Together, count all of the sticks by ones. Chorus the combination: "Ten and five is fifteen." Turn the mat around: "Five and ten is fifteen." Repeat with other numbers (9 or less) in a random order, but always keep 10 on the left side. After playing the game for a while, bundle the 10 sticks with a rubber band.

Activity 8.25 is designed to teach the often challenging number names in the "teens" and thus requires teacher modeling. Following this activity, explore numbers through

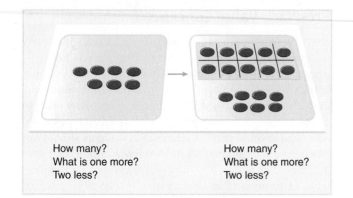

How many?
What is one more?
Two less?

How many?
What is one more?
Two less?

FIGURE 8.17 Extending relationships to the teens.

20 in a more open-ended manner. Provide each child with two ten-frames drawn one under the other on cardstock (see Blackline Master 11). In random order, have students show numbers up to 20 on the frames. Have students discuss how counters can be arranged on the mat so that it is easy to see how many are there. Not every student will use a full set of 10, but as this idea becomes more popular, they will develop the notion that 10 and some more is a teen amount. Then challenge students to find ways to show 26 counters or even more.

Extending More Than and Less Than Relationships

The relationships of one more than, two more than, one less than, and two less than are important for all numbers. However, these ideas are built on or connected to the same concepts for numbers less than 10. The fact that 17 is one less than 18 is connected to the idea that 7 is one less than 8. Students may need help in making this connection.

Activity 8.26

More and Less Extended

On the board, show seven counters and ask what is two more, or one less, and so on. Now add a filled ten-frame to the display (or 10 in any pattern) and repeat the questions. Pair up questions by covering and uncovering the ten-frame as in Figure 8.17.

Number Sense in Their World

Here we examine ways to broaden early knowledge of numbers. Relationships of numbers to real-world quantities and measures and the use of numbers in simple estimations can help students develop flexible, intuitive ideas about numbers. Here are some activities that can help students connect numbers to real situations.

Activity 8.27

Add a Unit to Your Number

Write a number on the board. Now suggest some units to go with it and ask the students what they can think of that fits. For example, suppose the number is 9. "What do you think of when I say nine *dollars*? Nine *hours*? Nine *cars*? Nine *kids*? Nine *meters*? Nine *o'clock*? Nine *hand spans*? Nine *gallons*?" Spend time discussing and exploring each. Let students suggest other appropriate units. Students from different cultures may bring different ideas to this activity, and including these ideas is a way to bring their culture into their school experience.

Activity 8.28

Is It Reasonable?

Select a number and a unit—for example, 15 feet. Could the teacher be 15 feet tall? Could a house be 15 feet wide? Can a man jump 15 feet high? Could three children stretch their arms 15 feet? Pick any number, large or small, and a unit with which students are familiar. Then make up a series of these questions. Also ask, "How can we find out if it is reasonable or not? Who has an idea about what we can do?" Then have the students select the number and unit.

These activities are problem based in the truest sense. Not only are there no clear answers, but students can easily begin to pose their own questions and explore the numbers and units most interesting to them.

Calendar Activities

The National Research Council (2009) has stated that "using the calendar does not emphasize foundational mathematics" (p. 241). They go on to remind early childhood teachers that although the calendar may be helpful in developing a sense of time, it does not align with the need to develop mathematical relationships related to the number 10 because the calendar is based on groups of seven. Although 90 percent of the classrooms surveyed reported using calendar-related activities (Hamre, Downer, Kilday, & McGuire, 2008), there are significant issues with this work being considered the kind of mathematics instruction that will support young learners in reaching mathematical literacy. They conclude, "Doing the calendar is not a substitute for teaching foundational mathematics" (p. 241). The key message is that doing calendar math should be thought of as an "add on" and not take time away from essential pre-K–2 math concepts. If you wish to keep track of the days of school, post and fill ten-frames.

Estimation and Measurement

One of the best ways for students to think of real quantities is to associate numbers with measures of things. Measures of length, weight, and time are good places to begin. Just measuring and recording results will not be very effective unless there is a reason for students to be interested in or think about the result. To help students think about what number might tell how long the desk is or how heavy the book is, it important if they could first write down or tell you an estimate. To produce an estimate is, however, a very difficult task for young children. They do not easily grasp the concept of "estimate" or "about." For example, suppose that you have cut out a set of very large footprints, each about 18 inches long. You would ask, "About how many footprints will it take to measure across the rug in our reading corner?" The key word here is *about*, and it is one that you will need to spend a lot of time helping your students understand. To this end, the request of an estimate can be made in ways that help with the concept of "about."

The following questions can be used with early estimation activities:

- *More or less than _____*? Will it be more or less than 10 footprints? Will the apple weigh more or less than 20 blocks? Are there more or less than 15 connecting cubes in this long bar?
- *Closer to _____ or to _____*? Will it be closer to 5 footprints or closer to 20 footprints? Will the apple weigh closer to 10 blocks or closer to 30 blocks? Does this bar have closer to 10 cubes or closer to 50 cubes?
- *About _____*? About how many footprints? About how many blocks will the apple weigh? About how many cubes are in this bar?

Asking for estimates using these formats helps students learn what you mean by "about." Every student can make a close estimate with some supportive questions and examples. However, rewarding students for the closest estimate in a competitive fashion will often result in their trying to seek precision and not actually estimate. Instead, discuss all answers that fall into a reasonable range. One of the best approaches is to give students ranges as their possible answers: Does your estimate fall between 10 and 30? Between 50 and 70? Or 100 and 130? Of course, you can make the choices more divergent until they grasp the idea.

Data Collection and Analysis

Graphing activities are good ways to connect students' worlds with number and relationships. Graphs can be quickly made from any student data, such as favorites (ice cream, sports team, pet), number of sisters and brothers, and transportation to school. Graphs can be connected to science, such as an investigation of objects that float or sink. Students can generate ideas for what data to gather.

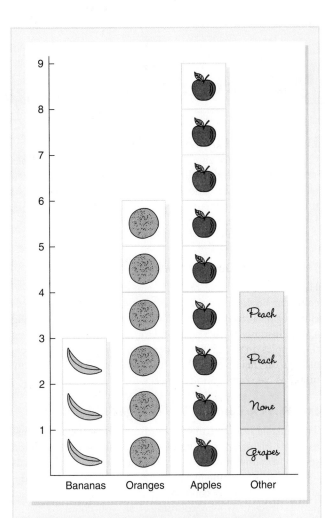

Class graph showing fruit brought for snack. Paper cutouts for bananas, oranges, apples, and cards for "others."

- Which snack (or refer to what the graph represents) is most, least?
- Which are more (less) than 7 (or some other number)?
- Which is one less (more) than this snack (or use fruit name)?
- How much more is _____ than _____ ? (Follow this question immediately by reversing the order and asking how much less.)
- How much less is _____ than _____ ? (Reverse this question after receiving an answer.)
- How much difference is there between _____ and _____ ?
- Which two bars together are the same as _____ ?

FIGURE 8.18 Relationships and number sense in a bar graph.

Once a simple bar graph is made, it is very important to take time to ask questions (e.g., "What do you notice about our class and our ice cream choices?"). In the early stages of number development, the use of graphs is primarily for developing number relationships and for connecting numbers to real quantities in the students' environment. The graphs focus attention on tallies and counts of realistic things.

Equally important, bar graphs clearly exhibit comparisons between numbers that are rarely made when only one number or quantity is considered at a time. See Figure 8.18 (p. 145) for an example of a graph and corresponding questions. At first, students may have trouble with questions involving differences, but these comparison concepts add considerably to students' understanding of number.

RESOURCES *for Chapter 8*

LITERATURE CONNECTIONS

Children's literature abounds with wonderful counting books and visually stimulating number-related books. Have children talk about the mathematics in the story. Begin by talking about the book's birthday (copyright date) and how old the book is. Here are a few ideas for making literature connections to concepts of number.

Ten Little Hot Dogs *Himmelman, 2010*

Here is an example of one of many predictable-progression counting books; this one highlights 10 dachshund puppies climbing on a chair. Children can create their own stories using a mat illustrated with a chair and move counters representing the puppies on or off. Two students can compare the numbers of dogs on their chairs. Who has more puppies? How many more? What combinations for each number are there?

Two Ways to Count to Ten *Dee, 1988*

This folktale is about King Leopard's search for the best animal to marry his daughter. The task devised involves throwing a spear and counting to 10 before the spear lands. Many animals try and fail as counting by ones proves too lengthy. Finally, the antelope succeeds by counting "2, 4, 6, 8, 10." The story is a perfect lead-in to skip counting. Can you count to 10 by threes? How else can you count to 10? How many ways can you count to 48? What numbers can you reach if you count by fives? A hundreds board or counters are useful in helping with these problems.

RECOMMENDED READINGS

Articles

Griffin, S. (2003). Laying the foundation for computational fluency in early childhood. *Teaching Children Mathematics, 9*(6), 306–309.
This useful article for assessment lays out five stages of number development with a simple addition story problem task followed by activities to develop number for each stage.

Losq, C. (2005). Number concepts and special needs students: The power of ten-frame tiles. *Teaching Children Mathematics, 11*(6), 310–315.

This article supports struggling learners in the use of a countable and visual model—the ten-frame tile. The ten-frames are positioned vertically to enhance subitizing and provide tools for formative assessment.

Moomaw, S., Carr, V., Boat, M., & Barnett, D. (2010). Preschoolers' number sense. *Teaching Children Mathematics, 16*(6), 333–340.
How can you best assess young learners? This article offers curriculum-based assessments that can capture number sense concepts through game-like activities.

Books

Dougherty, B., Flores, A., Louis, E., & Sophian, C. (2010). *Developing essential understanding of number and numeration for teaching mathematics in prekindergarten–grade 2.* Reston, VA: NCTM.
This book describes what big mathematical ideas a teacher needs to know about number, how number connects to other mathematical ideas, and how to teach and assess this pivotal topic.

Richardson, K. (2003). *Assessing math concepts: The hiding assessment.* Bellingham, WA: Mathematical Perspectives.
This is one of a series of nine assessment books with diagnostic interviews covering number topics from counting through two-digit numbers. Extensive explanations and examples are provided.

ONLINE RESOURCES

Let's Count to 5 (Grades K–2)
http://illuminations.nctm.org/LessonDetail.aspx?id=U57
Here are seven lessons where children make sets of zero through five objects and connect number words or numerals to the sets. Songs, rhymes, and activities that appeal to visual, auditory, and kinesthetic learners are included. See other Illuminations sites for counting to 10 and 20.

Toy Shop Numbers (Grades K–2)
http://illuminations.nctm.org/LessonDetail .aspx?id=L216
Using the setting of a toy shop, these activities focus on finding numbers in the real world.

REFLECTIONS *on Chapter 8*

WRITING TO LEARN

1. What must a child be able to do in order to accurately count a set of objects?
2. How can "Real Counting On" (Activity 8.8) be used as a diagnostic interview to determine whether children understand counting on or are still in a transitional stage?
3. What are three types of relationships for numbers 1 through 10? Explain briefly what each means, and suggest an activity for each.
4. How can a teacher assess part–whole number relationships?
5. How can a calculator be used to develop early counting ideas connected with number? How can it be used to help a child practice number relationships such as part-part-whole or one less than?
6. For numbers between 10 and 20, describe how to develop each of these ideas:
   a. The idea of the teens as a set of ten and some more
   b. Extension of the one-more/one-less concept to the teens

FOR DISCUSSION AND EXPLORATION

1. Examine the *Common Core State Standards* used in the United States (available at www.corestandards.org), the *Common Curriculum Framework* used in Canada (available at www.wncp .ca/media/38765/ccfkto9.pdf), or your own region's document. Look at the suggestions for K–2 children under headings such as "number," "counting and cardinality," "operations and algebraic thinking," and "number and operations in base ten." Compare these suggestions with the ideas presented in this chapter. What ideas are stressed? Did anything surprise you?
2. You've noticed that a student you are working with is counting objects with an accurate sequence of numbers words, but is not attaching one number to each object. Therefore, the student's final count is inconsistent and inaccurate. What would you plan to help this student develop a better grasp of one-to-one correspondence?

MyEducationLab™

Go to the MyEducationLab (www.myeducationlab.com) for Math Methods and familiarize yourself with the content. Much of the site content is organized topically. The topics include all of the following to support your learning in the course:

- Learning outcomes for important mathematics methods course topics aligned with the national standards
- Assignments and Activities, tied to these learning outcomes and standards, that can help you more deeply understand course content
- Building Teaching Skills and Dispositions learning units that allow you to apply and practice your understanding of the core mathematics content and teaching skills

Your instructor has a correlation guide that aligns the exercises on the topical portion of the site with your book's chapters.

On MyEducationLab you will also find book-specific resources including Blackline Masters, Expanded Lesson Activities, and Artifact Analysis Activities.

Field Experience Guide
CONNECTIONS

FEG Expanded Lessons 9.3, 9.12, 9.15, and 9.20 focus on early numbers, including concepts related to measurement and data. FEG Activity 10.1, "The Find!"; FEG Activity 10.2, "Move It, Move It"; and FEG Activity 10.3, "Odd or Even?" also engage children in thinking about number relationships.

Chapter 9

Developing Meanings for the Operations

*T*his chapter is about helping children connect different meanings, interpretations, and relationships to the four operations of addition, subtraction, multiplication, and division so that they can accurately and fluently apply these operations in real-world settings. This is part of the Operations Core (National Research Council, 2009), in which students learn to see mathematical situations in their day-to-day lives or in story problems and begin to identify and make models of these situations in words, pictures, models, and/or numbers. Students think about how many objects they have after changes take place or as they compare quantities. As they do this, they develop what might be termed *operation sense*, a highly integrated understanding of the four operations and the many different but related meanings these operations take on in real contexts.

As you read this chapter, pay special attention to the impact on number development, basic fact mastery, and computation. As children develop their understanding of operations, they can and should simultaneously be developing more sophisticated ideas about number and ways to think about basic fact combinations.

BIG IDEAS

1. Addition and subtraction are connected. Addition names the whole in terms of the parts, and subtraction names a missing part.

2. Multiplication involves counting groups of equal size and determining how many are in all (multiplicative thinking).

3. Multiplication and division are related. Division names a missing factor in terms of the known factor and the product.

4. Models can be used to solve contextual problems for all operations and to figure out what operation is involved in a problem regardless of the size of the numbers. Models also can be used to give meaning to number sentences.

Mathematics CONTENT CONNECTIONS

The ideas in this chapter are most directly linked to concepts of numeration and the development of invented computation strategies.

◆ **Number** (Chapter 8): As children learn to think about numbers in terms of the part-part-whole model, they should be relating this idea to addition and subtraction. Multiplication and division require students to think about numbers as units: In 3×6, each of the three sixes is counted as a unit.

◆ **Basic Facts** (Chapter 10): Understanding the meaning of operations can firmly connect addition and subtraction so that subtraction facts are a natural consequence of having learned addition. A firm connection between multiplication and division provides a similar benefit.

◆ **Place Value** (Chapter 11): Students develop ideas about the base-ten number system as they solve story problems involving two-digit numbers.

◆ **Computation** (Chapters 12 and 13): It is reasonable to have students invent strategies for computing with two-digit numbers as they build their understanding of the operations.

◆ **Algebraic Thinking** (Chapter 14): Representing contextual situations in equations is at the heart of algebraic thinking. This is exactly what students are doing as they learn to write equations to go with their solutions to story problems.

◆ **Fraction and Decimal Computation** (Chapters 16 and 17): These topics for the upper elementary and middle grades depend on a firm understanding of the operations.

Addition and Subtraction Problem Structures

We begin this chapter with a look at three categories of *problem structures* for additive situations (which include both addition and subtraction) and later explore four problem structures for multiplicative situations (which include both multiplication and division). These categories help students develop a schema to separate important information and to structure their thinking. In particular, researchers suggest that students with disabilities should be explicitly taught these underlying structures so that they can identify important characteristics of the situations and determine when to add or subtract (Fuchs, Fuchs, Prentice, Hamlett, Finelli, & Courey, 2004; Xin, Jitendra, & Deatline-Buchman, 2005). Students' thinking can be supported by identifying whether a problem fits a "join" or "separate" classification. When students are exposed to new problems, the familiar characteristics will assist them in generalizing from similar problems on which they have practiced. Furthermore, teachers who are not aware of the variety of situations and corresponding structures may randomly offer problems to students without the proper sequencing to support students' full grasp of the meaning of the operations. By knowing the logical structure of these problems, you will be able to help students interpret a variety of real-world contexts. More importantly, you will need to present a variety of problem types (within each structure) as well as recognize which structures cause the greatest challenges for students.

Researchers have separated addition and subtraction problems into structures based on the kinds of relationships involved (Verschaffel, Greer, & DeCorte, 2007). These include *change* problems (*join* and *separate*), *part-part-whole* problems, and *compare* problems (Carpenter, Fennema, Franke, Levi, & Empson, 1999). The basic structure for each of these three categories of problems is illustrated in Figure 9.1. Each structure involves a number "family" such as 3, 5, 8. Depending on which of the three quantities is unknown, a different problem type results.

Each of the problem structures is illustrated with the story problems that follow. The number family 4, 8, 12 is used in each problem and can be connected to the structure in Figure 9.1. Note that the problems are described in terms of their structure and interpretation and not as addition or subtraction problems. Contrary to what you may have thought, a joining action does not always mean addition, nor does separate or remove always mean subtraction.

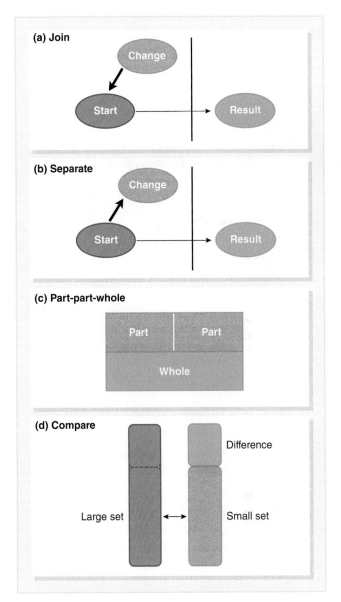

FIGURE 9.1 Basic structures for addition and subtraction story problem types. Each structure has three numbers. Any one of the three numbers can be the unknown in a story problem.

Examples of Change Problems

Join.   For the action of joining, there are three quantities involved: a start amount, a change amount (the part being added or joined), and the resulting amount (the total amount after the change takes place). In Figure 9.1(a), this is illustrated by the change being "added to" the start amount. Any one of these three quantities can be unknown in a problem, as shown here in these three types of joining problems.

Join: Result Unknown

Sandra had 8 pennies. George gave her 4 more. How many pennies does Sandra have altogether?

Join: Change Unknown

Sandra had 8 pennies. George gave her some more. Now Sandra has 12 pennies. How many did George give her?

Join: Start Unknown

Sandra had some pennies. George gave her 4 more. Now Sandra has 12 pennies. How many pennies did Sandra have to begin with?

Separate. In separating problems, the start amount is the whole or the largest amount, whereas in the joining problems, the result is the whole. In separating problems, the change is that an amount is being removed or taken away from the start value. Again, refer to Figure 9.1(b) as you consider these problems.

Separate: Result Unknown

Sandra had 12 pennies. She gave 4 pennies to George. How many pennies does Sandra have now?

Separate: Change Unknown

Sandra had 12 pennies. She gave some to George. Now she has 8 pennies. How many did she give to George?

Separate: Start Unknown

Sandra had some pennies. She gave 4 to George. Now Sandra has 8 pennies left. How many pennies did Sandra have to begin with?

Examples of Part-Part-Whole Problems

Part-part-whole problems involve two parts that are combined into one whole, as in Figure 9.1(c). In these situations, either the missing whole or one of the missing parts (unknown) must be found. The combining may be a physical action, or it may be a mental combination in which the parts are not physically combined. This structure links to the idea in the Number Core that numbers are embedded in other numbers (refer back to Figure 8.3). Students can break apart 7 into 5 and 2. Each of the addends (or parts) were embedded in the 7 (whole).

There is no meaningful distinction between the two parts in a part-part-whole situation, so there is no need to have a different problem for each part as the unknown. For both possibilities (whole unknown and part unknown), example problems are given. The first is a mental combination in which there is no action. The second problem involves a physical action.

Part-Part-Whole: Whole Unknown

George has 4 pennies and 8 nickels. How many coins does he have?

George has 4 pennies, and Sandra has 8 pennies. They put their pennies into a piggy bank. How many pennies did they put into the bank?

Part-Part-Whole: Part Unknown

George has 12 coins. Eight of his coins are pennies, and the rest are nickels. How many nickels does George have?

George and Sandra put 12 pennies into the piggy bank. George put in 4 pennies. How many pennies did Sandra put in?

Examples of Compare Problems

Compare problems involve the comparison of two quantities. The third amount does not actually exist but is the difference between the two amounts. Figure 9.1(d) illustrates the compare problem structure. There are three ways to present compare problems, corresponding to which quantity is unknown (smaller, larger, or difference). For each of these, two examples are given: one problem in which the difference is stated in terms of more and another in terms of less. Note that the language of "more" will often confuse students and thus presents a challenge in interpretation.

Compare: Difference Unknown

George has 12 pennies, and Sandra has 8 pennies. How many more pennies does George have than Sandra?

George has 12 pennies. Sandra has 8 pennies. How many fewer pennies does Sandra have than George?

Compare: Larger Unknown

George has 4 more pennies than Sandra. Sandra has 8 pennies. How many pennies does George have?

Sandra has 4 fewer pennies than George. Sandra has 8 pennies. How many pennies does George have?

Compare: Smaller Unknown

George has 4 more pennies than Sandra. George has 12 pennies. How many pennies does Sandra have?

Sandra has 4 fewer pennies than George. George has 12 pennies. How many pennies does Sandra have?

⏸ PAUSE and REFLECT

Go back through all of these examples and match the numbers in the problems with the components of the structures in Figure 9.1. For each problem, do two additional things. First, use a set of counters or coins to model (solve) the problem as you think children might do. Second, for each problem, write either an addition or subtraction equation that you think best represents the problem as you did it with counters. ⚫

In most curricula, the overwhelming emphasis is on the easiest problem types: join and separate with the result unknown. These become the de facto definitions of addition and subtraction: Addition is "put together" and subtraction is "take away." The fact is, these are *not* the definitions of addition and subtraction.

When students develop these limited put-together and take-away definitions for addition and subtraction, they often have difficulty later when addition or subtraction is called for but the structure is different from put together or take away. It is important that students be exposed to all forms within these different problem structures.

Problem Difficulty

Some of the problem types are more difficult than other problem types. The join or separate problems in which the start part is unknown (e.g., Sandra had some pennies) are often the most difficult, probably because students modeling the problems directly do not know how many counters to put down to begin modeling the problem. Problems in which the change amounts are unknown are also difficult. Compare problems are often challenging as the language often confuses students into adding instead of finding the difference.

Many children will solve compare problems as part-part-whole problems without making separate sets of counters for the two amounts. The whole is used as the large amount, one part for the small amount and the second part for the difference. As students begin to translate a story problem into an equation, they may be challenged to create a matching equation that emphasizes the corresponding operation. This is particularly important as students move into explorations that develop algebraic thinking. The structure of the equations also may cause difficulty for English language learners, who may not initially have the flexibility in creating equivalent equations due to reading

Quantity Unknown	Join Problems	Separate Problems
Result	8 + 4 = [ ]	12 − 4 = [ ]
Change	8 + [ ] = 12	12 − [ ] = 8
Start	[ ] + 4 = 12	[ ] − 4 = 8

FIGURE 9.2 The semantic equation for each of the six join and separate problems on pages 149–150. Notice that for results-unknown problems, the semantic form is also the computational form. The computational form for the other four problems is an equivalent equation that isolates the unknown quantity.

comprehension issues with the story situation. Therefore, we need to look at how knowing about computational and semantic forms of equations will help you help your students.

Computational and Semantic Forms of Equations

If you wrote an equation for each of the problems as just suggested, you may have some equations where the unknown quantity is not isolated on the right side of the equal sign. For example, a likely equation for the join problem with start part unknown is $\square + 4 = 12$. This is referred to as the *semantic* equation for the problem because the numbers are listed in the order that follows the meaning of the word problem. Figure 9.2 shows the semantic equations for the six join and separate problems on the previous pages. Note that the two result-unknown problems place the unknown alone on one side of the equal sign. An equation that isolates the unknown in this way is referred to as the *computational* form of the equation. The computational form is the one you would need to use if you were to solve these equations with a calculator. When the semantic form is not also the computational form, an equivalent equation can be written. For example, the equation $\square + 4 = 12$ can be written equivalently as $12 - 4 = \square$. Students need to see that there are several ways to represent a situation as an equation. As numbers increase in size and students are not solving equations with counters, they must learn to see the equivalence between different forms of the equations.

◆ Teaching Addition and Subtraction

So far, you have seen a variety of story problem structures for addition and subtraction, and you probably have attempted them using counters to help you understand how these problems can be solved by children. Combining the use of situations and models (counters, drawings, number lines) is important in helping students construct a deep understanding of these two operations. Let's examine how each approach can be used in the classroom. As you read this section, note that addition and subtraction are taught at the same time.

Contextual Problems

There is more to think about than simply giving students problems to solve. In contrast with the rather straightforward and brief contextual problems in the previous section, consider the following problem, which the student has solved in Figure 9.3.

> Yesterday we were measuring how tall we were. You remember that we used the connecting cubes to make a big train that was as long as we were when we were lying down. Dion and Rosa were wondering how many cubes long they would be together if they lie down head to foot. Dion had measured Rosa, and she was $49\frac{1}{2}$ cubes long. Rosa measured Dion, and he was 59 cubes long. Can we figure out how long they will be end to end?

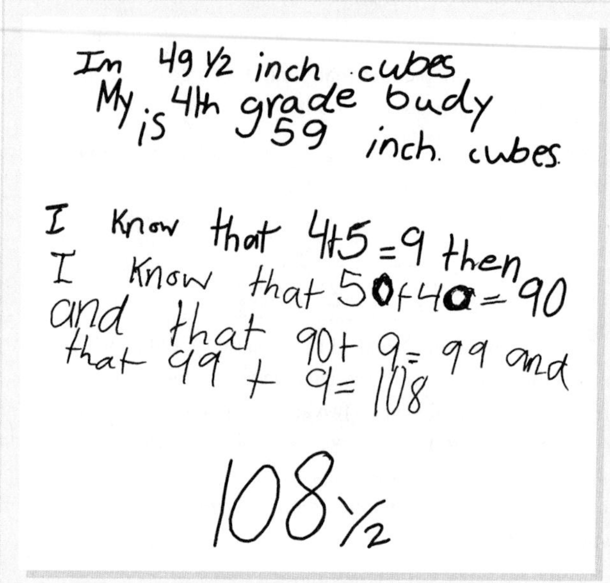

Fosnot and Dolk (2001) point out that in story problems, children tend to focus on getting the answer. "Context problems, on the other hand, are connected as closely as possible to children's lives, rather than to 'school mathematics.' They are designed to anticipate and to develop children's mathematical modeling of the real world" (p. 24). Contextual problems might derive from recent experiences in the classroom or on a field trip from a discussion in art, science, or social studies; or from children's literature. Because contextual problems connect to life experiences, they are important for English language learners, too, even though it may seem that the language presents a challenge to ELLs. To support their comprehension of such stories, the sentences can be structured using present and past tense; the word order adapted to noun-verb; terms like "his/her" and "it" replaced with a name; and unnecessary vocabulary words removed. For example, the preceding problem could be rewritten as:

> Yesterday, we measured how long you were using cubes. Dion and Rosa asked how many cubes long they are when they lie down head to foot. Rosa was $49\frac{1}{2}$ cubes long, and Dion was 59 cubes long. How long are Rosa and Dion when lying head to foot?

A visual or actual students modeling this story would also be an effective strategy for ELLs and students with disabilities.

Lessons Built on Context or Story Problems. What might a good lesson built around word problems look like? The answer comes more naturally if you think about students not just solving the problems but also using words, pictures, and numbers to explain how they went about solving the problem and justify why they are correct. In a single class period, try to focus on a few problems with an in-depth discussion rather than a lot of problems with little elaboration. Children

FIGURE 9.3 Student work shows a child's thinking as she calculates the total measurement of Rosa's and Dion's heights.

should be allowed to use whatever physical materials or drawings they feel they need to help them. Whatever they put on their paper should explain what they did well enough to allow someone else to understand their thinking.

The second-grade curriculum series *Investigations in Number, Data, and Space* places a significant emphasis on connecting addition and subtraction concepts. In the lesson shown here, you can see an activity involving word problems for subtraction. Take special note of the emphasis on students' visualizing the situation mentally and putting the problem in their own words.

Choosing Numbers for Problems. Pre-K and kindergarten children should be expected to solve story problems. Their initial methods of solution will typically involve using counters or role playing in a very direct modeling of the problems. Although the structure of the problems will cause the difficulty to vary, the numbers in the problems should be in accord with the number development of the children. Pre-K and kindergarten children can use numbers as large as they can grasp conceptually, which is usually to about 10 or 12.

First- and second-grade children are also learning about two-digit numbers and are beginning to understand how our base-ten system works, but these topics are not prerequisite knowledge for solving contextual problems with two-digit numbers. Rather, word problems can serve as an opportunity to learn about number and computation at the same time. For example, a problem involving the combination of 30 and 42 has the potential to help students focus on sets of ten. As they begin to think of 42 as 40 and 2, they might think, "Add 30 and 40 and then add 2 more." Invented strategies for computation in addition and subtraction are a focus of Chapter 12.

INVESTIGATIONS *in Number, Data, and Space*

Grade 2, *Counting, Coins, and Combinations*

Context

Counting, Coins, and Combinations is the first of nine curriculum units for the second grade. It is one of four units in which work on addition, subtraction, and the number system is undertaken. Children begin with the facts and move to two-digit problems using student-invented strategies. The focus on whole-number operations includes understanding problem structure to analyze situations; developing strategies to solve story problems; and using words, pictures, and numbers to communicate solutions. Over the series of units, the full variety of problem structures presented in this chapter will be developed. There is an emphasis on a variety of problem types to assist the students in thinking about different situations and perspectives rather than focusing on one action or visualization.

Task Description

Counting, Coins, and Combinations has students explore a range of addition and subtraction problems within story situations and then visualize and model the actions described. The discussions that follow these activities embody a definite effort to use the story problems to connect the concepts of addition and subtraction to the additive problem structures. The subtraction task shown here, for example, demonstrates a separate problem with the result unknown. To begin their work, students are told that they will be hearing a story and to visualize the situation in their minds and be ready to put the problem in their own words.

Because subtraction situations are often more challenging to follow, students are asked to think about the answer before solving the problem and estimate whether the answer will be more or less than 16. Then they share their thinking on how they thought about the answer. Students are to use whatever methods and materials they wish to solve the problem, but they are required to show their work: "Someone else should be able to look at your work and understand what you did to solve it" (p. 41).

In a full-class discussion following this activity, students share their problem-solving strategies while the teacher helps deepen their understanding by posing ques-

---

9 left

I used my cubes

$16 - 7 = 9$

I circled the 7 on
rhe Hundreds chart
and tnat was the
giving away group
then I counted
up to 16 8^1 9^2 10^3
11^4 12^5 13^6 14^7 15^8
16^9
(9)

Name _____ Date _____

Counting, Coins, and Combinations

How Many Cards? (page 1 of 2)

Solve the problem. Show your work.
Write an equation.

1. Kira had 16 baseball cards. She gave 7 of them away. How many baseball cards did Kira have left?

Trading Card

---

tions. The teacher also asks students to model a solution suggested by a classmate—such as using the cubes or hundreds chart as shown in the students' work samples. Students with disabilities may need to actually use cards as models to help them connect to the problem situation. Other students can then be asked to try the strategy. Poll students to see who also used a similar approach to give them ownership while you assess students' development. Before moving on, you can discuss strategies not already presented. Then carefully connect to the symbolic representation through writing the equation for the problem. Talk about how this can be linked to an addition story using the same numbers.

Take time to examine the two student work samples. What do you notice in their recording of their thinking? Can you follow their strategy use? Is one approach more prone to errors than the other? Does one work sample display a more sophisticated level of understanding than the other?

The *Principles and Standards for School Mathematics* authors make clear the value of connecting addition and subtraction. "Teachers should ensure that students repeatedly encounter situations in which the same numbers appear in different contexts. For example, the numbers 3, 4, and 7 may appear in problem-solving situations that could be represented by 4 + 3, 3 + 4, or 7 − 3, or 7 − 4. . . . Recognizing the inverse relationship between addition and subtraction can allow students to be flexible in using strategies to solve problems" (NCTM, 2000, p. 83).

Introducing Symbolism.   Very young children do not need to understand the symbols +, −, and = to begin to learn about addition and subtraction concepts. However, by first grade these symbolic conventions are important. When your students are engaged in solving story problems, introduce symbols as a way to record what they did as they share their thinking in the discussion portion of a lesson. Say, "You had the whole number of 12 in your problem, and the number 8 was one of the parts of 12. You found out that the part you did not know was 4. Here is a way we can write that: 12 − 8 = 4." The minus sign should be read as "minus" or "subtract" but not as "take away." The plus sign is easier because it is typically a substitute for "and."

Some care should be taken with the equal sign as it is a relational symbol, not an operations symbol (like + and −). That can confuse students. The equal sign means "is the same as." However, most children come to think of it as a symbol that tells you that the "answer is coming up." Students often interpret the equal sign in much the same way as the = on a calculator. That is, it is the key you press to get the answer. An equation such as 4 + 8 = 3 + 9 has no "answer" and is still true because both sides stand for the same quantity. A good idea is to often use the phrase "is the same as" in place of or in conjunction with "equals" as you record and read equations with students. Using equations like 9 = 5 + 4 and 3 + 3 = 2 + 4 is a way to help students understand the equal sign.

Another approach is to think of the equal sign as a balance; whatever is on one side of the equation "balances" or equals what is on the other side. This will support algebraic thinking in future grades if developed early (Knuth, Stephens, McNeil, & Alibali, 2006). (See Chapter 14 for a more detailed look at teaching the equal sign as "is the same as" rather than "give me the answer.")

FORMATIVE Assessment Notes   **Observing** how students solve story problems will give you a lot of information about children's understanding of number as well as the information about problem solving and their understanding of addition and

subtraction. The Cognitively Guided Instruction (CGI) project (Carpenter et al., 1999) found that children progress in their problem-solving strategies from kindergarten to grade 2. These strategies are a reflection of students' understanding of number and of their emerging mastery of basic fact strategies. For example, early on, students will use counters and count each addend and then recount the entire set for a join-result-unknown problem (this is called "count all"). With more practice, they will count on from the first set. This strategy will be modified to count on from the larger set; that is, for 4 + 7, the child will begin with 7 and count on, even though 4 is the start amount in the problem. Eventually, students should begin to use facts retrieved from memory, and their use of counters fades completely or counters are used only when necessary. Observing students solve problems provides evidence to help you decide what numbers to use in problems and what questions to ask that will focus students' attention on more efficient strategies. ■

Model-Based Problems

Many students will use counters, bar diagrams, or number lines (models) to solve story problems. The model is a thinking tool to help them both understand what is happening in the problem and use it as a means of keeping track of the numbers and solving the problem. Problems can also be posed using models when there is no context involved.

Addition.   When the parts of a set are known, addition is used to name the whole in terms of the parts. This simple definition of addition serves both action situations (join and separate) and static or no-action situations (part-part-whole).

Each of the models shown in Figure 9.4 represents 5 + 3 = 8. Some of these are the result of a definite put-together or joining action, and some are not. Notice that in every example, both of the parts are distinct, even after the parts are combined. If counters are used, the two parts should be in different piles, in different colors, or on different sections of a mat. For children to see a relationship between the two parts and the whole, the image of the 5 and 3 must be kept as two separate sets. This helps children reflect on the action after it has occurred. "These red chips are the ones I started with. Then I added these three blue ones, and now I have eight altogether."

The use of bar diagrams (also called strip or tape diagrams) as semi-concrete visual representations is a central fixture of both Japanese curriculum and what is known as Singapore mathematics. As with other tools, they support students' mathematical thinking by generating "meaning-making space" (Murata, 2008, p. 399) and are a precursor to the use of number lines. Murata states, "Tape diagrams are designed to bring forward the relational meanings of the quantities in a problem by showing the connections in context" (2008, p. 396).

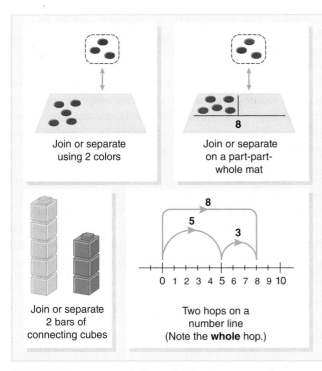

FIGURE 9.4 Part-part-whole models for 5 + 3 = 8 and 8 − 3 = 5.

A number line can initially present conceptual difficulties for children below second grade and students with disabilities (National Research Council, 2009). This is partially due to their difficulty in seeing the unit, which is a challenge when it appears in a continuous line. A number line is also a shift from counting a number of objects in a collection to length units. But there are ways to introduce and model number lines that support young learners. A number line measures distances from zero the same way a ruler does. If you don't actually teach the use of the number line through an emphasis on the unit (length), children may focus on the hash marks or numerals instead of the spaces (a misunderstanding that becomes apparent when their answers are consistently off by one). At first, children can build a number path by using a given length, such as a set of Cuisenaire rods of the same color. This will show each length unit is "one unit" and that same unit is repeated over and over to form the number line (Dougherty, 2008). Also, playing board games with number paths helped low SES students develop a better concept of number magnitude and helped them estimate more accurately on a number line (Siegler & Ramani, 2009). Furthermore, if arrows (hops) are drawn for each number in an expression, the length concept is more clearly illustrated. To model the part-part-whole concept of 5 + 3, start by drawing an arrow from 0 to 5, indicating, "This much is five." Do not point to the hash mark for 5, saying, "This is five." Then go on to show the three hops and count "six, seven, eight" (not "one, two, three") to demonstrate the counting-on model and reinforce the mental

process. Eventually, the use of a ruler or a scale in a bar graph will reinforce this model.

TECHNOLOGY There's a virtual number line at www .eduplace.com/kids/mw that illustrates the emphasis on the unit. It is free, and you go into the site, select a grade, select eManipulatives, and then select Number Line. Each grade level focuses on different skills—try grade 2 to do basic addition and subtraction or grade 4 to work with decimals. The student clicks on the number line at any number to start and then selects numbers on the keypad at the left to input the unit. The figure will jump forward (for addition) or backward (for subtraction) depending on whether the student selects the left-pointing arrow or right-pointing arrow.

Activity 9.1

Up and Down the Number Line

Create a large number line on the floor of your classroom, or display one in the front of the room. (Make sure you start with zero and have arrows at each end of the line.) Use a stuffed animal for hopping, or ask a student to walk the number line on the floor. Talk about the movement required for each of a variety of problem situations. This emphasizes the spaces (units of length) on the number line and is a wonderful mental image for thinking about the meaning of addition and subtraction.

Subtraction. In a part-part-whole model, when the whole and one of the parts are known, subtraction names the other part. This definition is consistent with the overused language of "take away." If you start with a whole set of 8 and remove a set of 3, the two sets that you know are the sets of 8 and 3. The expression 8 − 3, read "eight minus three," names the set of 5 that remains. Therefore, eight minus three is the same as five. Notice that the models in Figure 9.4 are models for subtraction as well as addition (except for the action). Helping children see that they are using the same models or pictures connects the two operations through their inverse relationship.

Activity 9.2

Missing-Part Subtraction

ENGLISH LANGUAGE LEARNERS

Use a situation about something that is hiding, as in the "lift the flap" book *What's Hiding in There?* (Drescher, 2008), where animals are concealed in various locations in the woods. Model the animals by using a fixed number of tiles placed on a mat. One student separates the tiles into two parts while another covers his or her eyes. The first student covers one of the two parts with a sheet of paper, revealing only the other part (see Figure 9.5(b)). The second student says the subtraction sentence. For example, "Nine minus four [the visible part] is five [the covered part]." The covered part can be revealed for the child to self-check. Record both the subtraction equation and the addition equation. ELLs may need sentence prompts such as "_____ minus _____ is _____."

Subtraction as Think-Addition.

Note that in Activity 9.2, the situation ends with two distinct parts, even when there is a remove action. The removed part remains on the mat as a model for an addition equation to be written after writing the subtraction equation. A discussion of how two equations can be written for the same situation is an important opportunity to connect addition and subtraction. The modeling and discussion of the relationship between addition and subtraction are significantly better than the activity of "fact families" in which children are given a family of numbers such as 3, 5, and 8 and are asked to write two addition equations and two subtraction equations. This often becomes a meaningless process of dropping the numbers into slots.

Thinking about subtraction as "think-addition" rather than "take-away" is significant for mastering subtraction facts. Because the counters for the remaining or unknown part are left hidden under the cover, when children do these activities, they are encouraged to think about the hidden part: "What goes with the part I see to make the whole?" For example, if the total or whole number of counters is 9, and 6 counters are removed from under the cover, the child is likely to think in terms of "6 and what makes 9?" or "What goes with 6 to make 9?" The mental activity is think-addition instead of "count what's left." Later, when working on subtraction facts, a subtraction fact such as $9 - 6 = \square$ should trigger the same thought pattern: "6 and what makes 9?"

Comparison Models.

Comparison situations involve two distinct sets or quantities and the difference between them. Several ways of modeling the difference relationship are shown in Figure 9.6. The same model can be used whether the difference or one of the two quantities is unknown.

Note that it is not immediately clear to students how to associate either the addition or subtraction operations with a comparison situation. From an adult vantage point, you can see that if you match part of the larger amount with the smaller amount, the large set is now a part-part-whole model that can help you solve the problem. In fact, many children do model compare problems in just this manner. But that is a very difficult idea to show students if they do not construct the idea themselves.

Have students make two amounts, perhaps with two bars of connecting cubes, to show how many pencils are in their backpacks. Discuss the difference between the two bars to generate the third number. For example, if the students make a bar of 10 and a bar of 6, ask, "How many more do we need to match the 10 bar?" The difference is 4. "What equations can we make with these three numbers?" Have children make up other story problems that involve the two amounts of 10 and 6. Discuss which equations go with the problems that are created.

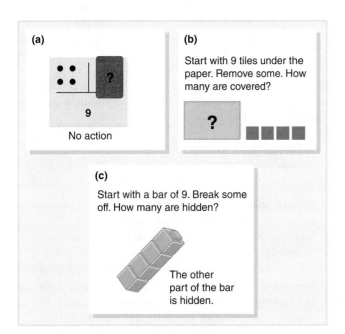

FIGURE 9.5 Models for $9 - 4$ as a missing-part problem.

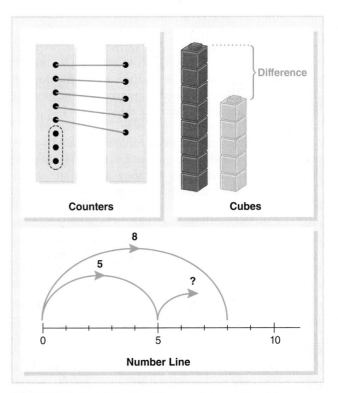

FIGURE 9.6 Models for the difference between 8 and 5.

Properties of Addition and Subtraction

The Commutative Property for Addition. The *commutative property* for addition means you can change the order of the addends and it does not change the answer. Although the commutative property may seem obvious to us (simply reverse the two piles of counters on the part-part-whole mat), it may not be as obvious to children. Because this property is essential in problem solving (counting on from the larger number), mastery of basic facts (if you know $3 + 9$, you also know $9 + 3$), and mental mathematics, there is value in spending time helping children construct the relationship (Baroody, Wilkins, & Tiilikainen, 2003). First-grade students do not need to be able to name the property as much as they need to understand and visualize the property, know why it applies to addition but not subtraction, and apply it.

Schifter (2001) describes students who discovered the "turn-around" property while examining sums to ten. Later, the teacher wondered if they really understood this idea and asked the children whether they thought it would always work. Many students were unsure if it worked all of the time and were especially unsure about it working with large numbers. The point is that children may see and accept the commutative property for sums they've experienced but not be able to explain or even believe that this simple yet important property works for all addition combinations. Asking students to think about when properties do (and don't) apply is the heart of mathematics, addressing numeration, reasoning, and algebraic thinking.

To help children focus on the commutative property, pair problems that have the same addends but in different orders. The context for each problem should be different. For example:

> Tania is on page 32 in her book. Tomorrow she hopes to read 15 more pages. What page will she be on if she reads that many pages?

> The milk tray in the cafeteria only had 15 cartons. The delivery person brought in some more milk and filled the tray with 32 more cartons. How many cartons are now on the milk tray?

Ask if anyone notices how these problems are alike. If done as a pair, some (not all) students will see that when they have solved one, they have essentially solved the other.

The Associative Property for Addition. The *associative property* for addition states that when adding three or more numbers, it does not matter whether the first pair is added first or if you start with any other pair of addends. There is much flexibility in addition, and students can change the order in which they group numbers to work with combinations they know. For example, knowing this property can help students with "making ten" from the numbers they are adding by mentally grouping numbers in an order different from just reading the expression from left to right.

Activity **9.3**

More Than Two Addends

STUDENTS with SPECIAL NEEDS

Give students six sums to find involving three or four addends. Prepare these on one page divided into six sections so that there is space to write beneath each sum. Within each, include at least one pair with a sum of 10 or perhaps a double: $4 + 7 + 6$, $5 + 9 + 9$, or $3 + 4 + 3 + 7$. Students should show how they added the numbers. If you are also working with students with disabilities, you may need to initially support them in their decision making, suggesting that they look for a 10 or a double and having them underline or circle those numbers as a starting point.

Figure 9.7 illustrates how students might show their thinking. As they share their solutions, there will be students who added using a different order but got the same result. From this discussion, you can help them conclude that they can add numbers in any order. You are also using the associative property, but it is the commutative property that is more important. This is also an excellent number-sense activity because many students will find combinations of ten in these sums or will use doubles. Learning to adjust strategies to fit the numbers is the beginning of the road to computational fluency.

The Zero Property. Story problems involving zero and using zeros in the three-addend sums are also good methods of helping students understand zero as an identity element in addition or subtraction (*Curriculum Focal Points* [CFP], Grade 1). Occasionally students believe that $6 + 0$ must be more than 6 because "adding makes numbers bigger" or that $12 - 0$ must be 11 because "subtracting makes

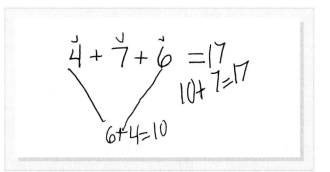

FIGURE 9.7 A student shows how she added. Note the check marks that helped her keep track of numbers added.

numbers smaller." Instead of making arbitrary-sounding rules about adding and subtracting zero, build opportunities for discussing zero into the problem-solving routine. Explore Franco's *Zero Is the Leaves on the Tree* (2009), a wonderful piece of children's literature to develop contexts for exploring situations with zero.

Although these properties are algebraic in nature (generalized rules), they are discussed here because the meanings of the properties are essential to understanding how numbers can be added. Explicit attention to these concepts (not the terminology) will help students become more flexible (and efficient) in how they combine numbers.

Multiplication and Division Problem Structure

Like addition and subtraction, there are problem structures that will help you as the teacher in formulating and assigning multiplication and division tasks. They will also help your students in generalizing as they solve familiar situations.

Most researchers identify four different classes of multiplicative structures (Greer, 1992). (The term *multiplicative* is used here to describe all types of problems that involve multiplication and division.) Of these, the two described in Figure 9.8, *equal groups* (*repeated addition*, *rates*) and *multiplicative comparison*, are by far the most prevalent in the elementary school. Problems matching these structures can be modeled with sets

of counters, number lines, or arrays. They represent a large percentage of the multiplicative problems in the real world.

In multiplicative problems, one number or *factor* counts how many sets, groups, or parts of equal size are involved. The other factor tells the size of each set or part. The third number in each of these two structures is the *whole* or *product* and is the total of all of the parts. The *parts and wholes* terminology is useful in making the connection to addition.

Examples of Equal-Group Problems

When the number and size of groups are known, the problem is a multiplication situation. When either the number of sets or the size of sets is unknown, then the problem is a division situation. But note that these division situations are not alike. Problems in which the size of the sets is unknown are called *fair-sharing* or *partition* problems. The whole is shared or distributed among a known number of sets to determine the size of each. If the number of sets is unknown but the size of the equal sets is known, the problems are called *measurement* or sometimes *repeated-subtraction* problems. The whole is "measured off" in sets of the given size. Use the illustrations in Figure 9.8 as a reference.

There is also a subtle difference between equal-group problems (also called *repeated-addition* problems, such as "If three children have four apples each, how many apples are there?") and those that might be termed *rate* problems ("If there are four apples per child, how many apples would three children have?").

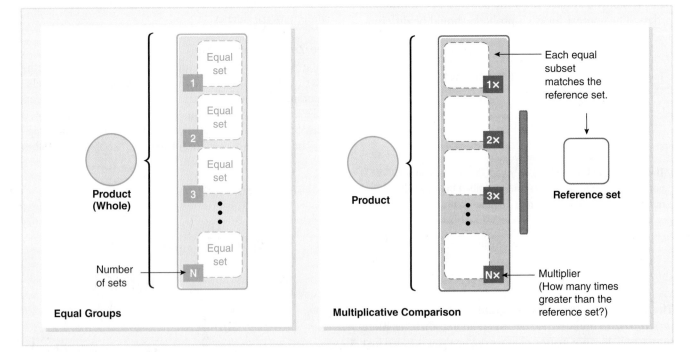

FIGURE 9.8 Two of the four problem structures for multiplication and division story problems. Each structure has three numbers. Any one of the three numbers can be the unknown in a story problem.

Equal Groups: Whole Unknown (Multiplication)

Mark has 4 bags of apples. There are 6 apples in each bag. How many apples does Mark have altogether? (*repeated addition*)

If apples cost 7 cents each, how much did Jill have to pay for 5 apples? (*rate*)

Peter walked for 3 hours at 4 miles per hour. How far did he walk? (*rate*)

Equal Groups: Size of Groups Unknown (Partition Division)

Mark has 24 apples. He wants to share them equally among his 4 friends. How many apples will each friend receive? (*fair sharing*)

Jill paid 35 cents for 5 apples. What was the cost of 1 apple? (*rate*)

Peter walked 12 miles in 3 hours. How many miles per hour (how fast) did he walk? (*rate*)

Equal Groups: Number of Groups Unknown (Measurement Division)

Mark has 24 apples. He put them into bags containing 6 apples each. How many bags did Mark use? (*repeated subtraction*)

Jill bought apples at 7 cents apiece. The total cost of her apples was 35 cents. How many apples did Jill buy? (*rate*)

Peter walked 12 miles at a rate of 4 miles per hour. How many hours did it take Peter to walk the 12 miles? (*rate*)

Examples of Comparison Problems

In multiplicative comparison problems, there are really two different sets, as there were with comparison situations for addition and subtraction. In additive situations, the comparison is an amount or quantity difference. In multiplicative situations, the comparison is based on one set being a particular multiple of the other. Two examples of each multiplicative comparison problem are provided here.

Comparison: Product Unknown (Multiplication)

Jill picked 6 apples. Mark picked 4 times as many apples as Jill. How many apples did Mark pick?

This month, Mark saved 5 times as much money as last month. Last month, he saved $7. How much money did Mark save this month?

Comparison: Set Size Unknown (Partition Division)

Mark picked 24 apples. He picked 4 times as many apples as Jill. How many apples did Jill pick?

This month, Mark saved 5 times as much money as he did last month. If he saved $35 this month, how much did he save last month?

Comparison: Multiplier Unknown (Measurement Division)

Mark picked 24 apples, and Jill picked only 6. How many times as many apples did Mark pick as Jill did?

This month, Mark saved $35. Last month, he saved $7. How many times as much money did he save this month as last?

 PAUSE and REFLECT

What you just read is complex yet important. Stop now and get a collection of about 35 counters to model the equal-groups examples starring "Mark." Match the story with the structure model in Figure 9.8. How are these problems alike, and how are they different? Repeat for "Jill" and "Peter" problems.

Repeat the same process with the comparison problems. Again, start with the first problem in all three sets and then the second problem in all three sets. Reflect on how they are the same and different. ●

Although the following two multiplicative structures are more complex and therefore not a good introductory point, it is important that you recognize them as two other categories of multiplicative situations.

Combinations (also called *Cartesian products*) and *area* (also called *product-of-measures*) problems are less frequently mentioned within the multiplication and division sections of most curricula but are used with older elementary and middle grade students.

Examples of Combination Problems

Combination problems involve counting the number of possible pairings that can be made between two or more sets.

Combinations: Product Unknown

Sam bought 4 pairs of pants and 3 jackets, and they all can be worn together. How many different outfits consisting of a pair of pants and a jacket does Sam have?

An experiment involves tossing a coin and rolling a die. How many different possible results or outcomes can this experiment have?

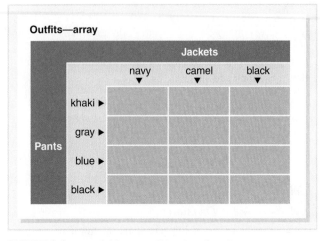

FIGURE 9.9 A model for a combination situation.

In these two examples, the product is unknown and the size of the two sets is given. It is possible—rarely—to have related division problems for the combinations concept. Figure 9.9 shows one common method of modeling combination problems: an array. Counting how many combinations of two or more things or events are possible is important in determining probabilities. The combinations concept is most often found in the probability strand.

Examples of Area and Other Product-of-Measures Problems

What distinguishes product-of-measures problems from the others is that the product is literally a different type of unit from the other two factors. In a rectangular shape, the product of two lengths (length × width) is an area, usually square units. Figure 9.10 illustrates how different the square units are from the two factors of length: 4 feet times 7 feet is not 28 feet but 28 square feet. The factors are each one-dimensional entities, but the product consists of *two*-dimensional units.

Two other fairly common examples in this category are number of workers × hours worked = worker-hours and kilowatts × hours = kilowatt-hours.

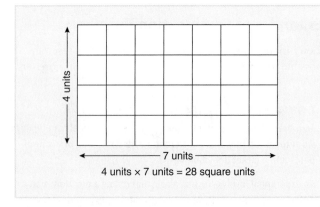

4 units × 7 units = 28 square units

FIGURE 9.10 Length times length equals area.

Teaching Multiplication and Division

Multiplication and division are often taught separately, with multiplication preceding division. It is important, however, to combine multiplication and division soon after multiplication has been introduced in order to help students see how they are related. In most curricula, these topics are first presented in grade 2 (as suggested by *Curriculum Focal Points* and *Common Core State Standards*) and then become a major focus of the third grade with continued development in the fourth and fifth grades. "In grades 3–5, students should focus on the meanings of, and relationship between, multiplication and division. It is important that students understand what each number in a multiplication or division expression represents. . . . Modeling multiplication problems with pictures, diagrams, or concrete materials helps students learn what the factors and their product represent in various contexts" (NCTM, 2000, p. 151).

A major conceptual hurdle in working with multiplicative structures is understanding groups of items as single entities while also understanding that a group contains a given number of objects (Blote, Lieffering, & Ouewhand, 2006; Clark & Kamii, 1996). Children can solve the problem, "How many apples in 4 baskets of 8 apples each?" by counting out four sets of eight counters and then counting all. To think multiplicatively about this problem as *four sets of eight* requires children to conceptualize each group of eight as a single item to be counted. Experiences with making and counting equal groups, especially in contextual situations, are extremely useful. (See the discussion of the article "Connecting Multiplication to Contexts and Language" at the end of this chapter.)

Contextual Problems

Many of the issues surrounding addition and subtraction also apply to multiplication and division and need not be discussed in depth again. It remains important, for example, to use interesting contextual problems instead of more sterile story problems whenever possible, use strategies to ensure they are comprehensible to ELLs, build lessons around only two or three problems, and encourage students to solve problems using whatever techniques they wish, using words, pictures, and numbers to explain their process.

Symbolism for Multiplication and Division. When students solve simple multiplication story problems before learning about multiplication symbolism, they will most likely write repeated-addition equations to represent what they did. This is your opportunity to introduce the multiplication sign and explain what the two factors mean.

The usual convention is that 4×8 refers to four sets of eight, not eight sets of four. There is no reason to be rigid about this convention. The important thing is that the students can tell you what each factor in *their* equations represents. In vertical form, it is usually the bottom factor that indicates the number of sets. Again, this distinction is not terribly important.

The quotient 24 divided by 6 is represented in three different ways: $24 \div 6$, $6\overline{)24}$, and $\frac{24}{6}$. Students should understand that these representations are equivalent. The fraction notation becomes important at the middle school level. Students often mistakenly read $6\overline{)24}$ as "6 divided by 24" due to the left-to-right order of the numerals. Generally this error does not match what they are thinking.

Compounding the difficulty of division notation is the unfortunate phrase "goes into," as in "6 goes into 24." This phrase carries little meaning about the division concept, especially in connection with a fair-sharing or partitioning context. The "goes into" terminology is simply engrained in adult parlance; it has not been in textbooks for years. Instead of this phrase, use appropriate terminology ("How many groups of 6 are in 24?") with students.

Choosing Numbers for Problems. When selecting numbers for multiplicative story problems or activities, there is a tendency to think that large numbers pose a burden to students or that 3×4 is somehow easier to understand than 4×17. An understanding of products or quotients is not affected by the size of numbers as long as the numbers are within the grasp of the students. A contextual problem involving 14×8 is appropriate for second or third graders. When given these challenges, children are likely to invent computational strategies (e.g., ten 8s and then four more 8s) or model the problem with manipulatives.

Remainders

More often than not in real-world situations, division does not result in a simple whole number. For example, problems with 6 as a divisor will result in a whole number only one time out of six. In the absence of a context, a remainder can be dealt with in only two ways: It can either remain a quantity left over or be partitioned into fractions. In Figure 9.11, the problem $11 \div 4$ is modeled to show fractions.

In real contexts, remainders sometimes have three additional effects on answers:

- The remainder is discarded, leaving a smaller whole-number answer.
- The remainder can "force" the answer to the next highest whole number.
- The answer is rounded to the nearest whole number for an approximate result.

The following problems illustrate all five possibilities.

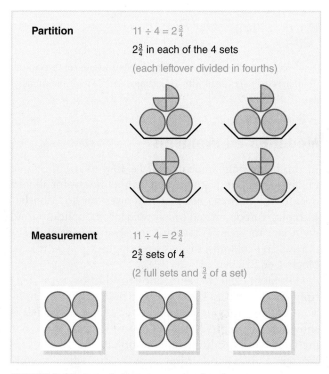

FIGURE 9.11 Remainders expressed as fractions.

1. You have 30 pieces of candy to share fairly with 7 children. How many pieces of candy will each child receive?
   Answer: 4 pieces of candy and 2 left over. (*left over*)

2. Each jar holds 8 ounces of liquid. If there are 46 ounces in the pitcher, how many jars will that be?
   Answer: 5 and $\frac{6}{8}$ jars. (*partitioned as a fraction*)

3. The rope is 25 feet long. How many 7-foot jump ropes can be made?
   Answer: 3 jump ropes. (*discarded*)

4. The ferry can hold 8 cars. How many trips will it have to make to carry 25 cars across the river?
   Answer: 4 trips. (*forced to next whole number*)

5. Six children are planning to share a bag of 50 pieces of bubble gum. About how many pieces will each child get?
   Answer: About 8 pieces for each child. (*rounded, approximate result*)

Students should not just think of remainders as "R 3" or "left over." Addressing what to do with remainders must be central to teaching about division. In fact, one of the most common errors students make on high-stakes assessments is to divide and then not pay attention to the context when selecting their answer. For example, in problem 4, answering with $3\frac{1}{8}$ trips doesn't make any sense.

PAUSE and REFLECT

It is useful for you to make up problems in different contexts. See if you can come up with division problems whose contexts would result in remainders dealt with as fractions, rounded up, and rounded down. ●

Model-Based Problems

In the beginning, students will be able to use the same models—sets, bar diagrams, and number lines—for all four operations. A model not generally used for addition but extremely important and widely used for multiplication and division is the array. An *array* is any arrangement of things in rows and columns, such as a rectangle of square tiles or blocks (see Blackline Master 12).

To make clear the connection to addition, early multiplication activities should also include writing an addition sentence for the same model. A variety of models is shown in Figure 9.12. Notice that the products are not included—only addition and multiplication "names" are written. This is another way to avoid the tedious counting of large sets. A similar approach is to write one sentence that expresses both concepts at once, for example, $9 + 9 + 9 + 9 = 4 \times 9$.

As with additive problems, students benefit from activities with models to focus on the meaning of the operation and the associated symbolism. Activity 9.4 has a good problem-solving spirit.

Activity 9.4

Finding Factors

Start by having students think about a context that involves arrays such as parade formations (see the Literature Connections at the end of the chapter), seats in a classroom, or patches of a quilt. Then assign a number that has several factors—for example, 12, 18, 24, 30, or 36. Have students find as many arrays (perhaps made from square tiles or cubes or drawn on grid paper) and corresponding multiplication and addition expressions for their assigned number as possible. (Students can also use counters and attempt to find a way to separate the counters into equal subsets.) For students with physical disabilities who may have limited motor skills to manipulate the materials, this activity is available as an applet at http://illuminations.nctm.org/ActivityDetail.aspx?id=64.

Activity 9.4 can also include division concepts. When students have learned that 3 and 6 are factors of 18, they can write the equations $18 \div 3 = 6$ and $18 \div 6 = 3$ along with $3 \times 6 = 18$ and $6 + 6 + 6 = 18$ (assuming that three sets of six were modeled). The following variation of the same activity focuses on division. Having students create word problems to fit what they did with the tiles, cubes, or counters is another excellent elaboration of this activity. Connecting the situation to the materials and to the equation is important in demonstrating understanding.

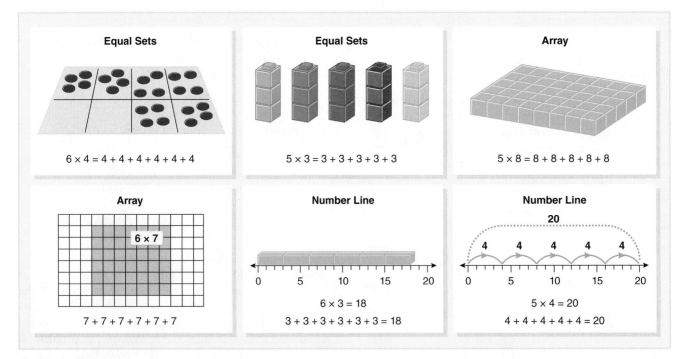

FIGURE 9.12 Models for equal-group multiplication.

Activity 9.5

Learning about Division

Using the context of a story about sharing such as *Bean Thirteen* (McElligott, 2007), provide children with a supply of counters (beans) and a way to place them into small groups (small paper cups). Have children count out a number of counters to be the whole or total set. They record this number. Next, specify either the number of equal sets to be made or the size of the sets: "Separate your counters into four equal-sized sets," or "Make as many sets of four as is possible." Next, have the students write the corresponding multiplication equation for what their materials show; under that, have them write the division equation. For ELLs, be sure they know what *sets, equal-sized sets,* and *sets of four* mean. For students with disabilities, consider having them start with a partition approach, in which they share the counters by placing one at a time into each cup.

STUDENTS *with* SPECIAL NEEDS

ENGLISH LANGUAGE LEARNERS

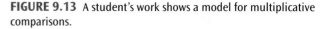

FIGURE 9.13 A student's work shows a model for multiplicative comparisons.

frequently found in the mathematics programs emerging from Singapore (Beckmann, 2004). See Figure 9.13 for a bar diagram related to this situation:

> Zane has 5 small toy cars. Madeline has 4 times as many cars. How many does Madeline have?

Be sure to have the class do both types of exercises: number of equal sets and size of sets. Discuss with the class how these two are different, how each is related to multiplication, and how each is written as a division equation. You can show the different ways to write division equations at this time. Do Activity 9.5 several times. Start with whole quantities that are multiples of the divisor (no remainders), but soon include situations with remainders. (Explain that it is technically incorrect to write $31 \div 4 = 7$ R 3.)

The activity can be varied by changing the model. Have children build arrays using square tiles or blocks or draw arrays on centimeter grid paper. Present the exercises by specifying how many squares are to be in the array. You can then specify the number of rows that should be made (partition) or the length of each row (measurement). How could students model the remainder using drawings of arrays on grid paper?

TECHNOLOGY The applet "Rectangle Division" from the National Library of Virtual Manipulatives website (http://nlvm.usu.edu/en/nav/frames_asid_193_g_2_t_1.html?from=category_g_2_t_1.html) is an interactive illustration of division with remainders. A division problem is presented with an array showing the selected number of squares in the product. The dimensions of the array can be modified, but the number of squares stays constant. If, for example, you model the problem $52 \div 8$, the squares will show an 8 by 6 array with 4 remaining squares in a different color ($8 \times 6 + 4$) as well as any other variation of 52 squares in a rectangular array plus a shorter column for the extra squares. This applet vividly demonstrates how division is related to multiplication.

Consider exploring the multiplicative comparison problems with the use of a bar diagram. These diagrams are

Activity 9.6

The Broken Multiplication Key

The calculator is a good way to relate multiplication to addition. Students can find various products on the calculator without using the ☒ key. For example, 6×4 can be found by pressing ⊞ 4 ⊜ ⊜ ⊜ ⊜ ⊜ ⊜. (Successive presses of ⊜ add 4 to the display each time. You began with zero and added 4 six times.) Students can be challenged to justify their result with sets of counters. This same technique can be used to determine products such as 23×459 (⊞ 459 and then 23 presses of ⊜). Students will want to compare to the same product using the ☒ key. Because the function of using the equal sign on the calculator may be abstract for some students with disabilities, you may need to actually carry out the repeated addition by adding 4 ⊞ 4 ⊞ 4 ⊞ 4 ⊞ 4 ⊞ 4 ⊜ on a scientific calculator so the student can see the full equation and the answer on the same screen.

Activity 9.7

The Broken Division Key

Have students work in groups to find methods of using the calculator to solve division exercises without using the divide key. "Find at least two ways to figure out $61 \div 14$ without pressing the divide key." If the problem is put in a story context, one method may actually match the problem better than another. Good discussions may follow different solutions with the same answers. Are they both correct? Why or why not?

Explore Broken Calculators at www.nctm.org/
eresources/view_article.asp?article_id=7457&
page=11&add=Y and www.fi.uu.nl/toepassingen/
00014/toepassing_rekenweb.en.html. These
two applets demonstrate the activities above, allowing for
problems at different levels.

PAUSE and REFLECT

Can you can find *three* ways to solve 61 ÷ 14 on a calculator
without using the divide key? For a hint, see the footnote.* ●

Properties of Multiplication and Division

As with addition and subtraction, there are some multiplicative properties that are useful and thus worthy of attention. The emphasis should be on the ideas and not
terminology or definitions.

Commutative and Associative Properties of Multiplication.
It is not obvious that 3 × 8 is the same as 8 × 3 or that, in
general, the order of the numbers makes no difference (the
commutative property). A picture of 3 sets of 8 objects cannot
immediately be seen as 8 piles of 3 objects, nor on a number
line are 8 hops of 3 noticeably the same as 3 hops of 8.

The array, by contrast, is quite powerful in illustrating
the commutative property, as shown in Figure 9.14a. Children should build or draw arrays and use them to demonstrate why each array represents two equivalent products.
As in addition, there is an *associative property* of multiplication that is fundamental in flexibly solving problems
(Ding & Li, 2010). This property allows that when you
multiply three numbers in an expression, you can multiply
either the first pair of numbers or the last pair and the product remains the same. A context is helpful, so here is an
example that could be shared with students. Each tennis ball
costs $2. There are 6 cans of tennis balls with 3 balls in each
can. How much will it cost if we need to buy 6 cans? After
analyzing the problem by showing actual cans of tennis
balls or illustrations, students should try to consider the
problem from two ways: (1) find out the cost for each can
and then the total cost (2 × 3) × 6; and (2) find out how
many balls in total and then the total cost 2 × (3 × 6) (Ding,
2010). See Figure 9.14(b).

Zero and Identity Properties.   Factors of 0 and, to a lesser
extent, 1 often cause conceptual challenges for students. In
textbooks, you may find that a lesson on factors of 0 and 1

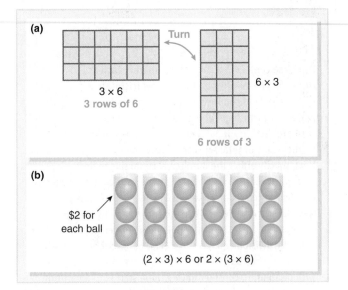

FIGURE 9.14 A model for the commutative property for
multiplication (a) and an illustration of a problem showing the
associative property of multiplication (b).

has students use a calculator to examine a wide range of
products involving 0 or 1 (423 × 0, 0 × 28, 1536 × 1, etc.)
and look for patterns. The pattern suggests the rules for
factors of 0 and 1 but not a reason. In another lesson, a word
problem asks how many grams of fat there are in 7 servings
of celery with 0 grams of fat in each serving. This approach
is far preferable to an arbitrary rule, because it asks students
to reason. Make up interesting word problems involving
0 or 1, and discuss the results. Problems with 0 as a first
factor are really strange. Note that on a number line, 5 hops
of 0 lands at 0 (5 × 0). What would 0 hops of 5 be? Another
fun activity is to try to model 6 × 0 or 0 × 8 with an array.
(Try it!) Arrays for factors of 1 are also worth investigating.
(Numbers that can only be made with an array with dimensions of 1 and itself are prime numbers!)

Distributive Property.   The *distributive property of multiplication over addition* refers to the idea that either one of the
two factors in a product can be split (decomposed) into two
or more parts and each part multiplied separately and then
added. The result is the same as when the original factors
are multiplied. For example, to find the number of yogurts
in 9 six-packs, use the logic that 9 × 6 is the same as (5 ×
6) + (4 × 6). The 9 has been split into 5 six-packs and 4 six-
packs. The concept involved is very useful in relating one
basic fact to another, and it is also involved in the development of two-digit computation. Figure 9.15 illustrates how
the array model can be used to demonstrate that a product
can be broken up into two parts.

The next activity is designed to help students discover
how to partition factors or, in other words, learn about the
distributive property of multiplication over addition.

---

*There are two measurement approaches to find out how many 14s
are in 61. A third way is essentially related to partitioning or finding
14 times what number is close to 61.

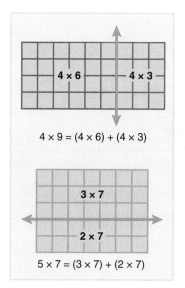

FIGURE 9.15 Models for the distributive property of multiplication over addition.

Activity **9.8**

Divide It Up

Supply students with several sheets of centimeter grid paper or color tiles to represent a small garden. Assign each pair of students a garden plot size such as 6 × 8. Garden sizes (products) can vary across the class to differentiate for varying skill levels. The task is to find all of the different ways to make a single slice or cut through the garden to divide the plot for two different vegetables. For each slice, students write an equation. For a slice of one row of 8, students would write 6 × 8 = (5 × 8) + (1 × 8). This might be a good time to discuss order of operations. The individual equations can be written in the arrays as shown in Figure 9.15.

Why Not Division by Zero?   Sometimes children are simply told, "Division by zero is not allowed," often because teachers do not fully understand this concept themselves (Quinn, Lamberg, & Perrin, 2008). Some students harbor misconceptions that the answer should be either zero or the number itself. How did you learn this information? To avoid an arbitrary rule, pose problems to be modeled that involve zero: "Take 30 counters. How many sets of 0 can be made?" or "Put 12 blocks in 0 equal groups. How many in each group?" or "Can you show me how to share 5 oranges with 0 children?" Then move students toward reasoned explanations (Crespo & Nicol, 2006) that consider the inverse relationship of multiplication and division and take the answer and put it back into a multiplication problem as a check. Then, with the orange problem you would ask, "What when multiplied by 0 produces an answer of 5?" Right, there is no answer. If you have students think of it as

repeated subtraction, they would take 0 from the original 5 oranges, leaving 5 and so forth. Therefore, division by 0 is undefined; it just doesn't make sense when we use our definition of division and its inverse relationship to multiplication.

Strategies for Solving Contextual Problems

Often students see context or story problems and are at a loss for what to do. Also, struggling readers or ELL students may need support in understanding the problem. In this section, you will learn some techniques for helping them.

Analyzing Context Problems

Consider the following problem:

> In building a road through a neighborhood, workers filled in large holes in the ground with dirt brought in by trucks. To completely fill the holes required 638 truckloads of dirt. The average truck carried $6\frac{1}{4}$ cubic yards of dirt, which weighed 7.3 tons. How many tons of dirt were used to fill the hole?

Typically, in textbooks, this kind of example is presented in a series of problems revolving around a single context or theme. Data may be found in a graph or chart or perhaps a short news item or story. Students may have difficulty deciding on the correct operation and are often challenged to identify the appropriate data for solving the problem. Sometimes they will find two numbers in the problem and guess at the correct operation. Instead, students need tools for analyzing problems. At least two strategies can be taught that are very helpful: (1) thinking about the answer before solving the problem, or (2) working a simpler problem.

Think about the Answer Before Solving the Problem. Students who struggle with problem solving need to spend adequate time thinking about the problem and what it is about. In addition, ELLs need to comprehend both the contextual words (like *dirt, filled,* and *road*) and the mathematical terminology (*cubic yards, weighed, tons, how many*). Instead of rushing in and beginning to do calculations, with the belief that "number crunching" is what solves problems, they should spend time talking about (and, later, thinking about) what the answer might look like. In fact, one great strategy for differentiation is to pose the problem with the numbers missing or covered up. This eliminates the tendency to number crunch. For our sample problem, it might go as follows:

What is happening in this problem? Some trucks were bringing dirt in to fill up big holes.

Is there any extra information we don't need? We don't need to know about the cubic yards in each truck.

What will the answer tell us? It will tell how many tons of dirt were needed to fill the holes. My answer will be some number of tons.

Will that be a small number of tons or a large number of tons? Well, there were 7.3 tons on a truck, but there were a lot of trucks, not just one. It's probably going to be a lot of tons.

About how many tons do you think it will be? It's going to be a lot. If there were 1000 trucks, it would be about 7300 tons, so it will be less than that. But it will be more than half of 7300, so the answer is more than 3650 tons.

In this type of discussion, three things are happening. First, students are asked to focus on the problem and the meaning of the answer instead of on numbers. The numbers are not important in thinking about the structure of the problem. Second, with a focus on the structure of the problem, students identify the numbers that are important as well as numbers that are not important. Third, the thinking leads to a rough estimate of the answer and the unit of the answer (tons in this case). In any event, thinking about what the answer tells and about how large it might be is a useful starting point.

Work a Simpler Problem. The reason that models are rarely used with problems such as the dirt problem is that the large numbers are very challenging to model. Distances in thousands of miles and time in minutes and seconds—data likely to be found in the upper grades—are difficult to model. The general problem-solving strategy of "try a simpler problem" can almost always be applied to problems with unwieldy numbers.

A simpler-problem strategy has the following steps:

1. Substitute small whole numbers for all relevant numbers in the problem.
2. Model the problem (with counters, drawings, number lines, or arrays) using the new numbers.
3. Write an equation that solves the simpler version of the problem.
4. Write the corresponding equation substituting back the original numbers.
5. Calculate or use a calculator to do the computation.
6. Write the answer in a complete sentence, and decide whether it makes sense.

Figure 9.16 shows how the dirt problem might be made simpler. It also shows an alternative in which only one

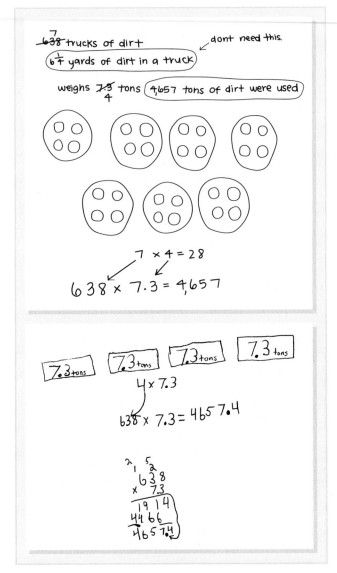

FIGURE 9.16 Two ways students created a simpler problem.

of the numbers is made smaller and the other number is illustrated symbolically. Both methods are effective.

The idea is to provide a tool students can use to analyze a problem and not just guess at what computation to do. It is much more useful to have students do a few problems in which they must use a model of a drawing to justify their solution than to give them a lot of problems in which they guess at a solution but don't use reasoning and sense making.

Caution: Avoid Relying on the Key Word Strategy! It is often suggested that students should be taught to find "key words" in story problems. Some teachers even post lists of key words with their corresponding meanings. For example, "altogether" and "in all" mean you should add, and "left" and "fewer" indicate you should subtract. The word "each" suggests multiplication. To some extent, teachers have been reinforced by the overly simple and formulaic story problems sometimes found in textbooks and other times by their own reading skills (Sulentic-Dowell, Beal, & Capraro, 2006). When problems are written in this way, it may appear that the key word strategy is effective.

In contrast with this belief, researchers and mathematics educators have long cautioned against the strategy of key words (e.g., Clement & Bernhard, 2005; Kenney, Hancewicz, Heyer, Metsisto, & Tuttle, 2005; Sowder, 1988). Here are four arguments against relying on the key word approach.

1. The key word strategy sends a terribly wrong message about doing mathematics. The most important approach to solving any contextual problem is to analyze it and make sense of it. The key word approach encourages students to ignore the meaning and structure of the problem and look for an easy way out. Mathematics is about reasoning and making sense of situations. Sense-making strategies always work!

2. Key words are often misleading. Many times, the key word or phrase in a problem suggests an operation that is incorrect. The following problem shared by Drake and Barlow (2007) demonstrates this possibility:

> There are three boxes of chicken nuggets on the table. Each box contains six chicken nuggets. How many chicken nuggets are there in all? (p. 272)

Drake and Barlow found that one student generated the answer of 9, using the words "how many in all" as a suggestion to add 3 + 6. Instead of making sense of the situation, the student used the key word approach as a shortcut in making an operational decision.

3. Many problems have no key words. Except for the overly simple problems found in primary textbooks, a large percentage of problems have no key words. A student who has been taught to rely on key words is left with no strategy. Here's an example:

> Aidan has 28 goldfish. Twelve are orange and the rest are yellow. How many goldfish are yellow?

4. Key words don't work with two-step problems or more advanced problems, so using this approach on simpler problems sets students up for failure as they are not learning how to read for meaning.

Two-Step Problems

Students often have difficulty with multistep problems. First, be sure they can analyze the structure of one-step problems in the way that we have discussed. The following ideas, adapted from suggestions by Huinker (1994), are designed to help students see how two problems can be linked together.

1. Give students a one-step problem and have them solve it. Before discussing the answer, have the students use the answer to the first problem to create a second problem. The rest of the class can then be asked to solve the second problem, as in the following example:

> *Given problem:* It took 3 hours for the Morgan family to drive the 195 miles to Washington, D.C. What was their average speed?
>
> *Second problem:* The Morgan children remember crossing the river at about 10:30, or 2 hours after they left home. About how far from home is the river?

2. Make a "hidden question." Repeat the approach above by giving groups of students a one-step problem. Give different problems to different groups. Have them solve it and write a second problem. Then they should write a single combined problem that leaves out the question from the first problem. That question from the first problem is the "hidden question," as in this example:

> *Given problem:* Toby bought three dozen eggs for 89 cents a dozen. How much was the total cost?
>
> *Second problem:* How much change did Toby get back from $5?
>
> *Hidden-question problem:* Toby bought three dozen eggs for 89 cents a dozen. How much change did Toby get back from $5?

Have other students identify the hidden question. Since all students are working on a similar task but with different problems (be sure to mix the operations), they will be more likely to understand what is meant by *hidden question*.

3. Pose standard two-step problems, and have the students identify and answer the hidden question. Consider the following problem:

> The Marsal Company bought 275 widgets wholesale for $3.69 each. In the first month, the company sold 205 widgets at $4.99 each. How much did the company make or lose on the widgets? Do you think the Marsal Company should continue to sell widgets?

Begin by considering the questions that were suggested earlier: "What's happening in this problem?" (Something is being bought and sold at two different prices.) "What will the answer tell us?" (How much profit or loss there was.) These questions will get you started. If students are stuck, you can ask, "Is there a hidden question in this problem?" While the examples given here provide a range of contexts, using the *same* (and familiar) context across this three-step process would reduce the linguistic demands for ELLs and therefore make the stories more comprehensible—and the mathematics more accessible.

The value of student discussion, described in the preceding paragraph, is quite evident in the NCTM *Standards*. The K–2 level states the following: "When students struggle to communicate ideas clearly, they develop a better understanding of their own thinking" (2000, p. 129). According to the grades 3–5 level of the standards, "The use of models and pictures provides a further opportunity for understanding and conversation. Having a concrete referent helps students develop understandings that are clearer and more easily shared" (2000, p. 197).

FORMATIVE Assessment Notes

One of the best ways to assess students' knowledge of the meaning of the operations is to have them generate story problems for a given equation or result (Drake & Barlow, 2007; Whitin & Whitin, 2008). Use a

diagnostic interview to see whether your students can flexibly think about an operation. Fold a sheet of paper into quarters. Give the students an expression such as 5×7; ask that they record the question and answer it in the upper left-hand quarter, write a story problem representing the expression in another quarter of the paper, draw a picture (or model) in the third section, and describe how they would tell a younger student how to solve this problem in the last section. (For a student with disabilities, the student could dictate the story problem and the description of the solving process while the teacher transcribes.) Students who can ably match scenarios, models, and explanations to the computation will demonstrate their understanding, whereas struggling students will reveal areas of weakness. This assessment can be adapted by giving students the result (e.g., "24 cents") and asking them to write a subtraction problem (or a division problem or any other appropriate type of problem) that will generate that answer, along with models and word problems written in the remaining quarters. Another option is to use a piece of children's literature to write a word problem that emphasizes the meaning of one of the four operations; each student then has to complete the other three sections. ∎

RESOURCES *for Chapter 9*

LITERATURE CONNECTIONS

There are many books with stories or pictures concerning sets, purchase items, measures, and so on that can be used to pose problems or, better, to stimulate children to invent their own problems. Perhaps the most widely mentioned book in this context is *The Doorbell Rang* by Pat Hutchins (1986). You can check that one out yourself, as well as the following three additional suggestions.

Guinea Pigs Add Up *Cuyler, 2010*

Appropriate for the pre-K–2 reader, this is a fun story of a growing and changing population of guinea pigs that are class pets. Starting with the addition of a set of babies, then multiplication by litters of baby guinea pigs and finally the distribution of pets to children who adopt them, there are many scenarios that engage the students. Of special note is the opportunity for students to use missing-part thinking for subtraction. Children can pose their own questions about the illustrations and record the appropriate number sentences.

One Hundred Hungry Ants *Pinczes, 1999*

This book, written by a grandmother for her grandchild, helps students explore the operation of multiplication (and division). It

tells the tale of 100 ants on a trip to a picnic. In an attempt to speed their travel, the ants move from a single-file line of 100 to two rows of 50, four rows of 25, and so forth. This story uses the visual representation of arrays to explore the options. Students can be given different sizes of ant groups to explore factors and products.

Remainder of One *Pinczes, 2002*

Similar to her other book, Pinczes describes the trials and tribulations of a parade formation of 25 bugs. As the queen views the rectangular outline of the parading bugs, she notices that 1 bug is trailing behind. The group tries to create different numbers of rows and columns (arrays), but again 1 bug is always a "leftover" (remainder). Students can be given different parade groups and can generate formations that will leave 1, 2, or none out of the group.

RECOMMENDED READINGS

Articles

Clement, L., & Bernhard, J. (2005). A problem-solving alternative to using key words. *Mathematics Teaching in the Middle School, 10*(7), 360–365.
This article explores the use of sense making in solving word problems as a replacement for using key words. The emphasis is

on the meanings of the operations as common student misconceptions are analyzed.

Sullivan, A. D., & Roth McDuffie, A. (2009). Connecting multiplication to contexts and language. *Teaching Children Mathematics, 15*(8), 502–512.
This article examines a way to give meaning to multiplication. By avoiding the word times *and moving toward collective nouns (e.g., a pride of lions), the students (including students with disabilities) explored photos of real-world groupings and created their own word problems.*

Books

Carpenter, T. P., Fennema, E., Franke, M. L., Levi, L., & Empson, S. (1999). *Children's mathematics: Cognitively guided instruction.* Portsmouth, NH: Heinemann.
This is the classic book for understanding the CGI approach to number and operations. Word-problem structures for all operations, as discussed in this chapter, are explained in detail along with methods for using these problems with students. The book comes with videos of classrooms and children modeling strategies.
Caldwell, J., Karp, K., & Bay-Williams, J. M. (2011). *Developing essential understanding of addition and subtraction for teaching mathematics in prekindergarten–grade 2.* Reston, VA: NCTM.
Otto, A., Caldwell, J., Lubinski, C., & Hancock, S. (2011). *Developing essential understanding of multiplication and division for teaching mathematics in grades 3–5.* Reston, VA: NCTM.

These two books offer the big ideas about the four operations using a three-part approach: the mathematical content teachers need to know, connections to other topics, and how to teach these topics. These are essential resources in any teacher's professional library.

ONLINE RESOURCES

All About Multiplication (Grades 3–5)
http://illuminations.nctm.org/LessonDetail
.aspx?id=U109
Four lessons with links to other activities and student recording sheets highlight the models of the number line, equal groups, arrays, and balanced equations.

Thinking Blocks: Addition and Subtraction
www.thinkingblocks.com/ThinkingBlocks_AS/TB_AS_Main.html

Thinking Blocks: Multiplication and Division
www.thinkingblocks.com/ThinkingBlocks_MD/TB_MD_Main.html
These teacher-developed tools link to the various problem structures. They use two-digit numbers and problems with multiple steps, including compare, part-part-whole, and change examples. Because the ideas are presented as games, view the introduction to be able to play.

REFLECTIONS *on Chapter 9*

WRITING TO LEARN

1. Make up a compare story problem. Alter the problem to provide an example of all six different possibilities for compare problems.
2. Explain how missing-part activities prepare students for mastering subtraction facts.
3. Make up multiplication story problems to illustrate the difference between equal groups and multiplicative comparison. Create a story problem involving rates or products of measures.
4. Make up two different story problems for 36 ÷ 9. Create one problem as a measurement problem and one as a partition problem.
5. Make up realistic measurement and partition division problems in which the remainder is dealt with in each of these three ways: (a) it is discarded (but not left over); (b) it is made into a fraction; (c) it forces the answer to the next whole number.
6. Why is the use of key words not a good strategy to teach children?

FOR DISCUSSION AND EXPLORATION

1. The National Mathematics Advisory Panel (2008) deemed number properties as a critical foundation for school mathematics. What is the importance of students learning the underlying principles of the fundamental properties of the operations (commutative, associative, distributive, etc.)? How does the knowledge of these "rules of arithmetic" prepare students for making generalizations and thereby develop their ability to reason algebraically?
2. See how many different story problem structures you can find in a textbook. In the primary grades, look for join, separate, part-part-whole, and compare problems. For grades 3 and up, look for the four multiplicative types. (Examine the multiplication and division chapters and also any special problem-solving lessons.) Are the various problem structures well represented?

MyEducationLab™

Go to the MyEducationLab (www.myeducationlab.com) for Math Methods and familiarize yourself with the content. Much of the site content is organized topically. The topics include all of the following to support your learning in the course:

- Learning outcomes for important mathematics methods course topics aligned with the national standards
- Assignments and Activities, tied to these learning outcomes and standards, that can help you more deeply understand course content
- Building Teaching Skills and Dispositions learning units that allow you to apply and practice your understanding of the core mathematics content and teaching skills

Your instructor has a correlation guide that aligns the exercises on the topical portion of the site with your book's chapters.

You'll also find a Study Plan written specifically to align with the chapters of this book. The pre-test, Review Practice and Enrichment Activities, and post-test offer feedback and support that allow you to check and enhance your understanding of the content in each chapter.

Field Experience Guide
C O N N E C T I O N S

The formative assessment discussed at the end of this chapter is detailed in FEG 3.4, "Student Interview: Assessing Mathematical Proficiency," with the accompanying Link Sheet already divided into quarters. Also, use FEG Field Experiences 3.1 and 3.6, which target conceptual and procedural understanding. FEG Activity 10.3, "Odd or Even?" and Activity 10.5, "The Other Part of 100," are problem-based activities that look for patterns/regularities in number as it relates to addition. FEG Expanded Lesson 9.1 focuses on subtraction, and FEG Expanded Lesson 9.4 focuses on connecting subtraction to division. Skip counting—a precursor to multiplication—is the focus of FEG Activity 10.1, "The Find!" Factors, which are important in division, are the focus of FEG Activity 10.4, "Factor Quest." FEG Activity 10.7, "Target Number," helps students develop number sense for all the operations.

Chapter 10

Helping Students Master the Basic Facts

*B*asic facts for addition and multiplication are the number combinations where both addends or both factors are less than 10. Basic facts for subtraction and division are the corresponding combinations. Thus, $15 - 8 = 7$ is a subtraction fact because the corresponding addition parts are less than 10.

Mastery of a basic fact means that a student can give a quick response (in about 3 seconds) without resorting to inefficient means, such as counting by ones. According to the *Curriculum Focal Points* (NCTM, 2006) and the *Common Core State Standards* (CCSSO, 2010), addition and subtraction concepts should be learned in first grade, with quick recall of basic addition and subtraction facts mastered by the end of grade 2. According to *Curriculum Focal Points*, concepts of multiplication and division should be learned in third grade, with quick recall of the one-digit facts (up through 9×9) mastered in grade 4, but in the *Common Core State Standards*, the one-digit facts are to be known by memory by the end of grade 3.

Developing quick and accurate recall with the basic facts is a developmental process—just like every topic in this book! It is critical that students know their basic facts well—and teaching them effectively requires much more than flash cards and timed tests. This chapter explains strategies for helping students learn their facts, including instructional approaches to use—and others to avoid. The key point: Focus on number sense! Research indicates that early number sense predicts school success more than other measures of cognition like verbal, spatial, or memory skills or reading ability (Jordan, Kaplan, Locuniak, & Ramineni, 2007; Locuniak & Jordan, 2008; Mazzocco & Thompson, 2005).

BIG IDEAS

1. Number relationships provide the foundation for strategies that help students remember basic facts. For example, knowing how numbers are related to 5 and 10 helps students master facts such as $3 + 5$ (think of a ten-frame) and $8 + 6$ (because 8 is 2 away from 10, take 2 from 6 to make $10 + 4 = 14$).

2. Because mastery of the basic facts is a developmental process, students move through phases, starting with counting, then to reasoning strategies, and eventually to quick recall. Instruction must help students through these phases without rushing them to know their facts from memory.

3. When students are not developing fluency with the basic facts, they may need to drop back to the foundational ideas. Just more drill will not resolve their struggles and can negatively affect their confidence and success in mathematics.

Mathematics CONTENT CONNECTIONS

As described previously, basic fact mastery is not really new mathematics; rather, it is the development of fluency with ideas already learned.

◆ **Number and Operations** (Chapters 8 and 9): Fact mastery relies significantly on how well students have constructed relationships about numbers and how well they understand the operations.

◆ **Computation and Estimation** (Chapters 12 and 13): Fact mastery is essential in the ability to use number sense to estimate and compute successfully. Fluency with basic facts allows for ease of computation, especially mental computation, and therefore aids in the ability to reason numerically in every number-related area. Although calculators and counting by ones are available for students who do not have command of the facts, reliance on these methods for simple number combinations is a serious handicap to computational fluency.

Developmental Nature of Basic Fact Mastery

Teaching basic facts requires the essential understanding that students progress through stages that eventually result in "just knowing" that $2 + 7$ is 9 or that 5×4 is 20. Arthur

	Addition	**Subtraction**
Counting	Direct modeling (counting objects and fingers) • Counting all • Counting on from first • Counting on from larger	Counting objects • Separating from • Separating to • Adding on
	Counting abstractly • Counting all • Counting on from first • Counting on from larger	Counting fingers • Counting down • Counting up Counting abstractly • Counting down • Counting up
Reasoning	Properties • $\alpha + 0 = \alpha$ • $\alpha + 1 =$ next whole number • Commutative property	Properties • $\alpha - 0 = \alpha$ • $\alpha - 1 =$ previous whole number
	Known-fact derivations (e.g., $5 + 6 = 5 + 5 + 1$; $7 + 6 = 7 + 7 - 1$)	Inverse/complement of known addition facts (e.g., $12 - 5$ is known because $5 + 7 = 12$)
	Redistributed derived facts (e.g., $7 + 5 = 7 + (3 + 2) = (7 + 3) + 2 = 10 + 2 = 12$)	Redistributed derived facts (e.g., $12 - 5 = (7 + 5) - 5 = 7 + (5 - 5) = 7$)
Retrieval	Retrieval from long-term memory	Retrieval from long-term memory

FIGURE 10.1 The developmental process for basic fact mastery for addition and subtraction.

Source: Henry, V. J., & Brown, R. S. (2008). "First-Grade Basic Facts: An Investigation into Teaching and Learning of an Accelerated, High-Demand Memorization Standard." *Journal for Research in Mathematics Education, 39*(2), p. 156.

Baroody, a mathematics educator who does research on basic facts, describes three phases in the process of learning facts (2006, p. 22):

Phase 1: counting strategies—using object counting (e.g., blocks or fingers) or verbal counting to determine the answer (Example: $4 + 7 =$ ___. Student starts with 7 and counts on verbally 8, 9, 10, 11.)

Phase 2: reasoning strategies—using known information to logically determine an unknown combination (Example: $4 + 7$. Student knows that $3 + 7$ is 10, so $4 + 7$ is one more, 11.)

Phase 3: mastery—producing answers efficiently (fast and accurately) (Example: $4 + 7$. Student quickly responds, "It's 11; I just know it.")

Figure 10.1 outlines the developmental methods for solving basic addition and subtraction problems.

Research over many years supports the notion that basic fact mastery is dependent on the development of reasoning strategies (Baroody, 2003, 2006; Brownell & Chazal, 1935; Carpenter & Moser, 1984; Fuson, 1992; Henry & Brown, 2008). Counting strategies (like counting on) are addressed in Chapter 8 and 9. This chapter focuses on reasoning strategies and effective ways to teach students to use reasoning to master the basic facts (phases 2 and 3).

FORMATIVE Assessment Notes

When are students ready to work on reasoning strategies? Based on the research, they are ready to apply reasoning strategies when they are able to use counting-on strategies (start with the largest and count up) and to see that numbers can be decomposed (e.g., that 6 is $5 + 1$). Pose one-digit addition problems to students in a one-on-one setting to see whether they show evidence of these skills. Use a **checklist** for these prerequisite skills. Once they have all needed skills, begin work on reasoning strategies. If they are lacking one skill, provide more experiences to develop it. ■

Approaches to Fact Mastery

In attempting to help students master their basic facts, three somewhat different approaches can be identified. First is to work on memorization of each fact in isolation. A second approach can be traced at least as far back as the 1970s. Rathmell (1978) suggests that for various classes of basic facts, we teach students a collection of strategies or thought patterns that have been found to be efficient and teachable. The third approach, "guided invention," also focuses on the use of strategies to learn facts; however, the strategies are generated, or reinvented, by students. Each of these approaches is briefly discussed in the following sections.

Knowing Facts from Memory. Some textbooks and teachers move from presenting concepts of addition and multiplication straight to memorization of facts, feeling that developing strategies is not essential in this process (Baroody, Bajwa, & Eiland, 2009). This "passive storage view" (the idea that students can just store the facts when practiced extensively) means that students have 100 separate addition facts (just for the various combinations of 0 through 9) and 100 separate multiplication facts that must be memorized and practiced frequently. They may even have to memorize subtraction and division separately—bringing the total to over 300! However, many fourth and fifth graders have not mastered addition and subtraction facts, and often middle school students do not know their multiplication facts. This is strong evidence that this method simply does not work. You may be tempted to respond that you learned your facts in this manner, as did many other students. However, studies by Brownell and Chazal as long ago as 1935 concluded that students develop a variety of different thought processes or strategies for basic facts in spite of the amount of isolated drill that they experience. Unfortunately, drill does not encourage or support the refinement of these strategies. Moreover, Baroody (2006) notes that this approach to basic fact instruction works against the development of the five strands of mathematics proficiency (see pp. 26–28), pointing out the following limitations:

- *Inefficiency.* There are too many facts to memorize.
- *Inappropriate applications.* Students misapply the facts and don't check their work.
- *Inflexibility.* Students don't learn flexible strategies for finding the sums (or products) and therefore continue to count by ones.

Struggling learners and students with disabilities often have difficulty memorizing so many isolated facts (but can be *very* successful at using strategies). In fact, many students with learning disabilities are stuck in phase 1 (Mazzocco et al., 2008). In addition, drill can cause unnecessary anxiety and undermine student interest and confidence in mathematics. Just as with all learning (see Chapter 2), connecting to what students know and building on that knowledge allow all students to learn the basic facts and learn them for life.

Explicit Strategy Instruction. For approximately three decades, basic fact instruction has focused on explicitly teaching efficient strategies that are applicable to a collection of facts. Students then practice these strategies as they were shown to them. There is strong evidence to indicate that such methods can be effective (e.g., Baroody, 1985;

Bley & Thornton, 1995; Fuson, 1984, 1992; Rathmell, 1978; Thornton & Toohey, 1984). Many of the ideas developed and tested by these researchers are discussed in this chapter.

Explicitly teaching strategies is intended to *support* student thinking rather than give the students something new to remember. Sometimes textbooks or teachers focus on memorizing the strategy and which facts work with that strategy. This doesn't work (for the same reason that memorizing isolated facts doesn't work). In reality, a recent study found that teachers who relied heavily on textbooks (that focused on memorizing basic fact strategies) had students with lower number-sense proficiency (Henry & Brown, 2008). The key is to help students see the possibilities and then let them *choose* strategies that help them get to the solution without counting.

Guided Invention. The third option might be called "guided invention" (Gravemeijer & van Galen, 2003). In this approach, fact mastery is intricately connected to students' collection of number relationships. Some students may think of $6 + 7$ as "double 6 is 12 and one more is 13." In the same class, others may note that 7 is 3 away from 10 and so take 3 from the 6 to put with the 7 to make 10. They then add on the remaining 3. Still other students may take 5 from each addend to make 10 and then add the remaining 1 and 2. The key is that students are using number combinations and relationships that make sense to them.

Gravemeijer and van Galen call this approach *guided invention* because many of the strategies that are efficient will not be developed by all students without some guidance. That is, we cannot simply place all of our efforts on number relationships and the meanings of the operations and assume that fact mastery will magically happen. The teacher's job is to design tasks and problems that will promote the invention of effective strategies by students and to be sure that these strategies are clearly articulated and shared in the classroom. They will also need to share their thinking in think-alouds to help students understand the decisions they are making and share counterexamples.

Guiding Strategy Development

In order for you to guide your students to use effective strategies, you need to have a command of as many successful strategies as possible. With this knowledge, you will be able to recognize effective strategies as your students develop them and help others capitalize on their peers' ideas.

Plan experiences that help students move from counting to strategies to recall. One effective approach is to use story problems with numbers selected in such a manner that students are most likely to develop a strategy as they solve them. In discussing student strategies, you can focus attention on the methods that are most useful.

Take the 6 + 7 example from earlier. Some students may count on from 7 (7 . . . 8, 9, 10, 11, 12, 13). Others will use the Up Over 10 strategy (7 to 10 is a jump of 3 and 3 more is 13). Help the students who are counting on to see the connections to Up Over 10. This helps students move from counting (phase 1) to reasoning strategies (phase 2). To move from reasoning strategies to recall (phase 3), continue to develop stories that have numbers that go "up over 10." The more students use it, the quicker they respond. These mental strategies eventually become so fluent that students will say, "I just knew it."

Explicitly teach reasoning strategies like Up Over 10. This can help students expand their own collection of mental strategies and move away from counting. Do not, however, require students to apply a particular strategy—this is the opposite of what you are trying to accomplish as it takes the reasoning right out of the strategy development. In fact, the more you can emphasize making good choices, the more efficient and accurate students will become.

Story Problems.   Story problems provide context that can help students understand the situation and apply flexible strategies for doing computation. Some teachers are hesitant to use story problems with ELLs or students with disabilities because of the additional language or reading required, but because language supports understanding, it is important for all students. It is necessary, however, to be sure that the contexts selected are relevant and understood. Consider, for example, that the class is working on the × 3 facts. The teacher poses the following question:

> **In 3 weeks we will be going to the zoo. How many days until we go to the zoo?**

Suppose that Aidan explains how she figured out 3 × 7 by starting with double 7 (14) and then adding 7 more. She knew that 6 added onto 14 equals 20 and one more is 21. You can ask another student to explain what Aidan just shared. This requires students to attend to ideas that come from their classmates. Now explore with the class to learn what other facts would work with Aidan's strategy. This discussion may include a variety of strategies. Some may notice that all of the facts with a 3 in them will work for the double-and-add-one-more strategy. Others may say that you can always add one more set on if you know the smaller fact. For example, for 6 × 8, you can start with 5 × 8 and add 8. Students with disabilities may be challenged to keep all of their peers' ideas in working memory, so recording the ideas in a display is an effective support.

Posing one problem like the one above each day, followed by a brief discussion of the strategies that students used, can improve student accuracy and efficiency with basic

---

Grade 1, Unit 6, Number Games and Crayon Puzzles
Lesson: Addition and Subtraction Story Problems
1. Max's soccer team has 15 balls.
    His team let Rosa's team borrow 6 balls.
    How many balls does Max's team have left?

Grade 4, Unit 1, Factors, Multiples, and Arrays
Lesson: Making Arrays
2. A package of juice boxes has 8 juice boxes.
    How many juice boxes are in 3 packages?
    How many juice boxes are in 6 packages?
    How many juice boxes are in 9 packages?

FIGURE 10.2 Story problems from the *Investigations in Number, Data, and Space* curriculum to develop basic fact reasoning strategies.

facts (Rathmell, Leutzinger, & Gabriele, 2000). A similar approach is shown in Figure 10.2, which includes story examples intended to support reasoning strategies from grade 1 and grade 4 of *Investigations in Number, Data, and Space*. Research has found that when a strong emphasis is placed on students' solving problems, they not only become better problem solvers but also master more basic facts than students in a drill program (National Research Council, 2001).

Reasoning Strategies.   A second approach is to directly model a reasoning strategy. A lesson may be designed to have students examine a specific collection of facts for which a particular type of strategy is appropriate. You can discuss how these facts are all alike in some way, or you might suggest an approach and see whether students are able to use it on similar facts.

Continue to discuss strategies invented in your class and plan lessons that encourage strategies. Don't expect to have a strategy introduced and understood with just one word problem or one exposure. Students need lots of opportunities to make a strategy their own. Many students will simply not be ready to use an idea the first few days, and then all of a sudden something will click and a useful idea will be theirs.

It is a good idea to write new strategies on the board or make a poster of strategies students develop. Give the strategies names that make sense so that students know when to apply them (e.g., "Strategy for × 3s: Double and add one more set. Ex: $3 \times 7 = (2 \times 7) + 7 = 14 + 7 = 21$").

Reasoning Strategies for Addition Facts

The strategies that students can and will invent for addition facts are directly related to one or more number relationships. In Chapter 8, numerous activities were suggested to develop these relationships. Now the teaching task is to help students connect these number relationships to the basic facts.

The "big idea" behind using reasoning strategies is for students to make use of known facts and relationships to solve unknown facts. Of the two ways students might do this, one is to use a *known fact* (like 7 + 3 = 10) to solve an unknown fact (like 7 + 5), which is two more than the known fact. The second is to use *derived facts*. In this case, the student might solve 7 + 5 by taking 7 apart into 5 + 2, then adding the 5 + 5 and then 2 more (Henry & Brown, 2008). Keep this "big idea" in mind as you review each of the reasoning strategies described in this section.

One More Than and Two More Than

Each of the 36 facts highlighted in the following chart has at least one addend of 1 or 2. These facts are a direct application of the one-more-than and two-more-than relationships described in Chapter 8. Being able to count on, then, is a necessary prerequisite to being able to apply this strategy (Baroody et al., 2009).

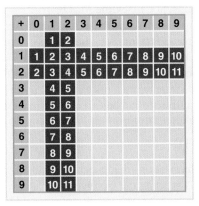

Story problems in which one of the addends is a 1 or a 2 are easy to make up. For example, *Seven children were waiting for the slide. Then 2 more children got in line. How many children were waiting for the slide?* Ask different students to explain how they got the answer of 9. Some will count on from 7. Some may still need to count 7 and 2 and then count all. Others will say they knew that 2 more than 7 is 9. Helping students see the connection between counting on and adding two will help students move from counting strategies to reasoning strategies.

Activity 10.1

How Many Feet in the Bed?

Read *How Many Feet in the Bed?* by Diane Johnston Hamm. On the second time through the book, ask students how many more feet are in the bed when a new person gets in. Ask students to record the equation (e.g., 6 + 2) and tell how many. Two less can be considered as family members get out of the bed. If you find that students are resorting to

ENGLISH LANGUAGE LEARNERS

STUDENTS *with* SPECIAL NEEDS

counting all, provide a ten-frame or number line to show how skip counting might help. For ELLs, be sure that they know what the phrases "two more" and "two less" mean (and clarify the meaning of *foot,* which is also used for measuring). Acting out with students in the classroom can be a great illustration for both ELLs and students with disabilities.

The different responses will provide you with a lot of information about students' number sense. As students are ready to use the two-more-than idea without "counting all," they can begin to practice with activities such as the following.

Activity 10.2

One More Than and Two More Than with Dice and Spinners

STUDENTS *with* SPECIAL NEEDS

Make a die labeled +1, +2, +1, +2, "one more," and "two more." Use with another die labeled 3, 4, 5, 6, 7, and 8 (or whatever values students need to practice). After each roll of the dice, students should say the complete fact: "Four and two more is six." Alternatively, roll one die and use a spinner with +1 on one half and +2 on the other half. For students with disabilities, you may want to start with a die that just has +1 on every side and then another day move on to a +2 die. This will help emphasize and practice one approach.

Figure 10.3 illustrates the ideas in Activity 10.2. Notice that activities such as these can be modified for almost all of the strategies in the chapter.

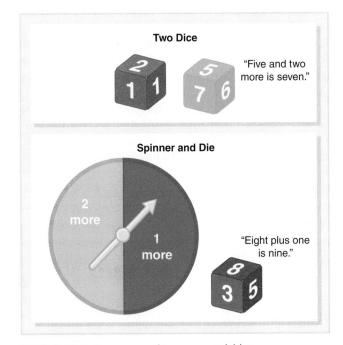

FIGURE 10.3 One-more and two-more activities.

Adding Zero

Nineteen addition facts have zero as one of the addends. Though such problems are generally easy, some students overgeneralize the idea that answers to addition problems are bigger than the addends. Word problems involving zero will be especially helpful. In the discussion, use drawings that show two parts with one part empty.

+	0	1	2	3	4	5	6	7	8	9
0	0	1	2	3	4	5	6	7	8	9
1	1									
2	2									
3	3									
4	4									
5	5									
6	6									
7	7									
8	8									
9	9									

Asking students to generalize from a set of problems is a good way to reinforce reasoning and avoid overgeneralization. You can write about 10 zero facts on the board, some with the zero first and some with the zero second. Discuss how the equations are alike. Ask students to create their own stories and/or to model the problems.

Using 5 as an Anchor

The use of an anchor (5 or 10) is a reasoning strategy that builds on students' knowledge of number relationships and is therefore a great way to both reinforce number sense and learn the basic facts. Using 5 as an anchor means looking for fives in the numbers in the problem. For example, in $6 + 7$, a student may see that 7 is $5 + 2$ and that 6 is $5 + 1$. The student would add $5 + 5$ and then the extra 2 from the 7 and the extra 1 from the 6, adding up to 13.

The ten-frames discussed in Chapter 8 can help students see numbers as 5 and some more. And because the ten-frame is a visual model, it may be a strategy that visual learners and students with disabilities find particularly valuable.

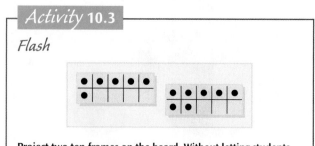

Activity **10.3**

Flash

Project two ten-frames on the board. Without letting students see, place counters on each—for example, six on one and seven on the other—so that the top row is full (five counters) and the

extras are in the next row of each ten-frame. Flash (uncover) for about three to five seconds and recover. Ask students how many counters they saw. Then uncover and have students explain how they saw it. See Blackline Masters 11 and 16.

Make 10

Perhaps the most important strategy for students to know is the Make 10 strategy, or the combinations that make 10. Story problems using two numbers that make 10 or that ask how many are needed to make 10 can assist this process.

The ten-frame is a very useful tool for creating a visual image for students. Place counters on one ten-frame and ask, "How many more to make 10?" This activity can be done over and over until students have mastered all the combinations to make 10. Later, display a blank ten-frame and say a number less than 10. Students start with that number and complete the "10 fact." If you say, "four," they say, "four plus six is ten." This can also be done individually or in small groups. See Blackline Master 16.

Knowing number combinations that make 10 not only helps with basic fact mastery but builds foundations for working on addition with higher numbers and understanding place-value concepts. Consider, for example, $28 + 7$. Using the Make 10 strategy, students can add 2 up to 30 and then 5 more. This strategy can be extended to make 100.

Up Over 10

Many facts have sums greater than 10, and all of those facts can be solved by using the Up Over 10 strategy. That makes this the most useful strategy, especially considering that the "toughies" for students tend to be those sums over 10. Students use their known facts that equal 10 and then add the rest of the number onto 10. For example, students solving $6 + 8$ might start with the larger number and see that 8 is 2 away from 10; therefore, they take 2 from the 6 to get 10 and then add on the remaining 4 to get 14. This process is also aptly called Break Apart to Make Ten, or BAMT (Sarama & Clements, 2009). This aligns with their previous experiences with ten-frames.

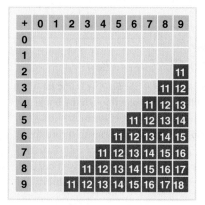

+	0	1	2	3	4	5	6	7	8	9
0										
1										
2										11
3									11	12
4								11	12	13
5							11	12	13	14
6						11	12	13	14	15
7					11	12	13	14	15	16
8				11	12	13	14	15	16	17
9			11	12	13	14	15	16	17	18

This reasoning strategy is extremely important and often not emphasized enough in U.S. textbooks or classrooms (Henry & Brown, 2008). Yet this strategy is heavily emphasized in high-performing countries (Korea, China, Taiwan, and Japan), where students learn facts sooner and more accurately than U.S. students. A recent study of California first graders found that the Make 10 strategy contributed more to developing fluency with Up Over 10 facts (e.g., 7 + 8) than using doubles (even though using doubles had been emphasized by teachers and textbooks in the study). Also, notice how many of the basic addition facts (about a third!) can be solved using the Up Over 10 strategy. Moreover, this strategy can be later applied to adding up over 20 or 50 or other benchmark numbers. Thus, this reasoning strategy deserves significant attention in teaching addition (and subtraction) facts.

Like the two strategies above (5 as an anchor and Make 10), double ten-frames can help students visualize the Up Over 10 strategy, so it is conceptually meaningful and not just a memorized procedure. For example, cover two ten-frames with a problem, like 6 + 8. Ask students to visualize moving counters from one frame (e.g., the one with 6 in it) to fill the other ten-frames (e.g., the one with 8). Ask, "How many moved?" "How many remain in the unfilled frame?" After students have found a total, have students share and record the equations. (See Blackline Master 11.) Students who are still in phase 1 of learning the facts (using counting strategies) or students with disabilities may need additional experience or one-on-one time working on this process. Activity 10.4 is designed for this purpose.

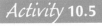

Activity 10.4

Move It, Move It

Give students a mat with two ten-frames. Flash cards are placed next to the ten-frames, or a fact can be given orally. The students cover each frame with counters to represent the problem (9 + 6 would mean covering nine places on one frame and six on the other). Ask students to "move it"—to decide a way to move the counters so that they can find the total without counting. Get students to explain what they did and connect to the new equation. For example, 9 + 6 may have become 10 + 5 by moving one counter to the first ten-frame. Emphasize strategies that are working for that student (5 as an anchor and/or Make 10 and/or Up Over 10). See Blackline Master 11.

Activity 10.5

Frames and Facts

STUDENTS with SPECIAL NEEDS

Make little ten-frame cards (Blackline Masters 15 and 16), and display them to the class on a projector. Show an 8 (or 9) card. Place other cards beneath it one at a

time as students respond with the total. Have students say orally what they are doing. For 8 + 4, they might say, "Take 2 from the 4 and put it with 8 to make 10. Then 10 and 2 left over is 12." Move to harder cards, like 7 + 6. The activity can be done independently with the little ten-frame cards. Ask students to record each equation, as shown in Figure 10.4. Especially for students with disabilities, highlight how they should explicitly think about filling in the little ten-frame starting with the higher number. Show and talk about how it is more challenging to start with the lower number as a counterexample.

Doubles

There are ten doubles facts from 0 + 0 to 9 + 9, as shown here. Students often know doubles, perhaps because of their rhythmic nature. These facts can be anchors for other facts.

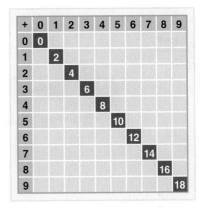

Students with disabilities or difficulties with memorizing can benefit from picture cards for each of the doubles

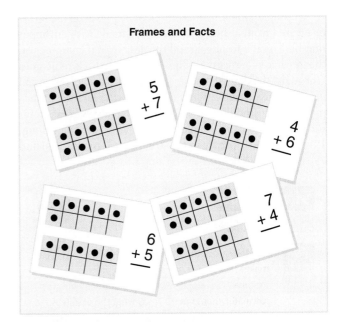

FIGURE 10.4 Frames and Facts activity.

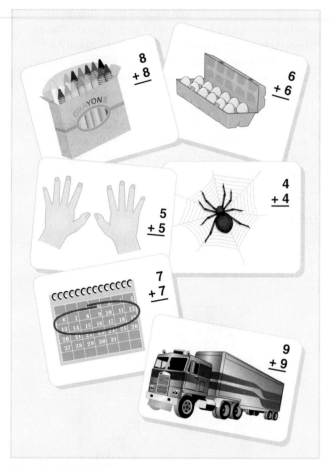

FIGURE 10.5 Doubles facts.

as shown in Figure 10.5. Story problems can focus on pairs of like addends: "Alex and Zack each found 7 seashells at the beach. How many did they find together?"

A simple "doubling machine" can be drawn on the board or created from a shoe box. Cards are made with an "input number" on the front side and the double of the number on the reverse. The card is flipped front to back as it goes "through" the double machine. A pair of students or a small group can use input/output machines, with one student flipping the card and the other(s) stating the fact. A great literature connection for doubling is *Two of Everything* (Hong, 1993), a Chinese folktale in which a couple (the Haktaks) find a magic pot that doubles everything that goes into it.

Activity 10.6

ENGLISH LANGUAGE LEARNERS

Calculator Doubles

Use the calculator and enter the "double maker" (2 ⨯). Let one student say, for example, "Seven plus seven." The student with the calculator should press 7, say what the double is, and then press = to see the correct double (14) on the display. For ELLs who are just learning English, invite them to say the

---

double in their native language or in both their native language and English. (Note that the calculator is also a good way to practice +1 and +2 facts.)

Near-Doubles

Near-doubles are also called "doubles-plus-one" or "doubles-minus-one" facts and include all combinations where one addend is one more or less than the other. This is a strategy that uses a known fact to derive an unknown fact. The strategy is to double the smaller number and add 1 or to double the larger and then subtract 1. Be sure students know the doubles before you focus on this strategy.

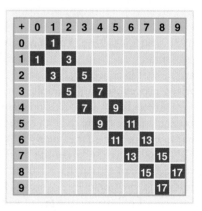

You can also introduce the strategy to the class by writing several near-doubles facts on the board. Place the smaller addend first for some of the problems and second for others. Have students solve independently, and then discuss their strategies. Some may double the smaller number and add one, and others may double the larger and subtract one. If no one uses a near-doubles strategy (they may instead use the Up Over 10 strategy), write the corresponding doubles for some of the facts and ask how these facts could help. This strategy is more difficult for students to recognize and therefore may not be a strategy that all students find useful. In that case, do not force it.

Activity 10.7

On the Double!

Create a display (on the board or on paper) that illustrates the doubles (see Figure 10.6). Prepare cards with near-doubles (e.g., 4 + 5). Ask students to find the fact that could help them solve the fact they have on the card and place it on that spot. Ask students if there are other doubles that could help.

Reinforcing Reasoning Strategies

The big idea of developing reasoning strategies is helping students move away from counting to becoming more efficient in recalling facts quickly and correctly. Also, it is very

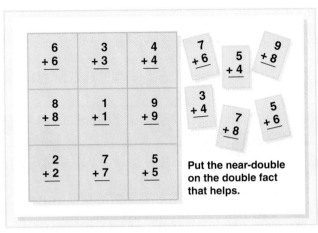

Put the near-double on the double fact that helps.

FIGURE 10.6 Near-doubles fact activity.

important to note that while the strategies above are explained individually, there is no one "best" strategy for any fact. For example, 7 + 8 could be solved using Up Over 10 or near-doubles. The more you emphasize choice, the more students will be able to find strategies that work for them, and that will lead to their own fact fluency.

Activity 10.8 is good for helping students realize that if they don't "just know" a fact, they can fall back on reasoning strategies to figure it out.

Activity **10.8**

If You Didn't Know

ENGLISH
LANGUAGE
LEARNERS

Pose the following task: If you did not know the answer to 8 + 5 [or any fact that you want students to think about], how could you figure it out without counting? Encourage students to come up with more than one way (hopefully using the strategies suggested above). ELLs and reluctant learners benefit from first sharing their ideas with a partner and then with the class.

FORMATIVE Assessment Notes

Using **diagnostic interviews** on basic facts is critical. Many students will be stuck in phase 1 (counting strategies). Some students can be so adept at counting that you may not be aware that they are doing so. Speed in counting is not a substitute for fact mastery! Use a short diagnostic interview that includes various facts that lend themselves to different strategies. Once the student records or states the answer, say, "Tell me how your thinking led to this answer." ■

⏸ *PAUSE and REFLECT*

Most of the addition facts lend themselves to a variety of different reasoning strategies. Name three strategies students might use to get the answer to 8 + 6. ●

Reasoning Strategies for Subtraction Facts

Subtraction facts prove to be more difficult than addition. This is especially true when students have been taught subtraction through a "count-count-count" approach; for 13 − 5, *count* 13, *count* off 5, *count* what's left. As discussed earlier in the chapter, counting is the first phase in reaching basic fact mastery.

Figure 10.1 at the beginning of the chapter lists the ways students might subtract, moving from counting to mastery. Without opportunities to learn and use reasoning strategies, students continue to rely on counting strategies to come up with subtraction facts, a slow and often inaccurate approach. Therefore, spend sufficient time working on the reasoning strategies outlined below to help students move to phase 2 and eventually on to mastery (phase 3).

Subtraction as Think-Addition

In Figure 10.7, subtraction is modeled in such a way that students are encouraged to think, "What goes with this part to make the total?" When done in this *think-addition* manner, the student uses known addition facts to produce the unknown quantity or part. If this important relationship between parts and wholes—between addition and subtraction—can be made, subtraction facts will be much easier. As with addition facts, it is helpful to begin with facts that have totals of 10 or less (e.g., 8 − 3, 9 − 7) before working on facts that have a total (minuend) higher than 10 (e.g., 13 − 4).

The value of think-addition cannot be overstated; however, if think-addition is to be used effectively, it is

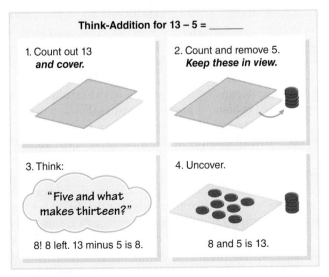

FIGURE 10.7 Using a think-addition model for subtraction facts.

essential that addition facts be mastered first. Evidence suggests that students learn very few, if any, subtraction facts without first mastering the corresponding addition facts. In other words, mastery of $3 + 5$ can be thought of as prerequisite knowledge for learning the facts $8 - 3$ and $8 - 5$.

Story problems that promote think-addition are those that sound like addition but have a missing addend: *join, initial part unknown; join, change unknown;* and *part-part-whole, part unknown* (see Chapter 9). Consider this problem: "Janice had 5 fish in her aquarium. Grandma gave her some more fish. Then she had 12 fish. How many fish did Grandma give Janice?" Notice that the action is *join*, which suggests addition. There is a high probability that students will think, "Five and how many more makes 12?" In the discussion in which you use problems such as this, your task is to connect this thought process with the subtraction fact, $12 - 5$. Students may use an Up Over 10 strategy to solve this, just as they did with addition facts ("It takes 5 to get to 10 and 2 more to 12 is . . . 7").

PAUSE and REFLECT

Before reading further, look at the three subtraction facts shown here, and try to reflect on what thought process you use to get the answers. Even if you "just know them," think about what a likely process might be.

$$
\begin{array}{ccc}
14 & 12 & 15 \\
-9 & -6 & -6 \\
\end{array}
$$

Down Over 10

You may have applied a think-addition strategy to any of the problems in the previous Pause and Reflect. Or you may have started with the 14 and counted down to 10 (4) and then down 1 more to 9, for a total difference of 5. This reasoning strategy is called Down Over 10. If you didn't already use this strategy, try it with one of the examples.

This reasoning strategy is a derived fact strategy, as students use what they know (that 14 minus 4 is 10) to figure out a related fact ($14 - 5$). Like the Make 10 and Up Over 10 strategies discussed previously, this strategy is one emphasized in high-performing countries (Fuson & Kwon, 1992). This strategy shows great promise for helping students move to mastery while supporting their number sense, yet it does not receive the attention it should in U.S. textbooks and classrooms.

One way to develop the Down Over 10 strategy is to write five or six pairs of facts in which the difference for the first fact is 10 and the second fact is either 8 or 9: for example, $16 - 6$ and $16 - 7$ or $14 - 4$ and $14 - 6$. Have students solve each problem and discuss their strategies. If students do not naturally see the relationship, ask them to think about how the first fact can help solve the second.

Reinforce with story problems use Down Over 10, such as this one:

> Becky had 16 toy animals. She gave 7 to a friend. How many does Becky have left?

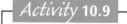

Activity 10.9

Apples in the Trees

Project a double ten-frame as a display with chips covering the first ten-frame and some of the second (e.g., for 16, cover 10 in the first frame and 6 on the second frame). Tell students some apples have fallen to the ground—you will tell them how many and they will tell you how many are still in the trees. Repeat the activity, asking students to explain their thinking. For ELLs or culturally diverse students, you can change to a context that is familiar or timely. See Blackline Master 11.

Take from the 10

This strategy is not as well known or commonly used in the United States but is consistently used in high-performing countries. It also takes advantage of students' knowledge of the combinations that make 10. It works for all subtraction problems in which the starting value (minuend) is more than 10. For example, take the problem $16 - 8$. Students take the minuend apart into $10 + 6$. Subtracting from the 10 (because they know this fact), $10 - 8$ is 2. Then they add the 6 back on to get 8. Try it on these examples:

$$15 - 8 = \qquad 17 - 9 = \qquad 14 - 8 =$$

You can see that while this may seem uncomfortable at first, it is a great reasoning strategy. And if you have students from other countries, they may already know this strategy and can share it with others. It can be used for all subtraction facts having minuends greater than 10 (the "toughies") by just knowing how to subtract from 10 and knowing addition facts with sums less than 10.

Activity 10.10

Apples in Two Trees

Adapting Activity 10.9, explain that each ten-frame is a different tree. Tell students you will tell them how many apples fall out of the "full" tree and they will tell you how many apples are left (on both trees). Each time, ask students to explain their thinking.

In the discussion of addition and subtraction strategies, you have seen a lot of activities. Activities and games provide a low-stress approach to practicing strategies and working toward fluency. More games and activities for all operations can be found later in this chapter.

Reasoning Strategies for Multiplication and Division Facts

Using a problem-based approach and focusing on reasoning strategies are just as important, if not more so, for developing mastery of the multiplication and related division facts (Baroody, 2006; Wallace & Gurganus, 2005). As with addition and subtraction facts, start with story problems as you develop reasoning strategies.

It is imperative that students completely understand the commutative property. This can be visualized by using arrays. For example, a 2×8 array can be described as 2 rows of 8 or 8 rows of 2. In both cases, the answer is 16. Understanding the commutative property cuts the basic facts to be memorized in half! For a virtual site to connect arrays to multiplication facts, go to www.haelmedia.com/OnlineActivities_txh/mc_txh3_002.html.

Doubles

Facts that have 2 as a factor are equivalent to the addition doubles and should already be known by students. Help students realize that 2×7 is the same as double 7, but so is 7×2. Try word problems in which 2 is the number of sets. Later, use problems in which 2 is the size of the sets. "George was making sock puppets. Each puppet needed 2 buttons for eyes. If George makes 7 puppets, how many buttons will he need for the eyes?"

×	0	1	2	3	4	5	6	7	8	9
0			0							
1			2							
2	0	2	4	6	8	10	12	14	16	18
3			6							
4			8							
5			10							
6			12							
7			14							
8			16							
9			18							

Fives

This group consists of all facts with 5 as the first or second factor, as shown here.

Practice skip counting by fives to at least 45. Connect counting by fives with arrays that have rows of 5 dots. Point

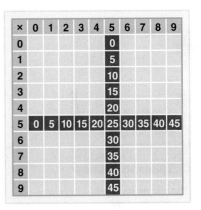

×	0	1	2	3	4	5	6	7	8	9
0						0				
1						5				
2						10				
3						15				
4						20				
5	0	5	10	15	20	25	30	35	40	45
6						30				
7						35				
8						40				
9						45				

out that such an array with six rows is a model for 6×5, eight rows is 8×5, and so on.

Activity 10.11

Clock Facts

Focus on the minute hand of the clock. When it points to a number, how many minutes after the hour is it? See Figure 10.8(a). Connect this idea to multiplication facts with 5. Hold up a flash card as in Figure 10.8(b), and then point to the number on the clock corresponding to the other factor. In this way, the fives facts become the "clock facts."

Zeros and Ones

Thirty-six facts have at least one factor that is either 0 or 1. These facts, though apparently easy on a procedural level, tend to get confused with "rules" that some students learned for addition. The fact $6 + 0$ stays the same, but 6×0 is always zero. The $1 + n$ fact is the next counting number, but $1 \times n$ stays the same. The concepts behind these facts can be developed best through story problems. Alternatively, ask students to put words to the equations. For example, say that 6×0 is six groups with zero items in them (or six rows of chairs with no people in each). For 0×6, there are six in the group, but you have zero groups. For example, you worked 0 hours babysitting at $6 an hour. Avoid rules that aren't conceptually based, such as "Any number multiplied by zero is zero."

×	0	1	2	3	4	5	6	7	8	9
0	0	0	0	0	0	0	0	0	0	0
1	0	1	2	3	4	5	6	7	8	9
2	0	2								
3	0	3								
4	0	4								
5	0	5								
6	0	6								
7	0	7								
8	0	8								
9	0	9								

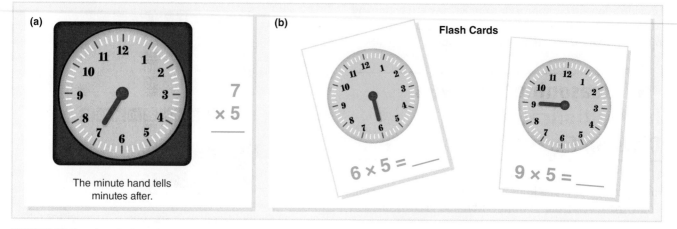

FIGURE 10.8 Using clocks to help learn fives facts.

Nifty Nines

Facts with a factor of 9 include the largest products but can be among the easiest to learn because there are several reasoning strategies and patterns that support their learning. First, students can derive that 7×9 is the same as 7×10 less one set of 7, or $70 - 7$. Because students can often easily multiply by 10 and subtract from a decade value (if they really learned their Make 10 combinations), this strategy makes sense. You might introduce this idea by showing a set of bars such as those in Figure 10.9 with only the end cube a different color. After explaining that every bar has 10 cubes, ask students if they can think of a good way to figure out how many are yellow.

Second, a table of nines facts includes some interesting patterns that lead to finding the products: (1) the tens digit of the product is always one less than the "other" factor (the one other than 9), and (2) the sum of the two digits in the product is always 9. For 7×9, 1 less than 7 is 6, and 6 and 3 makes 9, so the answer is 63.

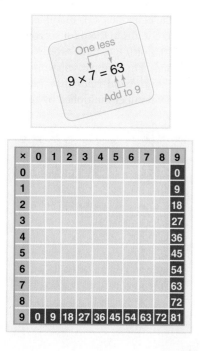

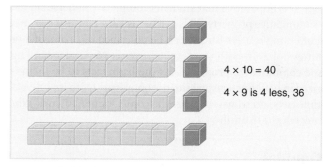

FIGURE 10.9 Using tens to think of the nines.

In order for students to explore and discover this pattern, ask students to record each fact for nines in order ($9 \times 1 = 9, 9 \times 2 = 18, \ldots, 9 \times 9 = 81$) and write down patterns they notice. After discussing all the patterns, ask students how these patterns can be used to figure out a product to a nines fact. (*Warning:* This strategy, grounded in the base-ten system, can be useful, but it also can cause confusion because the conceptual connection is not easy to see.) Challenge students to think about why this pattern works.

Once students have invented a strategy for the nines based on these patterns, a tactile way to help students remember the nifty nines is to use fingers—but not for counting. Here's how: Hold up both hands. Starting with the pinky on your left hand, count over for which fact you are doing. For example, for 4×9, you move to the fourth finger (your pointer). Bend it down. Look at your fingers: You have three to the left of the folded finger representing 3 tens and six to the right—36! (Barney, 1970). See Figure 10.10.

Using Known Facts to Derive Other Facts

The following chart shows the remaining 25 multiplication facts. It is worth pointing out to students that there are actually only 15 facts remaining to master because 20 of them consist of 10 pairs of turnarounds (e.g., 6×3 is the same as 3×6).

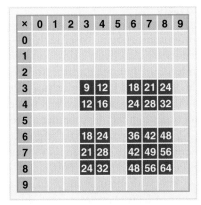

These 25 facts can be learned by relating each to an already known fact or *helping* fact. Because arrays are a powerful thinking tool for these strategies, provide students with copies of the 10×10 dot array (Figure 10.11) (see also Blackline Master 12). The lines in the array make counting the dots easier and often suggest the use of the easier fives facts as helpers. For example, 7×7 is 5×7 plus double 7, or $35 + 14$.

Doubling is a very effective reasoning strategy in helping students learn the difficult facts (Flowers & Rubenstein, 2010/2011). The Double and Double Again strategy shown in Figure 10.12(a) is applicable to all facts with 4 as one of the factors. Remind students that the idea works when 4 is the second factor as well as when it is the first. For 4×8, double 16 is also a difficult addition. Help students with this by noting, for example, that $15 + 15$ is 30, and $16 + 16$ is 2 more, or 32. Adding $16 + 16$ on paper defeats the development of reasoning.

The Double and One More Set strategy shown in Figure 10.12(b) is a way to think of facts with one factor of 3. With an array or a set picture, the double part can be circled, and it is clear that there is one more set. Two facts in this group involve more difficult mental additions: 8×3 and 9×3. Using doubling and one more, you can generate any fact. For the fact 6×7, think of 2×7 (14), then double it to get 4×7 (28), then add two more sets of 7 ($28 + 14 = 42$).

If either factor is even, a Half Then Double strategy as shown in Figure 10.12(c) can be used. Select the even factor, and cut it in half. If the smaller fact is known, that product is doubled to get the new fact.

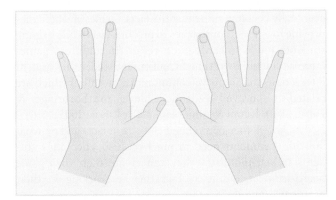

FIGURE 10.10 Nifty nines using fingers to show 4×9.

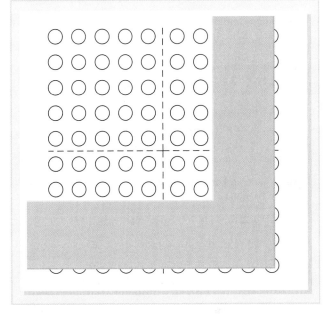

FIGURE 10.11 An array is a useful model for developing strategies for the hard multiplication facts (see Blackline Master 12).

Many students prefer to go to a fact that is "close" and then *add one more set* to this known fact, as shown in Figure 10.12(d). For example, think of 6×7 as 6 sevens. Five sevens is close: That's 35. Six sevens is one more seven, or 42. When using 5×8 to help with 6×8, the set language "6 eights" is very helpful in remembering to add 8 more and not 6 more. This "close" fact reasoning strategy is critically important. First, it has no limits—it can be used for any multiplication fact. Second, it reinforces students' sense of number and of relationships between numbers. Asking students whether they know a nearby fact to derive the new fact over time will help make this mental process become automatic for students.

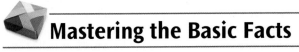

PAUSE and REFLECT

Select what you consider a "hard fact" and see how many of the reasoning strategies in Figure 10.12 you can use to derive the fact.

Division Facts

Mastery of multiplication facts and connections between multiplication and division are key elements of division fact mastery. For example, to solve $36 \div 9$, we tend to think, "Nine times what is thirty-six?" In fact, because of this, the reasoning facts for division are to (1) think multiplication and then (2) apply a multiplication reasoning fact, as needed.

Mastering the Basic Facts

The Common Core State Standards carefully state that students will know "from memory" their facts. This is a result of repeated experiences with reasoning strategies and not because

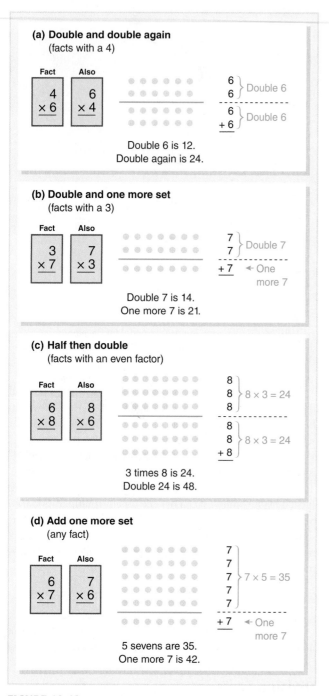

(a) Double and double again
(facts with a 4)

Double 6 is 12.
Double again is 24.

(b) Double and one more set
(facts with a 3)

Double 7 is 14.
One more 7 is 21.

(c) Half then double
(facts with an even factor)

3 times 8 is 24.
Double 24 is 48.

(d) Add one more set
(any fact)

5 sevens are 35.
One more 7 is 42.

FIGURE 10.12 Reasoning strategies for using a known fact to derive an unknown fact.

of time spent memorizing. This is an important distinction to make in mastering the facts (phase 3). Drill in the absence of accomplishing these phases has repeatedly been demonstrated as ineffective. However, drill strengthens memory and retrieval capabilities (Ashcraft & Christy, 1995). Students must master the basic facts (develop quick recall). Students who continue to struggle with the facts often fail to understand higher mathematics concepts; their cognitive energy gets pulled into computation when it should be focusing on the more sophisticated concept being developed (Forbringer & Fahsl, 2010).

Effective Drill

Drill—repetitive non-problem-based activity—is appropriate once students are effectively using reasoning strategies that they understand but with which they have not yet become facile. Pacing and focus are critical. Too often drill includes too many facts too quickly, and students become frustrated and overwhelmed. Also, students progress at different paces—gifted students tend to be good memorizers, whereas students with intellectual disabilities have difficulty memorizing (Forbringer & Fahsl, 2010).

When working with memorization, like with strategies, identify a group of facts that are related. Flash cards, for example, are much more effective if they are not covering all facts and strategies but are focused on a select group that the student is ready to memorize. For example, if given a stack of ×1 facts, some students will quickly learn these facts, noting the generalization described above, but for some students—in particular, students with disabilities—more discussion and illustration are often needed. Because many students need multiple experiences, it is important that instruction is differentiated and engaging. Technology and games can keep students engaged while supporting the mastery of the basic facts.

TECHNOLOGY A plethora of websites and software programs provide opportunities to drill on the basic facts. Though currently none exist that work on strategy development, these programs can be a great support to students who are near mastery or maintaining mastery, because they tend to be fun. One disadvantage of these software programs is that they tend to focus on all the facts at one time (rather than the set students are targeting). Two exceptions (sites that organize drill by fact family) are Fun 4 the Brain (www.fun4thebrain.com) and Math Fact Café (www.mathfactcafe.com). The key is to make wise choices about when and how to use available technology. See the suggestions at the end of the chapter for some good choices.

Games to Support Basic Fact Mastery

Playing games and doing activities in which students can choose from the strategies discussed in this chapter will allow them to become more fluent at picking strategies and eventually becoming fluent at the facts. Games and activities provide low-stress approaches to practice facts while helping students move toward quick recall. In addition, games increase student involvement, encourage student-to-student interaction, and improve communication—all of which are related to improved academic achievement (Forbringer & Fahsl, 2010; Kamii & Anderson, 2003; Lewis, 2005).

As noted, focus on related clusters of facts and on what individual students need to practice. Also, encourage students to self-monitor—they can create their own game board/game, including the facts they are working on (their personal "toughies").

Activity 10.12

STUDENTS with SPECIAL NEEDS

ENGLISH LANGUAGE LEARNERS

Salute!

Place students in groups of three, and give each group a deck of cards (omitting face cards and using aces as ones). Two students draw a card without looking at it and place it on their forehead facing outward (so the others can see it). The student with no card tells the sum (or product). The first of the other two to correctly say what number is on their forehead "wins" the card set. For ELLs, students with disabilities, and reluctant learners, speed can inhibit participation and increase anxiety. Speed of response can be removed as a variable by having each student write down the card they think they have (within five seconds) and getting a point if they are correct.

This can be differentiated by including only certain cards (e.g., addition facts using only the numbers 1 through 5).

Activity 10.13

Missing-Number Cards

Show students families of numbers with the sum [product] circled as in Figure 10.13(a). Ask why they think the numbers go together and why one number is circled. When this number family idea is understood, draw a different card and cover one of the numbers with your thumb, saying, "What's missing?" Ask students how they figured it out. After your modeling, students can do this with partners. Alternatively, you can create cards with one number replaced by a question mark, as in Figure 10.13(b).

When students understand this activity, explain that you have made some missing-number cards based on this idea, as in Figure 10.13(c). Ask students to name the missing number and explain their thinking.

As a follow-up to Activity 10.13, students can complete "cards" on a missing-number handout. Make copies of the Missing Part worksheet (Blackline Master 13) to make drill exercises for a cluster of facts, differentiated for varying student abilities. In a column of 13 "cards," put combinations with different numbers missing, some addends (factors) and some sums (products). Put blanks in different positions. An example for addition is shown in Figure 10.14. Have students write an equation for each missing-number card. This is an important step because many students are able to give the missing part in a family but do not connect this knowledge with subtraction.

Table 10.1 offers some ideas for how classic games can be adapted to focus on basic fact mastery, as well as how each can be differentiated.

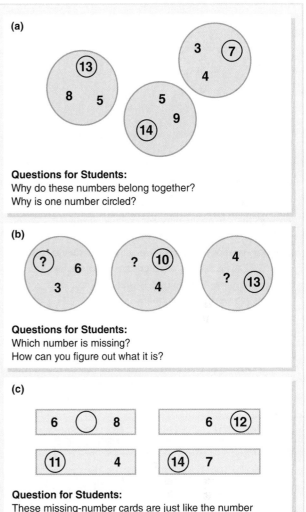

FIGURE 10.13 Introducing missing-number cards. Note: These are shown for addition/subtraction but work well for multiplication/division, too.

When all facts are learned, continued reinforcement through occasional games and activities is important. Consider the following activity that engages students in creatively applying all four operations.

Activity 10.14

Bowl a Fact

ENGLISH LANGUAGE LEARNERS

In this activity (suggested by Shoecraft, 1982), you draw circles placed in triangular fashion to look like bowling pins, with the front circle labeled 1 and the others labeled consecutively through 10. For culturally diverse classrooms, be sure that students are familiar with bowling. (If they are not, consider showing a YouTube clip or photographs.)

Take three dice and roll them. Students use the numbers on the three dice to come up with equations that result in answers that are on the pins. For example, if you roll 4, 2, and 3, they can "knock down" the 5 pin with $4 \times 2 - 3$. If they can produce equations to knock down all 10 pins, they get a strike. If not, roll again and see whether they can knock the rest down for a spare. After doing this with the whole class, students can work in small groups.

A good website to find additional basic facts games is www.kentuckymathematics.org/resources/pimser.asp.

[Make-10 facts]	[Near-doubles]	[Two-fact families (7, 8, 15) (4, 8, 12)]
4 ◯ 8	5 6 ◯	4 ⑫
◯ 9 6	⑬ 7	⑮ 8
8 7 ◯	⑮ 8	⑫ 4
⑮ 6	5 ⑪	7 8 ◯
5 ⑬	7 ⑮	⑫ 8
8 ⑰	⑨ 4	⑫ 8
6 ◯ 8	⑰ 8	4 ⑫
3 9 ◯	⑪ 6	8 ⑮
9 ⑯	5 ◯ 4	⑮ 7
◯ 6 8	3 ⑦	7 ◯ 8
7 ⑯	⑨ 5	4 ⑫
3 ◯ 9	6 ⑬	◯ 4 8
8 ◯ 8	⑰ 9	8 ⑮

FIGURE 10.14 Missing-number handouts. The blank version can be used to fill in any sets of facts you wish to emphasize (see Blackline Master 13). Labels (in brackets) are not included on student pages.

FORMATIVE Assessment Notes

As students are engaged in games and activities, **interview** students to find out whether they are using counting strategies, reasoning strategies, or quick recall. Ask students to tell what strategy they just used. If you observe counting, ask the student to try a reasoning strategy. If many students are counting, more experiences (with ten-frames, for example) are needed. ■

Fact Remediation

Students who have not mastered their addition facts by third grade or their multiplication facts by fifth grade are in need of something other than more drill. They have certainly seen and practiced facts countless times in previous grades and yet not remembered them. These students are likely in phase 1 (counting strategies) and lack number sense and reasoning strategies. The following key ideas can guide your efforts to help these students.

1. *Recognize that more drill will not work.* Students' fact difficulties are due not to a lack of drill but to a failure to develop or to connect concepts and relationships such as those that have been discussed in this chapter. At best, more drill will provide temporary results. At worst, it will cause negative attitudes about mathematics.

2. *Provide hope.* Students who have experienced difficulty with fact mastery often believe that they cannot learn facts or that they are doomed to use finger counting forever. Let these students know that you will help them and that you will provide some new strategies that will assist them.

3. *Inventory the known and unknown facts for each student in need.* Find out which facts are known quickly and comfortably and which are not. Fifth-grade or older students can do this diagnosis for themselves. Provide sheets of all facts for one operation in random order, and have the students answer the ones that they can and circle the facts they are hesitant about. To achieve an honest assessment, emphasize that you need this information so that you can help them.

4. *Diagnose strengths and weaknesses.* Observe what students do when they encounter one of their unknown facts. Do they count on their fingers? Add up numbers in the margins? Guess? Try to use a related fact? Write down times tables? Are they able to use any of the helpful strategies and reasoning suggested in this chapter?

You can conduct a 10-minute diagnostic interview with each student in need. Simply pose unknown facts and ask the student how he or she approaches them. Don't try to teach; just listen. Again, students can provide some of this information by writing about what they do when they don't know a fact.

5. *Focus on reasoning strategies.* Using a problem-solving strategy to focus on fact mastery is very effective (Baroody,

TABLE 10.1

CLASSIC GAMES ADAPTED TO BASIC FACT MASTERY		
Classic Game	**How to Use It with Basic Fact Mastery**	**Suggestions for Differentiation**
Bingo	Each bingo card has a fact problem (e.g., 2 × 3) in each box. The same fact will be on multiple bingo cards but in different locations on each card. You will call out an answer (e.g., 6), and the students will find a matching problem (or more than one problem) on their card.	Create bingo boards that focus on different clusters of facts (e.g., doubles or doubles + 1 on some boards, and Up Over 10 on other boards). Be sure that the answers you call out are an even mix of the clusters so that everyone has the same chance to win.
Concentration	Create cards that have a fact problem (e.g., 3 × 5) on one half and the answers (e.g., 15) on the other half. Shuffle the cards and turn them face-down in a 6 × 4 grid. (If you like, you can make the grid larger to use more cards.)	Select cards that focus on a particular cluster of facts (e.g., +1 and ×5 facts) for each round of the game. Multiple groups can play the game simultaneously—each group will use the parts of the deck that contain the facts they are working on. Also, consider making cards that show the ten-frames below the numbers to help provide a visual for students.
Dominoes	Create (or find online) dominoes that have a fact on one side and an answer (not to that fact) on the other. Each student gets the same number of dominoes (around eight). On his or her turn, they can play one of the dominoes in their hand only if they have an answer or a fact that can connect to a domino on the board.	As with other games, select the dominoes that focus on a particular clusters of facts.
Four in a Row	Create a 6 × 6 square game board with a sum (or product) written on each square. Below, list the numbers 0 through 9. Each of the two players has counters of a different color to use as their game pieces. On the first turn, Player 1 places a marker (paper clip) on two addends/factors and then gets to place his or her colored counter on the related answer. (If you have repeated the same answer on different squares of the board, the player only gets to cover one of them.) Player 2 can only move one paper clip and then gets to place his or her colored counter on the related answer. The first player to get four in a row wins.	Rather than list all the values below the chart, just list the related addends or factors. For example, use 1, 2, 6, 7, 8, 9 if you want to work on +1 and +2, or use 3, 4, 5, 6 if you are working on these multiplication facts.
Old Maid (retitled as Old Dog)	Create cards for each fact and each answer. Add one card that has a picture of an old dog (or use your school mascot). Shuffle and deal cards. On each player's turn, they draw from the person on their right, see whether that card is a match to a card in their hand (a fact and its answer), and, if so, lay down the pair. Then the person to their left draws from them. Play continues until all matches are found and someone is left with the Old Dog. Winner can be the person with (or not with) the Old Dog, or the person with the most pairs.	See Concentration (above).

Source: Adapted from Forbringer & Fahsl, 2010, and Kamii & Anderson, 2003.

2006; Crespo, Kyriakides, & McGee, 2005). Because students will likely be working alone or with a small group in this remediation program, they will not have the benefit of class discussion or the time required over weeks and months to develop their own strategies. Therefore, with these students, it is reasonable to share with them strategies that you "have seen other students use." Be certain that they have a conceptual understanding of the strategy and are able to use it. Flowers and Rubenstein (2010/2011) found that doubling was very effective in helping middle school students who had not yet mastered multiplication facts, increasing their facility with reasoning skills, as well as building their confidence.

6. *Build in success.* As you begin a well-designed fact program for a student who has struggled, be sure that successes come quickly and easily. Begin with easier and more useful reasoning strategies like Up Over 10 for addition. Success builds success! With strategies as an added assist, success comes more quickly. Point out to students how one idea, one strategy, is all that is required to learn many facts. Use fact charts to show the set of facts you are working on. It is surprising how the chart quickly fills up with mastered facts. Keep reviewing newly learned facts and those that were already known.

7. *Provide engaging activities for drill.* Many games and activities (including those previously discussed) can be used for drill.

What to Do When Teaching Basic Facts

We close this chapter with some important reminders in effectively teaching the basic facts. This is such an important life skill for all learners that it is important that we, as teachers, use what research suggests are the most effective practices. The following list of recommendations can support the development of quick recall.

1. *Ask students to self-monitor.* The importance of this recommendation cannot be overstated. Across all learning, having a sense of what you don't know and what you need to learn is important. It certainly holds true with memorizing facts. Students should be able to identify their "toughies" and continue to work on reasoning strategies to help them derive those facts.

2. *Focus on self-improvement.* This point follows from self-monitoring. If you are working on improving students' quickness at recalling facts, then the only persons the students should be competing with are themselves. Students can keep track of how long it took them to go through their "fact stack," for example, and then, two days later, pull the same stack and see whether they are quicker (or more accurate) than the last time.

3. *Drill in short time segments.* You can project numerous examples of double ten-frames in relatively little time. Or you can do a story problem a day—taking five minutes to share strategies. You can also have each student pull a set of flash cards, pair with another student, and go through each other's set in two minutes. Long periods (ten minutes or more) are not effective. Using the first five to ten minutes of the day, or extra time just before lunch, can provide continued support on fact development without taking up mathematics instructional time better devoted to other topics.

4. *Work on facts over time.* Rather than do a unit on fact memorization, work on facts over months and months, working on reasoning strategies, then on memorization, and then on continued review and monitoring.

5. *Involve families.* Share the big plan of how you will work on learning facts over the year. One idea is to let parents or guardians know that during the second semester of second grade (or third grade), for example, you will have one or two "Take Home Facts of the Week." Ask family members to help students by using reasoning strategies when they don't know a fact.

6. *Make drill enjoyable.* There are many games (including those in this chapter) designed to reinforce facts that are not competitive or anxiety inducing.

7. *Use technology.* When students work with technology, they get immediate feedback and reinforcement, helping them to self-monitor. See the Online Resources at the end of this chapter for ideas.

8. *Emphasize the importance of quick recall of facts.* Without trying to create pressure or anxiety, emphasize to students that in real life and in the rest of mathematics, they will be recalling these facts all the time—they really must learn them and learn them well. Celebrate student successes.

What Not to Do When Teaching Basic Facts

The following list describes strategies that may have been designed with good intentions but work against student recall of the basic facts.

1. *Don't use lengthy timed tests.* Students get distracted by the pressure and abandon their reasoning strategies in timed tests. If they miss some, they don't get the chance to see which ones they are having trouble with, so the assessment doesn't help them move forward. Students develop anxiety, which works against learning mathematics. Having students self-monitor the time it takes them to go through a small set of facts can help with their speed and avoid the negatives of long timed tests.

2. *Don't use public comparisons of mastery.* You may have experienced the bulletin board that shows which students are on which step of a staircase to mastering their multiplication facts. Imagine how the student who is on the step 3 feels when others are on step 6. Or imagine the negative emotional reaction with public competition with flash cards for the half who don't win. It is great to celebrate student successes, but avoid comparisons between students.

3. *Don't proceed through facts in order from 0 to 9.* It is better to work on collections based on the strategies and conceptual understanding and to "knock out" those that students know rather than proceed in a rigid fashion by going in numerical order.

4. *Don't work on all facts all at once.* Select a strategy (starting with easier ones) and then work on memorization of that set of facts (e.g., doubles). Be sure these are really learned before moving on. Differentiation is needed! Students should not move to new facts until one set is mastered—otherwise they will become confused and your goal for them to master all the facts will backfire.

5. *Don't move to memorization too soon.* This has been addressed throughout the chapter but is worth repeating. Quick recall or mastery can be obtained only after students are ready—meaning they have a robust collection of reasoning strategies to apply as needed.

6. *Don't use facts as a barrier to good mathematics.* Students who have total command of basic facts do not necessarily *reason better* than those who, for whatever reason, have not yet mastered facts. Mathematics is not solely about computation. Mathematics is about reasoning and using patterns and making sense of things. Mathematics is problem solving. There is no reason that a student who has not yet mastered all basic facts should be excluded from real mathematical experiences.

7. *Don't use fact mastery as a prerequisite for calculator use.* Insisting that students master the basic facts before allowing them to use a calculator denies them important learning

opportunities. For example, if your lesson goal is for students to discover the pattern (formula) for the perimeter of rectangles, then a good lesson would have students building and exploring different-shaped rectangles, recording the length, width, and perimeter and looking for patterns. A student who has not yet developed fact fluency will be too bogged down in computation without a calculator. With a calculator, the same student can participate and hopefully attain the learning goals of the lesson.

FORMATIVE
Assessment
Notes

If there is any purpose for a timed test of basic facts, it may be for diagnostic purposes—to determine which number combinations are mastered and which remain to be learned. For it to be diagnostic, the follow-up should include the teacher and the student identifying possible misconceptions or misapplication of strategies, as well as which facts are mastered and which need more practice. ■

RESOURCES *for Chapter 10*

LITERATURE CONNECTIONS

The children's books described in Chapters 8 and 9 are also good choices when working on the basic facts. In addition to those, consider these opportunities to develop and practice basic facts.

One Less Fish *Toft and Sheather, 1998*

This beautiful book with an important environmental message starts with 12 fish and counts back to zero fish. On a page with 8 fish, ask, "How many fish are gone?" and "How did you figure it out?" Encourage students to use the Down Over 10 strategy. Any counting-up or counting-back book can be used in this way!

The Twelve Days of Summer *Andrews and Jolliffe, 2005*

You will quickly recognize the style of this book with five bumble bees, four garter snakes, three ruffed grouse, and so on. The engaging illustrations and motions make this a wonderful book. Students can figure out how many of each item appear by the end of the book, applying multiplication facts. (For example, three ruffed grouse appear on days 3, 4, 5, and so on.)

RECOMMENDED READINGS

Articles

Baroody, A. J. (2006). Why children have difficulties mastering the basic fact combinations and how to help them. *Teaching Children Mathematics, 13*(1), 22–31.
Baroody suggests that basic facts are developmental in nature and contrasts "conventional wisdom" with a number-sense view. Great activities are included as exemplars.

Buchholz, L. (2004). Learning strategies for addition and subtraction facts: The road to fluency and the license to think. *Teaching Children Mathematics, 10*(7), 362–367.
A second-grade teacher explains how her students developed and named their strategies and even extended them to work with two-digit numbers. She found her "lower ability" students were very successful using reasoning strategies.

Crespo, S., Kyriakides, A. O., & McGee, S. (2005). Nothing "basic" about basic facts: Exploring addition facts with fourth graders. *Teaching Children Mathematics, 12*(2), 60–67.
This article provides evidence of the critical importance of addressing remediation through a focus on reasoning strategies and number sense.

Kamii, C., & Anderson, C. (2003). Multiplication games: How we made and used them. *Teaching Children Mathematics, 10*(3), 135–141.
Constance Kamii, a well-known constructivist, teams up with a third-grade teacher and describes a collection of games that were used to help students who were struggling to master multiplication facts.

ONLINE RESOURCES

Cross the Swamp (BBC)
**www.bbc.co.uk/schools/starship/maths/crosstheswamp
.shtml**
This British applet asks students to supply a missing operation (+/− or ×/÷) and a number to complete an equation (e.g., 4 __ __ = 12). There are five questions in a set, each with three levels of difficulty.

Deep Sea Duel (NCTM's Illuminations)
**http://illuminations.nctm.org/ActivityDetail.aspx?ID=
207**
The first person to choose a set of digit cards with a specified sum wins. You can choose how many cards, what types of numbers, and the level of strategy.

Diffy (NLVM—Applet/Game)
**http://nlvm.usu.edu/en/nav/frames_asid_326_g_1_
t_1.html**
Diffy is a classic mathematics puzzle that involves finding the differences of given numbers.

Factor Dazzle (NCTM's Calculation Nation)
http://calculationnation.nctm.org
A game in which a player identifies the factors of a number and picks numbers for the opponent to identify the factors. Registered players can play against others from all over the world.

Factorize (NCTM's Illuminations)
http://illuminations.nctm.org/ActivityDetail.aspx?ID=64

Visually explore the concept of factors by creating rectangular arrays. Choose your own number or one randomly selected.

IXL (IXL Learning)
www.ixl.com/math/practice

IXL contains interactive practice tools to monitor student progress toward basic fact mastery. Connections with the *Common Core State Standards*, Department of Defense Education Activity standards, and existing state standards are provided.

Let's Learn Those Facts (NCTM's Illuminations— Lessons, Grades 1–2)
http://illuminations.nctm.org/LessonDetail.aspx?id=U58

These six lessons, including links to resources and student recording sheets, target addition facts.

Multiplication: It's in the Cards (NCTM's Illuminations—Lessons, Grades 3–5)
http://illuminations.nctm.org/LessonDetail .aspx?id=U110

These four lessons, including links to resources and student recording sheets, use the properties of multiplication to help students master the multiplication facts. See also "Six and Seven as Factors" (NCTM's Illuminations— Lessons, Grades 3–5), two lessons on products where 6 or 7 is a factor (http://illuminations.nctm.org/LessonDetail .aspx?ID=U150).

The Product Game (NCTM's Illuminations—Lessons, Grades 3–8)
http://illuminations.nctm.org/LessonDetail .aspx?id=U100

These four lessons use the engaging and effective games "Factor Game" and "Product Game" to help students see the relationship between products and factors.

REFLECTIONS *on Chapter 10*

WRITING TO LEARN

1. Describe advantages of a developmental approach to helping students master basic facts.
2. For the fact $8 + 9$, list at least three reasoning strategies that a student might use.
3. What is meant by subtraction as think-addition? How can you help students develop a think-addition thought pattern for subtraction?
4. For the multiplication fact 6×7, describe three reasoning strategies a student might use.
5. Why are games and interactive software important in supporting basic fact mastery?
6. Describe methods to support basic fact mastery and practices to avoid.

FOR DISCUSSION AND EXPLORATION

1. Explore a Web-based program for drilling basic facts. What features does the program have that are good? Not so good? How would you use such programs in a classroom with only one or two available computers? How would you differentiate it to address those who are working on different fact strategies?
2. Assume you are teaching a grade that expects mastery of facts (grade 2 for addition and subtraction or grade 3 or 4 for multiplication and division). How will you design fact mastery across the semester or year? Include timing, strategy development, involvement of families, use of games, and so forth.

MyEducationLab™

Go to the MyEducationLab (www.myeducationlab.com) for Math Methods and familiarize yourself with the content. Much of the site content is organized topically. The topics include all of the following to support your learning in the course:

- Learning outcomes for important mathematics methods course topics aligned with the national standards
- Assignments and Activities, tied to these learning outcomes and standards, that can help you more deeply understand course content
- Building Teaching Skills and Dispositions learning units that allow you to apply and practice your understanding of the core mathematics content and teaching skills

Your instructor has a correlation guide that aligns the exercises on the topical portion of the site with your book's chapters.

You'll also find a Study Plan written specifically to align with the chapters of this book. The pre-test, Review Practice and Enrichment Activities, and post-test offer feedback and support that allow you to check and enhance your understanding of the content in each chapter.

Field Experience Guide
C O N N E C T I O N S

FEG Expanded Lesson 9.3 provides an exploration to help students develop and build fluency in a basic fact strategy of two more or two less. Similarly, FEG Expanded Lesson 9.12 helps students notice that $7 + 7$ is the same as $8 + 6$—relationships that help in memorizing the basic facts.

Chapter 11
Developing Whole-Number Place-Value Concepts

A complete understanding of place value, including extensions to decimal numeration, develops across the elementary and middle grades. In kindergarten and first grade, students count and are exposed to patterns in the numbers to 100. Most importantly, they begin to think about groups of ten objects as a unit. By second grade, these initial ideas of patterns and groups of ten are formally connected to our place-value system of numeration. In grades 3 and 4, students extend their understanding to numbers up to 10,000 in a variety of contexts. In fourth and fifth grades, the ideas of whole numbers are extended to decimals (CCSSO, 2010).

As a significant part of this development, students should begin to work at putting numbers together (composing) and taking them apart (decomposing) in a wide variety of ways as they solve addition and subtraction problems with two- and three-digit numbers. Students' struggles with the invention of their own computation strategies will both enhance their understanding of place value and provide a firm foundation for flexible methods of computation.

BIG IDEAS

1. Sets of 10 (and tens of tens) can be perceived as single entities or units. For example, three sets of 10 and two singles is a base-ten method of describing 32 single objects. This is the major principle of *base-ten* numeration.

2. The positions of digits in numbers determine what they represent and which size group they count. This is the major organizing principle of *place-value* numeration and is central for developing *number sense*.

3. There are patterns to the way that numbers are formed. For example, each decade has a symbolic pattern reflective of the 0-to-9 sequence (e.g., 20, 21, 22 . . . 29).

4. The groupings of ones, tens, and hundreds can be taken apart in different but equivalent ways. For example, beyond the typical way to decompose 256 of 2 hundreds, 5 tens, and 6 ones, it

can be represented as 1 hundred, 14 tens, and 16 ones but also 250 and 6. Decomposing and composing multidigit numbers in flexible ways is a necessary foundation for computational estimation and exact computation.

5. "Really big" numbers are best understood in terms of familiar real-world referents. It is difficult to conceptualize quantities as large as 1000 or more. However, the number of people who will fill the local sports arena is, for example, a meaningful referent for those who have experienced that crowd.

Mathematics CONTENT CONNECTIONS

The base-ten place-value system is the way that we communicate and represent anything that we do with whole numbers and later with decimals.

◆ **Whole-Number Computation and Estimation** (Chapters 12 and 13): Flexible methods of computation—including various mental methods, pencil-and-paper methods, estimation skills, and even effective use of technology—depend completely on understanding place value.

◆ **Decimal and Percents** (Chapter 17): Whole-number place-value ideas are extended to allow for representation of the full range of rational numbers and approximations of irrational numbers.

◆ **Measurement** (Chapter 19): Problem-based tasks involving real measures can be used to help students structure ideas about grouping by tens. Through measures, people develop benchmarks and meaningful referents for numbers.

Pre-Base-Ten Understandings

Students know a lot about numbers with two digits (10 to 99) as early as kindergarten. After all, most kindergartners can and should learn to count to 100 and count out sets with as many as 20 or 30 objects. They count students in the room, turn to specified page numbers in their books, and so on. However, their understanding is quite different from yours. It is based on a one-more-than or count-by-ones approach to quantity. This early phase is when students are not able to separate numbers into place-value groups—after counting 18 teddy bears, a young child might tell you that the 1 stands for 1 teddy and the 8 stands for 8 teddy bears. Such students have not had enough experiences to realize we are always grouping by tens. Let's look at a way to assess where students are in this trajectory.

FORMATIVE Assessment Notes

As a **diagnostic interview,** ask first or second graders to count out 53 tiles. Watch closely to note whether they count out the tiles one at a time and put them into a pile without any type of grouping or if they group them into tens. Have the students write the number that tells how many tiles they just counted. Some may write "35" instead of "53," a simple reversal. You will likely find that early on students count the tiles one by one and are therefore in a pre-place-value stage. ■

Counting by Ones

The students just described know that there are 53 tiles "because I counted them." Writing the number and saying the number are usually done correctly, but their understanding of 53 derives from and is connected to the count-by-ones approach. Students do not easily or quickly develop a meaningful use of groups of ten to represent quantities.

Even if students can tell you that in the numeral 53, the 5 "is in the tens place" or that there are "3 ones," they might just know the name of the positions without understanding that the "tens place" represents how many groups of ten. Similarly, if students use base-ten blocks, they may name a rod of ten as a "ten" and a small cube as a "one" but may not be able to tell how many ones are required to make a ten. It is easy to attach words to both materials and groups without realizing what the materials or symbols represent.

Students do know that 53 is "a lot" and that it's more than 47 (because you count past 47 to get to 53). They think of the "53" that they write as a single numeral. In this stage, they do not know that the 5 represents five groups of ten things and the 3 represents three single things (Fuson, 2006). Fuson and her colleagues refer to students' pre-base-ten understanding of number as "unitary." That is, there are no groupings of ten, even though a two-digit number is associated with the quantity. They initially rely on unitary counts to understand quantities.

Basic Ideas of Place Value

Place-value understanding requires an integration of new and sometimes difficult-to-construct concepts of grouping by tens (the base-ten concept) with procedural knowledge

of how groups are recorded in our place-value scheme, how numbers are written, and how they are spoken. Importantly, learners must understand the word *grouping*. Because the root word *group* is frequently used for instructing students to work together, this different use of the word may cause confusion, particularly for ELLs.

Integration of Base-Ten Groupings with Counting by Ones

Recognizing that students can count out a set of 53, we want to help them see that making groupings of tens and leftovers is a way of counting that same quantity. Each of the sets in Figure 11.1 has 53 tiles. We want students to construct the idea that all of these are the same and that the sameness is evident by virtue of the groupings of tens.

There is a subtle yet profound difference between students at this stage: Some know that set B is 53 because they understand the idea that 5 groups of ten and 3 more is the same amount as 53 counted by ones; others simply say, "It's 53," because they have been told that when things are grouped this way, it's called 53. The students who understand place value will see no need to count set B by ones. They understand the "fifty-threeness" of sets A and B to be the same. The students in the pre-place-value stage may not be sure how many they will get if they count the tiles in set B by ones or if the groups were "ungrouped" how many there would then be.

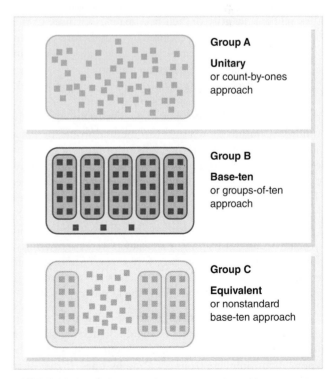

FIGURE 11.1 Three equivalent groupings of 53 objects. Group A is 53 because "I counted them (by ones)." Group B has 5 tens and 3 more. Group C is the same as B, but now some groups of ten are broken into singles.

PAUSE and REFLECT

The ideas in the preceding paragraph are important for you to understand so that the activities discussed later will make sense. What are some defining characteristics of "pre-place-value" students and those who understand place value? ●

Recognition of the equivalence of sets B and C is another step in students' conceptual development. Groupings with fewer than the maximum number of tens are referred to as *equivalent groupings* or *equivalent representations*. Understanding the equivalence of B and C indicates that grouping by tens is not just a rule that is followed but that any grouping by tens, including all or some of the singles, can help tell how many. Many computational techniques (e.g., regrouping in addition and subtraction) are based on equivalent representations of numbers.

Role of Counting

Counting plays a key role in constructing base-ten ideas about quantity and connecting these concepts to symbols and oral names for numbers.

Students can count sets such as those in Figure 11.1 using three distinct approaches. Each approach helps students think about the quantities in a different way (Thompson, 1990).

1. *Counting by ones.* Students usually begin with this method. Initially, a count-by-ones approach is the only way they name a quantity or "tell how many." All three of the sets in Figure 11.1 can be counted by ones. Before base-ten ideas develop, a count by ones is the only way students can be convinced that all three sets are the same.

2. *Counting by groups and singles.* In set B in Figure 11.1, counting by groups and singles would go like this: "One, two, three, four, five bunches of ten, and one, two, three singles." Consider how novel this method would be for a student who had never thought about counting a group of objects as a single item. Also notice how this approach to counting does not tell directly how many items there are. This counting must be coordinated with a count by ones before it can be a means of telling "how many."

3. *Counting by tens and ones.* This is the way adults would probably count set B and perhaps set C: "Ten, twenty, thirty, forty, fifty, fifty-one, fifty-two, fifty-three." Although this count ends by saying the number of items, it is not as explicit as the second method in counting the number of groups.

Regardless of the specific activity that you may be doing, your foremost objective should be helping students integrate the grouping-by-tens concept with what they know about numbers from counting by ones. If they first counted by ones, the question might be, "What will happen if we count these by groups and singles (or by tens and ones)?" If a set has been grouped into tens and ones and counted, then ask, "How can we be really certain that there

are 53 things here?" or "How many do you think we will get if we count by ones?" You cannot *tell* students that these counts will all be the same and hope that will make sense to them—it is a relationship they must construct themselves.

Integration of Groupings with Words

The way we say a number such as "fifty-three" must also be connected with the grouping-by-tens concept. The counting methods provide a connection. The count by tens and ones results in saying the number of groups and singles separately: "five tens and three." This is an acceptable, albeit nonstandard, way of naming this quantity. Saying the number of tens and singles separately in this fashion can be called *base-ten language*. Students can associate the base-ten language with the standard language: "five tens and three—fifty-three."

There are several variations of the base-ten language for 53: "5 tens and 3," "5 tens and 3 ones," "5 tens and 3 singles," and so on. Each may be used interchangeably with the standard name, "fifty-three." But if you have ELLs, it is best to select one base-ten approach (e.g., 5 tens and 3 ones) and consistently connect it to the standard approach. Other languages often use the base-ten phrase, so this can be a good cultural connection for students.

Integration of Groupings with Place-Value Notation

The symbolic scheme that we use for writing numbers (ones on the right, tens to the left of ones, and so on) must be coordinated with the grouping scheme. Activities can be designed so that students physically associate a tens and ones grouping with the correct recording of the individual digits, as Figure 11.2 indicates.

Language again plays a key role in making these connections. The explicit count by groups and singles matches the individual digits as the number is written in the usual left-to-right manner. A similar coordination is necessary for hundreds and other place values. "Making a transition from viewing 'ten' as simply the accumulation of 10 ones to seeing it both as 10 ones *and* as 1 ten is an important first step for students toward understanding the structure of the base-ten number system" (NCTM, 2000, p. 33).

Figure 11.3 summarizes the ideas of an integrated place-value understanding that have been discussed so far. Note that in addition to counting by ones, students use two other ways of counting: by groups and singles separately and by tens and ones. All three methods of counting are coordinated as the principal method of integrating the base-ten concepts, the written names, and the oral names.

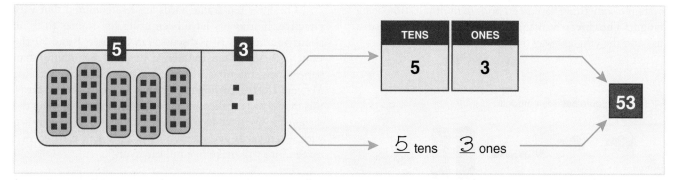

FIGURE 11.2 Groupings by 10 are matched with numerals, placed in labeled places, and eventually written in standard form.

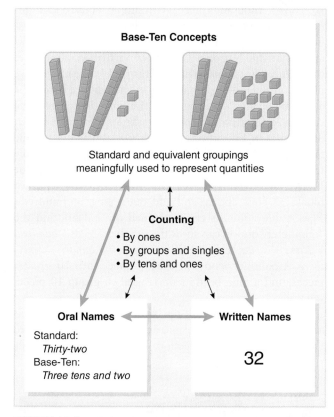

FIGURE 11.3 Relational understanding of place value integrates three components, shown as the corners of the triangle: base-ten concepts, oral names for numbers, and written names for numbers.

Base-Ten Models for Place Value

Physical models for base-ten concepts play a key role in helping students develop the idea of "a ten" as both a single entity and as a set of 10 units. Remember, though, that the models do not "show" the concept to the students; the students must mentally construct the "ten makes one

relationship" and impose it on the model. A good base-ten model for ones, tens, and hundreds is one that is *proportional.* That is, a model for ten is physically 10 times larger than the model for a one, and a hundred model is 10 times larger than the ten model. Base-ten models can be categorized as *groupable* and *pregrouped.*

Groupable Models

Models that most clearly reflect the relationships of ones, tens, and hundreds are those for which the ten can actually be made or grouped from the single pieces. When students put 10 beans in a small cup, the cup of 10 beans literally *is the same as* the 10 single beans. Examples of these groupable models are shown in Figure 11.4(a). These could also be called "put-together-take-apart" models.

Of the groupable models, beans or counters in cups are inexpensive and easy for students to use. Plastic connecting cubes also provide a good transition to pregrouped ten rods as they form a similar shape. Bundles of wooden craft sticks or coffee stirrers can be grouped with rubber bands, but small hands may have trouble using rubber bands.

As students become more and more familiar with these models, collections of tens can be made in advance by the students and kept as ready-made tens (e.g., craft sticks can be left prebundled). This is a good transition to the pregrouped models described next.

Pregrouped or Trading Models

Models that are pregrouped are commonly shown in textbooks and are often used in instructional activities. Pregrouped models, such as those in Figure 11.4(b), cannot be taken apart or put together. When 10 single pieces are accumulated, they must be exchanged or *traded* for a ten, and likewise, tens must be traded for hundreds. With pregrouped models, we need to make an extra effort to confirm that students understand that a ten piece really is the same as 10 ones. Here students combine multiplicative understanding (each place is 10 times the value of the place to the right) with a positional (each place has a value) system—something hard to do prior to multiplication being taught! The chief advantage of these models is their ease of use and the efficient way they model large numbers.

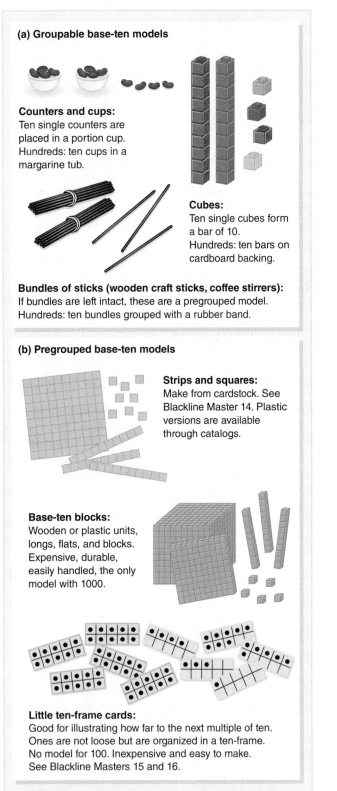

(a) Groupable base-ten models

Counters and cups:
Ten single counters are placed in a portion cup. Hundreds: ten cups in a margarine tub.

Cubes:
Ten single cubes form a bar of 10. Hundreds: ten bars on cardboard backing.

Bundles of sticks (wooden craft sticks, coffee stirrers):
If bundles are left intact, these are a pregrouped model. Hundreds: ten bundles grouped with a rubber band.

(b) Pregrouped base-ten models

Strips and squares:
Make from cardstock. See Blackline Master 14. Plastic versions are available through catalogs.

Base-ten blocks:
Wooden or plastic units, longs, flats, and blocks. Expensive, durable, easily handled, the only model with 1000.

Little ten-frame cards:
Good for illustrating how far to the next multiple of ten. Ones are not loose but are organized in a ten-frame. No model for 100. Inexpensive and easy to make. See Blackline Masters 15 and 16.

FIGURE 11.4 Groupable and pregrouped base-ten models.

The little ten-frame cards are less common, but very effective. If students have been using ten-frames to think about numbers to 20 as discussed in Chapters 8 and 10, the value of the filled ten-frame may be more meaningful than paper strips and squares of base-ten materials (see Blackline Masters 15–16). Although the ones are fixed on the cards, this model has the distinct advantage of always showing the distance to the next decade. For example, when 47 is shown with 4 ten cards and a seven card, a student can see that three more will make five full cards, or 50.

TECHNOLOGY Electronic versions of base-ten manipulatives are computer representations of the three-dimensional base-ten blocks, including the thousands piece. With simple mouse clicks, students (including those with disabilities) can place ones, tens, hundreds, or thousands on the screen. In the *Base Blocks* applets at the National Library of Virtual Manipulatives (http://nlvm.usu.edu/en/nav/vlibrary.html), the models are placed on a place-value mat. If 10 of one type are lassoed by a rectangle, they snap together; if a piece is dragged one column to the right, the piece breaks apart into 10 of that unit. Pearson Education's *eTools* has a similar place-value tool with a bit more flexibility. This applet is available free at www.kyrene.org/mathtools. Choose "Place Value Blocks," as shown in Figure 11.5. Then select the base-ten blocks of your choice and add ones, tens, or hundreds. Place-value columns can be turned on and off, and the "odometer" option can show the number 523 as *5 hundreds + 2 tens + 3 ones*, as *500 + 20 + 3*, or as *five hundred twenty-three*. A hammer icon will break a piece into 10 smaller pieces, and a glue bottle icon is used to group 10 pieces together.

Compared to real base-ten blocks, these virtual materials are free, are easily grouped and ungrouped, can be shown to the full class on a projection device, and are available

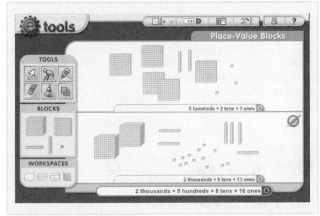

FIGURE 11.5 Pearson Scott Foresman's *eTools* includes a computer model of base-ten blocks.

in "endless" supply, even the thousands blocks. Computer models allow students to print their work and, thus, create a written record of what they've done. On the other hand, the computer model is no more conceptual than a physical model and, like the physical model, is only a representation for students who understand the relationships involved.

Nonproportional Models

Nonproportional models can be used by students who understand that 10 units make "a ten" or by students who need to return to place-value concepts because they are struggling with computation or other content that requires place-value understanding. These are models, such as money, where the ten is not physically 10 times larger than the one. Many students can grasp place-value relationships using pennies, dimes, and dollars to represent the ones, tens, and hundreds on their place-value mat. Using coin representations, they can display amounts and exchange 10 dimes for a dollar and represent and carry out a variety of calculations. Like a bead-frame that has same-sized beads in different columns (on wires) or chips that are given different place values by color, these nonproportional representations are *not* used for introducing place-value concepts. They are used when students already have a conceptual understanding of the numeration system and need additional reinforcement. Oftentimes money is a useful tool for students with special needs who understand the relationships between the place values yet need support in developing other mathematical concepts.

Developing Base-Ten Concepts

Now that you have a sense of the important place-value concepts, we turn to activities that assist students in developing these concepts. This section focuses on the top of the triangle of ideas in Figure 11.3: base-ten concepts or grouping by tens. The connections of this most important component with writing numbers and with the way we say numbers—the bottom two corners of the triangle in Figure 11.3—are discussed separately to help you focus on how to do each. However, in the classroom, the oral and written names for numbers can and should be developed in concert with conceptual ideas.

Grouping Activities

Because students come to their development of base-ten concepts with a count-by-ones idea of number, you must begin there. You cannot arbitrarily impose grouping by ten on students. Students need to experiment with showing amounts in groups of like size and perhaps come to an agreement that ten is a very useful size to use. The following activity could be done in late first grade or early second grade and is designed as an example of a first effort at developing grouping concepts.

Activity **11.1**

Counting in Groups

Find a collection of items that students might be interested in counting—perhaps the number of shoes in the classroom, a jar of cubes, a long chain of plastic links, or the number of crayons in the classroom crayon box. The quantity should be countable, somewhere between 25 and 100. Pose the question, "How could we count our shoes in some way that would be easier than counting by ones?" Whatever suggestions you get, try to implement them. After trying several methods, you can have a discussion of what worked well and what did not. If no one suggests counting by tens, you might casually suggest that as an idea to try.

One teacher had her second-grade students find a good way to count all the connecting cubes being held by the students after each had been given a cube for each of the pockets they had on their clothes that day. The first suggestion was to count by sevens. That was tried but did not work very well because none of the second graders could easily count by sevens. In search of a more efficient way, the next suggestion was to count by twos. This did not seem to be much better than counting by ones. Finally, they settled on counting by tens and realized that this was a pretty good method.

This and similar activities provide you with the opportunity to suggest that materials actually be arranged into groups of tens before the "fast" way of counting is begun. Remember that students may count "ten, twenty, thirty, thirty-one, thirty-two" but not fully realize the "thirty-two-ness" of the quantity. To connect the count-by-tens method with their understood method of counting by ones, the students need to count both ways and discuss why they get the same result.

The idea in the next activity is for students to make groupings of ten and record or say the amounts. Number words are used so that students will not mechanically match tens and ones with individual digits. It is important that students confront the actual quantity in a manner meaningful to them.

Activity **11.2**

Groups of Ten

STUDENTS with SPECIAL NEEDS

Prepare bags of counters of different types such as toothpicks, buttons, beans, plastic chips, connecting cubes, craft sticks, or other items. Students should have a recording sheet similar to Figure 11.6 (top left). The bags can be placed at stations around the room or given to pairs of students. Students empty the bags and count the contents. The amount is recorded as a number word. Then the counters are grouped in as many tens as possible. The groupings are recorded on the form. After returning the counters to the bags, bags are traded, or students move to another station. Note that students with disabilities may initially need to use a ten-frame to support their counting. Then the use of the ten-frame eventually should fade.

Variations of the "Groups of Ten" activity are suggested by the three other recording sheets in Figure 11.6. On the "Get this many" sheet, students count the dots and then count out the corresponding number of counters. Provide small cups to put the groups of ten in. Notice that the

activity requires students to first count the set in a way they understand (count by ones), record the amount in words, and then make the groupings. The "Fill the tens" and "Loop this many" sheets begin with a verbal name (number word), and students must count the indicated amount and then make groups. Look at Figure 11.7, which is a recording sheet that can be used with any items. Notice that all three place-value components are included.

 **FORMATIVE Assessment Notes**

As you watch students doing these activities, you can learn a lot about their base-ten concept development. For example, how do students count out the objects? Do they make groupings of ten? Do they count to 10 and then start again at 1? Students who do that

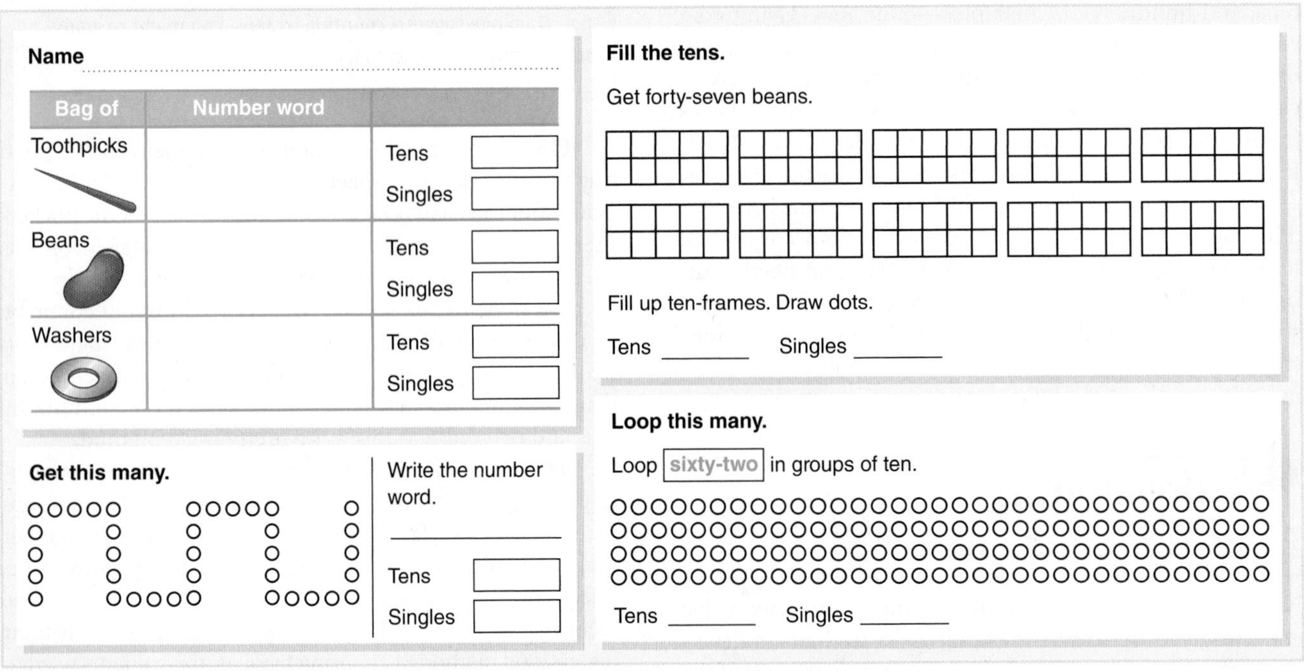

FIGURE 11.6 Activities involving number words and making groups of ten.

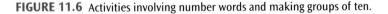

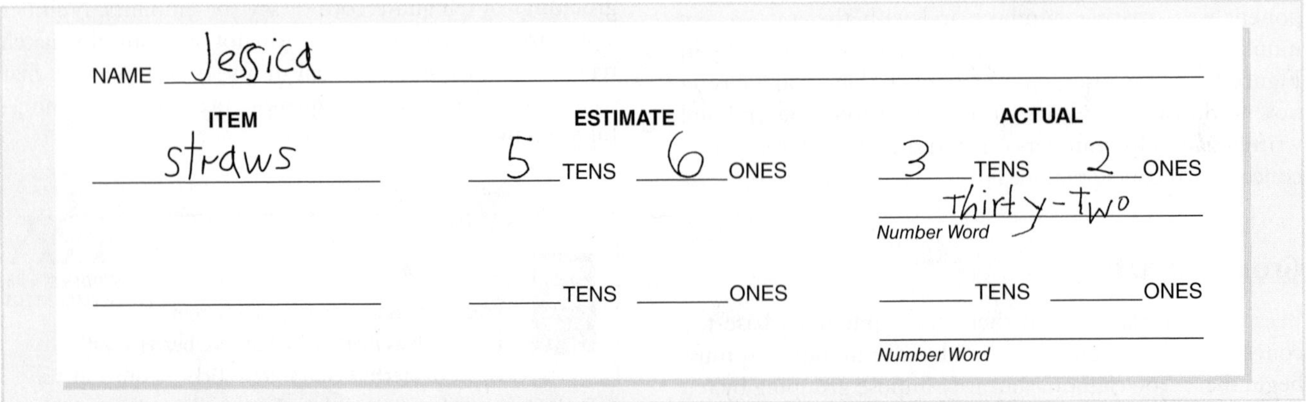

FIGURE 11.7 Recording sheet for estimating groups of tens and ones.

are already using the base-ten structure. But what you will more likely see early on is students counting a full set without any stopping at tens and without any effort to group the materials in piles. For example, ask a student in a **diagnostic interview** to count a jar of small beans. Then ask the student to record the number. Ask the student, "If you are to place a group of 10 beans in each small cup, how many cups would you need?" If a student has no idea or makes random guesses, what would you know about the student's knowledge of place value? ■

The Strangeness of *Ones, Tens,* and *Hundreds*

Reflect for a moment on how strange it must sound to say "seven ones." Certainly students have never said they were "seven ones" years old. The use of the word *ten* as a singular group name is even more mysterious. Consider the phrase "Ten ones makes one ten." The first *ten* carries the usual meaning of 10 things, the amount that is 1 more than 9 things. But the other *ten* is a singular noun, a thing. How can something the student has known for years as the name for a lot of things suddenly become one thing? And if you think this is confusing for native speakers, imagine the potential difficulty for ELLs.

As students begin to make groupings of ten, start introducing the language of "tens." In the beginning, use language that matches the objects, such as "cups of tens and ones" or "bundles of tens and singles." Then graduate to a general phrase, such as "groups of tens and ones." Eventually you can abbreviate this simply to "tens." There is no hurry to use the word "ones" for the leftovers. Language such as "four tens and seven" works very well.

The word *hundred* is equally strange and yet usually gets less attention. It must be understood in multiple ways, including as 100 single objects, as 10 tens, and as a singular thing. These word names are not as simple as they seem!

Grouping Tens to Make 100

So far, we have focused mainly on helping students move from counting by ones to understanding how groups of ten can be used more effectively. In second grade, numbers up to 1000 become important (CCSSO, 2010). Here the issue is not one of connecting a count-by-ones concept to a group of 100 but rather seeing how a group of 100 can be understood as a group of 10 tens as well as 100 single ones. In textbooks, this connection is often illustrated on one page showing how 10 sticks of ten can be put together to make 1 hundred. This quick demonstration may be lost on many students.

As a means of introducing hundreds as groups of 10 tens and also 100 singles, consider the following estimation activity.

Activity 11.3

Too Many Tens

Show students any quantity with 150 to 1000 items. For example, you might use a jar of lima beans or a grocery bag full of straws. Alternatives include a long chain of connecting links or paper clips or a box of Styrofoam packing peanuts. First, have students make and record estimates of how many beans are in the jar. Discuss with students how they selected their estimates. Give portions of the beans to pairs or triads of students to put into cups of 10 beans. Collect leftover beans and put these into groups of ten as well. Now ask, "How can we use these groups of ten to tell how many beans we have? Can we make new groups from the groups of ten? What is 10 groups of ten called?" If using cups of beans, be prepared with some larger containers or baggies into which 10 cups can be placed. When all groups are made, count the hundreds, the tens, and the ones separately. Record on the board as "4 hundreds + 7 tens + 8 ones."

In this activity, it is important to use a groupable model so that students can see how the 10 groups are the same as the 100 individual items. This connection is often lost in the rather simple display of a 100 flat or a paper hundreds square in the pregrouped base-ten models.

Equivalent Representations

An important variation of the grouping activities is aimed at the equivalent representations of numbers. For example, ask students who have just completed the "Groups of Ten" activity (Activity 11.2) with a bag of counters, "What is another way you can show 42 besides 4 groups and 2 singles? Let's see how many ways you can find." Interestingly, most students will go next to 42 singles. The following activities focus on creating equivalent representations.

Activity 11.4

Can You Make the Link?

Show a collection of materials that are only partly grouped in sets of ten. For example, you may have 5 chains of 10 links and 17 additional unconnected links. Be sure the students understand that each chain has 10 links. Have students count the number of chains and the number of singles in any way they wish to count. Ask, "How many in all?" Record all responses, and discuss how they got their answers. Next, change the groupings (make a ten from the singles, or break apart one of the tens) and repeat. Do not change the total number from one time to the next. Once students begin to understand that the total does not change, ask in what other ways the items could be grouped if you use tens and ones.

If you are teaching in grade 2 or 3, equivalent representations for hundreds as groups of tens can help with the concept of a hundred as 10 tens. The next activity is similar to "Can You Make the Link?" but is done using pregrouped materials and includes hundreds.

Activity 11.5

Three Other Ways

Students work in groups or pairs. First, they show 463 on their desks with base-ten materials in the standard representation. Next, they find and record at least three other ways of representing this number.

A variation of "Three Other Ways" is to challenge students to find a way to show an amount with a specific number of pieces. "Can you show 463 with 31 pieces?" (There is more than one way to do this.) Students in grade 3 can get quite involved with finding all the ways to show a three-digit number.

After students have sufficient experiences with pregrouped materials, a semi-abstract square-stick-dot notation can be used for recording ones, tens, and hundreds (see Figure 11.8). When needed, students can use small squares for hundreds. Use the drawings as a means of telling the students what materials to get out to solve the problems and also as a way for students to record results.

The next activity begins to incorporate oral language with equivalent representation ideas.

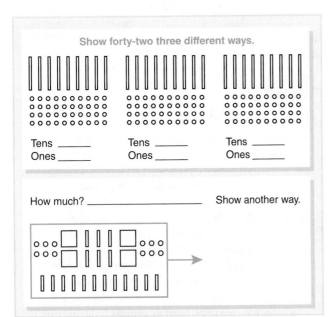

FIGURE 11.8 Equivalent representation exercises using square-stick-dot pictures.

Activity 11.6

Base-Ten Riddles

Base-ten riddles can be presented orally or in written form. In either case, students should use base-ten materials to help solve them. The examples here illustrate a variety of different levels of difficulty. Have students write new riddles when they complete these.

I have 23 ones and 4 tens. Who am I?

I have 4 hundreds, 12 tens, and 6 ones. Who am I?

I have 30 ones and 3 hundreds. Who am I?

I am 45. I have 25 ones. How many tens do I have?

I am 341. I have 22 tens. How many hundreds do I have?

I have 13 tens, 2 hundreds, and 21 ones. Who am I?

If you put 3 more tens with me, I would be 115. Who am I?

I have 17 ones. I am between 40 and 50. Who am I? How many tens do I have?

Oral and Written Names for Numbers

In this section, we focus on helping students connect the bottom two corners of the triangle in Figure 11.3—oral and written names for numbers—with their emerging base-ten concepts of using groups of ten or one hundred as efficient methods of counting. Note that the ways we say and write numbers are conventions rather than concepts. Students must learn these by being told rather than through problem-based activities. It is also worth remembering that for ELL students, the convention or pattern in our English number words is probably not the same as it is in their native language. This is especially true of the numbers 11 to 19.

Two-Digit Number Names

In first and second grades, students need to connect the base-ten concepts with the oral number names they have used many times. They know the words but have not thought of them in terms of tens and ones. In fact, early on they may want to write twenty-one as 201.

Almost always use base-ten materials while teaching oral names. Initially, rather than using standard number words, the more explicit *base-ten language* can be used. In base-ten language, rather than saying "forty-seven," you would say "four tens and seven ones." Base-ten language is rarely misunderstood. As it seems appropriate, begin to pair base-ten language with standard language. Emphasize the teens as exceptions. Acknowledge that they are formed "backward" and do not fit the patterns. The next activity helps introduce oral names for numbers.

Activity **11.7**

Counting Rows of Ten

ENGLISH LANGUAGE LEARNERS

Use a 10 × 10 array of dots on the projector. Cover up all but two rows, as shown in Figure 11.9. "How many tens? [2.] Two tens is called *twenty.*" Have the class repeat. Show another row. "Three tens is called *thirty.* Four tens is *forty.* Five tens could have been *fivety* but is just *fifty.* How many tens does sixty have?" The names *sixty, seventy, eighty,* and *ninety* all fit the pattern. Slide the cover up and down the array, asking how many tens and the name for that many. ELLs may not hear the difference between fifty and fifteen, sixty and sixteen, and so on, so explicitly comparing these words is important, and clearly enunciating is also important.

Use the same 10 × 10 array to work on names for tens and ones. Show, for example, four full lines, "forty." Next, expose one dot in the fifth row. "Four tens and one. Forty-one." Add more dots one at a time. "Four tens and two. Forty-two." "Four tens and three. Forty-three." This is shown in Figure 11.9. When that pattern is established, repeat with other decades from 20 through 90.

Repeat this basic approach with other base-ten models. The next activity shows how this might be done.

Activity **11.8**

Counting with Base-Ten Models

ENGLISH LANGUAGE LEARNERS

STUDENTS *with* SPECIAL NEEDS

Show some tens on the projector, or just place them on the carpet in a mixed arrangement. Ask how many tens. Add a ten or remove a ten, and repeat the question. Next, add some ones. Always have students give the base-ten name and the standard name (for ELLs and students with disabilities, as well as other students, it is helpful to post examples of base-ten names and the corresponding standard names on the math word wall). Continue to make changes in the materials displayed by adding or removing 1 or 2 tens and by adding and removing ones. By avoiding the standard left-to-right order for tens and ones, the emphasis is on the names of the materials, not the order they are in.

Reverse the activity by having students use base-ten blocks at their desks. For example, say, "Make 78." The students make the number with the models and then give the base-ten name and standard name. Students can also record their work (see Figure 11.10).

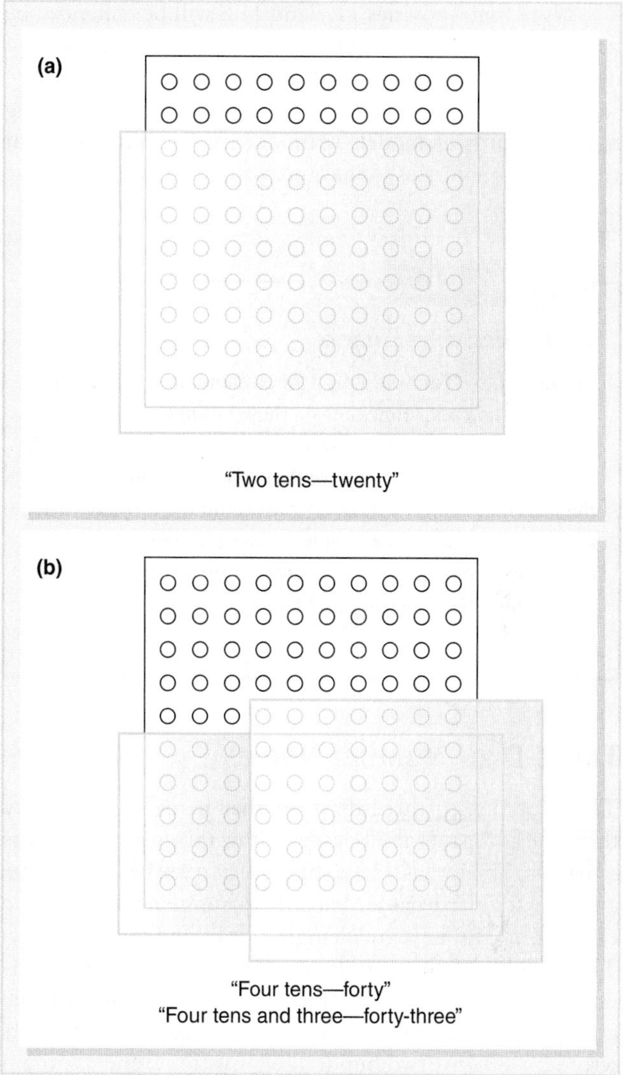

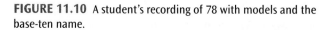

(a)

"Two tens—twenty"

(b)

"Four tens—forty"
"Four tens and three—forty-three"

FIGURE 11.9 10 × 10 dot arrays are used to model sets of tens and ones (Blackline Master 12).

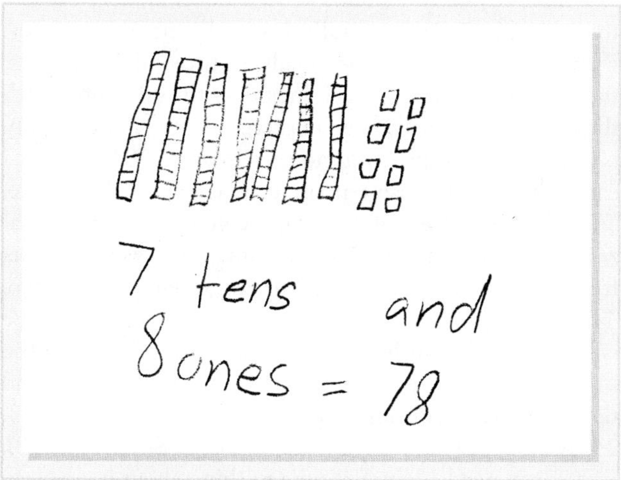

7 tens and
8 ones = 78

FIGURE 11.10 A student's recording of 78 with models and the base-ten name.

Note that Activities 11.7 and 11.8 will be enhanced by discussion. Have students explain their thinking. If you don't require students to reflect on their responses, they soon learn how to give the response you want, matching number words to models without actually thinking about the total quantities. The next activity has the same objective.

Activity 11.9

Tens, Ones, and Fingers

Ask your class, "Can you show 6 [or any amount less than 10] fingers?" Then ask, "How can you show 37 fingers?" Some students will figure out that at least four students are required. Line up four students, and have three hold up 10 fingers and the last child 7 fingers. Have the class count the fingers by tens and ones. Ask for other students to show different numbers. Emphasize the number of sets of ten fingers and the single fingers (base-ten language), and pair this with standard language.

Three-Digit Number Names

The approach to three-digit number names is essentially the same as for two-digit names. Show mixed arrangements of base-ten materials. Have students give the base-ten name and the standard name. Vary the arrangement from one example to the next by changing only one type of piece. That is, add or remove only ones or only tens or only hundreds. It is important for students with disabilities to see counterexamples, so actively point out that some students wrote 200803 for two hundred eighty-three, and ask them whether that is correct. These conversations allow students to explore their misunderstandings and focus on the place-value system more explicitly.

Similarly, have students at their desks model numbers that you give to them orally using the standard names. By the time that students are ready for three-digit numbers, the two-digit number names, including the difficulties with the teens, have usually been mastered. The major difficulty is with numbers involving no tens, such as 702. As noted earlier, the use of base-ten language is quite helpful here. The difficulty of zero-tens (or more generally the internal zero) is more pronounced when writing numerals. Students frequently incorrectly write 7002 for seven hundred two. The emphasis on the meaning in the oral base-ten language will be a significant help. At first, students do not see the importance of zero in place value and do not understand that zero helps us distinguish between such numbers as 203, 23, and 230 (Dougherty, Flores, Louis, & Sophian, 2010). ELLs may need additional time to think about how to say and write the numerals, because they are translating all the terms within the number.

Researchers note that there are significantly more errors with four-digit number names than three-digit numbers, so do not think that students will easily generalize to larger numbers without actually exploring examples and tasks (Cayton & Brizuela, 2007).

Written Symbols

Place-value mats are simple mats divided into two or three sections to hold ones and tens or ones, tens, and hundreds pieces as shown in Figure 11.11. You can suggest to your students that the mats are a good way to organize their materials when working with base-ten blocks. Explain that the standard way to use a place-value mat is with the space for the ones on the right and the tens and hundreds places to the left.

Although not commonly seen in textbooks, it is strongly recommended that two ten-frames be drawn in the ones place as shown (see Blackline Master 17). That way, the amount of ones on the ten-frames is always clearly evident, eliminating the need for repeatedly counting the ones. The ten-frame also makes it very clear how many additional counters would be needed to make the next set of ten. If students are modeling two numbers at the same time, one ten-frame could be used for each number.

As students use their place-value mats, they can be shown how the left-to-right order of the pieces is also the way that numbers are written. To show how the numbers are "built," have a set of 27 cards—one for each of the

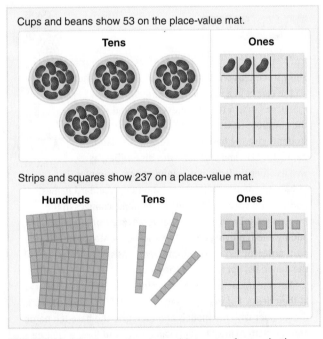

FIGURE 11.11 Place-value mats with two ten-frames in the ones place organize the counters and promote the concept of groups of ten.

FIGURE 11.12 Building numbers with a set of cards.

hundreds (100–900), one for each of the tens (10–90), and ones cards for 1 through 9 (see Figure 11.12). Notice that the cards are made so that the tens card is two times as long as the ones card and the hundreds card is three times as long as the ones card.

As students place the materials for a number (e.g., 457) on the mat, have them also place the matching cards (e.g., 400, 50, and 7) below the materials. Then starting with the hundreds card, layer the others on top, right aligned. This approach will show how the number is built while allowing the student to see the individual components of the number. This is especially helpful if there are zero tens. The place-value mat and the matching cards demonstrate the important link between the base-ten models and the written form of the numbers.

The next two activities are designed to help students make connections between all three representations: models, oral language, and written forms. They can be done with two- or three-digit numbers depending on students' needs.

Activity **11.10**

Say It/Press It

ENGLISH LANGUAGE LEARNERS

Display models of ones and tens (and hundreds) in a mixed arrangement. (Use a projector or simply draw on the board using the square-stick-dot method.) Students say the amount shown in base-ten language ("four hundreds, one ten, and five ones") and then in standard language ("four hundred fifteen"); next, they enter it on their calculators. Have someone share his or her display and defend it. Make a change in the materials and repeat. You can also do this activity as "Show It/Press It" and start by saying the standard name for a number (with either two or three digits). At their desks, students use base-ten materials to show that number and press it on their calculators (or write it). Again, pay special attention to numbers in the teens and the case of zero tens. ELLs may need additional time to think of the words that go with the numbers, especially as the numbers get larger.

These activities are especially good for numbers that pose a problem for students, like the teens and three-digit numbers with zero tens. If you show (or say) 7 hundreds and 4 ones, the class says, "Seven hundreds, zero tens, and four ones—seven hundred (*slight pause*) four." The pause and the base-ten language suggest the correct three-digit number to press, write, or model.

The next activity is a wonderful challenge for students in early stages of place-value development.

Activity **11.11**

Digit Change

STUDENTS *with* SPECIAL NEEDS

Have students enter a specific two- or three-digit number on the calculator.

The task is to change one of the digits in the number without simply entering the new number. For example, change 48 to 78. Change 315 to 305 or to 295. Changes can be made by adding or subtracting an appropriate amount. Students should write or discuss explanations for their solutions. Students with disabilities may need the visual support of having cards that say "add ten" or "add one" first to explore how the number changes. They may also need support with materials to be able to conceptualize the number and then move to more abstract work on the calculator alone.

Assessing Place-Value Concepts

Now that the three components of the place-value ideas shown in Figure 11.3 have been developed, you need to assess how students are integrating these ideas. Students are often able to disguise their lack of understanding of place value by following directions, using the tens and ones pieces in prescribed ways, and using the language of place value.

The diagnostic tasks presented here are designed to help you look more closely at students' understanding of the integration of the three place-value components. Designed as diagnostic interviews rather than full-class activities, these tasks have been used by several researchers and are adapted primarily from Labinowicz (1985), Kamii (1985), and Ross (1986).

FORMATIVE Assessment Notes

The first **diagnostic interview**, referred to as the Digit Correspondence Task, has been used widely in the study of place-value development. Take out 36 blocks. Ask the student to count the blocks, and then have the student write the number that tells how many there are. Circle the 6 in 36 and ask, "Does this part of your 36 have anything to do with how many blocks there are?" Then circle the 3 and repeat the question. As with all diagnostic interviews, do not give clues. Based on responses to the task, Ross (1989, 2002) has identified five distinct levels of understanding of place value:

1. *Single numeral.* The student writes 36 but views it as a single numeral. The individual digits 3 and 6 have no meaning by themselves.
2. *Position names.* The student correctly identifies the tens and ones positions but still makes no connections between the individual digits and the blocks.
3. *Face value.* The student matches 6 blocks with the 6 and 3 blocks with the 3.
4. *Transition to place value.* The 6 is matched with 6 blocks and the 3 with the remaining 30 blocks but not as 3 groups of 10.
5. *Full understanding.* The 3 is correlated with 3 groups of ten blocks and the 6 with 6 single blocks.

In the next **diagnostic interview,** write the number 342. Have the student read the number. Then have the student write the number that is 1 more. Next, ask for the number that is 10 more. You may wish to explore further with models. One less and 10 less can be checked the same way. Watch to see whether the student is counting on or counting back or if he immediately knows that ten more is 352.

This third **diagnostic interview** is also revealing. Ask the student to write the number that represents 5 tens, 2 ones, and 3 hundreds. Note that the task does not give the places in order. What do you think will be a common misunderstanding? If the student doesn't write 352, then ask them to show you the number with base-ten materials. What information can you get from the results of this interview? ■

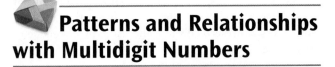

Patterns and Relationships with Multidigit Numbers

In this section, we move beyond this snapshot view of individual numbers toward an orientation that looks at the full number rather than just the digits. Here the focus will be on the patterns in our number system and how numbers are related. We are interested in the relationships of numbers to important special numbers—relationships that begin to overlap with or provide a basis for computation.

The Hundreds Chart

The hundreds chart (Figure 11.13) is such an important tool in the development of place-value concepts that it deserves special attention. K–2 classrooms should have a hundreds chart displayed prominently.

An extremely useful version of the chart is made of transparent pockets into which each of the 100 numeral cards can be inserted. You can hide a number by inserting

1	2	3	4	5	6	7	8	9	10
11	12	13	14	15	16	17	18	19	20
21	22	23	24	25	26	27	28	29	30
31	32	33	34	35	36	37	38	39	40
41	42	43	44	45	46	47	48	49	50
51	52	53	54	55	56	57	58	59	60
61	62	63	64	65	66	67	68	69	70
71	72	73	74	75	76	77	78	79	80
81	82	83	84	85	86	87	88	89	90
91	92	93	94	95	96	97	98	99	100

FIGURE 11.13 A hundreds chart (Blackline Master 22).

a blank card in front of a number in the pocket. You can also insert colored pieces of paper in the slots to highlight various number patterns. And you can remove the number cards and have students replace them in their correct positions.

A projection of a hundreds chart (www.crickweb.co.uk/ks2numeracy-tools.html) is almost as flexible as the pocket chart version. Numbers can be hidden by placing opaque counters on them. A blank 10 × 10 grid (see Blackline Master 21) serves as an empty hundreds chart on which you can write numbers.

At the kindergarten and first-grade levels, students can count and recognize two-digit numbers with the hundreds chart. In second grade and beyond, students use the hundreds chart to develop a base-ten understanding, noticing that jumps up or down are jumps of ten, while jumps to the right or left are jumps of one.

There are lots of patterns on the hundreds chart. In a discussion, different students will describe the same pattern in several ways. Accept all ideas. Here are some of the important place-value-related patterns they may notice:

- The numbers in a column all end with the same number, which is the same as the number at the top.
- In a row, the numbers "count" from left to right (the ones digit goes 1, 2, 3, . . . 9, 0); or the "second" number goes up by 1, but the first number (tens digit) stays the same.
- In a column, the first number (tens digit) "counts" or goes up by ones.
- You can count by tens going down the right-hand column.

For students, these patterns are not obvious or trivial. For example, one student may notice the pattern in the column under the 4—every number ends in a 4. Two minutes later, another student will "discover" the parallel pattern in the column headed by 7. That there is a pattern like this in every column may not be completely obvious.

Once you've discussed some of the patterns, try this next activity.

Activity 11.12

Missing Numbers

STUDENTS with SPECIAL NEEDS

Provide students with a hundreds chart on which some of the number cards have been removed. Use the classroom pocket chart, or for a full-class activity, you can use a projection. The students' task is to replace the missing numbers or tell what they are. To begin, have only a random selection of individual numbers removed. Later, remove sequences of several numbers from three or four different rows. Finally, remove all but one or two rows or columns. Eventually, challenge students to replace all of the numbers in a blank chart. (See Blackline Master 21.) For students with disabilities, model the placement of a number using a "think-aloud" to describe how you make your decision and what key features of the number you think about as you place the number properly on the chart.

Replacing the number cards or tiles from a blank chart is a good station activity for two students to try. By listening to how students go about finding the correct places for numbers, you can assess how well they have constructed an understanding of the 1-to-100 sequence.

Activity 11.13

Finding Neighbors on the Hundreds Chart

Begin with a blank or nearly blank hundreds chart. Circle a particular missing number. Students are to fill in the designated number and its "neighbors," the numbers to the left, to the right, above, and below. This can be done with the full class on a projection or with blank hundreds chart worksheets. After students become comfortable naming the neighbors of a number, ask what they notice about the neighboring numbers. The numbers to the left and right are one less and one more than the given number. Those above and below are ten less and ten more, respectively. What about those on the diagonal? By discussing these relationships on the chart, students begin to see how the sequence of numbers is related to numerical relationships.

Notice that students will first use the hundreds chart to learn about the patterns in the sequence of numbers.

Many students, especially at the K or grade 1 level, will not understand the corresponding numeric relationships such as those discussed in the last activity. In the following activity, number relationships on the chart are made more explicit by modeling the numbers with base-ten materials.

Activity 11.14

Models with the Hundreds Chart

Use any base-ten model for two-digit numbers with which the students are familiar. The little ten-frame cards are recommended (see Blackline Master 16).

- Give students one or more numbers to first make with the models and then find on the chart. Use groups of two or three numbers in either the same row or the same column.
- Indicate a number on the chart. What would you have to change to make each of its neighbors (the numbers to the left, to the right, above, and below)?

TECHNOLOGY

Several Web-based resources include hundreds charts that allow students to explore patterns. Learning about Number Relationships is an e-Example from NCTM's e-Standards that has a calculator and hundreds chart and allows for a variety of explorations. (There are extensions to thousands charts, too.) Students can skip-count by any number and also begin their counts at any number. Any two patterns can be overlapped using two colors. The *Number Patterns* applet from NLVM (http://nlvm.usu.edu/en/nav/vlibrary.html) presents students with number patterns to complete.

It is also helpful for students to have a chart that extends to 200, even in the first grade. Perhaps a more powerful idea is to extend the hundreds chart to 1000.

Activity 11.15

The Thousands Chart

Provide students with several sheets of the blank hundreds charts (Blackline Master 21). Assign groups of three or four students the task of creating a 1-to-1000 chart. The chart is made by taping 10 hundreds charts together in a long strip. Students should decide how they are going to divide up the task, with different students taking different parts of the chart.

The thousands chart should be discussed as a class to examine how numbers change as you count from one hundred to the next, what the patterns are, and so on. In fact, all of the earlier hundreds chart activities can be extended to thousands charts.

Relationships with Landmark Numbers

One of the most valuable features of both the hundreds chart and the little ten-frame cards is how clearly they illustrate the distance to the next multiple of 10—the end of the row on the chart or the blank spaces on the ten-frame card. Multiples of 10, 100, and occasionally other special numbers, such as multiples of 25, are referred to as *landmark numbers*. Students learn to use this term as they work with informal methods of computation. When finding the difference between 74 and 112, a student might say, "First, I added 6 onto 74 to get to a landmark number. Then I added 2 more tens onto 80 to get to 100 because that's another landmark number." Whatever terminology is used, understanding how numbers are related to these special numbers is an important step in students' development of number sense and place value.

In addition to the hundreds chart, the number line is an excellent way to explore these relationships. The next two activities are suggestions for using number lines.

Activity **11.16**

Who Am I?

Sketch a long line (or use a piece of cash register tape) and label 0 and 100 at opposite ends. Mark a point with a "?" that corresponds to your secret number. (Estimate the position the best you can.) Students try to guess your secret number. For each guess, place and label a mark on the line. Continue marking each guess until your secret number is discovered. As a variation, the end points can be different from 0 and 100. For example, try 0 and 1000, 200 and 300, or 500 and 800.

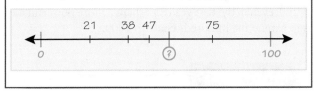

Activity **11.17**

Who Could They Be?

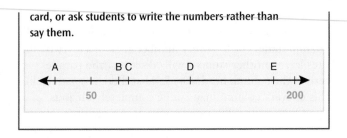

ENGLISH LANGUAGE LEARNERS

Label two points on a number line (not necessarily the ends) with landmark numbers. Show students different points labeled with letters, and ask what numbers they might be and why they think that. In the example shown here, B and C are less than 100 but probably more than 60. E could be about 180. You can also ask where 75 might be or where 400 is. About how far apart are A and D? Why do you think D is more than 100? For ELLs, rather than just saying the numbers, also write them on a note card, or ask students to write the numbers rather than say them.

Connecting Place Value to Addition and Subtraction

As you can see, there is much more to learning about place value than having students state how many ones, tens, or hundreds are in a number. Some research shows that learning place value is a prerequisite for learning operations with those numbers (Baroody, 1990), while other research suggests that problems involving addition and subtraction are a good context for learning place-value concepts (Wright, Stanger, Stafford, & Martland, 2006). Regardless, we know that students who only understand computation as a digit-by-digit exercise and not with the full understanding of the numbers involved make many errors and have little judgment of the reasonableness of their answers. So here we will lay the groundwork for both conceptual and procedural knowledge as we connect place value to addition and subtraction. The key component in the following activities is whether students can apply their emerging understanding of place value to computation. The next two activities are extensions of part-part-whole ideas that were explored in Chapter 9. In the first of these, the landmark number is one of the parts. In the second, the landmark number is the whole.

Activity **11.18**

50 and Some More

Say or write a number between 50 and 100. Students respond with "50 and ____." For 63, the response is "50 and 13." Any landmark number can be used instead of 50. For example, you could use any number that ends in 50. You can also do this with numbers such as 70 or 230.

Landmark numbers are often broken apart in computations. The next activity is aimed at what may be the most important landmark number, 100.

Activity **11.19**

The Other Part of 100

Two students work together with a set of little ten-frame cards. One student makes a two-digit number. Then both students work mentally to determine what goes with that ten-frame amount to make 100. They write their solutions on paper and then check by making the other part with the cards to see whether the total is 100. Students take turns making the original number. Figure 11.14 shows three different thought processes that students might use.

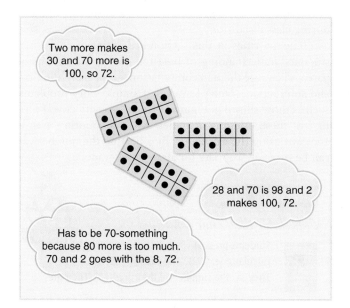

FIGURE 11.14 Using little ten-frames to help think about the "other part of 100."

If your students are adept at finding parts of 100, you can change the whole from 100 to another number. At first, try other multiples of 10 such as 70 or 80. Then extend the whole to any number less than 100.

 PAUSE and REFLECT

Suppose that the whole is 83. Sketch four little ten-frame cards showing 36. Looking at your "cards," what goes with 36 to make 83? How did you think about it? ⬤

What you just did in finding the other part of 83 was subtract 36 from 83. Notice that you did not regroup. Most likely you did it in your head. With more practice you (and students as early as second grade) can do this without the aid of the cards.

Compatible numbers for addition and subtraction are numbers that go together easily to make landmark numbers. Numbers that make tens or hundreds are the most common examples. Compatible sums also include numbers that end in 5, 25, 50, or 75, because these numbers are easy to work with as well. The teaching task is to get students accustomed to looking for combinations that work together and then looking for these combinations in computational situations.

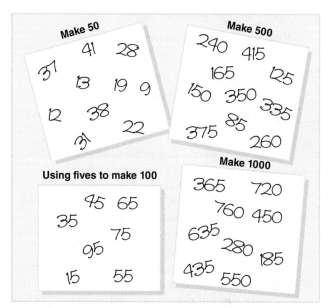

FIGURE 11.15 Compatible-pair searches.

Activity **11.20**

Compatible Pairs

Searching for compatible pairs can be done as an activity with the full class. Project the four suggested searches in Figure 11.15 (one at a time) on the board. The four possibilities are at different difficulty levels. Students name or connect the compatible pairs as they see them.

The next activity has students apply some of the same ideas about landmark numbers that we have been exploring.

Activity **11.21**

ENGLISH LANGUAGE LEARNERS

Close, Far, and In Between

Put any three numbers on the board. If more appropriate for your students, use two-digit numbers.

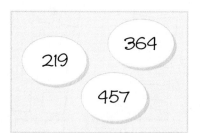

With these three numbers as referents, ask questions such as the following, encouraging discussion of all responses:

Which two numbers are closest? How do you know?

Which is closest to 300? To 250?

Name a number between 457 and 364.

Name a multiple of 25 between 219 and 364.

Name a number that is greater than all of these.

About how far apart are 219 and 500? 219 and 5000?

If these are "big numbers," what are some small numbers? Numbers that are about the same? Numbers that make these seem small?

For ELLs, this activity can be modified by using prompts that are similar to each other (rather than changing the prompts each time, which increases the linguistic demand). Also, ELLs will benefit from using a visual, such as a number line, and from writing the numbers rather than just hearing/saying them.

The NCTM *Standards* suggests a blending of numeration and computation. "It is not necessary to wait for students to fully develop place-value understandings before giving them opportunities to solve problems with two- and three-digit numbers. When such problems arise in interesting contexts, students can often invent ways to solve them that incorporate and deepen their understanding of place value, especially when students have the opportunities to discuss and explain their invented strategies and approaches" (NCTM, 2000, p. 82).

For example, Jerrika, in January of the first grade, solves a story problem for 10 + 13 + 22 using connecting cubes. Her written work is shown in Figure 11.16. She is beginning to use the idea of "1 ten" but most likely counted on the remaining cubes by ones. Her classmate, Monica, solved the same problem but has clearly utilized more base-ten ideas (Figure 11.16). Ideas such as these continue to grow with additional problem solving and sharing of ideas during class discussion.

The activities in this section are designed to further students' understanding of base-ten concepts and to prepare and engage them in computation—especially addition and subtraction. (Don't forget that simple story problems such as those shown in Figure 11.16 are also effective.) The first of these bridging activities involves counting with a constant using the calculator. By adjusting the numbers, it can be made appropriate for almost any grade.

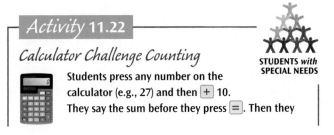

Activity 11.22

Calculator Challenge Counting

Students press any number on the calculator (e.g., 27) and then [+] 10. They say the sum before they press [=]. Then they

STUDENTS with SPECIAL NEEDS

FIGURE 11.16 The work of two first graders in January. They both solved the problem 10 + 13 + 22. Jerrika's work shows she does not yet use tens in her computation, whereas Monica is clearly adding groups of ten.

continue to add 10 mentally, challenging themselves to say the number before they press $=$. Challenge them to see how far they can go without making a mistake. You may want to begin with a starting number less than 10 (e.g., 6) for students with disabilities or start with a number such as 327 for students who need a challenge.

The constant addend ($+$ 10 in the example above) can be any number, with one, two or three digits. Some students will even find jumps of 5 can be fairly challenging if the starting number is not also a multiple of 5. Skip counting by 20 or 25 will be easier than counting by 7 or 12 and will help develop important patterns and relationships. "Calculator Challenge Counting" can also go in reverse. That is, enter a number such as 123 in the calculator and press $-$ 6. As before, students say the result before pressing $=$. Each successive press will subtract 6 or whatever constant was entered.

Two students can work together quite profitably on this activity. The flexibility of the activity allows for it to be used over and over at various skill levels, always challenging students and improving their mental skills with numbers.

The next activity combines symbolism with base-ten representations.

Activity 11.23

Numbers, Squares, Sticks, and Dots

As illustrated in Figure 11.17, prepare a worksheet or a display that includes a numeral and some base-ten pieces. Use small squares (hundreds), sticks (tens), and dots (ones) to keep the drawings simple. The task is to mentally compute the totals.

If this activity is done as a full class, discuss each exercise before going to the next. If you use a worksheet format, include only a few examples and have students write how they went about solving them. It is still important to have a discussion with the class. Students can also show these representations as a way to calculate or check answers, as shown in the work of a second grader in Figure 11.18.

The next activity extends the use of the hundreds chart.

Activity 11.24

Hundreds Chart Addition

For this activity, it is best to have a display of a hundreds chart (or a thousands chart) that all students can see. An alternative is to provide individual hundreds charts (see Blackline Master 22). Students are to use the hundreds chart to add two numbers. Because there are many ways that the hundreds chart can be used for addition, the value is in class discussions. Therefore, it is a good idea to do only one sum at a time and then have a discussion of different methods.

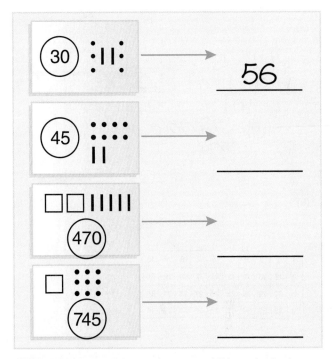

FIGURE 11.17 Flexible counting on or addition using both models and numerals.

The hundreds chart can be seen as a folded-up number line—one that accentuates the distance from any number to the next multiple of 10. A jump down a row is the same as adding 10, and a jump up a row is 10 less. As illustrated in Figure 11.19(a), you will see a student add 13 + 12 by just counting by ones. Many students will simply count on 12 individual squares from 25—an indication they may not understand how to count by tens from any starting value (an important place-value concept). Consider how a student might use the hundreds chart to help think about the sum of 27 and 12. This next student's approach (Figure 11.19(b)) is to begin at 27, jump down one row, and count over 2 to 39. Figure 11.19(c) shows a subtraction problem with a

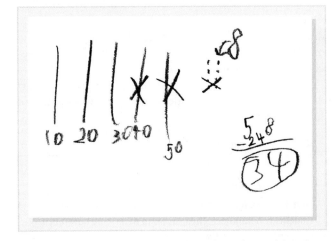

FIGURE 11.18 A student shows subtraction using a stick and dot model.

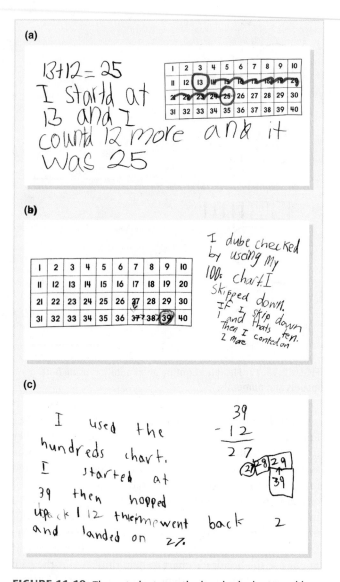

(a)

$13 + 12 = 25$
I startd at 13 and I counted 12 more and it was 25

(b)

I dube checked by useing my 100s chart. I skipped down. If I skip down 1 and thats ten. Then I counted on 2 more.

(c)

I used the hundreds chart. I started at 39 then hopped up back 1 12 then went back 2 and landed on 27.

$$39 - 12 = 27$$

FIGURE 11.19 Three students use the hundreds chart to add or subtract. Note that the first student is not using place-value concepts but is counting by ones. The other two students are jumping down or up one row to show adding or subtracting 10.

drawing of a hundreds chart, beginning at 39, jumping up one row, and backing off 2. Notice how the child double-checked by using an equation.

The following activity is similar to "Hundreds Chart Addition" but explores the idea of adding up as a method of subtraction.

Activity 11.25

How Much Between?

Students must have access to a hundreds chart. Give the students two numbers. Their task is to determine how much from one number to the next.

In "How Much Between?" the choice of the two numbers will have an impact on the strategies that students will use. The easiest pairs are those in the same column on the chart, such as 24 and 64. This may be a good place to begin. If the larger number is in a different column from the first (e.g., 24 and 56), students will likely add on tens to get to the target number's row and then add ones. Of course, this is also a reasonable strategy for any two numbers. But consider 17 and 45—the column that 45 is in on the chart is to the left of the column that 17 is in. With this pair, a reasonable strategy is to move down 3 rows (+ 30) to 47 and then count back 2 (– 2) to 45. The total count is now 30 – 2 or 28. There are also other possible approaches.

The next two activities are mathematically parallel to the previous two but use little ten-frame cards instead of the hundreds chart.

Activity 11.26

Little Ten-Frame Sums

Provide pairs of students with two sets of little ten-frame cards. Each student chooses a number. An example (47 + 36) is shown in Figure 11.20(a). Students then work together to find the total number of dots. Each pair of numbers and the sum should be written on paper when they agree on an answer.

The activity can also be done by showing the two numbers on the projector and having students work in pairs at their desks.

Activity 11.27

How Far to My Number?

Students work in pairs with a single set of little ten-frame cards. One student uses the cards to make a number less than 50. In the meantime, the other student writes a number greater than 50 on a piece of paper, as shown in Figure 11.20(b). You may choose to limit the size of this number, but it is not necessary. The task is for the students to work together to find out how much more must be added to the number shown with the ten-frames to get to the written number and write the equation. Students should try to do this without using any more cards. Once an answer is determined, they should demonstrate their answer with cards and see whether the total matches the written numbers.

Chapter 12 will discuss a variety of solution strategies that students use to add and subtract numbers. Students should have ample opportunities to develop their ideas in activities like the preceding ones. Notice, however, that students may still be developing their ideas about numbers and the distances between them. These ideas are as much about place-value understanding as about addition and subtraction.

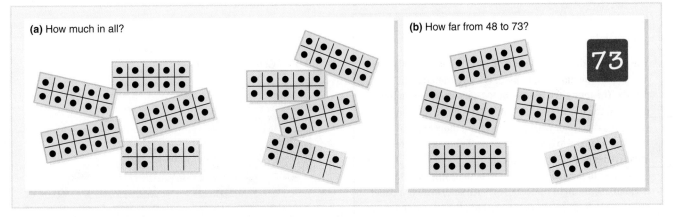

FIGURE 11.20 Two tasks that can be done with little ten-frame cards.

FORMATIVE Assessment Notes

Students who exhibit difficulty with any of these activities may also be challenged with invented computation strategies. For example, conduct a **diagnostic interview** to find how students go about the exercises in Activity 11.23, "Numbers, Squares, Sticks, and Dots." That activity requires that students have sufficient understanding of base-ten concepts to use them in meaningful counts. If students are counting by ones, perhaps on their fingers, then more practice with Activity 11.23 may be misplaced. Rather, consider additional counting activities in which students have opportunities to see the value of grouping by ten. Using the little ten-frame cards may help.

"How Far to My Number?" (Activity 11.27) is also a useful task for a **diagnostic interview**. As you listen to how students solve these problems, you will realize that there is a lot more information to be found about their thinking beyond simply getting the correct answer. ■

Connections to Real-World Ideas

We should not permit students to study place-value concepts without encouraging them to see numbers in the world around them. You do not need a prescribed activity to bring real numbers into the classroom.

Students in the second grade should be thinking about numbers under 100 first and, soon after, numbers up to 1000. Where are numbers like this? Look around your school: the number of children in the third grade, the number of minutes devoted to mathematics each week, or the number of days since school has started. And then there are measurements, numbers at home, numbers on a field trip, numbers in the news, and so on.

What do you do with these numbers? Turn them into interesting graphs, write stories using them, and make up problems.

As students get a bit more skilled, the interest in numbers can expand beyond the school and classroom. All sorts

of things can and should be measured to create graphs, draw inferences, and make comparisons. For example, how many cartons of chocolate and plain milk are served in the cafeteria each month? Collecting data and grouping them into tens and hundreds (or thousands) will help cement the value of grouping to count and compare. Can students estimate how many cartons will be sold in a year?

The particular way you bring number and the real world together in your class is up to you. But do not underestimate the value of connecting the real world to the classroom.

Numbers Beyond 1000

For students to have good concepts of numbers beyond 1000, the place-value ideas that have been carefully developed must be extended. This is sometimes difficult to do because physical models for thousands are not readily available, or you may just have one large cube to show. At the same time, number-sense ideas must also be developed. In many ways, it is these informal ideas about very large numbers that are the most important.

Extending the Place-Value System

Two important ideas developed for three-digit numbers should be extended to larger numbers. First, the grouping idea should be generalized. That is, ten in any position makes a single thing (group) in the next position, and vice versa. Second, the oral and written patterns for numbers in three digits are duplicated in a clever way for every three digits to the left. These two related ideas are not as easy for students to understand as adults seem to believe. Because models for large numbers are so difficult to demonstrate or visualize, textbooks must deal with these ideas in a predominantly symbolic manner. That is not sufficient!

Activity 11.28

What Comes Next?

Use paper models of base-ten strips and squares (see Blackline Master 14). The unit or ones piece is a 1-centimeter (cm) square. The tens piece is a 10-cm × 1-cm strip. The hundreds piece is a square, 10 cm × 10 cm. What is next? Ten hundreds is called a thousand. What shape would a thousand be? Tape together a long strip made of 10 paper hundreds squares. What comes next? (Reinforce the idea of "10 makes 1" that has progressed to this point.) Ten one-thousand strips would make a square measuring 1 meter (m) on each side, making a paper ten-thousands model. Once the class has figured out the shape of each piece, the problem posed to them is, "What comes next?" Let small groups work on the dimensions of a hundred-thousand piece.

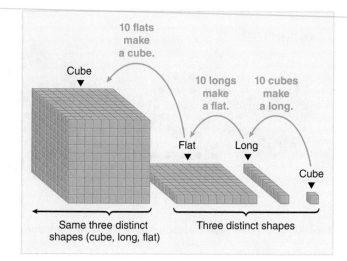

FIGURE 11.21 With every three places, the shapes repeat. Each cube represents a 1, each long represents a 10, and each flat represents a 100.

If your students become interested in seeing the big pieces from "What Comes Next?" engage them in measuring them out on paper. Ten ten-thousand squares (100,000) go together to make a huge strip. Draw this strip on a long sheet of butcher paper, and mark off the 10 squares that make it up. You will have to go out in the hall.

How far you want to extend this square-strip-square-strip sequence depends on your class. The idea that 10 in one place makes 1 in the next can be brought home dramatically. It is quite possible with older students to make the next 10-m × 10-m square using chalk lines on the playground. The next strip is 100 m × 10 m. This can be measured out on a large playground with students marking the corners. By this point, the payoff includes an appreciation of both the increase in size of each successive amount and the 10-makes-1 progression. The 10-m × 10-m square models 1 million, and the 100-m × 10-m strip is the model for 10 million. The difference between 1 million and 10 million is dramatic. Even the concept of 1 million tiny centimeter squares is impressive.

Try the "What Comes Next?" discussion in the context of three-dimensional models. The first three shapes are distinct: a *cube*, a *long*, and a *flat*. What comes next? Stack 10 flats and they make a cube—the same shape as the first one, only 1000 times larger. What comes next? (See Figure 11.21.) Ten cubes make another long. What comes next? Ten big longs make a big flat. The first three shapes have now repeated! Ten big flats will make an even bigger cube, and the trio of shapes begins again. Note that students with disabilities have difficulty interpreting spatial information, which plays into their challenges with interpreting the progression of place-value materials (Geary & Hoard, 2005). Although we are using the terms *cube*, *long*, and *flat* to describe the shape of the materials, students will see the shape pattern made as each gets 10 times larger. In fact, it is still critical to call these "ones,

tens, and hundreds," particularly for students with disabilities. We need to name them by the number they represent rather than their shape. This reinforces conceptual understanding and is less confusing for students who may struggle with these concepts.

Each cube has a name. The first one is the *unit* cube, the next is a *thousand*, the next a *million*, then a *billion*, and so on. Each long is 10 cubes: 10 units, 10 thousands, 10 millions. Similarly, each flat shape is 100 cubes.

To read a number, first mark it off in triples from the right. The triples are then read, stopping at the end of each to name the unit for that triple (see Figure 11.22). Leading zeros in each triple are ignored. If students can learn to read numbers like 059 (fifty-nine) or 009 (nine), they should be able to read any number. To write a number, use the same scheme. If first mastered orally, the system is quite easy. Remind students not to use the word "and" when reading a whole number. For example, 106 should be read as "one hundred six," not "one hundred *and* six." The word "and" will be needed to signify a decimal point. Please make sure you read numbers accurately.

It is important for students to realize that the system does have a logical structure, is not totally arbitrary, and can be understood.

Conceptualizing Large Numbers

The ideas just discussed are only partially helpful in thinking about the actual quantities involved in very large numbers. For example, in extending the paper square-strip-square-strip sequence, some appreciation for the quantities of 1000 or of 100,000 is acquired. But it is hard for anyone to translate quantities of small squares into quantities of other items, distances, or time.

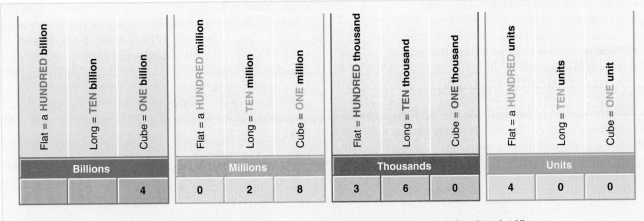

Billions			Millions			Thousands			Units		
Flat = a HUNDRED billion	Long = TEN billion	Cube = ONE billion	Flat = a HUNDRED million	Long = TEN million	Cube = ONE million	Flat = HUNDRED thousand	Long = TEN thousand	Cube = ONE thousand	Flat = a HUNDRED units	Long = TEN units	Cube = ONE unit
		4	0	2	8	3	6	0	4	0	0

"Four billion, twenty-eight million, three hundred sixty thousand, four hundred."

FIGURE 11.22 The triples system for naming large numbers.

PAUSE and REFLECT

How do you think about 1000 or 100,000? Do you have any real concept of a million? ●

Creating References for Special Big Numbers. In the following activities, numbers like 1000, 10,000 (see Blackline Master 29), or even 1,000,000 are translated literally or imaginatively into something that is easy or fun to think about. Interesting quantities become lasting reference points or benchmarks for large numbers and thereby add meaning to numbers encountered in real life.

Activity 11.29

Collecting 10,000

Collections. As a class or grade-level project, collect some type of object with the objective of reaching some specific quantity—for example, 1000 or 10,000 bread tabs or soda can pop tops. If you begin aiming for 100,000 or 1,000,000, be sure to think it through. One teacher spent nearly 10 years with her classes before amassing a million bottle caps. It takes a small dump truck to hold that many!

Activity 11.30

Showing 10,000

Illustrations. Sometimes it is easier to create large amounts than to collect them. For example, start a project in which students draw 100 or 200 or even 500 dots on a sheet of paper. Each week, different students contribute a specified number. Another idea is to cut up newspapers into pieces the same size as dollar bills to see what a large quantity would look like. Paper chain links can be constructed over time and hung down the hallways with special numbers marked. Let the school be aware of the ultimate goal.

Activity 11.31

How Long?/How Far?

Real and imagined distances. How long is a million baby steps? Other ideas that address length: a line of toothpicks, dollar bills, or candy bars end to end; students holding hands in a line; blocks or bricks stacked up; students lying down head to toe. Real measures can also be used: feet, centimeters, meters.

Activity 11.32

A Long Time

Time. How long is 1000 seconds? How long is a million seconds? A billion? How long would it take to count to 10,000 or 1,000,000? (To make the counts all the same, use your calculator to do the counting. Just press the ⊨.) How long would it take to do some task like buttoning a button 1000 times?

Estimating Large Quantities. Activities 11.29 through 11.32 focus on specific numbers. The reverse idea is to select a large quantity and find some way to measure, count, or estimate how many.

Activity 11.33

Really Large Quantities

Ask how many

- Candy bars would cover the floor of your classroom
- Steps an ant would take to walk around the school building

- Grains of rice would fill a cup or a gallon jug
- Quarters could be stacked in one stack from floor to ceiling
- Pennies can be laid side by side down the entire hallway
- Pieces of notebook paper would cover the gym floor
- Seconds you have lived

Big-number projects need not take up large amounts of class time. They can be explored over several weeks as take-home projects, done as group projects, or, perhaps best

of all, translated into great schoolwide estimation events. The NCTM *Standards* also recognizes the need for relating large numbers to the real world: "A third-grade class might explore the size of 1000 by skip-counting to 1000, building a model of 1000 using ten hundred charts, gathering 1000 items such as paper clips and developing efficient ways to count them, or using strips that are 10 or 100 centimeters long to show the length of 1000 centimeters" (NCTM, 2000, p. 149).

RESOURCES *for Chapter 11*

LITERATURE CONNECTIONS

Books that emphasize groups of things, even simple counting books, are a good beginning to the notion of ten things in a single group. Many books have wonderful explorations of large quantities and how they can be combined and separated.

100th Day Worries *Cuyler, 2005*

100 Days of School *Harris, 2000*

Both of these books focus on the 100th day of school, which is one way to recognize the landmark number of 100. Through a variety of ways to think about 100 (such as collections of 100 items or 10 salty peanuts every minute for 10 minutes), students will be able to use these stories to think about the relative size of 100 or ways to make 100 using a variety of combinations.

How Much Is a Million? *Schwartz, 2004*

If You Made a Million *Schwartz, 1994*

On Beyond a Million: An Amazing Math Journey *Schwartz, 2001*

The Magic of a Million Activity Book—Grades 2–5
Schwartz & Whitin, 1999

David Schwartz has generated a series of entertaining and conceptually sound children's books about the powers of ten or what makes a million—from visual images of students standing on one another's shoulders in a formation that reaches the moon to various monetary collections. In addition, the activity book by Schwartz and Whitin provides a series of powerful activities to help students interpret large numbers.

A Million Fish . . . More or Less *McKissack, 1996*

This story, which takes place in lower Louisiana, is a tall tale of a boy who catches three fish . . . and then a million more. The story is full of exaggerations such as a turkey that weighs 500 pounds and a jump-rope contest (using a snake) where the story's hero wins with 5553 jumps.

RECOMMENDED READINGS

Articles

Ellett, K. (2005). Making a million meaningful. *Mathematics Teaching in the Middle School*, *10*(8), 416–423.
This is an amazing collection of ideas for helping students think about large numbers, especially 1,000,000. Ellett gives examples of ways for students to conceptualize a million, shows student work, and connects many of these ideas to literature.

Kari, A. R., & Anderson, C. B. (2003). Opportunities to develop place value through student dialogue. *Teaching Children Mathematics*, *10*(2), 78–82.
Two teachers describe a mixed first-/second-grade classroom illustrating in vivid detail how students' understanding of two-digit numbers can at first be quite mistaken but can be developed conceptually with the aid of discussion. Much of the conversation revolves around a student's belief that any 1 in a number stands for ten. The student in the article is convinced that $11 + 11 + 11$ is 60. Reading this article emphasizes the wide range of student ideas and the value of classroom discourse.

Books

Richardson, K. (2003). *Assessing math concepts: Grouping tens*. Bellingham, WA: Mathematical Perspectives.
This is one of a nine-part series on using diagnostic interviews and other assessment tools to understand students' grasp of a concept—in this case, grouping by tens. Tips are shared about conducting careful observations, with suggestions for instruction. Blackline Masters are included to support the assessments.

ONLINE RESOURCES

Let's Count to 20 (NCTM Illuminations Lesson)
http://illuminations.nctm.org/LessonDetail .aspx?id=U153

This set of six lessons provides students with opportunities to connect groups of items to number names, compose and decompose numbers, and use numerals to record the size of a group.

Mega Penny Project
www.kokogiak.com/megapenny/default.asp

This is a fascinating look at large numbers in terms of stacks of pennies. Stacks from one penny to a trillion pennies are shown with visual referents, value, weight, height if stacked, and more. Great for large-number concepts.

Numbers and the Number System: Place Value (Primary Resources)
www.primaryresources.co.uk/maths/mathsB4.htm#1

A collection of templates, activities, and games, contributed by mathematics teachers, supports place-value concepts.

Place-Value Centers (Annenberg Foundation)
www.learner.org/resources/series32.html

A video resource shows first graders developing an understanding of the numeration system by relating counting, grouping, and place-value concepts. Activities include measuring with connecting cubes and using base-ten blocks.

Place-Value Game (Jefferson Lab)
http://education.jlab.org/placevalue/index.html

The goal of this online game is to make the largest possible number from the digits the computer gives you. Digits are presented one at a time. The player must place the digit in the number without knowing what the next digits will be.

REFLECTIONS *on Chapter 11*

WRITING TO LEARN

1. Name the three ways one can count a set of objects, and explain how these methods of counting can be used to coordinate concepts and oral and written names for numbers.
2. Describe the three types of physical models for base-ten concepts. What is the significance of the differences between these models?

3. How can students learn to write two- and three-digit numbers in a way that is connected to the base-ten meanings of ones and tens or ones, tens, and hundreds?
4. What are some of the ways the hundreds chart can be used to identify and use place-value concepts?
5. What are landmark numbers? Describe the relationships you want students to develop concerning landmark numbers. Describe an activity that addresses these relationships.
6. How can place-value concepts and computation skills be developed at the same time? Describe two activities that can be used to address these dual agendas.

FOR DISCUSSION AND EXPLORATION

1. Based on the suggestions in this chapter, conduct a diagnostic interview for a student at a particular grade level. It is a good idea to take a colleague to act as an observer or to use a video recorder to keep track of how the interview went. Analyze the student's understanding of the concepts, and suggest your next instructional steps.

MyEducationLab™

Go to the MyEducationLab (www.myeducationlab.com) for Math Methods and familiarize yourself with the content. Much of the site content is organized topically. The topics include all of the following to support your learning in the course:

- Learning outcomes for important mathematics methods course topics aligned with the national standards
- Assignments and Activities, tied to these learning outcomes and standards, that can help you more deeply understand course content
- Building Teaching Skills and Dispositions learning units that allow you to apply and practice your understanding of the core mathematics content and teaching skills

Your instructor has a correlation guide that aligns the exercises on the topical portion of the site with your book's chapters.

On MyEducationLab you will also find book-specific resources including Blackline Masters, Expanded Lesson Activities, and Artifact Analysis Activities.

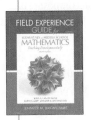

Field Experience Guide
C O N N E C T I O N S

FEG Expanded Lesson 9.5 focuses on estimating tens and ones, which builds important concepts in place value. In FEG Expanded Lesson 9.2, "Close, Far, and In Between," students estimate the relative size of a number between 0 and 100, strengthening their conceptual understanding of number size and place value. FEG Activity 10.5, "The Other Part of 100," builds place-value understanding as well as addition concepts.

Chapter 12

Developing Strategies for Addition and Subtraction Computation

Much of the public sees computational skills as the hallmark of what it means to know mathematics at the elementary school level. Although this is far from the truth, the issue of computational skills with whole numbers is, in fact, a very important part of the curriculum, especially in grades K to 6.

Rather than a single method of adding or subtracting, the most appropriate method can and should change flexibly as the numbers and the context change. In the spirit of the NCTM *Standards*, the issue is no longer a matter of "knows how to subtract three-digit numbers"; rather, it is the development over time of an assortment of flexible skills, including the ability to compute mentally, that will best serve students in the real world.

It is possible that you learned a single way to add or subtract, rather than multiple flexible approaches. If you haven't developed these on your own, you will learn them as you read this chapter and as you teach!

BIG IDEAS

1. Flexible methods of addition and subtraction computation involve taking apart (decomposing) and combining (composing) numbers in a wide variety of ways. Most of the decomposing of numbers is based on place value or "compatible" numbers—number pairs that work easily together, such as 25 and 75.

2. "Invented" strategies are flexible methods of computing that vary with the numbers and the situation. Successful use of the strategies requires that they be understood by the one who is using them—hence the term *invented*.

3. Flexible methods for computation require a strong understanding of the operations and properties of the operations, especially the commutative property and the associative property. How addition and subtraction are related as inverse operations is also an important ingredient.

4. The standard algorithms are elegant strategies for computing that have been developed over time. Each is based on performing the operation on one place value at a time with transitions to an adjacent position (trades or regrouping). Standard algorithms tend to make us think in terms of digits rather than the composite number that the digits make up. These algorithms work for all numbers but are often not the most efficient or useful methods of computing.

5. Multidigit numbers can be built up or taken apart in a variety of ways. When the parts of numbers are easier to work with, these parts can be used to estimate answers in calculations rather than using the exact numbers involved. For example, 36 is 30 and 6 or 25 and 10 and 1. Also, 483 can be thought of as $500 - 20 + 3$.

6. Nearly all computational estimations involve using easier-to-handle parts of numbers or substituting difficult-to-handle numbers with close "compatible" numbers so that the resulting computations can be done mentally.

Mathematics CONTENT CONNECTIONS

Flexible computation is built on the ideas found in the preceding three chapters. Flexible methods for computing, especially mental methods, allow students to reason much more effectively in every area of mathematics involving numbers.

◆ **Operation Meanings and Fact Mastery** (Chapters 9 and 10): Students explore contextual problems involving multidigit numbers as they develop their understanding of the operations. Without basic facts, students will be severely disadvantaged in any computational endeavor. Furthermore, many strategies and number concepts used to master basic facts can be extended to computation with larger numbers.

◆ **Place Value** (Chapter 11): Place value is not only a basis for computation; students also develop place-value understanding as a *result* of finding their own methods of computing.

◆ **Algebra** (Chapter 14): Algebra and number are strongly connected, which is explicitly described in the *Common Core State Standards* (CCSSO, 2010). The properties and algorithms mentioned previously are based on generalized "rules"—algebra. Helping students see patterns in their addition and subtraction, and then generalizing these patterns into rules, is *doing* algebra.

Toward Computational Fluency

With today's technology, the need for most adults to do paper-and-pencil computations by hand has essentially disappeared. You may think that means we can just rely on technology, but that is not the case. A study found that adults used mental computation methods for 85 percent of the calculations they did in their daily lives (Northcote & McIntosh, 1999). We now know that there are numerous methods of computing that can be handled either mentally or with paper-and-pencil support. In most everyday instances, these alternative strategies for computing are easier and faster, can often be done mentally, and contribute to overall number sense. The standard algorithms (procedures for computing) do not have these benefits. Therefore, it is best to have students learn a variety of methods that they can pull from as needed.

Consider the following problem:

> Mary has 114 spaces in her photo album. So far, she has placed 89 photos in the album. How many more photos can she put in before the album is full?

 ## PAUSE and REFLECT

Try solving the photo album problem using a method other than the one you were taught in school. If you are tempted to begin with the 9 and the 4, try a different approach. Can you do it mentally? Can you do it in more than one way? Work on this before reading further. ●

Here are just four of many methods that have been used by students in the primary grades to solve the computation in the photo album problem:

89 + 11 is 100. 11 + 14 is 25.
90 + 10 is 100 and 14 more is 24 plus 1 (for 89, not 90) is 25.
Take away 14 and then take away 11 more, or 25 in all.
89, 99, 109 (that's 20), 110, 111, 112, 113, 114 (keeping track on fingers) is 25.

Strategies such as these can be done mentally, are generally faster than standard algorithms, and make sense to

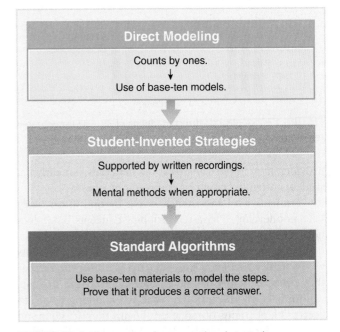

FIGURE 12.1 Three types of computational strategies.

the person using them. Every day, students and adults resort to often error-prone standard algorithms when other, more meaningful methods would be faster and less susceptible to mistakes. Flexibility with a variety of computational strategies is an important tool for a mathematically literate citizen to be successful in daily life. It is time to broaden our perspective of what it means to compute. As stated in the NCTM *Standards*, "Regardless of the particular methods used, students should be able to explain their method, understand that many methods exist, and see the usefulness of methods that are efficient, accurate, and general" (NCTM, 2000, p. 32).

Figure 12.1 lists three general types of computing. The direct modeling methods can, with guidance, develop into an assortment of more flexible and useful student-invented strategies. Many of these methods can be carried out mentally. The standard paper-and-pencil algorithms remain in the mainstream curricula; however, an emphasis on a variety of strategies is critical to developing procedural proficiency.

Direct Modeling

The developmental step that usually precedes invented strategies is called *direct modeling*: the use of manipulatives or drawings along with counting to represent directly the meaning of an operation or story problem. Figure 12.2

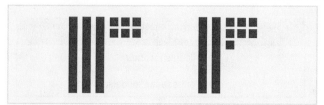

FIGURE 12.2 A possible direct modeling of 36 + 27 using base-ten models.

provides an example using base-ten materials, but early on, students often use counters and count by ones.

Students who consistently count by ones most likely have not developed base-ten grouping concepts. That does not mean that they should not continue to solve problems involving two-digit numbers. As you work with students who are still struggling with seeing ten as a unit, suggest that they group counters by tens as they count. Some students will initially use the base-ten block as a counting device to keep track of counts of ten, even though they are counting each segment of the block by ones. Make sure students write down the corresponding numbers for memory support (perhaps as they complete each intermediate step).

Students using direct modeling will soon transfer their ideas to methods that do not rely on materials or counting. The direct modeling phase provides a necessary background of ideas. These developmental strategies are also important because they provide students who are not ready for more efficient methods a way to explore the same problems as classmates who have progressed beyond this stage. It is important not to push students prematurely to abandon concrete approaches using materials.

Student-Invented Strategies

Carpenter and colleagues (1998) refer to any strategy other than the standard algorithm or that does not involve the use of physical materials or counting by ones as an *invented strategy*. We will use this term also. At times, invented strategies become mental methods after the ideas have been explored, used, and understood. For example, 75 + 19 is not difficult to do mentally (75 + 20 is 95, less 1 is 94). For 847 + 256, some students may write down intermediate steps to aid remembering as they work through the problem. (Try that one yourself.) In the classroom, written support is often encouraged as strategies develop. Written records of thinking are more easily shared and help students focus on the ideas. The distinction between written, partially written, and mental is not important, especially in the development period.

A number of research studies have focused attention on how students handle computational situations when they have been given options for multiple strategies (Keiser, 2010; Rittle-Johnson, Star, & Durkin, 2010; Verschaffel, Greer, & De Corte, 2007). "There is mounting evidence that students both in and out of school can construct

methods for adding and subtracting multi-digit numbers without explicit instruction" (Carpenter et al., 1998, p. 4). Not all students invent their own strategies. Strategies invented by class members are shared, explored, and tried out by others. However, students should not be permitted to use any strategy without understanding it (Campbell, Rowan, & Suarez, 1998).

Contrasts with Standard Algorithms. There are significant differences between student-invented strategies and standard algorithms.

1. *Invented strategies are number oriented rather than digit oriented.* Using the standard algorithm for 45 + 32, students think of 4 + 3 instead of 40 and 30. Kamii, long a crusader against standard algorithms, claims that they "unteach" place value (Kamii & Dominick, 1998).
2. *Invented strategies are left-handed rather than right-handed.* Invented strategies often begin with the largest parts of numbers, those represented by the leftmost digits. For 263 + 126, invented strategies will begin with 200 + 100 is 300, providing some sense of the size of the eventual answer in just one step. The standard algorithm begins with 3 + 6 is 9. By beginning on the right with a digit orientation, standard algorithms may hide the result until the end. (In Chapter 13, you will find that long division is an exception.)
3. *Invented strategies are a range of flexible options rather than "one right way."* Invented strategies tend to change with the numbers involved in order to make the computation easier. Try each of these mentally: 465 + 230 and 526 + 98. Did you use the same method? The standard algorithm suggests using the same tool on all problems. The standard algorithm for 7000 − 25 typically leads to student errors, yet a mental strategy is relatively simple.

Benefits of Student-Invented Strategies. The development and use of invented strategies deliver more than computational proficiency. The positive benefits are difficult to ignore:

- *Students make fewer errors.* Research indicates that students using methods they understand make many fewer errors than when strategies are learned without understanding (Gravemeijer & van Galen, 2003). After decades of good intentions with the standard algorithms, many students do not understand the concepts that support them. Not only do these students make errors, but the errors are often systematic and difficult to remediate. Errors with invented strategies are less frequent and almost never systematic.
- *Less reteaching is required.* Teachers often are concerned when students' early efforts with invented strategies are slow and time consuming. But the extended struggle in these early stages results in a meaningful and well-integrated network of ideas that are robust and long lasting. The increase in development time is

made up for with a significant decrease in reteaching and remediation.

- *Students develop number sense.* "More than just a means to produce answers, computation is increasingly seen as a window on the deep structure of the number system" (National Research Council, 2001, p. 182). Students' development and use of number-oriented, flexible algorithms offer them a rich understanding of the number system. In contrast, students who frequently use standard algorithms are unable to explain why they work. Such rules without reasons have few benefits.

- *Invented strategies are the basis for mental computation and estimation.* When invented strategies are the norm for computation, there is no need to talk about mental computation as if it were a separate skill. Often students who record their thinking with invented strategies or learn to jot down intermediate steps will ask if this writing is really required, because they find they can do the procedures more efficiently mentally.

- *Flexible methods are often faster than standard algorithms.* Consider 76 + 46. A simple invented strategy might involve 70 + 40 = 110 and 6 + 6 = 12. The sum of 110 and 12 is 122. This is easily done mentally, or even with some recording, in much less time than the steps of the standard algorithm. Those who become adept with invented strategies will consistently perform addition and subtraction computations more quickly than those using a standard algorithm.

- *Algorithm invention is itself a significantly important process of "doing mathematics."* Students who invent a strategy for computing, or who adopt a meaningful strategy shared by a classmate, are involved intimately in the process of sense making. They also develop a confidence in their ability. This development of procedures is a process that was often hidden from students (possibly yourself included). By engaging in this aspect of mathematics, a significantly different and valuable view of "doing mathematics" is revealed to learners.

Data collected from school systems using invented strategies show that those students consistently outperform their counterparts who were taught only standard algorithms on measures of understanding and problem solving. In the area of multidigit computation, most studies find that students using invented strategies either are on a par with students using standard algorithms or outperform them (Fuson, 2003). Students in other countries such as the Netherlands are not taught to use standard algorithms, and they perform significantly better than U.S. students in international measures of proficiency such as those of the Program for International Student Assessment (PISA) (Fleischman, Hopstock, Pelczar, & Shelley, 2010).

Mental Computation. A mental computation strategy is simply any invented strategy that is done mentally. What may be a mental strategy for one student may require

written support by another. Initially, students should not be asked to do computations mentally, as this may threaten students who have not yet developed a reasonable invented strategy or who are still at the direct modeling stage. As your students become more adept, they can and should be challenged from time to time to do computations mentally. You may be quite amazed at the ability of students (and at your own ability) to do mental math.

Try mental computation with this example:

$$342 + 153 + 481$$

PAUSE and REFLECT

For this addition task, try the following method: Begin by adding the hundreds, saying the totals as you go—*3 hundred, 4 hundred, 8 hundred.* Then add on to this the tens in successive manner and finally the ones. Give it a try. ●

When computations are a bit more complicated, the challenge is more interesting, and generally there is a wider range of alternatives.

Standard Algorithms

Most textbooks teach standard algorithms. More than a century of tradition combined with pressures from families who were taught that way may result in the thinking that there is only one best approach and one "right" algorithm. Arguments for a single algorithm generally revolve around efficiency and the need for methods that will work with all numbers. For addition and subtraction, one can easily counter that well-understood and practiced invented strategies are more than adequate and sometimes more efficient.

Teaching only the standard algorithm doesn't allow students to explore other useful approaches, yet including it among the strategies that students learn is very important. Understanding how it works and when it is a good choice (over an invented approach) is central to student development of procedural proficiency. The main focus in teaching the standard algorithm is not as a memorized series of steps but as making sense of the procedure as a process.

Standard Algorithms Must Be Understood. Students often pick up the standard algorithms from older siblings and family members ("My dad showed me this way"). Such students who already know the standard algorithm may resist the invention of more flexible strategies. What do you do then?

First and foremost, apply the same rule to standard algorithms as to all strategies: *If you use it, you must understand why it works and be able to explain it.* In an atmosphere that says, "Let's figure out why this works," students can profit from making sense of standard algorithms just as they should be able to reason about other approaches. But the responsibility for the explanations should be theirs, not yours. Remember, "Never say anything a kid can say!" (Reinhart, 2000).

The standard algorithm (once it is understood) is one more strategy to put in the students' "toolbox" of methods. But reinforce the idea that just like the other strategies, it may be more useful in some instances than in others. Pose problems in which a mental strategy is much more useful, such as $504 - 498$. Discuss which method seems best. Point out that for a problem such as $4568 + 12,813$, the standard algorithm has advantages. But in the real world, most people do those computations on a calculator.

Delay! Delay! Delay! Students are not likely to invent the standard algorithms. You will need to introduce and explain each algorithm to them and help them understand how and why they work. No matter how carefully you introduce these algorithms into your classroom as simply another alternative, students are likely to sense that "this is the real way" or the "one right way" to compute. Once having begun with standard algorithms, it is extremely difficult to suggest to students that they learn other methods. Notice how difficult it is for you to begin computations by working from the left rather than the right and to think in terms of whole numbers rather than digits. These habits, once established, are difficult to change.

First, spend a significant time with invented strategies—months, not weeks. Do not feel that you must rush to the standard algorithms. Delay! The understanding students gain from working with invented strategies will make it much easier for you to teach the standard algorithms. If you think you are wasting precious time by holding back, think of how many years teachers teach the same standard algorithms over and over to students who are still unable to understand them and use them without making errors.

Cultural Differences in Algorithms. Some teachers (falsely) assume that mathematics is easier than other subjects for immigrants who may not be native English speakers, thinking that mathematics is universal. The reality is that there are many international differences in notation, conventions, and algorithms. Knowing more about the diverse algorithms students bring to the classroom and their ways of recording symbols for "doing mathematics" will assist you in supporting students and responding to families (see also "Students Who Are Culturally and Ethnically Diverse" in Chapter 6). It is important to realize that an algorithm we call "standard" may not be not customary in other countries. Encouraging a variety of algorithms is important in valuing the experiences of all students.

For example, one popular subtraction algorithm used in many Latin and European countries is known as "equal addition" or "add tens to both" and is based on the knowledge that adding the same amount to both the minuend and the subtrahend will not change the difference (answer). Therefore, if the expression to be solved is $15 - 5$, there is no change to the answer (or the difference) if you add 10 to the minuend and subtrahend and solve $25 - 15$. There is still a

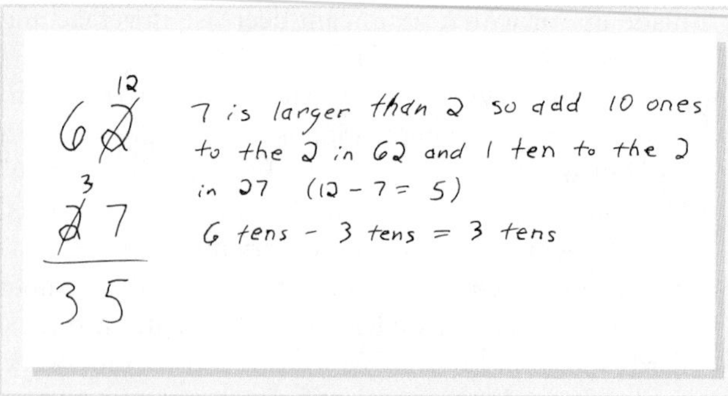

FIGURE 12.3 The "equal addition" algorithm.

difference of 10. Let's look at $62 - 27$ to think about this. Using the familiar algorithm that you may think of as "standard," you would likely regroup by crossing out the 6 tens, adding the 10 with a small "1" to the 2 in the ones column (making 12), and then subtracting the 7 from the 12 and so forth. In the "equal addition" approach (see Figure 12.3), you add 10 to 62 by just mentally adding a small "1" (to represent 10) to the 2 in the ones column and thereby having 12. You would then counteract that addition of 10 to the minuend by mentally adding 10 to the 27 (subtrahend), but doing that by increasing the tens column by one and then subtracting 37. This may sound confusing to you—but try it. Especially when there are zeros in the minuend (e.g., $302 - 178$), you may find this an interesting approach. More importantly, your possible confusion can give you the sense of how your students (and their families) may react to a completely different procedure from the one they know and find successful.

Another key component to understanding cultural differences in algorithms is the emphasis on mental mathematics in other countries (e.g., Latin America). This often surprises teachers, especially when a student writes down just an answer with no apparent intermediate calculations or notations. This can be misinterpreted by teachers as copying another student's work (Perkins & Flores, 2002). In fact, students are taught to pride themselves on their ability to do math mentally. Learning more about what your students, particularly those from other cultural backgrounds, are doing and thinking as they explore operations with numbers is often an opportunity to expand your own repertoire.

Development of Student-Invented Strategies

Students do not spontaneously invent wonderful computational methods while the teacher sits back and watches. In various experimental programs, students tended to develop or gravitate toward different strategies, suggesting that teachers and the programs do have an effect on the methods students develop (Verschaffel et al., 2007). The following section discusses general pedagogical methods for establishing an environment that will help students develop invented strategies that are appropriate at all grades and for all four operations.

Creating an Environment for Inventing Strategies

Invented strategies are developed out of a strong understanding of numbers. The development of place-value concepts must begin to prepare students for the challenges of inventing computational strategies. For example, the CCSSO (2010) suggests that first graders should be able to use mental math to name a number that is 10 more or 10 less than a given two-digit number without resorting to counting. This standard calls for young learners to publicly share emerging ideas. Therefore, students need a classroom environment where they can act like mathematicians and explore ideas without trepidation.

Students who are attempting to investigate new ideas in mathematics need to find their classroom a safe and nurturing place for expressing naïve or rudimentary thoughts. Some of the very characteristics described earlier in this book regarding the development of a problem-solving environment need to be reiterated here to establish the climate for taking risks, testing conjectures, and trying new approaches. Here are some factors to keep in mind:

- Avoid immediately identifying the right answer when a student states it. Give other students a chance to consider whether they think it is correct.
- Expect and encourage student-to-student interactions, questions, discussions, and conjectures.
- Encourage students to clarify previous knowledge and make attempts to construct new ideas.
- Promote curiosity and openness to trying new things.
- Talk about both right and wrong ideas in a nonevaluative or nonthreatening way.
- Move unsophisticated ideas to more sophisticated thinking through coaxing, coaching, and strategic questioning.
- Use familiar contexts and story problems to build background and connect to students' experiences.

Models to Support Invented Strategies

There are three common types of invented-strategy models that students come up with to solve addition and subtraction situations: split strategy (which can also be thought of as decomposition), jump strategy (similar to counting on or counting back), and shortcut strategy (sometimes known as *compensation*) (Torbeyns, De Smedt, Ghesquiere, & Verschaffel, 2009). The notion of "splitting" a number into parts is a useful strategy for all operations. Both the word *split* and the use of a visual diagram have been found to help students develop strategies (Verschaffel et al., 2007). Try using arrows or lines to indicate how two computations are joined together, as shown in Figure 12.4(a).

(a) How much is 86 and 47?

S: I know that 80 and 20 more is 100.

T: Where do the 80 and the 20 come from?

S: I split the 47 into 20 and 20 and 7 and the 86 into 80 and 6.

T: (illustrates the splitting with lines)
    So then you added one of the 20s to 80?

S: Yes, 80 and 20 is 100. Then I added the other 20 and got 120.

T: (writes the equations on the board)

S: Then I added the 6 and the 7 and got 13.

T: (writes this equation)

S: Then I added the 120 to the 13 and got 133.

T: Indicates with joining lines.

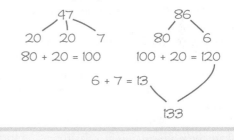

(b) What is 84 minus 68?

S: I started at 84. First, I jumped back 4 to make 80.

T: Why did you subtract 4 first? Why not 8?

S: It was easier to think about 80 than 84. I will save the other part of 8 until later. Then I jumped back 60 to get 20.

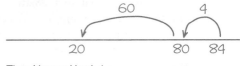

S: Then I jumped back 4.

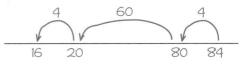

T: Why 4?

S: That was how much I still had left over from 68.

FIGURE 12.4 Two methods of recording students' thought processes on the board so that the class can follow the strategy.

The *empty number line* shown in Figure 12.4(b) incorporates a sequential *jump strategy* developed in the Netherlands that is increasingly being suggested for all learners (Gravemeijer & van Galen, 2003; Klein, Beishuizen, & Treffers, 2002; Verschaffel et al., 2007). Initially, the empty number line (also called an *open number line*) is a good way to help you model a student's thinking for the class (see a virtual version at www.dreambox.com/teachertools/open_number_line). With time and practice, students will find the empty number line to be an effective tool to use in supporting their thinking. The aforementioned researchers found that the empty number line is much more flexible than the usual number line because it can be jotted down anywhere, works with any numbers, and eliminates confusion with hash marks and the spaces between them. They also found that it is less prone to computational errors. The jumps on the line can be recorded as the students share or explain each step of their solution as they count up or down from an initial number.

The *shortcut strategy* involves the flexible adjustment of numbers. For example, just as students used 10 as an anchor in learning their facts, they can move numbers such as 38 or 69 to the nearest 10 and then take the 2 or 1 off to compensate later. As another example, 51 − 37 can be thought of as 37 + 10 = 47 and 47 + 4 more equals 51. Remember, students need to share these approaches in a classroom culture where the flexible adaptation of number is the classroom norm.

Student-Invented Strategies for Addition and Subtraction

Students should be able to use strategies that they understand and can use efficiently and effectively. Your goal might be that each of your students has at least one or two methods that are reasonably efficient, mathematically correct, and useful with lots of different numbers. Expect different students to settle on different strategies that play to their strengths.

The numbers involved in a computation and also the type of story problems used will tend to influence how students approach a problem. The following sections suggest a variety of invented strategies that students often use. These are presented not as a curriculum but rather to give you some idea of the range of possibilities.

Adding and Subtracting Single-Digit Numbers

When adding or subtracting a small amount, or finding the difference between two reasonably close numbers, many students will use counting to solve the problems. One goal

should be to extend students' knowledge of basic facts and the ten-structure of the number system so that counting is not required. When the calculation crosses a ten (e.g., 58 + 6), using the decade number (60) and thinking 58 + 2 + 4, for example, extends students' use of the Up Over 10 strategy.

> Tommy was on page 47 of his book. Then he read 8 more pages. What page did he end up on?

> How far is it from 68 to 75?

> Ruth had 52 cents. She bought a small toy for 8 cents. How much does she have left?

Each of these problems crosses a ten and involves a change or a difference of less than 10. Listen for students who are counting on or counting back without paying attention to the ten. For these students, suggest they use either the hundreds chart or the little ten-frames as shown in Figure 12.5. Also, find out how they solve fact combinations such as 8 + 6 or 13 − 5. The use of tens for these facts is essentially the same as for the higher-decade problems. Related activities in Chapter 11 are "Calculator Challenge Counting" (Activity 11.22), "How Much Between?" (Activity 11.25), and "Little Ten-Frame Sums" (Activity 11.26).

As you move students from single-digit to two-digit numbers, adding and subtracting tens and hundreds is an important transition. Sums and differences involving multiples of 10 or 100 are easily computed mentally. Write a problem such as the following:

$$300 + 500 + 20$$

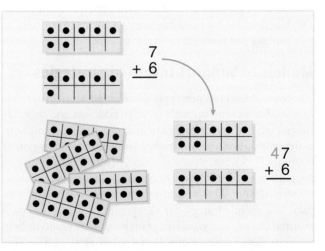

FIGURE 12.5 Little ten-frame cards can help children extend the Up Over 10 idea to larger numbers (see Blackline Masters 15–16).

Challenge students to solve it mentally. Ask students to share how they did it. Look for use of place-value words: "3 *hundred* and 5 *hundred* is 8 *hundred*, and 20 is 820."

Use base-ten models to help students begin to think in terms of units of tens and hundreds. Early examples should not include any trades. The exercise 420 + 300 involves no trades, whereas 70 + 80 may be more difficult.

Adding Two-Digit Numbers

Problems involving the sum of 2 two-digit numbers will usually produce a wide variety of strategies. Some of these will involve starting with one or the other number and working from that point, either by adding on to get to the next ten or by adding tens from one number to the other.

FORMATIVE Assessment Notes Try the following problem with a student in a **diagnostic interview**: 46 + 35. Note how your student solves this problem. See if they begin by splitting the numbers. That is, for 46 + 35, a student may add on 4 to the 46 to get to 50 and then add 31 more, or first add 30 to 46 and then add 4 to get to 80 and then add 1 more. In either case, you can see whether they are taking advantage of the utilization of tens. Many students will count past these multiples without stopping at ten. Another approach they may use involves splitting the numbers into parts and adding the easier parts separately. Usually the split will involve tens and ones, or students may use other parts of numbers such as 50 or 25 as an easier "compatible

number" to work with. Students will often use a counting-by-tens-and-ones technique. That is, instead of "46 + 30 is 76," they may use an open number line and count up "46, 56, 66, 76." These jumps can be written down as they are said to help students keep track. In each case, be mindful of how flexibly the students use ten as a unit or how they use the shortcut strategy. If they are not seeing the ten as a unit, you may need more work on place-value activities. ■

Figure 12.6 illustrates four different strategies for addition of 2 two-digit numbers. The ways that the solutions are recorded are suggestions. Note the use of the empty number line.

The following story problem is a suggestion.

> **Two Scout troops went on a field trip. There were 46 Girl Scouts and 38 Boy Scouts. How many Scouts went on the trip?**

The move to the shortcut strategy and compensation strategies focusing on making ten is useful when one of the numbers ends in 8 or 9. To promote that strategy, present problems with addends like 39 or 58. Note that it is only necessary to adjust one of the two numbers.

PAUSE and REFLECT

Try adding 367 + 155 in as many different ways as you can. How many of your ways are like those in Figure 12.6? ●

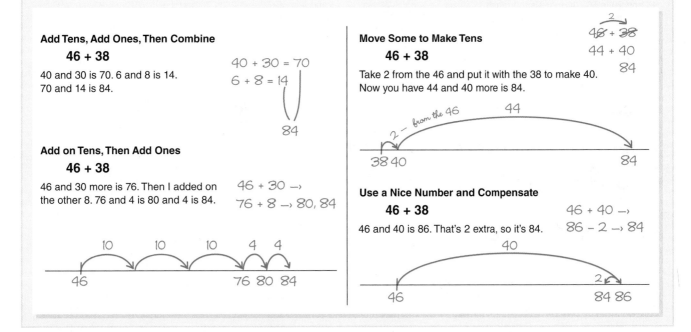

FIGURE 12.6 Four different invented strategies for addition with two-digit numbers.

Subtracting by Counting Up

This is an amazingly powerful way to subtract. Students working on the *think-addition* strategy for their basic facts can also be solving problems with larger numbers. The concept is the same. For $38 - 19$, the idea is to think, "How much do I add to 19 to get to 38?" Notice that this strategy is probably not as efficient for $42 - 6$. Using *join with change unknown* problems or *missing-part* problems (discussed in Chapter 9) will encourage the use of the counting-up strategy. Here is an example of each.

> Sam had 46 baseball cards. He went to a card show and got some more cards for his collection. Now he has 73 cards. How many cards did Sam buy at the card show?

> Juanita counted all of the teacher's pencils. Some were sharpened and some not. She counted 73 pencils in all; 46 pencils were not sharpened. How many were sharpened?

The numbers in these problems are used in the strategies illustrated in Figure 12.7. Simply asking for the difference between two numbers may also prompt these strategies.

Take-Away Subtraction

Using a take-away action is considerably more difficult to do mentally. However, take-away strategies are common, probably because many textbooks emphasize take-away as the meaning of subtraction. When the subtracted number is a multiple of 10 or close to a multiple of 10, take-away can be an easy method to use. Four different strategies are shown in Figure 12.8.

> There were 73 students on the playground. The 46 second-grade students came in first. How many students were still on the playground?

The two methods that begin by taking tens from tens are reflective of what most students do with base-ten pieces. The other two methods leave one of the numbers intact and subtract from it. Try $83 - 29$ in your head by first taking away 30 and adding 1 back. This is a good mental method when subtracting a number that is close to a multiple of ten.

Sometimes we need to be reminded of what comes naturally to students. Campbell (1997) tested over 2000 students in Baltimore who had not been taught the standard algorithm for subtraction. Not one student began with the ones place!

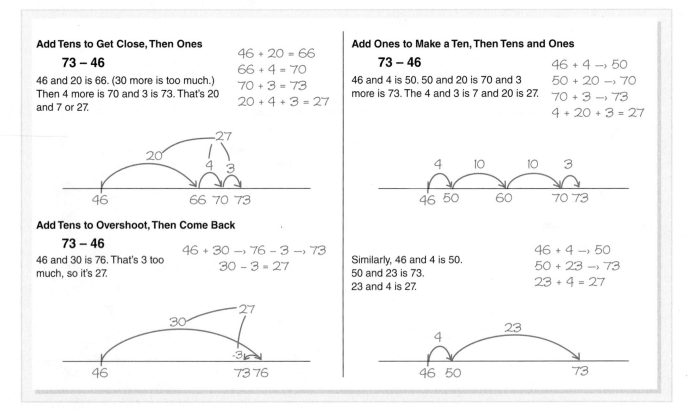

FIGURE 12.7 Three different invented strategies for subtraction by counting up.

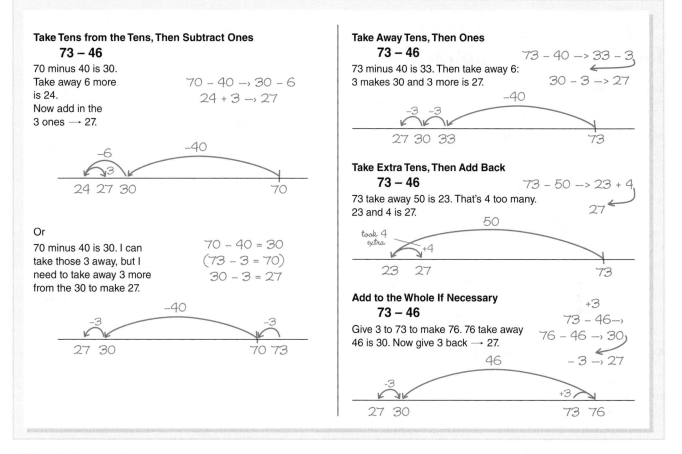

FIGURE 12.8 Four different invented strategies for take-away subtraction.

 PAUSE and REFLECT

Try computing 82 − 57. Use both take-away and counting-up methods. Can you use all of the strategies in Figures 12.7 and 12.8 without looking? ●

For many subtraction problems, especially those with three digits, adding on is significantly easier than a take-away approach. Try not to force the issue for students who do not use an add-on method. However, you may want to return to simple missing-part activities that are more likely to encourage that type of thinking. Try Activity 11.27, "How Far to My Number?" or simply show a number such as 28 with little ten-frame cards and ask, "What goes with 28 to make 53?" You can do the same with three-digit numbers without the use of models.

Extensions and Challenges

Each of the examples in the preceding sections involved sums less than 100, and all involved *bridging* or *crossing a ten;* that is, if done with a standard algorithm, they required regrouping or trading. Bridging, the size of the numbers, and the potential for doing problems mentally are all issues to consider.

Bridging. For most of the strategies, it is easier to add or subtract when bridging is not required. Try each strategy with 34 + 52 or 68 − 24 to see how it works. Easier problems instill confidence. They also permit you to challenge your students with a "harder one." There is also the issue of bridging 100 or 1000. Try 58 + 67 with different strategies. Bridging across hundreds is also an issue for subtraction. Problems such as 128 − 50 or 128 − 45 are more difficult than ones that do not cross a hundred.

Larger Numbers. Most curricula will expect third graders to add and subtract three-digit numbers, and perhaps four-digit numbers. Try seeing how *you* would do these without using the standard algorithms: 487 + 235 and 623 − 247. For subtraction, a counting-up strategy is usually the easiest. Occasionally, other strategies appear with larger numbers. For example, "chunking off" multiples of 50 or 25 is often a useful method. For 462 + 257, use 450 and 250 to make 700. That leaves 12 and 7 more, making 719.

Standard Algorithms for Addition and Subtraction

Because your students will not likely invent the standard algorithms, your instruction will necessarily be more directed. What is critical is that you teach it in a conceptual manner, helping students see the tens and ones as they work.

The standard algorithms require an understanding of *regrouping*, exchanging 10 in one place-value position for 1 in the position to the left—or the reverse, exchanging 1 for 10 in the position to the right. The corresponding terms *carrying* and *borrowing* are obsolete and conceptually misleading. The word *regroup* may have little meaning for young students. A preferable term to use initially is *trade*. Ten ones are *traded* for a ten. A hundred is *traded* for 10 tens. Notice that none of the invented strategies involves regrouping.

Standard Algorithm for Addition

Two things to remember in teaching the standard algorithm for addition: (1) Be sure students continue to view it as one possible algorithm that is a good choice in some situations (just as invented strategies are good choices in some situations), and (2) as with any procedure (algorithm), it must begin with the concrete, and then explicit connections must be made between the concept (regrouping) and the procedure.

Begin with Models Only. In the beginning, simply focus on regrouping without recording the numerical process. Provide students with place-value mats and base-ten models (see, for example, Blackline Master 17).

Have students make one number at the top of the mat and a second beneath it as shown in the top portion of Figure 12.9. If students are still developing base-ten concepts, a groupable model such as counters in cups is helpful.

Explain this one rule: *You begin in the ones column.* Let students solve the problem on their own. Provide plenty of time, and then have students explain what they did and why. Let students display their work on the overhead or use interactive whiteboard models to help with their explanations.

One or two problems in a lesson with lots of discussion are much more productive than a lot of problems based on rules students don't understand.

Develop the Written Record. Reproduce pages with simple place-value charts similar to those shown in Figure 12.10 (see Blackline Master 19). The charts will help students record numerals in columns as they model each step of the

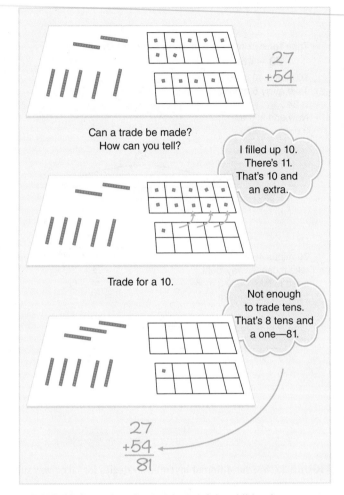

FIGURE 12.9 Working from right to left in addition (see Blackline Master 17).

procedure they do with the base-ten models. The first few times you do this, guide each step carefully through questioning, as shown in Figure 12.11. A similar approach would be used for three-digit problems.

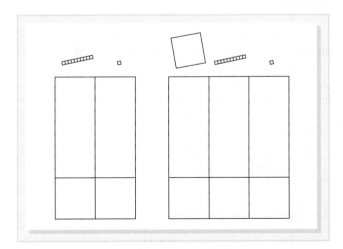

FIGURE 12.10 Blank recording charts are helpful (see Blackline Master 19).

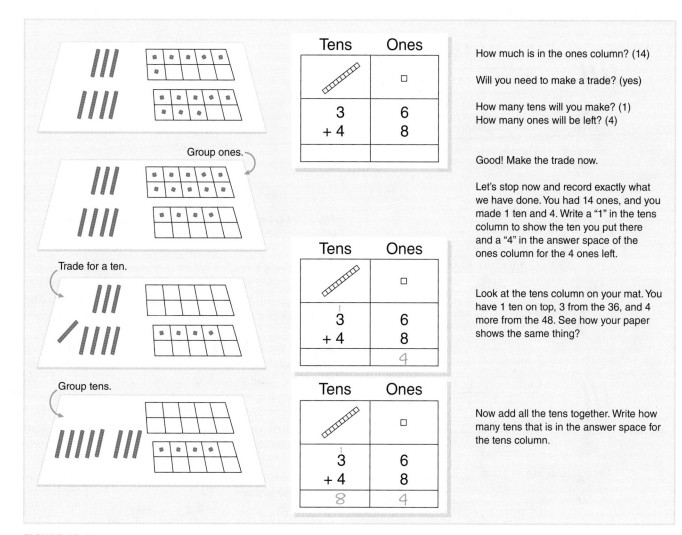

Tens	Ones
╱▨▨▨▨	□
3	6
+4	8

How much is in the ones column? (14)

Will you need to make a trade? (yes)

How many tens will you make? (1)
How many ones will be left? (4)

Good! Make the trade now.

Let's stop now and record exactly what we have done. You had 14 ones, and you made 1 ten and 4. Write a "1" in the tens column to show the ten you put there and a "4" in the answer space of the ones column for the 4 ones left.

Tens	Ones
▨▨▨▨	□
3	6
+4	8
	4

Look at the tens column on your mat. You have 1 ten on top, 3 from the 36, and 4 more from the 48. See how your paper shows the same thing?

Tens	Ones
▨▨▨▨	□
3	6
+4	8
8	4

Now add all the tens together. Write how many tens that is in the answer space for the tens column.

FIGURE 12.11 Help students record on paper each step they do on their place-value mats (see Blackline Masters 17 and 19).

A suggestion is to have students work in pairs. One student is responsible for the models, and the other records the steps. They can reverse roles with each problem.

Figure 12.12 shows a variation of the traditional recording scheme that is quite reasonable, at least for up to three digits. It avoids the "carried ones" and focuses attention on the actual value of the digits. If students were permitted to start adding on the left as they are inclined to do, this would just be a vertical recording scheme for the invented strategy "Add tens, add ones, then combine" (Figure 12.6). This slight adaptation can be particularly effective with students with disabilities.

Standard Algorithm for Subtraction

The general approach to developing the subtraction algorithm is the same as for addition. When the procedure is completely understood with models, a do-and-write approach connects it with a written form.

Begin with Models Only.   Start by having students model the top number in a subtraction problem on the top half of their place-value mats. For the amount to be subtracted,

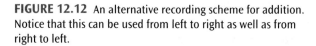

$$
\begin{array}{r}
358 \\
+276 \\
\hline
500 \\
120 \\
14 \\
\hline
634
\end{array}
$$

FIGURE 12.12 An alternative recording scheme for addition. Notice that this can be used from left to right as well as from right to left.

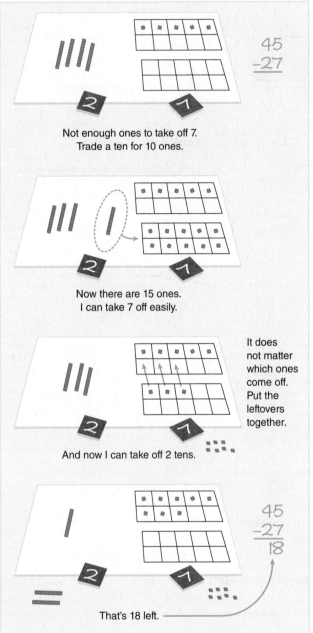

FIGURE 12.13 Two-digit subtraction with models.

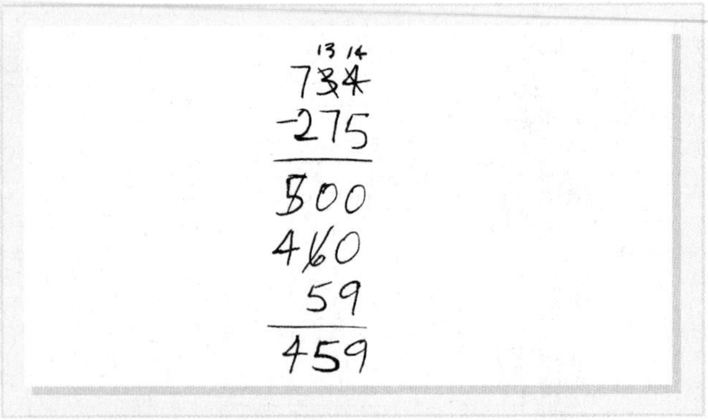

have students write each digit on a small piece of paper and place these pieces near the bottom of their mats in the respective columns, as in Figure 12.13. To avoid errors, suggest making all trades first. That way, the full amount on the paper slip can be taken off at once. Also explain to students that they are to begin working with the ones column first, as they did with addition.

Anticipate Difficulties with Zeros. Exercises in which zeros are involved anywhere in the problem tend to cause special difficulties. Give extra attention to these cases while still using models.

FIGURE 12.14 A left-hand recording scheme for subtraction. Other methods can also be devised.

The very common errors that emerge when "regrouping across zero" are best addressed at the modeling stage. For example, in 403 − 138, a double trade must be made: trading a hundreds piece for 10 tens and then a tens piece for 10 ones.

Develop the Written Record. The process of recording each step as it is done is the same as was suggested for addition. The same recording sheets (Figure 12.10) are also recommended.

When students can explain the use of symbols involved in the recording process, that is a signal for you to move them away from the use of physical materials on to a completely symbolic level. Again, be attentive to problems with zeros.

If students are permitted to follow their natural instincts and begin with the biggest pieces (from the left instead of the right), recording schemes similar to that shown in Figure 12.14 are possible. The trades are made from the pieces remaining *after* the subtraction in the column to the left has been done. A "regroup across zero" difficulty will still occur in problems like 462 − 168. Try it.

PAUSE and REFLECT

Contrast the difficulties of teaching students to regroup in subtraction, especially regrouping across zero, with the ease of adding on. For example, try solving this: 428 and how much makes 703? Now think about teaching students to regroup across zero to solve 703 − 428. ●

Introducing Computational Estimation

Whenever we are faced with a computation in real life or in school, we have a variety of choices to make concerning how we will find a reasonable answer. A first decision is: "Do we need an exact answer, or will an approximate answer be okay?" If precision is called for, we can use an invented strategy, a standard algorithm, or a calculator. Often, an estimate will suffice. How close an estimate must be to the actual computation is a matter of context, as was the original decision to use an estimate.

The goal of computational estimation is to be able to flexibly and quickly produce an approximate result that will work for the situation and give a sense of reasonableness. In everyday life, estimation skills are valuable. Many situations do not require an exact answer, so reaching for a calculator or a pencil is not necessary if one has good estimation skills. However, computational estimation is a higher-level thinking skill that requires many decisions. The NCTM *Standards* states, "Teachers should help students learn how to decide when an exact answer or an estimate would be more appropriate, how to choose the computational methods that would be best to use, and how to evaluate the reasonableness of answers to computations" (NCTM, 2000, p. 220). Students are not as good at computational estimation as they are at producing exact answers and find computational estimation uncomfortable (Reys, Reys, & Penafiel, 1991; Siegler & Booth, 2005).

Good estimators tend to employ a variety of computational strategies they have developed over time. As early as grade 2, we teach these strategies and help students develop an understanding of what it means to estimate a computation and start to develop some early strategies. From then on through middle school, students should continue to develop and add to their estimation strategies and skills.

Understanding Computational Estimation

An *estimate* refers to a number that is a suitable approximation for an exact number given the particular context. This concept of an estimate applies to measures and quantities as well as computation.

Three Types of Estimation. In the K–8 mathematics curriculum, *estimation* refers to three quite different ideas:

- *Measurement estimation*—determining an approximate measure without making an exact measurement. For example, we can estimate the length of a room or the weight of a watermelon.
- *Quantity estimation*—approximating the number of items in a collection. For example, we might estimate the number of students in the auditorium or jelly beans in the "estimation jar."
- *Computational estimation*—determining a number that is an approximation of a computation that we cannot or do not wish to determine exactly. For example, we might want to know the approximate amount we are spending at a store and need to add the cost of several items to see whether $20.00 will cover the amount.

Is It an Estimate or a Guess? Many students confuse the idea of estimation with guessing. None of the three types of estimation involves guessing. Each involves reasoning and sense making. Computational estimation, for example, involves computation; it is not a guess at all. It is therefore important to (1) avoid using the words *guess* and *guessing* when working on estimation and (2) explicitly help students see the difference between a guess and a reasonable estimate.

Computational estimation may be underemphasized in textbooks that focus on the standard algorithm, but it appears in the *Common Core State Standards* and is an important part of being able to do mathematics. If you recall the problem-solving process, the last of the four steps is to look back. If students practice estimating when they are computing and "look back" at the end of a computation, they should be able to see whether the answer is in the ballpark. Take $403 - 138$, mentioned above. At a glance, this answer has to be over 200, so an incorrect answer of 175 (a common error) would be recognized as impossible.

Suggestions for Teaching Computational Estimation

Here are some general principles that are worth keeping in mind as you help your students develop computational estimation skills.

Use Real Examples of Estimation. Discuss real-life situations in which computational estimations are used. Some common examples include comparative shopping (which store has the item for less); adding up distances in planning a trip; determining approximate monthly totals (school supplies, haircuts, lawn-mowing income, time watching TV); and figuring the cost of going to a sporting event or movie including transportation, tickets, and snacks. Discuss why exact answers are not necessary in some instances but are necessary in others. Look at newspaper headlines to find where numbers are the result of estimation and where they are the result of precision (e.g., "Hundreds of Students Leave School Ill" versus "Fourteen Students Injured in Bus Accident"). Students are more motivated with real examples—for example, asking older students, "Are you a million seconds old? How can you find out?"

Use the Language of Estimation. Words and phrases such as *about, close, just about, a little more* (or *less*) *than*, and *between* are part of the language of estimation. Students should understand that they are trying to get as close as possible using efficient methods, but there is no "one correct" or "winning" estimate. Language can help convey that idea.

Use Context to Help with Estimates. Situations play a role in estimation. For example, it is important to know whether the cost of a car would likely be $950 or $9500. Could attendance at the school play be 30 or 300 or 3000? A simple computation can provide the important digits, with knowledge of the context providing the rest.

Accept a Range of Estimates, and Offer a Range as an Option. Since estimates are based on computation, how can there be different answers? The answer, of course, is that any particular estimate depends on the strategy used and the kinds of adjustments in the numbers that might be made. Estimates also vary with the need for the estimate. Estimating someone's age from an approximate year they were born is quite different from trying to decide whether your last $5 will cover the three items you need at the Fast Mart. These are new and difficult ideas for young students.

What estimate would you give for 270 + 325? If you use 200 + 300, you might say 500. Or you might use 250 for the 270 and 350 for the 325, making 600. You could also use 300 for 270 and add 325, getting 625. Is only one of these "right"?

By sharing students' estimates and letting them discuss how and why different estimates resulted, they can begin to see that estimates generally fall in a range around the exact answer. And don't forget the context. Some situations call for more careful estimates than others, and all results should be judged on their reasonableness.

Important teacher note: Do not reward or emphasize the estimate that is the closest. It is already very difficult for students to handle "approximate" answers; worrying about accuracy and pushing for the closest answer only exacerbate this problem. Instead, focus on whether the answers given are *reasonable* for the situation or problem at hand. Offer ranges for answers that are estimates. Ask whether the answer will be between 300 and 400, 450 and 550, or 600 and 700.

Focus on Flexible Methods, Not Answers. Remember that your primary goal is to help students develop strategies for making computational estimates quickly. Reflection on the strategies therefore will lead to strategy development. Class discussion of strategies for estimation is just as important as it was for the development of invented methods of computation. For any given estimation, there are often several very good but different methods of estimation. Students will learn strategies from one another. The discussion of different strategies will also help students understand that there is no "right" estimate. Here is an activity in which a specific number is not required to answer the questions.

Activity 12.1

Over or Under?

Prepare several estimation exercises to display on a document projector. With each, provide an "over or under" number. In Figure 12.15, each is either over or under $1.50, but the number need not be the same for each task. You can add an interesting context to make the activity accessible to more learners, but remember that using multiple contexts can be difficult for ELLs, who must learn each new

context. Consider playing "Over or Under?" by picking one context (e.g., the price of candy bars or fruit) and then varying the values (5 at 43 cents each, then 6 at 37 cents each, etc.).

The "Over or Under?" activity need not be very elaborate. Here are some more over/under examples:

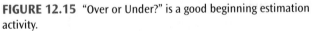

37 + 75	over/under 100
712 − 458	over/under 300

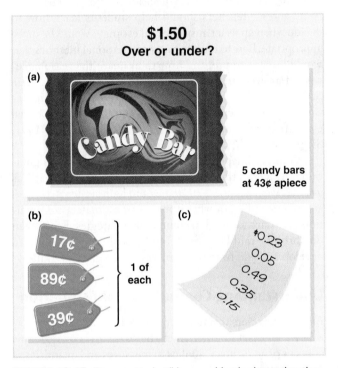

FIGURE 12.15 "Over or Under?" is a good beginning estimation activity.

Activity 12.2

Best Choice

For any single estimation task, offer three or four possible estimates.

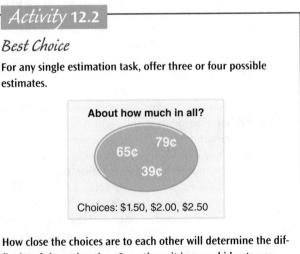

How close the choices are to each other will determine the difficulty of the estimation. Sometimes it is a good idea to use multiples of ten, such as $21, $210, and $2100.

Computational Estimation Strategies

Computational estimation is a real-world skill used by students to adapt multiple strategies to get approximate (and reasonable) answers. There are numerous strategies that are helpful in computing estimates in addition and subtraction. Here are a few to present to students.

Front-End Methods

A front-end approach is reasonable for addition or subtraction when all or most of the numbers have the same number of digits. Figure 12.16 illustrates the idea. Notice that when a number has fewer digits than the rest, that number is initially ignored. Also note that only the front (leftmost) number is used and the computation is then done as if there were zeros in the other positions.

After adding or subtracting the front digits, an adjustment is made to correct for the digits or numbers that were ignored. Making an adjustment is actually a separate skill. For young students, practice first just using the front digits.

The front-end strategy can be easy to use because it does not require rounding or changing numbers. The numbers used are there and visible, so students can estimate without changing the numbers. You do need to be sure that students pay close attention to place value and only consider digits in the largest place, especially when the numbers vary in the number of digits in each.

Rounding Methods

When several numbers are to be added, it is usually a good idea to round them to the same place value. Keep a running sum as you round each number. Figure 12.17 shows an example of rounding.

For addition and subtraction problems involving only two terms, one strategy is to round only one of the two numbers. For example, you can round only the subtracted number (e.g., 6724 − 1863 becomes 6724 − 2000, resulting in 4724). You can stop here, or you can adjust. Adjusting might go like this: You took away a bigger number, so the result must be too small. Adjust to about 4800.

Rounding to "compatible" numbers close to the actual number depends on what you, the estimator, consider an easy number to compute with. For example, in 625 + 385, you may want to round 385 to 375 or 400. The point is that there are no rigid rules. Choices depend on the relationships held by the estimator, on how quickly the estimate is needed, and on how precise an estimate needs to be.

Compatible Numbers

It is sometimes useful to look for two or three compatible numbers that can be grouped to make benchmark values (e.g., 10, 100, 500). If numbers in the list can be adjusted slightly to produce these groups, that will make finding an estimate easier. This approach is illustrated in Figure 12.18.

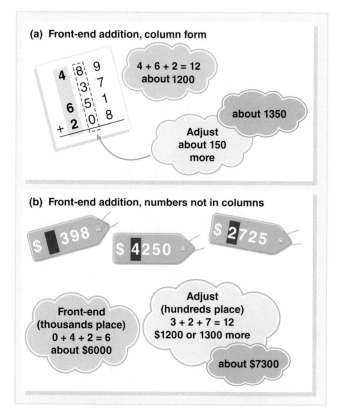

FIGURE 12.16 Front-end estimation in addition.

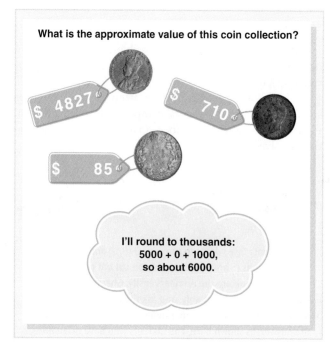

FIGURE 12.17 Rounding in addition.

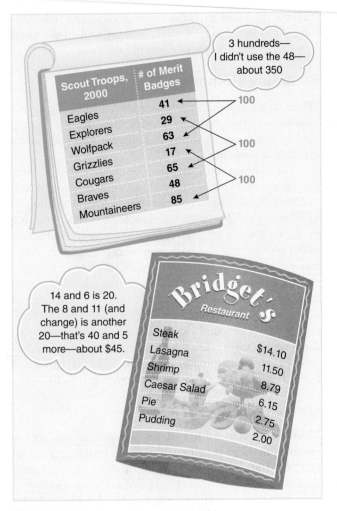

FIGURE 12.18 Compatibles used in addition.

box that generate the answer 42). These fixed problems will reduce the amount of decision making and allow them to focus on the numbers.

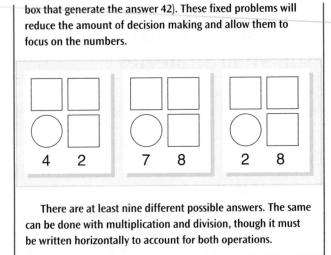

There are at least nine different possible answers. The same can be done with multiplication and division, though it must be written horizontally to account for both operations.

FORMATIVE Assessment Notes Using a **diagnostic interview,** ask a student to solve the following: "Charlie wants an estimate of how much he needs to save to buy two video games." One game is $99 and the other is $118. About how much does he need to save to purchase the two games?" Ask the student how they came up with their estimate. If you find that students are trying to mentally carry out the standard algorithm in the air or on the table with their finger, they likely have limited ability with estimation strategies. Because $99 is so close to $100, it would be important for the student to use that fact in combining the two prices. If the student is unclear as to whether to change 99 to 100 or to 98 (as it is equally as close), that would pinpoint a lack of understanding of the purpose of estimation. Estimation cannot be easily assessed with paper-and-pencil tasks, so interviews that require explanations give more substantial evidence of student performance. ■

In subtraction, it is often possible to adjust only one number to produce an easily observed difference, as illustrated in Figure 12.19.

The following activity (adapted from Coates & Thompson, 2003) is a blend of mental computation and estimation. Figuring out where the numbers go to create the exact solution involves estimation.

Activity **12.3**

Box Math

STUDENTS *with* SPECIAL NEEDS

Give students three digits to use (e.g., 3, 5, 7) and two operations (+ and −), preferably on cut out card stock so they can manipulate the numbers easily. Give students a set of equations with answers only, and ask them to use only their digits (in the squares) and operations (in the circle) to get to the answer, as shown here. For students who have disabilities, you may want to have the operation signs built into the displays of answers (such as an addition box and a subtraction

FIGURE 12.19 Compatibles can help find the difference.

RESOURCES *for Chapter 12*

LITERATURE CONNECTIONS

Children's literature plays a useful role in helping you develop problems that lead to invented strategies and mental computation.

The Great Math Tattle Battle *Bowen, 2006*

This entertaining book is largely about correcting errors in double-digit addition calculations. You can share a "student's worksheet" from it that contains lots of mistakes and see whether your class can find and correct the paper. There's also an interesting message about tattling!

The Breakfast Cereal Gourmet *Hoffman, 2005*
The History of Everyday Life *Landau, 2006*
National Geographic Kids Almanac 2012 *National Geographic, 2011*

These nonfiction books include interesting facts that can be used for a variety of calculations. Hoffman's book provides data about breakfast eating habits; for example, the average person eats 160 bowls of cereal a year. Such facts can be used to create word problems. In the *History of Everyday Life*, household inventions such as the toilet are discussed. If the toilet uses about 3 or 4 gallons of water for every flush, how much water are you using at home (repeated addition)? The *National Geographic Kids Almanac* combines information and numerical data. If the country of Malta has 3,393 people per square mile and Monaco has 48,231, what is the difference? Explore the local newspaper to get students thinking about calculations that naturally emerge from real situations.

Alice Ramsey's Grand Adventure *Brown, 2000*
Wilma Unlimited *Krull, 2000*
We Were There, Too! Young People in U.S. History *Hoose, 2001*

Brown and Krull both write about strong females who made their mark in history and sports. Alice Ramsey was the first woman to drive across the continental United States, and Wilma Rudolph was an Olympic track athlete who had polio as a young child. The Hoose book looks at stories of children who made history. Again, these represent opportunities to link factual information to calculations and estimations. The first book can lead to considering car trips, where road maps can be used to identify distances between locations. These can then be added. Alice's first trip (of 31 trips) took 59 days; that can be compared to cross-country car trips today. In *Wilma Unlimited*, you can make connections to the lengths of her races or add the lengths of each segment of a relay race. Additional problems can emerge as students calculate how long ago these people lived.

RECOMMENDED READINGS

Articles

O'Loughlin, T. A. (2007). Using research to develop computational fluency in young mathematicians. *Teaching Children Mathematics, 14*(3), 132–138.
Written by a second-grade teacher, this article describes her journey to improve her students' computational fluency through research-based practice. She encourages student-invented strategies to explore her students' thinking and understanding. The interesting collection of student work and related thought-provoking debriefing by the teacher will demonstrate various methods, such as split and jump strategies.

Russell, S. J. (2000). Developing computational fluency with whole numbers. *Teaching Children Mathematics, 7*, 155–158.
In just four pages, Russell provides an articulate view of what the NCTM Principles and Standards for School Mathematics means by computational fluency. She accompanies each point with examples from students. She explains that teaching for fluency is complex and requires teachers understanding mathematics, selecting appropriate tasks, and recognizing when to capitalize on students' ideas.

Books

Duncan, N., Geer, C., Huinker, D., Leutzinger, L., Rathmell, E., & Thompson, C. (2007). *Navigating through number and operations in grades 3–5*. Reston, VA: NCTM.
Chapter 3, Fluency with Algorithms, is a perfect companion to this chapter, reflecting on how to introduce and develop the four operations with the ultimate goal of developing computational fluency and mathematical proficiency. There is also follow-up on how to assess and interpret student work. Included with the book is a CD that includes blackline masters that correspond to a variety of activities in the book and a collection of related articles and chapters from NCTM publications.

ONLINE RESOURCES

Base Blocks Addition
http://nlvm.usu.edu/en/nav/frames_asid_154_g_2_t_1 .html

Base Blocks Subtraction
http://nlvm.usu.edu/en/nav/frames_asid_155_g_2_t_1 .html

These two similar applets use base-ten blocks on a place-value chart. You can form any problem you wish up to four digits. The subtraction model shows the bottom number in red instead of blue. When the top blocks are dragged onto the red blocks, they disappear. Although you can begin in any column, the model forces a regrouping strategy as well as a take-away model for subtraction. Good for reinforcing the standard algorithms.

Computational Algorithms (Everyday Mathematics)
http://everydaymath.uchicago.edu/educators/
computation

This site provides video examples of various computational algorithms including the research base, advice for use, and other information.

Estimate Sums
www.ixl.com/math/practice/grade-2-estimate-sums

This site has various applets to practice skills for pre-K–3 students. There is a range of rounding and estimating activities.

Number Line Boxes, Number Line Jump Maker, and Number Line
www.ictgames.com/addition.htm

This site supporting the English National Mathematics Curriculum has various applets to practice the jump strategy for young students. There is a range of rounding and estimating activities.

Thinking Blocks: Addition and Subtraction
www.thinkingblocks.com/ThinkingBlocks_AS/TB_
AS_Main.html

This teacher-developed tool links to the various types of problems discussed earlier in the chapter. It includes two-digit numbers and problems with multiple steps, including compare, part-part-whole, and change examples. There is an emphasis on identifying and solving for an unknown quantity. Because the ideas are presented in game formats, you should view the introduction to be able to play.

REFLECTIONS *on Chapter 12*

WRITING TO LEARN

1. How are standard algorithms different from student-invented strategies? Explain the benefits of invented strategies over standard algorithms.
2. Illustrate three different strategies for adding $46 + 39$. Which ones are easy to do mentally? Is there a strategy that is easier because 39 is close to 40? For each strategy you work with, think about how you could record it on the board so that students will be able to follow what is being done. What models (empty number line, etc.) would work best?
3. Use two different adding-up strategies for $93 - 27$ and for $545 - 267$. Make up a story problem that would encourage an adding-up strategy.
4. Why is an assessment that gets at student understanding so important when teaching standard algorithms?

5. How is computational estimation different from other types of estimation?
6. Why might computational estimation be uncomfortable for students?
7. What are some important considerations for teaching computational estimation?
8. What is the purpose of activities like "Over or Under?" in which students do not actually produce an answer?

FOR DISCUSSION AND EXPLORATION

1. What is the importance of mental mathematics and computational estimation for daily living? What are the advantages of being able to estimate in public situations and settings?

MyEducationLab™

Go to the MyEducationLab (www.myeducationlab.com) for Math Methods and familiarize yourself with the content. Much of the site content is organized topically. The topics include all of the following to support your learning in the course:

- Learning outcomes for important mathematics methods course topics aligned with the national standards
- Assignments and Activities, tied to these learning outcomes and standards, that can help you more deeply understand course content
- Building Teaching Skills and Dispositions learning units that allow you to apply and practice your understanding of the core mathematics content and teaching skills

Your instructor has a correlation guide that aligns the exercises on the topical portion of the site with your book's chapters.

On MyEducationLab you will also find book-specific resources including Blackline Masters, Expanded Lesson Activities, and Artifact Analysis Activities.

Field Experience Guide
C O N N E C T I O N S

There are a number of Expanded Lessons and activities that support student understanding of computation for whole numbers. FEG Activity 10.3, "Odd or Even?" is a problem-based activity that includes using addition and looking for patterns. In FEG Activity 10.5, students find the missing addend to make 100. FEG Expanded Lesson 9.1 focuses on building meaning for subtraction. Computational estimation is an excellent topic for a student interview. See FEG 7.2 for a template to design a diagnostic interview with a student about their understanding of addition and subtraction concepts.

Chapter 13

Developing Strategies for Multiplication and Division Computation

Recall that *Principles and Standards for School Mathematics* defined computational fluency as "having and using efficient and accurate methods for computing" (NCTM, 2000, p. 32). As students enter the intermediate grades, they begin to focus on computation strategies with multiplication and division. Researchers suggest that invented strategies for multiplication and division are less well documented (Verschaffel et al., 2007). But they go on to say that an instructional environment that rewards flexibility must be created if students will successfully explore and test new ideas. As it was with addition and subtraction, students who only have knowledge of the standard algorithm often have difficulty following steps they do not fully understand (Biddlecomb & Carr, 2011). When students can compute multidigit multiplication and division problems in a variety of ways, complete written records of their work, explain their thinking, and discuss the merits of one strategy over another, they are developing as independent learners.

BIG IDEAS

1. Flexible methods of computation in multiplication and division involve decomposing and composing numbers in a wide variety of ways.

2. Flexible methods for computation require a strong understanding of the operations and the properties of the operations, especially the commutative property, the associative property, and the distributive property of multiplication over addition. How multiplication and division are related as inverse operations is also critical knowledge.

3. Invented strategies provide flexible methods of computing that vary with the numbers and the situation. Successful use of the strategies requires that they be understood by those who are using them—hence, they must grasp that the process and the outcome of that process are related.

4. The standard algorithms are clever strategies for computing that have been developed over time. Each is based on performing the operation on one place value at a time with transitions to an adjacent position. Unfortunately, standard algorithms tend to make students think in terms of digits rather than the composite number that the digits make up, so students lose the essence of the actual place value of a digit.

5. Multidigit numbers can be built up or taken apart in a variety of ways. These parts can be used to create estimates in calculations rather than using the exact numbers involved.

6. Nearly all computational estimations involve using easier-to-handle parts of numbers or substituting difficult-to-handle numbers with close compatible numbers so that the resulting computations can be done mentally.

Mathematics CONTENT CONNECTIONS

Computation and estimation skills developed for multiplication and division are tools for everyday living as well as tools for sense making in other areas of mathematics.

◆ **Operations, Place Value, and Computation with Addition and Subtraction** (Chapters 9, 11, and 12): Many computing skills with multiplication and division grow directly out of the habits developed while inventing strategies for adding and subtracting. To multiply and divide using two-digit numbers requires an understanding of place value. Understanding how multiplication can help with the estimations required in division emphasizes how multiplication and division are related.

◆ **Algebra** (Chapter 14): Algebra and number are strongly connected. Helping students see patterns in multiplicative situations, and then generalizing these patterns into rules, is *doing* algebra.

◆ **Fractions, Decimals, and Percents** (Chapters 16 and 17): Once students understand computation with multiplication and division, that knowledge will support their understanding with other types of numbers. To calculate 7×24.06 requires no new skills, only a good conceptual understanding of multiplication and the estimation skills to know where to place the decimal point in the product. Similar statements are true of fractions and percents.

Student-Invented Strategies for Multiplication

Students are successful in the construction of useful methods for solving multiplication and division problems (Ambrose, Baek, & Carpenter, 2003; Baek, 2006; Fosnot & Dolk, 2001; Van Putten, van den Brom-Snijders, & Beishuizen, 2005). For multiplication, the ability to break numbers apart in flexible ways is even more important than in addition or subtraction. This skill hinges on the full understanding of the distributive property of multiplication over addition. For example, to multiply 43×5, one might think about breaking 43 into 40 and 3, multiplying each by 5, and then adding the results. Students require ample opportunities to develop these concepts by making sense of their own ideas and those of their classmates.

Useful Representations

The problem 6×34 may be represented in a number of ways, as illustrated in Figure 13.1. Often the choice of a model is influenced by a story problem. To determine how many oranges 6 classes need if there are 34 students in each class, students may model 6 sets of 34. If the problem is about the area of a rectangle that is 34 cm by 6 cm, then some form of an array is likely. But each representation is appropriate for thinking about 34×6 regardless of the context, and students should get to a point where they select ways to think about multiplication that are meaningful to them.

How students represent a product is directly related to their methods for determining answers. The equal groups of 34 students in a class might suggest repeated additions—perhaps taking the sets two at a time. Double 34 is 68 and there are three of those, so $68 + 68 + 68 = 204$. Or the six sets of base-ten pieces might suggest breaking the numbers into tens and ones: 6 times 3 tens or 6×30 and 6×4. Or some students use the tens individually: 6 tens make 60. So that's 60 and 60 and 60 (180); then add on the 24 to make 204.

All of these ideas should be part of students' repertoire of models for multidigit multiplication computation. Introduce different representations as ways to explore multiplication until you are comfortable that the class has a collection of useful ideas. Although teachers may worry that presenting multiple methods to solve problems will overwhelm and confuse students, researchers found that comparing a variety of methods from the start helped students

gain flexibility and that process enhanced learning (Rittle-Johnson et al., 2010).

Multiplication by a Single-Digit Multiplier

As with addition and subtraction, it is helpful to place multiplication tasks in context. (Be sure students, in particular ELLs, understand the context that is selected.) Let students model the problems in ways that make sense to them. Do not be concerned about reversing factors (6 sets of 34 or 34 sets of 6). Nor should you be timid about the numbers you use. The problem 3×24 may be easier than 7×65, but the latter provides a challenge. The types of strategies that students use for multiplication are much more varied than for addition and subtraction. The three categories described here are strategies grounded in student reasoning, as described in research on multiplicative reasoning (Baek, 2006; Confrey, 2008; Petit, 2009).

Complete-Number Strategies (Including Doubling). Students who are not yet comfortable breaking numbers into parts will approach the numbers in the sets as single groups. Most likely, these early strategies will be based on repeated addition. Often students will list long columns of numbers and add them up. In an attempt to shorten this process, students soon realize that if they add two numbers, the next two

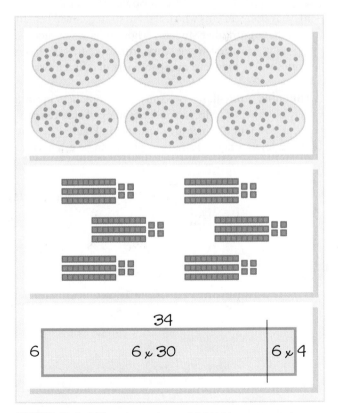

FIGURE 13.1 Different ways to model 6×34 may support different computational strategies.

Complete-Number Strategies for Multiplication

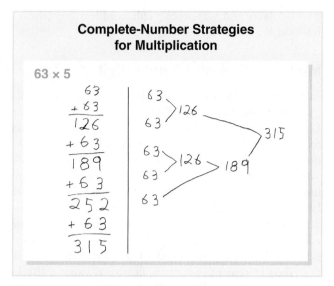

FIGURE 13.2 Students who use a complete-number strategy do not break numbers apart into decades or tens and ones.

will have the same sum and so on down the line. This doubling can become the principal approach for many students (Flowers & Rubenstein, 2010/2011). Doubling capitalizes on the distributive property, whereby doubling 47 is double $40 +$ double 7, and the associative property, in which doubling 7 tens—or $2 \times (7 \times 10)$—is the same as 10 times double 7 or $(2 \times 7) \times 10$. Figure 13.2 illustrates two methods students may use. Students who use these strategies will benefit from listening to other students who use base-ten models. They may also need more work with base-ten grouping activities where they take numbers apart in different ways.

Partitioning Strategies. Students break numbers up in a variety of ways that reflect an understanding of base-ten concepts, at least four of which are illustrated in Figure 13.3. The By Decades partitioning strategy (which can be extended to

Compensation Strategies for Multiplication

27 × 4

$$27 + 3 \rightarrow 30 \times 4 \rightarrow 120$$
$$3 \times 4 = 12 \rightarrow -12$$
$$\overline{108}$$

250 × 5

I can split 250 in half and multiply by 10.

$$125 \times 10 = 1250$$

17 × 70

$$20 \times 70 \rightarrow 1400 - 210 \rightarrow 1190 \quad {}^{3 \times 70}$$

FIGURE 13.4 Compensation methods use a product related to the original. A compensation is made in the answer, or one factor is changed to compensate for a change in the other factor.

By Hundreds, By Thousands, etc.) is the same as the standard algorithm except that students always begin with the largest values. It extends easily to three digits and is very powerful as a mental strategy. Another valuable strategy for mental methods is to compute mentally with multiples of 25 and 50 and then add or subtract a small adjustment. All partition strategies rely on knowledge of the distributive property.

Compensation Strategies. Students and adults look for ways to manipulate numbers so that the calculations are easy. In Figure 13.4, the problem 27×4 is changed to an easier one, and then an adjustment or compensation is made. In the second example, one factor is cut in half and the other doubled. This is often used when a 5 or a 50 is involved. Because these

Partitioning Strategies for Multiplication

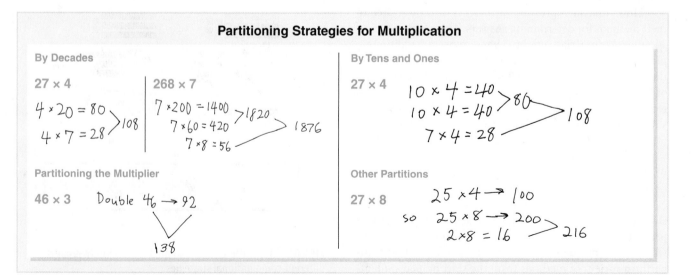

FIGURE 13.3 Four different ways to make easier partial products.

strategies are so dependent on the numbers involved, they can't be used for all computations. However, they are powerful strategies, especially for mental math and estimation.

Multiplication of Larger Numbers

As you move students from single-digit to two-digit factors, there is a value in exposing students early to products involving multiples of 10 and 100. This supports the importance of place value and an emphasis on the number rather than the separate digits. Consider the following problem:

> A Scout troop wants to package up 400 fire starter kits as a fundraising project. If each package will have 12 fire starters, how many fire starters are the Scouts going to need?

Students will use $4 \times 12 = 48$ to figure out that 400×12 is 4800. There will be discussion around how to say and write "forty-eight hundred." Be aware of students who simply tack on zeros without understanding why. Try problems such as 30×60 or 210×40 in which tens are multiplied by tens.

A problem such as this one can be solved in many different ways:

> The parade had 23 clowns. Each clown carried 18 balloons. How many balloons were the clowns carrying in the parade?

Some students look for smaller products such as 6×23 and then add that result three times. Another method is to do 20×23 and then subtract 2×23. Others will calculate four separate partial products: $10 \times 20 = 200$, $8 \times 20 = 160$, $10 \times 3 = 30$, and $8 \times 3 = 24$. And still others may add up a string of 23s. Two-digit multiplication is both complex and challenging. But students can solve these problems in a variety of interesting ways, many of which will contribute to the development of the standard algorithm. Figure 13.5 shows

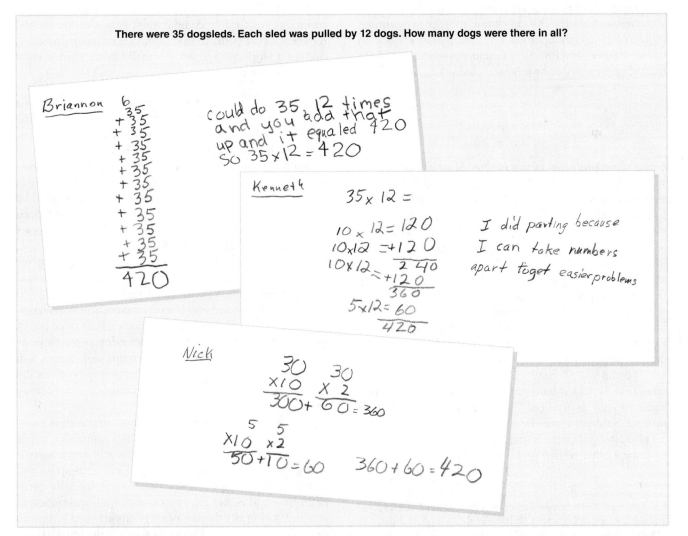

FIGURE 13.5 Three fourth-grade students solve a multiplication problem using their own invented strategies. Each is at a different place in developing a reasonably efficient method.

the work of three fourth-grade students who had not been taught the standard algorithm for multiplication. Kenneth's "parting" refers to *partitioning*, a strategy label provided earlier by his teacher. Briannon is content with adding. She needs to see and hear about other strategies developed by her classmates. Nick's method is conceptually very similar to the standard algorithm. As students begin partitioning numbers along place-value lines, the strategies are often like the standard algorithm but without the traditional recording schemes.

The NCTM *Standards* suggests, "Having access to more than one method for each operation allows students to choose an approach that best fits the numbers in a particular problem. For example, 298×42 can be thought of as $(300 \times 42) - (2 \times 42)$, whereas 41×16 can be computed by multiplying 41×8 to get 328 and then doubling 328 to get 656" (NCTM, 2000, p. 155).

Cluster Problems. In the fourth and fifth grades, one approach to multidigit multiplication is called "cluster problems." This approach encourages students to use facts and combinations they already know in order to figure out more complex computations. For example, in a lesson in which the goal is to find 57×6, students might record the following cluster of known facts:

$$7 \times 6 = 42$$
$$5 \times 6 = 30$$
$$10 \times 6 = 60$$
$$50 \times 6 = 300$$

Using these problems as support, students can analyze to see which ones can be used in finding the product. They can also consider adding other problems that might be helpful. In this case, lines 1 and 4 are added to get 342. Notice the distributive property at work here: $6(50 + 7) = (6 \times 50) + (6 \times 7)$. While the label "distributive property" may not be important, recognizing that this property always works (and understanding why) is critical to understanding multiplication (and its close ties to algebraic thinking).

It is useful to have students make an estimate of the final product before doing any of the problems in the cluster. For example, in a cluster for 34×50, 3×50 and 10×50 may be helpful in thinking about 30×50. The results of 30×50 and 4×50 combine to give you 34×50. It may seem that 34×25 is harder than 34×50. However, if you know 34×25, it need only be doubled to get the desired product. Students should be encouraged to create their own set of cluster problems. Think how you could use 10×34 (and some other related problems) to find 34×25.

PAUSE and REFLECT

Try your hand at making up a cluster of problems for 86×42. Include all possible problems that you think might be helpful, even if they are not all related to one approach to finding the product. Then use your cluster to find the product. Is there more than one way?

Here are some of the problems that might be in your cluster:

2×80 4×80 2×86 40×80
6×40 10×86 40×86

Of course, your cluster may have included products not shown here. All that is required to begin the cluster problem approach is that your cluster eventually leads to a solution. Besides your own cluster, see if you can use the problems in this cluster to find 86×42.

Cluster problems help students think about ways that they can break factors apart—or split numbers—into easier parts. The strategy of splitting numbers and multiplying the parts—the distributive property—is an extremely valuable technique for flexible computation. It is also fun to find different clever paths to the solution. For many problems, finding a workable cluster is actually faster than using a standard algorithm.

Area Models. The area model or the connected array is a key visual representation that can support students' multiplicative understanding and reasoning (Barmby, Harries, Higgins, & Suggate, 2009; Iszak, 2004). Using the repeated addition approach, the area model encourages a visual demonstration of the commutative and distributive properties (unlike the number line or a model of equal groups). The area model can also be linked to successful representations of the standard multiplication algorithm and future topics such as multiplication of fractions.

A valuable exploration is to prepare large rectangles for each group of two or three students. The rectangles should be measured carefully, with dimensions between 25 cm and 60 cm, and drawn accurately with square corners. The students' task is to determine how many small ones pieces (base-ten materials) will fit inside. Wooden or plastic base-ten pieces are best, but cardboard strips and squares will also work. Alternatively, students can simply be given the task verbally: *What is the area of a rectangle that is 47 cm by 36 cm?*

Most students will fill the rectangle first with as many hundreds pieces as possible. One obvious approach is to put the 12 hundreds in one corner. This will leave narrow regions on two sides that can be filled with tens pieces and a final small rectangle that will hold ones. Especially if students have had earlier experiences with finding products in arrays, figuring out the size of each subrectangle is not too difficult. The sketch in Figure 13.6 shows the four regions.

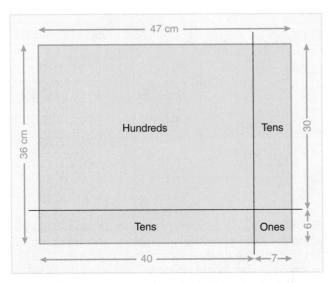

FIGURE 13.6 Ones, tens, and hundreds pieces fit exactly into the four sections of this 47 × 36 rectangle. Figure the size of each section to determine the size of the whole rectangle.

Activity **13.1**

Build It and Break It

ENGLISH LANGUAGE LEARNERS

Select a problem such as the previous example with the clowns and balloons (on page 239): 23 × 18. Use base-ten blocks or grid paper to build the corresponding array/area model. Then show and record as many ways as possible to "slice" the array into pieces. For example, with this problem, they could cut the array into 23 × 10 + 23 × 8. What other vertical or horizontal slices can be made? What property does this link to? Before engaging in this activity, provide students, particularly ELLs, a labeled visual of an array (or area model) that includes the terms *array, area model, slice, vertical*, and *horizontal*. In the *after* phase of the lesson, be sure to focus on the vocabulary of the key concepts (*distributive property, decompose, strategy*, etc.).

PAUSE and REFLECT

If you did not already know the standard algorithm, how would you determine the size of the rectangle? Use your method (not the standard algorithm) on a rectangle that measures 68 cm × 24 cm. Make a sketch to show and explain your work. ●

As you will see in the discussion of the standard algorithm, the area model leads to a reasonable approach to multiplying numbers. Recent research analyzed sixth graders' varied strategies for solving multiplication problems on the factors of flexibility, accuracy, and efficiency. Given the problem 13 × 7, only 11 percent of the students used the standard algorithm. When multiplying 2 two-digit numbers, 20 percent tried using the standard algorithm, with less than half of them reaching the correct answer (Keiser, 2010). Interestingly this work confirmed the researcher's prior observations that the standard algorithm for multiplication was not the most popular approach for two-digit factors when students had been taught other options. The array or area model was most often selected.

Standard Algorithm for Multiplication

Unlike addition and subtraction, in which you can argue that all problems can be solved with invented strategies, multiplication problems such as 486 × 372 can be difficult with invented strategies. Like addition and subtraction, instruction should focus on making good choices on when to use an invented strategy, when to use the standard algorithm, and when to use a calculator.

The standard multiplication algorithm is probably the most difficult of the four algorithms if students have not had plenty of opportunities to explore their own strategies first. The multiplication algorithm can be meaningfully developed using either a repeated addition model or an area model (connected array). For single-digit multipliers, the difference is minimal. When you move to two-digit multipliers, the area model has some advantages. For that reason, the discussion here will use the area model. Again, you are reminded of the need for a more directed approach than when developing invented strategies.

One-Digit Multipliers

As with the other algorithms, as much time as necessary should be devoted to the conceptual development of the algorithm with the recording or written part coming later. In contrast, many textbooks spend less time on development and more time on memorizing steps.

Begin with Models. Give students a drawing of a rectangle 47 cm by 6 cm. *How many small square centimeter pieces will fit in the rectangle?* (What is the area of the rectangle in square centimeters?) Let students solve the problem in groups before discussing it as a class. Challenge them to find a way to determine the number of unit squares on the inside of the rectangle by slicing it into two or more parts in such a way that they can tell the size of each part. For example, it could be sliced into two sections of 20 × 6 and one of 7 × 6.

As shown in Figure 13.7, the rectangle can be sliced or separated into two parts so that one part will be 6 ones by 7 ones, or 42 ones, and the other will be 6 ones by 4 tens,

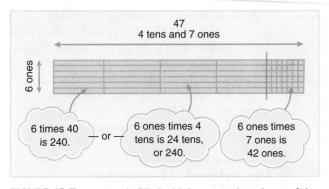

FIGURE 13.7 A rectangle filled with base-ten pieces is a useful model for two-digit-by-one-digit multiplication.

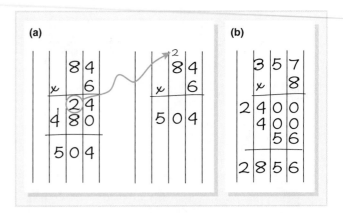

FIGURE 13.8 (a) In the standard algorithm, the product of ones is recorded first. The tens digit of this first product can be written as a "carried" digit above the tens column. (b) It is quite reasonable to abandon the carried digit and permit the partial products to be recorded in any order. (See Blackline Master 20.)

or 24 tens. Notice that the base-ten language "6 ones times 4 tens is 24 tens" tells how many *pieces* (strips of ten) are in the big section. To say "6 times 40 is 240" is also correct and tells how many units or square centimeters are in the section. Each section is referred to as a *partial product*. By adding the two partial products, you get the total product or area of the rectangle.

To avoid the tedium of drawing large rectangles and arranging base-ten pieces, use the base-ten grid paper found in Blackline Master 18. On the grid paper, students can easily draw accurate rectangles showing all of the pieces. Do not force any recording technique on students until they understand how to use the two dimensions of a rectangle to get a product.

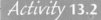

Make It Easy

Computer versions of the area model for multiplication can ease some of the difficulties of physically filling in base-ten blocks into rectangular grids. Go to the NLVM website and find the *Rectangle Multiplication* applet (http://nlvm.usu.edu/en/nav/frames_asid_192_g_2_t_1.html). Model a multiplication problem of your choice up to 30 × 30. See how the rectangle is split into two parts rather than four, corresponding to the tens and ones digits in the multiplier. How does this representation correlate to the standard algorithm? Try another problem. For students with disabilities, you may need to have a set of base-ten blocks nearby to show how the concrete version corresponds to the computer illustration.

Develop the Written Record. To help with a recording scheme, provide sheets with base-ten columns on which students can record problems. When the two partial products are written separately as in Figure 13.8(a), there is little new to learn. Students simply record the products and add them together. As illustrated, it is possible to teach students how to write the first product with a carried digit so that the combined product is written on one line. This recording scheme is known to be a source of errors. The little carried digit is often the difficulty—it often gets added in before the second multiplication or is forgotten.

Students should be encouraged to record both partial products and avoid the errors related to the carried digit. Then it makes no difference in which order the products are written. See how students do written multiplication as shown in Figure 13.8(b). When the factors are in a word problem, chart, or other format, all that is really necessary is to write down all the partial products and add. Furthermore, that is precisely how this is done mentally.

Most traditional curricula progress from two digits to three digits with a single-digit multiplier. Students can still write all three partial products separately, which may make more sense than carrying a digit.

Two-Digit Multipliers

With the area model, the progression to a two-digit multiplier is relatively straightforward. Rectangles can be drawn on base-ten grid paper, or full-sized rectangles can be filled in with base-ten pieces. Now there will be four partial products, corresponding to four different sections of the rectangle.

Several variations in language might be used. Consider the product 47 × 36 as illustrated in Figure 13.9. In the partial product 40 × 30, if base-ten language is used—*4 tens times 3 tens is 12 hundreds*—the result tells how many hundreds pieces are in that section. Try to avoid "four times three," which promotes thinking about digits rather than numbers. It is important to stress that a product of *tens times tens is hundreds*.

Figure 13.9 also shows the recording of four partial products in the traditional order and how these can be collapsed to two lines if carried digits are used. Here the

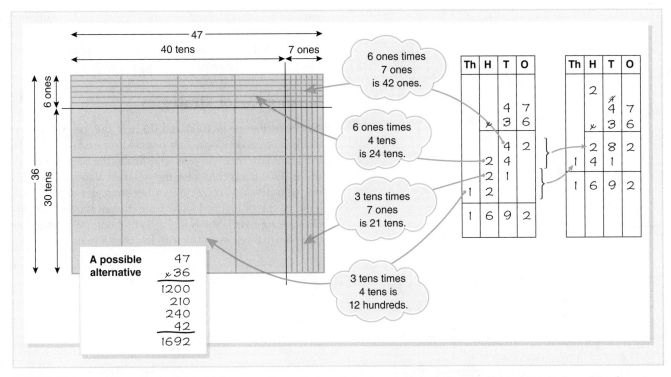

FIGURE 13.9 47 × 36 rectangle filled with base-ten pieces. Base-ten language connects the four partial products to the written format of the standard algorithm. Note the possibility of recording the products in some other order.

second "carry" technically belongs in the hundreds column, but it rarely is written there. Often it gets confused with the first and is thus an additional source of student errors. The lower left of the figure shows the same computation with all four products written in a different order. This is quite an acceptable algorithm. In the rare instance when someone multiplies numbers such as 538 × 29 with pencil and paper, there would be six partial products. But far fewer errors would occur, requiring less instructional time and much less remediation.

Student-Invented Strategies for Division

Even though many adults think division is the most onerous of the computational operations, some students find it considerably easier than multiplication. Division computation strategies are developed in third through fifth grade (CCSSO, 2010).

Recall that there are two concepts of division. First, there is the partition or fair-sharing idea, illustrated by this story problem:

> The bag has 783 jelly beans, and Eileen and her 4 friends want to share them equally. How many jelly beans will Eileen and each of her friends get?

Then there is the measurement or repeated subtraction concept:

> Jumbo the elephant loves peanuts. His trainer has 625 peanuts. If he gives Jumbo 20 peanuts each day, how many days will the peanuts last?

Students should be challenged to solve both types of problems. However, the fair-share problems are often easier to solve with base-ten pieces. Furthermore, the standard algorithm is built on this idea of partitioning. Eventually, students will develop strategies that they will apply to both types of problem, even when the process does not match the action of the story.

Figure 13.10 shows strategies that three fourth graders have used to solve division problems. The first example illustrates 92 ÷ 4 using base-ten blocks and a sharing process. A ten is traded when no more tens can be passed out. Then the 12 ones are distributed, resulting in 23 in each set. This direct modeling approach with base-ten pieces is quite easy to understand and use, even for third-grade students.

In Figure 13.10(b), the student sets out the base-ten pieces and draws a "bar graph" with six columns. After noting that there are not enough hundreds for each child, he splits the 3 hundreds in half, putting 50 in each column. That leaves him with 1 hundred, 5 tens, and 3 ones. After trading the hundred for tens (now 15 tens), he gives 20 to each, recording 2 tens in each bar. Now he is left with 3 tens

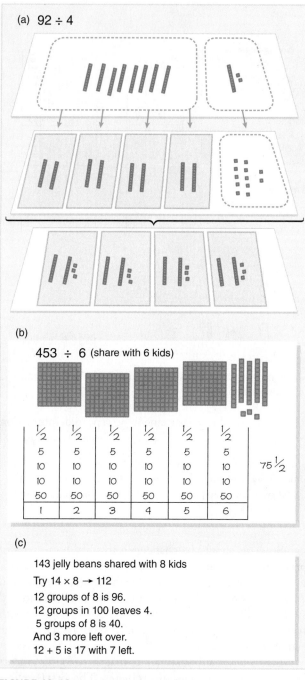

FIGURE 13.10 Students use both models and symbols to solve division tasks.

Source: Adapted from *Developing Mathematical Ideas: Numbers and Operations, Part I, Casebook,* by Deborah Schifter, Virginia Bastable, and Susan Jo Russell. Copyright © 2000 by the Education Development Center, Inc. Used by permission of Pearson Education, Inc. All rights reserved.

and 3 ones, or 33. He knows that 5×6 is 30, so he gives each child 5, leaving him with 3. These he splits in half and writes in each column.

The student in Figure 13.10(c) is solving a sharing problem but tries to do it as a measurement process. She wants to find out how many eights are in 143. Initially she

guesses. By multiplying 8 first by 10, then by 20 (work not shown), and then by 14, she knows the answer is more than 14 and less than 20. Then she rethinks the problem as how many eights in 100 and how many eights in 40.

Missing-Factor Strategies

Notice in Figure 13.10(a) and (b) how the use of base-ten blocks tends to develop a digit-oriented approach—first share the hundreds, then the tens, and finally the ones. Although this is good background for the standard algorithm, it does not help develop complete-number strategies that are also quite useful. In Figure 13.10(c), the student is using a multiplicative approach. She is trying to find out, "What number times 8 will be close to 143 with less than 8 remaining?"

> **PAUSE and REFLECT**
>
> Try to determine the quotient of $318 \div 7$ by figuring out *what number times 7* (or *7 times what number*) is close to 318 without going over. Do not use the standard algorithm. ●

There are several places to begin solving this problem. For instance, because 10×7 is only 70 and 100×7 is 700, the answer has to be between 10 and 100. You might start with multiples of 10. Thirty sevens are 210. Forty sevens are 280. Fifty sevens are 350. So 40 is not enough and 50 is too much. It has to be forty-something. At this point, you could guess at numbers between 40 and 50. Or you might add on sevens. Or you could notice that 40 sevens (280) leaves you with 20 plus 18 or 38. Five sevens will be 35 of the 38 with 3 left over. In all, that's $40 + 5$ or 45 with a remainder of 3.

This missing-factor approach is likely to be invented by some students if they are solving measurement problems such as the following:

> Grace can put 6 pictures on one page of her photo album. If she has 82 pictures, how many pages will she need?

Alternatively, you can simply pose a task such as $82 \div 6$ and ask students, "What number times 6 would be close to 82?" and continue from there.

Cluster Problems

Another approach to developing missing-factor strategies is to use cluster problems, as discussed for multiplication. Here are two examples:

100×4	10×72
$500 \div 4$	5×70
4×25	2×72
6×4	4×72
$\mathbf{527 \div 4}$	5×72
	$\mathbf{381 \div 72}$

Notice that the missing-factor strategy works equally well for one-digit divisors as for two-digit divisors. Also notice that it is okay to include division problems in the cluster. In the first example, 400 ÷ 4 could easily have replaced 100 × 4, and 125 × 4 could replace 500 ÷ 4. The idea is to capitalize on the inverse relationship between multiplication and division.

Cluster problems provide students with a sense that problems can be solved in different ways and with different starting points. Therefore, rather than cluster problems, you can provide students with a variety of first steps for solving a problem. Their task is to select one of the starting points and solve the problem from there. For example, here are four possible starting points for 514 ÷ 8:

$$10 \times 8 \qquad 400 \div 8 \qquad 60 \times 8 \qquad 80 \div 8$$

When students are first asked by the teacher to solve problems using two methods, they often use a primitive or completely inefficient method for their second approach (or revert to a standard algorithm). For example, to solve 514 ÷ 8, a student might perform a very long string of repeated subtractions (514 − 8 = 506, 506 − 8 = 498, 498 − 8 = 490, and so on) and count how many times he or she subtracted 8. Others will actually draw 514 tally marks and loop groups of 8. These students have not developed sufficient flexibility to think of other efficient methods. The idea just suggested of posing a variety of starting points can nudge students into other more profitable alternatives. Class discussions will also help students begin to see more flexible approaches.

Standard Algorithm for Division

Long division is the one standard algorithm that starts with the left-hand or biggest pieces. The conceptual basis for the algorithm most often taught in textbooks is the partition or fair-share method, the method we will explore in detail here. Another well-known algorithm is based on repeated subtraction and may be viewed as a good way to record the missing-factor approach with partial products recorded in a column to the right of the division computation. This may be the preferred strategy for some students, especially students from other countries and students with learning disabilities. Keep in mind that students from different countries learn other "standard" algorithms, and these should be valued and shared with other students as successful options for doing division. As shown by the two examples in Figure 13.11, one advantage of the standard algorithm that's used in the United States is that there is total flexibility in the factors selected at each step of the way. This is important for students who struggle, as they can select facts they know and work from that point.

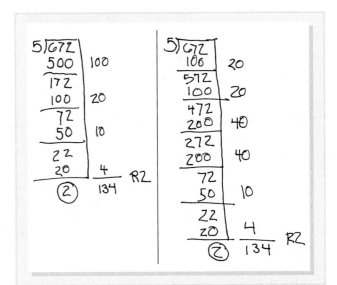

FIGURE 13.11 In the division algorithm shown, the numbers on the side indicate the quantity of the divisor being subtracted from the dividend. As the two examples indicate, the divisor can be subtracted repeatedly from the dividend in groups of any amount.

One-Digit Divisors

Typically, the division algorithm with one-digit divisors is introduced in the third grade, and it should provide the basis for two-digit divisors. Students in the upper grades who are struggling with the division algorithm can also benefit from a conceptual development.

Begin with Models.   Traditionally, if we were to do a problem such as 4)583, we might say, "4 goes into 5 one time." This is quite mysterious to students. How can you just ignore the "83" and keep changing the problem? Preferably, you want students to think of the 583 as 5 hundreds, 8 tens, and 3 ones, not as the independent digits 5, 8, and 3. One idea is to use a context such as candy bundled in boxes of ten with 10 boxes (100) to a carton. Then the problem becomes as follows: *We have 5 cartons, 8 boxes, and 3 pieces of candy to share evenly between 4 schools.* In this context, it is reasonable to share the cartons first until no more can be shared. Those remaining are "unpacked," and the boxes shared, and so on. Money ($100, $10, and $1) can be used in a similar manner.

PAUSE and REFLECT

Try this yourself using base-ten pieces, four paper plates (or pieces of paper), and the problem 583 ÷ 4. Try to talk through the process without using "goes into." Think sharing. ●

Language plays an enormous role in thinking about the standard algorithm conceptually. Most adults are so accustomed to the "goes into" language that it is hard to let it go. For the problem 583 ÷ 4, here is some suggested language:

- I want to share 5 hundreds, 8 tens, and 3 ones among these four sets. There are enough hundreds for each set to get 1 hundred. That leaves 1 hundred that I can't share.
- I'll trade the hundred for 10 tens. That gives me a total of 18 tens. I can give each set 4 tens and have 2 tens left over. Two tens are not enough to go around the four sets.
- I can trade the 2 tens for 20 ones and put those with the 3 ones I already had. That makes a total of 23 ones. I can give 5 ones in each of the four sets. That leaves me with 3 ones as a remainder. In all, I gave out to each group 1 hundred, 4 tens, and 5 ones with 3 left over.

Develop the Written Record.   The recording scheme for the long-division algorithm is not completely intuitive. You will need to be quite directive in helping students learn to record the fair sharing with models. There are essentially four steps:

1. *Share* and record the number of pieces put in each group.
2. *Record* the number of pieces shared in all. Multiply to find this number.
3. *Record* the number of pieces remaining. Subtract to find this number.
4. *Trade* (if necessary) for smaller pieces, and combine with any that are there already. Record the new total number in the next column.

When students model problems with a one-digit divisor, steps 2 and 3 seem unnecessary. Explain that these steps really help when you don't have the pieces there to count.

Record Explicit Trades.   Figure 13.12 details each step of the recording process just described. On the left, you see the standard algorithm. To the right is a suggestion that matches the actual action with the models by explicitly recording the trades. Instead of the somewhat mysterious "bring-down" step of the standard algorithm, the traded pieces are crossed out, as is the number of existing pieces in the next column. The combined number of pieces is written in this column using a two-digit number. In the example, 2 hundreds are traded for 20 tens, combined with the 6 that were there for a total of 26 tens. The 26 is, therefore, written in the tens column.

Students who are required to make sense of the long-division procedure find this *explicit-trade* method easier to follow. (*Author note:* The explicit-trade method is an invention of John Van de Walle. It has been used successfully in grades 3 to 8. You will not find it in other textbooks.) Blank division charts with wide place-value columns are highly recommended for this method. Such charts can be found in Blackline Master 20. Without the charts, it is important to spread out the digits in the dividend when writing down the problem.

Both the explicit-trade method and the use of place-value columns will help with the problem of leaving out a middle zero in a problem (see Figure 13.13).

Two-Digit Divisors

The *Common Core State Standards* states that fifth-grade students should be able to find "whole-number quotients of whole numbers with up to four-digit dividends and two-digit divisors, using strategies based on place value, the properties of operations, and/or the relationship between multiplication and division." The CCSSO goes on to state that the student should "[i]llustrate and explain the calculation by using equations, rectangular arrays, and/or area models" (p. 35). In the past, a large chunk of the fourth, fifth, and sometimes sixth grade was spent on this skill (long division), with the results often being that students acquire negative attitudes toward mathematics and many students not mastering the skill.

An Intuitive Idea.   Suppose that you were sharing a large pile of candies with 36 friends. Instead of passing them out one at a time, you conservatively estimate that each person could get at least 6 pieces. So you give 6 to each of your friends. Now you find there are more than 36 pieces left. Do you have everyone give back the 6 pieces so you can then give them 7 or 8? That would be silly! You simply pass out more.

The candy example gives us two good ideas for sharing in long division. First, always underestimate how much can be shared. You can always pass out some more. To avoid ever overestimating, always pretend there are more sets among which to share than there really are. For example, if you are dividing 312 by 43 (sharing among 43 sets or "friends"), pretend you have 50 sets instead. Round *up* to the next multiple of 10. You can easily determine that 6 pieces can be shared among 50 sets because 6×50 is an easy product. Therefore, since there are really only 43 sets, clearly you can give *at least* 6 to each. Always consider a larger divisor; *always round up*.

Using the Idea Symbolically.   These ideas are used in Figure 13.14. Both the standard algorithm and the explicit-trade method of recording are illustrated. The rounded-up divisor, 70, is written in a little "think bubble" above the real divisor. Rounding up has another advantage: It is

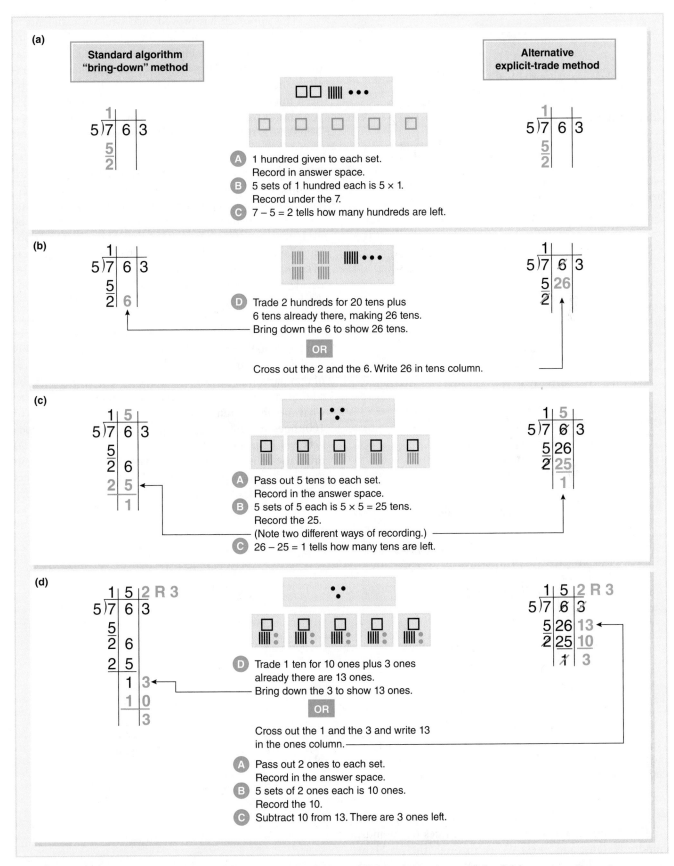

(a)

Standard algorithm "bring-down" method

Alternative explicit-trade method

(A) 1 hundred given to each set. Record in answer space.

(B) 5 sets of 1 hundred each is 5 × 1. Record under the 7.

(C) 7 − 5 = 2 tells how many hundreds are left.

(b)

(D) Trade 2 hundreds for 20 tens plus 6 tens already there, making 26 tens. Bring down the 6 to show 26 tens.

OR

Cross out the 2 and the 6. Write 26 in tens column.

(c)

(A) Pass out 5 tens to each set. Record in the answer space.

(B) 5 sets of 5 each is 5 × 5 = 25 tens. Record the 25.

(Note two different ways of recording.)

(C) 26 − 25 = 1 tells how many tens are left.

(d)

(D) Trade 1 ten for 10 ones plus 3 ones already there are 13 ones. Bring down the 3 to show 13 ones.

OR

Cross out the 1 and the 3 and write 13 in the ones column.

(A) Pass out 2 ones to each set. Record in the answer space.

(B) 5 sets of 2 ones each is 10 ones. Record the 10.

(C) Subtract 10 from 13. There are 3 ones left.

FIGURE 13.12 The standard algorithm and explicit-trade methods are connected to each step of the division process. Every step can and should make sense (see Blackline Master 20).

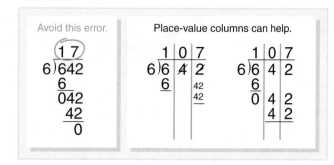

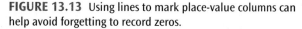

FIGURE 13.13 Using lines to mark place-value columns can help avoid forgetting to record zeros.

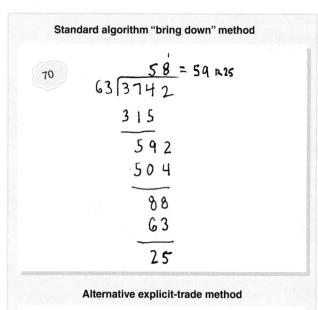

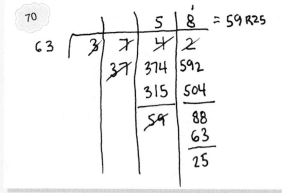

FIGURE 13.14 Round the divisor up to 70 to think with, but multiply what you share by 63. In the ones column, share 8 with each set. Oops! 88 left over. Just give 1 more to each set.

easy to run through the multiples of 70 and compare them to 374. Think about sharing base-ten pieces (thousands, hundreds, tens, and ones). Work through the problem one step at a time, saying exactly what each recorded step stands for.

This approach has proved successful with students in the fourth grade learning division for the first time, with students in the sixth to eighth grades in need of remediation, and with students with disabilities. It reduces the mental strain of making choices and essentially eliminates the need to erase. If an estimate is too low, that's okay. And if you always round up, the estimate will never be too high. The same is true of the explicit-trade notation.

A Low-Stress Approach. With a two-digit divisor, it is hard to come up with the right amount to share at each step. First, start with a conceptual approach based on place value by asking students to consider whether their answer will be in the thousands, hundreds, tens, etc. Then create a "doubling" sidebar chart (Martin, 2009) that shows the products of key multiples by the divisor. So, for the problem $3842 \div 14$, decide first whether the answer is in the thousands, hundreds, or tens. Selecting hundreds in this case, the students will then develop a chart of 100, 200, 400, and 800 times 14 (see Figure 13.15). Can you see how knowing 100 times 14 can help you figure out 200 and other products? Using this doubling sidebar chart can help students with the products of that particular divisor multiplied by 100 through 900 by adding the products in combinations. For example, to know what the divisor multiplied by 300 is, add the products of 100 times and 200 times the divisor. Knowing these products will help the student also know what 10 through 90 times the divisor is! Then the division becomes focused on the equal groups within the dividend and, as such, lowers stress. This scaffolding will help students (particularly

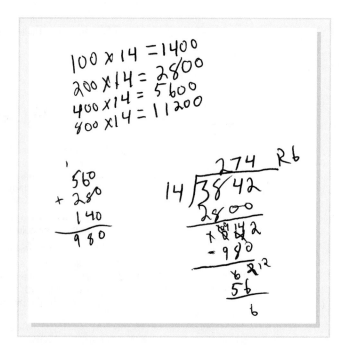

FIGURE 13.15 A student uses doubling to generate useful estimates in a sidebar chart.

students who struggle and those who have learning disabilities) estimate more successfully while allowing them to concentrate on the division process.

Activity 13.3

Double, Double—No Toil or Trouble!   **STUDENTS with**
                                                       SPECIAL NEEDS

Select a division problem with a two-digit divisor such as 936 ÷ 18. Display a corresponding sidebar chart (Martin, 2009) of the products of the divisor (in this case, 10, 20, 40, and 80 times 18) by the appropriate place value of the answer. Then try to think about the division as repeated subtraction. See if this helps in the estimation process. When working with students with learning disabilities, you may need to progress in a structured way to support their use of this approach. At first, you may want to supply them with the appropriate sidebar chart with the products filled in; on the next day, supply them with the chart and have them fill in the products, moving toward their independently creating and completing the chart. This "fading" of support moves students in an organized and systematic way to more responsibility for the learning.

When teaching a standard algorithm for any operation, you may give short assessments or use chapter-end tests found in your textbook. Whether students do well or not so well, it is important to ask yourself whether you really can assess what students understand or do not understand from a strictly computational test. When students make a systematic error in an algorithm, it will likely be repeated in the same way in other problems. What you do not know is what conceptual knowledge students are using—or not using. Don't mistake correct use of a standard algorithm for conceptual understanding. Instead, consider an assessment that captures student thinking.

FORMATIVE Assessment Notes   To assess this very important background understanding for algorithms, during class discussions, call on different students to explain individual steps using the appropriate terminology that connects to the concept of division. Use a **checklist** to keep track of students' responses, indicating how well they seem to understand the algorithm you are working on. For struggling students, you may want to conduct a short **diagnostic interview** to explore in more detail their level of understanding. An interview might begin by having the student complete a computation such as 115 ÷ 9. When finished, ask for explanations for specific steps in the process. If there is difficulty explaining the symbolic process, have the student use base-ten blocks to perform the same computation. Then ask for connections between what was done with the models and what was done symbolically. ■

Computational Estimation in Multiplication and Division

Computational estimation skills in multiplication and division round out a full development of flexible and fluent thinking with whole numbers. *Curriculum Focal Points* (NCTM, 2006) includes computational estimation with whole numbers alongside the expectations for related computation across grades, stating that the goal is for students to be able to "select and apply appropriate methods."

Mental computation and computational estimation are highly related yet quite different skills. Estimates are made using mental computations with numbers that are easier to work with than the actual numbers involved. Thus, estimation depends on students' mental computational skills.

Understanding Computational Estimation

As mentioned in Chapter 12, an *estimate* refers to a number that is a suitable approximation for an exact number, given the particular context. Particularly in multiplicative situations, computational estimation is useful in daily events such as calculating a tip or figuring out miles per gallon of gasoline. As students move to a more technological world where calculations are carried out by devices, never before has judging reasonableness been more important. Those who can estimate well use a variety of strategies based on the numbers and the context of the situation will rarely be tricked by a mistake in using a calculator.

Suggestions for Teaching Computational Estimation

Here are some general principles that are worth keeping in mind as you help your students develop computational estimation skills.

What estimate would you give for 27 × 325? If you use 20 × 300, you might say 6000. Or you might use 25 for the 27, noting that four 25s make 100. Because 325 ÷ 4 is about 81, that would make 8100. If you use 30 × 300, your estimate is 9000, and 30 × 320 gives an estimate of 9600. Is one of these "right"?

PAUSE and REFLECT

Estimate this product: 438 × 62. Use the first idea that comes to your head, and write down the result. Then return to the task and try a different approach, perhaps using different numbers in your approach to the estimate. ●

Sometimes different strategies produce the same estimates. For 438 × 62, you might have thought about using 450 × 60 as a first step. Then suppose you think 10 × 450 is

4500. Double 4500 is 9000 and 3×9000 is 27,000. You might also have thought 6×45 is $240 + 30$ or 270. But this is not 6×45 but 60 times 450 so you multiply by 100 and get 27,000.

Alternatively, you could have used 400×60 and gotten 24,000 and then recognized that you rounded both numbers down. You lost at least 38 sets of 62 or about 40×60. So add 2400 to the 24,000 to get 26,400.

If just a "ballpark" estimate were OK, you might have thought 500×60 is 30,000 and realized that it was a bit high. But the exact answer is also at least 400×60 or 24,000. So it's between 24 and 30 thousand.

You've just seen four of many possible estimation strategies for one computation. The more strategies students experience, the more they will learn. The more strategies they have, the better they can select one that best suits the situation at hand. In contrast, if you tell students to use a given strategy (e.g., round each number to one significant digit and multiply), they won't develop the skills to pick different strategies for different situations. Sometimes rounding is cumbersome and other strategies are quicker or more accurate.

Ask for Information, But No Answer. Consider the threat a third-grade student perceives when you ask for an estimate of the product $7 \times \$89.99$. The requirement to come up with *a number* can result in students trying to quickly calculate an exact answer and then round it—a common strategy, especially among poor estimators (Hanson & Hogan, 2000). To counter this, ask questions that provide a possible result, using prompts like "Is it more than or less than 1000?" or "Will \$500 be enough to pay for the tickets?" For the three prices, the question "About how much?" is quite different from "Is it more than \$600?" How would you answer each of those questions? Or ask if the answer is between \$100 and \$400, \$500 and \$800, or \$900 and \$1200. Narrow your ranges as students become more adept.

Each activity that follows suggests a format for estimation in which a specific numeric response is not required. The next activity is adapted from fifth-grade materials from *Investigations in Number, Data, and Space*.

Activity 13.4

High or Low?

Display a computation and three or more possible computations that might be used to create an estimate. The students' task is to decide whether the estimation will be higher or lower than the actual computation. For example, present the computation 736×18. For each of the following, decide whether the result will be higher or lower than the exact result and explain why you think so.

$$750 \times 10 \qquad 730 \times 15$$
$$700 \times 20 \qquad 750 \times 20$$

Computational Estimation from Invented Strategies

Estimation, like invented strategies, depends on using number relationships (Menon, 2003). Suppose that you were asked to compute the product of 64 and 28. You might begin by multiplying 60 and 20 or 60 and 30. From each of these starting points, you would need to make one or two additional computations before arriving at the answer. However, either of these beginnings is actually a reasonable estimate.

Stop Before the Details

Often it is the first step or two in an invented computation that are good enough for the estimate. In the 64×28 example, even a third grader would probably continue to the exact answer. But estimations are generally called for because an exact answer is too tedious or not necessary. When students have a good repertoire of invented strategies, one approach to an estimate is to simply begin to compute until they've gotten close to the exact answer.

Activity 13.5

STUDENTS with SPECIAL NEEDS

That's Good Enough

Present students with a computation that is reasonably difficult for their skills. For example: T-shirts with the school logo cost \$6 wholesale. The Pep Club has saved \$257. How many shirts can they buy for their fundraiser? The task is to describe the steps they would take to get an exact answer but not do them. For students with disabilities, you may want to have a series of examples of the steps (and counterexamples of steps) that they must choose from and put in order.

Share students' ideas. Next, have students actually do one or two steps. Stop and see whether that is a good estimate.

If you have ELLs, consider posing the situation without numbers first to be sure the context is understood. Then provide the numerical information and ask for estimates. If the numbers in Activity 13.5 are too difficult for a first estimate, use smaller values, but be sure the focus is on estimation and not exact answers. Another way to scaffold is to begin with multiplication—for example, asking the total cost for 86 hoodies that cost \$29 each. The methods that students will suggest will be based on the ideas that they have learned for computing. In most instances, the beginnings of these computations are good estimates. By using the first steps of an invented strategy, students are also improving their understanding and enhancing their number sense.

Use Related Problem Sets

The use of related cluster problem sets, or cluster problems, was explained above as a technique to help students develop invented strategies for multiplication and division. The cluster problem approach, adapted from the *Investigations in Number, Data, and Space* curriculum, has students solve a collection of problems related to but easier than the target problem. These problems are then used to solve the harder problem. An important aspect of the cluster problem approach is that students first make (and write down) an estimate of the target computation.

PAUSE and REFLECT

What follows are some cluster problems. The last problem is the target problem. Give these a try. Don't forget to first make an estimate of the target. Then solve all of the problems in the set. Use problems in the set to estimate the target. Which choices lead to good estimates? ●

$10 \div 7$	6×7
$70 \div 7$	6×8
7×11	70×7
7×12	60×7
$87 \div 7$	**68×7**

40×20	5×20
50×4	5×22
48×2	5×10
48×4	22×10
50×20	2×22
48×24	**$147 \div 22$**

There are many possible paths to the results. Notice, however, that some of the related cluster problems (not the target) are actually good problems to use in making estimates. Once students are comfortable with sets of problems, try the following task.

Make a Little Cluster

Give students a target problem for a related problem set. It can be any operation that you are working on. The task is to create a set of two to three problems that will help produce a reasonable estimate. Once students have made the little set cluster, they should use their problems to estimate the target.

Computational Estimation Strategies

Mental calculations using estimations are more complex than just the application of a procedure in that they require a deep knowledge of how numbers work (Hartnett, 2007). Estimation strategies are specific approaches that produce approximate results. They are not mentally carrying out standard algorithms with an image in your mind of the paper-and-pencil version. As you work through the strategies in this section, you may recognize many of the same approaches students developed from their invented methods. It is also likely that some of the strategies in this section will not have been developed, and you will need to introduce these to your students. Be very clear whenever you suggest a strategy that the intention is to create a collection of strategies to be used in different situations with different numbers. The NCTM *Standards* suggests, "Instructional attention and frequent modeling by the teacher can help students develop a range of computational estimation strategies including flexible rounding, the use of benchmarks, and front-end strategies. Students should be encouraged to frequently explain their thinking as they estimate" (NCTM, 2000, p. 156).

Front-End Methods

Front-end methods focus on the leading or leftmost digits in numbers, ignoring the rest. It is also called the *trunc* strategy, as it involves truncation or covering up all digits other than the first (Star & Rittle-Johnson, 2009). After an estimate is made on the basis of only these front-end digits, an adjustment can be made by noticing how much has been ignored.

For students who have had a lot of experience with invented strategies, the front-end strategy will make a lot of sense because invented strategies often begin with the "leftmost part" of the numbers involved. The front-end approach is an especially good place to begin the topic of estimation for students who only use standard algorithms. They will have to work hard at the idea of looking first at the left portion of numbers in a computation rather than starting at the rightmost digits. The front-end method has been shown to be one of the easiest for students to learn (Star & Rittle-Johnson, 2009).

For multiplication and division, the front-end method uses the first digit in each factor. The computation is then done using zeros in the other positions. For example, a front-end estimation of 48×7 is 40 times 7, or 280. When both numbers have more than one digit, the front ends of both are used. For 452×23, consider 400×20, or 8000. Because of the greater error that occurs in estimating with multiplication, it is important to adjust these estimates in a second step.

For division, one approach is to "think multiplication." Avoid presenting problems using the computational form $(7\overline{)3482})$ because this format tends to suggest a computation rather than an estimate and encourages a "goes into" approach. Present problems in context or use the algebraic form: $3482 \div 7$. For this problem, the front-end digit is determined by first deciding the correct position. (100×7 is too low. 1000×7 is too high. It's in the hundreds.) There are 34 hundreds in the dividend, so since $34 \div 7$ is between 4 and 5, the front-end estimate is 400 or 500. In this example, because $34 \div 7$ is almost 5, the closer estimate is 500.

Rounding Methods

The most familiar form of estimation is rounding, which is a way of changing the numbers in the problem to others that are easier to compute mentally. To be useful in estimation, rounding should be flexible and well understood conceptually. Like front-end methods, answers can be adjusted in a follow-up adjustment in order to get a closer estimate. In multiplication, students can either round one number or round both (Star & Rittle-Johnson, 2009).

Rounding Concept.   To round a number simply means to substitute a compatible number that is close so that some computation can be done more easily. (Note that the term *compatible* is not a mathematical term. It refers to numbers that would make the problem easier to compute mentally.) The compatible number can be any close number and need not be a multiple of 10 or 100. It should be whatever makes the computation or estimation easier or simplifies numbers sufficiently in a story, chart, or even conversation. You might say, "Last night, it took me 57 minutes to do my homework" or "Last night, it took me about one hour to do my homework." The first expression is more precise; the second substitutes a rounded number for better communication.

A number line with close numbers highlighted can be useful in helping students select compatible numbers. An empty number line like the one shown in Figure 13.16 can be made using strips of poster board (or cash register tape) taped end to end. Labels are written above the line. The ends can be labeled 0 and 100, 100 and 200, . . . , 900 and 1000. The other markings then show multiples of 25, 10, and 5. Indicate a number above the line that you want to round. Discuss the marks (or compatible numbers) that are close.

Rounding in Multiplication and Division.   The rounding strategy for multiplication is similar to the one for addition and subtraction with the exception that the error involved from rounding in multiplication can be significant. This is especially true when both factors are rounded. In Figure 13.17, several multiplication situations are illustrated, and rounding is used to estimate each.

If one number can be rounded to 10, 100, or 1000, the resulting product is easy to determine without adjusting the other factor. Figure 13.17(a) shows such a process.

When one factor is a single digit, examine the other factor. Consider the product 7×485. If 485 is rounded to 500, the estimate is relatively easy but is too high by the amount of 7×15. If a more precise result is required, subtract about 100 (an estimate of 7×15). See Figure 13.17(b).

Another good rounding strategy for multiplication is to round one factor up and the other down (even if that is not the closest round number). When estimating 86×28, 86 is between 80 and 90, but 28 is very close to 30. Try rounding 86 down to 80 and 28 up to 30. The actual product is 2408, only 8 off from the 80×30 estimate. If both numbers were rounded to the nearest 10, the estimate would be based on 90×30, with an error of nearly 300. (See Figure 13.17(c) for another example.)

When rounding in division, the key is to find two compatible numbers rather than round to the nearest benchmark. For example, $4325 \div 7$ can be estimated by rounding to the close compatible number, 4200, to yield an estimate

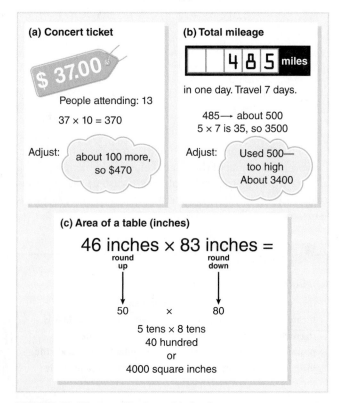

FIGURE 13.17 Rounding in multiplication.

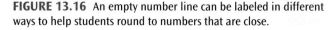

FIGURE 13.16 An empty number line can be labeled in different ways to help students round to numbers that are close.

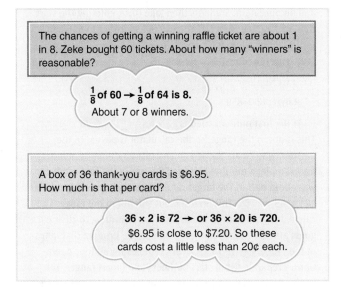

FIGURE 13.18 Using compatible numbers in division.

of 600. Rounding to the nearest hundred results in a dividend of 4300, which does not make the division easier to do mentally.

Compatible Numbers

One of the best uses of the compatible-numbers strategy is in division. Adjusting the divisor or dividend (or both) to close numbers to create a division that results in a whole number is easy to do mentally. Many percent, fraction, and rate situations involve division, and the compatible-numbers strategy is quite useful, as shown in Figure 13.18.

Using Tens and Hundreds

Sometimes one of the numbers in the problem can be changed to take advantage of how easy it is to multiply or divide by tens, hundreds, and thousands (Menon, 2003). For example, take 456×5. Five is really 10/2 (so substitute $10 \div 2$ to solve mentally). Multiply 456 by 10 to get 4560 and then estimate what half of that is—about 2300. See if you can apply this strategy to larger numbers: 786×48. You may first reason that 48 is almost 50, which is the same as $100 \div 2$. Because 786 times 100 equals 78,600, that is about 80,000 and half of that equals 40,000. Alternatively, you can divide by the 2 first and then multiply by 10 or 100. In the last example, that would mean taking half of 786, which is about 400, and multiplying by 100 to get 40,000.

This works with division, too. Consider $429 \div 5$. Think: $429 \div 10 \times 2$ (or $429 \times 2 \div 10$). The answer to $429 \div 10$ is about 42, and double that is 84. This can be a particularly useful strategy as the numbers get larger, like the following:

$$2309 \div 53$$
$$45,908 \div 517$$

This strategy can also be extended to numbers close to 25 (which is 100/4). For example, $786 \div 23$ can be thought of this way: $786 \times 4 \div 100$. So 786 is close to 800, times 4 is 3200, then divided by 100 is 32.

Because computational estimation involves an element of speed, teachers often wonder how they can assess it so that students are not computing on paper and then just rounding the answer to make it look like an estimate. One method is to prepare **performance-based tasks** that include about three estimation exercises ready for display. Students have their paper ready as you very briefly show one exercise at a time, perhaps for 20 seconds, depending on the task. Students write their estimate immediately and indicate whether they think their estimate is "low" or "high"—that is, lower or higher than the exact computation. They are not to do any written computation. Continue until you are finished. Then show all the exercises and have students write down how they did each estimate. They should indicate whether they think the estimate was a good estimate or not so good and why. By only doing a few estimates but having the students reflect on them in this way, you actually receive more information than you would with just the answers to a longer list. ■

Estimation Experiences

The examples presented here are not designed to teach estimation strategies but offer useful formats to provide your students with practice using their developing estimation skills. These activities support the reasoning and sense making students need when estimating or when finding exact answers.

Because students are less comfortable (and have less ability) with estimation as opposed to calculation, it is important to include regular experiences and activities that help students improve their estimation skills. Students from other countries are often very good at mental math and may feel compelled to find the exact answer. The following activity works well with the whole class and is also good for engaging students in discussions of estimation strategies. Limiting time to figure the estimates is one way to discourage exact computations, but for ELLs and for students who struggle with mathematics, additional time may be needed for reading the numbers and applying an estimation strategy. To monitor this, focus on follow-up by asking students how they thought about the problems.

Activity 13.7

What Was Your Method?

Select a problem with an estimation given. For example, say, "Juan estimated that 139×43 is about 6000. How do you think he came up with 6000? Was that a good approach? Is the estimate larger or smaller than the actual answer, and how do you know? How should it be adjusted? Why might someone select 150 instead of 140 as a substitute for 139?" Almost every estimate can involve different choices and methods. Alternatives make for good discussion points, helping students see different methods and learn that there is no single correct estimate.

Calculator Activities

The calculator is not only a good source of estimation activities but also one of the reasons estimation is so important. In the real world, we frequently hit a wrong key, leave off a zero or a decimal, or simply enter numbers incorrectly. An estimate of the expected result alerts us to the unreasonableness of these errors. The calculator as an estimation teaching tool lets students work independently or in pairs in a challenging, fun way without fear of embarrassment.

Activity 13.8

STUDENTS *with* SPECIAL NEEDS

Jump to It

This activity focuses on division. Students begin with a start number and estimate how many times they will add that start number to reach the goal. The numbers can vary to meet the needs and experiences of your students, but here are a few to get you started:

Jump Number	Goal	Estimate of Jumps	Was Estimate Reasonable?
5	72		
11	97		
7	150		
14	135		
47	1200		

To check estimates on the calculator, students can enter 0 + [jump number] and press = once for every estimated jump, or multiply [jump number] × [estimate of jumps]. Students with learning disabilities may need to have a number line close by. Then they can mark their goal number with a sticky dot and use another color dot to mark their first estimate. This will support them in the process of deciding whether they need to lower or raise their estimation of the number of jumps.

Activity 13.9

The Range Game

This is an estimation game that can be used for any of the four operations. First, pick a start number

and an operation. Students then take turns entering the start number, ×, a number of choice, and = to try to make the result land in the target range. The following example for multiplication illustrates the activity:

Start Number: 17

Range: 800–830

If the first number tried is 25, pressing 17 × 25 gives 425. This is not in the range, so the calculator is passed to the partner, who clears the screen and picks a different number—for example, a number close to 50 because the first product was about half of the target range. A second guess might be 17 × 45, or 765. This is closer, but still not in the range. The calculator goes back to the first person. Continue to clear each guess and start again until someone gets a product that lands in the range. Figure 13.19 gives examples for all four operations. Prepare a list of start numbers and target ranges. Let students play in pairs to see who can hit the most targets on the list (Wheatley & Hersberger, 1986).

The range game can also be played on a projection device with the whole class. The span of the range and the type of numbers used can all be adjusted to suit the level of

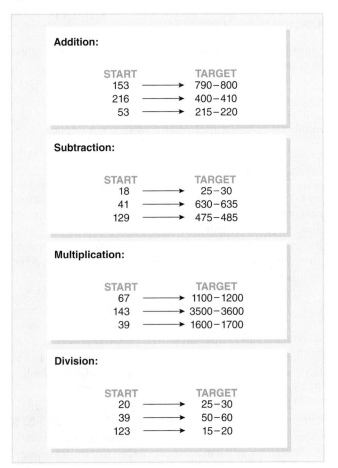

Addition:

START		TARGET
153	→	790–800
216	→	400–410
53	→	215–220

Subtraction:

START		TARGET
18	→	25–30
41	→	630–635
129	→	475–485

Multiplication:

START		TARGET
67	→	1100–1200
143	→	3500–3600
39	→	1600–1700

Division:

START		TARGET
20	→	25–30
39	→	50–60
123	→	15–20

FIGURE 13.19 Possible starting numbers and targets for the range game.

the students. Make sure you record estimates that have been given with the answer so that students who have trouble with working memory can keep track of the previous selections and outcomes.

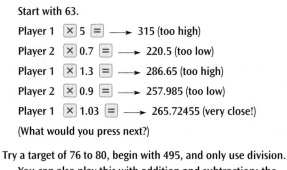

Activity 13.10

The Range Game: Continuous Input

Select a target range. Next, enter the starting number in the calculator, and hand it to the first player. For multiplication or division, only one operation is used through the whole game. After the first or second turn, decimal factors are usually required. This variation provides excellent understanding of multiplication or division by decimals. A sequence for a target of 262 to 265 might be like this:

Start with 63.

Player 1 ⊠ 5 = ⟶ 315 (too high)
Player 2 ⊠ 0.7 = ⟶ 220.5 (too low)
Player 1 ⊠ 1.3 = ⟶ 286.65 (too high)
Player 2 ⊠ 0.9 = ⟶ 257.985 (too low)
Player 1 ⊠ 1.03 = ⟶ 265.72455 (very close!)

(What would you press next?)

Try a target of 76 to 80, begin with 495, and only use division.
You can also play this with addition and subtraction; the first player then presses either ⊞ or ⊟ followed by a number and then =.

Using Whole Numbers to Estimate Rational Numbers

It might be argued that much of the estimation in the real world involves fractions, decimals, and percents. A few examples are suggested here:

> Sale! Original price of a jacket is $51.99. It is marked one-fourth off. What is the sale price?
> About 62 percent of the 834 students bought their lunch last Wednesday. How many bought lunch?
> Tickets sold for $1.25. If attendance was 3125, about how much was the total income?

> I drove 337 miles on 12.35 gallons of gas. How many miles per gallon did my car get?

⏸ PAUSE and REFLECT

Suppose you were to make estimates in each of the previous situations. Without actually getting an estimate, decide what numbers you would use in each case. For instance, in the first example, you would not use 51.99 but perhaps 50 or 52. What about the fractions, decimals, and percentages in the other problems? Think about that now before reading on. ●

The first example is basically asking for an estimate of $\frac{1}{4}$ off or $\frac{3}{4}$ of $51.99. To get $\frac{3}{4}$ of a quantity requires dividing by 4 and multiplying by 3. Those are whole-number computations, but they require an understanding of fraction multiplication.

In the next example, the problem is finding a way to deal with 62 percent. Well, that's close to 60 percent, which is $\frac{3}{5}$ or, equivalently, 6 times 10 percent. In either case, the required computations involve whole numbers. The translation of 62 percent requires an understanding of percents.

In the third example, an understanding of decimals and fractions converts the problem to $1\frac{1}{4}$ of 3125. The computations involve dividing 3125 (perhaps 3200) by 4 and adding that to 3125—all whole-number computations. Similarly, the final example requires an understanding of decimals followed by whole-number computations.

The point is that when fractions, decimals, and percentages are involved, an understanding of numeration is often the first thing required to make an estimate. That understanding often translates the situation into one involving only whole-number computations.

Of course, this is not always the case for fractions and decimals. Consider what is required to make estimates for the following:

$$2\frac{3}{8} \div \frac{1}{12}$$

$$42.5 \times 0.46$$

A reasonable estimate in each case requires an understanding of rational numbers. There are very few new estimation skills required. These problems are discussed in greater depth in Chapters 16 and 17.

RESOURCES *for Chapter 13*

LITERATURE CONNECTIONS

Literature often provides excellent contexts for computation and estimates, as in the following two engaging examples.

Is a Blue Whale the Biggest Thing There Is? *Wells, 2005*

This is one of the most intriguing books you will find about large objects and large distances. Blue whales look small next to Mount Everest, which in turn looks small next to the earth. The data in the book allow students to make other comparisons, such as the number of fourth graders who would have the same weight or volume as a blue whale or would fill the gymnasium. These comparisons are the perfect place for estimations and discussions about how much precision is necessary to make a meaningful comparison.

Counting on Frank *Clement, 1991*

This popular book has a narrator who uses his dog, Frank, as a counting reference. For example, he explains that 24 Franks would fit in his room. Because the book offers approximations, there are limitless opportunities to do computational estimation. For example, how many Franks would fit in five rooms? If there were 24 Franks, how many cans of dog food (discussed on a later page) might be needed? The back of the book offers a series of estimation questions to get you started.

RECOMMENDED READINGS

Books

Fosnot, C. T., & Dolk, M. (2001). *Young mathematicians at work: Constructing multiplication and division.* Portsmouth, NH: Heinemann.
  This is one in a series of three books (one book is on addition and subtraction and the third is on fractions and decimals). The books are products of a collaborative research effort of working with teachers to examine how students learn and how to support that learning. They show students' work constructing ideas about number, operations, and computation in ways not found elsewhere.

ONLINE RESOURCES

Factorize (NCTM)
http://illuminations.nctm.org/ActivityDetail.aspx?ID=64
  Use the grid to draw rectangular arrays for a given product. Record the factors for each array. Can you find all of the factors?

Meanings and Models for Operations
www.learner.org/courses/learningmath/number/session4/index.html
  This module examines the various models for multiplication and division of whole numbers and features video-based professional development, sample problems and solutions, and classroom activities.

Primary Krypto (NCTM)
http://illuminations.nctm.org/ActivityDetail.aspx?ID=173
  Arrange five number cards and combinations of the four operations to arrive at a target number.

Rectangle Division
http://nlvm.usu.edu/en/nav/frames_asid_193_g_1_t_1.html
  This applet uses an array model to represent any two-digit number as a product of two numbers. Remainders are included.

REFLECTIONS *on Chapter 13*

WRITING TO LEARN

1. Draw pictures showing how 57×4 could be modeled: with counters, with base-ten blocks, with arrays, or with areas on base-ten grids.
2. What would you do if your students seemed to persist in using repeated addition for multiplication problems without really doing any multiplication?
3. Which division concept, measurement or partition, is easier for direct modeling and is also the one used to develop the standard long-division algorithm? Make up an appropriate word problem to go with $735 \div 6$.
4. Use the standard algorithm for $735 \div 6$, and then repeat the process using the text's suggestion of recording trades explicitly. With the two algorithms side by side, explain every recorded number in terms of what it stands for when sharing base-ten blocks.

5. Describe each of these estimation strategies. Be able to make up an example and use it in your explanation.
   a. Front-end
   b. Rounding
   c. Compatibles
   d. Adapting to use tens, hundreds, and so forth

FOR DISCUSSION AND EXPLORATION

1. You notice a student is estimating by doing the computation and rounding the answer. Why might the student be using this strategy? What experiences might you plan to improve the student's ability to estimate?

MyEducationLab™

Go to the MyEducationLab (www.myeducationlab.com) for Math Methods and familiarize yourself with the content. Much of the site content is organized topically. The topics include all of the following to support your learning in the course:

- Learning outcomes for important mathematics methods course topics aligned with the national standards
- Assignments and Activities, tied to these learning outcomes and standards, that can help you more deeply understand course content
- Building Teaching Skills and Dispositions learning units that allow you to apply and practice your understanding of the core mathematics content and teaching skills

Your instructor has a correlation guide that aligns the exercises on the topical portion of the site with your book's chapters.

On MyEducationLab you will also find book-specific resources including Blackline Masters, Expanded Lesson Activities, and Artifact Analysis Activities.

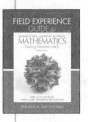

Field Experience Guide
C O N N E C T I O N S

Expanded Lesson 9.4 focuses on building meaning for division. FEG Activity 10.6, "Interference," focuses on multiples; FEG Activity 10.4, "Factor Quest," focuses on factors. Computational estimation is the focus of FEG Activity 10.7, "Target Number," as students use numbers on dice to try to reach a desired target number. Finally, the FEG Balanced Assessment Item 11.1, "Magic Age Rings," is an excellent assessment for order of operations.

Chapter 14

Algebraic Thinking: Generalizations, Patterns, and Functions

lgebra is an established content strand in most, if not all, state standards for grades K–12 and is one of the five content standards in NCTM's *Principles and Standards for School Mathematics*. Although there is much variability in the algebra requirements at the elementary and middle school levels, one thing is clear: The algebra envisioned for these grades—and for high school as well—is not the algebra that you most likely experienced. That typical algebra course of the eighth or ninth grade consisted primarily of symbol manipulation procedures and artificial applications with little connection to the real world. The focus now is on the type of thinking and reasoning that prepares students to think mathematically across all areas of mathematics.

Algebraic thinking or algebraic reasoning involves forming generalizations from experiences with number and computation, formalizing these ideas with the use of a meaningful symbol system, and exploring the concepts of pattern and functions. Far from a topic with little real-world use, algebraic thinking pervades all of mathematics and is essential for making mathematics useful in daily life. As Fosnot and Jacob (2010) write in their *Constructing Algebra* edition of *Young Mathematicians at Work*, "It is human to seek and build relations. The mind cannot process the multitude of stimuli in our surroundings and make meaning of them without developing a network of relations" (p. 12).

BIG IDEAS

1. Algebra is a useful tool for generalizing arithmetic and representing patterns and regularities in our world.

2. Symbolism, especially involving equality and variables, must be well understood conceptually for students to be successful in mathematics, particularly algebra.

3. Methods we use to compute and the structures in our number system can and should be generalized. For example, the generalization

that $a + b = b + a$ tells us that $83 + 27 = 27 + 83$ without computing the sums on each side of the equal sign.

4. Patterns, both repeating and growing, can be recognized, extended, and generalized.

5. Functions in K–8 mathematics describe in concrete ways the notion that for every input, there is a unique output.

6. Understanding of functions is strengthened when they are explored across representations, as each representation provides a different view of the same relationship.

Mathematics CONTENT CONNECTIONS

It is difficult to find an area of mathematics that does not involve generalizing and formalizing in some central way. In fact, this type of reasoning is at the heart of mathematics as a science of pattern and order. And this is a particular emphasis in both the *Standards for Mathematical Practice* and the content standards in the *Common Core State Standards* (CCSSO, 2010).

◆ **Number, Place Value, Basic Facts, and Computation** (Chapters 8–13): The most important generalizations at the core of algebraic thinking are those made about number and computation—arithmetic. Not only does algebraic thinking generalize from number and computation, but also the generalizations themselves add to understanding and facility with computation. We can use our understanding of 10 to add $5 + 8$ ($5 + 8 = 3 + 2 + 8 = 3 + 10$) or $5 + 38$ ($5 + 38 = 3 + 2 + 38 = 3 + 40$). The generalized idea is that 2 can be taken from one addend and moved to the other: $a + b = (a - 2) + (b + 2)$. Although students may not symbolize this general idea, seeing that this regularly works is algebraic thinking. Making these regularities explicit supports students' conceptual and procedural development of number as well as prepares them for the algebra they will explore in high school.

◆ **Proportional Reasoning** (Chapter 18): Every proportional situation gives rise to a linear (straight-line) function with a graph that goes through the origin. The constant ratio in the proportion is the slope of the graph.

◆ **Measurement** (Chapter 19): Measures are a principal means of describing relationships in the physical world, and these relationships are often algebraic. Measurement formulas, such as circumference of a circle, are functions. You can say that the height of a building is a function of how many stories it has.

◆ **Geometry** (Chapter 20): Geometric patterns are some of the first that students experience. Growing patterns generate functional relationships. And functions are graphed on the coordinate plane to visually show algebraic relationships.

◆ **Data Analysis** (Chapter 21): When data are gathered, the algebraic thinker is able to examine them for regularities and patterns. Functions are used to approximate trends or describe the relationships.

Algebraic Thinking

Algebraic thinking begins in prekindergarten and continues through high school. According to *Curriculum Focal Points* (NCTM, 2006), in prekindergarten, "Children recognize and duplicate simple sequential patterns (e.g., square, circle, square, circle, square, circle, . . .)" (p. 11). Algebraic thinking continues to be included in every grade level, with the primary topics being the use of patterns leading to generalizations (especially with operations), the study of change, and the concept of function.

In the *Common Core State Standards* (CCSSO, 2010), the close connections between arithmetic and algebra are noted in every grade from kindergarten through fifth grade, where number and algebra are combined in the discussions of clusters and standards under the domain of "Operations and Algebraic Thinking." In middle school (grades 6–8), students begin to study algebra in more abstract and symbolic ways, extending what was learned in K–5. This chapter follows the number concept chapters so that you can see the close relationship between number concepts, operations, and algebraic thinking.

James Kaput (2008), an expert in algebra in K–12 curriculum, suggests that there are three strands of algebraic reasoning, all three infusing the central notions of generalization and symbolization:

1. Study of structures in the number system, including those arising in arithmetic (algebra as generalized arithmetic)
2. Study of patterns, relations, and functions
3. Process of mathematical modeling, including the meaningful use of symbols

Thus, algebraic thinking is composed of different forms of thought and an understanding of symbols. It is a separate strand of the curriculum but is also embedded in all areas of mathematics. We initiate the development of these forms of thinking from the very beginning of school so that students will learn to think productively with these powerful mathematical ideas.

These three big strands are presented in this chapter. In each section, we share developmentally appropriate tasks and effective instructional activities across the pre-K–8 curriculum.

Generalization from Arithmetic

The process of creating generalizations from number and arithmetic begins as early as prekindergarten and continues as students learn about all aspects of number and computation, including basic facts and meanings of the operations.

Generalization with Operations

Young students explore addition families and in the process learn how to decompose and recompose numbers. The monkeys and trees problem illustrated in Figure 14.1 provides students a chance not only to consider ways to decompose 7 but also to see generalizable characteristics, such as that increasing the number in the small tree by one means reducing the number in the large tree by one.

Students may be asked to find all the ways the monkeys can be in the two trees. The significant algebra question is how to decide when all of the solutions have been found. At one level, students will just not be able to think of any more

FIGURE 14.1 Seven monkeys want to play in two trees, one big and one small. Show all the different ways that the seven monkeys could play in the two trees.

Source: Adapted from Yackel, E. (1997). "A Foundation for Algebraic Reasoning in the Early Grades." *Teaching Children Mathematics, 3*(6), 276–280. A similar task was explored in Carpenter, T. P., Franke, M. L., and Levi, L. (2003). *Thinking Mathematically: Integrating Arithmetic and Algebra in Elementary School.* Portsmouth, NH: Heinemann.

ways. At the next level, students will strategically use each number from 0 to 7 for one tree (and the corresponding number for the other tree). The student who explains that for each number 0 to 7 there is one solution is no longer partitioning 7 into parts (finding solutions by applying addition) but is making a *generalization* for how to determine the number of solutions without listing them. In this case, students might say, "There is always one more way than the number of monkeys." That reasoning can be applied to other numbers, which is an important step in generalization and later symbolization. The vignette below follows a similar exploration with seven mice in two cages and captures second graders' thinking as the teacher presses them to apply their generalization.

MS. S: How about 324 mice?

JAMIE: It would be 325.

ANNA: Yeah, it's always just one more than the number of mice. These are easy.

MS. S: Oh, how about if there are *n* mice?

ANNA: It would be just one more than that.

MS. S: How would we write this? [The children struggle with this question for a while.]

CARLA: Would it be *n* + 1? (Carpenter, Franke, & Levi, 2003, p. 69).

Generalizing can be extended to symbols, something that elementary students can do (as seen in this vignette), and middle school students must do. For example, in the monkeys and trees problem, the teacher might ask, "If I have some monkeys in the little tree, let's use an *l* for little. How might you describe how many monkeys are in the big tree?" Students might answer "Seven minus *l*." If the students answer "*b*," then the teacher can ask how *l* and *b* are related in an equation. Middle school students doing a similar problem with 8 mice in blue and green cages, for example, discovered three equations to describe the situation: $b + g = 8$, $8 - g = b$, and $8 - b = g$ (Stephens, 2005).

Slight shifts in how arithmetic problems are presented can open up opportunities for generalizations (Blanton, 2008). For example, instead of a series of unrelated two-digit multiplication problems, consider the following list:

$$\begin{array}{cccc} 35 & 52 & 23 & 46 \\ \times\,52 & \times\,35 & \times\,46 & \times\,23 \end{array}$$

Once students have solved these problems, you can focus attention on the factors, asking questions like "What do you notice?" "Will this always be true?" and "How could we write that using symbols?" In their own words, students will explain that the numbers can be multiplied in any order. While students may already understand commutativity of single-digit addends in learning their facts, they may not recognize the *generalizability* of the property, and this interaction can help them recognize the power of this critical property.

Exploring numerical situations, rather than just computing, is an effective way to infuse algebraic thinking and strengthen understanding of number, not just in addition, but all the operations (and with all types of numbers). For example, when working on multiplication concepts and related facts, ask students to decide whether the following conjecture is true or false: *If you multiply any whole number by 2, the answer will be an even number.* Or, *If you multiply any whole number by 9, the answer has digits that add up to 9.* Encourage students to make their own generalizations. For example, Schifter, Russell, and Bastable (2009) tell of a third-grade classroom where a student suggested that if a factor is doubled, then the product is also doubled. Students illustrated this conjecture by sketching rectangles on grid paper to show why it worked.

If students are to be successful in algebra, which is more abstract and symbolic, such discussions must be a part of the daily elementary and middle school experience (Mark, Cuoco, Goldenberg, & Sword, 2010). This is important in supporting the learning of those who struggle as well as those who excel (Schifter et al., 2009). To do so requires planning in advance—thinking of what questions you can ask to help students think about generalized characteristics within the problem they are working (e.g., when the number of monkeys in one tree goes down by 1, the number in the other goes up by 1) and to think about other problems that have the same pattern.

Generalization in the Hundreds Chart

The hundreds chart is a rich representation for exploring number relationships and should not be thought of as only useful for teaching numeration. You can use a hard copy or an interactive virtual hundreds chart (see, for example, Crickweb (www.crickweb.co.uk/ks1numeracy.html). In Chapter 11, students explored the hundreds chart and looked for patterns (see Activities 11.14–11.19 and Activity 11.28). In connecting arithmetic to algebra in the operations, you can ask students, "What did I add to get from 72 to 82? From 5 to 15? From 34 to 44?" When students stop counting and note the generalized idea that they are adding 10 and moving exactly one row down, they are deepening their understanding of number concepts and generalizing the idea of what +10 looks like. In the hundreds chart, moves can be represented with arrows (for example, → means right one column or plus 1, and ↑ means up one row or less 10). Consider asking students to complete these problems:

$$14 \rightarrow\ \rightarrow\ \leftarrow\ \leftarrow \qquad 63\uparrow\uparrow\downarrow\downarrow \qquad 45 \rightarrow\uparrow\leftarrow\downarrow$$

What do you anticipate students will do? At the most basic level, students may count up and back using a counting by ones approach. Or they may know to jump 10 (up or down) but still do all four moves. Students who are reasoning and moving toward generalizations may recognize that a downward arrow "undoes" an upward arrow (Blanton, 2008). In other words, $+ 10 - 10$ nets a zero change. Students can write the equations for the arrow moves with numbers or with variables—for example, for the first problem, $n + 1 + 1 - 1 - 1 = n + (1 - 1) + (1 - 1) = n$.

FORMATIVE Assessment Notes
As students work on such tasks, you can observe while using a **checklist** to note which students are solving by counting by ones, by jumping, or by noticing the "doing" and "undoing." What you observe can help your discussion as you can have students start by first sharing the more basic strategies and then have students who have generalized the situation share how they think about it. ■

Here are some additional tasks you might explore on the hundreds chart.

- When skip counting, which numbers make diagonal patterns? Which make column patterns? Can you describe a rule for explaining when a number will have a diagonal or column pattern?
- If you move down two and over one on the hundreds chart, what is the relationship between the original number and the new number?
- Can you find two skip-count patterns with one color marker "on top of" the other (that is, all of the shaded values for one pattern are part of the shaded values for the other)? How are these two skip-count numbers related? Is this true for any pair of numbers that have this relationship?
- Find a value on the hundreds chart. Add it to the number to the left of it and the one to the right; then divide by 3. What did you get? Why?

These examples extend number concepts to algebraic thinking. "When will this be true?" and "Why does this work?" questions require students to generalize (and strengthen) the number concepts they are learning.

Generalization Through Exploring a Pattern

One of the most interesting and perhaps most valuable methods of searching for generalization is to find it in the growing pattern represented with visual or concrete materials. One method of identifying the pattern is to examine only one growth step and ask students to find a method of counting the elements without simply counting each by one. The following problem is a classic example of a task that involves such a growing pattern, described in many resources, including Burns and McLaughlin (1990) and Boaler and Humphreys (2005).

Activity 14.1

The Border Tiles Problem

ENGLISH LANGUAGE LEARNERS

TECHNOLOGY Have students use color tiles to build an 8×8 square representing a swimming pool, with different color tiles around the border (see Figure 14.2). The task is to find at least two ways to get the number of border tiles without counting them one by one. Students should use their tiles, words, and number sentences to show how they counted the squares. Ask students to illustrate their solution on centimeter grid paper. For ELLs, the drawing will be a useful support, but be sure the instructions are clear and that they understand that they are counting the outside tiles and need to find more than one way. There are at least five different methods of counting the border tiles around a square other than counting them one at a time.

A great tool to help students explore the border tiles problem is the site Plan Your Room (www.planyourroom.com). Input your dimensions (e.g., 8' 0" × 8' 0") and click "Start with a Room . . ."

⏸ *PAUSE and REFLECT*

Before reading further, see if you can find four or five different counting schemes for the border tiles problem. Apply your method to a square border of other dimensions. ●

A very common solution to the border tiles problem is to notice that there are ten squares across the top and also across the bottom, leaving eight squares on either side. This might be written as:

$$10 + 10 + 8 + 8 = 36 \text{ or } (2 \times 10) + (2 \times 8) = 36$$

Each of the following expressions can likewise be traced to looking at the squares in various groupings:

$$4 \times 9$$
$$4 \times 8 + 4$$
$$4 \times 10 - 4$$
$$100 - 64$$

FIGURE 14.2 How many different ways can you find to count the border tiles of an 8×8 pool without counting them one at a time?

More expressions are possible, since students may use addition instead of multiplication. In any case, once the generalizations are created, students need to justify how the elements in the expression map to the physical representation.

Another approach to the border tiles problem is to have students build a series of pools in growth steps, each with one more tile on the side (3×3, 4×4, 5×5, etc.). Then students can find a way to count the elements of each step using an algorithm that handles the step numbers in the same manner. Students can find, for example, number sentences parallel to what they wrote for the 8×8 to find a 6×6 pool and a 7×7 pool. Eventually, this can result in a generalized statement, for example, taking $(2 \times 10) + (2 \times 8)$ and generalizing it to $2 \times (n + 2) + 2(n)$.

One important idea in generalization is recognizing a new situation in which it can apply and adapting it appropriately. For example, students may explore other perimeter-related growing patterns, such as a triangle made of dots with 3, 4, and 5 dots on each side. Students should reason that this is the same type of pattern, except that it has three sides, and be able to use their previous generalization (Steele, 2005).

Meaningful Use of Symbols

Perhaps one reason that students are unsuccessful in algebra is that they do not have a strong understanding of the symbols they are using. For many adults, the word *algebra* elicits memories of simplifying long equations with the goal of finding *x*. These experiences of manipulating symbols were often devoid of meaning and resulted in such a strong dislike for mathematics that algebra has become a favorite target of cartoonists and Hollywood writers. In reality, symbols represent real events and should be seen as useful tools for solving important problems that aid in decision making (e.g., calculating how many cookies we need to sell to make *x* dollars or at what rate do a given number of employees need to work to finish the project on time). Students cannot make sense of such questions without meaningful instruction on two very important (and poorly understood) topics: the equal sign and variables.

The Meaning of the Equal Sign

The equal sign is one of the most important symbols in elementary arithmetic, in algebra, and in all mathematics using numbers and operations. At the same time, research dating from 1975 to the present indicates clearly that $=$ is a very poorly understood symbol (RAND Mathematics Study Panel, 2003) and rarely represented in U.S. textbooks in a way that encourages students to understand the equivalence relationship—an understanding that is critical to understanding algebra (McNeil et al., 2006).

PAUSE and REFLECT

In the following expression, what number do you think belongs in the box?

$$8 + 4 = \Box + 5$$

How do you think students in the early grades or in middle school typically answer this question? ●

In one study, no more than 10 percent of students from grades 1 to 6 put the correct number (7) in the box. The common responses were 12 and 17. (How did students get these answers?) In grade 6, not one student out of 145 put a 7 in the box (Falkner, Levi, & Carpenter, 1999).

Where do such misconceptions come from? Most, if not all, equations that students encounter in elementary school look like this: $5 + 7 = \_\_\_$ or $8 \times 45 = \_\_\_$. Naturally, students come to see $=$ as signifying "and the answer is" rather than a symbol to indicate equivalence (Carpenter et al., 2003; McNeil & Alibali, 2005; Molina & Ambrose, 2006). Subtle shifts in the way you approach teaching computation can alleviate this major misconception. For example, rather than ask students to solve a problem (like $45 + 61$ or 4×26), ask them to find an equivalent expression and use that expression to write an equation (Blanton, 2008). So, for $45 + 61$, students might write $45 + 61 = 40 + 66$. For a multiplication problem, students might write $4 \times 26 = 4 \times 25 + 4$ or $4 \times 26 = 2 \times (2 \times 26)$. Activity 14.2 is a way to apply this idea to learning the basic facts and emphasize the Up Over 10 strategy.

Activity 14.2

Capture Ten

In this activity (adapted from Fosnot & Jacob, 2010), you will label 10 note cards with the equations from $10 + 1$ to $10 + 8$ and have students lay them out on their desks.

10 + 1

10 + 2

10 + 3

10 + 4

10 + 5

10 + 6

10 + 7

10 + 8

Place students with a partner, and give each a deck of cards from which all face cards, aces, and ten cards have been removed. Each partner draws one playing card from the deck. Together the partners decide which note card is equivalent to the sum of their playing cards and place it there. If the sum of the playing cards is less than 10, place the cards back in the deck. Note that the students do not need to actually add their cards; they just find the equivalent expression—but you can ask students to verbally state the sum matching them. Students can also play independently.

As an alternative, you can prepare a game board whose spaces are all the equations from 10 + 1 to 10 + 10. The student partners will then match the sum of the playing cards drawn to the space on the game board.

Why is it so important that students correctly understand the equal sign? First, it is important for students to understand and symbolize relationships in our number system. The equal sign is a principal method of representing these relationships. For example, $6 \times 7 = 5 \times 7 + 7$ shows a basic fact strategy. When these ideas, initially and informally developed through arithmetic, are generalized and expressed symbolically, powerful relationships are available for working with other numbers in a generalized manner.

A second reason is that when students fail to understand the equal sign, they typically have difficulty with algebraic expressions (Knuth et al., 2006). Consider the equation $5x - 24 = 81$. It requires students to see both sides of the equal sign as equivalent expressions. It is not possible to "do" the left-hand side. However, if both sides are understood as being equivalent, students will see that $5x$ must be 24 more than 81 or $5x = 81 + 24$.

Conceptualizing the Equal Sign as a Balance. Helping students understand the idea of equivalence can be developed concretely. The next two activities illustrate how kinesthetic approaches, tactile objects, and visualizations can reinforce the "balancing" notion of the equal sign (ideas adapted from Mann, 2004).

Activity 14.3

Seesaw Students

Ask students to raise their arms to look like a seesaw. Explain that you have big juicy oranges, all weighing the same, and tiny little apples, all weighing the same. Ask students to imagine that you have placed an orange in each of their left hands (students should bend to lower left side). Ask students to imagine that you place another orange on the right side (students level off). Next, with oranges still there, ask students to imagine an apple added to the left.

Finally, say you are adding another apple, which is going on the left (again). Then ask them to imagine the apple

moving over to the right. This is a particularly important activity for students with disabilities, who may be challenged with the abstract idea of balancing values of expressions.

After acting out the seesaw several times, ask students to write Seesaw Findings (e.g., "If you have a balanced seesaw and add something to one side, it will tilt to that side," and "If you take away the same object from both sides of the seesaw, it will still be balanced").

Activity 14.4

TECHNOLOGY

What Do You Know about the Shapes?

Present a scale with objects on both sides. Here is an example:

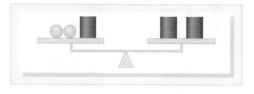

Ask students what they know about the shapes: "The red cylinders weigh the same. The yellow balls weigh the same. What do you know about how the weights of the balls and the cylinders compare?" Figure 14.3 illustrates how a third grader explained what she knew. (Notice that these tasks, appropriate for early grades, are good beginnings for the more advanced balancing tasks later in this chapter.)

For more explorations like this, see "Pan Balance—Shapes" on NCTM's Illuminations website: http://illuminations.nctm.org/ActivityDetail.aspx?id=33.

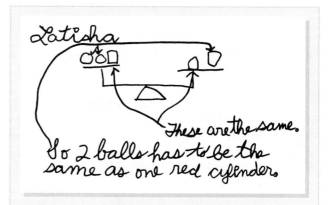

FIGURE 14.3 Latisha's work on the problem.

Source: Figure 4 from Mann, R. L. (2004). "Balancing Act: The Truth Behind the Equals Sign." *Teaching Children Mathematics, 11*(2), p. 68. Reprinted with permission. Copyright © 2004 by the National Council of Teachers of Mathematics. All rights reserved.

STUDENTS *with* SPECIAL NEEDS

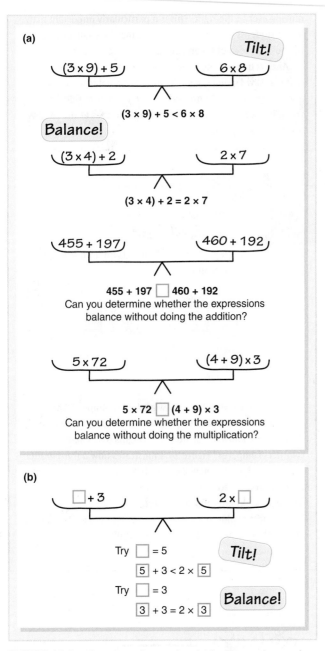

(a)

Tilt!

(3 × 9) + 5   6 × 8

(3 × 9) + 5 < 6 × 8

Balance!

(3 × 4) + 2   2 × 7

(3 × 4) + 2 = 2 × 7

455 + 197   460 + 192

455 + 197 ☐ 460 + 192
Can you determine whether the expressions
balance without doing the addition?

5 × 72   (4 + 9) × 3

5 × 72 ☐ (4 + 9) × 3
Can you determine whether the expressions
balance without doing the multiplication?

(b)

☐ + 3   2 × ☐

Try ☐ = 5   Tilt!
⑤ + 3 < 2 × ⑤

Try ☐ = 3   Balance!
③ + 3 = 2 × ③

FIGURE 14.4 Using expressions and variables in equations and
inequalities. The two-pan balance helps develop the meaning of =.

After students have experiences with these shapes,
they can then explore numbers, eventually moving on to
variables. Figure 14.4 offers examples that connect the
balance to the related equation. This two-pan balance
model also illustrates that the expressions on each side
represent a number.

Activity **14.5**

Tilt or Balance

On the board, draw or project a simple two-pan
balance. In each pan, write a numeric expression
and ask which pan will go down or whether the two will balance

(see Figure 14.4(a)). Challenge students to write expressions for
each side of the scale to make it balance. For each, write a
corresponding equation to illustrate the meaning of =. Note
that when the scale "tilts," either a "greater than" or "less than"
symbol (> or <) is used. Include examples (like the third and
fourth balances) for which students can make the determination
by analyzing the relationships on both sides rather than doing
the computation. For students with disabilities, instead of
having them write expressions for each side of the scale, share
a small collection of cards with expressions, and have them
identify the ones that will make the scale balance.

After a short time, add variables to the expressions, and
allow students to solve them using whatever methods they
wish (see Figure 14.4(b)).

TECHNOLOGY   The balance is a concrete tool that can help students understand that if you add or subtract a
value from one side, you must add or subtract a
like value from the other side to keep the equation balanced. An NCTM Illuminations applet titled "Pan
Balance—Expressions" (http://illuminations.nctm.org/
ActivityDetail.aspx?id=10) provides a virtual balance where
students can enter what they believe to be equivalent
expressions (with numbers or symbols) each in a separate
pan to see whether, in fact, the expressions balance.

Figure 14.5 shows solutions for two equations, one in a
balance and the other without. Even after you have stopped
using the balance, it is a good idea to refer to the pan-balance
concept of equality and the idea of keeping the scales balanced.
This use of concrete (actual balance) or semi-concrete (drawings of a balance) representations supports the abstract concept of equality. Students with intellectual disabilities, as well
as other students, benefit from this approach to learning.

In middle school, students begin to manipulate equations so that they are easier to graph and/or to compare to
other equations. These experiences help ground a student's
understanding of how to preserve equivalence when moving numbers or variables across the equal sign.

True/False and Open Sentences. Carpenter and colleagues (2003) suggest that a good starting point for helping
students with the equal sign is to explore equations as either
true or false. Clarifying the meaning of the equal sign is just
one of the outcomes of this type of exploration, as seen in
the following activity.

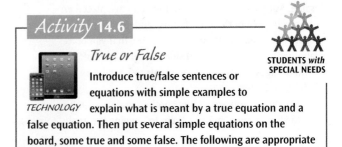

Activity **14.6**

True or False

TECHNOLOGY   Introduce true/false sentences or
equations with simple examples to
explain what is meant by a true equation and a
false equation. Then put several simple equations on the
board, some true and some false. The following are appropriate
for primary grades:

$$5 + 2 = 7 \qquad 4 + 1 = 6$$
$$4 + 5 = 8 \qquad 8 = 10 - 1$$

ENGLISH LANGUAGE LEARNERS

Your collection might include other operations, but keep the computations simple. The students' task is to decide which of the equations are true equations and which are not. For each response, they must explain their reasoning.

After this initial exploration of true/false sentences, have students explore equations that are in a less familiar form:

$$3 + 7 = 7 + 3 \qquad 10 - 3 = 11 - 4 \qquad 9 + 5 = 0 + 14$$
$$8 = 8 \qquad 9 \times 5 = 40 \qquad 4 \times 15 = 2 \times 30$$

Listen to the types of reasons that students use to justify their answers, and plan additional equations accordingly. ELLs and students with disabilities will benefit from first explaining (or showing) their thinking to a partner (a low-risk speaking opportunity) and then sharing with the whole group. "Pan Balance—Numbers" on NCTM's Illuminations website (http://illuminations.nctm.org/ActivityDetail.aspx?id=26) can be used to model and/or verify equivalence.

Students will generally agree on equations when there is an expression on one side and a single number on the other, although initially the less familiar form of $7 = 2 + 5$ may generate discussion. For an equation with no operation ($8 = 8$), the discussion may be lively. Students often believe that there must be an operation on one side and an "answer" on the other side. Reinforce that the equal sign means "is the same as" by using that language when you read the symbol. Inequalities should be explored in a similar manner.

After students have experienced true/false sentences, introduce an open sentence—one with a box to be filled in or letter to be replaced. To develop an understanding of open sentences, encourage students to look at the number sentence holistically and discuss in words what the equation represents.

Activity 14.7

Open Sentences

Write several open sentences on the board. To begin with, these can be similar to the true/false sentences that you have been exploring. Here is a sampling for addition (grades 1 and 2) and multiplication (grades 3–5).

$$5 + 2 = \square \qquad 4 + \square = 6 \qquad 4 + 5 = \square - 1$$
$$6 - n = 7 - 4 \qquad n + 5 = 5 + 8 \qquad 15 + 27 = n + 28$$
$$3 \times 7 = 7 \times \square \qquad \square \times 4 = 48 \qquad \square = 23 - 5$$
$$3 \times 7 = 7 \times \square \qquad \square \times 4 = 48 \qquad 12 \times \square = 24 \times 5$$
$$6 \times n = 3 \times 8 \qquad 15 \times 27 = n \times 27 + 5 \times 27$$

Ask students to decide what number can replace the box (or letter) to make the sentence true. They should be ready to

---

explain their thinking. For grades 3 and above, include multiplication as well as addition and subtraction.

Relational Thinking. Once students understand that the equal sign means that the quantities on both sides are the same, they can use relational thinking in solving problems. Relational thinking takes place when a student observes and uses numeric relationships between the two sides of the equal sign rather than actually computing the amounts. Relational thinking of this sort is a first step toward generalizing relationships found in arithmetic to relationships used when variables are involved.

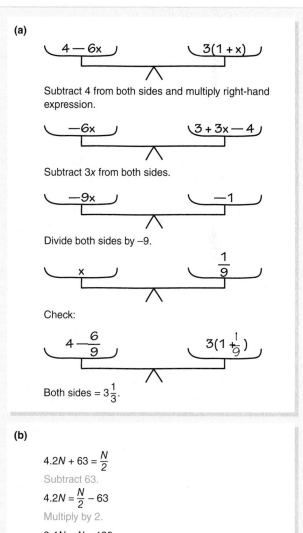

FIGURE 14.5 Using a balance scale to think about solving equations.

Consider two distinctly different explanations for placing an 8 in the box for the open sentence $7 + n = 6 + 9$.

a. Since $6 + 9$ is 15, I need to figure out 7 plus what equals 15. It is 8, so n equals 8.

b. Seven is one more than the 6 on the other side. That means that n should be one less than 9, so it must be 8.

The first student computes the result on one side and adjusts the result on the other to make the sentence true. The second student uses a relationship between the expressions on either side of the equal sign. This student does not need to compute the values on each side. When the numbers are large, the relationship approach is much more useful.

PAUSE and REFLECT

How are the two students' correct responses for $7 + n = 6 + 9$ different? How would each of these students solve this open sentence?

$$534 + 175 = 174 + \square$$

The first student will do the computation and will perhaps have difficulty finding the correct addend. The second student will reason that 174 is one less than 175, so the number in the box must be one more than 534.

FORMATIVE Assessment Notes As students work on these types of tasks, you can **interview** them one-on-one (though you may not get to everyone). Listen for whether they are using relational thinking. If they are not, ask, "Can you find the answer without actually doing any computation?" This questioning helps nudge students toward relational thinking and helps you decide what instructional steps are next. ■

In order to nurture relational thinking and the meaning of the equal sign, continue to explore an increasingly complex series of true/false and open sentences with your class. Select challenging equations designed to elicit relational thinking rather than computation. Use large numbers that make computation difficult (not impossible) as a means to push them toward relational thinking. Here are some examples:

True/False

$674 - 389 = 664 - 379$	$5 \times 84 = 10 \times 42$
$37 + 54 = 38 + 53$	$64 \div 14 = 32 \div 28$

Open Sentences

$73 + 56 = 71 + \square$	$126 - 37 = \square - 40$
$20 \times 48 = n \times 24$	$68 + 58 = 57 + 69 + n$

PAUSE and REFLECT

One of the true/false statements is false. Can you explain why using relational thinking? ●

Molina and Ambrose (2006), researchers in mathematics education, used the true/false and open-ended prompts with third graders, none of whom understood the equal sign in a relational way at the start of their study. For example, all 13 students answered $8 + 4 = \_\_\_ + 5$ with 12. They found that asking students to write their own open sentences was particularly effective in helping students solidify their understanding of the equal sign. The following forms were provided as guidance (though students could use multiplication and division if they wanted):

$$\_\_ + \_\_ = \_\_ + \_\_$$
$$\_\_ - \_\_ = \_\_ - \_\_$$
$$\_\_ + \_\_ = \_\_ - \_\_$$

Activity 14.8

Writing True/False Sentences

After students have had ample time to discuss true/false and open sentences, ask them to make up their own true/false sentences that they can use to challenge their classmates. Each student should write a collection of three or four sentences with at least one true and at least one false sentence. Encourage them to include one "tricky" one. Their equations can be either traded with a partner or used in full-class discussions.

Repeat for open sentence problems.

When students write their own true/false sentences, they often are intrigued with the idea of using large numbers and lots of numbers in their sentences. This encourages them to create sentences involving relational thinking.

The Meaning of Variables

Expressions or equations with variables are a means for expressing patterns and generalizations. When students can work with expressions involving variables without even thinking about the specific number or numbers that the letters may stand for, they have achieved what Kaput (1999) refers to as manipulation of opaque formalisms—they can look at and work with the symbols themselves. Variables can be used as unique unknown values or as quantities that vary. Unfortunately, students often think of the former (the variable is a place holder for one exact number) and not the latter (that a variable could represent multiple, even infinite values). Experiences in elementary and middle school should focus on building meaning for both, as delineated in the next two sections.

Variables Used as Unknown Values. In the open sentence explorations, the $\square$ is a precursor of a variable used in this way. Even in the primary grades, you can use letters instead of a box in your open sentences, such as an n standing for the missing number. Rather than ask students what number goes in the box, ask what number the letter could be to make the sentence true. Initial work with finding the value of the variable that makes the sentence true—solving the equation—should rely on relational thinking (reasoning). Starting in sixth grade, students will begin developing specific techniques for solving equations when relational thinking or reasoning is insufficient.

Consider the following open sentence: $\Box + \Box + 7 = \Box + 17$ (or, equivalently, $n + n + 7 = n + 17$). A convention for the use of multiple variables is that the same symbol or letter in an equation stands for the same number every place it occurs. Carpenter and colleagues (2003) refer to it as "the mathematician's rule." In the preceding example, the $\Box$ or n must be 10.

Many story problems involve a situation in which the variable is a specific unknown, as in the following basic example:

Gary ate 5 strawberries and Jeremy ate some, too. The container of 12 was gone! How many did Jeremy eat?

Although students can solve this problem without using algebra, they can begin to learn about variables by expressing it in symbols: $5 + s = 12$. These problems can grow in difficulty over time.

With a context, students can even explore three variables, each one standing for an unknown value, as in the following activity (adapted from Maida, 2004).

Activity 14.9

Balls, Balls, Balls

Students will figure out the weight of three balls, given the following three facts:

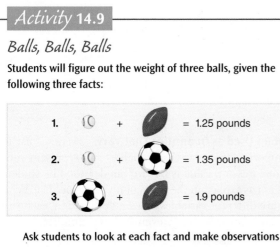

Ask students to look at each fact and make observations that help them generate other facts. For example, they might notice that the soccer ball weighs 0.1 pound more than the football. Write this in the same fashion as the other statements. Continue until these discoveries lead to finding the weight of each ball. Encourage students to use models to represent and explore the problem.

One possible approach: Add equations 1 and 2:

Then take away the football and soccer ball, reducing the weight by 1.9 pounds (based on the information in equation 3), and you have two baseballs that weigh 0.7 pound. Divide by 2, so one baseball is 0.35 pound.

You may recognize this last example as a system of equations presented in a visual. In this format, it can be solved by reasoning, making it accessible to upper elementary and middle school students.

Another concrete way to work on systems of equations is through balancing. Notice the work done in building the concept of the equal sign is now applied to understanding and solving for variables.

In Figure 14.6, a series of examples shows problems in which each shape on the scales represents a different value. Two or more scales for a single problem provide different information about the shapes or variables.

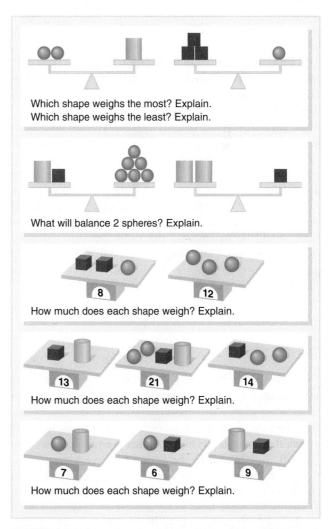

FIGURE 14.6 Examples of problems with multiple variables and multiple scales.

Problems of this type can be adjusted in difficulty for students across the grades.

When no numbers are involved, as in the top two examples of Figure 14.6, students can find combinations of numbers for the shapes that make all of the balances balance. If an arbitrary value is given to one of the shapes, then values for the other shapes can be found accordingly.

In the second example, if the sphere equals 2, then the cylinder must be 4 and the cube equals 8. If a different value is given to the sphere, the other shapes will change accordingly.

 PAUSE and REFLECT

How would you solve the last problem in Figure 14.6? Can you solve it in two ways? ●

You (and your students) can tell whether you are correct by checking your solutions against the original scale positions. Believe it or not, you have just solved a series of simultaneous equations, a skill generally found in a formal algebra class.

Simplifying Expressions and Equations. Simplifying equations and solving for x have often been meaningless tasks, and students are unsure of why they need to know what x is or what steps to do and in what order. This must be taught in a more meaningful way! Knowing how to simplify and recognizing equivalent expressions are essential skills to working algebraically. Students are often confused about what the instruction "simplify" means. (Imagine an ELL wondering why the teacher is asking students to change the original problem to an easier one.) The border tiles problem in Activity 14.1 provides a nice context for thinking about simplifying and equivalence. Recall that there are five (or more) possibilities for finding the number of border tiles. If the pool had different dimensions than 8×8, those equations would be structurally the same, but with different values. If the square has a side (of the pool) of p, the p:

$(p+2) + (p+2) + p + p$	$10 + 10 + 8 + 8$
$2 \times (p+2) + (2 \times p)$	$(2 \times 10) + (2 \times 8)$
$4 \times (p+1)$	4×9
$(p+2)^2 - p^2$	$100 - 64$

Students can also use the TABLE function on their graphing calculator to enter these expressions and then graph them to see whether they are equivalent (Brown & Mehilos, 2010).

Students need an understanding of how to apply mathematical properties and how to preserve equivalence as they simplify. In addition to the ideas that have been offered (open sentences, true/false sentences, etc.), one way to do this is to have students look at simplifications that have errors and explain how to fix the errors (Hawes, 2007). Figure 14.7 shows how three students have corrected the simplification of $(2x + 1) - (x + 6)$.

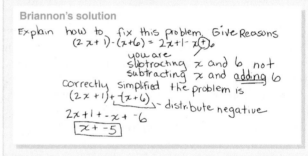

FIGURE 14.7 Three students provide different explanations for fixing the flawed simplification given.

Source: Figure 3 from Hawes, K. (2007). "Using Error Analysis to Teach Equation Solving." *Mathematics Teaching in the Middle School, 12*(5), p. 241. Reprinted with permission. Copyright © 2007 by the National Council of Teachers of Mathematics. All rights reserved.

Variables Used as Quantities That Vary. As noted earlier, the important concept that variables can represent more than one missing value is not well understood by students and is not as explicit in the curriculum as it should be. When there are different variables in a single equation, each variable can represent many, even infinite, numbers. In the middle school grades, variables that are used to describe functions (e.g., $y = 3x - 5$) are variables that have many possible numeric solutions. This shift from the variable as an unknown representing a single value to a variable representing a relationship can be difficult for students. This difficulty can be alleviated if students have experiences with variables that vary early in the elementary curriculum.

The number line is an important model in developing the concept of variable. As illustrated in Figure 14.8, finding where variables are in relation to numbers and in relation to other variables helps to build meaning (Darley, 2009).

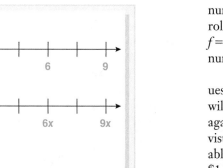

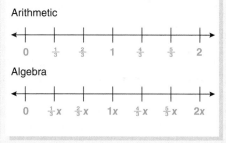

FIGURE 14.8 Using the number line to build meaning of variables.

When students are looking at the number line, ask questions like, "What is the value of x? Can it be any number? If we don't know what x is, how can we place $\frac{1}{3}x$ on the number line?" "Think of a value that x cannot be." Notice that in the two examples, x really can be any positive value. However, if you place $x + 2$ on the number line somewhere close to x, the space between these is 2, and you can use this distance as a "measure" to approximate the size of x. Because students use the number line extensively with whole numbers, it is a good way to bridge to algebra. Having an algebra number line posted in your room, where you can trade out what values are posted, can provide many opportunities to think about the relative value of variables.

Context is important in developing meaning for variables. As Blanton (2008) suggests, use slight alterations to a number task. Instead of "If Marta has $6 and Nathan has $3 more than Marta, how much more money does Nathan have?" use "If Marta has some money in her bank and Nathan has $3 more than Marta, how much more money does Nathan have?" (p. 18). Notice that in the new version, there is no student computation—the students just find ways to represent a varying situation. Primary grade students can list possible ways in a table and eventually represent the answer as *Marta + 3 = Nathan*.

The following example is appropriate for middle school students as a context for exploring variables that vary:

If you have $10 to spend on $2 granola bars and $1 fruit rolls, how many ways can you spend all your money without receiving change?

To begin exploring this problem, students record data in a table and look for patterns. They notice that when the number of granola bars changes by 1, the number of fruit rolls changes by 2. Symbolically, this representation is $2g + f = \$10$, where g is the number of granola bars and f is the number of fruit rolls.

It is also important to include decimal and fraction values in the exploration of variables. As any algebra teacher will confirm, students struggle most with these numbers— again resulting from the lack of earlier, more concrete, and visual experiences mixing fractions and decimals with variables. For example, if you were buying $1.75 pencils and $1.25 erasers from the school store and spent all of $35.00, how many combinations are possible? What equation represents this situation?

For students with special needs or students who might be unfamiliar with using a table, it is helpful to adapt the table to include both how many and how much, as shown in Figure 14.9. Reinforce the two elements with each entry (how many and how much). In addition, calculators can facilitate exploration of possible solutions. To increase the challenge for advanced or gifted students, ask students to graph the values or to consider more complex situations.

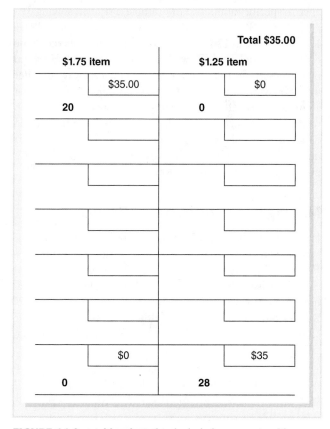

FIGURE 14.9 A table adapted to include how many and how much for each row.

Source: Hyde, A., George, K., Mynard, S., Hull, C., Watson, S., and Watson, P. (2006). "Creating Multiple Representations in Algebra: All Chocolate, No Change," *Mathematics Teaching in the Middle School, 11*(6), 262–268. Reprinted with permission. Copyright © 2006 by the National Council of Teachers of Mathematics. All rights reserved.

Once students have the expression in symbols (in this case, $1.75x + 1.25y = 35.00$), ask students to tie each number and variable back to the context. In this way, students can make sense of what is normally poorly understood and really develop a strong foundation for the algebra they will study in secondary school.

Making Structure in the Number System Explicit

Chapter 9 discusses several properties for each operation (see pp. 157–158 and pp. 164–165) that are important for students as they learn basic facts and computational strategies. For example, understanding the commutative property for both addition and multiplication reduces substantially the number of facts to be memorized. These and other properties are likely to be used informally as students develop relational thinking as they learn about computation.

A next step is to have students examine these properties explicitly and express them in general terms without reference to specific numbers. For example, a student solving $394 + 176 = N + 394$ may say that N must be 176 because $394 + 176$ is the same as $176 + 394$. This is a specific instance of the commutative property. To articulate this (and other structural properties of our number system) in a general way, in either words or symbols (e.g., $a + b = b + a$), noting that it is true for all numbers, is what making structure explicit means. When made explicit and understood, these structures not only add to students' tools for computation but also enrich their understanding of the number system, providing a base for even higher levels of abstraction (Carpenter et al., 2003).

Making Conjectures about Properties

Properties of the number system can be built into students' explorations with true/false and open number sentences. For example, third-grade students will generally agree that the true/false sentence $41 \times 3 = 3 \times 41$ is true. The pivotal question, however, asks, "Is this true for any numbers?" Some students will argue that although it seems to be true all of the time, there may be two numbers that haven't been tried yet for which it does not work.

The following problem and discussion were focused on investigating the distributive and associative properties, not on whether the equation was true or false (from Baek, 2008, pp. 151–152):

MS. J: [*Pointing at* $(2 \times 8) + (2 \times 8) = 16 + 16$ *on the board*] Is it true or false?

LEJUAN: True, because two 8s is 16 and two 8s is 16.

LIZETT: $(2 \times 8) + (2 \times 8)$ is 32 and $16 + 16$ is 32.

CARLOS: 8 plus 8 is 16, so 2 times 8 is 16, and 8 plus 8 is 16, and 2 times 8 is 16.

MS. J: [*Writing* $4 \times 8 = (2 \times 8) + (2 \times 8)$ *on the board*] True or false?

STUDENTS: True.

MS. J: What does the 2 stand for?

REGGIE: Two boxes of eight.

MS. J: So how many boxes are there?

STUDENTS: Four.

MS. J: [*Writing* $32 + 16 = (4 \times 8) + (a \times 8)$ *on the board*] What is a?

MICHAEL: Two, because 4 times 8 is 32, and 2 times 8 is 16.

MS. J: [*Writing* $(4 \times 8) + (2 \times 8) = (b \times 8)$ *on the board*] What is b?

STUDENTS: 6

Notice how the teacher is developing the aspects of these properties in a conceptual manner—focusing on exemplars to guide students to generalize, rather than asking students to memorize the properties as they appear in Table 14.1 as their first experience, which can be a meaningless, rote activity.

You can follow specific examples, such as those used in the preceding dialogue, by asking students to try to state the idea in words without using a specific number. For example, when multiplying a number by a second number, you can split the first number and multiply each part by the second number, and you will get the same answer. If a generalization is not clear or entirely correct, have students discuss the wording until all agree that they understand. Write this verbal statement of the property on the board. Call it a conjecture and explain that it is not necessarily a true statement just because we think that it is true. Until someone either proves it or finds a counterexample—an instance for which the conjecture is not true—it remains a conjecture.

Students can make conjectures about properties as early as first or second grade. By third or fourth grade, students should be challenged to translate verbal conjectures into open sentences. For example, in learning the multiplication facts, students might conjecture that if they have a product, like 5×8, they can split up the 5 however they like and multiply its parts by 8 and then put it back together (e.g., $(3 \times 8) + (2 \times 8) = 5 \times 8$). They may justify this with the following rectangles:

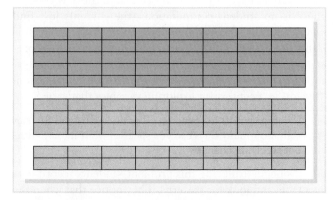

TABLE 14.1

PROPERTIES OF THE NUMBER SYSTEM	
Number Sentence	Student Statement of Conjecture
Addition and Subtraction	
$a + 0 = a$	When you add zero to a number, you get the same number you started with.
$a - 0 = a$	When you subtract zero from a number, you get the number you started with.
$a - a = 0$	When you subtract a number from itself, you get zero.
$a + b = b + a$	You can add numbers in one order and then change the order and you will get the same number.
Multiplication and Division	
$a \times 1 = a$	When you multiply a number by 1, you get the number you started with.
$a \div 1 = a$	When you divide a number by 1, you get the number you started with.
$a \div a = 1, a \neq 0$	When you divide a number that is not zero by itself, you get 1.
$a \times 0 = 0$	When you multiply a number times zero, you get zero.
$0 \div a = 0, a \neq 0$	When you divide zero by any number except zero, you get zero.
$a \times b = b \times a$	When you multiply two numbers, you can do it in any order and you will get the same number.
Conjectures Derived from Basic Properties	
$a + b - b = a$	When you add a number to another number and then subtract the number that you added, you will get the number that you started with.
$a \times b \div b = a, b \neq 0$	When you multiply a number by another number that is not zero and then divide by the same number, you get the number you started with.

Source: Adapted from Carpenter, T. P., Franke, M. L., and Levi, L. (2003). *Thinking Mathematically: Integrating Arithmetic and Algebra in Elementary School.* Portsmouth, NH: Heinemann.

Challenge students to think about this idea *in general.* For example, the preceding conjecture can be written described in words (at first) and even as symbols: $a \times b = (c \times b) + (d \times b)$, where $c + d = a$. Be sure students can connect the examples to general ideas and the general ideas back to examples. This is the distributive property, and it is perhaps the most important central idea in elementary school arithmetic (Goldenberg, Mark, & Cuoco, 2010). As an example of this, one strategy that has been successful in learning facts is using doubles (see Chapter 10). So if you have any product, you can solve it by using doubles,

applying the distributive property. For example, 6×8 can be expressed as $(2 + 2 + 2) \times 8 = 16 + 16 + 16 = 48$.

Activity **14.10**

Conjecture Creation

STUDENTS with SPECIAL NEEDS

ENGLISH LANGUAGE LEARNERS

Once students have seen conjectures developed out of your explorations of true/false sentences, challenge students to make up conjectures on their own—creating statements about numbers and computation that they believe are always true. It is best to have them state the conjectures in words. The full class should discuss the various conjectures, asking for clarity or challenging conjectures with counterexamples. Conjectures can be added to a class list written in words and in symbols. All students, but particularly ELLs, may struggle with correct and precise terms. You can "revoice" their ideas using appropriate phrases to help them learn to communicate mathematically, but be careful to not make this the focus—the focus should be on the ideas presented. Importantly, students with disabilities are helped by the presentation and discussion of counterexamples. They cement their thinking by focusing on the critical elements.

Table 14.1 lists basic properties of the number system for which students may make conjectures. Students are almost certainly not going to know or understand why division by zero is not possible. You will need to provide contexts for them to make sense of this property.

Justifying Conjectures

Attempting to justify or prove that a conjecture is true is a significant form of algebraic reasoning and is at the heart of what it means to do mathematics (Ball & Bass, 2003; Carpenter et al., 2003; Schifter, 1999; Schifter, Monk, Russell, & Bastable, 2007). Researchers and recent standards (*Curriculum Focal Points* and *Common Core State Standards*) argue that making conjectures and justifying that they are always true are central to reasoning and sense making. Therefore, when conjectures are made in class, rather than respond with an answer, ask, "Do you think that is always true? How can we find out?" Students need to reason through ideas based on their own thinking rather than simply relying on the word of others.

The most common form of justification, especially in elementary school, is the use of examples. Students will try lots of specific numbers in a conjecture. "See? It works for any number you try." They may try very large numbers as substitutes for "any" number, and they may try rational fractions or decimal values. Proof by example will hopefully lead to someone asking, "How do we know there aren't some numbers that it doesn't work for?"

Second, students may reason with physical materials or illustrations to show the reasoning behind the conjecture (like the rectangles showing the distributive property). What moves this beyond "proof by example" is an explanation such as "It would work this way no matter what the numbers are."

Odd and Even Relationships

An interesting category of number structures is that of odd and even numbers. Students will often observe that the sum of two even numbers is even, that the sum of two odd numbers is even, or that the sum of an even and an odd number is always odd. Similar statements can be made about multiplication.

 PAUSE and REFLECT

Before reading on, think for a moment about how you might prove that the sum of two odd numbers is always even. ●

Students will provide a variety of interesting proofs of odd/even conjectures. As with other conjectures, they typically begin by testing lots of numbers. But here it is a bit easier to imagine that there just might be two numbers "out there" that don't work. Then students turn to the definition or a model that illustrates the definition. For example, if a number is odd and you split it in two, there will be a leftover. If you do this with the second odd number, it will have a leftover also. So if you put these two numbers together, the two leftovers will go together so there won't be a leftover in the sum. Students frequently use models such as bars of connecting cubes to strengthen their arguments.

Activity 14.11 explores properties of odd and even numbers using the calculator.

Activity 14.11

Broken Calculator: Can You Fix It?

Explore these two challenges; afterward ask students for conjectures they might make about odds and evens.

1. If you cannot use any of the even keys (0, 2, 4, 6, 8), can you create an even number in the calculator display? If so, how?
2. If you cannot use any of the odd keys (1, 3, 5, 7, 9), can you create an odd number in the calculator display? If so, how?

 # Study of Patterns and Functions

Patterns are found in all areas of mathematics. Learning to search for patterns and how to describe, translate, and extend them is part of doing mathematics and thinking algebraically.

Repeating Patterns

The concept of a repeating pattern and how a pattern is extended or continued can be introduced to the full class in several ways. One possibility is to draw simple shape patterns on the board and extend them in a class discussion. Oral patterns can be recited. For example, "do, mi, mi, do, mi, mi" is a simple singing pattern. Body movements such as waving the arm up, down, and sideways can make patterns: up, side, side, down, up, side, side, down.

 There are numerous sites on the Web for exploring repeating patterns. For example, NLVM has several resources that support the **TECHNOLOGY** exploration of repeating (and growing) patterns, including Attribute Trains, Block Patterns, Color Patterns, Pattern Blocks, and Space Blocks (http://nlvm .usu.edu). For very young children, see PBS Kids (www.pbs .org/teachers/connect/resources/7661/preview).

Children's books often have patterns in repeating rhymes, words, or phrases. For example, a very long repeating pattern can be found in *If You Give a Mouse a Cookie* (Numeroff, 1985), in which each event eventually leads back to giving a mouse a cookie, with the implication that the sequence would be repeated.

Identifying and Extending Repeating Patterns. An important concept in working with repeating patterns is for students to identify the core of the pattern (Warren & Cooper, 2008). The *core* of a repeating pattern is the string of elements that repeats. It is important to use knowledge of the core to extend the pattern.

Activity 14.12

Making Repeating Patterns

STUDENTS with SPECIAL NEEDS

Students can work independently or in groups of two or three to extend patterns made from simple materials: buttons, colored blocks, connecting cubes, toothpicks, geometric shapes—items you can gather easily. For each set of materials, draw or build two or three complete repetitions so the core is obvious. The students' task is to extend it. Figure 14.10 illustrates one possible pattern for various manipulatives. Students can build their own patterns and then trade with a partner and work on identifying the core and extending the new pattern. In follow-up discussions, students should be able to identify the patterns as AB, ABC, ABBA, or whatever core is represented. For students with disabilities, you may need to ask them to say the name of the color or shape as they look at the pattern to help support their identifying the regularity.

Predicting with Repeating Patterns: Linking to Divisibility.

Prediction is an important part of algebraic thinking. The next activity focuses on prediction as a forerunner to looking at functions.

Activity 14.13

Predict Down the Line

For most repeating patterns, the elements of the pattern can be numbered 1, 2, 3, and so on (often referred to as *terms* or *steps*). Provide students with a pattern to extend. Before students begin to extend the pattern, have them predict exactly what elements will be in, say, the fifteenth step. Students should be required to provide a reason for their prediction, preferably in writing.

Notice in an ABC pattern that the third, sixth, ninth, and twelfth terms are the C element. Students can use their developing concepts of multiplication and division to predict what the eighteenth and twenty-fifth term would be. Ask them to predict what the element will be in the hundredth term. Since 100 ÷ 3 = 33 remainder 1, it would be the A element in the pattern. If predicting the hundredth element, students will not be able to check the prediction by extending the pattern. Justification focuses on students' knowledge of multiplication and division (Warren & Cooper, 2008).

Using Real Contexts. Though geometric patterns and motions like clapping are good ways to introduce patterns, it is important that students see patterns in the world around them. The seasons, days of the week, and months of the year are just a beginning. Students might be able to think of AB patterns in their daily activities—for example, "to school, home from school" or "set table before eating, clear table after eating."

Predicting has some interesting real-world contexts appropriate for upper elementary and middle school students. One context is the Olympics (Bay-Williams & Martinie, 2004). The Summer Olympics are held in 2012, 2016, and every four years after that. The Winter Olympics are held in 2014, 2018, and so on. This pattern can be described several ways: ABAC pattern (No Olympics, Summer Olympics, No

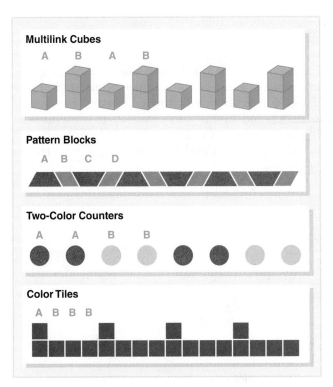

FIGURE 14.10 Examples of repeating patterns using manipulatives.

Olympics, Winter Olympics); AB (Olympics, No Olympics); or ABCD (the four-year rotation of the core pattern).

A second context is the names of hurricanes, which are in an ABCDEF repeating pattern by letter in the alphabet. For each letter of the alphabet, there are six names that are used cyclically (except that a name is retired when a major hurricane, like Katrina, has been given that name) (Fernandez & Schoen, 2008). The six A names, for example, will be used as follows: Alberto in 2012, Andrea in 2013, Arthur in 2014, Ana in 2015, Alex in 2016, and Arlene in 2017. (Good for you if you noticed the AB pattern regarding gender!) Assuming the names don't get retired, students can answer questions such as these:

- In what year will the first hurricane of that year be named Alex?
- What will the first hurricane's name be in the year 2020? 2050?
- Can you describe in words how to figure out the name of a hurricane, given the year?

Growing Patterns

Beginning in the primary grades and extending through the middle school years, students can explore patterns that involve a progression from step to step. In technical terms, these are called *sequences;* we will simply call them *growing patterns.* With these patterns, students not only extend or identify the core but also look for a generalization or an algebraic relationship that will tell them what the pattern will be at any point along the way (e.g., the *n*th term). Figure 14.11(a) is a growing pattern in which design 1 requires three triangles, design 2 requires six triangles, and so on—so we can say that the number of triangles needed is a function of which design it is (which happens to be the function triangles = 3 × design number).

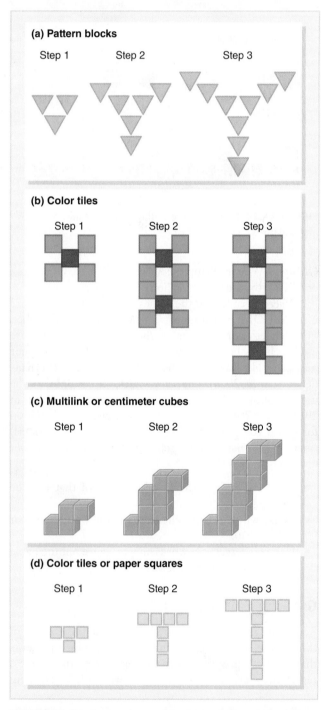

(a) Pattern blocks

Step 1   Step 2   Step 3

(b) Color tiles

Step 1   Step 2   Step 3

(c) Multilink or centimeter cubes

Step 1   Step 2   Step 3

(d) Color tiles or paper squares

Step 1   Step 2   Step 3

FIGURE 14.11 Geometric growing patterns using manipulatives.

The border tiles problem discussed earlier in this chapter can be adapted to be a growing pattern by simply having a swimming pool that is 5 × 5, then 6 × 6, then 7 × 7, and so on. The Magic Pot scenario from Chapter 3 can also become a growing pattern. In this example from children's literature (*Two of Everything*), the Haktaks' magic pot doubled anything that fell into it. Second graders can determine a rule for explaining how much will come out (output) if you tell them how much will go in (input) (McNamara, 2010).

Geometric patterns make good exemplars because the pattern is easy to see and because students can manipulate the objects. Figure 14.11 shows one growing pattern for four different manipulatives, though the possibilities are endless.

The questions in Activity 14.14, mapped to the pattern in Figure 14.11(a), are good ones to help students begin to think about the functional relationship.

ENGLISH LANGUAGE LEARNERS

Activity 14.14

Predict How Many

Working in pairs or small groups, have students explore a pattern and respond to these questions:

- **Complete a table that shows the number of triangles for each step.**

Step Number (Term)	1	2	3	4	5…	10	20
Number of Triangles (Element)							

- **How many triangles are needed for step 10? Step 20? Step 100? Explain your reasoning.**
- **Write a rule (in words and/or symbols) that gives the total number of pieces to build any step number (*n*).**

Keep in mind that ELLs need clarification on the specialized meanings of *step* and *table* because these words mean something else outside of mathematics.

Analyzing growing patterns should include the developmental progression of reasoning by looking at the visuals, then reasoning about the numerical relationships, and then extending to a larger (or *n*th) case (Friel & Markworth, 2009). Students' experiences with growing patterns should start with fairly straightforward patterns (such as in Figure 14.11) and continue with patterns that are somewhat more complicated (see Figure 14.12).

It is also important to include fractions and decimals in working with growing patterns. In 2003, the National Assessment of Educational Progress (NAEP) tested 13-year-olds on the item in Figure 14.13. Only 27 percent of students answered correctly (Lambdin & Lynch, 2005).

When looking for relationships, some students will focus on the table and others will focus on the physical pattern. It is important for students to see both forms. So if a relationship is found in a table, challenge students to see how that plays out in the physical version and vice versa.

Recursive Patterns and Formulas. For most students, it is easier to see the patterns from one step to the next. In Figure 14.12(a), the number in each step can be determined from the previous step by adding successive even numbers. The description that tells how a pattern changes from step to step is known as a *recursive* pattern (Bezuszka & Kenney, 2008; Blanton, 2008).

The recursive pattern can also be observed in the physical pattern and in the table. In Figure 14.12(b), notice that in each step, the previous step has been outlined. That lets you examine the amount added and see how it creates the pattern of adding on even numbers.

Explicit Formulas. To find the table entry for the hundredth step, the only way a recursive formula can help is to find all of the prior 99 entries in the table. If a formula can be discovered that connects the number of the step to the number of objects at that step, any table entry can be determined without building or calculating all of the previous entries. A rule that determines the number of elements in a step from the step number is called the *explicit formula*. The *Common Core State Standards* refer to an explicit formula as the "mathematical model."

Can you determine an explicit formula for the pattern in Figure 14.12? How did you find the formula?

There is no single best method for finding this relationship between step number (term) and element, and students are likely to see it different ways. Some will analyze the table and notice that if they multiply the step number by the next step number, they will get the number of circles for that step. This leads to the explicit formula or mathematical model: $d = n(n + 1)$, where d is number of dots and n is the step number.

Some will examine the physical pattern to see what is changing. In Figure 14.12(c), a square array is outlined for each step. Each successive square is one larger on a side. In this example, the side of each square is the same as the step number. The column to the right of each square is also the step number. At this point, writing a numeric expression for each step number can help students write the explicit formula. For example, the first four steps in Figure 14.12 are $1^2 + 1$, $2^2 + 2$, $3^2 + 3$, and $4^2 + 4$. The explicit formula is therefore $d = n^2 + n$.

Regardless of whether students use the table or the manipulatives, they will likely be able to describe the explicit formula in words before they can write it in symbols. If the goal of your lesson is to find the "rule," then stopping with the verbal formula is appropriate. In this case, you may have some students who are ready to represent the formula in symbols, and they can be challenged to do so as a form of differentiating your instruction. If your instructional goal is to write formulas using symbols, then ask students to first write the formula, or rule, in words and then think about

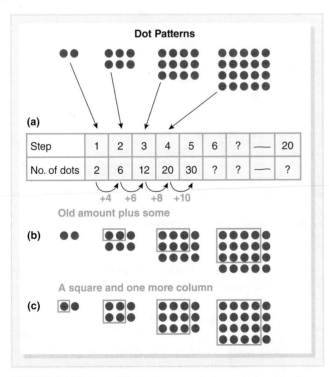

FIGURE 14.12 Two different ways to analyze relationships in the "dot pattern."

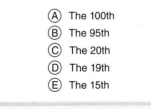

Term	1	2	3	4
Fraction	$\frac{1}{2}$	$\frac{2}{3}$	$\frac{3}{4}$	$\frac{4}{5}$

If the list of fractions above continues in the same pattern, which term will be equal to 0.95?

Ⓐ The 100th
Ⓑ The 95th
Ⓒ The 20th
Ⓓ The 19th
Ⓔ The 15th

FIGURE 14.13 NAEP item for 13-year-olds.

Source: Lambdin, D. V., & Lynch, K. (2005). "Examining Mathematics Tasks from the National Assessment of Educational Progress." *Mathematics Teaching in the Middle School, 10*(6), 314–318. Reprinted with permission. Copyright © 2005 by the National Council of Teachers of Mathematics. All rights reserved.

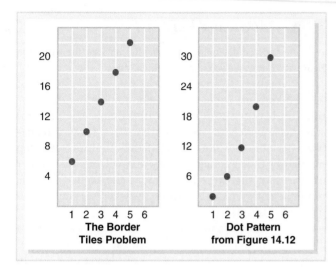

FIGURE 14.14 Graphs of two growing patterns.

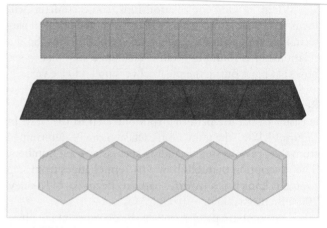

FIGURE 14.15 For each string of pattern blocks, can you determine the perimeter for *N* pattern blocks?

how they can translate that statement to numbers and symbols.

Graphs of Functions.   So far, growing patterns have been represented by (1) the physical materials or drawings, (2) a table, (3) words, and (4) symbols. A graph adds a fifth representation. Figure 14.14 shows the graph for the border tiles problem and the dot pattern from Figure 14.12. Notice that the first is a straight-line (linear) relationship and the other is a curved line that would make half of a parabola if the points were joined. The horizontal axis is always used for the step numbers, the independent variable.

Graphs provide visuals that allow students to readily see relationships between growing patterns. Consider strings of a single color of pattern blocks (Figure 14.15) and the corresponding perimeters. This is a good pattern to explore in the same manner as the border tiles problem, beginning with a string of seven or eight blocks and finding equivalent ways to determine the perimeter without counting.

Having graphs of three related growing patterns offers the opportunity to compare and connect the graphs to the patterns and to the tables (see Figure 14.16). For example, ask students to discuss how to get from one coordinate to the next (up six, over one), and then ask how that information can be found in the table. Second, identify a particular point on the graph and ask what it tells about the pattern.

See if you can answer the following questions, which you can also pose to students to help them understand the graphical representation of the function:

- How does each graph represent each of the string patterns?
- Why is there not a line connecting the dots?
- Why is one line steeper than the others?

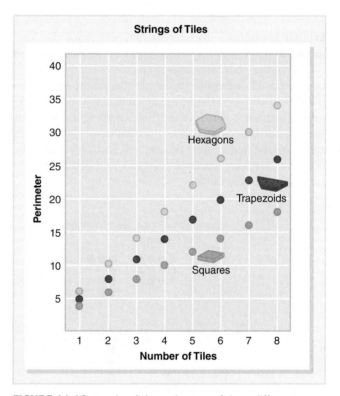

FIGURE 14.16 Graphs of the perimeters of three different pattern-block strings. The lines are not drawn because, for this context, there are no solutions between the points.

- What does this particular point on the graph match up to in the model and the table?

FORMATIVE Assessment Notes   Being able to make connections across representations is important for understanding functions, and the only way to know if a student is seeing the connections is to ask. In a **diagnostic interview,** ask questions like the ones just listed and look to see whether students

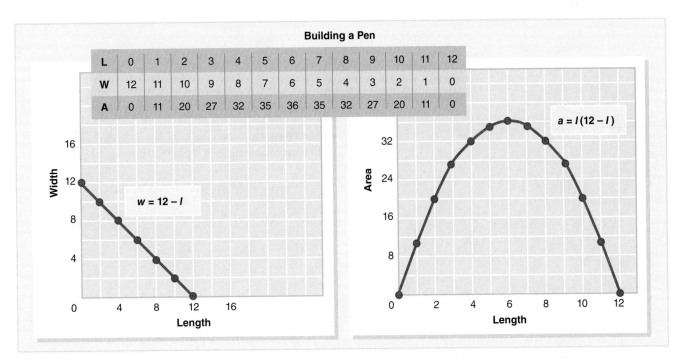

Building a Pen

L	0	1	2	3	4	5	6	7	8	9	10	11	12
W	12	11	10	9	8	7	6	5	4	3	2	1	0
A	0	11	20	27	32	35	36	35	32	27	20	11	0

$w = 12 - l$

$a = l(12 - l)$

FIGURE 14.17 The width and area graphs as functions of the length of a rectangle with a fixed perimeter of 24 units.

are able to link the graph to the context, to the table, and to the formula. ■

Not all functions have straight-line graphs. For example, in building a rectangular pen with 24 yards of fence, if you increase the width, you will decrease the length. The area will vary accordingly (see Figure 14.17). An explicit formula for the width is $w = 12 - l$ (l is the length), which decreases at a constant rate, therefore looking like a line. By contrast, the explicit formula for area of the pen is $a = l(12 - l)$—it rises in a curve, reaches a maximum value, and then goes back down.

Graphs and Contexts. It is important for students to be able to interpret and construct graphs related to real situations, including sketching the shape of a graph without using any specific data, equations, or numbers or looking at the shape of the graph and telling a possible story about the data. The advantage of activities such as these is the focus on how a graph can express the relationships involved.

Activity **14.15**

Sketch a Graph

STUDENTS with SPECIAL NEEDS

Sketch a graph for each of these situations. No numbers or formulas are to be used.

a. The temperature of a frozen dinner from 30 minutes before it is removed from the freezer until it is removed from the microwave and placed on the table. (Consider time 0 to be the moment the dinner is removed from the freezer.)

ENGLISH LANGUAGE LEARNERS

b. The value of a 1970 Volkswagen Beetle from the time it was purchased to the present. (It was kept by a loving owner and is in top condition.)
c. The level of water in the bathtub from the time you begin to fill it to the time it is completely empty after your bath.
d. Profit in terms of number of items sold.
e. The height of a thrown baseball from when it is released to the time it hits the ground.
f. The speed of the same baseball.

Be sure that the contexts you pick are familiar to ELLs (and other students). If they are not, change the context or illustrate what it is. For students with disabilities, you may want to have them match graphs (see Figure 14.18) first before drawing graphs.

PAUSE and REFLECT

Stop for a moment and sketch graphs for each situation in the last activity. ●

It is fun to have students sketch their graphs without identifying which situation they selected (no labels on the graphs). Then display them on a projector. Let students examine the graph to see whether they can determine the matching situation. Figure 14.18 contains six graphs that match the six situations described in the "Sketch a Graph" activity. Can you match these graphs with the six situations?

Graphs and Rate of Change. Notice that the analysis of the graphs focuses on how the graphs increase or decrease

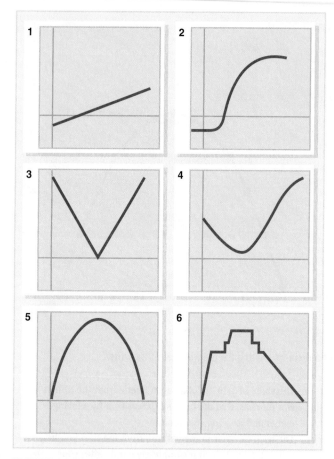

FIGURE 14.18 Match each graph with the situations described in Activity 14.15. Talk about what change is happening in each case.

and how rapidly or gradually. A graph is a picture of the rate of change of one variable in terms of the other. Essentially, graphs can only have one of the seven characteristics shown in Figure 14.19 or some combination of these. These types of change will be seen in the following activity.

Activity 14.16

Vases and Volume Graphs

Figure 14.20 shows six vases and six graphs. Assume that the vases are filled at a constant rate. Because of their shapes, the height of the liquid in the vases will increase either more slowly or more quickly as the vase gets wider or narrower. Match the graphs with the vases.

Find some vases or glasses that have different shapes. Give each group or pair one vase to use for the activity. Fill a small container (e.g., medicine cup or test tube) with water, and empty it into the vase, recording in a table the number of containers used and the height of the water after pouring. After each group gathers the data, they graph their findings. Graphs are collected, and then students try to match the graph with the vase.

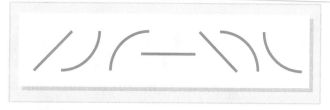

FIGURE 14.19 Seven ways that graphs can change. A graph often has combinations of these characteristics.

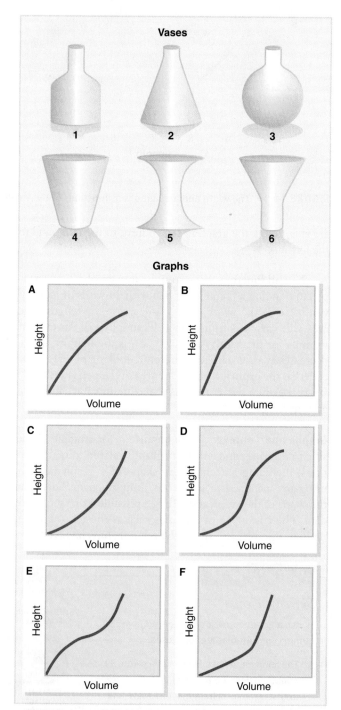

FIGURE 14.20 Assuming vases are filled at a constant rate, match the graphs with the vases.

Linear Functions

Linear functions are a subset of growing patterns and functions, which can be linear or nonlinear. But because linearity is a major focus of middle school mathematics, and because growing patterns in elementary school tend to be linear situations, it appears here in its own section. *Curriculum Focal Points* and the *Common Core State Standards* emphasize the importance of linear functions across the middle grades, with a strong focus on linearity in seventh and eighth grade (CCSSO, 2010; NCTM, 2006). Linear functions are defined quite simply as functions that grow in a linear or constant manner. In a graph, this can be easily established by seeing that the plotted points lie on one line.

Linearity can be established by looking at other representations. If you make a table for the hexagon pattern blocks perimeter problem in Figure 14.15, you will notice that the recursive pattern is + 4 each time. The rate of change from one step to the next is constant (+ 4). You can always look at the recursive relationship to determine whether the function is growing at a constant rate and therefore linear.

In the equation, linearity can be determined by looking at the part of the expression that changes. Compare the two formulas from the rectangular pen problem. One was $w = 12 - l$, and the other was $a = l(12 - l)$ or $a = 12l - l^2$. Notice that in the first case, the change is related to l and each time l changes by 1, w changes by the same amount—a constant rate of change, as in linear situations. In the area formula, when l changes by the same amount, the area changes in varying amounts. This is not linear but is a quadratic situation. Figure 14.17 shows these graphs.

Rate of Change and Slope. An analysis of change is one of the four components in the NCTM algebra standard (NCTM, 2000). Rate, whether constant or varying, is a type of change often associated with how fast something is traveling. Rate is an excellent context for exploring linearity, because constant rates can be seen in a wide range of contexts, such as the geometric model of the pattern block perimeters or the rate of growth of a plant. Other rate contexts in numerical situations include hourly wages, gas mileage, profit, and even the cost of an item, such as a bus ticket.

TECHNOLOGY The NCTM e-Examples from *Principles and Standards for School Mathematics* include two applets that target rate, making the connection between a real-world context and graphs. In Applet 5.2, students can adjust the speed, direction, and starting position of two runners. As the runners are set in motion, a time–distance graph is generated dynamically for each runner (see Figure 14.21). In Applet 6.2, phone call rates are explored.

These explorations of rate develop the concept of *slope*, which is the numeric value that describes the rate of change for a linear function. For example, one of the explicit

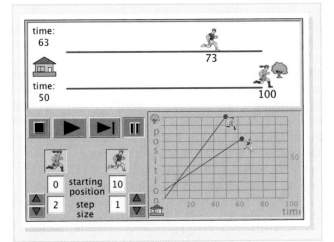

FIGURE 14.21 Applet 5.2, "Understanding Distance, Speed, and Time Relationships Using Simulation Software."

formulas for the hexagon perimeter growing pattern is $y = 4x + 2$. Note that the rate of change is 4 because the perimeter increases by 4 with each new piece. All linear functions can be written in this form: $y = mx + b$ (including $y = mx$ when $b = 0$).

Conceptually, then, slope signifies how much y increases when x increases by 1. If a line contains the points $(2, 4)$ and $(3, -5)$, then you can see that as x increases by 1, y decreases by 9. So the rate of change, or slope, is -9. For the points $(4, 3)$ and $(7, 9)$, you can see that when x increases by 3, y increases by 6. Therefore, an increase of 1 in x results in a change of 2 in y (dividing 6 by 3). After further exploration and experiences, your students will begin to generalize that you can find the rate of change or slope by finding the difference in the y values and dividing by the difference in the x values. Exploring this first through reasoning is important for students if they are to be able to make sense of and remember the formula for calculating slope when given two points.

Zero Slope and No Slope. Understanding these two easily confused slopes requires contexts, such as walking rates. Consider this story:

> You walk for 10 minutes at a rate of 1 mile per hour, stop for 3 minutes to watch a nest of baby birds, then walk for 5 more minutes at 2 miles per hour.

What will the graph look like for the 3 minutes when you stop? What is your rate when you stop? In fact, your rate is 0, and since you are at the same distance for 3 minutes, the graph will be a horizontal line.

Let's say that you see a graph of a walking story that includes a vertical line—a line with no slope. What would this mean? That there is no change in the x variable—that you traveled a distance with no time passing! Now, even if you were a world record sprinter, this would be impossible. Remember that rate is based on a change of 1 in the x value.

Proportional and Nonproportional Situations. Linear functions can be proportional or nonproportional. The rate example just described is *proportional*. The distance you walk is proportional to how much time you have walked. As another example, as a babysitter your pay is proportional to the hours you work. But it is not the case that the perimeter of the hexagon pattern blocks is proportional to the number of blocks used. Although you have a constant increase factor of 4, there are 2 extra units of perimeter (the heights of the two end blocks). Said another way, you cannot get from the input (number of blocks) to the perimeter by multiplying by a factor as you can in proportional situations.

All proportional situations, then, are equations in the form $y = mx$. Notice that the graphs of all proportional situations are straight lines that pass through the origin. Students will find that the slope of these lines is also the rate of change between the two variables.

Figure 14.11(d) demonstrates a nonproportional situation—for every square added to the horizontal portion, it grows by two squares in the vertical. Proportional representations are shown in Figure 14.11(a)–(c). However, if you slightly altered the patterns, they would become nonproportional. For example, in pattern (a), if the triangles were added on to only two of the prongs, like an upside-down V, then you could no longer find the nth term simply by multiplying the step number by a factor.

In nonproportional situations, one value is constant. In the pattern blocks perimeter problem, for example, no matter which step number you are on, there are 2 units (one on each end) that must be added. Similarly, the border tiles problem always has exactly 4 corners. If you were walking but had a head start of 50 meters, or if you were selling something and had an initial expense, those values are constants in the linear function that make it not proportional. The constant value, or initial value, can be found across representations beyond the contexts described here. In the table, it is the value when $x = 0$, which means it is the point where the graph crosses the y-axis.

Nonproportional situations are more challenging for students to generalize. Students want to use the recursive value (e.g., $+4$) as the factor ($\times 4$). Students often make the common error of using the table to find the tenth step and doubling it to find the twentieth step, which works in proportional situations but not in nonproportional situations. Mathematics education researchers have found that having students analyze errors such as these is essential in helping support their learning of mathematics concepts (Lannin, Arbaugh, Barker, & Townsend, 2006).

Parallel, Same, and Perpendicular Lines. Students in eighth grade should be comparing different linear situations

that result in parallel, same, or perpendicular lines (CCSSO, 2010). Using a context is necessary to build understanding. Consider the situation of Larry and Mary, each earning $30 a week for the summer months. Mary starts the summer $50 in debt and Larry already has $20. When will Mary and Larry have the same amount of money? In week 3, how much more money does Larry have? How much more does he have in week 7? In any week, what is the difference in their wealth? The rates for Larry's and Mary's earnings are the same—and the graphs would therefore go up at the same rate; that is, the slopes would be the same. We can tell that the graphs of $y = 30x + 20$ (Larry's money) and $y = 30x - 50$ (Mary's money) are parallel without even making the graphs because the rates (or slopes) are the same.

Can you think of what change in Larry's and Mary's situations might result in the same line? Remember the equivalent expressions discussed earlier? As illustrated on the calculator, they will have the same line. Slopes can also tell us when two lines are perpendicular, but it is less obvious. A little bit of analysis using similar triangles will show that for perpendicular lines, the slope of one is the negative reciprocal of the other.

Mathematical Modeling

Modeling with mathematics is one of the eight Standards for Mathematical Practices in the *Common Core State Standards*.

> Modeling links classroom mathematics and statistics to everyday life, work, and decision-making. Modeling is the process of choosing and using appropriate mathematics and statistics to analyze empirical situations, to understand them better, and to improve decisions. (CCSSO, 2010, p. 72)

Mathematical models are not to be confused with visual models such as manipulatives or drawings for building a pattern (such as pattern blocks or centimeter grid paper).

We have already seen many examples of mathematical models (e.g., the model or equation for describing the number of tiles required for a pool of various dimensions). How is modeling used to make decisions? Take the example of selling widgets marked up at some percentage over wholesale. Once a formula is derived for a given price and markup, it can be used to determine the profit at different sales levels. Furthermore, it is relatively easy to make adjustments in the price and markup percentage, allowing for further predictions. That is, the equation, or mathematical model, allows us to find values that cannot be observed in the real phenomenon.

Consider creating a mathematical model to describe the depreciation of a car at 20 percent each year. Determining the mathematical model might progress in the following steps: If the car loses 20 percent of its value in 1 year, then it must be worth 80 percent of its value after a year. So after 1 year, the $15,000 car is worth $15,000 × 0.8. In the second year, it loses 20 percent of that value, so it will be worth only 80 percent of its value at the end of year one, which was $15,000 × 0.8. The value at the end of year 2 would be ($15,000 × 0.8) × 0.8, and so on. At the end of y years, the value of the car can be expressed in this equation: value = $15,000 × 0.8^y$. Figure 14.22 shows the graph and the table of values on a graphing calculator.

The next activity provides another context appropriate for developing a mathematical model.

Activity 14.17

How Many Gallons Left?

ENGLISH LANGUAGE LEARNERS

A car gets 23 miles per gallon of gas. It has a gas tank that holds 20 gallons. Suppose that you were on a trip and had filled the tank at the outset. Determine a mathematical model that describes the gallons left for given miles traveled. ELLs may be more familiar with kilometers per liter, which means you can adapt the problem to those units or connect the meaning of the two.

Notice that the word *rule* or *explicit formula* could replace "mathematical model." In this case, one possible equation is $g = 20 - \frac{m}{23}$. Use the model, or equation, to make predictions. For example, "How can you tell from the model how much gas will be left after driving 300 miles?" "How many miles can you drive before the gas tank has only 3 gallons left?" Two more engaging contexts are provided in Figure 14.23.

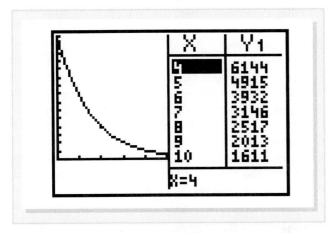

FIGURE 14.22 The graph and table for $V = 15,000 × 0.8^y$. Years, the independent variable, are shown under X, and value, the dependent variable, is shown under Y₁.

---

1. Pleasant's Hardware buys widgets for $4.17 each, marks them up 35 percent over wholesale, and sells them at that price. Create a mathematical model to relate widgets sold (w) to profit (p). The manager asks you to determine the formula if she were to put the widgets on sale for 25 percent off. What is your formula or mathematical model for the sale, comparing widgets sold (s) to profit (p)?
2. In Arches National Park in Moab, Utah, there are sandstone cliffs. A green coating of color, called cyanobacteria, covers some of the sandstone. Bacteria grow by splitting into two (or doubling) in a certain time period. If the sandstone started with 50 bacteria, create a mathematical model for describing the growth of cyanobacteria on the sandstone.

FIGURE 14.23 Mathematical modeling problems for further exploration.

Source: Adapted from Buerman, M. (2007). "The Algebra of the Arches." *Mathematics Teaching in the Middle School, 12*(7), 360–365.

Sometimes a model is provided, and the important task is for students to understand and use the formula. Consider the following pumping water problem and related equation from the Michigan Algebra Project (Herbel-Eisenmann & Phillips, 2005):

Suppose you turn a pump on and let it run to empty the water out of a pool. The amount of water in the pool (W, measured in gallons) at any time (T, measured in hours) is given by the following equation: $W = {}^{-}350\,(T - 4)$.

⏸ *PAUSE and REFLECT*

What questions might you pose to middle school students to help them make sense of this equation? Try to think of three. ●

In the Michigan Algebra Project, students were asked to solve several problems and explain how the equation was used to find the answer. Those questions and one student's responses are provided in Figure 14.24.

◆ Teaching Considerations

It is important to emphasize some key considerations that will lead students to feel empowered to do algebra. Some of these ideas have already been embedded in the previous discussions of algebraic concepts.

Emphasize Appropriate Algebra Vocabulary

A large part of understanding mathematics is the ability to communicate mathematically, so it is important to use appropriate terminology in teaching algebra. This is far more

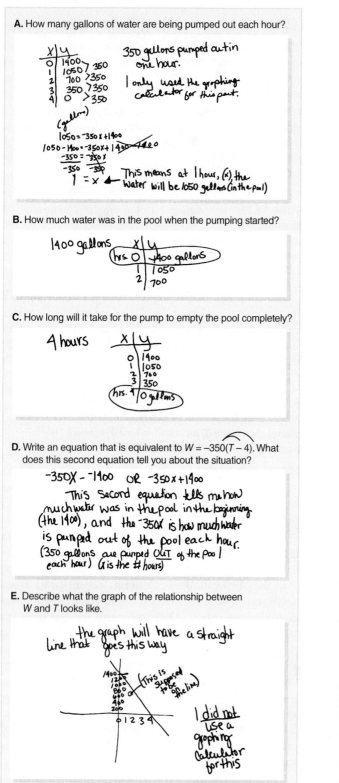

A. How many gallons of water are being pumped out each hour?

B. How much water was in the pool when the pumping started?

C. How long will it take for the pump to empty the pool completely?

D. Write an equation that is equivalent to $W = -350(T - 4)$. What does this second equation tell you about the situation?

E. Describe what the graph of the relationship between W and T looks like.

FIGURE 14.24 One student's explanations of questions regarding what a mathematical model means.

Source: Figure 3 from Herbel-Eisenmann, B. A., & Philips, E. D. (2005). "Using Student Work to Develop Teachers' Knowledge of Algebra." *Mathematics Teaching in the Middle School, 11*(2), p. 65. Reprinted with permission. Copyright © 2005 by the National Council of Teachers of Mathematics. All rights reserved.

than a vocabulary list; it is the practice of consistently using, and having students use, appropriate words for situations. Creating word walls and keeping a journal of terms are ways to help all students but especially English language learners (ELLs). Having graphs, models, or tables to illustrate the words is essential. Here we briefly share some important concepts that involve new or unfamiliar vocabulary.

Independent and Dependent Variables. Although the meanings of *independent variables* and *dependent variables* are implied by the words themselves, the concepts can still be challenging for students. The independent variable is the step number, or the input, or whatever value is being used to find another value. For example, in the case of the strings of pattern blocks, the independent variable is the number of blocks in the string. The dependent variable is the number of objects needed, the output, or whatever value you get from using the independent variable. In the pattern blocks problem, it is the perimeter. You can say that the perimeter of the block structure depends on the number of blocks. Recall the two equations and graphs representing a pen of 24 meters in Figure 14.17. In this case, the length has been selected as the independent variable (though it could have as easily been the width), and the dependent variable is width. What are the independent and dependent variables for the problem in Figure 14.24?

Discrete and Continuous. Even in elementary school, the discussion of functions, especially graphical representations, should include a discussion of whether the points plotted on the graph should be connected or not and why. In the pattern blocks perimeter problem, the answer is no; the points should not be connected because you will only use whole-number values for counting blocks. When isolated or selected values are the only ones appropriate for a context, the function is *discrete*. If all values along a line or curve are solutions to the function, then it is *continuous*. The problem in Activity 14.17 is an example of continuous because there can be any value for miles and gallons (within the appropriate domain).

Domain and Range. The *domain* of a function comprises the possible values for the independent variable. If it is discrete, like the pattern blocks perimeter problem, it may include all positive whole numbers. For the 24-meter rectangular pen, the domain is all real numbers between 0 and 12.

The *range* is the corresponding possible values for the dependent variable. In the pattern blocks perimeter problem, the range is the positive whole numbers. In the rectangular pen, the range for the length is the same as the domain—real numbers between 0 and 12.

Connecting Representations

Functions can be represented in any of five ways: (1) the pattern itself, which we can refer to as the *context*, (2) the table, (3) the verbal description, (4) the symbolic equation, and

(5) the graph. You have seen these representations throughout the chapter. Each representation is a way of looking at the function, each providing a different way of looking at or thinking about patterns and functions, leading to deeper understanding and more flexible reasoning. Students *must* understand the connections between these representations; it is not enough to just teach each one separately (Hackbarth & Wilsman, 2008). That means the teacher must pose tasks and questions that help students make these connections. To illustrate this point, we will use the context of a hot dog vendor.

> Brian is trying to make money to help pay for college by selling hot dogs from a cart at the coliseum during music performances and ball games. He pays the cart owner $35 per night for the use of the cart. He sells hot dogs for $1.25 each. His costs for the hot dogs, condiments, napkins, and other paper products are about 60 cents per hot dog on average. The profit from a single hot dog is, therefore, 65 cents.

Context. This function begins with a context: selling hot dogs and the resulting profit. We are interested in Brian's profit in terms of the number of hot dogs sold. The more hot dogs Brian sells, the more profit he will make. Brian does not begin to make a profit immediately because he must pay the $35 rent on the vending cart.

The context helps students make sense of what changes (number of hot dogs sold) and what stays the same ($35 rental), which can help them figure out the explicit formula. The context supports students' conceptual understanding of the other more abstract representations and illustrates that algebra is a tool for describing real-world phenomena. The context alone, though, is not sufficient—carefully selected prompts to connect the context to other representations are needed to support students' algebraic thinking (Earnest & Balti, 2008).

Table. Brian might sit down and calculate some possible figures based on anticipated hot dog sales. This will give him some idea of how many hot dogs he must sell to break even and what his profit might be for an evening. A table of values might resemble Table 14.2.

TABLE 14.2

NUMBER OF HOT DOGS SOLD (INDEPENDENT VARIABLE) AND THE PROFIT (DEPENDENT VARIABLE)	
Hot Dogs Sold	**Profit**
0	−35.00
50	−2.50
100	30.00
150	62.50

The number of hot dogs shown in the table is purely a matter of choice. One could calculate the profit for 10,000 hot dogs (10,000 × 0.65 − 35), even though it is not reasonable in this context. The table provides a concise way to look at the recursive pattern and the explicit pattern. The recursive pattern can lead to seeing what changes, whether it changes at a constant rate, and how that can help find the explicit formula.

Verbal Description. In the hot dog vendor situation, Brian's profit depends on the number of hot dogs that are sold. In functional language, we can say, "Profit is a function of the number of hot dogs sold." The phrase "is a function of" expresses the dependent relationship. The profit depends on—is a function of—the hot dog sales. The verbal description of the explicit formula for the hot dog stand might be stated by students as, "You multiply each hot dog sold by $0.65; then you subtract the $35 for the cart."

The verbal explanation of the explicit formula provides a connection from the context to the symbolic representation. Students may struggle with using variables, and being able to first describe the formula in words is an important stepping-stone for being able to use symbols (Lannin, Townsend, Armer, Green, & Schneider, 2008).

Symbols. Suppose that we pick a letter—say, h—to represent the number of hot dogs Brian sells. Brian's profit is represented by the equation $p = (0.65 \times h) - 35$, where p is the letter selected to stand for profit. This equation defines a mathematical relationship (i.e., is the mathematical model) between two values, profit and hot dogs.

By expressing a function as an equation, it is possible to find the profit for any number of hot dogs. Conversely, if Brian wants to make $100, he can figure out how many hot dogs he needs to sell. It is particularly important that students explain what each number and each variable represent.

The equation can be entered into a graphing calculator, and the calculator can do the calculations to produce a table and a graph. This enables students to make connections across representations without having to do the work of creating each one by hand.

Graphs. In Figure 14.25, four different values of hot dog sales are plotted on a graph. The horizontal axis represents the number of hot dogs sold, and the vertical axis, the profit. As we have already established, the profit goes up as the sales go up. There is, in this situation, a linear pattern to the six values. In this context, it means that the profit is going up at a constant rate, namely, at 0.65 per hot dog.

The graphical representation allows one to see "at a glance" that the relationship between sales and profits is linear—a straight line—and is increasing. It also can be used to get quick approximate answers to questions about Brian's profits, such as, "How many hot dogs must be sold to break even?" "How many will need to be sold to earn $100?" (It looks to be near 210 or 215.) The context gives

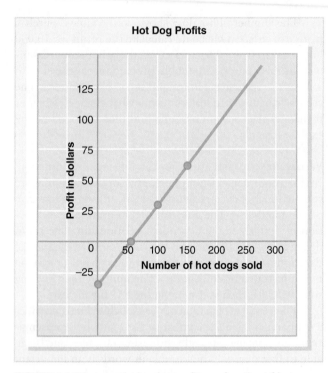

FIGURE 14.25 A graph showing profit as a function of hot dogs sold.

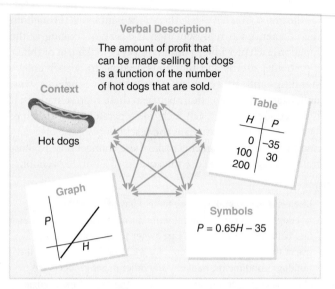

FIGURE 14.26 Five different representations of a function. For any given function, students should see that all these representations are connected and illustrate the same relationship.

meaning to the graph, and the graph adds understanding to the context.

TECHNOLOGY Graphs are easily created using technology. For example, GraphSketch (http://graphsketch .com) works very much like a graphing calculator and is great for graphing functions of any type.

The graph indicates the pattern in the data, but in terms of the context, all values may not make sense. In this case, it would not make sense to extend the line to the left of the vertical axis, as this would mean selling a negative quantity of hot dogs. Nor is it reasonable to talk about sales of millions of hot dogs—unless he starts a national chain!

Figure 14.26 illustrates the five representations of functions for the hot dog context. The most important idea is to see that, for a given function, each of these representations illustrates the same relationship and that students should be able to explain connections across representations in a conceptual manner. This is a different experience from one you might have experienced in an Algebra I class when you received instructions such as, "Graph the function, given the equation," along with a set of steps to follow. The difference lies in whether the movement among representations is about following a rote procedure or about making sense of the function. The latter is your goal as a teacher.

FORMATIVE Assessment Notes The hot dog problem is a good **performance assessment.** A good question (which can be adapted to any task) is, "Can you show me where in the table, the graph, and the equation you can find the profit for selling 225 hot dogs?" ■

The seventh-grade *Connected Mathematics Project* (CMP II) has an entire unit titled "Variables and Patterns," in which students explore and use different representations of functions in real contexts. The lesson shown here focuses on tables and graphs.

Algebraic Thinking Across the Curriculum

One reason the phrase "algebraic thinking" is used instead of "algebra" is that the practice of looking for patterns, regularity, and generalizations goes beyond curriculum topics that are usually categorized as algebra topics. You have already experienced some of this integration—looking at geometric growing patterns and working with perimeter and area. In fact, in *Curriculum Focal Points* (NCTM, 2006), many of the focal points that include algebra connect it to other content areas. In the sections that follow, the emphasis of the content moves to the other content areas, with algebraic thinking used as a tool for discovery. This brief discussion will be developed more fully in later chapters.

Measurement and Algebra. Soares, Blanton, and Kaput (2006) describe how to "algebraify" the elementary curriculum. One measurement example they give uses the children's book *Spaghetti and Meatballs for All* (by Burns and Tilley), looking at the increasing number of chairs needed given the growing number of tables.

Geometric formulas relate various dimensions, areas, and volumes of shapes. Each of these formulas involves at least one functional relationship. Consider any familiar formula for measuring a geometric shape. For example, the circumference of a circle is $c = 2\pi r$. The radius is the independent variable, and circumference is the dependent

CONNECTED MATHEMATICS

Grade 7, *Variables and Patterns*
Investigation 3: Analyzing Graphs and Tables

Context

Much of this unit is built on the context of a group of students who take a multiday bike trip from Philadelphia to Williamsburg, Virginia, and who then decide to set up a bike tour business of their own. Students explore a variety of functional relationships between time, distance, speed, expenses, profits, and so on. When data are plotted as discrete points, students consider what the graph might look like between points. For example, what interpretations could be given to each of these five graphs showing speed change from 0 to 15 mph in the first 10 minutes of a trip?

Task Description

In this investigation, the students in the unit began gathering data in preparation for setting up their tour business. As their first task, they sought data from two different bike rental companies as shown here, given by one company in the form of a table and by the other in the form of a graph. The task is interesting because of the way in which students experience firsthand the value of one representation over another, depending on the need of the situation. In this unit, students are frequently asked whether a graph or a table is the better source of information.

In the tasks that follow, students are given a table of data showing results of a phone poll that asked at which price former tour riders would take a bike tour. Students must find the best way to graph this data. After a price for a bike tour is established, graphs for estimated profits are created with corresponding questions about profits depending on different numbers of customers.

The investigations use no formulas at this point. The subsequent investigation is called "Patterns and Rules"

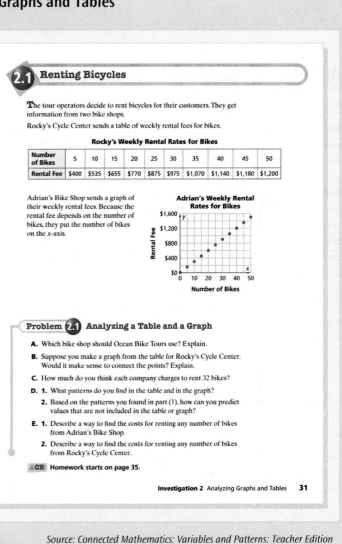

2.1 Renting Bicycles

The tour operators decide to rent bicycles for their customers. They get information from two bike shops.

Rocky's Cycle Center sends a table of weekly rental fees for bikes.

Rocky's Weekly Rental Rates for Bikes

Number of Bikes	5	10	15	20	25	30	35	40	45	50
Rental Fee	$400	$535	$655	$770	$875	$975	$1,070	$1,140	$1,180	$1,200

Adrian's Bike Shop sends a graph of their weekly rental fees. Because the rental fee depends on the number of bikes, they put the number of bikes on the *x*-axis.

Adrian's Weekly Rental Rates for Bikes

Problem 2.1 Analyzing a Table and a Graph

A. Which bike shop should Ocean Bike Tours use? Explain.

B. Suppose you make a graph from the table for Rocky's Cycle Center. Would it make sense to connect the points? Explain.

C. How much do you think each company charges to rent 32 bikes?

D. 1. What patterns do you find in the table and in the graph?

    2. Based on the patterns you found in part (1), how can you predict values that are not included in the table or graph?

E. 1. Describe a way to find the costs for renting any number of bikes from Adrian's Bike Shop.

    2. Describe a way to find the costs for renting any number of bikes from Rocky's Cycle Center.

ACE Homework starts on page 35.

Investigation 2 Analyzing Graphs and Tables   **31**

Source: Connected Mathematics: Variables and Patterns: Teacher Edition by Glenda Lappan, James T. Fey, William M. Fitzgerald, Susan N. Friel, & Elizabeth Difanis Phillips. Copyright © 2006 by Michigan State University. Used by permission of Pearson Education, Inc. All rights reserved.

and begins the exploration of connecting equations or rules to the representations of graphs and tables. In the final investigation, students use graphing calculators to explore how graphs change in appearance when the rules that produce the graphs change.

variable. We can say that the circumference is dependent on the radius. Even nonlinear formulas like volume of a cone ($V = \frac{1}{3}\pi r^2 h$) are functions. Here the volume is a function of both the height of the cone and the radius. If the radius is held constant, the volume is a function of the height. Similarly, for a fixed height, the volume is a function of the radius.

The following activity explores how the volume of a box varies as a result of changing the dimensions.

Activity 14.18

Designing the Largest Box

Begin with a rectangular sheet of card stock. From each corner, cut out a square, making them all the same size. Fold up the four resulting flaps, and tape them together to form an open box. The volume of the box will vary depending on the size of the squares (see Figure 14.27). Write a formula that gives the volume of the box as a function of the size of the cutout squares. Use the function to determine what size the squares should be to create the box with the largest volume. Alternatively, make origami boxes using squares with various side lengths, and see what the relationship is between the side length and the volume of the open box. (See DeYoung, 2009, for instructions for making the box and more on this idea. Or look on the Web.)

Data and Algebra. Data can be obtained from sports records, census reports, the business section of the newspaper, and many other sources. Students can gather data such as measurement examples or survey data. The Internet has many sites where data can be found.

Experiments. There are many experiments that students can explore to see the functional relationships, if any, that exist between two variables. Gathering real data is an excellent way to engage a range of learners and to see how mathematics can be used to describe phenomena.

Data should be collected and then represented in a table or on a graph. The goal is to determine whether there is a relationship between the independent and dependent variables, and if so, whether it is linear or nonlinear, as in the following engaging experiments:

- How long would it take for 100 students standing in a row to complete a wave similar to those seen at football games? Experiment with different numbers of students from 5 to 25. Can the relationship predict how many students it would take for a given wave time?
- How far will a Matchbox car roll off of a ramp, based on the height the ramp is raised?
- How is the flight time of a paper airplane affected by the number of paper clips attached to the nose of the plane?
- What is the relationship between the number of dominoes in a row and the time required for them to fall over? (Use multiples of 100 dominoes.)
- Make wadded newspaper balls using different numbers of sheets of newspaper, using a constant number of rubber bands to help hold the paper in a ball. What is the relationship between the number of sheets and the distance the ball can be thrown?
- What is the relationship between the number of drops of colored water dropped on a paper towel and the diameter of the spot? Is the relationship different for different brands of towels?
- How much weight can a toothpick bridge hold? Lay toothpicks in a bunch to span a 2-inch gap between two boards. From the toothpicks, hang a bag or other container into which weights can be added until the toothpicks break. Begin with only one toothpick (McCoy, 1997).

Experiments like these are fun and accessible to a wide range of learners. They also provide an opportunity for students to engage in experimental design. Students need practice in identifying independent and dependent variables, controlling experiments for other variables, measuring and recording results, and analyzing data. This is a perfect blend of mathematics and science.

Scatter Plots. Often in the real world, phenomena are observed that seem to suggest a functional relationship but not necessarily as clean or as well defined as some of the situations we have described so far. Certainly this would be true of the experiments described above. However, even in the case of measuring the increasing height of a stack of identical books as each new one is added—a linear situation—measuring error will lead to values that are not exactly on a line. In such cases, the data are generally plotted on a graph to produce a scatter plot of points.

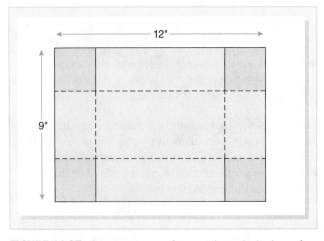

FIGURE 14.27 If squares are cut from a 9-by-12-inch piece of cardboard so that the four flaps can be folded up, what size squares should be cut so that the volume of the box is the largest possible?

TECHNOLOGY Two very good scatter plot generators can be found at NLVM's website (http://nlvm.usu.edu/en/nav/frames_asid_144_g_4_t_5.html?open=activities) and the NCES Kids' Zone (http://nces.ed.gov/nceskids/createagraph).

A visual inspection of the graphed data may suggest what kind of relationship, if any, exists. If a linear relationship seems to exist, for example, students can approximate a line of best fit or use graphing technology to do a linear regression to find the line of best fit (along with the equation).

They can use the regression function on the graphing calculator to support their identification of the line of best fit.

Not all scatter plots will show a straight-line relationship. Suppose students were figuring out the time it takes for balloons of various diameters to deflate (another engaging experiment). A parabolic or cubic function might better approximate the shape of the data. Graphing calculators can also find best-fitting curves. These brief examples of algebraic thinking in other content areas illustrate the importance of algebra in the K–8 curriculum.

RESOURCES *for Chapter 14*

LITERATURE CONNECTIONS

The following three examples of books are excellent beginnings for patterns and chart building.

Anno's Magic Seeds *Anno, 1994*

Anno's Magic Seeds has several patterns. A wise man gives Jack two magic seeds, one to eat and one to plant. The planted seed will produce two new seeds by the following year. Several years later, Jack decides to plant both seeds. Then he has a family and starts to sell seeds. At each stage of the story, there is an opportunity to develop a chart and extend the current pattern into the future. Austin and Thompson (1997) describe how they used the story to develop patterns and charts with sixth- and seventh-grade students.

Bats on Parade *Appelt and Sweet, 1999*

This story includes the pattern of bats walking 1 by 1, then 2 by 2, and so on. One activity from this enjoyable book is determining the growing pattern of the number of bats given the array length (e.g., 3 for the 3 × 3 array). There is also one mouse, so this can be included in a second investigation. Activity sheets for these two ideas and two others can be found in Roy and Beckmann (2007).

Two of Everything: A Chinese Folktale *Hong, 1993*

The magic pot discovered by Mr. Haktak doubles whatever goes in it, including his wife! This idea of input–output is great for exploring functions from grades 2 through 8; just vary the rule of the magic pot from doubling to something more complex. For more details and handouts, see Suh (2007a) and Wickett and colleagues (2002).

RECOMMENDED READINGS

Articles

Kalman, R. (2008). Teaching algebra without algebra. *Mathematics Teaching in the Middle School, 13*(6), 334–339.

This article includes three contexts that involve simplifying equations and effectively explains how to make sense of the simplification by relating it to the context. An excellent resource for helping middle school students make sense of symbols and properties.

Molina, M., & Ambrose, R. C. (2006). Fostering relational thinking while negotiating the meaning of the equals sign. *Teaching Children Mathematics, 13*(2), 111–117.
This article helps us understand the conceptual considerations related to the equal sign while simultaneously illustrating the value of errors and misconceptions in creating opportunities for learning.

Books

Blanton, M. L. (2008). *Algebra and the elementary classroom.* Portsmouth, NH: Heinemann.
This is an excellent book for teachers at all levels—full of rich problems to use and helpful for expanding the reader's understanding of algebra. Great for book study.

Carpenter, T. P., Franke, M. L., & Levi, L. (2003). *Thinking mathematically: Integrating arithmetic and algebra in elementary school.* Portsmouth, NH: Heinemann.
This book is a detailed look at helping students in the primary grades develop the thinking and create the generalizations of algebra. The included CD shows classroom-based examples of the ideas discussed.

Fosnot, C. T., & Jacob, B. (2010). *Young mathematicians at work: Constructing algebra.* Portsmouth, NH: Heinemann.
Like the other books in the series, this is a gem. Full of classroom vignettes and examples that will enrich your understanding of how algebra can support arithmetic (and vice versa).

Greenes, C. E., & Rubenstein, R. (Eds.). (2008). *Algebra and algebraic thinking in school mathematics.* NCTM 70th Yearbook. Reston, VA: NCTM.
NCTM yearbooks are always excellent collections of articles for grades pre-K–12. This one is no exception, offering a wealth of thought-provoking and helpful articles about algebraic thinking.

ONLINE RESOURCES

Algebra Balance Scales and Algebra Balance Scales—Negative
http://nlvm.usu.edu/en/nav/category_g_3_t_2.html

Linear equations are presented on a two-pan balance with variables on each side. The user can solve equations in the same way as described in the text. The negative version uses balloons for negative values and negative variables.

GraphSketch
http://graphsketch.com

Works very much like a graphing calculator for graphing functions of any type. A good demonstration tool for making graphs of equations.

Inside Mathematics (Noyce Foundation)
www.insidemathematics.org

This site contains sample lessons, formative assessment items, rubrics, student work samples, and professional development resources that support various levels and topics such as patterns, functions, and algebraic properties and relationships.

Interactive Linear Equation Activity (Math Warehouse)
www.mathwarehouse.com/algebra/linear_equation/linear-equation-interactive-activity.php

An interactive tool for the graph and equation of a line using the form $y = mx + b$. The user can adjust the slope of the line to see the equation and graph change dynamically.

Learning Math: Patterns, Functions, and Algebra (Annenberg Media)
www.learner.org/resources/series140.html

A video-based course for K–8 teachers that explores finding, describing, and using patterns; using functions to make predictions; understanding linearity and proportional reasoning; understanding nonlinear functions; and understanding and exploring algebraic structure.

Modeling Middle School Mathematics (MMMMath)
http://mmmproject.org/algebra.htm

See video clips, such as "V-Patterns, Beans, Hair & Nails," where students explore patterns with formulas and represent solutions using linear equations, graphs, and tables.

Patterns, Relations, and Functions (eNLVM module)
http://enlvm.usu.edu/ma/nav/toc.jsp?sid=__
shared&cid=emready@patterns_relations_
functions&bb=course

This site encourages students to generate rules and functions for geometric sequences, describing relationships between the pattern number and characteristics of the pattern.

Function Machine Applets
Function Machine (NLVM)
http://nlvm.usu.edu/en/nav/frames_asid_191_g_3_t_1.html

Function Machine (Math Playground)
www.mathplayground.com/functionmachine.html

This is a nice Flash-based tool.

Stop That Creature! (PBS Kids' CyberChase)
http://pbskids.org/cyberchase/games/functions/functions.html

In this fun game, figure out the rule that runs the game to shut down the creature-cloning machine.

Linear Function Machine (Shodor Project Interactivate)
www.shodor.org/interactivate/activities/LinearFunctMachine

REFLECTIONS *on Chapter 14*

WRITING TO LEARN

1. Kaput argues that generalization and symbolization are essential aspects of algebraic thinking. Describe what you think each is and give an example.
2. What misconceptions or limited conceptions do students have regarding the equal sign? What causes these misconceptions, and how can instruction clear these up?
3. What misconceptions or limited conceptions do students have regarding variables? What causes these misconceptions, and how can instruction clear these up?
4. Explain how to solve the equation $4x + 3 = x + 12$ on the pan balance.
5. What is a recursive relationship? An explicit relationship? Where in a table for a growing pattern would you look for the recursive relationship? What would it mean in terms of the pattern itself?

FOR DISCUSSION AND EXPLORATION

1. The idea of having students make connections from arithmetic to algebra is the emphasis of algebra in the elementary grades. What examples can you find in the curriculum for taking an algorithm and presenting it in a way that it becomes a process for generalizing a rule? Read the *Common Core State Standards*, focusing on the Standards for Mathematical Practices and the "Operations and Algebraic Thinking" items. What do you notice about the connections between arithmetic and algebra?
2. Explore some of the online applets that focus on functions (see "Online Resources" at the end of the chapter). For each applet, consider what the technology provides in terms of learning opportunities. How might the technology be used to support the diversity in a classroom?

MyEducationLab™

Go to the MyEducationLab (www.myeducationlab.com) for Math Methods and familiarize yourself with the content. Much of the site content is organized topically. The topics include all of the following to support your learning in the course:

- Learning outcomes for important mathematics methods course topics aligned with the national standards
- Assignments and Activities, tied to these learning outcomes and standards, that can help you more deeply understand course content
- Building Teaching Skills and Dispositions learning units that allow you to apply and practice your understanding of the core mathematics content and teaching skills

Your instructor has a correlation guide that aligns the exercises on the topical portion of the site with your book's chapters.

On MyEducationLab you will also find book-specific resources including Blackline Masters, Expanded Lesson Activities, and Artifact Analysis Activities.

Field Experience Guide
C O N N E C T I O N S

The focus on multiple representations and meaning in this chapter is a good match for FEG Field Experiences 3.2 and 4.1. Number patterns and geometric growing patterns are the focus of FEG Expanded Lessons 9.12 and 9.13 and FEG Activity 10.8. Expanded Lesson 9.14 for grades 6–8 connects graphs to stories—an excellent integration of writing. In addition, Activities 10.9 ("Compensation Decision") and 10.10 ("Solving the Mystery") are excellent applications of algebra. Balanced Assessment Item 11.2 ("Grocery Store") is an excellent assessment for finding a rule to describe a growing pattern.

Chapter 15

Developing Fraction Concepts

F ractions have always represented a considerable challenge for students, even into the middle grades. NAEP test results have consistently shown that students have a weak understanding of fraction concepts (Sowder & Wearne, 2006; Wearne & Kouba, 2000). This lack of understanding is then translated into difficulties with fraction computation, decimal and percent concepts, and the use of fractions in other content areas, particularly algebra (Brown & Quinn, 2007; National Mathematics Advisory Panel, 2008).

Curriculum Focal Points (NCTM, 2006) places initial development of foundational fraction concepts in grade 3 as one of three focal points: *Developing an understanding of fractions and fraction equivalence.* Similarly, the grade 3 *Common Core State Standards* (CCSSO, 2010) includes developing an understanding of fractions, especially unit fractions (fractions with numerator 1), as a critical area. Fraction concepts are also emphasized in both documents at grades 3 through 7, focusing on topics such as equivalence, the operations, and proportional reasoning. This emphasis over years of time is an indication of both the complexity and the importance of fraction concepts. We must provide students with adequate time and experiences to develop a deep conceptual understanding of this important area of the curriculum.

BIG IDEAS

1. For students to really understand fractions, they must experience fractions across many constructs, including part of a whole, ratios, and division.

2. Three categories of models exist for working with fractions—area (e.g., $\frac{1}{3}$ of a garden), length (e.g., $\frac{3}{4}$ of an inch), and set or quantity (e.g., $\frac{1}{2}$ of the class).

3. Partitioning and iterating are ways for students to understand the meaning of fractions, especially numerators and denominators.

4. Students need many experiences estimating with fractions.

5. Understanding equivalent fractions is critical. Two equivalent fractions are two ways of describing the same amount by using different-sized fractional parts.

Mathematics CONTENT CONNECTIONS

What students bring to the topic of fractions is an understanding of fair sharing. Other whole-number ideas can actually interfere in early fraction development, as discussed later in this chapter. Fraction concepts are intimately connected to other areas of the curriculum. In addition to the content connections listed below, fractions are used frequently in measurement (Chapter 19) and in probability (Chapter 22).

◆ **Algebraic Thinking** (Chapter 14): As described in Chapter 14, fractions are a part of algebra. Equations with variables often involve fractions or can be solved using fractions. For example, $\frac{x}{4} = \frac{5}{16}$ is an equation involving equivalent fractions.

◆ **Fraction Computation** (Chapter 16): Without a firm conceptual understanding of fractions, computation with fractions is relegated to rules without reasons.

◆ **Decimals and Percents** (Chapter 17): A key idea for students is that decimal notation and percent notation are simply two other representations of numbers. By making the connections between these three representations, students can move flexibly among them.

◆ **Ratio and Proportion** (Chapter 18): A part-to-whole concept of a fraction is just one form of ratio. The same fraction notation can be used for part-to-part ratios (e.g., the ratio of boys to girls in the room is 3 to 5 or $\frac{3}{5}$).

Meanings of Fractions

Fractions are a critical foundation for students, as they are used in measurement across various professions, and they are essential to the study of algebra and more advanced mathematics. This understanding must go well beyond recognizing that $\frac{3}{5}$ of an area is shaded. This chapter begins with a look at the multiple concepts related to fractions and how these relate to students' knowledge of whole numbers.

Fraction Constructs

Understanding fractions means understanding all the possible concepts that fractions can represent. One of the commonly used meanings of fraction is part-whole, including examples when part of a whole is shaded. In fact, part-whole is so ingrained in elementary textbooks as the way to represent fractions, it may be difficult for you to think about what else fractions might represent. Although the part-whole model is the most used in textbooks, many who research fraction understanding believe students would understand fractions better with more emphasis across other meanings of fractions (Clarke, Roche, & Mitchell, 2008; Siebert & Gaskin, 2006).

PAUSE and REFLECT

Beyond shading a region of a shape, how else are fractions represented? Try to name three ideas. ●

Part-Whole.   Using the part-whole construct is an effective starting point for building meaning of fractions (Cramer & Whitney, 2010). Part-whole goes well beyond shading a region. For example, it could be part of a group of people ($\frac{3}{5}$ of the class went on the field trip), or it could be part of a length (we walked $3\frac{1}{2}$ miles). Cramer, Wyberg, and Leavitt (2008), researchers on rational numbers, note that the circle model is particularly effective in illustrating the part-whole relationship. Perhaps these were among the ideas you listed in responding to the Pause and Reflect. The following paragraphs present some other meanings that are important for students to experience to achieve a deep understanding with many connections among ideas, as discussed in Chapter 2.

Measurement.   Measurement involves identifying a length and then using that length as a measurement piece to determine the length of an object. For example, in the fraction $\frac{5}{8}$, you can use the unit fraction $\frac{1}{8}$ as the selected length and then count or measure to show that it takes five of those to reach $\frac{5}{8}$. This concept focuses on how much rather than how many parts, which is the case in part-whole situations (Behr, Lesh, Post, & Silver, 1983; Martinie, 2007).

Division.   Consider the idea of sharing $10 with 4 people. This is not a part-whole scenario, but it still means that each person will receive one-fourth ($\frac{1}{4}$) of the money, or $2\frac{1}{2}$ dollars. Division is often not connected to fractions, which is unfortunate. Students should understand and

feel comfortable with the example here written as $\frac{10}{4}$, $4\overline{)10}$, $10 \div 4$, $2\frac{2}{4}$, and $2\frac{1}{2}$ (Flores, Samson, & Yanik, 2006). Division of fractions is addressed in detail in the next chapter.

Operator.   Fractions can be used to indicate an operation, as in $\frac{4}{5}$ of 20 square feet or $\frac{2}{3}$ of the audience was holding banners. These situations indicate a fraction of a whole number, and students may be able to use mental math to determine the answer. Researchers note that this construct is not emphasized enough in school curricula (Usiskin, 2007) and that just knowing how to represent fractions doesn't mean students will know how to operate with fractions, such as when working in other areas of the curriculum where fractions occur (Johanning, 2008).

Ratio.   Discussed at length in Chapter 18, the concept of ratio is yet another context in which fractions are used. For example, the fraction $\frac{1}{4}$ can mean that the probability of an event is one in four.

Ratios can be part-part or part-whole. For example, the ratio $\frac{3}{4}$ could be the ratio of those wearing jackets (part) to those not wearing jackets (part), or it could be part-whole, meaning those wearing jackets (part) to those in the class (whole). When working with ratios, students have to attend to part-part and part-whole relationships, which require attention to the context.

These constructs appear to be developmental in nature.

Why Fractions Are So Difficult

As described in Chapter 2, students build on their prior knowledge, meaning that when they encounter situations with fractions, they naturally use what they know about whole numbers to solve the problems. Based on the research, there are a number of reasons students struggle with fractions. They include:

- There are many meanings of fractions (as described above in the "Fraction Constructs" section).
- Fractions are written in an unusual way.
- Instruction does not focus on a conceptual understanding of fractions.
- Students overgeneralize their whole-number knowledge. (McNamara & Shaughnessy, 2010)

It is important for a teacher to help students see how fractions are like and different from whole numbers. The following list shows some common misapplications of whole numbers to fractions:

1. Students think that the numerator and denominator are separate values and have difficulty seeing them as a single value (Cramer & Whitney, 2010). It is hard for them to see that $\frac{3}{4}$ is one number. Finding fraction values on a number line or ruler can help students develop this notion.

Also, avoid the phrase "three *out of* four" (unless talking about ratios or probability) or "three over four" and instead say "three *fourths*" (Siebert & Gaskin, 2006).

2. In thinking of the numbers separately, students may think that $\frac{2}{3}$ means any two parts, not equal-sized parts. For example, students may think that the following shape shows $\frac{3}{4}$ green, rather than $\frac{1}{2}$ green:

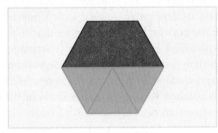

3. Students think that a fraction such as $\frac{1}{5}$ is smaller than a fraction such as $\frac{1}{10}$ because 5 is less than 10. Many visuals and contexts that show parts of the whole are essential in helping students understand. For example, ask students if they would rather go outside for $\frac{1}{2}$ of an hour, $\frac{1}{4}$ of an hour, or $\frac{1}{10}$ of an hour. Conversely, students may be told that fractions are the reverse—the bigger the denominator, the smaller the fraction. Teaching such rules, without providing the reason, may lead students to overgeneralize that $\frac{1}{5}$ is more than $\frac{7}{10}$.

4. Students mistakenly use the operation "rules" for whole numbers to compute with fractions, for example, $\frac{1}{2} + \frac{1}{2} = \frac{2}{4}$. The explorations in the estimation section of this chapter can help students understand that this answer is not reasonable.

Students who make these errors do not understand fractions. Until they understand fractions meaningfully, they will continue to make errors by overapplying whole-number concepts (Cramer & Whitney, 2010; Siegler et al., 2010). This chapter is designed to help you help students deeply understand fractions.

Models for Fractions

There is substantial evidence to suggest that the effective use of models in fraction tasks is important (Cramer & Henry, 2002; Siebert & Gaskin, 2006). Unfortunately, textbooks rarely use manipulatives, and when they do, they tend to be only area models (Hodges, Cady, & Collins, 2008). This means that students often do not get to explore fractions with a variety of models and/or do not have sufficient time to connect the models to the related concepts. In fact, what appears to be critical in learning is that the use of physical tools leads to the use of mental models, and this builds students' understanding of fractions (Cramer & Whitney, 2010; Petit, Laird, & Marsden, 2010).

Properly used, tools can help students clarify ideas that are often confused in a purely symbolic mode. Sometimes it is useful to do the same activity with two different representations and ask students to make connections between them. Different representations offer different opportunities to learn. For example, an area model helps students visualize parts of the whole. A linear model shows that there is always another fraction to be found between any two numbers—an important concept that is underemphasized in the teaching of fractions. Also, some students are able to make sense of one representation, but not another. Importantly, students need to experience fractions in real-world contexts that are meaningful to them (Cramer & Whitney, 2010). These contexts may align well with one representation and not as well with another. For example, if students are being asked who walked the farthest, a linear model is more likely to support their thinking than an area model.

Using appropriate representations and different categories of models broaden and deepen students' (and teachers') understanding of fractions. This section focuses on three categories of models: area, length, and set.

To begin, review Table 15.1, which provides an at-a-glance explanation of each type of model, with particular attention to defining the wholes and their related parts.

TABLE 15.1

MODELS FOR FRACTION CONCEPTS AND HOW THEY COMPARE			
Model	**What Defines the Whole**	**What Defines the Parts**	**What the Fraction Means**
Area	The area of the defined region	Equal area	The part of the area covered, as it relates to the whole unit
Length or Number Line	The unit of distance or length	Equal distance/length	The location of a point in relation to 0 and other values on the number line
Set	Whatever value is determined as one set	Equal number of objects	The count of objects in the subset, as it relates to the defined whole

Source: Adapted from Petit, Laird, & Marsden (2010).

An increasing number of web resources are available to help represent fractions. One excellent source, though subscription based, is Conceptua Fractions, developed by Conceptua Math (www.conceptuamath.com). This site offers free tools that help students explore various fraction concepts using area, set, and length models (including the number line). The activities can be prescribed by the teacher and contain formative assessment resources.

Area Models

In the discussion of sharing, all of the tasks involve sharing something that could be cut into smaller parts. The fractions are based on parts of an area. This is a good place to begin and is almost essential when doing sharing tasks. There are many good area models, as shown in Figure 15.1.

Circular fraction piece models are the most commonly used area model. (See Blackline Masters 24–26.) One advantage of the circular model is that it emphasizes the part-whole concept of fractions and the meaning of the relative size of a part to the whole (Cramer et al., 2008). The other models in Figure 15.1 demonstrate how different shapes can be the whole. Paper grids, several of which can be found in the blackline masters, are especially flexible and do not require management of materials. Commercial versions of area models are available in a wide variety, including circular and rectangular pieces. The following activity is an example of how area models can be used to help students develop concepts of equal shares.

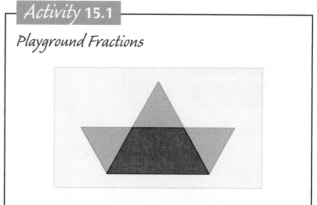

Activity 15.1

Playground Fractions

Create this "playground" with your pattern blocks. It is the whole. For each fraction below, find the pieces of the playground and draw it on your paper:

$\frac{1}{2}$ playground $\frac{1}{3}$ playground

$1\frac{1}{2}$ playgrounds $\frac{2}{3}$ playground

2 playgrounds $\frac{4}{3}$ playground

Source: Adapted from Roddick, C., & and Silvas-Centeno, C. (2007). "Developing Understanding of Fractions Through Pattern Blocks and Fair Trade." *Teaching Children Mathematics,* *14*(3), 140–145.

Length Models

With length models, lengths or measurements are compared instead of areas. Either lines are drawn and subdivided or physical materials are compared on the basis of

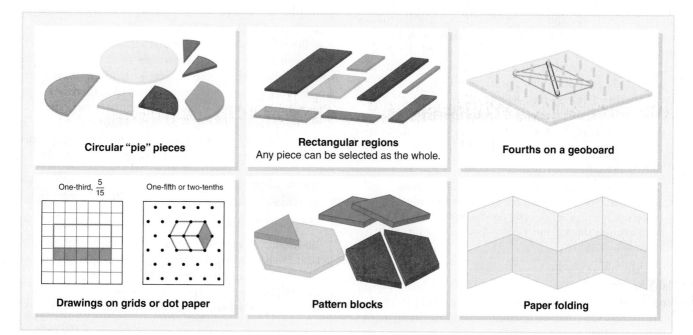

FIGURE 15.1 Area or region models for fractions.

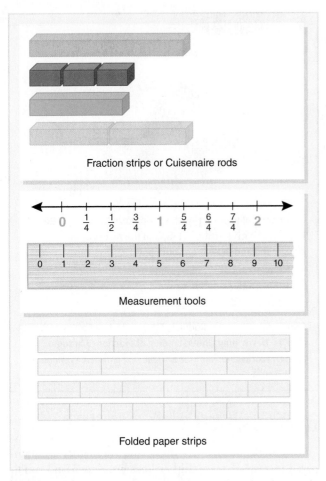

FIGURE 15.2 Length or measurement models for fractions.

length, as shown in Figure 15.2. Length models are very important in developing student understanding of fractions, and yet they are not widely used in classrooms. Recent reviews of research on fractions (Petit et al., 2010; Siegler et al., 2010) report that the number line helps students understand a fraction as a number (rather than one number over another number) and helps develop other fraction concepts. In a report completed by the Institute of Educational Sciences (IES), the researchers prepared recommendations for supporting the learning of fractions (Siegler et al., 2010), advising teachers to:

> Help students recognize that fractions are numbers and that they expand the number system beyond whole numbers. Use number lines as a central representational tool in teaching this and other fraction concepts from the early grades on. (p. 1)

One linear model, Cuisenaire rods, has pieces in lengths of 1 to 10 measured in terms of the smallest strip or rod. Each length is a different color for ease of identification. Virtual Cuisenaire rods can be found at http://nrich.maths.org/4782.

Another linear model, strips of paper or adding-machine tape, can be folded to produce student-made fraction strips.

Rods or strips provide flexibility because any length can represent the whole. For example, if you wanted students to work with $\frac{1}{4}$s and $\frac{1}{8}$s, select the brown Cuisenaire rod, which is 8 units long. Therefore, the four rod (purple) becomes $\frac{1}{2}$, the two rod (red) becomes $\frac{1}{4}$, and the one rod (white) becomes $\frac{1}{8}$. For exploring twelfths, put the orange rod and red rod together to make a whole that is 12 units long.

Cuisenaire rods consist of the following colors and lengths:

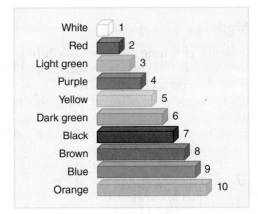

The number line is a significantly more sophisticated measurement model (Bright, Behr, Post, & Wachsmuth, 1988). In fact, many researchers in mathematics education have found it to be an essential model that should be emphasized more in the teaching of fractions (Clarke et al., 2008; Flores et al., 2006; Siegler, 2010; Usiskin, 2007; Watanabe, 2006). Linear models are closely connected to the real-world contexts in which fractions are commonly used—measuring. Music, for example, is an excellent opportunity to explore $\frac{1}{2}$s, $\frac{1}{4}$s, $\frac{1}{8}$s, and $\frac{1}{16}$s in the context of notes (Goral & Wiest, 2007).

In addition to emphasizing that a fraction is one number, the number line allows comparisons in its relative size to other numbers, which is not as clear when using area models. Importantly, the number line reinforces that there is always one more fraction to be found between two fractions. The following activity (adapted from Bay-Williams & Martinie, 2003) is a fun way to use a real-world context to engage students in thinking about fractions through a linear model.

Activity **15.2**

Who Is Winning?

The friends below are playing "Red Light–Green Light." Who is winning? The fractions tell how much of the distance they have already moved. Can you place these friends on a line to show where they are between the start and finish?

ENGLISH LANGUAGE LEARNERS

STUDENTS *with* SPECIAL NEEDS

Mary—$\frac{3}{4}$	Harry—$\frac{1}{2}$	Larry—$\frac{5}{6}$
Han—$\frac{5}{8}$	Miguel—$\frac{5}{9}$	Angela—$\frac{2}{3}$

The game of "Red Light–Green Light" may not be familiar to ELLs. Modeling the game with people in the class and using estimation are good ways to build background and support students with disabilities.

Set Models

In set models, the whole is understood to be a set of objects, and subsets of the whole make up fractional parts. For example, 3 objects are one-fourth of a set of 12 objects. The set of 12, in this example, represents the whole or 1. The idea of referring to a collection of counters as a single entity makes set models difficult for some students. Students will frequently focus on the size of the set rather than the number of equal sets in the whole. For example, if 12 counters make a whole, then a set of 4 counters is one-*third*, not one-fourth, because 3 equal sets make the whole. However, the set model helps establish important connections with many real-world uses of fractions and with ratio concepts. Figure 15.3 illustrates several set models for fractions.

Counters in two colors on opposite sides are frequently used. They can easily be flipped to change their color to model various fractional parts of a whole set. Also, students with disabilities may be supported by putting a piece of yarn in a loop around the items in the set to help "see" the whole.

The activity below can be done as an energizer or as a quick activity when you find you have five minutes.

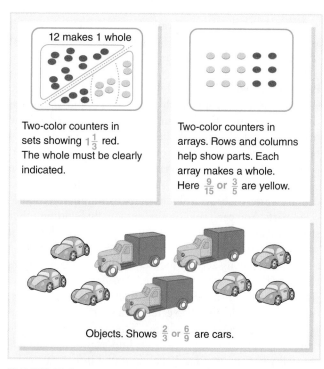

Two-color counters in sets showing $1\frac{1}{3}$ red. The whole must be clearly indicated.

Two-color counters in arrays. Rows and columns help show parts. Each array makes a whole. Here $\frac{9}{15}$ or $\frac{3}{5}$ are yellow.

Objects. Shows $\frac{2}{3}$ or $\frac{6}{9}$ are cars.

FIGURE 15.3 Set models for fractions.

Activity 15.3

Class Fractions

Use a group of students as the whole—for example, six students if you want to work on $\frac{1}{3}$s, $\frac{1}{2}$s, and $\frac{1}{6}$s. Ask students, "What fraction of our friends [are wearing tennis shoes, have brown hair, etc.]?" Change the number of people over time.

Students must be able to explore fractions across the three categories of models. If they never see fractions represented as a length, they will struggle to solve any problem or context that is linear. As a teacher, you will not know whether they really understand the meaning of a fraction such as $\frac{1}{4}$ unless you have seen a student represent one-fourth using area, length, and set models.

 FORMATIVE Assessment Notes A straightforward way to assess students' knowledge of a fractional amount is to give them a piece of paper folded into thirds; write *area*, *length*, and *set* at the top of each section and **observe** as they draw a picture and write a sentence describing a context or example in all three ways for a selected fraction (e.g., $\frac{3}{4}$). This can be done exactly for commonly used fractions or can be an estimation activity with fractions like $\frac{31}{58}$. ■

Concept of Fractional Parts

The first goal in the development of fractions should be to help students construct the idea of *fractional parts of the whole*—the parts that result when the whole or unit has been partitioned into *equal-sized portions* or *fair shares*. See Table 15.1 for meanings of parts and wholes across each type of model.

Students seem to understand the idea of separating a quantity into two or more parts to be shared fairly among friends. They eventually make connections between the idea of fair shares and fractional parts. Sharing tasks are, therefore, good places to begin the development of fractions.

Fraction Size Is Relative

A key idea about fractions that students must come to understand is that a fraction does not say anything about the size of the whole or the size of the parts. A fraction tells us only about the *relationship between* the part and the whole. Consider the following situation:

Mark is offered the choice of a third of a pizza or a half of a pizza. Because he is hungry and likes pizza, he chooses the half. His friend Jane gets a third of a pizza but ends up with more than Mark. How can that be?

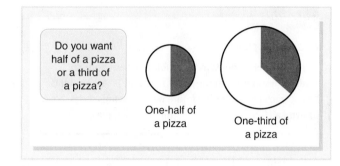

The visual illustrates how Mark got misdirected in his choice. The point of the "pizza fallacy" is that whenever two or more fractions are discussed in the same context, one cannot assume (as Mark did in choosing a half of a pizza) that the fractions are all parts of the same size whole.

Comparing two fractions with any representation can be made only if both fractions are parts of the same size whole. For example, when using Cuisenaire rods, $\frac{2}{3}$ of a light green strip cannot be compared to $\frac{2}{5}$ of an orange strip.

Fraction Language

During the discussions of students' solutions (and discussions are essential!) is a good time to introduce the vocabulary of fractional parts. When a brownie or other area has been broken into four equal shares, simply say, "We call these *fourths*. The whole is cut into four parts. All of the parts are the same size—fourths."

When partitioning a whole into fractional parts, students need to be aware that (1) the fractional parts must be the same size, though not necessarily the same shape; and (2) the number of equal-sized parts that can be partitioned within the unit determines the fractional amount (e.g., partitioning into 4 parts means each part is $\frac{1}{4}$ of the unit). It is important for students to understand, however, that sometimes visuals do not *show* all the partitions. For example, consider the picture below:

Referring back to the two criteria, a student might think, "If I partitioned this so that all pieces were the same size, then there will be four parts; therefore, the smaller partitioned region represents one-fourth"—not one-third, as many students without a conceptual understanding might suggest.

Emphasize that the number of parts that make up a whole determines the name of the fractional parts or shares. They will be familiar with halves but should quickly learn to describe thirds, fourths, fifths, and so on.

In addition to helping students use the words *halves*, *thirds*, *fourths*, *fifths*, and so on, be sure to make regular comparison of fractional parts to the whole. Make it a point to use the terms *whole*, or *one whole*, or simply *one* so that students have a language that they can use regardless of the model involved.

A physical model, like color tiles, can mislead students to believe that fractional parts must be the same *shape* as well as the same size. For example, students looking at this model may not see that the blue square is equivalent to the yellow and green rectangles:

Class discussions that challenge students' thinking and expose their ideas are the best ways both to help students develop accurate concepts and to find out what they understand.

Partitioning

Sectioning a shape into equal-sized pieces is called *partitioning*, a major part of developing fraction concepts with young students. You can partition regions or shapes, which fall under area models. It is also important to partition lengths and sets. A number line with only 0 and 1 at the ends, as well as paper strips, can be used. Students can partition sets of objects such as coins, counters, or baseball cards.

Partitioning with Area Models. Too often, students see shapes that are already all the same shape and size when they are asked questions about what fraction is shaded. The result is that students think that equal shares might need to be the same shape, which is not the case. Young students, in particular, tend to focus on shape, when the focus should be on equal-*sized* parts. Activity 15.1 is an example of how you can use pattern blocks to focus on partitioning into equal-sized parts. You can build on this activity by building other shapes that use different pattern block pieces and then have students figure out how much each piece is of the whole.

The following activity focuses on this, having examples that are (1) same shape, same size; (2) different shape, same size; (3) different shape, different size; and (4) same shape, different size. The first two categories are then examples of fair shares, or equivalent shares. The activity is a simple extension of the sharing tasks. It is important that students can tell when an area has been separated into a particular type of fractional part.

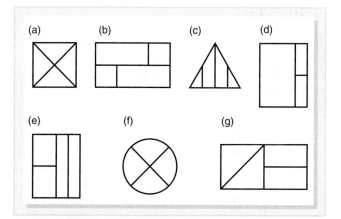

FIGURE 15.4 Students learning about fractional parts should be able to tell which of these figures are correctly partitioned in fourths. They should also be able to explain why the other figures are not showing fourths.

Activity 15.4

Correct Shares

STUDENTS *with* SPECIAL NEEDS

Draw regions like the ones in Figure 15.4, showing examples and non-examples (which are very important to use with students with disabilities) of fractional parts. Have students identify the wholes that are correctly divided into requested fractional parts and those that are not. For each response, have students explain their reasoning.

In the "Correct Shares" activity, it is important to have students explain why they do or do not think the shape is partitioned correctly. The diagrams in the task fall in each of the following categories:

1. Same shape, same size: (a) and (f) [equivalent]
2. Different shape, same size: (e) and (g) [equivalent]
3. Different shape, different size: (b) and (c) [not equivalent]
4. Same shape, different size: (d) [not equivalent]

FORMATIVE Assessment Notes

The "Correct Shares" task is a good **diagnostic interview** to assess whether students understand that it is the *size* that matters, not the shape. If students get all correct except (e) and (g), they do not have this concept and you need to plan future tasks that focus on equivalence—for example, asking students to take a square and subdivide a picture themselves, as in Activity 15.5. ■

Activity 15.5

Finding Fair Shares

ENGLISH LANGUAGE LEARNERS

Give students dot paper and have them find halves, fourths, or other fractional parts of an enclosed area. The activity is especially interesting when different

shapes represent equivalent areas. For ELLs, fraction parts sound like whole numbers (e.g., fourths and fours). Be sure to emphasize the *th* on the end and explicitly discuss the difference between four areas and a *fourth of* an area.

Partitioning with Length Models. As with area models, it is important to see whether students can recognize and create accurately partitioned linear models. On a number line, students may ignore the distance or length of each part (McNamara & Shaughnessy, 2010; Petit et al., 2010). Students can develop these skills by folding their own paper strips. Also, as with the area models, providing examples where the partitioning isn't already illustrated can help students develop a stronger understanding of equal parts. Activity 15.6 provides such an opportunity.

Activity 15.6

How Far Did She Go?

Give students number lines partitioned such that only some of the partitions are showing. Use a context such as walking to school. For each number line, ask, "How far has Nicole gone? How do you know?"

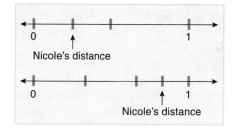

Students can justify their reasoning by measuring the size of the sections that have been partitioned.

Partitioning is a strategy commonly used in Singapore (a high-performing country on international mathematics assessments) as a way to solve story problems. Consider the following story problem (Englard, 2010):

A nurse has 54 bandages. Of those, $\frac{2}{9}$ are white and the rest are brown. How many of them are brown?

Students who have learned the Singapore bar diagram model solve the problem by partitioning a strip into nine parts and figuring out how many bandages go in two of the nine parts:

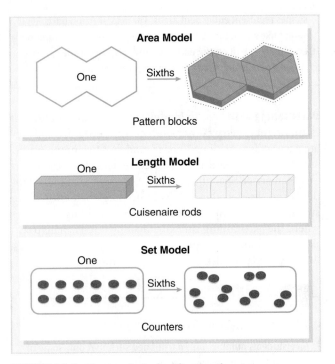

FIGURE 15.5 Given a whole, find fractional parts.

Partitioning with Set Models. When partitioning sets, students may confuse the number of counters in a share with the name of the share. In the example in Figure 15.5, the 12 counters are partitioned into 6 sets—*sixths*. Each share or part has two counters, but it is the number of shares that makes the partition show *sixths*. As with the other models, when the equal parts are not already figured out, then students may not see how to partition. Students seeing a picture of two cats and four dogs might think $\frac{2}{4}$ are cats (Bamberger, Oberdorf, & Schultz-Ferrell, 2010). Consider the following problem:

> Eloise has 6 trading cards, Andre has 4 trading cards, and Lu has 2 trading cards. What fraction of the trading cards does Lu have?

A student who answers "one-third" is not thinking about equal shares but about the number of people with trading cards.

Understanding that parts of a whole must be partitioned into equal-sized pieces across different models is an important step in conceptualizing fractions and provides a foundation for exploring sharing and equivalence tasks, which are prerequisite to performing fraction operations (Cramer & Whitney, 2010).

Sharing Tasks

A second recommendation by the IES research team on ways to help students learn fractions states, "Build on students' informal understanding of sharing and proportionality to develop initial fraction concepts" (Siegler et al., 2010, p.1). In particular, they suggest using equal-sharing activities to develop the concepts of fraction, equivalence, and ordering of fractions.

Students in the early grades partition by thinking about fair shares (division). Sharing tasks are generally posed in the form of a simple story problem. *Four friends are sharing two pizzas. How much pizza will each friend get?* Then problems become slightly more difficult: *Suppose there are four square brownies to be shared among three children so that each child gets the same amount. How much will each child get?* Students initially perform sharing tasks by distributing items one at a time. When this process leaves leftover pieces, students must figure out how to subdivide so that every group (or person) gets a fair share. Contexts that lend to subdividing an area include brownies, sandwiches, pizzas, and so on. The problems and variations that follow are adapted from Empson (2002).

> Four friends are sharing ten brownies so that each one will get the same amount. How much can each friend have?

Problem difficulty is determined by the relationship between the number of things to be shared and the number of sharers. Because students' initial strategies for sharing involve halving, a good place to begin is with two, four, or even eight sharers. For ten brownies and four sharers, many students will deal out two to each child and then halve each of the remaining brownies (see Figure 15.6).

Consider these variations in numbers:

5 brownies shared with 2 children
2 brownies shared with 4 children
5 brownies shared with 4 children
7 brownies shared with 4 children
4 brownies shared with 8 children
3 brownies shared with 4 children

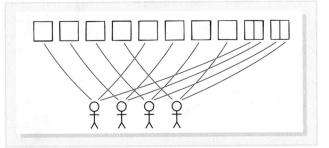

FIGURE 15.6 Ten brownies shared with four children.

Tier 1 task: for students who still need experience with halving	Tier 2 task: for students comfortable with halving and ready to try other strategies	Tier 3 task: for students ready to solve tasks in which students combine halving with new strategies
How can 2 people share 3 brownies?	How can 4 people share 3 brownies?	How can 3 people share 5 brownies?
How can 2 people share 5 brownies?	How can 3 people share 4 brownies?	How can 3 people share 2 brownies?
How can 4 people share 3 brownies?	How can 3 people share 5 brownies?	How can 6 people share 4 brownies?
How can 3 people share 4 brownies?	How can 6 people share 4 brownies?	How can 5 people share 4 brownies?

FIGURE 15.7 Example of a tiered lesson for the brownie-sharing problem.

PAUSE and REFLECT

Try drawing pictures for each of the preceding sharing tasks. Which do you think is most difficult? Which of these represent essentially the same degree of difficulty?

The last example, three brownies shared with four children, is significantly more challenging. When the numbers allow for some items to be distributed whole (five shared with two), some students will first share whole items and then cut up the leftovers. Others will partition every piece in half and then distribute the halves. When there are more sharers than items, some partitioning must happen at the beginning of the solution process.

When students who are still using a halving strategy try to share five things among four children, they will eventually get down to two halves to give to four children. For some, the solution is to cut each half in half; that is, "each child gets a whole (or two halves) and a half of a half."

As always, it is important to meet the needs of the range of learners in your classroom. The level of difficulty of these tasks varies, so a tiered lesson can be implemented to provide appropriate tasks for different students while still enabling all students to learn the important mathematics of the lesson (fair sharing as a meaning of fractions). Figure 15.7 shows how one teacher offers these three tiers for her lesson on sharing brownies (Williams, 2008).

As students report their answers, it is important to emphasize the equivalence of different representations (Flores & Klein, 2005). For example, in the case of three people sharing four brownies, the answer might be noted on the board this way:

$$\tfrac{4}{3} = 1\tfrac{1}{3} = 1 + \tfrac{1}{3}$$

It is a progression to move to three or six sharers because this will force students to confront their halving strategies.

PAUSE and REFLECT

Try solving the following variations using drawings. Can you do them in different ways?

4 pizzas shared with 6 children
7 pizzas shared with 6 children
5 pizzas shared with 3 children
5 pizzas shared with 4 children

Partitioning an area into a number of parts other than a power of two (four, eight, etc.) is more challenging for students. Figure 15.8 shows how a student partitioned to solve the third pizza problem. This took much guess and check, at which point the teacher asked, "Can you see a pattern in how you have divided the pizza and how many people are eating?" At this point, the student noticed a pattern: If there are three people, the remaining pizzas need to be partitioned into thirds. She used this fact to quickly solve the fourth problem. Notice that the context and the model match—both are circles. It is important to use a range of contexts and to encourage a range of representations across the different types of models (area, length, and set).

Fraction bars, Cuisenaire rods, and fraction circles can be subdivided. Another possibility is to cut out construction paper circles or squares. Some students who struggle may need to cut and physically distribute the pieces on a number of plates. Students can use connecting cubes to make bars that they can separate into pieces. Or they can use more traditional fraction models such as circular "pie" pieces.

Iterating

In whole-number learning, counting precedes and helps students to add and later subtract. This is also true with fractions. Counting fractional parts to see how multiple parts compare to the whole helps students to understand the relationship between the parts (the numerator) and the whole (the denominator). Students should come to think of counting fractional parts in much the same way as they might count apples or any other objects. If you know the kind of part you are counting, you can tell when you get to one, when you get to two, and so on. Students should be able to answer the question, "How many fifths are in one whole?" just as they know how many ones are in ten. However, the 2008 National Assessment of Education Progress (NAEP)

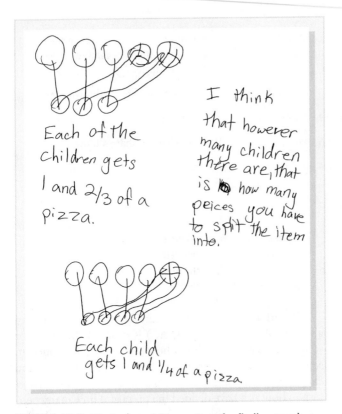

Each of the children gets 1 and 2/3 of a pizza.

I think that however many children there are, that is how many peices you have to split the item into.

Each child gets 1 and 1/4 of a pizza.

FIGURE 15.8 Elizabeth explains a pattern for finding equal shares of a pizza.

results indicated that only 44 percent of students answered this question correctly (Rampey, Dion, & Donahue, 2009).

This counting or repeating a piece is called *iterating*. Like partitioning, iterating is an important part of being able to understand and use fractions. Understanding that $\frac{3}{4}$ can be thought of as a count of three parts called *fourths* is an important idea for students to develop (Post, Wachsmuth, Lesh, & Behr, 1985; Siebert & Gaskin, 2006; Tzur, 1999). The iterative concept is most clear when focusing on these two ideas about fraction symbols:

- The top number *counts*. (numerator)
- The bottom number tells *what is being counted*. (denominator)

The *what* of fractions are the fractional parts. They can be counted. Fraction symbols are just a shorthand for saying *how many* and *what*.

Iterating makes sense with length models because iteration is much like measuring. Consider that you have $2\frac{1}{2}$ feet of ribbon and are trying to figure out how many fourths you have. You can draw a strip and start counting (iterating) the fourths:

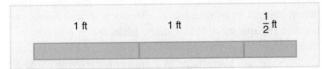

Using a ribbon that is $\frac{1}{4}$ of a foot long as a measuring tool, a student marks off ten fourths:

Students can participate in many tasks that involve iterating lengths, progressing in increasing difficulty. For example, give the students a strip of paper and tell them that it is $\frac{3}{4}$ of the whole. Ask them to find $\frac{1}{2}$, $1\frac{1}{2}$, $2\frac{1}{4}$, 3, and so on. To find these, students should partition the piece into three sections to find $\frac{1}{4}$ and then iterate the $\frac{1}{4}$ to find the fractions listed.

Iterating can be done with area models as well. Display some circular fractional pieces in groups as shown in Figure 15.9. For each collection, tell students what type of piece is being shown and simply count them together: "*One*-fourth, *two*-fourths, *three*-fourths, *four*-fourths, *five*-fourths." Ask, "If we have five-fourths, is that more than one whole, less than one whole, or the same as one whole?" To reinforce the piece size even more, you can slightly alter your language to say, "One $\frac{1}{4}$, two $\frac{1}{4}$s, three $\frac{1}{4}$s," and so on.

As students count each collection of parts, discuss the relationship to one whole. Make informal comparisons between different collections. "Why did we get almost two wholes with seven-fourths, and yet we don't even have one whole with ten-twelfths?"

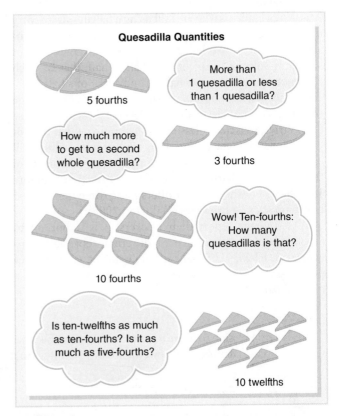

FIGURE 15.9 Iterating fractional parts in an area model. (See Blackline Masters 24–26.)

Also take this opportunity to lay verbal groundwork for mixed fractions. "What is another way that we could say seven-thirds?" (two wholes and one more third or one whole and four-thirds)

With this introduction, students are ready for the following activity.

Activity 15.7

More, Less, or Equal to One Whole

Give students a collection of fractional parts (all the same size pieces) and indicate the kind of fractional part they have. Parts can be drawn on a worksheet, or physical models can be placed in plastic baggies with an identifying card. For example, if done with Cuisenaire rods or fraction strips, the collection might have seven light green rods/strips with a caption or note indicating "each piece is $\frac{1}{8}$." The task is to decide if the collection is less than one whole, equal to one whole, or more than one whole. Ask students to draw pictures or use symbols to explain their answer.

Try Activity 15.7 with several different fraction models and then with no model, using mental imagery only.

Iteration can also be done with set models, although it tends to be more difficult for students. For example, show a collection of two-color counters and ask questions such as, "If 5 counters is one-fourth, how much is 15 counters?" These problems can be framed as engaging puzzles for students. For example: "Three counters represent $\frac{1}{8}$ of my set; how big is my set?" "Twenty counters represents $\frac{2}{3}$ of my set; how big is my set?"

Similar activities can be adapted to meet a range of learners. For example, adding a context such as people, candy, crayons, or an item familiar to students will help them understand the problem. Students who are very strong at doing these puzzles can create their own "puzzle statements" and pose them to the class.

Activity 15.8

Calculator Fraction Counting

STUDENTS with SPECIAL NEEDS

Calculators that permit fraction entries and displays are now quite common in schools. Many, like the TI-15, now display fractions in correct fraction format and offer a choice of showing results as mixed numbers or simple fractions. Counting by fourths with the TI-15 is done by first storing $\frac{1}{4}$ in one of the two operation keys: [Op1] [+] 1 [n] 4 [d̄] [Op1]. To count, press 0 [Op1], [Op1], [Op1], repeating to get the number of fourths wanted. The display will show the counts by fourths and also the number of times that the Op1 key has been pressed. Ask students questions such as the following: "How many $\frac{1}{4}$s to get to 3?" "How many

---

$\frac{1}{5}$s to get to 5?" These can get increasingly more challenging: "How many $\frac{1}{4}$s to get to $4\frac{1}{2}$?" "How many $\frac{2}{3}$s to get to 6? Estimate and then count by $\frac{2}{3}$s on the calculator." Students, particularly students with disabilities, should coordinate their counts with fraction models, adding a new fourths piece to the pile with each count. At any time, the display can be shifted from mixed form to simple fractions with a press of a key. The TI-15 can be set so that it will not simplify fractions automatically, the appropriate setting prior to the introduction of equivalent fractions.

Fraction calculators provide a powerful way to help students develop fractional symbolism. A variation on Activity 15.8 is to show students a mixed number such as $3\frac{1}{8}$ and ask how many counts of $\frac{1}{8}$ on the calculator it will take to count that high. The students should try to stop at the correct number ($\frac{25}{8}$) before pressing the mixed-number key.

⏸ PAUSE and REFLECT

Work through the exercises in Figures 15.10 and 15.11. If you do not have access to Cuisenaire rods or counters, just draw lines or circles. What can you learn about student understanding if they are able to solve problems in Figure 15.10 but not 15.11? What if students are able to use paper but not the Cuisenaire rods? If students are stuck, what contexts for each model can be used to support their thinking? ●

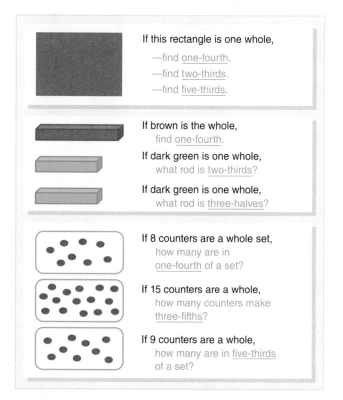

FIGURE 15.10 Given the whole and the fraction, find the part.

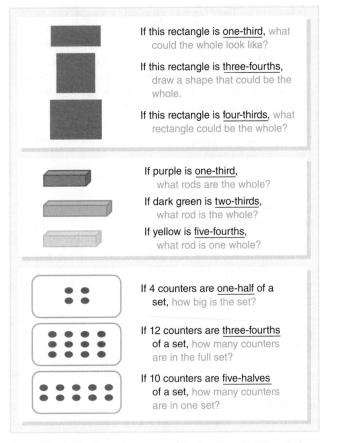

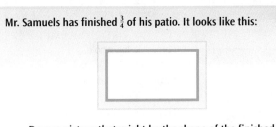

FIGURE 15.11 Given the part and the fraction, find the whole.

As noted throughout this book, it is a good idea to create simple story problems or contexts that ask the same questions.

> Mr. Samuels has finished $\frac{3}{4}$ of his patio. It looks like this:
>
> Draw a picture that might be the shape of the finished patio.

Questions involving unit fractions are generally the easiest. The hardest questions usually involve fractions greater than 1. For example, *If 15 chips are five-thirds of one whole set, how many chips are in a whole set?* However, in every question, the unit fraction plays a significant role. If you have $\frac{5}{3}$ and want the whole, you first need to find $\frac{1}{3}$.

The parts-and-whole questions are challenging yet very effective at helping students reflect on the meanings of the numerator and denominator.

The tasks in Figures 15.10 and 15.11 can be used as **performance assessments**. If students are able to solve these types of tasks, they can partition and iterate. That means they are ready to do equivalence and comparison tasks. If they are not able to solve problems such as these, provide a range of similar tasks, using real-life contexts and involving area, length, and set models. ∎

Fraction Notation

The way that we write fractions with a top and a bottom number and a bar between is a convention—an arbitrary agreement for how to represent fractions. However, understanding of the convention can be clarified by giving explicit attention to the meaning of the numerator and the denominator as part of iterating activities. Include sets that are more than one, but write them as simple or "improper" fractions and not as mixed numbers. Include at least two pairs of sets with the same numerators such as $\frac{4}{8}$ and $\frac{4}{3}$. Likewise, include sets with the same denominators. After the class has counted and you have written the fraction for at least six sets of fractional parts, pose the following questions:

> What does the denominator in a fraction tell us?
> What does the numerator in a fraction tell us?

Here are some likely explanations for the top and bottom numbers from second or third graders:

- Top number: This is the counting number. It tells how many shares or parts we have. It tells how many have been counted. It tells how many parts we are talking about. It counts the parts or shares.
- Bottom number: This tells what is being counted. It tells how big the part is. If it is a 4, it means we are counting *fourths;* if it is a 6, we are counting *sixths;* and so on.

This formulation of the meanings of the numerator and denominator may seem unusual to you. It is often said that the top number tells "how many." (This phrase seems unfinished. How many *what?*) The bottom number is said to tell "how many parts it takes to make a whole." This may be correct but can be misleading. For example, a $\frac{1}{6}$ piece is often cut from a cake without making any slices in the remaining $\frac{5}{6}$ of the cake. That the cake is only in two pieces does not change the fact that the piece taken is $\frac{1}{6}$. Or if a pizza is cut in 12 pieces, two pieces still make $\frac{1}{6}$ of the pizza. In neither of these instances does the bottom number tell how many pieces make a whole.

Fractions Greater Than 1

Throughout this chapter, fractions less than and greater than 1 were mixed together. This was done intentionally and should similarly be done with students as they are learning fractions. Too often, students aren't exposed to numbers greater than 1 (e.g., $\frac{5}{2}$ or $4\frac{1}{4}$), so when they are added into the mix (no pun intended!), students find them confusing.

The term *improper fraction* is used to describe fractions such as $\frac{5}{2}$ that are greater than one. This term can be a source of confusion as the word *improper* implies that this representation is not acceptable, which is not the case at all—in fact, it is often the preferred representation in algebra. Instead, try not to use this phrase and instead use "fraction" or "fraction greater than 1." If you do use the term (because it is in the state standards, for example), then be sure to share with students that it is really not improper to write fractions greater than one as a single fraction.

It is important that students understand the many ways to represent fractions greater than 1. In the fourth National Assessment of Educational Progress, about 80 percent of seventh graders could change a mixed number to an improper fraction, but fewer than half knew that $5\frac{1}{4}$ was the same as $5 + \frac{1}{4}$ (Kouba et al., 1988). The result indicates that many students are using procedures without understanding them.

If you have counted fractional parts beyond a whole, as in the previous section, your students already know how to write $\frac{13}{6}$ or $\frac{13}{5}$. Ask students to use a model to illustrate these values and find equivalent representations using wholes and fractions (mixed numbers). Neumer (2007), a fifth-grade teacher, found that using connecting cubes was the most effective way to help students see both forms for recording fractions greater than 1. (Multilink cubes could also be used.) Figure 15.12 illustrates how to use connecting cubes. Students identify one cube as the unit fraction ($\frac{1}{5}$) for the problem ($\frac{12}{5}$). They count out 12 fifths and build wholes. Conversely, they could start with the mixed number, build it, and find out how many total cubes (or fifths) were used. This procedure is an example of a length model. Repeated experiences in building and solving these tasks will lead students to see a pattern of multiplication and division that closely resembles the algorithm for moving between these two forms.

Context can help students understand the equivalence of these two ways to record fractions, which is the focus of Activity 15.9.

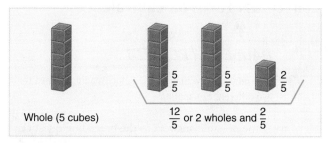

FIGURE 15.12 Connecting cubes are used to represent the equivalence of $\frac{12}{5}$ and $2\frac{2}{5}$.

Activity **15.9**

Pitchers and Cups

Show students a pitcher that can hold enough to fill six cups with juice. You can even use an actual pitcher and actual cups for sharing with the class. Ask questions such as the following: "If I have $3\frac{1}{2}$ pitchers, how many cups will I be able to fill?" "If we have 16 students in our class, how many pitchers will I need?" Alter the amount the pitcher can hold to involve other fractions.

It is important to help students move from models to mental images. Challenge students to figure out the two equivalent forms without using models. A good explanation for $3\frac{1}{4}$ might be that there are 4 fourths in one whole, so there are 8 fourths in two wholes and 12 fourths in three wholes. The extra fourth makes 13 fourths in all, or $\frac{13}{4}$. (Note the iteration concept playing a role.)

Do not push the standard algorithm (multiply the bottom by the whole number and add the top) as it can interfere with students making sense of the relationship between the two and their equivalence. This procedure can readily be developed by the students in their own words and with complete understanding by looking at patterns in their work.

Estimating with Fractions

The focus on fractional parts is an important beginning, but number sense with fractions demands more—it requires that students have some intuitive feel for fractions. They should know "about" how big a particular fraction is and be able to tell easily which of two fractions is larger.

As with whole numbers, students are less confident and less capable of estimating than they are at computing exact answers. Therefore, you need to provide many opportunities for students to estimate. Even in daily classroom conversations, you can work on estimation with fractions, asking questions like "About what fraction of your classmates are wearing sweaters?" Or after tallying survey data about a topic like favorite dinner, ask, "About what fraction of our class picked spaghetti?" Activity 15.10 offers some examples of visual estimating activities.

Activity **15.10**

About How Much?

STUDENTS with SPECIAL NEEDS

Draw a picture like one of those in Figure 15.13 (or prepare some ahead of time for the overhead). Have each student write down a fraction that he or she thinks is a good estimate of the amount shown (or the indicated

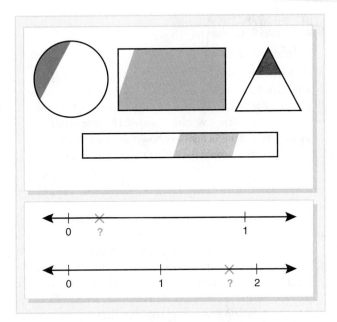

FIGURE 15.13 About how much? Name a fraction for each drawing and explain why you chose that fraction.

mark on the number line). Listen to the ideas of several students, and ask them whether a particular estimate is a good one. There is no single correct answer, but estimates should be in the "ballpark." If students have difficulty coming up with an estimate, ask whether they think the amount is closer to 0, $\frac{1}{2}$, or 1. For students with disabilities, you may want to give them a set of cards with possible options for estimates. Then they can match the card to one of the pictures.

As suggested in Activity 15.10, the most important reference points or benchmarks for fractions are 0, $\frac{1}{2}$, and 1. For fractions less than 1, simply comparing them to these three numbers gives quite a lot of information. The number line is a good model for helping students develop a better understanding for the relative size of a fraction (Petit, Laird, & Marsden, 2010). For example, $\frac{3}{20}$ is small, close to 0, whereas $\frac{3}{4}$ is between $\frac{1}{2}$ and 1. The fraction $\frac{9}{10}$ is quite close to 1. Because any fraction greater than 1 is a whole number plus an amount less than 1, the same reference points are just as helpful: $3\frac{3}{7}$ is almost $3\frac{1}{2}$.

Activity 15.11

Zero, One-Half, or One

ENGLISH LANGUAGE LEARNERS

On a set of cards, write a collection of 10 to 15 fractions, one per card. A few should be greater than 1 ($\frac{9}{8}$ or $\frac{11}{10}$), with the others ranging from 0 to 1. Let students sort the fractions into three groups: those close to 0, close to $\frac{1}{2}$, and close to 1. For those close to $\frac{1}{2}$, have them decide whether the fraction is more or less than half. The difficulty of this task largely depends on the fractions you select. The first time you

try this, use fractions such as $\frac{1}{20}$, $\frac{53}{100}$, or $\frac{9}{10}$ that are very close to the three benchmarks. On subsequent days, mostly use fractions with denominators less than 20. You might include one or two fractions such as $\frac{2}{8}$ or $\frac{3}{4}$ that are exactly in between the benchmarks. Ask students to explain how they are using the numerator and denominator to decide. For ELLs, be sure the term "benchmark" is understood and encourage illustrations as well as explanations.

The next activity is also aimed at developing the same three reference points. In "Close Fractions," however, the students must come up with the fractions rather than sort fractions already provided.

Activity 15.12

Close Fractions

Have your students name a fraction that is close to 1 but not more than 1. Next, have them name another fraction that is even closer to 1 than the first. For the second response, they have to explain why they believe the fraction is closer to 1 than the previous fraction. Continue for several fractions in the same manner, each one being closer to 1 than the previous fraction. Similarly, try close to 0 or close to $\frac{1}{2}$ (either under or over). The first several times you try this activity, let the students use models to help with their thinking. Later, see how well their explanations work when they cannot use models or drawings.

Focus discussions on the important idea that there are infinitely many fractions, so they can always find one in between.

Equivalent Fractions

As discussed in Chapter 14, equivalence is a critical but often poorly understood concept. This is particularly true with fraction equivalence.

Conceptual Focus on Equivalence

PAUSE and REFLECT

How do you know that $\frac{4}{6} = \frac{2}{3}$? Before reading further, think of at least two different explanations. ●

Here are some possible answers to the preceding question:

1. They are the same because you can simplify $\frac{4}{6}$ and get $\frac{2}{3}$.
2. If you have a set of 6 items and you take 4 of them, that would be $\frac{4}{6}$. But you can make the 6 into 3 groups, and

the 4 would be 2 groups out of the 3 groups. That means it's $\frac{2}{3}$.

3. If you start with $\frac{2}{3}$, you can multiply the top and the bottom numbers by 2, and that will give you $\frac{4}{6}$, so they are equal.
4. If you had a square cut into 3 parts and you shaded 2, that would be $\frac{2}{3}$ shaded. If you cut all 3 of these parts in half, that would be 4 parts shaded and 6 parts in all. That's $\frac{4}{6}$, and it would be the same amount.

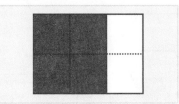

All of these answers are correct. But let's think about what they tell us. Responses 2 and 4 are conceptual, although not as efficient. The procedural responses, 1 and 3, are efficient but do not indicate conceptual understanding. All students should eventually be able to write an equivalent fraction for a given fraction. At the same time, the procedures should never be taught or used until the students understand what the result means. Consider how different the procedure and the concept appear to be:

Concept: Two fractions are equivalent if they are representations for the same amount or quantity—if they are the same number.
Procedure: To get an equivalent fraction, multiply (or divide) the top and bottom numbers by the same nonzero number.

In a problem-based classroom, students can develop an understanding of equivalent fractions and also develop from that understanding a conceptually based algorithm. As with most algorithms, it is a serious instructional error to rush too quickly to the rule. Be patient! Intuitive methods are always best at first.

Equivalent-Fraction Models

The general approach to helping students create an understanding of equivalent fractions is to have them use contexts and models to find different names for a fraction. Consider that this is the first time in their experience that a fixed quantity can have multiple names (actually an infinite number of names). Area models are a good place to begin understanding equivalence.

Activity 15.13

Different Fillers

Using an area model for fractions that is familiar to your students, prepare a worksheet with two or three outlines of different fractions, as in Figure 15.14. Do not limit yourself to unit fractions. For example, if the model is circular fraction pieces, you might draw an outline for $\frac{2}{3}$, $\frac{1}{2}$, and $\frac{3}{4}$. The students' task is to use their own fraction pieces to find as many equivalent fractions for the area as possible. After completing the three examples, have students write about the ideas or patterns they may have noticed in finding the names.

In the class discussion following the "Different Fillers" activity, a good question to ask involves what names could be found if students had other sized pieces. For example, ask students, "What equivalent fractions could you find if we had sixteenths in our fraction kit? What names could you find if you could have a piece of any size at all?"

The following activity is a variation of "Different Fillers." Instead of using a manipulative, the task is constructed on dot paper.

Activity 15.14

Dot Paper Equivalences

Create a worksheet using a portion of either isometric or square dot grid paper (Blackline Masters 37–40). On the grid, draw the outline of an area and designate it as one whole. Draw a part of the area within the whole. The task is to use different parts of the whole determined by the grid to find names for the part. See Figure 15.14, which includes an example drawn on an isometric grid. Students should draw a picture of the unit fractional part that they use for each fraction name. The larger the size of the whole, the more names the activity will generate.

The "Dot Paper Equivalences" activity is a form of what Lamon (2002) calls "unitizing," that is, given a quantity, finding different ways to chunk the quantity into parts in order to name it. She points out that this is a key ability related not only to equivalent fractions but also to proportional reasoning, especially in the comparison of ratios.

Length models should be used in activities similar to the "Different Fillers" task. Asking students to locate $\frac{2}{5}$ and $\frac{4}{10}$ on a number line, for example, can help them see that the two fractions are equivalent (Siegler et al., 2010). Rods or paper strips can be used to designate both a whole and a part, as illustrated in Figure 15.15. Students use smaller rods to find fraction names for the given part. To have larger wholes and, thus, more possible parts, use a train of

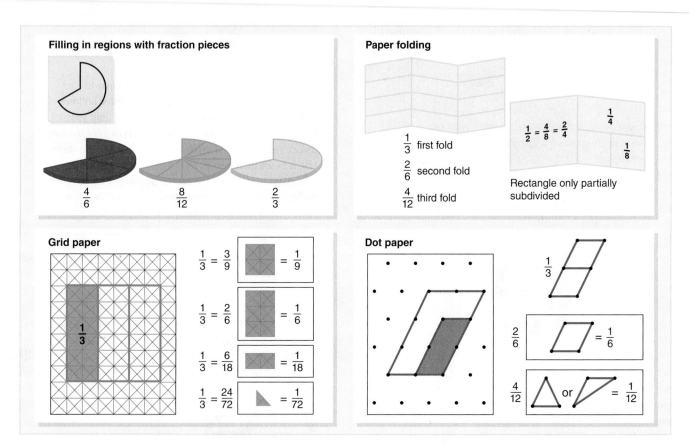

FIGURE 15.14 Area models for equivalent fractions.

two or three rods for the whole and the part. Folding paper strips is another method of creating fraction names. In the example shown in Figure 15.15, one-half is subdivided by successive folding in half. Other folds would produce other names, and these possibilities should be discussed if no one

tries to fold the strip in an odd number of parts. As noted earlier, research indicates the importance of fractions in learning algebra.

One excellent way to make a direct connection is to have students think of fractions as slope and find their locations on a coordinate axis (Cheng, 2010). For example, the fraction $\frac{3}{4}$ can represent the rise/run for slope (rise is the y value, and run is the x value). So $\frac{3}{4}$ is plotted at (4, 3). Similarly, the fraction $\frac{6}{8}$ is plotted at (8, 6).

 FORMATIVE Assessment Notes Consider using a **diagnostic interview** to see whether students are making the connection between equivalence and slope. Ask students to find other values that lie on this line. Ask what they know about the fraction they selected. Students should be able to explain that they are equivalent fractions and that they are fractions that represent the same slope. Conversely, you can give students fractions and ask, "Is this fraction equivalent to $\frac{3}{4}$?" "Will this fraction be on the same line with $\frac{3}{4}$?" ▪

Set models can also be used to develop the concept of equivalence. The following activity is also a unitizing activity in which students look for different units or chunks of the whole in order to name a part of the whole in different ways.

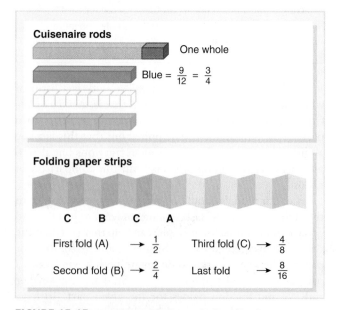

FIGURE 15.15 Length models for equivalent fractions.

Activity 15.15

Apples and Bananas

Have students set out a specific number of counters in two colors—for example, 24 counters, with 16 of them red (apples) and 8 of them yellow (bananas). The 24 counters make up the whole. The task is to group the counters into different fractional parts of the whole and use the parts to create fraction names for the fractions that are apples and fractions that are bananas. In Figure 15.16, 24 counters are arranged in different groups. You might also suggest arrays (see Figure 15.17). ELLs may not know what is meant by the term *group* because when used in classrooms, the word usually refers to arranging students. Spend time before the activity modeling what it means to group objects.

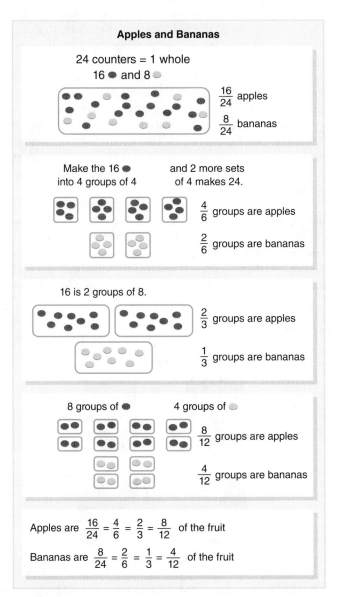

FIGURE 15.16 Set models for illustrating equivalent fractions.

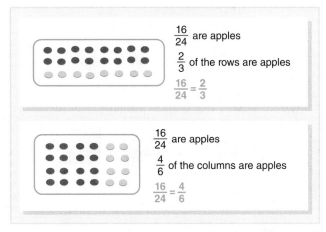

FIGURE 15.17 Arrays for illustrating equivalent fractions.

Ask questions such as, "If we make groups of four, what part of the set is red?" With these prompts, you can suggest fraction names that students are unlikely to suggest.

In the activities so far, there has only been a hint of a rule for finding equivalent fractions. The following activity moves a bit closer but should still be done before developing an algorithm.

Activity 15.16

Missing-Number Equivalences

Give students an equation expressing an equivalence between two fractions, but with one of the numbers missing. Ask them to draw a picture to solve. Here are four different examples:

$$\frac{5}{3}=\frac{}{6} \quad \frac{2}{3}=\frac{6}{} \quad \frac{8}{12}=\frac{}{3} \quad \frac{9}{12}=\frac{3}{}$$

The missing number can be either a numerator or a denominator. Furthermore, the missing number can be either larger or smaller than the corresponding part of the equivalent fraction. (All four possibilities are represented in the examples.) Figure 15.18 illustrates how Zachary represented the equivalences with equations and partitioning rectangles. The examples shown involve simple whole-number multiples between equivalent fractions. Next, consider pairs such as $\frac{6}{8}=\frac{}{12}$ or $\frac{9}{12}=\frac{6}{}$ In these equivalences, one denominator or numerator is not a whole-number multiple of the other.

When doing "Missing-Number Equivalences" you may want to specify a particular model, such as sets or pie pieces. Alternatively, you can allow students to select whatever methods they wish to solve these problems. Students who have learning disabilities and other students who struggle with mathematics may benefit from using clocks to do equivalence. Chick, Tierney, and Storeygard (2007) found that clocks were very helpful in a highly diverse classroom. Students were able to use the clocks to find equivalent fractions for $\frac{10}{12}, \frac{3}{4}, \frac{4}{6}$, and so on.

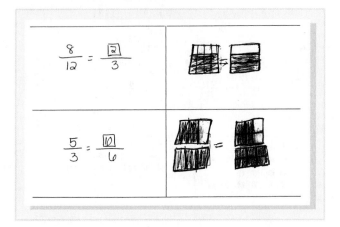

FIGURE 15.18 A student illustrates equivalence fractions by partitioning rectangles (notice that one equivalence is less than one and the other is greater than one).

TECHNOLOGY NCTM's Illuminations website offers an excellent set of three units called "Fun with Fractions." Each unit uses one of the model types (area, length, or set) and focuses on comparing and ordering fractions and equivalences. The five to six lessons in each unit incorporate a range of manipulatives and engaging activities to support student learning.

Area Model Unit: http://illuminations.nctm.org/LessonDetail.aspx?id=U113

Set Model Unit: http://illuminations.nctm.org/LessonDetail.aspx?id=U112

Length Model Unit: http://illuminations.nctm.org/LessonDetail.aspx?id=U152

Developing an Equivalent-Fraction Algorithm

When students understand that fractions can have different (but equivalent) names, they are ready to develop a method for finding equivalent names for a particular value. An area model is a good visual for connecting the concept of equivalence to the standard algorithm for finding equivalent fractions (multiply both the top and bottom numbers by the same number to get an equivalent fraction). The approach suggested here is to look for a pattern in the way that the fractional parts in both the part and the whole are counted. Activity 15.17 is a beginning, but a good class discussion following the activity will also be required.

Activity 15.17

Garden Plots

Have students draw a square "garden" on blank paper, or give each student a square of paper (like origami paper). Begin by explaining that the garden is divided into rows of various

vegetables. In the first example, you might illustrate four rows (fourths) and designate $\frac{3}{4}$ as corn. Ask students to partition their square into four rows and shade three-fourths as in Figure 15.19. Then explain that the garden is going to be shared with family and friends in a way that each person gets a harvest that is $\frac{3}{4}$ corn. Show how the garden can be partitioned horizontally to represent two people sharing the corn (i.e., $\frac{6}{8}$). Ask what fraction of the newly divided garden is corn. Next, tell students to come up with other ways that friends can share the garden (they can choose how many friends, or you can). For each newly divided garden, ask students to record an equation showing the equivalent fractions.

After students have prepared their own examples, provide time for them to look at their fractions and gardens and notice patterns about the fractions and the diagrams. Once they have time to do this individually, ask students to share. Figure 15.20 provides student explanations that illustrate the range of "noticing."

As you can see, for some of these students more experiences are needed. You can also assist in helping students make the connection from the partitioned square to the procedure by displaying a square (for example, partitioned to show $\frac{4}{5}$) (see Figure 15.21). Turn off or cover the display and partition the square vertically into six parts. Cover most of the square as shown in the figure. Ask, "What is the new name for my $\frac{4}{5}$?"

The reason for this exercise is that many students simply count the small regions and never think to use multiplication. This also helps students develop mental images of models that are critical to understanding equivalence. With the covered square, students can see that there are four columns and six rows to the shaded part, so

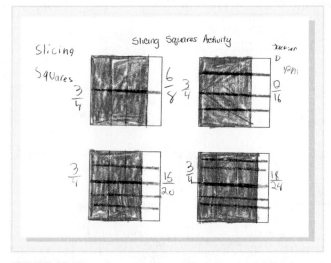

FIGURE 15.19 Jackson partitions a garden to model fraction equivalences.

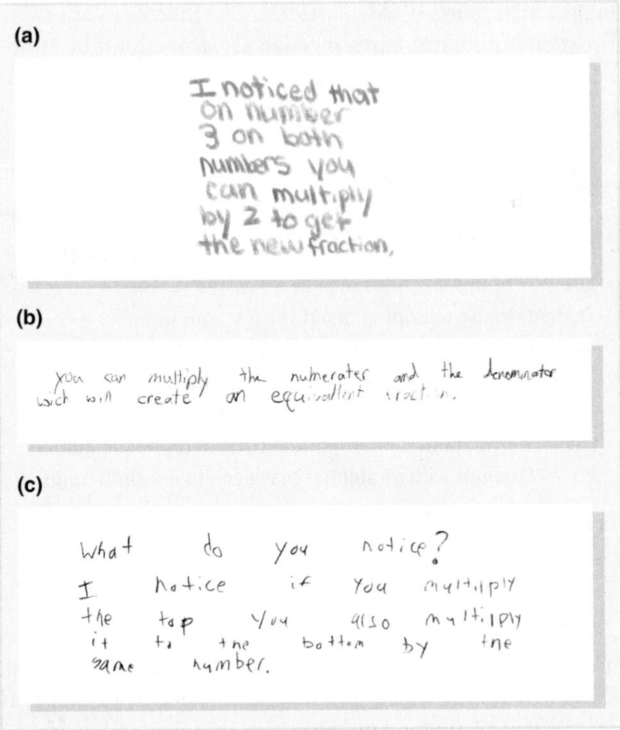

(a)

I noticed that on number 3 on both numbers you can multiply by 2 to get the new fraction,

(b)

you can multiply the numerater and the denominator wich will create an equivallent fraction.

(c)

What do you notice?
I notice if you multiply the top you also multiply it to the bottom by the same number.

FIGURE 15.20 Students explain what they notice about fraction equivalences based on partitioning "gardens" in different ways.

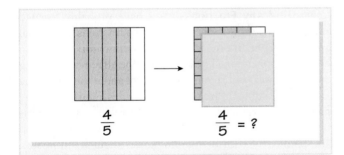

FIGURE 15.21 How can you count the fractional parts if you cannot see them all?

there must be 4×6 parts shaded. Similarly, there must be 5×6 parts in the whole. Therefore, the new name for $\frac{4}{5}$ is $\frac{4 \times 6}{5 \times 6}$, or $\frac{24}{30}$.

Using this idea, have students return to the fractions on their worksheet to see if the pattern works for other fractions.

Examine examples of equivalent fractions that have been generated with other models, and see if the rule of multiplying top and bottom numbers by the same number holds. If the rule is correct, how can $\frac{6}{8}$ and $\frac{9}{12}$ be equivalent?

Writing Fractions in Simplest Terms.   The multiplication scheme for equivalent fractions produces fractions with larger denominators. To write a fraction in *simplest terms* means to write it so that numerator and denominator have no common whole-number factors. (Some texts use the name *lowest terms* instead of *simplest terms*.) One meaningful approach to this task of finding simplest terms is to reverse the earlier process, as illustrated in Figure 15.22. The search for a common factor or a simplified fraction should be connected to grouping. Texas Instruments offers a comparing fractions activity using the number line on their Classroom Activities Exchange (go to http://education.ti.com/educationportal/sites/US/homePage/index.html).

Two additional things should be noted regarding fraction simplification:

1. Notice that the phrase *reducing fractions* was not used. Because this would imply that the fraction is being made smaller, this terminology should be avoided. Fractions are simplified, *not* reduced.
2. Teachers sometimes tell students that fraction answers are incorrect if not in simplest or lowest terms. This also misinforms students about the equivalence of fractions. When students add $\frac{1}{6} + \frac{1}{2}$, both $\frac{2}{3}$ and $\frac{4}{6}$ are correct. It is best to reinforce that they are both correct and are equivalent.

Multiplying by One.   Many textbooks and websites use a strictly symbolic approach to equivalent fractions. It is based on the multiplicative property that any number multiplied by 1 remains unchanged. Any fraction of the form $\frac{n}{n}$ can be used as the identity element. Therefore, $\frac{3}{4} = \frac{3}{4} \times 1 = \frac{3}{4} \times \frac{2}{2} = \frac{6}{8}$. Furthermore, the numerator and denominator of the identity element can also be fractions. In this way, $\frac{6}{12} = \frac{6}{12} \times \left(\frac{1/6}{1/6}\right) = \frac{1}{2}$.

This explanation relies on an understanding of the multiplicative identity property, which most students in grades 4 to 6 do not fully appreciate. It also relies on the procedure for multiplying two fractions. Finally, the argument uses solely deductive reasoning based on an axiom of the rational number system. It does not lend itself to intuitive modeling. A reasonable conclusion is to delay this important explanation until at least seventh or eighth grade

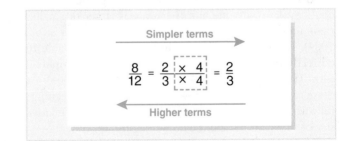

FIGURE 15.22 Using the equivalent-fraction algorithm to write fractions in simplest terms.

in an appropriate prealgebra context and not as a method or a rationale for producing equivalent fractions.

TECHNOLOGY Developing the concept of equivalence can be supported with the use of technology. In the NCTM e-Examples, there is a fraction game (Fraction Track) for two players (Applet 5.1, *Communicating about Mathematics Using Games*). The game uses a number-line model, and knowledge of equivalent fractions plays a significant role. The Equivalent Fractions tool from NCTM's Illuminations website is designed to help students create equivalent fractions by dividing and shading square or circular regions and then match each fraction to its location on a number line. Students can use the computer-generated fraction or build their own. Once the rectangular or circular shape is divided, the student fills in the parts or fractional region and then builds two models equivalent to the original fraction. The three equivalent fractions are displayed in a table and in the same location on a number line.

Comparing Fractions

When students are looking to see whether two or more fractions are equivalent, they are comparing them. If they are not equivalent, then students can determine which ones are smaller and which ones are larger. The ideas described previously for equivalence across area, length, and set models are therefore also appropriate for comparing fractions. Remember that students should be moving from real models to mental images to reasoning strategies. Just as students can become overreliant on the calculator when they could solve a problem mentally, they can become too reliant on a model (such as circle pieces) and not reason about the size of the fraction. Instead, the use of contexts, models, and mental imagery can help students build a strong understanding of the relative size of fractions (Bray & Abreu-Sanchez, 2010; Petit et al., 2010). The next section offers ways to support students' understanding of the relative size of fractions.

Comparing Fractions Using Number Sense

In the National Assessment of Educational Progress (NAEP) test, only 21 percent of fourth-grade students could explain why one unit fraction was larger or smaller than another—for example, $\frac{1}{5}$ and $\frac{1}{4}$ (Kloosterman et al., 2004). For eighth graders, only 41 percent were able to correctly put in order three fractions given in simplified form (Sowder, Wearne, Martin, & Strutchens, 2004). As these researchers note, "How students can work meaningfully with fractions if they do not have a sense of the relative size of the fractions is difficult to imagine" (p. 116).

Comparing Unit Fractions. As noted earlier, whole-number knowledge can interfere with comparing fractions. Students think, "Seven is more than four, so sevenths should be

bigger than fourths" (Mack, 1995). The inverse relationship between number of parts and size of parts cannot be "told" but must be a creation of each student's own thought process through many experiences.

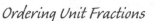

Activity 15.18

Ordering Unit Fractions

STUDENTS *with* SPECIAL NEEDS

List a set of unit fractions such as $\frac{1}{3}$, $\frac{1}{8}$, $\frac{1}{5}$, and $\frac{1}{10}$. Ask students to use reasoning to put the fractions in order from least to greatest. Challenge students to explain their reasoning with an area model (e.g., circles) *and* on a number line. Ask students to connect the two representations. ("What do you notice about $\frac{1}{3}$ of the circle and $\frac{1}{3}$ on the number line?") Students with disabilities may need to use clothespins with the fractions written on them and place them on the line first.

Students may notice that larger bottom numbers mean smaller fractions, but this is not a rule to be memorized. Revisit this basic idea periodically. You may find that students seem to understand this idea one day and revert to their more comfortable notions about big numbers a day or two later. Repeat Activity 15.18 with all numerators equal to some number other than 1. You may be surprised to see that this is much harder for students.

Comparing Any Fractions. You have probably learned rules or algorithms for comparing two fractions. The usual approaches are finding common denominators and using cross-multiplication. These rules can be effective in getting correct answers but require no thought about the size of the fractions. If students are taught these rules before they have had the opportunity to think about the relative sizes of various fractions, there is little chance that they will develop any familiarity with or number sense about fraction size. The goal is reflective thought, not the memorization of an algorithmic method of choosing the correct answer.

PAUSE and REFLECT

Assume for a moment that you do not know the common-denominator or cross-multiplication techniques. Now examine the pairs of fractions in Figure 15.23 and select the larger of each pair using a reasoning approach that a fourth grader might use. ●

Figure 15.24 provides explanations from two students on the first column (A–F). Both students are able to reason to determine which is larger, though one student is better able to articulate those ideas.

The list here summarizes ways that the fractions in Figure 15.23 might have been compared:

1. *Same-size whole (same denominators).* To compare $\frac{3}{8}$ and $\frac{5}{8}$, think about having 3 parts of something and also

Which fraction in each pair is greater?
Give one or more reasons. Try not to use drawings or models.
<u>Do</u> not <u>use</u> common denominators or cross-multiplication.

A. $\frac{4}{5}$ or $\frac{4}{9}$ G. $\frac{7}{12}$ or $\frac{5}{12}$

B. $\frac{4}{7}$ or $\frac{5}{7}$ H. $\frac{3}{5}$ or $\frac{3}{7}$

C. $\frac{3}{8}$ or $\frac{4}{10}$ I. $\frac{5}{8}$ or $\frac{6}{10}$

D. $\frac{5}{3}$ or $\frac{5}{8}$ J. $\frac{9}{8}$ or $\frac{4}{3}$

E. $\frac{3}{4}$ or $\frac{9}{10}$ K. $\frac{4}{6}$ or $\frac{7}{12}$

F. $\frac{3}{8}$ or $\frac{4}{7}$ L. $\frac{8}{9}$ or $\frac{7}{8}$

FIGURE 15.23 Comparing fractions using concepts.

5 parts of the same thing. (This method can be used for problems B and G.)

2. *Same number of parts (same numerators) but different-sized wholes.* Consider the case of $\frac{3}{4}$ and $\frac{3}{7}$. If a whole is divided into 7 parts, the parts will certainly be smaller than if divided into only 4 parts. (This strategy can be used with problems A, D, and H.)

3. *More than/less than one-half or one.* The fraction pairs $\frac{3}{7}$ versus $\frac{5}{8}$ and $\frac{5}{4}$ versus $\frac{7}{8}$ do not lend themselves to either of the previous thought processes. In the first pair, $\frac{3}{7}$ is less than half of the number of sevenths needed to make a whole, and so $\frac{3}{7}$ is less than a half. Similarly, $\frac{5}{8}$ is more than a half. Therefore, $\frac{5}{8}$ is the larger fraction. The second pair is determined by noting that one fraction is greater than 1 and the other is less than 1. (This method could be used on problems A, D, F, G, and H.)

4. *Closeness to one-half or one.* Why is $\frac{9}{10}$ greater than $\frac{3}{4}$? Each is one fractional part away from one whole, and tenths are smaller than fourths. Similarly, notice that $\frac{5}{8}$ is smaller than $\frac{4}{6}$ because it is only one-eighth more than a half, while $\frac{4}{6}$ is a sixth more than a half. Can you use this basic idea to compare $\frac{3}{5}$ and $\frac{5}{9}$? (*Hint:* Each is half of a fractional part more than $\frac{1}{2}$.) Also try $\frac{5}{7}$ and $\frac{7}{9}$. (This is a good strategy for problems C, E, I, J, K, and L.)

How did your reasons for choosing fractions in Figure 15.23 compare to these ideas? It is important that you are comfortable with these informal comparison strategies as a major component of your own number sense as well as for helping students develop theirs. Notice that some of the comparisons, such as problems D and H, could have been solved using more than one of the strategies listed.

Tasks you design for your students should assist them in developing these and possibly other methods of comparing two fractions. It is important that the ideas come from your students and their discussions. To teach "the four ways

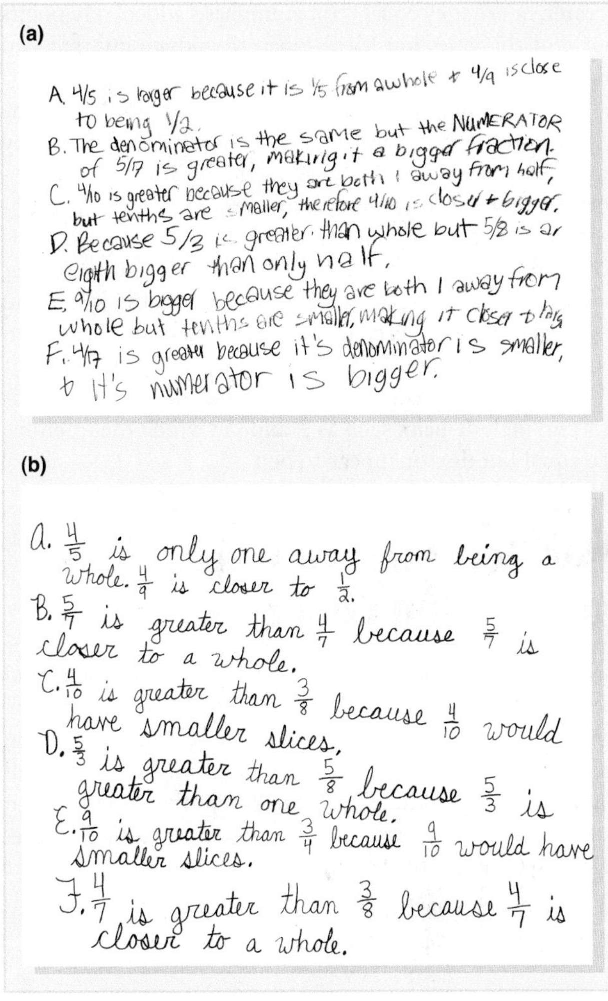

(a)

(b)

FIGURE 15.24 Two students explain how they compared the fractions in problems A through F from Figure 15.23.

to compare fractions" would be adding four more mysterious rules and defeats the purpose of encouraging students to apply their number sense.

To develop these methods for comparing fractions, select pairs of fractions that will likely elicit desired comparison strategies. On one day, for example, you might have two pairs with the same denominators and one with the same numerators. On another day, you might pick fraction pairs in which each fraction is exactly one part away from a whole. Try to build strategies over several days by the strategic choice of fraction pairs.

The use of an area or number-line model may help students who are struggling to reason mentally. Place greater emphasis on students' reasoning and connect it to the visual models.

Using Equivalent Fractions to Compare

Equivalent-fraction concepts can be used in making comparisons. Smith (2002) suggests that the comparison question to ask is, "Which of the following two (or more) fractions is greater, or are they equal?" (p. 9, emphasis added). He points out that this question leaves open the possibility that two fractions that may look different can, in fact, be equal.

In addition to this point, with equivalent-fraction concepts, students can adjust how a fraction looks so that they can use ideas that make sense to them. Burns (1999) describes how fifth graders compared $\frac{6}{8}$ to $\frac{4}{5}$. (You might want to stop for a moment and think how you would compare these fractions.) One child changed the $\frac{4}{5}$ to $\frac{8}{10}$ so that both fractions would be two parts away from the whole and he reasoned from there. Another changed both fractions to a common *numerator* of 12.

Be absolutely certain to revisit the comparison activities and include pairs such as $\frac{8}{12}$ and $\frac{2}{3}$ in which the fractions are equal but do not appear to be.

Teaching Considerations for Fraction Concepts

Because the teaching of fractions is so important, and because fractions are often not well understood even by adults, a recap of the big ideas is needed. Hopefully you have recognized that one reason fractions are not well understood is that there is a lot to know about them—from part–whole relationships to division constructs. And understanding includes representing across area, length, and set

models—and includes contexts that fit these models. Using estimation activities can support student understanding of fractions and is an important skill in and of itself. Many of these strategies may not have been part of your own learning experience, but they must be part of your teaching experience so that your students can fully understand fractions and be successful in algebra and beyond.

Equivalence, including comparisons, is a central idea for which students must have sound understanding and skill. Connecting visuals with the procedure and not rushing the algorithm too soon are important aspects of the process.

Clarke and colleagues (2008) and Cramer and Whitney (2010), researchers of fraction teaching and learning, offer research-based recommendations that provide an effective summary of this chapter:

1. Give a greater emphasis to number sense and the meaning of fractions, rather that rote procedures for manipulating them.
2. Provide a variety of models and contexts to represent fractions.
3. Emphasize that fractions are numbers, making extensive use of number lines in representing fractions.
4. Spend whatever time is needed for students to understand equivalences (concretely and symbolically), including flexible naming of fractions.
5. Link fractions to key benchmarks and encourage estimation.

RESOURCES *for Chapter 15*

LITERATURE CONNECTIONS

Context takes students away from rules and encourages them to explore ideas in a more open and meaningful manner. The way that students approach fraction concepts in these contexts may surprise you.

How Many Snails? A Counting Book *Giganti, 1988*

Each page of this book has a similar pattern of questions. For example, the narrator wonders how many clouds there are, how many of them are big and fluffy, and how many of them are big and fluffy and gray. Students can look at the pictures and find the fraction of the objects (e.g., clouds) that have the particular characteristic (big and fluffy). Whitin and Whitin (2006) describe how a class used this book to write their own stories in this pattern and record the fractions for each subset of the objects.

The Doorbell Rang *Hutchins, 1986*

Often used to investigate whole-number operations of multiplication and division, this book is also an excellent early intro-

duction to fractions. The story is a simple tale of two children preparing to share a plate of 12 cookies. Just as they have figured out how to share the cookies, the doorbell rings and more children arrive. You can change the number of children to create a sharing situation that requires fractions (e.g., 5 children).

The Man Who Counted: A Collection of Mathematical Adventures *Tahan, 1993*

This book contains a story, "Beasts of Burden," about a wise mathematician, Beremiz, and the narrator, who are traveling together on one camel. They are asked by three brothers to solve an argument. Their father has left them 35 camels to divide among them: half to one brother, one-third to another, and one-ninth to the third brother. The story provides an excellent context for discussing fractional parts of sets and how fractional parts change as the whole changes. However, if the whole is changed from 35 to, say, 36 or 34, the problem of the indicated shares remains unresolved. The sum of $\frac{1}{2}$, $\frac{1}{3}$, and $\frac{1}{9}$ will never be one whole, no matter how many camels are involved. Bresser (1995) describes three days of activities with his fifth graders.

RECOMMENDED READINGS

Articles

Clarke, D. M., Roche, A., & Mitchell, A. (2008). Ten practical tips for making fractions come alive and make sense. *Mathematics Teaching in the Middle School, 13*(7), 373–380.
Each of the excellent tips is discussed, and favorite activities are shared. An excellent overview of teaching fractions.

Flores, A., & Klein, E. (2005). From students' problem-solving strategies to connections in fractions. *Teaching Children Mathematics, 11*(9), 452–457.
This article offers a very realistic view (complete with photos of student work) of how children develop initial fraction concepts and an understanding of notation as they engage in sharing tasks like those described in this chapter.

Books

Burns, M. (2001). *Teaching arithmetic: Lessons for introducing fractions, grades 4–5.* Sausalito, CA: Math Solutions Publications.
This book offers well-designed lessons with lots of details, sample student dialogue, and blackline masters. These are introductory ideas for fraction concepts. Five lessons cover one-half as a benchmark. Assessments are also included.

McNamara, J., & Shaughnessy, M. M. (2010). *Beyond pizzas and pies: 10 essential strategies for supporting fraction sense (grades 3–5).* Sausalito, CA: Math Solutions Publications.
This book has it all—classroom vignettes, discussion of research on teaching fractions, and many activities, including student work.

ONLINE RESOURCES

Cyberchase (PBS)
http://pbskids.org/cyberchase
Cyberchase is a very popular television series targeting important mathematics. The site offers videos that model fractions with real-world connections. Also offered are activities such as "Make a Match" (http://pbskids.org/cyberchase/games/equivalentfractions), in which students examine the concept of equivalent fractions and match a fraction with a graphic representation of that fraction. Another activity is "Thirteen Ways of Looking at a Half" (http://pbskids.org/cyberchase/games/fractions), in which students explore fractions of geometric shapes—in particular, the thirteen ways half of an eight-piece square can be arranged.

Fraction Bars (Math Playground)
http://mathplayground.com/Fraction_bars.html
The user sets the total parts and then the shaded parts for each bar. Explore fractional parts, the concepts of numerator and denominator, and equivalence. The user can turn the numbers on or off.

Fractions Model (Illuminations)
http://illuminations.nctm.org/ActivityDetail.aspx?ID=11
Explore length, area, region, and set models of fractions including improper fractions, mixed numbers, decimals, and percentages.

Fraction Track
www.nctm.org/standards/content.aspx?id=26975
Players position fractions on number lines with different denominators. Fractions can be split into parts. A challenging game involving equivalent-fraction concepts.

National Library of Virtual Manipulatives
http://nlvm.usu.edu
This site offers numerous models for exploring fractions, including fraction bars and fraction pieces. There is also an applet for comparing and visualizing fractions.

REFLECTIONS *on Chapter 15*

WRITING TO LEARN

1. What is the goal of activities involving the concept of sharing? When would you implement sharing activities?
2. Give examples of manipulatives and contexts that fall into each of the three categories of fraction models (area, length, and set).
3. What does partitioning mean? Explain and illustrate.
4. What does iteration mean? Explain and illustrate.
5. What are two ways you can support students' development of estimating with fractions?
6. Describe two ways to compare $\frac{5}{12}$ and $\frac{5}{8}$ (not using common denominator or cross-product methods).
7. What are two ways to build the conceptual relationship between $\frac{11}{4}$ and $2\frac{3}{4}$?

FOR DISCUSSION AND EXPLORATION

1. A common error that students make is to write $\frac{3}{5}$ for the fraction represented here:

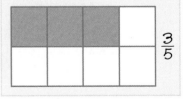

Why do you think they do this? What activity or strategy would you use to try to address this misconception?

2. Fractions are often named by adults (and depicted in cartoons) as a dreaded math topic. Why do you think this is true? How might your fraction instruction alter this perception for your students?

MyEducationLab™

Go to the MyEducationLab (www.myeducationlab.com) for Math Methods and familiarize yourself with the content. Much of the site content is organized topically. The topics include all of the following to support your learning in the course:

- Learning outcomes for important mathematics methods course topics aligned with the national standards
- Assignments and Activities, tied to these learning outcomes and standards, that can help you more deeply understand course content
- Building Teaching Skills and Dispositions learning units that allow you to apply and practice your understanding of the core mathematics content and teaching skills

Your instructor has a correlation guide that aligns the exercises on the topical portion of the site with your book's chapters.

On MyEducationLab you will also find book-specific resources including Blackline Masters, Expanded Lesson Activities, and Artifact Analysis Activities.

Field Experience Guide
C O N N E C T I O N S

Because fractions are not as well understood as whole numbers, they are a good content area for the Chapter 3 field experiences, especially 3.1, 3.2, 3.4, 3.5, and 3.6, which target conceptual and procedural understanding and mathematical proficiency. FEG Expanded Lesson 9.6 is a dot paper activity focused on fraction equivalences. FEG Expanded Lesson 9.6 and FEG Activity 10.11 ("Fraction Find") target an important concept of fractions—the idea that you can always find one more fraction between any two fractions.

Chapter 16

Developing Strategies for Fraction Computation

A fifth-grade student asks, "Why is it when we times 29 times two-ninths that the answer goes down?" (Taber, 2002, p. 67). Although generalizations to fraction computation from whole-number computation can confuse students, you should realize that their ideas about the operations were developed with whole numbers. We can use their prior understanding of the whole-number operations to give meaning to fraction computation. This, combined with a firm understanding of fractions (including relative size and equivalence), provides the foundation for understanding fraction computation (Petit et al., 2010; Siegler et al., 2010). Fraction computation is too often taught as a series of rules or algorithms. What we know about effectively developing whole-number operations must also be applied to instruction of fraction operations. This includes incorporating meaningful contexts and examples, using appropriate models and manipulatives, valuing invented strategies, using estimation, and explicitly addressing misconceptions.

BIG IDEAS

1. The meanings of each operation with fractions are the same as the meanings for the operations with whole numbers. Operations with fractions should begin by applying these same meanings to fractional parts.

   - For addition and subtraction, the numerator tells the number of parts and the denominator the unit. The parts are added or subtracted.

   - Repeated addition and area models support development of concepts and algorithms for multiplication of fractions.

   - Partition and measurement models lead to two different thought processes for division of fractions.

2. Estimation should be an integral part of computation development to keep students' attention on the meanings of the operations and the expected sizes of the results.

Mathematics CONTENT CONNECTIONS

As just noted, computation with fractions is built on an understanding of the operations for whole numbers and on fraction sense (Chapters 12, 13, and 15). Understanding fraction computation has connections in these areas as well.

- **Algebraic Thinking** (Chapter 14): Equations with variables often involve fractions or can be solved using fractions. For example, $\frac{3}{4}x = 15$ can be solved mentally if the student understands fraction multiplication *and* that the procedure for solving the problem requires multiplication (or division) of fractions.

- **Decimals and Percents** (Chapter 17): Because decimals and percents are alternative representations for fractions, they can often help with computational fluency, especially in the area of estimation. For example, 2.452×0.513 is about $2\frac{1}{2} \times \frac{1}{2}$ or $1\frac{1}{4} = 1.25$. Twenty-five percent off a \$132 list price is easily computed as $\frac{1}{4}$ of 132.

- **Proportional Reasoning** (Chapter 18): Fraction multiplication helps us to think about fractions as operators. This in turn is connected to the concepts of ratio and proportion, especially the ideas of scaling and scale factors.

- **Measurement** (Chapter 19): Not only does measuring often involve adding, subtracting, multiplying, and dividing with fractions, but the models for understanding the operations include a measurement interpretation (How many $\frac{1}{2}$ inch segments can you get from 5 inches of string?).

Understanding Fraction Operations

It is critically important to be able to flexibly and accurately compute with fractions. Success with fractions, in particular computation, is closely related to success in Algebra I.

If students enter formal algebra with a weak understanding of fraction computation (in other words, they have only memorized the four procedures but do not understand them), they are at risk of struggling in algebra, which in turn can limit college and career opportunities.

Conceptual Development Takes Time

It is important to give students ample opportunity to develop fraction number sense prior to and during instruction about common denominators and other procedures for computation. This is recognized by research and national curriculum documents. For example, the *Common Core State Standards* (CCSSO, 2010) suggests the following developmental process:

> Grade 4: Adding and subtracting of fractions with like denominators, and multiplication of fractions by whole numbers (p. 27).
>
> Grade 5: Developing fluency with addition and subtraction of fractions, and developing understanding of the multiplication of fractions and of division of fractions in limited cases (unit fractions divided by whole numbers and whole numbers divided by unit fractions) (p. 33).
>
> Grade 6: Completing understanding of division of fractions (p. 39).

Similarly, the *Curriculum Focal Points* (NCTM, 2006) places addition and subtraction of fractions (and decimals) as one of three focal points in grade 5 and multiplication and division of fractions as one of three focal points in grade 6. Collectively, these guides recognize that developing understanding and gaining procedural proficiency for fraction operations are priorities in late elementary and that they require significant time to develop. This is a significant point of departure from what you may have experienced as a student when your textbook addressed fraction operations through one designated (standard) algorithm. Unfortunately, since this has been the norm in the United States for many years, most adults, including teachers, don't have a strong conceptual understanding of fraction operations. If this applies to you, this chapter will be a great learning experience and an excellent resource to you when you teach grades 4–6.

Some teachers may argue that they can't or don't need to devote so much time to fraction operations—that sharing one algorithm is quicker and leads to less confusion for students. This approach does not work. First, none of the algorithms helps students think conceptually about the operations and what they mean. When students follow a procedure they do not understand, they have no means for

knowing when to use it and no way of assessing whether their answers make sense. Second, mastery of poorly understood algorithms in the short term is quickly lost, particularly with students who struggle in mathematics. When combined with the differing procedures for each operation, they all soon become a meaningless jumble. Students ask, "Do I need a common denominator, or do I just add or multiply the bottom numbers?" "Which one do you invert, the first or the second number?" Third, students can't adapt to slight changes in the fractions. For example, if a mixed number appears, students don't know how to apply the algorithm.

A Problem-Based Number-Sense Approach

Students should understand and have access to a variety of ways to solve fraction computation problems. In many cases, a mental or invented strategy can be applied, and a standard algorithm is not needed. The goal is to prepare students who are *flexible* in how they approach fraction computation. *Principles and Standards for School Mathematics* (NCTM, 2000) states, "The development of rational-number concepts . . . should lead to informal methods for calculating with fractions. For example, a problem such as $\frac{1}{2} + \frac{1}{4}$ should be solved mentally with ease because students can picture $\frac{1}{2}$ and $\frac{1}{4}$ or can use decomposition strategies, such as $\frac{1}{4} + \frac{1}{2} = \frac{1}{4} + (\frac{1}{4} + \frac{1}{4})$" (p. 35). In order for students to flexibly apply fraction algorithms, they must understand why they are doing what they are doing.

In a report that summarizes findings on fraction learning, researchers suggest that teachers "help students understand why procedures for computations with fractions make sense" (Siegler et al., 2010). They suggest four steps to effective fraction computation instruction: (1) use contexts, (2) use a variety of models, (3) include estimation and informal methods, and (4) address misconceptions. Each is briefly described here and then elaborated within the discussion of each operation throughout the chapter.

The following guidelines should be kept in mind when developing computational strategies for fractions:

1. *Use contextual tasks.* This should seem like déjà vu, as this recommendation applies to nearly every topic in this book. Huinker (1998) makes an excellent case for using contextual problems and letting students develop their own methods of computation with fractions. Problem contexts need not be elaborate. What you want is a context that fits both the meaning of the operation and the fractions involved.

2. *Explore each operation with a variety of models.* Have students defend their solutions using models, including simple student drawings. And have students connect the models to the symbolic operations. The ideas will help students learn to think about the fractions and the operations, contribute to mental methods, and provide a useful background for developing the standard algorithms.

3. *Let estimation and informal methods play a big role in the development of strategies.* "Should $2\frac{1}{2} \times \frac{1}{4}$ be more or less than 1? More or less than 2?" Estimation keeps the focus on the meanings of the numbers and the operations, encourages reflective thinking, and helps build informal number sense with fractions. Can you reason to get an exact answer without using the standard algorithm? One way is to apply the distributive property, splitting the mixed number and multiplying both parts by $\frac{1}{4}$: $(2 \times \frac{1}{4}) + (\frac{1}{2} \times \frac{1}{4})$. Two $\frac{1}{4}$s are $\frac{2}{4}$ or $\frac{1}{2}$ and a half of a fourth is $\frac{1}{8}$. So add an eighth to a half and you have $\frac{5}{8}$.

4. *Address common misconceptions regarding computational procedures.* Students apply their prior knowledge—in this case whole-number computation—to new knowledge. Using whole-number knowledge can be a support to learning. For example, ask, "What does 2×3 mean?" Follow this with "What might $2 \times 3\frac{1}{2}$ mean?" The concepts of each operation are the same, but the procedures are different. This means that whole-number knowledge also leads to errors (e.g., adding denominators when adding fractions). Teachers should present common misconceptions and discuss why some approaches lead to right answers and why others do not (Siegler et al., 2010).

These four instructional strategies are embedded in each of the sections in this chapter.

Computational Estimation

Estimation is one of the most effective ways to build understanding and procedural fluency with fractions. There are different ways to estimate fraction sums and differences (Siegler et al., 2010):

1. *Benchmarks.* Decide whether the fractions are closest to 0, $\frac{1}{2}$, or 1 (or 3, $3\frac{1}{2}$, or 4 for mixed numbers). After making the determination for each fraction, mentally add or subtract.

Example: $\frac{7}{8} + \frac{1}{10}$. Think, "$\frac{7}{8}$ is close to 1, $\frac{1}{10}$ is close to 0, the sum is about $1 + 0$ or close to 1."

Example: $5\frac{1}{3} \div \frac{3}{5}$. Think, "$5\frac{1}{3}$ is close to five, and $\frac{3}{5}$ is close to $\frac{1}{2}$. How many halves in five? Ten."

2. *Relative size of unit fractions.* Decide how big the fraction is, based on its unit (denominator), and apply this information to adding or subtracting.

Example: $\frac{7}{8} + \frac{1}{10}$. Think, "$\frac{7}{8}$ is just $\frac{1}{8}$ away from a whole (one) and $\frac{1}{8}$ is a close to (but bigger than) $\frac{1}{10}$, so the sum will be close to, but less than, 1."

Example: $\frac{1}{3} \times 3\frac{4}{5}$. Think, "I need a third of this value. A third of 3 is 1 and $\frac{1}{3}$ of $\frac{4}{5}$ is going to be just over $\frac{1}{5}$ (since there are four parts), so about $1\frac{1}{5}$."

Addition and Subtraction. Do you think students are better at computing with fractions or estimating? If you said

computing, you are correct! A frequently quoted result from the second National Assessment of Educational Progress (NAEP) (Post, 1981) concerns the following item:

Estimate the answer to $\frac{12}{13} + \frac{7}{8}$. You will not have time to solve the problem using paper and pencil.

Here is how 13-year-olds answered:

Response	Percent of 13-Year-Olds
1	7
2	24
19	28
21	27
Don't know	14

A study of sixth- and eighth-grade Taiwanese students included this same item. The results were nearly identical to those in the NAEP study (Reys, 1998). In the Taiwanese study, a significantly higher percentage of students (61 percent and 63 percent) were able to correctly compute the sum, a process that requires finding the common denominator of thirteenths and eighths! Notice that to estimate this sum requires no skill whatsoever with computation—only a feeling for the size of the two fractions. The following activity can be done regularly as a short full-class warm-up or be a focus activity for a full lesson.

 Activity **16.1**

STUDENTS with SPECIAL NEEDS

Over or Under 1

Tell students that they are going to estimate a sum or difference of two fractions. They are to decide only whether the exact answer is more than 1 or less than 1. Project a sum or difference for no more than 10 seconds. Then hide or remove it. Ask students to write down on paper or a mini whiteboard their choice of "over" or "under" one. You can also ask students to show you "thumbs up" and "thumbs down" to indicate over or under. Do several problems. (Figure 16.1 offers several possible problems.) Then return to each problem and discuss how students decided on their estimates. Students with disabilities should have a number line to use to try to think about the amounts. They may also need more than 10 seconds to think about the amounts. During the discussion, ask students to refer to an example (real-life situation), a number line, or an area model (e.g., rectangular region) to justify their decision.

Over time, Activity 16.1 can include tasks that are more challenging, or it can be differentiated with different groups of students working on different over/under values. Consider the following variations:

- Use a target answer that is different from 1. For example, estimate more or less than $\frac{1}{2}$, $1\frac{1}{2}$, 2, or 3.
- Adapt to multiplication or division problems.

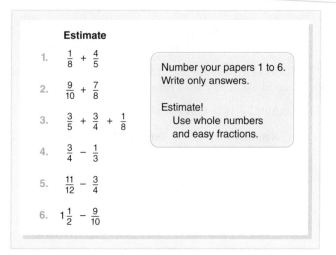

Estimate

1. $\frac{1}{8} + \frac{4}{5}$

2. $\frac{9}{10} + \frac{7}{8}$

3. $\frac{3}{5} + \frac{3}{4} + \frac{1}{8}$

4. $\frac{3}{4} - \frac{1}{3}$

5. $\frac{11}{12} - \frac{3}{4}$

6. $1\frac{1}{2} - \frac{9}{10}$

Number your papers 1 to 6. Write only answers.

Estimate!
Use whole numbers and easy fractions.

FIGURE 16.1 Example of fraction estimation expressions.

- Choose fraction pairs that are both less than 1 or both greater than 1. Estimate sums or differences to the nearest half.
- Ask students to create equations that are slightly less than or slightly more than 1 (or other values). They can trade equations with other students, who in turn need to decide whether the sum or difference is over 1 or under 1 (or other value).

 PAUSE and REFLECT

Test your own estimation skills with the sample problems in Figure 16.1. Look at each computation for only about 10 seconds and write down an estimate. After writing down all six of your estimates, look at the problems and decide whether your estimate is higher or lower than the actual computation. ●

A more challenging estimation activity is shared in Activity 16.2, adapted from Fung & Latulippe (2010) and Hynes (1996). This activity can be used after students have some experience with adding. It is an excellent opportunity to reinforce the relationship between the numerator and denominator.

Activity **16.2**

Can You Make It True?

Share equations with two missing values (in the numerators or denominators, or one of each). Explain that students cannot use the digits already in the problem. Encourage students to use fraction benchmarks (0, $\frac{1}{2}$, 1) to support their thinking. A few examples are shared here:

$\square/6 + \square/8 = 1$ $\square/5 - \square/3 = 1$ $9/\square + \square/8 = 1$

$\square/6 + 5/\square = 1/2$ $1/\square - 5/\square = 2$ $\square/7 - 5/\square = 1/2$

Can you find values for all of these equations? One of them is impossible. Any of these equations require reasoning and thinking about the relative size of fractions, which builds a critical foundation for success in developing and understanding fraction operations.

Multiplication. In the real world, there are many instances when whole numbers and fractions must be multiplied and mental estimates or even exact answers are quite useful. For example, sale items are frequently listed as "half off," or we read of a "one-third increase" in the number of registered voters. Also, fractions are excellent substitutes for percents, as you will see in the next chapter. To get an estimate of 60 percent of $36.69, it is useful to think of 60 percent as $\frac{3}{5}$ or as a little less than $\frac{2}{3}$.

These products of fractions and large whole numbers can be calculated mentally by thinking of the meanings of the top and bottom numbers. For example, $\frac{3}{5}$ is 3 *one*-fifths. So if you want $\frac{3}{5}$ of 350, for example, first think about *one*-fifth of 350, or 70. If *one*-fifth is 70, then *three*-fifths is 3×70, or 210. Although this example has very compatible numbers, it illustrates a process for mentally multiplying a large number by a fraction: First determine the unit fractional part, and then multiply by the number of parts you want.

When numbers are more complex, encourage students to use compatible numbers. To estimate $\frac{3}{5}$ of $36.69, a useful compatible number is $35. One-fifth of 35 is 7, so three-fifths is 3×7, or 21. Now adjust a bit—perhaps add an additional 50 cents, for an estimate of $21.50.

Division. Understanding division can be greatly supported by using estimation. Consider the problem $12 \div 4$. This can mean "How many fours in 12?" Similarly, $12 \div \frac{1}{4}$ means "How many fourths in 12?" There are 48 fourths in 12. With this basic idea in mind, students should be able to estimate problems like $4\frac{1}{3} \div \frac{1}{2}$ and even $3\frac{4}{5} \div \frac{2}{3}$. Asking students to first use words to describe what these equations are asking (e.g., "how many halves in $4\frac{1}{3}$") can help them think about the meaning of division and then develop an estimate. As with the other operations, using context is important in estimating with division. An example is: "We have 5 submarine sandwiches. A serving for one person is $\frac{2}{5}$ of a sandwich. About how many people can get a full serving?" Activity 16.3 uses a context of servings to take on the misconception that dividing always leads to a smaller answer.

Activity **16.3**

Sandwich Servings

Super Sub Sandwiches is starting a catering business. They know that a child's serving is $\frac{1}{6}$ of a Super Sub and an adult serving can be either $\frac{1}{3}$ or $\frac{1}{2}$ of a Super Sub, depending on whether the catering customer requests small or medium. The employees must be quick at deciding the number of subs for an event based on serving size. See how you do—make a decision without computing.

$$6 \div \frac{1}{6} \qquad 6 \div \frac{1}{3} \qquad 6 \div \frac{1}{2}$$

Which portion size serves the most people—child size, small, or medium? Why?

$$8 \div \frac{1}{6} \qquad 5 \div \frac{1}{6} \qquad 9 \div \frac{1}{6}$$

Which serves the most people—a child's serving of 8 sandwiches, 5 sandwiches, or 9 sandwiches? Why?

$$8 \div \frac{1}{3} \qquad 5 \div \frac{1}{2} \qquad 9 \div \frac{1}{6}$$

Which combination of sandwiches and portion sizes serves the most people? Why?

Addition and Subtraction

Addition and subtraction of fractions are usually taught together. As with whole-number computation, provide computational tasks in a context without giving rules or procedures for completing them. Expect that students will use a variety of methods and that the methods will vary with the contexts and the way the problems are framed. Students should find a variety of ways to solve problems with fractions, and their invented approaches will contribute to the development of the standard algorithms (Huinker, 1998; Lappan & Mouck, 1998; Schifter, Bastable, & Russell, 1999b).

Contextual Examples and Invented Strategies

Just like with whole numbers, invented strategies are important for students because they build on student understanding of fractions and fraction equivalence, and they can eventually be connected to the standard algorithm in such a way that the standard algorithm makes sense. Initially, contexts are needed to help students reason about the problem.

Consider the real-life example of measuring something in inches (sewing, cutting molding for a doorway, hanging a picture, etc.). These measures are in halves, fourths, eighths, and/or sixteenths—fractions that can be added mentally by considering the relationship between the sizes of the parts (e.g., $\frac{1}{2} = \frac{2}{4} = \frac{4}{8} = \frac{8}{16}$). If you can easily find the equivalent fraction, then you can count parts—no algorithm needed, though informally, you did find a common denominator and add.

Problems posed in a familiar context should also include whole numbers and mixed numbers, as in the four problems posed here:

> Magan gathered 4 pounds of walnuts and Aimee gathered another $2\frac{7}{8}$ pounds. How many pounds did they gather?

> On Saturday, Lisa walked $1\frac{1}{2}$ miles, and on Sunday she walked $2\frac{1}{8}$ miles. How far did she walk over the weekend?

> Jacob ordered $4\frac{1}{4}$ pizzas. Before his guests arrived, he ate $\frac{7}{8}$ of one pizza. How much was left for the party?

> In measuring the wood needed for a picture frame, Elise figured that she needed two pieces that were $5\frac{1}{4}$ inches and two pieces that were $7\frac{3}{4}$ inches. What length of wood board does she need to buy to build her picture frame?

Notice that these contextual problems (1) use a mix of area and linear models; (2) use a mix of whole numbers, mixed numbers, and fractions; (3) use a variety of different contexts; and (4) include both addition and subtraction situations. Did you notice that the last problem involves adding *four* fractions, not just two fractions? Adding a series is important with fractions, just as it is with whole numbers. Encourage students to model each problem or solve it in a way that makes sense to them.

A fifth-grade class was asked to solve the third problem (Jacob's pizza) in two ways. Many students attempted or correctly used a standard subtraction algorithm for mixed numbers as one method. They used pictures as their second method. As shown in Figure 16.2, Christian makes an error with the algorithm but draws a correct picture showing $4\frac{1}{4} = \frac{34}{8}$ and gets a correct answer of $\frac{27}{8}$. However, he is not confident in his drawing and crosses it out. Brandon used a drawing in which he takes $\frac{7}{8}$ from a whole, then takes the $\frac{1}{8}$ left from the whole, and adds it onto the $\frac{1}{4}$. DaQuawn did what Brandon did, but with numbers rather than pictures. His "second method" is a drawing supporting his work. Asking students to solve the problem two ways provided good insights to the teacher about what each student understood and helped students begin to see the important connection between a concrete model and an abstract algorithm.

FORMATIVE Assessment Notes

A simple problem like $4\frac{1}{4} - \frac{7}{8}$ can be used as a formative assessment and assessed using an **observation checklist**. On the checklist would be such concepts as "Recognizes equivalences between fourths and eighths" and "Can connect symbols to a model." As you can see in the work samples in Figure 16.2, students could find equivalences but struggled with using models and explaining their process. In particular, the students seem limited to a circle model and would benefit from shading other areas, like a rectangle, or using a linear or set model. The next steps in instruction should be explicit attention to using other models and directly connecting models and symbols. ■

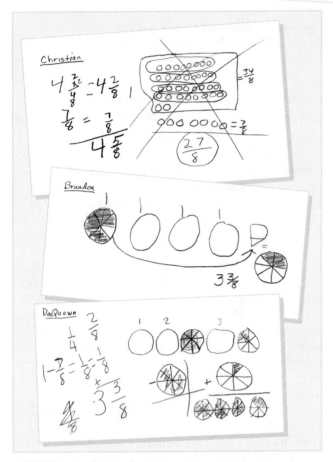

FIGURE 16.2 Fifth-grade students show how they solved the problem $4\frac{1}{4} - \frac{7}{8}$. For most students, their methods based on drawings have little to do with their symbolic algorithms. The work of DaQuawn is an exception.

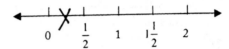

Estimate first by putting an **X** on the number line.

Solve with Fraction Circles. Draw pictures of what you did with the circles below.

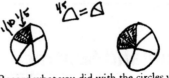

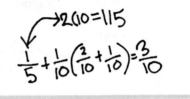

Record what you did with the circles with symbols.

FIGURE 16.3 A student estimates and then adds fractions using a fraction circle.

Source: Cramer, K., Wyberg, T., & Leavitt, S. (2008). "The Role of Representations in Fraction Addition and Subtraction." *Mathematics Teaching in the Middle School, 13*(8), p. 495. Reprinted with permission. Copyright © 2008 by the National Council of Teachers of Mathematics. All rights reserved.

Models

Recall that there are area, length, and set models for modeling fractions (see Chapter 15). Set models can be confusing in adding fractions, as they can reinforce the adding of the denominator. Therefore, instruction should initially focus on area and linear models.

Area Models. Students seem to have a preference for drawing circles to represent fractions. Perhaps that says something about an overuse of that model. The drawings in Figure 16.2 are not carefully drawn—the partitioning does not show equal parts. However, the students are not making conclusions based on the size of the pieces, but rather they are drawing to count sections.

Cramer, Wyberg, and Leavitt (2008), well-known researchers in the area of rational numbers, have found circles to be the best model for adding and subtracting fractions because circles allow students to develop mental images of the sizes of different pieces (fractions) of the circle. Figure 16.3 shows how students estimate first (including marking a

number line) and then explain how they added the fraction using fraction circles.

How you ask students to solve a problem can make a difference in what occurs in the classroom. For example, consider this problem:

> Jack and Jill ordered two medium pizzas, one cheese and one pepperoni. Jack ate $\frac{5}{6}$ of a pizza, and Jill ate $\frac{1}{2}$ of a pizza. How much pizza did they eat together?

PAUSE and REFLECT

Try to think of two ways that students might solve this problem without using a common-denominator symbolic approach. ●

If students draw circles as in the earlier example, some will try to fill in the $\frac{1}{6}$ gap in the pizza. Then they will need to figure out how to get $\frac{1}{6}$ from $\frac{1}{2}$. If they can think of $\frac{1}{2}$ as $\frac{3}{6}$, they can use one of the sixths to fill in the gap. Another approach, after drawing the two pizzas, is to notice that there is a half plus two more sixths in the $\frac{5}{6}$ pizza. Put the two halves together to make one whole, and there are $\frac{2}{6}$ more—$1\frac{2}{6}$. These are certainly good solutions that represent the type of thinking you want to encourage.

There are many other area models that can be used. Pattern blocks, for example, have pieces such that the hexagon can be one whole, the blue parallelogram $\frac{1}{3}$, the green triangle $\frac{1}{6}$, and the red trapezoid $\frac{1}{2}$. Like circles, rectangles can be drawn for any fractional value, depending on how it is partitioned. In addition, the partitioning can be easier and more accurate in a rectangle. The key is to have models that align with the contexts so that students can more readily make the connection between the model, the situation, and the symbols. The following task, for example, lends to a rectangular area model:

Al, Bill, Carrie, Danielle, Enrique, and Fabio are each given a portion of the school garden for spring planting. Here are the portions:

Al = $\frac{1}{4}$ Bill = $\frac{1}{8}$ Carrie = $\frac{3}{16}$
Danielle = $\frac{1}{16}$ Enrique = $\frac{1}{4}$ Fabio = $\frac{1}{8}$

They decide to pair up to share the work. What fraction of the garden will each of the following pairs or groups have if they combine their portions of the garden? Show your work.

Bill and Danielle   Al and Carrie
Fabio and Enrique   Carrie, Fabio, and Al

Linear Models. An important model for adding or subtracting fractions is the number line (Siegler et al., 2010). One advantage of the number line is that it can be connected to the ruler, which is a familiar context and perhaps the most common real context for adding or subtracting fractions. The number line is also a more challenging model than the circle model, because it requires that the student understand $\frac{3}{4}$ as 3 parts of 4, and also as a value between 0 and 1 (Izsák, Tillema, & Tunc-Pekkam, 2008). Using the number line in addition to area representations can strengthen student understanding (Clarke et al., 2008; Cramer et al., 2008; Petit et al., 2010).

Activity **16.4**

Jumps on the Ruler

ENGLISH LANGUAGE LEARNERS

Tell students to model the given examples on the ruler. A linear context can be added (length of grass in the yard, hair growing/getting cut), but if students have been doing many contextual tasks, it is important to see whether they can also add and subtract without a context. Use the ruler as a visual, and find the results of these three problems without applying the common denominator algorithm.

ELLs may not be as familiar with inches, because most countries measure in metric. In this case, be sure to spend time prior to the activity discussing how the inch is partitioned and/or add labels for fourths as a reminder that it is different from the metric system.

$\frac{3}{4} + \frac{1}{2}$ $2\frac{1}{2} - 1\frac{1}{4}$ $1\frac{1}{8} + 1\frac{1}{2}$

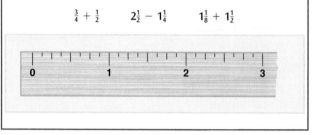

Can you think of different ways that the examples in Activity 16.4 might be solved? In the first problem, students might use 1 as a benchmark (in the way that 10 or 100 is used as a benchmark with whole numbers). They use $\frac{1}{4}$ from the $\frac{1}{2}$ to get to one whole and then have $\frac{1}{4}$ more to add on—so $1\frac{1}{4}$. Similarly, they could take the $\frac{1}{2}$ from the $\frac{3}{4}$ to make a whole with the $\frac{1}{2}$ and then add on the $\frac{1}{4}$, or they might just know that $\frac{1}{2}$ is $\frac{2}{4}$ and then count to get $\frac{5}{4}$ (or $1\frac{1}{4}$).

The context and measure can be adapted to steer students toward specific strategies. For example, consider two ways to pose the subtraction problem, one that is comparison and one that is how many more (see Chapter 9 for more on whole-number subtraction models):

1. Desmond runs $2\frac{1}{2}$ miles a day. If he has just passed the $1\frac{1}{4}$ mile marker, how far does he still need to go? Students may first subtract the whole numbers to get $1\frac{1}{2} - \frac{1}{4}$ and then know that $\frac{1}{2} - \frac{1}{4}$ is $\frac{1}{4}$, or they might prefer to change $\frac{1}{2}$ to $\frac{2}{4}$.

2. Desmond is at mile marker $2\frac{1}{2}$, and James is at mile marker $1\frac{1}{4}$. How far does James need to go to catch up to where Desmond is? In this case, students may use a counting-up strategy, noting that it takes $\frac{3}{4}$ to get to 2 and then another $\frac{1}{2}$ added to $\frac{3}{4}$ would be $1\frac{1}{4}$.

The more students can share strategies and illustrate them on the number line, the more flexible they will become in choosing how to add or subtract fractions.

Suppose that you had asked the students to solve the Jack and Jill pizza problem but changed the context to submarine sandwiches (linear context), suggesting students use Cuisenaire rods or fraction strips to model the problem. The first decision that must be made is what strip to use as the whole. That decision is not required with a circular model, where the whole is already established as the circle. The whole must be the same for both fractions. In this case, the smallest rod that will work is the 6 rod or the dark green strip, because it can be partitioned into sixths (1 rod/white) and into halves (3 rod/light green). Figure 16.4(a) illustrates a solution.

What if you instead asked students to compare the quantity that Jack and Jill ate? Figure 16.4(b) illustrates

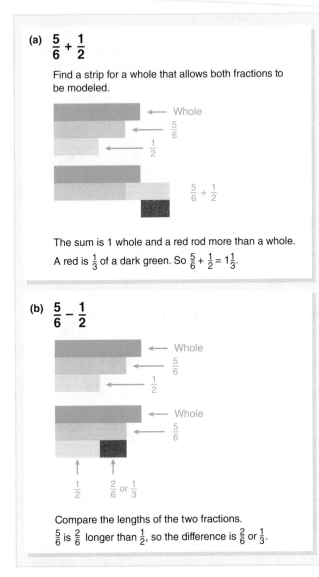

(a) $\frac{5}{6} + \frac{1}{2}$

Find a strip for a whole that allows both fractions to be modeled.

The sum is 1 whole and a red rod more than a whole.
A red is $\frac{1}{3}$ of a dark green. So $\frac{5}{6} + \frac{1}{2} = 1\frac{1}{3}$.

(b) $\frac{5}{6} - \frac{1}{2}$

Compare the lengths of the two fractions.
$\frac{5}{6}$ is $\frac{2}{6}$ longer than $\frac{1}{2}$, so the difference is $\frac{2}{6}$ or $\frac{1}{3}$.

FIGURE 16.4 Using rods to add and subtract fractions.

lining up the "sandwiches" to compare their lengths. Recall that subtraction can be thought of as "separate" where the total is known and a part is removed, "comparison" as two amounts being compared to find the difference, and "how many more are needed" as starting with a smaller value and asking how much more to get to the higher value (think addition). This sandwich example is a comparison—be sure to include more than "take away" examples in the stories and examples you create.

As we saw in the very first example (Figure 16.2), students can and do use invented methods for subtraction as well as addition. This reasoning is extremely important. Students should become comfortable with different methods of taking simple fractions apart and recombining them in ways that make sense.

Developing the Algorithms

Students can build on their invented strategies and knowledge of equivalence to develop the common-denominator approach for adding and subtracting fractions. As discussed in Chapter 15 in the section on equivalent fractions, having a strong conceptual foundation of equivalence is important in many other mathematics topics, one of which is computation of fractions. Students who have a level of fluency in moving between $\frac{1}{2}, \frac{2}{4}, \frac{4}{8}$ and $\frac{8}{16}$ or $\frac{3}{4}, \frac{6}{8}$, and $\frac{12}{16}$ can adjust the fractions as needed to combine or subtract fractions. Whether using an area, length, or set model, establishing equivalence is foundational and needs continued reinforcement during instruction on addition and subtraction of fractions. For example, have students complete a sum such as $\frac{3}{8} + \frac{4}{8}$ and write the finished equation on the board. Then, beneath this equation, write a second sum made of easily seen equivalents for each fraction as shown here:

$$\frac{3}{8} + \frac{4}{8} = \frac{7}{8}$$
$$\frac{6}{16} + \frac{1}{2} = ?$$

Discuss briefly the fact that $\frac{3}{8}$ is equivalent to $\frac{6}{16}$, as is $\frac{4}{8}$ to $\frac{1}{2}$. Now have students write the answer to the second equation and give a reason for their answer. Students should see that the answer is $\frac{7}{8}$. The second sum is the same as the first because although the fractions *look* different, they are actually the same numbers.

Like Denominators. Fraction addition and subtraction begin with situations using like denominators. In the *Common Core State Standards* (CCSSO, 2010), this is suggested for grade 4. *Curriculum Focal Points* (NCTM, 2006) recommends grade 5. If students have a good foundation with fraction concepts (part–whole, for example), they should be able to add or subtract fractions with like denominators. Students who are not confident solving problems such as $\frac{3}{4} + \frac{2}{4}$ or $3\frac{7}{8} - 1\frac{3}{8}$ may lack underlying fraction concepts and need more concrete and contextualized experiences. The idea that the top number counts and the bottom number tells what is counted makes addition and subtraction of like fractions the same as adding and subtracting whole numbers. When working on adding with like denominators, however, it is important to be sure that students are focusing on the key idea—the units are the same, so they can be combined (Mack, 2004).

FORMATIVE Assessment Notes

The ease with which students can or cannot add like-denominator fractions should be viewed as an important concept assessment before moving students to an algorithm. A **diagnostic interview** that asks students to (1) explain the meaning of the numerators and denominators, (2) connect the addition problems to a situation, and (3) illustrate with a model can help you to

determine whether they have a deep understanding of the numerator and denominator. If student responses are rule oriented and not grounded in understanding parts and wholes, then encourage students to focus on the meaning of the fractions by emphasizing the unit: "Three *fifths* plus one *fifth* is how many *fifths*?" This must be well understood before moving to adding with unlike denominators. Otherwise, any further symbolic development will almost certainly be without understanding. ∎

Unlike Denominators. Begin adding and subtracting fractions with unlike denominators with tasks where only one fraction needs to be changed, such as $\frac{5}{8} + \frac{1}{4}$. Let students use an invented strategy and representations to solve the problem. As students explain how they solved it, someone is likely to explain that $\frac{1}{4}$ is the same as $\frac{2}{8}$. Write equations on the board that show the initial equation and the equation rewritten with $\frac{2}{8}$ in place of $\frac{1}{4}$. Ask, "Is this still the same equation? Why would we want to change the $\frac{1}{4}$?" Have students use manipulatives or drawings to explain why the original problem and the converted problem are equivalent and that the reason for changing is so that equal-sized parts can be combined.

Next, try some examples in which both fractions need to be changed—for example, $\frac{2}{3} + \frac{1}{4}$ (or $\frac{2}{3} - \frac{1}{4}$). Initially, encourage students to solve these problems using models or drawings, but eventually students should be able to apply their understanding of equivalent fractions to solve these problems. In the discussion of student solutions, focus attention on the idea of *rewriting an equivalent problem* to make it possible to add or subtract *equal-sized parts*. If students express doubt about the equivalence of the two problems ("Is $\frac{8}{12} + \frac{3}{12}$ really the answer to $\frac{2}{3} + \frac{1}{4}$?"), that should be a cue that the concept of equivalent fractions is not well understood, and more experience using examples, visuals, or concrete tools is needed.

As students continue to explore solutions to sums and differences of fractions, models should remain available for use. The three examples in Figure 16.5 show how tools might be used. Note that each tool requires students to think about the size of a whole that can be partitioned into the units of both fractions (e.g., fifths and halves require tenths).

Are Common Denominators "Required"? Teachers commonly tell students, "In order to add or subtract fractions, you must first find common denominators." The explanation usually goes something like, "After all, you can't add apples and oranges." This well-intentioned statement is essentially false. A correct statement might be, "Remember that we must add equal-sized parts. The algorithm is designed to find common denominators because that means the parts that are being added or subtracted are the same size."

Using their own invented strategies, students will see that many correct solutions are found without ever getting

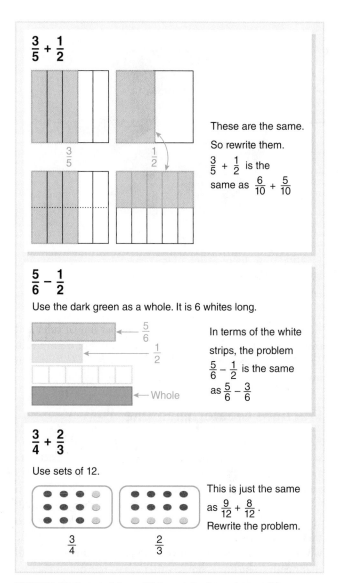

FIGURE 16.5 Rewriting addition and subtraction problems involving fractions so they have a common denominator.

a common denominator (Taber, 2009). Consider these expressions:

$$\frac{3}{4} + \frac{1}{8} \qquad \frac{1}{2} - \frac{1}{8} \qquad \frac{2}{3} + \frac{1}{2} \qquad 1\frac{1}{2} - \frac{3}{4} \qquad 1\frac{2}{3} + \frac{3}{4}$$

Working with the ways different fractional parts are related one to another often provides solutions without common denominators. For example, halves, fourths, and eighths are easily related because $\frac{1}{8}$ is half of $\frac{1}{4}$ and $\frac{1}{4}$ is half of $\frac{1}{2}$. Also, picture three-thirds making up a whole in a circle as in Figure 16.6. Have you ever noticed that one-half of the whole is a third plus a half of a third or a sixth? Similarly, the difference between a third and a fourth is a twelfth.

As noted, the number line is also a tool that can be used to mentally solve addition and subtraction situations without finding a common denominator. Students instead may

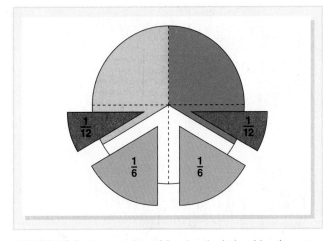

FIGURE 16.6 There are lots of fractional relationships that can be observed simply by looking at how halves, thirds, fourths, sixths, and twelfths fit into a partitioned circle.

start by finding one fraction on the number line or ruler and then "jump" the value of the other fraction. For example, in $3\frac{1}{4} - 1\frac{1}{2}$, students can find $3\frac{1}{4}$, jump down one to $2\frac{1}{4}$, and then jump $\frac{1}{2}$, which takes them to $1\frac{3}{4}$.

Fractions Greater Than One

A separate algorithm for mixed numbers in addition and subtraction is not necessary even though mixed numbers are often treated as separate topics in traditional textbooks and in some lists of objectives. Include mixed numbers in all of your activities with addition and subtraction, and let students solve these problems in ways that make sense to them. Students will tend to naturally add or subtract the whole numbers and then the fractions. Sometimes this is all that needs to be done, but in other cases, regrouping across the whole number and fraction is needed. In subtraction, this happens when the second fraction is larger than the first, and it occurs in addition when the answer of the fraction sum is more than 1.

Dealing with the whole numbers first makes sense. Consider this problem: $5\frac{1}{8} - 3\frac{5}{8}$. After subtracting 3 from 5, students will need to deal with the $\frac{5}{8}$. Some will take $\frac{5}{8}$ from the whole part, 2, leaving $1\frac{3}{8}$, and then $\frac{1}{8}$ more is $1\frac{4}{8}$. Others may take away the $\frac{1}{8}$ that is there and then take $\frac{4}{8}$ from the remaining 2. A third but less likely method is to trade one of the wholes for $\frac{8}{8}$, add it to the $\frac{1}{8}$, and then take $\frac{5}{8}$ from the resulting $\frac{9}{8}$. This last method is the same as the standard algorithm.

One underemphasized technique that is nevertheless a great strategy is to change the mixed numbers to single, or improper, fractions. You may have been taught that this was the process used for multiplication, but that is part of the "rules without reason" approach of having one way to do one procedure. Let's revisit $5\frac{1}{8} - 3\frac{5}{8}$. This can be rewritten as $\frac{41}{8} - \frac{29}{8}$. (See Chapter 15 for conceptual ways for helping

students do this.) Because $41 - 29$ is 12, the solution is $\frac{12}{8}$ or $1\frac{1}{2}$. This is certainly efficient and will always work. The message here is to provide options to students and you will find that more students understand and are able to solve these problems successfully.

Addressing Misconceptions

It is important to explicitly talk about common misconceptions, regardless of the topic. This is particularly important with fraction operations because students overgeneralize rules from whole-number operations.

Adding Both Numerators and Denominators. The most common error in adding fractions is to add both numerators and denominators. Consider the following task:

> Ms. Rodriguez baked a pan of brownies for the bake sale and cut the brownies into 8 equal-sized parts. In the morning, three of the brownies were sold; in the afternoon, two more were sold. What fractional part of the brownies had been sold? What fractional part is still for sale?

Students solving this task are able to effectively draw a rectangle partitioned into eighths and are able to shade $\frac{3}{8}$ and $\frac{2}{8}$, as shown here.

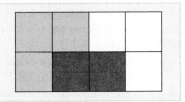

However, about half of students will write $\frac{3}{8} + \frac{2}{8} = \frac{5}{16}$, even after drawing the model correctly. And they won't seem to be bothered that the two answers ($\frac{5}{8}$ and $\frac{5}{16}$) are different (Bamberger et al., 2010). In such a case, ask students to decide whether both answers could be right. Ask them to defend which is right and why the other answer is not right. You cannot just tell students which is right—the key is for them to be able to overcome their misconceptions (influenced by their knowledge of how to add whole numbers) and for them to connect the model to the symbols.

Even after students have more experience with adding and subtracting, they can forget about the meaning of the denominator, so it is important to challenge potential misconceptions. For example, one teacher asked her fifth graders if the following were correct: $\frac{3}{8} + \frac{2}{8} = \frac{5}{16}$. A student correctly replied, "No, because they are eighths (*holds up one-eighth of a fraction circle*). If you put them together you still have eighths (*shows this with the fraction circles*). See, you didn't make them into sixteenths when you put them together. They're still eighths" (Mack, 2004, p. 229).

Failing to Find Common Denominators. Less common, but still prevalent, is the tendency to just ignore the denominator and add the numerators (Siegler et al., 2010). For example, $\frac{4}{5} + \frac{4}{10} = \frac{8}{10}$. This is an indication that students do not understand that the different denominators indicate different-sized pieces. Using a number line or fraction strip, where students must pay attention to the relative size of the fraction, can help develop a stronger understanding of the role of the denominator in adding.

Difficulty Finding Common Multiples. Many students have trouble finding common denominators because they are not able to quickly come up with common multiples of the denominators. This skill requires having a good command of multiplication facts. Activity 16.5 is aimed at the skill of finding least common multiples or common denominators. Least common denominators are preferred because the computation is more manageable with smaller numbers, and there is less simplifying to do after adding and subtracting. But *any* common denominator will work, whether it is the smallest or not. Do not require least common multiples—support all common denominators, and in discussion students will see that finding the smallest multiple is more efficient.

Activity 16.5

Common Multiple Flash Cards

STUDENTS with SPECIAL NEEDS

Make flash cards with pairs of numbers that are potential denominators. Most should be less than 12 (see Figure 16.7). Place students in partners and give them a deck of cards. On a student's turn, he or she turns over a card and states a common multiple (e.g., for 6 and 8, a student might suggest 48). The partner gets a chance to suggest a smaller common multiple (e.g., 24). The student suggesting the least common multiple (LCM) gets to keep the card. Be sure to include pairs that are prime, such as 9 and 5; pairs in which one is a multiple of the other, such as 2 and 8; and pairs that have a common divisor, such as 8 and 12. Start students with disabilities with the card where one member of the pair is a multiple of the other. Color code the cards so that they are easily located.

Difficulty with Mixed Numbers. Too often, instruction with mixed numbers is not well integrated into fraction instruction, and therefore students find these values particularly troubling. Here are three misconceptions described in the research (Petit et al., 2010; Siegler et al., 2010):

1. When given a problem like $3\frac{1}{4} - 1\frac{3}{8}$, students subtract the smaller fraction from the larger ($\frac{3}{8} - \frac{1}{4}$). While this occurs with whole-number subtraction, it is more prevalent with mixed numbers.

2. When given a problem like $4 - \frac{7}{8}$, students don't know what to do with the fact that one number is not a

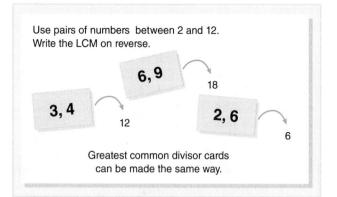

Use pairs of numbers between 2 and 12.
Write the LCM on reverse.

6, 9

18

3, 4

12

2, 6

6

Greatest common divisor cards
can be made the same way.

FIGURE 16.7 Least common multiple (LCM) flash cards.

fraction. They will tend to place an 8 under the four ($\frac{4}{8} - \frac{7}{8}$) in order to find a solution.

3. When given a problem like $14\frac{1}{2} - 3\frac{1}{8}$, students focus only on the whole-number aspect of the problem and don't know what to do with the fractional part.

There are ways to avoid and to address these misconceptions. Include more mixed numbers and whole numbers with fractions less than one. Use models and contexts. And, importantly, take on these misconceptions by making them part of public discussions about whether it is correct and why.

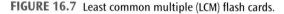

Multiplication

Can you think of a situation that requires using multiplication of whole numbers? Multiplication of fractions? For many, the answer to the first is yes but to the second is no. This is a result of not really understanding what fraction multiplication is and when we are using it in real situations. Here we will share contexts, models, ways to develop the algorithm so that it is understood, and common misconceptions that must be addressed. Fluency in fraction multiplication means that a student can not only do the algorithm but also model problems, estimate, and solve situations that involve multiplication.

Contextual Examples and Models

When working with whole numbers, we would say that 3×5 means "3 sets of 5" (equal sets) or "3 rows of 5" (area or array) or "5 three times" (number line). Notice the set, area, and linear models fitting with the multiplication structures. Different models must be used and aligned with contexts so that students get a comprehensive understanding of multiplication of fractions. The story problems that you use to pose multiplication tasks to students need not be elaborate, but it is important to think about the numbers and contexts that you use in the problems. A possible progression of problem difficulty is developed in the sections that follow.

Fractions of Whole Numbers. Students' first experiences with multiplication should involve finding fractions of whole numbers. In Chapter 15, several examples of finding fractions of the whole are provided, such as, "If the whole is 45, how much is $\frac{1}{5}$ of the whole?" A more challenging example is, "If the whole is 24, what is $\frac{3}{8}$ of the whole?" These reasoning tasks lead into discussions of what multiplication of fractions means. Activity 16.6 provides some great starting tasks.

Activity 16.6

Walking, Wheels, and Water

ENGLISH LANGUAGE LEARNERS

Ask students to use any manipulative or drawing to figure out the answers to the next three tasks. As you will notice, they represent area, linear, and set models in different contexts.

1. The walk from school to the public library takes 15 minutes. When Anna asked her mom how far they had gone, her mom said that they had gone $\frac{2}{3}$ of the way. How many minutes have they walked? (Assume a constant walking rate.)
2. There are 15 cars in Michael's matchbox car collection. Two-thirds of the cars are red. How many red cars does Michael have?
3. Wilma filled 15 glasses with $\frac{2}{3}$ cup of water in each. How much water did Wilma use?

Rather than have three different contexts, ELLs will benefit from three stories using the same context (vocabulary). This should still include three different models; for example, all three could be about cars but include parking lot (area), line of cars (linear), and collection (set).

How might students think through each problem? For problems 1 and 2, students might partition 15 into three groups (or partition a line into three parts) and then see how many are in two parts. Recording this in symbols ($\frac{2}{3}$ of 15) gives the following result: $15 \div 3 \times 2$.

Notice that problem 3 is "15 groups of $\frac{2}{3}$" and not "$\frac{2}{3}$ of a group of 15." Although the commutative property means that these numbers can be switched, it is important that students understand each type as representations whose meanings are different. The problem might be solved in a counting-up strategy. It may be solved by repeated addition: $\frac{2}{3} + \frac{2}{3} + \frac{2}{3} + \ldots + \frac{2}{3} = 30/3 = 10$. Students may notice that what they did was multiply the numerator by 15, so $(15 \times 2)/3 = 30/3 = 10$.

FORMATIVE Assessment Notes

These "fraction of a whole" problems can be used as a **performance assessment**. From their written solutions and from what you observe as students work, record your insights on a checklist about which of these models (area, linear, and set) are easy or challenging

for different learners. This will provide valuable insights in terms of planning instruction that builds on student strengths, because you can select examples and models that make sense to students. Also, you can identify which models need more attention so that they are better understood.

Fractions of Fractions—No Subdivisions. Once students have had experiences with fractions of a whole ($\frac{2}{3}$ of 15) or wholes of fractions (15 groups of $\frac{2}{3}$), a next step is to introduce fraction of a fraction, but carefully pick tasks where no additional partitioning is required. See if you can mentally answer the next three problems (again, using each model type):

> You have $\frac{3}{4}$ of a pizza left. If you give $\frac{1}{3}$ of the leftover pizza to your brother, how much of a whole pizza will your brother get?

> Someone ate $\frac{1}{10}$ of the loaf of bread, leaving $\frac{9}{10}$. If you use $\frac{2}{3}$ of what is left of the loaf to make French toast, how much of a whole loaf will you have used?

> Gloria used $2\frac{1}{2}$ tubes of blue paint to paint the sky in her picture. Each tube holds $\frac{4}{5}$ ounce of paint. How many ounces of blue paint did Gloria use?

In these problems, fractional parts have been chosen that do not need to be subdivided further. The first problem is $\frac{1}{3}$ of three things, the second is $\frac{2}{3}$ of nine things, and the last is $2\frac{1}{2}$ of four things. Figure 16.8 shows how problems of this type might be modeled. However, it is important for students to model and solve these problems in their own way, using whatever models or drawings they choose as long as they can explain their reasoning. In fact, there is more than one way to partition. In $\frac{3}{4} \times \frac{1}{3}$, for example, you can find one-third of the three-fourths (as in Figure 16.8), or you could find $\frac{1}{3}$ of *each* fourth and then combine the pieces (Izsák, 2008).

Subdividing the Unit Parts. When the pieces must be subdivided into smaller unit parts, the problems become more challenging.

> Zack had $\frac{2}{3}$ of the lawn left to cut. After lunch, he cut $\frac{3}{4}$ of the lawn he had left. How much of the whole lawn did Zack cut after lunch?

> The zookeeper had a huge bottle of the animals' favorite liquid treat, Zoo Cola. The monkey drank $\frac{1}{5}$ of the bottle. The zebra drank $\frac{2}{3}$ of what was left. How much of the bottle of Zoo Cola did the zebra drink?

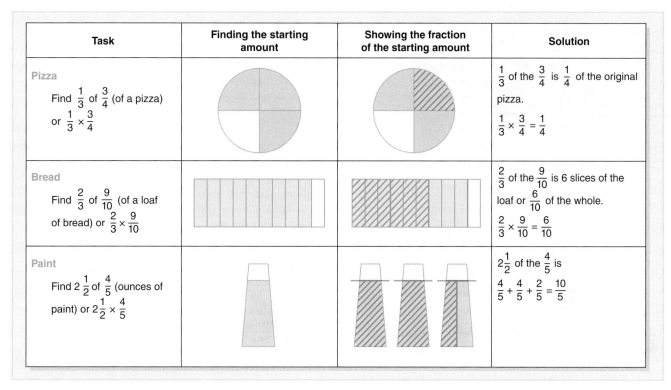

Task	Finding the starting amount	Showing the fraction of the starting amount	Solution
Pizza Find $\frac{1}{3}$ of $\frac{3}{4}$ (of a pizza) or $\frac{1}{3} \times \frac{3}{4}$			$\frac{1}{3}$ of the $\frac{3}{4}$ is $\frac{1}{4}$ of the original pizza. $\frac{1}{3} \times \frac{3}{4} = \frac{1}{4}$
Bread Find $\frac{2}{3}$ of $\frac{9}{10}$ (of a loaf of bread) or $\frac{2}{3} \times \frac{9}{10}$			$\frac{2}{3}$ of the $\frac{9}{10}$ is 6 slices of the loaf or $\frac{6}{10}$ of the whole. $\frac{2}{3} \times \frac{9}{10} = \frac{6}{10}$
Paint Find $2\frac{1}{2}$ of $\frac{4}{5}$ (ounces of paint) or $2\frac{1}{2} \times \frac{4}{5}$			$2\frac{1}{2}$ of the $\frac{4}{5}$ is $\frac{4}{5} + \frac{4}{5} + \frac{2}{5} = \frac{10}{5}$

FIGURE 16.8 Connecting representation to the procedure for three problems involving multiplication.

 PAUSE and REFLECT

Pause for a moment and figure out how you would solve each of these problems. Draw pictures to help you, but do not use a computational algorithm. ●

In Zack's lawn problem, it is necessary to find fourths of two things, the 2 *thirds* of the grass left to cut. In the Zoo Cola problem, you need thirds of four things, the 4 *fifths* of the cola that remain. Again, the concepts of the top number counting and the bottom number naming what is counted play an important role. Figure 16.9 shows a possible solution for Zack's lawn problem. A similar approach can be used for the Zoo Cola problem. You may have used different drawings, but the ideas should be the same.

Using a paper strip and partitioning is an effective way to solve multiplication problems, especially when they require additional partitioning (Siebert & Gaskin, 2006). Figure 16.9 illustrates how to use paper strips for the problem $\frac{3}{4} \times \frac{2}{3}$. (*Three-fourths of $\frac{2}{3}$ of a whole is how much of a whole?*) Solving this problem requires that the thirds be subdivided.

 The NLVM website (http://nlvm.usu.edu) has a nice collection of fraction applets. *Number Line Bars—Fractions* allows the user to place *TECHNOLOGY* bars of any fractional length along a number line. The number line can be adjusted to have increments from $\frac{1}{2}$ to $\frac{1}{15}$, but the user must decide. For example, if bars

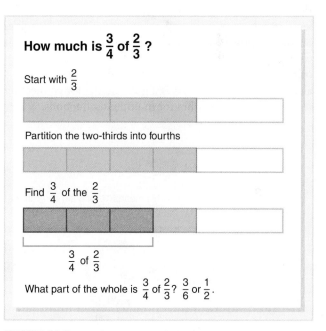

FIGURE 16.9 Solutions to a multiplication problem when the parts must be subdivided.

of $\frac{1}{4}$ and $\frac{1}{3}$ are placed end to end, the result cannot be read from the applet until the increments are in twelfths.

Multiplication of fractions can be modeled with counters (see Figure 16.10). Do not discourage students from

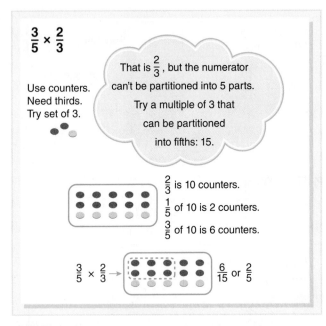

FIGURE 16.10 Modeling multiplication of fractions with counters.

using counters, but be prepared to help them find ways to determine the whole.

Area Model. The area model for modeling fraction multiplication has several advantages. First, it works for problems in which partitioning a length can be challenging. Second, it provides a powerful visual to show that a result can be quite a bit smaller than either of the fractions used or that if the fractions are both close to 1, then the result is also close to one. Third, it is a good model for connecting to the standard algorithm for multiplying fractions.

Provide students with a square as in Figure 16.11 and ask them to illustrate the first fraction. For example, in $\frac{3}{5} \times \frac{3}{4}$, you are finding $\frac{3}{5}$ of $\frac{3}{4}$, so you first must show $\frac{3}{4}$ (see Figure 16.11(a)). To find fifths of the $\frac{3}{4}$, draw four horizontal lines through the $\frac{3}{4}$ (see Figure 16.11(b)) or all the way across the square so that the whole is in the same-sized partitions (see Figure 16.11(c)).

Using a context and building on whole-number knowledge can support student reasoning about a fraction of a fraction. Quilting is a good context, since quilts are rectangles and the individual rectangles (or squares) within the quilt are a fraction of the whole quilt. Activity 16.7 provides a two-step activity with quilts adapted from Tsankova & Pjanic (2009/2010).

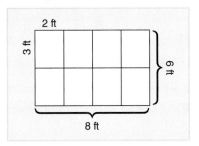

Activity 16.7

Quilting Pieces

Have students use grid paper to sketch a drawing of a quilt that will be 8 feet by 6 feet—or create a full-sized one for your class! Explain that each group will prepare a picture that is 3 feet by 2 feet for the quilt. Ask students to tell you what fraction of the quilt a group will provide.

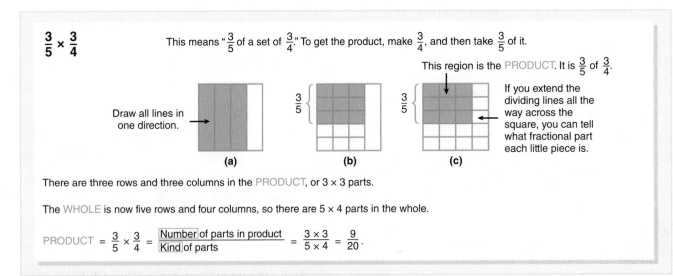

FIGURE 16.11 Development of the standard algorithm for multiplication of fractions.

Second, rephrase the task. Explain that in the quilt, each group is to prepare a section of the quilt that is $\frac{1}{4}$ of the length and $\frac{1}{2}$ of the width. Ask students to sketch the quilt and the portion that their group will prepare.

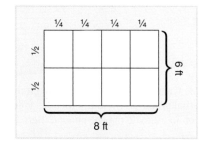

Help students make the connection that $\frac{1}{4}$ the length $\times$ $\frac{1}{2}$ the width $= \frac{1}{8}$ of the area $(\frac{1}{4} \times \frac{1}{2} = \frac{1}{8})$.

The following activity (adapted from Imm, Stylianou, & Chae, 2008, p. 459) engages students in exploring multiplication of fractions and the commutative property.

Activity 16.8

Playground Problem

Show students the problem below. Ask students to predict which community will have the bigger playground. Record predictions. Place students in partners, and ask one to solve the problem for community A and the other to solve for community B. Once they have completed their illustrations and solutions, ask students to compare their responses and to be ready to report to the class what they decided.

Two communities, A and B, are building playgrounds in grassy lots that are 50 yards by 100 yards. In community A, they have been asked to convert $\frac{3}{4}$ of their lot to a playground, and $\frac{2}{5}$ of that playground should be covered with blacktop. In community B, they are building their playground on $\frac{2}{5}$ of the lot, and $\frac{3}{4}$ of the playground should be blacktop. In which park is the grassy playground bigger? In which lot is the blacktop bigger? Illustrate and explain.

TECHNOLOGY

Area models can also be found at the NLVM site. The Fractions Rectangle Multiplication applet allows you to explore multiplication of any two fractions up to 2 × 2. Another wonderful interactive site to explore the area model is IMAP: www.sci.sdsu.edu/CRMSE/IMAP/applets/IE_Win/FracFracStory33_IE_WIN_jar/FracFracClass.html.

Developing the Algorithms

With enough experiences using the area model (or the linear model), students will start to notice a pattern. Remem-ber that "enough" is probably a lot more than is usually provided—in other words, this does not mean two or three examples, but several weeks working with different examples and representations. These exercises will lead students to focus on how the denominators relate to how the grid (or line) is partitioned and how the numerator affects the solution to the problem.

When students are ready to start using the standard algorithm, ask them to solve three examples such as the following:

$$\frac{5}{6} \times \frac{1}{2} \qquad \frac{3}{4} \times \frac{1}{5} \qquad \frac{1}{3} \times \frac{9}{10}$$

For each one, use a square and partition it vertically and horizontally to model the problems. Ask, "How did you figure out what the unit of the fraction [the denominator] was?" Or more specifically, on the first problem, you can ask, "How did you figure out that the denominator would be twelfths? Is this a pattern that is true for the other examples?" Then ask students to see whether they can find a similar pattern for how the number of parts (the numerator) is determined.

As you help students focus on the pattern and learn to use the algorithm, do not forget to emphasize the meaning of what they are doing. Ask students to estimate how big they think the answer will be and why. In the first example here, a student might note that the answer will be slightly less than $\frac{1}{2}$ since $\frac{5}{6}$ is close to, but less than, 1.

Factors Greater Than One

As students explore multiplication, begin to include tasks in which one of the factors is a mixed number—for example, $\frac{3}{4} \times 2\frac{1}{2}$. The more these are integrated into multiplication with fractions less than one, the more it will help students think about the impact of multiplying by a number less than one and a number more than one. Activity 16.9 (adapted from Thompson, 1995) is a way to focus on this reasoning.

Activity 16.9

Can You See It?

Post a partially shaded illustration like the one shown here.

Ask students the following questions, and have them explain how they see it.

Can you see $\frac{3}{5}$ of something?   Can you see $\frac{5}{3}$ of $\frac{3}{5}$?

Can you see $\frac{5}{3}$ of something?   Can you see $\frac{2}{3}$ of $\frac{3}{5}$?

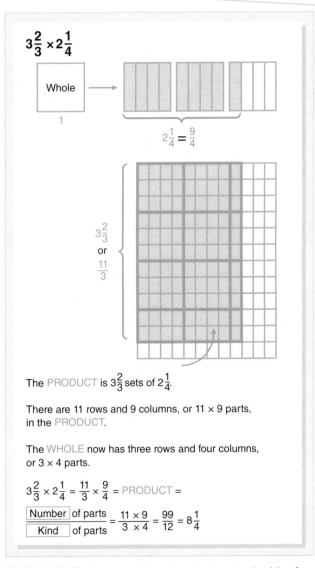

The PRODUCT is $3\frac{2}{3}$ sets of $2\frac{1}{4}$.

There are 11 rows and 9 columns, or 11 × 9 parts, in the PRODUCT.

The WHOLE now has three rows and four columns, or 3 × 4 parts.

$$3\frac{2}{3} \times 2\frac{1}{4} = \frac{11}{3} \times \frac{9}{4} = \text{PRODUCT} =$$

$$\frac{\boxed{\text{Number}} \text{ of parts}}{\boxed{\text{Kind}} \text{ of parts}} = \frac{11 \times 9}{3 \times 4} = \frac{99}{12} = 8\frac{1}{4}$$

FIGURE 16.12 The approach used to develop the algorithm for fractions less than 1 can be expanded to mixed numbers.

Many textbooks have students change mixed numbers to fractions (often referred to as *improper fractions*) in order to multiply them. In fact, students can multiply either way. Area representations can be used to model the problem in both cases, as illustrated in Figure 16.12. This is an efficient way to solve these types of problems, but it is not the only way. Students who understand that $2\frac{1}{2}$ means $2 + \frac{1}{2}$ might multiply $\frac{3}{4} \times 2$ and $\frac{3}{4} \times \frac{1}{2}$ and add the results—the distributive property.

When both factors are mixed numbers, there are four partial products, just as there are when multiplying 2 two-digit numbers.

 PAUSE and REFLECT

Find the four partial products in this multiplication: $3\frac{2}{3} \times 2\frac{1}{4}$. ●

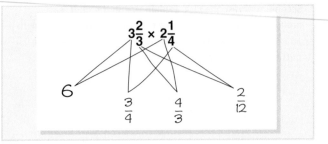

FIGURE 16.13 When multiplying two mixed numbers, there will be four partial products. These can then be added to get the total product, or an estimate may be enough. Here the answer is about 8.

Figure 16.13 shows how this product might be worked out by multiplying the individual parts. In most cases, the partial products can be solved mentally. More importantly, the process is more conceptual and also lends itself to estimation—either before the partial products are determined or after. Notice that the same four partial products of Figure 16.13 can be found in the rectangle in Figure 16.12.

Addressing Misconceptions

When students begin working with fraction multiplication, they already have internalized concepts of whole-number multiplication and fraction addition and subtraction that can lead to confusion. This is exacerbated when students are not given adequate time to explore multiplication of fractions conceptually and when they are too quickly pressed to memorize rules, such as "multiply both the bottom and the top." The result of memorizing rules that don't make sense is an inability to solve multiplication problems. This becomes a significant barrier for solving proportions and algebraic expressions.

Treating the Denominator the Same as in Addition/Subtraction Problems.   Why does the denominator stay the same when adding fractions and get multiplied when multiplying fractions? Do you have a conceptual explanation for this? You need one. In adding, the process is counting parts of a whole, so those parts must be the same size. In multiplication, you are actually finding a part of a part, so the part may change size. Compare the two operations with a rectangle, circle, or number line to see how these are conceptually different.

Inability to Estimate Approximate Size of the Answer. Some students have been told that multiplication makes bigger. So they have difficulty deciding whether their answers make sense. On one hand, they may never even think about fraction size, so any answer looks good to them (e.g., $\frac{1}{2} \times 6\frac{1}{4} = 12\frac{1}{8}$). On the other hand, they might actually notice the answer ($\frac{1}{2} \times 6\frac{1}{4} = 3\frac{1}{8}$) but become concerned that this can't be right because the answer should be bigger.

Estimation, contexts, and visuals are needed to better understand fraction multiplication.

Matching Multiplication Situations with Multiplication (and Not Division). Multiplication and division are closely related, and our language is sometimes not as precise as it needs to be. In the question, "What is $\frac{1}{3}$ of \$24?" students may correctly decide to divide by 3 or multiply by $\frac{1}{3}$. But they may (incorrectly) divide by $\frac{1}{3}$, confusing the idea that they are finding a fraction of the whole. This is more evident when the numbers are more complex or the story is more involved. Estimation can help students. This is particularly true for ELLs, who become confused by language such as "divide it *in* half" and "divide it *by* half" (Carr et al., 2009). Ask, "Should the result be larger or smaller than the original amount?" Also, having students rewrite a phrase to more clearly state the problem can help them determine whether the appropriate operation is multiplication or division.

Division

Can you think of a real-life example for dividing by a fraction? Few people can, even though we conceptually use division by fractions in many real-life situations. Do you know the "invert and multiply" algorithm? Have you used it in real situations? Division of fractions remains one of the most mysterious algorithms in elementary mathematics. We want to avoid this mystery at all costs and help students really understand when and how to divide fractions.

Contextual Examples and Models

As with the other operations, begin by building on students' prior knowledge of division with whole numbers. Recall that there are two meanings of division: partitive and measurement (Gregg & Gregg, 2007; Kribs-Zaleta, 2008; Tirosh, 2000). We will review each separately here and look at story problems in each problem type. In the classroom, the types of problems should eventually be mixed. As with multiplication, how the numbers relate to each other in the problems tends to affect the level of difficulty.

Measurement Interpretation of Division. The measurement interpretation is also called *repeated subtraction* or *equal groups* (NCTM, 2006). In these situations, an equal group is taken away from the total repeatedly. For example, *If you have 13 quarts of lemonade, how many canteens holding 3 quarts each can you fill?* Notice that this is not a sharing situation but rather an equal subtraction situation.

The measurement interpretation is a good way to begin fraction division because students can draw illustrations to show the measures (Cramer et al., 2010). And measurement interpretation will be used to develop an algorithm

for dividing fractions, so it is important for students to explore this idea in contextual situations.

Students readily understand problems such as this (adapted from Schifter, Bastable, & Russell, 1999a, p. 120):

> You are going to a birthday party. From Mitch and Bob's Ice Cream Factory, you order 6 pints of ice cream. If you serve $\frac{3}{4}$ of a pint of ice cream to each guest, how many guests can be served?

Students typically draw pictures of six items divided into fourths and count out how many servings of $\frac{3}{4}$ can be found. The difficulty is in seeing this as $6 \div \frac{3}{4}$, and that part will require some direct guidance on your part. One idea is to compare the problem to one involving whole numbers (6 pints, 2 per guest) and make connections.

Gregg and Gregg (2007) produced a method for developing the concept of division of fractions through servings, a measurement context. In tasks that progress in difficulty, they pose problems and include visuals of the size of the pieces. Figure 16.14 includes a subset of these tasks.

As the figure shows, moving slowly to more complex examples will enable students to use their whole-number concepts to build an understanding of division with fractions. Over time, students will be able to take on problems that are more complex both in the context and in the numbers involved, as in the following example:

> Farmer Brown found that he had $2\frac{1}{4}$ gallons of liquid fertilizer concentrate. It takes $\frac{3}{4}$ gallon to make a tank of mixed fertilizer. How many tankfuls can he mix?

Try solving this problem yourself. Use any model or drawing you wish to help explain what you are doing. Notice that you are trying to find out *How many sets of 3 fourths are in a set of 9 fourths?* Your answer should be 3 tankfuls (not 3 fourths).

Partitive Interpretation of Division. In this model, the problem asks us to partition or share the whole. Too often, we think of the partition problems strictly as sharing problems: 24 apples to be shared with 4 friends. But it also applies to rate problems: If you walk 12 miles in 3 hours, how many miles do you walk per hour? Both of these problems, in fact, are partition problems, asking, "How much is the amount for *one* friend?" "How many miles are walked in *one* hour?"

Fraction Divided by a Whole Number. This is not really a big leap from whole-number division. However, as you work through these questions, notice that you are answering the question, "How much is the whole?" or "How much for one?"

FIGURE 16.14 Tasks that use the measurement interpretation of "How many servings?" to develop the concept of division.

Source: Gregg, J., & Gregg, D. W. (2007). "Measurement and Fair-Sharing Models for Dividing Fractions." *Mathematics Teaching in the Middle School, 12*(9), p. 491. Reprinted with permission. Copyright © 2007 by the National Council of Teachers of Mathematics. All rights reserved.

Cassie has $5\frac{1}{3}$ yards of ribbon to make four bows for birthday packages. How much ribbon should she use for each bow if she wants to use the same length of ribbon for each?

When the $5\frac{1}{3}$ is thought of as fractional parts, there are 16 thirds to share, or 4 thirds for each ribbon. Alternatively, one might think of allotting 1 yard per bow, leaving $1\frac{1}{3}$ yards. These 4 thirds are then shared, one per bow, for a total of $1\frac{1}{3}$ yards for each bow. The unit parts (thirds) required no further partitioning in order to do the division. In the following problem, the parts must be split into smaller parts:

Mark has $1\frac{1}{4}$ hours to finish his three chores. If he divides his time evenly, how many hours can he give to each chore?

Note that the question is, "How many hours for one chore?" The 5 fourths of an hour that Mark has do not split neatly into three parts. So some or all of the parts must be partitioned. Figure 16.15 shows how to model these with each type of model (area, linear, and set). In each case, all of the fourths are subdivided into three equal parts, producing twelfths. There are a total of 15 twelfths, or $\frac{5}{12}$ hour for each chore. (Test this answer against the solution in minutes: $1\frac{1}{4}$ hours is 75 minutes, which divided among 3 chores is 25 minutes per chore. $\frac{25}{60} = \frac{5}{12}$.)

Fraction Divided by a Smaller Fraction. The sharing concept appears to break down when the divisor is a fraction. It is enormously helpful to keep in mind that for partition and rate problems, the fundamental question is, "How much is one?" However, the activities on finding the

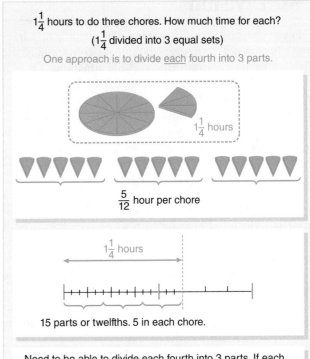

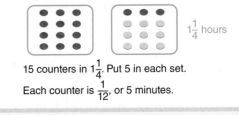

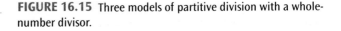

FIGURE 16.15 Three models of partitive division with a whole-number divisor.

whole (see Chapter 15, Figure 15.11) build a foundation for finding a fraction of a fraction. For example, if 18 counters represents $2\frac{1}{4}$ sets, how much is one whole set? In solving these problems, the first task is to find the number in one-fourth and then multiply by 4 to get 4 fourths or *one*. Let's see if we can see the same process in the following activity.

Activity 16.10

How Much for 1?

Pose contextual problems, like the ones here, where the focus question is, "How much for one ____?"

   a. Dan paid $3.00 for a $\frac{3}{4}$ pound box of cereal. How much is that per pound?

   b. Andrea found that if she walks quickly during her morning exercise, she can cover $2\frac{1}{2}$ miles in $\frac{3}{4}$ of an hour. She wonders how fast she is walking in miles per hour.

With both problems, first find the amount of one-fourth (partitioning) and then the value of one whole (iterating). Andrea's walking problem is a bit harder because the $2\frac{1}{2}$ miles, or 5 half miles, do not neatly divide into three parts. If this was difficult for you, try dividing each half into three parts. Draw pictures if that will help.

Answers That Are Not Whole Numbers

Most problems are not going to come out evenly. If Cassie had 5 yards of ribbon to make bows, and each needs $1\frac{1}{6}$ yards each, she could make only four bows because a part of a bow does not make sense. But other contexts, like the Farmer Brown problem, don't require the student to disregard the leftover. If Farmer Brown begins with 4 gallons of concentrate and makes five tanks of mix, he uses $\frac{15}{4}$, or $3\frac{3}{4}$ gallons, of the concentrate. With the $\frac{1}{4}$ gallon of remaining concentrate, he can make a *partial* tank of mix. He can make $\frac{1}{3}$ of a tank of mix, because it takes *3* fourths to make a whole, and he has *1* fourth of a gallon (he has one of the three parts he needs for a tank).

Here is another problem to try:

John is building a patio. Each patio section requires $\frac{1}{3}$ of a cubic yard of concrete. The concrete truck holds $2\frac{1}{2}$ cubic yards of concrete. If there is not enough for a full section at the end, John can put in a divider and make a partial section. How many patio sections can John make with the concrete in the truck?

 PAUSE and REFLECT

You should first try to solve this problem in some way that makes sense to *you*. Stop and do this now. ●

One way to do this is counting how many thirds there are in $2\frac{1}{2}$.

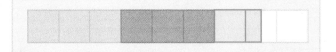

Here you can see that you get 3 patio sections from the yellow whole and 3 more from the orange whole, and then you get 1 more full section and $\frac{1}{2}$ of what you need for another patio section. So the answer is $7\frac{1}{2}$. Students will want to write the "remainder" as $\frac{1}{3}$ because they were measuring in thirds, but the question is how many sections can be made—$7\frac{1}{2}$.

Will common denominators work for division? Let's see. In the problem you just solved, $2\frac{1}{2} \div \frac{1}{3}$, the problem would become $2\frac{3}{6} \div \frac{2}{6}$, or it could be $\frac{15}{6} \div \frac{2}{6}$. The question becomes, *How many sets of 2 sixths are in a set of 15 sixths? Or, How many twos in 15?* This produces the correct answer of $7\frac{1}{2}$. This is as efficient as the standard algorithm, and it may make more sense to students to do it this way.

Figure 16.16 shows two division problems solved this way, each with a different representation. That is, both the dividend or given quantity and the divisor are expressed in the same type of fractional parts. This results in a whole-number division problem.

Developing the Algorithms

There are two different algorithms for division of fractions. Methods of teaching both algorithms are discussed here.

Common-Denominator Algorithm. The common-denominator algorithm relies on the measurement or repeated subtraction concept of division. Consider the problem $\frac{5}{3} \div \frac{1}{2}$. As shown in Figure 16.17, once each number is expressed in terms of the same fractional part, the answer is exactly the same as the whole-number problem $10 \div 3$. The name of the fractional part (the denominator) is no longer important, and the problem is one of dividing the numerators. The resulting algorithm, therefore, is as follows: *To divide fractions, first get common denominators, and then divide numerators.* For example, $\frac{5}{3} \div \frac{1}{4} = \frac{20}{12} \div \frac{3}{12} = 20 \div 3 = \frac{20}{3} = 6\frac{2}{3}$.

Try using circular fraction pieces, fraction strips, and then sets of counters to model $1\frac{2}{3} \div \frac{3}{4}$ using a common-denominator approach.

Invert-and-Multiply Algorithm. Providing a series of tasks and having students look for patterns in how they are finding the answers can help students discover this poorly understood and commonly taught algorithm. For example, consider this first set, in which the divisor is a unit fraction. Remember to pose the related question that goes with each equation. Servings of food can be the context.

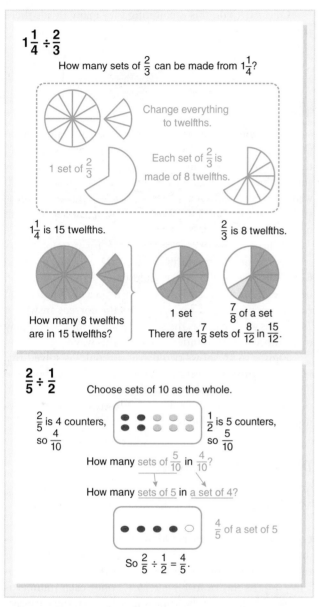

FIGURE 16.16 Common denominators can be used to solve division of fraction problems.

$3 \div \frac{1}{2} =$ (How many servings of $\frac{1}{2}$ in 3 containers?)

$5 \div \frac{1}{4} =$ (How many servings of $\frac{1}{4}$ in 5 containers?)

$8 \div \frac{1}{5} =$ (How many servings of $\frac{1}{5}$ in 8 containers?)

$3\frac{3}{4} \div \frac{1}{8} =$ (How many servings of $\frac{1}{8}$ in $3\frac{3}{4}$ containers?)

In looking across these problems (and others) and looking for a pattern, students will notice they are multiplying by the denominator of the second fraction. For example, in the third example, a student might say, "You get five for every whole container, so 5×8 is 40."

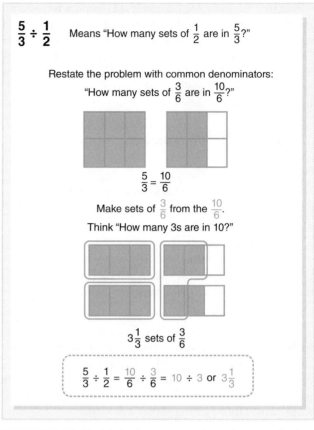

FIGURE 16.17 Models for the common-denominator method for fraction division.

Then move to similar problems, but with a second fraction that is not a unit fraction:

$5 \div \frac{3}{4} =$

$8 \div \frac{2}{5} =$

$3\frac{3}{4} \div \frac{3}{8} =$

Have students solve these problems and compare these responses to the problems in the first set. Notice that if there are 40 one-fifths in 8, then when you group the fifths in pairs (two-fifths), you will have half as many—20. Stated in servings, if the serving is twice as big, you will have half the number of servings. Similarly, if the fraction is $\frac{3}{4}$, after finding how many fourths, you will group in threes, which means you will get $\frac{1}{3}$ the number of servings. You can see that this means you must divide by 3.

The examples given were measurements because the size of the group (serving) was known, but not the number of groups. Partitioning or sharing examples nicely illustrate the standard algorithm. Consider this example:

> **You have $1\frac{1}{2}$ oranges, which is $\frac{3}{5}$ of an adult serving. How many oranges (and parts of oranges) make up 1 adult serving? (Kribs-Zaleta, 2008)**

You may be thinking that you first need to find what a fifth would be—which would be one-third of the oranges you have—or $\frac{1}{2}$ an orange (notice you are dividing by the numerator). Then, to get the whole serving, you multiply $\frac{1}{2}$ by 5 (the denominator) to get $2\frac{1}{2}$ oranges in 1 adult serving.

In either the measurement or the partitive interpretations, the denominator leads you to find out how many fourths, fifths, or eighths you have, and the numerator tells you the size of the serving, so you group according to how many are in the serving. So the process is *multiply by the denominator and divide by the numerator*. At some point, someone reasoned that just flipping the fraction would be more straightforward—multiplying by the top and dividing by the bottom—and that is why we have learned to "invert and multiply."

Addressing Misconceptions

The biggest misunderstanding with division of fractions is just not knowing what the algorithm means. Once students realize the meaning of division, they are able to begin thinking of different ways to approach problems and decide whether their answers make sense. Within division, there are some common misconceptions that need to be addressed.

Thinking the Answer Should Be Smaller.   Based on their experiences with whole-number division, students think that when dividing by a fraction, the answer should be smaller. This is true if the divisor is a fraction greater than one (e.g., $\frac{5}{3}$), but it is not true if the fraction is less than one. One way to help students address the misconception is to ask them to estimate. Estimation can be a final product, like in Activity 16.3, or it can just be a beginning to doing a computation as a way to help students decide whether their answer is reasonable.

Connecting the Illustration with the Answer.   Students may understand that $1\frac{1}{2} \div \frac{1}{4}$ means "How many fourths are in $1\frac{1}{2}$?" So they may set out to count how many fourths and get 6. But in recording their answer, they can confuse the fact that they were using fractions and instead record $\frac{6}{4}$ (Cramer et al., 2010).

Writing Remainders.   As noted above, knowing what the unit is (the divisor) is critical and must be understood in giving the remainder (Coughlin, 2010/2011; Lamon, 2006). In the problem $3\frac{3}{8} \div \frac{1}{4}$, students are likely to count 4 fourths for each whole (12 fourths) and one more for $\frac{2}{8}$ but then not know what to do with the extra eighth. It is important to be sure they understand the measurement concept of division. Ask, "How much of the next piece do you have?" Context can also help, in particular, servings. In this case, if this problem were about pizza servings, there would be 13 full servings and $\frac{1}{2}$ of the next serving.

 **RESOURCES** *for Chapter 16*

LITERATURE CONNECTIONS

Alice's Adventures in Wonderland *Carroll and Gray, 1865/1992*

This well-known children's story needs no introduction. Because Alice shrinks in the story, there is an opportunity to explore multiplication by fractions. Taber (2007) describes in detail how she used this story to engage students in understanding the meaning of multiplication of fractions. She begins by asking how tall Alice would be if she were originally 54" tall but was shrunk to $\frac{1}{9}$ of her height. What height will Alice be if she is later restored to only $\frac{5}{6}$ her original height? The students write their own Alice multiplication-of-fractions equations.

The Man Who Made Parks *Wishinsky and Zhang, 1999*

This nonfiction book explains the remarkable story of Frederick Olmsted, who designed Central Park in New York City.

Creating a park design, students can be given fractional amounts for what needs to be included in the park—for example, $\frac{2}{5}$ gardens, $\frac{1}{10}$ playgrounds, $\frac{1}{2}$ natural habitat (streams and forest), and the rest special features (like a zoo or outdoor theater). Students can build the plan for their park on a rectangular grid. To include multiplication of fractions, include guidelines such as that $\frac{3}{4}$ of the park is natural habitat, with $\frac{1}{3}$ of that to be wooded and $\frac{1}{6}$ to be water features, and so on.

RECOMMENDED READINGS

Articles

Cramer, K., Wyberg, T., & Leavitt, S. (2008). The role of representations in fraction addition and subtraction. *Mathematics Teaching in the Middle School, 13*(8), 490–496. *Illustrations and student work are used to show how to teach addition and subtraction using the fraction circle. Essential considerations of effective instruction are emphasized.*

Gregg, J., & Gregg, D. U. (2007). Measurement and fair-sharing models for dividing fractions. *Mathematics Teaching in the Middle School, 12*(9), 490–496.

These authors provide a series of tasks to develop the concept of division of fractions—a must-read for a teacher needing more experiences exploring division or trying to plan a good instructional sequence.

Huinker, D. (1998). Letting fraction algorithms emerge through problem solving. In L. J. Morrow (Ed.), *The teaching and learning of algorithms in school mathematics* (pp. 170–182). Reston, VA: NCTM.

Huinker takes the idea of students inventing algorithms and applies it to problems involving fractions. With examples of children's work, this article makes a good case for avoiding rules and letting students work with ideas that make sense.

Imm, K. L., Stylianou, D. A., & Chae, N. (2008). Student representations at the center: Promoting classroom equity. *Mathematics Teaching in the Middle School, 13*(8), 458–463.

Using a park context, these authors explain how to model multiplication of fractions. Equity and a culture for learning are emphasized.

ONLINE RESOURCES

Diffy
http://nlvm.usu.edu/en/nav/frames_asid_326_g_3_t_1 .html

The goal in a Diffy puzzle is to find differences between the numbers on the corners of the square, working to a desired difference in the center. When working with fractions, the difference of two fractions is a fraction that can be written in many different ways, and students must recognize equivalent forms.

Fractions—Adding
http://nlvm.usu.edu/en/nav/frames_asid_106_g_2_t_1 .html

Two fractions and an area model for each are given. The user must find a common denominator to rename and add the fractions.

Fraction Bars
http://nlvm.usu.edu/en/nav/frames_asid_203_g_2_t_1 .html

Much like Cuisenaire rods, this applet places bars over a number line on which the step size can be adjusted, providing a flexible model that can be used for all four operations.

REFLECTIONS *on Chapter 16*

WRITING TO LEARN

1. Why is it important to teach computational estimation with fractions?
2. A student adds $\frac{4}{5} + \frac{2}{3}$ and gets $\frac{6}{8}$. How will you help the student understand that this is incorrect? How would you redirect him or her to do it correctly?
3. For the problem $3\frac{1}{4} - 1\frac{1}{2}$, think of a story problem that would be a "take away" situation and one that would be a "comparison" situation.
4. Explain at least one mental method (estimation or mental computation) for each of these:

$$\frac{3}{4} \times 5\frac{1}{2} \qquad 1\frac{1}{8} \text{ of } 40$$

5. Make up a word problem with a fraction as a divisor. Is your problem a measurement problem or a partition problem? Make up a second word problem with fractions of the other type (measurement or partition).

FOR DISCUSSION AND EXPLORATION

1. Imagine you are about to start teaching fraction computation. You quickly find that your students have a very weak understanding of fractions. Your textbook primarily targets the algorithms. Some teachers argue that there is no time to reteach the concepts of fractions. Others would argue that it is necessary to teach the meanings of numerators and denominators and equivalent fractions or else all the computation will be meaningless rules. How will you plan for instruction? Justify your approach.
2. Several calculators are now available that do computations in fractional form as well as in decimal form. If you have access to such a calculator, discuss how it might be used in teaching fraction operations. If such calculators become commonplace, should we continue to teach fraction computation?

MyEducationLab™

Go to the MyEducationLab (www.myeducationlab.com) for Math Methods and familiarize yourself with the content. Much of the site content is organized topically. The topics include all of the following to support your learning in the course:

- Learning outcomes for important mathematics methods course topics aligned with the national standards
- Assignments and Activities, tied to these learning outcomes and standards, that can help you more deeply understand course content
- Building Teaching Skills and Dispositions learning units that allow you to apply and practice your understanding of the core mathematics content and teaching skills

Your instructor has a correlation guide that aligns the exercises on the topical portion of the site with your book's chapters.

On MyEducationLab you will also find book-specific resources including Blackline Masters, Expanded Lesson Activities, and Artifact Analysis Activities.

Field Experience Guide
C O N N E C T I O N S

The link sheet in FEG 3.4 is an excellent planning tool and an assessment tool, as it focuses on four representations for a topic such as multiplication of fractions. Both FEG 3.4 and FEG 7.2 could be used to interview students to find out what they know about fraction computation. FEG Expanded Lessons 9.7 and 9.9 are designed to help students understand fraction multiplication and division, respectively. In addition, FEG 10.4 ("Factor Quest"), which targets factors, and FEG 10.6 ("Interference"), which targets multiples, are good activities to use when teaching computation of fractions.

Chapter 17

Developing Concepts of Decimals and Percents

People need to be able to interpret decimals for such varied needs as reading precise metric measures, calculating distances, interpreting output on a calculator, or understanding sports statistics such as those at the Olympics, where winners and losers are separated by hundredths of a second. Decimals are critically important in many occupations: For nurses, pharmacists, and workers building airplanes, for example, the level of precision affects safety for the general public. Because students and teachers have been shown to have greater difficulty understanding decimals than fractions (Martinie, 2007; Ubuz & Yayan, 2010), conceptual understanding of decimals and their connections to fractions must be carefully developed.

The *Common Core State Standards* align with the *Curriculum Focal Points* (NCTM, 2006) in stating that fourth-grade students should "understand decimal notation for fractions and compare decimal fractions" (CCSSO, 2010, p. 31). (The phrase "decimal fractions" is often shortened to "decimals," and in this chapter we will use these terms interchangeably.) Both documents also suggest that most work on decimal computation should occur in the fifth grade and repeat later in grades 6 and 7. Fraction instruction initially precedes decimal fractions, but it is very important that the concepts of decimals, fractions, and place value are integrated and connected, both from a pedagogical view as well as a practical view.

BIG IDEAS

1. The base-ten place-value system extends infinitely in two directions: to tiny values as well as to large values. Between any two place values, the 10-to-1 ratio remains the same.

2. The decimal point is a convention that has been developed to indicate the units position. The position to the left of the decimal point is the unit that is being counted as singles or ones.

3. Decimal fractions are simply another way of writing fractions. Both notations have value. Maximum flexibility is gained by understanding how the two symbol systems are related.

4. Percents are simply hundredths and as such are a third way of writing both fractions and decimals.

5. Addition and subtraction with decimals are based on the fundamental concept of adding and subtracting the numbers in like position values—a simple extension from whole numbers.

6. Multiplication and division of two numbers will produce the same digits, regardless of the positions of the decimal point. As a result, the computations can be performed as whole numbers with the decimal placed by way of estimation.

Mathematics CONTENT CONNECTIONS

The most important connections for decimals are built between decimal numbers and the concepts of fractions.

◆ **Fraction Concepts** (Chapter 15): Both decimal and fraction symbolism represent the same ideas—the rational numbers.

◆ **Proportional Thinking** (Chapter 18): Percents are a part-to-whole ratio and can be extended to proportion concepts.

◆ **Measurement** (Chapter 19): The metric system is modeled after the base-ten system, and metric measures are expressed in decimals. Conversion from one metric measure to another depends on understanding the decimal system.

◆ **Real Number System** (Chapter 23): Decimal numeration is helpful in characterizing and understanding the density of the rational numbers and for approximating irrational numbers.

Extending the Place-Value System

Before exploring decimal numerals with students, it is advisable to review ideas of whole-number place value. One of the most basic of these ideas is the 10-to-1 multiplicative relationship between the values of any two adjacent positions. In terms of a base-ten model such as paper strips and squares, 10 of any one piece will make 1 of the next larger (to the immediate left), and movement of a piece to the immediate right involves division by 10 (1 divided by 10 is one-tenth).

A Two-Way Relationship. The 10-makes-1 rule continues indefinitely to larger and larger pieces or positional values. As you learned in Chapter 11, if you are using the paper strip-and-square model, for example, the strip and square shapes alternate in an infinite progression as they get larger. Likewise, each piece to the right in this continuum gets smaller by one-tenth. The critical question becomes "Is there ever a smallest piece?" In the students' experience, the smallest piece is the centimeter square or unit piece. But couldn't that piece be divided into 10 small strips? And couldn't those small strips be divided into 10 very small squares, and so on?

The goal of this discussion is to help students see that a 10-to-1 relationship can extend infinitely in two directions. There is no smallest piece and no largest piece. The symmetry of the system is around the ones place—not the decimal point. (Tens are to the left of the ones place, tenths are to the right, and so on.) The relationship between adja-

cent pieces is the same regardless of which two adjacent pieces are being considered. Figure 17.1 illustrates this idea.

Regrouping. Even at this stage, students need to be reminded of the powerful concept of regrouping. Flexible thinking about place values should be practiced prior to exploring decimals. Students should revisit not just making 1 ten from 10 units, but thinking about regrouping 2,451 into 24 hundreds, 245 tens or 2,451 ones. As you can see, this process will be essential in thinking about 6 tenths as 60 hundredths and so on.

The Role of the Decimal Point. Students must know that the decimal point marks the location of the ones (or units) place. On many calculators, when there is a whole number answer no decimal point appears—only when the ones place needs to be identified will the decimal point show in the display. Students also need to see that adding zeros to the left of a whole number will have no consequence and adding zeros to the right of a decimal fraction will not change the number.

An important idea to be realized in this discussion is that there is no built-in reason why any one position (or

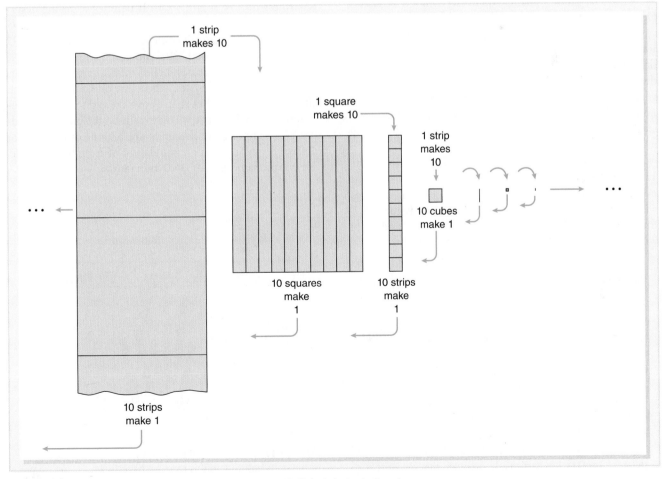

FIGURE 17.1 Theoretically, the strips and squares extend infinitely in both directions.

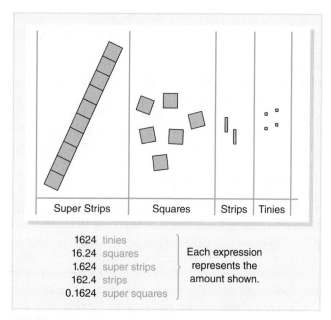

Super Strips	Squares	Strips	Tinies

1624	tinies	
16.24	squares	Each expression
1.624	super strips	represents the
162.4	strips	amount shown.
0.1624	super squares	

FIGURE 17.2 The placement of the decimal point indicates which position is the units.

base-ten piece) should be chosen to be the unit or ones position. In terms of strips and squares, for example, which piece is the ones piece? The small centimeter square? Why? Why not a larger or a smaller square? Why not a strip? *Any piece could effectively be chosen as the ones piece.*

As shown in Figure 17.2, a given quantity can be written in different ways, depending on the choice of the unit or what piece is used to count the entire collection. The decimal point is placed between two positions with the convention that the position to the left of the decimal is the units or ones position. Thus, the role of the decimal point is to designate the units position, and it does so by sitting just to the right of that position.

A fitting caricature for the decimal is shown in Figure 17.3. The "eyes" of the decimal always focus up toward the name of the units or ones. If the "smiling" decimal point were placed between the squares and strips in Figure 17.2, the squares would then be designated as the units, and 16.24 would be the correct written form for the model.

Activity 17.1

The Decimal Point Names the Unit

ENGLISH LANGUAGE LEARNERS

Have students display a certain number of base-ten pieces on their desks. For example, using the units from Figure 17.2, put out three squares, seven strips, and four tinies. For this activity, refer to the pieces as "squares," "strips," and "tinies," and reach an agreement on names for the theoretical pieces both smaller and larger. To the right of tinies can be "tiny strips" and "tiny squares." To the left of squares can be "super strips" and "super squares." For ELLs, it is particularly important that you write

these labels with the visuals in a prominent place in the classroom (and in student notebooks) so that they can refer to this terminology as they participate in the activity. Each student should also have a smiling decimal point. Now ask students to write and say how many squares they have, how many super strips, and so on. The students position their decimal point accordingly and both write and say the amounts.

Activity 17.1 illustrates vividly the convention that the decimal indicates the named unit and that the unit can change without changing the quantity.

The Decimal Point with Measurement and Monetary Units. The notion that the decimal identifies the units place is useful in a variety of contexts. For example, in the metric system, seven place values have names. As shown in Figure 17.4, the decimal point can be used to designate any of these places as the unit without changing the actual measure. Our monetary system is also a decimal system. In the amount $172.95, the decimal point designates the dollars position as the unit. There are 1 hundred (of dollars), 7 tens, 2 singles, 9 dimes, and 5 pennies in this amount of money, regardless of how it is written. If pennies were the designated unit, the same amount would be written as 17,295 cents or 17,295.0 cents. It could just as correctly be 0.17295 thousands of dollars or 1729.5 dimes.

In the case of measures such as metric lengths or weights or the U.S. monetary system, the name of the unit is written after the number rather than above the digit as on a place-value chart. In the paper, we may read about Congress spending $7.3 billion. Here the units are billions of dollars, not dollars. A city may have a population of 2.4 million people. That is the same as 2,400,000 individuals.

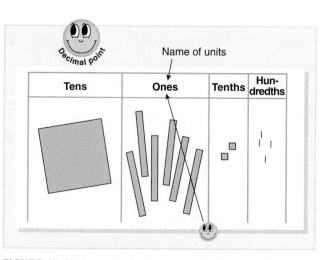

FIGURE 17.3 The decimal point always "looks up at" the name of the units position. In this case, we have 16.24.

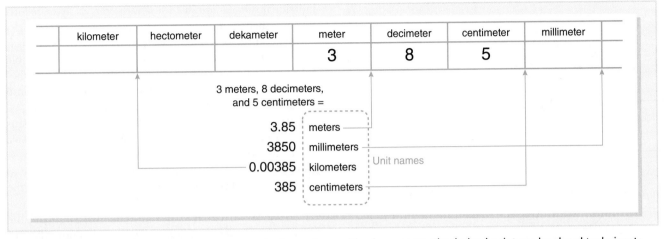

	kilometer	hectometer	dekameter	meter	decimeter	centimeter	millimeter
				3	**8**	**5**	

3 meters, 8 decimeters,
and 5 centimeters =

3.85 meters
3850 millimeters
0.00385 kilometers
385 centimeters

Unit names

FIGURE 17.4 In the metric measurement system, each place-value position has a name. The decimal point can be placed to designate which length is the unit length. Again, the decimal point will "look up" at the unit length. The arrows point to the corresponding location of the decimal point.

Connecting Fractions and Decimals

The symbols 3.75 and $3\frac{3}{4}$ represent the same quantity, yet on the surface they appear quite different. For students, the world of fractions and the world of decimals are very distinct. Even adults tend to think of fractions as sets or areas (e.g., three-fourths of something), but decimals as values or numbers (e.g., weight). When we tell students that 0.75 is the same as $\frac{3}{4}$, this can be confusing because the denominators are hidden in decimal fractions. Even though there are different ways of writing the numbers, the numbers themselves are not different. A significant goal of instruction in decimal and fraction numeration should be to help students see that both systems represent the same concepts.

There are important ways to help students see the connection between fractions and decimals. First, we can use familiar fraction concepts and models to explore rational numbers that are easily represented by decimals: tenths, hundredths, and thousandths. Then, we can help students use models to make meaningful translations between fractions and decimals. These components are discussed in turn.

Base-Ten Fractions

Fractions with denominators of 10, 100, 1000, and so on will be referred to in this chapter as *base-ten fractions*. This is simply a convenient label and is not one commonly found in the literature. Fractions such as $\frac{7}{10}$ or $\frac{63}{100}$ are examples of base-ten fractions.

Say Decimal Fractions Correctly. You must make sure you are reading and saying decimals in ways that support students' understanding. Always say "five and two tenths" instead of "five point two." Using the "point" terminology results in a disconnect to the fractional part that exists in every decimal. This is not unlike the ill-advised reading of fractions as "two over ten" instead of correctly saying "two tenths." This level of precision in language will provide your students with the opportunity to *hear* the connections between decimals and fractions, so that when they hear "two tenths," they think of both 0.2 and $\frac{2}{10}$.

Use Base-Ten Fraction Models. Many fraction manipulatives are not useful for depicting base-ten fractions because they cannot show hundredths or thousandths. It is important to provide models for base-ten fractions using the same conceptual approaches that were used for fractions such as thirds and fourths.

Two area models that can be used as representations of base-ten fractions are circular disks and a square grid. Circular disks such as the one shown in Figure 17.5 can be printed on card stock (see Blackline Master 28). Each disk is marked with 100 equal intervals around the edge and is cut along one radius. Two disks of different colors, slipped together as shown, can be used to model any fraction less than 1. Fractions modeled on this rational number wheel can be read as base-ten fractions (by noting the spaces around the edge) but can also be stated as non-base-ten fractions (e.g., $\frac{3}{4}$), helping students further make the connection between fractions and decimal fractions.

The most common area model for base-ten fractions is a 10×10 grid (see Figure 17.6 and Blackline Master 27). Another variation is to use base-ten place-value strips and squares. As a fraction model, the 10-cm square that was used as the hundreds model for whole numbers is taken as the whole or 1. Each strip is then 1 tenth, and each small square (now referred to as a tiny) is 1 hundredth. Blackline Master 29 provides a large square that is subdivided into 10,000 tiny squares. When displayed on a projector,

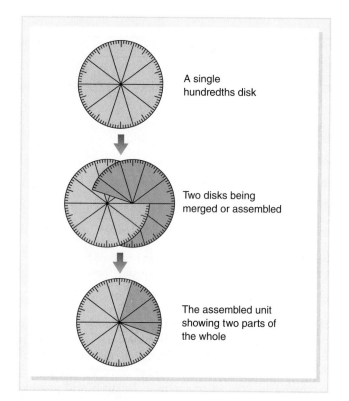

FIGURE 17.5 Rational number wheel. For example, turn the wheel to show $\frac{25}{100}$ on the blue plate (also $\frac{1}{4}$ of the circle) (see Blackline Master 28).

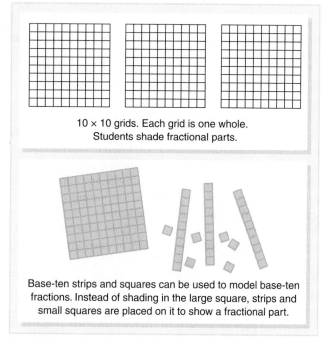

FIGURE 17.6 10 × 10 grids model base-ten fractions (see Blackline Master 27).

individual squares or ten-thousandths can easily be identified and shaded in.

One of the best length models for decimal fractions is a meter stick. Each decimeter is one-tenth of the whole stick, each centimeter is one-hundredth, and each millimeter is one-thousandth. Any number-line model broken into 100 subparts is likewise a useful model for hundredths.

Empty number lines are also useful in helping students compare decimals and think about scale and place value (Martinie & Bay Williams, 2003). Given two or more decimals, students can use an empty number line to position the values, revealing what they know about the size of these decimals using zero, one, other whole numbers, or other decimal values as benchmarks. Again, the use of multiple representations will broaden not only students' understanding but your understanding of their level of performance.

Many teachers use money as a model for decimals, and to some extent this is helpful. However, for students, money is almost exclusively a two-place system and is non-proportional. Numbers like 3.2 or 12.1389 do not relate to money and can cause confusion (Martinie, 2007). Students' initial contact with decimals should be more flexible, and so money is not recommended as an initial model for decimals although it is certainly an important application of decimal numeration.

Multiple Names and Formats. Early work with base-ten fractions is designed to acquaint students with the models to help them begin to think of quantities in terms of tenths and hundredths, and to learn to read and write base-ten fractions in different ways.

Have students show a base-ten fraction using any base-ten fraction model. Once a fraction, say $\frac{65}{100}$, is modeled, the following ideas can be explored:

- Is this fraction more or less than $\frac{1}{2}$? Than $\frac{2}{3}$? Than $\frac{3}{4}$? Some familiarity with base-ten fractions can be developed by comparison with fractions that are easy to think about.
- What are some different ways to say this fraction using tenths and hundredths? ("6 tenths and 5 hundredths," "65 hundredths") Include thousandths when appropriate.
- Show two ways to write this fraction ($\frac{65}{100}$ or $\frac{6}{10} + \frac{5}{100}$).

The last two points are very important in building the connection to decimal fractions. When base-ten fractions are written as decimals, they are usually read as a single value. That is, 0.65 is read "sixty-five hundredths." But to understand them in terms of place value, the same number must be thought of as 6 tenths and 5 hundredths. A mixed number such as $\frac{513}{100}$ is usually read the same way as a decimal: 5.13 is "five and thirteen-hundredths." Please note that it is accurate to use the word "and," which represents the decimal point. For purposes of place value, it should also be understood as $5 + \frac{1}{10} + \frac{3}{100}$.

Expanded forms will be helpful in translating fractions to decimals. Given a model or a written or oral fraction, students should be able to give the other two forms of the fraction, including equivalent forms where appropriate.

Activity 17.2

STUDENTS with SPECIAL NEEDS

Base-Ten Fractions to Decimals

For this activity, have students use their paper place-value strips and squares (Blackline Master 14). Agree that the large square represents one. Have students cover a base-ten fractional amount of the square using their strips and tinies (remember to call the pieces "tenths" and "hundredths"). For example, have them cover $2\frac{35}{100}$ of the square. Whole numbers require additional squares. The task is to decide how to write and say this fraction as a decimal and demonstrate the connection using their physical models. For students with disabilities, you may want to have the amount shaded rather than have the students try to cover the exact amount; then ask them to name and write the decimal fraction.

For the last activity, $2\frac{35}{100}$ is the same as 2.35 because there are 2 wholes, 3 tenths, and 5 hundredths. It is important to see this physically. The same materials that are used to represent $2\frac{35}{100}$ of the square can be rearranged or placed on a place-value chart with a paper decimal point used to designate the units position, as shown in Figure 17.7. Of course base-ten materials can be used too.

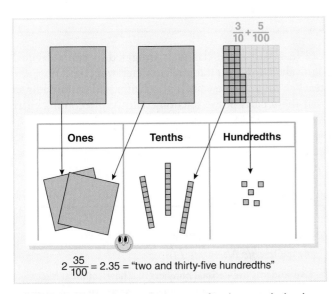

FIGURE 17.7 Translation of a base-ten fraction to a decimal.

Although these translations between decimals and base-ten fractions are rather simple, the main agenda is for students to learn from the beginning that decimals are simply fractions.

The calculator can also play a significant role in developing decimal concepts.

Activity 17.3

ENGLISH LANGUAGE LEARNERS

STUDENTS with SPECIAL NEEDS

Calculator Decimal Counting

Recall how to make the calculator "count" by pressing [+] 1 [=] [=] . . . Now have students press [+] 0.1 [=] [=] . . . When the display shows 0.9, stop and discuss what this means and what the display will look like with the next count. Many students will predict 0.10 (thinking that 10 comes after 9). This prediction is even more interesting if, with each press, the students have been accumulating base-ten strips as models for tenths. One more press would mean one more strip, or 10 strips. Why doesn't the calculator show 0.10? When the tenth press produces a display of 1 (calculators are not usually set to display trailing zeros to the right of the decimal), the discussion should revolve around trading 10 strips for a square. Continue to count to 4 or 5 by tenths. How many presses to get from one whole number to the next? For students with disabilities and ELLs, counting out loud along with the calculator "one tenth, two tenths, . . ." supports the concept (e.g., 10 tenths as being the same as 1 whole) while reinforcing appropriate mathematical language. They may need to be reminded that a place is "full" when it has 9 of any unit and the addition of another unit will push to the position that is one unit to the left (like the mileage in a car). Once students are working well with tenths, try counting by 0.01 or by 0.001. These counts illustrate dramatically how small one-hundredth and one-thousandth really are. It requires 10 counts by 0.001 to get to 0.01 and 1000 counts to reach 1.

The fact that the calculator counts 0.8, 0.9, 1, 1.1 instead of 0.8, 0.9, 0.10, 0.11 should give rise to the question "Does this make sense? If so, why?"

Calculators that permit entry of fractions also have a fraction-decimal conversion key. On some calculators, a decimal such as 0.25 will convert to the base-ten fraction $\frac{25}{100}$ and allow for either manual or automatic simplification. Graphing calculators can be set so that the conversion is either with or without simplification. The ability of fraction calculators to go back and forth between fractions and decimals makes them a valuable tool for connecting fraction and decimal symbolism.

Developing Decimal Number Sense

So far, the discussion has focused on the connection of decimals with base-ten fractions. Number sense implies more. It means having intuition about or a flexible understanding of decimal numbers. To this end, it is useful to connect decimals to the fractions with which students are familiar, to be able to compare and order decimals, and to approximate decimals with useful benchmarks.

Results of NAEP exams reveal that students have difficulties with the fraction-decimal relationship. In 2004, fewer than 30 percent of high school students were able to translate 0.029 as $\frac{29}{1000}$ (Kloosterman, 2010). In 2009, Shaughnessy found that more than 46 percent of the sixth graders she studied could not write $\frac{3}{5}$ as a decimal. Instead many wrote $\frac{3}{5}$ as 3.5, 0.35, or 0.3. She also found that more than 25 percent could not write $\frac{3}{10}$, a base-ten fraction, as a decimal. This misconception was also reversed when students wrote the decimal 4.5 as the fraction $\frac{4}{5}$. Division of the numerator by the denominator may be a means of converting fractions to decimals, but it contributes little to understanding the resulting equivalence.

Familiar Fractions Connected to Decimals

Chapter 15 showed how to help students develop a conceptual familiarity with common fractions, especially halves, thirds, fourths, fifths, and eighths. We should extend this familiarity to the same concepts expressed as decimal fractions. One way to do this is to have students translate familiar fractions to decimals in a conceptual manner, which is the focus of the next two activities.

Activity 17.4

Familiar Fractions to Decimals

Students are given a "familiar" or commonly used fraction to convert to a decimal. They first model the fraction using a 10 × 10 square grid and strips and "tinies." Covering the grid with the materials, they model then write the fraction and decimal equivalent. A good sequence is to start with halves and fifths, then fourths, and possibly eighths. Thirds are best done as a special activity.

Figure 17.8 shows how translations in the last activity might go with a 10 × 10 grid. For fourths, students will often cover a 5 × 5 section (half of a half). The question then becomes how to translate this to decimals. Ask these students how they would cover $\frac{1}{4}$ with tenths (strips) and hundredths (tinies) if they were only permitted to use nine or

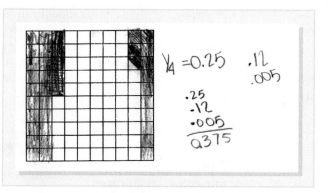

FIGURE 17.8 A student uses a 10 × 10 grid to convert $\frac{3}{8}$ to a decimal.

fewer hundredths. The fraction $\frac{3}{8}$ represents a wonderful challenge. A hint might be to find $\frac{1}{4}$ first and then notice that $\frac{1}{8}$ is half of a fourth. Remember that the next smaller pieces are tenths of the "tinies" (or thousands). Therefore, a half of a "tiny" is $\frac{5}{1000}$. Note how the student found that $\frac{2}{8} + \frac{1}{8} = \frac{37}{100} + \frac{5}{1000} = 0.375$.

Because the circular model carries such a strong mental link to fractions, it is worth the time to do some fraction-to-decimal conversions with the rational number wheel shown in Figure 17.5 (see Blackline Master 28).

Activity 17.5

Estimate, Then Verify

With the blank side of the wheel facing them, have students adjust the wheel to show a common fraction, for example $\frac{3}{4}$. Next they turn the wheel over and record how many hundredths they estimate were in the section. Finally, they should make an argument for the correct number of hundredths and the corresponding decimal equivalent.

In a fifth-grade class that struggled to find a decimal equivalent for their rational number wheel fraction, the teacher cut up some wheels into tenths and hundredths so that these parts of the fraction could be placed on a chart (see Figure 17.9).

The number line is another good connecting model to connect decimals and fractions. The following activity continues the development of fraction-decimal equivalences.

Activity 17.6

Decimals and Fractions on a Double Number Line

Give students five decimal numbers that have common fraction equivalents. Keep the numbers between two consecutive whole numbers. For example, use 3.5, 3.125, 3.4, 3.75, and 3.66. Show a number line starting from 3.0 to 4.0 with subdivisions on the number line of only fourths, only thirds, or only fifths but without labels. The students' task is to locate each of the decimal numbers on the fraction number line and to provide the fraction equivalent for each.

The exploration of modeling $\frac{1}{3}$ as a decimal is a good introduction to the concept of an infinitely repeating decimal, which is a standard for seventh grade (CCSSO, 2010). Try to partition the whole 10×10 grid into 3 parts using strips and tinies. Each part receives 3 strips with 1 strip left over. To divide the leftover strip, each part gets 3 tinies with 1 left over. To divide the tiny, each part gets 3 tiny strips with 1 left over. (Recall that with base-ten pieces, each smaller piece must be $\frac{1}{10}$ of the preceding size piece.) It becomes obvious that this process is never-ending. As a result, $\frac{1}{3}$ is the same as $0.333333\ldots$ or $0.\overline{3}$. For practical purposes, $\frac{1}{3}$ is about 0.333. Similarly, $\frac{2}{3}$ is a repeating string of sixes, or about 0.667. Later, students will discover that many fractions cannot be represented by a finite decimal.

FORMATIVE Assessment Notes A powerful **performance assessment** to evaluate decimal understanding has students represent two related decimal numbers, such as 0.6 and 0.06, using multiple representations: an empty number line, a 10×10 grid, and base-ten materials (Martinie & Bay-Williams, 2003). Ask students to describe their representations. If students have significantly more difficulty with one model than another, this may mean that they have not developed full conceptual understanding of decimal fractions. Placement of decimals on an empty number line is perhaps the most interesting task—and provides the most revealing information (see Figure 17.10). ∎

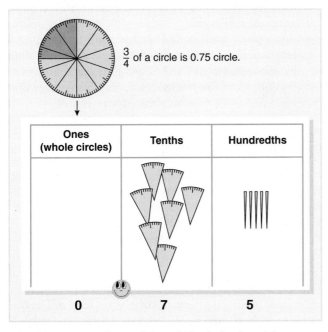

FIGURE 17.9 Fraction models could be decimal models.

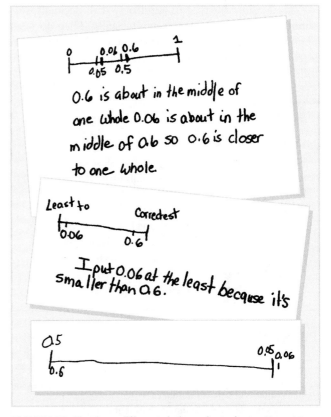

FIGURE 17.10 Three different sixth-grade students attempt to draw a number line and show the numbers 0.6 and 0.06.

Source: Reprinted with permission from Martinie, S. L., & Bay-Williams, J. (2003). "Investigating Students' Conceptual Understanding of Decimal Fractions Using Multiple Representations." *Mathematics Teaching in the Middle School, 8,* p. 246. Copyright © 2003 by the National Council of Teachers of Mathematics. All rights reserved.

Approximation with a Compatible Fraction. In the real world, decimal numbers are rarely those with exact equivalents to common fractions. What fraction would you say approximates the decimal 0.52? In the sixth NAEP exam, only 51 percent of eighth graders selected $\frac{1}{2}$. The other choices were $\frac{1}{50}$ (29 percent), $\frac{1}{5}$ (11 percent), $\frac{1}{4}$ (6 percent), and $\frac{1}{3}$ (4 percent) (Kouba, Zawojewski, & Strutchens, 1997). Again, a possible explanation for this performance is a reliance on rules. Students need to wrestle with the size of decimal fractions and begin to develop a sense of familiarity with them.

As with fractions, the first benchmarks that should be developed are 0, $\frac{1}{2}$, and 1. For example, is 7.3962 closer to 7 or 8? Why? (Would you accept this response: "Closer to 7 because 3 is less than 5"?) Is it closer to 7 or $7\frac{1}{2}$? Often the 0, $\frac{1}{2}$, or 1 benchmarks are good enough to make sense of a situation. If a closer approximation is required, encourage students to consider other common fractions (thirds, fourths, fifths, and eighths). In this example, 7.3962 is close to 7.4, which is $7\frac{2}{5}$. A good number sense with decimals entails the ability to think quickly of a fraction that is a close equivalent.

To develop this type of familiarity with decimals, students do not need new concepts or skills. They do need opportunities to apply and discuss the related concepts of fractions, place value, and decimals in activities such as the following.

Activity 17.7

Close to a Familiar Fraction

Make a list of about five decimals that are close to but not exactly equal to a familiar or commonly used fraction equivalent. For example, use 24.8025, 6.59, 0.9003, 124.356, and 7.7.

The students' task is to decide on a decimal number that is close to each of these decimals and that also has a common fraction equivalent that they know. For example, 6.59 is close to 6.6, which is $6\frac{3}{5}$. They should write an explanation for their choices. Different students may select different equivalent fractions, providing for a discussion of which is closer.

Activity 17.8

Best Match

STUDENTS *with* SPECIAL NEEDS

Create a deck of cards of familiar fractions and decimals that are close to the fractions but not exact. Students are to pair each fraction with the decimal that best matches it in a memory game in which they must flip over matching cards to make a pair. The difficulty is determined by how close the various fractions are to one another. Students with disabilities may need to be prompted to reflect each time whether what they've turned over is close to 0, close to $\frac{1}{2}$, or close to 1 to help support their matchmaking.

In Activities 17.7 and 17.8, students will have a variety of reasons for their answers. Sharing their thinking with the class provides a valuable opportunity for all to learn. Do not focus on the answers but on the rationales.

FORMATIVE Assessment Notes   The connections between models and the two symbol systems for rational numbers—fractions and decimals—are a good topic for a **diagnostic interview**. Provide students with a number represented in any one of these three ways (fraction, decimal, or model), and have them provide the other two along with an explanation. Here are a few examples:

- Write the fraction $\frac{5}{8}$ as a decimal. Use a drawing or a physical model (meter stick or 10×10 grid) and explain why your decimal equivalent is correct.
- What fraction is represented by the decimal 2.6? Use a model to explain your answer.

- Use a fraction and a decimal to tell what point might be indicated on this number line. Explain your reasoning.

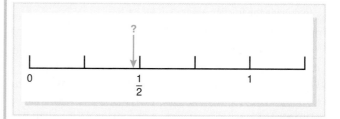

In the last example, it is especially interesting to see which representation students select first—fraction or decimal. Furthermore, do they then translate this number to the other representation or make a second independent estimate? ■

Other Fraction-Decimal Equivalents. Recall that the denominator is a divisor and the numerator is a multiplier. For example, $\frac{3}{4}$ means the same as $3 \times (1 \div 4)$ or $3 \div 4$. So how would you express $\frac{3}{4}$ on a simple four-function calculator? Simply enter $3 \div 4$. The display will read 0.75.

Too often, students think that dividing the denominator into the numerator is simply an algorithm for converting fractions to decimals, and they have no understanding of why this might work. Use the opportunity to help students develop the idea that in general $\frac{a}{b} = a \div b$, where b is not 0. (See Chapter 15, p. 291.)

The calculator is an important tool when developing familiarity with decimal concepts. Finding decimal equivalents with a calculator can produce interesting patterns. Here are some questions to explore:

- Which fractions have decimal equivalents that terminate? Is the answer based on the numerator, the denominator, or both?
- For a given fraction, how can you tell the maximum length of the repeating part of the decimal? Try dividing by denominators of 7 and 11 and 13 to reach an answer.
- Explore all of the ninths: $\frac{1}{9}, \frac{2}{9}, \frac{3}{9}, \ldots \frac{8}{9}$. Remember that $\frac{1}{3}$ is $\frac{3}{9}$ and $\frac{2}{3}$ is $\frac{6}{9}$. Use only the pattern you discover to predict what $\frac{9}{9}$ should be. But doesn't $\frac{9}{9} = 1$?
- How can you find what fraction produces this repeating decimal: 3.454545 . . . ?

The last question can be generalized for any repeating decimal, illustrating that every repeating decimal is a rational number.

Comparing and Ordering Decimal Fractions. Comparing decimal fractions and putting them in order from least to greatest is a skill closely related to comparing fractions and decimals. In the real world, we rarely think about the order of "ragged" decimals—decimals of unequal length. The real purpose of these exercises is to create a better understanding of decimal numeration and place-value concepts.

FORMATIVE Assessment Notes Consider the following list: 0.36, 0.058, 0.375, 0.97, 0, 2.0, and 0.4. Ask students to order these decimals from least to greatest. There are six common errors and misconceptions that students exhibit when comparing and ordering decimals (Desmet, Gregoire, & Mussolin, 2010; Steinle & Stacey, 2004a, 2004b). Knowing these will help you pinpoint ways to improve their conceptual understanding as they overcome these misconceptions.

1. *Longer is larger.* This is the most common initial error—students select the number with more digits as largest. This is an incorrect application of whole-number ideas, as students just look at the number beyond the decimal point and judge it as they would a whole number. Under this misconception, they would say that 0.375 is greater than 0.97.

2. *Shorter is larger.* Here the student thinks that because the digits far to the right represent very small numbers, hence, longer numbers are smaller. For example, they would choose 0.4 as larger than 0.97 because "a tenth is larger than a hundredth." This error is very persistent.

3. *Internal zero.* In this case, students are confused by a zero in the tenths position like 0.078. Here they would see 0.58 as less than 0.078 thinking that "zero has no impact" when written to the left, as is the case with a whole number. This has also shown to be an issue when placing decimals on the number line.

4. *Less than zero.* When some students compare 0.36 to 0, they choose 0 as larger. This is due to the thinking that zero is a whole number positioned in the ones column (to the left of the decimal point) and therefore greater than a decimal fraction (to the right of the decimal point). They are unsure whether a decimal fraction is greater than zero.

5. *Reciprocal thinking.* This error usually takes teachers by surprise. If students are asked to compare 0.4 and 0.6, some incorrectly select 0.4 as larger. Using their knowledge that decimals are like fractions, they connect 0.4 to $\frac{1}{4}$ and 0.6 to $\frac{1}{6}$ and erroneously decide 0.4 is greater.

6. *Equality.* Another surprise is that students don't integrate the idea of regrouping decimals and that 4 tenths is equal to 40 hundredths or 400 thousandths. This misconception has them thinking that the 0.4 in the group above is not close to 0.375 and/or that 0.3 is smaller than 0.30. ■

All of these common errors reflect a lack of conceptual understanding of how decimal numbers are constructed. The following activities can help promote discussion about the relative sizes of decimal numbers.

Activity 17.9

Line 'Em Up

Prepare a list of four or five decimal numbers that students might have difficulty putting in order. Use a context such as the height of plants. They should all be between the same two consecutive whole numbers. Have students first predict the order of the numbers, from least to greatest. Require students to use a model of their choice to defend their ordering. As students wrestle with representing the numbers with a model (perhaps a number line with 100 subdivisions or a 100 × 100 [10,000]) grid, they will necessarily confront the idea of which digits contribute the most to the size of a decimal.

For students who are struggling, some explicit instruction might be helpful. Write a four-digit decimal on the board—3.0917, for example. Start with the whole numbers: "Is it closer to 3 or 4?" Then go to the tenths: "Is it closer to 3.0 or 3.1?" Repeat with hundredths and thousandths. At each answer, challenge students to defend their choices with the use of a model or other conceptual explanation. A large, empty number line, shown in Figure 17.11, is useful.

When students only see decimals rounded to two places, this may reinforce the notion that there are no numbers between 2.37 and 2.38 (Steinle & Stacey, 2004b). Finding the decimal located between any two decimals requires that students understand the density of decimals. Using a linear model helps to show that there is always another decimal to be found between any two decimals—an important concept that is emphasized in the following activity.

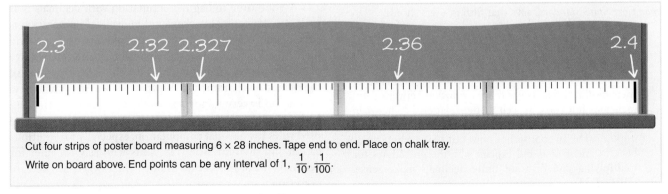

Cut four strips of poster board measuring 6 × 28 inches. Tape end to end. Place on chalk tray.

Write on board above. End points can be any interval of 1, $\frac{1}{10}$, $\frac{1}{100}$.

FIGURE 17.11 Decimal fractions on an empty number line.

Activity **17.10**

Close Decimals

STUDENTS *with* SPECIAL NEEDS

Have your students name a decimal between 0 and 1.0. Next have them name another decimal that is even closer to 1.0 than the first. Continue for several more decimals in the same manner, each one being closer to 1.0 than the previous decimal. Similarly, try close to 0 or close to 0.5. Let students with disabilities use models or a number line to help them with their decision making. Later, see how they can explain their thinking without representations.

Confusion over the density of decimals also plays out when students try to find the nearest decimal (Ubuz & Yayan, 2010). Many times when having students find which decimal is closer to a given decimal, students revert to thinking that tenths are comparable to tenths and that there are no hundredths between. When asked which decimal is closer to 0.19—0.2 or 0.21—they select 0.21. They also are not sure that 0.513 is near 0.51 but just a little larger. They may also think that 0.3 is near 0.4 but far away from 0.31784. These examples are evidence that students are in need of additional experiences and probably not yet ready for operations with decimals.

Computation with Decimals

Certainly, students should develop computational fluency with decimal fractions. In the past, decimal computation was dominated by the following rules: Line up the decimal points (addition and subtraction), count the decimal places (multiplication), and shift the decimal point in the divisor and dividend so that the divisor is a whole number (division). Some textbooks continue to emphasize these rules, but specific rules for decimal computation are not always necessary if computation is built on a firm understanding of place value and a connection between decimals and fractions. The *Common Core State Standards* says that fifth graders should

> apply their understandings of models for decimals, decimal notation, and properties of operations to add and subtract decimals to hundredths. They develop fluency in these computations, and make reasonable estimates of their results. Students use the relationship between decimals and fractions, as well as the relationship between finite decimals and whole numbers (i.e., a finite decimal multiplied by an appropriate power of 10 is a whole number), to understand and explain why the procedures for multiplying and dividing finite decimals make sense. (2010, p. 33)

The Role of Estimation

Students should become adept at estimating decimal computations well before they learn to compute with pencil and paper. For many decimal computations, rough estimates can be made by rounding the numbers to whole numbers or simple base-ten fractions. A minimum goal for your students should be to have the estimate contain the correct number of digits to the left of the decimal—the whole-number part. Start your instruction by selecting problems for which estimates are not terribly difficult.

 PAUSE and REFLECT

Before continuing, try making whole-number estimates of the following computations. ●

1. $4.907 + 123.01 + 56.1234$
2. $459.8 - 12.345$
3. 24.67×1.84
4. $514.67 \div 3.59$

Your estimates might be in the following ranges:

1. Between 175 and 200
2. More than 400, or about 425 to 450
3. More than 25, closer to 50 (1.84 is more than 1 and close to 2)
4. More than 125, less than 200 ($500 \div 4 = 125$ and $600 \div 3 = 200$)

In these examples, an understanding of decimal numeration and basic whole-number estimation skills can produce rough estimates. When estimating, focus on the meanings of the numbers and the operations and not on counting decimal places. Many students who are taught to focus on poorly understood rules for decimal computation do not even consider the actual values of the numbers, much less estimate.

Therefore, a good place to begin decimal computation is with estimation. Not only is it a practical skill, but it also helps students look at answers in terms of a reasonable range and can act as a check on calculator computation.

A good time to begin computation with decimals is as soon as a conceptual background in decimal numeration is developed. As with fractions, until students have a sound understanding of place value, equivalence, and relative size of decimals, they are not ready to develop understanding of the operations (Cramer & Whitney, 2010). An emphasis on estimation is very important, even for students in the seventh and eighth grades who have been exposed to and have used rules for decimal computation, especially for multiplication and division. Many students who rely on rules for decimals make mistakes without being aware, as they are not using number sense.

Addition and Subtraction

Consider this problem:

> Jessica and MacKenna each timed their own quarter-mile run with a stopwatch. Jessica says that she ran the quarter mile in 74.5 seconds. MacKenna was more accurate in her timing, reporting that she ran the quarter mile in 81.34 seconds. Who ran it the fastest and how much faster was she?

Students who understand decimal numeration should be able to tell approximately what the difference is—close to 7 seconds. Then they should be challenged to figure out the exact difference. The estimate will help them avoid the common error of lining up the 5 under the 4. A variety of student strategies are possible. For example, students might note that 74.5 and 7 is 81.5 and then figure out how much extra that is. Others may count on from 74.5 by adding 0.5 and then 6 more seconds to get to 81 seconds and then add on the remaining 0.34 second. These and other strategies will eventually confront the difference between the 0.5 and 0.34. Students can resolve this issue by returning to their understanding of place value. Similar story problems for addition and subtraction, some involving different numbers of decimal places, will help develop students' understanding. Always require an estimate prior to computation.

After students have had several opportunities to solve addition and subtraction story problems, it is important to see if they can reason without a context, as in the next activity.

> **Activity 17.11**
>
> ### Exact Sums and Differences
>
> Give students a sum involving different numbers of decimal places. For example: 73.46 + 6.2 + 0.582. The first task is to make an estimate and explain how the estimate was made. The second task is to compute the exact answer and explain how that was done (no calculators). In the third and final task, students devise a method for adding and subtracting decimal numbers that they can use with any two numbers.
>
> When students have completed these three tasks, have students share their strategies for computation and test them on a new computation that you provide. The same task can be repeated for subtraction.

The earlier estimation practice will focus students' attention on the meanings of the numbers. Remember, students can rewrite decimals as fractions with the same denominator to make connections. It is reasonable to expect that students will develop an algorithm that is essentially the same as aligning the decimal points.

FORMATIVE Assessment Notes As students complete Activity 17.11, use a **checklist** to record whether they are showing evidence of having an understanding of decimal concepts and the role of the decimal point. Note whether students get a correct sum by using a rule they learned in an earlier grade but have difficulty with their explanations. Rather than continue to focus on how to add or subtract decimals, struggling students should shift their attention to basic decimal concepts. ■

Multiplication

Explore multiplication of decimals by using problems in a context and by returning to a model that was successful with multiplying whole numbers—the area model (Rathouz, 2011). Use a scenario such as this one:

> A gardener has 1.5 m² of her garden where she can plant flowers. She decides to plant bluebells on an area that's 0.6 of the garden. On how many total square meters did she plant bluebells?

See a student's solution (Figure 17.12) using a grid diagram to model the problem. Each large square represents 1 square meter with each row of 10 small squares as 0.1 of a square meter and each small square as 0.01 of a square meter. The shaded section shows 0.6 m² + 0.3 m² = 0.9m². Notice that this is a proportional model, allowing students to "see" the values of the factors.

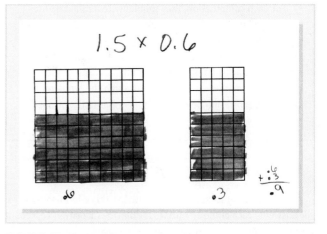

FIGURE 17.12 A student's use of grids to reason about 1.5 × 0.6.

Estimation should play a significant role in developing a multiplication algorithm. As a beginning, consider this problem:

> The farmer fills each jug with 3.7 liters of cider. If you buy 4 jugs, how many liters of cider is that?

Begin with an estimate. Is it more than 12 liters? What is the most it could be? Could it be 16 liters? Once an estimate of the result is decided on, let students use their own methods for determining an exact answer. Many will use repeated addition: 3.7 + 3.7 + 3.7 + 3.7. Others may begin by multiplying 3 × 4 and then adding up 0.7 four times. Eventually, students will agree on the exact result of 14.8 liters. Explore other problems involving whole-number multipliers. Multipliers such as 3.5 or 8.25 that involve common fractional parts—here, one-half and one-fourth—are also reasonable.

As a next step, have students compare a decimal product with one involving the same digits but no decimal. For example, how are 23.4 × 6.5 and 234 × 65 alike? Interestingly, both products have exactly the same digits: 15210. (The zero may be missing from the decimal product.) Using a calculator, have students explore other products that are alike except for the location of the decimals involved. The digits in the answer are always alike. After seeing how the digits remain the same for these related products, do the following activity.

Activity 17.12

Where Does the Decimal Go? Multiplication

ENGLISH LANGUAGE LEARNERS

Have students compute the following product:

24 × 63. Using only the result of this computation and estimation, have them give the exact answer to each of the following:

   0.24 × 6.3   24 × 0.63   2.4 × 63   0.24 × 0.63

   For each computation, they should write a rationale for how they placed the decimal point. They can check their results with a calculator. ELLs may apply a different mental strategy that is common in their country of origin. Even if they have trouble articulating their reasoning, it is important to consider alternative ways to reason through the problem. Discussing errors and how to avoid them is also important to discuss publicly.

 PAUSE and REFLECT

The product of 24 × 63 is 1512. Use this information to give the answer to each of the products in the previous activity. Do *not* count decimal places. Remember your fractional equivalents. ●

Another way to support full understanding of the algorithm is to rewrite the decimals in their fraction equivalent. So if you are multiplying 3.4 × 1.7, that is the same as $\frac{34}{10}$ × $\frac{17}{10}$. When multiplied, you would get $\frac{578}{100}$, which rewritten as a decimal fraction is 5.78, which corresponds to moving the decimal two places to the left (Rathouz, 2011).

The method of placing the decimal point in a product by way of estimation is more difficult as the product gets smaller.

For example, knowing that 54 × 83 is 4482 does not make it easy to place the decimal in the product 0.0054 × 0.00083. Even the product 0.054 × 0.83 is challenging. A reasonable algorithm for multiplication is the following: Ignore the decimal points, and do the computation as if all numbers were whole numbers. When finished, place the decimal by estimation. Even if students have already learned the standard algorithm, they need to know the conceptual rationale centered on place value and the powers of ten for "counting" and shifting the decimal places. By focusing on rote applications of rules, students lose out on opportunities to understand the meaning and effects of operations and are more prone to misapply procedures (Martinie & Bay-Williams, 2003).

Questions such as the following keep the focus on number sense and provide useful information about your students' understanding.

1. Consider these two computations: $3\frac{1}{2} \times 2\frac{1}{4}$ and 2.276 × 3.18. Without doing the calculations, which product do you think is larger? Provide a reason for your answer that can be understood by someone else in this class.
2. How much larger is 0.76 × 5 than 0.75 × 5? How can you tell without doing the computation? (Kulm, 1994)

Student discussions and explanations as they work on these or similar questions can provide insights into their decimal and fraction number sense and the connections between the two representations.

Division

Division can be approached in a manner exactly parallel to multiplication. In fact, the best approach to a division estimate generally comes from thinking about multiplication rather than division. Consider the following problem:

> The trip to Washington was 282.5 miles. It took exactly 4.5 hours to drive. What was the average miles per hour?

To make an estimate of this quotient, think about what times 4 or 5 is close to 280. You might think 60 × 4.5 = 240 + 30 = 270. So maybe about 61 or 62 miles per hour.

Here is a second example without context. Make an estimate of 45.7 ÷ 1.83. Think only of what times $1\frac{8}{10}$ is close to 46.

 PAUSE and REFLECT

Will the answer be more or less than 46? Why? Will it be more or less than 20? Now think about 1.8 being close to 2. What times 2 is close to 46? Use this to produce an estimate. ●

Because 1.83 is close to 2, the estimate is near 23. And because 1.83 is less than 2, the answer must be greater than 23—say 25 or 26. (The actual answer is 24.972677.)

23.5 ÷ 8

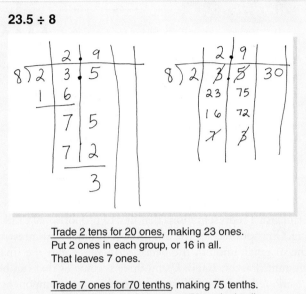

Trade **2 tens for 20 ones**, making 23 ones.
Put 2 ones in each group, or 16 in all.
That leaves 7 ones.

Trade **7 ones for 70 tenths**, making 75 tenths.
Put 9 tenths in each group, or 72 tenths in all.
That leaves 3 tenths.

Trade the **3 tenths for 30 hundredths**.

(Continue trading for smaller pieces as long as you wish.)

FIGURE 17.13 Extension of the division algorithm.

OK, so estimation can produce a reasonable result, but you may still require a standard algorithm to produce the digits the way it was done for multiplication. Figure 17.13 shows division by a whole number and how that can be carried out to as many places as you wish. (The explicit-trade method described in Chapter 13 is shown on the right.) It is not necessary to move the decimal point up into the quotient. Leave that to estimation.

Activity 17.13

Where Does the Decimal Go? Division

ENGLISH LANGUAGE LEARNERS

Provide a quotient correct to five digits but without the decimal point, such as 146 ÷ 7 = 20857. The task is to use only this information and estimation to give a fairly precise answer to each of the following:

146 ÷ 0.7   1.46 ÷ 7   14.6 ÷ 0.7   1460 ÷ 70

For each computation, students should write a rationale for their answers and then check their results with a calculator. Any errors should be acknowledged, and the rationale that produced the error adjusted. As noted in multiplication, ELLs may apply a different mental strategy, and it is important to value alternative approaches. Again, engage students in explicit discussions of common errors or misconceptions and how to fix them.

A reasonable algorithm for division is parallel to that for multiplication: Ignore the decimal points, and do the computation as if all numbers were whole numbers. When finished, place the decimal using estimation. This is reasonable for divisors greater than 1 or close to a familiar value (e.g., 0.1, 0.5, 0.01). If students have a method for dividing by 45, they can divide by 0.45 and 4.5.

Introducing Percents

The term *percent* is simply another name for *hundredths* and as such is a standardized ratio with a denominator of 100. If students can express fractions and decimals as hundredths, the term *percent* can be substituted for the term *hundredth*. Consider the fraction $\frac{3}{4}$. As a fraction expressed in hundredths, it is $\frac{75}{100}$. When $\frac{3}{4}$ is written in decimal form, it is 0.75. Both 0.75 and $\frac{75}{100}$ are read in exactly the same way, "seventy-five hundredths." When used as operators, $\frac{3}{4}$ of something is the same as 0.75 or 75 percent of that same thing. Thus, percent is merely a new notation and terminology, not a new concept.

The results of the 2005 NAEP exam revealed that only 37 percent of eighth graders could determine an amount following a given percent of increase. Many select the answer obtained by adding the percent itself to the original amount. That is, for a 10 percent increase, they would select an answer that was 10 more than the original amount. In another question, only 30 percent could accurately calculate the percent of the tip when given the cost of the meal and the amount of the tip left by the diners. A reason for this weak performance is a failure to develop percent concepts meaningfully. In this book, we explore percentages twice; here connected to fractions and decimals and in Chapter 18 as we explore percent as a ratio.

Models and Terminology

Models provide the main link between fractions, decimals, and percents, as shown in Figure 17.14 (see Blackline Masters 27 and 28). Base-ten models are suitable for fractions, decimals, and percents, because they all represent the same idea. The rational number wheel (Figure 17.5) with 100 markings around the edge is a model for percents as well as a fraction model for hundredths. The same is true of a 10×10 grid where each little square inside is 1 percent of the grid. Each row or strip of 10 squares is not only a tenth but also 10 percent of the grid.

Zambo (2008) suggests linking fractions to percent using a 10×10 grid. By marking one out of every four squares on the chart, students can discover the link between $\frac{1}{4}$ and $\frac{25}{100}$ or 25 percent. He goes on to suggest that even more complex representations such as $\frac{1}{8}$ can lead to interesting discussions about the remaining squares left at the end resulting in $12\frac{1}{2}$ out of 100 squares or $12\frac{1}{2}$ percent.

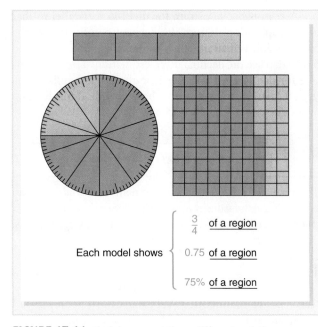

Each model shows
$$\frac{3}{4}$$ of a region

0.75 of a region

75% of a region

FIGURE 17.14 Models connect three different notations.

Similarly, the common fractions (halves, thirds, fourths, fifths, and eighths) should become familiar in terms of percents as well as decimals. Three-fifths, for example, is 60 percent as well as 0.6. One-third of an amount is frequently expressed as $33\frac{1}{3}$ percent instead of 33.3333 . . . percent. Likewise, $\frac{1}{8}$ of a quantity is $12\frac{1}{2}$ percent or 12.5 percent of the quantity. These ideas should be explored with base-ten models and with contexts rather than poorly understood rules about moving decimal points.

One representation that can be used to link percentages with data collection is a percent necklace. Using fishing cord or sturdy string, link 100 beads and knot them in a tight, circular necklace. Anytime a circle graph is displayed in class, the percent necklace can provide an estimation tool. Given any circle graph, even a human circle graph as shown in Figure 21.8 on page 442, place the necklace in a circle so that its center coincides with the center of the circle graph (don't try to align the necklace with the outside edge of the circle graph). If the necklace makes a wider concentric circle, students can use a straight edge to extend the lines distinguishing the different categories straight out to meet the necklace. If the circle graph is larger than the necklace, as it would be in Figure 21.8, use the radial lines marking off the categories. Have students count the number of beads between any two lines that represent a wedge of the circle. For example, they might find that 24 beads are in the section of the circle graph that shows how many students' favorite color is blue. That is an estimate that approximately 24 percent of the students favor blue. Counting the beads gives students an informal approach to estimating percent while investigating a meaningful model for thinking about the per-one-hundred concept.

Memory Match

STUDENTS with SPECIAL NEEDS

Create a deck of cards of circle graphs with a percentage shaded in and matching percents (like a circle with $\frac{1}{2}$ shaded and 50%). Students are to pair each circle graph with the percent that best matches it in a memory game in which they must flip over matching cards to make a pair. For students with disabilities, you may need to have rational number wheels (Figure 17.5) as a movable representation to help support their matchmaking.

Percent concepts can be developed through other powerful visual representations that link to proportional thinking. One option is the use of a three-part model to represent the original amount, the decrease/increase, and the final amount (Parker, 2004). Using three rectangles that can be positioned and divided, students can analyze components and consider each piece of the model. The rectangles can be a particularly useful representation for the often confusing problems that include a percentage increase to find an amount greater than the original. In a 2005 NAEP item, students were asked to calculate how many employees there were at a company whose workforce increased by 10 percent over the previous level of 90. Using Parker's approach, you can see in Figure 17.15 how a student used this proportional model to come up with a correct solution.

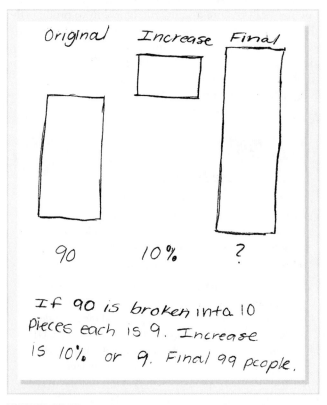

FIGURE 17.15 A student uses a proportional model for reasoning about percent.

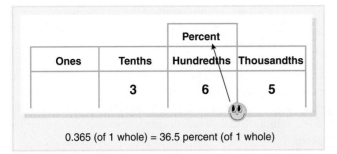

0.365 (of 1 whole) = 36.5 percent (of 1 whole)

FIGURE 17.16 Hundredths are also known as percents.

Another helpful approach to the terminology involved with percentages is through the role of the decimal point. Recall that the decimal point identifies the units position. When the unit is ones, a number such as 0.659 means a little more than 6 tenths of 1. The word *ones* is understood (6 tenths of 1 one or one whole). But 0.659 is also 6.59 tenths and 65.9 hundredths and 659 thousandths. The name of the unit must be explicitly identified. Because *percent* is another name for hundredths, when the decimal point identifies the hundredths position as the units, the word *percent* can be specified as a synonym for hundredths. Thus, 0.659 (of some whole or 1) is 65.9 hundredths or 65.9 percent of that same whole. As illustrated in Figure 17.16, the notion of placing the decimal point to identify the percent position is conceptually more meaningful than the rule: "To change a decimal to a percent, move the decimal two places to the right." A more conceptually focused idea is to equate hundredths with percent both orally and in notation.

Percent Problems in Context

Some middle school teachers may talk about "the three percent problems." The sentence "_____ is _____ percent of _____" has three spaces for numbers—for example, "20 is 25 percent of 80." The classic three percent problems come from this sterile expression; two of the numbers are given, and the students are asked to produce the third. Students tend to set up proportions but are not quite sure which numbers to put where. In other words, they are not connecting understanding with the procedure. Furthermore, commonly encountered percent situations, such as sales figures, taxes, food composition (% of fat), and economic trends are almost never in the " _____ is _____ percent of _____" format. Instead of these short, decontextualized prompts, engage students in more realistic contextual problems.

Chapter 15 explored equivalent fractions where one part was unknown (see Activity 15.16, for example). Developmentally, then, it makes sense to help students make the connection between the exercises done with fraction equivalences and percents. How? Emphasize equivalency, but add that you are seeking the equivalency for *hundredths*. Connect hundredths to percent, and replace fraction lan-

guage with percent language. In Figure 17.17, the three part–whole fraction exercises demonstrate the link between fractions and percents.

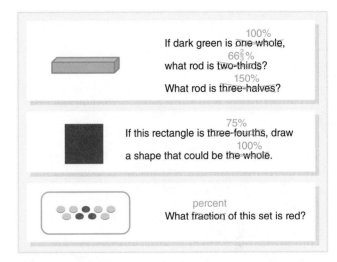

FIGURE 17.17 Part–whole fraction exercises can be translated into percent exercises.

Though students must have some experience with the noncontextual situations in Figure 17.17, it is important to have them explore percent relationships in real contexts. Find or make up percent problems, and present them in the same way that they appear in newspapers, on television, and in other real contexts. In addition to realistic problems and formats, follow these guidelines for your instruction on percents:

- Limit the percents to familiar fractions (halves, thirds, fourths, fifths, and eighths) or easy percents ($\frac{1}{10}$, $\frac{1}{100}$), and use numbers compatible with these fractions. The focus of these exercises is the relationships involved, not complex computational skills.
- Do not rush to developing rules or procedures for different types of problems—encourage students to notice patterns.
- Use the terms *part*, *whole*, and *percent* (or *fraction*). *Fraction* and *percent* are interchangeable. Help students see these percent exercises as the same types of exercises they did with simple fractions.
- Require students to use models, drawings, and contexts to explain their solutions. It is wiser to assign three problems requiring a drawing and an explanation than to give 15 problems requiring only computation and answers. Remember that the purpose is the exploration of relationships, not computational skill.
- Encourage mental computation.

The following problems meet these criteria for familiar fractions and compatible numbers. Try working each problem, identifying each number as a part, a whole, or a fraction. Draw bar diagrams to explain or work through your thought

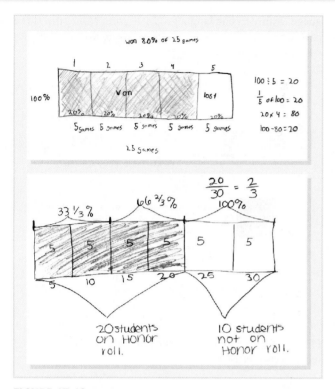

FIGURE 17.18 Students use bar diagrams to solve percent problems.

process. Examples of student reasoning using bar diagrams are illustrated in Figure 17.18.

1. The PTA reported that 75 percent of the total number of families were represented at the meeting. If students from 320 families go to the school, how many were represented at the meeting?
2. The baseball team won 80 percent of the 25 games it played this year. How many games were lost?
3. In Mrs. Carter's class, 20 students, or $66\frac{2}{3}$ percent, were on the honor roll. How many students are in her class?
4. Zane bought his new computer at a $12\frac{1}{2}$ percent discount. He paid $700. How many dollars did he save by buying it at a discount?
5. If Nicolas has read 60 of the 180 pages in his library book, what percent of the book has he read so far?
6. The hardware store bought widgets at 80 cents each and sold them for $1 each. What percent did the store mark up the price of each widget?

 PAUSE and REFLECT

Try each of the six problems just listed. Each can be done easily and mentally using familiar fraction equivalents. Use a model or drawing that you think your students might use. ●

These context-based percent problems are an effective **performance assessment** to evaluate students' understanding. Assign one or two, and have students explain why they think their answer makes sense. You might take a percent problem and substitute fractions for percents (e.g., use $\frac{1}{8}$ instead of $12\frac{1}{2}$ percent) to see how students handle these problems with fractions compared to percents.

FORMATIVE Assessment Notes

If your focus is on reasoning and justification rather than number of problems correct, you will be able to collect all the assessment information you need. ■

Estimation

Of course, many percent problems do not have simple (familiar) numbers. Frequently, in real life an approximation or estimate in percent situations is enough to help one think through the situation. Even if a calculator will be used to get an exact answer, an estimate based on an understanding of the relationship confirms that a correct operation was performed or that the decimal point was positioned correctly.

To help students with estimation in percent situations, two ideas that have already been discussed can be applied. First, when the percent is not a simple one, substitute a close percent that is easy to work with. Second, select numbers that are compatible with the percent involved to make the calculation easy to do mentally. In essence, convert the complex percent problem into one that is more familiar. Here are some examples.

1. The 83,000-seat stadium was 73 percent full. How many people were at the game?
2. The treasurer reported that 68.3 percent of the dues had been collected, for a total of $385. How much more money could the club expect to collect if all dues are paid?
3. Max McStrike had 217 hits in 842 at bats. What was his batting average?

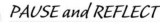 *PAUSE and REFLECT*

Use familiar percents, fractions, and compatible numbers to estimate solutions to each of these last three problems. Do this before reading on. ●

Possible Estimates

1. (Use $\frac{3}{4}$ and 80,000) → about 60,000
2. (Use $\frac{2}{3}$ and $380; will collect $\frac{1}{3}$ more) → about $190
3. ($4 \times 217 > 842$; $\frac{1}{4}$ is 25 percent, or 0.250) → a bit more than 0.250

Here are three percent problems with two sets of numbers. The first number in the set is a compatible number that allows the problem to be worked mentally using fraction equivalents. The second number requires a substitution with an approximation or estimation as in the last activity.

1. The school enrolls {480, 547} students. Yesterday {$12\frac{1}{2}$ percent, 13 percent} of the students were absent. How many came to school?
2. Mr. Carver sold his lawn mower for {$45, $89}. This was {60 percent, 62 percent} of the price he paid for it new. What did the mower cost when it was new?
3. When the box fell off the shelf, {90, 63} of the {720, 500} widgets broke. What percentage was lost in the breakage?

The first problem asks for a part (whole and fraction given), the second asks for a whole (part and fraction given), and the third asks for a fraction (part and whole given).

There are several common uses for estimating percentages in real-world situations. As students gain full conceptual understanding and flexibility, there are ways to think about percents that are useful as you are shopping or in situations that bring thinking about percents to the forefront.

Tips.   To figure a tip, you can find 10 percent of the amount and then half of that again to make 15 percent.

Taxes.   The same approach is used for adding on sales tax. Depending on the tax rate, you can find 10 percent, take half of that, and then find 1 percent and add or subtract that amount as needed. But encourage other approaches as well. Students should realize that finding percents is a process of multiplication; therefore, finding 8 percent (tax) of $50 will generate the same result as finding 50 percent (half) of 8, or $4.

Discounts.   A 30 percent decrease is the same as 70 percent of the original amount, and depending on the original amount, using one of those percents may be easier to use in mental calculations than the other. If a $48 outfit is 30% off, for example, you are paying 70%. Round $48 to $50 and you have $.70 \times 50$ (think 7×5), so your cost is less than $35.

Again, these are not rules to be taught but are reasoning activities to develop that require a full understanding of percent concepts and the commutative property.

RESOURCES *for Chapter 17*

LITERATURE CONNECTIONS

In newspapers and magazines, you will find decimal and percent situations with endless real-world connections. Money-related increases and decreases are interesting to project over several years. If the consumer price index rises 3 percent a year, how much will a $100 basket of groceries cost by the time your students are 21 years old?

The Phantom Tollbooth *Juster, 1961*

References to mathematical ideas abound in this story about Milo's adventures in Digitopolis, where everything is number-oriented. There, Milo meets a half of a boy, appearing in the illustration as the left half of a boy cut from top to bottom. As it turns out, the boy is actually 0.58 since he is a member of the average family: a mother, father, and 2.58 children. The boy is the 0.58. One advantage, he explains, is that he is the only one who can drive the 0.3 of a car, as the average family owns 1.3 cars. This story can lead to a great discussion of averages that result in decimals.

An extension of the story is to explore averages that are interesting to the students (average number of siblings, etc.) and see where these odd decimal fractions come from. Illustrating an average number of pets can be very humorous!

Piece = Part = Portion: Fraction = Decimal = Percent *Gifford & Thaler, 2008*

Illustrated with vivid photos, this book shows how fractions relate to decimals and percents. Written by a teacher, connections are made through common representations, such as one sneaker representing $\frac{1}{2}$ or 0.50 or 50 percent of a pair of shoes. Real-world links such as one-seventh of a week and one-eleventh of a soccer team will connect with students. Note that some decimals and percents are rounded.

RECOMMENDED READINGS

Articles

Cramer, K., Monson, D., Wyberg, T., Leavitt, S., & Whitney, S. B. (2009). Models for initial decimal ideas. *Teaching Children Mathematics, 16*(2), 106–116.
This article describes ways of using 10 × 10 grids and decimal addition and subtraction boards to enhance students' understanding of decimals. Several diagnostic interviews and an emphasis on having students use words, pictures, and numbers are included.

Suh, J. M., Johnston, C., Jamieson, S., & Mills, M. (2008). Promoting decimal number sense and representational fluency. *Mathematics Teaching in the Middle School, 14*(1), 44–50.
A group of fifth- and sixth-grade teachers in a lesson study group explored a variety of representations to develop students' proficiency with decimals. Ideas for games and strategies for ELLs and students with special needs are shared.

ONLINE RESOURCES

Base Blocks—Decimals
http://nlvm.usu.edu
Base-ten blocks can be placed on a place-value chart. The number of decimal places can be selected, thus designating any of the four blocks as the unit. Addition and subtraction problems can be created or can be generated randomly.

Circle 3 http://nlvm.usu.edu

This game challenges students to use logic as they combine decimals to add to 3. Not as easy as it sounds.

Concentration
http://illuminations.nctm.org/ActivityDetail.aspx?ID=73

This is an engaging matching game using representations of percents, fractions, and a regional model.

Fraction Model—Version 3
http://illuminations.nctm.org/activitydetail.aspx?ID=11

Explore equivalence of fraction, decimal, and percent representations using length, area, region, and set models.

REFLECTIONS *on Chapter 17*

WRITING TO LEARN

1. Describe three different base-ten models for fractions and decimals, and use each to illustrate how base-ten fractions can be represented.
2. How can we help students think about very small place values such as thousandths and millionths in the same way we get students to think about very large place values such as millions and billions?
3. Use an example involving base-ten pieces to explain the role of the decimal point in identifying the units position. Relate this idea to changing units of measurement as in money or metric measures.
4. Explain how the line-up-the-decimals rule for adding and subtracting can be developed through practice with estimation.

5. Give an example explaining how, in many problems, multiplication and division with decimals can be replaced with estimation and whole-number methods.

FOR DISCUSSION AND EXPLORATION

1. A way you may have learned to order a series of decimals is to annex zeros to each number so that all numbers have the same number of decimal places. For example, rewrite

   0.34 as 0.3400
   0.3004 as 0.3004
   0.059 as 0.0590

   Now ignore the decimal points and any leading zeros, and order the resulting whole numbers. This method was found to detract from students' conceptual understanding (Roche & Clarke, 2004). Why do you think that was the case? What should you try instead?

Go to the MyEducationLab (www.myeducationlab.com) for Math Methods and familiarize yourself with the content. Much of the site content is organized topically. The topics include all of the following to support your learning in the course:

- Learning outcomes for important mathematics methods course topics aligned with the national standards
- Assignments and Activities, tied to these learning outcomes and standards, that can help you more deeply understand course content
- Building Teaching Skills and Dispositions learning units that allow you to apply and practice your understanding of the core mathematics content and teaching skills

Your instructor has a correlation guide that aligns the exercises on the topical portion of the site with your book's chapters.

On MyEducationLab you will also find book-specific resources including Blackline Masters, Expanded Lesson Activities, and Artifact Analysis Activities.

Field Experience Guide
C O N N E C T I O N S

Expanded Lesson 9.8 is an engaging lesson that helps students fluently convert common fractions to their decimal equivalences. In Expanded Lesson 9.10 ("How Close Is Close?") students shade 10×10 grids to explore density of decimals, thus learning that for any two decimals, another decimal can be found between them.

Chapter 18

Proportional Reasoning

*I*n their book describing the essential understandings of ratios, proportions, and proportional reasoning, Lobato and Ellis (2010) write that it is really all one big idea: "When two quantities are related proportionally, the ratio of one quantity to the other is invariant as the numerical values of both quantities change by the same factor" (p. 11).

Proportional reasoning goes well beyond the notion of setting up a proportion to solve a problem—it is a way of reasoning about multiplicative situations. In fact, proportional reasoning, like equivalence, is considered a unifying theme in mathematics.

It is estimated that more than half the population of adults are not proportional thinkers (Lamon, 2006). This is a product of an overfocus on solving missing-value proportions without a focus on reasoning proportionally. Such rote practice is particularly troubling in the area of proportional reasoning because it is at the core of so many important concepts, including "similarity, relative growth and size, dilations, scaling, pi, constant rate of change, slope, speed, rates, percent, trigonometric ratios, probability, relative frequency, density, and direct and inverse variations" (Heinz & Sterba-Boatwright, 2008, p. 528). Wow!

BIG IDEAS

1. A ratio is a multiplicative comparison of two quantities or measures. A key developmental milestone is the ability of a student to begin to think of a ratio as a distinct entity, different from the two measures that made it up.

2. Ratios and proportions involve multiplicative rather than additive comparisons. Equal ratios result from multiplication or division, not from addition or subtraction.

3. Rate is a way to represent a ratio and in fact represents an infinite number of ratios.

4. Proportional thinking is developed through activities involving comparing and determining the equivalence of ratios and solv-

ing proportions in a wide variety of problem-based contexts and situations without recourse to rules or formulas.

Mathematics
CONTENT CONNECTIONS

Proportional reasoning is the cornerstone of a wide variety of essential topics in the middle grades and beyond.

- ◆ **Algebra** (Chapter 14): Rates of change (ratios) are central to algebra. Some linear situations are proportional and some are not.

- ◆ **Fractions** (Chapter 15) and **Percents** (Chapter 17): Part–whole relationships (fractions) are an example of ratio. Fractions are also one of the principal methods of representing ratios. Percents are part–whole ratios with a whole of 100.

- ◆ **Geometry** (Chapter 20): When two figures are the same shape but different sizes (i.e., similar), they constitute a visual example of a proportion. The ratios of linear measures in one figure will be equal to the corresponding ratios in the other.

- ◆ **Probability** (Chapter 22): A probability is a ratio that compares the number of outcomes in an event to the total possible outcomes.

Ratios

A *ratio* is a number that relates two quantities or measures within a given situation in a multiplicative relationship (in contrast to a difference or additive relationship). Reasoning with ratios involves paying attention to two quantities that covary. Reasoning about ratios should build on multiplicative reasoning and be a primary focus in sixth grade (CCSSO, 2010).

Types of Ratios

Part-to-Part Ratios. A ratio can relate one part of a whole (9 girls) to another part of the same whole (7 boys). This can be represented as $\frac{9}{7}$, meaning "a ratio of nine to seven" and not meaning nine-sevenths (the fraction). In other words, part-to-part ratios are not fractions, though they can be written using the fraction bar; the context is what tells you it is a part-to-part ratio. Part-to-part ratios occur across the curriculum. In geometry, corresponding parts of similar geometric figures are part-to-part ratios. The ratio of the diagonal of a square to its side is $\sqrt{2}$. In algebra, the slope of a line is a ratio of rise for each unit of horizontal distance (called the *run*). In probability, the likeliness of an event is a part-to-whole ratio, but the *odds* of an event is a part-to-part ratio.

Part–Whole Ratios. Ratios can express comparisons of a part to a whole—for example, the ratio of the number of girls in a class (9) to the number of students in the class (16). This can be written as the ratio $\frac{9}{16}$, or can be thought of as nine-sixteenths of the class (a fraction). Percentages are examples of part–whole ratios. Probabilities are ratios of a part of the sample space to the whole sample space.

Ratios as Quotients. Ratios can be thought of as quotients. For example, if you can buy four kiwis for $1.00, determining the cost for one kiwi is a rate problem that can be expressed as a quotient: $1.00 \div 4 = 0.25$. The cost of one kiwi is 25 cents.

Ratios as Rates. Miles per gallon, square yards of wall coverage per gallon of paint, passengers per busload, and roses per bouquet are all rates. Rates involve two different units and how they relate to each other. Relationships between two units of measure are also rates—for example, inches per foot, milliliters per liter, and centimeters per inch. It is important to understand that a rate is an infinite set of ratios (Lobato & Ellis, 2010). Rates will be discussed in more detail later in this chapter.

Ratios Compared to Fractions

Ratios are closely related to fractions but should be thought of as overlapping concepts with important distinctions (Lobato & Ellis, 2010). Because they are represented symbolically with a fraction bar, it is important to help students see that fractions and ratios are related. Here are three examples to make this point:

> *Example 1:* The ratio of cats to dogs at the pet store is $\frac{3}{5}$. This ratio is not a fraction, as fractions are not part-to-part.
>
> *Example 2:* The ratio of cats to pets at the pet store is $\frac{3}{8}$. This can be adapted to say three-eighths of the pets are cats. Since this is part–whole, this is both a ratio and a fraction.
>
> *Example 3:* Mario walked three-eighths of a mile ($\frac{3}{8}$ miles). This is a fraction of a length and is not a ratio, as there is not a multiplicative comparison.

Unfortunately, ratios are often addressed in a superficial manner, with students recording the symbols (3:5) to tell the ratio of girls to boys. Instead, ratios should be taught as relations that involve multiplicative reasoning.

Two Ways to Think about Ratios

Lobato and Ellis (2010) point out that "forming a ratio is a cognitive task—not a writing task" (p. 22). What they mean is that ratio is a relationship, and that relationship can be thought of in different ways, regardless of whether it is notated as $\frac{2}{5}$ or 2:5 or $2 \div 5$. It is important to understand two ways to think about ratios: as multiplicative comparisons and as composed units.

Multiplicative Comparison. A ratio represents a multiplicative comparison, and that comparison can go either way. Consider the following relationship: Wand A is 8 inches long, and Wand B is 10 inches long.

The ratio of the two wands is 8 to 10. But this statement does not necessarily communicate the *relationship* between the measures. There are two ways to compare the relationship multiplicatively:

> The short wand is eight-tenths as long as the long wand (or four-fifths the length).
> The long wand is ten-eighths as long as the short wand (or five-fourths or $1\frac{1}{4}$).

This multiplicative relationship is the ratio. This involves asking the question, "How many times greater is one thing than another?" Or "What fractional part is one thing of another?" (Lobato and Ellis, 2010, p. 18).

Composed Unit. *Composed unit* refers to thinking of the ratio as one unit. For example, if kiwi are 4 for $1.00, then you can think of this as a unit, and then think about other multiples that would also be true, like 8 for $2.00, 16 for $4.00, and so on. (Each of these would be a unit composed of the original ratio.) This is iterating (also discussed in Chapter 15). It can also be partitioned: 2 for $0.50 and 1 for $0.25. Any number of kiwis can be priced through using these composed units.

It is important that students can apply both types of ratios. Activity 18.1 provides a context for thinking of a composed unit and then a multiplicative comparison.

Activity 18.1

Birthday Cupcakes

STUDENTS *with* SPECIAL NEEDS

Explain to students that they are going to be icing cupcakes and selling them at school. In a recipe for icing, the instructions say that to ice one batch of cupcakes with aqua-colored icing, you will need 2 drops of green food coloring and 5 drops of blue food coloring. Ask students to figure out how many drops of food coloring will be needed for 1 batch of cupcakes, 2 batches, 5 batches, and so on. After students have explored and found a number of batches, ask if they can figure out how much blue for one drop of green, and how much green for one drop of blue. Ask students to think about how this information helps them in determining the number of color drops for various numbers of batches. Students—particularly students with disabilities—may need to model this situation by using green and blue color tiles or counters.

Proportional Reasoning

Ratios are extended to understanding and applying proportional reasoning—for example, investigating contexts such as interest, taxes, and tips as well as connecting to work with similar figures, graphing, and slope. Developing understanding of and applying proportional relationships is a focus in grade 7 (CCSSO, 2010; NCTM, 2006). But reasoning proportionally doesn't begin in middle school; one-to-one correspondence, place value, fraction concepts, and multiplicative reasoning are all topics that involve early ideas of proportional reasoning (Seeley & Schieleck, 2007).

Proportional reasoning is difficult to define in a simple sentence or two. It is not something that you either can or cannot do. According to Lamon (2006), proportional thinkers

- Understand *ratios as distinct entities* representing a relationship different from the quantities they compare (See earlier discussion about the composed units.)
- Recognize *proportional relationships as distinct from nonproportional relationships* in real-world contexts
- Have a sense of *covariation* (That is, they understand relationships in which two quantities vary together and are able to see how the variation in one coincides with the variation in another.)
- Develop *a wide variety of strategies* for solving proportions or comparing ratios, most of which are based on informal strategies rather than prescribed algorithms

Each of these last three areas is addressed in the sections that follow.

Proportional and Nonproportional Situations

Students should be able to compare situations and discuss whether the comparison is due to an *additive, multiplicative,* or *constant* relationship (Van Dooren, De Bock, Vleugels, & Verschaffel, 2010). Importantly, a ratio is a number that expresses a multiplicative relationship (part–part or part–whole) that can be applied to a second situation in which the relative quantities or measures are the same as in the first situation. For example, in the kiwi problem, the first situation was 4 kiwi for $1.00, and this relative quantity (4 for $1.00, or 1 for $0.25) is true regardless of how many kiwi you buy (the second situation).

PAUSE and REFLECT

Solve each of the following problems.

1. Janet and Jeanette were walking to school, each walking at the same rate. Jeanette started first. When Jeanette has walked 6 blocks, Janet has walked 2 blocks. How far will Janet be when Jeanette is at 12 blocks?
2. Lisa and Linda are planting corn on the same farm. Linda plants 4 rows and Lisa plants 6 rows. If Linda's corn is ready to pick in 8 weeks, how many weeks will it take for Lisa's corn to be ready?
3. Kendra and Kevin are baking cookies using the same recipe. Kendra makes 6 dozen and Kevin makes 3 dozen. If Kevin is using 6 ounces of chocolate chips, how many ounces will Kendra need?

The first situation is additive. Janet will still be 4 blocks behind, so 8 blocks. If incorrectly solved through multiplicative reasoning, however, you would have gotten 4 blocks. The second situation is constant. It will still take 8 weeks for the corn to grow, regardless of how many rows were planted. If solved through multiplicative reasoning, the incorrect answer would be 12 weeks. The final situation is multiplicative, and the answer is 12 ounces. How did you do?

The way to get students to distinguish between these types of reasoning is to provide opportunities for them to make the distinction between these problem types. Consider the following sample problem suggested by Cai and Sun in their discussion of how teachers in Chinese classrooms introduce the concept of ratio (2002, p. 196):

Miller Middle School has 16 sixth-grade students, and 12 of them say that they are basketball fans. The remaining students are not basketball fans. Describe as many relationships as you can about those who are basketball fans and those who are not.

Students should report several different relationships:

- There are eight more fans than nonfans.
- There are three times as many fans as nonfans.
- For every three students who like basketball, there is one who does not.

Of these, the first is an additive relationship—focusing on the difference between the two numbers. The other two are variations of the multiplicative relationship, each expressing the 3-to-1 ratio of fans to nonfans in a slightly different way. A discussion helps to contrast the multiplicative relationship with the additive one.

The following problem, adapted from the book *Adding It Up* (National Research Council, 2001), involves a comparison.

> Two weeks ago, two flowers were measured at 8 inches and 12 inches, respectively. Today they are 11 inches and 15 inches tall. Did the 8-inch or 12-inch flower grow more?

Additive reasoning would lead to the response that they both grew the same amount—3 inches. Reasoning multiplicatively leads to a different conclusion: The first flower grew $\frac{3}{8}$ of its height while the second grew $\frac{3}{12}$. So the first flower grew more. This is a proportional view of this change situation. Here, both the additive reasoning and multiplicative reasoning produce valid, albeit different, answers.

The following activities provide more opportunities for students to make the distinction between additive reasoning and multiplicative reasoning.

Activity 18.2

Which Has More?

ENGLISH LANGUAGE LEARNERS

Provide students with situations similar to those in Figure 18.1. Ask students to decide which has more and share a rationale for their thinking. As students share their reasoning, help students to see the difference between looking at the difference (additive reasoning) and looking at the ratio (multiplicative reasoning). For ELLs, take time to build meaning for what these terms mean—connect *additive* with the

(a) Which team has more girls?

The Stars   The Comets

(b) Which set has more circles?

A   B

FIGURE 18.1 Two pictorial situations that can be interpreted with either additive or multiplicative comparisons.

word *add,* and *multiplicative* with *multiple* and *multiply.* Reasoning can be modeled through illustrations or explanations. If no one suggests one of the options, introduce it. For example, say, "Amy says it is the second group. Can you explain why she made that choice?" or "Which class team has a larger proportion of girls?"

Activity 18.3

Weight Loss

Show students the data in the following chart:

Week	Max	Moe	Minnie
0	210	158	113
2	202	154	107
4	200	150	104

Max, Moe, and Minnie are each on a diet and have recorded their weight at the start of their diet and at two-week intervals. After four weeks, which person is the most successful dieter?

Ask students to make three different arguments—each favoring a different dieter. (The argument for Moe is that he is the most steady in his loss.)

Additive and Multiplicative Comparisons in Problems

When comparisons are embedded in a story situation, they may be additive *or* multiplicative. Using additive reasoning in a situation that calls for multiplicative, or vice versa, leads to incorrect answers. Solve the five-item assessment shown in Figure 18.2, devised to examine students' appropriate use of additive or multiplicative reasoning (Bright, Joyner, & Wallis, 2003). Which ones are multiplicative situations? Additive? What is the difference between items 2 and 4?

Notice that the items involving rectangles (1, 2, and 5) cannot be answered correctly using additive reasoning. Students are often challenged to determine which type of reasoning to use. When these questions were asked to 132 eighth- and ninth-grade students, scores on items 1 through 4 ranged from 45 percent to 67 percent correct. Item 5 proved quite difficult (37 percent correct for most square, 28 percent correct for least square).

FORMATIVE Assessment Notes

All five of these items could be used as a **performance assessment,** or a few of these (at least one additive) can be used as a **diagnostic interview.** For example, item 5 was given to an eighth grader, who first solved it incorrectly using an additive strategy (subtracting the sides). When asked if a very large rectangle 1,000,000

For each problem, circle the correct answer.

1. Mrs. Allen took a 3-inch by 5-inch photo of the Cape Hatteras Lighthouse and made an enlargement on a photocopier using the 200% option. Which is "more square," the original photo or the enlargement?

   a. The original photo is "more square."
   b. The enlargement is "more square."
   c. The photo and the enlargement are equally square.
   d. There is not enough information to determine which is "more square."

2. The Science Club has four separate rectangular plots for experiments with plants:

   1 foot by 4 feet   7 feet by 10 feet
   17 feet by 20 feet   27 feet by 30 feet

   Which rectangular plot is most square?

   a. 1 foot by 4 feet
   b. 7 feet by 10 feet
   c. 17 feet by 20 feet
   d. 27 feet by 30 feet

3. Sue and Julie were running equally fast around a track. Sue started first. When Sue had run 9 laps, Julie had run 3 laps. When Julie completed 15 laps, how many laps had Sue run?

   a. 45 laps
   b. 24 laps
   c. 21 laps
   d. 6 laps

4. At the midway point of the basketball season, you must recommend the best free-throw shooter for the all-star game. Here are the statistics for four players:

   Novak: 8 of 11 shots   Peterson: 22 of 29 shots
   Williams: 15 of 19 shots   Reynolds: 33 of 41 shots

   Which player is the best free-throw shooter?

   a. Novak   b. Peterson   c. Williams   d. Reynolds

5. Write your answer to this problem.

   A farmer has three fields. One is 185 feet by 245 feet, one is 75 feet by 114 feet, and one is 455 feet by 508 feet. If you were flying over these fields, which one would seem most square? Which one would seem least square? Explain your answers.

FIGURE 18.2 Five items to assess proportional reasoning.

Source: Reprinted with permission from Bright, G. W., Joyner, J. J., & Wallis, C. (2003). "Assessing Proportional Thinking." *Mathematics Teaching in the Middle School, 9*(3), p. 167. Copyright © 2003 by the National Council of Teachers of Mathematics. All rights reserved.

feet by 1,000,050 feet would look less square, he replied, "No—*ob*, this is a proportional situation." He then solved it using a novel strategy (see Figure 18.3). ■

Return for a moment to item 3 in Figure 18.2. This item has been used in other studies showing that students try to solve this as a proportion problem, when it is strictly an additive situation (The two runners will end up six laps apart, which is how they began). Watson and Shaughnessy

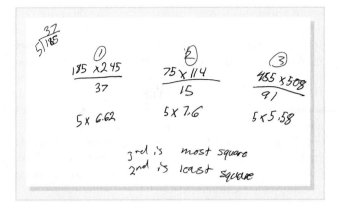

FIGURE 18.3 Jacob noticed that each length was divisible by 5; therefore, he simplified each ratio to have a side of 5 and then compared the widths.

(2004) note that often the way that we word problems is a clue that a proportion is involved. Students become accustomed to this wording being related to proportions and automatically arrange four quantities (three known and one unknown) into a proportion, without paying attention to whether there is a multiplicative relationship between the numbers. They are focused on the structure of the proportion, not the concept of the proportion (Heinz & Sterba-Boatwright, 2008).

Activity 18.4 describes an activity (adapted from Che, 2009) that can help students move from additive to multiplicative reasoning. See the end-of-chapter Literature Connections for ideas of books about giants to connect to this activity.

Activity 18.4

Pencil-to-Pencil

Hold up a cutout of a very large pencil (e.g., 30 inches in length). Explain to students that this is the exact size of a pencil used by a giant. Ask, "If this is her pencil, what else can you tell me about her?" For students (particularly those with disabilities) who need more structure or guidance, ask specific questions like "How tall is the giant?" "How long would her hand be?" After students have found out things about the giant, have them post their findings on posters, and have them illustrate or explain how they found the measures. ELLs are likely to be more familiar with centimeters, so have students choose what measurement system they use, or have all students use centimeters.

ENGLISH LANGUAGE LEARNERS

STUDENTS with SPECIAL NEEDS

When students first engage in this activity, they may focus on the difference between the pencil they are shown and a real pencil they have. If they reason about this difference, then they will find that the giant is only 24 inches taller than they are. Thinking about this should raise some doubt about this line of reasoning, because there are real people who are two feet taller, and a 30-inch pencil would still be too big for them to manage. They might then start thinking of how many of their pencils equal the pencil you have created. By counting (iterating), they may notice it takes about 5 of their pencils. In debriefing this activity with students, it is important to discuss these thought processes and why the situation is multiplicative and not additive.

Contrasting two very similar problems can also support students' emerging skills at reasoning proportionally (Lim, 2009). Consider these two tasks and how they are the same and how they are different:

---

1. A red car and a silver car are traveling at the same constant rate. When the red car has traveled 20 miles, the silver car has traveled 12 miles. How far will the red car be when the silver car has traveled 32 miles?
2. A red and a silver car are traveling at different but constant rates. They pass Exit 95 at the same time. When the red car has traveled 20 miles, the silver car has traveled 16 miles. How far will the red car be when the silver car has traveled 32 miles?

Lim (2009) suggests that having students write the relationships in variables can further help students see the difference. In the first case, the relationship is red = silver + 8 because the red car is 8 miles in front of the silver car. In the latter case, the relationships is red $= \frac{5}{4}$ silver because for every five miles the red car travels, the silver car travels four.

Covariation

Covariation means that two quantities (a ratio) vary together. For example, five mangos cost $2.00 (two quantities in a multiplicative relationship); as the number of mangos varies (for example, to 10 mangos), so does the cost. And as the cost changes, so does the number of mangos you will get. Once you know either a new price or a new number of mangos, you can determine the missing variable.

Within and Between Ratios. A ratio of two measures in the same setting is a *within* ratio. For example, in the case of the mangos, the ratio of mango to money is a within ratio; that is, it is "within" the context of that example.

A *between* ratio is a ratio of two corresponding measures in different situations. In the case of the mangos, the ratio of the original number of mangos (5) to the number of mangos in a second situation (10) is a between ratio; that is, it is "between" the two situations.

The drawing in Figure 18.4 is an effective way of looking at two ratios and determining whether a ratio is between or within. A drawing similar to this will be very helpful to students in setting up proportions, especially students who struggle with abstract representations.

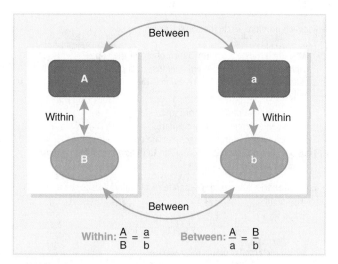

FIGURE 18.4 Given a proportional situation, the two between ratios will be equivalent, as will the two within ratios.

Different Objects, Same Ratios

Prepare cards with distinctly different objects, as shown in Figure 18.5. Given one card, students are to select a card on which the ratio of the two types of objects is the same. This task moves students toward a numeric approach rather than a visual one and introduces the notion of ratios as rates. In this context, it makes the most sense to find the boxes per truck as the rate (rather than trucks per box). Finding the rate (amount for 1 unit) for pairs of quantities facilitates comparisons (just as the unit prices provided in grocery stores allow you to compare different brands).

Covariation in Geometry and Measurement. Within and between ratios are particularly relevant in exploring similarity with geometric shapes. Students often struggle to determine which features to compare to which features. The following activity can help students begin to analyze which features to compare.

STUDENTS *with* SPECIAL NEEDS

Look-Alike Rectangles

Provide students with a copy of Blackline Masters 30 and 31, shown in Figure 18.6, and have them cut out the ten rectangles. Three of the rectangles (A, I, and D) have sides in the ratio of 3 to 4. Rectangles C, F, and H have sides in the ratio of 5 to 8. Rectangles J, E, and G have sides in the ratio of 1 to 3. Rectangle B is a square, so its sides are in the ratio of 1 to 1.

Ask students to group the rectangles into three sets that "look alike." If your students know the word *similar* from geometry, you can use that instead of "look alike." To explain what "look alike" means, draw three rectangles on the board,

with two that are similar and one that is clearly dissimilar to the other two, as in the following example. Have students use their language to explain why rectangles 1 and 3 are alike.

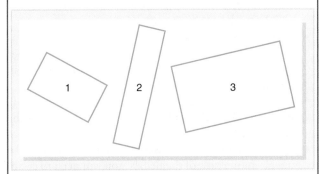

When students have decided on their groupings, stop and discuss the reasons they classified the rectangles as they did. Be prepared for some students to try to match sides or look for rectangles that have the same amount of difference between them. Next have the students measure and record the sides of each rectangle to the nearest half-centimeter. Blackline Master 31 can be used to record the data. Discuss these results and ask students to offer explanations of how the ratios and groupings are related. If the groups are formed of proportional (similar) rectangles, the ratios within each group will be equivalent. Students with disabilities may need to have examples of one rectangle from each grouping as a starting point for the groupings.

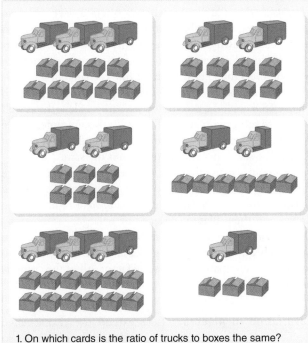

1. On which cards is the ratio of trucks to boxes the same?
2. What is the rate of boxes per truck for each card?

FIGURE 18.5 Ratio cards for exploring ratios and rates.

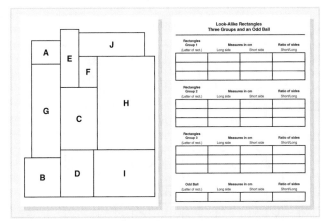

FIGURE 18.6 Blackline Masters 30 and 31 for use with Activity 18.6.

The connection between proportional reasoning and the geometric concept of similarity is very important. Similar figures provide a visual representation of proportions, and proportional thinking enhances the understanding of similarity. Discussion of the similar figures should focus on the ratios between and within the figures. The next activity is aimed at this connection.

Activity 18.7

Scale Drawings

ENGLISH LANGUAGE LEARNERS

On grid or dot paper (see Blackline Masters 34–37), have students draw a simple shape using straight lines with vertices on the dots. After one shape is complete, have them draw a larger or smaller shape that looks similar to the first. This can be done on a grid of the same size or a different size, as shown in Figure 18.7. First compare ratios within (see the first problem in Figure 18.7). Then compare ratios between the figures (see the second problem in Figure 18.7).

Corresponding sides from one figure to the next should all be in the same ratio. The ratio of two sides within one figure should be the same as the ratio of the corresponding two sides in another figure. With ELLs, be sure the term *scale* is understood, so they don't confuse this use of the word with a machine that weighs things and what fish have.

The third problem in Figure 18.7 involves area as well as length. Comparisons of corresponding lengths, areas, and volumes in proportional figures lead to some interesting patterns. If we know the length of a figure, we can create the ratio of 1 to *k*, for example, to represent the relationship to a proportional figure. (The variable *k* is often used with proportions, whereas *m* is used with equations to describe slope—both refer to the rate or ratio between two values, which is called the *scale factor*.) If two

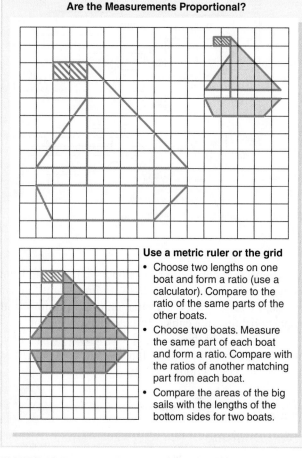

Are the Measurements Proportional?

Use a metric ruler or the grid
- Choose two lengths on one boat and form a ratio (use a calculator). Compare to the ratio of the same parts of the other boats.
- Choose two boats. Measure the same part of each boat and form a ratio. Compare with the ratios of another matching part from each boat.
- Compare the areas of the big sails with the lengths of the bottom sides for two boats.

FIGURE 18.7 Comparing similar figures drawn on grids.

figures are proportional (similar), then any corresponding linear dimensions will have the same scale factor. If the similar figure is three times the area of the original figure (scale of 3), then the ratio of the sides of the original to the sides of the new figure is 1:3, or we can write it symbolically as $y = 3x$, where x is the original figure and y is the new figure.

Imagine you have a square that is 3 by 3 and you create a new square that is 6 by 6. The ratio between the lengths is 1:2. What is the ratio between the two areas? Why is it 1:4? Try the same idea with the volume of a cube—what is the relationship of the original to the new volume when you double the length of the edges? Why? Returning to the sailboat in Figure 18.7, what would you conjecture is the ratio between the areas of the two sailboats? Measure and test your hypothesis.

Here are some interesting situations to consider for scale drawings:

- If you wanted to make a scale model of the solar system and use a Ping-Pong ball for the earth, how far away should the sun be? How large a ball would you need?

- What scale should be used to draw a scale map of your city (or some interesting region) so that it will nicely fit onto a standard piece of poster board?
- Use the scale on a map to estimate the distance and travel time between two points of interest.
- Roll a toy car down a ramp, timing the trip with a stopwatch. How fast was the car traveling in miles per hour? If the speed is proportional to the size of the car, how fast would this have been for a real car?
- Your little sister wants a table and chair for her doll. Her doll is 14 inches tall. How big should you make the table?
- Determine the various distances that a 10-speed bike travels in one turn of the pedals. You will need to count the sprocket teeth on the front and back gears.

TECHNOLOGY Google Earth (www.google.com/earth) is a great resource for doing authentic scaling activities (Roberge & Cooper, 2010). If you get a Google Earth diagram that includes something for which the measure is known, students can figure out other measures. For example, you know that a standard football field is 100 yards from end zone to end zone (120 yards if you include the end zone), so zoom in on your school football field. By zooming to different levels, students can build an understanding of scale factor in an interesting context. You can even do some interdisciplinary teaching by exploring regions that align with what is being studied in social studies!

Dynamic geometry software such as *GeoGebra* (a free download from www.geogebra.org/cms) or *The Geometer's Sketchpad* (Key Curriculum Press) offers a very effective method of exploring the idea of ratio. In Figure 18.8, two lengths are drawn on a grid using the software's "snap-to-grid" option. The lengths are measured, and two ratios are computed. As the length of either line is changed, the measures and ratios are updated instantly. A screen similar to Figure 18.8 could be used to discuss ratios of lengths as well as inverse ratios with your full class. In this example, notice that the difference between the first pair and second pair of lines is the same, but the ratios are not the same.

You can also use dynamic geometry software to explore similar figures and corresponding measures. Using the Dilate feature in *The Geometer's Sketchpad*, a figure can be drawn and then dilated (reduced or enlarged proportionally) according to any scale factor of your choosing. The ratios of beginning and ending measures (lengths and areas) can then be compared to the scale factor. All of the computations can be done within the software program.

Covariation in Algebra. Let's extend the "Look-Alike Rectangles" activity (Activity 18.6). Stack like rectangles so that that they are aligned at one corner, as in Figure 18.9. Place a straightedge across the diagonals, and you will see

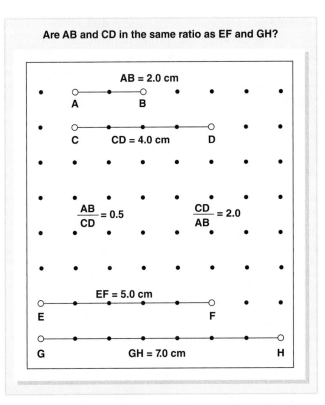

Are AB and CD in the same ratio as EF and GH?

AB = 2.0 cm

A   B

C   CD = 4.0 cm   D

$$\frac{AB}{CD} = 0.5 \qquad \frac{CD}{AB} = 2.0$$

EF = 5.0 cm

E   F

G   GH = 7.0 cm   H

FIGURE 18.8 Dynamic geometry software can be used to discuss ratios of two lengths.

Source: From *The Geometer's Sketchpad,* Key Curriculum Press, 1150 65th Street, Emeryville, CA 94608, 1-800-995-MATH, www.keypress.com. Reprinted by permission.

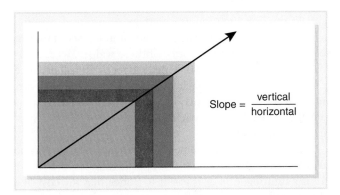

$$\text{Slope} = \frac{\text{vertical}}{\text{horizontal}}$$

FIGURE 18.9 The slope of a line through a stack of proportional rectangles is equal to the ratio of the two sides.

that opposite corners also line up. If the rectangles are placed on a coordinate axis with the common corner at the origin, the slope of the line joining the corners is the ratio of the sides. A great connection to algebra!

Proportional situations are linear situations. In fact, ratios are a special case of linear situations that will always go through the origin, since they are multiplicative relationships. The ratio or rate is the slope of the graph.

Activity 18.8

Rectangle Ratios—Revisited

Have students make a graph of the data from a collection of equal ratios that they have scaled or discussed. The graph in Figure 18.10 is based on the ratios of two sides of similar rectangles. If only a few ratios have actually been plotted, the graph can be drawn carefully and then used to determine other equivalent ratios. In the rectangle example, students can draw rectangles with sides determined by the graph and compare them to the original rectangles. A unit ratio can be found by locating the point on the line at $x = 1$ or at $y = 1$. Ask students to find the rate each way. Ask students to see if they can find a rectangle that has a noninteger side (e.g., $4\frac{1}{2}$ units). Ask students how, if they know the short side, they could find the long side (and vice versa).

Graphs provide another way of thinking about proportions, and they connect proportional thought to algebraic interpretations. All graphs of equivalent ratios fall along straight lines that pass through the origin. If the equation of one of these lines is written in the form $y = mx$, the slope m is always one of the equivalent ratios.

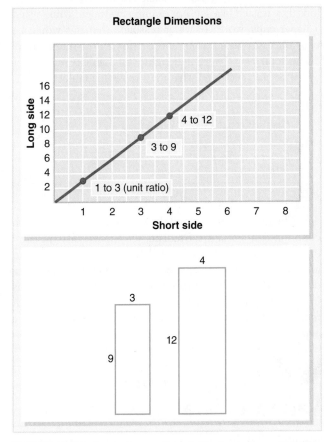

Rectangle Dimensions

Long side

4 to 12

3 to 9

1 to 3 (unit ratio)

Short side

3

9

4

12

FIGURE 18.10 Graph shows ratios of sides in similar rectangles.

The following is a relevant context that applies algebraic thinking to develop proportional reasoning.

Activity **18.9**

Dripping Faucet

Pose the following problem to students (adapted from Williams, Forrest, & Schnabel, 2006):

If you brush your teeth twice a day and leave the water running when you brush, how many gallons of water will you waste in one day? In two days? In a week? A month? Any number of days?

Have students actually gather real data, if possible. Then compute the mean. Ask students to figure out the answers to the questions posed and be able to justify their answers.

This environmental investigation involves real measurement and authentic data. Stemn (2008) implemented this investigation with students and found that it aided their understanding of multiplicative versus additive situations. Students in her class were challenged to figure out how many of the paper cups that they used to measure would fill a gallon. The class figured out that 2 paper cups were equal to one-quarter gallon. Each student reasoned how many gallons they wasted in a day. For example, a student who wasted 5 paper cups' worth of water reasoned that this would be two-fourths, plus a half of another fourth (or one-eighth). So, in total, there were five-eighths of a gallon wasted per day. The class recorded what they knew in a table:

Paper cups of water wasted	1	2	3	4	5
Gallons of water wasted	$\frac{1}{8}$	$\frac{1}{4}$	$\frac{3}{8}$	$\frac{2}{4}$	$\frac{5}{8}$

The teacher encouraged them to rewrite the table with common denominators. Students recognized that the ratio of paper cups to gallons was $1{:}\frac{1}{8}$. Notice the connection to algebraic reasoning and to measurement. The formula $y = \frac{1}{8}x$ describes the number of paper cups (x) to gallons (y). This investigation also showed the students how to reason through measurement conversions with a nonstandard measure (the paper cup), which is a very challenging concept for students.

Develop a Wide Variety of Strategies

An understanding of proportional situations includes being able to compare two ratios as well as being able to identify equivalent ratios. Posing problems that have multiple solution strategies can help students. Strategies for solving missing value proportions include unit rate, scaling up or down, scale factors (within or between measures), ratio tables, graphs, and cross multiplication (Berk, Taber, Gorowara, & Poetzl, 2009; Ercole, Frantz, & Ashline, 2011). It is worth repeating that all of these are *reasoning* strategies and any one of them may be useful in a particular situation.

Mental Strategies

Unit rate and scale factor can be used to mentally solve many proportional situations. The key is to know both strategies and pick the one that best fits the particular numbers in the problem, as the next examples illustrate.

Tammy bought 3 widgets for $2.40. At the same price, how much would 10 widgets cost?

Tammy bought 4 widgets for $3.75. How much would a dozen widgets cost?

 PAUSE and REFLECT

Before reading further, solve these two problems using an approach other than the cross-product algorithm. ●

In the first situation, it is perhaps easiest to determine the cost of one widget—the unit rate or unit price. This can be found by dividing the price of three widgets by 3. Multiplying this unit rate of $0.80 per widget by 10 will produce the answer. This approach is referred to as the *unit-rate* method of solving proportions. Notice that the unit rate is a within ratio. This approach applies the ratio as a multiplicative comparison.

In the second problem, a unit-rate approach could be used, but the division does not appear to be easy. Because 12 is a multiple of 4, it is easier to notice that the cost of a dozen is 3 times the cost of 4, or that the scale factor between the ratios is 4. This is called a *buildup strategy*. (This strategy could have been used on the first problem but would have been more difficult because the scale factor between 3 and 10 is $3\frac{1}{3}$.) Notice that the buildup approach applies the ratio as a composed unit. Although using scale factors (the buildup strategy) is a useful way to think about proportions, it is most frequently used when the numbers are compatible (i.e., the scale factor is a whole number). Students should be given problems in which the numbers lend themselves to both approaches so that they will explore both methods.

Try using the unit-rate method or scale factors to solve the next two problems.

At the Office Super Store, you can buy 4 pencils for 59 cents, or you can buy the same pencils in a large box of 5 dozen for $7.79. How much will you save per pencil if you buy the large box?

The price of a box of 2 dozen gumballs is $4.80. Bridget wants to buy 5 gumballs. What will she have to pay?

To solve the pencil problem, you might notice that the between ratio of pencils to pencils is 4 to 60 (5 dozen), or 1 to 15. If you multiply the 59 cents by 15, the factor of change, you will get the price of the box of 60 if the pencils were sold at the same price. In the gumball problem, the within ratio of 24 to $4.80 lends to finding the unit rate of $0.20 per gumball, which can then be multiplied by 5.

It is important to follow these tasks with problems that have more difficult numbers, asking students to still apply the same strategies to reason to an answer. For example, try to apply both strategies to the next problem.

Brian can run 5 km in 18.4 minutes. If he keeps on running at the same speed, how far can he run in 23 minutes?

Selecting problems that can be solved many ways is important. The following activity has been used in various studies and curricula because it can be approached in so many ways.

Activity 18.10

Lemonade Recipes

Show students a picture of two lemonade pitchers as in Figure 18.11. The little squares indicate the recipes used in each pitcher. A yellow square is a cup of lemonade concentrate and a blue square is a cup of water. Ask which pitcher will have the stronger lemonade flavor or whether they will both taste the same. Ask them to justify their answers.

 PAUSE and REFLECT

Solve the lemonade problem and write down your reasoning. Is there more than one way to justify the answer? ●

The task in "Lemonade Recipes" is interesting because of how many ways there are to make the comparison. A common method is to figure out how much water goes with each cup of concentrate. As we will see later, this is using a unit rate: cups of water per cup of lemonade concentrate ($1\frac{1}{2}$ vs. $1\frac{1}{3}$). Other approaches use fractions instead of unit rates and attempt to compare the fractions: concentrate compared to

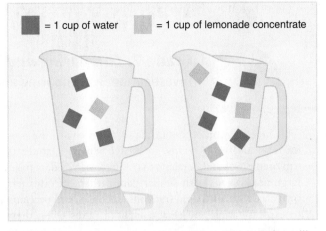

FIGURE 18.11 A comparing ratios problem: Which pitcher will have the stronger lemon flavor, or will they be the same?

water ($\frac{2}{3}$ vs. $\frac{3}{4}$) or the reverse, and also lemonade concentrate as a fraction of the total ($\frac{2}{5}$ vs. $\frac{3}{7}$). This can also be done with water as a fraction of the total. Some students may also use percentages instead of fractions, creating the same arguments. Another way to justify is to use multiples of one or both of the pitchers until either the water or the lemonade concentrate is equal in both.

One interesting argument is that the pitchers will taste the same: If the concentrate and water are matched up in each pitcher, then there will be one cup of extra water in each recipe. Although this is incorrect (can you tell why?), your class will likely have a spirited discussion of these ideas.

The lemonade task can be adjusted for difficulty. As given, there are no simple relationships between the two pitchers. If the solutions are 3 to 6 and 4 to 8 (equal flavors), the task is much simpler. For a 2-to-5 recipe versus a 4-to-9 recipe, it is easy to double the first and compare it to the second. When a 3-to-6 recipe is compared to a 2-to-5 recipe, the unit rates are perhaps more obvious (1 to 2 vs. 1 to $2\frac{1}{2}$). The Connected Mathematics (CMP II) lesson provides a fully developed way to engage students in the mixing juice problem.

The following problem provides another context for comparing ratios using a variety of approaches.

Two camps of Scouts are having pizza parties. The Bear camp ordered enough so that every 3 campers will have 2 pizzas. The leader of the Raccoons ordered enough so that there would be 3 pizzas for every 5 campers. Did the Bear campers or the Raccoon campers have more pizza to eat?

Figure 18.12 (p. 369) shows two different reasoning strategies. When the pizzas are sliced up into fractional parts as in Figure 18.12(a), the approach is to look for a unit rate—pizzas per camper. A partitioning approach has been used for each ratio (as in division). But notice that this

CONNECTED MATHEMATICS

Grade 7, *Comparing and Scaling*
Investigation 3: Comparing and Using Ratios

Context

This investigation occurs in the second week of the unit on ratio and proportions. In earlier activities, students explored ratios and percents to compare survey data from large populations with similar data gathered from their own class. Students used fractions, decimals, and percents to express ratios, and they compared ratios using their own strategies.

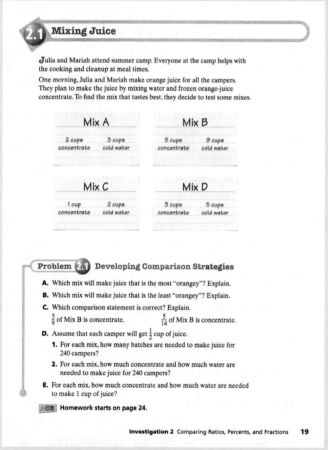

Task Description

In the juice problem shown (2.1: Mixing Juice), students apply proportional reasoning to figure out which recipe is

the orangeiest and which is the least orangey. Students are to apply their knowledge of ratios to reason to a solution. Students might solve this task in a variety of ways:

1. Make equal amounts of each recipe to compare (e.g., make 120 cups of each).
2. Make the cups of concentrate the same and look at how much water goes with each (e.g., for 30 cups of concentrate, how much water is needed for each recipe?).
3. Find part-to-whole fractions, find common denominators, and compare.
4. Find part-to-whole fractions, convert to percents, and compare.
5. Draw pictures to show how much water per cup of concentrate. For example, the following could be drawn for Mix D:

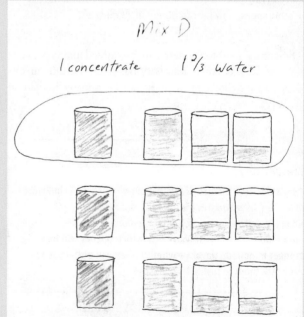

The context of this problem, a familiar one, allows students to apply their own creative and clever strategies to solve a proportional situation without instructions on *how* to solve the problem.

The full unit contains six investigations, each with numerous real contexts. Scaling, the use of unit rates, and percentages are suggested techniques for solving the proportional situations. A similar problem application can be found online at http://nrich.maths.org/6870.

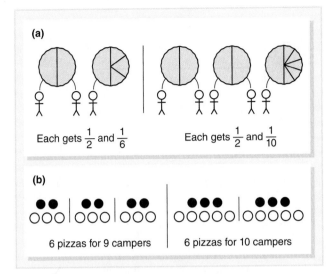

Each gets $\frac{1}{2}$ and $\frac{1}{6}$ Each gets $\frac{1}{2}$ and $\frac{1}{10}$

6 pizzas for 9 campers | 6 pizzas for 10 campers

FIGURE 18.12 Two reasoning methods for comparing two ratios.

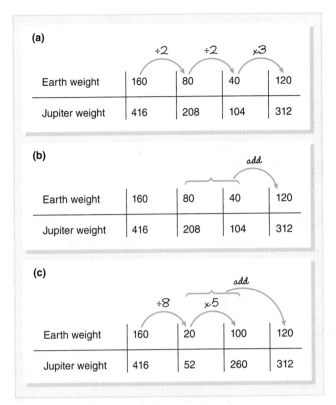

FIGURE 18.13 Something weighing 160 pounds on Earth is 416 pounds on Jupiter. If something weighs 120 pounds on Earth, how many pounds would it weigh on Jupiter? Three solutions using ratio tables.

problem does not say that the camps have only 3 and 5 campers, respectively. Any multiples of 2 to 3 and 3 to 5 can be used to make the appropriate comparison, the same as making multiple pitchers of lemonade. The iterative approach is illustrated in Figure 18.12(b). Three "clones" of the 2-to-3 ratio and two clones of the 3-to-5 ratio are made so that the number of campers getting a like number of pizzas can be compared. From the vantage of fractions, this is like getting common numerators. Because there are more campers in the Raccoon ratio (larger denominator), there is less pizza for each camper. These strategies, and the strategies in the lemonade activity, emerge through students' reasoning multiplicatively about the situations.

Hopefully you have noticed that some of the problems shared in this section include all the values and ask students to compare, while others ask for a missing value. Some lend to a unit-rate, some to a buildup, and some to a picture. The more experiences students have in comparing and solving situations that are proportional in nature, the more they will be able to reason proportionally.

Ratio Tables

Ratio tables or charts that show how two variable quantities are related are good ways to organize information. They serve as a tool for applying the buildup strategy but can be used to determine unit rate. Consider the following table:

Acres	5	10	15	20	25
Pine trees	75	150	225		

If the task is to find the number of trees for 65 acres of land or the number of acres needed for 750 trees, students can proceed by using addition. That is, they can add fives along the top row until they reach 65. This is a recursive

pattern, or repeated addition strategy. The pattern that connects acres to pine trees ($\times 15$) is the generative pattern and the multiplicative relationship between the values. This is the rate (15 pine trees per acre). The equation for this situation is $y = 15x$, where x is number of acres and y is the number of pine trees. Once this is discovered, students can figure out that 15×65 acres $= 975$ pine trees. But the nice thing about the ratio table is that neither variables nor equations are needed to solve it.

Ratio tables can be used to find a specific equivalent ratio. Then the ratio table can be used as a strategy for solving a proportion. The following activity provides examples, and Figure 18.13 gives illustrations of this use of a ratio table.

Activity **18.11**

Using Ratio Tables

ENGLISH LANGUAGE LEARNERS

Build a ratio table, and use it to answer the question (based on Dole, 2008, and Lamon, 2006). Be sure the context is relevant to the ELLs and other students in the classroom. If the examples below are not relevant to your students, select something of interest from their culture or experiences.

- Plants come in boxes of 35 plants. How many plants would be in 16 boxes?

- Five wheel rotations on a bike take you 8 yards. How many wheel rotations to go 50 yards?
- A person who weighs 160 pounds on Earth will weigh 416 pounds on the planet Jupiter. How much will a person weigh on Jupiter who weighs 120 pounds on earth?
- At the local college, 5 out of every 8 seniors live in apartments. How many of the 30 seniors are likely to live in an apartment?
- The tax on a purchase of $20 is $1.12. How much tax will there be on a purchase of $45.50?

The tasks in this activity are typical "solve the proportion" tasks. One ratio and part of a second are given, with the task being to find the fourth number. Figure 18.13 shows three different ways to solve the Jupiter weight task using ratio tables. As this example illustrates, the ratio table has several advantages over the missing value proportion. Students label each row and are more successful at placing the values appropriately, and therefore able to compare. And working within the ratio table is more directly connected to the concept of seeking an equivalent ratio than solving a missing value proportion. For all of these reasons, the ratio table should be introduced prior to missing value proportions and then used as a bridge to understanding them.

In applying this technique, students are using multiplicative relationships to transform a given ratio into an equivalent ratio. And students see that there are infinitely many equivalent ratios, an important concept of ratio and rate.

FORMATIVE Assessment Notes Because there are many ways to reason about proportional situations, it is important to capture *how* students are reasoning. **Writing** is an effective way to do this. You can simply ask students to tell how they solved a problem or to explain how they used the ratio table, or you can provide more structure by using specific writing prompts or sentence starters. ■

Double Line (Strip) Comparison

In Figure 18.14, a line segment is partitioned in two different ways: in fourths on one side and in twelfths on the other.

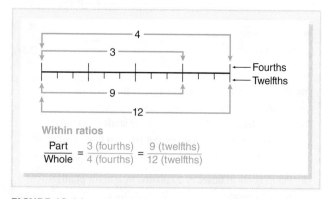

FIGURE 18.14 Equivalent fractions as proportions.

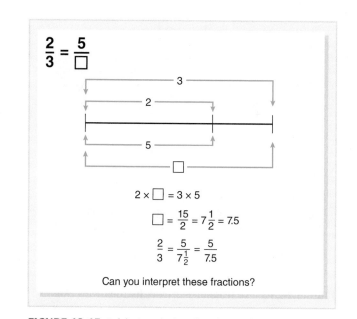

Can you interpret these fractions?

FIGURE 18.15 Solving equivalent-fraction problems as equivalent ratios using cross-products.

In previous examples in this chapter, proportions were established based on two categories of students, two flowers, and two different Scout camps. Here only one thing is measured—the part of a whole—but it is measured or partitioned two ways: in fourths and in twelfths.

A simple line segment drawing similar to the one in Figure 18.14 could be drawn to set up a proportion to solve any equivalent-fraction problem, even ones that do not result in whole-number numerators or denominators. An example is shown in Figure 18.15.

TECHNOLOGY For a nice virtual model that compares two strips, go to Math Playground (www.mathplayground.com/thinkingblocks.html) and scroll down to "Ratio Models." This site has instructions and practice that connects the two strips to different types of proportional situations.

Percents

All percent problems can be set up as equivalent fractions. They involve a part and a whole measured in some unit and the same part and whole measured in hundredths—that is, in percents. A simple line segment drawing can be used for each of the three types of percent problems. Let the measures on one side of the line correspond to the numbers or measures in the problem. On the opposite side of the line, indicate the corresponding values in terms of percents. Examples are shown in Figure 18.16.

Notice how flexible this double line model is for different types of percent problems. It allows modeling of not only part–whole scenarios but also increase–decrease situations and those in which there is a comparison between two distinct quantities. Another advantage of the line model is that it does not restrict students from thinking about percents

In 1960, U.S. railroads carried 327 million passengers. Over the next 20 years, there was a 14 percent decrease in passengers. How many passengers rode the railroads in 1980?

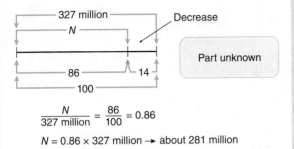

$$\frac{N}{327\text{ million}} = \frac{86}{100} = 0.86$$

$$N = 0.86 \times 327\text{ million} \rightarrow \text{about 281 million}$$

Sylvia's new boat cost $8950. She made a down payment of $2000. What percent of the sales price was Sylvia's down payment?

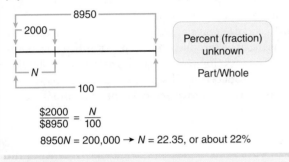

$$\frac{\$2000}{\$8950} = \frac{N}{100}$$

$$8950N = 200{,}000 \rightarrow N = 22.35, \text{ or about } 22\%$$

The seventh- and eighth-grade classes at Robious Middle School had a contest to see which class would sell more raffle tickets at the school festival. The eighth grade sold 592 tickets. However, this turned out to be only 62.5 percent of the number of tickets sold by the seventh grade. How many tickets did the seventh grade sell?

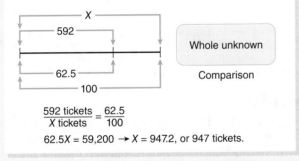

$$\frac{592\text{ tickets}}{X\text{ tickets}} = \frac{62.5}{100}$$

$$62.5X = 59{,}200 \rightarrow X = 947.2, \text{ or } 947 \text{ tickets.}$$

FIGURE 18.16 Percentage problems solved by setting up a proportion using a simple line-segment model.

greater than 100, since the line could represent more than 100 percent (not true for a circle model) (Parker, 2004).

Cross-Products

Traditional textbooks show students how to set up an equation of two ratios involving an unknown, "cross-multiply," and solve for the unknown. "The central challenge of devel-

oping students' capacity to think with ratios (to reason proportionally) is to teach ideas and restrain the quick path to computation" (Smith, 2002, p. 15). Even when using cross-products, students should be encouraged to reason in order to find the missing value, not just apply the cross-product algorithm.

Sixth- and seventh-grade students rarely use cross-multiplication to solve proportion problems, even when that method has been taught (Smith, 2002). A possible reason is that although the method is relatively efficient, it does not look like the earlier conceptual approaches.

Create a Visual Model.   Rather than tell students to cross-multiply, build understanding through visuals. In Figure 18.17, a simple model is drawn for a typical rate or price problem. The two equations in the figure come from setting up within and between ratios. Providing visual cues to set up proportions is a very effective way to support a wide range of learners. Figure 18.18 shows a different visual that integrates the double number line. Different students will find different strategies more logical—encourage students to select a strategy that makes sense to them.

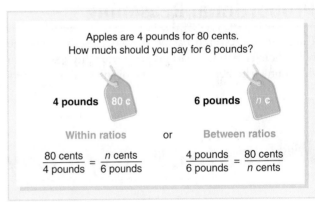

FIGURE 18.17 A simple drawing helps to establish correct proportion equations.

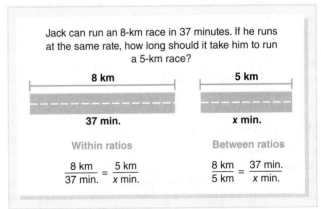

FIGURE 18.18 Line segments can be used to model both time and distance.

Solve the Proportion. Look at the situation in Figure 18.17. As students (and adults) often do naturally, you can determine the *unit rate* or the price for 1 pound by dividing the 80 cents by 4 and then multiplying this result by 6 to determine the price of 6 pounds. The equation is $(0.80 \div 4) \times 6 = 1.20$. Or you can examine the *scale factor* from 4 to 6 pounds (within ratio), which is 1.5. Multiply 0.80 by the same scale factor to get $1.20. The equation is $([6 \div 4] \times .80) = 1.20$. One equation uses 80 in a multiplication and the other equation uses 80 in division. These are exactly the two devices we employed in the line segment and picture approaches: (1) *scale factor* and (2) *unit rate*. If you cross-multiply the between ratios, you get exactly the same result. Furthermore, you get the same result if you had written the two ratios inverted, that is, with the reciprocals of each fraction. Try it!

The cross-product is not the only way to solve proportions, but if it is used, it should be understood. This is useful when numbers are more challenging and finding unit rate or scale factor is not as easy to calculate.

Teaching Proportional Reasoning

Considerable research has been conducted to determine how students reason in various proportionality tasks and to determine whether developmental or instructional factors are related to proportional reasoning (for example, see Bright et al., 2003; Lamon, 2006, 2007; Lobato and Ellis, 2010; Siegler et al., 2010). The findings are shared here as a way to summarize the chapter.

1. Use composed unit and multiplicative comparison ideas in building understanding of ratio. Multiplicative comparisons should lead to an understanding of rate, which is a strategy to be applied to proportions.
2. Help students distinguish between proportional and nonproportional comparisons by providing examples of each and discussing the differences.
3. Provide ratio and proportion tasks in a wide range of contexts, including situations involving measurements, prices, geometric and other visual contexts, and rates of all sorts.
4. Engage students in a variety of strategies for solving proportions. In particular, use ratio tables, visuals, and equations to solve problems—always expecting students to apply reasoning strategies.
5. Recognize that symbolic or mechanical methods, such as the cross-product algorithm, for solving proportions do not develop proportional reasoning and should not be introduced until students have had many experiences with intuitive and conceptual methods.

RESOURCES *for Chapter 18*

LITERATURE CONNECTIONS

Literature brings an exciting dimension to the exploration of proportional reasoning. Many books and stories discuss comparative sizes, concepts of scale as in maps, giants and miniature people who are proportional to regular people, comparative rates (especially rates of speed), and so on. For example, Beckman, Thompson, and Austin (2004) explore the popular *Harry Potter* stories, *The Lord of the Rings*, and *The Perfect Storm* for exciting contexts for proportional reasoning activities. Here are a few more, but many more exist beyond this list!

If You Hopped Like a Frog *Schwartz, 1999*

David Schwartz compares features of various creatures to humans. For example, in the title comparison, Schwarts deduces that if a person had a frog's jumping ability, he could jump from home plate to first base in one hop. This short picture book contains 12 more fascinating comparisons. Schwartz also provides the factual data on which the proportions are based. Students can figure out how strong or tall they would be if they were one of the featured animals.

Holes *Sachar, 1998*

A popular book and movie, this novel tells the story of boys in a "camp" digging holes every day, which provides an opportunity to look at daily rates of dirt removal. Pugalee and colleagues (2008) describe an excellent activity with this book that involves not only proportional reasoning but also measurement and algebra.

Literature with Large and/or Small People

There is a plethora of literature involving very little or very big people (or animals). With any of these books, body parts can be compared as a way to explore within and between ratios. The following list of some great literature can lead to wonderful lessons on proportional reasoning:

Alice's Adventures in Wonderland *Carroll, 1865/1982*

In this classic, Alice becomes very small and very tall, opening doors to many ratio and proportion investigations.

The Borrowers *Norton, 1953*

A classic tale of little folk living in the walls of a house. Furnishings are created from odds and ends of the full-sized human world.

Gulliver's Travels *Swift and Winterson, 1726/1999*

Yet another classic story. In this case, Gulliver first visits the Lilliputians, where he is 12 times their size, and then goes to Brobdingnag, where he is a tenth the size of the inhabitants.

Jim and the Beanstalk *Briggs, 1970*

What happened to the giant after Jack? Jim comes along. Jim wants to help the poor, pessimistic giant. This heartwarming story is great for multiplicative or proportional reasoning.

Kate and the Beanstalk *Osborne and Potter, 2000*

This version of the traditional "Jack and the Beanstalk" tale includes a giantess. The giantess falls to earth, and Kate finds out that the castle belongs to her family.

"One Inch Tall" in Where the Sidewalk Ends
Silverstein, 1973

Shel Silverstein is a hit with all ages. This poem asks what it would be like if you were one inch tall.

Swamp Angel *Isaacs and Zelinsky, 1994*

A swamp angel named Angelica grows into a giant. Students can explore birth height to current height or compare Angelica's measurements to their own.

RECOMMENDED READINGS

Articles

Ercole, L. K., Frantz, M., & Ashline, G. (2011). Multiple ways to solve proportions. *Mathematics Teaching in the Middle School, 16*(8), 482–490.
This article shares the many ways of reasoning to solve proportions: unit rate, factor of change, building up, ratio tables, and cross-multiplication. Student work is shared throughout.

Langrall, C. W., & Swafford, J. (2000). Three balloons for two dollars. *Mathematics Teaching in the Middle School, 6*(4), 254–261.

The authors describe and give examples of four levels of proportional reasoning using examples from the classroom. A good article on a difficult topic.

Books

Litwiller, B. (Ed.). (2002). *Making sense of fractions, ratios, and proportions: 2002 yearbook.* Reston, VA: NCTM.
Eleven of the 26 short chapters discuss explicitly the issue of multiplicative relationships and/or proportional reasoning. Accompanying the yearbook is a book of Classroom Activities complete with Blackline Masters.

Lobato, J., & Ellis, A. (2010). *Developing essential understanding of ratios, proportions, and proportional reasoning for teaching mathematics: Grades 6–8.* Reston, VA: NCTM.
If you want to really understand the important nuances of ratios and proportions, this is a phenomenal resource. Ten essential understandings are explained, along with excellent activities for students and teaching suggestions.

ONLINE RESOURCES

Figure This! Math Index: Ratio and Proportions (NCTM)
www.figurethis.org/challenges/math_index.htm
Several challenging ratio and proportion problems found in work and everyday life tasks.

Fish Simulation Applet I
http://mathforum.org/escotpow/puzzles/fish/applet.html
A collection of two colors of fish is to be placed into three ponds to create specified ratios within each pond. Students should find out whether there is more than one solution and then make up similar problems for their classmates.

Using Scale City to Teach Proportional Reasoning (Kentucky Educational Television)
www.teachersdomain.org/special/scl
An online mathematics resource for middle grades students featuring fun and engaging videos and interactive simulations to teach the mathematics of scale and scaling with connections to the *Common Core State Standards*. This site helps teachers learn how to use the student version of Scale City (www.ket.org/scalecity).

Rational Numbers and Proportional Reasoning and Fractions, Percents, and Ratios (Annenberg Foundation)
www.learner.org/courses/learningmath/number/session8
www.learner.org/courses/learningmath/number/session9
These two multisession modules examine several topics related to fractions, percents, ratios, and the basics of proportional reasoning.

REFLECTIONS *on Chapter 18*

WRITING TO LEARN

1. Describe the idea of a ratio in your own words. Explain how your idea fits with each of the following statements:

   a. A fraction is a ratio.
   b. Ratios can compare things that are not at all alike.
   c. Ratios can compare two parts of the same whole.
   d. Rates such as prices or speeds are ratios.

2. Describe a situation in which the comparison involved could be interpreted both additively and multiplicatively. Why is it important to include both types of reasoning when introducing ratios?

3. What is covariation? Give an algebraic and geometric example of covariation.

4. Make up a realistic proportional situation that can be solved mentally by a scale-factor approach and another that can be solved mentally by a unit-rate approach.

5. Consider this problem: *If 50 gallons of fuel oil cost $56.95, how much can be purchased for $100?* Draw a sketch to illustrate the proportion, and set up the equation in two different ways. One equation should equate within ratios and the other between ratios.

FOR DISCUSSION AND EXPLORATION

1. Proportional reasoning is a unifying theme in mathematics. For each of the content strands (number, algebra, measurement, geometry, and data analysis and probability), think about content that involves proportional reasoning, and explain the connections among all of these ideas.

2. In Chapter 17, the percentage problems were developed around the theme of which element was missing—the part, the whole, or the fraction that related the two. In this chapter, percent is related to proportions, an equality of two ratios with one of these ratios a comparison to 100. How are these two approaches alike? How are they different?

MyEducationLab™

Go to the MyEducationLab (www.myeducationlab.com) for Math Methods, and familiarize yourself with the content. Much of the site content is organized topically. The topics include all of the following to support your learning in the course:

- Learning outcomes for important mathematics methods course topics aligned with the national standards
- Assignments and Activities, tied to these learning outcomes and standards, that can help you more deeply understand course content
- Building Teaching Skills and Dispositions learning units that allow you to apply and practice your understanding of the core mathematics content and teaching skills

Your instructor has a correlation guide that aligns the exercises on the topical portion of the site with your book's chapters.

On MyEducationLab you will also find book-specific resources including Blackline Masters, Expanded Lesson Activities, and Artifact Analysis Activities.

Field Experience Guide
CONNECTIONS

Because ratios and proportions are important to many topics in the curriculum, they are the topic for many of the field experiences in Part I of the *Field Experience Guide*. For example, any of the proportional reasoning tasks in this chapter (including the assessment in Figure 18.2) can be used for FEG 7.2. FEG 3.5 ("Create a Web of Ideas") can be done by you to prepare for a lesson, or by students to see whether they connect ideas of ratio, fraction, division, and rate. This chapter includes many literature links; see Field Experience 2.6 for designing (and teaching) a lesson using children's literature. In Part II, FEG Expanded Lesson 9.11 provides interesting problem-solving contexts to explore proportional situations. FEG Activity 10.7 helps students connect representations for ratios.

Chapter 19

Developing Measurement Concepts

Measurement is one of the most useful mathematics content strands, as it is an important component in everything from occupational tasks to life skills for the mathematically literate citizen. From gigabytes that measure amounts of information to font size on computers, from miles per gallon to recipes for a meal, people are surrounded daily with measurement concepts that apply to a variety of real-world contexts and applications.

Measurement is not an easy topic for students to understand. Data from international studies consistently indicate that U.S. students are weaker in the area of measurement than any other topic in the mathematics curriculum (Thompson & Preston, 2004).

In this chapter, you will learn how to help students develop a conceptual understanding of the measurement process and the tools of measurement. You will also learn about nonstandard and standard units of measurement, estimation in measurement including the use of benchmarks, and the development of measurement formulas.

 BIG IDEAS

1. Measurement involves a comparison of an attribute of an item or situation with a unit that has the same attribute. Lengths are compared to units of length, areas to units of area, time to units of time, and so on.

2. Estimation of measures and the development of benchmarks for frequently used units of measure help students increase their familiarity with units, preventing errors and aiding in the meaningful use of measurement.

3. Measurement instruments (e.g., rulers) are devices that replace the need for actual measurement units (e.g., a physical foot measure).

4. Area and volume formulas provide a method of measuring these attributes by using only measures of length.

5. Area, perimeter, and volume are related. For example, as the shapes of regions or three-dimensional objects change while maintaining the same areas or volumes, there is an effect on the perimeters and surface areas.

Mathematics CONTENT CONNECTIONS

Students need to engage in meaningful integrations of measurement in all subject areas.

◆ **Number and Place Value** (Chapters 8 and 11): Measuring familiar objects connects ideas of number to the real world, enhancing number sense. The metric system of measurement is built on the base-ten system of numeration.

◆ **Geometry** (Chapter 20): Developing perimeter, area, and volume formulas requires understanding shapes and their relationships. Measures help describe shapes, and angular measures play a significant role in the properties of shapes.

◆ **Data** (Chapter 21): Statistics and graphs help answer questions about and describe our world. Often this description is in terms of measures.

The Meaning and Process of Measuring

Suppose that you asked your students to measure an empty bucket as in Figure 19.1. The first thing they would need to know is *what* about the bucket is to be measured. They might measure the height, depth, diameter (distance across), or circumference (distance around). All of these are length measures. The surface area of the side could be determined. A bucket also has volume (or capacity) and weight. Each aspect that can be measured is an *attribute* of the bucket.

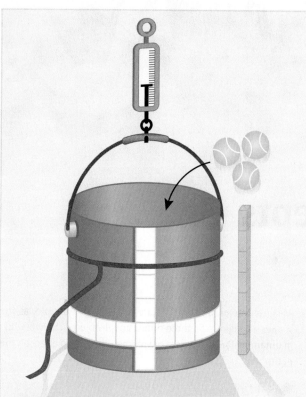

Attribute: Weight
Units: objects that <u>stretch</u> the spring in the scale
How many units will pull the spring as far as the bucket will?

Attribute: Volume/Capacity
Units: cubes, balls, cups of water
How many units will <u>fill</u> the bucket?

Attribute: Length
Units: rods, toothpicks, straws, string
How many units are <u>as tall as</u> the bucket?
How much string is needed to <u>go around</u> the bucket?

Attribute: Area
Units: index cards, squares of paper, tiles
How many cards will <u>cover</u> the surface of the bucket?

FIGURE 19.1 Measuring different attributes of a bucket.

Once students determine the attribute to be measured, they then choose a unit that has the attribute being measured. Length is measured with units that have length, volume with units that have volume, and so on.

Technically, a *measurement* is a number that indicates a comparison between the attribute of the object (or situation, or event) being measured and the same attribute of a given unit of measure. We commonly use small units of measure to determine a numeric relationship (the measurement) between what is measured and the unit. For example, to measure a length, the comparison can be done by lining up copies of the unit directly against the length being measured. For most attributes measured in schools, we can say that *to measure* means that the attribute being measured is

"filled" or "covered" or "matched" with a unit of measure with the same attribute.

In summary, to measure something, one must perform three steps:

1. Decide on the attribute to be measured.
2. Select a unit that has that attribute.
3. Compare the units—by filling, covering, matching, or using some other method—with the attribute of the object being measured. The number of units required to match the object is the measure.

Concepts and Skills

If a typical group of first graders attempts to measure the length of their classroom by laying strips 1 meter long end to end, the strips sometimes overlap and the line can weave in a snakelike fashion. Do they understand the concept of length as an attribute of the classroom? Do they understand that each 1-meter strip has this attribute of length? They most likely understand that they are counting a line of strips stretching from wall to wall. The skill of measuring with a unit must be explicitly linked to the concept of measuring as a process of comparing attributes, using measuring units and using measuring instruments as outlined in Figure 19.2.

Making Comparisons. Sometimes with a measure such as length, a direct comparison can be made where one object can be lined up and matched to another. But often an indirect method using a third object must be used. For example, if students compare the volume of one box to another, they must devise an indirect way to compare. They may fill one box with beans and then pour the beans into the other box. Another example using length would use a string to compare the height of a wastebasket to the distance around. The string is the intermediary, as it is impossible to directly compare these two lengths.

Remember to use precise language when helping students make comparisons. Avoid using "bigger than," and instead use language such as "longer than" or "holds more than."

Using Physical Models of Measuring Units. For most attributes measured in elementary schools, it is possible to have physical models of the units of measure. Time and temperature are exceptions. Many other attributes not commonly measured in school also do not have physical units of measure, such as light intensity, speed, and loudness. Unit models can be found for both nonstandard (sometimes referred to as *informal*) units and standard units. For length, for example, drinking straws (nonstandard) or card stock strips 1 foot long (standard) might be used as units.

The most easily understood use of unit models is actually to use as many copies of the unit as are needed to fill or match the attribute measured (this is called *tiling*). To measure the area of the desktop with an index card as your

Step One—Making Comparisons

Goal: Students will understand the attribute to be measured.

Type of Activity: Make comparisons based on the attribute. For example, longer/shorter, heavier/lighter. Use direct comparisons whenever possible.

Notes: When it is clear that the attribute is understood, there is no further need for comparison activities.

Step Two—Using Models of Measuring Units

Goal: Students will understand how filling, covering, matching, or making other comparisons of an attribute with measuring units produces a number called a *measure*.

Type of Activity: Use physical models of measuring units to fill, cover, match, or make the desired comparison of the attribute with the unit.

Notes: Begin with nonstandard units. Progress to the direct use of standard units when appropriate and certainly before using formulas or measuring tools.

Step Three—Using Measuring Instruments

Goal: Students will use common measuring tools with understanding and flexibility.

Type of Activity: Make measuring instruments and use them in comparison with the actual unit models to see how the measurement tool is performing the same function as the individual units. Be certain to make direct comparisons between the student-made tools and the standard tools. Standard measuring instruments such as rulers, scales, and protractors devices make the filling, covering, or matching process easier.

Notes: Student-made tools are usually best made with nonstandard units. Without a careful comparison with the standard tools, much of the value in making the tools can be lost. Make sure to highlight the switch to standard measurement tools that are used by many people as compared to manipulatives (paper clips and blocks) that have been used to support their development.

FIGURE 19.2 Measurement instruction—a sequence of experiences.

unit, you can literally cover the entire desk with index cards. Somewhat more difficult is to use a single copy of the unit (this is called *iteration*). That means measuring the same desktop with a single index card by repeatedly moving it from position to position and keeping track of which areas the card has covered.

It is useful to measure the same object with different-sized units. Estimate the measure in advance and discuss the estimate afterward. This will help students understand that the unit used is important. The fact that smaller units produce larger numeric measures, and vice versa, is hard for some students to understand. This inverse relationship can only be mentally constructed by estimating, then experimenting, and finally reflecting on the measurements.

Using Measuring Instruments. In the 2003 National Assessment of Educational Progress (NAEP) exam (Blume, Galindo, & Walcott, 2007), only 20 percent of fourth graders could give the correct measure of an object not aligned with the end of a ruler, as in Figure 19.3. Only 56 percent of eighth graders answered the same situation accurately (Kloosterman, Rutledge, & Kenney, 2009a). These results

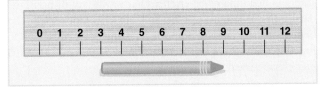

FIGURE 19.3 "How long is this crayon?"

point to the difference between using a measuring device and understanding how it works. Students also experienced difficulty when the increments on a measuring device were not one unit.

If students construct simple measuring instruments using unit models with which they are familiar, it is more likely that they will understand how an instrument measures. A ruler is a good example. If students line up individual physical units along a strip of card stock and mark them off, they can see that it is the *spaces* on rulers and not the hash marks or numbers that are important. It is essential that students discuss how measurement with iterating individual units compares with measurement using an instrument. Without this comparison and discussion, students may not understand that these two methods are essentially the same. Then they are ready to compare their "ruler" with standard rulers (or other instruments like scales) and can compare the use of these devices.

Introducing Nonstandard Units

It is common in primary grades to use nonstandard units to measure length and sometimes area. Unfortunately, measurement activities in the upper grades, where other attributes are measured, often do not begin with nonstandard units. The use of nonstandard units for beginning measurement activities is beneficial at all grade levels for the following reasons:

- Nonstandard units make it easier to focus directly on the attribute being measured. For example, when discussing how to measure the area of an irregular shape, units such as square tiles or circular counters may be suggested. Each unit covers area, and each will give a different result. The discussion can focus on what it means to measure area.

- The use of nonstandard units avoids conflicting objectives in introductory lessons. Is your lesson about what it means to measure area or about understanding square centimeters?

- Nonstandard units provide a good rationale for using standard units. The need for a standard unit has more meaning when your students measure the same objects with their own units and arrive at different and sometimes confusing answers.

The amount of time that should be spent using nonstandard units varies with students' age and level of understanding and with the attributes being measured. Pre-K–grade 1 students need many experiences with a variety of nonstandard units of length, weight, and capacity. Conversely, the benefits of nonstandard units may last only a day or two when fourth graders learn to measure angles. When nonstandard units have served their purpose, move on.

Developing Standard Units

Measurement sense demands that students be familiar with standard measurement units, be able to make estimates in terms of these units, and meaningfully interpret measures depicted with standard units. As you teach the standard units, review necessary words and symbols and include these on your math word wall.

Perhaps the biggest error in measurement instruction is the failure to recognize and separate two types of objectives: (1) understanding the meaning and technique of measuring a particular attribute and (2) learning about the standard units commonly used to measure that attribute.

Instructional Goals

Teaching standard units of measure can be organized around three broad goals:

1. *Familiarity with the unit.* Students should have a basic idea of the size of commonly used units and what they measure. Knowing approximately how much 1 liter of water is or being able to estimate a shelf as 5 feet long is as important as measuring either of these accurately.

2. *Ability to select an appropriate unit.* Students should know both what is a reasonable unit of measure in a given situation and the precision that is required. (Would you measure your lawn to purchase grass seed with the same precision as you would use in measuring a window to buy a pane of glass?) Students need practice in selecting appropriate standard units and judging the level of precision.

3. *Knowledge of relationships between units.* Students should know the relationships that are commonly used, such as those between inches, feet, and yards or milliliters and liters.

Developing Unit Familiarity. Two types of activities can develop familiarity with standard units: (1) comparisons that focus on a single unit and (2) activities that develop personal referents or benchmarks for single units or easy multiples of units.

Activity 19.1

Familiar References

Use the book *Measuring Penny* (Leedy, 2000) to get students interested in the variety of ways familiar items can be measured. In this book, the author bridges between nonstandard (e.g., dog biscuits, swabs, etc.) and stan-

ENGLISH LANGUAGE LEARNERS

dard units (inches, centimeters, etc.) to measure Penny the pet dog. Have students use the idea of measuring Penny to find something at home (or in class) to measure in as many ways as they can think of using standard units. The measures can be rounded to whole numbers or to a fractional unit to be more precise. Discuss in class the familiar items chosen and their measures so that different ideas and benchmarks are shared. Many of the units in the book are used in the United States, but not in other countries, but this book can be used to connect to the ways in which students from other countries do measure length and volume.

Of special interest for length are benchmarks found on our bodies. These become quite familiar over time and can be used in many situations as approximate rulers.

Activity 19.2

Personal Benchmarks

Measure your body. About how long are your foot, your stride, your hand span (stretched and with fingers together), the width of your finger, your arm span (finger to finger and finger to nose), and the distance around your wrist and around your waist? What is the height to your waist, shoulder, and head? Some may prove to be useful benchmarks for standard units, and some may be excellent models for single units. (The average child's fingernail width is about 1 cm, and most people can find a 10-cm length somewhere on their hands.)

Choosing Appropriate Units. Should the room be measured in feet or inches? Should the concrete blocks be weighed in grams or kilograms? The answers to questions such as these involve more than simply knowing how big units are, although that is certainly required. Another consideration involves the need for precision. If you were measuring your wall in order to cut a piece of molding to fit, you would need to measure it very precisely. The smallest unit would be an inch or a centimeter, and you would also use small fractional parts. But if you were determining how many 8-foot molding strips to buy, the nearest foot would probably be sufficient.

STUDENTS with SPECIAL NEEDS

Activity 19.3

Guess the Unit

Find examples of measurements of all types in newspapers, on signs, or in other everyday situations. Present the context and measures, but without units. The task is to predict what units of measure were used. Have students discuss their choices. For students with disabilities, you may want to provide the possible units so they can sort the real-world measures into groups.

Important Standard Units and Relationships

Your state or local curriculum is the best guide to help you decide which units your students should learn. The NCTM's position statement on the metric system (2011) states: "Because the metric system is an effective, efficient, base-ten measurement system used throughout the world, students need to develop an understanding of its units, and their relationship as well as fluency in its application to real world situations." They go on to say that because we are still using customary measures in day-to-day life, students must work in that system as well. Countries worldwide have passed laws stating that international commerce must use metric units, so if U.S. students are going to be prepared for the global workplace, they must be knowledgeable and comfortable with metric units. Results of the 2004 NAEP reveal that only 40 percent of fourth graders were able to identify how many kilograms a bicycle weighed given the choices of 1.5, 15, 150, and 1500 kg. Among eighth graders, only 37 percent knew how many milliliters were in a liter (Perie, Moran, & Lutkus, 2005). Interestingly, U.S. students do better on metric units than customary units (Preston & Thompson, 2004).

The relationships between units within either the metric or customary system are conventions. As such, students must simply be told what the relationships are, and instructional experiences must be devised to reinforce them. It can be argued that knowing about how much liquid makes a liter, or being able to pace off 3 meters—unit familiarity—is more important than knowing how many cubic centimeters are in a liter. Another approach to unit familiarity is to begin with common items and use their measures as references or benchmarks. A doorway is a bit more than 2 meters high, and a doorknob is about 1 meter from the floor. A bag of flour is a good reference for 5 pounds. A paper clip weighs about a gram and is about 1 centimeter wide. A gallon of milk weighs a little less than 4 kilograms. However, in the intermediate grades, knowing basic relationships becomes more important. Your curriculum should be your guide.

The customary system has few patterns or generalizable rules to guide students in converting units. In contrast, the metric system was systematically created around powers of ten. Understanding of the role of the decimal point as indicating the units position is a powerful concept for making metric conversions (see Figure 17.4). As students grasp the structure of decimal notation, develop the metric system with all seven places: three prefixes for smaller units (*deci-*, *centi-*, *milli-*) and three for larger units (*deka-*, *hecto-*, *kilo-*). Avoid mechanical rules such as "To change centimeters to meters, move the decimal point two places to the left." Instead create conceptual, meaningful methods for conversions rather than rules that are often misused and forgotten.

The Role of Estimation and Approximation

Measurement estimation is the process of using mental and visual information to measure or make comparisons without using measuring instruments. It is a practical skill used almost every day. Do I have enough sugar to make cookies? Can you throw the ball 15 meters? Is this suitcase over the weight limit? Here are several reasons for including estimation in measurement activities:

- Estimation helps students focus on the attribute being measured and the measuring process. Think how you would estimate the area of the cover of this book using playing cards as the unit. To do so, you have to think about what area is and how the units might be placed on the book cover.
- Estimation provides an intrinsic motivation for measurement activities. It is interesting to see how close you can come in your estimate.
- When standard units are used, estimation helps develop familiarity with the unit. If you estimate the height of the door in meters before measuring, you must think about the size of a meter.
- The use of a benchmark to make an estimate promotes multiplicative reasoning. The width of the building is about one-fourth of the length of a football field—perhaps 25 yards.

In all measuring activities, emphasize the use of approximate language. The desk is *about* 15 orange rods long. The chair is *a little less than* 4 straws high. Approximate language is very useful for students because many measurements do not result in whole numbers. As they develop, students will begin to search for smaller units or use fractional units to try to be more precise. That is an opportunity to develop the idea that all measurements include some error. Acknowledge that each smaller unit or subdivision produces a greater degree of *precision*. For example, a length measure can never be more than one-half unit in error. And yet, since there is mathematically no "smallest unit," there is always some error. The Standards for Mathematical Practices in the *Common Core State Standards* (CCSSO, 2010) include, "Attend to precision." Within that standard, they expect students to be "careful about specifying units of measure" and to "express numerical answers with a degree of precision appropriate for the problem context" (p. 7).

Strategies for Estimating Measurements

Always begin a measurement activity with students making an estimate. This is true with both nonstandard and standard units. Just as for computational estimation, specific strategies exist for estimating measures. Here are four strategies that can be taught:

1. *Develop and use benchmarks or referents for important units.* Research shows that students who have acquired mental benchmarks or reference points for measurements *and* have practiced using them in class activities are much better estimators than students who have not learned to use benchmarks (Joram, 2003). Students must pay attention to the size of the unit to estimate well (Towers & Hunter, 2010). Referents should be things that are easily envisioned by the student. One example is the height of a child (see Figure 19.4). Students should have a good referent for single units and also useful multiples of standard units.

2. *Use "chunking" when appropriate.* Figure 19.4 shows an example. It may be easier to estimate the shorter chunks along the wall than to estimate the whole length. The weight of a stack of books is easier if some estimate is given for an "average" book.

3. *Use subdivisions.* This is a similar strategy to chunking, with the chunks imposed on the object by the estimator. For example, if the wall length to be estimated has no useful chunks, it can be mentally divided in half and then in fourths or even eighths by repeated halving until a more manageable length is arrived at. Length, volume, and area measurements all lend themselves to this technique.

4. *Iterate a unit mentally or physically.* For length, area, and volume, it is sometimes easy to mark off single units visually. You might use your hands or make marks or folds to keep track as you go. If you know, for example, that your stride is about $\frac{3}{4}$ meter, you can walk off a length and then multiply to get an estimate. Hand and finger widths are useful for shorter measures.

Tips for Teaching Estimation

Each strategy just listed should be taught directly and discussed with students. Suggested benchmarks for useful measures can be developed and recorded on a class chart. Include items found at home. But the best approach to improving estimation skills is to have students do a lot of estimating. Keep the following tips in mind:

1. Help students learn strategies by having them first try a specified approach. Later activities should permit students to choose whatever techniques they wish.

2. Discuss how different students made their estimates. This will confirm that there is no single right way to estimate while reminding students of other useful approaches.

3. Accept a range of estimates. Think in relative terms about what is a good estimate. Within 10 percent for length is quite good. Even 30 percent off may be reasonable for weights or volumes. Do not promote a "winning" estimate.

4. Encourage students to give a range of estimates that they believe includes the actual measure. This not only is a practical approach in real life but also helps focus on the approximate nature of estimation.

5. Make measurement estimation an ongoing activity. Post a daily measurement to be estimated. Students can record their estimates and discuss them in a five-minute period. Older students can even determine the daily measurements to estimate, with a student or team of students assigned this task each week.

6. Be precise with your language, and do not use the word *measure* interchangeably with the word *estimate* (Towers & Hunter, 2010). Randomly substituting one word for the other will cause uncertainty and possibly confusion in students.

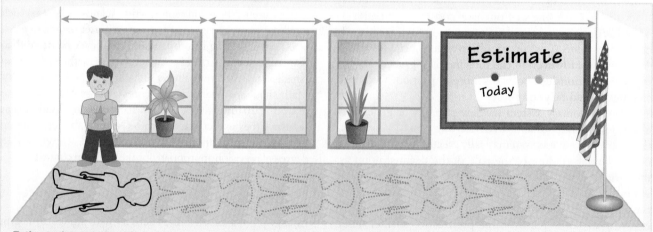

Estimate the room length.

Use: windows, bulletin board, and spaces between as "chunks."
Use: mental benchmark—"My height is about 5 feet long. I could get 5 kids lying down in here plus maybe 3 more feet. Say, 28 feet."

FIGURE 19.4 Estimating measures using benchmarks and chunking.

Measurement Estimation Activities

Estimation activities need not be elaborate. Any measurement activity can have an "estimate first" component. For more emphasis on the process of estimation itself, simply think of measures that can be estimated, and have students estimate. Here are two suggestions.

Activity **19.4**

Estimation Quickie

Select a single object such as a box, a pumpkin, a jar, or even the principal. Each day, select a different attribute or dimension to estimate. For a pumpkin, for example, students can estimate its height, circumference, weight, volume, and surface area. If you have ELLs, then be sure to include metric measures, or be sure to help students connect the centimeter to the inch (about 2.4 centimeters per inch, so about two and a half times more centimeters than inches).

Activity **19.5**

Estimation Scavenger Hunt

Conduct estimation scavenger hunts. Give teams a list of either nonstandard or standard measurements, and have them find things that are close to having those measurements. Do not use measuring instruments. A list might include the following items:

A length of 3.5 m

Something that is as long as your math book

Something that weighs more than 1 kg but less than 2 kg

A container that holds about 200 ml

An angle of 45 degrees or 135 degrees

Let students suggest how to judge results in terms of accuracy.

FORMATIVE
Assessment
Notes
Estimation tasks are a good way to assess students' understanding of both measurement and units. Use a **checklist** while students estimate measures of real objects and distances inside and outside the classroom. Prompt students to explain how they arrived at their estimates to get a more complete picture of their measurement knowledge. Asking only for a numeric estimate can mask a lack of understanding and will not give you the information you need to provide appropriate remediation. ■

Length

Length is usually the first attribute students learn to measure. Length measurement is not immediately understood by young students. Likewise, older students may be challenged by the concept of length as they investigate problems that include perimeter and circumference.

Comparison Activities

As noted in the process of measuring, students in pre-K–kindergarten should begin with direct comparisons of two or more lengths and then move to indirect comparisons (CCSSO, 2010; NCTM, 2006). Students can go to learning stations, for example, and explore which objects in a group are longer, shorter, or about the same as a specified "target" object. Change the target object and students will find the shorter item is now longer than the target. A similar task can involve putting a set of objects in order from shortest to longest.

Activity **19.6**

Length (or Unit) Hunt

Give pairs of students a strip of card stock, a stick, a length of rope, or some other object with an obvious length dimension. The task is to find five things in the room that are shorter than, longer than, or about the same length as their target unit. They can record what they find in pictures or words. Allow students with disabilities to have a copy of the "target" to carry with them as they make actual comparisons.

By making the target length a standard unit (e.g., a meter stick or a 1-meter length of rope), the activity can be repeated to provide familiarity with important standard units.

Also compare lengths that are not in straight lines. One way to do this is by using indirect comparisons, which means using another object to help make the measure. For example, students can wrap string around objects in a search for things that are, for example, as long around as the distance from the floor to their belly button or as long as the distance around their head or waist.

Activity **19.7**

Crooked Paths

Make some crooked or curvy paths on the floor (or outside) with masking tape or chalk. The task is to determine which path is longest, next longest, and so on. The students should suggest ways to measure the crooked paths so that they can be compared easily. If you wish to offer a hint, provide pairs of students with a long piece of string (at first make it longer than the path). Have students explain how they solved the problem. For students with disabilities, you may need to tape the end of the string to the beginning of the path and help them mark the final measurement on the string with a marker. Use another string for the other path in the same way. Then compare the string lengths.

Students may have trouble estimating lengths of crooked paths. You might want to show an example of two paths on the floor (one crooked and one straight) and have students walk each to see which takes longer to walk.

Using Models of Length Units

There are four important principles of iterating units of length, whether they are nonstandard or standard (Dietiker, Gonulates, Figueras, & Smith, 2010, p. 2):

- All units must have equal length—if not, you cannot accumulate units by counting.
- All units must be placed on the path being measured—otherwise, a different quantity is being measured.
- The units must be without gaps—if not, part of the quantity is not being measured.
- The units must not overlap—otherwise, part of the quantity is measured more than once.

Students can begin to measure length using a variety of nonstandard units, including these:

- *Giant footprints:* Cut out about 20 copies of a large footprint about $1\frac{1}{2}$ to 2 feet long on poster board.
- *Measuring ropes:* Cut rope into lengths of 1 m. These can measure the perimeter and the circumference of objects such as the teacher's desk, a tree trunk, or the class pumpkin.
- *Drinking straws:* Straws provide large quantities of a useful unit as they are easily cut into smaller units or linked together with a long string. The string of straws is an excellent bridge to a ruler or measuring tape.
- *Short units:* Connecting cubes and paper clips are useful nonstandard units for measuring shorter lengths. Cuisenaire rods are also useful, as they are easy to place end to end and are also metric (centimeters) and thus make an excellent bridge to a ruler.

The following activity encourages students to develop their own approach to measuring lengths.

Activity 19.8

How Long Is the Teacher?

Explain that you have received an important request from the principal. She needs to know exactly how tall each teacher in

the building is. The students are to decide how to measure the teachers and write a note to the principal explaining how tall their teacher is and detailing the process that they used. If you wish to give a hint, have students make marks at your feet and head and draw a straight line between these marks.

Explain that the principal says they can use any *one* of several nonstandard units to measure with (provide choices). For each choice of unit, supply enough units to more than cover your length. Put students in pairs and allow them to select one unit with which to measure. Ask students to make an estimate. Then have them use their unit to measure.

After students complete their measuring, follow up with questions like "How did you get your measurement?" "Did students who measured with the same unit get the same answers? Why not?" "How could the principal make a line that was as long as the teacher?" Focus on the value of carefully lining units up end to end. Discuss what happens if you overlap units, have a gap in the units, or don't follow in a straight line.

The following activity adds an estimation component.

Activity 19.9

STUDENTS with SPECIAL NEEDS

Estimate and Measure

Make lists of items in the room to measure, including which units to use (see Figure 19.5). For younger students, run a piece of masking tape along the dimension of objects to be measured. Include curves or other distances that are not straight lines. Have students estimate before they measure. Remember that young students have probably had limited experiences with estimating distances, and student with disabilities may need support in making estimates. If needed, have students make a row or chain of exactly 10 of the units to help them with their estimates. They first lay 10 units against the object and then make their estimate.

It is a challenge to explain to students that larger units will produce a smaller measure and vice versa. Instead, engage students in activities like the following, where this issue is emphasized.

Activity 19.10

Changing Units

Have students measure a length with a specified unit. Then provide them with a different unit that is either twice as long or half as long as the original unit. Their task is to predict the measure of the same length using the new unit. Students should write down their estimations and discuss how they made their estimations. Then have them make the actual

Name _____

Around your outline

Unit: ≡≡≡≡≡≡≡
straw

Estimate _____ straws

Measured _____ straws

The teacher's desk

Teacher's desk →

Unit: ▱▱▱▱▱
orange rod

Estimate _____ rods

Measured _____ rods

Around math book

Math Book

Unit: ⬯
paper clip

Estimate _____ clips

Measured _____ clips

FIGURE 19.5 Example of a recording sheet for measuring with nonstandard length units.

measurement. Cuisenaire rods are excellent for this activity. Some students can be challenged with units that are more difficult multiples of the original unit.

In "Changing Units," you are looking first for the basic idea that when the unit is longer, the measure is smaller and vice versa. This is a good activity to do just to introduce unit conversion with standard units (this is in the *Common Core State Standards* in grades 4 and 5), and is an excellent proportional reasoning task for middle school students.

Notice that the term *units* is used throughout this section. A physical object (like a cut-out "inch-worm") can be used to transition from nonstandard units to standard units. The Cuisenaire rod units are also standard, as the white cube is actually 1 centimeter in length.

 FORMATIVE Assessment Notes Observation and discussion during activities such as those just described provide evidence of how well your students understand length measurement. Additional tasks that can be used as assessments in a **diagnostic interview** format are:

- Ask students to draw a line or mark off a distance of a prescribed number of units. Observe whether students

know to align the units in a straight line without overlaps or gaps.
- Have students measure two different objects. Then ask how much longer the longer object is. Observe whether students can use the measurements to answer or whether they need to make a third measurement to find the difference. ■

Fractional Parts of Units. Students are sometimes perplexed when measurements do not result in a whole number. As early as first grade, students are exploring halves; this is an excellent context for students to apply their developing concepts of fractions. Students can relate the idea of unit to the whole, and partition to see half units. The use of fractional units helps students understand subdivision marks on a ruler.

Making and Using Rulers

The jump from measuring with actual units to using standard rulers is challenging. One method to help students understand rulers is to have them make their own rulers.

Activity **19.11**

Make Your Own Ruler

Use two colors of precut narrow strips of construction paper, 5 cm long and about 2 cm wide. Discuss how the strips could be used to measure by laying them end to end. Provide long strips of card stock about 3 cm wide. Have students make their own ruler by gluing the units onto the card stock. Have students use their new rulers to measure items on a list that you provide. Discuss the results. It is possible that there will be discrepancies due to rulers that were not made properly or to a failure to understand how a ruler works.

Also consider using larger nonstandard units such as tracings of students' footprints glued onto strips of cash register tape. Older students can use standard units (centimeter, inch, foot) to make marks on the strips and color in the spaces with alternating colors.

Students should use their rulers to measure lengths that are longer than their rulers and discuss how that can be done. Another challenge is to find more than one way to measure a length with a ruler. Do you have to begin at the end? What if you begin at another unit in the center? Students can eventually put numbers on their handmade rulers, as shown in Figure 19.6. For students who struggle, numbers can be written in the center of each unit to make it clear that the numbers are a way of precounting the units. When numbers are written in the standard way, at the ends of the units, the ruler becomes a number line.

Be explicit in making this connection from the handmade rulers to standard rulers. Give students a standard ruler,

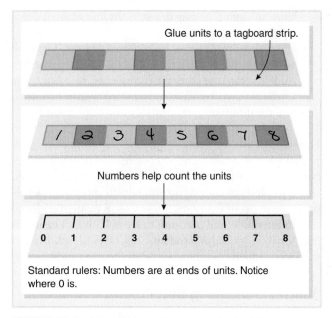

Glue units to a tagboard strip.

Numbers help count the units

Standard rulers: Numbers are at ends of units. Notice where 0 is.

FIGURE 19.6 Give meaning to numbers on rulers.

and discuss how it is like and how it differs from the ones they have made. What are the units? Could you make a ruler with units the same as this? What do the numbers mean? What are the other marks for? Where do the units begin?

FORMATIVE Assessment Notes

Research indicates that when students see standard rulers with the numbers on the hash marks, they often believe that the numbers are counting the marks rather than indicating the units or spaces between the marks. This is an incorrect understanding of rulers that can lead to wrong answers. As a **performance assessment**, provide students a ruler with hash marks but no numbers. Have students use the ruler to measure an item that is shorter than the ruler. Use a **checklist** to record whether students count spaces between the hash marks.

Another good **performance assessment** of ruler understanding is to have students measure with a "broken" ruler, one with the first two units broken off. Use your **checklist** to note whether students say that it is impossible to measure with such a ruler because there is no starting point. Also note those who match and count the units meaningfully. The dynamic GeoGebra worksheet at www.geogebra.org/en/upload/files/english/duane_habecker/broken_ruler.html is a good tool for this.

Observing how students use a ruler to measure an object that is longer than the ruler is also informative. Students who simply read the last mark on the ruler may struggle because they do not understand how a ruler is a representation of a continuous row of units. ■

The same activity can be done with other unit lengths. Families can be enlisted to help students find familiar

distances that are about 1 mile or about 1 kilometer. Suggest in a take-home letter that families check the distances around the neighborhood, to the school or shopping center, or along other frequently traveled paths. If possible, send home (or use in class) a 1-meter or 1-yard trundle wheel to measure distances.

Activity **19.12**

About One Unit

Give students a model of a standard unit, and have them search for objects that measure about the same as that one unit. For example, to develop familiarity with the meter, give students a piece of rope 1 meter long. Have them make lists of familiar things in their life that are about 1 meter. Keep separate lists for things that are a little less (or a little more) or twice as long (or half as long). Be sure to include curved or circular lengths. Later, students can try to predict whether a particular object is more than, less than, or close to 1 meter.

There are other measures of length, such as perimeter and circumference, that will be discussed in subsequent sections.

Area

Area is the two-dimensional space inside a region. As with other attributes, students must first understand the attribute of area before measuring. Data from the 2003 NAEP suggest that fourth- and eighth-grade students have an incomplete understanding of area (Blume et al., 2007). Estimating area and measuring area are critical areas in third grade (CCSSO, 2010).

Comparison Activities

One purpose of comparison activities with areas is to help students distinguish between size (or area) and shape, length, and other dimensions. A long, skinny rectangle may have less area than a triangle with shorter sides. This is an especially difficult concept for students to understand. Many 8- or 9-year-olds do not understand that rearranging areas into different shapes does not affect the amount of area.

Direct comparison of two areas is frequently impossible except when the shapes involved have some common dimension or property. For example, two rectangles with the same width can be compared directly, as can any two circles. Comparison of these special shapes, however, fails to deal with the attribute of area. Instead, activities in which one area is rearranged (conservation of area) are suggested. Cutting a shape into two parts and reassembling it into a different shape can show that the before and after shapes have the same area, even though they are different shapes. This idea is not at all obvious to students in the K–grade 2 range.

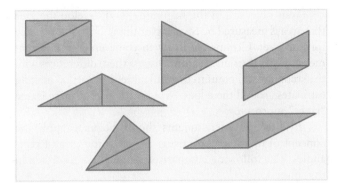

FIGURE 19.7 Different shapes, same area.

Two-Piece Shapes

Cut a large number of rectangles of the same area, about 3 inches by 5 inches. Each pair of students will need six rectangles. Have students fold and cut the rectangles on the diagonal, making two identical triangles. Next, have them rearrange the triangles into different shapes, including back into the original rectangle. The rule is that only sides of the same length can be matched up and they must be matched exactly. Have students work in pairs to find all the shapes that can be made this way, gluing the triangles on paper as a record (see Figure 19.7). Discuss the area and shape of each different response. Does one shape have a greater area than the rest? How do you know? Did one take more paper to make? Help students conclude that although each figure is a different shape, all the figures have the same *area*.

Tangrams, an ancient puzzle, can be used for the same purpose. The standard set of seven tangram pieces is cut from a square, as shown in Figure 19.8, in Blackline Master 51, or in the online version at http://nlvm.usu.edu/en/nav/frames_asid_268_g_1_t_3.html?open=activities. The two small triangles can be used to make the parallelogram, the square, and the medium triangle. This permits a similar discussion about the pieces having the same size (area) but different shapes.

Tangram Areas

Draw the outline of several shapes made with tangram pieces, as in Figure 19.9, duplicate them, and give them to groups of students. Ask groups to estimate which one they think is the largest (or smallest). Let students use tangrams to decide which shapes are the same size, which are larger, and which are smaller. Let students explain how they came to their conclusions. Use the animal shapes from *Grandfather Tang's Story* (Tompert, 1997) for additional investigations.

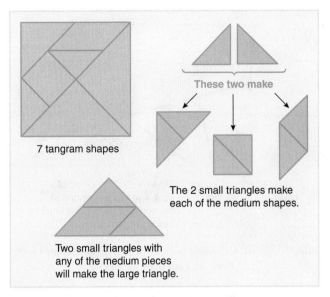

FIGURE 19.8 Tangrams provide an opportunity to investigate area concepts (see Blackline Master 51).

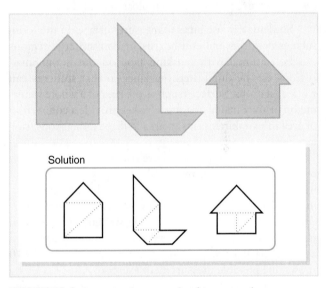
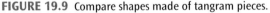

FIGURE 19.9 Compare shapes made of tangram pieces.

Using Models of Area Units

Although squares are the most common area units, any tile that conveniently fills up a plane region can be used. Non-standard units, such as same-sized circles or lima beans, can be used initially to explore the concept of area. Here are some suggestions for nonstandard area units:

- *Round counters, chips, or pennies.* It is not necessary at a beginning stage that the area units fit with no gaps.
- *Cardboard squares.* Squares that are about 20 cm per side work well for large areas. Smaller units should be about 5 to 10 cm per side.
- *Sheets of newspaper.* These make excellent units for very large areas.

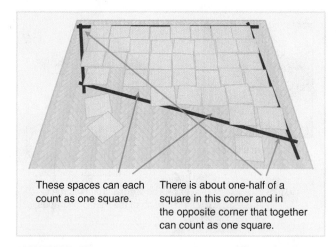

These spaces can each count as one square.

There is about one-half of a square in this corner and in the opposite corner that together can count as one square.

FIGURE 19.10 Measuring the area of a large shape drawn with tape on the floor. Units are card stock squares of the same size.

In addition, standard units can be used:

- Color tiles (1 inch sides)
- Cuisenaire rod or base-ten blocks (1 cm sides)

Students can use units to measure surfaces in the room such as desktops, bulletin boards, or books. Large regions can be outlined with masking tape on the floor. Small regions can be duplicated on paper so that students can work at stations. Surfaces such as the rind of a whole watermelon or the outside of a wastebasket provide a connection of area in two dimensions to area in three dimensions (surface area).

In area measurements, there may be lots of units that only partially fit. You may wish to begin with shapes in which the units fit by building a shape with units and drawing the outline. According to the *Common Core State Standards* (CCSSO, 2010), in third grade, students should begin to wrestle with partial units and mentally put together two or more partial units to count as one unit. Figure 19.10 shows one possible measurement exercise.

The following activity is a good starting point to see what ideas your students have about units of area.

Activity 19.15

Fill and Compare

Draw two rectangles and a blob shape on a sheet of paper. Make it so that the three areas are not the same but with no area that is clearly largest or smallest. The students' first task is to estimate which is the smallest and the largest area of the three shapes. After recording their estimate, they are to figure it out using square units. This can be done by tracing or gluing the same two-dimensional unit on the shapes, or by cutting the shapes out and placing them over grid paper. Students should explain their strategy and justification of the largest and smallest shape in writing.

Your objective in the beginning is to develop the idea that area is measured by covering or tiling. Do not introduce formulas yet. Groups are likely to come up with different measures for the same region. Discuss these differences with the students, and point to the difficulties involved in making estimates around the edges. Avoid the idea that there is one "right" approach.

By fourth grade, students should begin to apply the concept of multiplication using arrays to the area of rectangles. The following comparison activity is a good step in that direction.

Activity 19.16

STUDENTS with SPECIAL NEEDS

Rectangle Comparison—Square Units

Students are given a pair of rectangles that are the same or very close in area. They are also given a model of a single square unit and a ruler that measures the appropriate unit. The students are not permitted to cut out the rectangles, but they may draw on them if they wish. The task is to use their rulers to determine, in any way that they can, which rectangle is larger or whether they are the same. They should use words, pictures, and numbers to explain their conclusions. Some suggested pairs are as follows:

4×10 and 5×8

5×10 and 7×7

4×6 and 5×5

Some students with disabilities may need to have modified worksheets of the figures on grid paper that matches the square units to be used.

The goal of this activity is not to develop an area formula but to apply students' developing concepts of multiplication to the area of rectangles. Not all students will use a multiplicative approach. In order to count a single row of squares along one edge and then multiply by the length of the other edge, the first row must be thought of as a single unit that is then replicated to fill in the rectangle (Outhred & Mitchelmore, 2004). Many students will attempt to draw in all the squares. However, some may use their rulers to determine the number of squares that will fit along each side and, from that, use multiplication to determine the total area (see Figure 19.11). By having students share strategies, more students can be exposed to the use of multiplication in this context.

Grids. Grids of various types can be thought of as "area rulers." A grid of squares does for area what a ruler does for length. It lays out the units for you. Square grids on transparencies can be made from Blackline Masters 34–36. Have students place the clear grid over a region to be measured

INVESTIGATIONS *in Number, Data, and Space*

Grade 3, *Perimeter, Angles, and Area*

Context

This perimeter activity continues the development of ideas about linear measurement. At this point in the curriculum, it is assumed that students understand the need for standard units and can use tools that measure length in both the metric and customary systems. Students should recognize that perimeter is the measure around the outside edges of a two-dimensional shape.

Task

In this investigation, students select real-world objects and measure the perimeter. (A hint given to students: the word *rim* is in *perimeter*.) Key in this process will be the choices the students make, such as whether the object they choose has a perimeter that is regular (like the top of a desk) or more challenging (like the top of a wastebasket). They also need to choose the tool that will be best for measuring, given yardsticks, metersticks, cash register tape, or string. First, students are asked to suggest an object all will measure. Then one student traces with a finger the perimeter that will be measured. All students include this object so students will be able to compare the results of at least one common item. That will provide a basis for discussing any measurement errors. Prior to measuring, ask students to include an estimate of the perimeter on their chart. During the "after" period of the lesson, students should discuss how they measured objects that were larger than the tool they were using and how they knew when to use a flexible measuring tool such as the string or paper tape.

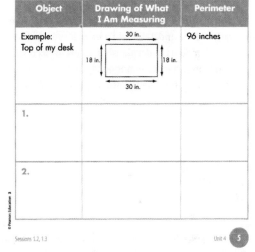

and count the units inside. An alternative method is to trace around a region on a paper grid.

The Relationship Between Area and Perimeter

Area and perimeter (the distance around a region) are a continual source of confusion for students. Although perimeter is a standard (CCSSO, 2010) and focal point (NCTM, 2006) at grade 3, of the eighth-grade students given an illustration on the NAEP exam of a rectangle with side lengths, only 71 percent accurately identified the perimeter. Perhaps it is because both area and perimeter involve

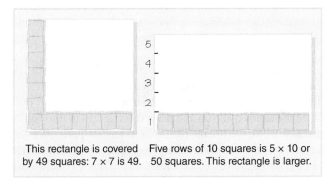

This rectangle is covered by 49 squares: 7 × 7 is 49.   Five rows of 10 squares is 5 × 10 or 50 squares. This rectangle is larger.

FIGURE 19.11 Some students use multiplication to tell the total number of square units.

regions to be measured or because students are taught formulas for both concepts at about the same time that they tend to get formulas confused. Teaching these two concepts during a close time frame is particularly challenging for students with disabilities (Parmar, Garrison, Clements, & Sarama, 2011). Whatever the reason, anticipate that even fifth- and sixth-grade students will confuse these two ideas or have misconceptions. The next activities are designed to help students develop a deeper understanding of the relationship between perimeter and area.

Activity 19.17

Fixed Perimeters

Give students a loop of nonstretching string that is 24 centimeters in circumference and 1-cm grid paper, or just use the grid paper alone. The task is to decide what different-sized rectangles can be made with a perimeter of 24 cm. Each different rectangle can be recorded on the grid paper with the area noted inside the figure (area = 20 cm^2).

Activity 19.18

Fixed Areas

Provide students with 1-cm grid paper. The task is to see how many rectangles can be made with an area of 36—that is, to make filled-in rectangles, not just borders. Each new rectangle should be recorded by sketching the outline and the dimensions on grid paper. For each rectangle, students should determine and record the perimeter inside the figure. (See the "Fixed Areas" Expanded Lesson at the end of Chapter 4.)

 PAUSE and REFLECT

Let's think about the two preceding activities. For "Fixed Areas," will all of the perimeters be the same? If not, what can you say about the shapes with longer or shorter perimeters? For "Fixed Perimeters," will the areas remain the same? Why or why not? ●

When students complete Activities 19.17 and 19.18, have them cut out all the figures. Label either two charts or locations on the board with "Perimeter" and "Area," and have the teams come up and place their figures (left to right) from smallest perimeter (or area) to largest perimeter (or area) on the appropriate chart. Ask students to state what they observe, make conjectures, and see if any conclusions can be drawn. Students may be surprised to find out that rectangles having the same areas do not necessarily have the

same perimeters and vice versa. And, of course, this fact is not restricted to rectangles.

Students will notice an interesting relationship. When the area is fixed, the shape with the smallest perimeter is "square-like," as is the rectangle with the largest area. If you allowed for any shapes whatsoever, the shape with the smallest perimeter for a fixed area is a circle. Also, they will notice that the "fatter" a shape, the smaller its perimeter; the skinnier a shape, the larger its perimeter. (This is true in three dimensions—replace perimeter with surface area and area with volume.)

Developing Formulas for Area

Do not make the mistake of bypassing formula development with your students, even if your annual testing programs allow students access to formulas during the test. When students develop formulas, they gain conceptual understanding of the ideas and relationships involved, and they engage in "doing mathematics." Also, there is less likelihood that students will confuse area and perimeter or that they will select the incorrect formula on the test. Students form general relationships when they see how all area formulas are related to one idea: length of the base times the height. And students who understand where formulas come from do not see them as mysterious; they tend to remember the formulas. This reinforces the idea that mathematics makes sense.

Student Misconceptions

The results of NAEP testing indicate clearly that students do not have a very good understanding of formulas. For example, in the 2007 NAEP, only 39 percent of fourth-grade students were able to give the area of a carpet 15 feet long and 12 feet wide. A common error is to confuse the formulas for area and perimeter. Such results are largely due to an overemphasis on formulas with little or no conceptual background. The tasks in Figure 19.12 cannot be solved

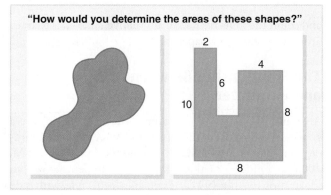

"How would you determine the areas of these shapes?"

FIGURE 19.12 Understanding the attribute of area.

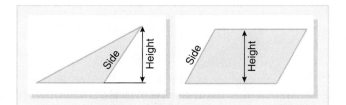

FIGURE 19.13 Heights of two-dimensional figures are not always measured along an edge.

with simple formulas; they require an understanding of concepts and how formulas work. "Length times width" is not a definition of area.

Another common error when students use formulas comes from failure to conceptualize the meaning of height and base in two-dimensional geometric figures. The shapes in Figure 19.13 each have a slanted side and a height given. Students tend to confuse these two. Any side of a figure can be called a *base*. For each base that a figure has, there is a corresponding height. If the figure were to slide into a room on a selected base, the *height* would be the height of the shortest door it could pass through without tipping—that is, the perpendicular distance to the base. The confusion may be because students have a lot of early experiences with the length-times-width formula for rectangles, in which the height is exactly the same as the length of a side. Before formulas involving heights are discussed, students should identify where a height could be measured for any base on a figure.

Areas of Rectangles, Parallelograms, Triangles, and Trapezoids

The formula for the area of a rectangle is one of the first that is developed and is usually given as $A = L \times W$, which is "area equals length times width." Thinking ahead to other area formulas, an equivalent but more unifying idea might be $A = b \times h$, or "area equals *base* times *height*." The base-times-height formulation can be generalized to all parallelograms (not just rectangles) and is useful in developing the area formulas for triangles and trapezoids. Furthermore, the same approach can be extended to three dimensions—volumes of cylinders are given in terms of the *area of the base* times the height. Therefore, base times height connects a large family of formulas that otherwise must be mastered independently.

Rectangles. Research suggests that it is a significant leap for students to move from counting squares inside of a rectangle to a conceptual development of a formula. Battista (2003) found that students often try to fill in empty rectangles with drawings of squares and then count the result one square at a time.

An important concept to review is the meaning of multiplication as seen in arrays. Show students the structure of

rows and columns of squares and discuss why multiplication tells the total amount. We count either a single row or column and then find out how many columns or rows there are in all. This is the same concept that they will apply to the area of a rectangle. When we multiply a length times a width, we are not multiplying "squares times squares." Rather, the *length* of one side indicates how many squares will fit on that side. If this set of squares is taken as a unit, then the *length* of the other side (not a number of squares) will determine how many of these *rows of squares* can fit in the rectangle. Then the amount of square units covering the rectangle is the product of the length of a row and the number of rows (column × row = area).

A good activity to begin your exploration of area formulas is to revisit Activity 19.16, "Rectangle Comparison—Square Units." Students who draw in all of the squares and count them have not thought about a row of squares as a single row that can be replicated.

When your students have formulated an approach to area based on the idea of a row of squares (determined by the length of a side) multiplied by the number of these rows that will fit the rectangle (determined by the length of the other side), it is time to consolidate these ideas. Explain to students that you like the idea of measuring one side to tell how many squares will fit in a row along that side. You would like them to call or think of this side as the *base* of the rectangle even though some people call it the *length* or the *width*. Then the other side can be called the *height*. But which side is the base? Be sure that students conclude that either side could be the base. If you use the formula $A = b \times h$, then the same area will result using either side as the base.

From Rectangles to Other Parallelograms. Once students understand the base-times-height formula for rectangles, the next challenge is to determine the areas of parallelograms. Rather than provide a formula, use the following activity, which asks students to devise their own formula, building on what they know about rectangles.

> *Activity* **19.19**
>
> *Area of a Parallelogram*
>
> Give students two or three parallelograms either drawn on grid paper or, for a slightly harder challenge, drawn on plain paper with all dimensions—the lengths of all four sides and the height. Ask students to use what they have learned about the area of rectangles to determine the areas of these parallelograms. Students should find a method that will work for any parallelogram, even if not drawn on a grid.

If students are stuck, ask them to examine ways that the parallelogram is like a rectangle or how it can be changed

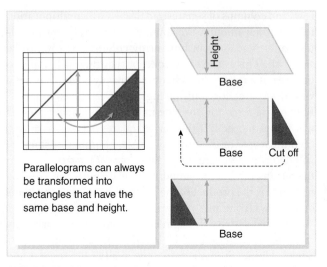

FIGURE 19.14 Transforming a parallelogram into a rectangle.

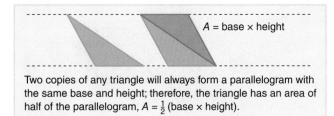

$A = \text{base} \times \text{height}$

Two copies of any triangle will always form a parallelogram with the same base and height; therefore, the triangle has an area of half of the parallelogram, $A = \frac{1}{2}(\text{base} \times \text{height})$.

FIGURE 19.15 Two congruent triangles always make a parallelogram.

into a rectangle. As shown in Figure 19.14, a parallelogram can always be transformed into a rectangle with the same base, the same height, and the same area. Thus, the formula for the area of a parallelogram is exactly the same as for a rectangle: base times height.

From Parallelograms to Triangles.   With that background, the area of a triangle can logically follow. Again, use a problem-based approach as in the next activity.

Activity 19.20

Area of a Triangle

STUDENTS *with* SPECIAL NEEDS

Provide students with at least two triangles drawn on grid paper. Avoid right triangles because they are an easier special case. Challenge the students to use what they have learned about the area of parallelograms to find the area of each of the triangles and to develop a method that will work for any triangle. They should be sure that their method works for all the triangles given to them as well as at least one more that they draw. For students with disabilities or those that need more structure, ask, "Can you find a parallelogram that is related to your triangle?" Then suggest that they fold a piece of paper in half, draw a triangle on the folded paper, and cut it out, making two identical copies. Use the copies to fit the triangles together into a parallelogram. This provides a nice visual of how a triangle is related to a parallelogram.

As shown in Figure 19.15, two congruent triangles can always be arranged to form a parallelogram with the same base and the same height as the triangle. The area of the triangle will, therefore, be one-half as much as that of the parallelogram. Have students further explore all three

possible parallelograms, one for each triangle side that serves as a base. Will the computed areas always be the same?

From Parallelograms to Trapezoids.   After developing formulas for parallelograms and triangles, your students may be interested in tackling trapezoids. There are at least 10 different methods of arriving at a formula for trapezoids, each related to the area of parallelograms or triangles. One method uses the same general approach that was used for triangles. Suggest that students work with two trapezoids that are identical, just as they did with triangles. Figure 19.16 shows how this method results in the formula. Not only are all of these formulas connected, but similar methods were used to develop them as well.

Here are a few suggestions, each leading to a different approach to finding the area of a trapezoid:

- Make a parallelogram inside the given trapezoid using three of the sides.
- Make a parallelogram using three sides that surround the trapezoid.
- Draw a diagonal forming two triangles.
- Draw a line through the midpoints of the nonparallel sides. The length of that line is the average of the lengths of the two parallel sides.
- Draw a rectangle inside the trapezoid, leaving two triangles, and then put those two triangles together.

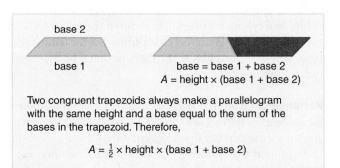

base 2

base 1

base = base 1 + base 2
$A = \text{height} \times (\text{base 1} + \text{base 2})$

Two congruent trapezoids always make a parallelogram with the same height and a base equal to the sum of the bases in the trapezoid. Therefore,

$$A = \frac{1}{2} \times \text{height} \times (\text{base 1} + \text{base 2})$$

FIGURE 19.16 Two congruent trapezoids always form a parallelogram.

PAUSE and REFLECT

Do you think that students should learn special formulas for the area of a square? Why or why not? Do you think students need formulas for the perimeters of squares and rectangles? ⬤

TECHNOLOGY The relationship between the areas of rectangles, parallelograms, and triangles can be dramatically illustrated using dynamic geometry programs such as *The Geometer's Sketchpad* (Key Curriculum Press) or *GeoGebra* (free public domain software). Draw two congruent segments on two parallel lines, as shown in Figure 19.17. Then connect the end points of the segments to form a parallelogram and two triangles. The height is indicated by a segment perpendicular to the parallel lines. Either of the two line segments can be dragged left or right to slant the parallelogram and triangle without changing the base or height. All area measures remain fixed! Also, explore the applet at http://illuminations.nctm.org/ActivityDetail .aspx?ID=108 to test how changes in the base and height of these shapes affect the area.

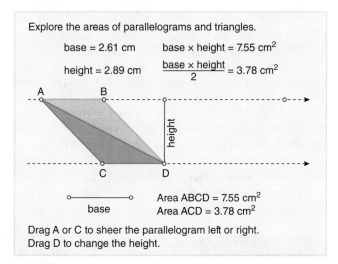

Explore the areas of parallelograms and triangles.

base = 2.61 cm   base × height = 7.55 cm²

height = 2.89 cm $\frac{\text{base} \times \text{height}}{2}$ = 3.78 cm²

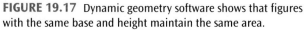

base

Area ABCD = 7.55 cm²
Area ACD = 3.78 cm²

Drag A or C to sheer the parallelogram left or right.
Drag D to change the height.

FIGURE 19.17 Dynamic geometry software shows that figures with the same base and height maintain the same area.

Surface Area. According to the *Common Core State Standards* (CCSSO, 2010), sixth-grade students begin the exploration of surface area of prisms and triangles. Build on the knowledge students have of the areas of two-dimensional figures. If they think of each face of a solid as its two-dimensional counterpart, they can find the area of each face and add the areas. One of the best approaches to teaching the surface area of three-dimensional figures is to create several card-stock rectangular prisms, cubes, or cylinders that have sides held together by small pieces of Velcro. In this way, students can think about the components or the "net" of the figure as they break the figure into faces and calculate the surface area. See www.shodor.org/interactivate/activities/ SurfaceAreaAndVolume to explore how changing dimensions of polyhedrons changes the surface area (and volume) or www.learner.org/interactives/geometry/index.html for explorations of surface area through animations (under the "surface area and volume" tab).

Circumference and Area of Circles

The relationship between the *circumference* of a circle (the distance around or the perimeter) and the length of the *diameter* (a line through the center joining two points on the circle) is one of the most interesting that students can discover and is a topic appropriate for seventh grade according to the *Common Core State Standards* (CCSSO, 2010). The circumference of every circle is about 3.14 times as long as the diameter. The exact ratio is an irrational number close to 3.14 and is represented by the Greek letter π. So $\pi = C/D$, the circumference divided by the diameter. In a slightly different form, $C = \pi D$. Half the diameter is the radius (r), so the same equation can be written $C = 2\pi r$. (Activity 20.10 in Chapter 20 will discuss the concept of π and how students can discover this important ratio.)

Students should be challenged to figure out the area formula for circles on their own. For example, give a hint by showing students how to arrange 8 or 12 sectors of a circle into an approximate parallelogram. You may need to help them notice that the arrangement of sectors is an approximate parallelogram and that the smaller the sectors used, the closer the arrangement gets to a rectangle. But the complete argument for the formula should come from your students. Figure 19.18 presents a common development of the area formula $A = \pi r^2$.

Volume and Capacity

Volume and *capacity* are both terms for measures of the "size" of three-dimensional regions—a topic for fifth grade according to the *Common Core State Standards* (CCSSO, 2010). The term *capacity* is generally used to refer to the amount that a container will hold. Standard units of capacity include quarts, gallons, liters, and milliliters. The term *volume* can be used to refer to the capacity of a container but is also used for the size of solid objects. Standard units of volume are expressed in terms of length units, such as cubic inches or cubic centimeters.

Comparison Activities

Comparing the volumes of solid objects can be challenging. For primary students, it is appropriate to focus on capacity. A simple method of comparing capacity is to fill one container with something and then pour this amount into the

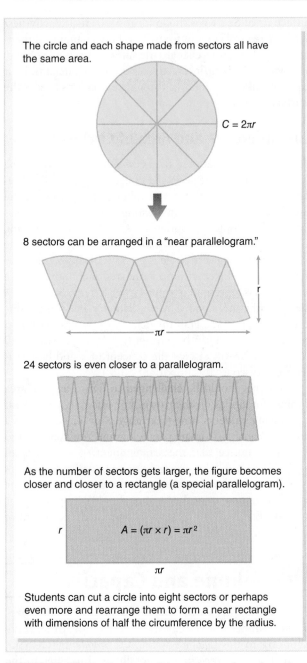

The circle and each shape made from sectors all have the same area.

$C = 2\pi r$

8 sectors can be arranged in a "near parallelogram."

πr

24 sectors is even closer to a parallelogram.

As the number of sectors gets larger, the figure becomes closer and closer to a rectangle (a special parallelogram).

$A = (\pi r \times r) = \pi r^2$

πr

Students can cut a circle into eight sectors or perhaps even more and rearrange them to form a near rectangle with dimensions of half the circumference by the radius.

FIGURE 19.18 Development of the circle area formula.

comparison container. By third grade, most students understand the concept of "holds more" with reference to containers. The concept of volume for solid objects may not be as readily understood.

In pre-K settings, students should compare the capacities of different containers as in the following activity:

Activity 19.21

Capacity Sort

Provide a variety of containers, with one marked as the "target." The students' task is to sort the collection into those that

hold more than, less than, or about the same amount as the target container. Provide a recording sheet on which each container is listed and a place to circle "holds more," "holds less," and "holds about the same." List the choices twice—one to record an estimate and one for the actual measure. Provide a filler (such as beans, rice, or Styrofoam peanuts), scoops, and funnels. Working in pairs, have students measure and record results. Discuss what students noticed in their estimating and measuring (e.g., that fatter/rounder shapes seem to hold more, etc.).

Students and adults can have difficulty accurately predicting which of two containers holds more. The apparent volumes of solid objects are sometimes misleading, and a method of comparison is also difficult. To compare volumes of solids such as a ball and an apple, a displacement method must be used. Again, you can have students predict which object has the smaller or greater volume and then place it in a measuring cup or beaker to see how much the water rises.

Try the following task yourself as well as with students. Take two sheets of construction paper. Make a tube shape (cylinder) by taping the two long edges together. Make a shorter, fatter cylinder from the other sheet by taping the short edges together. When placed upright, which cylinder holds more? Or do they have the same capacity?

Survey students first to see how many select which option. To test the conjectures, use a filler such as beans. Place the skinny cylinder inside the fat one. Fill the inside tube and then lift it up, allowing the filler to empty into the fat cylinder. Surprising to many, the volume is different even though the size of the paper holding the filler is the same.

Just as students should understand the relationship between perimeter and area (see Activity 19.18), they should also understand the relationship between volume and surface area, as in Activity 19.22.

Activity 19.22

ENGLISH LANGUAGE LEARNERS

Fixed Volume: Comparing Prisms

Give each pair of students a supply of centimeter cubes or wooden cubes. If you have ELLs, provide a visual of a rectangular solid, labeling all the key words they will need for the lesson (*length, width, height, surface area, cube, volume, side*). Ask students to use 64 cubes (or 36, if you prefer) to build different rectangular prisms and record the surface area for each prism formed in a table. Then ask students to describe any patterns that they notice. In particular, what happens to the surface area as the prism becomes less like a tall, skinny box and more like a cube?

The goal here is for students to realize that volume does not dictate surface area and to recognize that the pattern between surface area and volume is similar to the one found between area and perimeter. Namely, prisms that are more cubelike have less surface area than prisms with the same volume that are long and narrow.

Once students have developed formulas for computing area and volume, they can continue to explore the relationships between surface area and volume without actually building the prisms.

Using Models of Volume and Capacity Units

Two types of units can be used to measure volume and capacity: solid units and containers. Solid units are objects like wooden cubes or old tennis balls that can be used to fill the container being measured. The other type of unit model is a small container that is filled and poured repeatedly into the container being measured. The following are a few examples of units that you might want to collect:

- Liquid medicine cups
- Plastic jars and containers of almost any size
- Wooden cubic blocks or blocks of any shape (as long as you have a lot of the same size)
- Styrofoam packing peanuts (which still produce conceptual measures of volume despite not packing perfectly)

The following activity is similar to Activity 19.16, "Rectangle Comparison—Square Units."

Activity 19.23

Box Comparison—Cubic Units

Provide students with a pair of small boxes that you have folded up from poster board (see Figure 19.19). Use unit dimensions that match the cube blocks that you have for units. Students are given two boxes, one block, and an appropriate ruler. (If you use 2-cm cubes, make a ruler with the unit equal to 2 centimeters.) Ask students to decide which box has the greater volume or if they have the same volume.

Here are some suggested box dimensions ($L \times W \times H$):

6×3×4   5×4×4   3×9×3   6×6×2   5×5×3

Students should use words, drawings, and numbers to explain their conclusions.

A useful hint in the last activity is to first figure out how many cubes will fit on the bottom of the box. Some students will discover a multiplicative rule for the volume. The boxes can be filled with cubes to confirm conclusions.

Using Measuring Cups

Instruments for measuring capacity are generally used for small amounts of liquids or pourable materials such as rice or water. These tools are commonly found in kitchens and

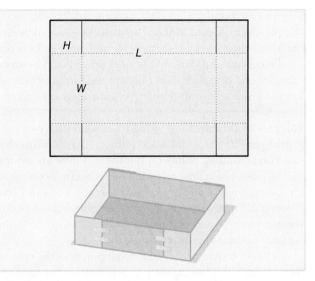

FIGURE 19.19 Make small boxes by starting with a rectangle and drawing a square on each corner as shown. Cut on the solid lines and fold the box up, wrapping the corner squares to the outside and taping them to the sides as shown.

laboratories. Students should use measuring cups to explore recipes for foods, papier-mâché, or Oobleck for science experiments (google "making Oobleck" for recipes). Books such as the *Better Homes and Gardens New Junior Cookbook* (2004) provide student-friendly recipes and multiple opportunities to use units of capacity.

Developing Formulas for Volumes of Common Solid Shapes

A common error that repeats from two- to three-dimensional shapes is when students confuse the meaning of height and base in their use of formulas. Note that the shapes in Figure 19.20 each have a slanted side and a height given. The base of the figure can be any flat surface of a figure. As mentioned before, to visualize the height, have students think of the figure sliding under a doorway: The *height* would be the height of the shortest door it could pass through. Keep this in mind as you work to use precise language to develop formulas for volume.

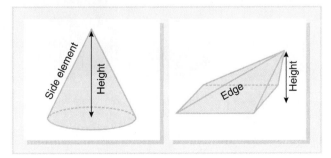

FIGURE 19.20 Heights of three-dimensional figures are not always measured along a surface.

The relationships between the formulas for volume are completely analogous to those for area. As you read, notice the similarities between rectangles and prisms, between parallelograms and slanted (oblique) prisms, and between triangles and pyramids. Not only are the formulas related, but the processes for developing the formulas are similar.

Volumes of Cylinders. A *cylinder* is a solid with two congruent parallel bases and sides with parallel elements that join corresponding points on the bases. There are several special classes of cylinders, including *prisms* (with polygons for bases), *right prisms*, *rectangular prisms*, and *cubes* (see Chapter 20). Interestingly, all of these solids have the same volume formula, and that one formula is analogous to the area formula for parallelograms.

Review Activity 19.23. The development of the volume formula from this box exploration is parallel to the development of the formula for the area of a rectangle, as shown in Figure 19.21. The *area* of the base (instead of *length* of the base for rectangles) determines how many *cubes* can be placed on the base, forming a single unit—a layer of cubes. The *height* of the box then determines how many of these *layers* will fit in the box, just as the height of the rectangle determined how many *rows* of squares would fill the rectangle.

Recall that a parallelogram can be thought of as a slanted rectangle, as was illustrated with the dynamic geometry software (see Figure 19.17). Show students a stack of three or four decks of playing cards (or a stack of books). When stacked straight, they form a rectangular solid. The volume, as just discussed, is $V = A \times H$, with A equal to the area of one playing card. Now if the stack is slanted to one side as shown in Figure 19.22, what will the volume of this new figure be? Students should be able to argue that this figure has the same volume (and same volume formula) as the original stack.

What if the cards in this activity were some other shape? If they were circular, the volume would still be the area of the base times the height; if they were triangular,

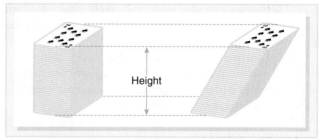

FIGURE 19.22 Two prisms with the same base and height have the same volume.

still the same. The conclusion is that the volume of *any* cylinder is equal to the *area of the base* times the *height*.

Volumes of Cones and Pyramids. Recall that when parallelograms and triangles have the same base and height, the areas are in a 2-to-1 relationship. Interestingly, the relationship between the volumes of cylinders and cones with the same base and height is 3 to 1. That is, *area* is to *two*-dimensional figures what *volume* is to *three*-dimensional figures. Furthermore, triangles are to parallelograms as cones are to cylinders.

To investigate this relationship, use plastic models of these related shapes (e.g., translucent Power Solids from Learning Resources). Have students estimate the number of times the pyramid will fit into the prism. Then have them test their predictions by filling the pyramid with water or rice and emptying it into the prism. They will discover that exactly three pyramids will fill a prism with the same base and height (see Figure 19.23). The volume of a cone or pyramid is exactly one-third the volume of the corresponding cylinder with the same base and height.

Using the same idea of base times height, it is possible to explore the surface area of a sphere (4 times the area of a circle with the same radius) and the volume of a sphere ($\frac{1}{3}$ times the surface area times the radius). That is, the surface area of a sphere is $4\pi r^2$ and the volume is $\frac{1}{3}(4\pi r^2)r$ or $\frac{4}{3}\pi r^3$.

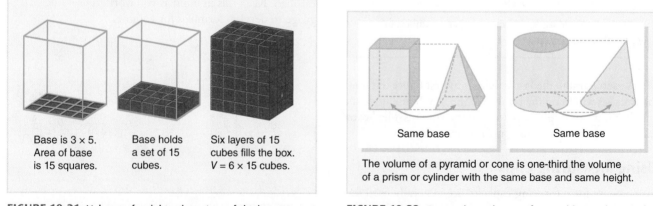

Base is 3 × 5. Area of base is 15 squares.

Base holds a set of 15 cubes.

Six layers of 15 cubes fills the box. $V = 6 \times 15$ cubes.

FIGURE 19.21 Volume of a right prism: *Area* of the base × height.

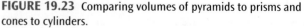

Same base

Same base

The volume of a pyramid or cone is one-third the volume of a prism or cylinder with the same base and same height.

FIGURE 19.23 Comparing volumes of pyramids to prisms and cones to cylinders.

Connections Between Formulas

The connectedness of mathematical ideas can hardly be better illustrated than with the connections of all of these formulas to the single concept of *base times height*.

A conceptual approach to the development of formulas helps students understand that they are meaningful and efficient ways to measure different attributes of the objects around us. After developing formulas in conceptual ways, students can derive formulas from what they already know. Mathematics does make sense!

Weight and Mass

Weight is a measure of the pull or force of gravity on an object. *Mass* is the amount of matter in an object and a measure of the force needed to accelerate it. On the moon, where gravity is much less than on earth, an object has a smaller weight than on earth but the identical mass. For practical purposes, on the earth, the measures of mass and weight will be about the same. In this discussion, the terms *weight* and *mass* will be used interchangeably.

Comparison Activities

The most conceptual way to compare weights of two objects is to hold one in each hand, extend your arms, and experience the relative downward pull on each—effectively communicating to a pre-K–grade 1 student what "heavier" or "weighs more" means. This personal experience can then be transferred to one of two basic types of scales—balances and spring scales.

When students place the objects in the two pans of a balance, the pan that goes down can be understood to hold the heavier object. Even a relatively simple balance will detect small differences. If two objects are placed one at a time in a spring scale, the heavier object pulls the pan down farther. Both balances and spring scales have real value in the classroom. (Technically, spring scales measure weight and balance scales measure mass. Why?)

With either scale, estimating, sorting, and ordering tasks are possible with very young students. For older students, comparison activities for weight are not necessary. Why?

Using Models of Weight or Mass Units

Any collection of uniform objects with the same mass can serve as weight units. For very light objects, large paper clips, wooden blocks, or plastic cubes work well. Large metal washers found in hardware stores are effective for weighing slightly heavier objects. You will need to rely on standard weights to weigh things as heavy as a kilogram or more.

Weight cannot be measured directly. Either a two-pan balance or a spring scale must be used. In a balance scale, place an object in one pan and weights in the other until the two pans balance. In a spring scale, first place the object in and mark the position of the pan on a piece of paper taped behind the pan. Remove the object and place just enough weights in the pan to pull it down to the same level. Discuss how equal weights will pull the spring with the same force.

Although the concept of heavier and lighter begins to be explored in kindergarten, the notion of units of weight or mass appears in third-grade standards (CCSSO, 2010). At any grade level, experiences with informal unit weights are good preparation for standard units and scales.

Angles

Understanding the concept (or attribute) of angle and measuring angles is one of the mathematical standards in the *Common Core State Standards* (CCSSO, 2010), beginning at grade 4 and developing in middle school. Angle measurement can be a challenge for two reasons: The attribute of angle size is often misunderstood, and protractors are commonly introduced and used without students understanding how they work.

Comparison Activities

The attribute of angle size might be called the "spread of the angle's rays." Angles are composed of two rays that are infinite in length with a common vertex. The only difference in their size is how widely or narrowly the two rays are spread apart.

To help students conceptualize the attribute of the spread of the rays, two angles can be directly compared by tracing one and placing it over the other. Be sure to have students compare angles with sides of different lengths. A wide angle with short sides may seem smaller than a narrow angle with long sides. This is a common misconception among students (Munier, Devichi, & Merle, 2008). As soon as students can tell the difference between a large angle and a small one, regardless of the length of the sides, you can move on to measuring angles.

Using Models of Angular Measure Units

A unit for measuring an angle must be an angle. Nothing else has the same attribute of spread that we want to measure. (Contrary to what many people think, you do not need to use degrees to measure angles.)

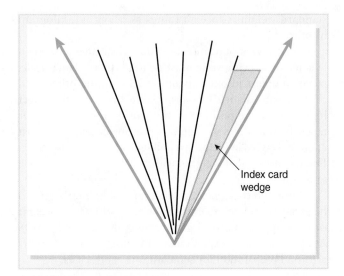

FIGURE 19.24 Using a small wedge cut from an index card as a unit angle, this angle measures about $7\frac{1}{2}$ wedges. Accuracy of measurement with these nonstandard angles is less important than the idea of how an angle is used to measure the size of another angle.

Activity **19.24**

A Unit Angle

Give each student an index card. Have students draw a narrow angle on the card using a straightedge and then cut it out (or use wedges made from Blackline Master 32). The resulting wedge can then be used as a unit of angular measure by counting the number that will fit in a given angle as shown in Figure 19.24. Distribute a pre-made page with assorted angles on it, and have students use their angle unit to measure the angles. Because students made different unit angles, the results will differ and can be discussed in terms of unit size.

Activity 19.24 illustrates that measuring an angle is the same as measuring length or area; unit angles are used to fill or cover the spread of an angle just as unit lengths fill or cover a length. Once this concept is well understood, move on to the use of measuring instruments.

Using Protractors and Angle Rulers

The protractor is one of the most poorly understood measuring instruments. Part of the difficulty arises because the units (degrees) are so small. It would be physically impossible for students to cut out and use a single degree to measure an angle accurately. In addition, the numbers on most protractors run clockwise and counterclockwise along the edge, making the scale hard to interpret without a strong conceptual foundation. Note that the units of degrees are based on an angle where the vertex of the rays is located at the midpoint of a circle creating an arc. A "one degree"

angle is one where the arc is 1/360 of the circle (see Blackline Master 32). These small angles are used to measure.

Students can make nonstandard waxed-paper protractors (see Figure 19.25), but soon move them to standard instruments. To understand measures on a protractor or angle ruler (see Figure 19.26), students need an approximate mental image of angle size. Then false readings of the protractor scale will be eliminated. One approach is to use a wheel like the rational number wheel in Figure 17.5 on page 342. Rather than measuring hundredths, use the wheel as an "angle fixer." Cut and merge two different colored paper dessert plates as in Figure 17.5. You can then rotate the plates to match angles of interest and to estimate important benchmark angles such as 30, 45, 60, 90, 135, 180, and 270 degrees. If students have a strong grasp of the approximate sizes of angles, that will give them the background needed to move to standard measuring tools such as the protractor and angle ruler.

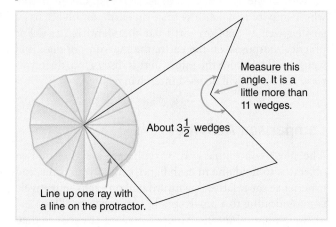

FIGURE 19.25 Measuring angles in a polygon using a waxed-paper protractor.

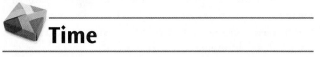

Time

Time is different from most other attributes that are commonly measured in school because it cannot be seen or felt and because it is more difficult for students to comprehend units of time or how those units are matched against a given time period or duration.

Comparison Activities

Time can be thought of as the duration of an event from its beginning to its end. As with other attributes, for students to adequately understand the attribute of time, they should make comparisons of events that have different durations. If two events begin at the same time, the shorter duration will end first and the other last longer. For example, which top spins longer? However, this form of comparison focuses on the ending of the duration rather than the duration itself. In order to think of time as something that can be

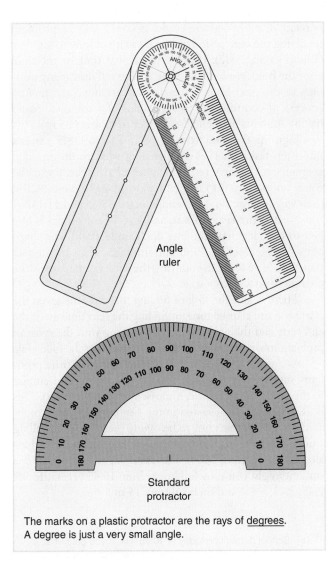

Angle ruler

Standard protractor

The marks on a plastic protractor are the rays of <u>degrees</u>. A degree is just a very small angle.

FIGURE 19.26 Different tools to measure angles.

Be Ready for the Bell

Give students a recording sheet with a set of clock faces (see Blackline Master 33). Secretly set a timer to go off at the hour, half hour, or minute. When the bell rings, students should look up and record the time on the clock face and in numerals on the recording sheet. This highly engaging activity motivates students not only to think about telling time but to consider the relationship between the analog clock reading and digital recording. Elapsed time can also be explored by discussing the time between timer rings.

Reading Clocks

The common instrument for measuring time is the clock. However, learning to tell time has little to do with time measurement and more to do with the skills of learning to read a dial-type instrument. Clock reading can be a difficult skill to teach. Starting in first grade, students are usually taught first to read clocks to the hour, then the half hour, and finally to 5- and 1-minute intervals in second and third grades (CCSSO, 2010). In the early stages of this sequence, students are shown clocks set exactly to the hour or half hour. Thus, many students who can read a clock at 7:00 or 2:30 are initially challenged by 6:58 or 2:33.

Digital clocks permit students to read times easily but do not relate times very well. To know that a digital reading of 7:58 is nearly 8 o'clock, the student must know that there are 60 minutes in an hour, that 58 is close to 60, and that 2 minutes is not a very long time. These concepts are challenging for many first-grade and second-grade students. The analog clock (with hands) shows "close to" times visually without the need for understanding big numbers or even how many minutes in an hour.

The following suggestions can help students understand and read analog clocks.

1. Begin with a one-handed clock, which can be read with reasonable accuracy. (Break off the minute hand from a regular clock.) Use lots of approximate language: "It's about 7 o'clock." "It's a little past 9 o'clock." "It's halfway between 2 o'clock and 3 o'clock" (see Figure 19.27).

measured, it is helpful to compare two events that do not start at the same time. This requires that some form of measurement of time be used from the beginning.

Engaging tasks that address duration include the following:

- Stacking 10 blocks one at a time and then removing them one at a time
- Saying your full name
- Walking on a designated path

Students need to learn about seconds, minutes, and hours and to develop some concept of how long these units are. You can help by making a conscious effort to note the duration of short and long events during the day. Have students time familiar events in their daily lives: brushing teeth, eating dinner, riding to school, spending time doing homework.

Timing small events of $\frac{1}{2}$ minute to 2 minutes is fun and useful and can be adapted from the following activity.

"About 7 o'clock"   "A little bit past 9 o'clock"   "Halfway between 2 o'clock and 3 o'clock"

FIGURE 19.27 Approximate time with one-handed clocks.

2. Discuss what happens to the big hand as the little hand goes from one hour to the next. When the big hand is at 12, the hour hand is pointing precisely to a number. If the hour hand is about halfway between numbers, about where would the minute hand be? If the hour hand is a little past or before an hour (10 to 15 minutes), about where would the minute hand be?

3. Use two real clocks, one with only an hour hand and one with two hands. Cover the two-handed clock. Periodically during the day, direct attention to the one-handed clock. Discuss the time in approximate language. Have students predict where the minute hand should be. Uncover the other clock and check.

4. Teach time after the hour in 5-minute intervals. After step 3 has begun, count by fives going around the clock. Instead of predicting that the minute hand is "pointing at the 4," transition to the language "it is about 20 minutes after the hour." As skills develop, suggest that students look first at the little or hour hand to learn approximately what time it is and then focus on the minute hand for precision.

5. Predict the reading on a digital clock when shown an analog clock, and vice versa; set an analog clock when shown a digital clock.

6. Relate the time after the hours to the time before the next hour. This is helpful not only for telling time but for number sense as well.

The following activity assesses students' ability to read a clock.

Activity **19.26**

One-Handed Clocks

Prepare a page of clock faces (see Blackline Master 33). On each clock draw an hour hand. Include placements that are approximately a quarter past the hour, a quarter until the hour, half past the hour, and some that are close to but not on the hour. For each clock face, the students' task is to write the digital time and draw the corresponding minute hand on the clock. If you have ELLs, it is important to note that time-telling is done differently in different cultures. For example, in Spanish any time past 30 minutes is stated as the next hour minus the time until that hour. For example, 10:45 is thought of as 15 minutes before 11, or eleven minus a quarter. It is important to be explicit about the fact that in English it can be said either way— "10:45" or "a quarter till 11."

Elapsed Time

Determining time intervals or elapsed time is a skill required starting in grade 3 (CCSSO, 2010). It is also a skill that students can find challenging, especially when the period of time includes noon or midnight. On the 2003 NAEP assessment, only 26 percent of fourth graders and 55

percent of eighth-grade students could solve a problem involving the conversion of one measure of time to another (Blume et al., 2007). If given the digital time or the time after the hour, students must be able to tell how many minutes to the next hour. This should certainly be a mental process of counting on for multiples of 5 minutes. Avoid having students use pencil and paper to subtract 25 from 60.

Figuring the time from, say, 8:15 A.M. to 11:45 A.M. is a multistep task that requires deciding what to do first and keeping track of the intermediate steps. In this case you could count hours from 8:15 to 11:15 and add on 30 minutes. But then what do you do if the endpoints are 8:45 and 11:15?

Next is the issue of A.M. and P.M. The problem is due less to the fact that students don't understand what happens on the clock at noon and midnight than to the fact that they have trouble counting the interval that spans the change from A.M. to P.M.

There is also the task of finding the end time given the start time and elapsed time, or finding the start time given the end time and the elapsed time. In keeping with the spirit of problem solving and the use of models, consider the following.

As a general model for all of these elapsed time problems, suggest that students sketch an empty time line (similar to the empty number line, discussed for computation). This is also the model suggested in the *Common Core State Standards*. It is important not to be overly prescriptive in telling students how to use the time line since there are various alternatives (Dixon, 2008). For example, in Figure 19.28, a student might count by full hours from 10:45 (11:45, 12:45, 1:45, 2:45, 3:45) and then subtract 15 minutes.

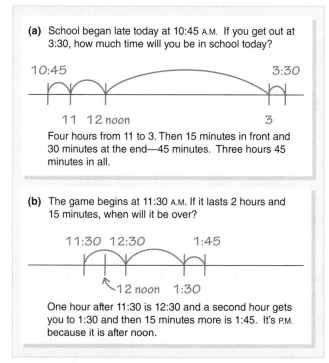

(a) School began late today at 10:45 A.M. If you get out at 3:30, how much time will you be in school today?

10:45   3:30

11 12 noon   3

Four hours from 11 to 3. Then 15 minutes in front and 30 minutes at the end—45 minutes. Three hours 45 minutes in all.

(b) The game begins at 11:30 A.M. If it lasts 2 hours and 15 minutes, when will it be over?

11:30 12:30   1:45

12 noon 1:30

One hour after 11:30 is 12:30 and a second hour gets you to 1:30 and then 15 minutes more is 1:45. It's P.M. because it is after noon.

FIGURE 19.28 A sketch of an empty time line can be useful in solving elapsed time problems.

Also explore "What Time Will It Be?" at http://nlvm.usu.edu/en/nav/frames_asid_318_g_2_t_4.html to find elapsed-time word problems.

Money

Here is a list of the money ideas and skills typically required in the primary grades:

- Recognizing coins
- Identifying and using the values of coins
- Counting and comparing sets of coins
- Creating equivalent coin collections (same amounts, different coins)
- Selecting coins for a given amount
- Making change
- Solving word problems involving money (starting in second grade [CCSSO, 2010])

The following sections support the learning of these ideas and skills.

Recognizing Coins and Identifying Their Values

The names of our coins are conventions of our social system. Students learn these names the same way that they learn the names of physical objects in their daily environment—through exposure and repetition.

The value of each coin is also a convention that students must simply be told. For these values to make sense, students must understand 5, 10, and 25 and think of these quantities without seeing countable objects. Where else do we say, "this is 5," while pointing to a single item? A student who remains tied to counting objects will be challenged to understand the values of coins. Coin value lessons should focus on purchase power—a dime can *buy the same thing* that 10 pennies can buy.

Counting Sets of Coins

Naming the total value of a group of coins is the same as mentally adding their values. Second-grade students can be asked to do the mental math required in counting a collection of different coins. Make sure students sort their coins and start counting from the highest values. Even though it is actually mental computation, the numbers are fortunately restricted to multiples of 5 and 10 with some ones added at the end. The next activity is a preparation for counting money.

ENGLISH LANGUAGE LEARNERS

Activity **19.27**

Money Skip Counting

Explain to students that they will start skip counting by one number, and at your signal they will shift to a count by a different number. Begin with only two different amounts, say, 25 and 10. Write these numbers on the board. Point to 25 and have students begin to skip-count. After three or more counts, raise your hand to indicate a pause in the counting. Then point to 10. Students continue the skip count from where they left off but now count by tens. Use any two of these numbers: 100, 50, 25, 10, 5, 1. Always start with the larger. Later, try three numbers in descending order. If you have ELLs and they are recent immigrants, invite them to share the coins from their country and see how they compare.

When discussing solutions to situations involving counting of coins, pay special attention to students who put combinations together utilizing thinking with tens.

Making Change

Because adding on to find a difference is such a valuable skill, it makes sense to give students experiences with adding on to find differences before asking them to make change. As students become more skillful at adding on, they can see the process of making change as an extension of a skill already acquired.

This sequence of suggested activities is not a surefire solution to the difficulties students experience with money. It is designed to build on prerequisite number and place-value skills and concepts without or before using coins.

RESOURCES *for Chapter 19*

LITERATURE CONNECTIONS

How Big Is a Foot? *Myller, 1991*

The story in this book is fun for young students. The king measures the queen using his feet and orders a bed made that is 6 feet long and 3 feet wide. The carpenter's apprentice, who is very small, makes the bed according to his own feet, demon-strating the need for standard units. (Another tale of nonstandard units is *Twelve Snails to One Lizard* [Hightower, 1997].)

Every Minute on Earth: Fun Facts That Happen Every 60 Seconds? *Murrie & Murrie, 2007*

This amazing book is not just about the concept of time. The authors provide fun facts about what can happen in 60 seconds:

a snow avalanche travels 4.2 miles (6.8 kilometers); the adult heart pumps 3.3 liters (3.5 quarts) of blood; movie film travels 90 feet (27.4 meters) through a projector; a garden snail moves 0.31 inches (7.8 millimeters); people in the United States discard 18,315 pounds (8325 kilograms) of food; and consumers spend $954.00 on chewing gum. Students can use the facts provided to explore and discuss these relationships.

RECOMMENDED READINGS

Articles

Austin, R., Thompson, D., & Beckmann, C. (2005). Exploring measurement concepts through literature: Natural links across disciplines. *Mathematics Teaching in the Middle School, 10*(5), 218–224.

This article includes a rich collection of almost 30 children's books that emphasize length, weight, capacity, speed, area, perimeter, and volume. Three books are described in detail as the authors share how to link measurement to science, history, geography, and economics.

Whitin, D. (2008). Learning our way to one million. *Teaching Children Mathematics, 14*(8), 448–453.

Through exploring the topic of one million, Whitin suggests ways for students in grades 2–5 to investigate several mathematics topics, including length, area, and money. All activities emphasize the need for problem solving in real-world contexts that reflect students' interests.

ONLINE RESOURCES

Google Earth's Measuring Tools
www.google.com/earth

Students can measure distances in centimeters, inches, feet, yards, kilometers, miles, degrees, and other measures. (Introductory information can be found at http://earth.google.com/support/bin/static.py?page=guide.cs&guide=22365&topic=23730&answer=148134). The polygon tool allows the user to chart a course using three or more points and calculates the length of the path.

Cubes
http://illuminations.nctm.org/ActivityDetail.aspx?ID=6

An excellent interactive applet that illustrates the volume of a rectangular prism (box). Units of single cubes, rows of cubes, or layers of cubes can be used to fill a prism.

Finding the Area and Perimeter of Rectangles (Math Playground)
www.mathplayground.com/area_perimeter.html

Amy and Ben explore the relationship between area and perimeter of rectangles. After the lesson, you can measure the lengths and widths of a variety of rectangles and calculate the area and perimeter of each.

REFLECTIONS *on Chapter 19*

WRITING TO LEARN

1. Explain what it means to measure something. Does your explanation work equally well for length, area, weight, volume, and time?

2. A general instructional plan for measurement has three steps. Explain how the type of activity used at each step accomplishes the instructional goal.

3. Four reasons were offered for using nonstandard units instead of standard units in instructional activities. Which of these seem most important to you, and why?

4. Develop in a connected way the area formulas for rectangles, parallelograms, triangles, and trapezoids. Draw pictures and provide explanations.

5. Explain how the area of a circle can be determined using the basic formula for the area of a parallelogram. (If you have a set of circular fraction pieces, use them as sectors of a circle.)

FOR DISCUSSION AND EXPLORATION

1. Get a teacher's edition of a textbook for any grade level, and look at the chapters on measurement. How well does the book cover metric measurement ideas? How would you modify or expand on the lessons found there?

MyEducationLab™

Go to the MyEducationLab (www.myeducationlab.com) for Math Methods and familiarize yourself with the content. Much of the site content is organized topically. The topics include all of the following to support your learning in the course:

- Learning outcomes for important mathematics methods course topics aligned with the national standards
- Assignments and Activities, tied to these learning outcomes and standards, that can help you more deeply understand course content
- Building Teaching Skills and Dispositions learning units that allow you to apply and practice your understanding of the core mathematics content and teaching skills

Your instructor has a correlation guide that aligns the exercises on the topical portion of the site with your book's chapters.

On MyEducationLab you will find book-specific resources including Blackline Masters, Expanded Lesson Activities, and Artifact Analysis Activities.

Field Experience Guide
C O N N E C T I O N S

Because measurement is so much a part of real-life experiences, lessons in measurement should be too. Use FEG Field Experiences 2.3 and 2.4 to assess whether lessons have authentic opportunities for students to explore measurement concepts. FEG Expanded Lesson 9.15, "Crooked Paths," explores length, and Expanded Lesson 9.16, "Fixed Areas" (also on pages 76–77 in this book), engages students in exploring area and perimeter. FEG Activity 10.13, "Cover All," uses manipulatives to explore area. Balanced Assessment Task 11.3, "Bolts and Nuts!" analyzes student thinking about measuring length and proportional thinking.

Chapter 20

Geometric Thinking and Geometric Concepts

eometry is a "network of concepts, ways of reasoning and representation systems" used to explore and analyze shape and space (Battista, 2007, p. 843). This critical area of mathematics appears in everything from global positioning systems to computer animation.

BIG IDEAS

1. What makes shapes alike and different can be determined by geometric properties. For example, shapes have sides that are parallel, perpendicular, or neither; they have line symmetry, rotational symmetry, or neither; they are similar, congruent, or neither.

2. Shapes can be moved in a plane or in space. These changes can be described in terms of translations (slides), reflections (flips), and rotations (turns).

3. Shapes can be described in terms of their location in a plane or in space. Coordinate systems can be used to describe these locations precisely. In turn, the coordinate view of shape offers ways to understand certain properties of shapes, changes in position (transformations), and how they appear or change size (visualization).

4. Three-dimensional shapes can be seen from various views. The ability to perceive shapes from different viewpoints helps us understand relationships between two- and three-dimensional figures and mentally change the position and size of shapes.

Mathematics CONTENT CONNECTIONS

A rich understanding of geometry has clear and important implications for other areas of the curriculum. Take advantage of these connections whenever possible.

Coordinate graphing provides an analytic cept of slope and, in turn, of perpendicular and

parallel relationships. Transformations of shapes (slides, flips, and turns) can be described in terms of coordinates, allowing for the digital manipulation of shapes.

◆ **Proportional Reasoning** (Chapter 18): Similar geometric objects have proportional dimensions and provide visual representations of proportionality.

◆ **Measurement** (Chapter 19): Measurement is central in developing area and volume formulas and in understanding area/perimeter and surface area/volume relationships. Coordinate geometry provides new ways to determine lengths, areas, and volumes. The Pythagorean relationship is at once an algebraic, geometric, and metric relationship.

◆ **Integers** (Chapter 23): Both positive and negative numbers are used describing positions in the plane and in space.

Geometry Goals for Students

It is useful to think about your geometry objectives in terms of two related frameworks: (1) spatial sense and geometric reasoning and (2) the specific geometric content found in your state or district objectives. The first framework has to do with the way students think and reason about shape and space. There is a well-researched theoretical basis for organizing the development of geometric thought that guides this framework. The second framework is content in the more traditional sense—knowing about symmetry, triangles, parallel lines, and so forth. The *Common Core State Standards* and *Curriculum Focal Points* help describe content goals across the grades. We need to understand both aspects of geometry—reasoning and content—so that we can best help students grow.

Spatial Sense and Geometric Reasoning

Spatial sense can be defined as an intuition about shapes and the relationships between shapes and is considered a core area of mathematical study, like number (Sarama & Clements, 2009). Spatial sense includes the ability to mentally visualize objects and spatial relationships—to turn things around in your mind. It includes a comfort with geometric descriptions of objects and position. People with well-developed spatial sense appreciate geometric form in art, nature, and architecture and they use geometric ideas to describe and analyze their world.

Some people say that you either are or are not born with spatial sense. This simply is not true! Meaningful experiences with shape and spatial relationships, when provided consistently over time, can and do develop spatial sense. Between 1990 and 2000, NAEP data indicated a steady, continuing improvement in students' geometric reasoning at grade 8 (Sowder & Wearne, 2006). Students did not just get smarter. Instead, there has been an increasing emphasis on geometry at all grades. The NCTM *Standards* supports the notion that all students can grow in their geometric skills and understandings. "The notion of building understanding in geometry across the grades, from informal to more formal thinking, is consistent with the thinking of theorists and researchers" (2000, p. 41).

Geometric Content

For too long, geometry curricula in the United States emphasized the learning of terminology. However, geometry has a number of content goals that apply to all grade levels:

- *Shapes and Properties* includes a study of the properties of shapes in two dimensions and three dimensions, as well as a study of the relationships built on properties.
- *Transformation* includes a study of translations, reflections, rotations (slides, flips, and turns), the study of symmetries, and the concept of similarity.
- *Location* refers primarily to coordinate geometry or other ways of specifying how objects are located in the plane or in space.
- *Visualization* includes the recognition of shapes in the environment, developing relationships between two- and three-dimensional objects, and the ability to draw and recognize objects from different viewpoints.

The content in this chapter is divided according to these four categories, with each category beginning with early experiences and moving through the grades to middle school experiences using van Hiele's levels of geometric thought.

Excerpt reprinted with permission from *Principles and Standards for School Mathematics*, copyright © 2000. The National Council of Teachers of Mathematics.

Developing Geometric Thinking

Although not all people think about geometric ideas in the same manner, we are all capable of developing the ability to think and reason in geometric contexts. The research of two Dutch educators, Pierre van Hiele and Dina van Hiele-Geldof, provides insights into the differences in geometric thinking and how the differences come to be. The van Hiele theory has been a major influence on geometry curricula worldwide.

The van Hiele Levels of Geometric Thought

The van Hiele model is a five-level hierarchy of ways of understanding spatial ideas (see Figure 20.1). Each level describes the thinking processes used in geometric contexts. Specifically, the levels describe how we think and what types of geometric ideas we think about (called *objects of thought*).

Level 0: Visualization

The objects of thought at level 0 are shapes and what they "look like."

Students at level 0 recognize and name figures based on the global visual characteristics of the figure. For example, a square is defined by a level-0 student as a square "because it looks like a square." Because appearance is dominant at this level, appearances can overpower properties of a shape. For example, a rotated square whose sides are all at a 45-degree angle to the vertical may now be a diamond and no longer a square according to a student at level 0. Students at this level will sort and classify shapes based on their appearance—"I put these together because they are all pointy" (or "fat," or "look like a house," and so on). Students are able to see how shapes are alike and different. As a result, students at this level can create and begin to understand classifications of shapes.

The products of thought at level 0 are classes or groupings of shapes that seem to be "alike."

The emphasis at level 0 is on shapes that students can observe, feel, build, take apart, or work with in some manner. The general goal is to explore how shapes are alike and different and to use these ideas to create classes of shapes (both physically and mentally). Some of these classes of shapes have names—rectangles, triangles, prisms, cylinders, and so on. Properties of shapes, such as parallel sides, symmetry, right angles, and so on, are included at this level but only in an informal, observational manner.

Although the van Hiele theory applies to students of all ages learning any geometric content, it may be easier to

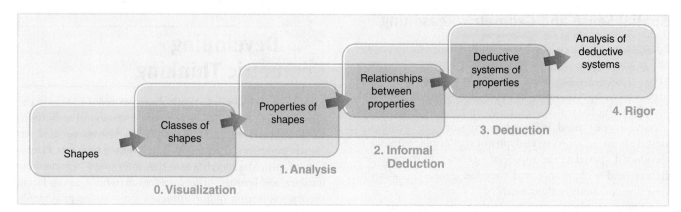

FIGURE 20.1 The van Hiele theory of geometric thought.

apply the theory to the shapes-and-property category. The following is a good representation of an activity appropriate for level-0 learners.

Activity 20.1

Shape Sorts

Have students work in groups of four with a set of 2-D shapes similar to those in Figure 20.2, doing the following related activities in order:

- Each student selects a shape. In turn, the students tell one or two things they find interesting about their shape.
- Students each randomly select two shapes and try to find something that is alike about their two shapes and something that is different.
- The group selects one target shape at random and places it in the center of the workspace. Their task is to find all other shapes that are like the target shape according to the same rule. For example, if they say "This shape is like the target shape because it has a curved side and a straight side," then all other shapes that they put in the collection must have these properties. Do a second sort with the same target shape but using a different property.
- Do a "secret sort." You (or one of the students) create a collection of about five shapes that fit a secret rule. Leave others that belong in your set in the pile. Students try to find additional pieces that belong to the set and/or guess the secret rule.

Depending on the grade level, these activities will elicit a wide variety of ideas as students examine the shapes. They may start describing the shapes with ideas such as "curvy" or "looks like a rocket" rather than typical geometric properties. But as students notice more sophisticated properties, you can attach appropriate names to them. For example, students may notice that some shapes have corners "like a square" (explain that those are also called *right angles*) or that "these shapes are the same on both sides" (symmetrical).

FIGURE 20.2 A collection of shapes for sorting. See Blackline Masters 41–47 for these shapes and others.

What makes this a level-0 activity is that students are operating on the shapes that they see in front of them and are beginning to see similarities and differences in shapes. By forming groups of shapes, they begin to imagine shapes belonging to classes that are not there.

Level 1: Analysis

The objects of thought at level 1 are classes of shapes rather than individual shapes.

Students at the analysis level are able to consider all shapes within a class rather than just the single shape on their desk. Instead of talking about this rectangle, they can talk about all rectangles. By focusing on a class of shapes, students are able to think about what makes a rectangle a rectangle (four sides, opposite sides parallel, opposite sides same length, four right angles, congruent diagonals, etc.). The irrelevant features (e.g., size or orientation) fade into the background, and students begin to appreciate that a collection of shapes goes together because of properties. If a shape belongs to a particular class such as cubes, it has the corresponding properties of that class. "All cubes have six congruent faces, and each of those faces is a square." These properties were only implicit at level 0. Students operating at level 1 may be able to list all the properties of squares, rectangles, and parallelograms but may not see that these are subclasses of one another—that all squares are rectangles and all rectangles are parallelograms. In defining a shape, level-1 thinkers are likely to list as many properties of a shape as they know.

The products of thought at level 1 are the properties of shapes.

While level-1 students will continue to use models and drawings of shapes, they begin to see these individual shapes as representatives of classes of shapes. Their understanding of the properties of shapes—such as symmetry, perpendicular and parallel lines, and so on—continues to be refined. The identification of properties is an important cognitive activity (Yu, Barrett, & Presmeg, 2009).

In the following activity, students use the properties of shapes they learned in earlier activities, possibly while operating at level 0. These include ideas such as symmetry, angle classification (right, obtuse, acute), parallel and perpendicular, and the concept of congruent line segments and angles.

with disabilities, provide a structured recording sheet with a table listing the four property headings. This will help organize their thinking around the many diverse possibilities.

What distinguishes this activity from the earlier level-0 activity is the object of students' thinking. Now students must assess whether the properties apply to all shapes in the category. If they are working on the squares, for example, their observations apply to a square mile as well as a square centimeter.

Level 2: Informal Deduction

The objects of thought at level 2 are the properties of shapes.

As students begin to think about properties of geometric objects without focusing on one particular object (shape), they are able to develop relationships between these properties. "If all four angles are right angles, the shape must be a rectangle. If it is a square, all angles are right angles. If it is a square, it must be a rectangle." With greater ability to engage in if-then reasoning, students can classify shapes using only a minimum set of defining characteristics. For example, four congruent sides and at least one right angle are sufficient to define a square. Rectangles are parallelograms with a right angle. Observations go beyond properties themselves and begin to focus on logical arguments about the properties. Students at level 2 will be able to follow and appreciate informal deductive arguments about shapes and their properties. "Proofs" may be more intuitive than rigorously deductive; however, there is an appreciation

Activity 20.2

Property Lists for Quadrilaterals

ENGLISH LANGUAGE LEARNERS

STUDENTS *with* SPECIAL NEEDS

Prepare handouts for parallelograms, rhombi, rectangles, and squares (see Blackline Masters 54–57 and Figure 20.3.) Assign groups of three or four students to work with one type of quadrilateral. Post labeled shapes for ELLs to use as a reference. Ask students to list as many properties as they can that apply to all of the shapes on their sheet. They will need tools such as index cards (to check right angles, to compare side lengths, and to draw straight lines), mirrors (to check line symmetry), and tracing paper (for identifying angle congruence and rotational symmetry). Encourage students to use the words "at least" when describing how many of something: for example, "rectangles have at least two lines of symmetry," because squares—included in the rectangles category—have four.

Have students prepare their property lists under these headings: Sides, Angles, Diagonals, and Symmetries. Be sure ELLs understand what each of these categories mean. Groups then share their lists with the class, and eventually a class list for each category of shape will be developed. For students

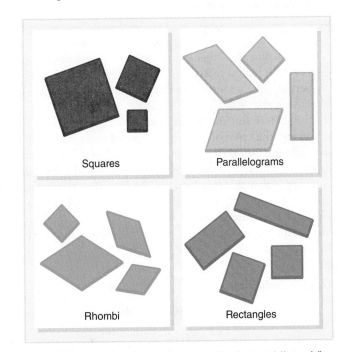

FIGURE 20.3 Shapes for the "Property Lists for Quadrilaterals" activity (see Blackline Masters 54–57).

that a logical argument is compelling. An appreciation of the axiomatic structure (an agreed-on set of rules) of a formal deductive system, however, remains under the surface.

The products of thought at level 2 are relationships between properties of geometric objects.

The hallmark of level-2 activities is the inclusion of informal logical reasoning. Because students have developed an understanding of various properties of shapes, it is now time to encourage conjecture and to ask "Why?" or "What if?"

Activity 20.3

Minimal Defining Lists

This activity is a sequel to Activity 20.2, "Property Lists for Quadrilaterals."

Once property lists for the parallelogram, rhombus, rectangle, and square (and possibly the kite and trapezoid) have been generated, post the lists. Have students work in groups to find "minimal defining lists," or MDLs, for each shape. An MDL is a subset of the properties for a shape that is defining and "minimal." "Defining" here means that any shape that has all the properties on the MDL must be that shape. "Minimal" means that if any single property is removed from the list, it is no longer defining. For example, one MDL for a square is a quadrilateral with four congruent sides and four right angles. Students should try to find at least two or three MDLs for their shape. A proposed list can be challenged as either not minimal or not defining. A list is not defining if a counterexample—a shape other than one being described—can be produced using only the properties on the list.

The hallmark of this and other level-2 activities is the emphasis on logical reasoning. "If a quadrilateral has these properties, then it must be a square." Logic is also involved in proving that a list is faulty—either not minimal or not defining. Here students begin to learn the nature of a definition and the value of counterexamples. In fact, any minimal defining list (MDL) is a potential definition. The other aspect of this activity that clearly sets it into the level-2 category is that students focus on the lists of properties of the shapes—the very factors that were products of the earlier level-1 activity. As a result of the MDL activity, students are creating a collection of new relationships that exist between properties.

Level 3: Deduction

The objects of thought at level 3 are relationships between properties of geometric objects.

At level 3, students move from thinking about properties to reasoning or proving related to the properties. As this

analysis of the informal arguments takes place, the structure of a system complete with axioms, definitions, theorems, corollaries, and postulates begins to develop and can be appreciated as the necessary means of establishing geometric truth. The student at this level is able to work with abstract statements about geometric properties and make conclusions based more on logic than intuition. A student operating at level 3 is not only aware that the diagonals of a rectangle bisect each other (level 2) but has an appreciation of the need to prove this from a series of deductive arguments.

The products of thought at level 3 are deductive axiomatic systems for geometry.

The type of reasoning that characterizes a level-3 thinker is the same reasoning required in high school geometry, where students build on a list of axioms and definitions to create theorems. In a very global sense, high school geometry students are working on the creation of a complete geometric deductive system.

Level 4: Rigor

The objects of thought at level 4 are deductive axiomatic systems for geometry.

At the highest level of the van Hiele hierarchy, the objects of thought are axiomatic systems themselves, not just the deductions within a system. There is an appreciation of the distinctions and relationships between different axiomatic systems. For example, spherical geometry is based on lines drawn on a sphere rather than in a plane or ordinary space. This geometry has its own set of axioms and theorems and is generally the level of college geometry courses.

Levels 3 and 4 are beyond the scope of this book.

Characteristics of the van Hiele Levels. The van Hiele levels have several common elements:

- The products of thought at each level are the same as the objects of thought at the next level, as illustrated in Figure 20.1. The objects (ideas) must be created at one level so that relationships between these objects of thought can become the focus of the next level.
- The levels are not age dependent. A third grader or a high school student could be at level 0.
- Advancement through the levels requires geometric *experiences*. Students should explore, talk about, and interact with content at the next level while increasing experiences at their current level.
- When instruction or language is at a level higher than that of the student, students will not be able to understand the concept being developed. They may memorize a fact (e.g., all squares are rectangles) but not construct the actual relationship of the properties of a square.

Implications for Instruction

If students are to be prepared for the deductive geometry of high school and beyond, reaching the van Hiele level 2 by the end of the eighth grade is critically important. All teachers should be aware that the experiences they provide are the single most important factor in moving students up this developmental ladder.

The van Hiele theory and the developmental perspective of this book highlight the necessity of teaching at the student's level of thought. However, almost any activity can be modified to span two levels of thinking. For many activities, you will need to adapt the activity to the level of individual students so you can challenge them to operate at the next higher level. At every level, the use of physical materials, drawings, and computer models is a must!

From Level 0 to Level 1. Students moving from level 0 to level 1 can be supported as follows:

- Challenge students to test ideas about shapes using a variety of examples from a particular category. Say, "Let's see if that is true for other rectangles," or "Can you draw a triangle that does not have a right angle?" In general, question students to see whether observations made about a particular shape apply to other shapes of a similar kind.
- Provide ample opportunities to draw, build, make, put together (compose), and take apart (decompose) shapes in both two and three dimensions. These activities should be built around understanding and using specific characteristics or properties.
- Focus on the properties of figures rather than on simple identification. As new geometric concepts are learned, the number of properties that figures have can be expanded.
- Apply ideas to entire classes of figures (e.g., *all* rectangles, *all* prisms) rather than to individual models. For example, find ways to sort all possible triangles into groups. From these groups, define types of triangles.

From Level 1 to Level 2. Students transitioning from level 1 to level 2 can be supported as follows:

- Challenge students with questions that involve reasoning, such as "If the sides of a four-sided shape are all congruent, will you always have a square?" and "Can you find a counterexample?"
- Encourage the making and testing of hypotheses or conjectures. "Do you think that will work all the time?" "Is that true for all triangles or just equilateral ones?"
- Examine properties of shapes to determine necessary and sufficient conditions for different shapes or concepts. "What properties of diagonals do you think will guarantee that you will have a square?"

- Using the language of informal deduction: *all, some, none, if . . . then, what if,* and so on.
- Encourage students to attempt informal proofs. As an alternative, require them to make sense of informal proofs that other students or you have suggested.

Task Selection and Levels of Thought. If you teach at the primary level, many of your students will be at level 0. In the upper grades, you may have students within the same classroom at two or even three levels. How do you discover the level of each student? How will you select the right activities to match your students' needs?

No simple assessment exists to identify the exact level at which a student is functioning. However, examine the descriptors for the first two levels. As you conduct an activity or do a diagnostic interview, listen to students' discuss their thinking. Can they talk about shapes as classes? Do they refer, for example, to "rectangles" rather than basing discussion around a particular rectangle? Do they understand that shapes do not change when the orientation or size changes? With careful observations such as these, you will soon be able to distinguish between students at levels 0 and 1.

At the upper grades, focus on moving students from level 1 to level 2. If students are not able to follow logical arguments and are not comfortable with making conjectures and using if-then reasoning, these students are likely still at or below level 1.

The remainder of this chapter offers a sampling of activities organized around the four content goals of the NCTM standards: Shapes and Properties, Location, Transformations, and Visualization. Within each of these content groupings, activities are further sorted according to the first three van Hiele levels. Understand that all of these subdivisions are quite fluid. An activity found at one level can easily be adapted to an adjacent level simply by the way it is presented to the students.

Learning about Shapes and Properties

This is the content area most often associated with geometry in pre-K–grade 8 classrooms; students are working with both two- and three-dimensional shapes. This is the time when young students begin to "perceive, say, describe/discuss and construct objects in 2-D space" (National Research Council Committee, 2009, p. 177). They are finding out what makes these shapes alike and different, and in the process they begin to discover properties of the shapes, including the conventional names for these properties. With sufficient experiences, students develop classifications of special shapes—triangles, parallelograms, cylinders, pyramids, and so on—and learn that some properties apply to

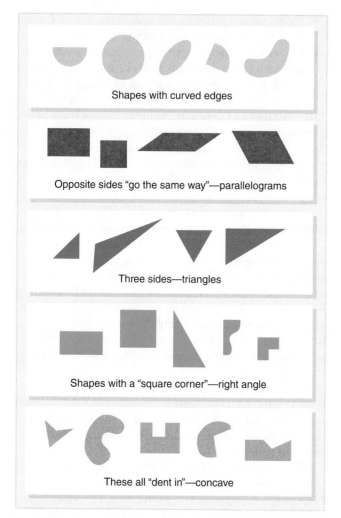

FIGURE 20.4 By sorting shapes, students begin to recognize properties.

full classes. Eventually, they will investigate how properties of shapes impose logical consequences on geometric relationships, and the ability to reason about shapes and properties will be developed.

Shapes and Properties for Level-0 Thinkers

Students need experience with a wide variety of two- and three-dimensional shapes. Triangles should be more than just equilateral and not always shown with the vertex at the top. Shapes should have curved sides, straight sides, and combinations of these. Along the way, the names of shapes and their properties can be introduced.

Sorting and Classifying. As young students work at classification of shapes, be prepared for them to notice features that you do not consider to be "real" geometric attributes, such as "dented" or "looks like a tree." Students at this level

will also attribute to shapes ideas that are not part of the shape, such as "points up" or "has a side that is the same as the edge of the board."

For variety in two-dimensional shapes, create your own materials. A good set of assorted shapes is found in Blackline Masters 41–47. Make multiple copies so that groups of students can all work with the same shapes. Once you have your sets constructed, try Activity 20.1, "Shape Sorts," on page 404.

In any sorting activity, the students—not the teacher—should decide how to sort. This allows students to do the activity using ideas they own and understand. By listening to the kinds of attributes that they use in their sorting, you will be able to tell what properties they know and use and how they think about shapes. Figure 20.4 illustrates a few of the many ways a set might be sorted.

The secret sort in Activity 20.1 is one option for introducing a new property. For example, sort the shapes so that all have at least one right angle or "square corner." When students discover your rule, you have an opportunity to talk more about that property and name the property "right angle."

The following activity is also done with the 2-D shapes.

Activity 20.4

What's My Shape?

STUDENTS *with* SPECIAL NEEDS

From Blackline Masters 41–47, make a double set of 2-D assorted shapes on card stock. Cut out one set of shapes and glue each shape inside a folded half-sheet of construction paper to make "secret-shape" folders.

In a group, one student is designated the leader and given a secret-shape folder. The other students are to find the shape that matches the shape in the folder by asking only "yes" or "no" questions. The group can eliminate shapes as they get answers that narrow down the possibilities. They are not allowed to point to a piece and ask, "Is it this one?" Rather, they must continue to ask questions about properties or characteristics that reduce the choices to one shape. The final piece is checked against the one in the leader's folder. Students with disabilities may need a list of possible properties and characteristics (e.g., number of sides) to help support their question asking.

The difficulty of Activity 20.4 is largely dependent on the shape in the folder. The more shapes in the collection that share properties with the secret shape, the more difficult the task.

FORMATIVE Assessment Notes

Adapt the activity "Shape Sorts" (Activity 20.1) using three-dimensional shapes and do a **diagnostic interview.** Make sure you have a collection of solids that has variability (curved surfaces, etc.). Power Solids and other collections of 3-D shapes are available through various catalogs. Another option is to collect real objects such as cans, boxes, balls, and Styrofoam shapes. Figure 20.5 illustrates some simple classifications of solids.

The ways students describe these three-dimensional shapes are good evidence of their level of thinking. The classifications made by level-0 thinkers are generally restricted to the shapes that they have in front of them. Level 1 thinkers will begin to create categories based on properties, and their language will indicate that there are many more shapes in the group than those that are physically present. Students may say things like "These shapes have square corners sort of like rectangles," or "These look like boxes. All the boxes have square [rectangular] sides." ■

Composing and Decomposing Shapes.   Students need to freely explore how shapes fit together to form larger shapes (compose) and how larger shapes can be made of smaller shapes (decompose). Among two-dimensional shapes for these activities, pattern blocks and tangrams are the best known. In a 1999 article, Pierre van Hiele describes an interesting set of tiles he calls the "mosaic puzzle" (see Figure 20.6). The value of van Hiele's puzzle is due to the fact that the set contains five different angles. You can use the

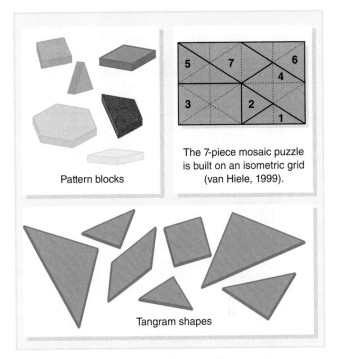

Pattern blocks

The 7-piece mosaic puzzle is built on an isometric grid (van Hiele, 1999).

Tangram shapes

FIGURE 20.6 Assorted materials for activities.

pieces to talk about square corners (right angles) and angles that are more and less than a right angle (obtuse and acute angles). Patterns for the mosaic puzzle and tangrams can be found in Blackline Master 51.

Figure 20.7 shows tangram puzzles in order of increasing difficulty. The National Library of Virtual Manipulatives (http://nlvm.usu.edu) has a tangram applet with a set of fourteen puzzle figures that can be made using all seven tangram pieces. The e-version of tangrams has the advantage of motivation and the fact that you must be much more deliberate in arranging the shapes.

The geoboard is one of the best devices for "constructing" two-dimensional shapes. Activity 20.5 offers several geoboard activities appropriate for level 0.

Activity **20.5**

Geoboard Copy

Students copy shapes, designs, and patterns from a geoboard projected by the teacher. Begin with designs using one band; then create more complex designs (see Figure 20.8).

Activity **20.6**

Congruent Parts

Copy a shape from a card, and have students decompose it into smaller shapes on their geoboards. Specify the number of smaller shapes. Also specify whether they are all to be congruent or simply of the same type as shown in Figure 20.9.

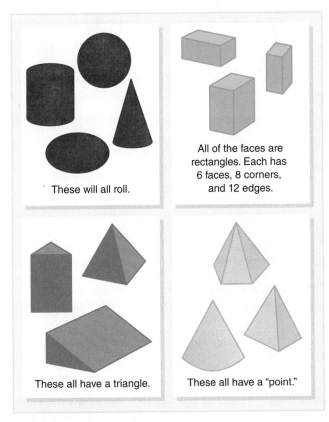

These will all roll.

All of the faces are rectangles. Each has 6 faces, 8 corners, and 12 edges.

These all have a triangle.

These all have a "point."

FIGURE 20.5 Early classifications of three-dimensional shapes.

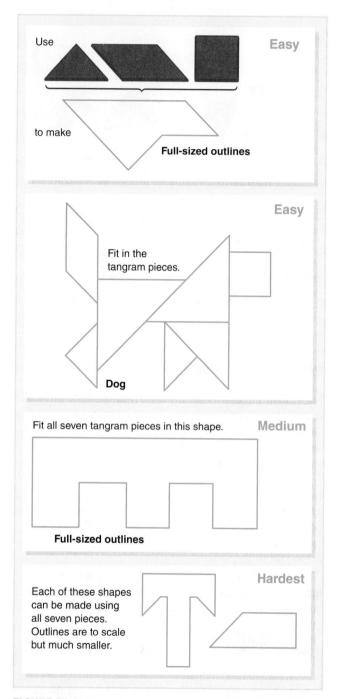

FIGURE 20.7 Four tangram puzzles (see Blackline Master 51).

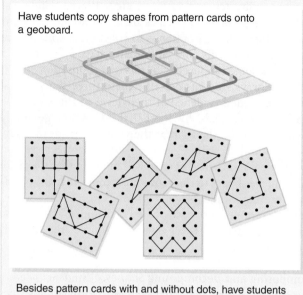

Besides pattern cards with and without dots, have students copy <u>real</u> shapes—tables, houses, letters of the alphabet, etc.

FIGURE 20.8 Shapes on geoboards (see Blackline Masters 49 and 50).

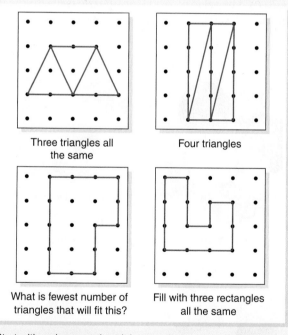

Start with a shape, and cut it into smaller shapes. Add special decompose conditions to make the activity challenging.

FIGURE 20.9 Decomposing shapes (see Blackline Masters 49 and 50).

Have lots of geoboards available in the classroom. It is better for two or three students to have 10 or 12 boards at a station than for each to have only one. That way, a variety of shapes can be made and compared before they are changed.

Teach students from the very beginning to record their geoboard designs (use Blackline Masters 49–50). To help students who struggle with this transfer, suggest that they first mark the dots for the corners of their shape ("second row, end peg"). With the corners identified, it is much easier

for them to draw lines between to make the shape. These drawings can be placed in groups for classification and discussion, made into booklets illustrating a new idea that is being discussed, or sent home to families.

TECHNOLOGY There are excellent electronic versions of the geoboard. One is found at National Library of Virtual Manipulatives (http://nlvm.usu.edu). One option includes instant calculation of perimeter and area by clicking the "measures" button. The Online Geoboard applet at the University of Illinois Office for Mathematics, Science, and Technology Education website (http://mste.illinois.edu/users/pavel/java/geoboard) is essentially the same but also has a clickable option that shows the lengths of the sides of the figure.

Building three-dimensional shapes is more difficult than building two-dimensional shapes. A variety of commercial materials permit fairly creative construction of geometric solids (e.g., Polydron and the Zome System). The following are three approaches to making homemade models.

- *Plastic coffee stirrers with twist ties or modeling clay.* Plastic stirrers can be cut into different lengths. Use twist ties inserted into the ends or small balls of clay to connect corners.
- *Plastic drinking straws.* Cut the straws lengthwise from the top down to the flexible joint. These slit ends can then be inserted into the uncut bottom ends of other straws, making a strong but flexible joint. Join straws in this fashion to form three-dimensional shapes.
- *Rolled newspaper rods.* Fantastic super-large skeletons can be built using newspaper and masking or duct tape (see Figure 20.10).

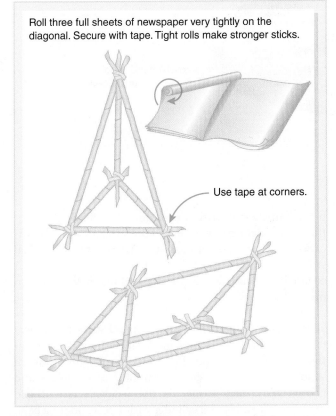

Roll three full sheets of newspaper very tightly on the diagonal. Secure with tape. Tight rolls make stronger sticks.

Use tape at corners.

FIGURE 20.10 Large skeletal structures and special shapes can be built with tightly rolled newspaper.

With these handmade models, point out that triangles are used in many bridges, in the long booms of construction cranes, and in the structural parts of buildings. Discuss why this may be so.

Shapes and Properties for Level-1 Thinkers

As students move to level-1 thinking, the attention turns more to properties of shapes. During this period, students learn the proper names for shapes and their properties.

For the sake of clarity, the important definitions of two- and three-dimensional shapes are provided here. You will notice that shape definitions include relationships between shapes.

Special Categories of Two-Dimensional Shapes.   Table 20.1 lists some important categories of two-dimensional shapes. Examples of these shapes can be found in Figure 20.11.

TABLE 20.1

CATEGORIES OF TWO-DIMENSIONAL SHAPES	
Shape	**Description**
Simple Closed Curves	
Concave, convex	An intuitive definition of concave might be "having a dent in it." If a simple closed curve is not concave, it is convex. A more precise definition of concave may be interesting to explore with older students.
Symmetrical, nonsymmetrical	Shapes may have one or more lines of symmetry and may or may not have rotational symmetry. These concepts will require more detailed investigation.

Polygons
  Concave, convex
  Symmetrical, nonsymmetrical
	Simple closed curves with all straight sides.

Regular	All sides and all angles are congruent.
Triangles	
Triangles	Polygons with exactly three sides.
Classified by sides	
Equilateral	All sides are congruent.
Isosceles	At least two sides are congruent.
Scalene	No two sides are congruent.
Classified by angles	
Right	Has a right angle.
Acute	All angles are smaller than a right angle.
Obtuse	One angle is larger than a right angle.
Convex Quadrilaterals	
Convex quadrilaterals	Convex polygons with exactly four sides.
Kite	Two opposing pairs of congruent adjacent sides.
Trapezoid	At least one pair of parallel sides.
Isosceles	A pair of opposite sides is congruent.
Parallelogram	Two pairs of parallel sides.
Rectangle	Parallelogram with a right angle.
Rhombus	Parallelogram with all sides congruent.
Square	Parallelogram with a right angle and all sides congruent.

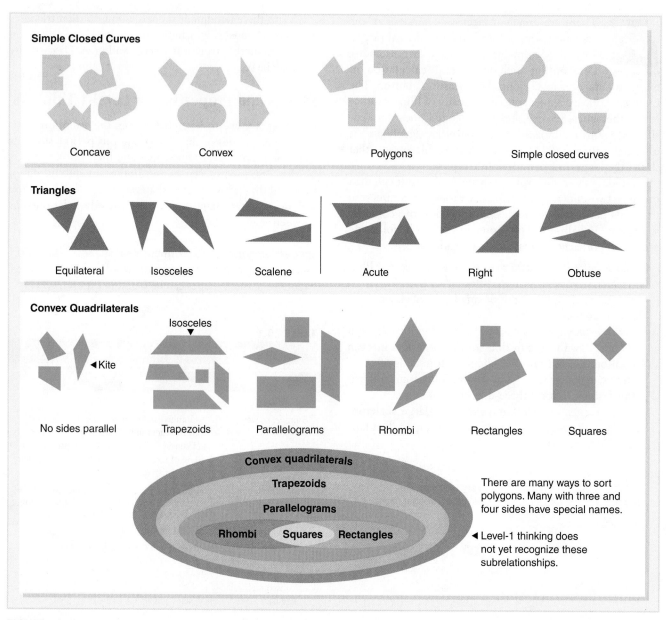

FIGURE 20.11 Classification of two-dimensional shapes.

In the classification of quadrilaterals and parallelograms, some subsets overlap. For example, a square is a rectangle and a rhombus. All parallelograms are trapezoids, but not all trapezoids are parallelograms.* Students at level 1 commonly have difficulty seeing this type of subrelationship. They may quite correctly list all the properties of a square, a rhombus, and a rectangle and still might classify a square as a "nonrhombus" or a "nonrectangle." By fourth or fifth grade, encourage students to be more

precise in their classifications. Burger (1985) points out that upper elementary students correctly use such classification schemes in other contexts. For example, individual students in a class can belong to more than one club. A square is an example of a quadrilateral that belongs to two other clubs.

Special Categories of Three-Dimensional Shapes. Important and interesting shapes and relationships also exist in three dimensions. Table 20.2 describes classifications of solids. Figure 20.12 shows examples of cylinders and prisms. Note that prisms are defined here as a special category of cylinder—a cylinder with a polygon for a base. Figure 20.13 (p. 414) shows a similar grouping of cones and pyramids.

*Some definitions of trapezoid specify *only one* pair of parallel sides, in which case parallelograms would not be trapezoids. The University of Chicago School Mathematics Project (UCSMP) uses the "at least one pair" definition, meaning that parallelograms and rectangles are trapezoids.

TABLE 20.2

CATEGORIES OF THREE-DIMENSIONAL SHAPES	
Shape	**Description**

Sorted by Edges and Vertices

Spheres and "egglike" shapes	Shapes with no *edges* and no *vertices* (corners). Shapes with *edges* but no *vertices* (e.g., a flying saucer). Shapes with *vertices* but no *edges* (e.g., a football).

Sorted by Faces and Surfaces

Polyhedron	Shapes made of all faces (a face is a flat surface of a solid). If all surfaces are faces, all the edges will be straight lines. Some combination of faces and rounded surfaces (circular cylinders are examples, but this is not a definition of a cylinder). Shapes with all curved surfaces. Shapes with and without edges and with and without vertices. Faces can be parallel. Parallel faces lie in planes that never intersect.

Cylinders

Cylinder	Two congruent, parallel faces called *bases*. Lines joining corresponding points on the two bases are always parallel. These parallel lines are called *elements* of the cylinder.
Right cylinder	A cylinder with elements perpendicular to the bases. A cylinder that is not a right cylinder is an oblique cylinder.
Prism	A cylinder with polygons for bases. All prisms are special cases of cylinders.
Rectangular prism	A cylinder with rectangles for bases.
Cube	A square prism with square sides.

Cones

Cone	A solid with exactly one face and a vertex that is not on the face. Straight lines (elements) can be drawn from any point on the edge of the base to the vertex. The base may be any shape at all. The vertex need not be directly over the base.
Circular cone	Cone with a circular base.
Pyramid	Cone with a polygon for a base. All faces joining the vertex are triangles. Pyramids are named by the shape of the base: *triangular* pyramid, *square* pyramid, *octagonal* pyramid, and so on. All pyramids are special cases of cones.

Many textbooks limit the definition of cylinders to just circular cylinders. These books do not have special names for other cylinders. Under that definition, the prism is not a special case of a cylinder. This points to the fact that definitions are conventions, and not all conventions are universally agreed on. If you return to the volume formulas in Chapter 19, you will see that the more inclusive definition of cylinders and cones allows one formula for any type of cylinder—hence, prisms—with a similar statement that is true for cones and pyramids.

Sorting and Classifying Activities. At level 1, classifying and sorting focus more deeply on the properties that make the shape what it is (not just that it looks like the others in its group).

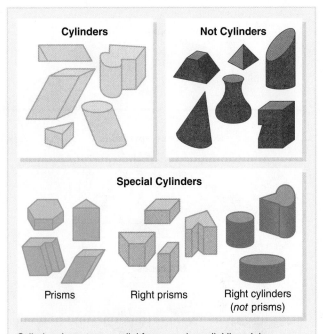

Cylinders have two parallel faces, and parallel lines join corresponding points on these faces. If the parallel faces are polygons, the cylinder can be called a prism.

FIGURE 20.12 Cylinders and prisms.

Activity **20.7**

Mystery Definition

Use a projection device to conduct logic activities such as the example in Figure 20.14 (p. 414). For your first collection, be certain that you have allowed for all possible variables. In Figure 20.14, for example, a square is included in the set of rhombi. Similarly, choose non-examples to be as close to the positive examples as is necessary to help with an accurate definition. The third or mixed set should also include those non-examples with which students are most likely to be confused. Students should justify their choices. Note that the use of non-examples is particularly important for students with disabilities.

STUDENTS *with* SPECIAL NEEDS

The value of the "Mystery Definition" approach is that students develop ideas and definitions based on their own concept development. After their definitions have been discussed and compared, you can offer the traditional definition for the sake of clarity.

For defining types or categories of triangles, the next activity is especially good and uses a different approach.

Activity **20.8**

Triangle Sort

Make copies of the Assorted Triangles sheet (see Blackline Master 58). Note the examples of right,

ENGLISH LANGUAGE LEARNERS

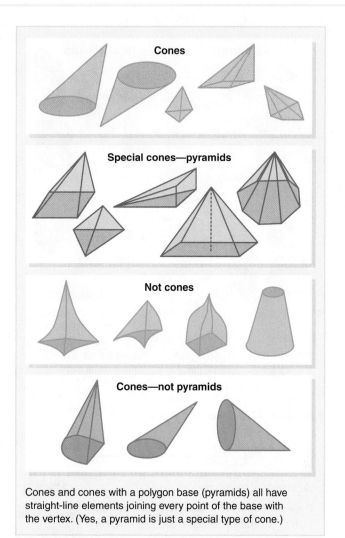

Cones and cones with a polygon base (pyramids) all have straight-line elements joining every point of the base with the vertex. (Yes, a pyramid is just a special type of cone.)

FIGURE 20.13 Cones and pyramids.

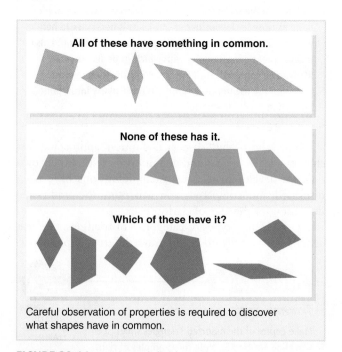

Careful observation of properties is required to discover what shapes have in common.

FIGURE 20.14 A mystery definition.

acute, and obtuse triangles; examples of equilateral, isosceles, and scalene triangles; and triangles that represent every possible combination of these categories. Have students cut them out. The task is to sort the entire collection into three discrete groups so that no triangle belongs to two groups. When this is done and descriptions of the groupings have been written, students should then find a second criterion for creating three different groupings. Students who struggle may need a hint to look only at angle sizes or only at the issue of congruent sides, but delay giving these hints if you can. Once the groups have been determined, provide appropriate terminology. For ELLs and other students who struggle, focusing on the specialized meaning of these terms is important (e.g., contrasting "acute pain" and "acute angle"), as well as root words (*equi-* meaning *equal* and *-lateral* meaning *side*). As a follow-up activity, challenge students to sketch a triangle in each of the nine cells of the chart.

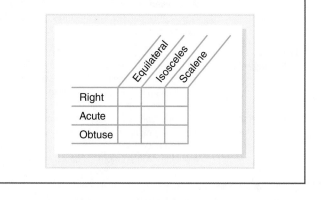

PAUSE and REFLECT

Of the nine cells in the chart, two of them are impossible to fill. Can you tell which ones and why? ●

Quadrilaterals (polygons with four sides) are a rich source of investigations. Once students are familiar with the concepts of right, obtuse, and acute angles, congruence of line segments and angles, and symmetry (both line and rotational), Activity 20.2, "Property Lists for Quadrilaterals," on page 405 is a good way to bring these ideas together and begin to see how different collections of properties apply to special classes of shapes.

The class must agree with everything that is put on the list. As new relationships come up in this presentation-and-discussion period, introduce proper terminology. For example, if two diagonals intersect in a square corner, then they are perpendicular. Other terms such as *parallel, congruent, bisect, midpoint,* and so on can be clarified as you help students write their descriptions. This is also a good time to introduce symbols such as ≅ for "congruent" or ∥ for "parallel."

Construction Activities. Students' building or drawing shapes continues to be important at level 1.

In the next activity, students examine the diagonals of various classes of quadrilaterals.

Activity 20.9

Diagonal Strips

For this activity, students need three strips of card stock about 2 cm wide. Two should be the same length (about 30 cm) and the third somewhat shorter (about 20 cm). Punch nine holes equally spaced along the strip. Use a brass fastener to join two strips. A quadrilateral is formed by joining the four end holes as shown in Figure 20.15. Provide students with the list of possible relationships for angles, lengths, and ratios of parts. Their task is to use the strips to determine the properties of diagonals that will produce different quadrilaterals. Students may want to make drawings on dot grids to test the various hypotheses.

Every type of quadrilateral can be uniquely described in terms of its diagonals using only the conditions of length, ratio of parts, and whether they are perpendicular.

Circles.   Many interesting relationships can be observed among measures of different parts of the circle. One of the most astounding and important is the ratio between measures of the circumference and the diameter.

Activity 20.10

Discovering Pi

Have groups of students carefully measure both the circumference and diameter of circular items such as jar lids, cans, and wastebaskets. To measure circumference, wrap string once around the object and then measure that length of string. Also measure the circumference of large circles marked on gym floors and playgrounds with a trundle wheel or rope.

Collect measures of circumference and diameter from all groups and enter them in a table. Ratios of the circumference to the diameter should also be computed for each circle. A scatter plot of the data should be made with the horizontal axis representing diameters and the vertical axis circumferences.

Most ratios should about 3.1 or 3.2. The scatter plot should approximate a straight line through the origin with the slope of the line close to 3.1. (Recall from Chapter 18 that graphs of equivalent ratios are always straight lines through the origin.) The exact ratio is an irrational number, about 3.14159, represented by the Greek letter π (pi).

What is most important in Activity 20.10 is that students develop a clear understanding of π as the ratio of circumference to diameter in any circle regardless of size. The quantity π is not some mystical number that appears in mathematics formulas; it is a naturally occurring and universal ratio.

Dynamic Geometry Software.   Activity 20.9 can be explored using dynamic geometry software. In these programs, points,

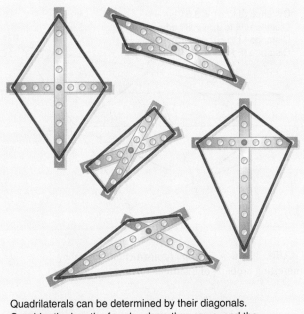

Quadrilaterals can be determined by their diagonals. Consider the length of each, where they cross, and the angles between them. What conditions will produce parallelograms? Rectangles? Rhombi? Challenge: What properties will produce a nonisosceles trapezoid?

FIGURE 20.15 Diagonals of quadrilaterals.

lines, and geometric figures are easily constructed on the computer using only a mouse or a stylus. Once drawn, the geometric objects can be moved about and manipulated in an endless variety. As figures are changed, the measurements of distances, lengths, areas, angles, slopes, and perimeters update instantly!

Additionally, lines can be drawn perpendicular or parallel to other lines or segments. Angles and segments can be drawn congruent to other angles and segments. A point can be placed at the midpoint of a segment. A figure can be produced that is a reflection, rotation, or dilation of another figure. The most significant idea is that when a geometric object is created with a particular relationship to another, that relationship is maintained no matter how either object is moved or changed.

The best known dynamic geometry programs are *The Geometer's Sketchpad* (Key Curriculum Press), *Geo-Gebra* (open source at www.geogebra.org/cms), and *Cabri Geometry II* (Texas Instruments). Originally designed for high school students, all can be used starting about grade 4.

Dynamic Geometry Activities.   To appreciate the potential (and the fun) of dynamic geometry software, you need to experience it. In Figure 20.16, the midpoints of a freely drawn quadrilateral ABCD have been joined. The diagonals of the resulting quadrilateral (EFGH) are also drawn and measured. No matter how the points A, B, C, and D are dragged around the screen, even inverting the quadrilateral,

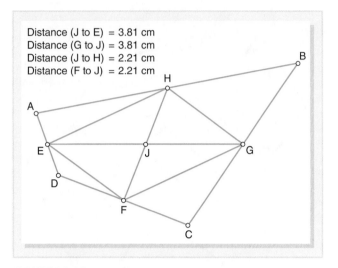

Distance (J to E) = 3.81 cm
Distance (G to J) = 3.81 cm
Distance (J to H) = 2.21 cm
Distance (F to J) = 2.21 cm

FIGURE 20.16 A *Sketchpad* construction illustrating an interesting property of quadrilaterals.

the other lines will maintain the same relationships (joining midpoints and diagonals), and the measurements will be instantly updated.

Remember that at level 1, the objects of thought are classes of shapes. In a dynamic geometry program, if a quadrilateral is drawn, only one shape is observed, as would be the case on paper or on a geoboard. But now that quadrilateral can be stretched and altered in endless ways, so students actually explore not one shape but an enormous number of examples from that class of shapes. If a property or constructed relationship does not change when the figure changes, the property is attributable to the class of shapes rather than any particular shape.

Shapes and Properties for Level-2 Thinkers

At level 2, the focus shifts from simply examining properties of shapes to explorations that include logical reasoning. As students develop an understanding of various geometric properties and attach these properties to categories of shapes, it is essential to encourage conjecture and to explore informal deductive arguments. Students should begin to attempt—or at least follow—simple proofs and explore ideas that connect directly to algebra.

Definitions and Proofs. The previously described activities of "Property Lists for Quadrilaterals" (Activity 20.2), which is a level-1 activity, and "Minimal Defining Lists" (Activity 20.3), a level-2 activity, clarify the distinction between these two levels. The parallelogram, rhombus, rectangle, and square each have at least four MDLs. One of the most interesting MDLs for each shape consists only of the properties of its diagonals. For example, a quadrilateral

with diagonals that bisect each other and are perpendicular (intersect at right angles) is a rhombus.

Notice that the MDL activity is actually more involved with logical thinking than with examining shapes. Students are engaged in the general process of deciding, "If we specify only this list of properties, will that guarantee this particular shape?" A second feature is the opportunity to discuss what constitutes a definition. In fact, any MDL could be the definition of the shape. We usually choose MDLs based on the ease with which we can understand them. A quadrilateral with diagonals that bisect each other does not immediately call to mind a parallelogram, even though that is a defining property.

PAUSE and REFLECT

Use the property list for squares and rectangles to prove "All squares are rectangles." Notice that you must use logical reasoning to understand this statement. It does little good to simply force definitions on students who are not ready to develop the relationship. ●

The next activity is also a good follow-up to Activities 20.2 and 20.3, although it is not restricted to quadrilaterals and can include three-dimensional shapes as well. Notice again the logical reasoning involved.

Activity 20.11

True or False?

Prepare a set of true/false statements of the following forms: "If it is a _____, then it is also a _____." "All _____ are _____." "Some _____ are _____."

A few examples are suggested here, but numerous possibilities exist.

- If it is a square, then it is a rhombus.
- All squares are rectangles.
- Some parallelograms are rectangles.
- All parallelograms have congruent diagonals.
- If it has exactly two lines of symmetry, it must be a quadrilateral.
- If it is a cylinder, then it is a prism.
- All prisms have a plane of symmetry.
- All pyramids have square bases.
- If a prism has a plane of symmetry, then it is a right prism.

Students determine whether the statements are true or false and present an argument to support the decision (see Figure 20.17). Four or five true/false statements will make a good lesson. Once this format is understood, let students challenge their classmates by making their own lists of statements. Each list should have a mix of true and false statements. See an article by Renne (2004) for additional ideas. Students' lists can then be used in subsequent lessons.

1. If it is a square, then it is a rhombus.

TRUE.. A square can be a rhombus Beacuse they are both paralleliograms and all the sides are the exact. ALSO if you rotate a square than it becums a rhombus.

2. If it is a pyramid, then it must have a square base.

FALSE... TO be a pyramid it does not have to have square base. I think this beacuse thair can be tryangular pyramids.

Net ·· ∆

FIGURE 20.17 True or false? A fifth-grade student presents an argument to support her decision.

FORMATIVE Assessment Notes

The "True or False?" activity is also a good **diagnostic assessment**. Note how the student's response shown in Figure 20.17 gives insights into her fully formed ideas and representations. She also reveals her emerging conceptions as she attempts to make arguments for her answers of true or false. ■

The following activity was designed by Sconyers (1995) to demonstrate that students can create proofs in geometry well before high school.

Activity 20.12

Two Polygons from One

Pose the following problem:

Begin with a convex polygon with a given number of sides. Connect two points on the polygon with a line segment, forming two new polygons. How many sides do the two resulting polygons have together?

Demonstrate with a few examples (see Figure 20.18). Have students explore by drawing polygons and slicing them. Encourage students to make a table showing sides in the original and resulting sides. Students should first make conjectures about a general rule. When groups are comfortable with their conjecture, they should try to reason why their statement is correct—that is, prove their conjecture.

The number of resulting sides depends on where the slice is made (from a vertex or from a side). With the exception of triangles, there are three possibilities. For each case, a pattern emerges. The problem is left for you to figure out, but trust that students can do this task.

Notice that in this task, as in others we have explored, the statements to be proved come from students. If you write a theorem on the board and ask students to prove it, you have

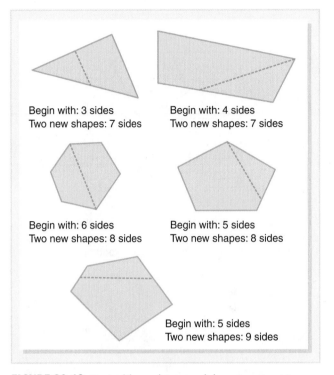

Begin with: 3 sides / Two new shapes: 7 sides

Begin with: 4 sides / Two new shapes: 7 sides

Begin with: 6 sides / Two new shapes: 8 sides

Begin with: 5 sides / Two new shapes: 8 sides

Begin with: 5 sides / Two new shapes: 9 sides

FIGURE 20.18 Start with a polygon, and draw a segment to divide it into two polygons. How many sides will the two new polygons have?

already told them that it is true. If, by contrast, a student makes a statement about a geometric situation the class is exploring, it can be written on the board with a question mark as a conjecture, a statement whose truth has not yet been determined. You can ask, "Is it true? Always? Can we prove it? Can we find a counterexample?" Reasonable deductive arguments can be forged out of discussions (Martin, 2009).

The Pythagorean Relationship. The *Pythagorean relationship* is so important that it deserves special attention. In geometric terms, this relationship states that if a square is constructed on each side of a right triangle, the areas of the two smaller squares will together equal the area of the square on the longest side, the hypotenuse.

Activity 20.13

The Pythagorean Relationship

Have students draw a right triangle on half-centimeter grid paper (see Blackline Master 36). Assign each student a different triangle by specifying the lengths of the two legs. Students are to draw a square on each leg and the hypotenuse and find the areas of all three squares. (For the square on the hypotenuse, the exact area can be found by making each of the sides the diagonal of a rectangle. See Figure 20.19.) Make a table of the area data (Sq. on leg 1, Sq. on leg 2, Sq. on hyp.), and ask students to look for a relationship between the squares.

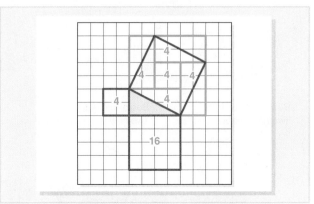

FIGURE 20.19 The Pythagorean relationship. Note that if drawn on a grid, the area of all squares is easily determined. Here 4 + 16 = area of the square on the hypotenuse.

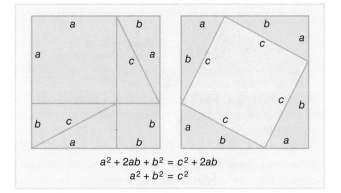

$$a^2 + 2ab + b^2 = c^2 + 2ab$$
$$a^2 + b^2 = c^2$$

FIGURE 20.20 The two squares together are a "proof without words." Can you supply the words?

What about proof? Both large congruent squares in Figure 20.20 together show a nonverbal proof of the Pythagorean theorem (Nelson, 2001). Note that both squares contain four triangles that are the same but arranged differently. By adding up the areas of the squares and the triangles and setting them equal, the Pythagorean relationship can be found by subtracting out the common areas in both squares. An algebraic recording of the thinking process is shown below the drawings.

 PAUSE and REFLECT

Use the two drawings in Figure 20.20 to create a proof of the Pythagorean relationship. ●

The NCTM e-Examples (Applet 6.5) is a dynamic proof without words that is worth sharing with your students.

Finding Versus Explaining Relationships. At level 2, the focus is on reasoning or deductive thinking. Can dynamic geometry software programs help students develop

deductive arguments to support the relationships they come to believe through inductive reasoning? Consider the following situation.

Suppose that you have students use a dynamic geometry program to draw a triangle, measure all of the angles, and add them up. As the triangle vertices are dragged around, the sum of the angles would remain steadfast at 180 degrees. Students can conjecture that the sum of the interior angles of a triangle is always 180 degrees, and they would be completely convinced of the truth of this conjecture based on this inductive experience. (Several noncomputer activities lead to the same conclusion.) However, the experience just described fails to explain why it is so. Consider the following activity to support the conjecturing that will lead to more formal proofs.

Activity **20.14**

Angle Sum in a Triangle

Have all students cut out three congruent triangles. (Stack three sheets of paper, and cut three shapes at one time.) Place one triangle on a line and the second directly next to it in the same orientation. Place the third triangle in the space between the triangles as shown in Figure 20.21(a). Based on this experience, what conjecture can you make about the sum of the angles in a triangle?

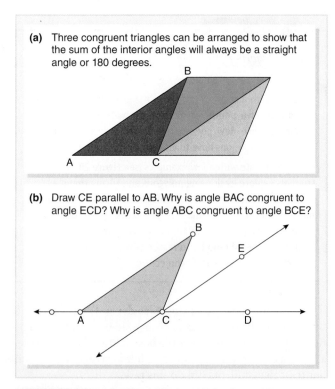

(a) Three congruent triangles can be arranged to show that the sum of the interior angles will always be a straight angle or 180 degrees.

(b) Draw CE parallel to AB. Why is angle BAC congruent to angle ECD? Why is angle ABC congruent to angle BCE?

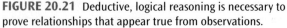

FIGURE 20.21 Deductive, logical reasoning is necessary to prove relationships that appear true from observations.

In a dynamic geometry program, the three triangles in Figure 20.21(a) can be drawn by starting with one triangle, translating it to the right the length of AC, and then rotating the same triangle about the midpoint of side BC. When vertices of the original triangle are dragged, the other triangles will change accordingly and remain congruent. Although this exploration demonstrates to students that the angle sum is always a straight angle, it does not show them why. In the figure, there are lines parallel to each side of the original triangle. By using properties of angles formed by cutting parallel lines with a transverse line, it is easy to argue that the sum of the angles will always be a straight line. See Figure 20.21(b); the proof is left to you.

At level 2, to help students move from observation of geometric relationships to making and testing conjectures that explore why these relationships hold, helping students observe geometric relationships and make conjectures is critical. The following activity further illustrates the point.

Activity 20.15

Triangle Midsegments

Using a dynamic geometry program, draw a triangle, and label the vertices A, B, and C. Draw the segment joining the midpoints of AB and AC, and label this segment DE, as in Figure 20.22. Measure the lengths of DE and BC. Also measure angles ADE and ABC. Drag points A, B, and C. What conjectures can you make about the relationships between segment DE (the *midsegment* of triangle ABC) and BC (the base of ABC)?

The midsegment is half the length of the base and parallel to it, but why is this so? If needed, provide some guidance. Suggest that they draw a line through A parallel to BC. List all pairs of angles that they know are congruent. Why are they congruent? Note that triangle ABC is similar to triangle ADE. Why is it similar? With hints such as these,

many students can begin to make logical arguments for why the things they observe to be true are in fact true.

Learning about Transformations

Transformations are changes in position or size of a shape. Movements that do not change the size or shape of the object moved are called "rigid motions." Usually, three rigid-motion transformations are discussed: *translations* or slides, *reflections* or flips, and *rotations* or turns. Interestingly, the study of symmetry is also included under the study of transformations. Do you know why?

Transformations for Level-0 Thinkers

Transformations at this level involve an introduction to the basic concepts of slides, flips, and turns and the initial development of line symmetry and rotational symmetry.

Slides, Flips, and Turns. At the primary level, the terms *slide, flip,* and *turn* are adequate. The early goal is to help students recognize these transformations and to begin to explore their effects on simple shapes. You can use a nonsymmetric shape to introduce these terms (see Figure 20.23). Most likely your textbook will use only the center of a shape as the point of rotation and restrict reflections to vertical and horizontal lines through the center. These restrictions are not necessary and may even be misleading.

The Motion Man activity described next can also be used to introduce students to the terms *slide, flip,* and *turn*. In the activity, rotations are restricted to $\frac{1}{4}$, $\frac{1}{2}$, and $\frac{3}{4}$ turns in a clockwise direction. The center of the turn will be the center of the figure. Reflections will be flips over vertical or horizontal lines. These restrictions are for simplicity. In the

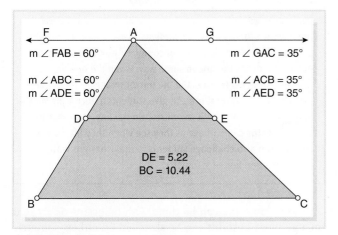

FIGURE 20.22 The midsegment of a triangle is always parallel to the base and half as long.

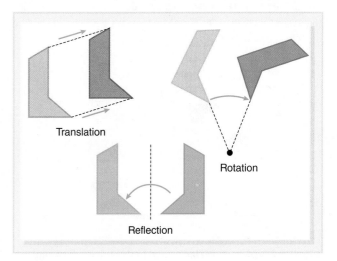

FIGURE 20.23 Translation (slide), reflection (flip), rotation (turn).

general case, the center of rotation can be anywhere on or off the figure. Lines of reflection can also be anywhere.

Activity 20.16

ENGLISH LANGUAGE LEARNERS

Motion Man

Using Blackline Masters 52–53, make copies of the first Motion Man, and then copy the mirror image on the backs of these copies. (See Figure 20.24.) You want the back image to match the front image when held to the light. Give all students a two-sided Motion Man.

Demonstrate each of the possible motions. A slide is simply that. The figure does not rotate or turn over. Demonstrate turns. Emphasize that only clockwise turns will be used for this activity. Similarly, demonstrate a horizontal flip (top goes to bottom) and a vertical flip (left goes to right). For all students, ELLs in particular, it is important that these demonstrations include explicit practice with the terms and that visuals are posted for reference. Practice by having everyone start with his or her Motion Man in the same orientation. As you announce one of the moves, students slide, flip, or turn Motion Man accordingly.

Then display two Motion Men side by side in any orientation. The task is to decide what motion or combination of motions will get the man on the left to match the man on the right. Students use their own man to work out a solution. Test the solutions that students offer. If both men are in the same position, call that a slide.

 ### PAUSE and REFLECT

Begin with the Motion Man in the left position shown in Figure 20.24. Now place a second Motion Man next to the first. Will it take one move or more than one move (transformation) to get from the first to the second Motion Man? Can you describe all of the positions that require more than one move? Are there any positions that require more than two moves? ●

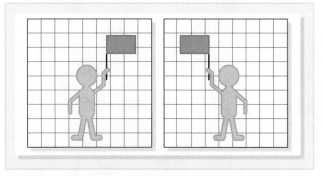

FIGURE 20.24 Motion Man is used to show slides, flips, and turns (see Blackline Masters 52 and 53).

At first, students will be confused when they can't get their Motion Man into the new position with one move. This causes an excellent problem. Don't be too quick to suggest that it may take two moves. If flips across each of the two diagonals are added to the motions along with vertical and horizontal flips, Motion Man can assume any new position in exactly one move. Then have two students begin with their Motion Man figures in the same position. One student then changes his or her Motion Man and challenges the other student to say what motion is required to make the two Motion Men match. The solution is then tested and the roles reversed.

Line and Rotational Symmetry. If a shape can be folded on a line so that the two halves match, then it is said to have *line symmetry* (or mirror symmetry). Notice that the fold line is actually a line of reflection—the portion of the shape on one side of the line is reflected onto the other side, demonstrating a connection between line symmetry and transformations (flip).

One way to introduce line symmetry to students is to show examples and non-examples using an "all-of-these" or "none-of-these" approach as in Figure 20.14 on page 414. Another possibility is to have students fold a sheet of paper in half and cut out a shape of their choosing. When they open the paper, the fold line will be a line of symmetry. A third way is to use mirrors or Miras. (The Mira is a red, plastic image reflector used to explore concepts of symmetry and congruence.) When you place a mirror on a picture or design so that the mirror is perpendicular to the table, you see a shape with symmetry when you look in the mirror. See http://illuminations.nctm.org/ActivityDetail .aspx?ID=24 for a wonderful symmetry activity with a virtual mirror.

Activity 20.17

Pattern Block Mirror Symmetry

Students need a plain sheet of paper with a straight vertical line through the middle. Ask students to use about six to eight pattern blocks to make a design completely on one side of the line that touches the line in some way. When the one side is finished, students try to make the mirror image on the other side of the line. After it is built, give students a mirror (or Mira) to check their work. With the mirror on the line, they should see exactly the same image as they see when they lift the mirror. You can also challenge students to make designs with more than one line of symmetry.

The same task can be done with tangrams or created on a geoboard. And it can be sketched on either isometric or square dot grids (Blackline Masters 34 and 38) as shown in Figure 20.25 or with dynamic geometry software.

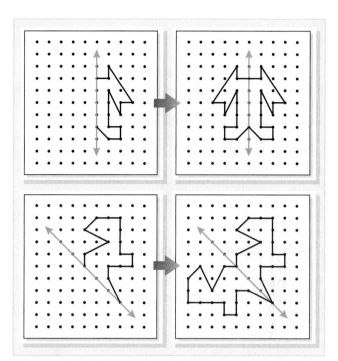

FIGURE 20.25 Exploring symmetry on dot grids (Blackline Masters 37 and 39).

A shape has rotational symmetry (also referred to as *point symmetry*) if it can be rotated about a point and land in a position exactly matching the one in which it began. A square has rotational symmetry, as does an equilateral triangle.

A good way to understand rotational symmetry is to take a shape with rotational symmetry, such as a square, and trace around it on a piece of paper. Call this tracing the shape's "footprint." The order of rotational symmetry will be the number of ways that the shape can fit into its footprint without flipping it over. The parallelogram in Figure 20.26 has rotational symmetry of order 2, also known as *180-degree rotational symmetry*. The degrees refer to the smallest angle of rotation required before the shape matches itself or fits into its footprint. A square has rotational symmetry of order 4 (or *90-degree rotational symmetry*), whereas an equilateral triangle has rotational symmetry of order 3.

FIGURE 20.26 This parallelogram fits in its footprint two ways without flipping it over. Therefore, it has rotational symmetry of order 2.

Activity 20.18

Pattern Block Rotational Symmetry

Have students construct designs with pattern blocks having different rotational symmetries. They should be able to make designs with order 2, 3, 4, 6, or 12 rotational symmetry. Which of the designs have mirror symmetry as well?

Transformations for Level-1 Thinkers

Within the context of transformations, students moving into level-1 thinking can begin to analyze transformations a bit more analytically and to apply them to shapes that they see. Two types of activities are appropriate at this level: compositions of transformations and using transformations to create tessellations.

Composition of Transformations. One transformation can be followed by another. For example, a figure can be reflected over a line, and then that figure can be rotated about a point. A combination of two or more transformations is called a *composition*.

Have students experiment with compositions of two or even three transformations using a simple shape on a rectangular dot grid. For example, have students draw an L shape on a dot grid and label it L_1 (refer to Figure 20.27). Reflect it through a line, and then rotate the image $\frac{1}{4}$ turn clockwise about a point not on the shape. Call this image L_2, the image of a composition of a reflection followed by a

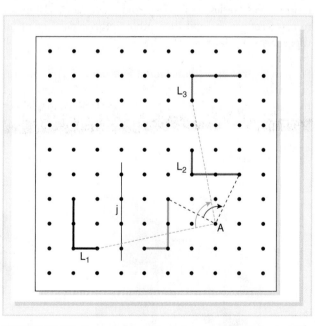

FIGURE 20.27 Shape L_1 was reflected across line j and rotated $\frac{1}{4}$ turn about point A, resulting in L_2. L_1 was also rotated $\frac{1}{4}$ turn about point A, resulting in L_3. How are L_2 and L_3 related? Will this always work?

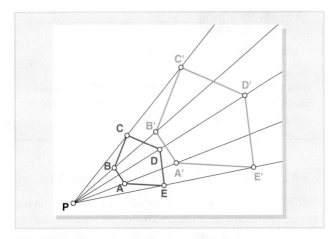

FIGURE 20.28 Begin with figure ABCDE and place point P anywhere. Draw lines from P through each vertex. Place point A' twice as far from P as A is from P (scale factor of 2). Do similarly for the other points. ABCDE is similar to A'B'C'D'E'.

rotation. Notice that if L_1 is rotated $\frac{1}{4}$ turn clockwise about the same point used before (the result of which we will call L_3), there is a relationship between L_2 and L_3. Continue to explore different combinations of transformations. Don't forget to include translations (slides) in the compositions.

TECHNOLOGY Compositions do not have to involve different types of transformations. For example, a reflection can be followed by another reflection. NCTM's e-Example, "Understanding Congruence, Similarity, and Symmetry" (Applet 6.4), at www.nctm.org/standards/content.aspx?id=26885 is one of the best applets to support students' understanding of all three rigid motions. In the last two parts, students explore compositions of reflections and then other compositions of up to three transformations.

Similar Figures and Proportional Reasoning. Two figures are *similar* if all of their corresponding angles are congruent and the corresponding sides are proportional. As noted in Chapter 18, proportional reasoning activities are good connections to geometry, such as Activity 18.7, which involves scale drawings and proportional relationships in similar figures.

A dilation is a nonrigid (can change size) transformation that produces similar two-dimensional figures. Figure 20.28 shows how a given figure can be dilated to make larger or smaller figures. If different groups of students dilate the same figure using the same scale factor, they will find that the resulting figures are all congruent, even with each group using different dilation points. Dynamic geometry software makes the results of this exercise quite dramatic. The software allows for the scale factors to be set at any value. Once a dilation is made, the dilation point can be dragged around the screen and the size and shape of the image clearly stay unchanged. Scale factors less than 1 produce smaller figures.

Tessellations. A *tessellation* is a tiling of the plane using one or more shapes in a repeated pattern with no gaps or overlaps (see Figure 20.29). A *regular tessellation* is made of a single tile that is a regular polygon (all sides and angles congruent). Each vertex of a regular tessellation has the same number of tiles meeting at that point. A checkerboard is a simple example of a regular tessellation. A *semiregular tessellation* is made of two or more tiles, each of which is a regular polygon. At each vertex of a semiregular tessellation, the same collection of regular polygons comes together in the same order. A vertex (and, therefore, the complete semiregular tessellation) can be described by the series of shapes meeting at a vertex. Students can figure out which polygons are possible at a vertex and design their own semiregular tessellations. Either by using transformations or by combining compatible polygons, students can create tessellations that are artistic and quite complex.

The Dutch artist M. C. Escher is well known for his tessellations, where the tiles are very intricate and often take the shape of things like birds, horses, or lizards. Escher took a simple shape such as a triangle, parallelogram, or hexagon and performed transformations on the sides. For example,

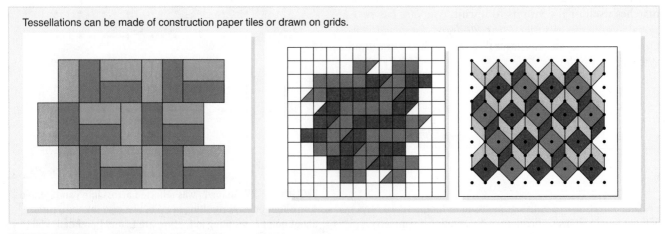

Tessellations can be made of construction paper tiles or drawn on grids.

FIGURE 20.29 Tessellations (see Blackline Masters 34–40).

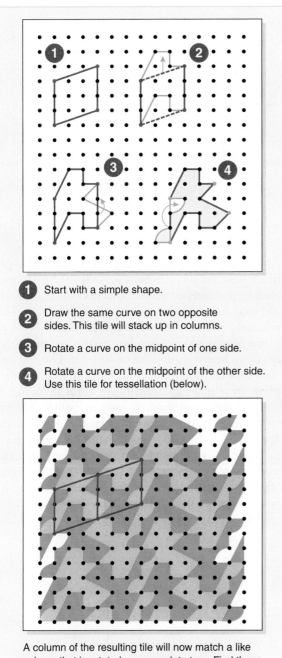

1. Start with a simple shape.

2. Draw the same curve on two opposite sides. This tile will stack up in columns.

3. Rotate a curve on the midpoint of one side.

4. Rotate a curve on the midpoint of the other side. Use this tile for tessellation (below).

A column of the resulting tile will now match a like column that is rotated one complete turn. Find these rotated columns in the tessellation shown here.

FIGURE 20.30 Creating an Escher-type tessellation (see Blackline Master 37).

a curve drawn along one side might be translated (slid) to the opposite side. Another idea was to draw a curve from the midpoint of a side to the adjoining vertex. This curve was then rotated about the midpoint to form a totally new side of the tile. These two ideas are illustrated in Figure 20.30. Dot paper is used to help draw the lines. Escher-type tessellations, as these have come to be called, are important applications of transformations for students in grades 5 and

up. Once a tile has been designed, it can be cut from two different colors of construction paper instead of drawing the tessellation on a dot grid.

Transformations for Level-2 Thinkers

The following activity is a challenge for students to use their understanding of symmetries and transformations to establish an interesting relationship between these two ideas. The shapes used for this activity are called *pentominoes*—shapes made from 5 squares, each square touching at least one other square by sharing a full side. A well-known geometry activity is to have students search to see how many different pentominoes they can find (see Activity 20.26). For our purposes in discussing transformations and symmetries, the collection of 12 pentominoes simply serves as a convenient collection of shapes, as in the following activity.

Activity 20.19

Pentomino Positions

Have students cut out a set of 12 pentominoes from 2-cm grid paper (see Figure 20.31). Mark one side of each piece to help remember whether it has been flipped over. The first part of the task is to determine how many different positions on the grid each piece has (Walter, 1970). Call positions "different" if a reflection or a turn is required to make them match. Therefore, the cross-shaped piece has only one position. The strip of five squares has two positions. Some pieces have as many as eight positions—can you find them? The second part of the task is to find a relationship between the line symmetries and rotational symmetries for each piece and the number of positions it can have on the grid. Students may need to make a table of what they know.

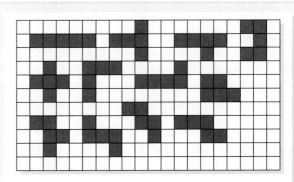

There are 12 pentominoes.

Finding all possible shapes made with five squares—or six squares (called "hexominoes") or six equilateral triangles and so on—is a good exercise in spatial problem solving.

FIGURE 20.31 There are 12 different pentomino shapes. An exploration to find these shapes is Activity 20.26.

Learning about Location

The CCSSO standard in grade 5 states that students should "Graph points on the coordinate plane to solve real-world and mathematical problems" (2010, p. 34). After early development of terms for how objects are located with respect to other objects (e.g., "the ball is under the table"), location activities involve analysis of paths from point to point as on a map and the use of coordinate systems.

In pre-K and kindergarten (CCSSO, 2010), students learn about everyday positional descriptions—*over*, *under*, *near*, *far*, *between*, *left*, and *right*. These "place learnings" (Sarama & Clements, 2009) are the beginnings of the goal of specifying locations. However, helping students refine the way they think and reason about direction, distance, and location enhances spatial understandings. Geometry, measurement, and algebra are all supported by the use of a grid system with numbers or coordinates attached that can specify location. Students at the primary level can begin to think in terms of a grid system to identify location. As students become more sophisticated thinkers, their use of coordinates progresses.

The next activity can serve as a readiness task for coordinates and help students see the value of having a way to specify location without pointing.

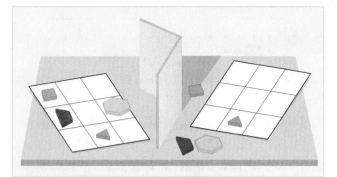

FIGURE 20.32 The "Hidden Positions" game.

The "Hidden Positions" game can be extended to grids up to 6×6. As the grid size increases, the need for a system of labeling positions increases. Students can begin to use a simple coordinate system as early as the first grade. Use a coordinate grid like the one shown in Figure 20.33 (see Blackline Master 48). Explain how to use two numbers to designate an intersection point on the grid. The first number tells how far to move to the right. The second number tells how far to move up. Initially use words along with the numbers: 3 right and 0 up. Be sure to include 0 in your introduction. Then select a point on the grid and have students decide what two numbers name that point. If your point is at (2,4) and students incorrectly say "four, two," then simply indicate where the point is that they named. Another way for students to visualize the difference is to compare students in the second row fourth seat to the fourth row second seat.

Activity 20.20

Hidden Positions

XXXX
**STUDENTS *with*
SPECIAL NEEDS**

For the game boards, draw an 8-inch square on card stock. Subdivide the squares into a 3×3 grid. Two students sit with a "screen" separating their desktop space so that neither student can see the other's grid (see Figure 20.32). Each student has four different pattern blocks. The first player places a block on four different sections of the grid. He then tells the other player where to put blocks on her grid to match his own. When all four pieces are positioned, the two grids are checked to see that they are alike. Then the players switch roles. Model the game once by taking the part of the first student. Use words such as *top row, middle, left*, and *right*. Students can play in pairs as a station activity. For students with disabilities, consider starting with just one shape. Then move to two and so on.

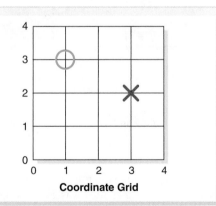

FIGURE 20.33 A simple coordinate grid. The X is at (3,2) and the O is at (1,3). Use the grid to play "Three in a Row" (like Tic-Tac-Toe). Put marks on intersections, not spaces (see Blackline Master 48).

The next activity explores the notion of different paths on a grid.

If you add a coordinate system on the grid in "Paths," students can describe their paths with coordinates: For example: $(1,2) \to (3,2) \to (3,5) \to (7,5) \to (7,7)$.

NCTM's e-Example (Applet 4.3) is similar to "Paths" but offers some additional challenges. Students move a ladybug by issuing directions. *TECHNOLOGY* The task is to make a list of directions to hide the ladybug beneath a leaf. When the directions are complete, the ladybug is set in motion to follow them. The ladybug is also used to draw shapes such as a rectangle in a tilted position or to travel through mazes.

Location for Level-1 Thinkers

At level 1, students examine transformations on a coordinate plane (a standard in grade 6 [CCSSO, 2010]). The activities here suggest how coordinates can be used to examine transformations.

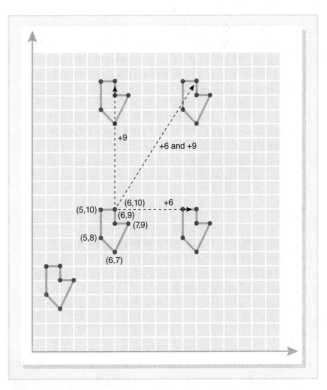

FIGURE 20.35 Begin with a simple shape and record the coordinates. By adding or subtracting from the coordinates, new shapes are found that are translations (slides) of the original.

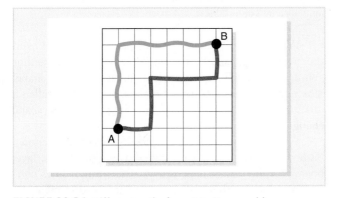

FIGURE 20.34 Different paths from A to B on a grid.

Ask students, "What does adding (or subtracting) a number from the first coordinates cause? What if the number is added or subtracted from the second coordinates? From both coordinates?" Have students draw lines connecting corresponding points in the original figure with one of those where both coordinates were changed. What do they notice? (The lines are parallel and the same length.)

In "Coordinate Slides," the figure did not twist, turn, flip over, or change size or shape. The shape "slid" along a path that matched the lines between the corresponding points. Reflections can be explored on a coordinate grid just as easily as translations. At this beginning level, it is advisable to restrict the lines of reflection to the x- or y-axis, as in the following activity.

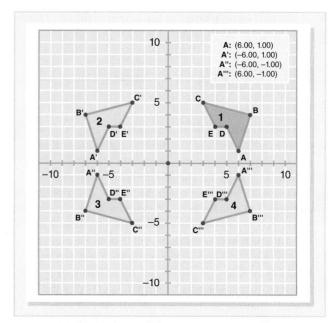

FIGURE 20.36 Exploring reflections on a coordinate grid.

Activity 20.23

Coordinate Reflections

Have students draw a five-sided shape in the first quadrant on coordinate grid paper. Label the Figure ABCDE, and call it Figure 1 (see Figure 20.36). Use the y-axis as a line of symmetry, and draw the reflection of the shape in the second quadrant. Call it Figure 2 (for second quadrant), and label the reflected points A'B'C'D'E'. Now use the x-axis as the line of symmetry. Reflect both Figure 2 and Figure 1 into the third and fourth quadrants, respectively, and call these Figures 3 and 4. Label the points of these figures with double and triple primes A″ and A‴, and so on). Write in the coordinates for each vertex of all four figures.

- How is Figure 3 related to Figure 4? How else could you have gotten Figure 3? How else could you have found Figure 4?
- How are the coordinates of Figure 1 related to its image in the y-axis, Figure 2? What can you say about the coordinates of Figure 4?
- Make a conjecture about the coordinates of a shape reflected in the y-axis and a different conjecture about the coordinates of a shape reflected in the x-axis.
- Draw lines from the vertices of Figure 1 to the corresponding vertices of Figure 2. What can you say about these lines? How is the y-axis related to each of these lines?

Students who have done the preceding activities should have a general way to describe translations and reflections across an axis, all in terms of coordinates. Rotations can also be explored with the use of coordinates. In the following activity, multiplying a constant times the coordinates is a transformation that is not a rigid motion.

Activity 20.24

Coordinate Dilations

Students begin with a four-sided shape in the first quadrant. They then make a list of the coordinates and make a new set of coordinates by multiplying each of the original coordinates by 2. They plot the resulting shape. What is the result? Now have students multiply each of the original coordinates by $\frac{1}{2}$ and plot that shape. What is the result? Next, students draw a line from the origin to a vertex of the largest shape on their paper. Repeat for one or two additional vertices, and ask for observations. (An example is shown in Figure 20.37.)

PAUSE and REFLECT

How do the lengths of sides and the areas of the shapes compare when the coordinates are multiplied by 2? What if they are multiplied by 3 or by $\frac{1}{2}$?

When the coordinates of a shape are multiplied as in the last activity, each by the same factor, the shape either gets larger or smaller. The size is changed but not the shape. The new shape is similar to the old shape. This is called a dilation, a transformation that is not rigid because the shape changes.

Your students may enjoy exploring this phenomenon a bit further. If they start with a line drawing of a simple face, boat, or some other shape drawn with straight lines connecting vertices, they will create an interesting effect by multiplying just the first coordinates, just the second coordinates, or using a different factor for each. When only the

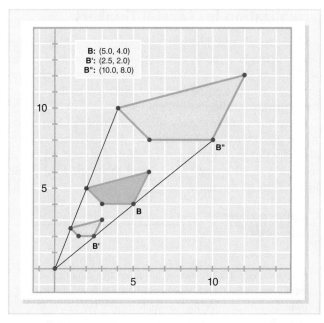

B: (5.0, 4.0)
B': (2.5, 2.0)
B": (10.0, 8.0)

FIGURE 20.37 Dilations with coordinates.

second coordinate is multiplied, the vertical dimensions alone are dilated, so the figure is proportionally stretched (or shrunk) in a vertical manner. Students can explore this process to distort shapes in various ways.

It is impressive to see how an arithmetic operation can control a figure. Imagine being able to control slides, flips, turns, and dilations, not just in the plane but also for three-dimensional figures. The process is identical to computer animation techniques.

Location for Level-2 Thinkers

The move to level-2 thinking is subtle, but it includes an explicit focus on logical reasoning and generalizations.

Coordinate Transformations Revisited.   It is common for a class to have both level-1 and level-2 thinkers or at least students who are ready to move on to logical reasoning. While exploring the transformation activities in the last section, students might be challenged with questions such as the following that are a bit more than simple explorations:

- How should the coordinates be changed to cause a reflection if the line of reflection is not the *y*-axis but is parallel to it?
- Can you discover a single rule for coordinates that would cause a reflection across one of the axes followed by a rotation of a quarter turn? Is that rule the same for the reverse order—a quarter turn followed by a reflection?
- If two successive slides are made with coordinates and you know what numbers were added or subtracted, what number should be added or subtracted to get the figure there in only one move?

- What do you think will happen if, in a dilation, different factors are used for different coordinates?

Applying the Pythagorean Relationship.   The geometric version of the Pythagorean relationship is about areas. The following activity has students use the coordinate grid and the Pythagorean relationship to develop a formula for the distance between points.

Activity 20.25

The Distance Formula

Have students draw a line between two points in the first quadrant that are not on the same horizontal or vertical line. Ask students to draw a right triangle using the line as the hypotenuse (the vertex at the right angle will share one coordinate with each end point). Students then apply the Pythagorean theorem to find the distance. Ask students to do two to four more examples, asking them to look for patterns across their examples.

Next, have them look through all of their calculations and see how the coordinates of the two end points were used. Challenge students to use the same type of calculations to get the distance between two new points without drawing any pictures.

Level-2 students do not necessarily independently construct proofs but should be able to follow the rationale if shown proofs. By using the Pythagorean theorem to find the length of one line (or the distance between the end points), you provide the opportunity for students to make an important connection between two big mathematical ideas. Level 2 thinkers can see the relationship between the Pythagorean theorem and the distance formula.

Slope.   The topic of slope connects geometry and algebra and does not immediately require the study of linear equations. To begin a discussion of slope, draw and compare several different slanted lines. Some are steeper than others. Some go up (sloping upward from left to right) and others go down. This "steepness" of a line is an attribute that can be measured like other measurable attributes. To measure slope requires a reference line (the *x*-axis) and the numbers to use in the measurement. Spend some time having students invent their own methods for attaching a number to the concept of steepness.

The convention for measuring the steepness of a line, or the slope, is based on the ideas of the rise and run between any two points on the line. The rise is the vertical change from the left point to the right point—positive if up, negative if down. The run is the horizontal distance from the left point to the right point. Slope is then defined as rise ÷ run, or the ratio of the vertical change to the horizontal

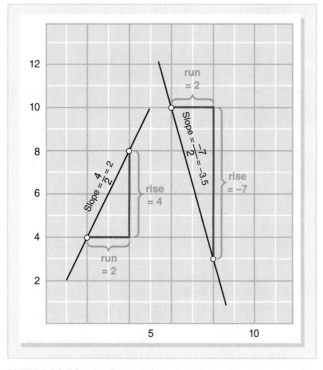

FIGURE 20.38 The slope of a line is equal to rise ÷ run.

Visualization for Level-0 Thinkers

Remember that at level 0, students are thinking about shapes in terms of the way they look. Visualization activities at this level will have students using a variety of physical shapes and drawings and will challenge them to think about these shapes in different orientations.

Finding out how many different shapes can be made with a given number of simple tiles demands that students mentally flip and turn shapes in their minds and find ways to decide whether they have found them all. That is the focus of the next activity.

Activity 20.26

Pentominoes

A pentomino is a shape formed by joining five squares as if cut from a square grid. Each square must have at least one side in common with another. Provide students with five square tiles and a sheet of square grid paper for recording. Challenge them to see how many different pentomino shapes they can find. Shapes that are flips or turns of other shapes are not considered different. Do not tell students how many pentomino shapes there are. Good discussions will come from deciding whether some shapes are really different and if all shapes have been found.

change (see Figure 20.38). By agreement, vertical lines have no slope, or the slope is said to be "undefined." Horizontal lines have a slope of 0 as a result of the definition.

Once students are given the definition, they should be able to compute the slope of any nonvertical line drawn on a coordinate grid without further assistance and without formulas. A good problem-based task is to have students ponder the slopes of parallel lines and perpendicular lines.

Learning about Visualization

Visualization might be called "geometry done with the mind's eye." It involves being able to create mental images of shapes and then turn them around mentally, thinking about how they look from different viewpoints—predicting the results of various transformations. It includes the mental coordination of two and three dimensions—predicting the unfolding of a box (or net) by understanding a two-dimensional drawing of a three-dimensional shape. Any activity that requires students to think about, manipulate, or transform a shape mentally or to represent a shape as it is seen visually will contribute to the development of students' visualization skills.

Once students have decided that there are just 12 pentominoes (revisit Figure 20.31), the 12 pieces can then be used in a variety of activities. Glue the grids with the students' pentominoes onto card stock, and let them cut out the 12 shapes.

Lots of activities can be done with pentominoes. For example, try to fit all 12 pieces into a 6 × 10 or 5 × 12 rectangle. Also, each of the 12 shapes can be used as a tessellation tile. Another task is to examine each of the 12 pentominoes and decide which will fold up to make an open box. (This two-dimensional representation of a three-dimensional object is called a *net*.) For those pentominoes that are "box makers," which square is the bottom?

Another aspect of visualization for young students is to be able to think about solid shapes in terms of their faces or sides. For these activities, you will need to make "face cards" by tracing around the different faces of a shape, making either all faces on one card or a set of separate cards with one face per card (see Figure 20.39).

Activity 20.27

Face Matching

There are two versions of the task: Given a face card, find the corresponding solid, or given a solid, find the face card. With a collection of single-face cards, students can select the cards

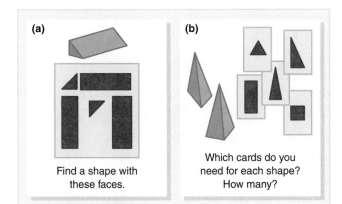

FIGURE 20.39 Matching face cards with solid shapes.

that go with a particular solid. For another variation, stack all of the single-face cards for one solid face down. Turn them up one at a time as clues to finding the solid.

The following activity has been adapted from NCTM's *Principles and Standards* and is found in the pre-K–grade 2 section on geometry (NCTM, 2000, p. 101).

Activity 20.28

Quick Images

Draw some simple sketches of figures that students can easily reproduce, such as the examples in Figure 20.40. Display one of the figures for about 5 seconds. Then have students attempt to reproduce it on their own. Show the same figure again for a few seconds, and allow students to modify their drawings. Repeat with additional figures.

Ask students to tell how they thought about the figure or to describe it in words that helped them remember what they saw. As students learn to verbally describe what they see, their visual memory will improve.

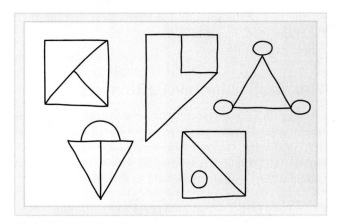

FIGURE 20.40 Examples to use in the "Quick Images" activity.

Visualization for Level-1 Thinkers

In identifying a visualization task as either level 0 or level 1, one consideration is the degree of attention that must be given to the particular properties of shapes. One of the main goals of the visualization strand is to be able to identify and draw two-dimensional images of three-dimensional figures and to build three-dimensional figures from two-dimensional images, which falls in level 1.

Activity 20.29

Building Views

For this activity, students will need paper for drawing a building plan and 1-inch blocks for constructing a building.

● **Version 1:** Students begin with a building made of the blocks and draw the left, right, front, and back views (these are called elevations). In Figure 20.41, the building plan shows a top view of the building and the number of blocks in each position. After students build a building from a plan like this, they draw the elevations (views) of the front, right, left, and back as shown in the figure.
● **Version 2:** Students are given right and front elevations. Ask students to build the corresponding building. To record their solution, they draw a building plan (top elevation with numbers).

Notice that front and back elevations are symmetric, as are the left and right elevations. That is why only one of each is given in the second part of the activity.

To expand "Building Views" into a significantly more challenging activity, students can draw 3-D drawings (isometric) of these block buildings or match 3-D drawings with

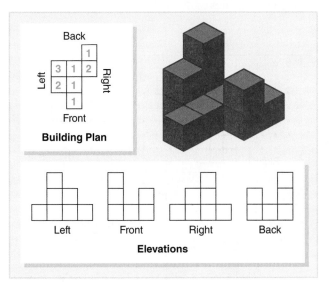

FIGURE 20.41 "Building Views" task.

a building. Isometric dot grids (Blackline Masters 38 and 39) are a form of *axonometric* drawing where the scale is preserved in all dimensions (height, depth, width). The next activity provides a glimpse at this form of visualization activity.

Activity 20.30

3-D Drawings

STUDENTS *with* SPECIAL NEEDS

- Version 1: Students begin with an isometric 3-D drawing of a building. The assumption is that there are no hidden blocks. From the drawing, the students build the actual building with their blocks. To record the result, they draw a building plan (top view) indicating the number of blocks in each position.
- Version 2: Students are given the four elevation views and a building plan (top view) (see Figure 20.42). They build the building accordingly and draw two or more of the elevation views. There are four possible views: the front left and right and the back left and right. For students who struggle, have them build the building on a sheet of paper with the words "front," "back," "left," and "right" written on the edges to keep from getting different views confused.

TECHNOLOGY

An amazing computer tool for drawing two- and three-dimensional views of block buildings is the Isometric Drawing Tool, available at Illuminations (http://illuminations.nctm.org/Activity Detail.aspx?ID=125). This applet uses mouse clicks to draw either whole cubes, any single face of a cube, or just lines. The drawings, however, are actually "buildings" and can be viewed as three-dimensional objects. They can be rotated in space so that they can be seen from any vantage point. Prepared investigations are informative and also lead students through the features of the tool.

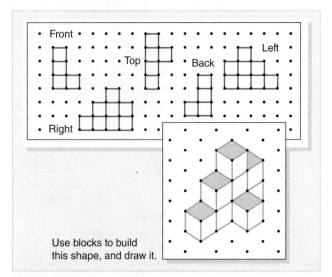

Use blocks to build this shape, and draw it.

FIGURE 20.42 Block "buildings" on isometric grids.

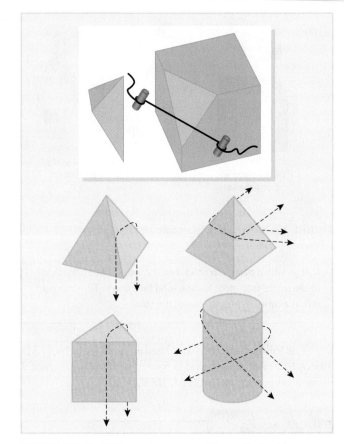

FIGURE 20.43 Cutting a clay model with a potter's wire.

Another interesting connection between two and three dimensions is found in slicing solids in different ways. This is a CCSSO standard for grade 7 (2010). When a solid is sliced into two parts, a two-dimensional figure is formed on the slice faces. Slices can be explored with solids made of clay that are sliced with a potter's wire. Figure 20.43 shows a cube being sliced off at the corner, leaving a triangular face. Another engaging method is to partially fill a plastic solid (such as Power Solids) with water. The surface of the water simulates a slice and models the face of the solid as if it were cut at that location. By tilting the shape in different ways, every possible "slice" can be observed.

Visualization for Level-2 Thinkers

Once again, logical reasoning is what distinguishes activities for level-2 thinkers from those for level 1. The activities described above for level 1 can easily be modified to challenge level-2 thinkers. Likewise, the activities in this section can push level-1 students forward in their thinking.

Connecting Earlier Activities to Level-2 Visualization. Students who are ready can be challenged to make predictions about the types of slices that are possible. For example, given a particular solid, prior to testing with water (as described previously), they might use a list of possible triangles and quadrilaterals to predict which can be made and which are impossible. In each case, they should offer a reason for that hypothesis.

The following are extensions of pentomino activities that are appropriate visualization tasks for level 2:

- How many *hexominoes* are there? A hexomino is made of six squares following the same rule as for pentominoes. Because there are quite a few hexominoes (35), devising a logical scheme for categorizing the shapes is one of the few ways students will know all the hexominoes have been found.
- Instead of putting together five squares, students can find all of the arrangements of five cubes. These shapes are called *pentominoids*. In general, shapes made of cubes in which adjoining cubes share a complete face are called *polyominoids*.

The Platonic Solids.   A *polyhedron* is a three-dimensional shape with polygons for all faces. Among the various polyhedra, *Platonic solids* is the name given to the set of completely regular polyhedrons. "Completely regular" means that each face is a regular polygon and every vertex has exactly the same number of faces joining at that point. An interesting visualization task appropriate for this level is to find and describe all of the Platonic solids.

Activity 20.31

Search for the Platonic Solids

Provide students with a supply of equilateral triangles, squares, regular pentagons, and regular hexagons from one of the plastic sets for building solids (e.g., Polydron or Geofix). Explain what a completely regular solid is. The task is to find as many different completely regular solids as possible. For students with disabilities, share the

STUDENTS with SPECIAL NEEDS

following explicit structure to support their search. The smallest number of sides a face can have is three, so begin with triangles, then squares, then pentagons, and so on. Furthermore, because every vertex must have the same number of faces, try three faces at a point, then four, and so on. They will find that it is clearly impossible to have only two faces at a point.

Students will find they can have three, four, or five triangles coming to a point. For each of these, they can begin with a "tent" of triangles and then add more triangles so that each vertex has the same number. With three at a point, you get a four-sided solid called a *tetrahedron* (in Greek, *tetra* is "four"). With four at each point, you get an eight-sided solid called an *octahedron* (*octa* = eight). It is really exciting to build the solid with five triangles at each point. It will have 20 sides and is called an *icosahedron* (*icosa* = twenty).

In a similar manner, students will find that there is only one solid made of squares—three at each point and six in all—a *hexahedron* (*hex* = six), also called a *cube*. And there is only one solid with pentagons—three at each point, and 12 in all. This is called a *dodecahedron* (*dodeca* = twelve).

 PAUSE and REFLECT

Why are there no regular polyhedra with six or more triangles or four or more squares? Why are there no regular polyhedra made with hexagons or with polygons with more than six sides? The best way to answer these questions is to experiment with the polygons and explain the answers in your own words.

A fantastic skeletal icosahedron can be built out of the newspaper rods described earlier (see Figure 20.10 on p. 411). Because five triangles converge at each point, there are also five edges at each point. Simply work at bringing five rods to each vertex and remember that each face is a triangle. This icosahedron will be about 4 feet across and will be amazingly sturdy.

RESOURCES *for Chapter 20*

LITERATURE CONNECTIONS

The Greedy Triangle *Burns, 1995*

This delightful book is the story of a triangle that is very busy being a sail, or a roof, or fitting into the crook of the arm of someone standing with hand on hip. Soon he becomes bored and travels to the local shape-shifter for a change. Adding a new side and angle and becoming a quadrilateral gives the Greedy Triangle new things to try as he fits into different four-sided figures in the environment. The triangle goes through several other shape-shifts. This book links well with activities at level 0 and level 1. Using a meter-long loop of yarn for every pair of students (or three ace bandages in a loop for a class

demonstration), have students follow and discuss events in the book by creating appropriate shapes with the loop (holding it in the air between their hands). First they can explore different triangles that were made, and eventually they can investigate properties as they shift from one shape to the next. They can also move to level-2 thinking, by providing proof that they have a square, for example.

I Spy Shapes in Art, *Micklethwait, 2007*
Museum Shapes, *Metropolitan Museum of Art, 2005*

Using artwork from such masters as Matisse and Warhol, students are challenged to look for particular shapes in paintings in an "I spy" approach. This activity can be extended to post-cards of artwork from local museums and then act as a catalyst for budding "mathematical" artists in the classroom.

Color Farm, *Ehlert, 1990*

Color Zoo, *Ehlert, 1989*

These visually motivating books can engage students in thinking about shapes. Using cut-out overlays of circles, rectangles, triangles, and other familiar shapes, images of either farm or zoo animals are created. The reader turns the page to remove a shape, transforming the image into a new animal. Because these books reinforce shapes, animals, and colors, they engage English language learners and their families.

Cubes, Cones, Cylinders and Spheres, *Hoban, 2000*

Shapes, Shapes, Shapes, *Hoban, 1996*

So Many Circles, So Many Squares, *Hoban, 1998*

These wordless books of dramatic photographs on a geometric theme will engage students of all ages in thinking about and locating shapes in the environment. Students can use digital cameras to create their own Hoban-like books that invite readers to seek and identify two- and three-dimensional shapes in the world around them. Student-made books are great for taking home to families or for students in upper grades to make for younger students.

RECOMMENDED READINGS

Articles

Edwards, M. T., & Harper, S. R. (2010). Paint bucket polygons. *Teaching Children Mathematics, 16*(7), 420–428.
To advance students' understanding of polygons, examples and non-examples are used to help refine definitions and thinking. Using the "paint bucket" feature found in most graphics programs, or the "fill color" feature found in Microsoft Word, students are able to quickly think about defining features of polygons.

Koester, B. A. (2003). Prisms and pyramids: Constructing three-dimensional models to build understanding. *Teaching Children Mathematics, 9*(8), 436–442.
Koester's explorations with third to fifth graders use straws and pipe cleaners to build models. The activities involve classification and definitions of shapes and seeking patterns in number of faces, vertices, and edges.

Renne, C. G. (2004). Is a rectangle a square? Developing mathematical vocabulary and conceptual understanding. *Teaching Children Mathematics, 10*(5), 258–263.
The voices of students in this article are clear examples of the difficulty that students at level-1 reasoning have in attempting to make logical conclusions about geometric properties and relationships.

ONLINE RESOURCES

Dynamic Paper (NCTM)
http://illuminations.nctm.org/ActivityDetail .aspx?ID=205

This multipurpose tool creates custom graph paper, number grids, nets, number lines, shapes, spinners, and tessellations that can be exported in .jpeg and .pdf formats.

Interactives: 3-D Shapes (Annenberg Foundation)
www.learner.org/interactives/geometry/index.html

Learn about the mathematical properties of three-dimensional polyhedra, including how to calculate their surface area and volume.

Shape Sorter (Illuminations)
http://illuminations.nctm.org/ActivityDetail.aspx?ID=34

Using a Venn diagram, select a "rule." Then sort each shape according to its properties by dragging it to the workspace.

Shapes and Space in Geometry
www.learner.org/teacherslab/math/geometry

Designed for teachers, this teachers' lab provides background into plane and three-dimensional geometry.

REFLECTIONS *on Chapter 20*

WRITING TO LEARN

1. Describe in your own words the first three van Hiele levels of geometric thought (levels 0, 1, and 2), including the object of thought and the product of thought. How would activities aimed at levels 0, 1, and 2 differ?

2. Briefly describe the nature of the content in each of the four geometric strands discussed in this chapter: Shapes and Properties, Location, Transformations, and Visualization.

3. What can you do when the students in your classroom are at different van Hiele levels of thought?

4. Find one of the suggested applets, or explore GeoGebra (www.geogebra.org) and explain how it can be used. What are the advantages of using the computer instead of hands-on materials or drawings?

5. How can you use the van Hiele theory to assess your students' geometric growth or spatial sense?

FOR DISCUSSION AND EXPLORATION

1. Examine the teacher's edition of a textbook and select a geometry lesson. How might the lesson be adapted for students who may be at several different van Hiele levels?

MyEducationLab™

Go to the MyEducationLab (www.myeducationlab.com) for Math Methods, and familiarize yourself with the content. Much of the site content is organized topically. The topics include all of the following to support your learning in the course:

- Learning outcomes for important mathematics methods course topics aligned with the national standards
- Assignments and Activities, tied to these learning outcomes and standards, that can help you more deeply understand course content
- Building Teaching Skills and Dispositions learning units that allow you to apply and practice your understanding of the core mathematics content and teaching skills

Your instructor has a correlation guide that aligns the exercises on the topical portion of the site with your book's chapters.

On MyEducationLab you will also find book-specific resources including Blackline Masters, Expanded Lesson Activities, and Artifact Analysis Activities.

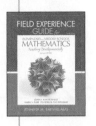

Field Experience Guide
C O N N E C T I O N S

This chapter includes many literature links; see Field Experience 2.7 for designing and teaching a lesson using children's literature. What van Hiele level have students achieved within an area such as shapes and properties? Use Field Experience 7.2 to prepare an interview to find out! FEG Expanded Lessons 9.17, 9.18, and 9.19 target explorations of shapes and their properties across the grades.

Chapter 21

Developing Concepts of Data Analysis

Graphs and statistics bombard the public in areas such as advertising, opinion polls, population trends, health risks, and progress of students in schools. We hear that the average amount of rainfall this summer is more than it was last summer or that the average American family consists of 3.19 people. We read on the U.S. Census website (www.census.gov) that the median home price in 2000 was $119,600, and in March 2011 it was $213,800. The mean home price in March 2011 was $246,800. Knowing these statistics should raise an array of questions: How were these data gathered? What was the purpose? What does it mean to have an average of 3.19 people? Why are the median and the mean for home sales so different? Which statistic makes more sense for communicating about the prices of homes?

Statistical literacy is critical to understanding the world around us, essential for effective citizenship, and vital for developing the ability to question information presented in the media (Shaughnessy, 2007). Misuse of statistics occurs even in trustworthy sources like newspapers, where graphs are often designed to exaggerate a finding. Students in pre-K through grade 8 should have meaningful experiences with basic concepts of statistics throughout their school years. At the pre-K–grade 1 level (CCSSO, 2010), students can begin this understanding by learning how data can be categorized and displayed in various graphical forms. In grades 2–5, students should collect and organize sets of data as well as represent data in frequency tables, bar graphs (scaled with one-to-many), line plots (including fractional units), and picture graphs (CCSSO, 2010). As they mature in understanding, they should be introduced to new data representations such as dot plots, histograms, box plots, scatter plots, and stem-and-leaf plots. Students should also study measures of center—for example, median and mean (NCTM, 2006; Schielack & Seeley, 2007) and measures of variability.

BIG IDEAS

1. Statistics is its own field different from mathematics; one key difference is focus on variability of data in statistical reasoning.

2. Doing statistics involves a four-step process: formulating questions, collecting data, analyzing data, and interpreting results.

3. Data are gathered and organized in order to answer questions about the populations from which the data come. With data from only a sample of the population, inferences are made about the population.

4. Different types of graphs and other data representations provide different information about the data and, hence, the population from which the data were taken. The choice of graphical representation can affect how well the data are understood.

5. Measures that describe data with numbers are called *statistics*. The use of a particular graph or statistic can mediate what the data tell about the population.

6. Both graphs and statistics can provide a sense of the shape of the data, including how spread out or how clustered they are. Having a sense of the shape of data is having a big picture of the data rather than a collection of numbers.

Mathematics CONTENT CONNECTIONS

Statistics involves using data in the form of numbers and graphs to describe our world. Certainly, there are connections to the areas of the curriculum that center on number. However, the connection to algebra is perhaps one of the most important mathematical connections.

◆ **Number Sense** (Chapter 8): Young students create graphs of class data (such as "What pets do you have at home?" or "How many buttons on your outfit?") and use the graphs to talk about quantity.

◆ **Algebra** (Chapter 14): Algebra is used to analyze and describe relationships. Whenever data are gathered on two related variables (e.g., height and arm span, age and growth), algebra can be used to describe the relationship between the variables. The resulting relationship can be used to predict outcomes for which no data have yet been gathered.

◆ **Proportional Reasoning** (Chapter 18): Statistical reasoning *is* proportional reasoning. When a population is sampled (a subset selected), that sample is assumed to be proportional to the larger population.

◆ **Measurement** (Chapter 19): Measurement can be interwoven with data analysis as students make measurements to gather data and answer real-world questions.

What Does It Mean to Do Statistics?

Doing statistics is, in fact, a different process from doing mathematics—a notion that has recently received much attention in standards documents and research (Burrill & Elliott, 2006; Franklin et al., 2005; Shaughnessy, 2003). As Richard Scheaffer, past president of the American Statistics Association, notes,

> Mathematics is about numbers and their operations, generalizations and abstractions; it is about spatial configurations and their measurement, transformations, and abstractions. . . . Statistics is also about numbers—but numbers in context: these are called data. Statistics is about variables and cases, distribution and variation, purposeful design or studies, and the role of randomness in the design of studies, and the interpretation of results. (Scheaffer, 2006, pp. 310–311)

Statistical literacy is needed by all students to interpret the world. This section describes some of the big ideas and essential knowledge regarding statistics and explains a general process for doing statistics. Each of the four steps in the process is used as a major section in the organization of this chapter.

Is It Statistics or Is It Mathematics?

Statistics and mathematics are two different fields; however, statistical questions are often asked in assessments with questions that are mathematical in nature rather than statistical. The harm in this is that students are not focusing on statistical reasoning, as shown by the following excellent exemplars from Scheaffer (2006).

> Read the following questions, and label each as "doing mathematics" or "doing statistics."

1. The average weight of 50 prize-winning tomatoes is 2.36 pounds. What is the combined weight, in pounds, of these 50 tomatoes? (NAEP sample question)
   a. 0.0472   b. 11.8   c. 52.36   d. 59   e. 118
2. Joe had three test scores of 78, 76, and 74, whereas Mary had scores of 72, 82, and 74. How did Joe's average (mean) compare to Mary's average (mean) score? (TIMSS eighth-grade released item)
   a. Joe's was one point higher.
   b. Joe's was one point lower.
   c. Both averages were the same.
   d. Joe's was 2 points higher.
   e. Joe's was 2 points lower.
3. Table 21.1 gives the times each girl has recorded for seven trials of the 100-meter dash this year. Only one girl may compete in the upcoming track meet. Which girl would you select for the meet and why?

TABLE 21.1

	RACE TIMES FOR THREE RUNNERS						
Runner	**Race**						
	1	**2**	**3**	**4**	**5**	**6**	**7**
Suzie	15.2	14.8	15.0	14.7	14.3	14.5	14.5
Tanisha	15.8	15.7	15.4	15.0	14.8	14.6	14.5
Dara	15.6	15.5	14.8	15.1	14.5	14.7	14.5

Which of these involves statistical reasoning? All of them? None of them? As explained by Schaeffer, only the last is statistical in nature. The first requires knowing the formula for averages, but the task required is to work backwards through a formula—mathematical thinking, not statistical thinking. Similarly in the second problem, one must know the formula for the mean, but the question is about the computational process of using the formula. In both of these, you might notice that the context is irrelevant to the problem. The final question is statistical in nature because the situation requires analysis—graphs or averages might be used to determine a solution. The mathematics here is basic; the focus is on statistics. Notice the context is central to responding to the question, which is an indication that it is statistical reasoning.

In statistics, the context is essential to analyzing and interpreting the data (Franklin & Garfield, 2006; Franklin et al., 2005; Langrall, Nisbet, Mooney, & Jansem, 2011; Scheaffer, 2006). Looking at the spread, or shape, of data and considering the meaning of unusual data points (outliers) are determined based on the context.

The Shape of Data

A big conceptual idea in data analysis can be referred to as the *shape of data*: a sense of how data are spread out or grouped, what characteristics about the data set as a whole can be described, and what the data tell us in a global way about the population from which they are taken.

There is no single technique that can tell us what the shape of the data is. Across the pre-K–8 curriculum, students begin looking at the shape of data by examining various graphs. Different graphing techniques or types of graphs can provide a different snapshot of the data as a whole. For example, bar graphs and circle graphs (percentage graphs) each show how the data cluster in different categories. The circle graph focuses more on the relative values of this clustering, whereas the bar graph adds a dimension of quantity. The choice of which and how many categories to use in these graphs will result in different pictures of the shape of the data.

Part of understanding the shape of data is being aware of how spread out or clustered the data are. In the early grades, this can be discussed informally by looking at almost any graph.

For numeric data, there are statistics that tell us how data are spread or dispersed. The simplest of these is the range. Averages (the mean and the median) tell us where the "center" of the data is. In high school, students will learn about the standard deviation statistic, which is also a measure of spread. At the middle school level, a simple graphical technique called the *box plot* is designed to give us visual information about the spread of data.

The Process of Doing Statistics

Just as learning addition involves much more than the procedure for combining, doing statistics is much more than the computational procedures for finding the mean or the process of creating a circle graph. To engage students *meaningfully* in learning and doing statistics, they should be involved in the full process, from asking and defining questions to interpreting results. This broad approach provides a framework and purpose under which students learn how to create graphs, compute the mean, and analyze data in other ways. This chapter is organized around this process, which is presented in Figure 21.1.

Formulating Questions

Statistics is about more than making graphs and analyzing data. It includes both asking and answering questions about our world. The first goal in the Data Analysis and Probability standard of *Principles and Standards* says that students should "formulate questions that can be addressed with data and collect, organize, and display relevant data to answer them" (NCTM, 2000, p. 48). Notice that data collection should be for a purpose, to answer a question, just as in the real world. Then the analysis of data actually adds information about some aspect of our world, just as political pollsters,

I. Formulate Questions
  • Clarify the problem at hand
  • Formulate one (or more) questions that can be answered with data
II. Collect Data
  • Design a plan to collect appropriate data
  • Employ the plan to collect the data
III. Analyze Data
  • Select appropriate graphical and numerical methods
  • Use these methods to analyze the data
IV. Interpret Results
  • Interpret the analysis
  • Relate the interpretation to the original question

FIGURE 21.1 Process of doing statistics.

Source: Franklin, C., Kader, G., Mewborn, D., Moreno, J., Peck, R., Perry, M., & Scheaffer, R. (2005, August). *Guidelines for Assessment and Instruction in Statistics Education (GAISE) Report: A Pre-K–12 Curriculum Framework,* p. 11. Reprinted with permission. Copyright © 2005 by the American Statistical Association. All rights reserved.

advertising agencies, market researchers, census takers, wildlife managers, medical researchers, and hosts of others gather data to answer questions and make informed decisions.

According to *Curriculum Focal Points* (NCTM, 2006) and the *Common Core State Standards* (CCSSO, 2010), students in the primary grades should be given opportunities to generate their own questions, decide on appropriate data to help answer these questions, and determine methods of collecting the data. For example, a second grader wanted to know how many houses were on her street (Russell, 2006). Or a teacher may ask, "How many sisters and brothers do you have?" Whether the question is teacher initiated or student initiated, students should engage in conversations about how well defined the question is. In the house example, students wondered whether they should include houses that weren't finished yet or whether apartments counted. In the second case, there may be a need to discuss half siblings.

When students formulate the questions, the data they gather become more meaningful. How they organize the data and the techniques for analyzing them have a purpose. They may start by just hand raising, a tally, or a ballot using both limited response (narrow range of possible answers) and then unlimited response options (Hudson, Shupe, Vasquez, & Miller, 2008).

Often the need to gather data will come from the class naturally in the course of discussion or from questions arising in other content areas. Science, of course, is full of measurements and, thus, abounds in data analysis possibilities. Social studies is also full of opportunities to pose questions requiring data collection. The next two sections suggest some additional ideas.

Classroom Questions

Students want to learn about themselves (what does the "typical" student look like or have an interest in?), their families and pets, measures such as arm span or time to get to school, their likes and dislikes, and so on. The easiest questions to begin with are those that can be answered by each class member contributing one piece of data. Here are a few ideas:

- *Favorites:* TV shows, games, movies, ice cream, video games, sports teams, music (When there are lots of possibilities, start by restricting the number of choices.)
- *Numbers:* number of pets, siblings; hours watching TV or hours of sleep; bedtime; time spent on the computer
- *Measures:* height, arm span, area of foot, long-jump distance, shadow length, seconds to run around the track, minutes spent traveling to school

Beyond One Classroom

The questions in the previous section are designed for students to contribute data about themselves. These questions can be expanded by asking, "How would this compare to another class?" Comparison questions are a good way to help students focus on the data they have collected and the variability within that data (Russell, 2006). As students get older, they can begin to think about various populations and differences between them. For example, how are fifth graders similar or different from middle school students? Students might examine questions where they compare responses of boys versus girls, adults or teachers versus students, or categories of full-time workers compared to college students. These situations involve issues of sampling and making generalizations and comparisons. In addition, students can ask questions about things beyond the classroom. Discussions about communities provide a good way to integrate social studies and mathematics.

The newspaper suggests all sorts of data-related questions. For example, how many full-page ads occur on different days of the week? What types of stories are on the front page? Which comics are really for kids and which are not?

Science is another area in which questions can be asked and data gathered. For example, what is the width of maple leaves that fall to the ground? How many times do different types of balls bounce when each is dropped from the same height? How many days does it take for different types of bean, squash, and pea seeds to germinate when kept in moist paper towels? Observations on a zoo field trip can be preceded with the development of questions that are used to gather data on the trip (Mokros & Wright, 2009).

TECHNOLOGY Because context is particularly important, and is particularly supportive when it is culturally meaningful (McGlone, 2008), the Internet is an important resource. Students may have interests in various sports, nature, or international events. Whatever their interests, data can be located on the Web. For example, students may wonder how athletes are chosen for the Olympics. Data can be gathered on swimmers' times at various meets and then students analyze which swimmers should be selected.

Data Collection

There are two main types of data—categorical and numerical. NCTM suggests that by the sixth grade, students should be able to sort these two data types (NCTM, 2000). Categorical data is information that can be collected about things that can be grouped by labels such as favorite vacations, colors of cars in the school parking lot, and the most popular suggestion for a name to give the class guinea pig. Categorical data may not have any order; the bars in a bar graph could be put in any arrangement, or they could be in an order when you rank something on a scale from 1 to 10. Numerical data, on the other hand, counts things or measures on a continuous scale. This includes how many miles to school, the temperature in your town over a one-week period, or the weight of the students' backpacks. Students need to have opportunities to explore the idea that statistics such as the mean or median involve using numerical data (Leavy, Friel, & Mamer, 2009).

Collecting Data

Gathering data is not easy for students, especially young students. In a first-grade class, a teacher asked students to gather data on "Are you 6?" Upon receiving the prompt, 18 eager students began asking others in the class if they were 6 and tallying the yes and no responses. The problem? They had no idea whom they had asked more than once or whom they had not asked at all. This provided an excellent entry into a discussion about how statisticians must gather data. Carolyn Cook, a kindergarten teacher, asked her students to help think of an organized manner to gather the data from their classmates on favorite ice cream flavors. These students decided a class list (see Figure 21.2) would allow them to keep track (Cook, 2008).

Gathering data also must take into consideration variability. Young students can understand that a survey of first graders on favorite TV show will produce different answers from a survey of fifth graders. Answers also may vary based on the day the question is asked or whether a particular show has been recently discussed.

Data can also be collected through observation. This makes a shared context for students in that they will all be a part of observing phenomena. For example, set up a bird feeder outside the classroom window and collect data at different times during the day to either count number or type of birds. Students can also conduct observational data collection events on field trips (Mokros & Wright, 2009) and in evening or weekend activities with their families.

For older students, planning data collection includes gathering data from more than one classroom to seek a

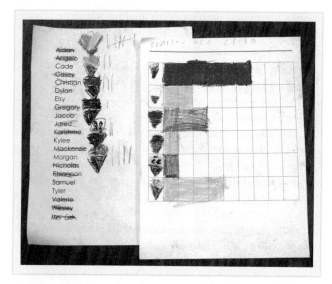

FIGURE 21.2 Kindergartners collect data on favorite ice cream flavors, keeping track of who they have surveyed, tallying the data, and then creating a horizontal bar graph.

Source: Cook, C. D. (2008). "I Scream, You Scream: Data Analysis with Kindergartners." *Teaching Children Mathematics, 14*(9), p. 539. Reprinted with permission. Copyright © 2008 by the National Council of Teachers of Mathematics. All rights reserved.

more representative sample, or even using random sampling. In fact, for middle school students, it is important that they engage in the whole process of doing statistics, including designing an experiment in which most variables are kept the same (controlled) so that one variable can be analyzed.

Using Existing Data Sources

Data do not have to be collected by survey; existing data abound in various places, such as the following sources of print and Web data.

Print Resources. Newspapers, almanacs, sports record books, maps, and various government publications are possible sources of data that may be used to answer student questions.

Children's literature is an excellent and engaging resource. Young students can tally words in a repeating verse like "Hickory, Dickory, Dock" (Niezgoda & Moyer-Packenham, 2005). Similarly, books like *Goodnight Moon* (by Margaret Wise Brown) or *Green Eggs and Ham* (by Dr. Seuss) have many repeated words or phrases. Nonfiction literature can be a source of data, especially for older students. For example, *Book of Lists: Fun Facts, Weird Trivia, and Amazing Lists on Nearly Everything You Need to Know!* (by James Buckley and Robert Stremme) reports on various statistics and includes surveys at the end of every section. Books on sports, such as *A Negro League Scrapbook* (by Carole Boston Weatherform), can have very interesting statistics about historic periods that students can explore and compare.

Websites. Students may be interested in facts about another country as a result of a social studies unit or a country in the news. Olympic records *TECHNOLOGY* in various events over the years or data related to environmental issues are other examples of topics around which student questions may be formulated. For these and hundreds of other questions, data can be found on the Web. Below are several websites with a lot of interesting data.

- USDA Economic Research Service (www.ers.usda.gov/data/foodconsumption) offers wonderful data sets on the availability and consumption of hundreds of foods. Annual per capita estimates often go back to 1909.
- Google Public Data Explorer (www.google.com/publicdata/home) makes large data sets available to explore, visualize, and interpret.
- Internet Movie Database (www.imdb.com) offers information about movies of all genres.
- State Data Map (http://illuminations.nctm.org/ActivityDetail.aspx?ID=151) is a source that displays state data on population, land area, political representation, gasoline use, and so on.
- World Fact Book (https://www.cia.gov/library/publications/the-world-factbook/index.html) provides demographic information for every nation in the world: population; age distributions; death and birth rates; and information on the economy, government, transportation, and geography.
- U.S. Census Bureau (www.census.gov) has copious statistical information by state, county, or voting district.

Data Analysis: Classification

Classification involves making decisions about how to categorize things, a basic activity that is fundamental to data analysis. In order to formulate questions and decide how to represent data that have been gathered, decisions must be made about how things might be categorized. Young students might group farm animals, for example, by number of legs; by type of product they provide; by those that work, provide food, or are pets; by size or color; by the type of food they eat; and so on. Each of these groupings is based on a different attribute of the animals.

Both *Curriculum Focal Points* (NCTM, 2006) and the *Common Core State Standards* (CCSSO, 2010) place classification by attributes as a kindergarten topic. Attribute activities are explicitly designed to develop flexible reasoning about the characteristics of data.

Attribute Materials

Attribute materials can be any set of objects that lend themselves to being sorted and classified in different ways—for example, seashells, leaves, the students themselves, or the set of the students' shoes. The *attributes* are the ways that

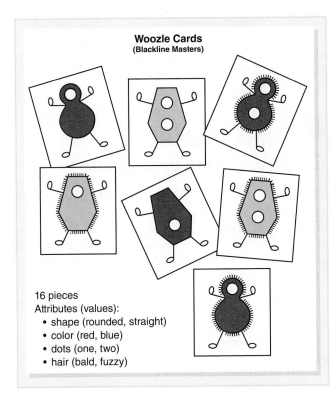

Woozle Cards
(Blackline Masters)

16 pieces
Attributes (values):
- shape (rounded, straight)
- color (red, blue)
- dots (one, two)
- hair (bald, fuzzy)

FIGURE 21.3 Woozle Cards can be duplicated on card stock colored with red and blue bodies, and then laminated and cut into individual cards (see Blackline Master 59).

the materials can be sorted. For example, hair color, height, and gender are attributes of students. Each attribute has a number of different *values:* for example, blond, brown, black, or red (for the attribute of hair color); tall or short (for height); male or female (for gender). An example of a teacher-made attribute set is displayed in Figure 21.3 (see also Blackline Master 59).

Commercially available attribute blocks are sets of 60 plastic attribute materials, with each piece having four attributes: color (red, yellow, blue), shape (circle, triangle, rectangle, square, hexagon), size (big, little), and thickness (thick, thin). The specific values, number of values, or number of attributes that a set may have is not important.

Activities with Attribute Materials. At least initially, attribute activities are best done by sitting in a large circle on the floor where all students can see and have access to the materials to be sorted. Kindergarten classes can have fun with simple Venn diagram activities. With the use of words such as *and, or,* and *not,* the loop activities become quite challenging, even for fifth graders.

pieces inside one string and all triangles inside the other. Let the students try to resolve the difficulty of what to do with the red triangles. When the notion of overlapping the strings to create an area common to both loops is clear, more challenging activities can be explored. Students with disabilities will need to use labels on each loop of string.

As shown in Figure 21.4, the labels need not be restricted to single attributes. If a piece does not fit in any region, it is placed outside all of the loops.

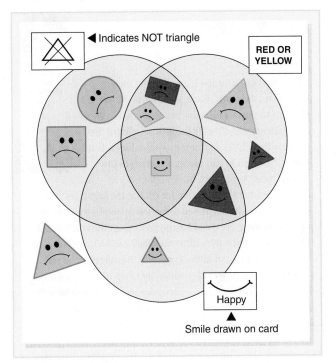

◀ Indicates NOT triangle

RED OR YELLOW

Happy

Smile drawn on card

FIGURE 21.4 A Venn diagram activity with attribute pieces. A rule is written on a card for each Venn diagram circle.

As students progress, it is important to introduce labels for negative attributes such as "not red" or "not small." Also important is the eventual use of *and* and *or* connectives, as in two-value rules such as "red and square" or "big or happy." This use of *and, or,* and *not* significantly widens students' classification schemes.

An engaging and challenging activity is to infer how things have been classified when the loops are not labeled. The following activities require students to make and test conjectures about how things are being classified.

and move the student to the left or right according to this secret rule. After a number of students have been sorted, have the next student come up and ask students to predict which group he or she belongs in. Before the rule is articulated, continue the activity for a while so that others in the class will have an opportunity to determine the rule. This same activity can be done with virtually any materials that can be sorted, such as students' shoes, shells, or buttons. Encourage ELLs to use their native language and English to describe the rule.

Activity 21.3

Hidden Labels

Select label cards for the loops of string used to make Venn diagrams. Place the cards facedown. Ask students to select a piece for you to place. For ELLs and students with disabilities, provide a list of the labels with pictures and/or translations for each as a reference. Begin to sort pieces according to the hidden rules. As you sort, have students try to determine what the labels are for each of the loops. Let students who think they have guessed the labels try to place a piece in the proper loop, but avoid having them guess the labels aloud. Students who think they know the labels can be asked to "play teacher" and respond to the guesses of the others. Point out that one way to test an idea about the labels is to select a piece that you think might go in a particular section. Wait to turn the cards up until most students have figured out the rule.

ENGLISH LANGUAGE LEARNERS

STUDENTS with SPECIAL NEEDS

"Hidden Labels" can and should be repeated with real-world materials connected to other content areas and to students' experiences. For example, if you were doing a unit on wildlife in the backyard, you can use pictures of creatures (see Figure 21.5) to sort by relevant attributes. The class can

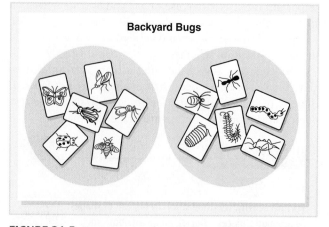

FIGURE 21.5 Can you guess the rule that was used to sort these bugs?

"graph" data about themselves by first placing information in loops with labels. A graph of "Our Pets" might consist of a picture of each student's pet or favorite stuffed animal (in lieu of a pet) and be affixed to a wall display showing how the pets were classified.

Data Analysis: Graphical Representations

How data are organized should be directly related to the question that caused you to collect the data in the first place. For example, suppose students want to know how many pockets they have on their clothing (Bus, 1996; Russell, 2008). Data collection involves each student counting his or her pockets.

PAUSE and REFLECT

If your second-grade class had collected these data, what methods might you suggest they use for organizing and graphing them? Is one of your ideas better than others for answering the question about how many pockets?

If a bar graph is made with one bar per student, that will certainly tell how many pockets each student has. However, is it the best way to answer the question? If the data were categorized by number of pockets, then a graph showing the number of students with two pockets, three pockets, and so on will easily show which number of pockets is most common and how the number of pockets varies across the class.

Students should be involved in deciding how they want to represent their data. However, for students lacking experience with the various methods of picturing data, you will need to introduce options.

Once students have made the display, they can discuss its value. Analyzing data that are numerical (number of pockets) versus categorical (color of socks) is an added challenge for students as they struggle to make sense of the graphs (Russell, 2006). If, for example, the graph has seven stickers above the five, students may think that five people have seven pockets or seven people have five pockets.

The goal is to help students see that graphs and charts tell about information and that different types of representations tell different things about the same data. The value of having students actually construct their own graphs is not so much that they learn the techniques but that they are personally invested in the data and that they learn how a graph conveys information. Once a graph is constructed, the most important activity is discussing what it tells the people who see it, especially those who were not involved in making the graph. Discussions about graphs of real data that the students have themselves been involved in gathering will help them analyze and interpret other graphs and charts that they see in newspapers and on TV.

What we should not do is only concentrate on the details of graph construction. Your objectives should focus on the issues of analysis and communication, which are much more important than the technique! In the real world, technology will take care of details.

Students should construct graphs or charts by hand and with technology. First, encourage students to make charts and graphs that make sense to them and that they feel communicate the information they wish to convey. The intent is to get the students involved in accurately communicating a message about their data.

TECHNOLOGY

Computer programs and graphing calculators can provide a variety of graphical displays. Use the time saved by technology to focus on the discussions about the information that each display provides. Students can make their own selections from among different graphs and justify their choice based on their own intended purposes. The graphing calculator puts data analysis technology in the hands of every student. The TI-73 calculator is designed for middle grade students. It will produce eight different kinds of plots or graphs, including circle graphs, bar graphs, and picture graphs and will compute and graph lines of best fit.

Bar Graphs and Tally Charts

Bar graphs and tally charts are some of the first ways to group and present data. In grades pre-K–1, teachers model and co-create the displays. In grades 2 and 3, students should be able to create their own displays (CCSSO, 2010). Initially, bar graphs should be made so that each bar consists of countable parts such as squares, objects, tallies, or pictures of objects. Figure 21.6 illustrates a few techniques that can be used to make a graph quickly with the whole class.

A "real graph" uses the actual objects being graphed. Examples include types of shoes, favorite apple, energy bar wrappers, and books. Each item can be placed in a square or on a floor tile so that comparisons and counts are easily made.

Picture graphs use a drawing that represents what is being graphed. Students can make their own drawings (on the same-size paper), or you can duplicate drawings to be colored or cut out to suit particular needs.

Symbolic graphs use something like squares, blocks, tallies, or Xs to represent the items being counted in the graph. An easy approach is to use sticky notes as elements of a graph. These can be stuck directly to the board or chart paper and rearranged if needed.

Recall that analyzing data in this way is step 3 of the process of doing statistics. A question is posed and data are

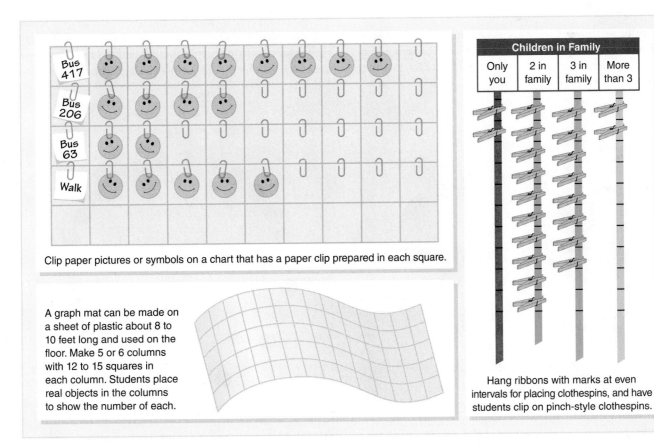

Clip paper pictures or symbols on a chart that has a paper clip prepared in each square.

A graph mat can be made on a sheet of plastic about 8 to 10 feet long and used on the floor. Make 5 or 6 columns with 12 to 15 squares in each column. Students place real objects in the columns to show the number of each.

Hang ribbons with marks at even intervals for placing clothespins, and have students clip on pinch-style clothespins.

FIGURE 21.6 Some ideas for quick graphs that can be used again and again.

collected based on the categories that will be graphed. Figure 21.6 illustrates two quick ways to gather information (step 2) and analyze it (step 3). A class of 25 to 30 students can make a graph in less than 10 minutes, leaving ample time to use it for interpreting results (step 4).

Once a graph has been constructed, engage the class in a discussion of what information the graph tells or conveys. "What can you tell about our class by looking at this shoe graph?" Graphs convey factual information (more students wear sneakers than any other kind of shoe) and also provide opportunities to make inferences that are not directly observable in the graph (kids in this class do not like to wear leather shoes). The difference between actual facts and the inferences that go beyond the data is an important idea in graph construction. Students can examine graphs found in newspapers or magazines and discuss the facts in the graphs and the message that may have been intended by the person who made the graph.

Students' conceptual ability to analyze data and draw conclusions and interpretations is often weak (Tarr & Shaughnessy, 2007), so work on emphasizing this higher-level skill. This emphasis will support the development of statistical thinking and links to the *Standards for Mathematical Practice* (CCSSO, 2010) of reasoning abstractly and quantitatively.

Circle Graphs

Typically, we think of circle graphs as showing percentages and, as such, these would probably not be appropriate for primary students. However, notice in Figure 21.7 that the circle graph could be set up to only indicate the number of data points (in this case, students) in each of five categories. And an understanding of percentages is not required when using computer software to create the graph.

Notice also that the circle graph shows information that is not as easily available from the other graphs. In Figure 21.7, the two graphs show the percentages of students with different numbers of siblings. One graph is based on classroom data and the other on schoolwide data. Because circle graphs display ratios rather than quantities, the small set of class data can be compared to the large set of school data, which could not be done with bar graphs.

Easily Made Circle Graphs. There are several fun and simple ways to make a circle graph. First, use students. Suppose, for example, that each student picked his or her favorite basketball team in the NCAA tournament's "Final Four." Line up all of the students in the room so that students favoring the same team are together. Now form the entire group into a circle of students. Tape the ends of four long strings to the floor in the center of the circle, and extend them to the circle at each point where the teams change. Voilà! You now have a life-sized circle graph with no measuring and no percentages. If you copy and cut out a rational number wheel (see Blackline Master 28) and place it on the center of the circle, the strings will show approximate percentages for each part of your graph (see Figure 21.8).

A second easy approach is to convert bar graphs into a circle graph. Once a bar graph is complete, cut out the bars themselves, and tape them together end to end. Next, tape the two ends together to form a circle. Estimate where the

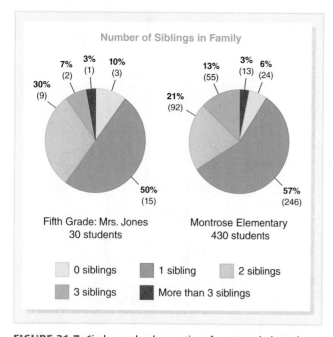

FIGURE 21.7 Circle graphs show ratios of part to whole and can be used to compare ratios.

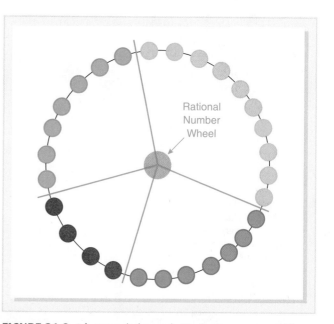

FIGURE 21.8 A human circle graph: Students are arranged in a circle, with string stretched from the center to show the divisions.

center of the circle is, draw lines to the points where different bars meet, and trace around the full loop. You can estimate percentages using the rational number wheel or percent necklace as described in Chapter 17.

Determining Percentages.   If students have experienced the methods just described, using their own calculations to make circle graphs will make more sense. The numbers in each category are added to form the total or whole. (That's the same as taping all of the strips together or lining up the students.) By dividing each of the parts by the whole, students will find the decimals and convert to percents. It is an interesting proportional problem for students to convert between percents and degrees because one is out of 100 and the other out of 360. It is helpful to start students with obvious values like 50 percent, 25 percent, and 10 percent before moving to more difficult values. A ratio table with one row for percent and one row for degrees can serve as an important tool to help students reason.

FORMATIVE Assessment Notes   Students should write in a **journal** about their graphs, explaining what the graph tells and why they selected that type of graph to illustrate the data. As you evaluate students' responses, it is important not to focus undue attention on the skills of constructing a graph, but instead to focus on whether they chose an appropriate representation and have provided a good rationale for its selection that connects back to their question (step 1). ∎

Continuous Data Graphs

Bar graphs or picture graphs are useful for illustrating categories of data that have no numeric ordering—for example, favorite colors or TV shows. On the other hand, when data are grouped along a continuous scale, they should be ordered along a number line. Examples of such information include temperatures that occur over time, height or weight over age, and percentages of test takers' scoring in different intervals along the scale of possible scores.

Line Plots.   *Line plots* are counts of things along a numeric scale. To make a line plot, a number line is drawn and an X is made above the corresponding value on the line for every corresponding data element. One advantage of a line plot is that every piece of data is shown on the graph. It is also a very easy type of graph for students to make. It is essentially a bar graph with a potential bar for every possible value. A simple example is shown in Figure 21.9.

Stem-and-Leaf Plots.   Stem-and-leaf plots (sometimes called *stem plots*) are a form of bar graph in which numeric data are graphed and displayed as a list. By way of example, suppose that the American League baseball teams had posted the following record of wins over the past season:

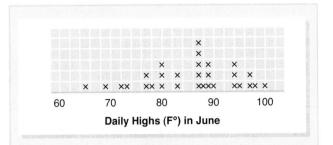

FIGURE 21.9 Line plot of temperatures.

Baltimore	45	Tampa Bay	91
Boston	94	Minnesota	98
Los Angeles	85	New York	100
Chicago	72	Oakland	101
Cleveland	91	Seattle	48
Detroit	102	Toronto	64
Kansas City	96	Texas	65

If the data are to be grouped by tens, list the tens digits in order and draw a line to the right, as shown in Figure 21.10(a). These form the "stem" of the graph. Next, go through the list of scores, and write the ones digits next to the appropriate tens digit, as shown in Figure 21.10(b). These form the "leaves." The process of making the graph groups the data for you. Furthermore, every piece of data can be retrieved from the graph. (Notice that stem-and-leaf plots are best made on graph paper so that each digit takes up the same amount of space.) The graph can be quickly rewritten, ordering each leaf from least to most, as shown in Figure 21.10(c).

Stem-and-leaf plots are not limited to two-digit data. For example, if the data ranged from 600 to 1300, the stem could be the numerals from 6 to 13 and the leaves made of two-digit numbers separated by commas.

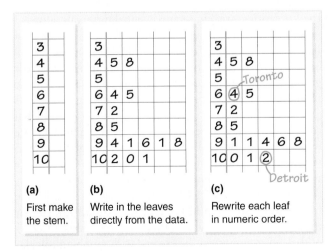

(a)
First make the stem.

(b)
Write in the leaves directly from the data.

(c)
Rewrite each leaf in numeric order.

FIGURE 21.10 Making a stem-and-leaf plot.

	Test Scores		
	Mrs. Day		**Mrs. Knight**
	4	5	
		•	9
	2 3	6	
7 7	8	•	5
3 0 4 2 4	7	1 0	
7 9 5	•	8 6 9 9	
3 4 1	8	4 0 1 3 1 2	
5 8 7	•	9 5	
	9	3 1 0	
9 6	•	7	
0 0	10	0	

FIGURE 21.11 Stem-and-leaf plots can be used to compare two sets of data.

Figure 21.11 illustrates two additional variations. When two sets of data are to be compared, the leaves can extend in opposite directions from the same stem. In this example, notice that the data are grouped by fives instead of tens. When plotting 62, the 2 is written next to the 6; for 67, the 7 is written next to the dot below the 6.

Notice that the stem-and-leaf plot in Figure 21.11 clearly shows the shape of the data. You can observe how the data spread and how they cluster. From observation, students can find the range, median, mode, and outliers. Using rows grouped by fives instead of by tens illustrates the spread of the data, perhaps to illustrate particular grades (e.g., B from B+). Determining how to set up the stem-and-leaf plot depends on the context and on the question being asked.

Histograms.   A histogram is a form of bar graph in which the categories are consecutive equal intervals along a numeric scale. The number of data elements falling into that particular interval determines the height or length of each bar. Histograms differ from bar graphs in that bar graphs can be used for categorical data and the bars can be placed in a different order without changing the results (Metz, 2010). Histograms are not difficult in concept but can be challenging to construct: What is the appropriate interval to use for the bar width? What is a good scale to use for the length of the bars? The need for all of the data to be grouped and counted within each interval causes further difficulty. Figure 21.12 shows a histogram for the same temperature data used in Figure 21.9. Notice how similar the two displays are in illustrating the spread and clustering of data. Histograms can be created with graphing calculators, computer software, or online at http://illuminations. nctm.org/ActivityDetail.aspx?ID=78.

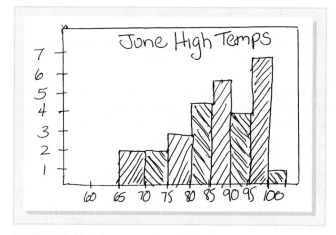

FIGURE 21.12 Histogram of June high temperatures.

Line Graphs.   A *line graph* is used to represent two related pieces of continuous data, and a line is drawn to connect the points. For example, a line graph might be used to show how the length of a flagpole shadow changed from one hour to the next during the day. The horizontal scale would be time, and the vertical scale would be the length of the shadow. Data can be gathered at specific points in time (e.g., every 15 minutes), and these points can be plotted. A straight line can be drawn to connect these points because time is continuous and data points do exist between the plotted points. See the example in Figure 21.13 for a line graph on temperature change.

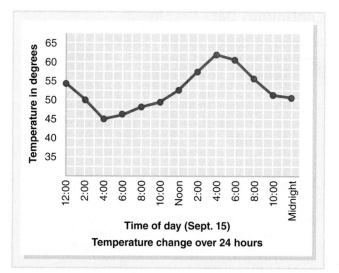

FIGURE 21.13 Line graph of one day's temperatures.

Scatter Plots

Scatter plots are an emphasis in grade 8 (CCSSO, 2010; NCTM, 2006). "Teachers should encourage students to plot many data sets and look for relationships in the [scatter] plots; computer graphing software and graphing calculators can be very helpful in this work. Students should see a range of examples in which plotting data sets suggests linear relationships, and no apparent relationships at all" (NCTM, 2000, p. 253). Data in scatter plots are often analyzed to search for or demonstrate relationships between two sets of data or phenomena. For example, what are the relationships, if any, between time spent watching television and overall grades?

All sorts of real situations exist in which we are interested in relationships between two variables or two numeric phenomena. How far does a toy car roll beyond an inclined plane as the angle of the plane varies? Is there a relationship between the air in a balloon and the time it takes to deflate? Such data are generally gathered from some sort of experiment that is set up and observed, with measurements taken.

Data that may be related are gathered in pairs. For example, if you were going to examine the possible relationship between hours of TV watched and grades, each person in the survey or sample would produce a pair of numbers, one for TV time and one for grade point average.

Data involving two variables can be plotted on a scatter plot, a graph of points on a coordinate grid with each axis representing one of the two variables. Each pair of numbers from the two sets of data, when plotted, produces a visual image of the data as well as a hint concerning any possible relationships. Suppose that the following information was gathered from 25 eighth-grade boys: height in inches, weight in pounds, and number of letters in their last name. The two graphs in Figure 21.14 show (a) a scatter plot of height to weight, and (b) a scatter plot of name length to weight.

The scatter plots indicate that there is a relationship in the boys' weights and heights, though there is some variation. But there is no relationship between name length and weight.

Best-Fit Lines.   If your scatter plot indicates a relationship, it can be simply described in words. "As boys get taller, they get heavier." This may be correct but is not particularly useful. What exactly is the relationship? If I knew the height of a boy, could I predict what his weight might be? Like much of statistical analysis, the value of a statistic is to predict what has not yet been observed. (For example, we poll a small sample of voters before an election to predict how the full population will vote.)

The relationship in this case is a ratio between the two measures. If the scatter plot seems to indicate a steadily increasing or steadily decreasing relationship (as in the height–weight graph), you can find the ratio between the variables by drawing a straight line through the data points that "best" represent the pattern or shape of all of the dots.

What determines best fit? From a strictly visual standpoint, the line you select defines the observed relationship and could be used to predict other values not in the data set. The more closely the dots in the scatter plot cluster around the line you select, the greater the confidence you would have in the predictive value of the line. Certainly you could try to draw a straight line somewhere in the name length–weight graph, but you would not have much confidence in its predictive capability because the dots would be quite dispersed from the line.

Activity 21.4

Best-Fit Line

Once students have collected related data and prepared a scatter plot, duplicate an accurate version of the plot for each group of students. Provide groups with one piece of uncooked spaghetti to use as a line. The task is to tape the spaghetti on the plot so that it is the "best" line to represent the relationship in the dots. Ask students to develop a rationale for why they positioned the line as they did, and write an equation for their line.

Using a projection device, compare the lines chosen by various groups and their rationales. Use the different choices to predict the data for a new value.

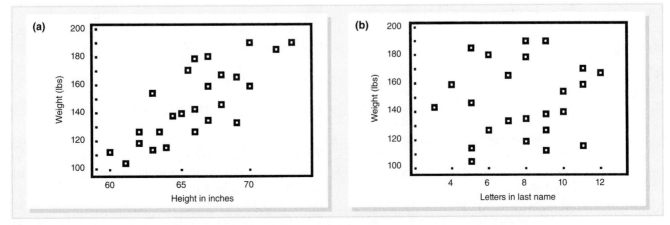

FIGURE 21.14 Scatter plots show potential relationships or lack of relationships.

PAUSE and REFLECT

Before reading further, return to the height–weight plot in Figure 21.14(a) and draw a straight line that you think would make a good line of best fit. (You may want to make an enlargement of that figure to use with your class.) Why did you draw the line where you did? ●

Encourage students to use a "mathematical" reason for why a line might be best. Since a good line is one around which most dots cluster, a good-fitting line is one where the distances from all of the dots to the line are minimal. This general notion of least distance to the line for all points can lead to an algorithm that will always produce a unique line for a given set of points. Two such algorithms are well known and used in statistics. The more complicated approach is called the *least squares regression line*. It is an algebraic procedure that is challenging for middle grade students and can be rather complicated for them to compute. The second algorithm produces the median-median line, which is easier to determine. It basically involves dividing the data into three sets and finding the medians of each. The medians are plotted and further manipulated to find a best-fit line.

These techniques are programmed into graphing calculators. Students can enter their data into the table feature, plot it on the graph, and TECHNOLOGY then find the line of best fit. If students have already drawn a line by hand, then the calculator provides a good opportunity to compare equations to see whether they are both reasonable.

Data Analysis: Measures of Center and Variability

Although graphs provide visual images of data, measures of the data are a different and important way to describe data. The most common numerical descriptions of a set of data relate to the spread (the *range*) and the center (a *mean*, *median*, or *mode*), and dispersion within the range (the *variance* or *dispersion*). Students can get an idea of the importance of these statistics by exploring the ideas informally.

Averages

The term *average* is heard quite frequently in everyday usage. Sometimes it refers to an exact arithmetic average, as in "the average daily rainfall." Sometimes it is used quite loosely, as in "She is about average height." In either situation, an average is a single number or measure that is descriptive of a larger collection of numbers. If your test average is 92, it is assumed that somehow this number reflects all of your test scores.

Students' understanding of average can be categorized into different ways of thinking: average as mode (what is

there most of?), average as something reasonable, average as the standard algorithm, average as mean point, and average as mathematical equilibrium (Garcia and Garret, 2006). As students avoid short-circuiting their thinking by merely using procedural knowledge (Russell & Mokros, 1991), they should widen their experiences with real-world contexts in an effort to explore the conceptual understanding of statistics (Jacobbe, 2008).

The mean, median, and mode are specific types of averages, also called *measures of center* or *measures of central tendency*. The mode is the value that occurs most frequently in the data set.

The mean is computed by adding all of the numbers in the set and dividing the sum by the number of elements added. A common misconception with the mean is that students use it to find a measure of center regardless of the context (McGatha, Cobb, & McClain, 1998).

The median is the middle value in an ordered set of data. Half of all values lie at or above the median and half at or below. The median is easier to understand and to compute and is not affected, as the mean is, by one or two extremely large or extremely small values outside the range of the rest of the data. The most common misconception using the median emerges when students neglect to order the numbers in the data set from least to greatest. The median and the mean first appear as standards in the sixth grade in the *Common Core State Standards* (CCSSO, 2010). *Curriculum Focal Points* places descriptive statistics as a focus in eighth grade, integrated with number and algebra (NCTM, 2006).

Students can investigate http://illuminations.nctm .org/ActivityDetail.aspx?ID=160 to find the mean and median for a set of data that they create.

As mentioned earlier, the context in statistics is important. The context of a situation will determine whether the mode, mean, or median is the measure you want to use. For example, in reporting home prices (see p. 434), the median is quite different from the mean, with the mean being higher. Which better portrays the cost of housing? Very expensive homes can drive the mean up, so typically the median is a more common measure for describing average housing costs. If a travel agent gathered data on the number of days that families usually travel as part of planning a vacation package, the agent would be more interested in the mode because the other measures would not be as helpful in answering the question.

Understanding the Mean: Two Interpretations

There are actually two different ways to think about the mean. First, it is a number that represents what all of the data items would be if they were leveled off. In this sense, the mean represents all of the data items. Statisticians prefer to think of the mean as a central balance point. This concept of the mean is more in keeping with the notion of a measure of the "center" of the data or a measure of central tendency. Both concepts are discussed in the following sections.

Leveling Interpretation.   Suppose that the average number of family members for the students in your class is 5. One way to interpret this is to think about distributing the entire collection of moms, dads, sisters, and brothers to each of the students so that each would have a "family" of the same size. To say that you have an average score of 93 for the four tests in your class is like spreading the total of all of your points evenly across the four tests. It is as if each student had the same family size and each test score were the same, but the totals matched the actual distributions. An added benefit of this explanation of the mean is that it connects to the algorithm for computing the mean.

Activity 21.5

Leveling the Bars

ENGLISH LANGUAGE LEARNERS

Have students make a bar graph of some data using connecting cubes (one cube per value). Choose a situation with 5 or 6 values. For example, Figure 21.15 shows bars for six toys. The task for students is to use the stacks of cubes (bars) to determine what the price would be if all of the toys were the same price. Encourage students to use various techniques to rearrange the cubes to "level" the prices, or make the price the same for each item. Be sure that ELLs understand the meaning of "leveling" the bars.

Explain to students that the size of the leveled bars is the mean of the data—the amount that each item would cost if all items cost the same amount but the total of the prices remained fixed.

Follow "Leveling the Bars" with the next activity to help students develop an algorithm for finding the mean.

Activity 21.6

The Mean Foot

ENGLISH LANGUAGE LEARNERS

STUDENTS *with* SPECIAL NEEDS

Pose the following question: What is the mean length of our feet in inches? This context needs to be clear to ELLs because *foot* is not being used as a measurement unit, but as an object. Also, consider measuring in centimeters rather than inches. Have each student cut a strip of cash register tape that matches the length of his or her foot. Students record their names and the length of their feet in inches on the strips. Suggest that before finding a mean for the class, you will first get means for smaller groups. Put students into groups of four, six, or eight students (use even numbers). In each group, have the students tape their foot strips end to end. The task for each group is to come up with a method of

finding the mean without using any of the lengths written on the strips. They can only use the combined strip. Each group will share their method with the class. From this work, they will devise a method for determining the mean for the whole class. For students with disabilities, help them fold the strip to see how to divide the cash register strip into equal lengths.

PAUSE and REFLECT

Before reading on, what is a method that the students could use in "The Mean Foot"? ●

To evenly distribute the inches for each student's foot among the members of the group, they can fold the strip into equal parts so that there are as many sections as students in the group. Then they can measure the length of any one part.

How can you find the mean for the whole class? Suppose there are 23 students in the class. Using the strips

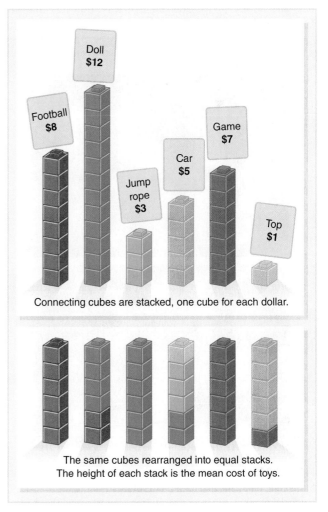

Connecting cubes are stacked, one cube for each dollar.

The same cubes rearranged into equal stacks. The height of each stack is the mean cost of toys.

FIGURE 21.15 Understanding the mean as a leveling of the data.

already taped together, make one very long strip for the whole class. It is not reasonable to fold this long strip into 23 equal sections. But if you wanted to know how long the resulting strip would be, how could that be done? The total length of the strip is the sum of the lengths of the 23 individual foot strips. To find the length of one section if the strip were actually folded in 23 parts, simply divide by 23. In fact, students can mark off "mean feet" along the strip. There should be very close to 23 equal-length "feet." This dramatically illustrates the algorithm for finding the mean.

Balance Point Interpretation.   Statisticians think about the mean as a point on a number line where the data on either side of the point are balanced. To help think about the mean in this way, it is useful to think about the data placed on a line plot. Notice that what is important includes how many pieces of data are on either side of the mean *and* their distances from the mean.

To illustrate, draw a number line on the board, and arrange eight sticky notes above the number 3 as shown in Figure 21.16(a). Each sticky note represents one family. The notes are positioned on the line to indicate how many pets the family owns. Stacked like this indicates that all families have the same number of pets. The mean is three pets. But different families are likely to have different

numbers of pets. So we could think of eight families with a range of numbers of pets. Some may have zero pets, and some may have ten pets or even more. How could you change the number of pets for these eight families so that the mean remains at 3? Students will suggest moving the sticky notes in opposite directions, probably in pairs. This will result in a symmetrical arrangement. But what if one of the families has eight pets, a move of five spaces from the 3? This might be balanced by moving two families to the left, one three spaces to the 0 and one two spaces to the 1. Figure 21.16(b) shows one way the families could be rearranged to maintain a mean of 3. Can you find at least two other distributions of the families, each having a mean of 3?

Use the next activity to find the mean or balance point given the data.

Finding the Balance Point

Have students draw a number line from 0 to 12 with about two inches between the numbers. Use six small sticky notes to represent the prices of six toys as shown in Figure 21.17. Have them place a light pencil mark on the line where they think the mean might be. For the moment, avoid the add-up-and-divide computation. Ask students to determine the mean by moving the sticky notes in toward the "center." That is, the students are to find out what price (point on the number line) balances out the six prices. For each move of a sticky one space to the left, a different sticky must be moved one space to the right. Eventually, all sticky notes should be stacked above the same number, the balance point or mean.

  PAUSE and REFLECT

Stop and try this exercise yourself. Notice that after any pair of moves that keep the distribution balanced, you actually have a new distribution of prices with the same mean. The same was true when you moved the sticky notes out from the mean when they were all stacked on the same point. ●

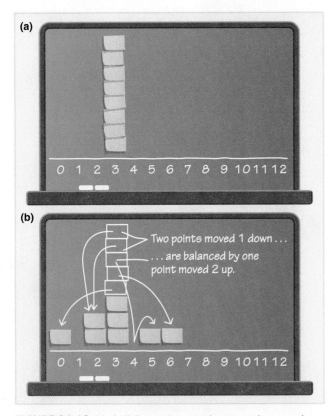

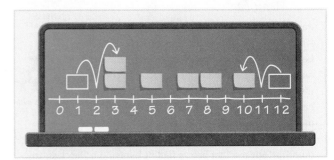

FIGURE 21.16 (a) If all data points are the same, the mean is that value. (b) By moving data points away from the mean in a balanced manner, different distributions can be found that have the same mean.

FIGURE 21.17 Move data points in toward the center or balance point without changing the balance around that point. When you have all points at the same value, that is the balance or the mean.

Changes in the Mean. The balance approach to finding the mean clearly illustrates different data distributions can have the same mean. Especially for small sets of data, the mean is significantly affected by extreme values. For example, suppose another toy with a price of $20 is added to the six we have been using in the examples. How will the mean change? If the $1 toy were removed, how would the mean be affected? Suppose that one new toy is added that increases the mean from $6 to $7. How much does the new toy cost? Students should be challenged with questions such as these using small sets of data and either the balance or the leveling concept.

TECHNOLOGY In the NCTM e-Examples, Applet 6.6, "Comparing Properties of the Mean and the Median," shows seven data points that can be dragged back and forth along a number line with the mean and median updated instantly. The applet allows students to see how stable the median is and how changing one point can affect the mean.

FORMATIVE Assessment Notes Consider using a **diagnostic interview** to assess whether students are able to determine the best measure of center to use in a given situation such as the average height of students in the class. You can begin with general questions such as these: What is an average? What does the mean represent? What does the median represent? What is the difference between the mean and the median? What is each useful for? Then move to more analytical questions: Which should we use for this set of data? Might we use a different measure of center in another class? When you've found the average height of the students in our class, is it possible that no one is that height? Why? ■

Variability

While measures of center are a long-standing topic, measures of variability also need explicit attention in the curriculum (Franklin & Garfield, 2006; Franklin et al., 2005; Rossman, Chance, & Medina, 2006; Scheaffer, 2006). In the *Common Core State Standards*, variability is a focus of seventh grade (CCSSO, 2010). Students often do not have a clear understanding of variability, because analyzing measure of center dominates the data analysis phase. Shaughnessy (2006) summarized the findings on what students should know about variability in the following list, starting with basic notions and progressing to more sophisticated ideas:

1. Focusing only on outliers or extremes (but not on the full distribution of the data)
2. Considering change over time (which can lead into discussions of other types of variation)
3. Examining variability as the full range of data (Range is everything that occurs, but it doesn't reveal the frequency of different events within the range.)
4. Considering variability as the likely range or expected value
5. Looking at how far data points are from the center (e.g., the mean)
6. Looking at how far off a set of data is from some fixed value

In order to be prepared to teach students variability beyond outliers and extremes, it is important to know about the way that variability occurs in statistics.

The Guidelines for Assessment and Instruction in Statistics Education (GAISE) report (Franklin et al., 2005) discusses three levels of statistical thinking that, although developmental in nature, can be roughly mapped to elementary, middle, and high school curriculum. At the first level, the focus is on variability within a group—for example, the varying lengths of students' names, varying family sizes, and so on. When students create a bar graph of class data and compare the data collected, they are discussing the variability within a group.

At the second level, variability within a group continues, but groups of data are also considered. Students might compare the variability of fifth graders' favorite music choices with eighth graders' music choices, an example of variability between groups. In addition, middle school students study how the change in one variable relates to change in another variable—yes, algebra! Students analyze two variables to see whether there is a relationship (as discussed in the section on scatter plots). Students also explore sampling variability (Franklin et al., 2005). When students flip a coin 10 times as a sample, they may get 5 heads and 5 tails, but they also may get many other results (even 0 heads and 10 tails). This is sampling variability. The larger the sample, the more the data reflect the expected values (50 percent heads, 50 percent tails).

At the third level, students can examine natural and induced variability. For example, plants grow at different rates. When one flower naturally grows taller than the one right next to it in the garden, that is natural variability. If the two plants were in two different gardens, then other variables come into play: fertilization, amount of sunlight, amount of water, and so on, which can "induce" different growth rates. Knowing these variability terms is less important than knowing that in designing an experiment, we must look at one factor (e.g., sunlight) and all other factors should be kept the same or controlled. This is at the heart of doing statistics (Franklin & Garfield, 2006).

One way to help students understand variability is to ask questions on variability in the discussion of data. Friel, O'Conner, and Mamer (2006), using the context of heart rates, suggest the following questions as examples of how to get students to focus on data and variability:

- If the average heart rate for 9- to 11-year-olds is 88 beats per minute, does this mean every student this age has a heart rate of 88 beats per minute? (Note that the range is actually quite large—from 60 to 110 beats per minute.)

- If we found the heart rate for everyone in the class (of 30), what might the distribution of data look like?
- If another class (of 30) was measured, would their distribution look like the one for our class? What if they just came in from recess?
- Would the distribution of data from 200 students look like the data from the two classes?

Comparing different data sets or playing a game repeatedly provides the opportunity for students to analyze the spread of data and think about variation in data (Franklin & Mewborn, 2008; Kader & Mamer, 2008).

Box Plots

Box plots (also known as *box and whisker plots*) are a method for visually displaying not only the center (median) but also the range and spread of data. Sixth graders should be able to create and analyze box plots (CCSSO, 2010). In Figure 21.18, the ages in months for 27 sixth-grade students are given, along with stem-and-leaf plots for the full class and the boys and girls separately. Box plots are shown in Figure 21.19.

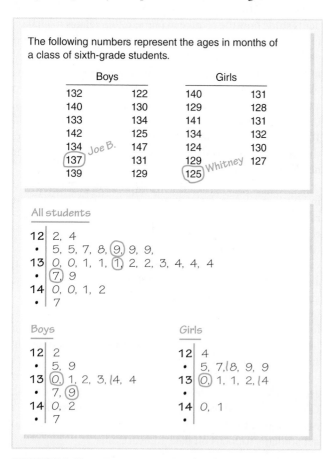

FIGURE 21.18 Ordered stem-and-leaf plots grouped by fives. Medians and quartiles are circled or are represented by a vertical bar if they fall between two elements.

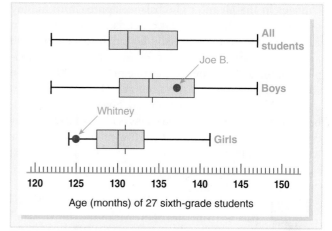

FIGURE 21.19 Box plots show a lot of information. In addition to showing how data are distributed, data points of particular interest can be shown.

Each box plot has these three features:

1. A box that contains the "middle half" of the data, one-fourth to the left and right of the median. The ends of the box are at the *lower quartile*, the median of the lower half of the data, and the *upper quartile*, the median of the upper half of the data.
2. A line inside the box at the median of the data.
3. A line (sometimes known as the *whisker*) extending from the end of each box to the *lower extreme* and *upper extreme* of the data. Each line, therefore, covers the upper and lower fourths of the data.

Look at the information these box plots provide at a glance! The box and the lengths of the lines provide a quick indication of how the data are spread out or bunched together. Because the median is shown, this spreading or bunching can be determined for each quarter of the data. The entire class in this example is much more spread out in the upper half than the lower half. The girls are much more closely grouped in age than either the boys or the class as a whole. The range of the data (the difference between upper and lower extremes) is represented by the length of the plot, and the extreme values can be read directly. The mean is indicated by the small marks above and below each box. A box plot provides useful visual information to help understand the shape of a data set.

To make a box plot, put the data in order. Next, find the median. This can be done on stem-and-leaf plots as in Figure 21.18. To find the two quartiles, ignore the median itself, and find the medians of the upper and lower halves of the data. Mark the two extremes, the two quartiles, and the median above an appropriate number line. Draw the box and the lines. See http://illuminations.nctm.org/Activity Detail.aspx?ID=77 for a way to use technology to create box plots.

Because box plots have so much information and proportional thinking, students may be challenged to interpret box plots (Bakker, Biehler, & Konold, 2004). Support in making these connections can be done by using contexts that are meaningful and asking questions about the various statistics that are shown on the plot. Understanding the proportional relationships can be supported through use of percent strips or ratio tables. (See Chapter 18 for more on models to support proportional thinking.)

Remember that a box plot, like any graph, is a tool for learning about the question posed, not an end in itself (McClain, Leckman, Schmitt, & Regis, 2006). Because a box plot offers so much information on the spread and center of the data, much can be learned from careful examination, and particularly from comparing two box plots with related data.

 Graphing calculators and several computer programs draw box plots, making this process even more accessible. The TI-73, TI-84, and TI-Nspire calculators can draw box plots for up to *TECHNOLOGY* three sets of data on the same axis.

 ## PAUSE and REFLECT

Notice that in Figure 21.19 the box for the boys is actually a bit longer than the box for the whole class. How can that be when there are clearly more students in the full class than there are boys? How would you explain this apparent discrepancy to a class of seventh graders?

 # Interpreting Results

Interpretation is the fourth step in the process of doing statistics. As seen in the sample test items shown earlier, sometimes questions focus on mathematical ideas rather than statistical ideas. Although it is helpful to ask mathematical questions, it is essential to ask questions that are statistical in nature. That means the questions focus on the context of the situation and seeing what can be learned or inferred from the data. In addition, they should focus on the key ideas of statistics, such as variability, center of the data, and the shape of the data. During interpretation, students might want to loop back and create a different data display to get a different look at the data, or gather data from a different population to see whether their results are representative.

Different researchers have recommended questions that focus on statistical thinking (Franklin et al., 2005; Friel, O'Conner, & Mamer, 2006; Russell, 2006; Shaughnessy, 2006). Here are some ideas from their lists to get you started on having meaningful discussions interpreting data:

- What do the numbers (symbols) tell us about our class (or other population)?
- If we asked another class (population), how would our data look? What if we asked a larger group, how would the data look?
- How do the numbers in this graph (population) *compare* to this graph (population)?
- Where are the data "clustering"? How much of the data are in the cluster? How much are *not* in the cluster? About what percent is or is not in the cluster?
- What kinds of variability might need to be considered in interpreting these data?
- Would the results be different if . . . [change of sample/population or setting]? (Example: Would gathered data on word length in a third-grade book be different from a fifth-grade book? Would a science book give different results from a reading book?)
- How strong is the association between two variables (scatter plot)? How do you know? What does that mean if you know *x*? If you know *y*?
- What does the graph *not* tell us? What might we infer?
- What new questions arise from these data?
- What is the maker of the graph trying to tell us?

These prompts apply across many data displays. It certainly should be a major focus of your instruction. Consider it the *after* phase of your lesson, though some of these questions will be integrated in the *during* phase as well. The emphasis of the questions in this phase is on getting students to notice differences in the data and provide possible reasons for those differences (Franklin & Mewborn, 2008).

Our world is inundated with data, from descriptive statistics to different graphs. It is essential that we prepare students to be literate about what can be interpreted from data and what cannot be interpreted from data, what is important to pay attention to and what can be discarded as misleading or poorly designed statistics. This is important for success in school, as well as for being a mathematically literate citizen.

RESOURCES *for Chapter 21*

LITERATURE CONNECTIONS

Literature is full of situations in which things must be sorted, compared, or measured. As noted earlier in this chapter, books of lists also are fruitful beginnings for data explorations. Students can use the data in the books and/or compare similar data collected themselves.

The Best Vacation Ever *Murphy, 1997*

In this book, appropriate for first or second grade, a little girl gathers data from her family on what is important to them to decide where the family would have the best vacation. This book nicely introduces the concept of gathering data to answer a question.

Frog and Toad Are Friends *Lobel, 1970*

When Frog and Toad go walking, Frog loses a button. As they search to find the button, they find many buttons. Whenever Frog's friends ask, "Is this your button?" Frog responds (with a touch of frustration), "No, that is not my button! That button is _____, but my button was _____."

    This classic story is a perfect lead-in to sorting activities as described in this chapter. Young students can model the story directly with sets of buttons, shells, attribute blocks, Woozle Cards (Blackline Master 59), or other objects with a variety of attributes.

200% of Nothing: An Eye-Opening Tour Through the Twists and Turns of Math Abuse and Innumeracy *Dewdney, 1993*

This middle school–friendly book has explanations of the many ways that "statistics are turned" to mislead people. Because the examples are *real*, provided by readers of *Scientific American*, this book is an excellent tool for showing how important it is to be statistically literate in today's society. Reading the examples can launch a mathematics project into looking for errors in advertisements and at how overlapping groups (as in a Venn Diagram) can be reported separately to mislead readers. (See Bay-Williams and Martinie, 2009, for more ways to use this book.)

If the World Were a Village: A Book about the World's People [Second Edition] *Smith, 2011*

This book explores global wealth, culture, language, and other influences. Each beautiful two-page spread shares the statistics for the topic (e.g., language). This book can give rise to other questions about the world, which can be researched and interpreted into the village metaphor. An article that links this idea to a project exploring concepts of statistics using 100 students is a great follow-up (Riskowski, Olbricht, & Wilson, 2010).

RECOMMENDED READINGS

Articles

Harper, S. R. (2004). Students' interpretations of misleading graphs. *Mathematics Teaching in the Middle Grades, 9*(6), 340–343.
    Harper explores some types of misleading graphing techniques that are often seen in the popular press and discusses how she used these graphs with students. This examines the kind of ideas found in the classic book How to Lie with Statistics *(Huff, 1954/1993).*

Franklin, C. A., & Mewborn, D. S. (2008). Statistics in the elementary grades: Exploring distribution of data. *Teaching Children Mathematics, 15*(1), 10–16.

Kader, G., & Mamer, J. (2008). Statistics in the middle grades: Understanding center and spread. *Mathematics Teaching in the Middle Grades, 14*(1), 38–43.
    Both of these articles use the process of doing statistics as a launching point to frame effective statistics instruction. Both include excellent examples of activities, including questions and data displays.

Books

Curcio, F. (2010). *Developing data-graph comprehension in grades K–8.* Reston, VA: NCTM.
    This NCTM book shares 30 graphing activities on exploring, investigating, reasoning, and communicating about data. Each activity includes procedures, discussion questions, writing and reading prompts, and ways to use technology.

Franklin, C., Kader, G., Mewborn, D., Moreno, J., Peck, R., Perry, M., & Scheaffer, R. (2005). *Guidelines for assessment and instruction in statistics education* (GAISE Report). Alexandria, VA: American Statistical Association.
    This excellent framework provides examples for teaching statistics including great tasks to use with students in pre-K–8.

ONLINE RESOURCES

Create a Graph (NCES Kids Zone)
http://nces.ed.gov/nceskids/createagraph
    This site provides tools for creating five different graphical displays.

Data Grapher and Advanced Data Grapher (Illuminations)
http://illuminations.nctm.org/ActivityDetail .aspx?ID=204 http://illuminations.nctm.org/ ActivityDetail.aspx?ID=220
    Analyze data from bar graphs, line graphs, circle graphs, and pictographs. Users can enter data, select which set(s) to display, and choose the type of representation.

REFLECTIONS *on Chapter 21*

WRITING TO LEARN

1. How is statistics different from mathematics? In a lesson on the mean, what mathematical questions and what statistical questions might you ask?
2. What is meant by the "shape of data"?
3. Data should be collected to answer questions. What are some examples of questions that students might explore with data at the K–2 level? 3–5? 6–8?
4. What kinds of graphs can be used for data that can be put into categories (categorical data)?
5. Give an example of a context in which you would you choose to use median over mean and when you would choose mean over median. (Use examples other than the ones given in the text.)
6. Describe two different ways to develop the concept of mean. How can each be developed? Which idea leads to the method of computing the mean?

FOR DISCUSSION AND EXPLORATION

1. Select a popular news magazine such as *Time* or *Newsweek*. Look through at least one issue carefully to find graphs and statistical information a typical reader would be expected to understand. Note that you will not be able to do this by simply looking for graphs. Statistics are frequently used without any corresponding graphs.
2. The process of doing statistics must be clear to students, even when they are working on a piece (e.g., circle graphs) within the process. Pick a grade, and consider possibilities for authentic and engaging (and researchable) questions. Then discuss how you would plan instruction in order to include the four-step process and engage students in statistical thinking.

MyEducationLab™

Go to the MyEducationLab (www.myeducationlab.com) for Math Methods, and familiarize yourself with the content. Much of the site content is organized topically. The topics include all of the following to support your learning in the course:

- Learning outcomes for important mathematics methods course topics aligned with the national standards
- Assignments and Activities, tied to these learning outcomes and standards, that can help you more deeply understand course content
- Building Teaching Skills and Dispositions learning units that allow you to apply and practice your understanding of the core mathematics content and teaching skills

Your instructor has a correlation guide that aligns the exercises on the topical portion of the site with your book's chapters.

On MyEducationLab you will also find book-specific resources including Blackline Masters, Expanded Lesson Activities, and Artifact Analysis Activities.

Field Experience Guide
C O N N E C T I O N S

Field Experiences 1.1, 1.3, and 1.4 focus on the learning environment and can be used to explore the extent to which lessons incorporate the process of doing statistics. FEG Expanded Lesson 9.20 uses the four-step process of doing statistics and can be used alone or with Field Experiences 1.6, "Implementing Mathematical Practice #1"; 2.5, "Incorporating the Standards for Mathematical Practice"; or 2.6, "Planning a Problem-Based Lesson." FEG Expanded Lesson 9.22 engages students in comparing and analyzing different ways to graph data. FEG Expanded Lesson 9.24 explores the impact of outliers in data sets.

Chapter 22

Exploring Concepts of Probability

References to probability are all around us: The weather forecaster predicts a 60 percent chance of snow; medical researchers predict people with certain diets have a high chance of heart disease; investors calculate risks of specific investments; and so on. Simulations of complex situations are frequently based on probabilities and are then used in decision making about such situations as airplane safety under different weather circumstances, highway traffic patterns after building new housing, and disaster plans.

Realistic concepts of chance require considerable development before students are ready to construct formal ideas about the probability of an event. Optimally, this development occurs as students consider and discuss with their peers the outcomes of a wide variety of probabilistic situations. The emphasis should be on exploration rather than rules and formal definitions. These informal experiences will provide a useful background from which more formal ideas can be developed in middle and high school. In *Curriculum Focal Points* (NCTM, 2006) and the *Common Core State Standards* (CCSSO, 2010), probability is one of the major concepts developed in seventh grade.

BIG IDEAS

1. Chance has no memory. For repeated trials of a simple experiment, the outcomes of prior trials have no impact on the next trial. The chance occurrence of six heads in a row has no effect on getting a head on the next toss of the coin. That chance remains 50–50.

2. The probability that a future event will occur can be characterized along a continuum from impossible (0) to certain (1).

3. The *probability* of an event is a number between 0 and 1 that is a measure of the chance that a given event will occur.

A probability of $\frac{1}{2}$ indicates an even chance of the event occurring.

4. The relative frequency of outcomes (from *experiments*) can be used as an estimate of the probability of an event. The larger the number of trials, the better the estimate will be. The results for a small number of trials may be quite different from those experienced in the long run.

5. For some events, the exact probability can be determined by an analysis of the event itself. A probability determined in this manner is called a *theoretical probability.*

6. *Simulation* is a technique used for answering real-world questions or making decisions in complex situations in which an element of chance is involved. To see what is likely to happen in the real event, a model must be designed that has the same probabilities as the real situation.

Mathematics CONTENT CONNECTIONS

Probability is grounded in concepts of rational number and data analysis.

◆ **Fractions and Percents** (Chapters 15 and 17): Students can see fractional parts of spinners or sets of counters in a bag and use these fractions to determine probabilities. Percents provide useful common denominators for comparing ratios (e.g., rolling a 7 three times in the first 20 rolls, or 15 percent, and 16 times in 80 rolls, or 20 percent).

◆ **Ratio and Proportion** (Chapter 18): Comparing probabilities means relating part-to-whole ratios. To understand these comparisons requires proportional reasoning.

◆ **Data Analysis** (Chapter 21): The purpose of probability is to answer statistics-related questions. When performing a probability experiment, the results are data—a sample of the theoretically infinite experiments that could be done.

Introducing Probability

Although probability does not appear as a major topic until seventh grade, it is critical to begin early with notions of chance and fairness. Young students' concept of the likeliness of a future event can be surprising. Students can be absolutely convinced that the next roll of the die will be a 3 "because I just know it's going to happen" or "because 3 is my lucky number." While intuitions such as this can be a positive thing, in probability it can be a preconception that works against understanding randomness of events (Abu-Bakare, 2008).

Likely or Not Likely

Probability is about how likely an event is. Therefore, a good place to begin is with a focus on possible and not possible (Activity 22.1) and later impossible, possible, and certain (Activity 22.2). In preparation for these activities, discuss the meaning of *impossible* and *certain*. These experiences can be woven into discussions across the curriculum, as in Activity 22.1, which is an idea for connecting to children's literature, or in science and social studies, as in Activity 22.2.

Activity 22.1

Nursery Rhyme Possibilities

Create a table, labeling one column "Impossible" and the other "Possible." Take a nursery rhyme verse, such as "Hey, Diddle, Diddle" (or a picture book) and for each line, ask students if it goes in the impossible or possible column. Record each statement in the appropriate column.

Activity 22.2

Is It Likely?

Ask students to judge various events as *certain, impossible,* or *possible* ("might happen"). Consider these examples:

ENGLISH LANGUAGE LEARNERS

STUDENTS *with* SPECIAL NEEDS

- It will rain tomorrow.
- Drop a rock in water and it will sink.
- A sunflower seed planted today will bloom tomorrow.
- The sun will rise tomorrow morning.
- A hurricane/tornado will hit our town.
- In an election, candidate A will be elected.
- If you ask someone who the first U.S. president was, they will know.
- You will have two birthdays this year.
- You will be in bed by 9:00 p.m.

For each event, they should justify their choice of how likely they think it is. Notice that the last two ideas are about the students. This is an opportunity to bring in students' identities and cultures. Ask students to work with their families to write events in their family that are certain, impossible, or possible. Encourage native language use, as appropriate, for ELLs. For students with disabilities, use a strip of cash register tape and label the ends with *impossible* and *certain* to assist them in organizing their thinking. Write the events above on cards so they can place them along the strip.

The key idea to developing chance or probability on a continuum is to help students see that some of these possible events are more likely or less likely than others. For instance, if a group of students is in a running race, the chance that Gregg, a really fast runner, will be first is not certain but is very likely. It is more likely that Gregg will be near the front of the group than near the back of the pack.

The use of random devices (tools) that can be analyzed (e.g., spinners, number cubes, coins to toss, colored cubes drawn from a bag) can help students make predictions about how likely a particular occurrence is. The process of exploring how likely an event is maps to the before, during, after lesson plan model. In the before phase, students make predictions of what they think will be likely; in the during phase, students experiment to explore how likely the event is; and in the after phase, students compile and analyze the experimental results to determine more accurately how likely the event is.

Begin with the use of random devices with which students can count the outcomes. Colored dots can be stuck on the sides of a wooden cube to create different color probabilities. Color tiles (e.g., eight red and two blue) can be placed in opaque bags. Students draw a tile from the bag and then return it after each draw. The following activity is a game of chance with unequal outcomes. However, students may not initially connect that having more of something means it is more likely. A common initial misconception is that there is a one-in-three chance of each of the values, because each one is possible.

Activity 22.3

1-2-3 How Likely?

Make number cubes with sides as follows: 1, 1, 2, 3, 3, 3. Ask students to predict what they might get when they roll the cube. What is likely? What is impossible? Have students roll the cube and record results in a bar graph (as in Figure 22.1, but with just the first three rows), marking an X for 1, 2, and 3 each time the cube shows that value). Stop when one row is full.

Add, Then Tally

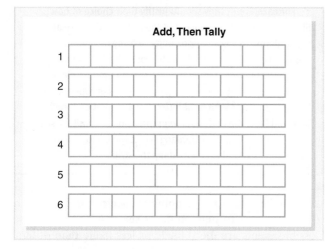

1

2

3

4

5

6

FIGURE 22.1 A recording sheet for "1-2-3 How Likely?"

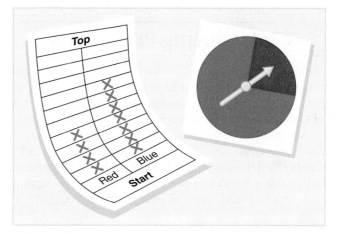

FIGURE 22.2 Students take turns spinning a spinner and recording the result. The first color to reach the top is the winner.

After exploring either 1-2-3 activity, ask, "Which numbers 'won' the most and the least often?" and "If you play again, which number would you pick to win and why?" In Activity 22.4, although an outcome of 1 is impossible, all of the other outcomes, 2 through 6, are possible. A sum of 4 is the most likely. Sums of 2 or 3 are not very likely.

Area models, such as spinners, are more challenging because students cannot count the possible outcomes as readily (Abu-Bakare, 2008). It is therefore important to connect counting to area, as in the following spinner activity.

Students can play "Race to the Top" several times. In the after phase, ask "Which color is likely to win if we play again? Why do you think so?" Spinners show the relative portion of the whole to each color or outcome, but that does not mean that students then draw the conclusion that $\frac{3}{4}$ blue means the probability of blue is 75 percent.

After trying this activity, move to using a variety of spinners. Use spinners that have two colors with the same area—and colors covering different areas, as shown here.

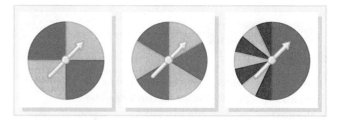

Students do not always see that the first two spinners, or a spinner divided into just two sections, have the same chance of getting blue (Cohen, 2006; Nicolson, 2005). Therefore, it is important to use spinners that are partitioned in different ways. Spinner faces can easily be made to adjust the chances of different outcomes. An effective way to connect the idea that the larger area or region on the spinner is more likely to have a spin land there is to have students use frequency charts to record data. In Figure 22.3 a student explains how she knows which frequency table goes with which circle graph.

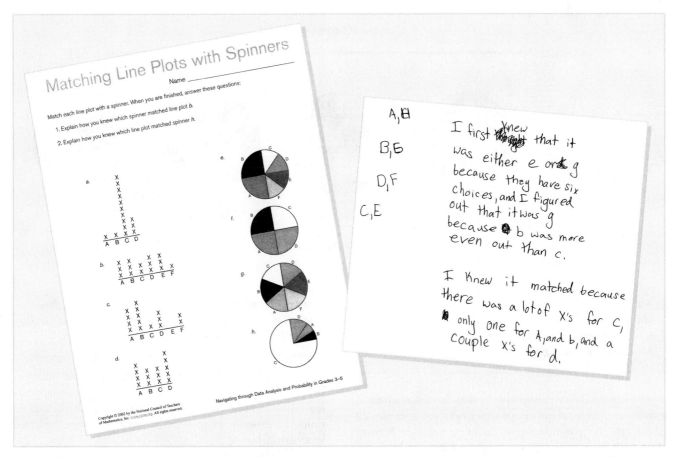

FIGURE 22.3 Student explanations connecting frequency charts to spinners.

Source: Adapted with permission from Chapin, S., Kozial, A., MacPherson, J., & Rezba, C. (2002). *Navigating Through Data Analysis and Probability in Grades 3–5.* Reston, VA: NCTM, p. 116. Copyright © 2002 by the National Council of Teachers of Mathematics. All rights reserved.

FORMATIVE Assessment Notes

Diagnostic interviews can uncover student misconceptions or preconceptions about the probability of an event. Ask students about the probability using color tiles or dice (countable objects). For example, ask, "If there are 3 red and 1 blue tile in this bag and I draw one out, what do you think I will get?" and "If I draw four times, and put the tile back each time, what do you think I will get?" Ask about the chance of rolling certain outcomes on a die. Some students may think 5 is a more likely outcome on a die than a 2 because 5 is bigger than 2. Or students may think a 1 is not as likely as rolling a 5 on a die, perhaps because they are familiar with a game in which 1 is desirable. The 1 is not likely compared to the combined possibility of the other 5 choices, but it is as likely as any other number (Nicolson, 2005; Watson & Moritz, 2003). Finally, ask about how likely outcomes are in an area model such as a spinner. These questions will help you know whether you need to focus on counting or area models, and what kinds of questions or experiences to prepare in order to help students understand that probability is based on knowing all the possible outcomes and how likely each one is. ■

The Probability Continuum

To begin refining the concept that some events are more or less likely to occur than others, introduce the idea of a continuum of probability between impossible and certain. Create a continuum as in Figure 22.4. Label the left end "Impossible" and the right end "Certain." Write "Chances of Spinning Blue" above the line. Discuss various positions on the line and what the corresponding spinner would look like. To review these ideas, show the spinners one at a time and ask which marks represent the chance of getting blue for that particular spinner.

Activity **22.6**

Create a Two-Color Spinner

Using two colors of construction paper or cardstock, cut out circles that are the same size (you can use Blackline Master 28 or create your own). Cut a radius. Slide one into the other and show students how they can create any one of the spinners in Figure 22.4. Have students select one of the spinners.

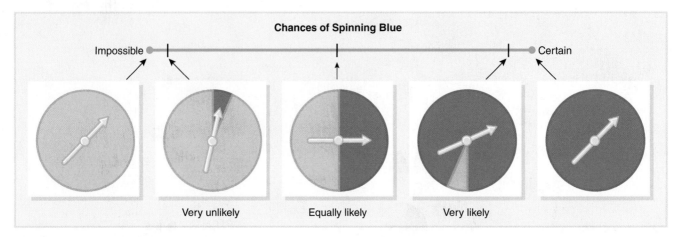

Chances of Spinning Blue

Impossible ● — — — — — — — — — — ● Certain

Very unlikely   Equally likely   Very likely

FIGURE 22.4 The probability continuum. Use these spinner faces to help students see how chance can be at different places on a continuum between impossible and certain.

A paper clip can be used as the spinner. Have students spin and record how many times out of 20 they get each color. Ask students to compare what they got in their experiment with what they expected to get.

Post the probability continuum in the classroom where it can be used as a reference for other opportunities to talk about how likely something is (see the questions in Activity 22.2 for a start to the many things you could ask). Some things change in their probability; for example, the chance of a snow day could be posted and moved from day to day.

In the next activity, students design a random device (color tiles in a bag) that represents various designated positions on the probability line.

Activity 22.7

Design a Bag

ENGLISH LANGUAGE LEARNERS

STUDENTS *with* SPECIAL NEEDS

Provide students with a copy of the recording sheet shown in Figure 22.5 (see Blackline Master 60). Ask students to mark a place on a probability line at roughly the 20 percent position. Students should color the square indicated by "Color" at the top of the page. Students must select 12 tiles, such that their selected color is likely to occur 20 percent of the time. For students with disabilities, begin with 50 percent instead of 20 percent. You can vary the percentages for different groups as a way to differentiate the lesson. Once selected, ask students to experiment by drawing out and recording how many times out of 50 draws their shape shows up. Remind students to shake the bag each time to ensure random sampling.

At the bottom of each sheet (and on the reverse if needed), students explain why they chose their tiles. ELLs and students with disabilities can benefit from sentence starters, such as: *In*

our bag, we explored the color _____. We put in _____ (how many) of _____ (color) and _____ (tell how many of other color tiles). We picked these numbers because_____.

The "Design a Bag" activity provides useful information about how your students conceive of chance as appearing on a continuum. The next follow-up activity focuses on doing an experiment to see whether the design predicted was reasonable.

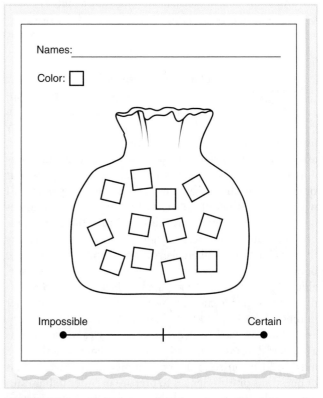

Names: _____

Color: ☐

Impossible ●————————|————————● Certain

FIGURE 22.5 A possible recording sheet for the "Design a Bag" activity (see Blackline Master 60).

Testing Bag Designs

Select a bag design (from Activity 22.7) that most students seem to agree on for the 20 percent mark. Distribute lunch bags and colored tiles or cubes to pairs of students to fill according to the selected design. Once filled, students shake the bag and draw out one tile. Tally marks are used to record a Yes (for the designated color) or No for any other color. This is repeated at least ten times. Be sure that students replace each tile after it is drawn.

Discuss with the class how their respective experiments turned out. Did it turn out about the way they expected? With the small number of trials, there will be groups that get rather unexpected results.

Next, make a large bar graph or tally graph of the data from all of the groups together. This should show many more nos than yeses. Discuss the important idea that if the experiment is repeated a lot of times (many trials), the results are closer to what is expected, which is often not true with a small number of trials.

The "Design a Bag" and "Testing Bag Designs" activities can and should be repeated for two or three other marks on the probability line. Try marks at about $\frac{1}{3}$, $\frac{1}{2}$, and $\frac{3}{4}$. These activities are particularly important because no numbers are used for the probabilities; there are no "right" answers. The testing of a design with only a small group demonstrates to students that chance is not an absolute predictor in the short run. The group graphs help students with the difficult concept that the chance tends to approach what is expected in the long run.

As a fun twist on this activity, have a group select a probability, design a bag, and then trade bags with another group. Each group conducts 50 draws and then predicts what is in the bag. They can compare results with the group who designed the bag.

Theoretical Probability and Experiments

The *probability* of an event is a measure of the chance of that event occurring (Franklin et al., 2005). Students to this point have only been asked to place events on a continuum from impossible to certain or to compare the probability of one event with another. So how do you measure chance of an event? In many situations, there are actually two ways to determine this measure.

Probability has two distinct types. The first type involves any specific event whose probability of occurrence is known (e.g., that a fair die has a $\frac{1}{6}$ chance of producing each number). When the probability of an event is known, probability can be established theoretically by examining all the possibilities.

The second case involves any event whose probability of occurrence isn't observable but can be established through empirical data or evidence from past experiments or data collection (Colgan, 2006; Nicolson, 2005). Examples include a basketball player's probability of making free throws in a game (based on the player's previous record), the chance that a salesperson will be successful (based on prior rates of success), or the chance of rain (based on how often it rained under equivalent conditions). Although this latter type of probability is less common in the school curriculum, it is the most applicable to fields that use probability and therefore important to include in your teaching (Franklin et al., 2005).

In both cases, experiments or simulations can be designed to explore the phenomena being examined. (Sometimes in the K–12 curriculum this is referred to as *experimental probability*, but because this terminology is not employed by statisticians, it is not used here.)

Coin flips have a known probability of occurrence. Logically, we can argue that if it is a fair coin, obtaining a head is just as likely as obtaining a tail. Because there are two possible outcomes that are equally likely, each has a probability of $\frac{1}{2}$. Hence, the theoretical probability of obtaining a head is $\frac{1}{2}$. When all possible outcomes of a simple experiment are equally likely, the theoretical probability of an event is

Number of outcomes in the event ÷ Number of possible outcomes

Instead, consider the question, "Is this coin fair?" This is a statistics problem that can only be answered by doing an experiment and establishing the frequency of heads and tails over the long run (Franklin et al., 2005). The answer requires empirical data and the probability will be:

Number of observed occurrences of the event ÷ Total number of trials

Because it is impossible to conduct an infinite number of trials, we can only consider the relative frequency for a very large number of trials as an approximation of the theoretical probability. This emphasizes the notion that probability is more about predictions over the long term than predictions of individual events.

Theoretical Probability

A problem-based way to introduce theoretical probability is to engage students in an activity with an unfair game. In the following activity, the results of the game will likely be contrary to students' intuitive ideas. This in turn will provide a real reason to analyze the game in a logical manner and find out why things happened as they did—theoretical probability.

Activity 22.9

Fair or Unfair?

Three students toss 2 like coins (e.g., 2 pennies or 2 nickels) and they record points according to the following rules: Player A gets 1 point if the coin toss results in "two heads"; player B gets 1 point if the toss results in "two tails"; and player C gets 1 point if the toss results are "mixed" (one head, one tail). The game is over after 20 tosses. The player who has the most points wins. Have students play the game at least two or three times. After each game, the players are to stop and discuss whether they think the game is fair and make predictions about who will win the next game.

When the full class has played the game several times, conduct a discussion on the fairness of the game. Challenge students to make an argument based on the data and game rules as to whether the game is fair or not. For ELLs, discuss the meaning of *fair* prior to beginning the game, and review the term when asking students to create an argument.

ENGLISH LANGUAGE LEARNERS

A common analysis of the game in Activity 22.9 might go something like this: At first students think that because there are three outcomes—two tails, one head and one tail, or two heads—that each has an equal chance. The game should be fair. However, after playing "Fair or Unfair?" students find that player C (the player who gets points for a mixed result) appears to have an unfair advantage (especially if they have played several games or the class pooled its data). This observation seems to contradict the notion that the outcomes are equally likely.

Rubel (2006, 2007) used a similar two-coin task with students from fifth to eleventh grades, asking for the probability of getting a head and a tail with two coins and found similar misconceptions. About 25 percent of the students said the probability was $\frac{1}{3}$—because three things could happen (two heads, one of each, two tails). And although more than half (54 percent) answered correctly about the probability, many of these students used faulty reasoning, explaining that they picked that answer because there is a 50–50 chance in any experiment. See, for example, Figure 22.6.

In order to help students connect how likely an event is to the possible outcomes, encourage students to analyze the situation and generate all the possible outcomes; for example, use a table such as in Figure 22.7. Getting a head and a tail happens in two out of the four possible outcomes. Figure 22.8 provides an example of a correct student explanation for "Fair or Unfair." This theoretical probability is based on a logical analysis of the experiment, not on experimental results.

Another great context is the game of "rock, paper, scissors," which can be played in the normal way, or adapted so "same" scores 1 point and "different" scores 1 point for the

> *I think that player C will win because a coin flip is a 50-50 chance and he's guessing a 50-50 chance. He's guessing that it will be one then, the other witch is 50-50. The game is unfair for player A and B. Player C had the advantage.*

FIGURE 22.6 Correct conclusion but incomplete reasoning on "Fair or Unfair."

First Coin	Second Coin
Head	Head
Head	Tail
Tail	Head
Tail	Tail

FIGURE 22.7 Four possible outcomes of flipping two coins.

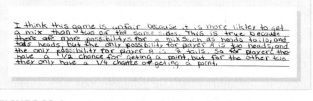

> *I think this game is unfair because it is more likley to get a mix than two of the same sides. This is true because there are more possibilitys for a mix such as heads tails, and tails heads, but the only possibility for player A is two heads, and the only possibility for player B is 2 tails. So for player C they have a 1/2 chance for geting a point, but for the other two they only have a 1/4 chance of geting a point.*

FIGURE 22.8 Student reasoning for "Fair or Unfair?" that connects outcomes to probability.

other player. Decide whether this is a fair game (Ellis, Yeh, & Stump, 2007–2008).

Experiments

As noted earlier, some probabilities cannot be analyzed by the analysis of possible outcomes of an event, but instead must be determined only through gathering empirical data. This data may be preexisting or may need to be established through an experiment, conducting a sufficiently large number of trials to become confident that the resulting relative frequency is an approximation of the theoretical probability. For example, the probability of a hurricane is based on historic data. (See http://landfalldisplay.geolab virtualmaps.com for an interesting look at the probability of hurricanes.) The following activities are examples of situations in which the only way to establish how likely an outcome is would be to do an experiment and use the results of a large number of trials to approximate how likely each outcome is.

Activity 22.10

Drop It!

In this activity, students drop an object to explore how likely various outcomes are. The number of possible outcomes varies with the different objects. Any object can be used. Here are a few ideas to try:

1. *Cup Toss.* Provide a small plastic cup to pairs of students. Ask them to list the possible ways that the cup could land if they tossed it in the air and let it land on the floor. Which of the possibilities (upside down, right side up, or on its side) do they think is most and least likely? Why? Have students toss the cup 20 times, each time recording how it lands. Students should agree on a uniform method of tossing the cups to ensure unbiased data (e.g., dropping the cups from the same height). Record each pair's data in a class chart. Discuss the differences and generate reasons for them. Have students predict what will happen if they pool their data. Pool the data and compute the three ratios (upside down, right side up, and on the side) to the total number of tosses. The relative frequency of the combined data should approximate the actual probability.
2. *Toy Animal Drop.* Bring in small plastic toys that can land in different ways. Repeat the activity above. (See Nelson & Williams, 2009, for an exploration with toy pigs.)
3. *Falling Kisses.* Using Hershey Kisses, conduct an experiment to see how often they land directly on their base (Gallego, Saldamando, Tapia-Beltran, Williams, & Hoopingarner, 2009). Alternative candies include Rolos or Reeses peanut butter cups. For a healthier option, consider goldfish crackers (using the position they face as the experiment).

In these experiments, there is no practical way to determine the results before you start. However, once you have results for 200 tosses (empirical data), you would undoubtedly feel more confident in predicting the results of the next 100 tosses. After gathering data for 1000 trials, you would feel even more confident. The more tosses that are made, the more confident you become. For example, in the cup dropping, you may have determined a probability of $\frac{4}{5}$ or 80 percent for the cup to land on its side. It is empirical data because it is based on the results of an experiment rather than a theoretical analysis of the cup.

The Law of Large Numbers.   The phenomenon that the relative frequency of an event becomes a closer approximation of the actual probability or the theoretical probability as the size of the data set (sample) increases is referred to as *the law of large numbers.* The larger the size of the data set, the more representative the sample is of the population. Thinking about statistics, a survey of 1000 people provides more reliable and convincing data about the larger population than a survey of 5 people. The larger the number of

trials (people surveyed), the more confident you can be that the data reflect the larger population. The same is true when you are attempting to determine the probability of an event through data collection.

Although critical to understanding probability, this concept is difficult for students to grasp. Students commonly think that a probability should play out in the short term, a misconception sometimes referred to as "the law of small numbers" (Flores, 2006; Tarr, Lee, & Rider, 2006). Comparing small data sets to large data sets is one way to help students think more deeply about the fact that the size of the trial matters. The next two activities are designed with this purpose in mind.

Activity 22.11

Get All 6!

Ask students to list the numbers 1 through 6 at the bottom of a frequency table. Students should roll a die and mark an X over each number until they have rolled each number at least once. Repeat five or six times. Discuss how the frequency charts compare in each case. Students will see that in some cases there are many fours, for example, and it took 25 rolls before getting all numbers, while in other cases they got all the numbers in only 10 rolls. Focus discussion on the fact that in the short run, data varies a lot—it is over the long run that the data "evens out." This activity can also be done on a graphing calculator (Flores, 2006).

Truly random events often occur in unexpected groups; a fair coin may turn up heads five times in a row. A 100-year flood may hit a town twice in 10 years. Using random devices such as spinners, dice, or cubes drawn from a bag gives students an intuitive feel for the imperfect distribution of randomness. The next activity is designed to help students with this difficult idea.

Activity 22.12

What Are the Chances?

Use a copy of Blackline Master 61, shown in Figure 22.9. Provide pairs of students with a spinner face that is half red and half blue. Discuss the chances of spinning blue. Mark the halfway point on the Impossible–Certain continuum and draw a vertical line down through all of the lines below this point. Then have each pair of students spin their spinner 20 times, tallying the number of red and blue spins. Mark the number of blue spins on the second line. For example, if there are 13 blue and 7 red, place a mark at about 13 on the 0-to-20 number line. If the results of these 20 spins were not exactly 10 and 10, discuss possible reasons why this may be so.

Repeat 20 more times. Add the tallies for the first 20 spins and again mark the total in the right-hand box of the third line.

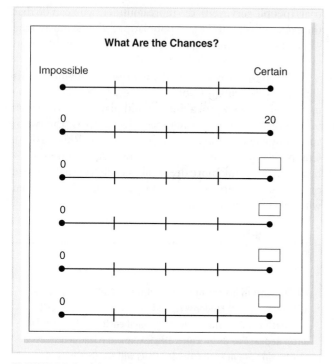

FIGURE 22.9 This activity is used to explore probability in the short run and the long run (see Blackline Master 61).

Repeat at least two more times, continuing to add the results of new spins to the previous results. Using a graphing calculator or applet, even 1000 trials are possible in a short amount of time. Ask students to reflect on what they notice in each number line.

The successive number lines used in "What Are the Chances?" each have the same length and each represent the total number of trials. When the results are plotted on any one number line, the position shows the fraction of the total spins as a visual portion of the whole line. With more trials, the marks will get closer and closer to the $\frac{1}{2}$ mark. Note that 240 blue spins out of 500 is 48 percent, or very close to one-half. This is so even though there are 20 more red spins (260) than blue.

The same Blackline Master and the same process of accumulating data in stages can and should be used for other experiments. For example, try using this approach with the "Cup Toss" experiment in Activity 22.10. Rather than draw a vertical line before collecting data, decide on the best guess at the actual probability after the numbers have gotten large, and then draw the vertical line in the appropriate position. Observe and record on the number lines 10 additional trials, 20 additional trials, and 50 additional trials. Compare these smaller data sets to the larger data set. Write the probabilities as percents and as fractions to show the connection between these representations.

FORMATIVE Assessment Notes

Pose the following **performance assessment** to assess students' ideas about long-run results versus short-run results. Have students write about their ideas.

Margaret spun the spinner 10 times. Blue turned up on three spins. Red turned up on seven spins. Margaret says that there is a 3-in-10 chance of spinning blue. Carla then spun the same spinner 100 times. Carla recorded 53 spins of blue and 47 spins of red. Carla says that the chance of spinning blue on this spinner is about even.

Who do you think is more likely to be correct: Margaret or Carla? Explain. Draw a spinner that you think they may have been using.

Look for evidence that students understand that even 10 spins is not very good evidence of the probability and that 100 spins tells us more about the chances. Also, to assess whether students understand the big idea that chance has no memory, have students write in their journal about the following:

Duane has a lucky coin that he has tossed many, many times. He is sure that it is a fair coin with an even chance of heads or tails. Duane tosses his coin six times and heads come up six times in a row. Duane is sure that the next toss will be tails. What do you think the chances are of Duane tossing heads on the next toss? Explain your answer.

In this case, you are looking for the idea that each toss of the coin is independent of prior tosses. ■

Why Use Experiments?

Actually conducting experiments and examining outcomes in teaching probability is important in helping students address common misconceptions and in building deeper understanding for why certain things are more likely than others. Specifically, experiments

- Model real-world problems that are actually solved by conducting experiments (doing simulations) (See, for example, The Futures Channel's "probability map," which is used to locate sunken ships that contained gold treasure: www.thefutureschannel.com/dockets/hands-on_math/undersea_treasure.)
- Provide a connection to counting strategies (lists, tree diagrams) to increase confidence that the probability is accurate
- Provide an experiential background for examining the theoretical model
- Help students see how the ratio of a particular outcome to the total number of trials begins to converge to a fixed number (For an infinite number of trials, the relative frequency and theoretical probability would be the same.)
- Help students learn more than students who do not engage in doing experiments (Gurbuz, Erdem, Catlioglu, & Birgin, 2010)

Try to use an experimental approach whenever possible, posing interesting problems to investigate. If a theoretical analysis (such as with the two-coin experiment in "Fair or Unfair?") is possible, it should also be examined, and the results compared to the expected outcomes.

Use of Technology in Experiments

Many simple calculators and graphing calculators are designed to produce random outcomes at the press of a button. Calculators produce random numbers that can then be interpreted relative to the possible outcomes in the experiment. For example, you can assign the final digit such that if it is odd it represents one outcome and if it is even it represents a second outcome. If there are four outcomes, you can look at the remainder when the last two digits are divided by 4 and assign a remainder to each outcome. In addition, some calculators, like the TI-73, TI-83, and TI-84, can run the free Probability Simulation App, an interactive tool that simulates tossing coins, rolling number cubes, using spinners, and generating random numbers. (Visit the Texas Instruments Education Portal at http://education .ti.com.)

Also, computer applets can be used to virtually flip coins, spin spinners, or draw numbers from a hat. NCTM's Illuminations website has a series of lessons called "Probability Exploration" in which students explore probability through virtual experiments, including graphing the results. (See http://illuminations.nctm.org/LessonDetail.aspx?ID=U190.)

As long as students accept the results generated by the technology as truly random or equivalent to the hands-on device, these virtual devices have the advantages of being quicker, more motivating to some students, and accessible when the actual devices (e.g., spinners with various partitions) are not. Web-based tools such as the National Library of Virtual Manipulative's Spinner (http://nlvm.usu.edu) have the advantage of generating many more trials in much less time. Due to the speed at which an experiment can be done, these virtual devices afford the opportunity for teachers to explore probability across a variety of tools (virtual dice, coins, cards, etc.), including the use of graphical displays of the trials. Also, in a virtual world, dice can be "loaded" and used to challenge students' thinking ("Are these fair dice? How can you find out?") (Beck & Huse, 2007; Phillips-Bey, 2004).

Sample Spaces and Probability of Two Events

Understanding the concepts of outcome and sample space is central to understanding probability. The *sample space* for an experiment or chance situation is the set of all possible outcomes for that experiment. For example, if a bag contains two red, three yellow, and five blue tiles, the sample space consists of all ten tiles. An *event* is a subset of the sample space. The event of drawing a yellow tile has three elements or outcomes in the sample space, and the event of drawing a blue tile has five elements in the sample space. For rolling a single common die, the sample space consists of the numbers 1 to 6.

Rolling a single die, drawing one colored tile from a bag, or the occurrence of rain tomorrow are all examples of one-event experiments. A two-event experiment requires two (or more) actions to determine an outcome. Examples include rolling two dice, drawing two tiles from a bag, or the combination of both the occurrence of rain and forgetting your umbrella.

When exploring two-event experiments, there is another factor to consider: Does the occurrence of the event in one stage have an effect on the occurrence of the event in the other? In the following sections, we will consider two-event experiments of both types—those with independent events and those with dependent events.

Independent Events

Recall that in Activity 22.9, "Fair or Unfair?," students explored the results of tossing two coins. The toss of one coin had no effect on the other. These were examples of *independent events*; the occurrence or nonoccurrence of one event has no effect on the other. The same is true of rolling two dice—the result on one die does not affect the other die. The common error for both tossing two coins or rolling two dice is a failure to distinguish between the two events, especially when the outcomes are combined, as in tossing "a head and a tail" or adding the numbers on two dice.

Let's explore rolling two dice and adding the results. Suppose that your students tally the sums that they get for two dice. The results might look like Figure 22.10. These events do not appear to be equally likely, and in fact the sum of 7 appears to be the most likely outcome. To explain this, students might look for the combinations that make 7: 1 and 6, 2 and 5, and 3 and 4. But there are also three combinations for 6 and for 8. It seems as though 6 and 8 should be just as likely as 7, and yet they are not.

Now suppose that the experiment is repeated. This time, for the sake of clarity, suggest that students roll two different-colored dice and that they keep the tallies in a chart like the one in Figure 22.10(b).

The results of a large number of dice rolls indicate what one would expect—namely, that all 36 cells of this chart are equally likely. But there are more cells with a sum of 7 than any other number. Notice that 3 red, 4 green is different from 4 red, 3 green. Students often do not see 3, 4 and 4, 3 as separate events and therefore don't count each of them separately. The color-coded dice can help address this misconception. There are six outcomes in the desired

Sum of Two Dice

2	𝍷𝍷𝍷 𝍷
3	𝍷𝍷𝍷𝍷 𝍷𝍷𝍷𝍷
4	𝍷𝍷𝍷 𝍷𝍷𝍷 𝍷𝍷𝍷 𝍷𝍷𝍷𝍷
5	𝍷𝍷𝍷 𝍷𝍷𝍷 𝍷𝍷𝍷 𝍷𝍷𝍷𝍷
6	𝍷𝍷𝍷 𝍷𝍷𝍷 𝍷𝍷𝍷 𝍷𝍷𝍷 𝍷𝍷𝍷 𝍷𝍷𝍷𝍷
7	𝍷𝍷𝍷 𝍷𝍷𝍷 𝍷𝍷𝍷 𝍷𝍷𝍷 𝍷𝍷𝍷 𝍷𝍷𝍷 𝍷𝍷𝍷 𝍷𝍷𝍷𝍷
8	𝍷𝍷𝍷 𝍷𝍷𝍷 𝍷𝍷𝍷 𝍷𝍷𝍷 𝍷𝍷𝍷 𝍷𝍷𝍷 𝍷𝍷𝍷𝍷
9	𝍷𝍷𝍷 𝍷𝍷𝍷 𝍷𝍷𝍷 𝍷𝍷𝍷 𝍷𝍷𝍷
10	𝍷𝍷𝍷 𝍷𝍷𝍷 𝍷𝍷𝍷 𝍷
11	𝍷𝍷𝍷 𝍷𝍷
12	𝍷𝍷𝍷 𝍷𝍷𝍷

(a)

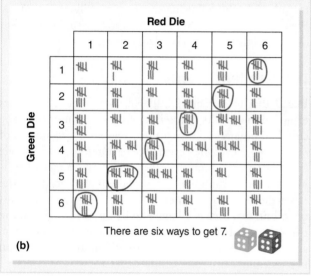

Red Die

There are six ways to get 7.

(b)

FIGURE 22.10 Tallies can account only for the total (a) or keep track of each die (b).

event (getting a 7) out of a total of the sample space (36), for a probability of $\frac{6}{36}$ or $\frac{1}{6}$.

To create the sample space for two independent events, use a chart or diagram that keeps the two events separate and illustrates all possible combinations. The matrix in Figure 22.10(b) is a suggestion when there are only two events. A tree diagram (Figure 22.11) is another method of creating sample spaces that can be used with any number of events. For example, consider the context of creating an ice cream cone. You can choose a waffle or regular cone, dipped or not dipped, and then any of three single flavors. This can be simulated using coins and a spinner, as illustrated in Figure 22.11.

PAUSE and REFLECT

Use a chart and/or tree diagram to analyze the sum of two number cubes each with sides 1, 1, 2, 3, 3, and 3. (These were the cubes used in Activity 22.4.) What is the probability of each sum, 1 through 6?

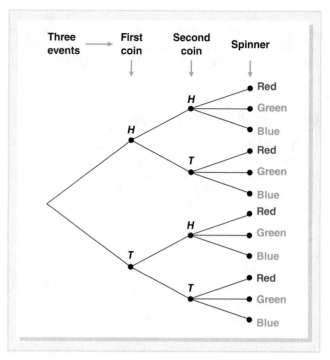

FIGURE 22.11 A tree diagram showing all possible outcomes for two coins and a spinner that is $\frac{1}{3}$ red.

A common process to help students connect sample space with probability is to ask students to first make a prediction of the probability of the event, second conduct an experiment with a large number of trials, and third compare the prediction to what happened. Then ask students to create the sample space and see how it compares to the predication and the results of the experiment.

Activity 22.13

Lu-Lu

ENGLISH LANGUAGE LEARNERS

This Hawaiian game involves tossing four stones and calculating the resulting score. (You can create stones like the ones pictured here by getting glass stones from a craft store and marking dots on one side.) The first player to reach fifty wins. (See McCoy, Buckner, & Munley [2007] for more on this game.) Invite students to play the game with a partner.

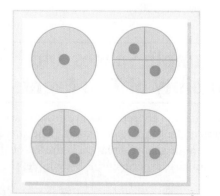

After they have played, ask what they notice about the sums they are getting. Ask questions such as, "What sums are possible?" "What sums were common?" "What scores are possible in a single turn?" and "What are all the outcomes (possible combinations of stones)?" "What is the probability of each score?"

ELLs may have games from their native countries. These games could be used to explore probability, using questions like the ones posed here.

The following are additional examples of probabilities of independent events. Any one of these could be explored as part of a full lesson.

- Rolling an even sum with two dice
- Spinning blue twice on a spinner
- Having a tack *or* a cup land up when each is tossed once
- Getting at *least* two heads from tossing four coins

Words and phrases such as *and, or, at least,* and *no more than* may cause students some confusion. Of special note is the word *or* because its everyday usage is generally not the same as its strict logical use in mathematics. In mathematics, *or* includes the case of both. So in the tack-and-cup example, the event includes tack up, cup up, and both tack and cup up.

Area Models

One way to determine the theoretical probability of a multistage event is to list all possible outcomes and count the number of outcomes that make up the event. This is effective but has some limitations. First, a list implies that all outcomes are equally likely. Second, lists can get tedious when there are many possibilities. Third, students can lose track of which possibilities they have included in the list and may leave off some of the possibilities. An area model is a good option for all of these reasons. The following activity uses information about students and applies it to the area model.

Activity 22.14

Are You a Spring Tiger?

Before doing this activity, determine which Chinese birth year animals are likely to be represented in the classroom (for example, the tiger and the rabbit). Begin by finding out what percent of the class is each animal. Ask, "If I name one of the Chinese birth year animals, what is the probability it will be your birth year animal?" Illustrate this percentage by partitioning a rectangle, as illustrated in Figure 22.12(a). (This particular illustration finds 64 percent of the class was born in the year of the tiger and 36 percent was born in the year of the rabbit.) Ask, "If I name one of the seasons, what is the probability it will be the season you were born in?" Ask students to illustrate their response by partitioning and shading a rectangle as in Figure 22.12(b). Then ask, "What is the probability of being both a spring and a tiger?"

In Figure 22.12(b), you can visually see that students in the year of the tiger and spring groups make up $\frac{1}{4}$ of 64 percent, or 16 percent of the population. This should look very familiar, as the same process is used for multiplying fractions. The area model is effective in solving "or" situations, as shown in Figure 22.12(c). Half of the students are born in summer or fall, and 36 percent are born in the year of the rabbit. Students can add up the percentages in the boxes, or they can think about the two situations separately: 50 percent are spring/fall and 36 percent are born in the year of the rabbit. Combining these results in 86 percent, but some students are both, and have therefore been double counted. The diagram shows this case as the overlap of the shaded columns with the shaded rows. In the situation under consideration, that amount is $\frac{1}{2}$ of 36, or 18 percent. Therefore, the population that is summer or fall or born in the year of the rabbit is $50 + 36 - 18 = 68$ percent of the population. This is approaching the formal formula for how you determine the formula of two independent events, which is the probability of each event, minus the overlap (or intersection):

$$P(A \text{ or } B) = P(A) + P(B) - P(A \text{ and } B)$$

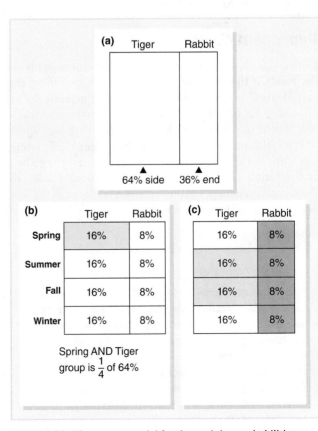

FIGURE 22.12 An area model for determining probabilities.

The area approach is accessible to a range of learners, as it is less abstract than equations or tree diagrams. For more than two independent events, further subdivision of each region is required, but it is still a useful model.

The following activity is a challenging and engaging way for students to think about the probability of independent events, but this time they design the random device (Ely & Cohen, 2010).

Activity 22.15

Design a Winning Spinner

Explain that each student is going to create a winning spinner, which means that when it is spun twice, the sum will be on a number strip with values 2, 3, 4, 5, 6, 7, and 8. Each student creates their own spinner, partitioning a circle however they like, and writing a number in each sector. Once students have their spinner, they pair with someone else and play the game using their own spinner: Student A spins twice and adds the two values. If the sum is 5, Student A covers 5 on his/her number strip. Student B takes a turn. The first partner to cover all numbers on their strip wins. Play 3 rounds. Next, ask students to redesign their spinner, find a new partner, and play 3 more rounds. If possible, repeat a third time. Afterwards, discuss how they designed a winning spinner.

In going backwards (from the desired outcome to the spinner), students can build a deeper understanding of how to determine the probability of independent events.

Dependent Events

Dependent events occur when the second event depends on the result of the first. For example, suppose that there are two identical boxes. One box contains one genuine dollar bill and two counterfeit bills. In the other box is one of each bill. You may choose one box and from that box select one bill without looking. What are your chances of getting a genuine dollar? Here there are two events: selecting a box and selecting a bill. The probability of getting a dollar in the second event depends on which box is chosen in the first event. These events are *dependent*, not independent.

Activity 22.16

Keys to a New Car

Pose the following problem: In a game show, you can win a car if you make it through the maze to the room where you have placed the car key. You can place the keys in either Room A or Room B (see maze in Figure 22.13). At the start and at each fork in the path, you must spin the spinner and follow the path that it points to. Once you've reached Room A or Room B, the game is over—there is no going back through the maze. In which room should you place the key to have the best chance of winning the car?

You can use the area model to determine the theoretical probabilities for dependent events too. An area model solution to the car problem is shown in Figure 22.14. How would the area model for the car problem be different if the spinner at Forks I and II were $\frac{1}{3}$ A and $\frac{2}{3}$ B spinners?

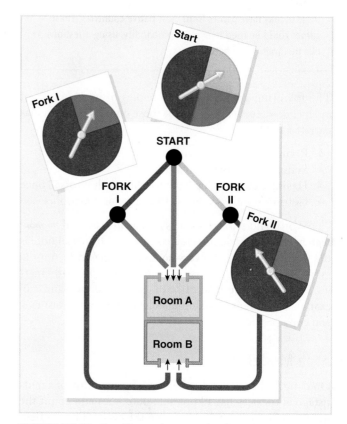

FIGURE 22.13 Should you place your key in Room A or Room B to have the best chance at winning?

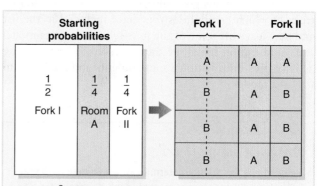

At Fork I, $\frac{3}{4}$ of the time you will go to Room B.

(Note: Not $\frac{3}{4}$ of the square but $\frac{3}{4}$ of the times you go to Fork I.)

At Fork II, $\frac{3}{4}$ of these times (or $\frac{3}{16}$ of total time) you will go to Room B.

Therefore, you will end up in Room A $\frac{7}{16}$ of the time and Room B $\frac{9}{16}$ of the time.

FIGURE 22.14 Using the area model to solve the maze problem.

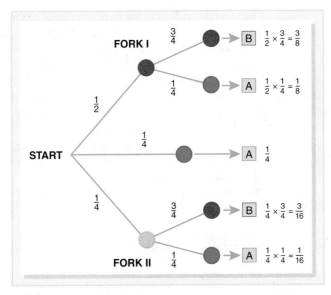

FIGURE 22.15 A tree diagram is another way to model the outcomes of two or more dependent events.

 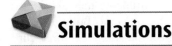

PAUSE and REFLECT

Try the area approach for the problem of the counterfeit bills. The chance of getting a genuine dollar is $\frac{5}{12}$. Can you get this result? ●

Figure 22.15 shows a tree diagram for the Keys to a New Car problem, with the probability of each path in the maze written on the "branch" of the tree. After some experience with probability situations, the tree diagram model can be easier to use and adapts to a wider range of situations. You should be able to match up each branch of the tree diagram in Figure 22.15 with a section of the square in Figure 22.14. Use the area model to explain why the probability for each complete branch of the tree is determined by multiplying the probabilities along the branch.

Simulations

Simulation is a technique used for answering real-world questions or making decisions in complex situations where an element of chance is involved. Many times simulations are conducted because it is too dangerous, complex, or expensive to manipulate the real situation. To see what is likely to happen in the real event, a model must be designed that has the same probabilities as the real situation. For example, in designing a rocket, a large number of related systems all have some chance of failure that might cause serious problems with the rocket. Knowing the probability of serious failures will help determine whether redesign or backup systems are required. It is not reasonable to make repeated tests of the actual rocket. Instead, a model that simulates all of the chance situations is designed and run repeatedly with the help of a computer. The computer model can simulate thousands of flights, and an estimate of the chance of failure can be made.

For example, water must be pumped from A to B within a system (see Figure 22.16). The five pumps that connect A and B are aging, and it is estimated that at any given time, the probability of pump failure is $\frac{1}{2}$. If a pump fails, water cannot pass that station. For example, if pumps 1, 2, and 5 fail, water flows only through 4 and 3. Consider the following questions that might well be asked about such a system:

- What is the probability that water will flow at any time?
- On the average, about how many stations need repair at any time? (Gnanadesikan, Schaeffer, & Swift, 1987).

For any simulation, the following steps can serve as a useful guide.

1. *Identify key components and assumptions of the problem.* The key component in the water problem is the condition of a pump. Each pump is either working or not. The assumption is that the probability that a pump is working is $\frac{1}{2}$.

2. *Select a random device for the key components.* Any random device can be selected that has outcomes with the same probability as the key component—in this case, the pumps. Here a simple choice might be tossing a coin, with heads representing a working pump.

3. *Define a trial.* A *trial* consists of simulating a series of key components until the situation has been completely modeled one time. In this problem, a trial could consist of tossing a coin five times, each toss representing a different pump (heads for pump is working; tails for pump is not working).

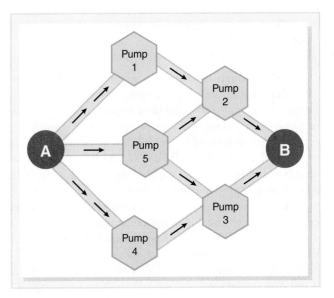

FIGURE 22.16 Each of these five pumps has a 50 percent chance of failure. What is the probability that some path from A to B is working?

4. *Conduct a large number of trials and record the information.* For this problem, it would be useful to record the number of heads and tails in groups of five because each set of five is one trial and represents all of the pumps.

5. *Use the data to draw conclusions.* There are four possible paths for the water, each flowing through two of the five pumps. As they are numbered in the drawing, if any one of the pairs 1–2, 5–2, 5–3, and 4–3 is open, it makes no difference whether the other pumps are working. By counting the trials in which at least one of these four pairs of coins both came up heads, we can estimate the probability of water flowing. To answer the second question, the number of tails (not working) per trial can be averaged.

Here are a few more examples of problems for which a simulation can be used to gather empirical data.

In a true-or-false test, what is the probability of getting 7 out of 10 questions correct by guessing alone? (*Key component:* Answering a question. *Assumption:* Chance of getting it correct is $\frac{1}{2}$.)
Simulation option: Flip a coin 10 times for one trial.

In a group of five people, what is the chance that two were born in the same month? (*Key component:* Month of birth. *Assumption:* All 12 months are equally likely.)
Simulation option: 12-sided dice or 12 cards. Draw/roll one, replace, and draw/roll again.

Casey's batting average is .350. What is the chance he will go hitless in a complete nine-inning game? (*Key component:* Getting a hit. *Assumptions:* Probability of a hit for each at-bat is .35. Casey will get to bat four times in the average game.)
Simulation option: Spinner with 35 percent shaded. Spin 4 times for one trial.

Students often have trouble selecting an appropriate random device for simulations. Spinners are a good choice because areas can be adjusted to match probabilities. Coins or two-colored counters are useful for probabilities of $\frac{1}{2}$. A standard die can be used for probabilities that are multiples of $\frac{1}{6}$. There are also dice with 4, 8, 12, and 20 sides available online and in smart phone apps. Many calculators include a key that will produce random numbers that can be used to simulate experiments (e.g., 1 means true and 2 means false). Usually, the random numbers generated are between 0 and 1, such as 0.8904433368. How could a list of decimals like this replace flipping a coin or spinning a spinner? Suppose each was multiplied by 2. The results would be between 0 and 2, as shown here:

$$0.8904433368 \times 2 = 1.7808866736$$
$$0.0232028877 \times 2 = 0.0464057754$$
$$0.1669322714 \times 2 = 0.3338645428$$

If you focus on the ones column, you have a series of zeros and ones that could represent heads and tails, boys and girls, true and false, or any other pair of equally likely outcomes. For three outcomes, the same as a $\frac{1}{4} - \frac{1}{4} - \frac{1}{2}$ spinner, you might decide to look at the first two digits of the number and assign values from 0 to 24 and 25 to 49 to the two quarter portions and values 50 to 99 for the one-half portion. Alternatively, each randomly generated number could be multiplied by 4 and the decimal part ignored, resulting in random numbers 0, 1, 2, and 3. These could then be assigned to the desired outcomes.

In this final activity, consider how you would design a simulation.

Activity 22.17

Chance of Triplet Girls

Ask students, "What is the chance that a woman having triplets will end up with all girls?" Record estimates. Ask students to create simulation to model this problem using the five steps previously described. Encourage students to use various tools to simulate (flipping three coins, random number generator, two-color spinner spun three times, etc.). After examining the results, ask questions to relate the predictions to the results. This may lead to creating a tree diagram of the options to make sense of the results.

"Chance of Triplet Girls" is a great task, as it can lead interesting conversations like, "Are three girls less likely or more likely than two girls and a boy?" and "If a family already has two girls, what do you think they will have for their third child?" (Tillema, 2010). These questions connect to two of the common misconceptions students have related to probability, the commutativity confusion and gambler's fallacy.

These misconceptions, and one shared earlier, are discussed briefly here.

1. *Commutativity confusion.* Students may think two girls and one boy is one possible outcome. But notice that if you list the eight possible combinations for three children, you have three girls only once (GGG), but two girls and one boy three times (GGB, GBG, BGG). Two girls and a boy are three times as likely. We refer to this as *commutativity confusion* because students, knowing that a + a + b is the same as a + b + a, think that that one boy and two girls is one event, not three. Students need to connect how likely with all the ways an event can occur.

2. *Gambler's fallacy.* The gambler's fallacy is the notion that what has already happened (two girls) influences the event. Students will argue a boy is more likely since there are already two girls. Similarly, students think that if a coin has had a series of 4 heads, it is more likely on the fifth flip to be tails (Ryan & Williams, 2007). But a coin has no memory, and the probability of heads or tails is still 50–50, just as the probability of a girl is still 50–50.

3. *Law of small numbers.* This misconception is like the gambler's fallacy in that it relates to small samples but, with this misconception, students expect small samples to be like the greater population (Flores, 2006; Tarr, Lee, & Rider, 2006). This is discussed previously in the section "The Law of Large Numbers" (see Activities 22.11 and 22.12). So in the case of the three girls, it is not so unusual—it is just a very small data set, so it is not likely to resemble the larger population.

Whether doing simulations, experiments, or theoretical probability, it is important for students to use many models (lists, area, tree diagrams) and to discuss developing conceptions and misconceptions explicitly. In addition to being more interesting, teaching probability in this way allows students to understand important concepts that have many real-world implications.

RESOURCES *for Chapter 22*

LITERATURE CONNECTIONS

The books described here offer both fanciful and real-life data for investigating probability. Also, these books can be paired with Activities in this chapter.

Go Figure! A Totally Cool Book about Numbers
Ball, 2005

This wonderful book could be placed in every chapter of this book. About 40 different topics are covered, one of which is called "Take a Chance." This two-page spread is full of interesting contexts for probability, including a match-dropping experiment and genetics.

Harry Potter Books *Rowling, 1998*

The game of Quidditch can lend itself to creating a simulation to explore the probability of winning. Wagner and Lachance (2004) suggest that sums of two dice be linked to Quidditch actions. For example, a roll of 7 means a player scores a Quaffle, which is worth 10 points. Rolls of 2 or 12 mean the player catches the Snitch and the game ends, 150 points; 3, 5, 9, 11 means hit by Bludger—lose a turn; 4, 6, 8, 10 means dodge a Bludger, no points. Students play and then can explore the probability of winning.

Do You Wanna Bet? Your Chance to Find Out about Probability *Cushman, 2007*

The two characters in this book, Danny and Brian, become involved in everyday situations both in and out of school. Each situation involves an element of probability. For example, two invitations to birthday parties are for the same day. What is the chance that two friends would have the same birthday? In another situation, Danny flips heads several times and readers are asked about Brian's chances on the next flip. Students can create simulations to examine some of the ideas.

My Little Sister Ate One Hare *Grossman, 1996*

This counting book will appeal to the middle school set as well as to young students due to the somewhat gross thought of a little girl eating one rabbit, two snakes, three ants, and so on, including bats, mice, worms, and lizards. Upon eating ten peas, she throws up everything she ate.

Bay-Williams and Martinie (2004b) used this tale to explore probability. If one of the things the little sister "spilled" on the floor is picked up at random in the process of cleaning up, what is the probability of getting a polliwog (or other animal or category of animal)? Students can use cards representing things eaten and approach the task experimentally.

RECOMMENDED READINGS

Articles

Coffey, D. C., & Richardson, M. G. (2005). Rethinking fair games. *Mathematics Teaching in the Middle School, 10*(6), 298–303.

Students explore the fairness of a matching game both experimentally and using a theoretical model. They then set out to create a variation of the game that would be fair by assigning points to a match and to a mismatch. A TI-73 program is included that simulates the revised game.

Edwards, T. G., & Hensien, S. M. (2000). Using probability experiments to foster discourse. *Teaching Children Mathematics, 6*(8), 524–529.

Fifth-grade students experiment with outcomes of flipping a coin, spinning a spinner, and rolling a die. The discourse is directed to the disparity between the observed outcomes and the theoretical probabilities. For example, is it reasonable that there are 77 heads out of 150 tosses?

McCoy, L. P., Buckner, S., & Munley, J. (2007). Probability games from diverse cultures. *Mathematics Teaching in the Middle School, 12*(7), 394–402.

As the title suggests, this article includes games from African, Hawaiian, Jewish, Mexican, and Native American cultures. Games include probability connections, handouts, and questions to pose to students.

McMillen, S. (2008). Predictions and probability. *Teaching Children Mathematics, 14*(8), 454–463.

This article provides a series of high-quality probability lessons—various contexts and models are used, as well as calculators. The lessons include a number of key concepts discussed in this chapter, and two handouts are provided.

Books

Shaughnessy, J. M. (2003). Research on students' understanding of probability. In J. Kilpatrick, W. G. Martin, & D. Schifter (Eds.), *A research companion to Principles and Standards for School Mathematics* (pp. 216–226). Reston, VA: NCTM. *Shaughnessy's chapter offers interesting insights from research and makes useful recommendations about successful ways to teach probability concepts.*

ONLINE RESOURCES

Adjustable Spinner (Illuminations)
http://illuminations.nctm.org/activitydetail.aspx?ID=79

A virtual spinner can be adjusted to have any number of sections of any size. It can then be spun any number of times and records the theoretical and experimental probabilities in a table.

A Better Fire! (Shodor's Project Interactivate)
www.shodor.org/interactivate/activities/ABetterFire

This site offers a realistic simulation of actual forest fires, with controls for wind speed and direction to add more realism. The simulation uses a virtual "die" to see whether a tree should be planted for each square. Then the fire is set and allowed to burn. An excellent authentic use of simulations.

Marble Mania
www.sciencenetlinks.com/interactives/marble/marblemania.html

This resource explores randomness and probability. You'll be able to control how many and what color marbles to place in a virtual marble bag. An advantage of this resource is that you can run a large number of different trials in a short amount of time.

TossingTossingData Analysis and Probability Manipulatives (NLVM) http://nlvm.usu.edu/en/nav/topic_t_5.html

This contains the entire collection of probability tools organized across grade bands.

REFLECTIONS *on Chapter 22*

WRITING TO LEARN

1. What are the first ideas about probability that students should develop? How can you help students with these ideas?
2. Activities 22.3 and 22.5 ("1-2-3 How Likely?" and "Race to the Top") are each designed to help students see that some outcomes are more likely than others. What is the difference between these two activities? Why might this difference be useful in helping students gain insights about how likely an event is?
3. What are the advantages of having students conduct experiments even before they attempt to figure out a theoretical probability?
4. Explain the law of large numbers. Describe an activity that might help students to appreciate this idea.
5. Describe the difference between an independent and dependent event. Give an example of each.
6. What are some misconceptions and challenges students have with learning probability?

FOR DISCUSSION AND EXPLORATION

1. The classic "Monty Hall Problem" is a favorite for studying probability. In the game show, one of three doors has a big prize. The contestant guesses one door, but, before revealing what is behind that door, Monty shows the contestant a goat behind one of the doors not selected. Then he offers the contestant the opportunity to switch doors. Does the contestant have a better chance of winning the big prize by *switching* or by *staying* with the original choice (or does it not matter)? There are numerous methods of answering this question. Make a convincing argument for your own answer based on the ideas and techniques in this chapter.
2. Go to the Illuminations website (http://illuminations.nctm.org) and explore one of the virtual experiments. Discuss (a) the advantages and disadvantages of virtual experiments and (b) the content within this chapter that could be discussed following student exploration of this experiment.
3. Use an area model and a tree diagram to determine the probability for the following situation:

   Dad puts a $5 bill and three $1 bills in the first box. In a second box, he puts another $5 bill with just one $1 bill. For washing the car, Junior gets to take one bill from the first box without looking and put it in the second box. After these are well mixed, he then gets to take one bill from the second box. What is the probability that he will get a $5 bill?

   Design a simulation for the problem and try it out. Does your simulation agree with your theoretical probability? Discuss responses you would anticipate from 7th graders doing this same task.

MyEducationLab™

Go to the MyEducationLab (www.myeducationlab.com) for Math Methods and familiarize yourself with the content. Much of the site content is organized topically. The topics include all of the following to support your learning in the course:

- Learning outcomes for important mathematics methods course topics aligned with the national standards
- Assignments and Activities, tied to these learning outcomes and standards, that can help you more deeply understand course content
- Building Teaching Skills and Dispositions learning units that allow you to apply and practice your understanding of the core mathematics content and teaching skills

Your instructor has a correlation guide that aligns the exercises on the topical portion of the site with your book's chapters.

On MyEducationLab you will also find book-specific resources including Blackline Masters, Expanded Lesson Activities, and Artifact Analysis Activities.

Field Experience Guide
C O N N E C T I O N S

Students have very interesting notions about probability. Use Diagnostic Interview 7.2 with activities from this chapter to find out what students think is likely or not likely and why they think so. Or adapt Student Interview 4.5 to focus on attitudes about probability. FEG Expanded Lesson 9.21, "Create a Game," engages students in designing a fair game, and FEG Expanded Lesson 9.23, "Testing Bag Designs," provides more details on using Activity 22.8 (see page 459 in this chapter).

Chapter 23

Developing Concepts of Exponents, Integers, and Real Numbers

Students in the middle grades need to develop a more complete understanding of the number system, which includes extending whole numbers to integers and starting to think of fractions as rational numbers (both positive and negative). In these ways and others, they can begin to appreciate the completeness of the real number system.

The ideas presented in this chapter build on ideas that have been developed throughout this book. Exponents are used in algebraic expressions and add to the operations. Scientific notation expands how large and small numbers are represented, building on place-value concepts. Integers move beyond the positive counting numbers to numbers less than 0 and therefore extend the number line (as well as operations) to include negative values. *Common Core State Standards* suggests that sixth graders, "extend their previous understandings of number and the ordering of numbers to the full system of rational numbers, which includes negative rational numbers, and in particular negative integers." (CCSSO, 2010, p. 39). *Curriculum Focal Points* (NCTM, 2006) states that seventh graders should be "developing an understanding of operations on all rational numbers and solving linear equations" (p. 19) and that in eighth grade, "Students use exponents and scientific notation to describe very large and very small numbers. They use square roots when they apply the Pythagorean theorem." (p. 20). These connections help students move to more sophisticated understandings of foundational topics presented previously.

 BIG IDEAS

1. Exponential notation is a way to express repeated products of the same number. Specifically, powers of 10 express very large and very small numbers in an economical manner.

2. Integers are the negative and positive counting numbers and 0. Positive and negative numbers are used together to describe quantities having opposite directions or values (e.g., temperature above or below zero).

3. Whole numbers, fractions, and integers are rational numbers. Every rational number can be expressed as a fraction.

4. Many numbers are not rational; the irrationals can be expressed only symbolically or approximately using a close rational number. Examples include $\sqrt{2} \approx 1.41421\ldots$ and $\pi \approx 3.14159.\ldots$

 Mathematics CONTENT CONNECTIONS

The ideas in this chapter represent an expansion of number concepts and algebraic thinking.

◆ **Whole-Number Place Value, Fractions, and Decimals** (Chapters 11, 15, and 17): When exponential notation is combined with decimal notation, very small and very large numbers can be written efficiently. Decimals and fractions help to describe the difference between rational and irrational numbers.

◆ **Algebra** (Chapter 14): The symbolic manipulation of numbers, including the rules for order of operations, is exactly the same as is used with variables. The study of integers helps with the notion of "opposite," represented by a negative sign: $^-6$ is the opposite of $^+6$ and ^-x is the opposite of ^+x, regardless of whether x is negative or positive. Exponents can also be variables, giving rise to exponential functions.

Exponents

As numbers in our increasingly technological world get very small or very large, expressing them in standard form is cumbersome. Exponential notation is more efficient for conveying numeric or quantitative information. For an illustration that compares the size of the Milky Way to the size of a plant cell using images and the distance measures in exponential notation (powers of 10), see http://micro.magnet.fsu.edu/primer/java/scienceopticsu/powersof10.

Exponents in Expressions and Equations

Sometimes students get confused trying to remember the rules of exponents. For example, they may not know whether you add or multiply the exponents when you raise a number to a given power. This is an example of procedural knowledge that may be learned without supporting conceptual knowledge. Students should have ample opportunity to explore exponents with whole numbers before they use exponents with letters or variables. By doing so, they are able to deal directly with the concept and actually generate the rules themselves.

A whole-number exponent is simply shorthand for repeated multiplication of a number times itself; for example, $3^4 = 3 \times 3 \times 3 \times 3$.

Special attention to the symbols related to exponents must also be given. The first is that an exponent applies to its immediate base. For example, in the expression $2 + 5^3$, the exponent 3 applies only to the 5, so the expression is equal to $2 + (5 \times 5 \times 5)$. However, in the expression $(2 + 5)^3$, the 3 is an exponent of the quantity $2 + 5$ and is evaluated as $(2 + 5) \times (2 + 5) \times (2 + 5)$, or $7 \times 7 \times 7$. Notice that the process follows the order of operations.

As with any topic, it is important to begin with what students know and what is concrete. With exponents, this means beginning with exploring squares and cubes—operations that can be represented geometrically. For example, consider the following problem:

> Minia knows that square animal pens are the most economical for the amount of space they provide (assuming straight sides). Can you provide a table for Minia that shows the areas of square pens that have between 4 meters and 10 meters of fence on each side?

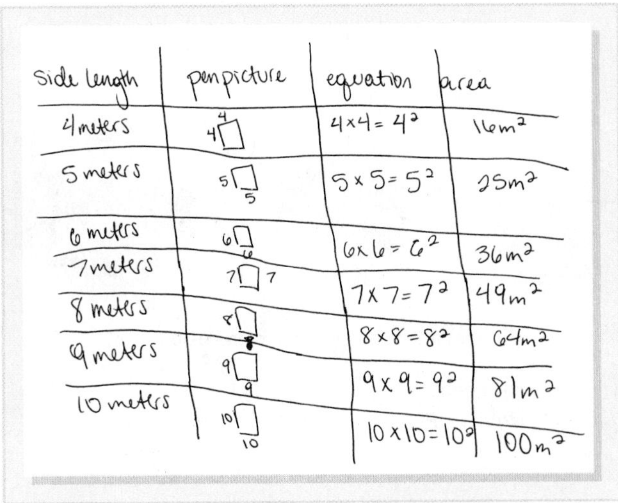

Students may set up a table similar to Figure 23.1, showing possible areas for the square pens.

Another way to explore exponents is to explore algebraic growing patterns involving squares and/or cubes. The Painted Cube Problem is a popular investigation that appears in such curricula as *Connected Mathematics* as seen in Figure 23.2. (See also http://connectedmath.msu.edu/CD/Grade8/Painted/PaintedCubes.html.) The six faces of the cube are squares and it is the faces (not including the edges) that will have little cubes with one side painted. As the painted cube grows, so does the size of each square face, meaning that the faces (squares) grow in a quadratic (squared) rate. The centimeter cubes with no sides painted are those hidden inside the large painted cube. In a $2 \times 2 \times 2$

FIGURE 23.1 A student records possibilities for making a square pen.

cube, there are 0 inside cubes, but in a $3 \times 3 \times 3$, there is one hidden cube inside that will not get painted. The number of "hidden cubes" grows at a cubic rate. In exploring the pattern, students get experience with algebraic rules that are linear, squared, and cubed.

Order of Operations

Working with exponents extends the *order of operations:* Because order of operations requires that multiplication and division are done before addition and subtraction, and exponents are repeated multiplication, exponents also precede addition and subtraction. In the expression $5 + 4^2 - 6 \div 3$, 4^2 and $6 \div 3$ are done first. Therefore, the expression is evaluated as $5 + 16 - 2 = 21 - 2 = 19$.

Parentheses are used to group operations that are to be done first. Therefore, in $(5 + 4) \times 2 - 6 \div 3$, the addition can be done inside the parentheses first, or the distributive property can be used, and the final result is 16. The phrase "Please excuse my dear Aunt Sally" or more simply, "PEMDAS" is sometimes used to help students remember the order of operations. Although these mnemonics are helpful, they may lead students to think that addition is done before subtraction and multiplication comes before division. An improvement involves writing the order in rows:

P = parenthesis
E = exponents
MD = multiplication and division (whichever is first from left to right)
AS = addition and subtraction (whichever is first from left to right)

But these mnemonics do not replace the need to understand the meaning of the order. Students continue to do poorly on order-of-operations items on high-stakes assessments, and this is due to a lack of understanding. While part

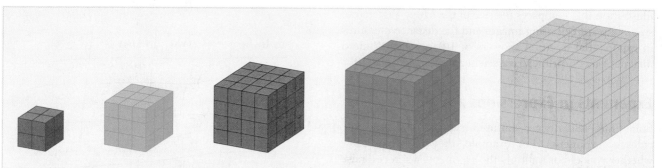

Organize your data in a table like the one below.

Edge Length of Large Cube	Number of Centimeter Cubes	Number of Centimeter Cubes Painted On			
		3 faces	2 faces	1 face	0 faces
2					
3					
4					
5					
6					

Study the patterns in the table.

1. Describe the relationship between the edge length of the large cube and the total number of centimeter cubes.

2. Describe the relationship between the edge length of the large cube and the number of centimeter cubes painted on.

   a. three faces   **b.** two faces   **c.** one face   **d.** zero faces

FIGURE 23.2 The Painted Cube Problem provides a context for exploring squares and cubes.

Source: Adapted from *Connected Mathematics: Frogs, Fleas and Painted Cubes: Quadratic Relationships* by Glenda Lappan, James T. Fey, William M. Fitzgerald, Susan N. Friel, & Elizabeth Difanis Phillips. Copyright © 2006 by Michigan State University. Used by permission of Pearson Education, Inc. All rights reserved.

of the order of operations is due to convention (e.g., working from left to right), it is largely due to the meaning of the operations. Because multiplication represents repeated addition, it must be figured first before adding on more. Because exponents represent repeated multiplication, these multiplications must be considered before multiplying or adding.

Consider writing $4^2 + 3 + 2 \times 5$ as all addition: $4^2 + 3 + 2 \times 5 = 4 + 4 + 4 + 4 + 3 + 5 + 5$. How would you combine? Add up all the fours ($4 \times 4 = 4^2$); then add $5 + 5$ (2×5), and add on 3. The order of operations is actually based on the meaning of the operations!

One applet, Rags to Riches (www.quia.com/rr/116044 .html), provides practice for doing the Order of Operations in a game format, something like the game show, "Who Wants to Be a Millionaire." You can also strengthen students' understanding of order of operations by having them record expressions, using appropriate symbols, as in the activity here.

Activity **23.1**

Guess My Number

This algebraic activity involves the teacher giving hints about a number and students thinking backwards to find it (using logical reasoning). For ELLs and students with disabilities, provide the statements in writing in addition to stating it. Students create equations, using parentheses appropriately to reflect the clues the teacher gives, as in the following three examples:

ENGLISH LANGUAGE LEARNERS

STUDENTS with SPECIAL NEEDS

- I am thinking of a number; I add 5, double it, and get 22. $[(n + 5) \times 2 = 22]$
- I am thinking of a number; I subtract 2, square it, and get 36. $[(n - 2)^2 = 36]$
- I am thinking of a number; I double it, add 2, cube it, and get 1000. $[(2n + 2)^3 = 1000]$

> For students with disabilities, you may want to start with a known number rather than an unknown number—for example, start with 5, square it, add 11, divide by 6. They should write $(5^2 + 11) \div 6 = n$.

FORMATIVE Assessment Notes   Students can be asked to write an expression using all the operations and parentheses—for example, $(4 + 2)^2 \times 2 \div 4$—and then write a matching story, using a context of their choice, to fit the expression. Writing these stories in **journals** provides an excellent assessment of students' understanding of the order of operations. Provide one format, and have students create the other. As students write expressions or stories, determine whether they realize that multiplication and division (and addition and subtraction) are equal in order and should be solved left to right. Also, use questioning to see whether they understand when parentheses are optional and when they are necessary. ■

Exponent Notation on the Calculator.   Most simple four-function calculators do not use algebraic logic, so operations are processed as they are entered. Calculators with algebraic logic usually have a negative (−) key, while those without have a +/− key. If you have to press the $\sqrt{\ }$ key *before* the number to find square root, the calculator probably has algebraic logic. On calculators without algebraic logic, the following two keying sequences produce the same results:

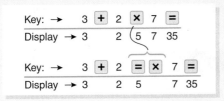

Whenever an operation sign is pressed, the effect is the same as pressing = and then the operation. Of course, neither result is correct for the expressions $3 + 2 \times 7$, which should be evaluated as $3 + 14$, or 17.

Calculators designed for middle grades use algebraic logic (follow the order of operations) and include parenthesis keys so that both $3 + 2 \times 7$ and $(3 + 2) \times 7$ can be keyed in the order that the symbols appear. See the difference in the following displays:

Key: →	3	+	2	×	7	=
Display →	3		2		7	17

Notice that the following display does not change when × is pressed and a right parenthesis is never displayed. Instead, the expression that the right parenthesis encloses is calculated and that result displayed.

Key: →	(	3	+	2	)	×	7	=
Display →	[	3		2	5		7	35

Some basic calculators and graphing calculators show the expression $3 + 2 \times (6^2 - 4)$. Nothing is evaluated until you press Enter or EXE. Then the result appears on the next line to the right of the screen:

$3 + 2 * (6^2 - 4)$	67

Moreover, the last expression entered can be recalled and edited so that students can see how different expressions are evaluated. Only minimum key presses are required.

$3 + 2 * (6^2 - 4)$	67
$(3 + 2) * (6^2 - 4)$	160
$(3 + 2) * 6^2 - 4$	176
$3 + 2 * 6^2 - 4$	71

The simple four-function calculator remains a powerful tool for exploration. For example, to evaluate 3^8, press 3 × = = = = = = =. (The first press of = will result in 9, or 3 × 3.) Students will be fascinated by how quickly numbers grow. Enter any number, press ×, and then repeatedly press =. Try two-digit numbers. Try 0.1.

Give students many opportunities to explore expressions involving exponents and the order of operations.

Activity **23.2**

Entering Expressions

Provide students with numeric expressions to evaluate with simple four-function calculators. Ask, "How will you have to enter these to correctly apply the order of operations?" Rewrite the expression the way it will be entered. Here are some examples of expressions:

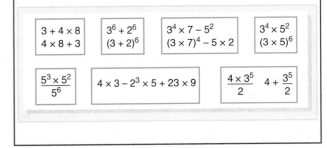

A common misconception with exponents is to think of the two values as factors, so 5^3 is thought of as 5×3, rather than the correct equivalent expression of $5 \times 5 \times 5$. This is further problematic when students hear things like "It is five three times," since the word "times" indicates multiplication. Avoid confusing language, and spend significant time having students state and write the equivalent expressions. When experiencing difficulty with exponents, students should write equivalent expressions without exponents or include parentheses to indicate explicit groupings. For example:

$$(7 \times 2^3 - 5)^3 = (7 \times (2 \times 2 \times 2) - 5)$$
$$\times (7 \times (2 \times 2 \times 2) - 5)$$
$$\times (7 \times (2 \times 2 \times 2) - 5)$$
$$= ((7 \times 8) - 5) \times ((7 \times 8) - 5) \times ((7 \times 8) - 5)$$
$$= (56 - 5) \times (56 - 5) \times (56 - 5) = 51 \times 51 \times 51$$

For many expressions, there is more than one way to proceed, and sharing different ways is important.

Of course, calculators with algebraic logic will automatically produce correct results. Yet it is critically important for students to know the order of operations. These rules apply to symbolic manipulation in algebra and must be understood for the many times that they will apply mental calculations to such computations.

Negative Exponents

When students begin to explore exponents and have also experienced negative integers, it is interesting to consider what it might mean to raise a number to a negative power. For example, what does 2^{-4} mean? The following two related options can help students explore the possibilities of negative exponents. The powers of 10 are good to explore because they directly relate to place value. First, have students consider 10^N as follows:

$$10^4 = 10,000$$
$$10^3 = 1000$$
$$10^2 = 100$$
$$10^1 = 10$$
$$10^0 = ?$$
$$10^{-1} = ?$$

To continue the pattern, 10^0 would be 1, which it is! (In fact, it is the definition of 10^0.) If the pattern is to continue, the next value would be one-tenth of 1. And, each successive number is one-tenth of the one that comes before it:

$$10^{-1} = 0.1 = \tfrac{1}{10}$$
$$10^{-2} = 0.01 = \tfrac{1}{100} = \tfrac{1}{10^2}$$
$$10^{-3} = 0.001 = \tfrac{1}{1000} = \tfrac{1}{10^3}$$

Here students might notice that the negative exponent is the reciprocal of the value it would be without the negative sign.

Second, students can explore negative exponents on a calculator. For example, tell students, "Use a calculator to see

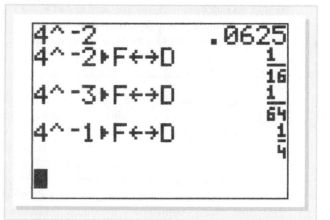

FIGURE 23.3 Graphing calculators evaluate expressions as decimals. However, they also convert decimals to fractions. This figure shows the screen of a TI-73 calculator. The F→D key converts fractions to decimals (and decimals to fractions) as shown here.

if you can figure out what 4^{-3} or 2^{-5} equal." If the calculator has decimal-to-fraction conversion, suggest that students use that feature to help develop the meaning of negative exponents. Figure 23.3 gives an example of how this might look on a graphing calculator. Ask students to notice patterns that they think are generalizable and test those conjectures.

Students often confuse exponent rules. Identifying a mistake in someone else's work is another effective way to help students think about the correct (and incorrect) order in a problem, as illustrated in Activity 23.3.

Activity 23.3

Find the Error

Create solved problems and ask students to explain what the student did wrong. Have them explain both what the person did wrong and how to do it correctly. A few examples are provided here:

Zach: $3(4)^2 = 24$

Yoli: $(5^3)^2 = 55$

Wilma: $\dfrac{20x^8}{5x^2} = 4x^4$

Examples can be increasingly more challenging, and can be mixed with correct solutions. For activity sheets with more examples, see Johnson and Thompson (2009).

Scientific Notation

The more common it becomes to find very large or very small numbers in our daily lives, the more important it is to have convenient ways to represent them. One option is to say and write numbers in their common form. However, this practice can be cumbersome. Another option is to use exponential notation and our base-ten place-value system—scientific notation. In scientific notation, a number is changed to be the product of a number greater than or equal to 1 and less than 10 (meaning only one digit in front of the decimal) multiplied by a multiple of 10. For example, 3,414,000,000 can also be written as 3.414×10^9. Since you have divided by one billion to place the decimal, to keep the number equivalent, you must multiply by one billion (10^9).

Different notations have different purposes and values. For example, the population of the world on 4/30/11 was estimated to be 6,915,518,006 (U.S. Census Bureau, n.d.). This can be expressed in various ways:

6,915 million
6.9×10^9
Nearly 7 billion

Each way of stating the number has value and purpose in different contexts. Rather than spend time with exercises converting numbers from standard form to scientific notation, consider large numbers found in newspapers, magazines, and atlases. How are they written? How are they said aloud? When are they rounded and why? What forms of the numbers seem best for the purposes? What level of precision is appropriate for the situation? And how do these numbers relate to other numbers? How does the population of the world relate to the population in your state or your continent? Websites like the U.S. Census Bureau (www.census.gov) make this timely data readily available.

Contexts for Very Large Numbers. The real world is full of very large quantities and measures. We see references to huge numbers in the media all the time. Unfortunately, most of us have not developed an appreciation for extremely large numbers, such as the following examples:

- A state lottery with 44 numbers from which to pick 6 has over 7 million possible combinations of 6 numbers. There are $44 \times 43 \times 42 \times 41 \times 40 \times 39$ possible ways that the balls could come out of the hopper (5,082,517,440). But generally the order in which they are picked is not important. Because there are $6 \times 5 \times 4 \times 3 \times 2 \times 1 = 720$ different arrangements of 6 numbers, each collection appears 720 times. Therefore, there are *only* 5,082,517,440 ÷ 720 possible lottery numbers, or 1 out of 7,059,052 chances to win.
- The estimated size of the universe is 40 billion light-years. One light-year is the number of miles light travels in *one year*. The speed of light is 186,281.7 miles per *second*, or 16,094,738,880 miles in a single day.
- The human body has about 100 billion cells.
- The distance to the sun is about 150 million kilometers.
- The population of the world in 2011 was about 6.96 billion. (Various population estimates can be found by seeking out worldometers on the Internet.)

Connecting these large numbers to meaningful points of reference can help students get a handle on their true magnitude. For example, suppose students determine the population in their city or town is about 500,000 people. They can then figure that it would take approximately 13,300 cities of the same population size to generate the population of the world. Or suppose students determine that it is about 4600 km between San Francisco, California, and Washington D.C. This would mean that it would take over 32,000 trips back and forth between these two cities to equal the distance between the earth and the sun. Building from such familiar or meaningful reference points helps students develop benchmarks to work with and make sense of large numbers.

The following activity uses real data to develop an understanding of scientific notation and the relative size of numbers.

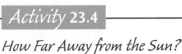

> ### Activity 23.4
>
> #### How Far Away from the Sun?
>
> **ENGLISH LANGUAGE LEARNERS**
>
> Explain to students that they are going to research planetary distances from the sun (in km), record the data in scientific notation, and create a scaled illustration of the distances. If data gathering is not practical, provide the following figures:
>
> | | | | |
> |---|---|---|---|
> | Mercury | 57,909,000 | Jupiter | 778,400,000 |
> | Venus | 108,200,000 | Saturn | 1,423,600,000 |
> | Earth | 149,600,000 | Uranus | 2,867,000,000 |
> | Mars | 227,940,000 | Neptune | 4,488,400,000 |
>
> Encourage students to develop strategies to figure out the relative distance between each planet. You can give a long strip of adding machine paper to each group and have them mark the sun on one end and Neptune on the other. For ELLs, reinforce the names of thousands, millions, and billions. (These terms are not the same in some countries.)

Contexts for Very Small Numbers. It is also important to use real examples of very small numbers. As with large numbers, connecting very small numbers to points of reference can help students conceptualize how tiny these numbers really are, as shown by the following real-world examples:

- The length of a DNA strand in a cell is about 10^{-7} m. This is also measured as 1000 *angstroms*. (Based on this information, how long is an angstrom?) For perspective, the diameter of a human hair is about 2.54×10^{-5} m.
- Human hair grows at the rate of 10^{-8} miles per hour.
- Garden snails have been clocked at about 3×10^{-2} mph.
- The chances of winning the Virginia lottery, based on selecting six numbers from 1 to 44, is 1 in 7.059 million. That is a probability of less than 1.4×10^{-7}.

- The mass of one atom of hydrogen is 0.000 000 000 000 000 000 000 001 675 g compared to the mass of one paper clip at about 1 g.
- It takes sound 0.28 second (2.8×10^{-1}) to travel the length of a football field. In contrast, a TV signal travels a full mile in about 0.000005368 second, or 5.3×10^{-6} second. A TV viewer at home hears the football being kicked before the receiver on the field does.

Activity 23.5

At a Snail's Pace

As noted previously, garden snails have been clocked at about 3×10^{-2} mph. Ask students to estimate how long it will take a snail to cover one mile. To explore, have them record the decimal equivalent of 3×10^{-2} (0.03). In the calculator, they can use the counting function (enter .03 + .03 =). On most calculators, when you hit = again, the calculator counts by the last value entered (.03). Each = represents one hour. Ask students figure it out mathematically or by counting. Share strategies. When students have shared their results, ask what it would mean if the rate would have been 3×10^{-3}. They can explore this problem, too, and should conclude that it would take ten times longer.

An activity like Activity 23.5 can help students understand the relative size of very small numbers.

Scientific Notation on the Calculator. Students may learn how to multiply by 10, by 100, and by 1000 by simply adding the appropriate number of zeros. Help students expand this idea by examining powers of 10 on a calculator that handles exponents.

Activity 23.6

Exploring Powers of 10

Have students use any calculator that permits entering exponents to explore some or all of the following:

- Explore 10^N for various values of N. What patterns do you notice? What does 1E15 mean? (1E15 is the typical calculator form of 1×10^{15}.) What does 1E–09 mean?
- What does 4.5E10 mean? 4.5E–10?
- What does 5.689E6 mean? Can you enter this another way?
- Try sums like $(4.5 \times 10^N) + (27 \times 10^K)$ for different values of N and K. What can you find out? Does it hold true when N and K are negative integers?
- What happens with products of numbers like those in the previous item?

It is useful to become comfortable with the power-of-ten expressions in written forms and the calculator form.

For example, on a TI-73, the product of $45,000,000 \times 8,000,000$ is displayed as 3.6E14, meaning 3.6×10^{14}, or 360,000,000,000,000 (360 trillion).

One misconception students can develop is that the exponent tells the numbers of zeros to add onto the number. Address this explicitly in discussions. For example, ask students, "Why are there 13 zeros and not 14?" "Is there a relationship between the exponent and the number of zeros?" (No, it depends on how many non-zero digits are in the number.)

 PAUSE and REFLECT

With each factor in the product expressed in scientific notation: $(4.5 \times 10^7) \times (8 \times 10^6)$, or 4.5E7 × 8.0E6, can you compute the result mentally? ●

Notice the advantages of scientific notation, especially for multiplication. Here the significant digits can be multiplied mentally ($4.5 \times 8 = 36$) and the exponents added to produce almost instantly 36×10^{13} or 3.6×10^{14}.

Integers

Almost every day, students have interactions with negative numbers or experience phenomena that negative numbers can model, as shown in the following list:

Temperature
Altitude (above and below sea level)
Golf (above and below par)
Money
Time lines (including B.C.)
Football yardage (gains/losses)

In fact, almost any concept that is quantified and has direction probably has both positive and negative values.

Generally, negative numbers are introduced with integers—the whole numbers and their negatives or opposites—instead of with fractions or decimals. However, it is a mistake to stop with integer values, because students must understand where numbers like -4.5 and $-1\frac{3}{4}$ belong in relation to the integers. In fact, because non-integer negative numbers are not addressed adequately, students have misconceptions about where non-integer negative numbers belong on the number line. For example, students will place $-1\frac{3}{4}$ between -1 and 0 instead of between -2 and -1.

Contexts for Exploring Integers

As with any new topic or type of number, it is important to start with familiar contexts so that students can use prior knowledge to build meaning. With integers, students often get confused as to which number is bigger or which direction they are moving when they do operations, so having a context is particularly important. For ELLs, it is important to include visuals with the contexts, to support language development (Swanson, 2010). As students learn to compare and compute, they can use the contexts to ground their thinking and justify their answers.

Quantity Contexts

Golf Scores. In golf, scores are often written in relationship to a number considered par for the course. So, if par is 70 for the course, a golfer who ends the day at 67 has a score of −3, or 3 strokes under par. Consider a player in a four-day tournament with day-end scores of +5, −2, −3, +1. What would be his or her final result for the tournament? How did you think about it? You could match up the positive and the negatives (in this case, +5 with −2 and −3 to get a net result of 0), and then see what is left (in this case, +1). The notion that opposites (5 and −5) equal zero is a big idea in the teaching of integers. You can post a mixed-up leader board of golf scores and ask students to order the players from first through tenth place. Emphasize that first place is the *lowest* score—and therefore the *smallest* number.

Money: Payments and Deposits. Suppose that you have a bank account. At any time, your records show how many dollars are in your account. The difference between the payments and deposit totals tells the amount of money in the account. If there is more deposited than paid out, the account has a positive balance, or "in the black." If there are more payments than deposits, the account is in debt, showing a negative cash value, or is "in the red." This is a good context for exploring addition and subtraction of integers, as in the example illustrated in Figure 23.4. Net worth is a similar way to look at integers (assets and debts). Considering the net worth of famous people can engage students in making sense of integers (Stephan, 2009).

Activity 23.7

What Is Her Net Worth?

STUDENTS with SPECIAL NEEDS

On the Internet, look up the net worth of someone interesting to your students (e.g., Lady Gaga). Make up two to three assets and two to three debts that will total that net worth, and ask your students to figure out her net worth. Then, with students, look up the net worth of other people of their choice. Have them suggest possible assets and debts for that person. One clever way to do this is to have a net worth page filled out with two to three assets and two to three debts, but include a smudge on the paper so that all students can see the total net worth (Stephan, 2009). This visual is particularly important for students with disabilities.

Eventually debts can be represented as negative values, and a bridge is created to integer addition and subtraction.

Item	Payments or Deposits	Balance
Mowing lawn	+12.00	$34.00
Phone bill	−55.00	−21.00
iTunes downloads	−9.00	−30.00
Paycheck	+120.00	90.00

FIGURE 23.4 A checkbook as a context for adding and subtracting integers.

Linear Contexts

Many of the real contexts for negative numbers are linear. In addition, the number line provides a good tool for learning the operations and relate well to what the students have done with whole number and fraction operations. See www.mathgoodies.com/lessons/vol5/intro_integers.html for a good introduction to integers on a number line.

Temperature. The "number line" measuring temperature is vertical. This context demonstrating negative integers may be the most familiar to students, as they have either experienced temperatures below zero or know about temperatures at the North or South Pole. A good starting activity for students is finding where various temperatures belong on a thermometer. For example, Figure 23.5 displays a thermometer marked in increments of five degrees, and students are asked to place on the number line the following temperatures from a week in North Dakota: 8°, −2°, −12°, 4°, −8°. Ask students

FIGURE 23.5 Thermometers provide an excellent tool for exploring positive and negative numbers.

to order the temperatures from the coldest to the warmest (least to greatest). Temperatures as a context have the advantage that you can also use fractional and decimal values.

Altitude. Another vertical number-line model, altitude, is also a good context for integers. The altitudes of sites below sea level are negative, such as the town of Dead Sea, Israel (with an altitude of ⁻1371 feet), and Badwater, California, in Death Valley (which has an altitude of ⁻282 feet). Positive values for altitude include Mount McKinley (the tallest mountain in North America) at 20,322 feet. Students can order the altitudes of various places around the world (data easily found through a Google search on the Web) or find the difference between the altitudes of two different places—a good context for subtraction of integers.

Time Lines. Asking students to place historical events on a time line is an excellent interdisciplinary opportunity. The time line is useful for examples with larger values (e.g., 1950) as well as negative values (e.g., ⁻3000). Or students can explore their own personal time line (Weidemann, Mikovch, & Hunt, 2001), in which students find out key events that happened before they were born (e.g., the birth of an older sibling) and since they have been alive (e.g., the move to a new house). Students place these events on a number line with 0 representing the day they were born. By partitioning a year into months, students can gain experience with rational numbers (halves, fourths, or twelfths) on the number line. Continue to reinforce the connection to the size of numbers, asking students, "Which number (year) is the smallest (earliest)?"

Football. A statistic reported on every play in a football game is yards gained and yards lost, which provides a good context for exploring integers, especially when it comes to comparing and adding integers. Students can be asked questions like "If the Steelers started their drive on the 20 yard line and the first three plays were recorded as ⁻4, ⁺9, ⁺3, did they get a first down?" or "On the Ravens first play, the yardage is ⁻4. Where are they in relation to the line of scrimmage (using negatives, if behind the line of scrimmage, in this case ⁻4), and where are they in relation to the first down marker (⁻14)?"

Activity 23.8

Football Statistics

ENGLISH LANGUAGE LEARNERS

Look up the average yards gained for some of the best running backs in the NFL or from college teams popular with your students. Ask students to use average yards gained per down to create a possible list of yardage gains and losses for that player. For example, if a player had an average of 4 yards per carry in a game, the following could have been his data:

10, ⁻3, ⁻2, 21, ⁻5, 3, ⁻1, 5, ⁻1, 13

You may want to do one like this together and then have students create their own. The football context provides an excellent way to *use* integers meaningfully, integrated with the important concept of averages. ELLs may not be familiar with (American) football, because football in most countries is what is called *soccer* in the United States. Modeling the game using students is a fun way to be sure the game is understood by all. Also, a yard is a U.S. measurement that may not be familiar and could be confused with the other meaning of *yard*. Comparing a yard to a meter can provide a point of reference that will help build meaning for this activity.

Meaning of Negative Numbers

Negative numbers are defined in relation to their positive counterparts. For example, the definition of negative 3 is the solution to the equation $3 + ? = 0$. In general, the *opposite of n* is the solution to $n + ? = 0$. If n is a positive number, the *opposite of n* is a negative number. The set of integers, therefore, consists of the positive whole numbers, the opposites of the whole numbers (or negative integers), and 0, which is neither positive nor negative. Like many aspects of mathematics, abstract or symbolic definitions are best understood when conceptual connections link to the formal mathematics.

Absolute Value. Knowing the distance between two points, either on a number line or on a plane, is often needed in applications of mathematics. For example, we need to be able to determine how far a helicopter is from a hospital, regardless of its direction. The *absolute value of a number* is defined as the distance between that number and zero. The notation for absolute value consists of two vertical bars on either side of the number. Thus, the absolute value of a number n is $|n|$. Opposites, such as -12 and 12, are the same distance from zero, and therefore have the same absolute value.

Experiences in absolute value should not be limited to simplifying expressions such as $|{-8}|$ or $|6 - 10|$. The unfortunate consequence of this approach to absolute value is that students do not connect the procedure with the meaning of absolute value, or see real purposes for doing this. In the example $|6 - 10|$, add in a context to make it meaningful. In this case, what is the distance between the 10-mile marker and the 6-mile marker? $10 - 6$ or $6 - 10$ can lead to the answer, and distance is positive (absolute value), so the answer is 4.

Notations. Because students have only seen the negative sign when doing subtraction, the symbolic notation for integers may be confusing. It is important to help students understand and use the appropriate symbols. Students may find it confusing that sometimes the negative sign appears at different heights (e.g., -7 and ⁻7). Also, sometimes parentheses are placed around the number so that it is separate from the operation—for example, $8 - (-5)$. Students have not seen parentheses used in this way and may think they should multiply. It is important to connect to their prior knowledge and explicitly build meaning for the new symbols. In this case, you might ask students, "When do we use parentheses in mathematics?" Students might say they are used for grouping a series of computations to show what to do first and that it can also mean multiplication. Point out that parentheses are also used to make a number sentence more readable—separating the negative number from the operation.

Models for Teaching Integers

Two models, one denoted by quantity and the other by linear operations, are popular for helping students understand comparisons and the four operations (+, −, ×, and ÷) with integers.

Counters. One model consists of two-color counters, one color for positive counts and one for negative counts. Two counters of each type result in zero ($^{+}1 + {^{-}}1 = 0$). Consider money: If yellows are credits and reds are debits, 5 yellows and 7 reds is the same as 2 reds or 2 debits and is represented as $^{-}2$ (see Figure 23.6). It is important for students to understand that it is always possible to add to or remove from a pile any number of pairs consisting of one positive and one negative counter without changing the value of the pile. (Intuitively, this is like adding equal quantities of debits and credits.)

Number Lines. The number line is the second model. A number line has several advantages. First, it shows the distance from 0 (or the absolute value of the number). In addition, it is an excellent tool for modeling the operations. Jumps can be shown in the same way as with whole numbers and fractions (see Chapters 12, 13, and 16). To add a context, consider using small cutouts of grasshoppers that jump up and down the line (Swanson, 2010). Students can see that integer moves to the left go to smaller numbers and moves to the right go to larger numbers. Also, the number line allows students to explore non-integer negative and positive values (e.g., $^{-}4\frac{1}{2} + 3\frac{1}{4}$) that cannot be modeled very well with counters.

In modeling operations, arrows can be used to show distance and direction. For example, 4 can be modeled with an arrow four units long pointing to the right, and $^{-}3$ can be modeled with an arrow three units long pointing to the left (see Figure 23.7). The arrows help students think of

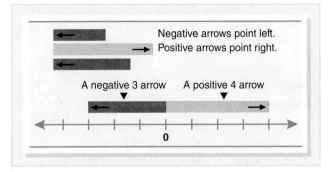

FIGURE 23.7 Number-line model for integers.

integer quantities as directed distances. A positive arrow never points left, and a negative arrow never points right. Furthermore, each arrow is a quantity with both length (magnitude or absolute value) and direction (sign). These properties are constant for each arrow regardless of its position on the number line.

Which Model to Use. Although the two models appear quite different, they are alike mathematically. Integers involve two concepts—*quantity* and *opposite*. Quantity is modeled by the number of counters or the length of the arrows. Opposite is represented as different colors or different directions.

Many teachers decide to use only the model that students like or understand better. This is a mistake! Remember that the concepts are not in the models but rather must be constructed by the students and imposed on the models. Seeing how integers are represented across two models can help students extract the intended concepts. And, students should make connections between the two models.

Operations with Integers

Once your students understand how integers are represented by each of the models, you can present the operations for the integers in the form of problems. In other words, rather than explaining how addition of integers works and showing students how to solve exercises with the models, you pose an integer computation and let students use their models to find a solution. When solutions have been reached, the groups can compare and justify their results using one of the contexts or models described earlier in this chapter.

Addition and Subtraction

In order to understand how to use the two models, it is good to begin with positive whole numbers. After a few examples to help students become reacquainted with the model for addition or subtraction with whole numbers, have them work through an example with integers using exactly the same reasoning. Remember, it is important to focus on the

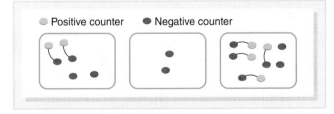

FIGURE 23.6 Each collection is a model of negative 2.

meaning of opposites. Activity 23.9 provides an excellent strategy for helping students use opposites as they think about integer addition (Friedmann, 2008).

Activity 23.9

Find the Zero

STUDENTS with SPECIAL NEEDS

Before beginning the activity, ask students to tell you the sums of several opposites (e.g., $4 + {}^-4$).
Then, ask students to look at a sum that is not opposites (e.g., $7 + {}^-4$) and ask if they can "find a zero" by partitioning one of the numbers (e.g., $(3 + 4) + {}^-4$)) and solve. Students, particularly students with disabilities, may benefit from creating a "zero box" below each problem as they solve it, as illustrated below.

$12 + {}^-5 =$

Zero Box: $\boxed{5 + {}^-5}$

$(7 + 5) - {}^-5) = 7 + (5 + {}^-5) = 7 + 0 = 7$

Introduce negative values using one of the contexts discussed earlier, such as golf scores. Personalize the story

by telling students that each weekend you golf a round on Saturday and on Sunday. The first weekend your results were $^+3$ and $^+5$, the next weekend you scored $^+3$ and $^-5$, and on the last weekend you scored $^-6$ and $^+2$. How did you do each weekend? Overall? Because this is a quantity model, counters are a good choice for modeling (though number lines can also be used). A linear context could be football yards gained and lost on two plays. See Figure 23.8 for illustrations of how to use both models for addition.

Conversely, ask students to create their own stories for integer operations. One way to scaffold this is to ask students the following three prompts: Where did you start? How far did you go? Where are you now? (Swanson, 2010). So, for example, a student might write, "I was three feet under water, then dove down 5 feet. Where am I now?"

In Figure 23.8, several examples of addition are modeled each in two ways: with positive and negative counters and with the number line and arrows. First, examine the counter model. After the two quantities are joined, any pairs of positive and negative counters combine to equal zero, and students can remove these, making it easier to see the result.

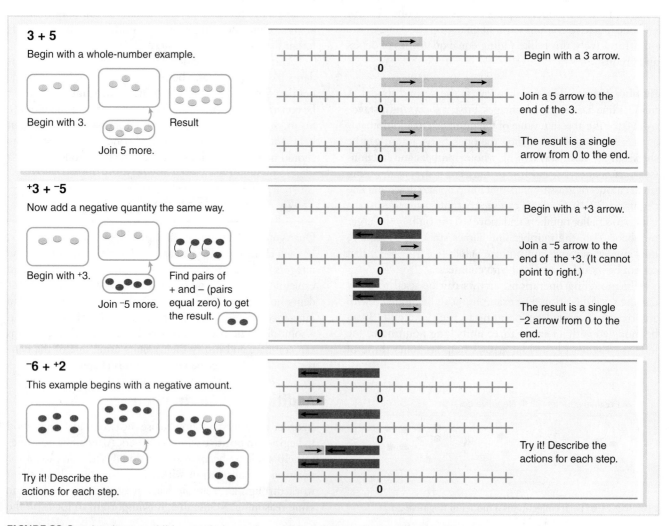

FIGURE 23.8 Relate integer addition to whole-number addition with counters and number lines.

To add using the number-line model, note that each added arrow begins at the arrowhead end of the previous arrow. Recall that subtraction can be used for take-away situations (e.g., start with 7 and take away 10) or in comparisons (What is the difference between 7 and ⁻3?). An advantage to the number-line model is that it can be used for both take-away and comparison situations.

Consider the problem ⁻5 − ⁺2, the second example modeled in Figure 23.9. If using a quantity model, the context could be money, such as, "I start with a debit of $5 and then withdraw (take out) $2 more from my account. What balance will my bank account show (if no fees have been charged yet for my overdrawn account)?" To model this problem, you start with the five red counters. To remove two positive counters from a set that has none, a different representation of ⁻5 must first be made. Because any number of neutral pairs (one positive, one negative) can be added without changing the value of the set, two pairs are added so that two positive counters can be removed. The net effect is to have more negative counters.

In the number-line model, subtraction can be modeled using arrows for take-away and for comparisons. Consider

take-away as a way to think about the second example in Figure 23.9. Using temperature as a context, the explanation could be: "The day begins at 5 below zero. Then the temperature drops +2°, which means it just got colder and is now −7°. The difficulty in the take-away thinking comes when trying to provide an authentic explanation of subtracting a negative value. For example, for ⁻4 − ⁻7 (see the third example in Figure 23.9) you start with taking away, but because it is negative temperature (or coldness) that is being taken away, you are in fact doing the opposite—warming up by 7 degrees. Modeling on the number line, you start at ⁻4, then reverse the arrow going left to one going right 7 moves. Number lines can also be used for comparison or distance. For subtraction, this can make a lot more sense to students (Tillema, in press). In this example, the comparison question is "What is the difference between ⁻7 and ⁻4?" In other words, how do you get from ⁻7 to ⁻4? You count up 3.

 PAUSE and REFLECT

Before reading further, go through each example in Figures 23.8 and 23.9. Explain each problem using both a quantity and a linear

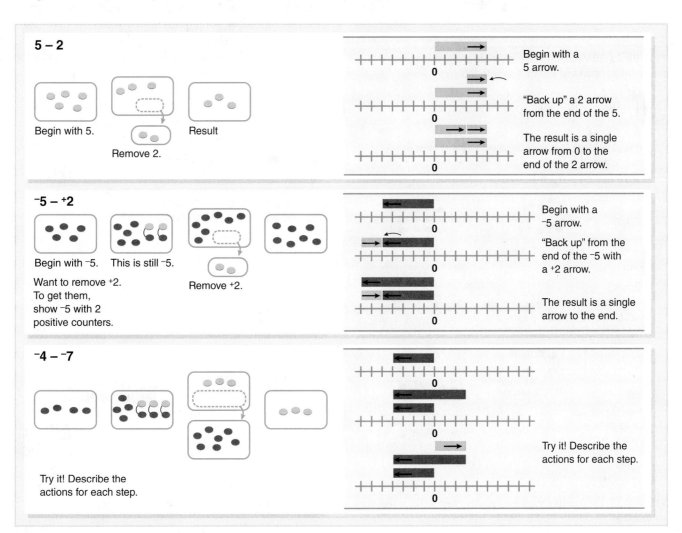

FIGURE 23.9 Integer subtraction is also related to whole numbers.

context. For subtraction, explain each using a take-away situation and a comparison situation. ●

Have your students draw pictures to accompany integer computations. Set pictures are easy enough; they may consist of Xs and Os, for example. For the number line, arrows can be used. Figure 23.10 illustrates how a student

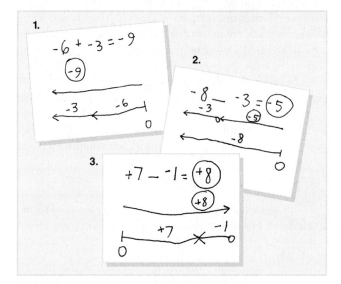

FIGURE 23.10 Students can use simple arrow sketches to represent addition and subtraction with integers.

might draw arrows for simple addition and subtraction exercises without even sketching the number line.

It is important for students to see that $^+3 + ^-5$ is the same as $^+3 - ^+5$ and that $^+2 - ^-6$ is the same as $^+2 + ^+6$. Modeling addition and subtraction problems in both ways will help students see the connection and recognize that while these expressions are quite distinguishable, they have the same result.

There are audio podcasts for adding and subtracting integers available via the Internet at http://itunes.apple.com/us/itunes-u/make-math-matter/id384510888. And, a video-cast of a teacher sharing how she uses Inspiration software is also on iTunesU: http://itunes.apple.com/us/podcast/adding-subtractingintegers/id402771898?i=90281736.

Multiplication and Division

Multiplication of integers should be a direct extension of multiplication for whole numbers, just as addition and subtraction were connected to whole-number concepts. We frequently refer to whole-number multiplication as *repeated addition*. The first factor tells how many sets there are or how many are added in all, beginning with 0. This translates to integer multiplication quite readily when the first factor is positive, regardless of the sign of the second factor. The first example in Figure 23.11 illustrates a positive first factor and a negative second factor.

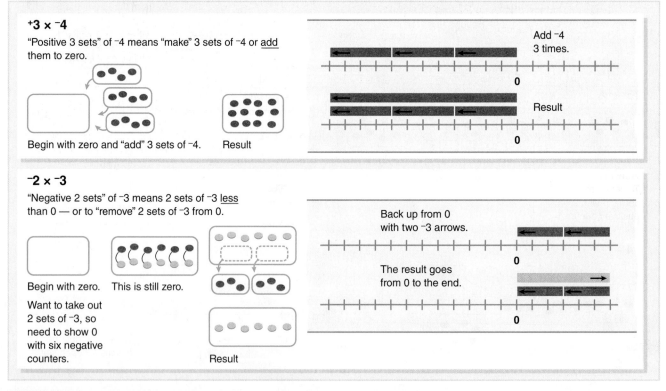

FIGURE 23.11 Multiplication by a positive first factor is repeated addition. Multiplication by a negative first factor is repeated subtraction.

What could the meaning be when the first factor is negative, as in ⁻2 × ⁻3? If a positive first factor means repeated addition (how many times added to 0), a negative first factor should mean repeated subtraction (how many times subtracted from 0). The second example in Figure 23.11 illustrates how multiplication with the first factor negative can be modeled.

With division of integers, again explore the whole-number case first. Recall that 8 ÷ 4 with whole numbers has two possible meanings corresponding to two missing-factor expressions: 4 × ? = 8 asks, "Four sets of what make eight?" whereas ? × 4 = 8 asks, "How many fours make eight?" Generally, the measurement approach (? × 4) is the one used with integers, although both concepts can be exhibited with either model. It is helpful to think of building the dividend with the divisor from 0, or repeated addition—to find the missing factor.

The first example in Figure 23.12 illustrates how the two models work for whole numbers. Following that is an example in which the divisor is positive but the dividend is negative.

PAUSE and REFLECT

Try using both models to compute ⁻8 ÷ ⁺2. Draw pictures using Xs and Os and also arrows. Check your understanding with the examples in Figure 23.12. Now try ⁺9 ÷ ⁻3 and ⁻12 ÷ ⁻4. ●

Understanding integer division rests on a good concept of a negative first factor for multiplication and knowledge of the relationship between multiplication and division.

Do not rush your students into difficult problems. It is much better that they first think about how to model the whole-number situation and then figure out, with guidance from you, how to connect that understanding to negative numbers.

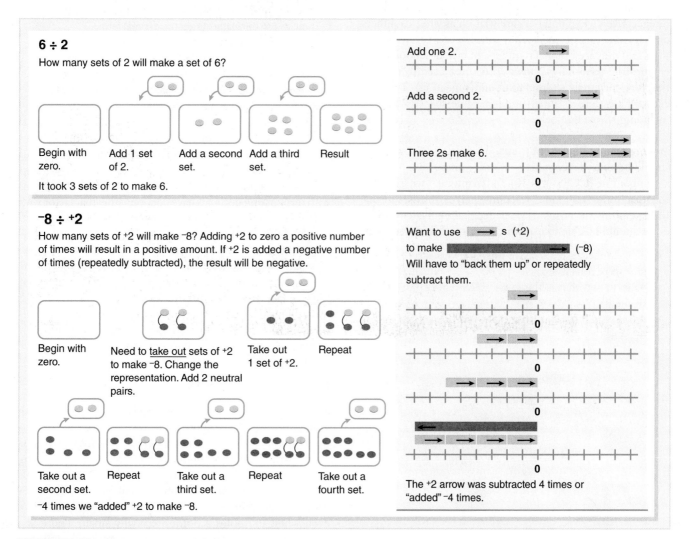

FIGURE 23.12 Division of integers following a measurement approach.

Real Numbers

Section II of this book began with whole numbers, then moved to fractions and decimals, and now, integers. All of these are rational numbers. *Irrational numbers* are numbers such as $\sqrt{2}$—numbers whose value cannot be written as a fraction and whose exact value can only be estimated. All these numbers are part of the *real numbers*, which are the only types of numbers students explore until high school, where they consider the square roots of negative numbers, called *imaginary numbers*. These sets of numbers are inter-related, and some are subsets of other sets. Figure 23.13 provides an illustration of the types of numbers and how they are interrelated.

Rational Numbers

Rational numbers comprise the set of all numbers that can be represented as a fraction—or a ratio of an integer to an integer. Even when numbers are written as whole numbers or as terminating decimals, they can also be written as fractions and thus are rational numbers. In fact, in school mathematics the term *rational numbers* is often used to refer to fractions, decimals (terminating and repeating), and per-cents. These are rational numbers, but so are integers, including whole numbers.

Moving among Representations. In sixth grade, students should be able to recognize a rational number as a point on a number line (CCSSO, 2010). In Chapter 17, we explored the idea of the "common" fractions (halves, thirds, fourths, fifths, eighths) in terms of their decimal equivalents. Students should be able to explain equivalence, as noted here:

- $4\frac{3}{5}$ is 4.6 because $\frac{3}{5}$ is six-tenths of a whole, so 4 wholes and six-tenths is 4.6.
- $4\frac{3}{5}$ is $\frac{23}{5}$, and that is the same as $23 \div 5$, or 4.6 if I use decimals.
- 4.6 is read "four and six-tenths," so I can write that as $4\frac{6}{10} = 4\frac{3}{5}$.

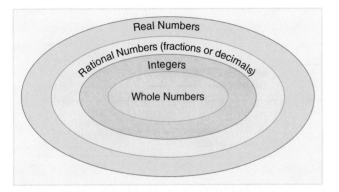

FIGURE 23.13 An illustration of the real numbers.

Similarly, compare these three expressions:

$$\tfrac{1}{4} \text{ of } 24 \qquad \tfrac{24}{4} \qquad 24 \div 4$$

This discussion can lead to a general development of the idea that a fraction can be thought of as division of the numerator by the denominator or that $\frac{a}{b}$ is the same as a $\div$ b.

When a fraction is converted to a decimal, the decimal either terminates (e.g., 3.415) or repeats (e.g., 2.5141414…). Is there a way to tell in advance whether a given fraction is a terminating decimal or a repeating decimal? The follow-ing activity can be used to discover why.

Activity 23.10

Repeater or Terminator?

Have students generate a table listing in one column the first 20 unit fractions ($\frac{1}{2}$, $\frac{1}{3}$, $\frac{1}{4}$, … $\frac{1}{21}$). In the second column, they list the prime factorization of the denominators; in the third column is the decimal equivalent for the fraction. Have students use calculators to get the decimal form.

After completing the table, the task is to see whether they can discover a rule that will tell in advance if the decimal will repeat or terminate. They can test the rule with fractions with denominators beyond 21. Also challenge students to confirm that their rule applies even if the numerator changes.

As students work on this task, they will notice various patterns, as can be seen in the student work provided in Fig-ure 23.14. As this student has discovered, the only fractions with terminating decimals have denominators that factor with only combinations of twos and fives. Why is this the case?

Middle school students must understand that any ratio-nal number, positive or negative, whole or not whole, can be written as a fraction and as a decimal. So, $^-8$ can be writ-ten as the fraction $\frac{^-8}{1}$ or $\frac{^-16}{2}$, or $\frac{^-800}{100}$ or as the decimal $^-8$ or $^-8.0$. In fact, there are infinite ways to write equivalencies for $^-8$. This fluency with equivalent representations is criti-cal and requires much more than teaching an algorithm for moving from one representation to another.

Irrational Numbers

Students have encountered *irrational numbers* as early as fifth grade when they learn about π. However, exploration of irra-tional numbers occurs in eighth grade (CCSSO, 2010). As noted earlier, *irrational* numbers are not rational, meaning they cannot be written in fraction form. The irrationals together with the rational numbers make up the *real num-bers*. The real numbers fill in all the holes on the number line even when the holes are infinitesimally small. There is a good YouTube video about rational, irrational, and real numbers at www.youtube.com/watch?v=oORCAz-V_Bg

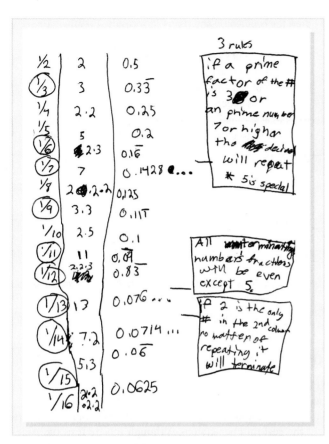

FIGURE 23.14 A student notes patterns as he explores the "Repeater or Terminator" activity.

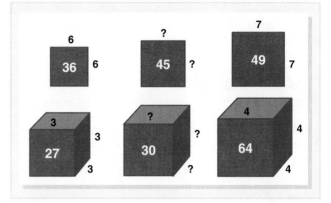

FIGURE 23.15 A geometric interpretation of square roots and cube roots.

Students' first experience with irrational numbers typically occurs when exploring square roots of whole numbers. The following activity provides a good introduction to square roots and cube roots.

Activity 23.11

Edges of Squares and Cubes

Show students pictures of three squares (or three cubes) as in Figure 23.15. The edges of the first and last figure are consecutive whole numbers. The areas (volumes) of all three figures are provided. The students' task is to use a calculator to find the edge of the figure in the center. Explain to students that they are not to use the square root key, but to estimate what they think the side would be and test it by squaring it. Ask students to continue to estimate until they have found a value to the hundredths place that gets as close to 45 as possible (or 30 in the case of the cube). Solutions will satisfy these equations:

$$\square \times \square = 45, \quad \text{or} \quad \square^2 = 45$$

and

$$\square \times \square \times \square = 30, \quad \text{or} \quad \square^3 = 30$$

To solve the cube problem, students might start with 3.5 and find that 3.5^3 is 42.875, much too large. Through trial and error, they will find that the solution is between 3.1 and 3.2. Continued use of strategic trial and error will lead to a close approximation. Although a calculator can find these square or cube roots quickly, the estimation activity strengthens students' understanding of squares and square roots and the relative sizes of numbers.

PAUSE and REFLECT

Use a calculator to continue getting a better approximation of the cube root of 30 to the hundredths place.

From this simple introduction, students can be challenged to find solutions to equations such as ($\square^2 = 8$). These students are now prepared to understand the general definition of the *n*th root of a number N as the number that when raised to the *n*th power equals N. The square and cube roots are simply other names for the second and third roots. The notational convention of the radical sign comes last. It is important to point out that $\sqrt{6}$ is a number rather than a computation (since it looks so much like a division problem). The cube root of eight is the same as $\sqrt[3]{8}$, which is equivalent to 2.

In middle school, students encounter irrational numbers primarily when working with the Pythagorean theorem ($a^2 + b^2 = c^2$), which is used to find the distance between two points (the distance being the diagonal, or *c*). If $a = 3$ and $b = 4$, then $c = 5$. All sides are rational numbers. But this case is the exception to the rule. More often sides will be something like 4 and 7 units, in which case $c = \sqrt{16 + 49} = \sqrt{65}$. Although sometimes there is a perfect square that can be simplified, in this case there is not one and the distance is $\sqrt{65}$, an irrational number.

An engaging middle school project applying the Pythagorean theorem and irrational numbers is a Wheel of Theodorus, as described in Activity 23.12. Theodorus was one of the early believers that irrational numbers existed (quite a contentious issue for the Pythagoreans, who were against the idea of irrationals!).

Activity 23.12

Wheel of Theodorus

Ask students to construct a right triangle that measures 1 centimeter on each side adjacent to the right angle and then draw the hypotenuse and record its measure. They then use the hypotenuse as a side and draw a new right triangle with this as side *a* along with a side *b* that is 1 cm. Draw and record the new hypotenuse ($\sqrt{3}$). Create the next triangle, which will have sides of $\sqrt{3}$ and 1 and a hypotenuse of $\sqrt{4}$ or 2, and so on. Doing this about 30 times will form a wheel. (See Bay-Williams & Martinie, 2009, for a complete lesson or search online for instructions and diagrams of a Wheel of Theodorus.)

RESOURCES *for Chapter 23*

LITERATURE CONNECTIONS

The Number Devil *Enzensberger, 1997*

Full of humor and wit, *The Number Devil* presents a collection of interesting ideas about numbers. Robert, a boy who hates mathematics, meets up with a crafty number devil in each of 12 dreams (one per chapter). On the fourth night's dream, Robert learns about infinitely repeating decimals and the "Rutabaga of two" (the square root of two), providing a connection to rational and irrational numbers.

Oh, Yikes! History's Grossest, Wackiest Moments *Masoff and Sirrell, 2006*

In this picture-rich reference book, the authors describe important historical events and people with facts that are interesting to middle schoolers (e.g., "Aztec Antics," "Cruel Constructions," "Humongous Hoaxes," "Pirates"). Selecting a topic, such as brushing teeth, the author describes how this was handled across all of history—an opportunity for time lines that include dates such as 2500 BC. Students can create a time line that is proportionally accurate to tell the events related to their topic. This lesson involves integers, measuring, proportional reasoning, and fractions.

RECOMMENDED READINGS

Articles

Reeves, C. A., & Webb, D. (2004). Balloons on the rise: A problem-solving approach to integers. *Mathematics Teaching in the Middle School, 9*(9), 476–482.
Expanding on a discussion of the possibility of helium party balloons making you weigh less if held while on a scale, the fifth-grade students in this article generalize the concepts of integers and use their ideas for addition and subtraction.

Swanson, P. E. (2010). The intersection of language and mathematics. *Mathematics Teaching in the Middle School, 15*(9), 516–523.

Weaving in many strategies to support ELLs, the author shares how she engaged students in real contexts to learn integer operations. Visuals and language support are used to ensure students understand.

ONLINE RESOURCES

The Evolution of the Real Numbers
www.themathpage.com/areal/real-numbers.htm
This is an interesting description of many topics related to the real number system. Although mostly text, the pages are filled with interactive questions.

National Library of Virtual Manipulatives (NLVM)
http://nlvm.usu.edu
Among the many applets on this site are "Color Chips—Addition," "Color Chips—Subtraction," "Rectangle Multiplication of Integers," and "Integer Arithmetic." These applets focus on using models for integer computation.

Volt Meter (Illuminations)
http://illuminations.nctm.org/ActivityDetail .aspx?ID=152
Click and drag batteries with negative and positive voltage to explore integer addition and subtraction.

Exponential Growth (Otherwise)
www.otherwise.com/population/exponent.html
This site offers an applet to experiment with population (exponential) growth.

The Next Billion (Illuminations)
http://illuminations.nctm.org/LessonDetail .aspx?id=L715
In 1999, the world population passed 6 billion. In this lesson, students predict when it will reach 7 billion. Students discuss their predictions, past trends in population growth, and social factors—a good interdisciplinary opportunity.

REFLECTIONS *on Chapter 23*

WRITING TO LEARN

1. What strategies can you use to help students understand and appropriately use the order of operations?

2. Explain how powers of 10 are used to write very small and very large numbers. What is the particular form of the power-of-10 symbolism used in scientific notation and on calculators?

3. Use a context and a model to solve the following:

$$^-10 + {}^+13 = {}^+3 \qquad ^-4 - {}^-9 = {}^+5 \qquad ^+6 - {}^-7 = {}^+13$$
$$^-4 \times {}^-3 = {}^+12 \qquad ^+15 \div {}^-5 = {}^-3 \qquad ^-12 \div {}^-3 = {}^+4$$

4. For each of the following numbers, tell all the kinds of numbers it is (real, rational, integer, whole). For example, $^-8$ is real and rational.

$$^-3 \qquad 120 \qquad \tfrac{4}{5} \qquad \sqrt{5} \qquad .323232\ldots \qquad {}^{-1}.4$$

5. How would you explain the difference between a rational and an irrational number to a middle school student?

FOR DISCUSSION AND EXPLORATION

1. Some exponent values are easily confused by students. Two of the most common cases are listed below. For each example,
   • Explain how the values are different in meaning.
   • Draw a representation to show how they are different.
   • Describe what investigation you would plan to help students see the differences in these values.
   Case 1: 2^3 and 2×3 and 3^2
   Case 2: $2n$ and n^2 and 2^n

MyEducationLab™

Go to the MyEducationLab (www.myeducationlab.com) for Math Methods and familiarize yourself with the content. Much of the site content is organized topically. The topics include all of the following to support your learning in the course:

• Learning outcomes for important mathematics methods course topics aligned with the national standards

• Assignments and Activities, tied to these learning outcomes and standards, that can help you more deeply understand course content

• Building Teaching Skills and Dispositions learning units that allow you to apply and practice your understanding of the core mathematics content and teaching skills

Your instructor has a correlation guide that aligns the exercises on the topical portion of the site with your book's chapters.

On MyEducationLab you will also find book-specific resources including Blackline Masters, Expanded Lesson Activities, and Artifact Analysis Activities.

Field Experience Guide
C O N N E C T I O N S

This chapter covers a range of topics, so there are numerous excellent lessons and resources in the *Field Experience Guide*. FEG 3.5 ("Create a Web of Ideas") can support the exploration of the relationships between rational numbers (integers, fractions, whole numbers, etc.). FEG Expanded Lesson 9.2 ("Close, Far, and In Between") focuses on the relative magnitude of numbers, and FEG Expanded Lesson 9.10 ("How Many In Between?") focuses on the density of rational numbers. FEG Activity 10.14 ("Find the Zero") focuses on addition and subtraction of integers. The order of operations is the focus of FEG Activity 10.7 ("Target Number") and Balanced Assessment Task 11.1 ("Magic Age Rings").

Appendix A

Standards for Mathematical Practice

The Standards for Mathematical Practice found in the *Common Core State Standards* describe varieties of expertise that mathematics educators at all levels should seek to develop in their students. These practices rest on important "processes and proficiencies" with longstanding importance in mathematics education. The first of these are the NCTM process standards of problem solving, reasoning and proof, communication, representation, and connections. The second are the strands for mathematical proficiency specified in the National Research Council's report *Adding It Up*: adaptive reasoning, strategic competence, conceptual understanding (comprehension of mathematical concepts, operations, and relations), procedural fluency (skill in carrying out procedures flexibly, accurately, efficiently, and appropriately), and productive disposition (habitual inclination to see mathematics as sensible, useful, and worthwhile, coupled with a belief in diligence and one's own efficacy).

1 Make sense of problems and persevere in solving them

Mathematically proficient students start by explaining to themselves the meaning of a problem and looking for entry points to its solution. They analyze givens, constraints, relationships, and goals. They make conjectures about the form and meaning of the solution and plan a solution pathway rather than simply jumping into a solution attempt. They consider analogous problems, and try special cases and simpler forms of the original problem in order to gain insight into its solution. They monitor and evaluate their progress and change course if necessary. Older students might, depending on the context of the problem, transform algebraic expressions or change the viewing window on their graphing calculator to get the information they need. Mathematically proficient students can explain correspondences between equations, verbal descriptions, tables, and graphs or draw diagrams of important features and relationships, graph data, and search for regularity or trends. Younger students might rely on using concrete objects or pictures to help conceptualize and solve a problem. Mathematically proficient students check their answers to problems using a different method, and they continually ask themselves, "Does this make sense?" They can understand the approaches of others to solving complex problems and identify correspondences between different approaches.

2 Reason abstractly and quantitatively

Mathematically proficient students make sense of quantities and their relationships in problem situations. They bring two complementary abilities to bear on problems involving quantitative relationships: the ability to *decontextualize*—to abstract a given situation and represent it symbolically and manipulate the representing symbols as if they have a life of their own, without necessarily attending to their referents—and the ability to *contextualize*, to pause as needed during the manipulation process in order to probe into the referents for the symbols involved. Quantitative reasoning entails habits of creating a coherent representation of the problem at hand; considering the units involved; attending to the meaning of quantities, not just how to compute them; and knowing and flexibly using different properties of operations and objects.

3 Construct viable arguments and critique the reasoning of others

Mathematically proficient students understand and use stated assumptions, definitions, and previously established results in constructing arguments. They make conjectures and build a logical progression of statements to explore the truth of their conjectures. They are able to analyze situations by breaking them into cases, and can recognize and use counterexamples. They justify their conclusions, communicate them to others, and respond to the arguments of others. They reason inductively about data, making plausible arguments that take into account the context from which the data arose. Mathematically proficient students are also able to compare the effectiveness of two plausible arguments, distinguish correct logic or reasoning from that which is flawed, and—if there is a flaw in an argument—explain what it is. Elementary students can construct arguments using concrete referents such as objects, drawings, diagrams, and actions. Such arguments can make sense and be correct, even though they are not generalized or made formal until later grades. Later, students learn to determine domains to which an argument applies. Students at all grades can listen or read the arguments of others, decide whether they make sense, and ask useful questions to clarify or improve the arguments.

4 Model with mathematics

Mathematically proficient students can apply the mathematics they know to solve problems arising in everyday life, society, and the workplace. In early grades, this might be as simple as writing an addition equation to describe a situation. In middle grades, a student might apply proportional reasoning to plan a school event or analyze a problem in the community. By high school, a student might use geometry to solve a design problem or use a function to describe how one quantity of interest depends on another. Mathematically proficient students who can apply what they know are comfortable making assumptions and approximations to simplify a complicated situation, realizing that these may need revision later. They are able to identify important quantities in a practical situation and map their relationships using such tools as diagrams, two-way tables, graphs, flowcharts, and formulas. They can analyze those relationships mathematically to draw conclusions. They routinely interpret their mathematical results in the context of the situation and reflect on whether the results make sense, possibly improving the model if it has not served its purpose.

5 Use appropriate tools strategically

Mathematically proficient students consider the available tools when solving a mathematical problem. These tools might include pencil and paper, concrete models, a ruler, a protractor, a calculator, a spreadsheet, a computer algebra system, a statistical package, or dynamic geometry software. Proficient students are sufficiently familiar with tools appropriate for their grade or course to make sound decisions about when each of these tools might be helpful, recognizing both the insight to be gained and their limitations. For example, mathematically proficient high school students analyze graphs of functions and solutions generated using a graphing calculator. They detect possible errors by strategically using estimation and other mathematical knowledge. When making mathematical models, they know that technology can enable them to visualize the results of varying assumptions, explore consequences, and compare predictions with data. Mathematically proficient students at various grade levels are able to identify relevant external mathematical resources, such as digital content located on a website, and use them to pose or solve problems. They are able to use technological tools to explore and deepen their understanding of concepts.

6 Attend to precision

Mathematically proficient students try to communicate precisely to others. They try to use clear definitions in discussion with others and in their own reasoning. They state the meaning of the symbols they choose, including using the equal sign consistently and appropriately. They are careful about specifying units of measure and labeling axes to clarify the correspondence with quantities in a problem. They calculate accurately and efficiently, express numerical answers with a degree of precision appropriate for the problem context. In the elementary grades, students give carefully formulated explanations to each other. By the time they reach high school, they have learned to examine claims and make explicit use of definitions.

7 Look for and make use of structure

Mathematically proficient students look closely to discern a pattern or structure. Young students, for example, might notice that three and seven more is the same amount as seven and three more, or they may sort a collection of shapes according to how many sides the shapes have. Later, students will see 7×8 equals the well-remembered $7 \times 5 + 7 \times 3$, in preparation for learning about the distributive property. In the expression $x^2 + 9x + 14$, older students can see the 14 as 2×7 and the 9 as $2 + 7$. They recognize the significance of an existing line in a geometric figure and can use the strategy of drawing an auxiliary line for solving problems. They also can step back for an overview and shift perspective. They can see complicated things, such as some algebraic expressions as single objects or as being composed of several objects. For example, they can see $5 - 3(x - y)^2$ as 5 minus a positive number times a square and use that to realize that its value cannot be more than 5 for any real numbers x and y.

8 Look for and express regularity in repeated reasoning

Mathematically proficient students notice if calculations are repeated, and look both for general methods and for shortcuts. Upper elementary students might notice when dividing 25 by 11 that they are repeating the same calculations over and over again, and conclude they have a repeating decimal. By paying attention to the calculation of slope as they repeatedly check whether points are on the line through $(1, 2)$ with slope 3, middle school students might abstract the equation $(y - 2)/(x - 1) = 3$. Noticing the regularity in the way terms cancel when expanding $(x - 1)(x + 1)$, $(x - 1)(x^2 + x + 1)$, and $(x - 1)(x^3 + x^2 + x + 1)$ might lead them to the general formula for the sum of a geometric series. As they work to solve a problem, mathematically proficient students maintain oversight of the process while attending to the details. They continually evaluate the reasonableness of their intermediate results.

Appendix B
Standards for Teaching Mathematics

STANDARD 1 Knowledge of Mathematics and General Pedagogy

Teachers of mathematics should have a deep knowledge of—

- sound and significant mathematics;
- theories of student intellectual development across the spectrum of diverse learners;
- modes of instruction and assessment; and
- effective communication and motivational strategies.

STANDARD 2 Knowledge of Student Mathematical Learning

Teachers of mathematics must know and recognize the importance of—

- what is known about the ways students learn mathematics;
- methods of supporting students as they struggle to make sense of mathematical concepts and procedures;
- ways to help students build on informal mathematical understandings;
- a variety of tools for use in mathematical investigation and the benefits and limitations of those tools; and
- ways to stimulate engagement and guide the exploration of the mathematical processes of problem solving, reasoning and proof, communication, connections, and representations.

STANDARD 3 Worthwhile Mathematical Tasks

The teacher of mathematics should design learning experiences and pose tasks that are based on sound and significant mathematics and that—

- engage students' intellect;
- develop mathematical understandings and skills;
- stimulate students to make connections and develop a coherent framework for mathematical ideas;
- call for problem formulation, problem solving, and mathematical reasoning;

- promote communication about mathematics;
- represent mathematics as an ongoing human activity; and
- display sensitivity to, and draw on, students' diverse background experiences and dispositions.

STANDARD 4 Learning Environment

The teacher of mathematics should create a learning environment that provides—

- the time necessary to explore sound mathematics and deal with significant ideas and problems;
- a physical space and appropriate materials that facilitate students' learning of mathematics;
- access and encouragement to use appropriate technology;
- a context that encourages the development of mathematical skill and proficiency;
- an atmosphere of respect and value for students' ideas and ways of thinking;
- an opportunity to work independently or collaboratively to make sense of mathematics;
- a climate for students to take intellectual risks in raising questions and formulating conjectures; and
- encouragement for the student to display a sense of mathematical competence by validating and supporting ideas with a mathematical argument.

STANDARD 5 Discourse

The teacher of mathematics should orchestrate discourse by—

- posing questions and tasks that elicit, engage, and challenge each student's thinking;
- listening carefully to students' ideas and deciding what to pursue in depth from among the ideas that students generate during a discussion;
- asking students to clarify and justify their ideas orally and in writing and by accepting a variety of presentation modes;
- deciding when and how to attach mathematical notation and language to students' ideas;

- encouraging and accepting the use of multiple representations;
- making available tools for exploration and analysis;
- deciding when to provide information, when to clarify an issue, when to model, when to lead, and when to let students wrestle with a difficulty; and
- monitoring students' participation in discussions and deciding when and how to encourage each student to participate.

STANDARD 6 Reflection on Student Learning

The teacher of mathematics should engage in ongoing analysis of students' learning by—

- observing, listening to, and gathering information about students to assess what they are learning so as to ensure that every student is learning sound and significant mathematics and is developing a positive disposition toward mathematics;
- challenging and extending students' ideas;

- adapting or changing activities while teaching;
- describing and commenting on each student's learning to parents and administrators; and
- providing regular feedback to the students themselves.

STANDARD 7 Reflection on Teaching Practice

The teacher of mathematics should engage in ongoing analysis of teaching by—

- reflecting regularly on what and how they teach;
- examining effects of the task, discourse, and learning environment on students' mathematical knowledge, skills, and dispositions;
- seeking to improve their teaching and practice by participating in learning communities beyond their classroom;
- analyzing and using assessment data to make reasoned decisions about necessary changes in curriculum; and
- collaborating with colleagues to develop plans to improve instructional programs.

Source: National Council of Teachers of Mathematics. (2007). *Mathematics Teaching Today.* Reston, VA: NCTM. Copyright © 2007 by the National Council of Teachers of Mathematics. All rights reserved.

Appendix C
Guide to Blackline Masters

This Appendix contains images of all of the Blackline Masters (BLM) that are listed below. The full-size masters can be found in either of two places:

- In hard copy at the end of the *Field Experience Guide* (Blackline Masters 62–77 are connected to Expanded Lessons provided in the *Field Experience Guide*.)
- On the MyEducationLab website (www.myeducationlab.com)

Suggestions for Use and Construction of Materials

CARD STOCK MATERIALS

A good way to have many materials made quickly and easily for students is to have them duplicated on card stock, laminated, and then cut into smaller pieces if desired. Once cut, materials are best kept in clear freezer bags with zip-type closures. Punch a hole near the top of the bag so that you do not store air.

The following list is a suggestion for materials that can be made from card stock using the masters in this section. Quantity suggestions are also given.

Dot Cards—3–8

One complete set of cards will serve four to six children. Duplicate each set in a different color so that mixed sets can be separated easily. Laminate and then cut with a paper cutter.

Five-Frames and Ten-Frames—9–10

Five-frames and ten-frames are best duplicated on light-colored card stock. Do not laminate; if you do, the mats will curl and counters will slide around.

10 × 10 Multiplication Array—12

Make one per student in any color. Lamination is suggested. Provide each student with an L-shaped piece of card stock to frame the array.

Base-Ten Materials—14

Run copies on white card stock. One sheet will make 4 hundreds and 10 tens or 4 hundreds and 100 ones. Cut into pieces with a paper cutter. It is recommended that you not laminate the base-ten pieces. A kit consisting of 10 hundreds, 30 tens, and 30 ones is adequate for each student or pair of students.

Little Ten-Frames—15–16

There are two masters for these materials. One has full ten-frames, and the other has one to nine dots, including two with five dots. Copy the 1-to-9 master on one color of card stock and the full ten-frames on another and then laminate. Cut into little ten-frames. Each set consists of 20 pieces: 10 full ten-frames and 10 of the 1-to-9 pieces, including 2 fives. Make a set for each student.

Place-Value Mat (with Ten-Frames)—17

Mats can be duplicated on any pastel card stock. It is recommended that you not laminate these because they tend to curl and counters slide around. Make one for every student.

Circular Fraction Pieces—24–26

Make three copies of each page of the master. To have a separate master for each size, cut the disks apart and tape onto blank pages with three of the same type on a page. Duplicate each master on a different color card stock. Laminate and then cut the circles out. A kit for one or two students should have two circles of each size piece.

Rational Number Wheel—28

These disks should be made on card stock. Duplicate the master on two contrasting colors. Laminate and cut the circles and also the slot on the dotted line. Make a set for each student.

Tangrams and Mosaic Puzzle—51

Copy the tangrams and the mosaic puzzle on card stock. For younger children, the card stock should be mounted on poster board to make the pieces thicker and easier to put together in puzzles. Prepare one set per student.

Woozle Cards—59

Copy the Woozle Card master on white card stock. You need two copies per set. Before laminating, color one set one color and the other a different color. An easy way to color the cards is to make one pass around the inside of each Woozle, leaving the rest of the creature white. If you color the entire Woozle, the dots may not show up. Make one set for every four students.

Many masters lend themselves to demonstration purposes. The 10 × 10 array, the blank hundreds board, and the large geoboard are examples. The place-value mat can be used with strips and squares or with counters and cups directly on the document camera or opaque projector. The missing-part blank and the record blanks for the four algorithms are pages that you may wish to write on as a demonstration.

The 10,000 grid is the easiest way there is to show 10,000 or to model four-place decimal numbers.

The degrees and wedges page is the very best way to illustrate what a degree is and also to help explain protractors.

All of the line and dot grids are useful for modeling. You may find it a good idea to have several copies of each easily available.

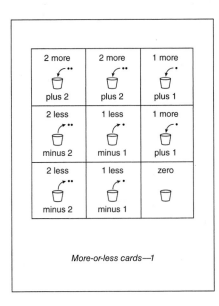

More-or-less cards—1

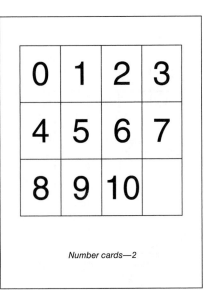

Number cards—2

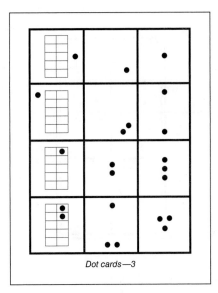

Dot cards—3

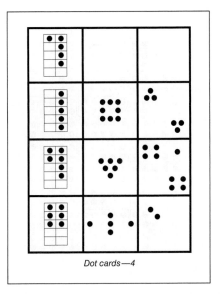

Dot cards—4

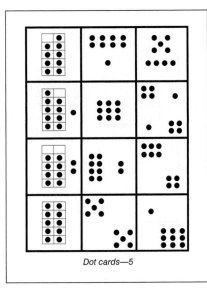

Dot cards—5

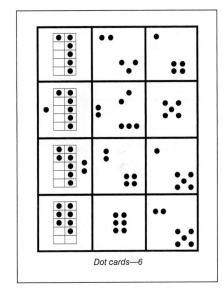

Dot cards—6

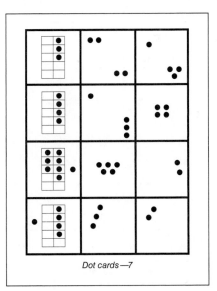

Dot cards—7

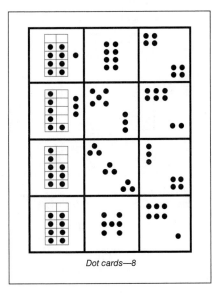

Dot cards—8

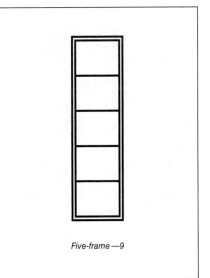

Five-frame—9

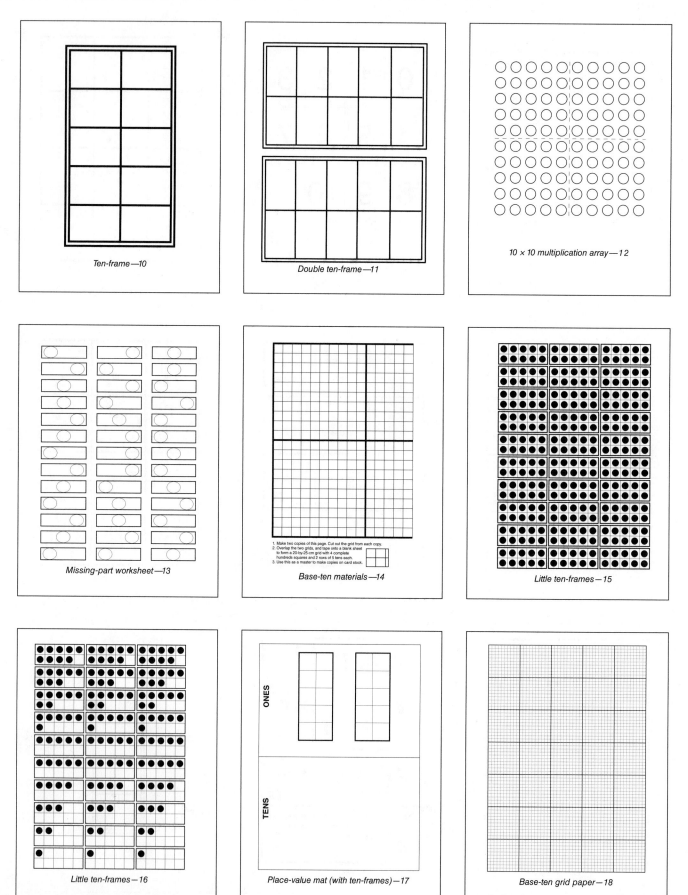

Ten-frame—10

Double ten-frame—11

10 × 10 multiplication array—12

Missing-part worksheet—13

Base-ten materials—14

Little ten-frames—15

Little ten-frames—16

Place-value mat (with ten-frames)—17

Base-ten grid paper—18

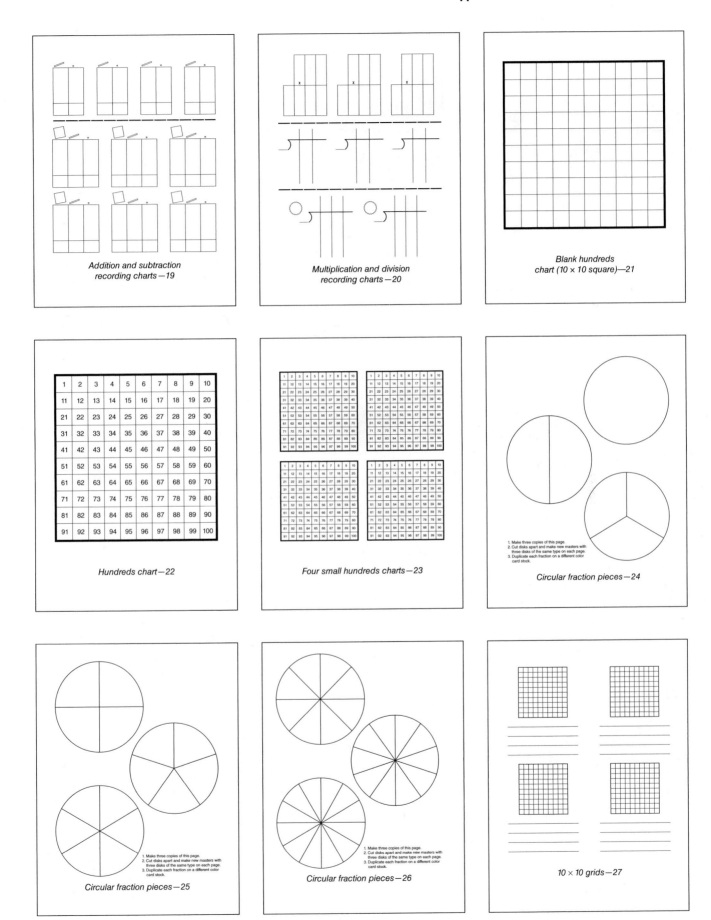

Addition and subtraction
recording charts—19

Multiplication and division
recording charts—20

Blank hundreds
chart (10 × 10 square)—21

Hundreds chart—22

Four small hundreds charts—23

Circular fraction pieces—24

Circular fraction pieces—25

Circular fraction pieces—26

10 × 10 grids—27

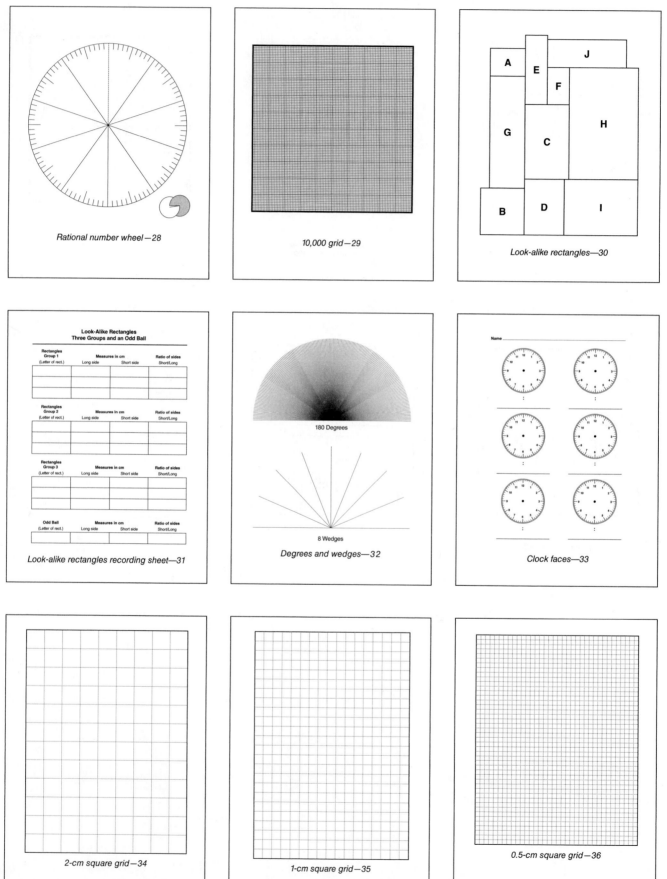

Rational number wheel—28

10,000 grid—29

Look-alike rectangles—30

Look-alike rectangles recording sheet—31

Degrees and wedges—32

Clock faces—33

2-cm square grid—34

1-cm square grid—35

0.5-cm square grid—36

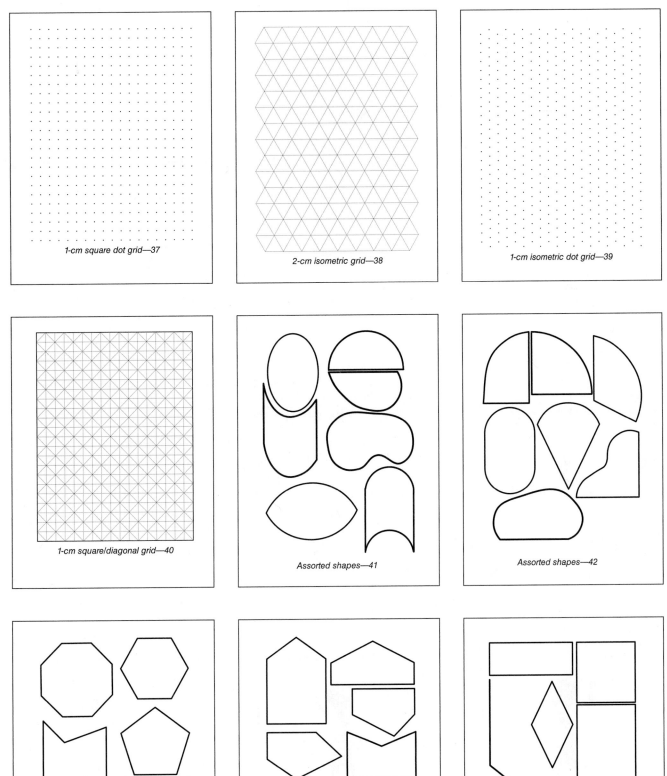

1-cm square dot grid—37

2-cm isometric grid—38

1-cm isometric dot grid—39

1-cm square/diagonal grid—40

Assorted shapes—41

Assorted shapes—42

Assorted shapes—43

Assorted shapes—44

Assorted shapes—45

Assorted shapes—46

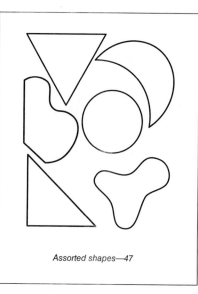

Assorted shapes—47

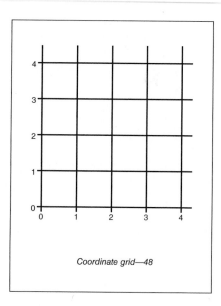

Coordinate grid—48

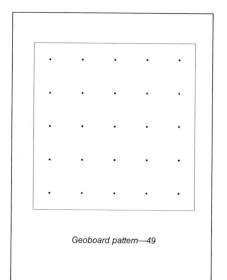

Geoboard pattern—49

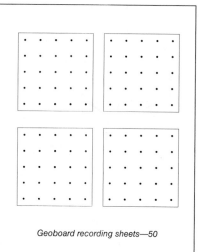

Geoboard recording sheets—50

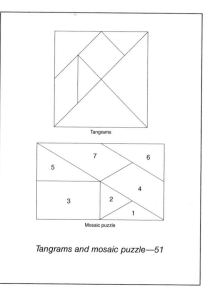

Tangrams

Mosaic puzzle

Tangrams and mosaic puzzle—51

Motion man—Side 1

Directions:

Make copies of Side 1. Then copy Side 2 on the reverse of Side 1. Check the orientation with one copy. When done correctly the two sides will match up when held to the light.

Motion man—52

Motion man—Side 2

(See directions on Side 1.)

Motion man—53

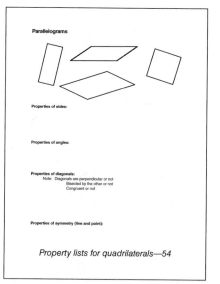

Parallelograms

Properties of sides:

Properties of angles:

Properties of diagonals:
Note: Diagonals are perpendicular or not
        Bisected by the other or not
        Congruent or not

Properties of symmetry (line and point):

Property lists for quadrilaterals—54

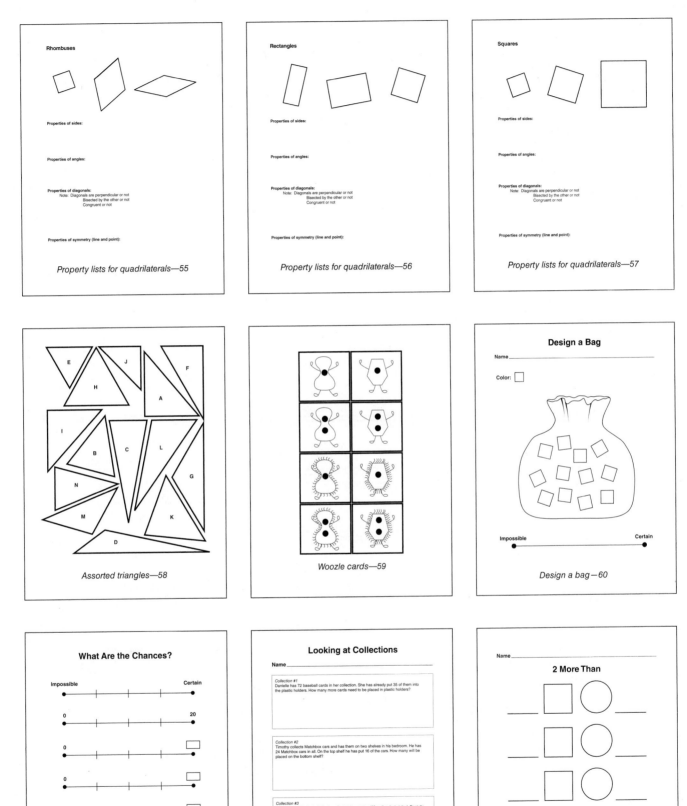

Rhombuses

Properties of sides:

Properties of angles:

Properties of diagonals:
Note: Diagonals are perpendicular or not
Bisected by the other or not
Congruent or not

Properties of symmetry (line and point):

Property lists for quadrilaterals—55

Rectangles

Properties of sides:

Properties of angles:

Properties of diagonals:
Note: Diagonals are perpendicular or not
Bisected by the other or not
Congruent or not

Properties of symmetry (line and point):

Property lists for quadrilaterals—56

Squares

Properties of sides:

Properties of angles:

Properties of diagonals:
Note: Diagonals are perpendicular or not
Bisected by the other or not
Congruent or not

Properties of symmetry (line and point):

Property lists for quadrilaterals—57

Assorted triangles—58

Woozle cards—59

Design a Bag

Name

Color:

Impossible   Certain

Design a bag—60

What Are the Chances?

Impossible   Certain

0   20

0

0

0

0

What are the chances?—61

Looking at Collections

Name

Collection #1
Danielle has 72 baseball cards in her collection. She has already put 35 of them into the plastic holders. How many more cards need to be placed in plastic holders?

Collection #2
Timothy collects Matchbox cars and has them on two shelves in his bedroom. He has 24 Matchbox cars in all. On the top shelf he has put 16 of the cars. How many will be placed on the bottom shelf?

Collection #3
Danielle and Timothy both like to collect state quarters. When they last visited, Danielle had 32 quarters and Timothy had 24 quarters. How many more does Danielle have than Timothy?

Looking at collections—62

Name

2 More Than

2 more than—63

Name_____

2 Less Than

2 less than—64

Name_____

How Long?

Object_____	Object_____
Estimate	Estimate
____ tens ____ ones	____ tens ____ ones
Actual	Actual
____ tens ____ ones	____ tens ____ ones
number word	number word
number	number

Object_____	Object_____
Estimate	Estimate
____ tens ____ ones	____ tens ____ ones
Actual	Actual
____ tens ____ ones	____ tens ____ ones
number word	number word
number	number

How long?—65

Name_____

Fraction Names

Find fraction names for each shaded region. Explain how you saw each name you found.

1.

2.

3.

Fraction names—66

Solving Problems Involving Fractions

Name_____

Solve these problems. Use words and drawings to explain how you got your answer.

1. You have 3/4 of a pizza left. If you give 1/3 of the leftover pizza to your brother, how much of a whole pizza will your brother get?

2. Someone ate 1/10 of the cake, leaving only 9/10. If you eat 2/3 of the cake that is left, how much of a whole cake will you have eaten?

3. Gloria used 2 1/2 tubes of blue paint to paint the sky in her picture. Each tube holds 4/5 ounce of paint. How many ounces of blue paint did Gloria use?

Solving problems involving fractions—67

It's a Matter of Rates

Solve each of these problems. Use pictures and words to show how you solved it.

1. Terry can run 4 laps in 12 minutes. Susan can run 3 laps in 9 minutes. Who is the faster runner?

2. Jack and Jill were at the bottom of a hill, hoping to fetch a pail of water. Jack walks uphill at 5 steps every 25 seconds, while Jill walks uphill at 3 steps every 10 seconds. Assuming a constant walking rate, who will get to the pail of water first?

3. Some of the hens in Farmer Brown's chicken farm lay brown eggs and some lay white eggs. Farmer Brown noticed that in the old hen house, she collected 4 brown eggs for every 10 white eggs. In the new hen house, the ratio of brown eggs to white eggs was 1 to 3. If both hen houses produce the same number of eggs, in which henhouse will there be more brown eggs?

4. The Play-a-Lot Video Game Store charges $2.00 for every 15 minutes to play on their wide selection of video games. Wired-for-Action Video Store charges $3.00 for 20 minutes of play on their video games. Where would you choose to go if you were basing your decision on pricing?

It's a matter of rates—68

Windows

Name_____

Step	1	2	3	4	5	6	7		20
No. of sticks	4	7	10						

Describe the pattern you see in the drawing:
_____

Describe the pattern you see in the table:
_____

Use words to describe the rule for finding out how many sticks you need to make any length of window:
_____

Use numbers and symbols to write an equation for your rule:
_____

Predict how many—69

Dot Arrays

Name_____

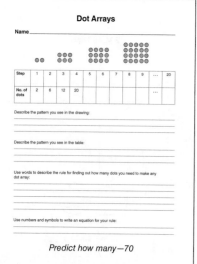

Step	1	2	3	4	5	6	7	8	9	...	20
No. of dots	2	6	12	20						...	

Describe the pattern you see in the drawing:
_____

Describe the pattern you see in the table:
_____

Use words to describe the rule for finding out how many dots you need to make any dot array:
_____

Use numbers and symbols to write an equation for your rule:
_____

Predict how many—70

Create a Journey Story

If possible, create a story about a journey that the graph could represent. If not possible, explain.

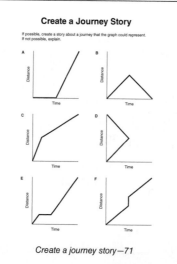

Create a journey story—71

Crooked Paths

Name_____

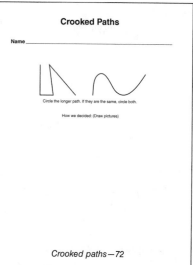

Circle the longer path. If they are the same, circle both.

How we decided: (Draw pictures)

Crooked paths—72

Rectangles Made with 36 Tiles

Name _____

Rectangle Dimensions	Area	Perimeter

Rectangles made with 36 tiles — 73

Fixed Area Recording Sheet

Name _____

Length	Width	Area	Perimeter

Fixed area recording sheet — 74

Properties of Quadrilateral Diagonals

Name _____

Name of Quadrilateral	Congruent Diagonals		Diagonals Bisected			Intersection of Diagonals	
	Yes	No	Both	One	Neither	Perpendicular	Not

Properties of quadrilateral diagonals — 75

Toy Purchases

Toy purchases — 76

Toying with Measures

Name _____

	Mean	Median	Mode
Original Set of 6			

Make predictions based on these changes. Give reasons for your predictions.

Add a $20 toy			
Reasons			
Return the $1 toy			
Reasons			
Get a free toy			
Reasons			
Buy a second $12 toy			
Reasons			
Your change:			
Reasons			

Calculate the actual statistics for each of the changes.

Add a $20 toy			
Return the $1 toy			
Get a free toy			
Buy a second $12 toy			
Your change:			

Toying with measures — 77

References

Abu-Bakare, V. (2008). *Investigating students' understandings of probability: A study of a grade 7 classroom.* (Master's thesis). Retrieved from http://hdl.handle.net/2429/4073

AIMS. (2001). *Looking at lines: Interesting objects and linear functions.* Fresno, CA: AIMS Education Foundation.

Ambrose, R., Baek, J., & Carpenter, T. P. (2003). Children's invention of multidigit multiplication and division algorithms. In A. J. Baroody & A. Dowker (Eds.), *The development of arithmetic concepts and skills: Constructing adaptive expertise* (pp. 305–336). Mahwah, NJ: Erlbaum.

Arbaugh, F., Herbel-Eisenmann, B., Ramirez, N., Kranendonk, H., Knuth, E., & Quander, J. R. (2010). *Linking research and practice: Practitioner community priorities for research in mathematics education.* Reston, VA: Report for the National Council of Teachers of Mathematics, Research Agenda Conference.

Ashcraft, M. H., & Christy, K. S. (1995). The frequency of arithmetic facts in elementary texts: Addition and multiplication in grades 1–6. *Journal for Research in Mathematics Education, 26*(5), 396–421.

Assouline, S. G., & Lupkowski-Shoplik, A. (2011). *Developing math talent: A comprehensive guide to math education for gifted students in elementary and middle school* (2nd ed.). Waco, TX: Prufrock Press.

Aud, S., Fox, M., & Kewalramani, A. (2010). *Status and trends in the education of racial and ethnic groups* (NCES 2010–015). U.S. Department of Education, National Center for Education Statistics. Washington, DC: U.S. Government Printing Office.

Austin, R., & Thompson, D. (1997). Exploring algebraic patterns through literature. *Mathematics Teaching in the Middle School, 2*(4), 274–281.

Averill, R., Anderson, D., Easton, H., Te Maro, P., Smith, D., & Hynds, A. (2009). Culturally responsive teaching of mathematics: Three models from linked studies. *Journal for Research in Mathematics Education, 40*(2), 157–186.

Backhouse, J., Haggarty, L., Pirie, S., & Stratton, J. (1992). *Improving the learning of mathematics.* Portsmouth, NH: Heinemann.

Baek, J. M. (2006). Children's mathematical understanding and invented strategies for multidigit multiplication. *Teaching Children Mathematics, 12*(5), 242–247.

Baek, J. M. (2008). Developing algebraic thinking through exploration in multiplication. In Greenes, C. E., & Rubenstein, R. (Eds.), *Algebra and algebraic thinking in school mathematics: 70th NCTM yearbook* (pp. 141–154). Reston, VA: NCTM.

Bakker, A., Biehler, R., & Konold, C. (2004). Should young students learn about box plots? In *Curricular development in statistics education* (pp. 163–173). Sweden: Curricular Development in Statistics Education.

Ball, D. L. (1992). Magical hopes: Manipulatives and the reform of math education. *American Educator, 16*(2), 14–18, 46–47.

Ball, D. L. (2008, February). *The work of teaching and the challenges for teacher education.* Presentation at the American Association of Colleges of Teacher Education annual meeting, New Orleans, LA.

Ball, D. L., & Bass, H. (2003). Making mathematics reasonable in school. In J. Kilpatrick, W. G. Martin, & D. Schifter (Eds.), *A research companion to Principles and Standards for School Mathematics* (pp. 27–44). Reston, VA: NCTM.

Ball, D. L., & Stacey, K. (2005). Teaching strategies for developing judicious technology use. In W. J. Masalski & P. C. Elliott (Eds.), *Technology-supported mathematics learning environments* (pp. 3–15). Reston, VA: NCTM.

Bamberger, H. J., Oberdorf, C., & Schultz-Ferrell, K. (2010). *Math misconceptions: From misunderstanding to deep understanding.* Portsmouth, NH: Heinemann.

Baratta-Lorton, M. (1976). *Mathematics their way.* Menlo Park, CA: AWL Supplemental.

Barlow, A. T. (2010). Building word problems: What does it take? *Teaching Children Mathematics, 17*(3), 140–148.

Barlow, A. T., & McCrory, M. (2011). Strategies for promoting math disagreements. *Teaching Children Mathematics, 17*(3), 530–539.

Barmby, P., Harries, T., Higgins, S., & Suggate, J. (2009). The array representation and primary children's understanding and reasoning in multiplication. *Educational Studies in Mathematics, 70,* 217–241.

Barnett, R. C. (2007, October). *As the twig is bent: Early and powerful influences on whether girls choose careers in math and science.* Presentation at Boston University.

Barney, L. (1970, April). Your fingers can multiply! *Instructor,* 129–130.

Baroody, A. J. (1985). Mastery of the basic number combinations: Internalization of relationships or facts? *Journal for Research in Mathematics Education, 16*(2), 83–98.

Baroody, A. J. (1987). *Children's mathematical thinking: A developmental framework for preschool, primary, and special education teachers.* New York: Teachers College Press.

Baroody, A. J. (1990). How and when should place value concepts and skills be taught? *Journal for Research in Mathematics Education, 21,* 281–286.

Baroody, A. J. (2003). The development of adaptive expertise and flexibility: The integration of conceptual and procedural knowledge. In A. J. Baroody & A. Dowker (Eds.), *The development of arithmetic concepts and skills: Constructing adaptive expertise* (pp. 1–34). Mahwah, NJ: Erlbaum.

Baroody, A. J. (2006). Why children have difficulties mastering the basic number combinations and how to help them. *Teaching Children Mathematics, 13*(1), 22–31.

Baroody, A. J. (2011). Learning: A framework. In F. Fennell (Ed.), *Achieving fluency: Special education and mathematics* (pp. 15–58). Reston, VA: NCTM.

Baroody, A. J., Bajwa, N. P., & Eiland, M. (2009). Why can't Johnny remember the basic facts? *Developmental Disabilities Research Reviews, 15,* 69–79.

Baroody, A. J., Feil, Y., & Johnson A. R. (2007). An alternative reconceptualization of procedural and conceptual knowledge. *Journal for Research in Mathematics Education, 38*(2), 115–131.

Baroody, A. J., Li, X., & Lai, M. L. (2008). Toddlers' spontaneous attention to number. *Mathematics Thinking and Learning, 10,* 1–31.

Baroody, A. J., Wilkins, J. L., & Tiilikainen, S. H. (2003). The development of children's understanding of additive commutativity: From protoquantitive concept to general concept? In A. J. Baroody & A. Dowker (Eds.), *The development of arithmetic concepts and skills* (pp. 127–160). Mahwah, NJ: Erlbaum.

Battista, M. T. (1999). The mathematical miseducation of America's youth: Ignoring research and scientific study in education. *Phi Delta Kappan, 80*(6), 424–433.

Battista, M. T. (2003). Understanding students' thinking about area and volume measurement. In D. H. Clements (Ed.), *Learning and teaching measurement* (pp. 122–142). Reston, VA: NCTM.

Battista, M. T. (2007). The development of geometric and spatial thinking. In F. Lester (Ed.), *Second handbook of research on mathematics teaching and learning* (pp. 843–908). Reston, VA: NCTM.

Bay-Williams, J. M. (2010). Influences on student outcomes: Teachers' classroom practices. In D. Lambdin (Ed.), *Teaching and learning mathematics: Translating research to the classroom* (pp. 31–36). Reston, VA: NCTM.

Bay-Williams, J. M., & Martinie, S. L. (2003). Thinking rationally about number in the middle school. *Mathematics Teaching in the Middle School, 8*(6), 282–287.

Bay-Williams, J. M., & Martinie, S. L. (2004a). What does algebraic thinking look like? *Mathematics Teaching in the Middle School, 10*(4), 198–199.

Bay-Williams, J. M., & Martinie, S. L. (2004b). *Math and literature: Grades 6–8.* Sausalito, CA: Math Solutions Publications.

Bay-Williams, J. M., & Martinie, S. L. (2009). *Math and nonfiction: Grades 6–8.* Sausalito, CA: Marilyn Burns Books.

Beck, S. A., & Huse, V. E. (2007). A virtual spin on probability. *Teaching Children Mathematics, 13*(9), 482–486.

Beckman, C. E., Thompson, D., & Austin, R. A. (2004). Exploring proportional reasoning through movies and literature. *Mathematics Teaching in the Middle School, 9*(5), 256–262.

Beckmann, S. (2004). Solving algebra and other story problems with simple diagrams: A method demonstrated in grade 4–6 texts used in Singapore. *The Mathematics Educator, 14*(1), 42–46.

Behr, M. J., Lesh, R., Post, T. R., & Silver, E. A. (1983). Rational number concepts. In R. Lesh & M. Landau (Eds.), *Acquisition of mathematics concepts and processes* (pp. 91–126). New York: Academic Press.

Beilock, S. L., Gunderson, E. A., Ramirez, G., & Levine, S. C. (2010). Female teachers' math anxiety affects girls' math achievement. *Proceedings of the National Academy of Sciences (PNAS), 107*(5), 1860–1963.

Bell, E. S., & Bell, R. N. (1985). Writing and mathematical problem solving: Arguments in favor of synthesis. *School Science and Mathematics, 85*(3), 210–221.

Benard, B. (1991). *Fostering resiliency in kids: Protective factors in the family, school and community.* Portland, OR: Northwest Regional Educational Laboratory.

Berk, D., Taber, S., Gorowara, C. C., & Poetzl, C. (2009). Developing prospective elementary teachers' flexibility in the domain of proportional reasoning. *Mathematical Thinking and Learning, 11*(3), 113–135.

Bezuszka, S. J., & Kenney, M. J. (2008). The three R's: Recursive thinking, recursion, and recursive formulas. In C. E. Greenes & R. Rubenstein (Eds.), *Algebra and algebraic thinking in school mathematics: 70th NCTM yearbook* (pp. 81–97). Reston, VA: NCTM.

Biddlecomb, B., & Carr, M. (2011). A longitudinal study of the development of mathematics strategies and underlying counting schemes. *International Journal of Science and Mathematics Education, 9,* 1–24.

Bishop, A. J. (2001). What values do you teach when you teach mathematics? *Teaching Children Mathematics, 7*(6), 346–349.

Blanton, M. L. (2008). *Algebra in the elementary classroom: Transforming thinking, transforming practice.* Portsmouth, NH: Heinemann.

Bley, N. S., & Thornton, C. A. (1995). *Teaching mathematics to students with learning disabilities* (3rd ed.). Austin, TX: Pro-Ed.

Bloom, B. S., Engelhart, M. D., Furst, E. J., Hill, W. H., & Krathwohl, D. R. (1956). *Taxonomy of educational objectives: The classification of educational goals. Handbook I: Cognitive domain.* New York: Longman, Green.

Blote, A., Lieffering, L., & Ouwehand, K. (2006). The development of many-to-one counting in 4-year-old children. *Cognitive Development, 21*(3), 332–348.

Blume, G., Galindo, E., & Walcott, C. (2007). Performance in measurement and geometry from the viewpoint of *Principles and Standards for School Mathematics.* In P. Kloosterman & F. Lester, Jr. (Eds.), *Results and interpretations of the 2003 mathematics assessment of the National Assessment of Educational Progress* (pp. 95–138). Reston, VA: NCTM.

Boaler, J. (1998). Open and closed mathematics: Student experiences and understandings. *Journal for Research in Mathematics Education, 29*(1), 41–62.

Boaler, J. (2002). *Experiencing school mathematics: Traditional and reform approaches to teaching and their impact on student learning.* Mahwah, NJ: Erlbaum.

Boaler, J. (2008, April). Promoting "relational equity" and high mathematics achievement through an innovative mixed ability approach. *British Educational Research Journal, 34,* 167–194.

Boaler, J., & Humphreys, C. (2005). *Connecting mathematical ideas: Middle school video cases to support teaching and learning.* Portsmouth, NH: Heinemann.

Bransford, J., Brown, A., & Cocking, R., Eds. (2000). *How people learn: Brain, mind, experience, and school: Expanded edition.* Washington, DC: National Academies Press.

Bray, W. S. (2009). The power of choice. *Teaching Children Mathematics, 16*(3), 178–184.

Bray, W. S., & Abreu-Sanchez, L. (2010). Using number sense to compare fractions. *Teaching Children Mathematics, 17*(2), 90–97.

Bresser, R. (1995). *Math and literature (grades 4–6)*. Sausalito, CA: Math Solutions.

Breyfogle, M. L., & Williams, L. E. (2008–2009). Designing and implementing worthwhile tasks. *Teaching Children Mathematics, 15*(5), 276–280.

Bright, G. W., Behr, M. J., Post, T. R., & Wachsmuth, I. (1988). Identifying fractions on number lines. *Journal for Research in Mathematics Education, 19*(3), 215–232.

Bright, G. W., Joyner, J. M., & Wallis, C. (2003). Assessing proportional thinking. *Mathematics Teaching in the Middle School, 9*(3), 166–172.

Brooks, J. G., & Brooks, M. G. (1993). *In search of understanding: The case for the constructivist classroom*. Alexandria, VA: Association for Supervision and Curriculum Development.

Brown, G., & Quinn, R. J. (2007). Investigating the relationship between fraction proficiency and success in algebra. *Australian Mathematics Teacher, 63*(4), 8–15.

Brown, S. A., & Mehilos, M. (2010). Using tables to bridge arithmetic and algebra. *Mathematics Teaching in the Middle School, 15*(9), 532–538.

Brownell, W., & Chazal, C. (1935). The effects of premature drill in third grade arithmetic. *Journal of Educational Research, 29*(1), 17–28.

Bruner, J. (1966). *Toward a theory of instruction*. Cambridge, MA: Harvard University Press.

Burger, W. F. (1985). Geometry. *Arithmetic Teacher, 32*(6), 52–56.

Burns, M. (1992). *Math and literature (K–3)*. Sausalito, CA: Math Solutions Publications.

Burns, M. (1996). *50 problem-solving lessons: Grades 1–6*. Sausalito, CA: Math Solutions.

Burns, M. (1999). *Making sense of mathematics: A look toward the twenty-first century*. Presentation at the annual meeting of the National Council of Teachers of Mathematics, San Francisco.

Burns, M., & McLaughlin, C. (1990). *A collection of math lessons from grades 6 through 8*. Sausalito, CA: Math Solutions Publications.

Burrill, G. F., & Elliot, P. (2006). *Thinking and reasoning with data and chance: 68th NCTM yearbook*. Reston, VA: NCTM.

Burris, C. C., & Welner, K. (2005). Closing the achievement gap by detracking. *Phi Delta Kappan, 86*(8), 594–598.

Buschman, L. (2003a). Children who enjoy problem solving. *Teaching Children Mathematics, 9*(9), 539–544.

Buschman, L. (2003b). Share and compare: A teacher's story about helping children become problem solvers in mathematics. Reston, VA: NCTM.

Butterworth, S., & Lo Cicero, A. M. (2001). Storytelling: Building a mathematics curriculum from the culture of the child. *Teaching Children Mathematics, 7*(7), 396–399.

Cai, J. (2003). What research tells us about teaching mathematics through problem solving. In F. K. Lester, Jr. (Ed.), *Research and issues in teaching mathematics through problem solving* (pp. 241–254). Reston, VA: NCTM.

Cai, J. (2010). Helping elementary school students become successful mathematical problem solvers. In D. Lambdin (Ed.), *Teaching and learning mathematics: Translating research to the classroom* (pp. 9–14). Reston, VA: NCTM.

Cai, J., & Sun, W. (2002). Developing students' proportional reasoning: A Chinese perspective. In B. Litwiller (Ed.), *Making sense of fractions, ratios, and proportions* (pp. 195–205). Reston, VA: NCTM.

Campbell, P. B. (1995). Redefining the "girl problem in mathematics." In W. G. Secada, E. Fennema, & L. B. Adajian (Eds.), *New directions for equity in mathematics education* (pp. 225–241). New York: Cambridge University Press.

Campbell, P. F. (1997, April). *Children's invented algorithms: Their meaning and place in instruction*. Presented at the annual meeting of the National Council of Teachers of Mathematics, Minneapolis, MN.

Campbell, P. F., & Johnson, M. L. (1995). How primary students think and learn. In I. M. Carl (Ed.), *Prospects for school mathematics* (pp. 21–42). Reston, VA: NCTM.

Campbell, P. F., Rowan, T. E., & Suarez, A. R. (1998). What criteria for student-invented algorithms? In L. J. Morrow (Ed.), *The teaching and learning of algorithms in school mathematics* (pp. 49–55). Reston, VA: NCTM.

Campione, J. C., Brown, A. L., & Connell, M. L. (1989). Metacognition: On the importance of understanding what you are doing. In R. I. Charles & E. A. Silver (Eds.), *The teaching and assessing of mathematical problem solving* (pp. 93–114). Reston, VA: NCTM.

Carpenter, T. P., Fennema, E., Franke, M. L., Levi, L., & Empson, S. B. (1999). *Children's mathematics: Cognitively guided instruction*. Portsmouth, NH: Heinemann.

Carpenter, T. P., Franke, M. L., Jacobs, V. R., Fennema, E., & Empson, S. B. (1998). A longitudinal study of invention and understanding in children's multidigit addition and subtraction. *Journal for Research in Mathematics Education, 29*(1), 3–20.

Carpenter, T. P., Franke, M. L., & Levi, L. (2003). *Thinking mathematically: Integrating arithmetic and algebra in elementary school*. Portsmouth, NH: Heinemann.

Carpenter, T. P., & Moser, J. M. (1984). The acquisition of addition and subtraction concepts in grades one through three. *Journal for Research in Mathematics Education, 15*(3), 179–202.

Carr, J., Carroll, C., Cremer, S., Gale, M., Lagunoff, R., & Sexton, U. (2009). *Making mathematics accessible to English learners, grades 6–12*. San Francisco: WestEd.

Carter, S. (2008). Disequilibrium & questioning in the primary classroom: Establishing routines that help students learn. *Teaching Children Mathematics, 15*(3), 134–137.

Cassone, J. D. (2009). Differentiating mathematics by using task difficulty. In D. Y. White & J. S. Spitzer (Eds.), *Mathematics for every student: Responding to diversity, grades Pre-K–5* (pp. 89–98). Reston, VA: NCTM.

Cayton, G. A., & Brizuela, B. M. (2007). First graders' strategies for numerical notation, number reading and the number concept. In J. H. Woo, H. C. Lew, K. S. Park, & D. Y. Seo (Eds.), *Proceedings of the 31st conference of the international group for the psychology of mathematics education* (Vol. 2, pp. 81–88). Seoul, South Korea: Psychology of Mathematics Education (PME).

CCSSO (Council of Chief State School Officers). (2010). *Common core state standards.* Retrieved from http://corestandards .org

Ceci, S. J., & Williams, W. M. (2010). Sex differences in math-intensive fields. *Current Directions in Psychological Science, 19*(5), 275–279.

Celedón-Pattichis, S. (2009). What does that mean? Drawing on Latino and Latina students' language and culture to make mathematical meaning. In M. W. Ellis (Ed.), *Responding to diversity: Grades 6–8* (pp. 59–74). Reston, VA: NCTM.

Chapin, S. H., O'Conner, C., & Anderson, N. C. (2009). *Classroom discussions: Using math talk to help students learn* (2nd ed.). Sausalito, CA: Math Solutions.

Che, S. M. (2009). Giant pencils: Developing proportional reasoning. *Mathematics Teaching in the Middle School, 14*(7), 404–408.

Checkley, K. (2006). "Radical" math becomes the standard: Emphasis on algebraic thinking, problem solving and communication. *Education Update, 48*(4), 1–2, 8.

Cheng, I. (2010). Fractions: A new slant on slope. *Mathematics Teaching in the Middle School, 16*(1), 35–41.

Chick, C., Tierney, C., & Storeygard, J. (2007). Seeing students' knowledge of fractions: Candace's inclusive classroom. *Teaching Children Mathematics, 14*(1), 52–57.

Clark, F. B., & Kamii, C. (1996). Identification of multiplicative thinking in children in grades 1–5. *Journal for Research in Mathematics Education, 27*(1), 41–51.

Clarke, B., & Clarke, D. (2004). Mathematics teaching in K–2: Painting a picture of challenging, supportive, and effective classrooms (pp. 67–81). In R. N. Rubenstein (Ed.), *Perspectives on the teaching of mathematics: Sixty-sixth yearbook.* Reston, VA: NCTM.

Clarke, D. (1997). *Constructive assessment in mathematics.* Berkeley, CA: Key Curriculum Press.

Clarke, D., Cheeseman, J., Clarke, B., Gervasoni, A., Gronn, D., Horne, M., . . . Sullivan, P. (2001, July). *Understanding, assessing and developing young children's mathematical thinking: Research as a powerful tool for professional growth.* Keynote paper at the annual conference of the Mathematics Education Research Group of Australia, Sydney.

Clarke, D., Roche, A., & Mitchell, A. (2008). 10 practical tips for making fractions come alive and make sense. *Mathematics Teaching in the Middle School, 13*(7), 373–380.

Cleaves, W. P. (2008). Promoting mathematics accessibility through multiple representations: Jigsaws. *Mathematics Teaching in the Middle School, 13*(8), 446–452.

Clement, L., & Bernhard, J. (2005). A problem-solving alternative to using key words. *Mathematics Teaching in the Middle School, 10*(7), 360–365.

Clements, D. H., & Battista, M. T. (1990). Constructivist learning and teaching. *Arithmetic Teacher, 38*(1), 34–35.

Clements, D. H., & Sarama, J. (2005). Young children and technology: What's appropriate? In W. Masalski & P. C. Elliott (Eds.), *Technology-supported mathematics learning environments: 67th NCTM yearbook* (pp. 51–73). Reston, VA: NCTM.

Clements, D. H., & Sarama, J. (2009). *Learning and teaching early math: The learning trajectories approach.* New York: Routledge.

Coates, G. D., & Thompson, V. (2003). *Family Math II: Achieving success in mathematics.* Berkeley, CA: EQUALS Lawrence Hall of Science.

Cobb, P. (1988). The tension between theories of learning and instruction in mathematics education. *Educational Psychologist, 23*(2), 87–103.

Cobb, P. (1994). Where is the mind? Constructivist and sociocultural perspectives on mathematical development. *Educational Researcher, 23*(7), 13–20.

Cobb, P., Gresalfi, M. S., & Hodge, L. L. (2009). An interpretive scheme for analyzing the identities that students develop in mathematics classrooms. *Journal for Research in Mathematics Education, 40*(1), 40–68.

Cobb, P., & Jackson, K. (2011). Assessing the quality of the common core state standards for mathematics. *Educational Researcher, 40*(4), 183–185.

Cohen, R. (2006). How do students think? *Mathematics Teaching in the Middle School, 11*(9), 434–436.

Colgan, M. D. (2006). March math madness: The mathematics of the NCAA basketball tournament. *Mathematics Teaching in the Middle School, 11*(7), 334–342.

Confrey, J. (2008). *Student and teacher reasoning on rational numbers, multiplicative structures, and related topics.* Presentation at ICME–11, Monterrey, Mexico.

Confrey, J., Maloney, A., & Nguyen, K. (2011). *Learning over time: Learning trajectories in mathematics education.* Charlotte, NC: Information Age Publishing.

Cook, C. D. (2008). I scream, you scream: Data analysis with kindergartners. *Teaching Children Mathematics, 14*(9), 538–540.

Cooper, H. (2007). *The battle over homework: Common ground for administrators, teachers, and parents* (3rd ed.). Thousand Oaks, CA: Corwin Press.

Corcoran, T., Mosher, F., & Rogat, A. (2009). *Learning progressions in science: An evidence-based approach to reform* (Research Report No. RR-63). Philadelphia, PA: Consortium for Policy Research in Education.

Correll, S. J. (2001). Gender and the career choice process: The role of biased self-assessment. *American Journal of Sociology, 106*(6), 1691–1730.

Coughlin, H. A. (2010–2011). Dividing fractions: What is the divisor's role? *Mathematics Teaching in the Middle School, 16*(5), 280–287.

Cramer, K., & Henry, A. (2002). Using manipulative models to build number sense for addition of fractions. In B. Litwiller (Ed.), *Making sense of fractions, ratios, and proportions* (pp. 41–48). Reston, VA: NCTM.

Cramer, K., Monson, D., Whitney, S., Leavitt, S., & Wyberg, T. (2010). Dividing fractions and problem solving. *Mathematics Teaching in the Middle School, 15*(6), 338–346.

Cramer, K., & Whitney, S. (2010). Learning rational number concepts and skills in elementary school classrooms. In D. V. Lambdin & F. K. Lester, Jr. (Eds.), *Teaching and learning mathematics: Translating research for elementary school teachers* (pp. 15–22). Reston, VA: NCTM.

Cramer, K., Wyberg, T., & Leavitt, S. (2008). The role of representations in fraction addition and subtraction. *Mathematics Teaching in the Middle School, 13*(8), 490–496.

Crespo, S., Kyriakides, A. O., & McGee, S. (2005). Nothing "basic" about basic facts: Exploring addition facts with fourth graders. *Teaching Children Mathematics, 12*(2), 60–67.

Crespo, S., & Nicol, C. (2006). Challenging preservice teachers' mathematical understanding: The case of division by zero. *School Science and Mathematics, 106*(2), 84–97.

Cross, C., Woods, T., & Schweingruber, H. (Eds.). (2009). *Mathematics in early childhood: learning paths toward excellence and equity.* Washington, DC: National Academies Press.

Cummins, J. (1994). Primary language instruction and the education of language minority students. In C. F. Leyba (Ed.), *Schooling and language minority students: A theoretical framework* (pp. 3–46). Los Angeles: California State University, National Evaluation, Dissemination and Assessment Center.

Darley, J. W. (2009). Traveling from arithmetic to algebra. *Mathematics Teaching in the Middle School, 14*(8), 458–464.

Darling-Hammond, L., & Bransford, J. (2005). *Preparing teachers for a changing world: What teachers should learn and be able to do.* New York: Wiley.

Daro, P., Mosher, F., & Corcoran, T. (2011). *Learning trajectories in mathematics: A foundation for standards, curriculum assessment and instruction.* Philadelphia, PA: Consortium for Policy Research in Education.

Davis, R. B. (1986). Learning mathematics: The cognitive science approach to mathematics education. Norwood, NJ: Ablex.

Dennis v. U.S., 339 U.S. 162 (1950).

Desmet, L. Gregoire, J., & Mussolin, C. (2010). Developmental changes in the comparison of decimal fractions. *Learning and Instruction, 20,* 521–532.

Dewdney, A. K. (1993). *200% of nothing: An eye-opening tour through the twists and turns of math abuse and innumeracy.* New York: Wiley.

DeYoung, M. J. (2009). Math in the box. *Mathematics Teaching in the Middle School, 15*(3), 134–141.

Dietiker, L., Gonulates, F., Figueras, J., & Smith, J. P. (2010, April). *Weak attention to unit iteration in U.S. elementary curriculum materials.* Presentation at the annual conference of the American Educational Research Association, Denver, CO.

Ding, M. (2010, October 7). Email interaction.

Ding, M., & Li, X. (2010, April). *The associative property: What do teachers know and how do textbooks help?* Paper presented at the annual meeting of the National Council of Teachers of Mathematics, San Diego, CA.

Diversity in Mathematics Education. (2007). Culture, race, power, and mathematics education. In F. Lester, Jr. (Ed.), *Second handbook of research on mathematics teaching and learning* (pp. 405–434). Charlotte, NC: Information Age Publishing and National Council of Teachers of Mathematics.

Dixon, J. (2008). Tracking time: Representing elapsed time on an open timeline. *Teaching Children Mathematics, 15*(1), 18–24.

Dougherty, B. (2008). Measure up: A quantitative view of early algebra. In J. Kaput, D. Carraher, & M. Blanton (Eds.), *Algebra in the early grades* (pp. 389–412). New York: Lawrence Erlbaum Associates.

Dougherty, B., Flores, A., Louis, E., & Sophian, C. (2010). *Developing essential understanding of number and numeration for teaching mathematics in prekindergarten–grade 2.* Reston, VA: NCTM.

Dole, S. (2008). Ratio tables to promote proportional reasonings in the primary classroom. *Australian Primary Mathematics Classroom, 13*(2), 18–22.

Drake, J., & Barlow, A. (2007). Assessing students' level of understanding multiplication through problem writing. *Teaching Children Mathematics, 14*(5), 272–277.

Dweck, C. (2006). *Mindset: The new psychology of success.* New York: Random House.

Earnest, D., & Balti, A. A. (2008). Instructional strategies for teaching algebra in elementary school: Findings from a research-practice partnership. *Teaching Children Mathematics, 14*(9), 518–522.

Echevarria, J., Vogt, M. E., & Short, D. (2008). *Making content comprehensible for English learners: The SIOP model* (3rd ed.). Boston: Allyn & Bacon.

Ellington, A. (2003). A meta-analysis of the effects of calculators on students' achievement and attitude levels in precollege mathematics classes. *Journal for Research in Mathematics Education, 34*(5), 433–463.

Ellis, M., Yeh, C., & Stump, S. (2007–2008). Rock-paper-scissors and solutions to the broken calculator problem. *Teaching Children Mathematics, 14*(5), 309–314.

Else-Quest, N. M., Hyde, J. S., Hejmadi, A. (2008). Mother and child emotions during mathematics homework. *Mathematical Thinking and Learning, 10,* 5–35.

Else-Quest, N. M., Hyde, J. S., & Linn, M. (2010). Cross-national patterns of gender differences in mathematics: A meta-analysis. *Psychological Bulletin, 136*(1), 103–127.

Ely, R. E., & Cohen, J. S. (2010). Put the right spin on student work. *Mathematics Teaching in the Middle School, 16*(4), 208–215.

Empson, S. B. (2002). Organizing diversity in early fraction thinking. In B. Litwiller (Ed.), *Making sense of fractions, ratios, and proportions* (pp. 29–40). Reston, VA: NCTM.

Englard, L. (2010). Raise the bar on problem solving. *Teaching Children Mathematics, 17*(3), 156–165.

Ercole, L. K., Frantz, M., & Ashline, G. (2011). Multiple ways to solve proportions. *Mathematics Teaching in the Middle School, 16*(8), 482–490.

Falkner, K. P., Levi, L., & Carpenter, T. P. (1999). Children's understanding of equality: A foundation for algebra. *Teaching Children Mathematics, 6*(4), 232–236.

Farmer, J. D., & Powers, R. A. (2005). Exploring Mayan numerals. *Teaching Children Mathematics, 12*(2), 69–79.

Fernandez, M. L., & Schoen, R. C. (2008). Teaching and learning mathematics through hurricane tracking. *Mathematics Teaching in the Middle School, 13*(9), 500–512.

Fey, J. T., Hollenbeck, R. W., & Wray, J. A. (2010). Technology and the teaching of mathematics: In B. Reys, R. Reys, & R. Rubenstein (Eds.) *Curriculum: Issues, trends, and future directions* (72nd Yearbook). Reston, VA: NCTM.

Fillingim, J. G., & Barlow, A. T. (2010). From the inside out. *Teaching Children Mathematics, 17*(2), 80–88.

Fleischman, H. L., Hopstock, P. J., Pelczar, M. P., & Shelley, B. E. (2010). *Highlights from PISA 2009: Performance of U.S. 15-Year-Old Students in Reading, Mathematics, and Science Literacy in an International Context* (NCES 2011–004). Washington, DC: U.S. Government Printing Office.

Flores, A. (2006). Using graphing calculators to redress beliefs in the "law of small numbers." *Thinking and reasoning about data and chance: 68th NCTM yearbook* (pp. 139–149). Reston, VA: NCTM.

Flores, A., & Klein, E. (2005). From students' problem solving strategies to connections with fractions. *Teaching Children Mathematics, 11*(9), 452–457.

Flores, A., Samson, J., & Yanik, H. B. (2006). Quotient and measurement interpretations of rational numbers. *Teaching Children Mathematics, 13*(1), 34–39.

Flowers, J. M., & Rubenstein, R. N. (2010–2011). Multiplication fact fluency using doubles. *Mathematics Teaching in the Middle School, 16*(5), 296–301.

Forbringer, L., & Fahsl, A. J. (2010). Differentiating practice to help students master basic facts. In D. Y. White & J. S. Spitzer (Eds.), *Responding to diversity: Grades pre-K–5* (pp. 7–22). Reston, VA: NCTM.

Forman, E. A. (2003). A sociocultural approach to mathematics reform: Speaking, inscribing, and doing mathematics within communities of practice. In J. Kilpatrick, G. Martin, & D. Schifter (Eds.), *A research companion to the NCTM Standards* (pp. 333–352). Reston, VA: NCTM.

Forman, E. A., & McPhail, J. (1993). A Vygotskian perspective on children's collaborative problem-solving activities. In E. A. Forman, N. Minick, & C. A. Stone (Eds.), *Contexts for learning: Sociocultural dynamics in children's development* (pp. 213–229). New York: Oxford University Press.

Fosnot, C. T. (1996). Constructivism: A psychological theory of learning. In C. T. Fosnot (Ed.), *Constructivism: Theory, perspectives, and practice* (pp. 8–33). New York: Teachers College Press.

Fosnot, C. T., & Dolk, M. (2001). *Young mathematicians at work: Constructing number sense, addition, and subtraction.* Portsmouth, NH: Heinemann.

Fosnot, C. T., & Jacob, B. (2010). *Young mathematicians at work: Constructing algebra.* Reston, VA: NCTM.

Franke, M. L., Kazemi, E., & Battey, D. (2007). Mathematics teaching and classroom practice. In F. K. Lester (Ed.), *Second handbook of research on mathematics teaching and learning* (pp. 225–256). Reston, VA: NCTM.

Franklin, C. A., & Garfield, J. B. (2006). The *GAISE* Project: Developing statistics education guidelines for grades PreK–12 and college courses. In G. F. Burrill & P. C. Elliott (Eds.), *Thinking and reasoning about data and chance: 68th NCTM yearbook* (pp. 345–376). Reston, VA: NCTM.

Franklin, C. A., Kader, G., Mewborn, D., Moreno, J., Peck, R., Perry, M., & Scheaffer, R. (2005). *Guidelines for assessment and instruction in statistics education (GAISE) report.* Alexandria, VA: American Statistical Association.

Franklin, C. A., & Mewborn, D. S. (2008). Statistics in the elementary grades: Exploring distribution of data. *Teaching Children Mathematics, 15*(1), 10–16.

Friedmann, P. (2008). The zero box. *Mathematics Teaching in the Middle School, 14*(4), 222–223.

Friedman, T. (2007). *The world is flat 3.0: A brief history of the twenty-first century.* New York: Picador.

Friel, S. N., & Markworth, K. A. (2009). A framework for analyzing geometric pattern tasks. *Mathematics Teaching in the Middle School, 15*(1), 24–33.

Friel, S. N., O'Conner, W., & Mamer, J. D. (2006). More than "meanmedianmode" and a bar graph: What's needed to have a statistical conversation? In G. F. Burrill & P. C. Elliott (Eds.), *Thinking and reasoning about data and chance: 68th NCTM yearbook* (pp. 117–138). Reston, VA: NCTM.

Fuchs, L. S., & Fuchs, D. (1986). Effects of systematic formative evaluation: A meta-analysis. *Exceptional Children, 53*(3), 199–208.

Fuchs, L. S., & Fuchs, D. (2001). Principles for the prevention and intervention of mathematics difficulties. *Learning Disabilities Research and Practice, 16*(2), 85–95.

Fuchs, L. S., & Fuchs, D. (2005). Enhancing mathematical problem solving for students with disabilities. *Journal of Special Education, 39*(1), 45–57.

Fuchs, L. S., & Fuchs, D. (2007). A framework for implementing responsiveness to intervention. *Teaching Exceptional Children, 39*(5), 14–20.

Fuchs, L. S., Fuchs, D., Prentice, K., Hamlett, C. L., Finelli, R., & Courey, S. J. (2004). Enhancing mathematical problem solving among third-grade students with schema-based instruction. *Journal of Educational Psychology, 96*(4), 635–647.

Fuchs, L. S., Fuchs, D., Yazdian, L., & Powell, S. R. (2002). Enhancing first-grade children's mathematics development with peer-assisted learning strategies. *School Psychology Review, 31*(4), 569–583.

Fung, M. G., & Latulippe, C. L. (2010). Computational estimation. *Teaching Children Mathematics, 17*(3), 170–176.

Fuson, K. C. (1984). More complexities in subtraction. *Journal for Research in Mathematics Education, 15*(3), 214–225.

Fuson, K. C. (1992). Research on whole number addition and subtraction. In D. A. Grouws (Ed.), *Handbook of research on teaching and learning* (pp. 243–275). Old Tappan, NJ: Macmillan.

Fuson, K. C. (2003). Developing mathematical power in whole number operations. In J. Kilpatrick, W. G. Martin, & D. Schifter (Eds.), *A research companion to Principles and Standards in School Mathematics* (pp. 68–94). Reston, VA: NCTM.

Fuson, K. C. (2006). Research on whole number addition and subtraction. In D. Grouws (Ed.), *Handbook of research on mathematics teaching and learning* (pp. 243–275). Charlotte, NC: Information Age Publishing.

Fuson, K. C., Kalchman, M., & Bransford, J. D. (2005). *How students learn: History, mathematics, and science in the classroom.* Washington, DC: The National Academies Press.

Fuson, K. C., & Kwon, Y. (1992). Korean children's single-digit addition and subtraction: Numbers structured by ten. *Journal for Research in Mathematics Education, 23*(2), 148–165.

Futrell, M. H., & Gomez, J. (2008). How tracking creates a poverty of learning. *Educational Leadership, 65*(8), 74–78.

Gagnon, J., & Maccini, P. (2001). Preparing students with disabilities for algebra. *Teaching Exceptional Children, 34*(1), 8–15.

Gallagher, A. M., & Kaufmann, J. C. (2005). *Gender differences in mathematics: an integrative psychological approach.* Cambridge, United Kingdom: Cambridge University Press.

Gallagher, J., & Gallagher, S. (1994). *Teaching the gifted child.* Boston: Allyn & Bacon.

Gallego, C., Saldamando, D., Tapia-Beltran, G., Williams, K., & Hoopingarner, T. C. (2009). Math by the month: Probability. *Teaching Children Mathematics, 15*(7), 416.

Garcia, C., & Garret, A. (2006). On average and open-end questions. In A. Rossman & B. Chance (Eds.), *Proceedings of the seventh international conference on teaching statistics.* Salvador, Brazil: International Statistical Institute.

Garofalo, J. (1987). Metacognition and school mathematics. *Arithmetic Teacher, 34*(9), 22–23.

Garrison, L. (1997). Making the NCTM's Standards work for emergent English speakers. *Teaching Children Mathematics, 4*(3), 132–138.

Gavin, M. K., & Sheffield, L. J. (2010). Using curriculum to develop mathematical promise in the middle grades. In M. Saul, S. Assouline, & L. J. Sheffield (Eds.), *The peak in the middle: Developing mathematically gifted students in the middle grades* (pp. 51–76). Reston, VA: NCTM, National Association of Gifted Children, & National Middle School Association.

Geary, D. C., & Hoard, M. K. (2005). Learning disabilities in arithmetic and mathematics: Theoretical and empirical perspectives. In J. Campbell (Ed.), *Handbook of mathematical cognition* (pp. 253–267). New York: Psychology Press.

Gelman, R., & Gallistel, C. R. (1978). *The child's understanding of number.* Cambridge, MA: Harvard University Press.

Gersten, R., Beckmann, S., Clarke, B., Foegen, A., Marsh, L., Star, J. R., & Witzel, B. (2009). *Assisting students struggling with mathematics: Response to Intervention (RtI) for elementary and middle schools* (NCEE 2009–4060). Washington, DC: National Center for Education Evaluation and Regional Assistance, Institute of Education Sciences, U.S. Department of Education. Retrieved from http://ies.ed.gov/ncee/wwc/publications/practiceguides

Gersten, R., Chard, D., Jayanthi, M., & Baker, S. (2006). *Experimental and quasi-experimental research on instructional approaches for teaching mathematics to students with learning disabilities: A research synthesis.* Signal Hill, CA: Center of Instruction Research Group.

Gilbert, M. C., & Musu, L. E. (2008). Using TARGETTS to create learning environments that support mathematical understanding and adaptive motivation. *Teaching Children Mathematics, 15*(3), 138–143.

Ginsburg, H. P. (1977). *Children's arithmetic: The learning process.* New York: Van Nostrand.

Gnanadesikan, M., Schaeffer, R. L., & Swift, J. (1987). *The art and techniques of simulation: Quantitative literacy series.* Palo Alto, CA: Dale Seymour.

Goldenberg, E. P., Mark, J., & Cuoco, A. (2010). An algebraic-habits-of-mind perspective on elementary school. *Teaching Children Mathematics, 16*(9), 548–556.

Gómez, C. L. (2010). Teaching with cognates. *Teaching Children Mathematics, 16*(8), 470–474.

González, N., Moll, L. C., & Amanti, C. (Eds.). (2005). *Funds of knowledge: Theorizing practices in households and classrooms.* Mahwah, NJ: Lawrence Erlbaum.

Goos, M. (2004). Learning mathematics in a classroom community of inquiry. *Journal for Research in Mathematics Education, 35*(4), 258–291.

Goral, M. B., & Wiest, L. R. (2007). An arts-based approach to teaching fractions. *Teaching Children Mathematics, 14*(2), 74–80.

Grandgenett, N., Harris, J., & Hofer, M. (2010–2011). An activity-based approach to technology integration in the mathematics classroom. *NCSM Journal of Mathematics Education Leadership, 13*(1), 19–28.

Gravemeijer, K., & van Galen, F. (2003). Facts and algorithms as products of students' own mathematical activity. In J. Kilpatrick, W. G. Martin, & D. Schifter (Eds.), *A research companion to Principles and Standards for School Mathematics* (pp. 114–122). Reston, VA: NCTM.

Greer, B. (1992). Multiplication and division as models of situations. In D. A. Grouws (Ed.), *Handbook of research on mathematics teaching and learning* (pp. 276–295). Old Tappan, NJ: Macmillan.

Gregg, J., & Gregg, D. U. (2007). Measurement and fair-sharing models for dividing fractions. *Mathematics Teaching in the Middle School, 12*(9), 490–496.

Guerrero, S. M. (2010). The value of guess & check. *Mathematics Teaching in the Middle School, 15*(7), 392–398.

Gutstein, E., Lipman, P., Hernandez, P., & Reyes, R. (1997). Culturally relevant mathematics teaching in a Mexican American context. *Journal for Research in Mathematics Education, 28*(6), 709–737.

Haas, E., & Gort, M. (2009). Demanding more: Legal standards and best practices for English language learners. *Bilingual Research Journal, 32*, 115–135.

Hackbarth, A. J., & Wilsman, M. J. (2008). 1P + 4R = 5D: An equation for deepening mathematical understanding. *Mathematics Teaching in the Middle School, 14*(2), 122–126.

Hamre, B. K., Downer, J. T., Kilday, C. R., & McGuire, P. (2008). *Effective teaching practices for early childhood mathematics.* White paper prepared for the National Research Council. Washington, DC.

Hanson, S. A., & Hogan, T. P. (2000). Computational estimation skill of college students. *Journal for Research in Mathematics Education, 31*(4), 483–499.

Hartnett, J. (2007). Categorisation of mental computation strategies to support teaching and to encourage classroom dialogue. In J. Watson & K. Beswick (Eds.), *Mathematics: essential research, essential practice: Proceedings of the 30th annual conference of the Mathematics Education Research Group of Australasia* (pp. 345–352). Hobart, Tasmania, Australia: MERGA.

Hattie, J. (2009). *Visible learning: A synthesis of over 800 meta-analyses relating to achievement.* New York: Routledge.

Hawes, K. (2007). Using error analysis to teach equation solving. *Mathematics Teaching in the Middle School, 12*(5), 238–242.

Hawkins, D. (1965). Messing about in science. *Science and Children, 2*(5), 5–9.

Heck, T. *Team building games on a shoestring.* Retrieved August 22, 2011, from www.teachmeteamwork.com

Heddens, J. (1964). *Today's mathematics: A guide to concepts and methods in elementary school mathematics.* Chicago, IL: Science Research Associates.

Heinz, K., & Sterba-Boatwright, B. (2008). The when and why of using proportions. *Mathematics Teacher, 101*(7), 528–533.

Hembree, R., & Dessert, D. (1986). Effects of hand-held calculators in precollege mathematics education: A meta analysis. *Journal for Research in Mathematics Education, 17*(2), 83–99.

Hembree, R., & Dessert, D. (1992). Research on calculators in mathematics education. In J. Fey & C. R. Hirsch (Eds.), *Calculators in mathematics education* (pp. 23–32). Reston, VA: NCTM.

Henry, V. J., & Brown, R. S. (2008). First grade basic facts: An investigation into teaching and learning of an accelerated, high-demand memorization standard. *Journal for Research in Mathematics Education, 39*(2), 153–183.

Herbel-Eisenmann, B. A., & Breyfogle, M. L. (2005). Questioning our patterns of questioning. *Mathematics Teaching in the Middle School, 10*(9), 484–489.

Herbel-Eisenmann, B. A., & Phillips, E. D. (2005). Using student work to develop teachers' knowledge of algebra. *Mathematics Teaching in the Middle School, 11*(2), 62–66.

Heritage, M., Kim, J., Vendlinski, T., & Herman, J. (2009). From evidence to action: A seamless process in formative assessment? *Education Measurement: Issues and Practice, 28,* 24–31.

Hiebert, J. (2003). What research says about the NCTM standards. In J. Kilpatrick, W. G. Martin, & D. Schifter (Eds.), *A research companion to Principles and Standards for School Mathematics* (pp. 5–23). Reston, VA: NCTM.

Hiebert, J., & Carpenter, T. P. (1992). Learning and teaching with understanding. In D. A. Grouws (Ed.), *Handbook of research on mathematics teaching and learning* (pp. 65–97). Old Tappan, NJ: Macmillan.

Hiebert, J., Carpenter, T. P., Fennema, E., Fuson, K., Human, P., Murray, H., . . . Wearne, D. (1996). Problem solving as a basis for reform in curriculum and instruction: The case of mathematics. *Educational Researcher, 25*(4), 12–21.

Hiebert, J., Carpenter, T. P., Fennema, E., Fuson, K., Wearne, D., Murray, H., . . . Human, P. (1997). *Making sense: Teaching and learning mathematics with understanding.* Portsmouth, NH: Heinemann.

Hiebert, J., Gallimore, R., Garnier, H., Givvin, K. B., Hollingsworth, H., Jacobs, J., . . . Stigler, J. (2003). *Teaching mathematics in seven countries: Results from the TIMSS 1999 video study.* Washington, DC: National Center for Education Statistics, U.S. Department of Education.

Hiebert, J., & Grouws, D. A. (2007). The effects of classroom mathematics teaching on students' learning. In F. K. Lester (Ed.), *Second handbook of research on mathematics teaching and learning* (pp. 371–404). Charlotte, NC: Information Age Publishing.

Hiebert, J., & Wearne, D. (1996). Instruction, understanding, and skill in multidigit addition and subtraction. *Cognition and Instruction, 14*(3), 251–283.

Hilliard, A. (1991). Do we have the will to educate all children? *Educational Leadership, 49*(1), 31–36.

Hodges, T. E., Cady, J., & Collins, R. L. (2008). Fraction representation: The not-so-common denominator among textbooks. *Mathematics Teaching in the Middle School, 14*(2), 78–84.

Hoffman, B. L., Breyfogle, M. L., & Dressler, J. A. (2009). The power of incorrect answers. *Mathematics Teaching in the Middle School, 15*(4), 232–238.

Howden, H. (1989). Teaching number sense. *Arithmetic Teacher, 36*(6), 6–11.

Hudson, P. J., Shupe, M., Vasquez, E., & Miller, S. P. (2008). Teaching data analysis to elementary students with mild disabilities. *TEACHING Exceptional Children Plus, 4*(3), Article 5. Retrieved from http://escholarship.bc.edu/education/tecplus/vol4/iss3/art5

Huff, D. (1954/1993). *How to lie with statistics.* New York: Norton.

Hughes, C., & Rusch, F. R. (1989). Teaching supported employees with severe mental retardation to solve problems. *Journal of Applied Behavior Analysis, 22*(4), 365–372.

Huinker, D. (1994, April). *Multi-step word problems: A strategy for empowering students.* Presented at the annual meeting of the National Council of Teachers of Mathematics, Indianapolis, IN.

Huinker, D. (1998). Letting fraction algorithms emerge through problem solving. In L. J. Morrow (Ed.), *The teaching and learning of algorithms in school mathematics* (pp. 170–182). Reston, VA: NCTM.

Hyde, J., Lindberg, S., Linn, M., Ellis, A., & Williams, C. (2008, July 25). Gender similarities characterize mathematics performance. *Science, 321*(5888), 494–495.

Hynes, M. C. (Ed.). (1996). *Ideas: NCTM Standards-based instruction, grades 5–8.* Reston, VA: NCTM.

Imm, K. L., Stylianou, D. A., & Chae, N. (2008). Student representations at the center: Promoting classroom equity. *Mathematics Teaching in the Middle School, 13*(8), 458–463.

Izsák, A. (2004). Teaching and learning two-digit multiplication: Coordinating analyses of classroom practices and individual student learning. *Mathematical Thinking and Learning, 6,* 37–79.

Izsák, A. (2008). Mathematical knowledge for teaching fraction multiplication. *Cognition and Instruction, 26*(1), 95–143.

Izsák, A., Tillema, E., & Tunc-Pekkam, Z. (2008). Teaching and learning fraction addition on number lines. *Journal for Research in Mathematics Education, 39*(1), 33–62.

Jacobbe, T. (2008). Elementary school teachers' understanding of the mean and median. In C. Batanero, G. Burrill, C. Reading, & A. Rossman (Eds.), *Joint ICMI/IASE Study Statistics in School Mathematics Challenges for Teaching and Teacher Education.* Proceedings of the ICMI Study 18 Conference and IASE Round Table Conference, Monterrey, MX.

Jacobs, V. R., & Ambrose, R. C. (2008). Making the most of story problems. *Teaching Children Mathematics, 15*(5), 260–266.

Jacobs, V. R., Lamb, L. L. C., & Philipp, R. A. (2010). Professional noticing of children's mathematical thinking. *Journal for Research in Mathematics Education, 41*(2), 169–202.

Janvier, C. (Ed.). (1987). *Problems of representation in the teaching and learning of mathematics.* Hillsdale, NJ: Erlbaum.

Janzen, J. (2008). Teaching English language learners in the content areas. *Review of Educational Research, 78*(4), 1010–1038.

Johanning, D. J. (2008). Learning to use fractions: Examining middle school students' emerging fraction literacy. *Journal for Research in Mathematics Education, 39*(3), 281–310.

Johnson, G., & Thompson, D. R. (2009). Reasoning with algebraic contexts. *Mathematics Teaching in the Middle School, 14*(8), 504–513.

Jones, A. (1999). *Team building activities for every group.* Richland, WA: Rec Room Publishing.

Joram, E. (2003). Benchmarks as tools for developing measurement sense. In D. H. Clements (Ed.), *Learning and teaching measurement* (pp. 57–67). Reston, VA: NCTM.

Jordan, N. C., Kaplan, D., Locuniak, M. N., & Ramineni, C. (2007). Predicting first grade math achievement from developmental number sense trajectories. *Learning Disabilities Research & Practice, 22*(1), 36–46.

Kader, G., & Mamer, J. (2008). Statistics in the middle grades: Understanding center and spread. *Mathematics Teaching in the Middle Grades, 14*(1), 38–43.

Kamii, C. K. (1985). *Young children reinvent arithmetic.* New York: Teachers College Press.

Kamii, C. K., & Anderson, C. (2003). Multiplication games: How we made and used them. *Teaching Children Mathematics, 10*(3), 135–141.

Kamii, C. K., & Dominick, A. (1998). The harmful effects of algorithms in grades 1–4. In L. J. Morrow (Ed.), *The teaching and learning of algorithms in school mathematics* (pp. 130–140). Reston, VA: NCTM.

Kaput, J. J. (1999). Teaching and learning a new algebra. In E. Fennema & T. A. Romberg (Eds.), *Mathematics classrooms that promote understanding* (pp. 133–155). Mahwah, NJ: Erlbaum.

Kaput, J. J. (2008). What is algebra? What is algebraic reasoning? In J. J. Kaput, D. W. Carraher, & M. L. Blanton (Eds.), *Algebra in the early grades.* Reston, VA: NCTM.

Karp, K. (1991). Elementary school teachers' attitudes towards mathematics: Impact on students' autonomous learning skills. *School Science and Mathematics, 91*(6), 265–270.

Karp, K., Brown, E. T., Allen, L., & Allen, C. (1998). *Feisty females: Inspiring girls to think mathematically.* Portsmouth, NH: Heinemann.

Karp, K., & Howell, P. (2004). Building responsibility for learning in students with special needs. *Teaching Children Mathematics, 11*(3), 118–126.

Keiser, J. M. (2010). Shifting our computational focus. *Mathematics Teaching in the Middle School, 16*(4), 216–223.

Kenney, J. M., Hancewicz, E., Heuer, L., Metsisto, D., & Tuttle, C. L. (2005). *Literacy strategies for improving mathematics instruction.* Alexandria, VA: Association for Supervision and Curriculum Development.

Kersaint, G., Thompson, D. R., & Petkova, M. (2009). *Teaching mathematics to English language learners.* New York: Routledge.

Khisty, L. L. (1997). Making mathematics accessible to Latino students: Rethinking instructional practice. In M. Kenney & J. Trentacosta (Eds.), *Multicultural and gender equity in the mathematics classroom: The gift of diversity* (pp. 92–101). Reston, VA: NCTM.

Kilic, H., Cross, D. I., Ersoz, F. A., Mewborn, D. S., Swanagan, D., & Kim, J. (2010). Techniques for small-group discourse. *Teaching Children Mathematics, 16*(6), 350–357.

Kingore, B. (2006, Winter). Tiered instruction: Beginning the process. *Teaching for High Potential,* 5–6.

Kinman, R. L. (2010). Communication speaks. *Teaching Children Mathematics, 17*(1), 22–30.

Klein, A. S., Beishuizen, M., & Treffers, A. (1998). The empty number line in Dutch second grade: *Realistic* versus *gradual* program design. *Journal for Research in Mathematics Education, 29*(4), 443–464.

Klein, A. S., Beishuizen, M., & Treffers, A. (2002). The empty number line in Dutch second grade. In J. Sowder and B. Schapelle (Eds.), *Lessons learned from research* (pp. 41–44). Reston, VA: NCTM.

Klein, P., Adi-Japha, E., & Hakak-Benizri, S. (2010). Mathematical thinking of kindergarten boys and girls: Similar achievement, different contributing processes. *Educational Studies in Mathematics, 73,* 233–246.

Kliman, M. (1999). Beyond helping with homework: Parents and children doing mathematics at home. *Teaching Children Mathematics, 6*(3), 140–146.

Kline, K. (2008). Learning to think and thinking to learn. *Teaching Children Mathematics, 15,* 144–151.

Kloosterman, P. (2010). Mathematics skills of 17-year-olds in the United States: 1978 to 2004. *Journal for Research in Mathematics Education, 41*(1), 20–51.

Kloosterman, P., Rutledge, Z., & Kenney, P. (2009a). Exploring the results of the NAEP: 1980s to the present. *Mathematics Teaching in the Middle School, 14*(6), 357–365.

Kloosterman, P., Rutledge, Z., & Kenney, P. A. (2009b). A generation of progress: Learning from NAEP. *Teaching Children Mathematics, 15*(6), 363–369.

Kloosterman, P., Warfield, J., Wearne, D., Koc, Y., Martin, W. G., & Strutchens, M. (2004). Fourth-grade students' knowledge of mathematics and perceptions of learning mathematics. In P. Kloosterman & F. K. Lester, Jr. (Eds.), *Results and interpretations of the 1990–2000 mathematics assessments of the National Assessment of Educational Progress* (pp. 71–103). Reston, VA: NCTM.

Knuth, E. J., Stephens, A. C., McNeil, N. M., & Alibali, M. W. (2006). Does understanding the equal sign matter? Evidence from solving equations. *Journal for Research in Mathematics Education, 37*(4), 297–312.

Kohn, A. (1993). *Punished by rewards: The trouble with gold stars, incentive plans, A's, praise, and other bribes.* Boston: Houghton Mifflin.

Kouba, V. L. (1989). Children's solution strategies for equivalent set multiplication and division word problems. *Journal for Research in Mathematics Education, 20*(2), 147–158.

Kouba, V. L., Brown, C. A., Carpenter, T. P., Lindquist, M. M., Silver, E. A., & Swafford, J. O. (1988). Results of the fourth NAEP assessment of mathematics: Number, operations, and word problems. *Arithmetic Teacher, 35*(8), 14–19.

Kouba, V. L., Zawojewski, J. S., & Strutchens, M. E. (1997). What do students know about numbers and operations? In P. A. Kenney & E. Silver (Eds.), *Results from the sixth mathematics assessment of the National Assessment of Educational Progress* (pp. 87–140). Reston, VA: NCTM.

Kribs-Zaleta, C. (2008). Oranges, posters, ribbons, and lemonade: Concrete computational strategies for dividing fractions. *Mathematics Teaching in the Middle School, 13*(8), 453–457.

Kulm, G. (1994). *Mathematics and assessment: What works in the classroom.* San Francisco: Jossey-Bass.

Labinowicz, E. (1985). *Learning from children: New beginnings for teaching numerical thinking.* Menlo Park, CA: AWL Supplemental.

Lambdin, D. V., & Lynch, K. (2005). Examining mathematics tasks from the National Assessment of Educational Progress. *Mathematics Teaching in the Middle School, 10*(6), 314–318.

Lamon, S. J. (1999). *More: In-depth discussion of the reasoning activities in "Teaching fractions and ratios for understanding."* Mahwah, NJ: Lawrence Erlbaum.

Lamon, S. J. (2002). Part-whole comparisons with unitizing. In B. Litwiller (Ed.), *Making sense of fractions, ratios, and proportions* (pp. 79–86). Reston, VA: NCTM.

Lamon, S. J. (2006). *Teaching fractions and ratios for understanding: Essential content knowledge and instructional strategies for teachers* (2nd ed.). Mahwah, NJ: Lawrence Erlbaum.

Lamon, S. J. (2007). Rational numbers and proportional reasoning: Toward a theoretical framework for research. In F. Lester (Ed.), *Second handbook of research on mathematics teaching and learning* (pp. 629–666). Reston, VA: NCTM.

Lampe, K. A., & Uselmann, L. (2008). Pen pals: Practicing problem solving. *Mathematics Teaching in the Middle School, 14*(4), 196–201.

Langrall, C., Nisbet, S., Mooney, E., & Jansem, S. (2011). The role of context expertise when comparing data. *Mathematical Thinking and Learning, 13*, 47–67.

Lannin, J. K., Arbaugh, F., Barker, D. D., & Townsend, B. E. (2006). Making the most of student errors. *Teaching Children Mathematics, 13*(3), 182–186.

Lannin, J. K., Townsend, B. E., Armer, N., Green, S., & Schneider, J. (2008). Developing meaning for algebraic symbols: Possibilities and pitfalls. *Mathematics Teaching in the Middle School, 13*(8), 478–483.

Lapp, D. (2001). *How do students learn with data collection devices?* Presentation given at the annual International Teachers Teaching with Technology Conference, Columbus, OH.

Lappan, G., & Even, R. (1989). *Learning to teach: Constructing meaningful understanding of mathematical content* (Craft Paper 89–3). East Lansing: Michigan State University.

Lappan, G., & Mouck, M. K. (1998). Developing algorithms for adding and subtracting fractions. In L. J. Morrow (Ed.), *The teaching and learning of algorithms in school mathematics* (pp. 183–197). Reston, VA: NCTM.

Leatham K. R., & Hill, D. S. (2010). Exploring our complex math identities. *Mathematics Teaching in the Middle School, 16*(4), 224–231.

Leatham, K. R., Lawrence, K., & Mewborn, D. S. (2005). Getting started with open-ended assessment. *Teaching Children Mathematics, 11*(8), 413–419.

Leavy, A., Friel, S., & Mamer, J. (2009). It's a fird! Can you compute a median of categorical data? *Mathematics Teaching in the Middle School, 14*(6), 344–351.

Leeming, C. (2007, November 3). *"Cool Cash" card confusion.* Manchester Evening News, Manchester, England. Retrieved from www.manchestereveningnews.co.uk/news/s/1022757_cool_cash_card_confusion

Leinwand, S. (2007). Four teacher-friendly postulates for thriving in a sea of change. *Mathematics Teacher, 100*(9), 582–584.

Lemons-Smith, S. (2009). Mathematics beyond the school walls project: Exploring the dynamic role of students' lived experiences. In D. Y. White & J. S. Spitzer (Eds.), *Responding to diversity: Grades pre-K–5* (pp. 129–136). Reston, VA: NCTM.

Leonard, J., & Guha, S. (2002). Creating cultural relevance in teaching and learning mathematics. *Teaching Children Mathematics, 9*(2), 114–118.

Lesh, R. A., Cramer, K., Doerr, H., Post, T., & Zawojewski, J. (2003). Model development sequences. In R. A. Lesh & H. Doerr (Eds.), *Beyond constructivism: A models and modeling perspective on mathematics teaching, learning, and problem solving* (pp. 35–58). Mahwah, NJ: Lawrence Erlbaum.

Lesh, R. A., & Zawojewski, J. S. (2007). Problem solving and modeling. In F. K. Lester, Jr. (Ed.), *The handbook of research on mathematics teaching and learning* (2nd ed., pp. 763–804). Reston, VA: NCTM; Charlotte, NC: Information Age Publishing.

Lester, F. K., Jr. (1989). Reflections about mathematical problem-solving research. In R. I. Charles & E. A. Silver (Eds.), *The teaching and assessing of mathematical problem solving* (pp. 115–124). Reston, VA: NCTM.

Lewis, T. (2005). Facts + fun = fluency. *Teaching Children Mathematics, 12*(1), 8–11.

Lim, K. H. (2009). Burning the candle at just one end. *Mathematics Teaching in the Middle School, 14*(8), 492–500.

Lobato, J., & Ellis, A.(2010). *Developing essential understanding of ratios, proportions, and proportional reasoning: Grades 6–8.* Reston, VA: NCTM.

Locuniak, M. N., & Jordan, N. C. (2008). Using kindergarten number sense to predict calculation fluency in second grade. *Journal of Learning Disabilities, 41*(5), 451–459.

Ma, L. (1999). *Knowing and teaching elementary mathematics: Teachers' understanding of fundamental mathematics in China and the United States.* Mahwah, NJ: Lawrence Erlbaum.

Mack, N. K. (1995). Confounding whole-number and fraction concepts when building on informal knowledge. *Journal for Research in Mathematics Education, 26*(5), 422–441.

Mack, N. K. (2004). Connecting to develop computational fluency with fractions. *Teaching Children Mathematics, 11*(4), 226–232.

Maida, P. (2004). Using algebra without realizing it. *Mathematics Teaching in the Middle School, 9*(9), 484–488.

Maldonado, L. A., Turner, E. E., Dominguez, H., & Empson, S. B. (2009). English language learning from, and contributing to, mathematical discussions. In D. Y. White & J. S. Spitzer (Eds.), *Responding to diversity: Grades pre-K–5* (pp. 7–22). Reston, VA: NCTM.

Mann, R. L. (2004). Balancing act: The truth behind the equals sign. *Teaching Children Mathematics, 11*(2), 68.

Mark, J., Cuoco, A., Goldenberg, E. P., & Sword, S. (2010). Developing mathematical habits of mind. *Mathematics Teaching in the Middle School, 15*(9), 505–509.

Martin, J. F. (2009). The goal of long division. *Teaching Children Mathematics, 15*(8), 482–487.

Martinie, S. L. (2007). *Middle school rational number knowledge* (Unpublished doctoral dissertation). Kansas State University.

Martinie, S. L., & Bay-Williams, J. M. (2003). Investigating students' conceptual understanding of decimal fractions using multiple representations. *Mathematics Teaching in the Middle School, 8*(5), 244–247.

Mathematical Sciences Education Board, National Research Council. (1989). *Everybody counts: A report to the nation on the future of mathematics education.* Washington, DC: National Academy of Sciences Press.

Matthews, M. E., Hlas, C. S., & Finken, T. M. (2009). Using lesson study and four-column lesson planning with preservice teachers. *Mathematics Teacher, 102*(7), 504–508.

Mau, T. S., & Leitze, A. R. (2001). Powerless gender or genderless power? The promise of constructivism for females in the mathematics classroom. In J. E. Jacobs, J. R. Becker, & G. F. Gilmer (Eds.), *Changing the faces of mathematics: Perspectives on gender* (pp. 37–41). Reston, VA: NCTM.

Mazzocco, M. M. M., Devlin, K. T., & McKenney, S. J. (2008). Is it a fact? Timed arithmetic performance of children with mathematical learning disabilities (MLD) varies as a function of how MLD is defined. *Developmental Neuropsychology, 33*(3), 318–344.

Mazzocco, M. M. M., & Thompson, R. E. (2005). Kindergarten predictors of math learning disability. *Learning Disabilities Research & Practice, 20*(3), 142–155.

McCallum, W. (2011). Illustrative mathematics project. Retrieved from http://illustrativemathematics.org/standards

McClain, K., Leckman, J., Schmitt, P., & Regis, T. (2006). Changing the face of statistical data analysis in the middle grades: Learning by doing. In G. F. Burrill & P. C. Elliott (Eds.), *Thinking and reasoning about data and chance: 68th NCTM yearbook* (pp. 229–240). Reston, VA: NCTM.

McCoy, L. P. (1997). Algebra: Real-life investigations in a lab setting. *Mathematics Teaching in the Middle School, 2*(4), 220–224.

McCoy, L. P., Buckner, S., & Munley, J. (2007). Probability games from diverse cultures. *Mathematics Teaching in the Middle School, 12*(7), 394–402.

McCulloch, A. W., Marshall, P. L., & DeCuir-Gunby, J. T. (2009). Cultural capital in children's number representations: Reflect and discuss—Youngsters' out-of-school knowledge influences their pictorial representations of number. *Teaching Children Mathematics, 16*(3), 184.

McGatha, M., Cobb, P., & McClain, K. (1998). *An analysis of students' statistical understandings.* Paper presented at the Annual Meeting of the American Educational Research Association, San Diego, CA.

McGlone, C. (2008, July). *The role of culturally-based mathematics in the general mathematics curriculum.* Paper presented at the Eleventh International Congress on Mathematics Education, Monterrey, Mexico.

McLean, D. L. (2002). Honoring traditions: Making connections with mathematics through culture. *Teaching Children Mathematics, 9*(3), 184–188.

McNamara, J. C. (2010). Two of everything. *Teaching Children Mathematics, 17*(3), 132–136.

McNamara, J. C., & Shaughnessy, M. M. (2010). *Beyond pizzas & pies: Ten essential strategies for supporting fraction sense (Grades 3–5).* Sausalito, CA: Math Solutions.

McNeil, N. M., & Alibali, M. W. (2005). Knowledge change as a function of mathematics experience: All contexts are not created equal. *Journal of Cognition and Development, 6,* 285–306.

McNeil, N. M., Grandau, L., Knuth, E. J., Alibali, M. W., Stephens, A. C., Hattikudur, S., & Krill, D. E. (2006). Middle-school students' understanding of the equal sign: The books they read can't help. *Cognition & Instruction, 24*(3), 367–385.

Menon, R. (2003). Using number relationships for estimation and mental computation. *Mathematics Teaching in the Middle School, 8*(9), 476–479.

Metz, M. L. (2010). Using GAISE and NCTM standards as framework for teaching probability and statistics to preservice elementary and middle school mathematics teachers. *Journal of Statistics Education, 18*(3), 1–27.

Midobuche, E. (2001). Building cultural bridges between home and the mathematics classroom. *Teaching Children Mathematics, 7*(9), 500–502.

Mishra, P., & Koehler, M. J. (2006). Technological pedagogical content knowledge: A new framework for teacher knowledge. *Teachers College Record, 108*(6), 1017–1054.

Mokros, J., Russell, S. J., & Economopoulos, K. (1995). *Beyond arithmetic: Changing mathematics in the elementary classroom.* Palo Alto, CA: Dale Seymour Publications.

Mokros, J., & Wright, T. (2009). Zoos, aquariums and expanding students' data literacy. *Teaching Children Mathematics, 15*(9), 524–530.

Molina, M., & Ambrose, R. C. (2006). Fostering relational thinking while negotiating the meaning of the equals sign. *Teaching Children Mathematics, 13*(2), 111–117.

Moschkovich, J. N. (1998). Supporting the participation of English language learners in mathematical discussions. *For the Learning of Mathematics, 19*(1), 11–19.

Moschkovich, J. N. (2009, March). *How do students use two languages when learning mathematics? Using two languages during conversations:* NCTM Research Clip. Reston, VA: NCTM.

Munier, V., Devichi, C., & Merle, H. (2008). A physical situation as a way to teach angle. *Teaching Children Mathematics, 14*(7), 402–407.

Murata, A. (2008). Mathematics teaching and learning as a mediating process: The case of tape diagrams. *Mathematical Thinking and Learning, 10,* 374–406.

Murrey, D. L. (2008). Differentiating instruction in mathematics for the English language learner. *Mathematics Teaching in the Middle School, 14*(3), 146–153.

National Association for Gifted Children (NAGC). (2007). What is giftedness? Retrieved from www.nagc.org

National Center for Education Statistics. (2009a). *NAEP Questions Tool.* Retrieved from http://nces.ed.gov/nationsreportcard/itmrlsx/detail.aspx?subject=mathematics

National Center for Education Statistics. (2009b). *The nation's report card: Mathematics 2009* (NCES 2010–451). Institute of Education Sciences, U.S. Department of Education, Washington, DC.

National Center for Technology Innovation. (2010). *Techmatrix.* Retrieved from www.techmatrix.org

National Geographic. (2010). *Kids Almanac 2011.* Washington, DC: National Geographic.

National Governors Association, & Council of Chief State School Officers. (2010, June). *Common Core State Standards Initiative.* Retrieved from www.corestandards.org

National Mathematics Advisory Panel. (2008). *Foundations for success*. Jessup, MD: U.S. Department of Education. (Also available online at www.ed.gov/MathPanel.)

National Research Council. (2001). *Adding it up: Helping children learn mathematics*. J. Kilpatrick, J. Swafford, & B. Findell (Eds.). Washington, DC: National Academies Press.

National Research Council Committee. (2009). *Mathematics learning in early childhood: Paths toward excellence and equity*. Washington, DC: The National Academies Press.

NCTM (National Council of Teachers of Mathematics). (1989). *Curriculum and evaluation standards for school mathematics*. Reston, VA: NCTM.

NCTM (National Council of Teachers of Mathematics). (1991). *Professional standards for teaching mathematics*. Reston, VA: NCTM.

NCTM (National Council of Teachers of Mathematics). (1995). *Assessment standards for school mathematics*. Reston, VA: NCTM.

NCTM (National Council of Teachers of Mathematics). (2000). *Principles and standards for school mathematics*. Reston, VA: NCTM.

NCTM (National Council of Teachers of Mathematics). (2006). Curriculum focal points for prekindergarten through grade 8 mathematics: A quest for coherence. Reston, VA: NCTM.

NCTM (National Council of Teachers of Mathematics). (2007a). *Mathematics teaching today*. Reston, VA: NCTM.

NCTM (National Council of Teachers of Mathematics). (2007b). *Research Brief: Effective Strategies for Teaching Students with Difficulties in Mathematics*. Retrieved from www.nctm.org/news/content.aspx?id=8452

NCTM (National Council of Teachers of Mathematics). (2008a, January). *Equity in Mathematics Education*. Retrieved from www.nctm.org/about/content.aspx?id=13490

NCTM (National Council of Teachers of Mathematics). (2008b, March). *The Role of Technology in the Teaching and Learning of Mathematics*. Retrieved from www.nctm.org/about/content.aspx?id=14233

NCTM (National Council of Teachers of Mathematics). (2009). *Focus in high school mathematics: Reasoning and sense making*. Reston, VA: NCTM.

NCTM (National Council of Teachers of Mathematics). (2011, July). *Position statement on calculator use in elementary grades*. Reston, VA: NCTM.

NCTM (National Council of Teachers of Mathematics). (2011, July). *Position statement on interventions*. Reston, VA: NCTM.

NCTM (National Council of Teachers of Mathematics). (n.d.). Statement of beliefs. Retrieved from www.nctm.org/about/content.aspx?id=210&LangType=1033

Nebesniak, A. L., & Heaton, R. M. (2010). Student confidence & student involvement. *Mathematics Teaching in the Middle School, 16*(2), 97–103.

Neel, K. S. (2005). Addressing diversity in the mathematics classroom with cultural artifacts. *Mathematics Teaching in the Middle School, 11*(2), 54–61.

Nelson, C. Q., & Williams, N. L. (2009). Mathematical explorations: Exploring unknown probabilities with min-iature toy pigs. *Mathematics Teaching in the Middle School, 14*(9), 557.

Nelson, R. (2001). *Proofs without words II: More exercises in visual thinking*. Washington, DC: Mathematical Association of America.

Neumann, M. D. (2005). Freedom quilts: Mathematics on the underground railroad. *Teaching Children Mathematics, 11*(6), 316–321.

Neumer, C. (2007). Mixed numbers made easy: Building and converting mixed numbers and improper fractions. *Teaching Children Mathematics, 13*(9), 488–492.

Nicolson, C. P. (2005). Is chance fair? One student's thoughts on probability. *Teaching Children Mathematics, 12*(2), 83–89.

Niess, M. (2008). Guiding preservice teachers in developing TPCK. In AACTE Committee on Innovation and Technology (Eds.), *Handbook of technological pedagogical content knowledge (TCPK) for educators* (pp. 223–250). New York: Routledge/Taylor & Francis Group.

Niezgoda, D. A., & Moyer-Packenham, P. S. (2005). Hickory, dickory, dock: Navigating through data analysis. *Teaching Children Mathematics, 11*(6), 292–300.

Noddings, N. (1988, December 7). Schools face crisis in caring. *Education Week*, p. 32.

Noddings, N. (1993). Constuctivism and caring. In R. B. Davis & C. A. Maher (Eds.), *Schools, mathematics, and the world of reality* (pp. 35–50). Boston: Allyn & Bacon.

Northcote, N., & McIntosh, A. (1999). What mathematics do adults really do in everyday life? *Australian Primary Mathematics Classroom, 4*(1), 19–21.

Norton, A., & D'Ambrosio, B. S. (2008). ZPC and ZPD: Zones of teaching and learning. *Journal for Research in Mathematics Education, 39*(3), 220–246.

Nosek, B., Banaji, M., & Greenwald, A. (2002). Math = male, me = female, therefore me math. *Journal of Personality and Social Psychology, 83*(1), 44–59.

Nyquist, J. B. (2003). *The benefits of reconstruing feedback as a larger system of formative assessment: A meta-analysis*. Unpublished master's thesis. Vanderbilt University, Nashville, TN.

Outhred, L., & Mitchelmore, M. (2004). Students' structuring of rectangular arrays. In M. J. Hoines & A. B. Fuglestad (Eds.), *Proceedings of the 28th PME International Conference, 3*, 465–472.

Parker, M. (2004). Reasoning and working proportionally with percent. *Mathematics Teaching in the Middle School, 9*(6), 326–330.

Parmar, R., Garrison, R., Clements, D., & Sarama, J. (2011). Measurement. In F. Fennell (Ed.), *Achieving fluency in special education and mathematics* (pp. 197–216). Reston, VA: NCTM.

Patall, E. A., Cooper, H., & Robinson, J. C. (2008). Parent involvement in homework: A research synthesis. *Review of Educational Research, 78*(4), 1039–1101.

Perie, M., Moran, R., & Lutkus, A. (2005). *NAEP 2004 trends in academic progress: Three decades of student performance in reading and mathematics*. Washington, DC: National Center for Education Statistics.

Perkins, I., & Flores, A. (2002). Mathematical notations and procedures of recent immigrant students. *Mathematics Teaching in the Middle School, 7*(6), 346–351.

Peterek, E., & Adams, T. L. (2009). Meeting the challenge of engaging students for success in mathematics by using culturally responsive methods. In D. Y. White & J. S. Spitzer (Eds.), *Responding to diversity: Grades pre-K–5* (pp. 149–160). Reston, VA: NCTM.

Petersen, J. (2004). *Math and nonfiction: Grades K–2.* Sausalito, CA: Math Solutions Publications.

Petit, M. (2009). *OGAP (Vermont mathematics partnership ongoing assessment project) multiplicative reasoning framework.* Communication with the author (September 2009).

Petit, M., Laird, R. E., & Marsden, E. L. (2010). A focus on fractions: Bringing research to the classroom. New York: Taylor & Francis.

Petit, M., & Zawojewski, J. (2010). Formative assessment in elementary school mathematics. In D. Lambdin & F. K. Lester, Jr. (Eds.), *Teaching and learning mathematics: Translating research for elementary school teachers* (pp. 73–79). Reston, VA: NCTM.

Philipp, R. A., Schappelle, B., Siegfried, J., Jacobs, V., & Lamb, L. (2008, April). *The effects of professional development on the mathematical content knowledge of K–3 teachers.* Paper presented at the American Educational Research Association annual meeting, New York City, NY.

Phillips-Bey, C. K. (2004). TI–73 calculator activities. *Mathematics Teaching in the Middle School, 9*(9), 500–508.

Piaget, J. (1976). *The child's conception of the world.* Totowa, NJ: Littlefield, Adams.

Pólya, G. (1945). *How to solve it.* Princeton, NJ: Princeton University Press.

Popham, W. J. (2008). *Transformative assessment.* Alexandria, VA: Association for Supervision and Curriculum Development.

Porter, A., McMaken, J., Hwang, J., & Yang, R. (2011). Common core standards: The new U.S. intended curriculum. *Educational Researcher, 40*(3), 103–116.

Post, T. R. (1981). Fractions: Results and implications from the national assessment. *Arithmetic Teacher, 28*(9), 26–31.

Post, T. R., Wachsmuth, I., Lesh, R. A., & Behr, M. J. (1985). Order and equivalence of rational numbers: A cognitive analysis. *Journal for Research in Mathematics Education, 16*(1), 18–36.

Preston, R., & Thompson, T. (2004). Integrating measurement across the curriculum. *Mathematics Teaching in the Middle School, 9*(8), 436–441.

Pugalee, D. K. (2005). *Writing for mathematical understanding.* Norwood, MA: Christopher Gordon.

Pugalee, D. K., Arbaugh, F., Bay-Williams, J. M., Farrell, A., Mathews, S., &. Royster, D. (2008). *Navigating through mathematical connections in grades 6–8.* Reston, VA: NCTM.

Pugalee, D. K., Harbaugh, A., & Quach, L. H. (2009). The human graph project: Giving students mathematical power through differentiated instruction. In M. W. Ellis (Ed.), *Responding to diversity: Grades 6–8* (pp. 47–58). Reston, VA: NCTM.

Quinn, R., Lamberg, T., & Perrin, J. (2008). Teacher perceptions of division by zero. *Clearing House, 81*(3), 101–104.

Rampey, B. D., Dion, G. S., & Donahue, P. L. (2009). *NAEP 2008 Trends in Academic Progress* (NCES 2009–479). Washington, DC: National Center for Education Statistics, Institute of Education Sciences, U.S. Department of Education.

RAND Mathematics Study Panel. (2003). *Mathematical proficiency for all students: Toward a strategic research and development program in mathematics education* (Issue 1643). Santa Monica, CA: Rand Corporation.

Rasmussen, C., Yackel, E., & King, K. (2003). Social and sociomathematical norms in the mathematics classroom. In H. L. Schoen & R. I. Charles (Eds.), *Teaching mathematics through problem solving: Grades 6–12* (pp. 143–154). Reston, VA: NCTM.

Rathmell, E. C. (1978). Using thinking strategies to teach the basic skills. In M. N. Suydam (Ed.), *Developing computational skills* (pp. 13–38). Reston, VA: NCTM.

Rathmell, E. C., Leutzinger, L. P., & Gabriele, A. (2000). *Thinking with numbers.* (Separate packets for each operation.) Cedar Falls, IA: Thinking with Numbers.

Rathouz, M. M. (2011). Making sense of decimal multiplication. *Mathematics Teaching in the Middle School, 16*(7), 430–437.

Reinhart, S. (2000). Never say anything a kid can say. *Mathematics Teaching in the Middle School, 5*(8), 478–483.

Reis, S., & Renzulli, J. S. (2005). *Curriculum compacting: An easy start to differentiating for high potential students.* Waco, TX: Prufrock Press.

Remillard, J. T., & Jackson, K. (2006). Old math, new math: Parents' experiences with standards-based reform. *Mathematical Thinking and Learning, 3*(6), 231–259.

Renne, C. G. (2004). Is a rectangle a square? Developing mathematical vocabulary and conceptual understanding. *Teaching Children Mathematics, 10*(5), 258–263.

Renzulli, J. S., Gubbins, E. J., McMillen, K. S., Eckert, R. D., & Little, C. A. (Eds.). (2009). *Systems & models for developing programs for the gifted & talented* (2nd ed.). Mansfield Center, CT: Creative Learning Press.

Resnick, L. B. (1983). A developmental theory of number understanding. In H. P. Ginsburg (Ed.), *The development of mathematical thinking* (pp. 109–151). New York: Academic Press.

Resnick, L. B., Nesher, P., Leonard, F., Magone, M., Omanson, S., & Peled, I. (1989). Conceptual bases of arithmetic errors: The case of decimal fractions. *Journal for Research in Mathematics Education, 20*(1), 8–27.

Reys, B. J., Reys, R. E., & Penafiel, A. F. (1991). Estimation performance and strategy use of Mexican 5th and 8th grade student sample. *Educational Studies in Mathematics, 22*(4), 353–375.

Reys, R. E. (1998). Computation versus number sense. *Mathematics Teaching in the Middle School, 4*(2), 110–113.

Reys, R. E., & Reys, B. J. (1983). *Guide to using estimation skills and strategies (GUESS)* (Boxes I and II). Palo Alto, CA: Dale Seymour.

Riegle-Crumb, C. (2006). The path through math: Course-taking trajectories and student performance at the intersection of gender and race/ethnicity. *American Journal of Education, 113*(1), 101–122.

Riegle-Crumb, C., & King, B. (2011). Questioning a white male advantage in STEM: Examining disparities in college major by gender and race/ethnicity. *Educational Researcher, 39*(9), 656–664.

Riordan, J. E., & Noyce, P. E. (2001). The impact of two *Standards*-based mathematics curricula on student achievement in Massachusetts. *Journal for Research in Mathematics Education, 32*(4), 368–398.

Riskowski, J. L., Olbricht, G., & Wilson, J. (2010). 100 students. *Mathematics Teaching in the Middle School, 15*(6), 320–327.

Rittle-Johnson, B., Star, J. R., & Durkin, K. (2010, April). *Developing procedural flexibility: When should multiple solution methods be introduced?* Paper presented at the Annual Conference of the American Educational Research Association, Denver, CO.

Roberge, M. C., & Cooper, L. L. (2010). Map scale, proportion, and Google™ Earth. *Mathematics Teaching in the Middle School, 15*(8), 448–457.

Robinson, J. P. (2010). The effects of test translation on young English learners' mathematics performance. *Educational Researcher, 39*(8), 582–590.

Roche, A., & Clarke, D. (2004). When does successful comparison of decimals reflect conceptual understanding? In I. Putt, R. Faragher, & M. McLean (Eds.), *Mathematics Education for the Third Millennium: Towards 2010. Proceedings of the 27th Annual Conference of the Mathematics Education Research Group of Australasia, 2,* 486–493.

Roddick, C., & Silvas-Centeno, C. (2007). Developing understanding of fractions through pattern blocks and fair trade. *Teaching Children Mathematics, 14*(3), 140–145.

Ross, S. H. (1986). *The development of children's place-value numeration concepts in grades two through five.* Presented at the annual meeting of the American Educational Research Association, San Francisco. (ERIC Document Reproduction Service No. ED 2773-482).

Ross, S. H. (1989). Parts, wholes, and place value: A developmental perspective. *Arithmetic Teacher, 36*(6), 47–51.

Ross, S. R. (2002). Place value: Problem solving and written assessment. *Teaching Children Mathematics, 8*(7), 419–423.

Rossman, A., Chance, B., & Median, E. (2006). Some important comparisons between statistics and mathematics, and why teachers should care. In G. F. Burrill & P. C. Elliott (Eds.), *Thinking and reasoning about data and chance: 68th NCTM yearbook* (pp. 323–334). Reston, VA: NCTM.

Rotigel, J., & Fellow, S. (2005). Mathematically gifted students: How can we meet their needs? *Gifted Child Today, 27*(4), 46–65.

Roy, J. A., & Beckmann, C. E. (2007). Batty functions: Exploring quadratic functions through children's literature. *Mathematics Teaching in the Middle School, 13*(1), 52–64.

Rubel, L. (2006). Students' probabilistic thinking revealed: The case of coin tosses. In G. Burrill & P. C. Elliott (Eds.), *Thinking and reasoning about data and chance: Sixty-eighth yearbook* (pp. 49–60). Reston, VA: NCTM.

Rubel, L. (2007). Middle school and high school students' probabilistic reasoning on coin tasks. *Journal for Research in Mathematics Education, 38*(5), 531–557.

Russell, S. J. (1997, April). *Using video to study students' strategies for whole-number operations.* Paper presented at the annual meeting of the National Council of Teachers of Mathematics, Minneapolis, MN.

Russell, S. J. (2006). What does it mean that "5 has a lot"? From the world to data and back. In G. F. Burrill & P. C. Elliott (Eds.), *Thinking and reasoning about data and chance: 68th NCTM yearbook* (pp. 17–30). Reston VA: NCTM.

Russell, S. J., & Economopoulos, K. (2008). *Investigations in number, data, and space.* New York: Pearson.

Russell, S. J., & Mokros, J. R. (1991). What's typical? Children's and teachers' ideas about average. In D. Vere-Jones (Ed.), *Proceedings of the 3rd International Conference on Teaching Statistics. Vol. 1. School and General Issues* (pp. 307–313). Voorburg, Netherlands: International Statistical Institute.

Ryan, J., & Williams, J. (2007). *Children's mathematics 4–15: Learning from errors and misconceptions.* New York: McGraw-Hill Open University Press.

Sadler, P., & Tai, R. (2007). The two pillars supporting college science. *Science, 317*(5837), 457–458.

Samara, T. R. (2007). *Obstacles to opportunity: Alexandria, Virginia students speak out.* Alexandria, VA: Alexandria United Teens, George Mason University.

Sarama, J., & Clements, D. H. (2009). *Early childhood mathematics education research: learning trajectories for young children.* New York: Routledge.

Sattler, J. (2008). *Assessment of children: Cognitive foundations.* La Mesa, CA: Jerome Sattler.

Saul, M., Assouline, S., & Sheffield, L. J. (Eds.). (2010). *The peak in the middle: Developing mathematically gifted students in the middle grades.* Reston, VA: NCTM, National Association of Gifted Children, & National Middle School Association.

Sawchuk, S. (2010, June 23). Three groups apply for race to top test grants. *Education Week.*

Scheaffer, R. L. (2006). Statistics and mathematics: On making a happy marriage. In G. F. Burrill & P. C. Elliott (Eds.), *Thinking and reasoning about data and chance: Sixty-eighth yearbook* (pp. 309–322). Reston, VA: NCTM.

Schielack, J., & Seeley, C. (2007). A look at the development of data representation and analysis in *Curriculum Focal Points: A Quest of Coherence. Mathematics Teaching in the Middle School, 13*(4), 208–210.

Schifter, D. (1999). Reasoning about operations: Early algebraic thinking, grades K through 6. In L. Stiff & F. Curcio (Eds.), *Developing mathematical reasoning in grades K–12* (pp. 62–81). Reston, VA: NCTM.

Schifter, D. (2001). Perspectives from a mathematics educator. In Center for Education, *Knowing and learning mathematics for teaching* (pp. 69–71). Washington, DC: National Academies Press.

Schifter, D., Bastable, V., & Russell, S. J. (1999a). *Developing mathematical understanding: Numbers and operations, Part 2, Making meaning for operations* (Casebook). Parsippany, NJ: Dale Seymour Publications.

Schifter, D., Bastable, V., & Russell, S. J. (1999b). *Developing mathematical understanding: Numbers and operations, Part 2, Making meaning for operations* (Facilitator's Guide). Parsippany, NJ: Dale Seymour Publications.

Schifter, D., & Fosnot, C. T. (1993). *Reconstructing mathematics education: Stories of teachers meeting the challenge of reform.* New York: Teachers College Press.

Schifter, D., Monk, G. S., Russell, S. J., & Bastable, V. (2007). Early algebra: What does understanding the laws of arithmetic mean in the elementary grades? In J. Kaput, D. Carraher, & M. Blanton (Eds.), *Algebra in the early grades.* Mahwah, NJ: Lawrence Erlbaum.

Schifter, D., Russell, S. J., & Bastable, V. (2009). Early algebra to reach the range of learners. *Teaching Children Mathematics, 16*(4), 230–237.

Schmidt, W. H., McKnight, C. C., & Raizen, S. A. (1996). *Executive summary of a splintered vision: An investigation of U.S. science and mathematics education.* Boston: Kluwer.

Schoenfeld, A. H. (1992). Learning to think mathematically: Problem solving, metacognition, and sense making in mathematics. In D. A. Grouws (Ed.), *Handbook of research on teaching and learning* (pp. 334–370). Old Tappan, NJ: Macmillan.

Schroeder, T. L., & Lester, F. K., Jr. (1989). Developing understanding in mathematics via problem solving. In P. R. Trafton (Ed.), *New directions for elementary school mathematics* (pp. 31–42). Reston, VA: NCTM.

Schwartz, S. L. (1996). Hidden messages in teacher talk: Praise and empowerment. *Teaching Children Mathematics, 2*(7), 396–401.

Sconyers, J. M. (1995). Proof and the middle school mathematics student. *Mathematics Teaching in the Middle School, 1*(7), 516–518.

Seattle Times News Services. (2008, July 25). In math, girls and boys are equal. *The Seattle Times.*

Seeley, C., & Schielack, J. F. (2007). A look at the development of ratios, rates, and proportionality. *Mathematics Teaching in the Middle School, 13*(3), 140–142.

Seidel, C., & McNamee, J. (2005). Teacher to teacher: Phenomenally exciting joint mathematics—English vocabulary project. *Mathematics Teaching in the Middle School, 10*(9), 461–463.

Setati, M. (2005). Teaching mathematics in a primary multilingual classroom. *Journal for Research in Mathematics Education, 36*(5), 447–466.

Shaughnessy, J. M. (2003). Research on students' understanding of probability. In J. Kilpatrick, W. G. Martin, & D. Schifter (Eds.), *A research companion to Principles and Standards for School Mathematics* (pp. 216–226). Reston, VA: NCTM.

Shaughnessy, J. M. (2006). Research on students' understanding of some big concepts in statistics. In G. F. Burrill & P. C. Elliott (Eds.), *Thinking and reasoning about data and chance: 68th NCTM yearbook* (pp. 77–98). Reston, VA: NCTM.

Shaughnessy, J. M. (2007). Research on statistics learning and reasoning. In F. Lester, Jr. (Ed.), *Second handbook of research on mathematics teaching and learning* (pp. 957–1010). Reston, VA: NCTM.

Shaughnessy, M. (2009). *Students' flexible use of multiple representations for rational numbers: Decimals, fractions, parts of area and number lines* (Doctoral dissertation). University of California–Berkeley.

Sheffield, L. J. (1997). From Doogie Howser to dweebs—or how we went in search of Bobby Fischer and found that we are dumb and dumber. *Mathematics Teaching in the Middle School, 2*(6), 376–379.

Sheffield, L. J. (Ed.). (1999). *Developing mathematically promising students.* Reston, VA: National Council of Teachers of Mathematics.

Sheffield, S. (1995). *Math and literature (K–3)* (Vol. 2). Sausalito, CA: Math Solutions Publications.

Sheffield, S., & Gallagher, K. (2004). *Math and nonfiction: Grades 3–5.* Sausalito, CA: Math Solutions Publications.

Shoecraft, P. (1982). Bowl-A-Fact: A game for reviewing the number facts. *Arithmetic Teacher, 29*(8), 24–25.

Shulman, L. (1986). Those who understand: Knowledge growth in teaching. *Educational Researcher, 15*(2), 4–14.

Siebert, D., & Gaskin, N. (2006). Creating, naming, and justifying fractions. *Teaching Children Mathematics, 12*(8), 394–400.

Siegler, R. S., & Booth, J. L. (2005). Development of numerical estimation: A review. In J. I. D. Campbell (Ed.), *Handbook of mathematical cognition* (pp. 197–212). New York Psychology Press.

Siegler, R. S., Carpenter, T., Fennell, F., Geary, D., Lewis, J., Okamoto, Y., . . . Wray, J. (2010). *Developing effective fractions instruction for kindergarten through 8th grade: A practice guide* (NCEE 2010-4039). Retrieved from www.whatworks.ed.gov/publications/practiceguides

Siegler, R. S., & Ramani, G. B. (2009). Playing linear number board games—but not circular ones—improves low-income preschoolers' numerical understanding. *Journal of Educational Psychology, 101,* 545–560.

Sikes, S. (1995). *Feeding the zircon gorilla and other team building activities.* Tulsa, OK: Learning Unlimited Corporation.

Silver, E. A., & Stein, M. K. (1996). The QUASAR project: The "revolution of the possible" in mathematics instructional reform in urban middle schools. *Urban Education, 30*(4), 476–521.

Simon, M. A. (2009). Amidst multiple theories of learning in mathematics education. *Journal for Research in Mathematics Education, 40*(5), 477–490.

Skemp, R. (1978). Relational understanding and instrumental understanding. *Arithmetic Teacher, 26*(3), 9–15.

Smith, A. (1997). Testing the surf: Criteria for evaluating Internet information resources. *The Public-Access Computer Systems Review, 8*(3), 5–23.

Smith, B. A. (1997). *A meta-analysis of outcomes from the use of calculators in mathematics education* (Doctoral dissertation). Texas A&M University. *Dissertation Abstracts International, 58,* 787A.

Smith, J. P., III. (2002). The development of students' knowledge of fractions and ratios. In B. Litwiller (Ed.), *Making sense of fractions, ratios, and proportions* (pp. 3–17). Reston, VA: NCTM.

Smith, M. S., Bill, V., & Hughes, E. K. (2008). Thinking through a lesson: Successfully implementing high-level tasks. *Mathematics Teaching in the Middle School, 14*(3), 132–138.

Smith, M. S., Hughes, E. K., Engle, R. A., & Stein, M. K. (2009). Orchestrating discussions. *Mathematics Teaching in the Middle School, 14*(9), 548–556.

Smith, M. S., & Stein, M. K. (1998). Selecting and creating mathematical tasks: From research to practice. *Mathematics Teaching in the Middle School, 3*(5), 344–350.

Smith, M. S., & Stein, M. K. (2011). *5 Practices for orchestrating productive mathematical discussions.* Thousand Oaks, CA: Corwin Press.

Soares, J., Blanton, M. L., & Kaput, J. J. (2006). Thinking algebraically across the elementary school curriculum. *Teaching Children Mathematics, 12*(5), 228–234.

Sowder, J. T., & Wearne, D. (2006). What do we know about eighth-grade student achievement? *Mathematics Teaching in the Middle School, 11*(6), 285–293.

Sowder, J. T., Wearne, D., Martin, W. G., & Strutchens, M. (2004). What do 8th-grade students know about mathematics? Changes over a decade. In P. Kloosterman & F. K. Lester, Jr., *Results and interpretations of the 1990–2000 mathematics assessments of the National Assessment of Educational Progress* (pp. 105–143). Reston, VA: NCTM.

Sowder, L. (1988). Children's solutions of story problems. *Journal of Mathematical Behavior, 7*(3), 227–238.

Spelke, E. S. (2005). *The science of gender and science: Pinker vs. Spelke, a debate.* Retrieved from www.edge.org/3rd_culture/debate05/debate05_index.html

Star, J. R., & Rittle-Johnson, B. (2009). The role of prior knowledge in the development of strategy flexibility: The case of computational estimation. In S. Swars, D. Stinson, & S. Lemons-Smith (Eds.), *Proceedings of the 31st annual meeting of the North American Chapter of the International Group for the Psychology of Mathematics Education* (pp. 577–584). Atlanta: Georgia State University.

Steele, D. F. (2005). Using schemas to develop algebraic thinking. *Mathematics Teaching in the Middle School, 11*(1), 40–46.

Steele, D. F. (2007). Understanding students' problem-solving knowledge through their writing. *Mathematics Teaching in the Middle School, 13*(2), 102–109.

Steen, L. A. (1997). Preface: The new literacy. In L. A. Steen (Ed.), *Why numbers count.* New York: College Entrance Examination Board.

Stein, M. K., & Bovalino, J. W. (2001). Manipulatives: One piece of the puzzle. *Teaching Children Mathematics, 6*(6), 356–359.

Stein, M. K., Remillard, J., & Smith, M. S. (2007). How curriculum influences student learning. In F. J. Lester, Jr. (Ed.), *Second handbook of research on mathematics teaching and learning* (pp. 319–369). Charlotte, NC: Information Age Publishing.

Stein, M. K., & Smith, M. S. (2010). The role of curricular materials in elementary school mathematics classrooms. In Lambdin, D. V., & Lester, F. K., Jr., *Teaching and learning mathematics: Translating research for elementary school teachers* (pp. 61–65). Reston, VA: NCTM.

Steinle, V., & Stacey, K. (2004a). Persistence of decimal misconceptions and readiness to move to expertise. *Proceedings of the 28th conference of the International Groups for the Psychology of Mathematics Education, 4*, 225–232.

Steinle, V., & Stacey, K. (2004b). A longitudinal study of students' understanding of decimal notation: An overview and refined results. In I. Putt, R. Faragher, & M. McLean (Eds.), *Mathematics Education for the Third Millennium: Towards 2010. Proceedings of the 27th Annual Conference of the Mathematics Education Research Group of Australasia, 2*, 541–548.

Stemn, B. (2008). Building middle school students' understanding of proportional reasoning through mathematical investigation. *Education, 36*(4), 3–13.

Stenmark, J. K. (1989). *Assessment alternatives in mathematics: An overview of assessment techniques that promote learning.* Berkeley: EQUALS, University of California.

Stenmark, J. K., & Bush, W. S. (Eds.). (2001). *Mathematics assessment: A practical handbook for grades 3–5.* Reston, VA: NCTM.

Stenmark, J. K., Thompson, V., & Cossey, R. (1986). *Family math.* Berkeley: University of California, Lawrence Hall of Science.

Stephan, M. L. (2009). What are you worth? *Mathematics Teaching in the Middle School, 15*(1), 16–24.

Stephan, M., & Whitenack, J. (2003). Establishing classroom social and sociomathematical norms for problem solving. In F. K. Lester, Jr. & R. I. Charles (Eds.), *Teaching mathematics through problem solving: Grades pre-K–6* (pp. 149–162). Reston, VA: NCTM.

Stephens, A. C. (2005). Developing students' understanding of variable. *Mathematics Teaching in the Middle School, 11*(2), 96–100.

Stevens, T., Wang, K., Olivarez, A., Jr., & Hamman, D. (2007). Use of self-perspectives and their sources to predict the mathematics enrollment intentions of girls and boys. *Sex Roles, 56*(3), 51–63.

Stigler, J., & Hiebert, J. (2009). Closing the teaching gap. *Phi Delta Kappan, 91*(3), 32–37.

Stoessiger, R., & Edmunds, J. (1992). *Natural learning and mathematics.* Portsmouth, NH: Heinemann.

Suh, J. M. (2007a). Developing "algebra-'rithmetic" in the elementary grades. *Teaching Children Mathematics, 14*(4), 246–253.

Suh, J. M. (2007b). Tying it all together: Building mathematics proficiency for all students. *Teaching Children Mathematics, 14*(3), 163–169.

Suh, J. M., Johnston, C., & Doud, J. (2008). Enhancing mathematics learning in a technology rich environment. *Teaching Children Mathematics, 15*(4), 235–241.

Sulentic-Dowell, M. M., Beal, G., & Capraro, R. (2006). How do literacy experiences affect the teaching propensities of elementary pre-service teachers? *Journal of Reading Psychology, 27*(2–3), 235–255.

Swanson, P. E. (2010). The intersection of language and mathematics. *Mathematics Teaching in the Middle School, 15*(9), 516–523.

Taber, S. B. (2002). Go ask Alice about multiplication of fractions. In B. Litwiller (Ed.), *Making sense of fractions, ratios, and proportions* (pp. 61–71). Reston, VA: NCTM.

Taber, S. B. (2007). Using Alice in Wonderland to teach multiplication of fractions. *Mathematics Teaching in the Middle School, 12*(5), 244–250.

Taber, S. B. (2009). Capitalizing on the unexpected. *Mathematics Teaching in the Middle School, 15*(3), 149–155.

Tarr, J. E., Lee, H. S., & Rider, R. L. (2006). When data and chance collide: Drawing inferences from empirical data. In G. Burrill & P. C. Elliott (Eds.), *Thinking and reasoning about data and chance: 68th NCTM yearbook* (pp. 139–149). Reston, VA: NCTM.

Tarr, J. E., & Shaughnessy, J. M. (2007). *Data and chance. Results from the 2003 National Assessment of Educational Process.* Reston, VA: NCTM.

Theissen, D., Matthias, M., & Smith, J. (1998). *The wonderful world of mathematics: A critically annotated list of children's books in mathematics* (2nd ed.). Reston, VA: NCTM.

Thomas, K. R. (2006). Students THINK: A framework for improving problem solving. *Teaching Children Mathematics, 13*(2), 86–95.

Thompson, C. S. (1990). Place value and larger numbers. In J. N. Payne (Ed.), *Mathematics for the young child* (pp. 89–108). Reston, VA: NCTM.

Thompson, P. W. (1994). Concrete materials and teaching for mathematical understanding. *Arithmetic Teacher, 41*(9), 556–558.

Thompson, P. W. (1995). Notation, convention, and quantity in elementary mathematics. In J. T. Sowder & B. P. Schappelle (Eds.), *Providing a foundation for teaching mathematics in the middle grades* (pp. 199–221). New York: State University of New York Press.

Thompson, T. D., & Preston, R. V. (2004). Measurement in the middle grades: Insights from NAEP and TIMSS. *Mathematics Teaching in the Middle School, 9*(9), 514–519.

Thornton, C. A., & Toohey, M. A. (1984). *A matter of facts: (Addition, subtraction, multiplication, division).* Palo Alto, CA: Creative Publications.

Tillema, E. S. (2010). Math for real: A three-girl family. *Mathematics Teaching in the Middle School, 48*(5), 304.

Tirosh, D. (2000). Enhancing prospective teachers' knowledge of children's conceptions: The case of division of fractions. *Journal for Research in Mathematics Education, 31*(1), 1, 5–25.

Tobias, S. (1995). *Overcoming math anxiety.* New York: Norton.

Tomlinson, C. A. (1999). *The differentiated classroom: Responding to the needs of all learners.* Alexandria, VA: Association for Supervision and Curriculum Development.

Tomlinson, C. A., & McTighe, J. (2006). *Integrating differentiated instruction.* Alexandria, VA: Association for Supervision and Curriculum Development.

Torbeyns, J., De Smedt, B., Ghesquiere, P., & Verschaffel, L. (2009). Acquisition and use of shortcut strategies by traditionally schooled children. *Educational Studies in Mathematics, 71*, 1–17.

Torgesen, J. K. (2002). The prevention of reading difficulties. *Journal of School Psychology, 40*(1), 7–26.

Tortolani, M. (2007, February). Presentation at the 2007 National Association of Multicultural Engineering Program Advocates National Conference, Baltimore, MD.

Towers, J., & Hunter, K. (2010). An ecological reading of mathematical language in a grade 3 classroom: A case of learning and teaching measurement estimation. *The Journal of mathematical Behavior, 29*, 25–40.

Tsankova, J. K., & Pjanic, K. (2009–2010). The area model of multiplication of fractions. *Mathematics Teaching in the Middle School, 15*(5), 281–285.

Turner, E. E., Celedón-Pattichis, S., Marshall, M., & Tennison, A. (2009). "Fijense amorcitos, les voy a contra una historia": The power of story to support solving and discussing mathematical problems among Latino and Latina kindergarten students. In D. Y. White & J. S. Spitzer (Eds.), *Responding to diversity: Grades pre-K–5* (pp. 23–42). Reston, VA: NCTM.

Tzur, R. (1999). An integrated study of children's construction of improper fractions and the teacher's role in promoting learning. *Journal for Research in Mathematics Education, 30*(4), 390–416.

Ubuz, B., & Yayan, B. (2010). Primary teacher' subject matter knowledge: Decimals. *International Journal of Mathematical Education in Science and Technology, 41*(6), 787–804.

U.S. Census Bureau. (n.d.). Population clocks. Retrieved from www.census.gov/population/international

U.S. Department of Education, Office of Educational Research and Improvement. (1997). *Introduction to TIMSS.* Washington, DC: U.S. Government Printing Office.

Usiskin, Z. (2007). Some thoughts about fractions. *Mathematics Teaching in the Middle School, 12*(7), 370–373.

Van Dooren, W., De Bock, D., Gillard, E., & Verschaffel, L. (2011). Add? Or multiply? A study on the development of primary school students' proportional reasoning skills. In M. Tzekaki, M. Kaldrimidou, & H. Sakonidis (Eds.), *Proceedings of the 33rd Conference of the International Group for the Psychology of Mathematics Education, 5*, 281–288.

Van Dooren, W., De Bock, D., Vleugels, K., & Verschaffel, L. (2010). Just answering . . . or thinking? Contrasting pupils' solutions and classifications of missing-value word problems. *Mathematical Thinking and Learning, 12*(1), 20–35.

van Hiele, P. M. (1999). Developing geometric thinking through activities that begin with play. *Teaching Children Mathematics, 5*(6), 310–316.

Van Putten, C. M., van den Brom-Snijders, P., & Beishuizen, M. (2005). Progressive mathematization of long division in Dutch primary schools. *Journal for Research in Mathematics Education, 36*, 44–73.

Van Tassel-Baska, J., & Brown, E. F. (2007). Toward best practice: An analysis of the efficacy of curriculum models in gifted education. *Gifted Child Quarterly, 51*(4), 342–358.

Verschaffel, L., Greer, B., & DeCorte, E. (2007). Whole number concepts and operations. In F. Lester, Jr. (Ed.), *Second handbook of research on mathematics teaching and learning* (pp. 557–628). Charlotte, NC: Information Age Publishing.

von Glasersfeld, E. (1990). An exposition of constructivism: Why some like it radical. In R. B. Davis, C. A. Maher, & N. Noddings (Eds.), *Constructivist views on the teaching and learning of mathematics* (pp. 19–29). Reston, VA: NCTM.

von Glasersfeld, E. (1996). Introduction: Aspects of constructivism. In C. T. Fosnot (Ed.), *Constructivism: Theory, perspectives, and practice* (pp. 3–7). New York: Teachers College Press.

Vygotsky, L. S. (1978). *Mind and society.* Cambridge, MA: Harvard University Press.

Wagner, M. M., & Lachance, A. (2004). Mathematical adventures with Harry Potter. *Teaching Children Mathematics, 10*(5), 274–277.

Wai, J., Cacchio, M., Putallaz, M. C., & Mackel, M. C. (2010). Sex differences in the right tail of cognitive abilities: A 20 year examination. *Intelligence, 38*(4), 412–423.

Wai, J., Lubinski, D., & Benbow, C. (2009). Spatial ability for STEM domains: Aligning over 50 years of cumulative psychological knowledge solidifies its importance. *Journal of Educational Psychology, 101,* 817–835.

Wallace, A. H. (2007). Anticipating student responses to improve problem solving. *Mathematics Teaching in the Middle School, 12*(9), 504–511.

Wallace, A. H., & Gurganus, S. P. (2005). Teaching for mastery of multiplication. *Teaching Children Mathematics, 12*(1), 26–33.

Walter, M. I. (1970). *Boxes, squares and other things: A teacher's guide for a unit in informal geometry.* Reston, VA: NCTM.

Ward, R. A. (2006). *Numeracy and literacy: Teaching K–8 mathematics using children's literature.* Colorado Springs, CO: PEAK Parent Center.

Wareham, K. (2005). *Hand-held calculators and mathematics achievement: What the 1996 national assessment of educational progress eighth-grade mathematics exam scores tell us.* (Unpublished doctoral dissertation). Utah State University.

Warren, E., & Cooper, T. J. (2008). Patterns that support early algebraic thinking in elementary school. In C. E. Greenes & R. Rubenstein (Eds.), *Algebra and algebraic thinking in school mathematics: 70th NCTM yearbook* (pp. 113–126). Reston, VA: NCTM.

Watanabe, T. (2006). The teaching and learning of fractions: A Japanese perspective. *Teaching Children Mathematics, 12*(7), 368–374.

Watson, J. M., & Moritz, J. B. (2003). Fairness of dice: A longitudinal study of students' beliefs and strategies for making judgments. *Journal for Research in Mathematics Education, 34*(4), 270–304.

Watson, J. M., & Shaughnessy, J. M. (2004). Proportional reasoning: Lessons learned from research in data and chance. *Mathematics Teaching in the Middle School, 10*(2), 104–109.

Wearne, D., & Kouba, V. L. (2000). Rational numbers. In E. A. Silver & P. A. Kenney (Eds.), *Results from the seventh mathematics assessment of the National Assessment of Educational Progress* (pp. 163–191). Reston, VA: NCTM.

Weidemann, W., Mikovch, A. K., & Hunt, J. B. (2001). Using a lifeline to give rational numbers a personal touch. *Mathematics Teaching in the Middle School, 7*(4), 210–215.

Welchman-Tischler, R. (1992). *How to use children's literature to teach mathematics.* Reston, VA: NCTM.

Wheatley, G. H., & Hersberger, J. (1986). A calculator estimation activity. In H. Schoen (Ed.), *Estimation and mental computation* (pp. 182–185). Reston, VA: NCTM.

Whiteford, T. (2009/2010). Is mathematics a universal language? *Teaching Children Mathematics, 16*(5), 276–283.

Whitin, D. J., & Whitin, P. (2004). *New visions for linking literature and mathematics.* Urbana, IL: National Council of Teachers of English; Reston, VA: NCTM.

Whitin, D. J., & Wilde, S. (1992). *Read any good math lately? Children's books for mathematical learning, K–6.* Portsmouth, NH: Heinemann.

Whitin, D. J., & Wilde, S. (1995). *It's the story that counts: More children's books for mathematical learning, K–6.* Portsmouth, NH: Heinemann.

Whitin, P., & Whitin, D. J. (2006). Making connections through math-related book pairs. *Teaching Children Mathematics, 13*(4), 196–202.

Whitin, P., & Whitin, D. (2008). Learning to solve problems in the primary grades. *Teaching Children Mathematics, 14*(7), 426–432.

Wickett, M., Kharas, K., & Burns, M. (2002). *Lessons for algebraic thinking.* Sausalito, CA: Math Solutions Publications.

Wieser, E. T. (2008). Students control their own learning: A metacognitive approach. *Teaching Children Mathematics, 15*(2), 90–95.

Wigfield, A., & Cambria, J. (2010). Expectancy-value theory: retrospective and prospective. In S. Karabenick & T. C. Urdan (Eds.), *The Decade Ahead: Theoretical Perspectives on Motivation and Achievement (Advances in Motivation and Achievement)* (Vol. 16, pp. 35–70). Bradford, UK: Emerald Group Publishing Limited.

Wiliam, D. (2007). Content *then* process: Teacher learning communities in the service of formative assessment. In D. B. Reeves (Ed.), *Ahead of the curve: The power of assessment to transform teaching and learning* (pp. 183–204). Bloomington, IN: Solution Tree.

Wiliam, D. (2008). Changing classroom practice. *Educational Leadership, 65*(4), 36–41.

Wiliam, D. (2010, September). *Practical techniques for formative assessment.* Presentation given in Boras, Sweden. Retrieved from www.slideshare.net/BLoPP/dylan-wiliam-bors-2010

Wilkins, M. M., Wilkins, J. L., & Oliver, R. (2006). Differentiating the curriculum for elementary gifted mathematics students. *Teaching Children Mathematics, 13*(1), 6–13.

Williams, L. (2008). Tiering and scaffolding: Two strategies for providing access to important mathematics. *Teaching Children Mathematics, 14*(6), 324–330.

Williams, M., Forrest, K., & Schnabel, D. (2006). Water wonders (math by the month). *Teaching Children Mathematics, 12*(5), 248–249.

Wilson, L. D., & Kenney, P. A. (2003). Classroom and large-scale assessment. In J. Kilpatrick, W. G. Martin, & D. Schifter (Eds.), *A research companion to Principles and Standards for School Mathematics* (pp. 53–67). Reston, VA: NCTM.

Witzel, B. S. (2005). Using CRA to teach algebra to students with math difficulties in inclusive settings. *Learning Disabilities—A Contemporary Journal, 3*(2), 49–60.

Wood, T., & Turner-Vorbeck, T. (2001). Extending the conception of mathematics teaching. In T. Wood, B. S. Nelson, & J. Warfield (Eds.), *Beyond classical pedagogy: Teaching elementary school mathematics* (pp. 185–208). Mahwah, NJ: Erlbaum.

Wood, T., Cobb, P., Yackel, E., & Dillon, D. (Eds.). (1993). Rethinking elementary school mathematics: Insights and issues [Monograph No. 6]. *Journal for Research in Mathematics Education* Reston, VA: NCTM.

Wood, T., Williams, G., & McNeal, B. (2006). Children's mathematical thinking in different classroom cultures. *Journal for Research in Mathematics Education, 37*(3), 222–255.

Woodward, J. (2006). Developing automaticity in multiplication facts: Integrating strategy instruction with timed practice drills. *Learning Disability Quarterly, 29*(4), 269–289.

Wright, R. J., Stanger, G., Stafford, A. K., & Martland, J. (2006). *Teaching number in the classroom with 4–8 year olds.* London: Paul Chapman Publications/Sage.

Wu, Z., An, S., King, J., Ramirez, M., & Evans, S. (2009). Second-grade "professors." *Teaching Children Mathematics, 16*(1), 34–41.

Wyner, J. S., Bridgeland, J. M., & DiIulio, J., Jr. (2007). *Achievement trap: How America is failing millions of high-achieving students from lower-income families.* Lansdowne, VA: Jack Kent Cooke Foundation.

Xin, Y. P., Jitendra, A. K., & Deatline-Buchman, A. D. (2005). Effects of mathematical word problem-solving instruction on middle school students with learning problems. *Journal of Special Education, 39*(3), 181–192.

Yackel, E., & Cobb, P. (1996). Sociomathematical norms, argumentation, and autonomy in mathematics. *Journal for Research in Mathematics Education, 27*(4), 458–477.

Ysseldyke, J. (2002). Response to "Learning Disabilities: Historical Perspectives." In R. Bradley, L. Danielson, & D. Hallahan (Eds.), *Identification of learning disabilities: Research to practice* (pp. 89–98). Mahwah, NJ: Erlbaum.

Yu, P., Barrett, J., & Presmeg, N. (2009). Prototypes and categorical reasoning: A perspective to explain how children learn about interactive geometry objects. In T. Craine & R. Rubenstein (Eds.) *Understanding geometry for a changing world.* Reston, VA: NCTM.

Zambo, R. (2008). Percents can make sense. *Mathematics Teaching in the Middle School, 13*(7), 418–422.

Zollman, A. (2009). Mathematical graphic organizers. *Teaching Children Mathematics, 16*(4), 222–229.

Children's Literature References

Andrews, J., & Jolliffe, S. (2005). *The twelve days of summer.* Victoria, BC: Orca Book Publishers.

Anno, M. (1994). *Anno's magic seeds.* New York: Philomel Books.

Appelt, K., & Sweet, M. (1999). *Bats on parade.* New York: Morrow Junior Books.

Ball, J. (2005). *Go figure! A totally cool book about numbers.* New York: DK Publishing.

Better Homes and Gardens. (2004). *New junior cookbook.* Des Moines, IA: Author.

Bowen, A. (2006). *The great math tattle battle.* Park Ridge, IL: Albert Whitman.

Briggs, R. (1970). *Jim and the beanstalk.* New York: Coward-McCann.

Brown, D. (2000). *Alice Ramsey's grand adventure.* Boston, MA: Sandpiper.

Brown, M. W. (1947). *Goodnight moon.* New York: Harper & Row.

Buckley, J., Jr., & Stremme, R. (2006). *Book of lists: Fun facts, weird trivia, and amazing lists on nearly everything you need to know!* Santa Barbara, CA: Scholastic.

Burns, M. (1995). *The greedy triangle.* New York: Houghton Mifflin.

Burns, M., & Tilley, D. (2008). *Spaghetti and meatballs for all! A mathematical story.* New York: Scholastic.

Carroll, L., & Gray, D. J. (1865/1992). *Alice in wonderland.* New York: Norton.

Clement, R. (1991). *Counting on Frank.* Milwaukee: Gareth Stevens Children's Books.

Cushman, R. (1991). *Do you wanna bet? Your chance to find out about probability.* New York: Clarion Books.

Cuyler, M. (2005). *100th day worries.* New York: Simon & Schuster.

Cuyler, M. (2010). *Guinea pigs add up.* New York: Walker.

Dee, R. (1988). *Two ways to count to ten.* New York: Holt.

DiSalvo-Ryan, D. (1994). *City green.* New York: William Morrow.

Drescher, D. (2008). *What's hiding in there?* Edinburgh, Scotland: Floris Books.

Ehlert, L. (1989). *Color zoo.* New York: HarperCollins.

Ehlert, L. (1990). *Color farm.* New York: HarperCollins.

Enzensberger, H. M. (1997). *The number devil.* New York: Metropolitan Books.

Franco, B. (2009). *Zero is the leaves on the tree.* Berkeley, CA: Tricycle Press.

Gifford, S., & Thaler, S. (2008). *Piece = part = portion: Fraction = decimal = percent.* New York: Tricycle Press.

Giganti, P. (1988). *How many snails? A counting book.* New York: Greenwillow.

Grossman, B. (1996). *My little sister ate one hare.* New York: Crown.

Hamm, D. J. (1991). *How many feet in the bed?* New York: Simon & Schuster.

Harris, T. (2000). *100 days of school.* Minneapolis, MN: Millbrook Press.

Hightower, S. (1997). *Twelve snails to one lizard: A tale of mischief and measurement.* New York: Simon & Schuster.

Himmelman, J. (2010). *Ten little hot dogs.* Tarrytown, NY: Pinwheel Books.

Hoban, T. (1996). *Shapes, shapes, shapes.* New York: Harper Trophy.

Hoban, T. (1998). *So many circles, so many squares.* New York: Greenwillow.

Hoban, T. (2000). *Cubes, cones, cylinders and shapes.* New York: Greenwillow.

Hoffman, D. (2005). *The breakfast cereal gourmet.* Riverside, NJ: Andrews McMeel Publishing.

Hong, L. T. (1993). *Two of everything: A Chinese folktale.* New York: Albert Whitman.

Hoose, P. (2001). *We were there, too! Young people in U.S. history.* New York: Farrar, Straus & Giroux.

Hutchins, P. (1986). *The doorbell rang.* New York: Greenwillow.

Isaacs, A., & Zelinsky, P. O. (1994). *Swamp angel.* New York: Dutton Children's Books.

Juster, N. (1961). *The phantom tollbooth.* New York: Random House.

Krull, K. (2000). *Wilma unlimited.* Boston: Sandpiper.

Landau, E. (2006). *The history of everyday life.* Minneapolis, MN: Lerner Classroom.

Leedy, L. (2000). *Measuring Penny.* New York: Holt.

Lobel, A. (1970). *Frog and Toad are friends.* New York: HarperCollins.

Masoff, J., & Sirrell, T. (2006). *Oh, yikes!: History's grossest, wackiest moments.* New York: Workman.

Mathis, S. B. (1986). *The hundred penny box.* New York: Viking Juvenile Books.

McElligott, M. (2007). *Bean thirteen.* New York: Putnam Juvenile.

McKissack, P. (1996). *A million fish . . . more or less.* New York: Dragonfly Books.

Metropolitan Museum of Art. (2005). *Museum shapes.* New York: Little Brown and Company.

Micklethwait, L. (2004). *I spy shapes in art.* New York: Greenwillow.

Murphy, S. (1997). *The best vacation ever.* New York: HarperCollins.

Murrie, S., & Murrie, M. (2007). *Every minute on earth.* New York: Scholastic.

Myller, R. (1991). *How big is a foot?* South Holland, IL: Yearling Books.

National Geographic. (2011). *Kids Almanac 2012.* Washington, DC: National Geographic Children's Books.

Norton, M. (1953). *The borrowers.* New York: Harcourt Brace.

Numeroff, L. J. (1985). *If you give a mouse a cookie.* New York: HarperCollins.

Osborne, M. P., & Potter, G. (2000). *Kate and the beanstalk.* New York: Atheneum Books for Young Readers.

Pinczes, E. (1999). *One hundred angry ants.* Boston: Sandpiper.

Pinczes, E. (2002). *Remainder of one.* Boston: Sandpiper.

Portis, A. (2007). *Not a stick.* New York: HarperCollins.

Rowling, J. K. (1998). *Harry Potter and the sorcerer's stone.* New York: A. A. Lewine.

Sachar, L. (1998). *Holes.* New York: Farrar, Straus & Giroux.

Schwartz, D. (1985). *How much is a million?* New York: Lothrop, Lee & Shepard.

Schwartz, D. (1994). *If you made a million.* New York: Lothrop, Lee & Shepard.

Schwartz, D. M. (1999). *If you hopped like a frog.* New York: Scholastic Press.

Schwartz, D. (2001). *On beyond a million: An amazing math journey.* New York: Random House.

Schwartz, D. (2004). *How much is a million?* New York: HarperCollins.

Schwartz, D., & Whitin, D. (1999). *The magic of a million activity book—Grades 2–5.* New York: Scholastic.

Seuss, Dr. (1960). *Green eggs and ham.* New York: Random House.

Silverstein, S. (1974). One inch tall. In *Where the sidewalk ends* (p. 55). New York: Harper & Row.

Slobodkina, E. (1938). *Caps for sale.* New York: Scholastic Books.

Smith, D. (2002). *If the world were a village: A book about the world's people.* Tonawanda, NY: Kids Can Press.

Stoeke, J. M. (1999). *Hide and seek.* New York: Dutton Juvenile Books.

Swift, J., & Winterson, J. (1726/1999). *Gulliver's travels.* Oxford: Oxford University Press.

Tahan, M. (1993). *The man who counted: A collection of mathematical adventures* (Trans. L. Clark & A. Reid). New York: Norton.

Toft, K. M., & Sheather, A. (1998). *One less fish.* Watertown, MA: Charlesbridge.

Tompert, A. (1997). *Grandfather Tang's story.* New York: Dragonfly Books.

Weatherform, C. B. (2005). *A Negro League scrapbook.* Honesdale, PA: Boyds Mills Press.

Wells, R. E. (1993). *Is a blue whale the biggest thing there is?* Morton Grove, IL: Whitman.

Wishinsky, F., & Zhang, S. N. (1999). *The man who made parks: The story of parkbuilder Frederick Law Olmsted.* Plattsburgh, NY: Tundra Books.

Index